PERGAMON GENERAL PSYCHOLOGY SERIES
EDITORS
Arnold P. Goldstein, Syracuse University
Leonard Krasner, Stanford University & SUNY at Stony Brook

HANDBOOK OF SOCIAL
AND CLINICAL PSYCHOLOGY

(PGPS-162)

Pergamon Titles of Related Interest

Hersen/Kazdin/Bellack THE CLINICAL PSYCHOLOGY HANDBOOK,
Second Edition

Higginbotham/West/Forsyth PSYCHOTHERAPY AND BEHAVIOR
CHANGE: Social, Cultural, and Methodological Perspectives

Winett/King/Altman HEALTH PSYCHOLOGY AND PUBLIC
HEALTH: An Integrative Approach

Related Journal
(Free sample copies available on request.)

CLINICAL PSYCHOLOGY REVIEW

HANDBOOK OF SOCIAL AND CLINICAL PSYCHOLOGY

The Health Perspective

C.R. SNYDER
University of Kansas

DONELSON R. FORSYTH
Virginia Commonwealth University

PERGAMON PRESS
Member of Maxwell Macmillan Pergamon Publishing Corporation
New York • Oxford • Beijing • Frankfurt
São Paulo • Sydney • Tokyo • Toronto

Pergamon Press Offices:

U.S.A.   Pergamon Press, Inc., Maxwell House, Fairview Park,
                     Elmsford, New York 10523, U.S.A.

U.K.   Pergamon Press plc, Headington Hill Hall,
                     Oxford OX3 0BW, England

PEOPLE'S REPUBLIC   Pergamon Press, 0909 China World Tower
OF CHINA   No. 1 Jian Guo Men Wei Avenue, Beijing 100004,
                     People's Republic of China

FEDERAL REPUBLIC   Pergamon Press GmbH, Hammerweg 6,
OF GERMANY   D-6242 Kronberg, Federal Republic of Germany

BRAZIL   Pergamon Editora Ltda, Rua Eça de Queiros,
                     346, CEP 04011, Paraiso, São Paulo, Brazil

AUSTRALIA   Pergamon Press Australia Pty Ltd., P.O. Box 544,
                     Potts Point, NSW 2011, Australia

JAPAN   Pergamon Press, 8th Floor, Matsuoka Central Building,
                     1-7-1 Nishishinjuku, Shinjuku-ku, Tokyo 160, Japan

CANADA   Pergamon Press Canada Ltd., Suite 271, 253 College Street,
                     Toronto, Ontario M5T 1R5, Canada

Library of Congress Cataloging-in-Publication Data

Handbook of social and clinical psychology : the health perspective /
  [edited by] C.R. Snyder, Donelson R. Forsyth.
      p.   cm. -- (Pergamon general psychology series : 162)
    Includes bibliographical references.
    ISBN 0-08-036128-5 :
    1. Clinical psychology. 2 Social psychology. I. Snyder, C.R.
  II. Forsyth, Donelson R., 1953- . III. Series.
      [DNLM: 1. Psychology, Clinical. 2. Psychology, Social. WM 105
  H2365]
  RC467.H29 1990
  616.89—dc20
  DNLM/DLC
  for Library of Congress   89-72133
                                                                   CIP

Printing: 1 2 3 4 5 6 7 8 9 10   Year: 1 2 3 4 5 6 7 8 9
Printed in the United States of America

⊗™ The paper used in this publication meets the minimum requirements of
    American National Standard for Information Sciences -- Permanence of
    Paper for Printed Library Materials, ANSI Z39.48-1984

To the third little pig, for building and sustaining a home where social and clinical psychologists can live and work together.

CONTENTS

PART IV.   NOW AND THEN: PRESENT PARADIGMS AND FUTURE DIRECTIONS

FOREWORD: MATURING OF AN INTERFACE

We were quite pleased to be asked to write the foreword for this first handbook of social and clinical psychology. Ever since the early handbooks in social and clinical psychology (e.g., the *Handbook of Social Psychology*, the *Clinical Psychology Handbook*), the connotation for such a volume has been that of a major collection of chapters authored by eminent scholars and representing state-of-the-art reviews of a mature body of scholarship. The present *Handbook of Social and Clinical Psychology* meets that criterion and in so doing makes an important statement about how far this integration of scholarship has come, albeit in stuttering steps, since developments in the first quarter of this century presaged such an explicit movement (e.g., the beginning of the *Journal of Abnormal and Social Psychology* in 1921). We believe that the editors Snyder and Forsyth have achieved a superb feat not only by bringing together a set of leading scholars of clinical, counseling, and social psychology, who in turn have produced interesting and useful manuscripts, but also because their volume comes at a time when interest in the possibilities of cross-fertiliza-

tion among these boundary fields is at an all time high in psychology. In this foreword, we will briefly examine what we believe are two basic questions involved in this integration and reflected in the present volume.

HOW FAR HAVE WE COME?

We may not be able to define precisely the boundaries of social-clinical/counseling psychology in 1989. Nonetheless, we should be able to recognize clear-cut signs that this interface has emerged as a background for developments such as a first handbook. As Snyder and Forsyth describe in the opening chapter, the historical course of this interface work between social and clinical (emphasizing "generic clinical") psychology has involved many landmark events. Certainly, the broadening of the *Journal of Abnormal Psychology* into the *Journal of Abnormal and Social Psychology* by Morton Prince and Floyd Allport in 1921 was a key historical event (Hill & Weary, 1983). Similarly, other publications signaled degrees of progress toward greater cross-disciplinary stimulation, including seminal works by Goldstein, Heller, and Sechrest (1966), Carson (1969), and Brehm (1976). Still, we believe that Snyder and Forsyth are correct in suggesting that the most fervent period of "interfacing" among these fields has occurred in the last decade. That decade has seen another string of influential and explicitly integrative works, including books by Sheras and Worchel (1979), Weary and Mirels (1982), Strong and Claiborn (1982), Leary and Miller (1986), Maddux, Stoltenberg, and Rosenwein (1987), Snyder and Ford (1987), and Higginbotham, West, and Forsyth (1988). Also, the *Journal of Social and Clinical Psychology* (Harvey, 1983) came on the scene early during this period and likely served as a catalyst for the vigor on display.

Over the first half of this century, many leading scholars cogently displayed the natural interplay among these fields of thought in their theoretical and empirical work. In addition to the historical works described by Snyder and Forsyth, a host of classic writings established a cogent foundation for integration. Several of the neo-Freudians (e.g., Horney, 1937) emphasized social processes in the etiology of psychopathology. Snyder and Forsyth are correct in pointing to Kurt Lewin's key role in providing a model of how to bridge theory and practice in psychology (see Patnoe, 1988). If Lewin had lived well into the epoch after World War II when clinical psychology started to grow and expand its horizon, it is tantalizing to imagine the scope of his contributions to this interface (and given Lewin's breadth, no doubt extending the interface to include other topics such as public policy). As Hill and Weary (1983) note, one of Lewin's students was Jerome Frank, who is a major figure in the theoretical analysis of psychopathology (e.g., Frank, 1961). So in many ways, Lewin's presence has been and continues to be felt in this domain of integrative work.

But the foundation is even deeper than these currents suggest. It extends to the field of sociological social psychology. Much of Erving Goffman's writing, which embraces Meadian social behaviorism (Mead, 1934), and symbolic interaction theory are highly relevant to contemporary work on self-evaluation (Shrauger & Schoeneman, 1979; Shrauger, 1982) and to work on labeling processes (e.g., Goffman's 1961 classic, *Asylums*). This latter work has been influential in the development of a major strand of current work on stigma (e.g., Jones, Farina, Hastorf, Markus,

Miller, & Scott, 1984) that represents another promising venue for social-clinical psychological research.

What conclusions can be drawn from this history of nourishment and the current situation of quite active interaction among these fields? It is a maturing, if not mature, domain with great promise because of the strength of its foundation. We also would suggest that Snyder's (1988) point about who represents the domain is right on the money, to wit: There are (and have been) many professionals working at this interface, but who do not know it. Indeed, it is a crowded intersection. We would, however, offer a slight modification of this point: There are many scholars who have adopted interdisciplinary (or intradisciplinary) approaches to understanding psychopathology and problems in living because such approaches provide broader methodological and conceptual perspectives. Further, these scholars may not know it, and that lack of recognition may not adversely affect progress at the boundary points. The ideas and methods deriving from this interdisciplinary work will continue to represent key contributions to the social-clinical/counseling interface, whether or not these scholars recognize the merit of this interface.

Yet, as many of us have experienced, increased specialization in psychology often has led to bias about which area is doing the most important work or has the highest "scientific" status and, in general, intellectual dogmatism (Harvey & Weary, 1979). Integrative and interdisciplinary endeavors are partial antidotes to such tendencies. Thus, even if the social-clinical/counseling psychology interface is seen as a somewhat arbitrary symbol of interdisciplinary movement in the social and behavioral sciences, we believe that it is a critically vital one in serving as a necessary counter to provincialism in understanding psychopathology and problems in living.

HOW FAR WILL WE GO?

As Fritz Heider (1976) once said about the importance of attribution (and the attribution theoretical perspective), "It is all-pervasive. I think it can go anywhere" (p. 18). We are tempted to make the same statement for the movement depicted in this volume. Certainly, Snyder and Forsyth reveal perspicacity in suggesting that the health scene is the greatest common ground for further integrations. The health arena (including work on prevention) is where a great many clinical/counseling and social psychologists now work. No end appears in sight partially because of increasing greater appreciation of their work by medical scientists, physicians, and the general public. The credence achieved by wholistic perspectives involving concern with social psychological processes in medicine portends well for decades of useful work by interdisciplinary teams of scholars, prominently including social, counseling, and clinical psychologists. This interdisciplinary health movement is a fait accompli in 1989 and is represented well in the chapters in this handbook.

Possible future steps to make the interface more clearly overlapping, as Snyder and Forsyth wisely suggest is necessary, might include the creation of a professional society with a newsletter, placement service, and other accoutrements focusing on these boundary areas, and formal lobbying for the creation of federal training grant programs that more explicitly involve social-clinical/counseling doctoral training (health training grants probably move programs some degrees in this direction as Snyder's own program at the University of Kansas has well-illustrated for several years).

The promise of greater development of and integration across the interface between social and clinical psychology comes across loudly and clearly in the final and interesting section of this volume, "The Interface Toward the Year 2000." At the same time, many of the issues that may stall clearcut, major integrative work also are revealed in the commentaries as well as in Snyder and Forsyth's accompanying, interpretive analysis. High on the list of issues is the never-ending problem of needing more and better theoretical work. The greatest inspiration of Lewin, first and foremost, was that of the power of theoretical analysis—even if the question was an applied one and concerned how to get people to eat more liver during a time of scarcity of other meat. Also, there is the practical issue of implementation of interdisciplinary training. As Hendrick and Hendrick and others note, some progress is being made toward relaxing artificially imposing training barriers. Nonetheless, there writers, as well as the editors of this volume, correctly observe that there are many obstacles which may preclude doctoral students' ease of movement across training areas in most psychology departments. Given the current disparate directions exhibited in organized psychology, we fear

that this training issue may continue to loom large despite the obvious intellectual and logical merit of greater cross-training across many areas of psychology.

While both of the above issues are formidable, the note of "challenges to be met" sounded by Snyder and Forsyth is the attitude that would be most productive for the future, we believe. Too much has already "gone down," to use a term of our time, for this movement to be significantly impaired in the future. There simply are too many scholars and practitioners endorsing the interplay, writing about it, and showing its value in their work for any imminent demise of the movement. Or to state this point in a voice more resonant with that of the editors, in Forsyth's wonderful concluding allegory, it might be argued that the third little pig survived because he or she had a more diversified portfolio of ideas!

Thus, in the end, we take our hats off, especially to editors Snyder and Forsyth, for such a major undertaking as this first handbook is and to each of the contributors and others working at this interface for providing the ideas and energy for one of the most exciting movements in psychology today.

John H. Harvey
University of Iowa
Gifford Weary
Ohio State University

REFERENCES

Brehm, S. S. (1976). *The application of social psychology to clinical practice*. Washington, DC: Hemisphere.

Carson, R. C. (1969). *Interaction concepts of personality*. Chicago: Aldine.

Frank, J. D. (1961). *Persuasion and healing*. Baltimore: Johns Hopkins University Press.

Goffman, E. (1961). *Asylums: Essays on the social situation of mental patients and other inmates*. Garden City, NJ: Anchor Books.

Goldstein, A. P., Heller, K., & Sechrest, L. B. (1966). *Psychotherapy and the psychology of behavior change*. New York: John Wiley & Sons.

Harvey, J. H. (1983). The founding of the *Journal of Social and Clinical Psychology*. *Journal of Social and Clinical Psychology, 1*, 1–3.

Harvey, J. H., & Weary, G. (1979). The integration of social and clinical psychology training programs. *Personality and Social Psychology Bulletin, 5*, 511–515.

Heider, F. (1976). A conversation with Fritz Heider. In J. H. Harvey, W. J. Ickes, & R. F. Kidd (Eds.), *New directions in attribution research* (Vol. 1, pp. 3–18). Hillsdale, NJ: Lawrence Erlbaum Associates.

Higginbotham, H. N., West, S. G., & Forsyth, D. R. (1988). *Psychotherapy and behavior change: Social, cultural, and methodological perspectives*. New York: Pergamon Press.

Hill, M. G., & Weary, G. (1983). Perspectives on the *Journal of Abnormal and Social Psychology*: How it began and how it was transformed. *Journal of Social and Clinical Psychology, 1*, 4–14.

Horney, K. (1937). *Neurotic personality of our times*. New York: W. W. Norton.

Jones, E. E., Farina, A., Hastorf, A. H., Marcus, H., Miller, D. T., & Scott, R. A. (1984). *Social stigma: The psychology of marked relationships*. San Francisco: W. H. Freeman.

Leary, M. R., & Miller, R. S. (1986). *Social psychology and dysfunctional behavior: Origins, diagnosis, and treatment*. New York: Springer-Verlag.

Maddux, J. E., Stoltenberg, C. D., & Rosenwein, R. (Eds.). (1987). *Social processes in clinical and counseling psychology*. New York: Springer-Verlag.

Mead, G. H. (1934). *Mind, self, and society*. Chicago: University of Chicago Press.

Patnoe, S. (1988). *A narrative history of experimental social psychology: The Lewin tradition*. New York: Springer-Verlag.

Sheras, P. L., & Worchel, S. (1979). *Clinical psychology: A social psychological approach*. New York: Van Nostrand Reinhold.

Shrauger, J. S. (1982). Selection and processing of self-evaluative information: Experimental evidence and clinical implications. In G. Weary & H. Mirels (Eds.), *Integrations of clinical and social psychology* (pp. 128–153). New York: Oxford University Press.

Shrauger, J. S., & Schoeneman, T. J. (1979). Symbolic interactionist view of self-concept: Through the looking glass darkly. *Psychological Bulletin, 86*, 549–572.

Snyder, C. R. (1988). On being where you already are: An invitation to the social/clinical/counseling interface. *Journal of Social and Clinical Psychology, 6*, i–ii.

Snyder, C. R., & Ford, C. E. (Eds.). (1987). *Coping with negative life events: Clinical and social psychological perspectives*. New York: Plenum Press.

Strong, S. R., & Claiborn, C. D. (1982). *Change through interaction: Social psychological processes of counseling and psychotherapy*. New York: Wiley-Interscience.

Weary, G., & Mirels, H. L. (Eds.). (1982). *Integrations of clinical and social psychology*. New York: Oxford University Press.

PREFACE

In 1986, Don Forsyth journeyed from Virginia Commonwealth University to undertake a sabbatical in the Department of Psychology at the University of Kansas, Lawrence. Don was sitting in his office on the fifth floor of Fraser Hall trying to organize his new workspace, when a knock at the door signaled his first business. In walked a fellow wearing jeans and a Jayhawk T-shirt, who introduced himself as a senior who had heard about the "new guy." Forsyth listened patiently for a few minutes to his visitor's rambling ideas for independent study projects, all the while thinking about the strangeness of this undergraduate Jayhawk. The undergraduate began to smile, and thereafter broke into raucous laughter. Sensing the unraveling of the masquerade, the senior introduced himself again, this time using his real name. This is how Don Forsyth and Rick Snyder met.

The rest is, as they say, history. Don, for all his social psychological blustering, was a closet clinician at heart. Rick, for all his apparent dedication to clinical psychology, was increasingly seduced by the power of social psychological theory build-

ing. In subsequent discussions, it was apparent that traditional boundaries between clinical and social psychology were being crossed freely without passports. Indeed, it was as if both of us were citizens of "Interfaceland." In a few short months, we had sketched an outline for what we believed would be the next logical step in the evolution of the social/clinical interface. This handbook represents that step.

Our colleagues immediately began to tell us about the Brobdingnagian nature of the task that we were beginning. We heard about the difficulty of getting 40 people to agree to write chapters and commentaries. Furthermore, we were warned about how authors would be one or more *years* late in delivering their chapters. All in all, a lot of crepe-hanging about the hazards of the project was brought to our attention. Of course, we stubbornly maintained that this need not happen with this project. Happily, it did not. Authors readily agreed to write, and the various drafts were delivered in a timely fashion. Although it is tempting to attribute this fortunate outcome to our editorial acumen, it is more accurate to give the credit to the present handbook authors for their remarkable attention to alacrity and quality. It has been a pleasure to work with this outstanding group of scholars, and we would like to deliver a full dose of praise and gratitude to them.

Our thanks also are extended to Jerry Frank and Arnold Goldstein at Pergamon for their unflagging support for this project since its inception. Arnold Goldstein was one of the founding fathers of the social/clinical interface, and his role in the past and present evolution of the interface deserves special acknowledgment.

C. R. Snyder
Lawrence, Kansas
Donelson R. Forsyth
Richmond, Virginia

HANDBOOK OF SOCIAL
AND CLINICAL PSYCHOLOGY

PART I

INTRODUCTION

CHAPTER 1

SOCIAL AND CLINICAL PSYCHOLOGY UNITED

C. R. Snyder
Donelson R. Forsyth

Until quite recently social psychologists were pre-occupied with the study of the interpersonal determinants of thought, feeling, and action. Their work was primarily theoretically driven, the behaviors they sought to explain were the sort that occurred in everyday settings, and they preferred to test their hypotheses through laboratory experimentation. Clinically oriented psychologists, in contrast, sought to understand the causes of and cures for dysfunctional behavior. Psychologists in counseling, community, and clinical settings were concerned with developing effective treatments and diagnostic techniques, the behaviors they puzzled over were abnormal ones, and they preferred to test their hypotheses in field settings.

A change, however, has been taking place at the borderline between social and clinical psychology. Although the benefits of an integrated social-clinical approach were recognized in 1966 by Goldstein, Heller, and Sechrest in their book *Psychotherapy and the Psychology of Behavior Change*, and were reiterated a decade later in Brehm's 1976 book *The Application of Social Psychology to Clinical Practice*, it was not until the 1980s that

this interface became truly viable. Now, for example, we find that social psychologists, who recognize the potential applicability of their theories to clinical practice, are exploring sources of dysfunction and suggesting socially based treatment strategies. Likewise, clinical, counseling, and community psychologists, who recognize the role of interpersonal dynamics in adjustment and therapy, have begun to synthesize social psychological principles and clinical practice. This collaborative, cross-disciplinary movement is producing a growing interface between psychology's helping professionals and social psychology (e.g., Brehm & Smith, 1986; Dorn, 1984; Higginbotham, West, & Forsyth, 1988; Leary & Maddux, 1987; Leary & Miller, 1986; Maddux, Stoltenberg, & Rosenwein, 1987; Sheras & Worchel, 1979; Snyder & Ford, 1987; Weary & Mirels, 1982).

In this chapter we present an overview of this interface. First we consider, in brief, the traditional goals of social and clinical psychology, where the word *clinical* is used in the "small c" sense, which includes such subspecialties as clinical, counseling, and community psychology. Second,

3

we enumerate the qualities that emerge when these two areas of psychology are linked together into a single perspective. This analysis maintains that the social/clinical interface not only provides insight into the factors that produce dysfunction and foundations of effective treatment, but also innumerable insights into the factors that operate to sustain psychological health on a day-to-day basis. In this latter vein, the chapter concludes with a presentation of a proposed health-help-health framework for understanding much of the recent work in the interface of social and clinical psychology.

A BRIEF HISTORY

The philosopher of science Thomas Kuhn, in his provocative book *The Structure of Scientific Revolutions*, argues that scientists working in a particular field often share a set of assumptions about the phenomena they study (Kuhn, 1970). His thesis is that when individuals are trained to be scientists, they learn not only the content of the science — important discoveries, general principles, facts, and so on — but also a way of looking at the world that is passed on from one scientist to another. This paradigm consists of a set of shared fundamental beliefs, exemplars, and symbolic generalizations, and it provides researchers with a world view that determines the questions they feel are worth studying and the methods that are most appropriate.

Historically, social and clinical psychologists have adopted differing paradigms. Although the two emerged within psychology at almost the same time, their differing concerns prompted them to develop divergent perspectives on human behavior. As the following brief review of historical trends in the two fields indicates, by tradition the questions raised by social psychologists focused their interest more on exogenous determinants of normal actions, whereas the questions raised by clinical psychologists drew them toward the study of endogenous determinants of abnormal actions.

Development of a Social Psychological Outlook

Social psychology, despite its ancient roots in the writings of philosophers and scholars, did not emerge as a unified subfield within psychology until the 1940s. Granted, certain social psycholog-

ical phenomena, such as individuals' performance in the presence of others (Triplett, 1897) and mob behavior (Le Bon, 1895), had been the target of scrutiny before the turn of the century. But as Cartwright's (1979) historical account of the field notes, these varied efforts remained relatively uncoordinated during the years that psychodynamic perspectives and behavioristic tenets shaped most psychologists' thinking.

The late 1930s and the 1940s, however, saw the gradual emergence of a set of core assumptions that provided the foundation for a contemporary social psychology. Moving away from the cultural perspective emphasized by anthropologists and the broad societal view embraced by sociologists, social psychologists within psychology firmly reiterated their focus on the individual. Social psychology, as Gordon W. Allport writes, was considered "above all else a branch of general psychology" (1985, p. 3). Social psychologists, however, claimed to be uniquely interested in how individuals influence and, in turn, are influenced by other people. Let other psychologists study neural structures, psychophysics, sensation and perception, and adjustment; social psychologists staked out the person in the social context as their domain.

Social psychologists did not, however, restrict themselves to the study of situations that required interaction among individuals. Although they were concerned with social behavior, their psychological bent led them to consider both endogenous and exogenous processes. An attitude, for example, was thought to be an affectively valenced mental state of readiness (Allport, 1985). Yet, this purely intrapsychic process became a "primary building stone in the edifice of social psychology" (Allport, 1985, p. 37) because researchers assumed that attitudes profoundly influenced, and were profoundly influenced by, the social world. Thus, rather than restrict their investigations to overtly social processes, social psychologists chose to investigate individual differences, personality traits, attitudes, values, motivation, emotion, and social cognition as well as attraction, influence, and group processes.

To some, the social psychologists' interest in intrapersonal factors seems misplaced. Carlson (1984), for example, criticized social psychologists for not restricting their investigations to the interpersonal realm. She argued that "solid social psychology" required studying naturally forming social groups, interaction among "real" individuals, the impact of social structural variables such as gender or race on behavior, and social issues such as political disputes or racism. Yet, as Kenrick (1986) explains in a rejoinder, most (but certainly not all) social psychologists adopt a broader, more balanced view of their field. Gordon W. Allport captured this outlook when he defined social psychology as "an attempt to understand and explain how the thought, feeling, and behavior of individuals are influenced by the actual, imagined, or implied presence of others" (1985, p. 3). Similarly, Kurt Lewin (1936, p. 12), a key figure in the founding of social psychology, wrote, "Every psychological event depends upon the state of the person and at the same time on the environment" and formalized this assumption in his equation $B = f(P, E)$. Although the P (person) in the equation is sometimes slighted relative to the E (environment), social psychologists continue to espouse the doctrine of interactionism.

With this growing recognition of the importance of both personal and situational factors came major advances in methodological sophistication (Cartwright & Zander, 1968). Reacting in part to Floyd Allport's influential 1924 text that demanded greater attention to scientific rigor, researchers managed to develop more precise measurement methods (Thurstone, 1928) and more elaborate experimental procedures (Murphy & Murphy, 1931). As Table 1.1 indicates, as early as 1928 Louis L. Thurstone published his precedent-setting paper titled "Attitudes Can Be Measured." In 1936 Muzafer Sherif demonstrated that a perceptual process can be influenced by an experimentally manipulated social norm. In 1939 Kurt Lewin, Ronald Lippitt, and Ralph White published their study of group members' reactions to leaders who adopt autocratic, democratic, and laissez-faire styles of leadership. And by 1943 Theodore Newcomb's so-called Bennington Study linked changes in attitudes to social pressure. These studies not only illustrated the potential of the social psychological perspective, but also provided models for how research should be carried out (Jones, 1985).

Social psychology's gradual development of a set of basic theoretical and methodological premises was accelerated by the Second World War. Scholars and researchers who were trained as social psychologists assisted in the war effort by examining a range of applied topics, including civilian and troop morale, changing attitudes through persuasion and propaganda, improving organiza-

tion in fighting units, and international relations. Dorwin Cartwright, in reflecting on this period, pointed out that this applied work changed the face of social psychology, for it "provided concrete examples of the practical usefulness of social psychology" (1979, p. 84). Moreover, it solidified the link between social psychology and social issues. Researchers expanded their investigations beyond theoretically interesting ideas to include the analysis of social problems, including conflict, racism, and environmental degradation.

Social psychology continued to develop during the postwar years, particularly in the realm of theory construction (see Table 1.1). Yet, in general these developments were consistent with the methodological and theoretical tenets established by earlier researchers and theorists: What was the goal of the field? Explain social behavior. What was the fundamental theoretical assumption? Social behavior depends on aspects of the individual (intrapersonal processes) and aspects of the situation (interpersonal processes). How should this assumption be tested? Through rigorous research; experimental, if possible. New ideas continued to influence the field, but the basic tenets that initially prompted the emergence of this subdiscipline continue to manifest themselves in contemporary social psychology.

Development of the Clinical Psychology Outlook

The era that witnessed the gradual growth of social psychology also watched clinical psychology develop into a dominant force within psychology and among the health-care professions. As was the case with social psychology, the seeds of the present-day field were sown gradually during the early part of this century (Table 1.2). At this time the treatment of psychological disorders was, in general, the physician's private domain. Some psychologists, such as Witmer, were actively treating clients with speech disorders and learning disabilities as early as 1896, but these practitioners were a rare breed (McReynolds, 1987). Their efforts were based on the then-radical idea that psychologists should not just generate information about human behavior, but also seek the "application of psychological principles and techniques to the problems of an individual" (Watson, 1951, p. 5). To the consternation of many psychologists (both then and perhaps even now), these clinicians

Table 1.1. Prominent Events in Social Psychology, 1897–1959

YEAR	EVENT
1897	Triplett publishes the results of a laboratory study of social facilitation
1908	Publication of the first texts in social psychology
1924	F. A. Allport presents a scientific framework for the study of social processes
1928	Thurstone proposes "Attitudes Can Be Measured"
1936	Sherif reports his study of conformity to group norms
1939	Lewin, Lippitt, and White publish an experimental study of leadership style and performance
1943	Newcomb reports his study of attitude change among students at Bennington College
1953	One of many monographs on communication and attitude change is published by Hovland, Janis, and Kelley
1954	Publication of G. W. Allport's *The Nature of Prejudice*
1954	The first modern edition of the *Handbook of Social Psychology* is published
1957	Festinger's *A Theory of Cognitive Dissonance* sparks two decades of research on attitude change
1958	Heider's *Psychology of Interpersonal Relations* set forth the tenets of attribution theory
1959	Thibaut and Kelley publish *The Social Psychology of Groups*

were suggesting that psychology was a profession as well as a science.

Psychologists also found considerable success when they used their psychometric skills to develop reliable measures of cognitive abilities and personality functions. At first, these tests were designed primarily for use in identifying children with special educational needs, but World War I stimulated the development of a number of batteries that could be used for measuring individual differences in adults. This emphasis on assessment, once established, continued into the 1920s with the publication of such tests as the Seashore Musical Ability Test (1919), the Woodworth Personal Data Sheet (1920), the Rorschach Inkblot Test (1921/1942), and the Goodenough Draw-A-Man Test (Buros, 1938).

Assessment, and its attendant focus on individual differences among individuals, stimulated theoretical analyses of the nature and function of personality. This intrapsychic perspective was all

the more reinforced by the advent of Freud's psychodynamic model of behavior disorders. Many clinicians worked closely with physicians at a time when Freud's views were revolutionizing the medical world's view of psychological abnormalities, so it is not surprising that clinical psychology began to link disordered behavior to disturbances in personality structure and development. Although clinicians weren't directly involved in treatment during these early years, the influence of Freud's thinking could be seen in their projective assessment methods and the rapid proliferation of personality theories that yielded clear predictions about the causes of abnormal behavior.

Despite continual advances in application, assessment, and theory, clinical psychology did not begin to thrive until World War II created a demand for trained mental health professionals. Clinical psychologists' specialized assessment skills proved invaluable to a nation at war; indeed, in 1944 alone nearly 20 million soldiers and civil-

Table 1.2. Prominent Events in Clinical Psychology, 1890–1953

YEAR	EVENT
1890	James McKeen Cattell describes the development of "mental tests"
1896	Witmer becomes the first "clinical" psychologist when he opens a clinic at the University of Pennsylvania
1909	Freud's lectures at Clark University spark widespread acceptance of his ideas by the medical community
1916	Publication of the Stanford-Binet test of intelligence
1924	A test-publishing firm, the Psychological Corporation, is founded by James McKeen Cattell
1936	Louttit publishes the first text titled *Clinical Psychology*
1938	The first *Buros Mental Measurement Yearbook* is published
1942	Carl Rogers' *Counseling and Psychotherapy* is published
1946	Veterans Administration supports the training of clinical psychologists in assessment, diagnosis, and treatment
1949	The "Boulder model" is adopted as the standard of training in clinical psychology

ians were assessed via written instrumentation or interview (Reisman, 1976). The war also took a huge toll in terms of psychological casualties, and this flood of persons in need of treatment opened the door for clinical psychologists to become therapists. This demand for human services prompted the Veteran's Administration, at the war's end, to recognize officially clinical psychology as a health-care profession. With this mantle and the promise of federal assistance in training clinical psychologists came the opening of the first Ph.D. programs in clinical psychology.

The bulk of these programs based their students' educational experiences on the recommendations offered by American Psychological Association's Committee on Training in Clinical Psychology (1947). Shakow, who was the chairperson of the committee, summarized the key principles as follows (1978, p. 151):

1. A clinical psychologist must be first and foremost a psychologist.
2. The program for doctoral education in clinical psychology should be as rigorous and as extensive as that for the traditional doctorate.
3. Preparation should be broad; it should be directed toward research and professional goals.
4. In order to meet the above requirements, a core program calls for the study of six major areas: general psychology, psychodynamics of behavior, diagnostic methods, research methods, related disciplines, and therapy.
5. Programs should consist mainly of basic courses in principles, rather than the multiplication of courses in technique. The specific program of instruction should be organized around a careful integration of theory and practice, of academic and field work, by persons representing both aspects.

This model of graduate training was subsequently adopted at a national training conference held in Boulder, Colorado, in 1949, and hence became known as the Boulder model (Raimy, 1950).

Clinical psychology continued to develop during the postwar years. New treatment perspectives, particularly those focusing on behavioral and phenomenological models, began to supplant the uniform reliance on psychodynamic models. Differences in emphasis resulted, in time, in the emergence of alternative models for understanding psychological problems and for delivering mental health services, including counseling psy-

chology, and community psychology. Overall, however, clinical psychology continued to expand along the philosophical lines established at the time of the Boulder Conference: What was the goal of the field? To identify and apply psychological principles to prevent and treat psychological problems. What was the fundamental theoretical assumption? That dysfunctional behavior stems from intrapersonal processes, including disturbances of personality and adjustment. How should this assumption be tested? Through rigorous research, with a strong emphasis on accurate assessment in clinical settings.

FOUNDATIONS OF THE SOCIAL/CLINICAL INTERFACE

When is a relationship between two people satisfying and long-lasting? Experts and laypersons tend to invoke one of two basic tenets in answer to this question. Some cite the principle of similarity; they note the striking unity of the characteristics, needs, and goals of the two parties involved and conclude that "birds of a feather flock together" (Byrne, 1971). Believers in the principle of complementarity, in contrast, attribute the relationship's longevity to the way each party's unique qualities mesh with the qualities of their partner (Snyder & Fromkin, 1980). The two can be so dissimilar as to be opposites, but when they join together a strong bond is formed; after all, "opposites attract."

Although social psychology and clinical psychology are two disciplines rather than two people, their interface is based on these two principles. As the historical trends described above suggest, social and clinical psychology's paradigmatic assumptions overlap to a degree, yet they also conflict. The two disciplines share important similarities in goals, methods, and theory. Both fields, for example, are branches of psychology, both seek to explain behavior, and both rely on a variety of empirical methods to achieve answers (Forsyth & Strong, 1986).

These similarities provide fundamental linkages between the two disciplines, but the value of their interface derives more from their dissimilarities. As the ancient concept of yin and yang argues, profound advances in knowledge often require the synthesis of opposites. In the historical differences between social and clinical psychology lies the present promise of the social/clinical interface. When integrated, the emergent interface embraces theoretical and methodological approaches that have previously typified only one or the other of social or clinical fields. In this section the unique metatheoretical and epistemological qualities of the interface's paradigm are considered.

Metatheoretical Assumptions

The social/clinical interface seeks to avoid the bifurcation of science into basic and applied. The boundary line between basic and applied research is not clear-cut, but philosophers of science highlight the different goals of basic and applied researchers (Bunge, 1974; Ziman, 1974). Simply put, the goal of basic researchers is the generation of knowledge. Guided by a particular theoretical system, they conduct research that provides critical information about the strengths and weakness of their hypotheses concerning the phenomena of interest. Applied scientists, in contrast, seek information that will increase knowledge while also proving itself to be relevant to some particular problem. In applied science, too, the research may spring from practical concerns as much as from theoretically relevant hypotheses.

This division of effort, however, leads to a variety of problems. On the basic side, researchers often gravitate unerringly toward elaborate theoretical models of behavior that have little or no applicability. Sommer (1982), for example, described a case of basic research gone awry in his analysis of historical trends in Prisoner's Dilemma (PD) research. As he noted, each study moved further and further away from the original questions concerning bargaining and negotiation. In consequence, "PD research has tended to be drawn from previous PD research, thus creating a hermetic laboratory system without the validity checks and enrichment of experimental conditions that could come from the study of actual cases" (p. 531). In a second example, Glasser (1982) found it odd that basic research in learning over the last three decades has yielded so little insight into the educational process. As he notes, as early as 1900 John Dewey recommended linking theory and educational practice to better understand learning processes. However, for many decades experimental learning theorists worked on their own questions in psychology departments, while educational researchers examined practical problems from positions in education programs. Glasser suggested that the slow progress of educational

psychology stems from this artificial separation of basic and applied research.

Hill and Weary (1983) noted that this drift toward increasing theoretical specificity accounted, in part, for the original split between social and clinical psychology. Considerable intermixing occurred in the early days of the *Journal of Abnormal and Social Psychology*; in time, though, social psychology grew away from application toward more theoretical pursuits. Zajonc, one-time editor of the journal, explained that the social psychological work became more theory-driven, whereas the clinical research "was mainly for professional purposes and seldom illustrated some theoretical point" (quoted in Hill & Weary, 1983, p. 9). As a result, the journal split into two, with one focusing on theoretical, mainstream social psychology (*Journal of Personality and Social Psychology*) and the second focusing on clinical topics (*Journal of Abnormal Psychology*).

Strong (1987), a long-time advocate of the interface of social and clinical psychology, similarly bemoaned the theoretical excesses in social psychology. Strong (p. 191) lamented that "social psychologists have become obsessed with methodological rigor, theory-driven research, and small-scope theories," with the result that the great promise of the field has turned into a false hope. Most social psychologists, when asked if their work can be applied to better understand social problems and processes, are quick to cite Lewin's (1951) maxim: There is nothing so useful as a good theory. What they forget, however, is that Lewin also charged basic researchers with the goal of developing powerful, comprehensive theories that could be tested by applying them in real-world settings. For the interface, if a theory is too narrow and trivial, too broad and general, or just too irrelevant to everyday issues, it is not a very good theory (Forsyth, 1988).

Applied research, too, suffers when separated from the basic (Hill & Weary, 1983; Weary, 1987). When findings are not placed in a larger scientific context, applied research can become too atheoretical. Indeed, when research becomes wholly applied, it also tends to drift toward technology. In science, applied problems may be the initial source of research questions, but these applied concerns are ultimately placed into a theoretical context, and the long-term goal of such research includes testing the adequacy of assumptions and hypotheses that make up the theory. In technology, on the other hand, theory and methods are used solely to develop some product — such as a new diagnostic instrument, an intake procedure that will satisfy the needs of some treatment agency, or a cost-effective structured training workshop. Technicians are concerned with solving a particular problem in a specific situation without concern for increasing our general understanding of human behavior. While technological researchers may borrow the theories of science to guide their problem-solving, their efforts are not designed to test generalizable propositions derived from these theories. Technological research may generate information that is useful in science — such as providing an indication of what variables are important in a given setting, stimulating research, or refining methodological tools and innovations — but the research is so problem and situation specific that generalizations to other settings are limited.

Without argument, the unique characteristics of psychotherapeutic settings pose special problems for researchers. Indeed, some have argued that the psychotherapy process and problems related to psychological adjustment are so special that they cannot be explained using principles of human behavior derived from the basic side of psychology. One proponent of this view wrote: "as counseling researchers we are interested in developing principles of human behavior only inasmuch as they tap principles of counseling" (Gelso, 1979, p. 14). He continued by suggesting that investigators must keep "actual counseling in central focus" with methodologies that closely approximate ongoing psychotherapy. To one who advocates such insularity, basing explanations of psychotherapeutic processes on principles drawn from basic studies of social psychological propositions is misguided (cf. Garfield, 1979, 1980; Gibbs, 1979).

The interface, however, is based on the premise that social and clinical psychologists share a similar goal: to develop and test generalizable principles of human behavior. Hence, if clinical psychologists explain behavior in terms of propositions that are essentially social psychological in nature, then findings obtained in basic studies of these general statements are necessarily relevant in evaluating the adequacy of these propositions. If, for example, basic researchers find that individuals who feel that they cannot control their outcomes on a laboratory task experience losses of motivation, then this finding lends support to the learned helplessness model of depression (Seligman, 1975). If an attitude change study shows that similarity between the communicator and the audience leads to increased persuasion, then this finding informs analyses of the client-therapist fit (Goldstein, 1971). If researchers discover that individuals who are fairly confident in their perceptions of another person tend to ask this person questions that confirm their original beliefs, then this finding offers insight into the clinical inference process (Murdock, 1988). For the interface, evidence concerning the adequacy of a general principle of human behavior should be drawn from all available sources, whether these sources be basic research or applied research within or outside clinical and counseling psychology.

In sum, if too basic, researchers sometimes develop elaborate theoretical conceptualizations that have little relationship to reality or lose sight of the social value of their findings. But if too applied, research can become theoretically simplistic, situationally restricted, and technologically oriented. The interface, recognizing the limitations of each pursuit, recommends that basic and applied research should be combined if the dynamics of health and abnormality are to be understood. The interface accepts the long-term goal of increasing knowledge and understanding, and insists that data should be relevant to some theoretical construct. The interface, too, assumes that the test of theory lies in objective, empirical methods rather than logical claims or subjective feelings, and it strives for consensus among members of the discipline concerning acceptable, unacceptable, and to-be-evaluated explanations of empirical observations.

The Role of Theory

Social psychologists have a penchant for erecting theoretical systems for understanding human behavior. Adopting a tradition that dates back to Allport's (1924) early insistence that our knowledge of social action must be systematized, social psychologists are skeptical of any observation or finding that cannot be put into a theoretical context. In consequence, much of social psychology's contribution to the analysis of clinical issues occurs at a theoretical level.

This emphasis on theoretical foundations is a potential point of dissension between clinical and social psychology (e.g., Rogers, 1973; Sarason, 1981; Strupp, 1975; Wachtel, 1980). Some clinical researchers, for example, argue that science progresses through the accumulation of evidence and fact rather than through theoretical accretion. Stressing the empirical side of science, they gather data that pertain to such questions as, Does therapy X work better than therapy Y? Is an elevated score on a certain subscale of the MMPI an indicant of psychopathology? Are therapists' religious values related to their clinical style?

Although all raise important issues, such studies cannot advance our understanding of psychotherapy unless the obtained findings are relevant to transituational statements dealing with behavior. Facts are used to spin theoretical systems or support existing frameworks, but because of their mutability and situational specificity, facts are of little long-lasting value in science. Specific facts — or, as in this case, empirical findings — are not themselves generalizable, but the hypotheses they either support or disconfirm are. For example, the investigator who finds that therapists who maintain eye contact 60% of the time are more effective than therapists who maintain eye contact 30% of the time may be tempted to tell practitioners to maintain a good deal of eye contact. Unfortunately, the specifics of the setting — the attractiveness of the therapists, the type of clients, the content of the therapists' statements during eye contact — all limit the generalizability of the "fact" that high eye contact makes counselors and clinicians more effective. If, however, the researcher had been studying a higher order theoretical proposition — such as (a) the greater the client's trust in the therapist, the more effective the therapy; (b) *ceteris paribus*, eye contact implies honesty and openness; and therefore (c) eye contact will create greater client-therapist trust and facilitate therapy — then the study has implications beyond the obtained data. In this latter case the researcher would be scientifically justified in suggesting that therapists establish a deep level of trust with clients, and that this trust could be created by appropriate nonverbal behaviors.

Thus, theory provides the organizing framework for conceptualizing problems, organizing knowledge, and suggesting solutions. Supporting this view, when decision-makers in mental health fields (federal and state administrators of psychological services programs) were asked "What makes research useful?" (Weiss & Weiss, 1981), the conceptualization of the problem (which could include the theoretical framework) was the most frequently noted attribute among both scientists (40%) and decision-makers (29%). Furthermore, when subjects actually evaluated sample studies, their judgments of usefulness were correlated with objectivity, in addition to practical, descriptive, causal, or theoretical knowledge.

Basic theory, too, provides the practitioner with an overall understanding of the therapeutic process. As Maddux (1987, p. 31) explained, because "clinical interventions without theoretical or empirical foundation are likely to be misdirected, a skillful clinical or counseling practitioner must be an astute theoretician and an empiricist."

Granted, this position contrasts sharply with the recommendation to avoid theory because it disrupts the spontaneity of the therapeutic process. As Strupp (1984, 1986) maintained, however, a "scientific attitude" is one of the key elements of a successful therapist. Indeed, Strupp (1975) worried that the erosion of excellence in applied psychotherapy programs was due to the rise of an anti-intellectualism that roadblocks the integration of science and application. Strupp wondered whether the rise of the humanistic, intuitive approaches to therapy results in such an emphasis on feelings over cognitions and emotions over reason to such a degree that models of therapy become little more than "dewy-eyed sentimentality, drivel, or worse" (p. 563). He was particularly strong in his criticism of many humanistic approaches for encouraging the viewpoint that "anyone who advocates study and scientific inquiry is perceived as an enemy of all that is good, open, spontaneous, authentic, beautiful, and enjoyable in human experience" (p. 571). He quoted in this context one sensitivity trainer who told Kurt Back (1972, p. 15), "Do not try to prove things; give yourself a chance to live the experience."

Strupp suggested that such a view makes for bad science and bad therapy. Although the actual practice of psychotherapy may not be science, it can be conducted with a "scientific attitude." A useful theory of psychological adjustment may state that increases in factors A, B, and C will benefit clients with D, E, and F characteristics, but experience in clinical settings may be needed to determine the optimal levels of A, B, and C, techniques to use in varying these factors, and ways to assess D, E, and F. Few theories in psychology are so precise that they yield mathematical statements describing the magnitude of important variables, so practitioners must be prepared to turn to situation-specific and client-specific research to obtain the precision they require.

Methodological Assumptions

A science's paradigm not only includes metatheoretical and theoretical beliefs about the phenomena under investigation, but also includes assumptions about the methodological practices that should be used in research. Traditional social psychologists, for example, prefer clearly manipulated independent variables, clever dependent measures, and the control afforded by a laboratory setting. Traditional clinical psychologists, in contrast, argue that the nature of clinical and counseling psychology requires field studies conducted in "real" therapy settings with "real" clients and "real" therapists, and that only findings that can be easily generalized to "real-life" psychotherapy are data worth discussing. Laboratory studies, to the clinician, are at best tangentially relevant to clinical practices and, at worst, completely irrelevant (e.g., Gibbs, 1979; Goldman, 1978).

The relative value of field versus laboratory is a complex question and has been debated in a number of areas of psychology (e.g., Berkowitz & Donnerstein, 1982; Bronfenbrenner, 1977; Dipboye & Flanagan, 1978; Gelso, 1979; Gibbs, 1979; Harre & Secord, 1972; Hernstein, 1977; Jenkins, 1974; McCall, 1977; McGuire, 1973; Mook, 1983; Rakover, 1980). When viewed from the holistic perspective derived from integrating social and clinical assumptions about behavior and basic and applied research strategies, however, the issue becomes less important. First of all, the context in which social behavior occurs must be thought of as only one more variable or dimension that must be interpreted within the larger theoretical scheme. Kazdin (1978, p. 684) made this point clearly when he stated that "research in psychotherapy and behavior therapy can differ from clinical application of treatment along several dimensions such as the target problem, the clients and the manner in which they are recruited, the therapists, the selection treatment, the client's set, and the setting in which treatment is conducted." Importantly, however, increasing the "similarity of an investigation to the clinical situation . . . does not necessarily argue for greater generality of the results." In essence, the importance of the setting must be established empirically (Bass & Firestone, 1980; Berkowitz & Donnerstein, 1982; Flanagan & Dipboye, 1980).

Second, as Mook (1983), Rakover (1980), and Forsyth and Strong (1986) maintained, where a study is conducted is not necessarily related to the theoretical import of the study. Studies conducted in laboratory settings, for example, may still be relevant to nonlaboratory behaviors (or so-called real behaviors, as if laboratory behaviors were not) if they examine theoretical generalizations that are relevant to these applied problems. Mook (1983, pp. 386–387) suggested that researchers should continually ask themselves, "Am I . . . trying to estimate from sample characteristics the characteristics of some population? Or am I trying to draw conclusions not about a population, but about a theory that specifies what these subjects ought to do?" If the investigator is concerned with theoretical issues, then generalizability is determined more by the structure of the theory—its scope, specificity, and universality—than by location of the supporting research.

There is little room for methodological snobbery in the interface of social and clinical psychology. The interface suggests that—like eclectic therapists who integrate many theories of psychological functioning when interacting with clients—researchers must also remain eclectic; they must use any and all scientific means possible to gather information concerning the theoretical system under investigation. Whether experimental, correlational, field, laboratory, role-play, or analogue, no opportunity to further our understanding of psychotherapy should be bypassed. As Hilgard (1971, p. 4) noted, in order to "satisfy the criteria of 'good science'" the researcher "must cover the world spectrum of basic and applied science by doing sound (and conclusive) work all along the line."

THE HEALTH PERSPECTIVE

Significant advances often occur in science when scientists in different fields abandon their independent efforts to understand a phenomenon and join together in a united effort. Biochemistry, astrophysics, biophysics, and the social/clinical interface are all examples of scientific fields that resulted from this melding process (Spring, Chiodo, & Bowen, 1987). As noted in earlier sections, the increased unification of social psychology and clinical psychology raises a number of metatheoretical, theoretical, and methodological issues. However, proponents of the social/clinical interface are united in their belief that significant scientific progress can be achieved through a collaborative, cross-disciplinary integration of social psychological principles and clinical diagnosis, prevention, and treatment (Dorn, 1984; Higginbotham, West, & Forsyth, 1988; Leary & Maddux, 1987; Leary & Miller, 1986; Maddux, Stoltenberg, & Rosenwein, 1987; Sheras & Worchel, 1979; Snyder & Ford, 1987; Weary & Mirels, 1982).

A number of assumptions provide the undergirding conceptual structure for much of the research and theoretical interface work. Without question, the field's emerging status and its multidisciplinary roots guarantee disagreements over these assumptions. Nevertheless, by identifying candidates for the conceptual cornerstones of this emerging field, we can better organize and integrate the various topics currently investigated by social and clinical psychologists, and identify directions for future growth.

Our view is that the concerns of the social/clinical psychologists are also the concerns of the health psychologist. Matazarro (1980, p. 815), who defined health psychology as the "aggregate of the . . . contributions of the discipline of psychology to the promotion and maintenance of health, the prevention and treatment of illness, and the identification of etiologic and diagnostic correlates of health, illness, and related dysfunctions," could have been defining the social/clinical interface.

Our belief is that health psychology is the wave of the future; in fact, the ripples from a health psychology perspective are already lapping at the shores of psychology. What is especially noteworthy in regard to health psychology is the fact that it has integrated social and clinical psychology from its inception. More than any other area of inquiry, social and clinical psychologists are working together to advance our understanding of health. In this vein, it should be noted that the ideas expressed in this paragraph are shared by leading thinkers at the social/clinical interface (e.g., Harvey, Bratt, & Lennox, 1987; Hendrick & Hendrick, 1984; Matarazzo, 1983; Meyerowitz, Burish, & Wallston, 1986; Rogers, 1983; Spring, Chiodo, & Bowen, 1987).

Although we will employ a health psychology perspective, the reader will recognize the rather easy fit of the social-clinical interface in the various sections of the book. Inherent in our general health approach is the belief that behaviors, including many of those that are often considered "abnormal" or "pathological," are best understood by examining processes that apply to most people. That certain forms of behavior have a genetic and biological underpinning cannot be denied; nor do we mean to argue against the view that a few behaviors are bizarre. Rather, our meaning is that the key to understanding the bulk of human behavior lies in normal processes that may or may not be working for people. As Maddux (1987, p. 30) put it:

> So-called "abnormal" . . . patterns are essentially distortions or exaggerations of normal patterns or normal patterns that are displayed at times and in places considered by those in charge (norm enforcers) to be inappropriate. Thus, the rules that govern normal . . . behavior—whatever those rules might be—also govern or can be used to explain and predict behaviors and social interactions that become identified as abnormal.

This general health psychology approach to the social-clinical interface suggests a health-help-health cycle that serves as organizing principle for arranging the individual chapters in this book. *Health*, when viewed from a social/clinical perspective, consists of the psychological/physical state that the person is motivated to sustain or change. Several points of elaboration are necessary at this point in order to clarify our use of the term *health*. Contrary to the conception of health as being a positive state of well-being, which is probably held by both laypeople and most psychologists (especially many of those in the health area), we employ this term in a more neutral sense. For example, the first definition of health in the unabridged Random House dictionary is "the general condition of the body or mind with reference to soundness and vigor." In this sense, one's health is not necessarily synonymous with "good health," but it may vary from very poor to very good health. Also, as we use the term *health*, we mean to convey, much like the "mind and body" phrasing of the dictionary definition, that the referent of health may either be psychological or physical; moreover, in most instances we would argue that the psychological/physical components are interactively and reciprocally bound up with each other.

For our present purposes, we would suggest that health may be relatively positive, or relatively negative; moreover, one's state of health may be temporarily confined or more enduring. Among the myriad of possible motivationally driven sequences, the following are most salient: good health→good health; bad health→good health; bad health→bad health; good health→bad health. In other words, different people may be motivated to act upon their present good or bad level of health so as to continue or change the present level of health. Help in this sense reflects the person's attempts to sustain or change the state of health (psychological/physical). Additionally, the helping process can originate within the person or it can derive from interpersonal sources. Whatever the outcome of the help, it impacts the person's initial sense of health. Thus, as the model shown in Figure 1.1 suggests, the health-help-health cycle is a cybernetic system that maintains health through a dynamic interlinking of the personal and environmental (e.g., interpersonal and therapeutic) processes.

As shown in Figure 1.1, the health-help-health model takes a holistic perspective in which health (including adaptive and dysfunctional states as we define it) and the various types of help are components of a unified system that cannot be fully understood by piecemeal examination. Rather than emphasizing endogenous factors relative to exogenous factors or vice versa, the interface considers the interaction of both intrapersonal and interpersonal factors. This view, of course, is consistent with the Gestalt principles that form the foundation of Kurt Lewin's field theory. Lewin (1936) believed that behavior (B) must be considered to be a function of both the personal qualities of the individual (P) and the characteristics of the environment (E), and he summarized this assumption in his formula $B = f(P, E)$. Applied to the health-help-health cycle, this formula implies that one's current level of health is a product of processes operating within the individual (e.g., affect, cognition, personality, temperament) interacting with such environmental factors as social support, stressors, and assistance provided by health-care professionals (Hendrick & Hendrick, 1984). All of these factors, when considered as a totality, form what Lewin called the lifespace.

The health-help-health framework that we have posited provides an organizational framework for examining much of the work that is evolving at the interface of social and clinical psychology. This organizing model contains both person-based processes (e.g., self-related and individual differences issues) and environment-based processes (e.g., interpersonal, diagnosis, and treatment issues).

In the first major section of the *Handbook*, entitled "Person-Based Processes," the reader will be given a sample of the new work that is redefining our views of the self, and the role that the self plays in maintaining health; moreover, some of the major individual difference dimensions for conceptualizing the person and health also will be presented in this section.

These person-based or intrapersonal processes may seem ordinary and mundane (and possibly of limited clinical interest), but they nonetheless serve crucial health-maintaining functions. Often psychologists implicitly adopt the medical world's view of the person as passive; an unfortunate individual who has "taken ill" and must be cured by experts. In the health-help-health model, however, people actively react to problems in living, seeking to maintain or enhance their level of well-being. As Califano (1979, p. viii) suggested in his analysis of health, "You, the individual, can do more for your own health and well-being than any doctor, any hospital, any drug, and exotic medical device."

In the second major section, entitled "Environment-Based Processes," the focus will move from the *intra*personal to the *inter*personal realm in order to examine external sources for garnering help. Individuals' success in coping with the large and small problems they invariably encounter on a near-daily basis also depends on their interrelationships with other individuals, including friends, acquaintances, and intimate companions (Brehm, 1984; Hendrick & Hendrick, 1984; Meyerowitz, Burish, & Wallston, 1986; Rogers, 1983, 1984). The first portion of the "Environment-Based Process" will contain chapters dealing with such interpersonal issues. Turning from the analysis of informal, day-to-day health-maintaining interpersonal processes to more formal, professional health-care processes, we will address the identification of problems and treatment approaches. In this latter vein, the second and third subsections of the "Environment-Based Processes" will include chapters describing diagnostic and treatment issues, respectively.

In summary, the health-help-health framework is a heuristic for organizing the ongoing interface research pertaining to the intrapersonal (person-based) and interpersonal (environment-based) processes whereby people obtain help to sustain or change their health.

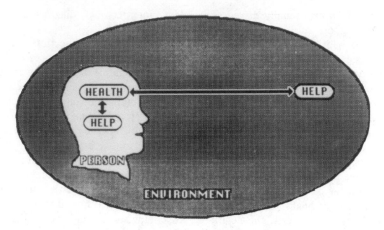

Figure 1.1. The health-help-health model of person-based and environment-based processes.

ON BEING WHERE
YOU ALREADY ARE

We are tempted to paint some bold new picture of the interface between social and clinical psychology, and to argue (like Kuhn, 1970) that some sort of major paradigm shift or revolution is taking place. But the nature of the "ah ha" experience for the present editors is somewhat more humble in regard to the present status of the interface. Remember the fable of the elephant and the blind men? A first blind man, putting his arms around the elephant's thick leg, says, "It must be a tree." The second, touching the elephant's vast side, concludes, "It must be a wall." And a third argues, "No, it is a snake" as he grasps the elephant's trunk. Indeed, as each successive blind man touches it, he finds a somewhat different "elephant." Ironically, each protagonist in this story does not realize that he is touching the same thing. In this parable, therefore, we would submit to the reader that the elephant is like the social/clinical interface. Our point is a simple one: There are many professionals who are already doing work at the social/clinical interface, but they do not know it (Snyder, 1988). For such people, reading the following pages may be like visiting rooms in a house that seems strangely familiar.

REFERENCES

Allport, F. A. (1924). *Social psychology*. Boston: Houghton Mifflin.

Allport, G. W. (1954). *The nature of prejudice*. Reading, MA: Addison-Wesley.

Allport, G. W. (1985). The historical background of modern social psychology. In G. Lindzey & E. Aronson (Eds.), *Handbook of social psychology* (Vol. 1, 3rd ed., pp. 1–46). New York: Random House.

American Psychological Association. (1947). Recommended graduate training programs in clinical psychology. *American Psychologist, 2*, 539–558.

Back, K. (1972). *Beyond words: The story of sensitivity training and the encounter movement*. New York: Russell Sage Foundation.

Bass, A. R., & Firestone, I. J. (1980). Implications of representativeness for generalizability of field and laboratory research findings. *American Psychologist, 35*, 463–464.

Berkowitz, L., & Donnerstein, E. (1982). External validity is more than skin deep. *American Psychologist, 37*, 245–257.

Brehm, S. S. (1976). *The application of social psychology to clinical practice*. Washington, DC: Hemisphere.

Brehm, S. S. (1984). New frontiers on the interface: Social support processes. *Society for the Advancement of Social Psychology Newsletter, 10*(1), 23–26.

Brehm, S. S., & Smith, T. W. (1986). Social psychological approaches to psychotherapy and behavior change. In S. L. Garfield & A. E. Bergin (Eds.), *Handbook of psychotherapy and behavior change* (3rd ed., pp. 69–115). New York: John Wiley & Sons.

Bronfenbrenner, U. (1977). Toward an experimental ecology of human development. *American Psychologist, 32*, 513–531.

Bunge, M. (1974). Towards a philosophy of technology. In A. C. Michalos (Ed.), *Philosophical problems of science and technology* (pp. 28–46). Boston: Allyn & Bacon.

Buros, O. K. (Ed.). (1938). *The mental measurements yearbook*. New Brunswick, NJ: Rutgers University Press.

Byrne, D. (1971). *The attraction paradigm*. New York: Academic Press.

Califano, J. A. (1979). *Healthy people: The Surgeon General's report on health promotion and disease prevention*. Washington, DC: U.S. Government Printing Office (Stock No. 017-001-00416-2).

Carlson, R. (1984). What's social about social psychology? Where's the person in personality research? *Journal of Personality and Social Psychology, 47*, 1304–1309.

Cartwright, D., & Zander, A. (Eds.). (1968). *Group dynamics* (3rd ed.). New York: Harper & Row.

Cartwright, D. (1979). Contemporary social psychology in historical perspective. *Social Psychology Quarterly, 42*, 82–93.

Dipboye, R. L., & Flanagan, M. R. (1978). Research settings in industrial and organizational psychology: Are findings in the field more generalizable than in the laboratory? *American Psychologist, 34*, 141–150.

Dorn, F. J. C. (1984). *Counseling as applied social psychology*. Springfield, IL: Charles C. Thomas.

Festinger, L. (1957). *A theory of cognitive dissonance*. Stanford, CA: Stanford University Press.

Flanagan, M. R., & Dipboye, R. L. (1980). Representativeness does have implications for the generalizability of laboratory and field research findings. *American Psychologist, 35*, 464–466.

Forsyth, D. R. (1988). Social psychology's three little pigs. *Journal of Social Behavior and Personality, 3*, 63–65.

Forsyth, D. R., & Strong, S. R. (1986). The scientific study of counseling and psychotherapy: A unificationist view. *American Psychologist, 41*, 113–119.

Garfield, S. L. (1979). Editorial. *Journal of Consulting and Clinical Psychology, 47*, 104.

Garfield, S. L. (1980). *Psychotherapy: An eclectic approach*. New York: John Wiley & Sons.

Gelso, C. J. (1979). Research in counseling: Methodological and professional issues. *The Counseling Psychologist, 8*, 7–36.

Gibbs, J. C. (1979). The meaning of ecologically oriented inquiry in contemporary psychology. *American Psychologist, 34*, 127–140.

Glasser, R. (1982). Instructional psychology. *American Psychologist, 37*, 292–305.

Goldman, L. (Ed.). (1978). *Research methods for counselors*. New York: John Wiley & Sons.

Goldstein, A. P. (1971). *Psychotherapeutic attraction*. New York: Pergamon Press.

Goldstein, A. P., Heller, K., & Sechrest, L. B. (1966). *Psychotherapy and the psychology of behavior change*. New York: John Wiley & Sons.

Harre, R., & Secord, P. F. (1972). *The explanation of social behavior*. Oxford, England: Blackwell.

Harvey, J. H., Bratt, A., & Lennox, R. D. (1987). The maturing interface of social-clinical-counseling psychology. *Journal of Social and Clinical Psychology, 5*, 8–20.

Heider, F. (1958). *The psychology of interpersonal relations*. New York: John Wiley & Sons.

Hendrick, C., & Hendrick, S. (1984). Toward a clinical social psychology of health and disease. *Journal of Social and Clinical Psychology, 2*, 182–192.

Hernstein, R. J. (1977). The evolution of behaviorism. *American Psychologist, 32*, 593–603.

Higginbotham, H. N., West, S. G., & Forsyth, D. R. (1988). *Psychotherapy and behavior change: Social, cultural, and methodological perspectives*. Elmsford, NY: Pergamon Press.

Hilgard, E. R. (1971). Toward a responsible social science. *Journal of Applied Social Psychology, 1*, 1–6.

Hill, M. G., & Weary, G. (1983). Perspectives on the Journal of Abnormal and Social Psychology: How it began and how it was transformed. *Journal of Social and Clinical Psychology, 1*, 4–14.

Hovland, C. I., Janis, I. L., & Kelley, H. H. (1953). *Communication and persuasion*. New Haven, CT: Yale University Press.

Jenkins, J. J. (1974). Remember that old theory of memory? Well, forget it! *American Psychologist, 29*, 785–795.

Jones, E. E. (1985). Major developments in social psychology during the past five decades. In G. Lindzey & E. Aronson (Eds.), *Handbook of social psychology* (Vol. 1, 3rd ed., pp. 47–108). New York: Random House.

Kazdin, D. E. (1978). Evaluating the generality of findings in analogue therapy research. *Journal of Consulting and Clinical Psychology, 46,* 673–686.

Kenrick, D. T. (1986). How strong is the case against contemporary social and personality psychology? A response to Carlson. *Journal of Personality and Social Psychology, 50,* 839–844.

Kuhn, T. S. (1970). *The structure of scientific revolutions* (2nd ed.). Chicago: University of Chicago Press.

Le Bon, G. (1895). *The crowd.* London: Ernest Benn.

Leary, M. R., & Maddux, J. E. (1987). Progress toward a viable interface between social and clinical-counseling psychology. *American Psychologist, 42,* 904–911.

Leary, M. R., & Miller, R. S. (1986). *Social psychology and dysfunctional behavior: Origins, diagnosis, and treatment.* New York: Springer-Verlag.

Lewin, K. (1936). *A dynamic theory of personality.* New York: McGraw-Hill.

Lewin, K. (1951). *Field theory in social science.* New York: Harper & Row.

Lewin, K., Lippitt, R., & White, R. (1939). Patterns of aggressive behavior in experimentally created "social climates." *Journal of Social Psychology, 10,* 271–299.

Louttit, C. M. (1936). *Clinical psychology: A handbook of children's behavior problems.* New York: Harper & Row.

Maddux, J. E. (1987). The interface of social, clinical, and counseling psychology: Why bother and what is it anyway? *Journal of Social and Clinical Psychology, 5,* 27–33.

Maddux, J. E., Stoltenberg, C. D., & Rosenwein, R. (1987). *Social processes in clinical and counseling psychology.* New York: Springer-Verlag.

Matarazzo, J. D. (1980). Behavioral health and health medicine: Frontiers for a new health psychology. *American Psychologist, 35,* 807–817.

Matarazzo, J. D. (1983). Interfaces of social, health, and clinical psychology. *Contemporary Social Psychology, 10,* 11.

McCall, R. B. (1977). Challenges to a science of developmental psychology. *Child Development, 48,* 333–344.

McGuire, W. J. (1973). The yin and yang of progress in social psychology: Seven Koan. *Journal of Personality and Social Psychology, 26,* 446–456.

McReynolds, P. (1987). Lightner Witomer: Little known founder of clinical psychology. *American Psychologist, 42,* 849–858.

Meyerowitz, B. E., Burish, T. G., & Wallston, K. A. (1986). Health psychology: A tradition of integration of clinical and social psychology. *Journal of Social and Clinical Psychology, 4,* 375–392.

Mook, D. G. (1983). In defense of external invalidity. *American Psychologist, 38,* 379–387.

Murdock, N. L. (1988). Category-based effects in clinical judgment. *Counseling Psychology Quarterly, 1,* 341–355.

Murphy, G., & Murphy, L. B. (1931). *Experimental social psychology.* New York: Harper & Row.

Newcomb, T. (1943). *Personality and social change.* New York: Dryden.

Raimy, V. C. (Ed.). (1950). *Training in clinical psychology.* Englewood Cliffs, NJ: Prentice-Hall.

Rakover, S. S. (1980). Generalization from analogue therapy to the clinical situation: The paradox and the dilemma of generality. *Journal of Consulting and Clinical Psychology, 48,* 770–771.

Reisman, J. M. (1976). *A history of clinical psychology.* New York: Irvington.

Rogers, C. R. (1942). *Counseling and psychotherapy.* Boston: Houghton Mifflin.

Rogers, C. R. (1973). Some new challenges. *American Psychologist, 28,* 379–387.

Rogers, R. W. (1983). Preventive health psychology: An interface of social and clinical psychology. *Journal of Social and Clinical Psychology, 1,* 120–127.

Rogers, R. W. (1984). Preventive health psychology: Reconciling the psychologist's and the health professional's perspectives. *Journal of Social and Clinical Psychology, 2,* 361–365.

Rorschach, H. (1921). *Psychodiagnostics: A diagnostic test based on perception.* P. Lemkau & B. Kronenburg (Trans., 1942). New York: Grune & Stratton.

Sarason, S. B. (1981). An asocial psychology and a misdirected clinical psychology. *American Psychologist, 36,* 827–836.

Seashore, C. E. (1919). *The psychology of musical talent*. New York: Silver, Burdett.

Seligman, M. E. P. (1975). *Human helplessness*. San Francisco: W. H. Freeman.

Shakow, D. (1978). Clinical psychology seen some 50 years later. *American Psychologist, 33*, 148–158.

Sheras, P. L., & Worchel, S. (1979). *Clinical psychology: A social psychological approach*. New York: Van Nostrand.

Sherif, M. (1936). *The psychology of social norms*. New York: Harper & Row.

Snyder, C. R. (1988). On being where you already are: An invitation to the social/clinical/counseling interface. *Journal of Social and Clinical Psychology, 6*, i–ii.

Snyder, C. R., & Ford, C. E. (Eds.). (1987). *Coping with negative life events: Clinical and social psychological perspectives*. New York: Plenum Press.

Snyder, C. R., & Fromkin, H. L. (1980). *Uniqueness: The human pursuit of difference*. New York: Plenum Press.

Sommer, R. (1982). The district attorney's dilemma: Experimental games and the real world of plea bargaining. *American Psychologist, 37*, 526–532.

Spring, B., Chiodo, J., & Bowen, D. J. (1987). The social-clinical-psychobiology interface: Implications for health psychology. *Journal of Social and Clinical Psychology, 5*, 1–7.

Strong, S. R. (1987). Social-psychological approach to counseling and psychotherapy: "A false hope?" *Journal of Social and Clinical Psychology, 5*, 185–194.

Strupp, H. H. (1975). Clinical psychology, irrationalism, and the erosion of excellence. *American Psychologist, 31*, 561–571.

Strupp, H. H. (1984). Psychotherapy research: Reflections on my career and the state of the art. *Journal of Social and Clinical Psychology, 2*, 3–24.

Strupp, H. H. (1986). Psychotherapy: Research, practice, and public policy (How to avoid dead ends). *American Psychologist, 41*, 120–130.

Thibaut, J. W., & Kelley, H. H. (1957). *The social psychology of groups*. New York: John Wiley & Sons.

Thurstone, L. L. (1928). Attitudes can be measured. *American Journal of Sociology, 33*, 529–554.

Triplett, N. (1897). The dynamogenic factors in pacemaking and competition. *American Journal of Psychology, 9*, 507–533.

Wachtel, P. J. (1980). Investigation and its discontents: Some constraints on progress in psychological research. *American Psychologist, 35*, 399–408.

Watson, R. I. (1951). *The clinical method in psychology*. New York: Harper & Row.

Weary, G. (1987). Natural bridges: The interface of social and clinical psychology. *Journal of Social and Clinical Psychology, 5*, 160–167.

Weary, G., & Mirels, H. L. (Eds.). (1982). *Integrations of clinical and social psychology*. New York: Oxford University Press.

Weiss, J. A., & Weiss, C. H. (1981). Social scientists and decision makers look at the usefulness of mental health research. *American Psychologist, 36*, 837–847.

Woodworth, R. S. (1920). *Personal data sheet*. Chicago: Stoelting.

Ziman, J. (1974). What is science? In A. C. Michalos (Ed.), *Philosophical problems of science and technology* (pp. 5–27). Boston: Allyn & Bacon.

PART II

PERSON-BASED PROCESSES

CHAPTER 2

TERROR MANAGEMENT THEORY OF SELF-ESTEEM

Sheldon Solomon
Jeff Greenberg
Tom Pyszczynski

Many researchers and clinicians would agree that self-esteem mediates many social behaviors and is a vitally important determinant of mental health. In addition, a number of quite fruitful theory-guided lines of research concerning self-esteem have been developed (e.g., Brockner's work on behavioral plasticity [1979], Bandura's work on self-efficacy [1982], and Tesser's work on self-evaluation maintenance [Tesser & Campbell, 1983]). Based on this research and on 10 to 11 thousand other studies that have investigated the relationship between feelings of self-esteem and various behaviors since the 1950s (cf. Scheff, 1990), we conclude that individuals are generally motivated to maintain self-esteem and that measures of self-esteem covary positively with other indicators of well-being.

Beyond that, however, little is known about what self-esteem is, what psychological purposes it serves, and how it is related to social behavior and mental and physical health. As Scheff (1990) and others (see, e.g., Diggory, 1966; Crandall, 1973; Savin-Williams & Demo, 1983; Jackson, 1984; Wells & Marwell, 1976; Wylie, 1979) have

forcefully contended, an exhaustive, empirically driven review of the self-esteem literature, with its hundreds of measures, procedures, and often contradictory results, would be a fruitless waste of paper demonstrating the "utter bankruptcy of it all" (Diggory, 1966) and leaving fundamental questions about the nature of self-esteem unbroached. Crandall (1973) neatly summed up the existing state of affairs in this area when he observed that "Despite the popularity of self-esteem, no standard theoretical or operational definition exists."

We have recently proposed a *terror management* theory of self-esteem and social behavior (Greenberg, Pyszczynski, & Solomon, 1986; Solomon, Greenberg, & Pyszczynski, in press) as a conceptual framework that offers answers to some basic questions about self-esteem and can be used to make sense of the existing literature and guide research and clinical practice in meaningful directions. In this chapter, we will present our conception of what self-esteem is and what functions it serves, followed by a summary of relevant empirical work. We will then explain how a variety of psychological and physical problems result from a lack of self-esteem. Finally, we will explore some of the implications of these notions for clinical practice and social science.

THE FUNCTION OF SELF-ESTEEM

Terror management theory is derived primarily from the work of Ernest Becker (1962, 1964, 1971, 1973, 1975). Becker attempted to synthesize the psychoanalytic work of Freud, Rank, Adler, Fromm, and Horney; the philosophical inquiry of Neitzche, Kierkegaard, and Norman Brown; the social psychiatry of Harry Stack Sullivan; and the sociological analyses of Erving Goffman, Peter Berger, and Thomas Luckmann into a broad integrated theoretical conception of human social behavior.

Starting from a basic evolutionary perspective, Becker hypothesized that human survival has been greatly facilitated by our intelligence, particularly our ability to think in symbolic or abstract terms, anticipate future events, and imagine what does not yet exist and then realize such possibilities. However, the complex structure of the brain that allows us to be intelligent also renders us self-conscious. Being directly aware of our existence includes the associated existential baggage of being aware of our inevitable ultimate fate: death and nonexistence. Not only are humans aware that they will all ultimately die, but they also are aware that death often occurs unexpectedly and uncontrollably. The lucky person is thus unwillingly born into a frenzied free-for-all where one competes against others for survival in a world with limited resources, destined to live for an infinitesimally small period of time (from an absolute perspective at least) followed by an inevitable death with its associated decay and physical decomposition. The unlucky person is born in similar circumstances, only to be negated unexpectedly by an earthquake, tidal wave, sniper's bullet, or an infinite number of other possible lethal experiences.

Becker speculated that human beings would be riddled with abject terror if they were constantly aware of their mortality and the possibility of death at any time. Consequently, cultural worldviews began to evolve as means to ameliorate the anxiety associated with the uniquely human awareness of death. For Becker, then, culture is a symbolic perceptual construction shared by groups of people to serve the essentially defensive function of minimizing the anxiety associated with the awareness of death.

The cultural worldview provides the basis for minimizing anxiety by imbuing the universe with order, stability, and permanence. Accordingly, all cultures have an explanation of how the earth was created, have prescriptions for how one should behave, and have explanations for what happens to people after they die. For example, in the Judeo-Christian tradition we are taught that God created the earth in 6 days and then took a break. The Fulani tribe in Mali believe that the earth was created out of a giant drop of milk. What all creation myths share in common is patent absurdity from a scientific point of view; they simply cannot be true. What is important here is the recognition that culture is not generally directed toward revealing the truth, but rather toward obscuring the horrifying possibility that we live in a random and indeterminant universe, in which the only certainty is death.

Two points should be noted here. First, we are not suggesting (nor is Becker) that culture is purely symbolic and only serves a death-denying function. Rather, we are claiming that this is a vitally important aspect of culture and that no adequate explanation of culture and/or of human behavior can be complete without a recognition of its death-denying symbolic qualities. This position is in marked contrast to some current anthropological conceptions of culture, especially Harris' cultural materialism (1979), which emphasizes the material aspects of culture while insisting on the ridiculous notion that the symbolic aspects of culture are of little use for understanding human behavior.

Second, terror management theory views the fear of death as the emotional manifestation of the instinct for self-preservation. Accordingly, all anxiety is ultimately derived from, and related to, the fear of death (see Solomon, Greenberg, & Pyszczynski, in press; Yalom, 1980; or Becker, 1973, for a more complete discussion of this idea).

Culture reduces anxiety for the individual by offering protection and hope of immortality, either symbolically or in reality, to those who live up to cultural prescriptions of value. Symbolically, culture provides opportunities for the production of tangible expressions of our existence that transcend our physical lives. Monuments, works of art and literature, estates, children, and so forth are all examples of symbolic immortality (Plato discussed this idea several thousand years ago). Additionally, cultures promote the notion that good things happen to good people and bad things do not (cf. Lerner, 1980). Finally, most organized religions claim that adherents who behave properly will literally be rewarded with eternal life. For example, Christianity promises eternal life for those who lead the "good life" on earth, whereas the Hindus promise eternal life unencumbered by bodily existence for those who reach nirvana.

Note that while perceiving oneself as a part of a meaningful universe is necessary for anxiety-free action, it is not sufficient. People must also feel that they are serving a uniquely valuable role in the context of that meaningful universe in order to qualify for safety and immortality and thus function with equanimity. To help individuals achieve this, all cultures provide prescriptions for "appropriate" behavior and valued roles; and people can feel valuable only by living up to those standards and role expectations.

The psychiatrist Alan Wheelis made a remarkably similar observation about the nature and function of culture in his novel *The Scheme of Things*:

> The scheme of things is a system of order. Beginning as our view of the world, it finally becomes our world. We live within the space defined by its coordinates. It is self-evidently true, is accepted so naturally and automatically that one is not aware of an act of acceptance having taken place. It comes with one's mother's milk, is chanted in school, proclaimed from the White House, insinuated by television, validated at Harvard. Like the air we breathe, the scheme of things disappears, becomes simply reality, the way things are. It is the lie necessary to life. The world as it exists beyond that scheme becomes vague, irrelevant, largely unperceived, finally nonexistent. . . .
>
> > No scheme of things has ever been both coextensive with the way things are and also true to the way things are. All schemes of things involve limitation and denial. . . .
>
> A scheme of things is a plan for salvation. How well it works will depend upon its scope and authority. If it is small, even great achievement in its service does little to dispel death. A scheme of things may be as large as Christianity or as small as the Alameda County Bowling League. We seek the largest possible scheme of things, not in a reaching out for truth, but because the more comprehensive the scheme the greater its promise of banishing dread. If we can make our lives mean something in a cosmic scheme we will live in the certainty of immortality. Those attributes of a scheme of things that determine its durability and success are its scope, the opportunity it

> offers for participation and contribution, and the conviction with which it is held as self-evidently true. . . . (cf. Hofstadter, 1985, p. 57)

Based on the preceding analysis, we propose that self-esteem consists of the perception that one is a valuable part of a meaningful universe, and that self-esteem serves the essentially defensive purpose of buffering anxiety. An important question to consider at this point is *how* the perception that one is a valuable part of a meaningful universe comes to serve an anxiety-reducing function for the individual.

Terror management theory asserts that as children we come to associate being good with being safe as a consequence of the socialization process. Specifically, as Freud and others (e.g., Bowlby, 1973) have suggested, little children become especially anxious when basic needs or wants are not met, and that part of this anxiety is due to the fear that their parents will abandon them. Darwin also felt that it made evolutionary sense for profoundly immature and utterly dependent creatures (human infants) to be especially anxious in such circumstances because their distress probably would be noticed by caretakers and would be attended to accordingly.

During socialization, children's behavior must be altered to conform to social dictates (e.g., no tap dancing on the white sofa with muddy shoes) and to protect their physical well-being (e.g., no sitting on the barbeque grill while the coals are lit). Consequently, children are rewarded for engaging in socially appropriate behaviors and punished for engaging in socially inappropriate behaviors. At this time in their lives, children view their parents as all-encompassing repositories of strength and wisdom. To be rewarded by parents for being good (i.e., for behaving according to cultural prescription) is thus functionally equivalent to basking in the omniscient glow of our parents' approval and its associated power. Hence, behaving according to cultural dictates (being good) results in parental approval, which results in feeling safe and secure. Not behaving according to cultural dictates renders children anxious and insecure by virtue of a loss of parental approval and the associated possibility of abandonment and annihilation. Consequently, children must learn to control their behavior so that they can maintain parental approval and thereby keep their anxieties to a minimum (i.e., by being a "good" person and behaving according to cultural demands). Children seem to accomplish this by internalizing the parental standards of value and learning to judge themselves accordingly; once having done so they are capable of viewing themselves as good and therefore protected, or as bad and therefore in danger (because of the threat of punishment or loss of protection). In this way, self-esteem (the perception that one is good) becomes an anxiety-buffer.

Theoretically, this analysis is generally consistent with the work of such diverse theorists as Cooley, Mead, Horney, Sullivan, and Kohut. While the agreement of psychoanalytic and symbolic interactionist theorists in this regard is noteworthy, perhaps even more impressive is that theorists concerned with artificial intelligence also have converged on these ideas. For example, Marvin Minsky (1987), who attempts to understand human behavior based on studies of artificial intelligence observed the following in *The Society of Mind*:

> Suppose a child were playing in a certain way, and a stranger appeared and began to scold and criticize. The child would become frightened and disturbed and try to escape. But if, in the same situation, the child's parent arrived and proceeded to scold and criticize, the result would be different. Instead of being frightened, the child would feel guilty and ashamed, and instead of trying to escape, the child would try to change what it was doing, in attempts to seek reassurance and approval. . . . If my theory is right, the presence of the attachment-person actually switches the effect of learning over to different sets of agents. . . . So far as I know, *this is a new theory about attachment. It asserts that there are particular types of learning that can proceed only in the presence of the particular individuals to whom one has become attached* [italics added]. . . . (p. 175)
> Then, our attachment mechanisms force us to focus on our parents' ways, and this leads us to build crude images of what those parents themselves are like. That way, the values and goals of a culture pass from one generation to the next. They are not learned the way skills are learned. We learn our earliest values under the influence of attachment-related signals that represent, not our own success or failure, but our parents' love or rejection. . . . Many people dislike the thought of being dominated from within by the image of a parent's wish. Yet, in exchange, that slavery is just what makes us relatively free (as compared with other animals) from being forced to obey so many other kinds of unlearned, built-in instinct-goals. (p. 181)

Children thus learn through the socialization process to equate being good with being safe by virtue of their interactions with their parents and/or significant others. Over time, however, children realize that their parents are imperfect and mortal and cannot protect them from all aversive experiences, especially their own inevitable deaths. It is at this point that a vague fear of annihilation via abandonment is replaced by an existential fear of death. From this point on the anxiety-buffering properties of self-esteem must be sufficient to minimize the terror of the ultimate threat of inevitable and absolute annihilation. This can only be accomplished by expanding the basis of self-esteem. Only then can self-esteem help one to transcend death.

Children respond to the realization of their parents' limitations and their own mortality in two ways: ambivalence toward the parents and a shift in the basis of self-esteem from the parents to the culture. Ambivalence is caused by our anger that our parents cannot really give us what we genuinely want and thought that they could provide — unlimited resources, permanent protection from all negative events now and in the future, and eternal life. Parents consequently lose the power to provide self-esteem, at least totally. Children experience terror as a result, and that terror impels the children to broaden their basis of self-esteem, primarily by attempting to adhere directly to the religious and secular values and standards espoused by their culture. In this way their goodness can earn them the approval and protection of God and powerful others (e.g., the president). For the vast majority of children, this transition is relatively easy because most parents teach their kids about religion, patriotism, and other death-denying symbolic possibilities before their first existential crisis. From this point on, self-esteem is a perception that one is fulfilling the requirements of value of the accepted cultural worldview.

Summary of the Terror Management Theory of Self-Esteem

To summarize, the uniquely human need for self-esteem is a consequence of the anxiety associated with the uniquely human awareness of mortality conferred by self-consciousness. Self-esteem is made possible by the development of cultural worldviews, which provide a stable and meaningful conception of the universe, social roles with specific prescriptions for behaviors that are deemed valuable, and the promise of safety and immortality to those who satisfy those prescriptions. Self-esteem is therefore a cultural contrivance consisting of two components: a meaningful conception of the universe combined with the perception that one is meeting the standards for value within that culturally contrived reality. The primary function of self-esteem is to buffer anxiety.

SELF-ESTEEM AS AN ANXIETY BUFFER

Both correlational and experimental research support the notion that self-esteem helps people minimize anxiety. First, there is a consistent relationship between chronic self-esteem and anxiety. Individuals with chronically low self-esteem are especially prone to anxiety in general (e.g., French, 1968; Lipsitt, 1958; Rosenberg & Simmons, 1972; Strauss, Frame, & Forehand, 1987), and death anxiety in particular (Templer, 1971); they also have particularly pessimistic views of the future (Coopersmith, 1967). Second, studies of the emotional mediation of the self-serving attributional bias (e.g., Fries & Frey, 1980; Gollwitzer, Earle, & Stephan, 1982) and affective reactions to self-esteem–threatening tests (e.g., Bennett & Holmes, 1975; Burish & Houston, 1979; Leary, Barnes, & Griebel, 1986) demonstrate that situationally imposed threats to self-esteem also engender anxiety.

DeLongis, Folkman, and Lazarus (1988) recently investigated the relationship between daily stress on health and mood as it is mediated by self-esteem and social support. Consistent with their predictions and with terror management theory, people with low self-esteem had significantly higher correlations between self-reported hassles on a given day and self-reported somatic symptoms on that day and on the following day, even when the effects of social support were partialed out, suggesting that people with low self-esteem are more likely to suffer physical ailments following stressful circumstances than are people with high self-esteem. DeLongis et al. interpreted these results by suggesting that people with high self-esteem are "less likely to feel overwhelmed when confronted with stressful demands than . . . people who do not have positive views." Our explanation for these findings is that, lacking an anxiety-buffer, people with low self-esteem experience far more debilitating anxiety when hassles occur than do people with high self-esteem.

Self-esteem did not influence the relationship between self-reported hassles and mood, but social support did. Specifically, subjects with strong social support networks felt better the same day when self-reported hassles were high (but not the day after self-reported hassles were high). Social support was not found to be related to somatic symptoms on or following stressful days.

Similar relationships between low self-esteem and ineffective responses to stress have been found for police officers (Lester, 1986), firemen (Petrie & Rotheram, 1982), recently widowed elderly people (Johnson, Lund, & Dimond, 1986), wives of soldiers sent to war (Hobfoll & London, 1986), women who have experienced difficult pregnancies (Hobfoll & Leiberman, 1987), recently unemployed individuals (Pearlin, Lieberman, Menaghan, & Mullan, 1981), medical students completing surgical internships (Linn & Zeppa, 1984), abused children (Zimrin, 1986), and new parents (Osofsky, 1985).

Although all of the above research is highly consistent with our proposal that self-esteem is an anxiety-buffer, it is all correlational and thus subject to a variety of alternative explanations. Indeed, any study that assesses the relationship between dispositional self-esteem and other variables will be inconclusive because so many personality and demographic variables covary with self-esteem. To provide stronger evidence concerning the terror management hypothesis that self-esteem functions to buffer anxiety, it is necessary to manipulate self-esteem in an experimental context. If self-esteem is an anxiety-buffer, then individuals whose self-esteem is raised should experience less anxiety than control subjects when exposed to anxiety-provoking stimuli.

To test this hypothesis, Greenberg, Solomon, Pyszczynski, Lyon, and Rosenblatt (1989, Study 1) gave subjects either positive or neutral personality feedback and then exposed them to either a gory videotape of death scenes or innocuous material. A postmanipulation Rosenberg self-esteem scale (Rosenberg, 1965) showed that the positive feedback subjects reported higher self-esteem than the neutral feedback subjects. In general, there was a main effect such that the death video led to higher self-reported anxiety on the Spielberger State Anxiety Inventory (Spielberger, Gorsuch, & Lushene, 1970) than the neutral video. However, this main effect was qualified by the predicted interaction, which showed that the death video led to an elevation in self-reported anxiety in the neutral personality feedback condition but not in the positive personality feedback condition.

In a second study (Greenberg et al., 1989, Study

2) subjects were given success or no feedback on an ego-relevant anagram test and then were led to expect either random electrical shocks or no shocks. The predicted interaction was found again, this time on galvanic skin response, a physiological indicator of anxiety. Under threat of shock, no feedback subjects exhibited greater arousal than success subjects; in the no shock conditions, arousal was similarly low for both groups. In a third study (Greenberg et al., 1989, Study 3), this interaction effect was replicated using false personality feedback rather than anagram test feedback to manipulate self-esteem. Although further research is needed to unambiguously establish that self-esteem is an anxiety buffer, these three experiments provide support for terror management theory through the consistent finding that raising self-esteem reduces the amount of anxiety engendered by threatening events.

Interestingly, in both studies 2 and 3, self-reports of anxiety, although in the predicted directions, did not yield the significant interactions found on GSR. We would speculate that the threat of shock places a high demand on subjects to report anxiety, whether felt or not; however, further research will be needed to determine the precise causes of this discrepancy between self-report and physiological measures of anxiety.

SELF-ESTEEM AND ADAPTATION

Our analysis suggests that adaptation can be conceptualized as the minimizing of anxiety through the perception that one is a valuable member of a meaningful universe. Accordingly, social behavior is primarily directed toward the acquisition and maintenance of self-esteem, which in turn can vary depending on transient or permanent changes in people's perceptions of their value and/or of the meaningfulness of the context in which they make such evaluative judgments about themselves. Put another way, self-esteem is a function of both value and meaning, and will change when either component is altered.

It is important to note that both the cultural worldview and one's value within it are purely social constructions (cf. Berger & Luckmann, 1967); therefore, these two components of the cultural anxiety buffer are validated and/or threatened primarily by other people. Thus, terror management theory suggests that a good deal of social behavior is directed toward seeking validation of, and avoiding threats to, value and meaning.

Only those who share one's basic worldview can threaten one's personal value directly, because only they use the same basis of judging value; thus, value is threatened primarily by others within the culture. In contrast, meaning is more commonly threatened by those outside the culture who espouse an alternative worldview of what is meaningful and valuable. It is worth noting that other theories, such as the social comparison theory (Festinger, 1954), posit that individuals seek social *assessment* of their beliefs, whereas terror management theory posits that individuals seek social *confirmation* of them.

When either value or meaning are undermined, individuals should experience anxiety and engage in compensatory responses, the character and duration of which would be determined by the locus and severity of the threat, whether the threat to value and meaning is chronic (stable) or acute (temporary), and the predispositions of the persons involved in conjunction with their specific prior experiences. Terror management theory thus posits that psychological problems (as well as some physical problems) can be understood as products of the anxiety resulting from an inability to acquire and/or maintain self-esteem.

Short-Term Consequences of Acute Threats to the Cultural Anxiety

Threats to Value

Terror management theory posits that (a) threats to self-esteem will lead to anxiety; (b) when self-esteem is threatened, individuals will be highly motivated to minimize the effects of the threat on self-esteem; and (c) when threats are minimized, the anxiety will be reduced. The available evidence is highly consistent with all three hypotheses. We have already noted that there is solid evidence that threats to self-esteem engender anxiety. There is also a large and continually growing literature documenting that such threats activate a variety of compensatory responses. Among the best documented self-esteem maintenance strategies are self-serving attributions (e.g., Miller, 1976), self-handicapping (e.g., Berglas & Jones, 1978), compensatory self-inflation (e.g., Greenberg & Pyszczynski, 1985), symbolic self-completion (e.g., Gollwitzer, Wicklund, & Hilton, 1982), basking and blasting (Cialdini & Richardson, 1980), downward social comparison (e.g., Hakmiller, 1966), false perceptions of uniqueness and consensus (e.g., Campbell, 1986), and altering perceptions of similarity to try to identify with and avoid comparison with superior others (e.g., Tesser, 1980). It has also been persuasively argued that many cognitive dissonance findings may have resulted from a need to defend self-esteem (e.g., Aronson, 1968; Bowerman, 1978; Steele & Liu, 1983). Additionally, in accord with our emphasis on the socially derived nature of self-esteem, it has been found that public failure activates particularly strong defensive reactions (e.g., Frey, 1978; Greenberg & Pyszczynski, 1985). For overviews of this literature, see Greenberg et al. (1986), Pyszczynski and Greenberg (1987), and Snyder and Higgins (1988).

The general tenor of these findings is that there are a variety of relatively easy cognitive and behavioral alterations that can be used to restore or protect one's self-esteem when it is threatened. Although not empirically established, there are probably also a variety of more active behavioral responses that are not uncommon; for example, increasing efforts to display one's prowess, whether via intellectual, athletic, social, or financial accomplishments, or, when appropriate, simply by eliminating or undermining the validity of the threatener.

For the most part, we would argue that to the extent these defenses are effective, they are short-term contributors to the threatened individual's mental and physical health because by restoring self-esteem they minimize the anxiety resulting from the threat.

We hedge a bit here because we can envision situations in which self-esteem defense might not be beneficial in the long run. For example, if the strategy led to negative reactions from others, such reactions from validators of one's self-worth could create more damage to self-esteem than the defensive strategy attempted to avert. Similarly, excessively unrealistic beliefs in the service of self-esteem maintenance could help perpetuate failure in both the social and achievement realms; for example, a male with poor social skills who cannot get dates but continually attributes his failures to the attributes of those who reject him. (See, for example, Greenberg, Pyszczynski, & Solomon, 1982; Pyszczynski & Greenberg, 1987; Schlenker, 1985.) There is surprisingly little empirical evidence on the consequences of self-esteem maintenance strategies; what does exist is, however, consistent with this analysis. McFarland and Ross

(1982) found that self-serving attributions after failure minimize the negative impact of failure on both self-esteem and affect. Other research suggests that non–self-protective attributions may contribute to long-term negative affect. A variety of correlational studies have shown that internal attributions for negative outcomes and the absence of a self-serving pattern of attributions are associated with depression (see Peterson & Seligman, 1984, for a review). In a particularly compelling example of this work, Rothwell and Williams (1983) found that an inclination toward internal attributions for failure predicted low self-esteem and depression in males who lost their jobs.

Affective responses to negative outcomes also seem to covary with the nature of self-esteem–relevant social comparisons. For example, Bennett and Holmes (1975) found that after failing an intelligence test, people who were encouraged to guess that their friends would have also done poorly on the test (which lessens the implications of the failure for self-esteem) were subsequently less anxious than those who were not. Similarly, Burish and Houston (1979) found that after a challenging intelligence test, individuals' subsequent anxiety was lowered if they were encouraged to engage in either of two defenses: claiming that the experimenter inhibited their performance or guessing that their friends would perform poorly on the test. Additionally, research on social comparison following negative outcomes indicates that comparing downward (i.e., with others worse than oneself), which casts the self in a relatively positive light, is associated with decreases in self-reported distress, anxiety, and depressive mood, and with increases in life satisfaction (Hakmiller, 1966; Crocker & Gallo, 1985).

Two studies have also found beneficial effects of providing people with excuses for future failure. Arkin and Baumgardner (1985, cited in Baumgardner & Arkin, 1987) had opposite-sex pairs engage in a conversation while they were exposed to white noise. They told half of the subjects that the noise would interfere with their social performance (thereby providing an excuse should they perform poorly). Socially anxious individuals (but not nonanxious individuals, who are unlikely to expect social failure) rated their interaction more enjoyable and themselves more relaxed when they believed the noise could serve as an excuse for failure than when they did not. In a similar study, Leary (1986) found that subjects who believed that noise would interfere with performance had lower pulse rates than did those who did not. As expected, this difference was especially great for socially anxious individuals.

Finally, Mehlman and Snyder (1985) demonstrated that simply giving people the opportunity to minimize a failure can be beneficial. Specifically, they manipulated performance outcome and then gave half of the subjects a questionnaire that allowed them to minimize the implications of failure for self-esteem. In addition, half of these subjects believed that they were attached to a lie detector while filling out the questionnaire. The opportunity to minimize the failure led to high anxiety and hostility among the failure subjects in the lie detector condition. Presumably, the lie detector undermined the utility of the opportunity to minimize the failure. In contrast, in the no lie detector condition, failure subjects reported less anxiety and hostility when they had the opportunity to minimize the failure than when they did not.

To summarize, research has found that threats to self-esteem cause anxiety and that people use a wide variety of strategies to defend self-esteem when it is threatened. In addition, when these defenses are used, or when conditions facilitate their use, anxiety and other forms of negative affect are reduced. The evidence to date is thus highly consistent with terror management theory. We are not suggesting that there are not other plausible theoretical accounts for the phenomena that we have just reviewed (usually the specific theoretical formulation used to generate a particular piece of research). What we are claiming instead is that while terror management theory can account for all of these findings, no other single conceptual framework that we are aware of is able to do so. Additionally, there are a number of empirical findings obtained from studies testing hypotheses derived from terror management theory (to be described later) that cannot be explained in terms of other theoretical perspectives.

Threats to Meaning

As with value, threats to meaning should engender anxiety and defenses, and such defenses should in turn reduce anxiety. Unfortunately, there is little research directly relevant to these hypotheses. In the one study we have found in which subjects' central beliefs were experimentally challenged, Batson (1975) presented Christian church-goers with evidence threatening the validity of their beliefs and found evidence of a compensatory increase in their reported faith. Festinger, Riecken, and Schachter (1956) observed a religious group's reaction when the day it predicted the world was going to end came and went. Similar to Batson's findings, they found that this rather blatant disconfirmation of their worldview seemed to lead to posthoc rationalizations, increased faith, and renewed efforts to gain more fellow validators of their faith.

More indirectly, there is substantial evidence that people react negatively to deviants, those with dissimilar attitudes, and outgroup members (e.g., Byrne, 1971; Miller & Anderson, 1979; Rokeach, 1968; Schachter, 1951). In addition, a number of studies suggest that negative reactions to outgroup members result primarily from the assumption that they have different values (Goldstein & Davison, 1972; Moe, Nacoste, & Insko, 1981). These findings are consistent with our analysis, in that those who do not conform to our values, those who do not agree with our attitudes, and those who accept an alternative worldview implicitly threaten our faith in the validity of our worldview. Consistent with the notion that derogation of outgroup members results from concerns about a threat to one's worldview, prior to the 1980 United States presidential election, Cooper and Mackie (1983) found that when members of a pro-Reagan group were induced to write arguments supporting the re-election of Carter, they subsequently derogated members of a pro-Carter group. Thus, threatening a central belief encouraged derogation of members of a group with contradictory views.

A number of studies have recently been conducted to directly assess the terror management explanation for negative reactions to those who do not conform to one's worldview. In the first set of six studies (Rosenblatt, Greenberg, Solomon, Pyszczynski, & Lyon, 1989), it was hypothesized that if derogation of deviants results in part from the implicit threat to the cultural worldview, then when subjects are made to think of their own deaths, they should be especially concerned with maintaining the cultural worldview and therefore should be especially punitive toward someone who violates cultural values. The six studies found consistent support for this hypothesis while eliminating mood congruency, arousal, and self-awareness alternative explanations.

A second set of three studies (Greenberg et al.,

in press) assessed whether mortality salience also would encourage derogation of outgroup members, dissimilar others, and those who directly criticize the accepted culture. In addition, these studies assessed whether mortality salience would encourage positive evaluations of fellow ingroup members, similar others, and those who directly praise the culture. In Study 1, as predicted, when mortality was salient, Christian subjects rated a fellow Christian especially positively and a Jew especially negatively. In Study 2, when mortality was salient, high authoritarians tended to rate an attitudinally similar other very favorably and clearly rated a dissimilar other very unfavorably. However, low authoritarians did not show this tendency (perhaps because open-mindedness and tolerance are part of their worldview). In Study 3, as predicted, mortality salience led to especially favorable ratings of one who praised the culture and especially unfavorable ratings of one who criticized the culture. Finally, our most recent study has shown that prior to the 1988 presidential election, mortality salience encouraged positive reactions to George Bush among Bush supporters, but not among Dukakis supporters (Pyszczynski, Becker, Gracey, Greenberg, & Solomon, 1989).

The 10 mortality salience studies conducted thus far support our contentions that (a) threats to meaning encourage negative reactions, compensatory responses, and derogation of threateners; and (b) that these responses are motivated by terror management concerns. None of these studies, however, has assessed whether such reactions actually reduce anxiety. In addition, there is no systematic evidence that implicit or explicit threats to the meaning component of the cultural anxiety buffer engender anxiety, although such a notion seems to fit a wide variety of historical events (e.g., reactions to Gallileo, Darwin and innumerable others whose ideas challenged accepted belief systems). Thus, overall the existing evidence concerning short-term threats to meaning is highly consistent with our analysis, but a number of important hypotheses have yet to be investigated.

Long-Term Consequences of Chronic Threats to the Cultural Anxiety Buffer

Terror management theory proposes that chronic low self-esteem results from an inability to maintain a sense that one is a valuable member of a meaningful universe. At this point it is impossible to determine if chronic low self-esteem is due to the chronic absence of value or meaning (recall that a terror management analysis would predict low self-esteem in either case). We can conceive of situations where people accept the cosmology given them by their culture, but are simply unable to perceive themselves as valuable persons within that context (e.g., a person who believes that all Americans who try hard enough can be financially successful, but who makes minimum wage and therefore sees him/herself as a failure).

Similarly, there may be circumstances where it is difficult or impossible for people to sustain a meaningful conception of the world at all (in which case there can be no sense of value). Available worldviews may simply be inadequate for acquiring meaning given specific individual circumstances. For example, members of minority groups may have an especially difficult time maintaining self-esteem because they are caught between two cultural contexts, neither of which provides a sufficient basis for self-worth. On the one hand their traditional worldviews have been severely distorted or threatened by the dominant culture; on the other hand, the dominant culture is either not acceptable because it historically treated the minority group horribly, or because it does not convince the minority individual that he or she will be given the opportunity to acquire value. Alternatively, other people may simply be constitutionally or experientially unable to sustain meaning entirely. Becker (1973) has suggested that this may be the case for schizophrenics.

Whatever the reason for the inability to sustain meaning, our theory suggests that the individual will either suffer chronic low self-esteem and its consequences (discussed below), or will find an alternative worldview that is more compelling (although the latter option may be problematic for schizophrenics). Interestingly, recent research on religious conversions is highly consistent with this analysis. Ullman (1982) found that religious conversions (to Judaism, Catholicism, and the Hare Krishna and Bahai faiths) are often preceded by acute stress and chronic low self-esteem, and the religious converts reported more markedly negative impressions of their parents than nonconverts. Additionally, Paloutzian (1981) found that people report having a greater purpose in life and a diminished fear of death directly following religious conversion.

Regardless of whether value or meaning is not being sustained, the lack of self-esteem will engender anxiety that results in maladaptive psychological and/or physical responses. Individuals with low self-esteem are likely to be very susceptible to anxiety when their value system is threatened. In addition, lacking much of an anxiety-buffer, they are likely to react to the anticipation and experience of minor and major negative life events with a great deal of anxiety. Thus, people with low self-esteem will suffer the effects of both long-term accumulations and extreme acute doses of anxiety.

Research suggests that this anxiety may contribute directly to psychological and physical problems (cf. Yalom, 1980); in addition, the anxiety may contribute indirectly to such problems via its relation to stress. Our analysis and research (e.g., the self-esteem anxiety-buffer studies reported above) indicate that individuals with low self-esteem will respond to stressful events with anxiety. This is likely to intensify the individual's level of stress in two ways. First, it is highly likely that anxiety is itself stressful (cf. Gray, 1982); thus, responding to stress with anxiety will add to the stress. Second, anxiety is likely to interfere with the implementation of adaptive coping strategies to alleviate the stress, thereby prolonging and amplifying the individual's exposure to stress.

Given that anxiety and ineffective coping with stress contribute to a variety of mental health problems, individuals with low self-esteem will be particularly vulnerable to such problems. Additionally, there is now a large body of evidence that suggests that anxiety and stress cause a host of physical problems (ranging in severity from nausea to cancer) by undermining the integrity of the immune system (see e.g., Jemmott, 1985; Tecoma & Huey, 1985, for reviews of current empirical work in psychoneuroimmunology—the study of how psychological factors influence immune-system function). Thus, low self-esteem may result in physical as well as psychological problems.

Research is highly consistent with this analysis. With regard to physical problems, studies have shown a relationship between low self-esteem and poor physical health (Antonucci & Jackson, 1983), headaches (Khouri-Haddad, 1984), children's visits to school sick bays (Harper & Field, 1986), hypochondriasis (Barsky & Klerman, 1983), and nervous breakdowns (Ingham, Kreitman, Miller, & Sasidharan, 1986). With regard to psychological problems, low self-esteem is associated with aggressive behavior in male children (Lochman & Lampron, 1986), bulimic behavior in

women (Crowther & Chernyk, 1986), smoking in adolescence (Penny & Robinson, 1986; Ahlgren, Norem, Hochhauser, & Garvin, 1982), male spouse abuse (Goldstein & Rosenbaum, 1985; Neidig, Friedman, & Collins, 1986), depression (e.g., Brown, Andrews, Harris, & Adler, 1986; Brown, Bifulco, Harris, & Bridge, 1986; Brown, Craig, & Harris, 1985; Mollon & Parry, 1984), anxiety-disorders (Strauss et al., 1987), and paranoid schizophrenia (Zigler & Glick, 1988). This is by no means a complete list of the correlational evidence linking self-esteem to a variety of psychological and physical problems. For a more complete review of this area, see Scheff et al., 1989.

Although understanding the precise nature of the relationship between self-esteem and psychological and physical adaptation will require further research, the impressive array of correlational findings indicates that the plausible terror management account of the relationship between self-esteem and anxiety and the role of self-esteem problems in psychological and psychosomatic disorders warrant serious consideration.

CLINICAL IMPLICATIONS OF TERROR MANAGEMENT THEORY

From a terror management perspective, people's psychological and physical well-being requires that they perceive themselves to be valuable members of a meaningful universe, which relieves the anxiety associated with the uniquely human awareness of death. Accordingly, health concerns are best considered as an interaction between individual and social factors. Specifically, one can ask about factors (genetic, biochemical, experiential) that make it difficult for people to acquire meaning and value regardless of specific social contexts. At the same time, one can consider how specific social contexts are more or less conducive to individual health. Effective interventions should therefore be directed toward facilitating the acquisition and maintenance of meaning and value, either at a broad social or individual level.

Individual Level

The individual therapeutic approach most consistent with a terror management analysis is described in Irvin Yalom's *Existential Psychotherapy* (1980). Yalom states his theoretical assumptions about psychopathology and psychotherapy as follows:

> 1. The fear of death plays a major role in our internal experience; it haunts us as does nothing else; it rumbles continuously under the surface; it is a dark, unsettling presence at the rim of consciousness.
> 2. The child, at an early age, is pervasively preoccupied with death, and his or her major developmental task is to deal with terrifying fears of obliteration.
> 3. To cope with these fears, we erect defenses against death awareness, defenses that are based on denial, that shape character structure, and that if maladaptive, result in clinical syndromes. In other words, psychopathology is the result of ineffective modes of death transcendence.
> 4. . . . a robust and effective approach to psychotherapy may be constructed on the foundation of death awareness. (pp. 27–28)

Yalom's conceptual analysis is very close to Becker's and our own. His clinical approach is to recognize that many (if not most) presenting symptoms when people begin therapy are maladaptive responses to the anxiety associated with the awareness of death, and to be aware that people coming to therapy are normally unaware that death concerns are related to their problems. Accordingly, Yalom tries to help clients become aware of their concerns regarding death, understand how their present problems are connected with those concerns, and agree that such responses are ineffective relative to other possibilities.

This is followed by an attempt to help clients acquire a meaningful conception of the world around them through which they can perceive themselves as valuable individuals. Yalom suggests that this can be achieved in a variety of ways, including (a) altruism (helping others), (b) dedication to a cause, (c) involvement in creative activities (or being creative regardless of what one does), (d) appreciation of life at all times (and "[retaining] one's sense of astonishment at the miracle of life"), and (e) devotion to self-actualization (the realization of one's own unique individual potential). A complete description of Yalom's approach to psychotherapy is beyond the scope of this paper.

Our recommendations for therapy are similar to Yalom's, but we are not as sure that making clients aware of their concerns about death is a necessary or useful step toward bolstering their mechanisms for minimizing such concerns. For many clients, simply strengthening their cultural anxiety buffers may be enough. Perhaps for other clients it would be necessary to strip their problems down to their essence to help them let go of maladaptive modes of coping and seek better solutions. However, this strategy is a dangerous one; accordingly, Becker (1973) advises that psychotherapists bent on providing self-knowledge to clients should provide a warning as well: "Danger: real probability of the awakening of terror and dread, from which there is no turning back." The problem is that decay and death are inescapable physical evils that we can only deal with via fragile symbolic social constructions; and prying someone from whatever such constructions in which they are imbedded would result in boundless terror unless a viable alternative was made readily available.

We also depart from Yalom in being guided more forcefully by the distinction between value and meaning. From the terror management perspective, a client's problems result from difficulties in sustaining one or both of the components of the cultural anxiety buffer. So for some clients, the question is, Why does the individual not have a sufficiently strong belief in his or her own value? For these clients, the solution is to help strengthen that belief, whether simply by altering cognitions about the self or, perhaps preferably, by helping the client work toward developing the skills and finding the surroundings necessary to achieve a sense of value within his or her accepted worldview (cf. Rogers, 1961).

For other clients, the problem may be the basis of self-evaluation; perhaps the client simply cannot derive value from the accepted worldview because the worldview involves excessively difficult, unrealistic standards (cf. Horney, 1950), or because the individual's attributes and situation are simply not well-suited to attaining value from that particular worldview. Either way, the solution is to help the individual alter his or her worldview so that it can be a fruitful basis of self-esteem. One common notion propagated in many clinical settings is that the client needs to shift his or her basis of self-worth from external sources to internal ones. However, our analysis suggests that this would not be a productive strategy. Self-worth is inherently a cultural construction and thus must always be validated externally; otherwise it cannot be sustained. Therefore the client should not be focused on deriving self-esteem internally, but on adopting values, roles, and behaviors that will provide compelling, consistent social validation of his or her self-worth.

Finally, for some clients the problem may be that they simply cannot sustain faith in the worldview itself. Here again, the solution is to guide the client toward a more beneficial worldview, one that is more compelling in providing a meaningful view of reality from which a sense of personal value can be derived (cf. Rank, 1936/1978). Of course, helping individuals construct a worldview carries with it serious ethical concerns for psychotherapists who are commonly taught to avoid value judgments (regardless of the impossibility of doing so). In addition, Rank (1931, 1936) has argued that psychology is particularly well-suited for destroying worldviews but rather ill equipped for helping individuals develop them: "However, psychology, which is gradually trying to supplant religious and moral ideology, is only partially qualified to do this, because it is a preponderantly negative and disintegrating ideology. . . . " (Rank, 1931, p. 192). Ideally, the hope is that informed psychotherapists can avoid this problem by working with the client's own beliefs and assumptions, and not imposing psychological analysis and ideology too heavily on the worldview that emerges from the therapeutic intervention.

Rank (1931, 1961), Becker (1971), and others (e.g., James, 1911) have argued that the best and highest level of meaning is what Becker refers to as the sacred level at which one links oneself to the highest power—some conception of a creator and the meaning of creation. Becker argues that this is the most psychologically beneficial level for a number of reasons. First, faith in some spiritual conception of reality offers the possibility of actual immortality, which, if one can sustain such faith, quiets the fear of death most effectively. Second, spiritual bases of meaning are less disconfirmable than more tangible bases (such as country, family, spouse, or material possessions). God cannot die, be disproven, or be found to be corrupt. Third, by serving the creator, or universal life force, or whatever, one can have a sense of cosmic value, which would certainly be the deepest sense of self-worth.

There are two problems in applying this notion to clinical issues. One is that it is not clear how an individual who was not deeply embedded in a spiritual system from early childhood on could be helped to acquire faith, or what the specific nature of that faith should be. There are, however, a wide variety of known spiritual conceptions. Perhaps the client's prior affinities for a particular approach might provide a base that can then be elaborated and strengthened (the problem then is how to help the client be courageous enough to be a "knight of faith" [Becker, 1973, based on an analysis of Kierkegaard] and maintain the security base, while acknowledging that in the modern scientific world [see our discussion of the social level] doubt is the knight's squire [cf. Bergman's 1957 film, *The Seventh Seal*]).

The other problem is that of the psychotherapist becoming a guru or religious authority in the client's life. Although gurus may be exactly what some people need, one most definitely would not want this to be the psychotherapist's role. However, the priests of self-insight and self-reliance must recognize that the strength of one's self-worth derives from the way in which the individual imbues the world with meaning. While it may seem that we have strayed across the line from psychology to philosophy/theology, as Rank points out, each school of psychology is a meaning system of its own, and usually (perhaps necessarily) not the most beneficial one. The reader may also wonder at this point what all of this has to do with the role of self-esteem in adaptation, but again, self-esteem is a sense of value made possible by some cultural conception of meaning that specifies what is (and is not) of value and what the requirements of being a good person are. If the goal is to help the client achieve a stronger, less vulnerable sense of self-worth, the basis of that self-worth must not be ignored as a possible cause of problems and a possible target of change.

Social Level

Freud was the first psychologist to note in *The Future of an Illusion* and *Civilization and Its Discontents* (Freud, 1961a, b) that to conform to social standards is by no means to be either healthy or normal, and that entire societies are by their very nature neurotic. Because culture is a humanly created social construction, all enculturated individuals are deluded to the extent that they believe their worldview to be absolutely correct and do not recognize the illusory nature of their perspectives. Enculturated individuals perceive the world as described by their culture rather than forming impressions directly based on their own interpretations of sensory information, resulting in a restricted range of potential life experiences according to cultural dictates.

This is potentially important from a clinical perspective; Becker recognized that whereas different cultures serve the same essential purpose — that of minimizing anxiety associated with the awareness of death — they do not all do so equally well and there are reasonably objective standards according to which the relative merits of different cultures might be compared. Specifically, Becker suggests that cultures can be evaluated in terms of the extent to which (a) physical needs for members of a group are satisfied given technical capabilities and natural resources; (b) adequate social roles are provided that allow for as many members of a group as possible to acquire and maintain self-esteem; and (c) physical and psychological needs are not satisfied at the expense of others.

Becker's second criterion is most relevant for the present discussion. If self-esteem is a vitally important component of human adaptation as we propose, and if self-esteem consists of the belief that one is a valuable member of a meaningful universe, then self-esteem is derived entirely from the cultural context in which one resides. There are two important implications of this notion. First, a behavior considered valuable and meaningful in one social milieu, and that would consequently confer immense self-esteem, might be deemed meaningless or humiliating in a different social context and would therefore confer no esteem or cause the loss of self-esteem. For example, in the Sambia tribe of New Guinea a normal part of the transition to heterosexual adulthood for boys includes performing fellatio on male elders of the tribe (Herdt, 1982). While most American males would find this ritual severely threatening to self-esteem, an American-born infant raised to adolescence in that culture would most likely gain self-esteem from it. Conversely, a male member of the Sambia tribe would not derive much self-esteem from wearing a suit and tie, and carrying a wallet full of little plastic cards, unless he were brought up by Americans.

Perhaps more importantly, recognizing that the bases of self-esteem are cultural contrivances allows direct comparisons between different cultures; a given culture's designation of what is meaningful and valuable provides opportunities for the greatest number of people to acquire and maintain self-esteem.

Rank observed, for example, that Christianity in the middle ages was an excellent worldview in terms of the potential for acquiring self-esteem, because Christians were told that they were all equally valuable in the eyes of God and that eternal life was dependent on living the good life re-

gardless of one's material or social status. Thus, all Christians had the opportunity to acquire self-esteem because they were potentially able to adhere to the standards of appropriate behavior mandated by their reference group. Conversely, many have observed (e.g., Albee, 1986; Sampson, 1985) that it is very difficult to feel good about oneself in America because the standards by which we are taught to judge ourselves are not realistically attainable for most of our population. In America, people are deemed successful only to the extent that they have acquired enormous material resources, power over others, or are the best at what they do. The problem is that in a hierarchically stratified society only a few can have money and power (they tend to go together), because money and power are derived from, and depend on, large numbers of people who have less of both. Consequently, we are a society that virtually ensures low self-esteem for many of its members by setting goals that most people, even with the best intentions, cannot fulfill.

Consider for example, a recent American Express television commercial where a businessman is feverishly trying to get home on a miserable rainy evening to see his daughter perform as a flower in the school play. His flight is canceled, and an inquiry to the airlines finds only first class seats on another flight, which he is able to get because he has the American Express card. When he arrives at his destination, he is able to get cash with the card to take a limousine directly to the school to watch the play, while the rabble wait in the rain hoping for cabs or buses. The commercial ends with the reminder that "membership has its privileges," the implication of course being that those with means deserve to be able to do these things, while those without such means are wretched failures who do not deserve to see their children grow up in the same fashion as their more worthy counterparts.

The general point here is that Americans are constantly reminded (a) that success consists of the increasing consumption of goods and services (and conversely that one who does not or cannot do this is a failure); (b) that we are also taught to believe that we all have an equal opportunity to acquire such wealth and are thus responsible for not doing so; and (c) that in fact the structure and organization of a capital-based economy depends on massive numbers of people engaged in relatively trivial occupations for meager compensation. The effect of this type of social arrangement is that it is very difficult to acquire and maintain self-esteem for many people, because the standards of value by which we are taught to judge ourselves are so difficult to obtain. This analysis may help account for the prevalence of depression and anxiety-related disorders in contemporary American society.

In addition to the difficulty of obtaining value within the context of contemporary western society, Becker and Rank have noted that current western worldviews are also especially ill-suited for deriving meaning. Specifically, for centuries western societies were dominated by a Christian cosmology, which offered all the possibility for acquiring meaning and value by living the good life. What a person had was unimportant relative to what one did and how one did it, because God did not discriminate between the president of a large corporation and a sewer worker; both would go to heaven as long as each behaved in a Christian fashion. Similarly, in traditional tribal cultures all members of the tribe had a role in the tribal rituals, which provided cosmic significance.

Such cosmologies are now very difficult to accept by many for four historical reasons. First, Darwin's theory of evolution made it extremely difficult for all but the willfully ignorant to accept a literal interpretation of the Christian worldview. In other words, Christianity has been massively undermined by the present Western conception of reality. Second, the scientific revolution has resulted in magnificent achievements in many physical domains (e.g., agriculture and medicine), making the scientific worldview extremely compelling. Centuries ago people would appeal to God when the crops failed or when they broke a leg; now the same problems would prompt a visit to a botanist and physician, respectively. Third, Christianity has never been able to deliver on earth what it promises in heaven, namely genuine equality for all (cf. Becker, 1975). The church has generally supported the powers that be, defending the privileges of few against the rights of many.

Finally, the division of labor and assembly lines resulting from the industrial revolution have changed what the average individual does on a daily basis. As Fromm (1941) argued, following the industrial revolution, division of labor and assembly line activities have improved our physical well-being, while at the same time divesting us of the sense of value that comes from creative work. The person who used to make a shoe or a car now puts a heel on a shoe or an ashtray in a car as it goes through an assembly line, or perhaps collects tolls in a small booth for 8 hours or works third shift in a gas station or convenience store, doing virtually nothing except generating revenue for someone else.

All of the factors mentioned above have transformed people from creative individuals encouraged to cooperate with each other in the service of higher powers into pathetic consumers who measure themselves against others by what they have instead of by what they do and how they do it. Because it is currently hard to sustain faith in an invisible dimension (i.e., spirits and deities), meaning and hence value can only be obtained through the accumulation of more things than those around you (i.e., tangible proof of your worth). This can at best provide a very fragile sense of meaning and self-worth that is difficult to maintain; whatever you have is not enough because it's not all of it, and someone else surely has more than you do anyway. Consequently, the only way to procure value in the context of this type of social arrangement is to perceive yourself as superior to others, and as Harry Stack Sullivan (1953) recognized:

> If you have to maintain self-esteem by pulling down the standing of others, you are extraordinarily unfortunate in a variety of ways. Since you have to protect your feeling of personal worth by noting how unworthy everybody around you is, you are not provided with any data that are convincing evidence of your having personal worth, so it gradually evolves into "I am not as bad as the other swine." To be the best of swine, when it would be nice to be a person, is not a particularly good way of furthering anything except security operations. (p. 242)

At this point the reader might be wondering about how all of this could possibly be relevant for clinical practice. Terror management theory suggests that mental health concerns cannot be properly understood without evaluating the social context in which those concerns occur, and that effective therapy requires constructive social change and/or convincing people in unhealthy social contexts that the basis of meaning and value prescribed by that context is by no means absolute, which then allows for the possibility that those people can seek meaning and value elsewhere. Albee (1982) has argued that social change directed at reducing unnecessary stress (access to basic resources necessary for physical survival) and enhancing social competence, self-esteem, and social support networks may be the only viable form of therapeutic intervention for most people, as there are many more people in need of psychological interventions (most lacking the financial resources to procure them) than there are people to provide such services.

One interesting implication of this conceptual analysis pertains to the role of the social sciences in the development and maintenance of cultural worldviews. As Skinner (see *Walden Two* [1948] and/or *Beyond Freedom and Dignity* [1971]) has forcefully argued for decades, the human race seems to be on a self-determined collision course with extinction caused by violence, overpopulation, and destruction of the environment, and solutions to these problems are best sought through science. Do we want our world described to us, our problems analyzed, and solutions suggested to us by the likes of Reagan, Kadaffi, and Khomeini, or should these concerns be relegated to the sciences?

Skinner argues that we stand a better chance of survival if these concerns are broached scientifically, but unfortunately his conceptual analysis does not lead to fruitful suggestions in that regard. Specifically, Skinner insists that because all behavior is determined by responses to external contingencies, that constructive social changes must be effected by altering those contingencies through positive reinforcement in order to get people to behave in a less destructive fashion. The problem is that Skinner cannot specify in advance what those contingencies are, although he insists that a retrospective analysis of any behavior would necessarily reveal the specific environmental factors responsible for the behavior. Because Skinner does not distinguish between the basic predispositions of a lizard and that of a person, he cannot make any informed predictions about what might be reinforcing. (A critical examination of Skinner's analysis of human behavior is far beyond the scope of this work. We believe that his perspective is wrong, but for the purposes of the present discussion we are confining our concerns to the argument that his perspective is simply not useful, which may be the only legitimate basis by which scientific claims can be evaluated. See, for example, Laudan, 1977.)

In contrast, terror management theory presumes that there is a fundamental difference between humans and other living organisms that renders us responsive to different types of reinforcement by virtue of our having different needs (i.e., meaning and value). Consequently, we suggest that inasmuch as people are motivated to reduce anxiety through the acquisition of meaning and value (i.e., self-esteem), applied social science should be directed toward the development and maintenance of worldviews that maximize the equitable distribution of material resources and development of nondestructive technologies, which emphasize social roles that confer the possibility of acquiring self-esteem to as many people as possible, and which do so at a minimum of expense to others.

When these standards are applied to our own culture, we must somberly recognize that the American way of life is not particularly conducive to mental health. Note that this is not a political judgment, but instead follows directly from our conceptual analysis of what mental health is and how it is acquired. While we have argued that American culture does not provide adequate opportunities to acquire value and meaning, Marcuse (1955) and others have also noted that American culture fails miserably in terms of Becker's two other criteria for evaluating the utility of specific cultures. Specifically, many of our citizens lack access to basic resources necessary for physical survival (e.g., adequate food, housing, medical care, education, etc.) despite the obvious fact that we possess the technology and resources to provide for the satisfaction of those needs. Additionally, others outside and inside American culture have paid a dear price for the psychological and physical comfort of the majority. Specifically, this comfort level was made possible in part by the support of and investment in innumerable tyrannical, racist, and oppressive activities in a variety of other countries, along with the wanton exploitation of immigrants and other minority group members within the United States.

REFERENCES

Ahlgren, A., Norem, A., Hochhauser, M., & Garvin, J. (1982). Antecedents of smoking among pre-adolescents. *Journal of Drug Education, 12*, 325–340.

Albee, G. (1982). Preventing psychopathology and promoting human potential. *American Psychologist, 37*, 1043–1050.

Albee, G. (1986). Toward a Just Society: Lessons from observations on the primary prevention of psychopathology. *American Psychologist, 41*, 891–898.

Antonucci, T., & Jackson, J. (1983). Physical health and self-esteem. *Family and Community Health, 6,* 1–9.

Aronson, E. (1968). Dissonance theory: Progress and problems. In R. P. Abelson, E. Aronson, W. J. McGuire, T. M. Newcomb, M. J. Rosenberg, & P. H. Tannenbaum (Eds.), *Theories of cognitive consistency: A source-book.* Chicago: Rand McNally.

Bandura, A. (1982). Self-efficacy mechanism in human agency. *American Psychologist, 37,* 122–147.

Barsky, A., & Klerman, G. (1983). Overview: Hypochondriasis, bodily complaints, and somatic styles. *American Journal of Psychiatry, 140,* 273–283.

Batson, C. D. (1975). Rational processing or rationalization? The effect of disconfirming information on a stated religious belief. *Journal of Personality and Social Psychology, 32,* 176–184.

Baumgardner, A. H., & Arkin, R. M. (1987). Coping with the prospect of disapproval: Strategies and sequelae. In C. R. Snyder & C. E. Ford (Eds.), *Coping with negative life events: Clinical and social psychological perspectives.* New York: Plenum Press.

Becker, E. (1962). *The birth and death of meaning.* New York: Free Press.

Becker, E. (1964). *The revolution in psychiatry: The new understanding of man.* London: Collier-Macmillian.

Becker, E. (1971). *The birth and death of meaning* (2nd ed.). New York: Free Press.

Becker, E. (1973). *The denial of death.* New York: Free Press.

Becker, E. (1975). *Escape from evil.* New York: Free Press.

Bennett, D. H., & Holmes, D. S. (1975). Influences of denial (situational redefinition) and projection on anxiety associated with threat to self-esteem. *Journal of Personality and Social Psychology, 32,* 915–921.

Berger, P. L., & Luckmann, T. (1967). *The social construction of reality: A treatise in the sociology of knowledge.* Garden City, NY: Anchor Books.

Berglas, S., & Jones, E. E. (1978). Drug choice as a self-handicapping strategy in response to a non-contingent success. *Journal of Personality and Social Psychology, 36,* 405–417.

Bergman, I. (Director). (1957). *The seventh seal* [Film]. Janus.

Bowlby, J. (1973). *Separation: Anxiety and anger.* New York: Basic Books.

Bowerman, W. (1978). Subjective competence: The structure, process, and function of self-referent causal attributions. *Journal for the Theory of Social Behavior, 8,* 45–75.

Brockner, J. (1979). The effects of self-esteem, success-failure and self-consciousness on task performance. *Journal of Personality and Social Psychology, 37,* 1732–1741.

Brown, G., Andrews, B., Harris, T., & Adler, Z. (1986). Social support, self-esteem and depression. *Psychological Medicine, 16,* 13–31.

Brown, G., Bifulco, A., Harris, T., & Bridge, L. (1986). Life stress, chronic subclinical symptoms and vulnerability to clinical depression. *Journal of Affective Disorders, 11,* 1–19.

Brown, G., Craig, T., & Harris, T. (1985). Depression: Distress or disease? Some epidemiological considerations. *British Journal of Psychiatry, 147,* 612–622.

Burish, T. G., & Houston, B. K. (1979). Causal projection, similarity projection, and coping with threat to self-esteem. *Journal of Personality, 47,* 57–70.

Byrne, D. (1971). *The attraction paradigm.* New York: Academic Press.

Campbell, J. D. (1986). Similarity and uniqueness: The effects of attribute type, relevance, and individual differences in self-esteem and depression. *Journal of Personality and Social Psychology, 50,* 281–294.

Cialdini, R. B., & Richardson, K. D. (1980). Two indirect tactics of image management: Basking and blasting. *Journal of Personality and Social Psychology, 39,* 406–415.

Cooper, J., & Mackie, D. (1983). Cognitive dissonance in an intergroup context. *Journal of Personality and Social Psychology, 44,* 536–544.

Coopersmith, S. (1967). *The antecedents of self-esteem.* San Francisco: W. H. Freeman.

Crandall, R. (1973). The measurement of self-esteem and related constructs. In J. Robinson & P. Shaver (Eds.), *Measures of social psychological attitudes.* Ann Arbor: Institute for Social Research.

Crocker, J., & Gallo, L. (1985). Self-enhancing effects of downward comparison: An experimental test. In T. A. Wills (Chair), *Self-esteem maintenance: Theory and evidence.* Symposium presented at the meeting of the American Psychological Association, Los Angeles.

Crowther, J., & Chernyk, B. (1986). Bulimia and

binge eating in adolescent females: A comparison. *Addictive Behaviors, 11*, 415–424.

DeLongis, A., Folkman, S., & Lazarus, R. (1988). The impact of daily stress on health and mood: Psychological and social resources as mediators. *Journal of Personality and Social Psychology, 54*, 486–495.

Diggory, J. (1966). *Self-evaluation: Concepts and studies*. New York: John Wiley & Sons.

Festinger, L. (1954). A theory of social comparison processes. *Human Relations, 7*, 117–140.

Festinger, L., Riecken, H., & Schachter, S. (1956). *When prophecy fails*. Minneapolis: University of Minnesota Press.

French, J. R. P. (1968). The conceptualization and measurement of mental health in terms of self-identity theory. In S. B. Bells (Ed.), *The definition and measurement of mental health*. Washington, DC: U.S. Department of Health, Education, and Welfare.

Freud, S. (1961a). Civilization and its discontents. In *The standard edition of the complete psychological works of Sigmund Freud* (Vol. 21). London: Hogarth Press. (Original work published 1930.)

Freud, S. (1961b). The future of an illusion. In *The standard edition of the complete psychological works of Sigmund Freud* (Vol. 22). London: Hogarth Press. (Original work published 1930).

Frey, D. (1978). Reactions to success and failure in public and private conditions. *Journal of Experimental Social Psychology, 14*, 172–179.

Fries, A., & Frey, D. (1980). Misattribution of arousal and the effects of self-threatening information. *Journal of Experimental Social Psychology, 16*, 405–416.

Fromm, E. (1941). *Escape from freedom*. New York: Holt, Rinehart & Winston.

Gollwitzer, P. M., Earle, W. B., & Stephan, W. G. (1982). Affect as a determinant of egotism: Residual excitation and performance attributions. *Journal of Personality and Social Psychology, 43*, 702–709.

Gollwitzer, P. M., Wicklund, R. A., & Hilton, J. L. (1982). Admission of failure and symbolic self-completion: Extending Lewinian theory. *Journal of Personality and Social Psychology, 43*, 358–371.

Goldstein, M., & Davison, E. E. (1972). Race and beliefs: A further analysis of the social determinants of behavioral intentions. *Journal of Personality and Social Psychology, 22*, 346–355.

Goldstein, D., & Rosenbaum, A. (1985). An evaluation of the self-esteem of maritally violent men. *Journal of Applied Family and Child Studies, 34*, 425–428.

Gray, J. A. (1982). *The neuropsychology of anxiety*. London: Oxford University Press.

Greenberg, J., & Pyszczynski, T. (1985). Compensatory self-inflation: A response to the threat to self-regard of public failure. *Journal of Personality and Social Psychology, 49*, 273–280.

Greenberg, J., Pyszczynski, T., Solomon, S., Rosenblatt, A., Veeder, M., Kirkland, S., & Lyon, D. (in press). Evidence for terror management theory II: The effects of mortality salience on reactions to those who threaten or bolster the cultural worldview. *Journal of Personality and Social Psychology*.

Greenberg, J., Pyszczynski, T., & Solomon, S. (1982). The self-serving attributional bias: Beyond self-presentation. *Journal of Experimental Social Psychology, 18*, 56–67.

Greenberg, J., Pyszczynski, T., & Solomon, S. (1986). The causes and consequences of the need for self-esteem: A terror management theory. In R. F. Baumeister (Ed.), *Public self and private self*. New York: Springer-Verlag.

Greenberg, J., Solomon, S., Pyszczynski, T., Lyon, D., & Rosenblatt, A. (1989). *The effects of raising self-esteem on physiological and affective responses to subsequent threat*. Unpublished manuscript, University of Arizona, Tucson.

Hakmiller, J. L. (1966). Threat as a determinant of downward comparison. *Journal of Experimental Social Psychology, 2*, 32–39.

Harris, M. (1979). *Cultural materialism: The struggle for a science of culture*. New York: Random House.

Harper, J., & Field, G. (1986). A preliminary study of children who visited a school sick bay. *Mental Health in Australia, 1*, 8–11.

Herdt, G. (1982). *Rituals of manhood*. Berkeley: University of California Press.

Hobfoll, S., & Leiberman, J. (1987). Personality and social resources in immediate and continued stress resistance among women. *Journal of Personality and Social Psychology, 52*, 18–26.

Hobfoll, S., & London, P. (1986). The relationship of self-concept and social support to emotional distress among women during war. *Journal of Social and Clinical Psychology, 4*, 189–203.

Hofstadter, D. R. (1985). *Metamagical themes:*

Questing for the essence of mind and pattern. New York: Basic Books.

Horney, K. (1950). *Neurosis and human growth.* New York: W. W. Norton.

Ingham, J., Kreitman, N., Miller, P., & Sasidharan, S. (1986). Self-esteem, vulnerability and psychiatric disorder in the community. *British Journal of Psychiatry, 148,* 373–385.

Jackson, M. (1984). *Self-esteem and meaning: A life-historical investigation.* Albany: SUNY Press.

James, W. (1911). *Essays on faith and morals.* New York: Meridian Books.

Jemmott, J. B. (1985). Psychoneuroimmunology: The new frontier. *American Behavioral Scientist, 28,* 497–509.

Johnson, R., Lund, D., & Dimond, M. (1986). Stress, self-esteem and coping during bereavement among the elderly. *Social Psychology Quarterly, 49,* 273–279.

Khouri-Haddad, S. (1984). Psychiatric consultation in a headache unit. *Headache, 24,* 322–328.

Laudan, L. (1977). *Progress and its problems.* Berkeley, Los Angeles, London: University of California Press.

Leary, M. R. (1986). The impact of interactional impediments on social anxiety and self-presentation. *Journal of Experimental Social Psychology, 22,* 122–135.

Leary, M. R., Barnes, B. D., & Griebel, C. (1986). Cognitive, affective, and attributional effects of potential threats to self-esteem. *Journal of Social and Clinical Psychology, 4,* 461–474.

Lerner, M. J. (1980). *The belief in a just world: A fundamental delusion.* New York: Plenum Press.

Lester, D. (1986). Subjective stress and self-esteem of police officers. *Perceptual and Motor Skills, 63,* 1334.

Linn, B., & Zeppa, R. (1984). Stress in junior medical students: Relationship to personality and performance. *Journal of Medical Education, 59,* 7–12.

Lipsitt, L. P. (1958). A self-concept scale for children and its relationship to the childrens' form of the manifest anxiety scale. *Child Development, 29,* 463–472.

Lochman, J., & Lampron, L. (1986). Situational social problem-solving skills and self-esteem of aggressive and nonaggressive boys. *Journal of Abnormal Child Psychology, 14,* 605–617.

Marcuse, H. (1955). *Eros and civilization.* Boston: Beacon Press.

McFarland, C., & Ross, M. (1982). Impact of causal attributions on affective reactions to success and failure. *Journal of Personality and Social Psychology, 43,* 937–946.

Mehlman, R. C., & Snyder, C. R. (1985). Excuse theory: A test of the self-protective role of attributions. *Journal of Personality and Social Psychology, 49,* 994–1001.

Miller, C. E., & Anderson, P. D. (1979). Group decision rules and the rejection of deviates. *Social Psychology Quarterly, 42,* 354–363.

Miller, D. T. (1976). Ego involvement and attribution for success and failure. *Journal of Personality and Social Psychology, 34,* 901–906.

Minksy, M. (1987). *The society of mind.* New York: Simon and Schuster.

Moe, J. L., Nacoste, R. W., & Insko, C. A. (1981). Belief versus race as determinants of discrimination: A study of Southern adolescents in 1966 and 1979. *Journal of Personality and Social Psychology, 41,* 1031–1050.

Mollon, P., & Parry, G. (1984). The fragile self: Narcissistic disturbance and the protective function of depression. *British Journal of Medical Psychology, 57,* 137–145.

Neidig, P., Friedman, D., & Collins, B. (1986). Attitudinal characteristics of males who have engaged in spouse abuse. *Journal of Family Violence, 1,* 223–233.

Osofsky, H. (1985). Transition to parenthood: Risk factors for parents and infants. *Journal of Psychosomatic Obstetrics and Gynecology, 4,* 303–315.

Paloutzian, R. F. (1981). Purpose in life and value changes following conversion. *Journal of Personality and Social Psychology, 41,* 1153–1160.

Pearlin, L., Lieberman, M., Menaghan, E., & Mullan, J. (1981). The stress process. *Journal of Health and Social Behavior, 22,* 337–356.

Penny, G., & Robinson, J. (1986). Psychological resources and cigarette smoking in adolescents. *British Journal of Psychology, 77,* 351–357.

Peterson, C., & Seligman, M. E. P. (1984). Causal explanations as a risk factor for depression: Theory and evidence. *Psychological Review, 91,* 247–274.

Petrie, K., & Rotheram, M. (1982). Insulators against stress: Self-esteem and assertiveness. *Psychological Reports, 50,* 963–966.

Pyszczynski, T., Becker, L., Gracey, L., Greenberg, J., & Solomon, S. (1989). *The terror management function of political attitudes: The effects of mortality salience on reactions to the 1988 presidential debates*. Unpublished manuscript, University of Colorado, Colorado Springs.

Pyszczynski, T., & Greenberg, J. (1987). Toward an integration of cognitive and motivational perspectives on social inference: A biased hypothesis-testing model. In L. Berkowitz (Ed.), *Advances in experimental social psychology* (Vol. 20). Hillsdale, NJ: Lawrence Erlbaum Associates.

Rank, O. (1931). *Psychology and the soul*. New York: Perpetua Books Edition, 1961.

Rank, O. (1936). *Truth and reality*. New York: W. W. Norton, 1978.

Rogers, C. R. (1961). *On becoming a person*. Boston: Houghton Mifflin.

Rokeach, M. (1968). *Beliefs, attitudes, and values*. San Francisco: Jossey-Bass.

Rosenberg, M. (1965). *Society and the adolescent self-image*. Princeton, NJ: Princeton University Press.

Rosenberg, M., & Simmons, R. G. (1972). *Black and white self-esteem: The urban school child*. Washington, DC: American Sociological Association.

Rosenblatt, A., Greenberg, J., Solomon, S., Pyszczynski, T., & Lyon, D. (1989). Evidence for terror management theory I: The effects of mortality salience on reactions to those who violate or uphold cultural values. *Journal of Personality and Social Psychology, 57*, 681–690.

Rothwell, N., & Williams, J. M. G. (1983). Attributional style and life events. *British Journal of Clinical Psychology, 22*, 139–140.

Sampson, E. (1985). The decentralization of identity: Toward a revised concept of personal and social order. *American Psychologist, 40*, 1203–1211.

Savin-Williams, R., & Demo, D. (1983). Conceiving or misconceiving the self: Issues in adolescent self-esteem. *Journal of Early Adolescence, 3*, 121–140.

Schachter, S. (1951). Deviation, rejection and communication. *Journal of Abnormal and Social Psychology, 46*, 190–207.

Scheff, T. (1990). *Crisis in the academic system: Is the emperor wearing clothes?* Unpublished manuscripts, University of California, Santa Barbara.

Schlenker, B. R. (1985). Identity and self-identification. In B. R. Schlenker (Ed.), *The self and social life*. New York: McGraw-Hill.

Skinner, B. F. (1948). *Walden two*. New York: Macmillan.

Skinner, B. F. (1971). *Beyond freedom and dignity*. New York: Knopf.

Snyder, C. R., & Higgins, R. L. (1988). Excuses: Their effective role in the negotiation of reality. *Psychological Bulletin, 104*, 23–35.

Solomon, S., Greenberg, J., & Pyszczynski, T. (in press). *A terror management theory of self-esteem and its role in social behavior*. In M. P. Zanna (Ed.), *Advances in experimental social psychology*.

Spielberger, C. D., Gorsuch, R. L., & Lushene, R. E. (1970). *Trait anxiety inventory (self-evaluation questionnaire)*. Palo Alto, CA: Consulting Psychologist Press.

Steele, C. M., & Liu, T. J. (1983). Dissonance processes as self-affirmation. *Journal of Personality and Social Psychology, 45*, 5–19.

Strauss, C., Frame, C., & Forehand, R. (1987). Psychosocial impairment associated with anxiety in children. *Journal of Clinical Child Psychology, 16*, 235–239.

Sullivan, H. S. (1953). *The interpersonal theory of psychiatry*. New York: W. W. Norton.

Tecoma, E. S., & Huey, L. Y. (1985). Psychic distress and the immune response. *Life Sciences, 36*, 1799–1812.

Templer, D. I. (1971). The relationship between verbalized and non-verbalized death anxiety. *Journal of Genetic Psychology, 119*, 211–214.

Tesser, A. (1980). Self-esteem maintenance in family dynamics. *Journal of Personality and Social Psychology, 39*, 77–91.

Tesser, A., & Campbell, J. (1983). Self-definition and self-evaluation maintenance. In J. Suls & A. G. Greenwald (Eds.), *Psychological perspectives on the self* (Vol. 2). Hillsdale, NJ: Lawrence Erlbaum Associates.

Ullman, C. (1982). Cognitive and emotional antecedents of religious concern. *Journal of Personality and Social Psychology, 43*, 183–192.

Wells, L., & Marwell, G. (1976). *Self-esteem: Its conceptualization and measurement*. Beverly Hills, CA: Sage Publications.

Wylie, R. (1979). *The self-concept*. Lincoln, NE: University of Nebraska Press.

Yalom, I. (1980). *Existential psychotherapy*. New York: Basic Books.

Zigler, E., & Glick, M. (1988). Is paranoid schizophrenia really camouflaged depression? *American Psychologist, 43*, 284–290.

Zimrin, H. (1986). A profile of survival. *Child Abuse and Neglect, 10*, 339–349.

CHAPTER 3

THE ROLE OF HUMOR AND THE SELF

Herbert M. Lefcourt
Karina Davidson-Katz

In a charming article entitled "A Laugh a Day: Can Mirth Keep Disease at Bay?" (Goldstein, 1982), quotations from physicians and philosophers throughout several centuries were presented as testimonies to the value of humor for retaining health. Humor has been said to be good for digestion, for recovery from surgery, for blood circulation, and for the release of tension. At the same time, Goldstein noted that certain puritanical religious figures perceived humor to be evil, a point discussed at some length by Robertson Davies (1975) in *World of Wonders* and Umberto Ecco in *The Name of the Rose* (Ecco, 1983).

More recently, the therapeutic value of humor has been affirmed by Norman Cousins, who, in a brief book entitled *Anatomy of an Illness* (Cousins, 1979), told of his recovery from a serious disintegrative disease through the powers of humor and Vitamin C. Cousins, the former editor of the *Saturday Review*, has been referred to as "the man

who laughed himself back to health." He described his experiences with a life-threatening collagen disorder (ankylosing spondylitis), which followed some severely frustrating and stressful experiences. He also described the procedures that he underwent during his hospitalization that seemed to be more debilitating than helpful. In response to acute pain and his self-perceived decline, Cousins took his treatment into his own hands. He began by seeking an antidote to the dysphoria that accompanied his pain and poor prognosis since he believed it would serve to worsen his already deteriorating condition. Cousins, therefore, arranged to view several comic films, including episodes from *Candid Camera* and various Laurel and Hardy movies, while he was hospitalized. After watching these funny films, Cousins noticed that he was able to sleep painlessly for a few hours without the use of sedative drugs. In addition, his sedimentation rate (an index of the

This chapter was written while the senior author was supported by a research grant from the Canadian Social Sciences and Humanities Research Council Grant No. 410-89-0926 and the second author held a fellowship from the same agency.

severity of inflammation) declined, which was a major reversal of trends before he began watching the humorous films. Eventually Cousins enjoyed a complete recovery from this disorder, which was thought to be a fatal condition. Sometime after his recovery he began discussing his experience in print and in public forums.

Testimonials such as those offered by Norman Cousins and the many physicians and philosophers noted in the article by Goldstein (1982) encourage us to examine the role that humor may play in the health process. It is obvious that humor has had a significant impact on health for certain individuals. It will be the purpose of this chapter to examine the empirical literature concerning humor to determine whether there is much evidence in support of the assumed salutary effects of humor.

In discussing humor's effects on health, we will review research with regard to different junctures in the process that proceed from the onset of stressful experiences to the development of illness. The first phase concerns the effects of stressful experiences on the creation of what some investigators call distress, or strain. That is, stressful events often result in what is phenomenologically experienced as emotional disturbance. However, despite the robust evidence that stressful life experiences are associated with dysphoria and illness, several investigators (Johnson & Sarason, 1979; Rabkin & Stuening, 1976) have pointed out that there is a good deal of variation in the responses of individuals to similar life events, and that as a consequence the relationship between stress and illness is rarely of a high magnitude. As a result, these authors and a number of others have undertaken the next logical step, that of exploring the individual characteristics that either moderate or exacerbate the deleterious effects of stress. There have been at least two recent and extensive reviews of this stress-moderator literature (Cohen & Edwards, 1988; Wheeler & Frank, 1988), indicating the degree of activity in this research area. Our first concern, then, will be to evaluate the literature concerned with the moderation or buffering of stressful experiences.

The question to be addressed is whether a sense of humor serves to lessen the impact of stressful events, perhaps through affecting what Lazarus and Folkman (1984) term the primary appraisal process wherein people evaluate stressors for their potential threat. Another way of phrasing this question is to ask whether those people who have

a good sense of humor are less likely to find stressful events threatening or distressing.

The second focus of the stress-illness connection to be explored concerns the ways in which people cope with distress or emotional upset once it has occurred following the experience of stress. That is, if an individual comes to suffer emotional turmoil following the occurrence of stressful events, does humor have a role to play in lessening that disturbance? Here we will examine the literature concerned with the relationship between humor and the ways in which individuals cope or come to terms with their personal duress. The question we will address is whether humor presages better management of emotional experience.

The third focus concerns the relationship between mood and illness. If a person experiences distress or emotional disturbance following the advent of a stressful event, is illness inevitable? Might the presence of humor indicate a positive mood state that would render the emotional disturbance and its physiological concomitants benign? Here we will examine the relationship between humor and mood states and, in turn, the accompanying physiological changes that are likely to have some influence on health and the development of illness.

Finally, if humor is found to have salubrious effects, we may ask what it is about humor that makes it protective. Here we will share some of our recent thoughts about humor as a "distance-producing" mechanism that allows us to remain somewhat aloof from our own experiences and less vulnerable to the daily "slings and arrows" that comprise stressful events.

HUMOR AS A MODERATOR BETWEEN STRESS AND MOOD DISTURBANCE

Though many writers have attested to the value of humor as a stress moderator, few have offered any elaborate theoretical conceptualizations or empirical data that support their contentions. Freud (1928) is one of the few who have discussed the role of humor at length. "The essence of humour," wrote Freud (1928) "is that one spares oneself the affects to which the situation would naturally give rise and overrides with a jest the possibility of such an emotional display" (p. 216). Thus, humor is a sort of defense mechanism that allows people to face a difficult situation without becoming overwhelmed by unpleasant emotion. In fact, Freud referred to humor as "the highest of the defense mechanisms." Humor is "the triumph of narcissism, the ego's victorious assertion of its own invulnerability. It refuses to be hurt by the arrows of reality or to be compelled to suffer. It insists that it is impervious to wounds dealt by the outside world, in fact, that these are merely occasions for affording it pleasure" (p. 217).

It is interesting to note in passing that in terms of dynamics, Freud considered humor to be the action of the superego assimilated from parental attempts to comfort and reassure the anxious child. By means of humor, wrote Freud (1928), "one refuses to undergo suffering, asseverates the invincibility of one's ego against the real world and victoriously upholds the pleasure principle, yet all without quitting the ground of mental sanity" (p. 217). A sense of humor to Freud was "a rare and precious gift" that in the face of hardships and anxieties, asserted "Look here! This is all that this seemingly dangerous world amounts to. Child's play—the very thing to jest about!" (p. 220).

Freud's focus on humor as a moderator of stress is mirrored in the writings of Dixon (1980), who regarded humor as a response that evolved in our species as a means of defusing negative arousal states. Since the physiological responses attendant upon laughing and being in funny circumstances are similar to those found during emotional arousal, Dixon argued that humor and mirth are "wired-in" alternative responses that may replace anxiety and anger.

Despite these testimonies to the value of humor, there are only four empirical investigations that have examined the function of humor as a moderator of the stress-mood disturbance relationship; and these four studies do not provide the kind of consistency that permits great confidence about the value of humor as a stress moderator. As is usually the case, more research is surely required.

Safranek and Schill (1982) were the first to report on the assumed moderator role of humor. These investigators used an unknown measure of humor, the Humor Use Inventory (Angell, 1970), to predict the effects of stress measured by Sarason's Life Events Scale (LES-Sarason, Johnson, & Siegel, 1978) on *Beck's Depression Inventory* ([BDI] Beck, Ward, Mendelson, Mock, & Erbaugh, 1961) and Spielberger's State-Trait Anxiety Inventory ([STAI] Spielberger, Gorsuch, & Lushene, 1970). The Humor Use Inventory as-

sesses how frequently and how funny a person tries to be in various situations. In addition, subjects were asked to rate the funniness of five types of jokes. With a fairly sizable sample (82 male and 79 female undergraduates) Safranek and Schill found the anticipated relationships between stress, anxiety, and depression. However, neither of their humor measures interacted with stress as a moderator variable. In fact, their humor appreciation measure was positively correlated with stress and depression among the female participants.

These latter findings are not terribly surprising. Some time ago Babad (1974) questioned the use of typical humor scales that make use of preferences and ratings for certain kinds of jokes because they seem to bear no relationship to validity criteria such as peer ratings of the subject's sense of humor. More recently reported studies (Mannell & McMahon, 1982) have also found humor appreciation scores unrelated to criteria of pertinence to humor, whereas laughing and noting humorous incidents were associated with such criteria as well-being. As for self-ratings of one's funniness, like those assessed by the Humor Uses Inventory, social desirability always has proven to be a major problem. When Gordon Allport (1961) attempted to study humor as a personal trait, he found that 94% of his subjects claimed to have an average or above-average sense of humor. Given the shortcomings of the devices used by Safranek and Schill (1982) to measure humor, it would seem wise not to put undue weight on their negative results.

In our own research we have developed two scales for the assessment of humor, the Situational Humor Response Questionnaire ([SHRQ] Martin & Lefcourt, 1984) and the *Coping Humor Scale* ([CHS] Martin & Lefcourt, 1983). The former was designed in a similar way as Endler, McV. Hunt, and Rosenstein's (1962) S-R Inventory of Anxiety. That is, subjects are not asked to directly evaluate their own sense of humor so much as to describe the magnitude of their potential humor responses to a number of situations that vary in their potential for evoking mirth. Thus, subjects describe how often and to what degree they are apt to exhibit mirth in situations that could be potentially irritating as well as funny. We have interpreted the scores on this measure as revealing a sense of bemusement, the likelihood that one will adopt a somewhat distant and humorous vantage point in situations that could be mildly irritating if they were taken as self-affronts.

The CHS, on the other hand, asks simply if the subject uses humor as a means of coping with stress. Both of these scales have been used with fair-sized samples so that there are well-established norms; and there is sufficient validity data for each scale to attest to its value as a measure of humor. Both of these scales have been used along with behavioral measures of humor and another humor questionnaire (Svebak, 1974) in the prediction of mood disturbance following stressful events.

In the first study (Martin & Lefcourt, 1983) conducted with 56 university undergraduates, the SHRQ, the CHS, and the Liking of Humor subscale from Svebak's Sense of Humor Questionnaire were each found to produce significant interactions with a measure of life stress (Life Events of College Students [Sandler & Lakey, 1982]) in the prediction of Total Mood Disturbance Scores from the Profile of Mood States ([POMS] McNair, Lorr, & Droppleman, 1971). The stress measure assessed life changes that had occurred throughout the year while the mood disturbances were from the month immediately prior to participation in the study. In subsequent analyses of these effects, humor was found to have acted as a stress moderator. That is, subjects whose scores on each of the humor measures indicated that they had a good sense of humor were less likely than those who had a lesser sense of humor to be predictable on the POMS from the stress measure. The relationship between stress and mood disturbance was much lower for those with a good sense of humor than for others who had a lesser sense of humor.

Subsequently, we conducted a second similar study with another sample of 62 university students. The measure of stress was the Life Experiences Survey (Sarason, Johnson, & Siegel, 1978) and the mood measure was again the POMS. In this study, however, instead of relying on scales, we obtained a measure of humor productivity using a technique described by Turner (1980). Participants were seated at a table on which there were about a dozen miscellaneous objects such as an old tennis shoe, a crushed beer can, a toothbrush, an aspirin bottle, and so forth. The participants were then asked to make up a 3-minute comedy routine incorporating any or all of the objects in as humorous a way as they could. The skits that had been tape recorded were later scored for number of witty remarks and overall wittiness. These two measures of humor were found to be strongly correlated and consequently were combined into a composite humor index.

Like the previous study, we found a significant interaction between stress and humor in predicting total mood disturbance on the POMS. In the analysis of that interaction, we once again found humor to operate as a moderating variable. Participants who were able to produce humor showed less of a relationship between stress and mood disturbance than did those who were less able to be humorous on this difficult and demanding task.

Finally, 25 of those who had participated in our first study and who had volunteered for further experimentation comprised the sample for our third investigation. The same life stress and mood disturbance scores were used. For humor scores, we again relied on a humor productivity measure, this time one that was most like producing humor in a stressful situation. Subjects watched the film *Subincision*, which had been used as a stressor in laboratory research conducted by Lazarus (1966). They were then asked to create a humorous monologue to accompany the film, which portrays ritual genital mutilation among the aboriginies in Australia. The monologues they created while watching the film were recorded and later scored for wittiness in the same way as humor productivity had been scored in the second study.

Once again, a significant interaction was obtained between stress and humor in the prediction of mood disturbance. When the interaction was further examined, the pattern of the results was the same as in the previous studies. Those who were unable to produce humorous monologues evinced a strong relationship between stress and mood disturbance scores. Mood disturbance scores for subjects who could produce humor in this exceedingly difficult situation, on the other hand, were unpredictable from the measure of stress.

The results of these studies provided considerable support for the hypothesized stress moderator role for humor. Five different measures of humor produced consistent effects: stress had less of a uniform impact among subjects who had a good sense of humor than it did for those bereft of humor. In other words, some of the subjects with a good sense of humor showed little emotional impact from stressful experiences while others did reveal mood disturbance. Among those with a lesser sense of humor, stressful experiences were more likely to arouse negative emotions in the larger number of subjects.

Following the presentation of our research, two

other investigations were published that found mixed results regarding the stress-moderator role of humor. Porterfield (1987) attempted to replicate our studies using both the SHRQ and CHS as measures of humor and the College Student Life Events Schedule (Sandler & Lakey, 1982), which we had used as the measure of stress. On the other hand, Porterfield used the depression scale from the Center for Epidemiological Studies Scales ([CES-D] Radloff, 1977) as opposed to the POMS. The sample size was also larger than ours: 220 Oberlin undergraduates.

The results in Porterfield's study were quite different from what we found in our investigations. First of all, both humor measures were found to produce main effects in the prediction of depression, with humor scores being inversely related to depression. In none of our samples did we obtain main effects between humor and mood disturbance. In addition, there were no interactions to be found between stress and humor and, therefore, no moderator effect to be attributed to humor. Porterfield concluded that the moderator effect of humor was questionable. There was one other difference, however, in Porterfield's study that might help to account for the discrepancies between the results found in his study and ours. Porterfield's sample had a rather high mean on the depression measure ($M = 19.42$), which was more than one standard deviation above that of Radloff's (1977) normative sample ($M = 9.25$, $SD = 8.58$). Quite conceivably, humor may not be an operative moderator for those who are at least moderately depressed. While there is no definitive way to interpret the negative findings in Porterfield's study, sample differences lead us to evaluate his findings with caution.

The one other major study which attempted to test the moderator effects of humor (Nezu, Nezu, & Blissett, 1988) did offer some support for the findings that we had obtained earlier. This study was particularly valuable because the investigators obtained both concurrent and prospective data in the prediction of depression and anxiety. Eighty-seven college undergraduates were administered the BDI, STAI, and LES twice with a 2-month interval. During the first testing they were also administered the CHS and SHRQ.

In the concurrent analysis, both the CHS and SHRQ produced significant main effects in the prediction of depression along with the LES. In addition, the product or interaction between the stress measure and each of the humor scales also was significant, adding predictive power beyond that produced by each variable itself. In a close examination of these results it was evident that while negative life experiences were associated with depression, and an absence of humor also betokened depression, it was particularly the less humorous individual undergoing highly stressful experiences who seemed most destined to become depressed.

When the prospective data were examined, similar findings were in evidence. With depression assessed during the first testing period parceled out, depression at the second testing session was predictable from LES scores for events that had transpired between the two assessments, from the humor measures obtained during the first session, and from the interactions between LES scores and each of the humor scales. Depression seemed most likely to occur among those who had the greater number of negative life experiences and who had a lesser sense of humor. In essence, the data from the concurrent investigation were replicated in the prospective data set.

In complete contrast, nothing was found in the data concerned with anxiety. Anxiety, like depression, was predictable following the experience of negative life events in both the concurrent and prospective data sets. However, humor, although negatively correlated with anxiety scores at both the first and second testing sessions, failed to add significant variance to that of stressful events in regression analyses predicting to anxiety.

The authors offered an interpretation for the divergent findings with anxiety and depression in temporal terms. They suggested that if anxiety may be regarded as an affect associated with the anticipation of negative events and depression can be considered a response to events that have already occurred, then the role of humor would be more of an aid in the coming to terms with past events. The absence of similar findings with anxiety may indicate that humor is not as much a tool for dealing with ongoing or upcoming threats as it is a means of coming to terms with stressful events once they have transpired. In other words, humor in this study would seem to reflect what has been termed emotion-focused coping as opposed to the more instrumentally focused type of coping that would be more useful in warding off potentially anxiety-arousing circumstances.

Finally, in a brief article Trice and Price-Greathouse (1986) reported that among 40 patients who had been assessed for humor with the

CHS and were observed for joking and laughter before dental surgery, those who gave greater evidence of humor had less stressful subjective experiences during surgery.

Though there obviously has been some variation in the results obtained in the aforementioned investigations, there is reason to believe that humor does play a role in the moderation of stress. In our studies, that we obtained interactions indicating stress moderation with five different measures of humor in two separate samples, lends substantial support for the hypothesized value of humor as a stress-moderating personality characteristic.

The results obtained by Nezu et al. (1988) likewise support the stress-moderating role of humor in the development of depression. That these investigators found support in both concurrent and prospective data adds substantially to the claims for the efficacy of humor as a stress moderator. On the other hand, that their results held true only for depression and not anxiety suggests that humor may indicate a style of coping that is more effective for coming to terms with already experienced events than it is for dealing with ongoing threatening circumstances.

Whereas these studies afford positive evidence in support of the stress-moderating role of humor, the studies by Porterfield (1987) and by Safranek and Schill (1982) at least give us reason to question the universality of these findings. Despite the sampling problems in one and the questionable instruments in the other study, the failure to find stress moderator effects in these investigations indicates that the moderator effects that have been reported are not always to be found. The nature of the measuring devices and the characteristics of the subject sample may serve to limit or enhance the likelihood of finding the moderator effects noted in the other studies.

HUMOR AND COPING WITH EMOTIONAL DISTRESS

The literature concerned with humor as a means of dealing with emotional duress is somewhat slender. However, in those studies that have explored the impact of humor on mood, the results are fairly consistent: Those who laugh more readily and are more apt to respond with humor to life's circumstances seem more likely to emerge from emotional duress and enjoy a restoration of positive mood states.

Among the earliest studies concerned with the power of humor to alter mood states were those by Dworkin and Efran (1967) and Berkowitz (1970). In the former, subjects were demeaned by an experimenter for the way in which they had completed autobiographical sketches that they had been asked to write. Following this deliberate arousal of anger, subjects completed a mood adjective checklist on which they readily acknowledged their anger. Subjects in the experimental condition were then asked to listen to one of two humor tapes; one that contained decidedly hostile and the other nonhostile humorous skits that subjects were to rate for humorousness. The control group, in contrast, listened to nonhumorous tapes that were to be rated for "interest level." A second measure of mood states was then obtained.

The resulting data revealed that there were significant decreases in hostility scores for subjects listening to either set of humor tapes, while no changes were found among those who had listened to the control tapes. Contrary to the investigators' hypotheses, hostile humor did not differ from nonhostile humor in serving to lessen the hostility scores. Similar effects were also found for anxiety scores obtained from the mood adjective checklist. That is, the humorous tapes served to lessen the anxiety reported by subjects after they had been berated by the experimenter. These findings led the authors to conclude that humor mitigates feelings of hostility and anxiety.

Berkowitz's (1970) study likewise dealt with the role of humor in the lessening of anger. In his study, the subjects who were female university students assumably listened to a job applicant who spoke rather disdainfully about college women. Given a ruse that the experimenter had to leave to get the correct forms to continue the study, subjects were asked as a favor to listen either to a tape of skits by a hostile (Don Rickles) or nonhostile (George Carlin) comedian, and to rate it for humor. These tapes were presumably going to be used in another study. After rating these tapes, the experimenter reappeared and gave the subject the correct forms on which she was to make judgments about the job applicant and then to record her affect states on the Nowlis Mood Scale (Nowlis, 1965).

The findings revealed that the subjects became more unfavorable to the irritating job applicant following their exposure to the hostile humor presentation. Descriptions and ratings were decidedly more negative. Most importantly, on the mood measure subjects who had listened to the hostile humor tape were characterized as forgiving-kindly, and refreshed-pleased in contrast to those who had heard the nonhostile humor tape, and were equivalent moodwise to those control subjects who had been exposed to a nonirritating job applicant. The hostile comedy skit then was seen as relatively tension reducing for the girls who had been angered.

More recently, Martin, Labott, and Stote (1987) reported similar findings about the effectiveness of humor as a mood reverser in a study of crying. In this investigation, subjects completed a depression adjective checklist and a measure of anger derived from the POMS before and after watching the movie *Brian's Song*. Following the presentation of the movie, subjects either waited for 15 minutes, listened to humorous skits by George Carlin and Robin Williams, or saw the last 15 minutes of the movie again.

As could have been anticipated, crying persisted the most if subjects were exposed to the climax of the movie for a second time. Those who simply had to wait for 15 minutes showed a partial recovery; that is, there were still some signs of sniffling and tears. The humor group, on the other hand, recovered completely, ceasing to cry at all. These findings also were borne out in mood measures. All subjects showed an increase in depression following the movie presentation. Only those subjects who had listened to the humorous sketches, however, evinced a complete recovery of premovie mood states.

Findings such as these have been found elsewhere as well. For example, Singer (1968) found a decrease in tension among black adults following the presentation of a humorous tape recording in which white segregationists were the targets of humorous monologues. Thus, in most studies, humor seems capable of altering prevailing negative mood states, eliminating feelings of depression, and decreasing feelings of anger or tension in the others.

Despite the consistency with which humor is found to alter mood states, there has been little work done that would elucidate the ways in which humor serves to relieve people from negative feelings. Assumably, emotion-focused coping skills would be involved, and it could be hypothesized that persons who more readily respond with humor are usually better able to cope with their own emotional responses than are persons less given to humorous responses. There has been some re-search concerned with the relationship between humor and coping processes that may help to shed some light on the processes by which a sense of humor may help alter mood states.

One of the more consistent findings concerned with individual differences in humor is that children who are adjudged or self-rated as having a good sense of humor are more likely to be assertive in their interactions with peers and in their social and academic activities. In some studies assertiveness has consisted of verbal and physical aggression, dominance, and talkativeness (McGhee, 1980; Bell, McGhee, & Duffey, 1986), whereas in others it has consisted of engagement in the school milieu, popularity, sociability, leadership (Masten, 1986; Pelligrini, Masten, Garmezy, & Ferrarese, 1987; Sherman, 1988) and communicative competence (Carson, Sharpness, Schultz, & McGhee, 1986). This association between humor, assertiveness, and activity level mirrors earlier findings that linked humor with locus of control (Lefcourt, Sordoni, & Sordoni, 1974; Lefcourt, Antrobus, & Hogg, 1974). In those studies, humor was more likely to be found in tense situations among people who perceived themselves to be active determiners of their own experiences (internals) than it was among more fatalistic people. Because internals are more likely to be active in pursuit of their purposes than externals, these earlier results seem to cohere with those from more recent studies focusing on children's assertiveness.

These observations indicate that individuals with a good sense of humor are more likely to take an active stance toward their own experiences than are those with a lesser sense of humor. Therefore, it is reasonable to assume that people with a good sense of humor also would be more active in attempting to alter their unpleasant mood states rather than to endure them passively. This assumption is supported in the above-mentioned studies in that children with a lesser sense of humor were found to be more shy, less engaged, and more socially distant from their peers, characteristics that seem to suggest passive endurance.

Further indications that humor is associated with more activity, or "approach" rather than "avoidance" coping styles, are found in two studies that have linked humor with self-monitoring. Turner (1980) found that high self-monitoring college students, who are presumed to be more socially astute and to have greater mastery of interpersonal skills than low self-monitors, were better able to produce humor on demand in one study; in a second study, where subjects engaged in group interactions, high self-monitoring subjects were most likely to make humorous remarks and to be adjudged as funny by their peers. Similarly, Bell, McGhee, and Duffey (1986) found that among college students, those who commonly engage in self-monitoring of their expressive behavior were more likely to describe themselves as frequent initiators of humor. In a regression analysis of their data, these investigators found self-monitoring to be their strongest predictor of humor.

From other studies directly concerned with coping styles associated with humor and/or positive affect, further evidence accrues regarding the relationship between activity levels and humor. Positive mood states have been found to be related to humor. Mannell and McMahon (1982), for example, found evidence that the number of humorous incidents and frequency of overt laughter recorded in a "humor diary" were positively correlated with elation and surgency and negatively with anxiety, fatigue, and hostility on the Nowlis Mood Adjective Check List (Nowlis, 1965). In our work with humor and moods (Lefcourt & Martin, 1986), we have repeatedly found our humor scales positively related to the Vigor subscale of the POMS (McNair et al., 1971). Therefore, humor may often be a correlate of positive affect, although positive affect states also may occur without any incident of humor.

Viney (1986) examined the coping behaviors of more than 500 patients undergoing medical treatment in Australian hospitals. She found that patients who scored higher on a measure of positive emotions were more competent and more likely to be engaged in satisfying social relationships despite their illness. Positive emotionality was also associated with less depression, or indirectly expressed anger. Viney raised the question of whether the expression of positive emotion among the physically ill was evidence of defensiveness (avoidance) or coping (approach) behavior. Though she found some evidence for both interpretations, Viney concluded from the balance of her findings that positive emotions can more easily be regarded as coping behavior because they help individuals preserve their psychological integrity, which, in turn, helps to sustain physical integrity.

In Viney's approach, coping seemed to be defined in terms of competence and effectiveness in the encounter with stress, whereas defensiveness

was inferred from a less than competent response to life ordeals. Viney then found evidence to the effect that positive emotions were related to more effective or competent reactions to illness, reactions that would offer better prognosis for recovery from illness.

In laboratory experimentation where positive affects were induced by humor or the receipt of small gifts, Isen, Daubman, and Nowicki (1987) found that subjects exhibited improved performance on tasks that required creative ingenuity for their solution: Duncker's (1945) candle task and the Remote Associates Test (Mednick, Mednick, & Mednick, 1964). In contrast, the arousal of negative affect or periods of physical exercise wherein affectless arousal occurred failed to have a similar impact. Positive affect, then, seems to be associated with more flexibility and/or ingenuity in problem-solving, which would mirror the findings of Viney regarding competence in the encounter with stressor.

In another study of coping styles associated with humor, Rim (1988) examined the relationships between an extensive measure of coping and both the SHRQ and CHS (Lefcourt & Martin, 1986) measures of humor. More than 100 students completed a measure of coping styles deriving from Plutchik's (1980, 1981) work on emotions as well as the two humor measures. Among the coping styles evaluated were "minimization," whereby people minimize the magnitude of their problems, "suppression," which denotes the avoidance of even thinking about displeasing things, and "replacement," which indicates flexibility when thwarted in the pursuit of usual activities. Five other coping styles also were described, but it was on the three aforementioned coping strategies that the results for both sexes and both humor scales were the most uniform. The humor scales were positively associated with minimization and replacement, and negatively with suppression.

These findings complement those described earlier. Minimization and replacement reflect a "carrying on" despite adversity, whereas suppression reflects an avoidance or failure to contend with the details of one's stressful experiences. Rim's findings, then, mirror the approach versus avoidance and activity versus passivity dimensions that characterized persons differing in their sense of humor in other investigations.

What may we conclude from these investigations with regard to the ways in which people come to terms with the affective consequences of stress? It seems as though people with a good sense of humor are less likely to passively accept the negative affects that accompany stressful experiences. Humor seems to signify an active and assertive orientation that augurs a readiness to change feelings and, perhaps, an impatience with negative affects such as anxiety and depression. The tendency to minimize and replace one pursuit with another suggests that the person with a good sense of humor does not as easily accept the experiencing of negative emotions for a lengthy time as might their less mirthful peers.

It is still somewhat mysterious and perhaps beyond the purview of psychological methods to know what exactly occurs when people deal with their immediate experience of negative affects. We are most often left with self-reports of events and experiences that have already transpired. To examine the moment in which a person shifts from one affective state to another, or to closely observe the process of recovery from mourning, for example, might more clearly reveal to us how humor plays a role in the response to emotional experiences.

HUMOR AND THE DEVELOPMENT OF ILLNESS

Stress has been implicated as a source of illness for a considerable length of time, and in the past two decades there has been much research reported indicating that negative life events, comprising the definition of stress, are often precursors of illness. However, as noted in the introduction to this chapter, although the relationship between stress and illness is significant and reliable, there is still considerable room for variation, which has provoked researchers to explore the effects of a number of moderator variables, such as beliefs about control and social support, that could account for differential susceptibility to illness.

Because negative life experiences assumably create dysphoric moods that in turn are said to eventuate in illnesses, it occurred to Norman Cousins (1979) that positive moods associated with humor might have the reverse effect of somehow strengthening people's resistance to and aiding in the recovery from illness. In his self-experimentation he found some supporting evidence to the effect that laughter served to ease his pain and enabled him to sleep. In addition, the sedimentation rates assessed from his blood samples, which indicate inflammation, decreased following laughter, when it had been steadily increasing before his therapeutic use of humor.

Recent evidence offers some support for the analgesic qualities of humor. Cogan, Cogan, Waltz, and McCue (1987) found that thresholds for pressure-induced discomfort increased following the presentation of a humorous tape recording that produced laughter among subjects. The humorous tape was contrasted with relaxing and boring tapes in one study, and with an interesting narrative, a boring narrative, a multiplication task, or simply waiting in a second investigation. In the first study both humor and relaxation had positive effects upon pain thresholds; in the second study it was only humor that served to raise the threshold for pain.

A study by Prerost and Ruma (1987) presented data suggesting that humor could play a role in facilitating muscle relaxation. In this investigation, which was designed to find facilitators of biofeedback, subjects who had looked at any of three series of cartoons showed a marked decrease in muscle tension as measured by electromyogram, and an increase in relaxation as the session progressed, compared with a control group that viewed slides that depicted forest scenery. On mood measures (Nowlis-Green Mood Adjective Checklist, Nowlis, 1965) administered after the relaxation experience, control subjects reported fatigue, whereas subjects exposed to humor reported elation and vigor. In these two studies, then, some evidence was found that at least indirectly supports Norman Cousin's conjectures regarding humor, pain, and relaxation.

In our own labs we have found some preliminary evidence suggesting that humor as a personality characteristic, measured by the SHRQ and CHS, affords some prediction of blood pressure changes among subjects undergoing stressful tasks. Throughout a set of tasks, including the Stroop Test (Manuck & Krantz, 1986), the Favorable Impressions Task (Borkovec, Stone, O'Brien, & Kaloupek, 1974), in which the subject is supposed to impress a nonresponsive member of the opposite sex, and the Mental Arithmetic Task (Williams, Lane, Kuhn, Melosh, White, & Schanberg, 1982), 20 measures of systolic and diastolic blood pressure were obtained. Thus far, we have found that our SHRQ has an average negative correlation of .30 with the 20 measures of blood pressure that were taken during these tasks. The results seem to be even more marked with females, among whom correlations have averaged in the .40 range.

Where the first two studies indicate that humor can help relieve pain and muscle tension, our developing work suggests that humor may also serve to lessen the arousability that can occur during stressful situations. The implications for health are apparent here. In the work with blood pressure we may be examining early indications of hypertension, which is a condition responsible for the development of various circulatory problems.

Another set of research findings have drawn attention to the role of humor and positive affect in the functioning of the immune system. In attempting to explain the relationship between stress, mood disturbance, and illness, immune system failure often is cited as the intervening step between mood and illness. A number of investigators have reported that distress and emotional upset can depress the functioning of the immune system, which would leave an individual more susceptible to illness (see, i.e., Glaser, Kiecolt-Glaser, Speicher, & Holliday, 1985; Jemmott & Magloire, 1988; Kiecolt-Glaser, Fisher, Ogrocki, Stout, Speicher, & Glaser, 1987; Kiecolt-Glaser, Kennedy, Malkoff, Fisher, Speicher, & Glaser, 1988; McClelland, Floor, Davidson, & Saron, 1980; McClelland, Ross, & Patel, 1985). Because negative mood states following stressful experiences have been found to be associated with a decline in immune system functioning and illness, it is not surprising that certain investigators recently have begun to explore the opposite side of the coin: the possible beneficial effects of humor and positive mood states on immune system functioning.

The first study to directly link humor with immune system activity was reported by Dillon, Minchoff, and Baker (1985). In this investigation with only nine subjects, humor was found to be associated with the production of salivary immunoglobulin A (S-IgA). S-IgA is often regarded as the body's first line of defense and is thought to defend against viral and bacterial infections, especially of the upper respiratory tract (Tomasi, 1976). In previous research, S-IgA concentrations have been found to be depressed when persons were undergoing stressful experiences such as examinations (Jemmott, Borysenko, Borysenko, McClelland, Chapman, Meyer, & Benson, 1983; Linn, Linn, & Jensen, 1984). Because S-IgA concentrations were found to be depressed following

stressful experiences, Dillon et al. reasoned that positive moods activated by laughter or a sense of humor are associated with elevations in S-IgA concentrations. As the first of their findings, Dillon et al. found a rather high correlation ($r = .75$, $p < .02$) between the CHS measure of humor and levels of S-IgA from each of four saliva samples obtained during this experiment. Following the presentation of a humorous film (*Richard Prior Live*) there was also a significant increase in S-IgA concentrations. In contrast, S-IgA concentrations did not vary at all when a control tape was presented which offered a didactic discussion about anxiety. This investigation, though limited in value because of the small number of subjects used, was exciting in that it showed the first positive linkage between humor and the kinds of physiological processes that could have implications for the development of illness.

Following this report by Dillon et al. (1985), Martin and Dobbin (1988) examined the role of humor as a moderator of the relationship between stressful experiences and S-IgA suppression. In their experiment, the Daily Hassles Scale (Kanner, Coyne, Schaeffer, & Lazarus, 1981) was used as the measure of stress, with S-IgA concentrations obtained during a second test session, 1 1/2 months later, serving as the dependent measure. Humor was assessed by the SHRQ, CHS, and scales from Svebak's Sense of Humor Questionnaire (Svebak, 1974). The first point of interest to be noted was that S-IgA concentration levels obtained during the first testing session were not significantly related to the Daily Hassles scores obtained at the same time. However, the Daily Hassles scores from the first testing session were related to the concentration levels of S-IgA obtained at the second testing session some 45 days later ($r = -.32$, $p < .05$).

Most importantly, both the SHRQ and CHS measures of humor interacted with the Daily Hassles scores in regression analyses predicting the concentration levels of S-IgA. These results also were found with one of the two scales of Svebak's humor measure (Meta-Message Sensitivity scale). In each case, it was found that subjects with low scores on the humor scales revealed a stronger negative relationship between hassles and S-IgA concentrations than did those with high humor scores.

Martin and Dobbin (1988) therefore found evidence to the effect that humor serves to moderate the physiological effects of stress in the same way that Lefcourt and Martin (1986) found humor to moderate the mood effects of stressful experiences: those who had a lesser sense of humor showed the greatest immunosuppressive effect following the experience of negative live events. Those with a good sense of humor, on the other hand, seemed to be less predictable from measures of stressful experiences.

In our own labs we also found evidence concerning the relationship between humor and S-IgA concentration levels (Lefcourt, Davidson-Katz, & Kueneman, 1989). We have thus far conducted three studies in which S-IgA has been assessed from salivary samples obtained before and after listening to or watching humorous tapes. We also have examined S-IgA responses as a function of sense of humor assessed by the SHRQ and CHS scales. In all three studies we have found S-IgA concentrations increased following the presentation of humorous tapes, whereas S-IgA levels remained stable in control conditions. In two of the three studies, subjects who scored higher on the humor scales showed larger increases in S-IgA concentrations following the exposure to the humorous tapes.

Although there is some dispute among investigators as to the ways in which S-IgA should be assessed, and there are questions as to the value of S-IgA itself as an indicator of immune system activity, these findings are impressive in linking paper-and-pencil measures of a phenomenon such as humor with physiological processes associated with health.

Although there are no other articles directly linking humor to immune system functioning, there are some investigations that provide indirect evidence of this relationship by examining the association between positive mood states and the activation of the immune system. As noted earlier, humor and positive mood states are usually correlated with one another in a positive direction.

Stone, Cox, Valdimarsdottir, Jandorf, and Neale (1987) found that the Nowlis Mood Adjective Check List completed thrice weekly for $8\frac{1}{3}$ weeks by dental students was significantly related to concentrations of S-IgA that were measured in a more elaborate fashion than had been done in the previous investigations. Antibody responses were found to be lower on days when high negative moods were reported in comparison with days when less negative moods were noted. Conversely, S-IgA antibody responses were higher on days when there were highly positive moods recorded

relative to days when less positive moods were recorded.

Although there have been no other studies directly linking humor, positive affect, and immune system activity, and there is a dearth of research using more profound immune system activity markers (natural killer cells, suppressor T lymphocytes, etc.), the studies described above are promising. Further work using a range of immune system markers, as in the research of Kiecolt-Glaser and her colleagues, may help to shed more light on the relationships between affect and immune system activity. In her studies of stressed individuals, Kiecolt-Glaser has found evidence indicating that husbands and wives in happier marriages have more active immune system responses than those experiencing discord or separation (Kiecolt-Glaser et al., 1987, 1988). Though her work is mostly concerned with immunosuppression among the distressed, the control groups who can be assumed to be happier are usually found to evince stronger immune system responses.

In sum, although we are only at the preliminary stages of exploration, there is reason to be optimistic regarding the role of humor in the relationship between mood and health. People with a better sense of humor, who are more likely to find things to laugh about, seem better equipped to survive the ordeal of pain and to resist intrusive illnesses, at least insofar as the data regarding immune system activity seems to indicate. Obviously, much more research is necessary before this assertion can be regarded as reliable. However, early indications would suggest that humor may prove to be valuable in the struggle to sustain health.

WHY HUMOR HAS BENEFICIAL EFFECTS ON HEALTH

Earlier in this chapter we alluded to the writings of Freud concerning humor as a means of perceiving our conundrums as "child's play." In his article on humor, Freud (1928) drew sharp differentiations between jokes, wit, the comic, and what he referred to as humor. The former kinds of humor more often seem to involve invidious comparisons and hostile expressions toward others. Humor, on the other hand, seems to be of a gentler sort, where the joke, if there is one, is self-directed; and it is this sort of humor that we have come to believe has the greatest potential for affecting health status. If witty joking does indeed contain the barbs of anger and hostility, then such forms of humor are probably abrasive and serve to solidify negative relationships between persons. The joker affirms his position with his joking and ascribes the targets of the joke to their positions. Much of the sociological study of joking reflects the role-maintaining behavior that is implicit in joking (Coser, 1959, 1960; Kaplan & Boyd, 1965).

In contrast, the discussion of humor as consisting of self-directed jesting offers a form of cognitive and affective activity that seems to be more congruent with the findings noted above than are the more hostile forms of humor comprising much of wit and joking. Humor may be viewed as an expression of not taking oneself terribly seriously. That is, humor may be in evidence when some stressful events, variations of moods, and our fates in general are regarded from a somewhat remote position wherein bemusement can also be experienced.

Rollo May (1953) described this form of humor:

It is an expression of our uniquely human capacity to experience ourselves as subjects who are not swallowed up in the objective situation. It is the healthy way of feeling a "distance" between oneself and the problem, a way of standing off and looking at one's problems with perspective. One cannot laugh when in an anxiety panic, for then one is swallowed up, one has lost the distinction between himself as subject and the objective world around him. (p. 54)

A similar position is advanced by the writer, George Mikes (1971):

There is nothing self-effacing in a sense of humor. Laughing at oneself does not mean that one is inferior to others; it means that we accept ourselves as erratic, foolish and bungling as all our fellow creatures are . . . to laugh at oneself does not mean to be modest, insecure, unsure. A man who is unsure usually takes himself deadly seriously and is given to watching himself anxiously at all times. (p. 36)

The SHRQ that we originally developed to assess humor as a kind of tendency to be bemused was designed to reflect the kinds of sentiments offered by Freud, May, and Mikes. In the scale we asked whether the subject would feel bemused by odd situations that might be embarrassing or annoying. One question, for example, dealt with the event of a waiter in a restaurant accidentally spilling a glass of water on the subject. It is quite

acceptable to become upset at such a circumstance, and some people might become furious at such a turn of events. But what if one can instantly see the event from afar, adapting a "Why me?" kind of expression. As May suggested, this would indicate that one is not totally caught up in this objective situation; and Mikes might interpret our momentary victimhood as somehow personifying the victimhood of us all for a person with a good sense of humor, and therefore not being as arousing as it would be for a more self-serious person.

Following these considerations, Rob Shepherd (1989) explored the role of humor in allowing us to tolerate thoughts about our own mortality. We have been examining the relationship between humor and a number of activities that concern death, such as agreeing to donate body parts following death, writing wills, visiting dying persons, and so forth. We have found evidence to the effect that people with a better sense of humor as measured by the SHRQ are less emotionally disturbed by thinking about death and are consequently more inclined to donate body parts and to be willing to do things that remind us of our own transience.

We have regarded thoughts about our own deaths as one of the missing items from most measures of life stress, and we have considered humor to be a moderating variable that can account for differential responses to that threat. Thus far, we have been encouraged by our results. It seems that humor may reflect our not regarding ourselves as overly important, despite the central position we occupy in our own lives. Such humility, in turn, may enable us to engage in potentially stressful circumstances as are inherent in considering our own mortality.

In our attempts to better measure this kind of self-directed humor, we have created another device that assesses whether subjects comprehend the meaning of certain cartoons from Gary Larsen's *The Far Side*. The cartoons selected all depict the absurdity of human conceit. We have developed a battery consisting of six of these cartoons, and have discovered that persons who can laugh and talk about the absurdity of human pretensions vis-a-vis other species reflected in the cartoon battery are less disturbed by exercises that make their own deaths quite salient (filling out one's own death certificate, writing an obituary for oneself, etc.).

Assumably, if we can accept our own mortality, if we are more tolerant and less serious about many of the absurd, embarrassing, or demeaning circumstances that we are bound to endure, we should experience less ire and negative affect, which exacts such a high price from our health status.

CONCLUSIONS

While the data we have presented indicates that humor may have an important and positive role to play with regard to health, it is obvious that much more needs to be known before we can join those nurses and clinicians who advocate the use of humor in medical and therapeutic settings (Fry & Salameh, 1987). It seems obvious, if only from the fact that people seek out exposure to comedians and generally prefer to be with people who have a good sense of humor, that humor is something good and desirable.

From the research described in this chapter, the liking of humor seems to be related to the fact that we feel better and enjoy more positive feeling states when we laugh and find things funny. In turn, these positive affect states seem to be associated with feelings of well-being and health. At each juncture of the process that begins with stress and ends with illness, there is evidence that positive affect states associated with humor play a facilitative role in enabling us to survive, if not totally unscathed, then at least less perturbed. There is evidence that mood disturbance may not follow as inevitably from stress among persons who have a good sense of humor; likewise, there is evidence that humor can reverse the affects in situations where stress has resulted in a degree of anguish; and finally, there is some evidence that humor and positive affective states have a physiological counterpart that seems to be positive in our resistance to illness. However, despite the optimism that such evidence can produce, we must remember that the evidence is all quite preliminary, and much more needs to be understood before we become too sanguine about the effectiveness of humor in affecting our health.

REFERENCES

Allport, G. (1961). *Pattern and growth in personality*. New York: Holt, Rinehart & Winston.

Angell, J. D. (1970). The effects of social success and social failure on the humor production of wits. *Dissertation Abstracts International, 10*, 375–376.

Babad, E. Y. (1974). A multimethod approach to the assessment of humor: A critical look at humor tests. *Journal of Personality, 42*, 618–631.

Beck, A. T., Ward, C. H., Mendelson, M., Mock, J., & Erbaugh, J. (1961). An inventory for measuring depression. *Archives of General Psychiatry, 4*, 561–571.

Bell, N. J., McGhee, P. E., & Duffey, N. S. (1986). Interpersonal competence, social assertiveness and the development of humor. *British Journal of Developmental Psychology, 4*, 51–55.

Berkowitz, L. (1970). Aggressive humor as a stimulus to aggressive responses. *Journal of Personality and Social Psychology, 16*, 710–717.

Borkovec, T. D., Stone, N. M., O'Brien, G. T., & Kaloupek, D. (1974). Evaluation of a clinically relevant target behavior for analog outcome research. *Behavior Therapy, 5*, 503–513.

Carson, D. K., Skarpness, L. R., Schultz, N. W., & McGhee, P. E. (1986). Temperament and communicative competence as predictors of young children's humor. *Merrill-Palmer Quarterly, 32*, 415–426.

Cogan, R., Cogan, D., Waltz, W., & McCue, M. (1987). Effects of laughter and relaxation on discomfort thresholds. *Journal of Behavioral Medicine, 10*, 139–143.

Cohen, S., & Edwards, J. R. (1988). Personality characteristics as moderators of the relationship between stress and disorder. In R. W. J. Neufeld (Ed.), *Advances in the investigation of psychological stress*. New York: John Wiley & Sons.

Coser, R. J. (1959). Some social functions of laughter. *Human Relations, 12*, 171–182.

Coser, R. J. (1960). Laughter among colleagues. *Psychiatry, 23*, 81–95.

Cousins, N. (1979). *Anatomy of an illness as perceived by the patient*. New York: W. W. Norton & Co.

Davies, R. (1975). *World of wonders*. New York: Viking-Penguin.

Dillon, K. M., Minchoff, B., & Baker, K. H. (1985). Positive emotional states and enhancement of the immune system. *International Journal of Psychiatry in Medicine, 15*, 13–17.

Dixon, N. F. (1980). Humor: A cognitive alternative to stress? In I. G. Sarason & C. D. Spielberger (Eds.), *Stress and anxiety: Vol. 7* (pp. 281–289). Washington, DC: Hemisphere.

Duncker, K. (1945). On problem solving. *Psychological Monographs, 58,* (5, Whole No. 270).

Dworkin, E. S., & Efran, J. S. (1967). The angered: Their susceptibility to varieties of humor. *Journal of Personality and Social Psychology, 6,* 233–236.

Ecco, U. (1983). *The name of the rose.* San Diego: Harcourt-Brace-Jovanovich.

Endler, N. S., McV. Hunt, J., & Rosenstein, A. J. (1962). An S-R inventory of anxiousness. *Psychological Monographs, 76* (17, Whole No. 536).

Freud, S. (1928). Humour. *International Journal of Psychoanalysis, 9,* 1–6.

Fry, W. F., & Salameh, W. A. (1987). *Handbook of humour and psychotherapy.* Sarasota, FL: Professional Resource Exchange.

Glaser, R., Kiecolt-Glaser, J. K., Speicher, C. E., & Holliday, J. (1985). Stress, loneliness and herpes virus latency. *Journal of Behavioral Medicine, 8,* 249–260.

Goldstein, J. H. (1982). A laugh a day. *The Sciences, 22,* 21–25.

Isen, A. M., Daubman, K. A., & Nowicki, G. P. (1987). Positive affect facilitates creative problem solving. *Journal of Personality and Social Psychology, 52,* 1122–1131.

Jemmott, J. B., Borysenko, J. Z., Borysenko, M., McClelland, D. C., Chapman, R., Meyer, D., & Benson, H. (1983). Academic stress, power motivation, and decrease in salivary secretory immunoglobulin A secretion rate. *Lancet, 1,* 1400–1402.

Jemmott, J. B., & Magloire, K. (1988). Academic stress, social support, and secretory immunoglobulin A. *Journal of Personality and Social Psychology, 55,* 803–810.

Johnson, J. H., & Sarason, I. G. (1979). Moderator variables in life stress research. In I. G. Sarason & C. D. Spielberger (Eds.), *Stress and Anxiety: Vol. 6* (pp. 151–167). Washington, DC: Hemisphere.

Kanner, A. D., Coyne, J. C., Schaeffer, C., & Lazarus, R. S. (1981). Comparison of two modes of stress measurement: Daily hassles and uplifts versus major life events. *Journal of Behavioral Medicine, 4,* 1–39.

Kaplan, H. B., & Boyd, I. H. (1965). The social functions of humor on an open psychiatric ward. *Psychiatric Quarterly, 39,* 502–515.

Kiecolt-Glaser, J. K., Fisher, L., Ogrocki, P., Stout, J. C., Speicher, C. E., & Glaser, R. (1987). Marital quality, marital disruption, and immune function. *Psychosomatic Medicine, 49,* 13–34.

Kiecolt-Glaser, J. K., Kennedy, S., Malkoff, S., Fisher, L., Speicher, C. E., & Glaser, R. (1988). Marital discord and immunity in males. *Psychosomatic Medicine, 20,* 2–17.

Lazarus, R. S. (1966). *Psychological stress and the coping process.* New York: McGraw-Hill.

Lazarus, R. S., & Folkman, S. (1984). *Stress, appraisal, and coping.* New York: Springer.

Lefcourt, H. M., Antrobus, P., & Hogg, E. (1974). Humor response and humor production as a function of locus of control, field dependence, and type of reinforcements. *Journal of Personality, 42,* 632–651.

Lefcourt, H. M., Davidson-Katz, K., & Kueneman, K. (1990). Humor and immune system functioning. *Humor: International Journal of Humor Research, 4.*

Lefcourt, H. M., Sordoni, C., & Sordoni, C. (1974). Locus of control, field dependence and expression of humor. *Journal of Personality, 42,* 130–143.

Lefcourt, H. M., & Martin, R. A. (1986). *Humor and life stress.* New York: Springer-Verlag.

Linn, B. S., Linn, M. W., & Jensen, J. (1984). Degree of depression and immune responsiveness. *Psychosomatic Medicine, 44,* 128.

Mannell, R. C., & McMahon, L. (1982). Humor as play: Its relationship to psychological well-being during the course of a day. *Leisure Sciences, 5,* 143–155.

Manuck, S. B., & Krantz, D. S. (1986). Psychophysiologic reactivity in coronary heart disease and essential hypertension. In K. A. Matthews, S. M. Weiss, B. Falkner, S. B. Manuck, & R. B. Williams, Jr. (Eds.), *Handbook of stress reactivity and cardiovascular disease* (pp. 11–34). New York: John Wiley & Sons.

Martin, R. A., & Dobbin, J. P. (1988). Sense of humor, hassles, and immunoglobulin A: Evidence for a stress-moderating effect of humor. *International Journal of Psychiatry in Medicine, 18,* 93–105.

Martin, R. A., & Lefcourt, H. M. (1983). Sense of humor as a moderator of the relation between stressors and moods. *Journal of Personality and Social Psychology, 45,* 1313–1324.

Martin, R. A., & Lefcourt, H. M. (1984). The situational humor response questionnaire: A quantitative measure of the sense of humor. *Journal of Personality and Social Psychology, 47,* 145–155.

Martin, R. B., Labott, S. M., & Stote, J. (1987). Emotional crying and exposure to humor as factors in the recovery from depressed mood. Paper presented at Eastern Psychological Association Convention, Arlington, VA.

Masten, A. S. (1986). Humor and competence in school-aged children. *Child Development, 57*, 461–473.

May, R. (1953). *Man's search for himself*. New York: Random House.

McClelland, D. C., Floor, E., Davidson, R. J., & Saron, C. (1980). Stressed power motivation, sympathetic activation, immune function, and illness. *Journal of Human Stress, 6*, 11–19.

McClelland, D. C., Ross, G., & Patel, V. (1985). The effect of an academic examination on salivary norepinephrine and immunoglobulin levels. *Journal of Human Stress, 11*, 52–59.

McGhee, P. E. (1980). Development of the sense of humour in childhood: A longitudinal study. In P. E. McGhee & J. H. Goldstein (Eds.), *Children's humor* (pp. 213–236). Chichester, England: John Wiley & Sons.

McNair, D. M., Lorr, M., & Droppleman, L. F. (1971). *The profile of mood states*. San Diego, CA: Educational and Industrial Testing Service.

Mednick, M. T., Mednick, S. A., & Mednick, E. V. (1964). Incubation of creative performance and specific associative priming. *Journal of Abnormal and Social Psychology, 69*, 84–88.

Mikes, G. (1971). *Laughing matter: Towards a personal philosophy of wit and humor*. New York: Liberty Press.

Nezu, A. M., Nezu, C. M., & Blissett, S. E. (1988). Sense of humor as a moderator of the relation between stressful events and psychological distress: A prospective analysis. *Journal of Personality and Social Psychology, 54*, 520–525.

Nowlis, V. (1965). Research with the mood adjective check list. In S. Tomkins & C. Izard (Eds.), *Affect, cognition, and personality*. New York: Springer.

Pelligrini, D. S., Masten, A. S., Garmezy, N., & Ferrarese, M. J. (1987). Correlates of social and academic competence in middle childhood. *Journal of Child Psychology and Psychiatry, 28*, 699–714.

Plutchik, R. (1980). *Emotion: A psychoevolutionary synthesis*. New York: Harper & Row.

Plutchik, R. (1981). Development of a scale for the measurement of coping styles: A preliminary report.

Porterfield, A. L. (1987). Does sense of humor moderate the impact of life stress on psychological and physical well-being? *Journal of Research in Personality, 21*, 306–317.

Prerost, F. J., & Ruma, C. (1987). Exposure to humorous stimuli as an adjunct to muscle relaxation training. *Psychology, A Quarterly Journal of Human Behavior, 24*, 70–74.

Rabkin, J. G., & Struening, E. L. (1976). Life events, stress, and illness. *Science, 194*, 1013–1020.

Radloff, L. S. (1977). The CES-D scale: A self-report depression scale for research in the general population. *Applied Psychological Measurement, 1*, 385–401.

Rim, Y. (1988). Sense of humor and coping styles. *Personality and Individual Differences, 9*, 559–564.

Safranek, R., & Schill, T. (1982). Coping with stress: Does humor help? *Psychological Reports, 51*, 222.

Sandler, I. N., & Lakey, B. (1982). Locus of control as a stress moderator: The role of control perceptions and social support. *American Journal of Community Psychology, 10*, 65–80.

Sarason, I. G., Johnson, J. H., & Siegel, J. M. (1978). Assessing the impact of life changes: Development of the life experiences survey. *Journal of Consulting and Clinical Psychology, 46*, 932–946.

Shepherd, R. (1989). Sense of humor and the ability to consider mortality. Doctoral Dissertation, University of Waterloo.

Sherman, L. W. (1988). Humor and social distance in elementary school children. *Humor: International Journal of Humor Research, 1*, 389–404.

Singer, D. L. (1968). Aggression arousal, hostile humor, catharsis. *Journal of Personality and Social Psychology, 8*, 1–14.

Spielberger, C. D., Gorsuch, R. L., & Lushene, R. E. (1970). *The state-trait anxiety inventory*. Palo Alto, CA: Consulting Psychologists Press.

Stone, A. A., Cox, D. S., Valdimarsdottir, H., Jandorf, J., & Neale, J. M. (1987). Evidence that secretory IgA is associated with daily mood. *Journal of Personality and Social Psychology, 52*, 988–993.

Svebak, S. (1974). Revised questionnaire on the sense of humor. *Scandinavian Journal of Psychology, 15*, 328–331.

Tomasi, T. B. (1976). *The immune system of secretions*. Englewood Cliffs, NJ: Prentice-Hall.

Trice, A. D., & Price-Greathouse, J. (1986). Joking under the drill: A validity study of the CHS. *Journal of Social Behavior and Personality, 1*, 265–266.

Turner, R. G. (1980). Self-monitoring and humor production. *Journal of Personality, 48*, 163–172.

Viney, L. L. (1986). Expression of positive emotion by people who are physically ill: Is it evidence of defending or coping? *Journal of Psychosomatic Research, 30*, 27–34.

Wheeler, R. J., & Frank, M. A. (1988). Identification of stress buffers. *Behavioral Medicine, 14*, 78–89.

Williams, R. B., Lane, J., Kuhn, C., Melosh, W., White, A., & Schaneberg, S. (1982). Type A behavior and elevated physiological and neuroendocrine responses to cognitive tasks. *Science, 218*, 483–485.

CHAPTER 4

SELF-EFFICACY

James E. Maddux

People tend to engage in behaviors that they believe will get them what they want and that they believe they can do. We are more likely to pursue those goals we value highly than those we value less; we are more likely to pursue those courses of actions we anticipate will lead to the desired goals than those courses of action that appear less likely to be profitable; and, all else being equal, we are more likely to attempt those actions and strategies we believe are within our capabilities than those means that seem to exceed our capacities. A number of important psychological theories have been based on some variation or another of these sound and simple premises concerned with the role of perceived competence, personal effectiveness, and control in psychological health and well-being (see chapters in this volume by Burns; Higgins; Karoly; Lefcourt; Schlenker; Seligman; Solomon; Thompson, & Snyder). *Self-efficacy theory* (Bandura, 1977, 1982, 1986a) is one of the more recent in a long tradition of personal competence or efficacy theories and probably has generated more research in clinical, social, and

personality psychology in the past dozen years than other similar models and theories. The crux of self-efficacy theory is found in the above premises: that the initiation of and persistence at behaviors and courses of action are determined largely by (a) *outcome value* (the importance of certain outcomes, consequences, or goals); (b) *outcome expectancy* (expectations concerning the effectiveness of certain behavioral means in producing those outcomes); and, most importantly, (c) *self-efficacy expectancy* (judgments and expectations concerning behavioral skills and capabilities and the likelihood of being able to successfully implement the selected courses of action). Self-efficacy theory also maintains that these same factors play an important role in psychological adjustment and dysfunction and in effective therapeutic interventions for emotional and behavioral problems.

The major purpose of this chapter is to describe and evaluate self-efficacy theory and the research most directly relevant to the interface of clinical and social psychology. The chapter will provide an overview of self-efficacy theory, describe the relationships between self-efficacy theory and other theories of personal competence and effectiveness, and discuss the role of self-efficacy and related constructs in psychological health and adjustment, and in psychotherapeutic interventions. One important assumption guiding this chapter is that self-efficacy theory is a true "bridging" theory between social and clinical psychology, a theory of social cognition on which there has been a tremendous amount of basic research and a theory of therapeutic behavioral and emotional change of great practical interest to clinical researchers and practitioners.

MODELS OF PERSONAL EFFICACY

A number of theorists have explored the nature of our feelings and beliefs about personal mastery and competence and the effects of these feelings and beliefs on behavior and psychological adjustment. Because understanding self-efficacy theory and research depends on the ability to place the theory in a larger context, several other models concerned with mastery and efficacy will be reviewed briefly before self-efficacy theory and research are presented in detail. The reviews to follow do not do justice to the richness, diversity, and complexity of this topic, and the reader is urged to consult related chapters in this volume and the other sources noted for more comprehensive presentations.

Effectance Motivation

In attempting to explain human behavior that is not directed toward the satisfaction of biological needs such as hunger, thirst, and sexual desire, White (1959) proposed that humans must be motivated by a different kind of goal, the goal of exploring, manipulating, and mastering the environment. White called this motivation *effectance motivation* and said that its satisfaction leads to a "feeling of efficacy." According to White, we are biologically driven to explore and master our environment, and we feel good when we explore new situations, learn about them, and deal with them effectively. White also proposed that this feeling of efficacy is an aim in itself, apart from the practical value of the things we learn about the environment.

Achievement Motivation

The motivation to strive for achievement, success, and excellence is referred to as *achievement motivation* or *achievement need* (McClelland, Atkinson, Clark, & Lowell, 1953; McClelland, 1985). Achievement motivation is similar to White's notion of effectance motivation in that each is an inherent (i.e., biologically based) traitlike tendency to set mastery-related goals, work toward them, and gain satisfaction from attaining them. Research has demonstrated that measures of achievement motivation predict performance on specific achievement-related tasks, as well as patterns of performance across time and situations (McClelland, 1985). Theory and research on achievement motivation are concerned more with what people want or need to accomplish than with what they expect to accomplish. The positing of a motive to achieve implies that achieving is satisfying and pleasurable and that feelings of efficacy and success have incentive value independent of the material by-products of success.

Level of Aspiration

Theory and research on level of aspiration (e.g., Festinger, 1942) are concerned with what people would like to achieve and how their aspirations influence their behavior. Level of aspiration is concerned with the goals that people set for themselves in situations relevant to achievement or mastery, not the levels of performance people *expect* to attain (Kirsch, 1986). In much of the early research on level of aspiration, however, investigators did not make this distinction clearly. Sometimes they asked people about what they would like to be able to do or achieve; other times they asked people what they expected to be able to achieve. The studies that made this important distinction found that people's levels of aspiration were usually greater than their expectancies for success (Kirsch, 1986). These older studies also found that expectancies concerning performance levels were more strongly correlated with past performance than was level of aspiration. Studies directly comparing the predictive utility (i.e., predicting behavior) of level of aspiration measures with expectancy measures have not been conducted, but a reasonable hypothesis based on these prior studies is that expectancies for success would predict future performance better than would level of aspiration.

Expectancy-Value Theory

Expectancy-value theories deal with the value placed on certain kinds of reward or reinforcement and with expectations for obtaining these rewards. These theories have a long tradition in psychology. Tolman's (1932) theory of animal learning, Lewin's (1938) field theory, and Edwards' (1954) theory of decision-making are all concerned with the importance of goals or rewards and subjective probabilities for obtaining them and share the basic assumption that people are likely to initiate behaviors that they believe will lead to desirable consequences. In his "social learning theory," Rotter (1954) proposed that the feeling of success and accomplishment itself is a form of reinforcement that is valued and sought for its own sake. Recent models in the expectancy-value tradition include protection motivation theory (Maddux & Rogers, 1983; Rogers, 1975), the theory of reasoned action (Fishbein & Ajzen, 1975), and control theory (Carver & Scheier, 1981).

Locus of Control

Locus of control (Rotter, 1966; Lefcourt, this volume) refers to the general belief that one's behavior can have an impact on the environment and that one is capable of controlling outcomes through one's own behavior. People who believe that their own behavior controls outcomes and that the environment is generally responsive to their behavior are said to have an *internal* locus of control. People who believe outcomes are determined by luck (good and bad) or powerful others (such as God) and that the environment is generally unresponsive to their own efforts are said to have an *external* locus of control. Locus of control is more concerned with what people believe they can control than with their need to control or what they want to control. Locus of control also is more similar to an outcome expectancy than to a self-efficacy expectancy because locus of control is concerned with beliefs about the effect of one's behavior on the environment rather than one's beliefs about one's ability to execute certain behaviors. Although measures of locus of control have been shown to be related to a large array of psychological and behavioral variables (see Lefcourt,

this volume), research on the role of causal attributions in depression (Burns & Seligman, this volume) suggests that the locus of perceived control (i.e., whether internal or external) may be less important in some cases than beliefs about degree of controllability (i.e., the source of control may be internal yet perceived as uncontrollable).

Self-Concept and Self-Esteem

Self-concept consists of the sum total of attitudes and beliefs about the self—the kind of person one is, one's likes and dislikes, and what one is capable or not capable of doing well. *Self-esteem* is one's evaluation of these beliefs, or how one feels about these beliefs—one's assessment of one's worth or value as a person. (See Solomon, this volume, & Higgins, this volume.) Beliefs about mastery and personal effectiveness are important aspects of self-concept and self-esteem. If one's sense of competence is high for an ability one values, then this will contribute to high self-esteem (or low self-esteem if perceived competence for the valued skill is low). Judgments of inefficacy in unvalued areas of competence are unlikely to significantly influence self-concept and self-esteem.

Mastery Orientation

Dweck and Leggett (1988) have offered a social-cognitive approach to personality and motivation that seeks to explain patterns of goal-directed behavior by referring to differences in individuals' "implicit theories" concerning the relative mutability or controllability of personal attributes (such as intelligence or social skillfulness) and characteristics of the world (including other people). According to this model, these implicit theories determine the types of goals people choose to pursue and how they respond to challenge and adversity in pursuing goals. Dweck and Leggett describe the *mastery-oriented* pattern (as opposed to the *helpless* pattern) as characterized by the belief or theory that aspects of oneself and the world are changeable and controllable rather than fixed, by the pursuit of development or learning goals (competence-enhancement goals) rather than judgment or performance goals (competence judgments from others), and by "the seeking of challenging tasks and the generation of effective strategies in the face of obstacles" (p. 257).

An Organizing Framework

The preceding paragraphs probably do not exhaust the list of terms and concepts in the psychological literature related to personal efficacy, mastery, and control (e.g., see Thompson, this volume). They do, however, provide a sense of the diversity of efficacy and mastery ideas and models. In fact, one of the most confusing aspects of the body of theory and research on efficacy and mastery is the diversity of terms that leave the impression of great diversity of and conflict among ideas. On closer examination, however, this apparent diversity fades. The basic notions employed in these models can be reduced to five:

1. *Motives* — inherent, biologically-based needs to explore, achieve, affiliate, or otherwise master one's environment
2. *Feelings of esteem* — pleasurable affective or emotional (rather than cognitive) states that result from mastery, achievement, or personal effectiveness
3. *Outcome value* — importance attached to specific goals or outcomes in specific contexts, sometimes referred to as reinforcement value (Rotter, 1954) or incentive value (McClelland, 1985)
4. *Outcome expectancies* — perceived subjective probabilities concerning the contingency between behavior and outcome, or consequence or set of consequences
5. *Self-efficacy expectancies* — perceived subjective probabilities or judgments concerning the effective execution of a behavior or course of action.

That the basic concepts concerning personal effectiveness can be reduced to so few that recur so often is a testimony to the power and importance of these ideas. Most models employ more than one of these notions without incorporating all five. In fact, one of the major differences between the various models of efficacy concerns which one or two of these five concepts or variables is most strongly emphasized.

Effectance motivation, for example, is concerned with two of the five variables noted above: a basic, biologically based motive or drive to master the environment, and a pleasurable affective response to mastery and success. It does not deal directly with the role of expectations for attaining mastery, either expectations concerning behaviors and outcomes or expectations concerning personal ability.

Expectancy-value models are concerned almost exclusively with cognitive rather than motivational factors or feelings of esteem. In addition, prior to self-efficacy theory, few expectancy-value models made clear the distinction between outcome expectancy and self-efficacy expectancy.

Level of aspiration is concerned with motives and outcome values — what people want or need to accomplish. As noted earlier, however, research on level of aspiration has focused sometimes on what people want to achieve and sometimes on what people expect to be able to achieve without making clear the distinction. Also, level of aspiration research has not made clear the distinction between motives and values demonstrated by Mc-Clelland (1985) to be important.

Work on achievement motivation has made clear the distinction between motives and values (McClelland, 1985) but is less concerned with expectations for success (i.e., self-efficacy expectancies and outcome expectancies). As noted earlier, the concept of a motive to achieve implies that achieving results in feelings of esteem that are sought for their own sake.

Locus of control is concerned with expectancies rather than motives, outcome values, or subjective feelings of effectance or esteem. At first glance, locus of control sounds similar to self-efficacy expectancy. Bandura (1986a) has argued, however, that locus of control is really a kind of outcome expectancy because it is concerned with whether one's behavior controls outcomes, not whether one can or cannot perform certain behaviors that might or might not have an effect on the environment. Empirical evidence for the distinction between self-efficacy and locus of control has been provided by Smith (1989) in a study that found that cognitive-behavioral coping skill strategies taught to test-anxious college students led to changes on a measure of general self-efficacy but not on a measure of locus of control. In addition, changes in general self-efficacy were unrelated to changes in locus of control.

Self-concept and self-esteem are generalized sets of beliefs and feelings about the self that consist of expectancies, motives, needs, values, and subjective feelings about one's skills and abilities. Self-esteem is perhaps most closely related to White's feeling of efficacy in that both are more affectively charged constructs, whereas expectancies for success and outcome value are more cognitive.

Dweck and Leggett's mastery-oriented pattern might be renamed a "generalized high expectancy for success" pattern and not lose much in the translation. What Dweck and Leggett offer is a model of the more basic and general psychological processes (i.e., the implicit theories) that underlie and explain how people process success and failure experiences, how and why some people develop a strong and relatively impervious sense of personal effectiveness in many aspects of life, and how and why others seem inordinately vulnerable to cessation of effort and demoralization in the face of adversity. In a study of managerial skills, for example, Wood and Bandura (1989) demonstrated that managers who viewed managerial effectiveness as an acquirable skill that could be improved through experience sustained their self-efficacy expectancies in the face of difficult challenges and set more difficult goals than managers who viewed managerial skill as a fixed entity. Dweck and Leggett's framework, however, does not emphasize the distinction between an outcome expectancy and a self-efficacy expectancy.

The various models also differ in the degree of generality or specificity of their constructs and their predictions. For example, effectance motivation, locus of control, and need to achieve are generalized, traitlike constructs proposed to predict long-term trends or patterns in a general class of mastery behaviors (e.g., achievement, affiliation), whereas self-efficacy expectancy and outcome expectancy are typically defined and measured with considerable behavioral and situational specificity and used to predict relatively specific behaviors in relatively specific contexts.

The organizational framework described above is far from novel. For example, in a recent review of theory and research on motivation, McClelland (1985) argued and provided empirical evidence for distinguishing among motivation, incentive value, and probability of success, and for the importance of each in predicting achievement performance and affiliation acts. In McClelland's framework, a motive is a biologically based tendency to work toward a certain class of goals. Thus, motives are physiological and affective rather than purely cognitive in nature. Incentive value, on the other hand, is defined by McClelland as more cognitive than affective and refers to the magnitude of the reward expected in a particular situation and the importance of that reward. Probability of success refers to the probability of goal attainment based on beliefs about skill. Atkinson's (1957) theory of motivation proposed a similar framework by postulating that choice of behavior and persistence are determined by expectancy for success; incentive value of success; and motive, the disposition to strive for particular kinds of satisfactions. Rotter (1954) also emphasized the distinction between expectancy for success and reinforcement value of success. Likewise, self-efficacy theory is concerned largely with expectancies for success but provides a distinction between an outcome expectancy and a self-efficacy expectancy.

Self-efficacy theory focuses on the more cognitive aspects of mastery and effectiveness — expectancies and values — rather than on more affective constructs such as needs, motives, and feelings of efficacy. Yet, to focus on cognitions and expectations is not to diminish the importance of needs, motives, and feelings. The various models and constructs described here are by no means incompatible with self-efficacy theory, nor with one another. Any model or explanation of human behavior and adjustment will be incomplete unless it considers the individual's inherent motivation toward a general class of goals, the feelings of satisfaction one achieves from meeting challenges and overcoming obstacles, the value attached to the specific goal or outcome sought at a given time and place, and the individual's assessment of the likelihood of attaining the goal or goals, an assessment that will include beliefs about behavior-outcome contingencies and beliefs about personal ability or skill. Therefore, each of the models described here, including self-efficacy theory, is incomplete because one or more important variables are not dealt with directly. Yet, this incompleteness is to be expected because a theorist's or researcher's choice of variables to investigate will depend on what he or she wishes to predict. Motives or needs may be more useful in predicting general trends in mastery-oriented behavior over relatively long periods of time. Predicting relatively specific behaviors in specific situations over relatively brief time frames is likely to be more successful when specific expectancies and values are assessed. In fact, self-efficacy theory's most important contribution to the body of theory and research on personal effectiveness and control — as the rest of chapter will attempt to demonstrate — is made not by offering an opposing alternative framework to other models of personal efficacy, but, first, by emphasizing the distinction between three important mastery/efficacy constructs — self-efficacy expectancy, outcome expectancy, and outcome value — and, second, by emphasizing their measurement with a greater degree of behavioral and situational specificity than has been the case in other theories and bodies of research.

OVERVIEW OF SELF-EFFICACY THEORY

Basic Cognitive Processes

Self-efficacy theory maintains that all processes of psychological and behavioral change operate through the alteration of the individual's sense of personal mastery or efficacy (Bandura, 1977, 1982, 1986a). According to Bandura (1977), "people process, weigh, and integrate diverse sources of information concerning their capability, and they regulate their choice behavior and effort expenditure accordingly" (p. 212). Expectations concerning mastery or efficacy are assumed to determine our choice of actions, the effort we expend, our persistence in the face of adversity, and our emotional or affective experiences. The self-efficacy model holds that three basic, cognitive, mediating processes are important in explaining and predicting which behaviors people initiate and to what degree they persist in actions that meet with barriers and obstacles. These same cognitive mediators also can be viewed as important components of psychological problems and effective clinical interventions: (a) self-efficacy expectancies, beliefs concerning one's ability to execute a specified course of action; (b) outcome expectancies, beliefs concerning the probability that this specified course of action will lead to certain consequences or outcomes; and (c) outcome value, the subjective value one places on certain outcomes or sets of outcomes.

Self-Efficacy Expectancy

Self-efficacy expectancy is presumed to have the more powerful influence on behavior (Bandura, 1977). Self-efficacy judgments are concerned "not with the skills one has but with judgments of what one can do with the skills one possesses" (p. 391) or with one's ability to execute courses of action to deal effectively with problematic situations or to obtain desired goals. The vast majority of studies on self-efficacy theory have demonstrated that self-efficacy expectancies are good predictors of behavior (e.g., Bandura, Adams, & Beyer, 1977; Bandura, Adams, Hardy, & Howell, 1980; Condiotte & Lichtenstein, 1981). Experimental research also has been supportive of the importance of self-efficacy expectancies in directly influencing behavioral intentions and behaviors (e.g., Bandura, Reese, & Adams, 1982; Maddux & Rogers, 1983; Maddux, Norton, & Stoltenberg, 1986; Maddux, Sherer, & Rogers, 1982; Stanley & Maddux, 1986a; Wurtele & Maddux, 1987) and mood states (e.g., Davis & Yates, 1982; Kanfer & Zeiss, 1983; Maddux, Norton, & Leary, 1988; Stanley & Maddux, 1986b).

Self-efficacy expectancies are not personality traits. They are relatively specific cognitions that can only be understood and defined in relation to specific behaviors in specific situations or contexts. Although self-efficacy sometimes is used to refer to one's general sense of competence and effectiveness (e.g., Smith, 1989), the term is most useful when defined, operationalized, and measured as an expectancy specific to a behavior or set of behaviors in a specific context (e.g., Kaplan, Atkins, & Reinsch, 1984; Manning & Wright, 1983). For example, the best way to predict a smoker's attempt and success at giving up cigarettes is to measure his self-efficacy expectancy for quitting, not his general self-confidence or self-esteem. In addition, measuring self-efficacy expectancies for quitting smoking will be more successful if we measure smokers' expectations for being able to refrain from smoking under specific situations (e.g., while at a party, after eating, when around other smokers [DiClemente, 1986]). Although "general self-efficacy" scales have been developed (Sherer et al., 1982; Tipton & Worthington, 1984), these scales have not resulted in much useful research on specific types of behavior change.

Despite the large number of studies supporting its utility, the self-efficacy expectancy construct has not escaped criticism (Maddux & Stanley, 1986a, b). For example, Kirsch (1982, 1983) has raised serious questions about the relationships between self-efficacy expectancy, fear, and intentions to attempt a feared behavior. Kirsch has demonstrated that self-efficacy expectancies for approaching a snake in a glass cage can be enhanced by providing small financial incentives for approach behavior. He argues that if self-efficacy ratings are of a ratings perceived ability, then incentives or rewards should not influence them. Kirsch (1982) found correlations as high as .90

between self-efficacy ratings and ratings of expected fear. He argued (Kirsch, 1986) that in situations involving fear, self-efficacy expectancy can be regarded as indirect measures of expected fear, rather than measures of performance capabilities.

Outcome Expectancy

A second controversy and area of criticism is the relationship between self-efficacy and outcome expectancy. In Bandura's framework, outcome expectancies are viewed as less important and as dependent primarily on self-efficacy expectancies (Bandura, 1986a), although good studies of their relationship and relative utility are rare. Bandura (1977) originally proposed that self-efficacy expectancy and outcome expectancy are independent. This proposed orthogonality was then and continues to be an important topic of discussion (Borkovec, 1978; Kazdin, 1978; Kirsch, 1986; Teasdale, 1978). Eastman and Marzillier (1984) have argued that Bandura does not provide a clear conceptual distinction between the two expectancies and "has failed to credit the importance of outcome expectations" (p. 227) as a cognitive mediator. Bandura (1984) has responded to these criticisms by insisting that self-efficacy expectancies and outcome expectancies are conceptually distinct but that the types of outcomes people anticipate are influenced strongly by self-efficacy expectancies (e.g., my expectations for consequences or results depend on my expectations concerning the skillfulness of the execution of the behavior in question).

Most studies that have examined both self-efficacy expectancy and outcome expectancy seem to suggest that the two are not orthogonal and that outcome expectancy does not add significant predictive utility beyond that offered by self-efficacy expectancy. Many of these studies, however, employed measures of self-efficacy expectancy and outcome expectancy that are somewhat questionable (see Maddux & Barnes, 1985; Maddux et al., 1986). For example, in some studies dependent measures of self-efficacy expectancy and outcome expectancy have failed to make a clear distinction between perceived ability to perform a behavior or behavior sequence and the perceived probability that the behavior will lead to certain outcomes (e.g., Davis & Yates, 1982; Manning & Wright, 1983; Taylor, 1989). In some studies, outcome expectancy has been measured as outcome value by items that assess the positive or negative valence of consequences instead of the probability of the occurrence of the consequences (e.g., Cooney, Kopel, & McKeon, 1982; Lee, 1984a, 1984b). In other studies, traitlike measures of outcome expectancy, such as locus of control, have been employed rather than situation-specific and behavior-specific measures (Devins et al., 1982; Meier, McCarthy, & Schmeck, 1984). Recent research, however, indicates that, when defined and measured carefully and in a manner consistent with the conceptual distinction, self-efficacy expectancy and outcome expectancy can be manipulated and assessed relatively independently and that outcome expectancy can make a significant independent contribution in predictive formulas (Maddux et al., 1986).

Outcome Value

Outcome value or importance has been proposed as an additional component of the self-efficacy model (Maddux et al., 1986; Maddux & Rogers, 1983; Teasdale, 1978), but has not been studied extensively in self-efficacy research. Most researchers seem to assume, logically, that outcome value needs to be high for self-efficacy expectancy and outcome expectancy to influence behavior. Considerable research in expectancy-value theory has shown that outcome value (reinforcement value, incentive value) is an important predictor of response strength and response probability (e.g., Kirsch, 1986; McClelland, 1985). Only a few studies, however, have investigated the role of outcome value in conjunction with self-efficacy expectancy and outcome expectancy (Maddux et al., 1986; Manning & Wright, 1983). The findings have been mixed. Maddux et al. (1986) found that outcome value did not add significantly to the prediction of behavioral intentions when examined in conjunction with self-efficacy expectancy and outcome expectancy. Maddux and Barnes (1989), however, corrected a problem in the measurement of outcome value found in Maddux et al. (1986) and found that outcome value did serve as a significant predictor variable independent of self-efficacy expectancy and outcome expectancy.

Dimensions of Self-Efficacy

Self-efficacy expectancies are viewed as varying along three dimensions: magnitude, strength, and generality (Bandura, 1977, 1982, 1986a). *Magnitude* of self-efficacy, in a hierarchy of behaviors, refers to the number of steps of increasing difficulty or threat a person believes himself capable of performing. For example, a person who is trying to abstain from smoking may believe that he can maintain abstinence under conditions in which he feels relaxed and in which no others present are smoking. He may doubt, however, his ability to abstain under conditions of higher stress and/or when in the presence of other smokers (DiClemente, 1986).

Strength of self-efficacy expectancy refers to the resoluteness of a person's convictions that he or she can perform a behavior in question. For example, each of two smokers may feel capable of abstaining from smoking at a party, but one may hold this belief with more conviction or confidence than the other. Strength of self-efficacy expectancy has been related repeatedly to persistence in the face of frustration, pain, and other barriers to performance (Bandura, 1986b).

Generality of self-efficacy expectancies refers to the extent to which success or failure experiences influence self-efficacy expectancies in a limited, behaviorally specific manner, or whether changes in self-efficacy expectancy extend to other similar behaviors and contexts (e.g., Smith, 1989). For example, the smoker whose self-efficacy expectancy for abstinence has been raised by successful abstinence in a difficult or high-risk situation (e.g., in a bar around other smokers) may extend his feelings of self-efficacy to other contexts in which he has not yet experienced success or mastery. In addition, successful abstinence might generalize to other contexts of self-control such as eating or maintaining an exercise regimen.

Although Bandura (1977) has stated that a thorough analysis of self-efficacy expectancy requires a detailed assessment of magnitude, strength, and generality, most studies rely on unidimensional measures of self-efficacy expectancy that most resemble Bandura's strength dimension (e.g., confidence in one's ability to perform a behavior under certain conditions).

Sources of Self-Efficacy Information

Four sources of information are posited to influence self-efficacy expectancies: performance or enactment experiences, vicarious experiences, verbal persuasion (or social persuasion), and emotional or physiological arousal (Bandura, 1977, 1986a). These four sources are presumed to differ in their power to influence self-efficacy expectancies.

Performance Experiences

Performance experiences, in particular clear success or failure, are proposed to be the most powerful sources of self-efficacy information (Bandura, 1977). Success at a task, behavior, or skill strengthens self-efficacy expectancies for that task, behavior, or skill, whereas perceptions of failure diminish self-efficacy expectancy. A person who once tried to quit smoking for a day but failed probably will doubt his or her ability to quit for a day in the future. On the other hand, a person who is able to go a full day without smoking may hold strong self-efficacy expectancies for abstaining for another day.

Vicarious Experiences

Vicarious experiences (observational learning, modeling, imitation) influence self-efficacy expectancy when we observe the behavior of others, see what they are able to do, note the consequences of their behavior, and then use this information to form expectancies about our own behavior. The effects of vicarious experiences depend on such factors as the observer's perception of the similarity between him- or herself and the model, the number and variety of models, the perceived power of the models, and the similarity between the problems faced by the observer and the model (Bandura, 1986a; Schunk, 1986). Vicarious experiences generally have weaker effects on self-efficacy expectancy than do direct personal experiences (e.g., Bandura, Adams, & Beyer, 1977).

Verbal Persuasion

Verbal persuasion (or social persuasion) is presumed to be a less potent source of enduring change in self-efficacy expectancy than performance experiences and vicarious experiences. The potency of verbal persuasion as a source of self-efficacy expectancies should be influenced by such factors as the expertness, trustworthiness, and attractiveness of the source, as suggested by decades of research on verbal persuasion and attitude change (see, Claiborn, Cacioppo, & Petty, this volume). Experimental studies have shown that verbal persuasion is a moderately effective means for changing both self-efficacy expectancies and outcome expectancies (e.g., Maddux & Rogers, 1983; Maddux et al., 1986).

Emotional Arousal

Emotional or physiological arousal influences self-efficacy expectancies when people associate aversive emotional states with poor behavioral performance, perceived incompetence, and perceived failure. Thus, when a person becomes aware of unpleasant physiological arousal, he or she is more likely to doubt his or her behavioral competency than if the physiological state were pleasant or neutral. Likewise, comfortable physiological sensations (e.g., feelings of relaxation) are likely to lead one to feel confident in one's ability in the situation at hand. Physiological indicants of self-efficacy expectancy, however, extend beyond autonomic arousal because, in activities involving strength and stamina, perceived efficacy is influenced by such experiences as fatigue and pain, or the absence thereof (e.g., Bandura, 1986b).

SELF-EFFICACY AND PROBLEMS OF ADJUSTMENT

A self-efficacy approach to psychological problems and their treatment assumes that people become distressed, unhappy, or anxious, get into conflicts with other people, and experience other emotional and behavioral problems in adjustment because they hold inaccurate and unrealistic expectations about their own behavior and the behavior of others, undervalue or overvalue certain outcomes or consequences, feel nothing can be done to control important life events and achieve valued life goals, or feel incapable of doing those things that might control events and obtain goals (things that others seem capable of doing). Also, a self-efficacy perspective suggests that people are motivated to seek professional help following the experience of a major failure or series of failures (or what they believe are failures) in one or more important areas of their lives such as in their jobs, at school, or in relationships. Because of these perceived failures, these people may come to hold a number of specific low self-efficacy expectancies about specific areas of life. These low self-efficacy expectancies may lead them to give up or stop trying to be effective in their lives.

Measures of self-efficacy expectancies (or measures of outcome expectancy and outcome value) are not direct measures of psychological adjustment. Low self-efficacy expectancies are not sufficient for diagnosing psychological dysfunction, nor are high self-efficacy expectancies a guarantee of psychological health. Instead, self-efficacy expectancies are important because of their influence on subjective distress (e.g., anxiety, depression, low self-esteem) and on the initiation of and persistence at adaptive behaviors and attempts at coping.

Self-efficacy theory has inspired a tremendous number of studies on the etiology, assessment, and treatment of emotional and behavioral problems (Maddux, Stanley, & Manning, 1987). Research has shown, for example, that low self-efficacy expectancies are an important feature of depression (see Stanley & Maddux, 1986a, for a review). Depressed people usually believe they are less capable than other people of performing effectively in their lives and feel little control over their environments. Low self-efficacy is also an important feature of anxiety problems and specific fears. Much of the work of Bandura and his associates has focused on understanding the role of self-efficacy in the development and treatment of extreme fears or phobias (Bandura, 1986a). Self-efficacy also seems to be important in social or interpersonal anxiety (Leary & Atherton, 1986; Maddux et al., 1988). Also, some research has examined the importance of self-efficacy in many other problems such as cigarette smoking, alcoholism, obesity, and eating disorders (e.g., bulimia).

The following section discusses research on the role of self-efficacy in five general types of problems commonly presented by psychotherapy and counseling clients: (a) specific fears and phobias; (b) interpersonal or social anxiety; (c) depression; (d) addictive behaviors and substance abuse; and (e) career choice. The selection of topics is not meant to be exhaustive but representative of the research on self-efficacy theory that can most readily be used by practitioners. Much good research has been conducted on several other topics that may also be of interest to clinicians, such as pain control (e.g., Manning & Wright, 1983), academic achievement (Schunk, 1986), athletic performance (Wurtele, 1986), and a variety of other health-related behaviors (Bandura, 1986b; O'Leary, 1985).

Anxiety and Fear

Problems involving anxiety, fear, and avoidance have provided fertile ground for self-efficacy research. In their earlier studies, Bandura and his colleagues used people with specific fears or phobias to test both the basic assumptions and hypotheses of self-efficacy theory and to demonstrate its practical clinical utility. A self-efficacy model of anxiety is concerned primarily with the anticipation or expectation that danger or harm is imminent and the expectation that one will not be able to prevent or otherwise cope effectively with the anticipated aversive event. Perceptions of coping ability can be viewed in terms of both outcome expectancy, the belief that the means for preventing the aversive event are at hand, and, most importantly, self-efficacy, the belief that one will be able to implement the course of action that seems likely to avert the threat.

According to Bandura (1986a), anxiety is the direct result of low self-efficacy expectancies. People who have confidence in their ability to deal effectively with a threatening situation will approach the situation with self-assurance and calm, whereas those who have serious doubts about their coping skills will anticipate catastrophes and generate a state of affective arousal that will then interfere with effective functioning. A recent study by Tilley and Maddux (1989) provides evidence for the *causal* link between self-efficacy expectancies and anxiety. This study induced self-efficacy for coping with imagined stressful life events (e.g., a difficult exam, an important social encounter) and found that low self-efficacy expectancies were associated with anticipated anxiety. Self-efficacy theory also hypothesizes that the key element common to all successful clinical interventions for anxiety disorders is increasing the client's sense of self-efficacy in mastering the anxiety-provoking situation (Bandura, 1977).

Beck's cognitive model of anxiety disorders (Beck, Emery, & Greenberg, 1985) includes elements identical to those of self-efficacy theory. In Beck's model, anxiety is elicited when a person anticipates danger or threat and anticipates that he or she will not be able to cope with the threat. The anxious person is viewed as following a set of "rules" about danger, vulnerability, and his or her inability to cope with perceived danger of threat. Beck et al. (1985) define vulnerability as "a person's perception of himself as subject to internal or external dangers over which his control is lacking or is insufficient to afford him a sense of safety" (p. 67). The vulnerable person lowers his assessment of his abilities and focuses on his weakness and ineptness and makes predictions about being unable to cope with the threatening situation. Thus, Beck's formulation gives a prominent role to low self-efficacy expectancies.

Barlow (1988) has noted that research on the power of self-efficacy in predicting anxiety as an emotional response has not been as compelling as research on the ability of self-efficacy to predict approach and avoidance behaviors. He also has noted, however, that Bandura proposed self-efficacy theory as a model for behavioral change, not of emotional experience. As Bandura (1984) has stated, "Self-efficacy scales ask people to judge their performance capabilities and not if they can perform nonanxiously" (p. 238). Barlow (1988) credits self-efficacy theory with generating considerable useful research on anxiety and fear problems, but he also suggests that application to the most common clinical anxiety disorders, panic disorder and generalized anxiety disorder, may be limited because these disorders are characterized primarily by anxiety states rather than behavioral avoidance patterns. A recent study suggests, however, that self-efficacy is related not just to control of behavior, but to control of cognitions related to anxiety. In a study of dental anxiety, Kent and Gibbons (1987) found that people low in dental anxiety had fewer negative thoughts about dental appointments than did people high in dental anxiety, and, more important, that low-anxiety people expressed having more control over their negative thoughts than high-anxiety people. If self-efficacy can be applied to the control of anxiety-related cognitions, then it also might be applied effectively to control of anxiety states.

Phobic Disorders

The earliest application of self-efficacy theory to clinical problems was the exploration of the relationship between self-efficacy expectancies and specific phobias and phobic avoidance behavior (Bandura, 1977). This research has found consistently that self-efficacy expectancies are significant predictors of phobic individuals' ability to approach feared stimuli. This effect has been reported for subjects who experience phobias of snakes and spiders (Bandura et al., 1977; Bandura et al., 1980; Bandura et al., 1982), heights (Williams & Watson, 1985), driving (Williams, Dooseman, & Kleinfield, 1984), and the dark (Biran & Wilson, 1981). The effect also has been demonstrated with agoraphobic subjects (Bandura et al., 1980) despite the controversy regarding the appropriateness of classifying agoraphobia as a true phobic disorder (Turner, McCann, Beidel, & Messick, 1986).

The relationship between self-efficacy expectancies and phobic approach and avoidance behavior has been reported following diverse types of treatment (Bandura, 1986a). Self-efficacy expectancy measures at posttreatment appear to be better predictors of approach behavior and therapeutic outcome than perceived danger and subjective anxiety measures (Williams, Dooseman, & Kleinfield, 1984; Williams, Turner, & Peer, 1985; Williams & Watson, 1985). Self-efficacy theory also has been invoked to explain the treatment-enhancing effect of imipramine (an antidepressant) in exposure-based behavioral interventions with agoraphobics. Research by Telch and his colleagues (e.g., Telch, 1988) suggests that, by elevating mood, imipramine leads agoraphobic clients to judge their behavioral success more positively, generating greater feelings of self-efficacy.

Social Anxiety

Anxiety or discomfort during social or interpersonal situations is one of the most common problems of behavioral and emotional adjustment (Buss, 1980; Leary, 1983). Schlenker and Leary's (1982) self-presentational model proposes that all instances of social anxiety arise from concerns with how we are perceived and evaluated by others. In this model, social anxiety occurs when we are motivated to make a particular impression on others but hold a low subjective probability that we will do so. Most existing research supports the hypothesized link between self-presentational concerns and social anxiety (Leary, 1983; Schlenker & Leary, 1982; Schlenker, this volume).

In an elaboration of the self-presentational model, Maddux et al. (1988) demonstrated that the subjective probability of making the impression one desires can be better understood as a combination of *self-presentational outcome expectancy* (the belief that certain interpersonal behaviors, if performed competently, will lead to the desired impression) and *self-presentational efficacy expectancy* (the belief that one is or is not capable of performing the necessary interpersonal behaviors). This distinction has implications for the situational and dispositional antecedents of social anxiety, other affective reactions that may accompany social anxiety, the attributions people make about the causes of their interpersonal difficulties, and the treatment of social anxiety and inhi-

bition (Leary, 1987). For example, a self-efficacy analysis suggests that social skills training should include explicit efforts to ensure that socially anxious clients perceive the improvement in their social skills (a focus on self-efficacy expectancy as well as skills) and that setting realistic interpersonal goals or outcomes also may be crucial (a focus on outcome expectancies). Finally, a self-efficacy approach suggests that successful social experiences will be the best source of efficacy information for the socially anxious client, perhaps even more important than systematic training in specific social skills (Leary, 1987; Leary & Atherton, 1986).

Depression

Depression is probably the most common diagnosis in the practice of clinical psychology and psychiatry (Goodwin & Guze, 1984). In recent years, cognitive approaches to the study and treatment of depression have dominated the literature (see Coyne & Gotlib, 1983, for review of theories). The two models that have received the most attention and support, the revised learned helplessness theory (Abramson, Seligman, & Teasdale, 1978) and Beck's cognitive theory (Beck, 1976), both emphasize the individual's perceptions of control over his or her own behavior and, more important, over environmental events. Also, both deal with general and specific expectancies and beliefs about the contingencies between personal behavior and positive and negative life events. Self-efficacy theory offers a third but related perspective on the role of cognitions, particularly expectancies for control, in depression.

In the self-efficacy model, depression is predicted under conditions of high outcome value, high outcome expectancy, and low self-efficacy expectancy (Bandura, 1982). Specifically, when people believe that highly valued outcomes are obtainable through the performance of certain behaviors (high outcome expectancy), and believe that they are incapable of performing the requisite behaviors (low self-efficacy expectancy), they will display performance deficits (e.g., lack of behavioral initiative and persistence), self-devaluation, and depressed affect. This perspective is compatible with other cognitive models of depression. For example, self-efficacy theory incorporates both an emphasis on perceptions of response-outcome noncontingency, which is important in the revised

68   HANDBOOK OF SOCIAL AND CLINICAL PSYCHOLOGY

learned helplessness theory, and an emphasis on perceptions of personal incompetence and self-devaluation, which is important in Beck's (1976) cognitive model.

Self-Efficacy and Learned Helplessness

The revised learned helplessness model of depression (Abramson et al., 1978) is concerned primarily with the perception of the controllability of aversive outcomes. According to Peterson and Seligman (1984), "the central prediction of the reformulation is that individuals who have an explanatory style that invokes internal, stable, and global causes for bad events tend to become depressed when bad events occur" (p. 347). Research on the model has demonstrated that depressed people are characterized by a particular style of causal attributions concerning the noncontingency or uncontrollability of past and present negative life events, that these attributions lead to expectancies of future uncontrollability, and that these expectancies concerning negative life events and their uncontrollability are the proximal cause of depressed mood (e.g., Riskind, Rholes, Brannon, & Burdick, 1987).

Self-efficacy expectancy and outcome expectancy are directly related to noncontingency and uncontrollability, which are often used interchangeably in the depression literature. A low outcome expectancy is a perception of noncontingency between a behavior and a desired consequence. A low self-efficacy expectancy, however, is a perception not of noncontingency but of inability to perform a behavior upon which a given outcome may or may not be contingent. Both low self-efficacy expectancies and low outcome expectancies can contribute to one's perceptions of the uncontrollability of outcomes because, to obtain desired outcomes or prevent aversive outcomes, one must believe that a particular behavioral strategy will have the desired consequence and that one is capable of implementing the course of action. From an attributional standpoint, people who attribute the causes of bad events to personal flaws and defects also are expressing low self-efficacy expectancies or lack of confidence in their skills and abilities. Such people are likely to believe that bad outcomes are uncontrollable not because they perceive responses and outcomes as noncontingent, but because they perceive themselves as incapable of implementing the necessary courses of action.

The distinction between self-efficacy expectancy and outcome expectancy may clarify the revised learned helplessness theory's distinction between "personal helplessness," the belief that one is uniquely deficient in the ability to control specific outcomes, and "universal helplessness," the belief that no one is able to control the outcome or outcomes in question. In self-efficacy theory, universal helplessness can be defined in terms of either universal low outcome expectancies (no responses can control the outcome) or universal self-efficacy expectancies (no one is capable of implementing the behaviors that might control the outcome). Personal helplessness, however, is a combination of high outcome expectancy and low self-efficacy expectancy; the personally helpless individual believes that certain behaviors might or will lead to the desired outcomes (or prevent a negative outcome), that others are capable of performing these behaviors, but that he or she is not.

Self-Efficacy and Cognitive Theory

According to Beck's (1976) cognitive theory, depressed people hold negative views of themselves (seeing themselves as defective and deficient), negative views of the world (seeing the world as difficult, uncaring, and fraught with obstacles and problems), and negative views of the future (viewing their condition as hopeless and their future as bleak). The depressed person's negative view of self can be seen as a generalized low self-efficacy expectancy that is the product of and is manifested in numerous situation-specific and behavior-specific low self-efficacy expectancies (e.g., Kanfer & Zeiss, 1983). The negative view of the world can be defined as a set of low outcome expectancies, a set of expectations about response-outcome noncontingency—the world is filled with obstacles that cannot be overcome because nothing works to change undesirable situations. Finally, the depressed person's negative view of the future can be expressed as a set of low outcome expectancies (the world will continue to be as it is) and low self-efficacy expectancies (he or she will remain incapable and incompetent).

Research on Self-Efficacy and Depression

Correlational studies provide evidence for the relationship between specific and general low self-efficacy expectancies and depressive symptoms (Devins et al., 1982; Kanfer & Zeiss, 1983; Rosenbaum & Hadari, 1985; Stanley & Maddux, 1986b). In addition, experimental studies that have attempted to induce self-efficacy expectancies (Stanley & Maddux, 1986b & c; Tilley & Maddux, 1989) have provided evidence a causal relationship between low self-efficacy expectancies and depressed mood. Perceived uncontrollability of outcomes seems to be the heart of the cognitive problem of depressed people, and low self-efficacy expectancies appear to be more important than low outcome expectancies in depressed people's perceptions of uncontrollability (Anderson, Horowitz, & French, 1983; Anderson & Arnoult, 1985). A self-efficacy analysis might aid the clinician in determining which component of a cognitive intervention program to emphasize for a particular client. For example, should unrealistic outcome expectancies or inappropriate outcome values be the primary target of change? Or should the client's inaccurate perceptions of his or her interpersonal skills be emphasized?

The low self-efficacy expectancies held by depressed people may be accurate estimations of skills deficits rather than cognitive errors or distortions (Lewinsohn, Mischel, Chaplin, & Barton, 1980). Therefore, research is needed on the accuracy of depressed people's low self-efficacy expectancies at different times during depression. This issue may have important treatment implications in that the clinician could focus either on enhancing an unskilled client's social skills or helping a relatively skilled client to recognize and take credit for the skills he or she is capable of exercising (or both approaches could be taken) (e.g., skills training vs. persuasion).

Addictive Behaviors and Substance Abuse

A number of recent studies indicate that self-efficacy theory is a useful model for exploring the process of addictive behavior change and the impact of clinical interventions, especially the prediction of relapse and maintenance (DiClemente, 1986). The role of self-efficacy expectancies in smoking cessation has been studied most thoroughly, but the application of self-efficacy theory to understanding alcohol abuse and eating disorders such as obesity and bulimia also has received good initial support.

DiClemente (1986) has proposed that addictive behavior change efficacy can best be conceptualized and assessed in terms of (a) treatment behavior efficacy (the client's ability to perform treatment behaviors such as self-monitoring and stimulus control); (b) recovery efficacy (the cli-

ent's ability to recover from a temporary relapse in addictive behavior control); (c) and control efficacy or abstinence efficacy (the client's confidence in his or her ability to abstain from engaging in the problem behavior in a variety of situations that typically serve as cues for the behavior).

Smoking has received the most attention from self-efficacy researchers. Scales based on self-efficacy theory have proven useful in predicting successful completion of a treatment program (Myerson, Foreyt, Hammond, & DiClemente, 1980), posttreatment relapse (Coehlo, 1984; Condiotte & Lichtenstein, 1981; DiClemente, 1981), and smoking rates following treatment (Coletti, Supnik, & Rizzo, 1981; DiClemente, Prochaska, & Gibertini, 1985; Godding & Glasgow, 1985; Nicki, Remington, & MacDonald, 1984). Research suggests, however, that self-efficacy for abstinence assessed at pretreatment may predict treatment program attendance but not treatment success. Also, efficacy ratings increase during successful treatment, and posttreatment self-efficacy assessments are significant predictors of maintenance of smoking cessation for at least 3 to 6 months after treatment. To the author's knowledge, the relationship between outcome expectancy and smoking behavior has been assessed in only one published study (Godding & Glasgow, 1985), and no significant correlation was found.

Efficacy scales designed for alcohol abuse (Annis, 1982; Chambliss & Murray, 1979; DiClemente, Gordon, & Gibertini, 1983; Marlatt & Gordon, 1985), obesity (O'Leary, 1985; Weinberg, Hughes, Critelli, England, & Jackson, 1984; Weinberg & Agras, 1984), and bulimic behavior (Schneider, O'Leary, & Agras, 1985) have shown some promise in predicting treatment success for these problems. Self-efficacy for weight loss has been a significant predictor of actual weight loss (Weinberg et al., 1984), and self-efficacy to resist bulimic behaviors has been found predictive of binge-and-purge episodes. In alcoholism treatment, self-efficacy expectancy measures have been related to relapse categories identified in previous research (Marlatt & Gordon, 1985), alcohol use patterns, and deterioration (DiClemente, 1986). These scales were developed primarily for research purposes and have been used mainly in research settings, but most are suitable for common clinical use. Utility of these scales in typical private practice clinical settings remains an important area for research. A clinician could use scales based on self-efficacy theory to determine which clients would benefit most from extensive relapse prevention. Self-efficacy scales might also be useful for planning appropriate individualized follow-up treatment.

Career and Vocational Choice

Although decision-making about career or vocation is not usually considered a topic for clinical or abnormal psychology, few decisions one makes about one's life can have such long-lasting effects on happiness and adjustment as one's choice of work. Research and theory on vocational and career choice have been dominated by trait and developmental approaches (Betz & Hackett, 1986). Only recently have social cognitive models been applied systematically to the explanation, prediction, and modification of career and vocational behavior. Among social cognitive models, self-efficacy theory has been the most thoroughly investigated, especially in relation to women's career and vocational issues. The concept of self-efficacy helps us understand two continuing problems in women's career development: (a) women's continued underrepresentation in many male-dominated career fields, such as mathematics, engineering, and the sciences; and (b) the underutilization of women's talents and skills in career pursuits (Betz & Hackett, 1986). Betz and Hackett (1981, 1986) propose that gender differences in self-efficacy expectancies significantly influence the career choices of young women and that these self-efficacy expectancies are derived from sex role socialization experiences that are different from those of men.

In their review of career self-efficacy, Lent and Hackett (1987) evaluate research relating self-efficacy to career entry behavior, college major choice, academic achievement, career choice, career decision-making, career adjustment, and gender differences in career behavior. They conclude that self-efficacy measures have been useful in predicting some aspects of career and vocational behavior, but that the "incremental contribution" of self-efficacy measures to interest and ability measures is questionable. They also point out that research is especially needed on the causal links between self-efficacy and career behavior.

Betz and Hackett (1986) suggest that self-efficacy theory may not lead to the development of completely new interventions in career decision-making but should lead to the enhancement of existing interventions by encouraging the develop-

ment of multiple-intervention packages. The self-efficacy model also should enhance these interventions by providing more focused goals (e.g., the enhancement of specific self-efficacy expectancies, more accurate and reliable measures of intervention success).

CLINICAL APPLICATIONS OF SELF-EFFICACY THEORY

In addition to contributing to the understanding of the etiology of emotional and behavioral problems, self-efficacy theory offers guidelines for their assessment and treatment. In trying to understand and help people who are experiencing emotional or psychological problems, evaluating specific self-efficacy expectancies about specific behaviors and specific life goals is usually more useful than simply examining a person's general sense of competence or effectiveness because specificity helps a clinician determine exactly what beliefs and behaviors need to be changed to help the person experience success and begin to feel and be more effective and productive. Once a client begins to experience some success in one or two aspects of his or her life, the client may develop stronger self-efficacy expectancies for behaviors in other areas of life. For example, an extremely shy client may be helped with calling a friend to arrange a lunch date, or a severely depressed person may be encouraged to simply get up and get dressed in the morning. According to self-efficacy theory, these small successes strengthen the client's sense of self-efficacy and his or her expectations for additional, more important successes. Most effective clinical interventions help people experience success as a way of restoring high self-efficacy expectancies and a general sense of personal efficacy (Goldfried & Robins, 1982).

Clinical Assessment

In assessing clients' problems, the self-efficacy model and the considerable research on measurement of self-efficacy expectancies may be useful in two ways. First, an assessment of self-efficacy before treatment, at various stages in treatment, and following treatment can help the clinician target specific competency-related beliefs and situations, predict areas of potential difficulty, and tailor interventions to meet a client's special needs. For example, a self-efficacy scale that provides detailed information about "at risk" situations for clients with eating problems or substance abuse problems (e.g., DiClemente, 1986; Schneider et al., 1985) can help the therapist clarify, anticipate, and prevent problems clients typically encounter when attempting new or anxiety-provoking behaviors such as being assertive, controlling food intake in the face of temptation, or refusing a drink when offered one at a party. Such information can also assist in the timing of interventions because the therapist and the client are better able to predict relapse.

Second, self-efficacy measures may be helpful in the evaluation of treatment effectiveness. Most theories and models of psychotherapy emphasize the importance of helping the client attain a greater sense of personal mastery or competence (Goldfried & Robins, 1982). Perceptions of personal mastery, if measured at all as a part of treatment outcome, usually have been measured as global traitlike constructs (e.g., locus of control, self-esteem). Self-efficacy theory has encouraged research on the development of assessment instruments that are more problem specific and therefore more useful clinically. Such measures should be of particular interest to behavioral and cognitive-behavioral clinicians.

Most measures of self-efficacy expectancies have been developed for research rather than for direct clinical use, but many of them share a number of characteristics that make them suitable for use in clinical settings. Most have good logical or face validity, are brief and straightforward, are highly specific regarding problem behaviors and problem situations, and lend themselves to use at frequent intervals to provide efficient monitoring of client progress. (See previous section on specific disorders and problems.)

Although a number of measures of self-efficacy expectancies have been developed that are suitable for clinical use, the measurement of outcome expectancy and outcome value has been largely ignored. Research suggests that outcome expectancy and outcome value can be useful predictor variables along with self-efficacy expectancy. Thus, the development of measures of these constructs deserves attention. For example, an outcome expectancy measure might consist of a list of possible coping strategies for a specific problem and allow for ratings of the client's perception of the potential effectiveness of these strategies. An outcome value measure might consist of a list of the anticipated consequences (both positive and negative) that might result from being more assertive or losing weight, and the extent to which these consequences are desired or feared (e.g., Saltzer, 1981). Both kinds of measures might assist the therapist in assessing a client's motivation for treatment in general, the value they place on attaining certain treatment goals, and their expectations about the effectiveness of specific intervention strategies (see Thompson, this volume, for additional information about the use of outcome expectancy in psychotherapy).

Enhancing Self-Efficacy in Psychotherapy

In social learning (e.g., cognitive-behavioral) approaches to clinical psychology, assessment and intervention are integrated activities rather than conceptually and procedurally distinct. Therefore, a self-efficacy theory approach to clinical interventions is guided by the same principle that guides the use of self-efficacy theory in assessment—that situational and behavioral specificity are crucial to understanding clinical problems and designing successful therapeutic procedures. Few theories or models provide explicit step-by-step guidelines for conducting clinical interventions, but a good theory should provide the clinician with a conceptual framework that serves as a general guide to understanding and conducting the clinical situation (Kanfer, 1984). Goldfried and Robins (1982) suggest that self-efficacy theory can be most useful not by suggesting new strategies for engineering initial behavior change but by providing an index of the way clients cognitively process behavior changes and experiences that occur in psychotherapy. They point out that many clients may encounter success experiences in certain areas of their lives but may fail to benefit fully from these experiences because they interpret these experiences in ineffective ways, such as by overlooking, ignoring, or discounting the importance of these success experiences. In other words, "self-efficacy expectancies often lag behind behavior change" (Goldfried & Robins, 1982, p. 373).

Sources of Efficacy Information

All four sources of self-efficacy information— verbal persuasion, vicarious experience, emotional arousal, and performance experience—are important in effective clinical interventions. Most forms of psychotherapy rely strongly on verbal persuasion as a means of enhancing a client's sense of self-efficacy and encouraging clients to take small risks that may lead to small successes (Harvey, Weary, Maddux, Jordan, & Galvin, 1985). Almost all psychotherapists rely initially upon their own powers of persuasion to convince clients that they can make some small changes in their behavior. In cognitive and cognitive-behavioral therapies, the therapist engages the client in a discussion of the client's dysfunctional beliefs, attitudes, and expectancies, and helps the client see the irrationality and self-defeating nature of such beliefs. The therapist encourages the client to adopt new, more adaptive beliefs, and the client is then encouraged to act on these new beliefs and expectancies and to encounter the success that will lead to more enduring alterations in self-efficacy expectancies and adaptive behavior. (See Hollon & Beck, 1986, and Ingram & Kendall, this volume, for reviews of cognitive and cognitive-behavioral psychotherapy.)

Some clinical interventions use vicarious means for enhancing self-efficacy. For example, modeling films and videotapes have been used successfully to encourage socially withdrawn children to interact with other children. In such films, the socially withdrawn child observes another child similar to himself or herself encounter and then master problems similar to his or her problems. The child model initially expresses some fear about approaching another group of children, but then takes a chance and starts talking to the children and joins in their play. The child watching the film sees the model child, someone much like himself or herself, experience success and comes to believe that he or she too can do the same thing (see Conger & Keane, 1981, for a review.) In vivo modeling has been used successfully in the treatment of phobic individuals. This research has shown that changes in self-efficacy expectancies for approach behaviors mediate therapeutic behavioral changes (Bandura, 1986a).

Biofeedback, relaxation training, and meditation are attempts to reduce emotional or physiological arousal (e.g., anxiety) and to reduce the association between this arousal and low self-efficacy. As noted above, actual performance of behaviors that lead to success is perhaps the most powerful way to enhance personal efficacy in psychotherapy. For example, the most effective treatments for phobias and fears involve in vivo experience with the feared object or situation during therapy sessions and between sessions as homework assignments (Bandura, 1986a; Barlow, 1988). In cognitively based treatments of depression, depressed clients are provided structured guidance in the arrangement of success experiences that will counteract low self-efficacy expectancies (Beck, Rush, Shaw, & Emery, 1979).

Most psychotherapy and counseling approaches involve combinations of more than one source of self-efficacy information. For example, successful treatment with agoraphobic clients may require intervention using all four sources of efficacy information: (a) emotional arousal, teaching the client to relax and feel less anxious when out in public; (b) verbal persuasion, encouraging the client to attempt feared behaviors and challenging the client's expectations of catastrophe; (c) vicarious experiences, observation of filmed or live models (such as the therapist) engaging in feared behaviors or participation in an agoraphobic group; (d) performance experiences, actual practice in engaging in feared behaviors such as leaving one's home and approaching a feared situation or setting, such as a supermarket.

A Self-Efficacy Focus for Psychotherapy

Goldfried and Robins (1982) suggest that a self-efficacy framework can be useful in helping clients process success experiences more beneficially in four specific ways. First, the self-efficacy model suggests that therapists should help clients discriminate between past and present behavior to more accurately gauge their progress. For example, therapists can help clients feel more self-efficacious by encouraging them to contrast recent successful coping strategies with past ineffective behaviors and view competence not as a trait but as a set of specific behaviors performed in specific situations, and by discouraging them from comparing their behavior with others who may seem more competent. Second, therapists can encourage clients to attribute successful behavioral changes to effort and competence rather than to environmental circumstances.

Third, therapists and counselors can encourage clients to retrieve past success experiences to use as a guide for future behavior. In other words, "clients must not only behave in competent ways but must also view these behavior patterns as being part of their personal history" (Goldfried & Robins, 1982, p. 371). Fourth, therapists can assist clients in aligning or attaining greater consonance among expectancies, anticipatory feelings, behaviors, objective consequences of behaviors, and their self-evaluation. For example, Goldfried and Robins point out that clients may perform adequately in threatening situations yet feel unpleasant emotional arousal and thus face two conflicting sources of self-efficacy information. In such situations, the therapist needs to emphasize that the emotional arousal did not predict the outcome of the situation and thereby discount a source of efficacy information that previously had great importance for the client but was maladaptive. (See Thompson, this volume, for additional strategies.)

FUTURE DIRECTIONS

Since the publication of Bandura's (1977) *Psychological Review* article, "self-efficacy" has become one of the most ubiquitous terms in the literature of social, clinical, counseling, health, and personality psychology and probably will continue to be the subject of considerable research by psychologists interested in the cognitive mediation of behavior and emotion. A sampling of this literature reveals that most researchers, regardless of their specialty field, are concerned with a relatively small number of questions on the role of basic cognitive processes in human behavior and affective experience, including the following:

1. What is the role of perceived ability or competence in the individual's decision to engage in certain behaviors and to persist in the face of obstacles or failure?
2. How are perceptions of competence related to the expected consequences of behavior?
3. How well can these "cognitive" factors predict behavior and affect?
4. How are these cognitions related to the development and treatment of psychological, behavioral, and emotional maladjustment?

Two different but overlapping research goals probably will continue to receive the most attention. The first of these concerns the relative utility of self-efficacy expectancy, outcome expectancy, and outcome value (including similar concepts with different names) in predicting and influencing a wide variety of behaviors. These studies are concerned with the relationships of various cognitive patterns and styles to behavior and emotion. The second line of research is concerned with the relationships among these cognitive mediators,

such as studies on the orthogonality of self-efficacy expectancy and outcome expectancy. These goals and lines of research are mutually informative. Studies of the relationship of cognition to affect and behavior will shed light on the relationships among the cognitive mediators. More important, assessing the utility of cognitive mediators, alone and in combination, in predicting behavior and emotion is dependent on a clear understanding of their relationships to one another, which itself is dependent on clear definition and measurement. The following goals and guidelines are suggested for future research on self-efficacy and related constructs.

Theory and research involving self-efficacy expectancy, outcome expectancy, and outcome value (and similar concepts) should begin to employ a common set of terms to avoid confusion and to facilitate communication among researchers in various areas. For example, Kirsch (1986) reviewed research on such topics as expectancy and achievement motivation and argued that much of this past research deals with self-efficacy expectancy but refers to the construct by various other terms. Thompson (this volume) provides additional evidence for this problem by noting the many terms in the literature on "control" that are used for similar concepts and by showing the similarity between control terms and self-efficacy theory's terms. The use of a common set of terms by researchers and theorists working in the broad area of personal competence, efficacy, and control (including researchers in clinical, social, health, and industrial/organizational psychology) would facilitate communication and enhance research efforts and theory development by allowing researchers to more easily see the links between their own work and that of others. The classification of personal efficacy concepts as (a) motives, (b) feelings of esteem, (c) outcome value, (d) outcome expectancies, and (e) self-efficacy expectancies may provide a starting point (see earlier discussion).

Further attention needs to be given to the role that behavioral intention, commitment, or behavioral plan may play in mediating the relationship between behavior and self-efficacy expectancy, outcome expectancy, and outcome value. The relationships among attitudes, beliefs, intentions, and behaviors continue to be the topic of research, most of which is based on Fishbein and Ajzen's (1975; Ajzen & Fishbein, 1980) *theory of reasoned action*. This theory proposes that the most powerful and immediate influence on behavior is behavioral intention, which in turn is determined by the attitude toward the behavior and perceptions of social norms regarding the behavior. (See Chaiken & Stangor, 1987, for review of recent research). If self-efficacy expectancies, outcome expectancies, and outcome value are viewed as beliefs and attitudes, then a model integrating self-efficacy theory with the theory of reasoned action, now revised as the theory of planned behavior (Ajzen, 1985), may be possible. Such an integration might involve measuring attitudes toward the behavior as self-efficacy expectancies and outcome expectancies for the behavior in question and the importance or value placed on the anticipated consequences. Social norms also might be measured in terms of expected social support for engaging in the behavior in question and the value of social support. In addition, theoretical and conceptual links need to be established between self-efficacy theory and related theories, such as learned helplessness theory (Abramson et al., 1978), control theories (Carver & Scheier, 1981; Thompson, this volume), attributional theories (e.g., Harvey, Ickes, & Kidd, 1978), and general behavior theory (McClelland, 1985). This chapter has explored briefly some of these links, but much more work is needed.

REFERENCES

Abramson, L. Y., Seligman, M. E. P., & Teasdale, J. D. (1978). Learned helplessness in humans: Critique and reformulation. *Journal of Abnormal Psychology, 87*, 49–74.

Ajzen, I. (1985). From intentions to actions: A theory of planned behavior. In J. Kuhl & J. Beckman (Eds.), *Action-control: From cognition to behavior* (pp. 11–39). Heidelberg: Springer.

Ajzen, I., & Fishbein, M. (1980). *Understanding attitudes and predicting social behavior*. New York: Prentice-Hall.

Anderson, C. A., & Arnoult, L. H. (1985). Attributional style and everyday problems in living: Depression, shyness, and loneliness. *Social Cognition, 3*, 16–35.

Anderson, C. A., Horowitz, L. M., & French, R. (1983). Attributional style of lonely and depressed people. *Journal of Personality and Social Psychology, 45*, 127–136.

Annis, H. M. (1982). *Situational confidence questionnaire*. Toronto: Addiction Research Foundation.

Atkinson, J. W. (1957). Motivational determinants of risk-taking behavior. *Psychological Review, 84*, 191–215.

Bandura, A. (1977). Self-efficacy: Toward a unifying theory of behavioral change. *Psychological Review, 84*, 191–215.

Bandura, A. (1982). Self-efficacy mechanism in human agency. *American Psychologist, 37*, 122–147.

Bandura, A. (1984). Recycling misconceptions of perceived self-efficacy. *Cognitive Therapy and Research, 8*, 231–255.

Bandura, A. (1986a). *Social foundations of thought and action*. New York: Prentice-Hall.

Bandura, A. (1986b). Self-efficacy mechanism in physiological activation and health-promoting behavior. In J. Madden IV, S. Mathysse, & J. Barchas (Eds.), *Adaptation, learning, and affect*. New York: Raven Press.

Bandura, A., Adams, N. E., & Beyer, A. (1977). Cognitive processes mediating behavior change. *Journal of Personality and Social Psychology, 35*, 125–139.

Bandura, A., Adams, N. E., Hardy, A. B., & Howell, G. N. (1980). Tests of the generality of self-efficacy theory. *Cognitive Therapy and Research, 4*, 39–66.

Bandura, A., Reese, L., & Adams, N. E. (1982). Microanalysis of action and fear arousal as a function of differential levels of perceived coping self-efficacy. *Journal of Personality and Social Psychology, 43*, 5–21.

Barlow, D. H. (1988). *Anxiety and its disorders: The nature and treatment of anxiety and panic*. New York: Guilford Press.

Beck, A. T. (1976). *Cognitive therapy and the emotional disorders*. New York: International Universities Press.

Beck, A. T., Emery, G., & Greenberg, R. L. (1985). *Anxiety disorders and phobias: A cognitive perspective*. New York: Basic Books.

Beck, A. T., Rush, A. J., Shaw, B. F., & Emery, G. (1979). *Cognitive therapy of depression: A treatment manual*. New York: Guilford Press.

Betz, N. E., & Hackett, G. (1981). The relationships of career-related self-efficacy expectations to perceived career options in college women and men. *Journal of Counseling Psychology, 28*, 399–410.

Betz, N. E., & Hackett, G. (1986). Applications of self-efficacy theory to understanding career choice behavior. *Journal of Social and Clinical Psychology, 4*, 279–289.

Biran, M., & Wilson, G. T. (1981). Treatment of phobic disorders using cognitive and exposure methods: A self-efficacy analysis. *Journal of Consulting and Clinical Psychology, 49*, 886–899.

Borkovec, T. D. (1978). Self-efficacy: Cause or reflection of behavioural change? In S. Rachman (Ed.), *Advances in behaviour therapy and research* (Vol. 1, pp. 163–170). Oxford: Pergamon Press.

Buss, A. H. (1980). *Self-consciousness and social anxiety*. San Francisco: W. H. Freeman.

Carver, C. S., & Scheier, M. F. (1981). *Attention and regulation: A control theory approach to human behavior*. New York: Springer-Verlag.

Chaiken, S., & Stangor, C. (1987). Attitudes and attitude change. In M. R. Rosenzweig & L. W. Porter (Eds.), *Annual review of psychology* (Vol. 38, pp. 575–630). Palo Alto, CA: Annual Reviews, Inc.

Chambliss, C. A., & Murray, E. J. (1979). Efficacy attribution, locus of control, and weight loss. *Cognitive Therapy and Research, 3*, 349–353.

Coelho, R. J. (1984). Self-efficacy and cessation of smoking. *Psychological Reports, 54*, 309–310.

Colletti, G., Supnick, J. A., & Rizzo, A. A. (1981, August). *An analysis of relapse determinants for treated smokers*. Paper presented at the 89th annual meeting of the American Psychological Association, Los Angeles.

Condiotte, M. M., & Lichtenstein, E. (1981). Self-efficacy and relapse in smoking cessation programs. *Journal of Consulting and Clinical Psychology, 49*, 648–658.

Conger, J. C., & Keane, S. P. (1981). Social skills intervention in the treatment of isolated or withdrawn children. *Psychological Bulletin, 90*, 478–495.

Cooney, N. L., Kopel, S. A., & McKeon, P. (1982, August). Controlled relapse training and self-efficacy in ex-smokers. Paper presented at the annual meeting of the American Psychological Association, Washington, DC.

Coyne, J. C., & Gotlib, I. H. (1983). The role of cognition in depression: A critical appraisal. *Psychological Bulletin, 94*, 472–505.

Davis, F. W., & Yates, B. T. (1982). Self-efficacy expectancies versus outcome expectancies as determinants of performance deficits and de-

pressive affect. *Cognitive Therapy and Research, 6*, 23–36.

Devins, G. M., Binik, Y. M., Gorman, P., Dattell, M., McClosky, B., Oscar, G., & Briggs, J. (1982). Perceived self-efficacy, outcome expectancies, and negative mood states in end-stage renal disease. *Journal of Abnormal Psychology, 91*, 241–244.

DiClemente, C. C. (1981). Self-efficacy and smoking cessation maintenance: A preliminary report. *Cognitive Therapy and Research, 5*, 175–187.

DiClemente, C. C. (1986). Self-efficacy and the addictive behaviors. *Journal of Social and Clinical Psychology, 4*, 302–315.

DiClemente, C. C., Gordon, J. R., & Gibertini, M. (1983, August). *Self-efficacy and determinants of relapse in alcoholism treatment*. Paper presented at the annual meeting of the American Psychological Association, Anaheim, CA.

DiClemente, C. C., Prochaska, J. O., & Gibertini, M. (1985). Self-efficacy and the stages of self-change of smoking. *Cognitive Therapy and Research, 9*, 181–200.

Dweck, C. S., & Leggett, E. L. (1988). A social-cognitive approach to motivation and personality. *Psychological Review, 95*, 256–273.

Eastman, C., & Marzillier, J. S. (1984). Theoretical difficulties in Bandura's self-efficacy theory. *Cognitive Therapy and Research, 8*, 213–229.

Edwards, W. (1954). The theory of decision making. *Psychological Bulletin, 51*, 380–417.

Festinger, L. (1942). A theoretical interpretation of shifts in level of aspiration. *Psychological Review, 49*, 235–250.

Fishbein, M., & Ajzen, I. (1975). *Belief, attitude, intention, and behavior: An introduction to theory and research*. Reading, MA: Addison-Wesley.

Godding, P. R., & Glasgow, R. E. (1985). Self-efficacy and outcome expectancy as predictors of controlled smoking status. *Cognitive Therapy and Research, 9*, 583–590.

Goldfried, M. R., & Robins, C. (1982). On the facilitation of self-efficacy. *Cognitive Therapy and Research, 6*, 361–380.

Goodwin, D. W., & Guze, S. B. (1984). *Psychiatric diagnosis* (3rd ed.). New York: Oxford University Press.

Harvey, J. H., Ickes, W., & Kidd, R. F. (1978). *New directions in attribution research* (Vol. 2). Hillsdale, NJ: Lawrence Erlbaum Associates.

Harvey, J. H., Weary, G., Maddux, J. E., Jordan, J., & Galvin, K. (1985). Attitude change theory, research, and clinical practice. In G. Stricker & R. Keisner (Eds.), *From research to clinical practice*. New York: Plenum Press.

Hollon, S. H., & Beck, A. T. (1986). Research on cognitive therapies. In S. L. Garfield & A. E. Bergin (Eds.), *Handbook of psychotherapy and behavior change* (pp. 443–482). New York: John Wiley & Sons.

Kanfer, F. H. (1984). Introduction. In R. P. McGlynn, J. E. Maddux, C. D. Stoltenberg, & J. H. Harvey (Eds.), *Social perception in clinical and counseling psychology*. Lubbock, TX: Texas Tech Press.

Kanfer, R., & Zeiss, A. M. (1983). Depression, interpersonal standard-setting, and judgements of self-efficacy. *Journal of Abnormal Psychology, 92*, 319–329.

Kaplan, R. M., Atkins, C. J., & Reinsch, S. (1984). Specific efficacy expectations mediate exercise compliance in patients with COPD. *Health Psychology, 3*, 223–242.

Kazdin, A. E. (1978). Conceptual and assessment issues raised by self-efficacy theory. In S. Rachman (Ed.), *Advances in behaviour research and therapy* (Vol. 1, pp. 177–185). Oxford: Pergamon Press.

Kent, G., & Gibbons, R. (1987). Self-efficacy and the control of anxious cognitions. *Journal of Behavior Therapy and Experimental Psychiatry, 18*, 33–40.

Kirsch, I. (1982). Efficacy expectations as response predictions: The meaning of efficacy ratings as a function of task characteristics. *Journal of Personality and Social Psychology, 42*, 132–136.

Kirsch, I. (1983). Self-efficacy and expectancy: Old wine with new labels. *Journal of Personality and Social Psychology, 49*, 824–830.

Kirsch, I. (1986). Early research on self-efficacy: What we already know without knowing we knew. *Journal of Social and Clinical Psychology, 4*, 339–358.

Leary, M. R. (1983). *Understanding social anxiety: Social, personality, and clinical perspectives*. Beverly Hills, CA: Sage Publications.

Leary, M. R. (1987). A self-presentational model for the treatment of social anxieties. In J. E. Maddux, C. D. Stoltenberg, & R. Rosenwein (Eds.), *Social processes in clinical and counseling psychology* (pp. 126–138). New York: Springer-Verlag.

Leary, M. R., & Atherton, S. C. (1986). Self-efficacy, social anxiety, and inhibition in social encounters. *Journal of Social and Clinical Psychology, 4*, 258–267.

Lee, C. (1984a). Accuracy of efficacy and outcome expectations in predicting performance in a simulated assertiveness task. *Cognitive Therapy and Research, 8*, 37–48.

Lee, C. (1984b). Efficacy expectations and outcome expectations as predictors of performance in a snake-handling task. *Cognitive Therapy and Research, 8*, 590–596.

Lent, R. W., & Hackett, G. (1987). Career self-efficacy: Empirical status and future directions. *Journal of Vocational Behavior, 30*, 347–382.

Lewin, K. (1938). The conceptual representation and the measurement of psychological forces. Durham, NC: Duke University Press.

Lewinsohn, P. M., Mischel, W., Chaplin, W., & Barton, R. (1980). Social competence and depression: The role of illusory self-perceptions. *Journal of Abnormal Psychology, 89*, 203–212.

Maddux, J. E., & Barnes, J. (1985). *The orthogonality and relative predictive utility of self-efficacy expectancy, outcome expectancy, and outcome value: A review of empirical studies*. Unpublished manuscript. George Mason University, Fairfax, VA.

Maddux, J. E., & Barnes, J. (1989). Self-efficacy theory and theory of reasoned action: Relative predictive utility of expectancies, values, and intentions. Unpublished manuscript. George Mason University, Fairfax, VA.

Maddux, J. E., Norton, L. W., & Leary, M. R. (1988). Cognitive components of social anxiety: An investigation of the integration of self-presentation theory and self-efficacy theory. *Journal of Social and Clinical Psychology, 6*, 180–190.

Maddux, J. E., Norton, L. W., & Stoltenberg, C. D. (1986). Self-efficacy expectancy, outcome expectancy, and outcome value: Relative effects on behavioral intentions. *Journal of Personality and Social Psychology, 51*, 783–789.

Maddux, J. E., & Rogers, R. W. (1983). Protection motivation and self-efficacy: A revised theory of fear appeals and attitude change. *Journal of Experimental Social Psychology, 19*, 469–479.

Maddux, J. E., Sherer, M., & Rogers, R. W. (1982). Self-efficacy expectancy and outcome expectancy: Their relationships and their effects on behavioral intentions. *Cognitive Therapy and Research, 6*, 207–211.

Maddux, J. E., & Stanley, M. A. (Eds.). (1986a). Self-efficacy theory in contemporary psychology (special issue). *Journal of Social and Clinical Psychology, 4*, 249–373.

Maddux, J. E., & Stanley, M. A. (1986b). Self-efficacy theory in contemporary psychology: An overview. *Journal of Social and Clinical Psychology, 4*, 249–255.

Maddux, J. E., Stanley, M. A., & Manning, M. M. (1987). Self-efficacy theory and research: Applications in clinical and counseling psychology. In J. E. Maddux, C. D. Stoltenberg, & R. Rosenwein (Eds.), *Social processes in clinical and counseling psychology* (pp. 39–55). New York: Springer-Verlag.

Manning, M. M., & Wright, T. L. (1983). Self-efficacy expectancies, outcome expectancies, and the persistence of pain control in childbirth. *Journal of Personality and Social Psychology, 45*, 421–431.

Marlatt, G. A., & Gordon, J. R. (Eds.). (1985). *Relapse prevention.* New York: Guilford Press.

McClelland, D. C. (1985). How motives, skills, and values determine what people do. *American Psychologist, 40*, 812–825.

McClelland, D. C., Atkinson, J. W., Clark, R. A., & Lowell, E. L. (1953). *The achievement motive.* New York: Appleton-Century-Crofts.

Meier, S., McCarthy, P. R., & Schmeck, R. R. (1984). Validity of self-efficacy as a predictor of writing performance. *Cognitive Therapy and Research, 8*, 107–120.

Myerson, W. A., Foreyt, J. P., Hammond, G. S., & DiClemente, C. C. (1980, November). *Self-efficacy: The development of a brief scale for prediction of success in a smoking cessation program.* Paper presented at the 14th annual convention of the Association for Advancement of Behavior Therapy, New York.

Nikki, R. M., Remington, R. E., & MacDonald, G. A. (1984). Self-efficacy, nicotine fading/self-monitoring and cigarette smoking behaviour. *Behaviour Research and Therapy, 22*, 477–485.

O'Leary, A. (1985). Self-efficacy and health. *Behavior Therapy and Research, 23*, 437–452.

Peterson, C., & Seligman, M. E. P. (1984). Causal explanations as a risk factor for depression: Theory and evidence. *Psychological Review, 91*, 347–374.

Riskind, J. H., Rholes, W. S., Brannon, A. M., & Burdick, C. A. (1987). Attributions and expectations: A confluence of vulnerabilities in mild depression in a college student population. *Journal of Personality and Social Psychology, 53*, 349–354.

Rogers, R. W. (1975). A protection motivation theory of fear appeals and attitude change. *Journal of Psychology, 91*, 93–114.

Rosenbaum, M., & Hadari, D. (1985). Personal efficacy, external locus of control, and perceived contingency of parental reinforcement among depressed, paranoid, and normal subjects. *Journal of Personality and Social Psychology, 49*, 539–547.

Rotter, J. B. (1954). *Social learning and clinical psychology.* Englewood Cliffs, NJ: Prentice-Hall.

Rotter, J. B. (1966). Generalized expectancies for internal versus external control of reinforcement. *Psychological Monographs, 80* (1, Whole No. 609).

Saltzer, E. B. (1981). Cognitive moderators of the relationship between behavioral intentions and behaviors. *Journal of Personality and Social Psychology, 41*, 260–271.

Schlenker, B. R., & Leary, M. R. (1982). Social anxiety and self-presentation: A conceptualization and model. *Psychological Bulletin, 92*, 641–669.

Schneider, J. A., O'Leary, A., & Agras, W. S. (1985). The role of perceived self-efficacy in recovery from bulimia. (1987). *Behaviour Research and Therapy, 25*, 429–432.

Schunk, D. H. (1986). Vicarious influences in self-efficacy on cognitive skill learning. *Journal of Social and Clinical Psychology, 4*, 302–327.

Sherer, M., Maddux, J. E., Mercandante, B., Prentice-Dunn, S., Jacobs, B., & Rogers, R. W. (1982). The self-efficacy scale: Construction and validation. *Psychological Reports, 51*, 663–671.

Smith, R. E. (1989). Effects of coping skills training on generalized self-efficacy and locus of control. *Journal of Personality and Social Psychology, 56*, 228–233.

Stanley, M. A., & Maddux, J. E. (1986a). Cognitive processes in health enhancement: Investigation of a combined protection motivation and self-efficacy model. *Basic and Applied Social Psychology, 7*, 101–113.

Stanley, M. A., & Maddux, J. E. (1986b). Self-efficacy expectancy and depressed mood: An investigation of causal relationships. *Journal of Social Behavior and Personality, 4,* 575–586.

Stanley, M. A., & Maddux, J. E. (1986c). Self-efficacy theory: Potential contributions to understanding cognitions in depression. *Journal of Social and Clinical Psychology, 4,* 268–278.

Taylor, J. (1989). The effect of personal and competitive self-efficacy and differential outcome feedback on subsequent self-efficacy and performance. *Cognitive Therapy and Research, 13,* 67–79.

Teasdale, J. D. (1978). Self-efficacy: Toward a unifying theory of behavioural change? In S. Rachman (Ed.), *Advances in behaviour research and therapy* (Vol. 1, pp. 211–215). Oxford: Pergamon Press.

Telch, M. J. (1988). Combined pharmacologic and psychological treatments for panic sufferers. In S. Rachman & J. D. Masur (Eds.), *Panic: Psychological perspectives.* Hillsdale, NJ: Lawrence Erlbaum Associates.

Tilley, C., & Maddux, J. E. (1989). *Self-efficacy for coping with anticipated negative life events: Relationship to depressed and anxious mood.* Unpublished manuscript. George Mason University, Fairfax, VA.

Tipton, R. M., & Worthington, E. L. (1984). The measurement of generalized self-efficacy: A study of construct validity. *Journal of Personality Assessment, 48,* 545–548.

Tolman, E. C. (1932). *Purposive behavior in animals and men.* New York: Appleton-Century-Crofts.

Turner, S. M., McCann, B. S., Beidel, D. C., & Messick, J. E. (1986). DSM-III classification of the anxiety disorders. *Journal of Abnormal Psychology, 95,* 168–172.

Weinberg, R. S., & Agras, W. S. (1984). *The Weight Reduction Efficacy Questionnaire.* Unpublished manuscript, Stanford University.

Weinberg, R. S., Hughes, H. H., Critelli, J. W., England, R., & Jackson, A. (1984). Effects of preexisting and manipulated self-efficacy on weight loss in a self-control program. *Journal of Research in Personality, 18,* 352–358.

White, R. W. (1959). Motivation reconsidered: The concept of competence. *Psychological Review, 66,* 297–333.

Williams, L. S., Dooseman, G., & Kleinfield, E. (1984). Comparative effectiveness of guided mastery and exposure treatments for intractable phobias. *Journal of Consulting and Clinical Psychology, 52,* 505–518.

Williams, L. S., Turner, S. M., & Peer, D. F. (1985). Guided mastery and performance desensitization treatments for severe acrophobia. *Journal of Consulting and Clinical Psychology, 53,* 237–247.

Williams, L. S., & Watson, N. (1985). Perceived danger and perceived self-efficacy as cognitive determinants of acrophobic behaviors. *Behavior Therapy, 16,* 136–146.

Wood, R., & Bandura, A. (1989). Impact of conceptions of ability on self-regulatory mechanisms and complex decision making. *Journal of Personality and Social Psychology, 56,* 407–415.

Wurtele, S. K. (1986). Self-efficacy and athletic performance: A review. *Journal of Social and Clinical Psychology, 4,* 290–301.

Wurtele, S. K., & Maddux, J. E. (1987). Relative contributions of protection motivation theory components in predicting exercise intentions and behavior. *Health Psychology, 6,* 453–466.

CHAPTER 5

REALITY NEGOTIATION AND EXCUSE-MAKING

Raymond L. Higgins
C. R. Snyder

Accurately perceiving reality has long been regarded as a hallmark of psychological health (e.g., Jahoda, 1953; Jourard & Landsman, 1980; Vaillant, 1977). Although a number of theorists have emphasized phenomenological perspectives on perception (e.g., Maslow, 1968; Rogers, 1965; Yalom, 1980), these authors have typically focused on the manner in which the individual's needs (especially self-esteem needs) distort their ability to accurately perceive reality and impair their adaptation or adjustment. While the above authors have written primarily from a clinical vantage point, others within the social psychological perspective have held similar views.

Although Heider (1944, 1958) theorized that the causal attributions people form about events of personal relevance may be influenced by their self-esteem needs, other early writers in both the attribution (e.g., Bem, 1972; Jones & Nisbett, 1972; Kelley, 1967, 1971; Miller & Ross, 1975) and social comparison (e.g., Festinger, 1957) literatures contended that people typically seek accurate, valid information about their characteristics and abilities. In recent years, however, evidence

has mounted that normal (and presumably mentally healthy) people systematically distort information they receive from (and deliver to) their environments about their "selves" (see Arkin, Cooper, & Kolditz, 1980; Bradley, 1978; Zuckerman, 1979 for reviews). In particular, it has become apparent that, far from being dispassionate or objective processors of information about themselves, people routinely distance themselves from acts or outcomes that would cast them in a negative light (i.e., would threaten their positive images or sense of control; Snyder, Higgins, & Stucky, 1983). Although it may be maladaptive or self-defeating in certain instances (Baumeister & Scher, 1988; Higgins & Berglas, in press; Higgins & Snyder, 1989), there is growing evidence that such distancing is frequently adaptive and linked to benefits in such areas as improved affect, performance, and health (see Snyder, in press; Snyder & Higgins, 1988a, 1988b for reviews).

In 1983, Snyder et al. presented a comprehensive theory of excuse-making in which we outlined the mechanisms and motivations underlying the aforementioned process of seeking distance from negative acts or outcomes. Subsequently, in reviews of the effects of excuse-making (Snyder & Higgins, 1988a, 1988b), we introduced the concept of "reality negotiation" to express our view that excuse-making, as one form of coping with negative life events, relates to a broader, more encompassing coping process that is aimed at mediating the change-inducing effects of self-relevant information. One purpose of the present chapter will be to provide a further elaboration of our thinking about reality negotiation and to examine how excuse-making relates to this more general hypothetical coping process. In closing, we will speculate about the role of excuse-making and reality negotiation in adaptive and maladaptive adjustment to serious illness.

REALITY NEGOTIATION

We have previously described reality negotiation as "*any* [italics added] coping process that involves the incorporation of change-inducing information into one's personal theory of self" (Snyder & Higgins, 1988a, p. 32). However, given our current focus on excuse-making as a means of coping with negative change-inducing information (i.e., illness), our attention here will be on reality negotiation within situations in which the individual is linked to threatening outcomes or actions.

As noted above, the idea that accurate reality perception is equivalent to good mental health has been challenged in recent years. Indeed, in a provocative review and analysis of this issue, Taylor and Brown (1988; also see Brown's chapter in this volume) concluded that mentally healthy individuals are characterized by "*overly positive* self-evaluations, *exaggerated* perceptions of control or mastery, and *unrealistic* optimism [italics added]" (p. 193). For such illusory specialness to be as pervasive and systematic as Taylor and Brown suggest it is, it would appear to require some equally pervasive and systematic mechanism through which reality-oriented information is processed. Furthermore, the fact that such illusory specialness involves a consistent bias in the individual's favor implicates a motivated process. As we have written elsewhere (e.g., Snyder, 1989, in press; Snyder & Higgins, 1988a, 1988b), we view reality negotiation as just such a motivated process designed to mediate the transformation of self-theories by serving the individual's underlying needs to maintain positive images and a sense of control.

Dynamic Self-Theories

As evidence of such phenomena as self-serving biases in causal attributions and "downward" social comparisons in the context of esteem threats has accumulated (see Wills, 1981, 1987, chapter in this volume for reviews), researchers have increasingly regarded the self-concept as a dynamic force in personality rather than as a simple reflection of a person's current attitudes toward him or herself. This elevation over the last two decades in the standing of the self-concept as a formative influence in personality can be seen in contrasting reviews. For example, whereas Wylie (1974) did not regard the self-concept as playing a significant role in instigating behavior, 13 years later Markus and Wurf (1987) wrote the following:

> The unifying premise of the last decade's research on the self is that the self-concept does not just reflect on-going behavior but instead mediates and regulates this behavior. In this sense the self-concept has been viewed as dynamic—as active, forceful, and capable of change. It interprets and organizes self-relevant actions and experiences; it has motivational consequences, providing the incentives, standards, plans, rules, and scripts for behavior; *and it adjusts in response to challenges from the social environment* [italics added]. (pp. 299–300)

Elsewhere (e.g., Snyder, 1989, in press; Snyder & Higgins, 1988a, 1988b), we have suggested that the self-concept may be thought of as a "self-theory," a set of beliefs, assumptions, and images that one holds about him or herself across contexts and time (for related ideas, see Bowlby, 1969; Epstein, 1984; Marris, 1975; Parkes, 1975; Schlenker, 1987). We have, in addition, likened our view of self-theories as both a means of representing ourselves and a process influencing our behaviors to Alfred Adler's concept of the "style of life" (e.g., Snyder, 1989):

> All inherited possibilities and all influences of the body, all environmental influences, including educational application, are perceived, assimilated, digested, and answered by a living and striving being, striving for a successful achievement in his view. The subjectiveness of the individual, his special style of life, and his conception of life mold and shape all influences. The individual life collects all these influences and uses them as provocative bricks in building a totality which aims toward a successful goal in relating itself to outside problems. (Adler, in Ansbacher & Ansbacher, 1967, p. 178)

The reader will notice a remarkable similarity between Adler's concept of the style of life and Markus and Wurf's (1987) view of the self-concept in terms of the degree of latitude afforded for subjective, self-creative action (see also Markus & Sentis, 1982; Neisser, 1976). Moreover, within our particular framework of discussing the role of reality negotiation in the process of coping with esteem- or control-threatening events, this self-creative potential extends to the self's involvement in the continuous modification and refinement of the self-theory in response to challenges from both the internal and external environments.

Revising Self-Theories

A self-theory reflects the cumulative influence of several self-representations. In other words, the self-representations that an individual makes on particular dimensions of appraisal are subcomponents of the larger, encompassing self-theory. The dimensions of appraisal, or schemas, are templates against which the person evaluates his or her behavior. Some schemas may be situation-specific, while others may transcend several arenas of human activity. (Snyder, 1989, p. 133)

As the above quotation implies, revisions in the self-theory are based on a continuous process of reappraising the goodness-of-fit between the individual's self-representations on relevant dimensions of appraisal and his or her ongoing activities and behaviors. Of particular interest here are two higher order dimensions of appraisal (i.e., linkage-to-act and valence-of-act) that we believe routinely come into play whenever individuals are confronted with information about themselves that is discrepant from (or, for that matter, consistent with) their current self-theories (Higgins & Snyder, 1989; Snyder & Higgins, 1990).

The Linkage-to-Act/Valence-of-Act Matrix

Figure 5.1 illustrates the interactive matrix formed by the linkage-to-act and valence-of-act dimensions of self-theory appraisal. Whereas the linkage-to-act dimension represents the degree to which the individual perceives him or herself to be linked (from no linkage to total linkage) to a particular act or outcome, the valence-of-act dimension represents the individual's qualitative assessment of the positiveness of the act or outcome (from positive to negative).

The reason that the linkage-to-act and valence-of-act dimensions form an interactive matrix derives from the fact that in isolation the dimensions do not provide the individual with sufficient information to judge whether revisions in the relevant aspects of his or her self-theory are warranted. For example, information that an individual is linked to an outcome has little meaning without knowing whether or not the outcome was desirable. By the same token, information that an outcome was desirable (or undesirable) has little personal significance to the individual (in terms of revising self-theories) in the absence of information concerning his or her level of linkage to the outcome. In combination, however, these two appraisal dimensions provide a powerful network of information for judging the viability of operative self-theories. In addition, the linkage and valence appraisal dimensions are reflected in what may be the two most influential (and interacting) motives underlying the maintenance of self-theories: the desire to promote positive images in the eyes of oneself and others, and the desire to promote and sustain a sense of control over one's destiny.

Mirrored Motives: Image and Control Maintenance

As we have indicated above, we believe that the linkage-to-act and valence-of-act appraisal dimensions are paralleled by motives to maintain positive images and a sense of control. This state of affairs can easily be understood by considering that one of the primary developmental tasks of the child is to gain a sense of instrumentality (White, 1959) and to distinguish between good and bad acts. In the words of Snyder (1989):

As we learn the importance of these dimensions in evaluating our own actions, we increasingly maximize the linkages to positive actions and minimize the linkages to more negative outcomes. In this sense, a normal person erects a self-theory that represents himself or herself as typically being a "good/in-control" person. (p. 135)

Furthermore, throughout our socialization, rewards and punishments are differentially dispensed to us based on how our behaviors measure up (or fail to measure up) to socially recognized standards of performance. We believe that, as a consequence of these learning experiences, the individual ultimately becomes *motivated* to preserve and promote the "good/in-control" self-theory (see also, Arkin & Baumgardner, 1986; Greenwald, 1980; Langer, 1983, Snyder et al., 1983; Tay-

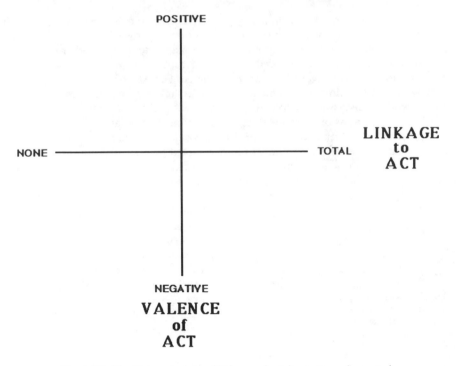

Figure 5.1. The Linkage-to-act and Valence-of-act dimensions of appraisal.

lor & Brown, 1988). Equally important is the apparent fact that people especially strive to maintain their "good/in-control" self-theories when they are confronted with disconfirming or contradictory evidence.

The Illusion Exchange

For purposes of conceptual clarity, control motives may be thought of as largely operating on the linkage-to-act appraisal dimension, while positive image motives may be thought of as largely operating on the valence-of-act appraisal dimension (Snyder, 1989). This bifurcated model, however, represents a simplification of a more complex, interactive system. Earlier, for example, we argued that, when considered in isolation from one another, neither valence-of-act appraisals nor linkage-to-act appraisals provide the individual with much useful information in judging the tenability of their personal theories of self. It is only when an outcome is "mapped" onto the matrix formed by crossing the two appraisal dimensions (see Figure 5.1) that the individual can determine whether his or her good/in-control self-theory is being threatened. Once this mapping has occurred, any alteration of the individual's position on either the linkage or valence dimensions will simultaneously affect the strength of the individual's motivation (need) to effect alterations in the other dimension. As an illustration of this, consider Figure 5.2.

Figure 5.2 essentially replicates Figure 5.1 with the exception that we now have an individual, "Fred," mapped onto the lower right quadrant of the matrix such that he is perceived (perceives himself) as being linked to a negative outcome. This represents a distinct challenge to Fred's self-theory of being a good/in-control person. Now, imagine that, through some psychological slight of hand (e.g., he denies any connection with the outcome), Fred successfully shifts his perceived position on the linkage dimension to the lower left quadrant of the matrix (i.e., to $Fred_1$). Even though the perceived negativeness (valence) of the act remains unaffected, the threat to Fred's self-theory has been assuaged and his motive (need) to alter the perceived negativeness of the act has been correspondingly diminished. Conversely, now imagine that Fred elects not to deny his role in the outcome but, rather, to lessen its perceived negativeness (e.g., through exonorative moral reasoning) and successfully locates himself in the upper-right quadrant of the matrix (i.e., at $Fred_2$).

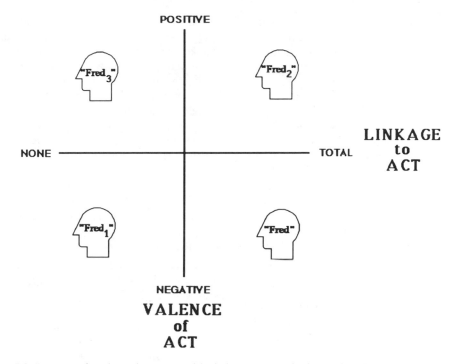

Figure 5.2. Excuse-mediated transformations of the linkage-to-act and valence-of-act dimensions of appraisal.

Here the threat to Fred's good/in-control self-theory has clearly been undermined and his motivation to cut his link to the outcome may collapse (indeed, he may now desire to increase perceptions of his linkage). Of course, Fred could elect to manipulate both the linkage (denial) and valence (exonorative moral reasoning) dimensions and relocate himself in the upper left quadrant of the matrix (i.e., at $Fred_3$).

Although it may be heuristically useful to think of the control and image motives as working primarily on the linkage and valence appraisal dimensions, respectively, in reality the interplay is more complex. In any event, the central thrust of this interactive matrix of appraisal dimensions and motives is that the individual attempts to increase his or her linkage to positive acts or outcomes and to decrease his or her linkage to negative acts or outcomes. Moreover, in the furtherance of these control and positive image motives, people not only perceive feedback from their environment in a self-servingly biased fashion, but they also actively attempt to manipulate their own and others' perceptions of self-relevant actions and outcomes in a process that has been called the *illusion exchange* (Snyder, 1989).

According to Snyder (1989), the linkage-to-act/valence-of-act matrix "is an exchange in the sense that it is where the individual 'negotiates' with the incoming reality of external feedback in order to preserve and enhance the personal theory of self" (p. 136). Although this statement places equal emphasis on preserving and enhancing the personal theory of self, our focus in this chapter is on excuse-making and, hence, on the self-protective use of the exchange to preserve the personal theory of self. In this vein, when people perceive that they are (or may be) linked to a negative outcome, they access the exchange in an attempt to (a) decrease their perceived linkage to the outcome and/or (b) decrease the perceived negativeness of the outcome to which they are linked.

Snyder's (1989) discussion of the illusion exchange focused both on excuse-making and hoping. In contrast to excuse-making, which is self-protective and largely seeks to decrease the individual's causal linkage to negative acts or outcomes, Snyder conceives of hoping as an acquisitive or self-enhancing process whereby the individual seeks to increase his or her causal linkage to positive outcomes or goals. Although there is one type of excuse-making, self-handicapping, which is theoretically capable of increasing an individual's causal linkage to positive outcomes (Berglas, 1988; Jones & Berglas, 1978), the effects of excuse-making are typically of the self-protective variety.

The linkage/valence exchange is an illusion exchange in the sense that the individual either perceives his or her linkage to (or the negativeness of) the "bad" act in a biased and esteem-preserving fashion (Higgins & Snyder, 1989; Snyder & Higgins, 1988a; Taylor & Brown, 1988), and/or attempts to create biased perceptions in the eyes of others (Snyder et al., 1983). It is also frequently an illusion exchange at a secondary level. As we have argued elsewhere, the excuse-making individual is motivated to remain unaware of his or her excuse efforts (Snyder et al., 1983) and, more often than not, self-deceptively regards them as reasons, explanations, or "truths" (Higgins & Snyder, 1989; Snyder, 1985a; Snyder & Higgins, 1988a, 1988b). In effect, then, the excuse-maker is negotiating a biased view of the excuses themselves. This secondary level of the illusion exchange appears to be especially successful when the individual is under no obligation to verbalize his or her excuse to an external audience or when the excuse resides in some relatively enduring physical or psychological attribute of the individual (Higgins & Snyder, 1989; Snyder & Higgins, 1988c).

Summary

In the preceding sections we have characterized reality negotiation as relating to the individual's motivated manipulation of linkage-to-act and valence-of-act appraisal dimensions, and have described the process as an "illusion exchange." In the words of Snyder (1989), "The process of employing the illusion exchange so as to uphold the personal theory of self *is* [italics added] reality negotiation" (p. 136).

The capacity for growth and development is one of the defining characteristics of all living things and, we would argue, of the psychological and physical health of people as well. However, the healthily developing individual's need for change must exist in some kind of balance with his or her countervailing need for stability and security (Maslow, 1968). When viewed in proper perspective, the reality-negotiation process we have described above should not be regarded as a means for the individual to maintain a kind of psychological stasis but, rather, as a means for the indi-

vidual to exercise some control over his or her rate and direction of change (cf. Janoff-Bulman & Timko, 1987). The very notion of *negotiation* implies that the "healthy" individual manages to maintain sufficient reality contact to continue to function reasonably. In the words of Snyder and Higgins (1990), the task of the individual is to "achieve a biased compromise between what we want to perceive about ourselves and what outside persons *will not seriously question* [italics added]" (pp. 212–213).

EXCUSE-MAKING AND REALITY NEGOTIATION

Definitional Issues

In several of our recent writings (e.g., Higgins & Snyder, 1989; Snyder & Higgins, 1988a), we have employed a definition of excuse-making that emphasizes the motivated "shifting of causal attributions for negative personal outcomes from sources that are relatively more central to the person's sense of self to sources that are relatively less central, thereby resulting in perceived benefits to the person's image and sense of control" (Snyder & Higgins, 1988a, p. 23). This definition clearly targets the linkage-to-act appraisal dimension as the focus of excuse-based efforts at reality negotiation and ignores the valence-of-act appraisal dimension. In effect, this definition returns to a definition of excuse-making that has been common in the impression-management literature, where a distinction has typically been made between excuses and justifications (Schlenker, 1980; Scott & Lyman, 1968). We say that this definition "returns" to the traditional impression management distinction between excuses and justifications because in our book, *Excuses: Masquerades in search of grace* (Snyder et al., 1983), we used a definition of excuse-making that subsumed justifications: "Excuses are explanations or actions that lessen the negative implications of an actor's performance, thereby maintaining a positive image for oneself and others" (p. 45). According to Tedeschi and Riess (1981), for example, "Excuses are explanations in which one admits that the disruptive act is bad, wrong, or inappropriate but dissociates himself from it. Justifications are explanations in which the actor takes responsibility for the action but denies that it has the negative quality that others might attribute to it" (p. 281). Within this framework, it is the justifications that target the valence-of-act appraisal dimension.

Previously, we have taken the position that excuse-making is an overarching self-protective process (Higgins & Snyder, 1990; Snyder & Higgins, 1990; Snyder et al., 1983), and we will employ a definition of excuse-making here that explicitly includes both the linkage-to-act and valence-of-act dimensions. Specifically, in the present context, we regard excuse making as the following:

> including the motivated processes of (a) diminishing the perceived negativity of esteem-threatening outcomes, and (b) shifting causal attributions for negative personal outcomes from sources that are relatively more central to the person's sense of self to sources that are relatively less central. (Higgins & Snyder, 1990, pp. 73–74)

Motivating Excuses: The Linkage/Valence Matrix

Excuse-making motives are stimulated whenever an individual perceives him or herself to be linked to an act or outcome that occupies a position on the negative end of the valence-of-act continuum. Such a situation is illustrated in Figure 2 for Fred (see lower right quadrant). Generally speaking, the strength of the excuse-making motives should be roughly proportional to (a) the strength of the individual's linkage to the act or outcome, and (b) the perceived negativeness of the act or outcome.

Factors Affecting Perceived Linkage

There appear to be a number of important determinants of the strength of the individual's perceived causal role in effecting outcomes. According to Kelley (1967), for example, attributions concerning the causes of events are most likely to focus on those aspects of the environment that covary with the outcomes of interest. Specifically, an individual is more likely to be seen as playing a causal role if he or she is associated with similar outcomes under differing circumstances (low distinctiveness), if he or she is often associated with similar outcomes in the same circumstances (high consistency), and if other people in the same situation are only rarely or never associated with similar outcomes (low consensus). (Also see Jones & Davis's, 1965, discussion of category- and target-based expectancies.) Subsequently, Kelley (1971)

added the principles of *discounting* and *augmentation* to his theory. The discounting principle states that when there is more than one plausible cause for an outcome the attribution to any one of those causes will be weaker than if it stands alone. Conversely, the augmentation principle states that causal attributions to an individual may be strengthened if the outcome he or she is associated with occurred despite the presence of inhibiting influences (cf., Jones & Berglas, 1978).

While Kelley's (1967) covariance theory focuses on the assignment of causality for oneself and others, Jones and Davis' (1965) theory of correspondent inferences largely concerns itself with how people form judgments about the intentions and dispositions of others. If, for example, an individual had the ability to produce certain consequences and foresaw them, Jones and Davis' theory predicts that external audiences will judge the individual as having intended to produce the consequences. Moreover, the audience might be expected to form a dispositional attribution — that is, a judgment regarding the individual's general tendencies to produce such consequences across situations and time. In a similar vein, if an action has unique consequences relative to those of other possible actions, there is an increased likelihood that those consequences will be regarded as the goal of the action (i.e., that the consequences were intentionally produced). Such judgments of intentionality and foreseeability, whether or not they lead to supplementary dispositional attributions, should be reflected in enhanced perceptions of causal linkages.

Finally, there is one other set of circumstances that appears to enhance perceptions of causal linkage and has special relevance to our focus on the role of excuses in coping with illness. Specifically, if external observers believe that a particular victimization experience could happen to them (i.e., it has situational relevance, Shaver, 1970), they tend to increase their assignment of causality to the victim, especially if they can construe themselves as being dissimilar to the victim (e.g., Burger, 1981; Chaiken & Darley, 1973). Attribution theorists typically explain victim-blaming as deriving from observer's efforts to cognitively defend themselves against the threat that similar misfortunes could befall *them* (e.g., Thornton, 1984). In other words, if victims are regarded as somehow responsible for their own victimization experiences, the observers can feel less personally threatened.

Factors Affecting Perceived Valence

We have previously defined a "bad" act as "any action or behavior on the part of a person that falls below the standards that have been established as being typical for that person or people in general" (Snyder et al., 1983, pp. 39–40). Obviously, the further an act or outcome falls short of accepted standards, the more negative it is perceived as being. By the same token, the more clearly defined the standards for acceptable performance become, the more likely it is that outcomes that fall short of those standards will be regarded negatively (Snyder, 1985b). Also, it can be expected that as a person's level of ego- or esteem-involvement in a performance increases, so will his or her perceptions of the negativeness of doing poorly (e.g., Carson, 1969; Walster, Walster, & Berscheid, 1978; Wicklund & Brehm, 1976). Perhaps more important, however, are a number of factors that increase perceived negativeness and illustrate the highly interactive nature of the valence-of-act/linkage-to-act matrix.

The most readily apparent tie-in between the valence and linkage dimensions can be seen in the interrelated factors of intentionality, controllability, and foreseeability. Certainly, a person who foresees an outcome, has control over it, and/or intends to produce it may be seen as having a strong causal link to it (see above discussion). Interestingly, these factors also are associated with increased perceptions of the negativeness of acts (e.g., Darley & Zanna, 1982; Rotenberg, 1980; Shaw, 1968; Shaw & Reitan, 1969; Sulzer & Burglass, 1968), as well as with greater anger and disliking toward the perpetrators of the acts (e.g., Weiner, Amirkhan, Folkes, & Verette, 1987). In this same vein, we have noted that Kelley's (1967) analysis of covariance theory of attributions specifies conditions under which an individual will be regarded as a causal agent. If such conditions as the consensus, distinctiveness, and consistency of .the outcomes become translated into inferences concerning foreseeability, intentionality, and controllability (Jones & Davis, 1965), it can be expected that causal inferences will be associated with increasingly severe judgments concerning the negativeness of the acts and their perpetrators (e.g., Weiner et al., 1987). Similarly, it might be expected that conditions that increase the likelihood of victim-blaming (see above discussion of factors increasing causal linkages) also will tend to increase the negativeness of reactions to illness victims and their illnesses.

Audiences for Excuse-Making

Once an individual's image and sense of control have been sufficiently threatened by actual or anticipated links to a negative outcome, the excuse-making/reality-negotiation process is set in motion. Perhaps one of the earliest and most significant discriminations the excuse-maker must make in terms of its impact on the subsequent course of the reality-negotiation process is whether or not external audiences are involved.

Relatively early in our thinking about excuse-making, we argued that excuse-makers would be motivated to remain unaware of their excuses if for no other reason than that remaining unaware would absolve them of having yet another negative act for which they must be accountable (Snyder et al., 1983). As our thinking has developed, however, we have come to regard excuse-making that is directed purely at the internal audience of the self to occur largely below the level of conscious awareness without the individual's having to "suppress" his or her awareness (e.g., Higgins & Snyder, 1989; Snyder & Higgins, 1988a). In effect, the individual's private excuse attributions tend to be reflexively honored because they are consistent with his or her good/in-control self-theory. The reality-negotiation process becomes more complicated primarily when external audiences enter the picture.

The presence of an external audience usually, though not always, requires the individual to give voice to his or her excuse attribution. (In many instances, excuse attributions may be physically (i.e., nonverbally) manifested. See Snyder and Higgins (1986c) for an additional discussion of this issue). This automatically curtails opportunities for reflexive self-deception regarding excuse-making and entails a more aware and active negotiation process both within and among the protagonists (Snyder & Higgins, 1988a). In this regard, there is growing evidence that people sometimes knowingly withhold the "true" reasons for their behavior (Folkes, 1982; Weiner et al., 1987, experiment 1) and instead present excuse attributions that effectively minimize negative responses on the part of their target audiences (e.g., Tetlock, 1981; Weiner et al., 1987).

The internal reality-negotiation process in such instances is revealed in findings such as those reported by Folkes (1982) in which the true reasons for social rejection were ostensibly withheld in order to avoid damaging a rejected individual's self-esteem (see also Weiner & Handel, 1985). The rejecting individuals appear to have negotiated their internal reality by identifying socially acceptable, even praiseworthy reasons for their deceit. Such excuses target the valence-of-act appraisal dimension and may go a long way toward explaining why external audiences often appear to be willing collaborators in the excuse-making individual's reality-negotiation efforts. In other words, people seem inclined to be particularly accepting of feedback or information that supports their own good/in-control self-theories (cf. Brown, this volume; Snyder, in press; Taylor & Brown, 1988). This dynamic may have particular relevance to illness victimization experiences where external audiences are "primed" to ego-defensively respond favorably to excuses that diminish the perceived severity of outcomes that *could* happen to them. However, even in situations when external audiences are not personally affected by the excuse-maker's excuse attributions, their tendency to be positively biased toward others (e.g., Schneider, Hastorf, & Ellsworth, 1979; Sears, 1983) and to deliver primarily positive feedback (e.g., Tesser & Rosen, 1975) typically makes them de facto collaborators with the excuse-maker's reality-negotiation efforts.

EXCUSE-MAKING, REALITY NEGOTIATION, AND HEALTH

We turn now to a consideration of the relationship of excuse-mediated reality negotiation to the process of coping adaptively with serious illness. We have recently reviewed evidence concerning the effects of excuse-making on such diverse concerns as negative affect, depression, self-esteem, performance, and health (Snyder, in press; Snyder & Higgins, 1988a, 1988b), but for our illustrative purposes we will focus only on findings related to health.

Health Maintenance

There are several findings suggesting that excuse-making may be positively related to the maintenance of health. One of these findings (i.e., Leary, 1986) stems from an experimental investigation of the effects on pulse-rates of having a handicapping excuse attribution available during a stressful social interaction. Self-handicapping has recently been defined by Snyder (in press) as follows:

Self-handicapping is a process of preserving the personal theory of self, wherein the person, experiencing uncertainty about success in an anticipated important performance arena, utilizes seeming impediments in order to (1) decrease the linkage to that impending performance should it prove to be poor (i.e., discounting), and (2) increase the linkage should the performance prove to be good (augmentation). (p. 16 in manuscript)

Leary (1986) examined the effects of a situation-imposed handicap on high and low socially-anxious subjects' responses to a social interaction task. College student subjects participated in a social interaction task in the presence of a background noise that was described as either distracting (handicapped condition) or not distracting (control condition). Pulse rates measured during the course of the social interaction revealed that subjects (particularly highly socially anxious subjects) in the distracting noise condition had lower pulse rates and lower pulse rate changes relative to baseline in comparison with subjects in the non-handicapping control condition.

A second body of literature relating excuse-making tendencies to health-maintenance effects derives from research flowing out of investigations of the reformulated theory of learned helplessness (Abramson, Seligman, & Teasdale, 1978; Burns & Seligman, in this volume; Peterson & Seligman, 1984; Seligman, Abramson, Semmel, & von Baeyer, 1979). In general, this theory states that learned helplessness in the wake of negative events is most likely to ensue if people make internal (I), stable (S), and global (G) attributions for those events and least likely to ensue if people make external (E), variable (V), and specific (S) attributions. Elsewhere, we have referred to this latter, EVS, pattern of attributions for negative events as the *prototypical excuse-making pattern* (Snyder & Higgins, 1988a, p. 25). Of course, learned helplessness is thought to be associated with the occurrence of depression (e.g., Peterson & Seligman, 1984), but it also is believed to have repercussions for performance and health. It is to consideration of this latter literature that we now turn.

Seligman (1986) reported the results of several studies relating excuse-making attributional styles to health maintenance effects. In a longitudinal study, 28 women were solicited in 1943 for their explanations of their worst events during 1942, and these explanations were subsequently rated on the attributional dimensions of global/specific and stable/variable (Elder, Bettes, & Seligman, 1982). Again, in 1970, these women provided attributional explanations for the events of 1969 and also reported their health. The women's attributional patterns for 1942 were significantly and positively correlated with their attributions for 1969 ($r = .44$) and, in addition, variable and specific attributions in 1942 significantly predicted health in 1970 (no statistics are reported for this latter effect).

Seligman (1986) also reported a second longitudinal study in which raters read the sports page quotations from Hall-of-Fame baseball players who played between 1900 and 1950 and generated ISG/EVS scores for both the good and bad performances of each player. The dependent variable was the players' ages at death, which, remarkably, correlated positively with both EVS attributional patterns for bad performances ($r = .26, p < .08$) and with ISG attributional patterns for good performances ($r = .45, p < .01$). Finally, Seligman (1986) reported a study that found that elderly people with EVS as opposed to ISG attributional patterns displayed better immune system functioning (no statistical analyses were reported for this result).

In yet another longitudinal study (Peterson, Seligman, & Vaillant, 1988; also see Seligman, 1986), 99 Harvard graduates in 1946 provided descriptions of difficult wartime experiences. These descriptions were subsequently rated for internal/external, stable/variable, and global/specific attributions. In addition, physical health scores (based on physician reports) were derived for the men beginning at age 25 (in 1946) and every 5 years thereafter until age 60. The results indicated that an excuse-making (EVS) attributional style for the wartime experiences reported in 1946 significantly predicted later physical health—especially from ages 45 to 60—even after health at age 25 was statistically controlled.

The findings from the above longitudinal studies provide strong support for the notion that an excuse-making explanatory style for negative life events is associated with superior health maintenance among people who were relatively healthy at the beginning of the studies (i.e., Peterson et al., 1988; Seligman, 1986). In addition, at least two potential mechanisms through which such excuse-mediated benefits may accrue have been identified (i.e., reduced pulse rates in stressful situations, [Leary, 1986] and enhanced immune system functioning [Seligman, 1986]). Although the correlational nature of most of these findings makes it hazardous to render conclusions regarding the causal role of excuse attributions in producing the observed health effects, the findings are, nonetheless, consistent with the hypothesized role of excuses in moderating the effects of threats to self-theories (Snyder & Higgins, 1988a, 1988b).

Coping with Existing Illness

Although the literature is fairly consistent with regard to the beneficial effects of excuse-related attributions on maintaining health, the picture with regard to the causal attributions that are associated with adaptive coping with existing illness is more differentiated. For example, Tennen, Affleck, Allen, McGrade, and Ratzan (1984) in a study of children with insulin-dependent diabetes found that those who viewed the onset of their disease as due to internal, variable, and specific factors were rated by their physicians as coping better than children who attributed the beginning of their disease to external, stable, and global factors. By the same token, the adjustment and rehabilitation of both severely disabled (Bulman & Wortman, 1977) and less severely disabled (Brewin, 1984) victims of industrial accidents has been found to be better for those who attributed causation to themselves than for those who attributed causation to others. In fact, Brewin (1984) reported that those workers whose injuries resulted from accidents that were the least foreseeable and controllable (i.e., most excusable within a personal framework) tended to have the least favorable rehabilitation, whereas workers who reported believing that they were causally responsible appeared to show superior adaptation.

Similar findings relating self-blame to better adaptation have been reported among mothers with acutely ill or handicapped children (Affleck, McGrade, Allen, & McQueeney, 1985) and among breast cancer patients (Timko & Janoff-Bulman, 1985). In other studies of breast cancer (Taylor, Lichtman, & Wood, 1984) and renal failure patients (Witenberg, Blanchard, Suls, Tennen, McCoy, & McGoldrick, 1983), no relationship has been observed between self-blame and adjustment, although Taylor et al. (1984) reported that current beliefs that one could control cancer were associated with good adjustment. In contrast to the above findings indicating that self-blame is associated with positive rehabilitation outcomes (or, at worst, has no association with outcome), it has been consistently found that blaming others is associated with poor adjustment and rehabilitation to illness (e.g., Affleck, Allen, McGrade, & McQueeney, 1982; Affleck, McGrade, Allen, & McQueeney, 1985; Affleck, Tennen, Croog, & Levine, 1987a; Bulman & Wortman, 1977; Taylor et al., 1984; Tennen, Affleck, & Gershman, 1986; Timko & Janoff-Bulman, 1985), though not necessarily to injury (e.g., Brewin, 1984; Frey, Rogner, Schuler, & Korte, 1985; Nelson & MacDonald, 1988).

Although findings such as these appear, at first glance, to contradict our model of excuse-making and reality negotiation in the process of coping with negative life events, we will develop the thesis that they fit rather comfortably within that model.

Illness and the Linkage/Valence Matrix

The advent of serious illness in an individual's life obviously is an outcome with a distinctly negative valence — and one to which the individual is indisputably linked. Moreover, within an attributional framework, it may often be the case that the affected individual, and/or external audiences, perceive the linkage to be a causal one. Heider (1958), for example, speculated that misfortunes will often be attributed to the individual's blameworthiness, and subsequent research on victim blaming has supported Heider's thinking (e.g., Burger, 1981; Howard, 1984; Janoff-Bulman, 1982; Thornton, 1984).

Historically, research on victim-blaming has been heavily influenced by the "just world" (Lerner, 1970, 1980) and defensive attribution hypotheses (Walster, 1966; Shaver, 1970), which have been regarded as reflecting two parts of the same attributional strategy (Burger, 1981; Thornton, 1984). Whereas the "just world" hypothesis states that people need to maintain a belief that they live in a just world where bad things only happen to those who deserve them, the defensive attribution hypothesis argues, in part, that people distort their causal attributions regarding negative outcomes in order to maintain the belief that the outcome was controllable and, therefore, avoidable for them (i.e., harm avoidance; Shaver, 1970). Moreover, the more negative the outcome is, the more causal responsibility will be assigned to the victim (Walster, 1966). To a large extent, such causal attributions should also characterize the victims themselves due to their attributional ef-

forts to maintain a sense of control over their worlds (e.g., Kelley, 1967; Taylor, 1983; Tennen et al., 1986). From the perspectives of both the affected individual and external audiences, therefore, illness (especially serious illness) should represent a threat to the individual's good/in-control self-theory and serve as an instigation for excuse-making in the service of reality negotiation.

Negotiating Linkages

Findings that self-blame is associated with better adjustment to misfortune are frequently attributed to the importance people place on maintaining a sense of behavioral control over their lives and destinies (e.g., Taylor, 1983; Tennen et al., 1986). From our perspective, however, such efforts to maintain a sense of primary control (Rothbaum, Weisz, & Snyder, 1982) also may be regarded as linkage excuses. Believing that one can control the course or outcome of an illness or disease, for example, may be regarded as a consistency-lowering and/or a distinctiveness-raising excuse, depending on one's point of view (Kelley, 1971; Snyder et al., 1983). In a similar vein, attributing one's illness or misfortune to one's behaviors or actions (behavioral self-blame) as opposed to one's character or enduring traits (characterological self-blame; Janoff-Bulman, 1979) may be regarded as "shifting causal attributions for negative personal outcomes from sources that are *relatively* more central to the person's sense of self to sources that are *relatively* less central" (see previous definition of excuse-making).

From the vantage point of reality negotiation, the above types of excuses seem especially well suited to serve the individual's need to preserve his or her good/in-control self-theory. Within the individual's personal frame of reference, for example, behavioral self-blame serves to simultaneously maintain the belief that he or she is capable of exercising effective control over his or her life and to delimit the search for causal explanations to aspects of the individual's behavior as opposed to aspects of the individual's dispositional characteristics. Perhaps equally important is that such behavioral self-blame honors an external audience's need to defensively regard such misfortunes as "deserved" (Lerner, 1970, 1980) while helping them nurture their own comforting illusions that similar misfortunes are somehow avoidable in their own lives (Shaver, 1970; Walster, 1966).

Earlier in this chapter we suggested that one of

the primary tasks facing the reality-negotiating individual is to arrive at a self-serving answer to his or her dilemma that will not be seriously questioned by external audiences. As noted above, engaging in behavioral self-blame appears to provide an elegant solution for this problem. It is a solution, moreover, that seems particularly well designed to maximize the individual's chances of maintaining his or her social support networks at a time that such support may be critical to adaptive coping or successful rehabilitation.

Negotiating Valences

To this point in our discussion, we have focused primarily on linkage and control issues as they relate to adaptation, excuse-making, and reality negotiation. As we have emphasized throughout this chapter, however, valence information plays a critical role in the appraisal of self-theories—and provides an important avenue of action for excuse-based reality negotiation. There is growing evidence that valence-shifting excuses may play an important role in successful adaptation to illness.

Taylor, Wood, and Lichtman (1983) have reviewed a number of cognitive coping strategies (e.g., downward social comparison, selecting self-serving comparison dimensions, creating hypothetical worse worlds, manufacturing standards of adjustment) that may be thought of as having valence-shifting properties for victims of various types of misfortunes. Affleck, Tennen, Pfeiffer, and Fifield (1988), for example, found that rheumatoid arthritis patients who made pronounced downward social comparisons were rated as displaying more positive adjustment.

Recent theory and research on coping with traumatic events has emphasized the adaptive value of finding meaning in those events (Thompson & Janigian, 1988). Successful efforts to find positive meaning have been associated with better adaptation following the loss of a child (Chodoff, Friedman, & Hamburg, 1964), following incest victimization (Silver, Boon, & Stones, 1983), following loss of homes in fires (Thompson, 1985), and having children with severe perinatal complications (Tennen et al., 1986) or experiencing a lightning strike (Dollinger, 1986). Of more direct relevance here, however (given our primary focus on coping with illness), are findings of better adaptation following successful searches for meaning in women with breast cancer (Taylor et al., 1984), and in heart attack (Affleck et al., 1987a) and stroke vic-

tims (Thompson, Sobolew-Shubin, Graham, & Janigian, 1989). Consistent with our thinking about the role of excuse-making and reality negotiation in the process of preserving personal self-theories, such findings as these have been theoretically linked to the role of finding meaning in preserving or restoring "positive assumptions about the world and the self" (Thompson & Janigian, 1988, p. 261).

Within our framework, efforts to exercise secondary control (Rothbaum et al., 1982) by finding positive meaning in adverse outcomes may be regarded as efforts at excuse-making aimed at the valence dimension of self-theory appraisal. By identifying positive aspects or benefits associated with a misfortune (a type of reframing, Snyder et al., 1983), its negativeness is lessened and the threat to the self-theory is diminished. Interestingly, one would typically expect the reality-negotiation process vis-a-vis both the internal audience of the self and any external audience to proceed quite smoothly in such instances. Concerning the internal audience, finding positive meaning in adversity clearly serves to preserve the good-self image and, in addition, may help to define positive goals (cf. Snyder, 1989). With regard to the external audience, one would expect them to react positively to any help the "victim" might give them in diminishing the severity of vicariously experienced threats to their own good/in-control self-theories (cf. Shaver, 1970; Walster, 1966). As-yet untested predictions flowing from this line of reasoning are that external audiences who are made aware of the positive meaning that illness victims find in their suffering (a) should rate the illness as being less serious and (b) should judge the victim to be less causally responsible for their illness (cf. Walster, 1966).

CONCLUDING SPECULATIONS

Within a temporal framework, it is likely that coping with illness often involves progressing through a series of stages, including the individual's appraisal of the severity of the threat and his or her resources for dealing with that threat (e.g., Lazarus & Folkman, 1984), as well as possibly having to disengage from previous goals and become invested in new goals (e.g., Klinger, 1977). During the early, threat-appraisal stages, the evidence suggests that people may engage in a concerted effort to identify potential causes and treatments for their disorder (e.g., Fay, 1983), with the number of causal attributions entertained being somewhat proportional to the severity of the perceived threat (e.g., Affleck, Tennen, Croog, & Levine, 1987b; see also Affleck, Allen, Tennen, McGrade, & Ratzan, 1985; Tennen et al., 1986). Ultimately, of course, many people settle on some subset of causal attributions that facilitate their adaptation, while others adopt attributions that appear to impair their adaptation (see above discussion of other-blame, for example). Our concluding remarks are addressed to a consideration of how the excuse-making/reality-negotiation process may ultimately serve this latter group of sufferers.

We have argued that being diagnosed as having an illness is tantamount to being linked (perhaps causally) to a negative outcome and represents a threat to the individual's good/in-control self-theory. It is apparent that, in the case of chronic or recurring illness, the original diagnosis or illness episode often represents only the first of a perhaps lengthy series of threatening experiences. Over time, many people will receive either interpersonal (e.g., from physicians, family members, or friends) or more tangible (e.g., recurrences of illness) feedback that they are not coping adequately. Each successive episode of such feedback once again links the individual to a negative outcome (now the act of not coping adequately) and threatens anew the good/in-control self-theory.

In theory, the excuse-making/reality-negotiation principles we have outlined apply as much to such recurrences as to the original illness episodes. The ability of the affected individuals to accommodate themselves to such threatening, change-inducing information, for example, may be significantly enhanced by such linkage-shifting attributions as, "I haven't been trying hard enough to follow the doctor's orders," or, "I've been using the wrong strategy." Similarly, such valence-shifting excuse strategies as downward social comparison (e.g., "Other people with similar problems aren't doing as well as I") or finding new meaning in the recurrence may often be employed. As an illustration of this latter point, Affleck et al. (1987a) reported that men who had survived a second heart attack were more likely than men who had not had second heart attacks to report benefits from their "experience."

In the end, of course, those individuals who cope satisfactorily with serious illness are likely to be more able to identify and invest themselves in pursuing positive life goals. As we have attempted

to demonstrate in this chapter, the potential of excuse-mediated reality negotiation may be one important avenue through which people are able to get beyond being preoccupied with the negative aspects of their experience and to productively live the lives they have. In this latter sense, our outcome in the game of life depends not only on the cards that we have been dealt, but also on how we play out our hands.

REFERENCES

Abramson, L. Y., Seligman, M. E. P., & Teasdale, J. D. (1978). Learned helplessness in humans: Critique and reformulation. *Journal of Abnormal Psychology, 87*, 49–74.

Affleck, G., Allen, D., McGrade, B. J., & McQueeney, M. (1982). Maternal causal attributions at hospital discharge of high risk infants. *American Journal of Mental Deficiency, 86*, 575–580.

Affleck, G., Allen, D., Tennen, H., McGrade, B., & Ratzan, S. (1985). Causal and control cognitions in parents coping with a chronically ill child. *Journal of Social and Clinical Psychology, 3*, 369–379.

Affleck, G., McGrade, B. J., Allen, D. A., & McQueeney, M. (1985). Mother's beliefs about behavioral causes for their developmentally disabled infant's condition: What do they signify? *Journal of Pediatric Psychology, 10*, 293–303.

Affleck, G., Tennen, H., Croog, S., & Levine, S. (1987a). Causal attribution, perceived benefits, and morbidity after a heart attack: An 8-year study. *Journal of Consulting and Clinical Psychology, 55*, 29–35.

Affleck, G., Tennen, H., Croog, S., & Levine, S. (1987b). Causal attribution, perceived control, and recovery from a heart attack. *Journal of Social and Clinical Psychology, 5*, 339–355.

Affleck, G., Tennen, H., Pfeiffer, C., & Fifield, J. (1988). Social comparisons in rheumatoid arthritis: Accuracy and adaptational significance. *Journal of Social and Clinical Psychology, 6*, 219–234.

Ansbacher, H. L., & Ansbacher, R. R. (1967). *The individual psychology of Alfred Adler.* New York: Harper & Row.

Arkin, R. M., & Baumgardner, A. H. (1986). Self-presentations and self-evaluation: Processes of self-control and social control. In R. F. Baumeister (Ed.), *Public self and private self* (pp. 75–97). New York: Springer-Verlag.

Arkin, R. M., Cooper, H., & Kolditz, T. (1980). A statistical review of the literature concerning the self-serving attribution bias in interpersonal influence situation. *Journal of Personality, 48*, 435–448.

Baumeister, R. F., & Scher, S. J. (1988). Self-defeating behavior patterns among normal individuals: Review and analysis of common self-destructive tendencies. *Psychological Bulletin, 104*, 3–22.

Bem, D. J. (1972). Self perception theory. In L. Berkowitz (Ed.), *Advances in experimental social psychology* (Vol. 6, pp. 1–62). New York: Academic Press.

Berglas, S. (1988). The three faces of self-handicapping: Protective self-presentation, a strategy for self-esteem enhancement, and a character disorder. In S. L. Zelen (Ed.), *Self-representation: The second attribution-personality theory conference, CSPP-LA, 1986* (pp. 133–169). New York: Springer-Verlag.

Bowlby, J. (1969). *Attachment and loss*. Vol. 1: Attachment. London: Hogarth.

Bradley, G. W. (1978). Self-serving biases in the attribution process: A reexamination of the fact or fiction question. *Journal of Personality and Social Psychology, 36*, 56–71.

Brewin, C. R. (1984). Attributions for industrial accidents: Their relationship to rehabilitation outcome. *Journal of Social and Clinical Psychology, 2*, 156–164.

Bulman, R. J., & Wortman, C. B. (1977). Attribution of blame and coping in the "real world": Severe accident victims react to their lot. *Journal of Personality and Social Psychology, 35*, 351–363.

Burger, J. M. (1981). Motivational biases in the attribution of responsibility for an accident: A meta-analysis of the defensive attribution hypothesis. *Psychological Bulletin, 90*, 496–512.

Carson, R. C. (1969). *Interaction concepts of personality*. Chicago: Aldine.

Chaiken, A. L., & Darley, J. M. (1973). Victim or perpetrator? Defensive attribution of responsibility and the need for order and justice. *Journal of Personality and Social Psychology, 25*, 268–275.

Chodoff, P., Friedman, S. B., & Hamburg, P. A. (1964). Stress defenses and coping behavior. *American Journal of Psychiatry, 120*, 433–439.

Darley, J. M., & Zanna, M. P. (1982). Making moral judgments. *American Scientist, 70*, 515–521.

Dollinger, S. J. (1986). The need for meaning following disaster: Attributions and emotional upset. *Personality and Social Psychology Bulletin, 12*, 300–310.

Elder, G., Bettes, B. A., & Seligman, M. E. P. (1982). Unpublished data. Cornell University. [Cited on p. 368 of Peterson, C., & Seligman, M. E. P. (1984). Causal explanations as a risk factor for depression: Theory and evidence. *Psychological Review, 91*, 347–374.]

Epstein, S. (1984). Controversial issues in emotion theory. In P. Shaver (Ed.), *Review of personality and social psychology: Emotions, relationships, and health* (pp. 64–88). Beverly Hills, CA: Sage Publications.

Fay, M. (1983). *A mortal condition*. New York: Coward-McCann, Inc.

Festinger, L. (1957). *A theory of cognitive dissonance*. Stanford, CA: Stanford University Press.

Folkes, V. S. (1982). Communicating the causes of social rejection. *Journal of Experimental Social Psychology, 18*, 235–252.

Frey, D., Rogner, O., Schuler, M., & Korte, C. (1985). Psychological determinants in the convalescence of accident patients. *Basic and Applied Social Psychology, 6*, 317–328.

Greenwald, A. G. (1980). The totalitarian ego: Fabrication and revision of personal history. *American Psychologist, 35*, 603–618.

Heider, F. (1944). Social perception and phenomenal causality. *Psychological Review, 51*, 358–374.

Heider, F. (1958). *The psychology of interpersonal relations*. New York: John Wiley & Sons.

Higgins, R. L., & Berglas, S. (in press). The maintenance and treatment of self-handicapping: From risk-taking to face-saving—and back. In R. L. Higgins, C. R. Snyder, & S. Berglas (Eds.), *Self-handicapping: The paradox that isn't*. New York: Plenum Press.

Higgins, R. L., & Snyder, C. R. (1989). Excuses gone awry: An analysis of self-defeating excuses. In R. C. Curtis (Ed.), *Self-defeating behaviors: Experimental research, clinical impressions, and practical implications* (pp. 99–130). New York: Plenum Press.

Higgins, R. L., & Snyder, C. R. (1990). The business of excuses. In R. A. Giacalone & P. Rosenfeld (Eds.), *Impression management in the organization* (pp. 73–85). Hillsdale, NJ: Lawrence Erlbaum Associates.

Howard, J. (1984). Societal influences on attribution: Blaming some victims more than others. *Journal of Personality and Social Psychology, 47,* 494–505.

Jahoda, M. (1953). The meaning of psychological health. *Social Casework, 34,* 349.

Janoff-Bulman, R. (1979). Characterological versus behavioral self-blame: Inquiries into depression and rape. *Journal of Personality and Social Psychology, 37,* 1798–1809.

Janoff-Bulman, R. (1982). Esteem and control bases of blame: "Adaptive" strategies for victims versus observers. *Journal of Personality, 50,* 180–191.

Janoff-Bulman, R., & Timko, C. (1987). Coping with traumatic events: The role of denial in light of people's assumptive worlds. In C. R. Snyder & C. E. Ford (Eds.), *Coping with negative life events: Clinical and social psychological perspectives* (pp. 135–159). New York: Plenum Press.

Jones, E. E., & Berglas, S. (1978). Control of attributions about the self through self-handicapping strategies: The appeal of alcohol and the role of underachievement. *Personality and Social Psychology Bulletin, 4,* 200–206.

Jones, E. E., & Davis, K. E. (1965). From acts to dispositions: The attribution process in person perception. In L. Berkowitz (Ed.), *Advances in experimental social psychology* (Vol. 2, pp. 219–266). New York: Academic Press.

Jones, E. E., & Nisbett, R. E. (1972). The actor and observer: Divergent perceptions of the causes of behavior. In E. E. Jones, D. Kanouse, H. H. Kelley, R. E. Nisbett, S. Valins, & B. Weiner (Eds.), *Attribution: Perceiving the causes of behavior* (pp. 79–94). Morristown, NJ: General Learning Press.

Jourard, S. M., & Landsman, T. (1980). *Healthy personality: An approach from the viewpoint of humanistic psychology* (4th ed.). New York: Macmillan.

Kelley, H. H. (1967). Attribution theory in social psychology. In D. Levine (Ed.), *Nebraska symposium on motivation, 1967* (pp. 192–238). Lincoln, NE: University of Nebraska Press.

Kelley, H. H. (1971). *Attribution in social interaction.* New York: General Learning Press.

Klinger, E. (1977). Consequences of commitment to and disengagement from incentives. *Psychological Review, 82,* 1–25.

Langer, E. J. (1983). *The psychology of control.* Beverly Hills, CA: Sage Publications.

Lazarus, R., & Folkman, S. (1984). *Stress, appraisal, and coping.* New York: Springer.

Leary, M. R. (1986). The impact of interactional impediments on social anxiety and self-presentation. *Journal of Experimental Social Psychology, 22,* 122–135.

Lerner, M. J. (1970). The desire for justice and reactions to victims. In J. Macaulay & L. Berkowitz (Eds.), *Altruism and helping behavior* (pp. 205–229). New York: Academic Press.

Lerner, M. J. (1980). *The belief in a just world: A fundamental delusion.* New York: Plenum Press.

Markus, H., & Sentis, K. (1982). The self in social information processing. In J. Suls (Ed.), *Psychological perspectives on the self* (pp. 41–70). Hillsdale, NJ: Lawrence Erlbaum Associates.

Markus, H., & Wurf, E. (1987). The dynamic self-concept: A social psychological perspective. *Annual Review of Psychology, 38,* 299–337.

Marris, P. (1975). *Loss and change.* Garden City, NJ: Anchor/Doubleday.

Maslow, A. H. (1968). *Toward a psychology of being.* New York: Van Nostrand-Reinhold.

Miller, D. T., & Ross, M. (1975). Self-serving bias in the attribution of causality: Fact or fiction? *Psychological Bulletin, 82,* 213–225.

Neisser, U. (1976). *Cognition and reality.* San Francisco: W. H. Freeman.

Nelson, W. R., & MacDonald, M. R. (1988). Attributions of blame and coping following spinal cord injury: Is self-blame adaptive? *Journal of Social and Clinical Psychology, 7,* 163–175.

Parkes, C. M. (1975). What becomes of redundant world models? A contribution to the study of adaptation to change. *British Journal of Medical Psychology, 48,* 131–137.

Peterson, C., & Seligman, M. E. P. (1984). Causal explanations as a risk factor for depression: Theory and evidence. *Psychological Review, 91,* 347–374.

Peterson, C., Seligman, M. E. P., & Vaillant, G. E. (1988). Pessimistic explanatory style is a risk factor for physical illness: A thirty-five-year longitudinal study. *Journal of Personality and Social Psychology, 55,* 23–27.

Rogers, C. R. (1965). *Client-centered therapy.* Boston: Houghton Mifflin. (Originally published by Riverside Press, Cambridge, MA, 1951.)

Rotenberg, K. (1980). Children's use of intentionality in judgements of character and disposition. *Child Development, 51*, 282–284.

Rothbaum, F., Weisz, J., & Snyder, S. (1982). Changing the world and changing the self: A two-process model of perceived control. *Journal of Personality and Social Psychology, 42*, 5–37.

Schlenker, B. R. (1980). *Impression management: The self-concept, social identity, and interpersonal relations*. Monterey, CA: Brooks/Cole.

Schlenker, B. R. (1987). Threats to identity: Self-identification and social stress. In C. R. Snyder & C. E. Ford (Eds.), *Coping with negative life events: Clinical and social psychological perspectives* (pp. 323–346). New York: Plenum Press.

Schneider, D. J., Hastorf, A. H., & Ellsworth, P. C. (1979). *Person perception*. Reading, MA: Addison-Wesley.

Scott, M. R., & Lyman, S. M. (1968). Accounts. *American Sociological Review, 33*, 46–62.

Sears, D. O. (1983). The person-positivity bias. *Journal of Personality and Social Psychology, 44*, 233–250.

Seligman, M. E. P. (1986, August). *Explanatory style: Depression, Lyndon Baines Johnson and the Baseball Hall of Fame*. Paper presented at the 94th Annual Convention of the American Psychological Association, Washington, DC.

Seligman, M. E. P., Abramson, L. Y., Semmel, A., & von Baeyer, C. (1979). Depressive attributional style. *Journal of Abnormal Psychology, 88*, 242–247.

Shaver, K. G. (1970). Defensive attribution: Effects of severity and relevance on the responsibility assigned for an accident. *Journal of Personality and Social Psychology, 14*, 101–113.

Shaw, M. E. (1968). Attribution of responsibility by adolescents in two cultures. *Adolescence, 3*, 23–32.

Shaw, M. E., & Reitan, H. T. (1969). Attribution of responsibility as a basis for sanctioning behavior. *British Journal of Social and Clinical Psychology, 8*, 217–226.

Silver, R. L., Boon, C., & Stones, M. H. (1983). Searching for meaning in misfortune: Making sense of incest. *Journal of Social Issues, 39*, 81–102.

Snyder, C. R. (1985a). Collaborative companions: The relationship of self-deception and excuse-making. In M. W. Martin (Ed.), *Self-deception and self-understanding* (pp. 35–51). Lawrence, KS: Regents Press of Kansas.

Snyder, C. R. (1985b). The excuse: An amazing grace? In B. R. Schlenker (Ed.), *The self and social life* (pp. 235–260). New York: McGraw-Hill.

Snyder, C. R. (1989). Reality negotiation: From excuses to hope and beyond. *Journal of Social and Clinical Psychology, 8*, 130–157.

Snyder, C. R. (in press). Self-handicapping processes and sequelae: On the taking of a psychological dive. In R. L. Higgins, C. R. Snyder, & S. Berglas, *Self-handicapping: The paradox that isn't*. New York: Plenum Press.

Snyder, C. R., & Higgins, R. L. (1988a). Excuses: Their effective role in the negotiation of reality. *Psychological Bulletin, 104*, 23–35.

Snyder, C. R., & Higgins, R. L. (1988b). Excuse attributions: Do they work? In S. L. Zelen (Ed.), *Self-representation: The second attribution-personality theory conference, CSPP-LA, 1986* (pp. 50–132). New York: Springer-Verlag.

Snyder, C. R., & Higgins, R. L. (1988c). From making to being the excuse: An analysis of deception and verbal/nonverbal issues. *Journal of Nonverbal Behavior, 12*, 237–252.

Snyder, C. R., & Higgins R. L. (1990). Reality negotiation and excuse-making: President Reagan's 4 March 1987 Iran arms scandal speech and other literature. In M. J. Cody & M. L. McLaughlin (Eds.), *Psychology of tactical communication* (pp. 207–228). Clevedon, England: Multilingual Matters, Ltd.

Snyder, C. R., Higgins, R. L., & Stucky, R. J. (1983). *Excuses: Masquerades in search of grace*. New York: John Wiley & Sons.

Sulzer, J. L., & Burglass, R. K. (1968). Responsibility attribution, empathy and punitiveness. *Journal of Personality, 36*, 272–282.

Taylor, S. (1983). Adjustment to threatening events: A theory of cognitive adaptation. *American Psychologist, 38*, 1161–1173.

Taylor, S. E., & Brown, J. D. (1988). Illusion and well-being: A social psychological perspective on mental health. *Psychological Bulletin, 103*, 193–210.

Taylor, S. E., Lichtman, R. R., & Wood, J. V. (1984). Attributions, beliefs about control, and adjustment to breast cancer. *Journal of Personality and Social Psychology, 46*, 489–502.

Taylor, S. E., Wood, J. V., & Lichtman, R. R. (1983). It could be worse: Selective evaluation as a response to victimization. *Journal of Social Issues, 39*, 19–40.

Tedeschi, J. T., & Riess, M. (1981). Verbal strategies in impression management. In C. Antaki (Ed.), *The psychology of ordinary explanations of social behavior* (pp. 271–309). London: Academic Press.

Tennen, H., Affleck, G., Allen, D. A., McGrade, B. J., & Ratzan, S. (1984). Causal attributions and coping with insulin-dependent diabetes. *Basic and Applied Social Psychology, 5*, 131–142.

Tennen, H., Affleck, G., & Gershman, K. (1986). Self-blame among parents of infants with perinatal complications: The role of self-protective motives. *Journal of Personality and Social Psychology, 50*, 690–696.

Tesser, A., & Rosen, S. (1975). The reluctance to transmit bad news. In L. Berkowitz (Ed.), *Advances in experimental social psychology* (Vol. 8, pp. 193–232). New York: Academic Press.

Tetlock, P. E. (1981). The influence of self-presentation goals in attributional reports. *Social Psychology Quarterly, 44*, 300–311.

Thompson, S. C. (1985). Finding positive meaning in a stressful event and coping. *Basic and Applied Social Psychology, 6*, 279–295.

Thompson, S. C., & Janigian, A. S. (1988). Life schemes: A framework for understanding the search for meaning. *Journal of Social and Clinical Psychology, 7*, 260–280.

Thompson, S. C., Sobolew-Shubin, A., Graham, M. A., & Janigian, A. S. (1989). Psychosocial adjustment following a stroke. *Social Science and Medicine, 28*, 239–247.

Thornton, B. (1984). Defensive attribution of responsibility: Evidence for an arousal-based motivational bias. *Journal of Personality and Social Psychology, 46*, 721–734.

Timko, C., & Janoff-Bulman, R. (1985). Attributions, vulnerability and psychological adjustment: The case of breast cancer. *Health Psychology, 4*, 521–546.

Vaillant, G. (1977). *Adaptation to life*. Boston: Little, Brown.

Walster, E. (1966). Assignment of responsibility for an accident. *Journal of Personality and Social Psychology, 3*, 73–79.

Walster, E., Walster, G. W., & Berscheid, E. (1978). *Equity: Theory and research*. Boston: Allyn & Bacon.

Weiner, B., Amirkhan, J., Folkes, V. S., & Verette, J. A. (1987). An attributional analysis of excuse giving: Studies of a naive theory of emotion. *Journal of Personality and Social Psychology, 52*, 316–324.

Weiner, B., & Handel, S. (1985). Anticipated emotional consequences of causal communications and reported communication strategy. *Developmental Psychology, 21*, 102–107.

White, R. W. (1959). Motivation reconsidered: The concept of competence. *Psychological Review, 66*, 297–335.

Wicklund, R. A., & Brehm, J. W. (1976). *Perspectives on cognitive dissonance*. Hillsdale, NJ: Lawrence Erlbaum Associates.

Wills, T. A. (1981). Downward social comparison principles in social psychology. *Psychological Bulletin, 90*, 245–271.

Wills, T. A. (1987). Downward comparison as a coping mechanism. In C. R. Snyder & C. E. Ford (Eds.), *Coping with negative life events: Clinical and social psychological perspectives* (pp. 243–268). New York: Plenum Press.

Witenberg, S. H., Blanchard, E. B., Suls, J., Tennen, H., McCoy, G., & McGoldrick, M. D. (1983). Perceptions of control and causality as predictors of compliance and coping in hemodialysis. *Basic and Applied Social Psychology, 4*, 319–336.

Wylie, R. C. (1974). *The self-concept*. (Vol. 1). Lincoln, NE: University of Nebraska Press.

Yalom, I. D. (1980). *Existential psychotherapy*. New York: Basic Books.

Zuckerman, M. (1979). Attribution of success and failure revisited, or: The motivational bias is alive and well in attribution theory. *Journal of Personality, 47*, 245–287.

CHAPTER 6

COPING WITH ACCOUNTABILITY: SELF-IDENTIFICATION AND EVALUATIVE RECKONINGS

Barry R. Schlenker
Michael F. Weigold
Kevin Doherty

It is our thesis that people's problems dealing with accountability are at the core of most dysfunctional behaviors. To be accountable is to be ready to answer for one's conduct. One undergoes an evaluative reckoning about how well one has lived up to particular prescriptions, including responsibilities, duties, and obligations at home, at work, and in social life in general. The result is a judgment and sanctioning of one's conduct by audiences (oneself included) that has repercussions for the outcomes one receives and for one's very identity.

Identity and accountability are intertwined, and the construction and evaluation of identity takes place in the context of accountability. Identity is a theory of self that is formed and maintained through actual or imagined interpersonal agreement about what the self is like (see Schlenker, 1985, 1986a). The identities people establish determine how they are regarded and treated in social life, so people have a stake in constructing and

preserving identities that mediate valued outcomes. According to self-identification theory (Schlenker, 1980, 1984, 1985, 1986a, 1987; Schlenker & Weigold, 1989), people strive to construct and maintain desired identity images. These images are neither idealistically glorifying nor faithful to the nuances of evidence as seen by an omniscient observer. Rather, desirable identity images represent a compromise between one's wishes (the personal beneficiality component, or the extent to which the image serves the holder's values and goals) and reality (the believability component, or the extent to which the image is perceived to be an accurate, defensible interpretation of evidence) (Schlenker, 1980; Schlenker & Weigold, 1989). These images represent what people believe they both should and can be on particular occasions, being "reality-edited" yet somewhat glorified views of the self. People attempt to construct and preserve these images, both privately and publicly, and are threatened when they might be

Preparation of this chapter was supported in part by a Research Development Award from the Division of Sponsored Research, University of Florida, Gainesville.

96

damaged by events. When potential threats to identity arise, stress is created and people take action to cope with the problem (Schlenker, 1987).

Self-identification is the process, means, or result of showing oneself to be a particular type of person, thereby specifying one's identity (Schlenker, 1984, 1985; Schlenker & Weigold, 1989). It is accomplished privately, through contemplation of oneself, and publicly, through self-disclosure, self-presentation, and other activities (e.g., task performances) that serve to construct one's identity for audiences. Fixing and expressing identity involves systematically defining and categorizing oneself, bringing relevant evidence and experiences to bear. As such, self-identification can be regarded as an accounting, conducted for a specific purpose on a specific occasion, in which one's assets and liabilities are selectively documented and evaluated for the benefit of an audience. When people are accountable for particular events, those events have potential implications for identity; when people are not accountable, the implications of events are less meaningful. Consequently, behavior that occurs under conditions of accountability has a greater potential impact on the actor's thoughts, feelings, and efforts (Schlenker, 1986b; Schlenker & Weigold, in press; Tetlock, 1985a).

When people confront threats to identity, as when they anticipate or experience failures, they increasingly attempt to change the timing, terms, and outcomes of their accountability. To do so, people use one or more of three primary strategies: (a) retreating from accountability by avoiding or selectively encountering situations and audiences to whom they would be accountable (e.g., agoraphobia permits avoidance of most external audiences while alcohol or drug use dulls the internal audience); (b) accounting for potential failures with excuses and justifications that try to avoid "worst case" interpretations (e.g., blaming one's troubles on factors other than one's personal skills, such as drugs or hostile coworkers); and (c) using apologies to mitigate the negative repercussions accompanying responsibility for a transgression (e.g., admitting responsibility for the event but expressing remorse and begging forgiveness). With frequent use, the first two strategies can build a wall between one's identity and one's actions, blocking the implications of one's behavior for one's identity. The third strategy involves chronic self-blame of the type seen in depression. The occurrence and communication of symptoms of "psychological problems" can be viewed in terms of their impact on accountability. The cognitive, affective, and behavioral symptoms of most mental illnesses ultimately function to modify the timing, terms, and outcomes of accountability and thereby protect, as best as possible under adverse conditions, the actor's desired identity.

The ideas that responsibility can be frightening (Fromm, 1941; Horosz, 1975), that people try to reduce their responsibility when failure looms (Austin, 1961; Carson, Butcher, & Coleman, 1988; Goffman, 1971; Schlenker, 1980, 1987; Schlenker & Leary, 1982; Scott & Lyman, 1968; Shea, 1988; Snyder & Higgins, 1988; Snyder, Higgins, & Stucky, 1983), and that symptoms of mental illness are communications that influence the reactions of others, often by reducing one's responsibilities (Braginsky, Braginsky, & Ring, 1969; Carson et al., 1988; Scheff, 1966; Schlenker, 1980; Snyder & Smith, 1982; Szasz, 1961; Wood, 1986) have been around for some time. Our goal in this chapter is to place these ideas in the larger social psychological context of people's problems dealing with the nature and implications of accountability. In so doing, we present a model of accountability and try to establish its relevance for clinical symptomology. Further, we examine how people arrange their environments so as to control, as best as possible, the timing, terms, and outcomes of accountability in order to preserve desired identities. The theoretical approach is based on self-identification theory (Schlenker, 1980, 1984, 1985, 1986a, 1987; Schlenker & Weigold, 1989), and the model of accountability is termed the *pyramid model* (Schlenker, 1986b; Schlenker & Weigold, in press).

ACCOUNTABILITY AND IDENTITY

Accountability has received relatively little explicit conceptual or empirical attention from psychologists until recently (Schlenker, 1986b; Schlenker & Weigold, in press; Tetlock, 1985a), despite the fact that it is one of the oldest and most important concepts in social science. Historically, accountability has been a central concept in analyses of justice and social control, and substantially predates the notion of personal responsibility, which was introduced in the 18th century as a component of accountability (McKeon, 1957). Any collective, ranging from a dyad to a civilization, must resolve how coordination and cooperation can emerge from a collection of individuals with diverse goals and interests. Accountability provides the mechanism through which people expect others to perform to certain prescriptions for conduct, judge the performance in relation to those prescriptions, and distribute rewards and punishments based on that performance. Because of accountability, people can exert legitimized control over one another's conduct. We watch, judge, and sanction others, and they do the same to us, thereby ensuring adherence to valued prescriptions for conduct.

Accountability also makes self-regulation possible. When appraising potential courses of action, people take into account how their actions will look in light of the relevant prescriptions, and how they might explain those actions in the event that questions or indictments arise. As C. Wright Mills (1940, p. 906) contended, "Often anticipations of acceptable justifications will control conduct. ('If I did this, what could I say? What would they say?') Decisions may be, wholly or in part, delimited by answers to such queries." Self-regulation — in the form of observing, monitoring, and controlling our behavior according to certain standards, evaluating the resulting performance, and administering self-reward or self-punishment (Bandura, 1982) — entails dealing with accountability.

The Pyramid Model of Accountability

Accountability involves evaluation, and all evaluative reckonings require information about three key elements and the linkages or connections between them: (a) the *prescriptions* that should be guiding the actor's conduct on the occasion (e.g., how one should treat one's children); (b) the *event* that occurred (or is anticipated) that is relevant to the prescriptions (e.g., how one has treated one's children); and (c) a set of *identity images* that are relevant (e.g., the type of parent one is). The three elements and their linkages depict a triangle when visualized, so we will call this the *triangle component* of accountability. When the evaluating audience is added as a hovering eye-in-the-sky, shown in Figure 6.1, the model becomes an iconic Pyramid, and hence is termed the *pyramid model* of accountability (Schlenker, 1986b; Schlenker & Weigold, in press). We propose that the actor's evaluation of the worth of the relevant elements of the triangle on the occasion combine with the strength of the linkages of the triangle to determine its impact on the actor's identity. A task is

ego involving to the extent that the elements are more important and the linkages are stronger. Briefly consider the constituents.

Elements

Prescriptions are criteria for performance that can be used to guide behavior and evaluate it. They include, implicitly or explicitly, information about what people should try to accomplish (goals), how they should go about doing so (rules), and what level of accomplishment is satisfactory (standards). Prescriptions are more important to the extent that they are regarded as valued principles for conduct (e.g., duties, obligations, moral or personal aspirations) or have high personal consequences (e.g., following shop rules because doing so brings promotions while failing to do so brings dismissal).

Events are the units of action actors and observers regard as a unified segment for purposes of some evaluation (e.g., performance on a task). Accountability has a greater impact when the relevant event is associated with more important consequences (e.g., a greater effect on the lives of other people; greater potential monetary gain or loss).

Finally, accountability has a greater impact when the performance pertains to images that the actor regards as more central and important to his or her identity. For example, accountability on an intellectual task will have a greater impact on people who have pretensions of being an intellectual than those who do not.

Linkages

The perceived strength of the linkages between the three elements represent the actor's *responsibility* for the event. That is, people are held responsible to the extent that (a) a clear set of prescriptions should be applied in the situation (the prescription-event linkage); (b) the actor is perceived to be bound by the prescriptions (the prescription-identity linkage); and (c) the actor seems to have (or to have had) control over the event, such as by intentionally producing the consequences with foreknowledge of what would happen (the identity-event linkage).

The *prescription-event link* refers to the extent to which a clear set of prescriptions is perceived to exist that should govern conduct (e.g., clear laws, commandments, imperatives, traditions, shop rules). The link is weaker to the extent that pre-

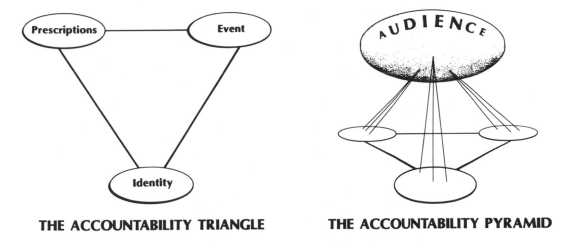

Figure 6.1. The pyramid model of accountability.

scriptions are perceived to be ambiguous, conflicting, obscure, or nonexistent, such that there is uncertainty about what should be done or how to go about doing it.

The *prescription-identity link* refers to the extent to which the actor is perceived to be bound by the prescriptions; that is, to fall under the domain of the particular set of laws, policies, etc. This linkage can exist because of the actor's resources and attributes (e.g., being of sound mind and capable of understanding the consequences of one's actions, so therefore having to obey the relevant laws), roles (e.g., being responsible for the actions of one's child by virtue of one's role as a parent), and personal convictions (e.g., Christian beliefs). The linkage is strong to the extent that the prescriptions clearly apply and the actor is supposed to be committed to following them.

The *identity-event link* refers to the extent to which the actor is perceived to have (or have had) control over the event. The link is stronger when the actor seems to have intended to produce the consequences of the event with foreknowledge of what would happen, and weaker when the consequences are unforeseeable, accidental, or uncontrollable (Fincham & Jaspars, 1980; Heider, 1958).

It is proposed that an actor's responsibility on any occasion is determined by the summed strength of the three linkages. If any of the links can be completely severed, responsibility is eliminated. Reductions in responsibility are associated with weakened or questionable linkages. Our view of responsibility explicitly describes the link-

ages that constitute it, and is more inclusive than most prior analyses that focus primarily on causality, role obligations, or other delimited aspects without integrating the overall picture. Table 6.1 summarizes the key points in our overview of the pyramid model and indicates for each linkage the state represented by a strong connection, major factors that strengthen the linkage, and accounts that can be used to weaken the linkage.

According to the model, ego involvement is a combination of the worth of the elements and the strength of the linkages. When these are high, the task will have a dramatic impact on the actor; when these are low, the task is trivial or irrelevant. Further, it is proposed that when an event (anticipated or *fait accompli*) is likely to be regarded positively (e.g., a success), actors will attempt to increase the strength of the linkages in order to create a greater impact on identity. Conversely, when an event (anticipated or *fait accompli*) is likely to be regarded negatively (e.g., a failure), actors will try to decrease the strength of the linkages or reinterpret the relevant elements. Before examining the ways in which people deal with accountability under threat, we will first consider the nature of threats to identity.

Accountability Is Aversive when Identities Are Threatened

Problems for identity arise when people encounter or anticipate undesired events, that is, events that might seem to contradict important prescriptions and identity images. The magnitude

Table 6.1. Implications of the Accountability Linkages

	ACCOUNTABILITY LINKAGE		
	IDENTITY-PRESCRIPTION	IDENTITY-EVENT	PRESCRIPTION-EVENT
State represented by a strong linkage	Obligation; duty; role responsibility	Personal responsibility as control	Task or action clarity; procedural clarity
Antecedents that strengthen the linkage	Clear role requirements; self-attention to salient standards; internalization of prescriptions	Feelings of internal or personal control; expectations of success; high need for achievement	Clear goals, rules, and standards; crystallized scripts or procedures
Accounts to weaken the linkage	Lower the relevance of prescriptions; "I'm sick, so I can't be expected to follow those rules"; "I'm old and my memory is poor, so you should do it for me"	Diminish personal responsibility: "It wasn't my fault"; "I couldn't help it"; "I was drunk"; "The devil made me do it"	Redefine task or make it appear to be ambiguous; "I didn't know what to do"; "Nobody ever taught me that"

of the problem is greater as a direct function of (a) the actor's apparent responsibility (i.e., the combined strength of the linkages) and (b) the absolute value of the elements that are involved (e.g., more negative consequences produced by the event, more important prescriptions or identity images) (Schlenker, 1980). Further, larger problems require more extreme actions in order to deal with accountability.

Problems are not threats in and of themselves. Whether a problem is perceived as a threat depends on the actor's expectations that it can be successfully handled (Schlenker, 1987). *Outcome expectations* reflect the perceived likelihood to the actor that goals will be achieved given the nature of the task (e.g., its difficulty or ambiguity), the audience (e.g., how demanding, critical, or supportive it is), and the actor's perceived skills and resources (e.g., perceived ability, supportive co-performers). (For discussion of factors that affect outcome expectations, see Schlenker, 1987; Schlenker & Leary, 1982; and Schlenker & Weigold, 1989.) When outcome expectations are low, actors feel threatened and become focused on the possibilities for failure and its costly consequences.

Threats create negative affect, potentially debilitating levels of stress and anxiety, and poorer performance (Lazarus, 1981; Lazarus & Launier, 1978; Schlenker, 1987; Schlenker & Leary, 1982). People with lower outcome expectations avoid the task or, if they cannot, procrastinate before starting, work less hard, give up if they encounter impediments to goal accomplishment, and have more negative feelings about the performance

(Bandura, 1977; Feather, 1982; Lazarus, 1981). Performance thus declines quantitatively and qualitatively.

Accountability Amplifies Threats

Accountability intensifies the cognitive, affective, and behavioral consequences of threats. Accountability is frequently described as an unpleasant social experience that produces anxiety, reduces creativity, generates task disengagement, and ultimately harms performance. Consistent with this view, accountability has been shown (a) to undermine intrinsic interest in a task and be detrimental to creativity (Amabile, 1979); (b) to distract people from concentrating on a task because of a concern for how they might look to the audience (Baumeister, 1984; Baumeister, Hamilton, & Tice, 1985); and (c) to produce "choking" and poor task performance when the audience has high expectations (Baumeister, 1984; Baumeister et al., 1985). When people try to please those to whom they are accountable, compromises often replace good judgment, and task performance suffers (Adelberg & Batson, 1978; Tetlock, 1985a).

Further, research indicates that people will engage in protective self-presentations when they are accountable and the audience's expectations are excessively high (Schlenker, 1986a, 1987; Schlenker & Leary, 1985). Protective self-presentations are designed to avoid losses for identity, and can be contrasted with acquisitive or assertive self-presentations, which are designed to achieve gains (Arkin, 1981; Tedeschi & Norman, 1985; Schlenker & Leary, 1985). Protective self-presentations are characterized by less communication, less self-disclosure, greater caution in judgments, and task disengagement in which people attempt to avoid the task if possible (Schlenker & Leary, 1985). On occasions when task avoidance is impossible, people become more self-focused, become obsessed with their frailties and limitations, and perform worse (Pyszczynski & Greenberg, 1987; Schlenker, 1987; Schlenker & Leary, 1982).

Accountability Can Be Beneficial

Accountability amplifies the unpleasant repercussions of threats, but it would be misleading to leave the impression that accountability always has a detrimental impact. Accountability also can spotlight one's strengths and secure the benefits of success. Achievements are more gratifying when people are accountable, and people seem to seek out accountability when they have high outcome expectations.

Research has demonstrated that accountability can have beneficial effects on performance (Schlenker, 1986b; Tetlock, 1985a). It has been found that accountability (a) generates greater learning and subsequent recall of information, provided that rewards are offered for successful task performance (Slavin, 1983); (b) produces more cognitively complex judgment and decision strategies instead of a reliance on simple heuristics (Chaiken, 1980; McAllister, Mitchell, & Beach, 1979; Tetlock, 1983a, 1985a; Tetlock & Kim, 1987; Weldon & Gargano, 1985, 1988); (c) produces data-driven processing of information in which judgments are influenced more by the relevant data than by pre-existing biases (Ford & Weldon, 1981; Mann & Taylor, 1970; Rozelle & Baxter, 1981; Tetlock, 1983b); (d) produces a greater awareness of the strategies that are being employed during decision-making and performance (Cvetkovich, 1978; Hagafors & Brehmer, 1983; Tetlock, 1985a); and (e) produces greater effort devoted to task completion (e.g., Latané, Williams, & Harkins, 1979; Williams, Harkins, & Latané, 1981). When people think they can perform well, accountability may activate resources in the interests of task accomplishment and increase the likelihood of success.

Heightening Threats and Challenges

Accountability seems to improve performance when people have higher outcome expectations

but seems to harm performance when people have lower outcome expectations. Doherty, Weigold, and Schlenker (1989) tested these hypotheses directly. They led subjects to believe they would serve as division heads in a simulated business enterprise. Performance of the company as a whole would be determined by how well each of the divisions did. Based on bogus feedback on a practice task, subjects were induced to have expectations of success or failure on the major task. Subjects also believed a company meeting would be held in which they would have to explain and defend the performance of their division (accountable condition) or would not have to do so (unaccountable condition). Accountability produced the hypothesized effects on measures of the creativity, quality, and quantity of subjects' responses. When they expected success, subjects performed better (i.e., more solutions that were judged as higher quality and more creative) if they were accountable than unaccountable. The reverse was true when subjects expected failure: They performed far worse when they were accountable than unaccountable. Accountability thus seems to intensify reactions to challenging and threatening situations.

In a second study, Schlenker, Weigold, and Doherty (1989) asked subjects to think of and evaluate occasions on which they did or did not feel accountable (answerable for one's actions or performance) and, if accountable, felt either good, bad, or indifferent. Being accountable for incidents that involved positive affect was associated with perceptions of better task performance, greater task effort, higher self-evaluations, and more positive feelings about being held accountable; subjects also said they sought out these incidents. In sharp contrast, being accountable for incidents that involved negative affect was associated with perceptions of poorer task performance, lower effort, lower self-evaluations, and less positive feelings about being held accountable. Situations in which subjects were accountable but indifferent were associated with intermediate perceptions on these dimensions, and with perceptions that the situation was relatively unimportant. Finally, although lack of accountability was associated with positive self-evaluations, unaccountable subjects also said they expended less effort and were less persistent in the face of obstacles than subjects who were accountable under conditions of positive affect or indifference. These results support the idea that accountability can be associated with positive feelings, approach, determination, and achievement, as well as with negative feelings, avoidance, lack of determination, and failure.

In sum, accountability seems to amplify the cognitive, affective, and behavioral reactions that otherwise occur. When people have high outcome expectations, they will work harder toward their goals, concentrate better, and be more likely to take effective remedial action when problems are encountered. In contrast, threats are associated with negative affect, stress and anxiety, self-focus, task distraction, and ineffective coping strategies.

MANAGING ACCOUNTABILITY UNDER THREAT

When people encounter threats to identity, they respond with remedial activities designed to cope with the threat (Austin, 1961; Goffman, 1971; Schlenker, 1980, 1982, 1987; Scott & Lyman, 1968; Snyder et al., 1983). We propose that these activities are ultimately aimed at changing the timing, terms, and outcomes of accountability, and can be grouped into three categories: accountability avoidance strategies, accounting strategies, and apology strategies. First, people can try to avoid being answerable, such as by avoiding threatening tasks and threatening audiences, concealing threatening information, and withdrawing prematurely from threatening situations. These will be termed accountability avoidance strategies. Second, people can deal with threats by providing their own account of what transpired, usually by generating excuses and justifications that protect their identities. These accounting strategies try to change the linkages and/or the elements in the accountability triangle. Third, people can apologize for the problem, thereby attempting to minimize damage to identity and negative sanctions. These apology strategies accept some blame for failure or wrong-doing and try to show, among other things, that one has already self-inflicted punishment, mitigating the need for maximum sanctioning by the audience.

The three types of strategies aim at different facets of what it means to be accountable (Schlenker, 1986b). Being held accountable involves (a) submitting to an inquiry by an audience who will evaluate one's conduct in relation to certain prescriptions (the *inquiry facet*); (b) presenting one's side of the story, in which the actor can describe, document, interpret, and explain rele-

vant information and construct a personal version of the events and why they occurred (the *accounting facet*); and (c) rendering a verdict, including judgment of the actor and positive or negative sanctions (the *verdict facet*). In attempting to deal with accountability, people will try to influence each facet as best they can. Accountability avoidance strategies are aimed at avoiding inquiries. Accounting strategies attempt to influence the verdict by constructing self-serving interpretations of events. Apology strategies assume some degree of blame and try to reduce the negative repercussions that will accompany the verdict. These strategies are not mutually exclusive, of course, and are often used in combination. We will now examine each of the strategies and their implications.

Accountability Avoidance Strategies

Accountability avoidance strategies aim at circumventing or eliminating accountability inquiries. In essence, the actor attempts to put off, avoid, or escape from tasks, situations, and audiences that would involve an accounting, especially when an undesired verdict is feared.

The tendency for people to avoid accountability when their identities are threatened is well documented. People avoid tasks that produce embarrassment or involve specific ego threats, even sacrificing monetary rewards to do so (Brown, 1970; Teichman, 1973). People also avoid situations in which they anticipate social difficulties and prematurely leave those that elicit social anxiety (Cheek & Buss, 1982; Pilkonis, 1977; Twentyman & McFall, 1975; Zimbardo, 1977). People also try to conceal events that are potentially embarrassing or out of character, hiding them from public view (Lewittes & Simmons, 1975), and prefer not to affiliate with evaluative others under these conditions (Fish, Karabenick, & Heath, 1978; Sarnoff & Zimbardo, 1961; Teichman, 1973; Watson & Friend, 1969).

Social anxiety, which arises when people perceive threats to their identities (Schlenker & Leary, 1982, 1985), is strongly associated with disaffiliation—behaviors that decrease the actor's social contact with others. When experiencing social anxiety, people initiate conversations less frequently, are more reluctant to speak freely, speak for a lower percentage of the time and, in general, participate less fully in conversations (Cheek & Buss, 1982; Leary, 1983, 1986; Slivken & Buss, 1984; Zimbardo, 1977). The tendency to maintain distance from others is also suggested by findings that socially anxious people decrease eye contact (Modigliani, 1971; Pilkonis, 1977; Zimbardo, 1977), disclose less information about themselves (Leary, Knight, & Johnson, 1987; Post, Wittmaier, & Radin, 1978), describe themselves in less unique terms (Leary et al., 1987), and generally act in a less sociable fashion (Cheek & Buss, 1982) than nonanxious people. Socially anxious people thereby minimize the extent to which they will be held accountable by selectively avoiding evaluative audiences and, when forced to interact, cautiously avoiding a more complete participation that would give audiences diagnostic information that could be judged.

The anxiety disorders (see American Psychiatric Association, 1987 [*Diagnostic and Statistical Manual of Mental Disorders*, 3rd ed., rev. (DSM-III-R)]), particularly social phobias and generalized anxiety, involve retreats from evaluative audiences. Because of their generalized disaffiliative tendencies, socially anxious people report a higher incidence of loneliness (Cheek & Busch, 1981). The generalized retreat from accountability thus involves a price—social isolation. A dramatic case is agoraphobia, in which people avoid public places, preferring to block social scrutiny from which they cannot escape except for that by family and close friends, whose regard is usually more assured. People with avoidant personality disorders (DSM-III-R) suffer a similar reluctance to participate in social life. They are fearful of criticism, interpret others' remarks as personal rejection and derogation, and develop a pattern of limited social relationships (Carson et al., 1988). Yet they experience distress because they would like to have friends and dislike their loneliness. Thus, their sensitivity to and fear of failure cause them to perceive most situations as threatening, causing a retreat, but are upset by the social cost that their strategy involves.

Avoiding Legitimate Inquiries

People can also be said to be avoiding accountability when they refuse, often belligerently or aggressively, to submit themselves to inquiries by audiences who otherwise have a legitimate right to demand an inquiry. This strategy is typified by the assertion, "You have no right to ask me that or to judge me," and justified by reference to the audience's inferior status (e.g., a parent to a child; an employer to an employee), rights (e.g., an employee asserts that the union contract or job description does not cover what is being asked), knowledge (e.g., a teenager tells her mother she just doesn't understand what it is like to be in high school today), or antagonist qualities (e.g., the audience is prejudiced, hostile, and out to persecute the actor, therefore disqualifying itself as a fair judge). In effect, the actor tries to blunt inquiries by eliminating as an appropriate judge the audience who would otherwise conduct an inquiry.

In milder form, the tactic is illustrated by people's tendency to derogate evaluators who deliver undesirable personal feedback, viewing them as stupid or prejudiced (Jones, 1973; Mettee & Aronson, 1974). In more extreme forms, the tactic is characterized by stronger attacks on anyone who disagrees with the actor. The paranoid personality (DSM-III-R), for example, is typified by a rebuking style in which others who disagree are confronted in an attempt to make them back down. The paranoid not only refuses to recognize potentially critical others as judges for his or her conduct, but also blames those others for personal failures (Carson et al., 1988; Marmar, 1988; Schlenker, 1987).

Dulling the Internal Audience

Even when people are able to rid themselves of the evaluative stare of an external audience, they must still account to themselves (Schlenker, 1986b; Schlenker & Weigold, 1989). People serve as audiences for their own self-identifications, using internalized prescriptions for guiding and judging their conduct (Greenwald & Breckler, 1985; Schlenker, 1980, 1985, 1986a; Snyder et al., 1983). When people's identities are threatened, the self-as-audience can be a potentially harsh judge. Self-focused attention then can be an unpleasant state that people want to terminate (Duval & Wicklund, 1972; Hull, 1981; Hull & Young, 1983; Wicklund, 1975). As such, people often take action to escape rumination about their own accountability for their problems. Self-evaluation can be reduced through drugs, intoxication, physical exercise, and meditation. Watching television, going to the theater, shopping in malls, and an array of other enjoyable activities may similarly claim attention and refocus it beyond the self.

Alcohol has historically functioned as a stress reducer. Hull (1981; Hull & Young, 1983) demonstrated that alcohol lowers self-focused attention, which in turn is reinforcing for people who have experienced recent failures or other negative events. In both experimental and field studies, the combination of threats to identity and chronic levels of self-focused attention leads to increased alcohol consumption (Hull & Young, 1983).

Similarly, Baumeister (1988) has argued that masochistic behavior is an attempt to escape from a higher order awareness of self by focusing attention on immediate sensations (Baumeister, 1988). Besides dulling the internal audience, masochism may also serve as self-punishment in expiation for real or imagined transgressions, thereby being a form of apology (see below).

Accountability Avoidance:
Pluses and Minuses

Although accountability avoidance can protect identity, it carries a price, and the price increases when it is used indiscriminately. Accountability avoidance leads to loneliness and isolation when people pull back from others and it leads to unfulfilled potential when people refuse to tackle potentially difficult tasks, thereby dooming themselves to mediocrity. Further, chronic use of accountability avoidance has an impact on the actor's identity. People who avoid others and appear nervous when they must interact gain reputations as being shy, anxious, and weak. People who assertively attack others to disqualify them as judges gain reputations as eccentrics, paranoids, or antisocial characters. These identity images then influence the future conduct of audiences toward the actor.

In addition, accountability avoidance is often not a viable strategy because of competing pressures to perform on schedule. A shy businessman may dread the speech he must give at the next meeting, but he dare not fail to show up because doing so would jeopardize his job. There are only so many responsibilities people can avoid without jeopardizing their status as viable actors on the stage of life.

Space does not permit an analysis of the factors that would facilitate or impede the use of the different accountability avoidance tactics, or the use of this strategy as compared with accounting or apology strategies. Considerations that are involved include (a) the believability or defensibility of the tactic (e.g., Can the actor construct an acceptable explanation for avoiding the task or audience that does not force an admission of fear of failure?); (b) the expected value of avoiding the task or audience (e.g., To what extent will avoidance protect identity? How great are the costs of avoidance?); and (c) the expected value of confronting the task or audience (e.g., How rewarding would it be to succeed? How costly would it be to fail? What are the likelihoods of success and failure?). (For discussion of factors that influence the choice of self-presentation strategies, see Schlenker, 1980; Schlenker & Weigold, 1989.) Clearly, such utilitarian considerations play an important role in the use of avoidance strategies. For example, social phobias, such as the fear of public places or crowds, are more common in females than males. Such excessive fears are more compatible with the traditional female role of being helpless and dependent (Carson et al., 1988), whereas males traditionally should be assertive and dominant, so use of such tactics is undoubtedly less costly to the identity of females.

Accounting Strategies

To be accountable is to stand ready to explain one's conduct. An explanation provides an interpretation of an event when its meaning is unclear or might be misinterpreted or misconstrued by audiences (Schlenker, 1982). When people confront impediments to their goals, such as when events threaten identity, they construct explanations that define the potential problem and specify its implications for identity. It is proposed that people attempt to explain events in ways that validate desired identity images and repudiate undesired images (Schlenker, 1980, 1982, 1987; Schlenker & Weigold, 1989). To the extent that this can be accomplished, threats and damage to identity are minimized, the affective consequences are more positive (or less negative), and people can continue to work toward their goals with reasonable expectations of success.

An *account* is a self-serving explanation that attempts to reconcile an event with the prescriptions that appear to have been violated or unfulfilled (Schlenker, 1982). The extensive literature on accounts offers a social psychological perspective on rationalization, and indicates that people attempt to construct reality in self-serving ways and negotiate that reality with others (Goffman, 1971; Schlenker, 1980, 1982; Scott & Lyman, 1968; Semin & Manstead, 1983; Tedeschi & Riess, 1981; Tetlock, 1985b). Accounts work to interpret selectively (a) the relevant elements in the accountability triangle (the prescriptions, the event, and the pertinent identity images), thereby influencing the apparent value of the incident and its consequences; and (b) the strength of the linkages in the accountability triangle, thereby influencing the actor's apparent responsibility.

Affecting the Linkages

When undesirable incidents occur, the "ideal" explanation from the actor's perspective is a *defense of innocence* (Schlenker, 1980). Defenses of innocence sever all connections between identity and event by showing that the actor did not commit the undesirable act or influence its commission in any way (i.e., cutting the identity-event link; e.g., "I didn't do it; I have a foolproof alibi"); or by showing that the undesirable act did not occur (i.e., reinterpreting the event itself; e.g., "His death was a suicide, not a homicide, so I didn't do anything wrong"). When actors use this defense during an accountability inquiry and the audience accepts its veracity, the actor is judged faultless. If the audience does not accept the defense, the actor is either judged guilty and a liar, or judged mentally ill, depending on whether the audience thinks the actor truly believes his or her account. Amnesia, denial, and repression can all function as defenses of innocence by cutting the actor's connection to undesired events, both to external audiences and to the self-as-audience.

Excuses are accounts that attempt to minimize the actor's personal responsibility for potentially threatening events without totally disconnecting the actor from the event. Excuses try to reduce the strength of the linkages between the three elements of the accountability triangle, thereby mitigating the actor's culpability. In a complementary fashion, people use *entitlements* to maximize their personal responsibility for potentially validating events, e.g., explaining why a promotion was merited and not, as some coworkers insinuate, a matter of politics or ingratiation (Schlenker, 1980). To examine these tactics in more detail, consider each of the linkages.

The identity-event link. The identity-event link is probably the most frequently analyzed facet of responsibility in the psychology literature because it deals with issues of free will, intentionality, causality, and blame. People are held most responsible for events when they appear to be able to foresee the consequences, intentionally act to produce those consequences, and are not under the influence of external pressures (e.g., coercion) or debilitating internal factors (e.g., drugs, sleep deprivation) that would reduce the actor's freedom. Weakening the identity-event link involves trying to show that the actor did not have full control over the event, in that the consequences were unintentional, unforeseeable (or at least unforeseen), accidental, or influenced by external pressures.

When people perceive themselves to be in control of events, this linkage is stronger, producing feelings of greater personal responsibility and therefore greater ego involvement with the task. A stronger identity-event link is associated with increased determination (evidenced by effort and persistence in the face of obstacles) on tasks, which more often than not results in improved task performance (Baumgardner, Heppner, & Arkin, 1986; Weiner, Russell, & Lerman, 1978). Further, feelings of personal control are associated with the effectiveness of problem-solving, as self-appraised (effective as compared with ineffective) problem-solvers see the etiology of their personal problems as largely within their own control and their failures as caused by insufficient effort (Baumgardner et al., 1986). Ineffective problem-solving is related to feelings of little personal control. Moreover, desire for personal control is associated with higher and more realistic levels of aspiration, higher outcome expectations, increased performance motivation on challenging tasks, increased task effort, persistence in the face of problems, and performance attributions that increase motivation on subsequent tasks (Burger, 1985). Finally, people who are high on perceived control are more likely to act on their stated intentions (Schifter & Ajzen, 1985), suggesting that the linkage engages a commitment for one's identity.

Similarly, people who are internally rather than externally controlled (based on scores on locus of control scales) tend to have higher mastery motivation, greater perceived self-worth, greater academic achievement, better job performance, and more work satisfaction, and they expend more effort on tasks and take more personal responsibility for task outcomes (e.g., Phares, 1976; Ryan & Grolnick, 1986; Spector, 1982). Externals are lower on motivation, effort, performance, and job satisfaction, and prefer directive approaches to goal and policy determination (instead of participative approaches), perhaps as a way of decreasing their responsibility and lessening the link between their identities and their job performance (Spector, 1982). These findings all support the proposition that a stronger identity-event link increases ego involvement, which, in combination with high outcome expectations, increases determination and thereby improves task performance.

When outcome expectations are low, the denial of control is a way of retreating from accountability, thereby disengaging identity from the implications of one's actions. When people fail (or anticipate failure), they attribute their performance to external factors (e.g., an unfair or difficult test, bad luck, a bad home environment, possession by demons, pressure from others) or unstable, potentially alterable, internal factors (e.g., lack of sleep, intoxication, drugs, lack of training, uncontrollable urges) (Schlenker, 1980; Snyder et al., 1983). These excuses attempt to weaken the link between identity and events and shield the actor from the ramifications of his or her own behavior.

Where excuses are concerned, it is often difficult to discern the truth from a convenient lie, even for the actor. Carson (1969) observed that "the alleged hallucinations of schizophrenic persons might sometimes be merely lies, not qualitatitively different from, 'I couldn't come to school yesterday because I was sick'" (p. 223). Such excuses permit the user both to avoid difficult tasks and blame possible failures on the symptom. People suffering from factitious disorders willfully produce the signs or symptoms of illness (Eisendrath, 1988). In mild forms, factitious disorders involve fabricating a personal history of medical or psychological symptoms. More serious cases involve elaborate simulations of illness (e.g., pricking one's finger and putting blood in a urine sample) or ingestion of foreign substances or drugs to produce abnormal physiological states. Factitious disorders are somewhat unusual in that they seem to be the only recognized psychiatric disorders in which psychiatrists concede that the symptoms are manipulatively produced to feign serious illness.

People are often able to convince themselves that their excuses describe real problems, even when the excuses may not have at one time. A paranoid's headache may keep him from accomplishing a task at work, and the headache is, in turn, blamed on the use of an invisible electric ray by a coworker who, the paranoid contends, is jealous. The headache is real; its etiology and impact are constructed. In the case of somatic disorders, stress created by threats produces real physiological symptoms which may, in turn, serve as excuses for subsequent problems. In still other cases, there

may be a physiological basis for the problem, which the actor can then employ for purposes of affecting accountability. We do not suggest that psychopathological symptoms are usually feigned or without biological basis. However, given that a person has strange thoughts or performs strange acts, for whatever reasons, an explanation is required. Psychopathological symptoms provide viable excuses for failures and transgressions.

Self-handicapping is a type of anticipatory excuse that paradoxically preserves identity by seeming to increase the chance of failure. Self-handicapping involves placing (or seeming to place) obstacles in one's own path so that one's performance cannot provide diagnostic information about relevant skills and abilities (Jones & Berglas, 1978; Snyder & Smith, 1982). Jones and Berglas (1978) suggested that heavy drinking may often function as a self-handicap. If an alcoholic fails, the bottle and not his (lack of) talent can be faulted; fantasies of glorified achievements, if and when he stops drinking, can thereby be maintained. If he succeeds, he must surely be talented, since how else could the obstacle have been overcome? Consistent with this reasoning, males have been shown to use alcohol as a self-handicapping tactic when doubts existed about their performance-related abilities (Higgins & Harris, 1988; Tucker, Vuchinich, & Sobell, 1981). Moreover, actors given the opportunity to self-handicap through alcohol consumption tend to attribute failure more to the alcohol than to personal abilities, and afterward evidence heightened self-esteem (Isleib, Vuchinich, & Tucker, 1988).

Self-handicapping is most likely to occur when people are publicly accountable and fear that their performance will damage their desired identities (Baumgardner, Lake, & Arkin, 1985; Kolditz & Arkin, 1982). In the face of potential failures for which they are accountable, people will cite as handicaps such things as (a) adverse past life experiences (Degree & Snyder, 1985); (b) anxiety (Greenberg, Pyszczynski, & Paisley, 1984; Leary & Schlenker, 1981; Smith, Snyder, & Handelsman, 1982; Snyder & Smith, 1982; Snyder, Smith, Augelli, & Ingram, 1985); (c) depression (Baumgardner et al., 1985); and (d) physical illness (Smith, Snyder, & Perkins, 1983).

Lack of effort can also be an excuse for failure, and it can function as a handicap when actors actually reduce how hard they try on a task. Decreased effort often follows initial task failures (Bandura, 1977; Feather, 1982; A. Miller, 1985), as actors begin to disengage their identities after disappointments. A. Miller (1985) suggested that this decrement in effort arises primarily as a means of self-protection. He found that sixth graders' performance on anagram problems was impaired after an initial failure when the problems were supposed to be moderately difficult but not when the problems were supposed to be extremely difficult. Failure on a moderately difficult task is threatening to the self because it would implicate low ability. Reducing effort provides a plausible excuse for continued failure that can preserve pretensions of ability. In comparison, if the evaluator defines the task as extremely difficult, that designation serves as both an excuse for failure and an indication that the evaluator has lower expectations for performance. Similar results have been reported among adult subjects by Frankel and Snyder (1978).

Many psychological symptoms are regarded by audiences as legitimate excuses for poor performance. For example, Schouten and Handelsman (1987) found that actors involved in domestic violence or job-related difficulties were viewed as less the cause of their behavior, less responsible for the consequences of their actions, and less worthy of sanctioning when the actor was described as experiencing depressive symptoms at the time of his actions than when no information was provided.

In sum, a stronger identity-event link increases ego involvement and, when outcome expectations are reasonably high, increases determination. When failures occur or are expected, however, people can retreat from responsibility by trying to weaken the link. It appears that many psychopathological symptoms function to achieve this goal.

The prescription-identity link. The prescription-identity link describes the extent to which the prescriptions apply to the actor because of external requirements (e.g., being bound by the laws of the land) or internalized commitments (e.g., pledging oneself to follow the Ten Commandments). To say that a person has certain duties, obligations, responsibilities, or moral or personal aspirations is to recognize the existence of a prescription-identity link.

The link is stronger—and hence ego involvement is greater—when the prescription can be clearly applied to the actor and the actor should be committed to following them. Research suggests that people will perform better when they personally accept group goals and rules (Locke, 1968; Locke, Shaw, Saari, & Latham, 1981) or choose their own treatment programs in therapy (W. R. Miller, 1985; Spector, 1982).

When identities are threatened by events, actors can try to reduce their responsibility by weakening the link. Prescriptions can be designated as inapplicable because of the actor's special identity ("I have diplomatic immunity;" or "I'm the boss's son") or because the actor never made a personal commitment to the prescriptions (e.g., "I never promised to do that;" "Those are your rules, not mine"). The "sick role" serves a dual purpose. By "being sick" (physically or mentally), the actor can reduce the identity-event link and blame failures on the "problem." Plus, the sick role excuses actors from many undesired duties and responsibilities until such time as they are "cured" and able to reassume a normal identity (Braginsky et al., 1969; Carson, 1969; Scheff, 1966).

The prescription-event link. The prescription-event link is stronger to the extent that a clear, well-defined set of prescriptions seems applicable on the occasion; these delineate the appropriate goals, rules, and levels of accomplishment required to perform satisfactorily. The linkage is weakened to the extent that the prescriptions are ambiguous, difficult to prioritize, conflicting, or obscure. A weaker prescription-event link is associated with uncertainty and anxiety, at least when people are expected to do well but do not know how to do so. Indeed, people are more anxious and perform more poorly when prescriptions for performance are unclear but they "should" do well (Hom & Murphy, 1985; Leary, Kowalski, & Bergen, 1988; W. R. Miller, 1985; Schlenker & Leary, 1982). Many excuses for poor performance are addressed to attenuating this linkage (e.g., "I didn't know what to do;" "You didn't give me proper instructions;" "The rules were confusing and contradictory").

Affecting the Elements

Explanations focusing on interpretations of the elements have been called justifications and enhancements. *Justifications* try to minimize the apparent undesirability of the elements when these could threaten desired identity images, whereas *enhancements* try to increase the desirability of the elements when these could potentially validate desired identity images (Schlenker, 1980, 1982).

This is done through selective interpretations of (a) the relevant principles and their priority of application (e.g., "I killed her because I loved her and she was in great pain with terminal cancer, not because I wanted the insurance money"); (b) the nature and consequences of the event (e.g., "I stopped her pain and she didn't suffer"); or (c) the identity images affected by the incident (e.g., "I am an altruist who reduced her agony, not a cold killer"). Through the self-serving interpretation of these elements, the seemingly undesirable consequences of events can be changed quantitatively (e.g., making the amount of harm seem to be less than it otherwise appears to be, as in "I broke the lamp, Mom, but you needed a new one anyway;" or "I hit him but he wasn't hurt so bad, he's just a bleeder") and qualitatively (e.g., transforming the act from one that seemingly violates prescriptions to one that is congruent with prescriptions, as in "It was self-defense, not murder").

Research amply documents people's proclivities for explaining events in ways that justify seemingly undesirable conduct. The literature on attitude change following counterattitudinal behavior (Schlenker, 1982; Wicklund & Brehm, 1976) shows that people will change their attitudes in order to justify their behavior when they appear to be personally responsible for producing harm. Similarly, subjects who are given high rather than low choice about administering electric shocks to a confederate, and who therefore appear to be more personally responsible for the harm, later say the shocks were less painful (Brock & Buss, 1962).

Another way to justify one's conduct is to embed the prescriptions in the context of what people actually do, not what they are supposed to do. The actor tries to show that although the prescriptions say one thing, most people do another (e.g., "Everybody misreports income or inflates deductions for tax purposes"), thereby justifying conduct through social comparison. The implication is that if everybody does it, the act must be reasonably normal and acceptable, and to single out the actor for punishment is unfair. Variations on this theme include (a) projecting one's own undesired characteristics onto others (Holmes, 1978), and (b) seeking out social comparison information after a failure only when subjects believe that others have done poorly (Pyszczynski, Greenberg, & LaPrelle, 1985).

People often set the stage for an upcoming performance by trying to influence the prescriptions that will be applied by audiences to evaluate their conduct. For instance, actors may try to lower the standards that will be used to evaluate them, thereby increasing the odds of success. Research indicates that people will try to lower the expectations of others when they doubt they will perform up to those standards (Baumgardner & Brownlee, 1987; Baumeister & Scher, 1988; Kanouse, Gumpert, & Canavan-Gumpert, 1981; Maracek & Mettee, 1972). Hill, Weary, and Williams (1986) have argued that a primary function of the communication of depressive symptoms is to reduce expectations about the caliber of future performance.

In sum, people often deal with problems created by accountability through their interpretations of the relevant prescriptions, identity images, and event itself. By so doing, they try to make the performance seem less undesirable or even desirable.

Apologies

Apologies provide a third major means of coping with accountability when threats to identity arise. Apologies are admissions of blameworthiness and regret for an undesired event, such as a transgression or failure. From a societal perspective, apologies serve several important functions, including recognizing that rules have been broken, reaffirming the value of the rules, and regulating social conduct by acknowledging the existence of interpersonal obligations and the legitimacy of sanctions (Darby & Schlenker, 1982; Goffman, 1971; Schlenker, 1980). From the perspective of the actor, an apology functions as a remedial behavior that aims to maintain the negative repercussions of an undesirable incident and repair the actor's damaged identity (Darby & Schlenker, 1982; Goffman, 1971; Schlenker, 1980; Schlenker & Darby, 1981). If the apology seems sincere, the actor appears (a) to be not as bad a person as the incident might otherwise suggest, (b) to have either repented or not intended the incident to occur, and (c) to not require further rehabilitative punishment because the actor has already suffered self-imposed punishment. Through apologies, the actor can appear to be a more self-policing, dependable, and cooperative social participant who does not require external control through sanctions.

In their more complete forms, apologies contain the following elements: (a) the communication of apologetic intent, such as saying, "I'm, sorry"; (b) clarification that one recognizes what the appropriate performance should have been and sympathizes with the application of negative sanctions for not fulfilling the prescriptions; (c) self-castigation, in which the actor disparages the "bad" self that behaved wrongly and rejects the "bad" conduct; (d) a vow to try to do better in the future; (e) an expression of guilt, remorse, or embarrassment, indicating that one has suffered; (f) the performance of penance and an offer to compensate any victims who may have been involved; and (g) an attempt to obtain forgiveness, as by saying, "Can you find it in your heart to forgive me?" (Goffman, 1971; Schlenker, 1980; Schlenker & Darby, 1981). The more of these elements that seem to be sincerely conveyed, the more rehabilitated the actor will appear to be. Minor incidents, such as a trivial breach of etiquette, can be resolved with a perfunctory apology ritual (e.g., a person bumps into someone on a movie line and responds with a quick, "I'm sorry"). More serious transgressions, though, require more elaborate apologies to minimize the potential negative repercussions (Schlenker & Darby, 1981).

Apologies are effective in controlling damage to identity and reducing punishment after transgressions. Even children as young as three regard situations in which the actor apologizes as better and more just than ones in which the actor is unapologetic (Irwin & Moore, 1971; Wellman, Larkey, & Sommerville, 1979; von Wright & Niemela, 1966). Darby and Schlenker (1982) found that apologetic actors are blamed less, forgiven more, liked more, seen as more remorseful, and actually punished less for their transgressions. Defendants who appear to be sad, guilt-ridden, and remorseful, as compared with those who do not, receive less punishment from jurors (Austin, Walster, & Utne, 1976; Kalven & Zeisel, 1966). The apology-forgiveness script may be such an ingrained aspect of social life that its appearance almost automatically improves the actor's position (Darby & Schlenker, 1989).

Apologies also can win over the audience and prompt them to terminate the actor's self-punishment, often by going so far as to argue the actor's case. As Goffman (1971) observed about the self-castigation that often accompanies apologies:

Were others to do to him what he is willing to do to himself, he might be obliged to feel affronted and to engage in retaliatory action to sustain his moral worth and autonomy. And he can overstate or overplay the case against himself, thereby giving the others the task of cutting the self-derogation short. . . . (p. 113)

Apologies are not without their disadvantages. Apologies always involve the admission of some blame for an undesirable event. As such, apologies communicate a willingness to assume, at least temporarily, an inferior status in a relationship, analogous to the misbehaving child who must await the verdict of the more powerful adult. This does not imply, however, that the actor gives up control in the relationship. The control merely shifts from a more assertive, direct approach to a more defensive, supplicant approach. In fact, apologies often communicate a desire to take an inferior role in a relationship, in which the audience is placed in the position of guiding and nurturing the contrite actor. The actor may communicate that he or she truly wants to do well and fulfill the prescriptions, but because of lack of skills, resources, or other deficits, must be aided by others. If played skillfully, the actor can even transfer responsibility for his or her future conduct to the audience, who then must assume a type of guardianship.

The apologetic self-flagellation employed by depressives and highly anxious individuals can be regarded as the use of an apology strategy to handle the pressures of accountability. People who are high in anxiety or high in depression tend to reverse the usual pattern of attributions by taking personal responsibility for failure but ascribing success to external factors such as luck (Arkin, Appelman, & Burger, 1980; Brewin, 1985; Seligman, Abramson, Semmell, & Von Baeyer, 1979). Further, depressives do not simply accept responsibility for failure, but blame it on their character, as opposed to their behavior or to other unstable, more modifiable factors such as lack of training or effort (Peterson, Schwartz, & Seligman, 1981). When accountability inquiry must be confronted, an apology strategy has high utility and defensibility for those who feel incapable of an assertive attack.

Stabilizing Strategies: Chronic Patterns

Everyone develops his or her own pattern of strategies and tactics for dealing with the pressures of accountability. These preferences can be due to the actor's (more or less) stable characteristics, such as personality dispositions and roles, or they may be guided and reinforced by repeated encounters with similar types of audiences or situations. Over time, these preferences become stabilized and habitual, and are used unthinkingly to influence the timing, terms, and outcomes of accountability whenever threats to identity arise.

Strategies and tactics become dysfunctional when they are used indiscriminately or extremely. Actors may retreat so far from accountability that their behavior is distressing to themselves and to others. Actors may begin to regret the costs they incur by (say) becoming social isolates, or they may avoid accountability in such an extreme manner that they lose their jobs or become irresponsible in caring for their families. In addition, when actors lose consensual validation for their tactics but persist anyway (e.g., other people do not accept the validity of the actor's excuses and justifications), they gain reputations as kooks, oddballs, or even threats to the community. We must all deal with accountability. The art is to deal in such a way as to protect and enhance identity without sacrificing opportunities or paying too high a price.

SUMMARY

Accountability is at the heart of social control and self-regulation. It refers to being answerable to audiences, oneself included, for performing up to prescribed standards. When people are accountable they must deal with inquiries about their performance, they must be ready to provide an account to explain or defend their performance, and they must experience a tacit or explicit verdict, including judgment and positive or negative sanctions. People's outcomes and their identities are influenced by these evaluative reckonings. In fact, identity is constructed via the layering of judgments that emerge from being accountable for events.

It is proposed that people will attempt to influence the timing, terms, and outcomes of their accountability. They will try to arrange their environments such that they validate and protect desired identity images, maximizing their accountability for desired events and minimizing it for undesired events. When identities are threatened by events, people will use one or more of three strategies in dealing with accountability: (a) avoiding accountability inquiries (e.g., avoid-

ing potentially threatening audiences and tasks, and attempting to disqualify certain audiences as judges); (b) using accounting strategies (e.g., excuses and justifications for failures and transgressions); and (c) using apology strategies (e.g., using self-derogation and self-punishment to atone for the violation and gain forgiveness). Everyone uses these strategies to protect and enhance identity and maximize their outcomes in social life. However, when the strategies are used indiscriminately or in an extreme fashion that is distressing to the actor or others, problems ensue. From this perspective, many psychopathological symptoms represent communications designed to deal with accountability in one of these three strategic manners.

REFERENCES

Adelberg, S., & Batson, C. D. (1978). Accountability and helping: When needs exceed resources. *Journal of Personality and Social Psychology, 36,* 343–350.

Amabile, T. M. (1979). Effects of external evaluation on artistic creativity. *Journal of Personality and Social Psychology, 37,* 221–233.

American Psychiatric Association. (1987). *Diagnostic and statistical manual of mental disorders* (3rd ed., rev.). Washington, DC: Author.

Arkin, R. (1981). Self-presentation styles. In J. T. Tedeschi (Ed.), *Impression management theory and social psychological research* (pp. 311–333). New York: Academic Press.

Arkin, R. M., Appelman, A. J., & Burger, J. M. (1980). Social anxiety, self-presentation, and the self-serving bias in causal attribution. *Journal of Personality and Social Psychology, 38,* 23–35.

Austin, J. L. (1961). *Philosophical papers.* New York: Oxford University Press.

Austin, W., Walster, E., & Utne, M. K. (1976). Equity and the law: The effects of harmdoer's "suffering in the act" on liking and punishment. In L. Berkowitz & E. Walster (Eds.), *Advances in experimental social psychology* (Vol. 9, pp. 163–190). New York: Academic Press.

Bandura, A. (1977). Self-efficacy: Toward a unifying theory of behavioral change. *Psychological Review, 84,* 191–215.

Bandura, A. (1982). The self and mechanisms of agency. In J. Suls (Ed.), *Psychological perspectives on the self* (Vol. 1, pp. 3–39). Hillsdale, NJ: Lawrence Erlbaum Associates.

Baumeister, R. F. (1984). Choking under pressure:

Self-consciousness and paradoxical effects of incentives on skillful performance. *Journal of Personality and Social Psychology, 46,* 610–620.

Baumeister, R. F. (1988). Masochism as escape from self. *Journal of Sex Research, 25,* 28–59.

Baumeister, R. F., Hamilton, J. C., & Tice, D. M. (1985). Public versus private expectancy of success: Confidence booster or performance pressure. *Journal of Personality and Social Psychology, 48,* 1447–1457.

Baumeister, R. F., & Scher, S. J. (1988). Self-defeating behavior patterns among normal individuals: Review and analysis of common self-destructive tendencies. *Psychological Bulletin, 104,* 3–22.

Baumgardner, A. H., & Brownlee, E. A. (1987). Strategic failure in social interaction: Evidence for expectancy disconfirmation processes. *Journal of Personality and Social Psychology, 52,* 525–535.

Baumgardner, A. H., Heppner, P. P., & Arkin, R. M. (1986). Role of causal attribution in personal problem solving. *Journal of Personality and Social Psychology, 50,* 636–643.

Baumgardner, A. H., Lake, E. A., & Arkin, R. M. (1985). Claiming mood as a self-handicap: The influence of spoiled and unspoiled public identities. *Personality and Social Psychology Bulletin, 11,* 349–358.

Braginsky, B. M., Braginsky, D. D., & Ring, K. (1969). *Methods of madness: The mental hospital as a last resort.* New York: Holt, Rhinehart & Winston.

Brewin, C. B. (1985). Depression and causal attributions: What is their relation? *Psychological Bulletin, 98,* 297–309.

Brock, T. C., & Buss, A. H. (1962). Dissonance, aggression, and evaluation of pain. *Journal of Abnormal and Social Psychology, 65,* 197–202.

Brown, B. R. (1970). Face-saving following experimentally induced embarrassment. *Journal of Experimental Social Psychology, 6,* 255–271.

Burger, J. M. (1985). Desire for control and achievement-related behaviors. *Journal of Personality and Social Psychology, 48,* 1520–1533.

Carson, R. C. (1969). *Interactional concepts of personality.* Chicago: Aldine.

Carson, R. C., Butcher, J. N., & Coleman, J. C. (1988). *Abnormal psychology and modern life* (8th ed.). Glenview, IL: Scott, Foresman.

Chaiken, S. (1980). Heuristic versus systematic information processing and the use of source versus message cues in persuasion. *Journal of Personality and Social Psychology, 39,* 752–766.

Cheek, J. M., & Busch, C. M. (1981). The influence of shyness on loneliness in a new situation. *Personality and Social Psychology Bulletin, 7,* 572–577.

Cheek, J. M., & Buss, A. H. (1982). Shyness and sociability. *Journal of Personality and Social Psychology, 41,* 330–339.

Cvetkovich, G. (1978). Cognitive accommodation, language, and social responsibility. *Social Psychology, 41,* 149–155.

Darby, B. W., & Schlenker, B. R. (1982). Children's reactions to apologies. *Journal of Personality and Social Psychology, 43,* 742–753.

Darby, B. W., & Schlenker, B. R. (1989). Children's reactions to transgressions: Effects of the actor's apology, reputation and remorse. *British Journal of Social Psychology, 28,* 353–364.

Degree, C. E., & Snyder, C. R. (1985). Adler's psychology (of use) today: Personal history of traumatic life events as a self-handicapping strategy. *Journal of Personality and Social Psychology, 48,* 1512–1519.

Doherty, K., Weigold, M. F., & Schlenker, B. R. (1989, August). *Accountability and performance: The mediating role of outcome expectations.* Paper presented at the 97th Annual Meeting of the American Psychological Association.

Duval, S., & Wicklund, R. A. (1972). *A theory of objective self-awareness.* New York: Academic Press.

Eisendrath, S. J. (1988). Factitious disorders. In H. H. Goldman (Ed.), *Review of general psychiatry* (2nd ed., pp. 470–476). Norwalk, CT: Appleton & Lange.

Feather, N. T. (1982). Actions in relation to expected consequences: An overview of a research program. In N. T. Feather (Ed.), *Expectations and actions: Expectancy-value models in psychology* (pp. 53–95). Hillsdale, NJ: Lawrence Erlbaum Associates.

Fincham, F. D., & Jaspars, J. M. (1980). Attribution of responsibility: From man the scientist to man as lawyer. In L. Berkowitz (Ed.), *Advances in experimental social psychology* (Vol. 13, pp. 81–138). New York: Academic Press.

Fish, B., Karabenick, S., & Heath, M. (1978). The effects of observation on emotional arousal and affiliation. *Journal of Experimental Social Psychology, 14*, 256–265.

Ford, J. K., & Weldon, E. (1981). Forewarning and accountability: Effects on memory-based interpersonal judgments. *Personality and Social Psychology Bulletin, 7*, 264–268.

Frankel, A., & Snyder, M. L. (1978). Poor performance following unsolvable problems: Learned helplessness or egotism? *Journal of Personality and Social Psychology, 12*, 1415–1423.

Fromm, E. (1941). *Escape from freedom*. New York: Avon.

Goffman, E. (1971). *Relations in public*. New York: Basic Books.

Greenberg, J., Pyszczynski, T. A., & Paisley, C. (1984). Effect of intrinsic incentives on use of test anxiety as an anticipatory attributional defense: Playing it cool when the stakes are high. *Journal of Personality and Social Psychology, 47*, 1136–1145.

Greenwald, A. G., & Breckler, S. J. (1985). To whom is the self presented? In B. R. Schlenker (Ed.), *The self and social life* (pp. 126–145). New York: McGraw-Hill.

Hagafors, R., & Brehmer, B. (1983). Does having to justify one's judgments change the nature of the judgment process? *Organizational Behavior and Human Performance, 31*, 223–232.

Heider, F. (1958). *The psychology of interpersonal relations*. New York: John Wiley & Sons.

Higgins, R. L., & Harris, R. N. (1988). Strategic "alcohol" use: Drinking to self-handicap. *Journal of Social and Clinical Psychology, 6*, 191–202.

Hill, M. G., Weary, G., & Williams, J. (1986). Depression: A self-presentation formulation. In R. F. Baumeister (Ed.), *Public self and private self* (pp. 213–239). New York: Springer-Verlag.

Holmes, D. S. (1978). Projection as a defense mechanism. *Psychological Bulletin, 85*, 677–688.

Hom, H. L., & Murphy, M. D. (1985). Low need achievers' performance: The positive impact of a self-determined goal. *Personality and Social Psychology Bulletin, 11*, 275–285.

Horosz, W. (1975). *The crisis of responsibility: Man as the source of accountability*. Norman: University of Oklahoma Press.

Hull, J. G. (1981). A self-awareness model of the causes and effects of alcohol consumption. *Journal of Abnormal Psychology, 90*, 586–600.

Hull, J. G., & Young, R. D. (1983). Self-consciousness, self-esteem, and success-failure as determinants of alcohol consumption. *Journal of Personality and Social Psychology, 44*, 1097–1109.

Irwin, D. M., & Moore, S. G. (1971). The young child's understanding of social justice. *Developmental Psychology, 5*, 406–410.

Isleib, R. A., Vuchinich, R. E., & Tucker, J. A. (1988). Performance attributions and changes in self-esteem following self-handicapping with alcohol consumption. *Journal of Social and Clinical Psychology, 6*, 88–103.

Jones, E. E., & Berglas, S. (1978). Control of attributions about the self through self-handicapping strategies: The appeal of alcohol and the role of underachievement. *Personality and Social Psychology Bulletin, 4*, 200–206.

Jones, S. C. (1973). Self- and interpersonal evaluations: Esteem theories versus consistency theories. *Psychological Bulletin, 79*, 185–199.

Kalven, J., Jr., & Zeisel, H. (1966). *The American jury*. Boston: Little, Brown.

Kanouse, D. E., Gumpert, P., & Canavan-Gumpert, D. (1981). The semantics of praise. In J. H. Harvey, W. J. Ickes, & R. F. Kidd (Eds.), *New directions in attribution research* (Vol. 3, pp. 97–115). Hillsdale, NJ: Lawrence Erlbaum Associates.

Kolditz, T., & Arkin, R. (1982). An impression management interpretation of the self-handicapping strategy. *Journal of Personality and Social Psychology, 43*, 492–502.

Latané, B., Williams, K., & Harkins, S. (1979). Many hands make light the work: The causes and consequences of social loafing. *Journal of Personality and Social Psychology, 37*, 823–832.

Lazarus, R. S. (1981). The stress and coping paradigm. In C. Eisdorfer, D. Cohen, A. Kleinman, & P. Maxim (Eds.), *Models for clinical psychopathology* (pp. 177–214). New York: Spectrum.

Lazarus, R. S., & Launier, R. (1978). Stress related transactions between person and environment. In L. A. Pervin & M. Lewis (Eds.), *Perspectives in interactional psychology* (pp. 287–327). New York: Plenum Press.

Leary, M. R. (1983). *Understanding social anxiety: Social, personality, and clinical perspectives*. Beverly Hills: Sage Publications.

Leary, M. R. (1986). The impact of interactional impediments on social anxiety and self-presentation. *Journal of Experimental Social Psychology, 22*, 122–135.

Leary, M. R., Knight, P. D., & Johnson, K. A. (1987). Social anxiety and dyadic conversation: A verbal response analysis. *Journal of Social and Clinical Psychology, 5*, 34–50.

Leary, M. R., Kowalski, R. M., & Bergen, D. J. (1988). Interpersonal information acquisition and confidence in first encounters. *Personality and Social Psychology Bulletin, 14*, 68–77.

Leary, M. R., & Schlenker, B. R. (1981). The social psychology of shyness. In J. T. Tedeschi (Ed.), *Impression management theory and social psychological research* (pp. 335–358). New York: Academic Press.

Lewittes, D. J., & Simmons, W. I. (1975). Impression management of sexually motivated behavior. *Journal of Social Psychology, 96*, 39–44.

Locke, E. A. (1968). Towards a theory of task motivation and incentive. *Organizational Behavior and Human Performance, 3*, 157–189.

Locke, E. A., Shaw, K. N., Saarı, L. M., & Latham, G. P. (1981). Goal setting and task performance: 1968–1980. *Psychological Bulletin, 90*, 125–152.

Mann, L., & Taylor, V. (1970). The effects of commitment and choice difficulty on predecision processes. *Journal of Social Psychology, 82*, 221–230.

Maracek, J., & Mettee, D. R. (1972). Avoidance of continued success as a function self-esteem, level of esteem certainty, and responsibility for success. *Journal of Social Psychology, 22*, 98–107.

Marmar, C. R. (1988). Personality disorders. In H. H. Goldman (Ed.), *Review of general psychiatry* (2nd ed., pp. 401–424). Norwalk, CT: Appleton & Lange.

McAllister, D. W., Mitchell, T. R., & Beach, L. R. (1979). The contingency model for the selection of decision strategies: An empirical test of the effects of significance, account-ability, and reversibility. *Organizational Behavior and Human Performance, 24*, 228–244.

McKeon, R. (1957). The development and the significance of the concept of responsibility. *Revue Internationale de Philosophie, 39*, 3–32.

Mettee, D. R., & Aronson, E. (1974). Affective reactions to appraisal from others. In T. L. Huston (Ed.), *Foundations of interpersonal attraction* (pp. 235–283). New York: Academic Press.

Miller, A. (1985). A developmental study of the cognitive basis of performance impairment after failure. *Journal of Personality and Social Psychology, 49*, 529–538.

Miller, W. R. (1985). Motivations for treatment: A review with special emphasis on alcoholism. *Psychological Bulletin, 98*, 84–107.

Mills, C. W. (1940). Situated actions and vocabularies of motive. *American Sociological Review, 5*, 904–913.

Modigliani, A. (1971). Embarrassment, facework, and eye contact: Testing a theory of embarrassment. *Journal of Personality and Social Psychology, 17*, 15–24.

Peterson, C., Schwartz, S. M., & Seligman, M. E. P. (1981). Self-blame and depressive symptoms. *Journal of Personality and Social Psychology, 41*, 253–259.

Phares, E. J. (1976). *Locus of control in personality*. Morristown, NJ: General Learning Press.

Pilkonis, P. A. (1977). The behavioral consequences of shyness. *Journal of Personality, 45*, 596–611.

Post, A. L., Wittmaier, B. C., & Radin, M. E. (1978). Self-disclosure as a function of state and trait anxiety. *Journal of Clinical and Counseling Psychology, 46*, 12–19.

Pyszczynski, T. A., & Greenberg, J. (1987). Depression, self-focused attention, and self-regulatory perseveration. In C. R. Snyder & C. E. Ford (Eds.), *Coping with negative life events: Clinical and social psychological perspectives* (pp. 105–129). New York: Plenum Press.

Pyszczynski, T. A., Greenberg, J., & LaPrelle, J. (1985). Social comparison after success and failure: Biased search for information consistent with a self-serving conclusion. *Journal of Experimental Social Psychology, 21*, 195–211.

Rozelle, R. M., & Baxter, J. C. (1981). Influence of role pressures on the perceiver: Judgments of videotaped interviews varying judge accountability and responsibility. *Journal of Applied Psychology, 66*, 437–441.

Ryan, R. M., & Grolnick, W. S. (1986). Origins and pawns in the classroom: Self-report and projective assessments of individual differences in children's perceptions. *Journal of Personality and Social Psychology, 50*, 550–558.

Sarnoff, I., & Zimbardo, P. G. (1961). Anxiety, fear, and social affiliation. *Journal of Abnormal and Social Psychology, 62*, 356–363.

Scheff, T. J. (1966). *Being mentally ill*. Chicago: Aldine.

Schifter, D. E., & Ajzen, I. (1985). Intention, perceived control, and weight loss: An application of the theory of planned behavior. *Journal of Personality and Social Psychology, 49*, 843–851.

Schlenker, B. R. (1980). *Impression management: The self concept, social identity, and interpersonal relations*. Monterey, CA: Brooks/Cole. (Distributed by Krieger Publishing Co., Melbourne, FL).

Schlenker, B. R. (1982). Translating actions into attitudes: An identity-analytic approach to the explanation of social conduct. In L. Berkowitz (Ed.), *Advances in experimental social psychology* (Vol. 15, pp. 193–247). New York: Academic Press.

Schlenker, B. R. (1984). Identities, identifications, and relationships. In V. Derlega (Ed.), *Communication, intimacy, and close relationships* (pp. 71–104). New York: Academic Press.

Schlenker, B. R. (1985). Identity and self-identification. In B. R. Schlenker (Ed.), *The self and social life* (pp. 65–99). New York: McGraw-Hill.

Schlenker, B. R. (1986a). Self-identification: Toward an integration of the private and public self. In R. F. Baumeister (Ed.), *Public self and private self* (pp. 21–62). New York: Springer-Verlag.

Schlenker, B. R. (1986b). *Personal accountability: Challenges and impediments in the quest for excellence*. Technical Report for the Navy Personnel Research and Development Center, San Diego.

Schlenker, B. R. (1987). Threats to identity: Self identification and social stress. In C. R. Snyder & C. Ford (Eds.), *Coping with negative life events* (pp. 275–323). New York: Academic Press.

Schlenker, B. R., & Darby, B. W. (1981). The use of apologies in social predicaments. *Social Psychology Quarterly, 44*, 271–278.

Schlenker, B. R., & Leary, M. R. (1982). Social anxiety and self-presentation: A conceptualization and model. *Psychological Bulletin, 92*, 641–669.

Schlenker, B. R., & Leary, M. R. (1985). Social anxiety and communication about the self. *Journal of Language and Social Psychology, 4*, 171–193.

Schlenker, B. R., & Weigold, M. F. (1989). Goals and the self-identification process: Constructing desired identities. In L. Pervin (Ed.), *Goals concepts in personality and social psychology* (pp. 243–290). Hillsdale, NJ: Lawrence Erlbaum Associates.

Schlenker, B. R., & Weigold, M. F. (in press). Self-identification and accountability. In R. A. Giacalone and P. Rosenfeld (Eds.), *Impression management in the organization*. Hillsdale, NJ: Lawrence Erlbaum Associates.

Schlenker, B. R., Weigold, M. F., & Doherty, K. (1989, March). *Accountability and affective associates of determination and success*. Paper presented at the meeting of the Southeastern Psychological Association.

Schouten, P. G. W., & Handelsman, M. M. (1987). Social basis of self-handicapping: The case of depression. *Personality and Social Psychology Bulletin, 13*, 103–110.

Scott, M. B., & Lyman, S. M. (1968). Accounts. *American Sociological Review, 33*, 46–62.

Seligman, M. E. P., Abramson, L. Y., Semmel, A., & von Baeyer, C. (1979). Depressive attributional style. *Journal of Abnormal Psychology, 88*, 242–247.

Semin, G. R., & Manstead, A. S. R. (1983). *The accountability of conduct: A social psychological analysis*. London: Academic Press.

Shea, S. C. (1988). Personality disorders: Reflection of the social history. In S. C. Shea (Ed.), *Psychiatric interviewing: The art of understanding*. Philadelphia: W. B. Saunders.

Slavin, R. E. (1983). When does cooperative learning increase student achievement? *Psychological Bulletin, 94*, 429–445.

Slivken, K. E., & Buss, A. H. (1984). Misattribution and speech anxiety. *Journal of Personality and Social Psychology, 47*, 1276–1283.

Smith, T. W., Snyder, C. R., & Handelsman, M. M. (1982). On the self-serving function of an academic wooden leg: Test anxiety as a self-handicapping strategy. *Journal of Personality and Social Psychology, 42*, 314–321.

Smith, T. W., Snyder, C. R., & Perkins, S. C. (1983). The self-serving function of hypochondriacal complaints: Physical symptoms as self-handicapping strategies. *Journal of Personality and Social Psychology, 44*, 787–797.

Snyder, C. R., & Higgins, R. L. (1988). Excuses: Their effective role in the negotiation of reality. *Psychological Bulletin, 104*, 23–35.

Snyder, C. R., Higgins, R. L., & Stucky, R. J. (1983). *Excuses: Masquerades in search of grace*. New York: John Wiley & Sons.

Snyder, C. R., & Smith, T. W. (1982). Symptoms as self-handicapping strategies: The virtues of old wine in a new bottle. In G. Weary & H. L. Mirels (Eds.), *Integrations of clinical and social psychology* (pp. 104–127). New York: Oxford University Press.

Snyder, C. R., Smith, T. W., Augelli, R. W., & Ingram, R. E. (1985). On the self-serving function of social anxiety: Shyness as a self-handicapping strategy. *Journal of Personality and Social Psychology, 48*, 970–980.

Spector, P. E. (1982). Behavior in organizations as a function of employee's locus of control. *Psychological Bulletin, 91*, 429–445.

Szasz, T. S. (1961). *The myth of mental illness.* New York: Harper & Row.

Tedeschi, J. T., & Norman, N. (1985). Social power, self-presentation, and the self. In B. R. Schlenker (Ed.), *The self and social life* (pp. 293–321). New York: McGraw-Hill.

Tedeschi, J. T., & Riess, M. (1981). Predicaments and verbal tactics of impression management. In C. Antaki (Ed.), *Ordinary language explanations of social behavior.* London: Academic Press.

Teichman, Y. (1973). Emotional arousal and affiliation. *Journal of Experimental Social Psychology, 9*, 591–605.

Tetlock, P. E. (1983a). Accountability and the complexity of thought. *Journal of Personality and Social Psychology, 45*, 74–83.

Tetlock, P. E. (1983b). Accountability and the perseverance of first impressions. *Social Psychology Quarterly, 46*, 285–292.

Tetlock, P. E. (1985a). Accountability: The neglected social context of judgment and choice. In B. M. Staw & L. Cummings (Eds.), *Research in organizational behavior* (Vol. 9, pp. 279–232). Greenwich, CT: JAI Press.

Tetlock, P. E. (1985b). Toward an intuitive politician model of the attribution process. In B. R. Schlenker (Ed.), *The self and social life* (pp. 203–234). New York: McGraw-Hill.

Tetlock, P. E., & Kim, J. I. (1987). Accountability and judgment processes in a personality prediction task. *Journal of Personality and Social Psychology, 52*, 700–709.

Tucker, J. A., Vuchinich, R. E., & Sobell, M. B. (1981). Alcohol consumption as a self-handicapping strategy. *Journal of Abnormal Psychology, 90*, 220–230.

Twentyman, C. T., & McFall, R. M. (1975). Behavioral training of social skills in shy males. *Journal of Consulting and Clinical Psychology, 43*, 381–395.

von Wright, J. M., & Niemela, P. (1966). On the ontogenic development of moral criteria. *Scandinavian Journal of Psychology, 7*, 65–75.

Watson, D., & Friend, R. (1969). Measurement of social-evaluative anxiety. *Journal of Consulting and Clinical Psychology, 33*, 448–457.

Weiner, B., Russell, D., & Lerman, D. (1978). Affective consequences of causal ascriptions. In J. H. Harvey, W. Ickes, & R. F. Kidd (Eds.), *New directions in attribution research* (Vol. 2, pp. 59–90). Hillsdale, NJ: Lawrence Erlbaum Associates.

Weldon, E., & Gargano, G. M. (1985). Cognitive effort in addictive task groups: The effects of shared responsibility on the quality of multiattribute judgments. *Organizational Behavior and Human Performance, 36*, 348–361.

Weldon, E., & Gargano, G. M. (1988). Cognitive loafing: The effects of accountability and shared responsibility on cognitive effort. *Personality and Social Psychology Bulletin, 14*, 159–171.

Wellman, H. M., Larkey, C., & Sommerville, S. C. (1979). The early development of moral criteria. *Child Development, 50*, 869–873.

Wicklund, R. A. (1975). Objective self-awareness. In L. Berkowitz (Ed.), *Advances in experimental social psychology* (Vol. 8, pp. 233–275). New York: Academic Press.

Wicklund, R. A., & Brehm, J. W. (1976). *Perspectives on cognitive dissonance.* Hillsdale, NJ: Lawrence Erlbaum Associates.

Williams, K., Harkins, S., & Latané, B. (1981). Identifiability as a deterrent to social loafing: Two cheering experiments. *Journal of Personality and Social Psychology, 40*, 303–311.

Wood, G. (1986). *The myth of neurosis.* New York: Harper & Row.

Zimbardo, P. G. (1977). *Shyness: What it is and what to do about it.* New York: Jove.

CHAPTER 7

THE SELF, APPRAISAL, AND COPING

Craig A. Smith

The focus of this chapter is on emotion and its role in coping and adaptation. When most social scientists think of affective phenomena associated with coping, they think of stress, not emotion. This association reflects a curious state of affairs. There are currently two distinct literatures, one on emotion (e.g., Frijda, 1986; Izard, 1977; Lazarus, 1982; Roseman, 1984; Scherer & Ekman, 1984; Smith & Ellsworth, 1985) and one on stress and coping (e.g., Fleming, Baum, & Singer, 1984; Folkman, Lazarus, Dunkel-Schetter, DeLongis, & Gruen, 1986; Holahan & Moos, 1985; McCrae, 1984; Schroeder & Costa, 1984; Selye, 1974, 1976; Stone & Neale, 1984); and with a few notable exceptions (e.g., Ellsworth & Smith, 1988a, 1988b; Folkman & Lazarus, 1985, 1988a, 1988b; Lazarus, Kanner, & Folkman, 1980), there has been little interchange between the two.

The segregation of these literatures is intriguing because the conceptual overlap between emotion and stress is enormous (cf. Lazarus, 1968, in press-b; Lazarus & Folkman, 1984; Lazarus & Launier, 1978; Smith & Lazarus, in press). In fact, there originally was a single literature, and emotion was the construct of choice for describing affective reactions to stressful conditions (e.g., Cannon, 1929). However, with the rise of behaviorism and the shift to unidimensional drive theories of emotion (e.g., Lindsley, 1951), the utility of the emotion construct was severely questioned (e.g., Duffy, 1941), and "emotion" was largely replaced by "stress" in the study of coping and adaptation. For obscure reasons the current resurgent interest in emotion, which began in the 1960s (e.g., Arnold, 1960; Lazarus, 1968; Tomkins, 1962, 1963), has not yet resulted in the reintegra-

The model advanced in this chapter has evolved over the past several years in close collaboration with Phoebe C. Ellsworth and Richard S. Lazarus. Their contributions to my developing theoretical perspective are immeasurable and gratefully acknowledged. I also thank Richard Lazarus and C. R. Snyder for their helpful comments on an earlier version of this chapter. Preparation of this chapter was supported in part by National Research Service Award (NRSA) Postdoctoral Fellowship MH-09445.

tion of a coherent literature concerned with emotion, coping, and adaptation.

Nonetheless, the overlap between emotion and stress is implicitly acknowledged within both contemporary literatures. Most emotions researchers view emotions as fulfilling important functions in the service of adaptation and survival (e.g., Ekman, 1984; Ellsworth & Smith, 1988a, 1988b; Epstein, 1984; Izard, 1977; Lazarus, 1968; Lazarus et al., 1980; Leventhal, 1980; Plutchik, 1980; Roseman, 1984; Scherer, 1984b; Tomkins, 1962). They consider emotion to be an evolutionary advance over reflex and instinct that mediates between environmental stimulation and behavioral response in a highly flexible manner (cf. Ellsworth & Smith, 1988a, 1988b; Epstein, 1984; Leeper, 1948, 1965; Scherer, 1984b; Smith & Ellsworth, 1987; Smith & Lazarus, in press). Emotions arise when the organism perceives itself to be in a relationship with its environment that has particular implications for its well-being (e.g., perceives itself to be facing a particular kind of stressor), and emotions physically prepare and motivate the organism to respond to (i.e., cope with) that situation in an adaptive manner. In a complementary fashion, subjective stress is universally considered an affective reaction, and measures of emotion and mood are often used as indices (e.g., Billings & Moos, 1984; Eckenrode, 1984; Holahan & Moos, 1985; Sarason, 1984). Given this overlap, each literature should have much to offer the other.

Although there are exceptions (e.g., Epstein, 1984; Larsen, Diener, & Emmons, 1986; Lazarus et al., 1980), many emotions researchers are social psychologists (e.g., Ekman, 1984; Ellsworth & Smith, 1988a, 1988b; Roseman, 1984; Schachter & Singer, 1962; Scherer, 1984b), whereas most research on stress and coping is conducted by personality and clinical psychologists (e.g., Ganellen & Blaney, 1984; Holahan & Moos, 1985; Scheier, Weintraub, & Carver, 1986; Snyder & Smith, 1982). Consistent with the mission of this handbook, this chapter will explore the potential benefits of a perspective that integrates emotion with stress and coping.

It will be argued that adopting a coping perspective provides the emotions researcher with invaluable conceptual tools for solving some of the perennial problems in emotion theory, including specification of both the appraisal processes producing emotion and the organization of patterned physiological activity in emotion. It will be also argued that coping researchers have as much to gain by replacing the essentially unidimensional construct of stress with the richer, broader, multidimensional construct of emotion depicted in recent theories. Consideration of specific emotions and their adaptive functions has direct implications for the variables to be included in coping research. These implications not only touch on appraisal, but also extend to the personality variables, including facets of the self, most likely to be relevant to stress and coping, as well as to the nature of coping itself.

These themes will be developed by examining a general model of the emotion system that is emerging from ongoing attempts (e.g., Lazarus & Smith, 1988; Smith & Lazarus, in press; Smith, Lazarus, & Novacek, in preparation) to explicitly integrate recent theoretical and empirical work on specific emotions (e.g., Ellsworth & Smith, 1988a, 1988b; Frijda, 1986, 1987; Roseman, 1984; Scherer, 1984b; Smith & Ellsworth, 1985, 1987; Weiner, 1985) into the more general theory of appraisal, stress, and coping developed by Lazarus and his colleagues (e.g., Lazarus, 1966, 1968; Lazarus, Averill, & Opton, 1970; Lazarus & Folkman, 1984). The outlines of this model are presented in Figure 7.1.

The centerpiece and foundation of the model is the role of appraisal in emotion (e.g., Lazarus & Smith, 1988; Smith, 1989; Smith et al., in preparation), and this issue will be considered first. However, as indicated in the figure, the model builds on this foundation to consider the joint contributions of the person and the situation to appraisal, the contributions of both personality and emotion to coping, and the effects of coping on both the person and the situation. Each of these issues will be considered in turn.

DIFFERENTIATION OF EMOTION THROUGH APPRAISAL

The view of emotion embraced by the model is relational. Emotion is considered a reaction to a person-environment relationship, not a response to a simple stimulus situation (cf. Lazarus, 1968, in press-a; Smith & Lazarus, in press). That is, the environmental demands, constraints, and resources confronting the individual are combined with the individual's motivations and beliefs to produce a cognitive evaluation—an appraisal—of the significance of the person-environment relationship for personal well-being. Each distinct

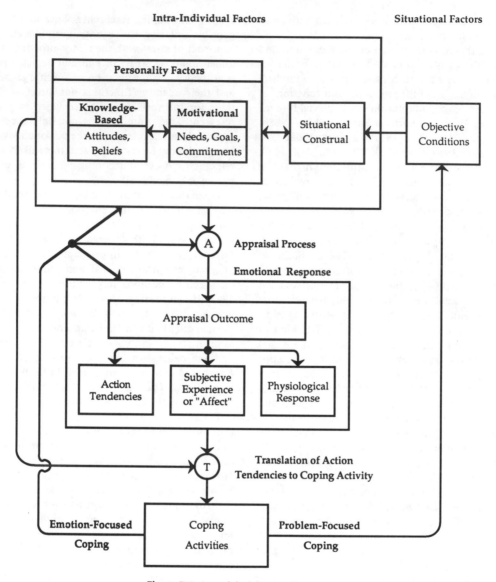

Figure 7.1. A model of the emotion system.

emotion reflects the appraisal of a different kind of adaptationally relevant person-environment relationship—a different kind of harm or benefit (Lazarus, 1968, 1982; Lazarus & Smith, 1988; Smith & Lazarus, in press). The outcome of the appraisal process—the cognitive evaluation itself—is a continuing part of the emotional response, but it is by no means the entire response. Instead, specific motivational urges (action tendencies) relevant to the appraised harm or benefit (Frijda, 1986; Scherer, 1984b) and a distinct subjective feeling state (subjective affect) follow from the appraisal outcome. The action tendencies are not abstract, but are embodied in a particular physiological pattern associated with the emotion (Lazarus, 1968; Smith & Lazarus, in press). The physiological changes producing this pattern serve the two general functions of communicating the person's emotional state to others in the social environment (Scherer, 1982, 1984a; Smith, 1989) and physically preparing the person to cope with the appraised environmental demands (Frijda, 1986; Lazarus, 1968; Smith, 1989).

In other words, the entire emotional response,

including action tendencies, physiological activity, and subjective affect, is hypothesized to be organized around and shaped by the appraisal of the person-environment relationship. Not surprisingly, considerable effort has been directed toward explicating the role of appraisal in emotion. A large portion of my own work, in collaboration with Phoebe Ellsworth (e.g., Ellsworth & Smith, 1988a, 1988b; Smith & Ellsworth, 1985, 1987) and Richard Lazarus (e.g., Lazarus & Smith, 1988; Smith & Lazarus, in press; Smith et al., in preparation), has been directed at specifying the appraisals that lead to each kind of emotion.

The only major claim about the organization of the emotional response advanced in the present model is that the action tendencies, physiological activity, and subjective affect are caused by and organized around the appraised significance of the person-environment relationship. The model does not attempt to depict further interrelationships among the response components. Both within and across theoretical perspectives there is considerable debate as to how these components are organized. For instance, the subjective experience of emotion has been conceived of as (a) a centrally mediated neuropsychological event that is distinct from, and causally prior to, the physiological activity (e.g., Cannon, 1927); (b) the conscious perception of the physiological activity (e.g., Izard, 1971; James, 1890/1950; Tomkins, 1962); and (c) the view I favor, a gestalt presented into consciousness that reflects all the other components combined (i.e., a conscious perception that combines the appraisal outcome, action tendencies, and physiological activity). Similarly, the action tendencies might be conceptualized as (a) purely centrally mediated and largely independent of the physiological activity; (b) the perception of the physiological activity; or (c) something that combines a centrally mediated motivational urge with the perception of physiological activity, perhaps with the physiological activity serving to intensify the urge. Obviously, a complete theory of emotion must resolve these ambiguities. However, their resolution is not central to the issues discussed in this chapter, and they will not be considered further here. Again, the important claim made by the present model is that, whatever their interrelationships, the action tendencies, physiological activity, and subjective experience of emotion are all caused by and organized around the outcome of the appraisal process.

The Nature of Appraisal

Although emotions are produced as a result of a cognitive evaluation, not all cognitive activity is relevant to emotion, and even relevant cognitive activities are not all equally relevant. The task of interpreting the adaptational significance of one's circumstances is quite difficult. The person must draw on a highly complicated and only partially reliable arrangement of cues to determine what, if anything, his or her relationship to the environment implies for personal well-being. There are at least two distinct types of cognition involved in this process, only one of which is directly related to emotion.

To assess adaptational significance, the person needs a representation of the factual nature of his or her circumstances. Considerable social psychological work has been devoted to describing a vast array of attributional and inferential strategies that people use to go beyond the often paltry data directly available to them and construct rich representations of their circumstances (e.g., Fiske & Taylor, 1984; Heider, 1958; Jones, Kanouse, Kelley, Nisbett, Valins, & Weiner, 1972; Lewin, 1936; Nisbett & Ross, 1980; Ross, 1977, 1987). These representations, or situational construals, reflect the person's knowledge and beliefs about their objective circumstances. They are highly relevant to emotion because they are the data the person evaluates to determine adaptational significance, but they do not directly produce emotion. Instead, an additional step—in which the person considers the perceived circumstances in relation to his or her personal goals, needs, and abilities to determine the implications, if any, for personal well-being—is needed to produce the emotion. This further evaluation, which directly produces the emotional reaction, is what is meant by *appraisal* (cf. Lazarus & Folkman, 1984; Lazarus & Smith, 1988; Smith & Lazarus, in press). Thus, it is often the case that two individuals, with different configurations of motivations and abilities, will construe their situations similarly (agree on all the facts) and yet react with different emotions because they have appraised the adaptational significance of those facts differently.

In mapping the relations between appraisal and emotion it is important to carefully distinguish appraisal from other cognitive activities, and in formulating our specific appraisal model, Richard Lazarus and I have been quite restrictive about what we include as appraisal. As we have detailed elsewhere (Lazarus & Smith, 1988), we have not included a number of cognitive variables previously proposed or found to be relevant to emotion because on close inspection we have found them to reflect either the construal-related cognitive activities discussed above (e.g., locus of causality/control [Roseman, 1984; Smith & Ellsworth, 1985; Weiner, 1985]), or the subjective properties of the emotional response itself (e.g., subjective pleasantness [Scherer, 1984b; Smith & Ellsworth, 1985]) instead of appraisal.

Core Relational Themes and Appraisal Components

Even when appraisal is considered by itself, it is probably best to include two distinct levels of analysis, one categorical and one dimensional. The ultimate goal of appraisal is to classify one's perceived circumstances in terms of a relatively small number of categories of adaptational significance, corresponding to different types of benefit or harm, each with different implications for coping. Each of these categories corresponds to a different emotion; each positive emotion reflects a particular kind of appraised benefit, and each negative emotion a particular kind of appraised harm (Lazarus & Smith, 1988; Smith & Lazarus, in press). Thus, one way to describe appraisal is at this categorical level. For each distinct emotion there should be a distinct *core relational theme*, which in a single categorical construct summarizes the person's relationship to the environment in terms of a particular type of harm or benefit. For instance, the global evaluation that one is facing a potential danger or threat produces anxiety, while the overall evaluation that one has suffered an irremedial loss produces sadness, and so on (cf. Abramson, Seligman, & Teasdale, 1978; Plutchik, 1980).

Analysis of appraisal at the level of core relational themes provides an economical summary of the appraised meaning leading to each distinct emotion. However, this level of description is incomplete because it reveals very little about the individual evaluations leading to the appraisal. For example, knowing that an appraisal of danger produces anxiety indicates very little about the issues considered in determining that the situation is dangerous. Therefore, the categorical level of analysis should be supplemented with a more molecular one that describes the particular issues or

questions evaluated in appraisal. These issues are the *components* of appraisal.

The present model considers appraisal in terms of both components and core relational themes. The components reflect the molecular questions evaluated in appraisal, the answers to which combine to produce the molar personal meanings — the core relational themes — that directly produce specific emotions (cf. Lazarus & Smith, 1988; Smith & Lazarus, in press). Past attempts to identify the component cognitions associated with particular emotions (e.g., Frijda, 1986; Roseman, 1984; Scherer, 1984b; Smith & Ellsworth, 1985, 1987; Weiner, 1985) have implicitly drawn on a coping perspective. The present model benefits from these previous efforts, but makes the connection to coping theory explicit. Each component addresses one of the two global appraisal issues originally proposed by Lazarus and his colleagues in their theory of appraisal, stress, and coping (e.g., Lazarus, 1966; Lazarus et al., 1970; Lazarus & Folkman, 1984): Primary appraisal, which concerns whether and how the encounter is relevant to the person's well-being, or secondary appraisal, which concerns the person's resources and options for coping with the encounter. Both of these issues can be further subdivided, and at present the model includes a total of six appraisal components, two related to primary appraisal and four to secondary appraisal (cf. Lazarus & Smith, 1988; Smith & Lazarus, in press).

The two components of primary appraisal are motivational relevance (or importance) and motivational congruence. Motivational relevance is an evaluation of the extent to which the encounter touches on personal goals and concerns, or in other words, issues the person cares about or has a stake in. This component also is included in the dimensional systems of Frijda (1986), Scherer (1984b), and Smith and Ellsworth (1987). Motivational congruence refers to the extent to which a transaction is consistent or inconsistent with what the person wants; that is, either thwarts or facilitates personal goals. It corresponds closely to Roseman's (1984) concept of motive consistency, Scherer's (1984b) goal conduciveness, and Smith and Ellsworth's (1985) perceived obstacle.

The four components of secondary appraisal are accountability, problem-focused coping potential, emotion-focused coping potential, and future expectancy. The *accountability* evaluation provides direction and focus to the emotional response and the coping efforts motivated by it. The outcome of the accountability judgment determines who (oneself or someone else) is to receive the credit (if the encounter is motivationally congruent) or the blame (if it is motivationally incongruent) for the encounter. The other three components all have to do with the evaluation of the potential for improvement of an undesirable situation or the maintenance of a desirable one. The two components of coping potential correspond to the person's evaluations of his or her abilities to engage in the two major types of coping identified by Folkman and Lazarus (1980, 1985; Folkman et al., 1986; Lazarus & Folkman, 1984). *Problem-focused coping potential* reflects evaluations of the person's ability to act directly on the situation to manage the demands of the encounter and actualize the personal commitments brought to it. This evaluation is closely related to the concepts of power as discussed by Roseman (1984), and control and power as discussed by Scherer (1984b). *Emotion-focused coping potential* refers to the perceived prospects of psychologically adjusting to the encounter or, in other words, of regulating the emotional state that harmful or threatening consequences generate. This evaluation is closely related to Scherer's concept of adjustment, which he defines as "the potential for adjustment to the final outcome via internal restructuring" (Scherer, 1984a, p. 39). *Future expectancy* refers to the perceived possibilities, for any reason (i.e., independent of whether the individual plays a role), for changes in the actual or psychological situation that could make the encounter more or less motivationally congruent.

Specific Appraisals in Specific Emotions

The two components of primary appraisal are involved in every emotional encounter. Evaluation of motivational relevance is necessary for strong emotion, because it indicates whether there is any personal stake in the encounter, and thus defines the person's level of affective involvement. In the absence of motivational relevance, the person's state is likely to be one of either apathy on the negative side of things, or of quiet tranquility on the positive side (cf. Ellsworth & Smith, 1988b). Assessments of motivational congruence combine with relevance to determine whether the encounter is stressful or benign (Lazarus et al., 1980). Benign encounters are ones that are appraised as both motivationally relevant and

motivationally congruent (i.e., both important and desired), whereas stressful ones are appraised as both relevant and motivationally incongruent (i.e., important but in some way not as desired).

Although sufficient to define the encounter as stressful or benign, the two components of primary appraisal are generally not sufficient to define the core relational themes associated with individual emotions. The components of secondary appraisal must be added to determine the specific emotions that will be experienced. Thus, examination of the appraisal components and core relational themes associated with specific emotions vividly illustrates how emotion is a much richer, more informative construct than stress.

First, consider the so-called negative or harm-related emotions, such as anger, guilt, anxiety, sadness, and so forth that tend to be equated with stress in many minds—those of layperson and researcher alike (cf. Lazarus, 1968; Lazarus & Launier, 1978; Lazarus et al., 1980). Table 7.1 depicts the specific appraisals for illustrative harm-related emotions. This analysis is generally consistent with the findings of a number of previous studies that examined the relationships between cognitive activities and emotions (e.g., Ellsworth & Smith, 1988a, 1988b; Frijda, 1987; Roseman, 1984; Scherer, Wallbott, & Summerfield, 1986; Smith & Ellsworth, 1985, 1987; Weiner, Graham, & Chandler, 1982), and has received direct support in an initial study explicitly designed to test it (Smith et al., in preparation). For each emotion, Table 7.1 first lists the emotion's proposed adaptive function, then the core relational theme corresponding to the particular relationship with environment in which that function is likely to be useful, and finally the major appraisal components that combine to define the core relational theme.

For instance, the proposed function of anger is to motivate the person to remove a source of harm from the environment, and to undo the harm, if possible (cf. Cannon, 1929; Ellsworth & Smith, 1988a; Izard, 1977; Plutchik, 1980; Tomkins, 1963). The core relational theme that defines the circumstances under which this motivation is likely to be useful is *other-blame*, which is defined by the components of motivational relevance, motivational incongruence, and other-accountability. In other words, anger arises when someone else is being blamed for a stressful situation, and it motivates the person to do something to remove the source of harm. Importantly, the as-

Table 7.1. Some Illustrative Harm-related Emotions

EMOTION	PROPOSED ADAPTIVE FUNCTION	CORE RELATIONAL THEME	IMPORTANT APPRAISAL COMPONENTS
Anger	Remove source of harm from environment and undo harm	Other-blame	Motivationally relevant Motivationally incongruent Other-accountability
Guilt	Reparation for harm to others/ motivate socially responsible behavior	Self-blame	Motivationally relevant Motivationally incongruent Self-accountability
Anxiety	Avoid potential harm	Ambiguous danger/ threat	Motivationally relevant Motivationally incongruent Low/uncertain (emotion-focused) coping potential
Sadness	Get help and support in the face of harm/disengage from a lost commitment	Irrevocable loss/ helplessness	Motivationally relevant Motivationally incongruent Low (problem-focused) coping potential Low future-expectancy

signment of accountability to someone else provides a target for these coping efforts.

In an analogous fashion, guilt has been proposed to contribute to the development of one's conscience and the maintenance of social order. It motivates the individual to make reparations for harm he or she has caused to others, and to generally engage in socially responsible behavior (cf. Ellsworth & Smith, 1988a; Izard, 1977). Consistent with these functions, the core relational theme producing guilt is *self-blame*. This theme is defined by holding oneself accountable for a stressful (important, motivationally incongruent) situation. Like anger, guilt is hypothesized to motivate the person to do something to remove the source of harm from the environment, but, because the focus in guilt is on oneself, this motivation takes the form of a desire to make reparations for any harm the self has caused (e.g., Carlsmith & Gross, 1969; Freedman, Wallington, & Bless, 1967). In addition, this motivation tends to be quite punishing (Wallington, 1973), and therefore reduces the probability that the person will continue to engage in the harmful behavior in the future.

Whereas the accountability component is important in differentiating the core relational themes responsible for anger and guilt, the three components addressing the potential for improving the stressful situation are important in defining the themes for anxiety and sadness. Both emotions are associated with stressful situations in which the prospects for improvement are uncer-

tain or poor. However, they have distinct motivational functions, and their core relational themes, as well as the appraisal components that define them, reflect these differences.

The proposed function of fear is to motivate the person to avoid potential harm (cf. Cannon, 1929; Izard, 1977; Plutchik, 1980; Tomkins, 1963), and appropriate to this function, the core relational theme is an appraisal of *danger* or *threat*. The component of secondary appraisal that defines this sense of danger is an assessment of uncertain or low coping potential. Although uncertainty about either problem- or emotion-focused coping potential can contribute to the appraisal of danger, the evaluation of emotion-focused coping potential appears to be especially relevant. This component reflects the person's assessment of his or her ability to adjust to a bad situation should things not work out as desired, and the person's sense of danger, and hence his or her anxiety, should be particularly acute when, beyond seeing potential or actual harm in the situation, the person believes that he or she may not be able to adjust to this harm in the event it occurs (or has occurred).

In contrast, the function proposed for sadness is to motivate the person to get help and support in the face of harm, and to motivate disengagement from any commitments destroyed by the harm (cf. Izard, 1977; Klinger, 1975; Plutchik, 1980). The theme that produces this emotion is an appraisal of *irrevocable loss* or *helplessness*—the perception that the person is in a bad situation that he or she is powerless to change, and in which there is little expectation for improvement (Abramson et al., 1978). The components of secondary appraisal hypothesized to produce the theme of loss/helplessness are a combination of low future expectancy and low coping potential. The appraisals of low coping potential in sadness can be distinguished from those in anxiety in two ways. First, they tend to be more pessimistic. In threat there is considerable doubt and uncertainty about whether the person can cope, but in loss/helplessness there is little doubt — the person is sure he or she cannot. Second, although emotion-focused coping potential is most relevant for threat and anxiety, problem-focused coping potential is more relevant for loss/helplessness and sadness, because in loss and helplessness the focus is on the inability to do anything to improve the situation.

These "negative" harm-related emotions are highly relevant to theories of stress and coping. They motivate the person to act in ways that will eliminate or reduce the harm, or to adapt to the harm if it cannot be avoided or undone. As such, they are vital to the survival of the individual and the species. The above descriptions of specific emotions and their associated appraisals illustrate how knowledge about a person's emotional state — that the person is experiencing anger, guilt, shame, anxiety, sadness, or so forth — can provide a wealth of information about how the person is interpreting and likely to cope with the encounter that is not available from knowledge that the person is undergoing "stress" (cf. Lazarus, 1968, in press-b; Lazarus & Folkman, 1984; Lazarus & Launier, 1978; Smith & Lazarus, in press).

Nonetheless, as some have argued in differentiating between harm, threat, and challenge (Lazarus et al., 1980), or between "eustress" and "distress" (Selye, 1974), stress and coping are not limited to the avoidance or amelioration of actual and potential harm. There is also a more positive side to stress, involving sustained striving toward mastery and gain, that enables the individual and the species to grow and flourish (Ellsworth & Smith, 1988b; Lazarus et al., 1980; Smith & Lazarus, in press). Motivational incongruence can involve the perceived absence of potential benefits and gains in addition to the presence of actual and potential harms. Just as consideration of specific harm-related emotions and their associated appraisals enriches one's understanding of the stress process, so does consideration of emotions asso-

ciated with potential benefit. Further, conditions of actual benefit, such as when a sought-after goal has been achieved, or a threat has been successfully removed, are outside the pale of stress, but are clearly encompassed by emotion (cf. Ellsworth & Smith, 1988b; Lazarus, 1968; Lazarus et al., 1980). Thus, consideration of emotion instead of stress not only provides more detail, but also expands the domain of inquiry in important, adaptationally relevant ways.

Table 7.2 describes the adaptive functions and appraisals associated with some illustrative emotions associated with potential and actual benefit. Both hope and challenge serve to *sustain* coping efforts to improve one's situation, and motivate striving toward mastery or gain (Ellsworth & Smith, 1988b; Lazarus et al., 1980). Of the two, hope is structurally simpler, and hence more general. The core relational theme producing hope is the *possibility of amelioration or success* — the belief that there is the possibility that things will improve. A high degree of future expectancy is what distinguishes this theme from most other core relational themes involving stress. In hope it is not necessary to personally be able to do anything to bring about the improvement, and evaluations of coping potential need not be involved. Thus, hope serves the very important function of motivating the person to maintain commitments, even under dire circumstances, so long as some chance for improvement is perceived (Lazarus et al., 1980).

In contrast, the function of challenge is to motivate more active coping toward mastery or gain. Hence, beyond the general sense of optimism leading to hope, the core relational theme leading to challenge is a more restrictive appraisal of *effortful optimism*, the belief that if the person tries hard enough, there is a good chance he or she will be able to improve the situation. Therefore, in challenge, positive future expectancy is accompanied by the additional appraisal that the person has the capability to act on the situation to bring about the improvement. In other words, a high degree of problem-focused coping potential, not required to sustain hope, is required to produce a strong sense of challenge.

Finally, there are a cluster of emotions to reward "success," that is, a change in an important situation that increases its degree of motivational congruence. Happiness appears to be a general response to this benign state of affairs, and all that seems necessary for happiness are the combined

Table 7.2. Some Illustrative Benefit-related Emotions

EMOTION	PROPOSED ADAPTIVE FUNCTION	CORE RELATIONAL THEME	IMPORTANT APPRAISAL COMPONENTS
Hope	Sustainer	Possibility of amelioration/success	Motivationally relevant Motivationally incongruent High future-expectancy
Challenge	Sustainer/motivate mastery	Effortful optimism	Motivationally relevant Motivationally incongruent High (problem-focused) coping potential High future-expectancy
Happiness	Reward success	Success	Motivationally relevant Motivationally congruent
Pride	Reinforce one's own successful efforts	Self-credit	Motivationally relevant Motivationally congruent Self-accountability
Gratitude	Reinforce pro-social behavior in others	Other-credit	Motivationally relevant Motivationally congruent Other-accountability

components of motivational relevance and motivational congruence (cf. Ellsworth & Smith, 1988b; Weiner, 1985). Secondary appraisals of coping potential and future expectancy do not appear to provide much differentiation among the benefit emotions, perhaps because it may be difficult to sustain appraisals of motivational congruence if one believes that the situation will soon deteriorate or that one will not be able to cope (Ellsworth & Smith, 1988b). However, the accountability component appears to provide some differentiation. If accountability is assigned to oneself, to produce a theme of *self-credit*, pride results. Feeling proud makes the situation particularly rewarding, and by strongly reinforcing successful coping efforts, increases the probability they will be repeated in the future. If accountability is assigned to someone else, to produce a theme of *other-credit*, gratitude results, which motivates the person to reinforce the other's prosocial behaviors.

These examples vividly illustrate some of the benefits of a theoretical perspective that combines emotion with stress and coping. The appraisal model draws heavily on a coping perspective to identify the individual appraisal components most relevant to emotion. The identification of these components is invaluable to emotions research. Once they have been identified it is a relatively straightforward matter to derive a host of specific, testable hypotheses regarding the appraisal patterns differentiating among the various

emotions. Knowledge of these patterns provides a firm foundation for further research on fundamental issues in emotion theory, including the nature of the appraisal process and the degree and organization of physiological patterning in emotion—both of which are considered briefly below. In return, the development of a specific appraisal model of emotion contributes substantial detail to theories of stress and coping. Moreover, the move from stress to emotion broadens the scope of the study of coping and adaptation. There is a shift from a bleak view of humanity that exclusively emphasizes the struggle against potential and actual harm, to a more balanced view that supplements this struggle with active striving for mastery and beneficial gain, and the enjoyment of that gain when achieved.

Nonetheless, these examples are not meant to be exhaustive, and they in no way represent the full range of human emotions. Instead, the attempt has been to provide a representative sample of some of the more basic categories of appraised harm and benefit, in order to illustrate both the broad range of adaptive functions the emotion system is designed to serve and the high degree of organization it brings to the task. The richness of emotion in our English vocabulary (cf. Averill, 1975; Ortony, Clore, & Foss, 1987; Shaver, Schwartz, Kirson, & O'Connor, 1987) suggests the existence of many more emotional states, each produced by distinctive appraisals and serving distinctive adaptive functions, than has been considered here. For example, within the general rubric of "sadness" there is a diverse range of states, ranging from distress to resignation, associated with various stages of disengagement from a harmed or lost commitment (cf. Klinger, 1975).

A Note on Process

The above examples have focused on the contents of the specific appraisals producing individual emotions, and very little has been said or implied about the formal cognitive processes that underlie these contents. In particular, it would be a mistake to assume that the model implies that appraisal along the individual components follows a predefined sequence, or that appraisal is necessarily conscious, volitional, verbally accessible, and time consuming (although it can be). To the contrary, proponents of this model have consistently maintained that appraisal can be automatic, nonverbal, instantaneous, and occur outside of consciousness (cf. Lazarus, 1966, 1968, 1982, 1984; Lazarus & Folkman, 1984; Lazarus & Smith, 1988; Smith & Lazarus, in press).

For example, the distinction between primary and secondary appraisal is not meant to imply a sequence in which primary appraisal necessarily precedes secondary appraisal. Instead, primary appraisal is primary because it establishes the personal relevance of the encounter, and, as discussed above, this relevance is a prerequisite for strong emotion. If the encounter is appraised as not relevant to well-being then secondary appraisal is relatively unimportant because there will be little emotion of any kind (cf. Lazarus, in press-a; Lazarus & Folkman, 1984; Lazarus & Smith, 1988; Smith & Lazarus, in press). However, if primary appraisal indicates that the situation is relevant to well-being then secondary appraisal plays a vital role in differentiating the emotional experience. Thus, secondary appraisal is secondary because its role in differentiating the emotional response is highly dependent on the outcome of primary appraisal, not because of its temporal characteristics (cf. Lazarus, 1968).

In understanding how appraisal can be unconscious and nearly instantaneous, and why it is often inappropriate to think of appraisal as following a predetermined sequence, it is useful to maintain a distinction advanced by Leventhal (1980, 1984; Leventhal & Scherer, 1987) between schematic and conceptual processing. These two forms of qualitatively distinct cognitive processing, which also have been discussed by others (e.g., Buck, 1985; Lazarus, 1982, 1984), provide the emotion system with the ability to react nearly instantaneously to adaptationally significant events, and yet to draw fully on the power and flexibility of human cognitive capacities (cf. Smith & Lazarus, in press).

In schematic processing the personal significance of an encounter is appraised automatically and nearly instantaneously on the basis of past experiences with similar encounters. How this is achieved can be understood using the concepts of activation and associative networks commonly invoked in the study of memory (e.g., Anderson & Bower, 1973), although alternative accounts also can describe this type of processing. When a person finds him or herself in an encounter similar to some in the past, memories of these past encounters are likely to become quickly activated. Personal meanings strongly associated with those memories also are likely to be activated, and hence to be available as contributors to the person's current emotional state. Through this activation process, complicated and involved appraisals can be arrived at quickly, automatically, and in a single step.

Schematic processing is passive, however, and human beings are sentient, problem-solving creatures who actively seek to understand the world and their reactions to it. Thus, schematic processing is accompanied by conceptual processing—a set of more abstract, conscious, deliberate, and time-consuming cognitive processes through which the person is able to evaluate the significance of the encounter more actively. This more deliberate evaluation process might follow a predetermined sequence of components (cf. Scherer, 1984b), but it seems more likely that whatever issues are especially salient or pressing at any given moment will preempt attention. Conceptual processing is an important kind of appraisal because it not only actively draws on the person's complex and highly symbolic knowledge, but also permits the evaluation of the adaptive significance of the encounter to be finely tuned to the specific, and often changing, environmental circumstances. To the extent that they become associated with the encounter in memory, the products of conceptual processing become available for subsequent schematic processing, and thus contribute to the power and flexibility of that faster, more automatic form of processing. In any case, appraisal is a set of complex processes that occur on multiple cognitive processing levels, and simple assumptions about the timing or sequencing of appraisal are unwarranted.

Appraisal and Physiological Activity in Emotion

In addition to its contributions to identifying the specific components of appraisal, use of a coping perspective may prove indispensable to understanding the organization of physiological activity in emotion. The questions of whether and how various emotions are distinguished by distinct patterns of physiological activity, particularly autonomic activity, have been enigmatic for decades (cf. Levenson, 1988; Smith, 1989).

There is good evidence that distinctive facial expressions are closely associated with a number of different emotions, and the specific facial actions that combine to produce these expressions have been well documented (e.g., Darwin, 1872/1965; Ekman & Freisen, 1975, 1978; Frois-Wittmann, 1930; Izard, 1971; reviewed in Ekman, Friesen, & Ellsworth, 1982). The evidence for autonomic patterning in emotion is less clear. There is considerable evidence that autonomic activity is differentiated along multiple dimensions (e.g., Ax, 1953; Ekman, Levenson, & Friesen, 1983; Elliott, Bankart, & Light, 1970; Lacey & Lacey, 1958; Schwartz, Weinberger, & Singer, 1981; Winton, Putnam, & Krauss, 1984), but the patterns of activity associated with different emotions have not yet been clearly specified (cf. Levenson, 1988; Smith, 1989). Further, for both facial and autonomic activity, it is unclear whether any emotion-specific patterns that might exist are organized at only the molar, categorical level of discrete emotions, or are further organized at a more molecular, dimensional level, such that the individual activities contributing to the global patterns are themselves meaningful.

However, appraisal theory, with its emphasis on the role of emotion in coping, not only predicts considerable patterned physiological activity, organized at both the categorical and dimensional levels, but also provides some basic principles for predicting the specific nature of this organization. As previously noted, the appraisal is hypothesized to cause and shape the physiological activity produced in emotion in a manner that serves two general functions: (a) communicating the person's appraisals and intentions to others (Scherer, 1982,

1984a; Smith, 1989) and (b) physically preparing the person to cope with the adaptive implications of the appraised person-environment relationship (Frijda, 1986; Lazarus, 1968; Smith, 1989). Thus, as Lazarus (1968, p. 206) has stated: "The physiological patterns should be associated with the different adaptive tasks which the appraisals leading to the different emotions seem to require." That is, for communication purposes appraisals should be at least partially encoded in the externally observable components of the emotion's physiological expression (e.g., facial expression, posture, vocal tone, etc.; see Ekman, 1984; Riskind, 1984; Scherer, 1986), and aspects of appraisal having direct implications for coping should be directly related to the properties of the physiological response that prepare the person to cope in particular ways (cf. Smith, 1989; Smith & Lazarus, in press).

The linkages between appraisal and physiological activity can occur at both the level of core relational themes and individual appraisal components. The existence of universally recognized facial expressions corresponding to individual emotions such as happiness, sadness, fear, anger, disgust, and surprise (Ekman et al., 1982) attests to a categorical organization of facial activity. It is also likely that autonomic and other activities related to the preparation for coping are partially organized in a categorical, emotion-specific manner. Because each core relational theme reflects the identification of a particular type of harm or benefit, with particular implications for coping, it is likely that the motivational action tendencies produced in emotion are emotion specific and linked to specific relational themes. Accordingly, any physiological activities specific to performing the behaviors motivated by the action tendency are also likely to be emotion specific and linked to the theme. For example, other-blame generates anger and the impulse to attack the blameworthy agent, whereas threat or danger generates anxiety and the impulse to avoid or escape the threat. Any physiological activities that meet requirements specific to attack, or specific to avoidance, are likely to be emotion specific and linked to the appropriate core relational theme.

Nonetheless, it is also likely that some physiological activities are directly linked to specific molecular components of appraisal. Beyond contributing to the global patterns of facial activity associated with specific emotions, some individual facial actions might convey specific information about the person's appraisals along particular component dimensions (cf. Darwin, 1872/1965; Scherer, 1984a; Smith, 1989). In addition, it is possible that secondary appraisals having direct implications for subsequent coping (e.g., evaluations related to the assessment of coping potential) have direct autonomic and postural effects consistent with the implied coping requirements (cf. Smith & Lazarus, in press).

Preliminary evidence that some facial and autonomic activities are linked directly to specific appraisal components was obtained in my dissertation research (Smith, 1987, 1989). For instance, activity of the *corrugator supercilii* to pull the eyebrows together and down into a frown was found to be produced by the perception of goal-obstacles (appraisals of motivational incongruence), and this relationship did not depend on the identity of the particular emotions experienced. The relationship between motivational incongruence and *corrugator* activity not only applied to an array of negative emotions, including anger, fear, and sadness, but also extended to highly pleasant experiences involving motivational incongruence, such as those associated with hope and challenge. Specific autonomic activities also were found to be differentially associated with cognitive outcomes related to evaluations of coping potential in ways that are consistent with previous proposals and findings (e.g., Elliott, 1969; Elliott et al., 1970; Kilpatrick, 1972). First, increasing the amount of effort believed to be required to contend with the situation produced increases in heart rate. Second, skin conductance level was not only elevated under conditions of high anticipated effort, but also was found to be positively correlated with the amount of attention and thought the person wanted to devote to his or her circumstances.

These findings only scratch the surface of the potential organization in emotional response. Although the global patterns of facial activity associated with various emotions have been fairly well described, the extent to which most of the individual facial actions are directly linked to particular appraisal components awaits investigation. For most other physiological parameters implicated in emotion, both the extent and organization of systematic activity remain to be specified (cf. Levenson, 1988; Smith, 1989). Nonetheless, appraisal theory offers considerable guidance as to how analyses might proceed. Quite simply, one should be able to derive specific relationships between appraisal and coping-related physiological activity

by carefully comparing the adaptive implications of particular appraisals with the adaptive functions of particular physiological activities or the physiological subsystems those activities represent. The prediction of specific relationships between appraisal and purely communicative physiological activity is less straightforward because such activities need not be directly linked to any physiological demands implied by the appraisals. However, a careful analysis of the functions once served by specific communicative actions, or their progenitors, in our evolutionary past may suggest some of the important appraisal-related meanings they currently convey (cf. Andrew, 1963, 1965; Darwin, 1872/1965; Fridlund, in press; Smith, 1989). Whatever the outcome of such analyses, it is evident that a consideration of emotion in light of its coping functions provides substantially richer leads into the difficult puzzle of physiological patterning than have previously been offered by less theoretical approaches.

THE SELF AND APPRAISAL

The analysis so far has focused on the affective response and what can be learned about it from a coping perspective, as well as what studying this response might offer to students of coping and adaptation. However, as suggested by Figure 1, the implications of the combined perspective extend beyond the properties of the affective response, and include the contributions of personality to appraisal, the contributions of both personality and emotion to coping, and the role of coping in adaptation. Each of these areas will now be considered.

An appreciation of the role of individual differences is fundamental to understanding both emotion and coping. One of the first harsh realities facing a student of emotion is that there is no such thing as a universal emotional stimulus. It is easy to demonstrate that under the appropriate circumstances just about any stimulus event can produce just about any emotion, and no single stimulus will always elicit the same emotion under all conditions (Ekman, 1984; Frijda, 1986). This property is often used to differentiate emotion from reflex and instinct (cf. Ekman, 1984; Ekman, Friesen, & Simons, 1985). In fact, the desire to understand the vast individual variation in emotional response provided much of the impetus for developing a cognitive-relational theory of emotion (cf. Lazarus, 1968, in press-a; Smith & Lazarus, in press). If an individual's emotional reaction could be adequately predicted and understood solely on the basis of a sufficiently developed description of the objective stimulus situation, then there would be little need to consider constructs like cognitive appraisal. Individual variation is no less important to understanding coping and adaptation. One of the central agendas in coping research is to understand how and why some people appear to thrive under conditions that are devastating to others, and, especially, to understand the nature and functioning of personal resources that make the individual especially vulnerable or resistant to particular sources of stress (cf. Cohen & Wills, 1985; Ganellen & Blaney, 1984; Holahan & Moos, 1985; Lazarus & Folkman, 1984; Scheier & Carver, 1987).

As indicated in the top portion of Figure 1, the present model implicates two general classes of personality variables, one motivational and one knowledge-based, as being especially relevant to appraisal, emotion, and coping. The identification of these person characteristics, and their hypothesized contributions to appraisal, are derived directly from the specific appraisal model that was outlined above. Figure 1 depicts these factors as contributing to both the construal of the factual representation of the situation and the appraisal of that representation as to its implications for well-being. The present focus will be on the latter contributions, but there is also ample documentation within the social psychological and personality literatures indicating that the motivations, goals, beliefs, and expectations one brings into a situation strongly influence how that situation is construed (e.g., Asch, 1946; Fiske & Taylor, 1984; Hastorf & Cantril, 1954; Ross, 1987; see Smith & Lazarus, in press, for a more complete discussion of these influences and their relevance to emotion).

The motivational factors relevant to appraisal include the values, goals, and commitments that the person brings into every encounter. These factors are closely related to such motivational constructs as "current concerns" (Klinger, 1975), "personal projects" (Little, 1983; Palys & Little, 1983), and "personal strivings" (Emmons, 1986). These factors, which are important components of the person's self-concept (Markus, 1977; Rosenberg, 1979), are indispensable to the appraisal process. The very construct of primary appraisal makes sense only when the person's circumstances are considered in relation to what the person wants, needs, or otherwise cares about in the situation. It is impossible to assess either the motivational relevance or motivational congruence of an encounter without referring to the personal goals and commitments that are, or might be, at stake in the encounter. If nothing the person cares about is at stake, then little or no emotion will result (cf. Lazarus, in press-a; Lazarus & Folkman, 1984; Lazarus & Smith, 1988; Smith & Lazarus, in press).

The theoretical relationship between goal commitments and primary appraisal suggests that knowledge of motivations, goals, and concerns should make it possible to identify both the individuals who will react to certain situations with especially strong emotion, and the particular kinds of situations to which a given individual is likely to react strongly. A number of studies illustrate the promise of this proposition (e.g., Bergman & Magnusson, 1979; Kasl, Evans, & Niederman, 1979). For example, Vogel, Raymond, and Lazarus (1959) found that subjects with strong achievement goals and weak affiliation goals react to achievement-related threats with more psychophysiological arousal than they do to affiliation-related threats, while the reverse pattern was found for subjects with strong affiliation and weak achievement goals. Similarly, Hammen, Marks, Mayol, and deMayo (1985) have recently found that students who consider interpersonal goals to be central to their self-concepts are more likely to experience depression in relation to negative events involving interpersonal relationships than they are to stressful events involving achievement concerns, and the reverse tends to be true for students who identify with strong achievement goals.

The second type of personality factor the model identifies as relevant to appraisal is the person's knowledge base, which consists of beliefs, both concrete and abstract, about the way things are, how they work, the nature of the world, and the person's place in it. It also contains attitudes, expectations, and intuitive theories about the self (cf. Epstein, 1983; Smith & Lazarus, in press). Whereas the motivational factors are most relevant to primary appraisal, these knowledge-based factors can contribute to both primary and secondary appraisal.

For instance, one's beliefs and expectations about the probable effectiveness of various courses of action, and one's ability to perform those actions, contribute to judgments of self-efficacy (Bandura, 1977, 1982) and, therefore, to appraisals of coping potential and future expectancy. Thus, these expectations partially determine whether a stressful situation will be appraised as a loss, a threat, or a potential gain, and hence will be reacted to with sadness, anxiety, or challenge. Similarly, beliefs about what is normatively appropriate, avoidable, legitimate, or excusable in a given situation influence whether, to what extent, and on whom an appraisal of accountability for a stressful encounter will be made (cf. Pastore, 1952; Shaver, 1985; Weiner, Amirkhan, Folkes, & Verette, 1987), and therefore, whether the encounter will result in any guilt or anger.

In addition, knowledge and beliefs can contribute to primary appraisal by helping to define what is relevant to particular goal-commitments and what constitutes harm or benefit. For example, beliefs and expectations about what it is normal to experience and what benefits are likely to result from a necessary but aversive procedure (e.g., surgery) can strongly influence the degree to which the encounter is appraised as motivationally incongruent, as well as influence appraisals of coping potential and future expectancy.

Obviously, these few examples do not exhaustively catalog the ways in which a person's knowledge and beliefs are relevant to appraisal and emotion. Nor are all knowledge and beliefs relevant. However, as the above examples illustrate, one good place to start a search for the most relevant knowledge and beliefs is with the individual appraisal components. Careful consideration of the types of information and beliefs that should influence how these specific issues are evaluated, perhaps drawing on the literatures on attribution and social cognition (e.g., Fiske & Taylor, 1984; Jones et al., 1972), should provide considerable guidance toward the most emotionally relevant kinds of knowledge, beliefs, and attitudes.

The recent work of Higgins and his colleagues (e.g., Higgins, 1987; Strauman & Higgins, 1987; Van Hook & Higgins, 1988) illustrates still another way that self-related goals and beliefs contribute to emotion. Their work builds on the observation that in addition to knowledge and beliefs about the way they actually are (actual selves), which comprise most of the self-relevant beliefs considered in the above examples, most people possess goals and beliefs regarding the way they would ideally like to be (ideal selves), the way they believe they should be in light of social norms and demands (ought selves), as well as beliefs

about numerous other possible selves (e.g., James, 1890/1950; Markus & Nurius, 1986). They have found that when discrepancies between the actual self and particular potential selves (self-guides), or even discrepancies among different potential selves, are made salient to the person, specific emotional consequences tend to follow. For example, salient discrepancies between the real and ideal selves tend to produce emotions related to sadness and depression, while discrepancies between the real and ought selves tend to produce emotions related to fear and anxiety (Higgins, 1987).

A future challenge is to integrate these findings with the model presented here. Such an integration should provide a more microanalytic, process-oriented view of the relationships between self-discrepancies and emotion. According to the present model, self-discrepancies do not directly produce particular emotional reactions. Instead, they represent particular kinds of knowledge or beliefs about the self that are available for appraisal, and it is how the discrepancies are appraised, not their objective properties, that determines the emotional reaction. In other words, appraisal is hypothesized to mediate between the self-discrepancy and the emotional reaction. Thus, actual-ideal discrepancies tend to result in sadness because they tend to be appraised as important, undesirable aspects of the self that the person feels powerless to change, whereas actual-ought discrepancies tend to result in anxiety because they are more likely to generate appraisals of uncertainty about what the person can and should do to resolve the discrepancy. To the extent that a particular individual appraises a particular discrepancy differently from the norm, that person would be expected to experience a nonnormative emotional reaction consistent with his or her appraisal. For example, someone who appraises an actual-ought discrepancy as an irremedial harm will react with sadness, whereas someone who appraises an actual-ideal discrepancy as a threat with uncertain coping implications will react with anxiety.

THE SELF AND EMOTION IN COPING

As the bottom portion of Figure 1 indicates, what the person actually does to cope with the adaptive implications of an encounter is a joint function of the person's current emotional state and his or her more stable personality characteristics. Importantly, the contributions of personality that directly influence coping are distinct from the personality contributions to appraisal that were discussed above.

A central tenet of emotion-theory is that each emotion produces it's own action-tendency, consisting of a motivational urge to respond to the encounter in a particular way—to cry in sadness, to flee or avoid in anxiety, to attack in anger, to make amends in guilt, and so on (cf. Frijda, 1986; Plutchik, 1980; Scherer, 1984b; Smith & Lazarus, in press).

However, these action tendencies are not the sole determinants of coping. At all but the most extreme levels of emotional arousal people have the ability to suppress the specific action tendency and select from a wide array of coping options. The person is free to engage in any number of problem-focused coping activities in an active attempt to increase or maintain the motivational congruence of the person-environment relationship. He or she is also free to engage in any of a number of emotion-focused coping strategies that attempt to regulate the emotional response itself (cf. Folkman & Lazarus, 1980, 1985; Lazarus & Folkman, 1984). The person is not constrained to engage in a single coping strategy, and under stressful circumstances most people tend to engage in complex combinations of both problem-focused and emotion-focused coping (Folkman & Lazarus, 1980; Lazarus & Folkman, 1984).

The person's knowledge and beliefs are important determinants of the actual coping strategies employed in any given encounter. For instance, knowledge and beliefs about the availability and likely effectiveness of various coping options, as well as beliefs concerning their social appropriateness and their congruence with the person's own self-concept, are likely to be important influences. The emotional response compellingly alerts the person that he or she is in an adaptationally important encounter, provides strong motivational incentive to react to the encounter in some way, and through the action tendency even suggests a particular approach to take. However, the person is left relatively free to draw on his or her powerful intellectual capacities to select the coping alternatives most likely to be effective under the particular circumstances.

This view of coping raises important issues for its study and measurement. The influence on coping of action tendencies and their interactions with knowledge and beliefs has been severely neglected as a research area. This is likely because coping has traditionally been studied within the framework of stress-theory rather than emotion-theory (cf. Folkman & Lazarus, 1988b). The unidimensional nature of the stress-construct encourages a view, quite at odds with the notion of discrete action tendencies, of the affective reaction merely providing a very diffuse mobilization to alleviate the source of motivational incongruence, with the specifics of the coping to be determined solely by the person's personality, knowledge, and skills. A shift from stress to emotion demands that the influences of specific emotion-driven action tendencies be taken into account as well.

One basic implication of this shift is that it is important to make sure that behaviors related to the various action tendencies are sufficiently represented in measures of coping, such as the Ways of Coping Scale (e.g., Folkman & Lazarus, 1980; Folkman et al., 1986). In addition, it would seem important not only to assess the actual coping activities the person engaged in, but also to measure the motivational urges they experienced, and to compare what the person wanted to do in the encounter with the coping activities he or she actually performed. The possibility of discrepancies between the coping activities motivated by the emotion and those actually employed raises a number of important issues.

For instance, an initial question is how often, or to what degree, the adaptive functions of the various emotions are still served when the action tendencies themselves are not directly acted on. For example, to what extent does experiencing anxiety increase the probability that a potential harm will be successfully averted—perhaps through increased vigilance or a preemptive attack—even though the specific urge to flee the threatening situation is not consummated? Or, to what extent does the experience of anger result in the effective removal of the identified source of harm, even though, as Averill (1983) has observed in college students, overt aggression may be relatively uncommon in angry encounters?

A further issue concerns the health implications of not performing the behaviors directly motivated by the action tendencies. For instance, are people who habitually suppress their aggressive urges and respond to anger-inducing provocations in a pacifistic manner necessarily placing themselves at a greater health risk than people who habitually act directly on those urges? Or, as seems more likely, is it the adequacy of the ultimate resolution of the underlying anger-inducing conflict that truly matters for long-term health and adaptation? These issues are fundamental to understanding coping, but they are difficult to conceptualize, let alone investigate, without a consideration of the role of emotion in the coping process.

COPING AND ADAPTATION

The model depicted in Figure 1 does not stop at coping, but depicts a continuous process in which coping activities influence the person's subsequent appraisals and emotions (cf. Lazarus, 1968, in press-a). This last step is very important because it emphasizes and clarifies the adaptive nature of the emotion-system. A major theme throughout this chapter has been that the emotion system evolved in the service of adaptation. Its purpose is to alert the person when he or she faces adaptationally relevant circumstances, and to motivate the person to react to those circumstances in an adaptationally beneficial manner. For instance, when the appraisal of the encounter reveals a significant incongruence, or mismatch, between the perceived circumstances and what the person needs or wants — be it a potential benefit that is not currently present, or a potential or actual harm that is — the resulting emotional response offers the person compelling motivation to attempt to bring the circumstances and his or her wants or needs into better alignment. The two types of coping depicted in the model reflect the two major avenues of change available to the person, and the effects of attempts for change along either will influence subsequent appraisals and emotions (cf. Folkman & Lazarus, 1988a, 1988b).

First, *problem-focused coping* consists of active attempts to alert the circumstances to bring them more in line with the person's wants and needs (Lazarus & Folkman, 1984). If the coping attempts are effective, and the harm or threat is alleviated or removed, or the potential benefit is achieved, the change is likely to be reflected in subsequent appraisal with consequent changes in emotion away from distress or challenge to more benefit-related emotions such as happiness or relief (see Folkman & Lazarus, 1988a). Ineffective attempts at problem-focused coping can influence subsequent appraisal as well. A nonresponsive environment will often alter the person's beliefs and

expectations about both the nature of the encounter and his or her efficacy in it. Encounters originally appraised as subject to beneficial change can be reappraised as irremedial harms, producing the corresponding emotional changes from hope or challenge to sadness or resignation.

Emotion-focused coping reflects the second major avenue for realignment of the person and environment — change within the person. Some forms of emotion-focused coping alter the emotional response directly without changing the meaning of what is happening (e.g., by affecting autonomic arousal through relaxation or exercise, or by avoiding thinking about the appraisal, etc.). But other forms, which are probably more significant for long-term adaptation, alter the appraised meaning of the encounter in one of several possible ways. Many of these emotion-focused coping strategies overlap those identified in a long tradition of research into cognitive dissonance (e.g., Festinger, 1957; Wicklund & Brehm, 1976), even though cognitive dissonance encompasses a much more restricted type of motivational incongruence than is relevant to emotion. For example, one can reconstrue the nature of the situation, such as by deciding that a perceived offense was really unintentional or unavoidable, or that an inferred event did not actually occur. Or one can alter personal beliefs and attitudes relevant to the meaning of the encounter, and hence the encounter's appraised implications for well-being. In the face of a seemingly intractable unpleasant person-environment relationship, one also can alter personal goals and values so that the encounter is no longer appraised as relevant to well-being, and no longer has the power to evoke strong emotion (cf. Klinger, 1975).

The fact that emotion-focused coping reduces motivational incongruence by altering the person instead of the environment, and often does so by distorting reality, does not imply that emotion-focused coping is inherently less adaptive than problem-focused coping, despite Western biases to the contrary. Even when considerable distortion of reality is involved, the illusions produced through emotion-focused coping can often provide the extra motivation, not available through a more realistic assessment, that might be needed to persevere through dire circumstances, to comply with difficult treatment regimens, or to buy the time necessary to accept and adapt to tragic losses (cf. Collins, Baum, & Singer, 1983; Janoff-

Bulman & Timko, 1987; Lazarus, 1983; Snyder & Higgins, 1988; Strentz & Auerbach, 1988; Taylor, 1983; Taylor & Brown, 1988).

Further, it is important not to overemphasize the role of distortions or illusions, adaptive or not, in emotion-focused coping. Often emotion-focused coping reflects realistic adjustments to a situation that was originally misperceived or is actually unchangeable. If one's circumstances are truly impervious to change, it is much more realistic to attempt to let go of any commitments that have been destroyed than it is to continue to fight for their recovery (cf. Janoff-Bulman & Brickman, 1982). By the same token, there is strong appreciation within both the clinical and social psychological literatures that one's objective social reality is often so ambiguous and complex that the individual has considerable power to define and shape it through his or her construals and appraisals of it, as is conveyed through the notions of "reality negotiation" (C. R. Snyder, 1989; Snyder & Higgins, 1988) and "self-fulfilling prophecies" (e.g., Jones, 1986; Snyder, 1984). For instance, it has been well documented that a person's expectations for success, and his or her beliefs about the likely effectiveness of their actions, strongly influence how much effort the person will expend in a given situation, which, in turn, strongly influences the ultimate probability of success (e.g., Bandura, 1977, 1982; Dweck, 1975; Dweck & Leggett, 1988; Weiner, 1985). Thus, much emotion-focused coping might, indeed, be better thought of as an active negotiation or construction of reality rather than as a distortion of it.

Both of the major forms of coping serve important functions in the service of human adaptation, and in the long term, adaptive functioning requires maintaining a delicate balance between the two (Lazarus, in press-a; Smith & Lazarus, in press). Consistent with the idea of balance, it is important to realize that the two basic coping strategies are not mutually exclusive. As previously noted, most people react to stressful conditions with complex combinations of both problem-focused and emotion-focused coping activities (Folkman & Lazarus, 1980; Lazarus & Folkman, 1984). The major point, however, is that a consideration of coping is fundamental to understanding emotion and its role in adaptation, just as a consideration of emotion is fundamental to understanding coping (cf. Folkman & Lazarus, 1988a, 1988b).

CONCLUDING THOUGHT

With the consideration of the role of coping in adaptation, the examination of emotion and coping has come full circle, and the benefits that might accrue to students of both emotion and coping from an integrated perspective should be evident. Consideration of emotion lends the study of coping a degree of specificity and guidance that is extremely difficult to derive from a consideration of stress. In return, consideration of coping places the study of emotion in context, and provides a coherent theoretical framework for interpreting the diverse, complex, and often puzzling phenomena encompassed by emotion. In short, emotion and coping are different sides of the same coin. They are both integral aspects of a single process that is of central importance to human health and adaptation — a process that combines consideration of the individual's needs, concerns, and abilities with consideration of the environmental realities confronting the individual in order to promote the individual's survival and personal growth. To consider one of these aspects without reference to the other is folly.

REFERENCES

Abramson, L. Y., Seligman, M. E. P., & Teasdale, J. D. (1978). Learned helplessness in humans: Critique and reformulation. *Journal of Abnormal Psychology, 87*, 49–74.

Anderson, J. R., & Bower, G. H. (1973). *Human associative memory*. Washington, DC: Hemisphere.

Andrew, R. J. (1963). Evolution of facial expression. *Science, 142*, 1034–1041.

Andrew, R. J. (1965). The origins of facial expressions. *Scientific American, 213*, 88–94.

Arnold, M. B. (1960). *Emotion and personality* (2 vols.). New York: Columbia University Press.

Asch, S. E. (1946). Forming impressions of personality. *Journal of Abnormal and Social Psychology, 41*, 258–290.

Averill, J. R. (1975). A semantic atlas of emotional concepts. *JSAS Catalogue of Selected Documents in Psychology, 5*, 330. (Ms. No. 421).

Averill, J. R. (1983). Studies on anger and aggression: Implications for theories of emotion. *American Psychologist, 38*, 1145–1160.

Ax, A. F. (1953). The physiological differentiation between fear and anger in humans. *Psychosomatic Medicine, 15*, 433–442.

Bandura, A. (1977). Self-efficacy: Toward a unifying theory of behavioral change. *Psychological Review, 84*, 191–215.

Bandura, A. (1982). Self-efficacy mechanism in human agency. *American Psychologist, 37*, 122–147.

Bergman, L. R., & Magnusson, D. (1979). Overachievement and catecholamine excretion in an achievement-demanding situation. *Psychosomatic Medicine, 41*, 181–188.

Billings, A. G., & Moos, R. H. (1984). Coping, stress, and social resources among adults with unipolar depression. *Journal of Personality and Social Psychology, 46*, 877–891.

Buck, R. (1985). Prime theory: An integrated view of motivation and emotion. *Psychological Review, 92*, 389–413.

Cannon, W. B. (1927). The James-Lange theory of emotion: A critical examination and an alternative theory. *American Journal of Psychology, 39*, 106–124.

Cannon, W. B. (1929). *Bodily changes in pain, hunger, fear, and rage* (2nd ed.). New York: Appleton-Century-Crofts.

Carlsmith, J. M., & Gross, A. E. (1969). Some effects of guilt on compliance. *Journal of Personality and Social Psychology, 11*, 232–239.

Cohen, S., & Wills, T. A. (1985). Stress, social support, and the buffering hypothesis. *Psychological Bulletin, 98*, 310–357.

Collins, D. L., Baum, A., & Singer, J. E. (1983). Coping with chronic stress at Three Mile Island: Psychological and biochemical evidence. *Health Psychology, 2*, 149–166.

Darwin, C. (1965). *The expression of the emotions in man and animals*. Chicago: University of Chicago Press. (Original work published 1872)

Duffy, E. (1941). An explanation of emotional phenomena without the use of the concept of "emotion." *Journal of General Psychology, 25*, 283–293.

Dweck, C. S. (1975). The role of expectations and attributions in the alleviation of learned helplessness. *Journal of Personality and Social Psychology, 31*, 674–685.

Dweck, C. S., & Leggett, E. L. (1988). A social-cognitive approach to motivation and personality. *Psychological Review, 95*, 256–273.

Eckenrode, J. (1984). Impact of chronic and acute stressors on daily reports of mood. *Journal of Personality and Social Psychology, 46*, 907–918.

Ekman, P. (1984). Expression and the nature of emotion. In K. R. Scherer & P. Ekman (Eds.), *Approaches to emotion* (pp. 329–343). Hillsdale, NJ: Lawrence Erlbaum Associates.

Ekman, P., & Friesen, W. V. (1975). *Unmasking the face: A guide to recognizing emotions from facial clues*. Englewood Cliffs, NJ: Prentice-Hall.

Ekman, P., & Friesen, W. V. (1978). *Investigator's guide to the facial action coding system*. Palo Alto, CA: Consulting Psychologists Press.

Ekman, P., Friesen, W. V., & Ellsworth, P. (1982). Research foundations. In P. Ekman (Ed.), *Emotions in the human face* (2nd ed., pp. 1–143). New York: Cambridge University Press.

Ekman, P., Friesen, W. V., & Simons, R. C. (1985). Is the startle reaction an emotion? *Journal of Personality and Social Psychology, 49*, 1416–1426.

Ekman, P., Levenson, R. W., & Friesen, W. V. (1983). Autonomic nervous system activity distinguishes among emotions. *Science, 221*, 1208–1210.

Elliott, R. (1969). Tonic heart rate: Experiments on the effects of collative variables lead to a hypothesis about its motivational significance. *Journal of Personality and Social Psychology, 12*, 211–228.

Elliott, R., Bankart, B., & Light, T. (1970). Differences in the motivational significance of heart rate and palmar conductance: Two tests of a hypothesis. *Journal of Personality and Social Psychology, 14*, 166–172.

Ellsworth, P. C., & Smith, C. A. (1988a). From appraisal to emotion: Differences among unpleasant feelings. *Motivation and Emotion, 12*, 271–302.

Ellsworth, P. C., & Smith, C. A. (1988b). Shades of joy: Patterns of appraisal differentiating pleasant emotions. *Cognition and Emotion, 2*, 301–331.

Emmons, R. A. (1986). Personal strivings: An approach to personality and subjective well-being. *Journal of Personality and Social Psychology, 51*, 1058–1068.

Epstein, S. (1983). A research paradigm for the study of personality and emotions. In M. M. Page (Ed.), *Personality: Current theory and research. Nebraska symposium on motivation, 1982* (pp. 91–154). Lincoln: University of Nebraska Press.

Epstein, S. (1984). Controversial issues in emotion theory. In P. Shaver (Ed.), *Review of personal-*

ity and social psychology: Vol. 5. Emotions, relationships, and health (pp. 64–88). Beverly Hills, CA: Sage Publications.

Festinger, L. (1957). A theory of cognitive dissonance. Stanford, CA: Stanford University Press.

Fiske, S. T., & Taylor, S. E. (1984). Social cognition. New York: Random House.

Fleming, R., Baum, A., & Singer, J. E. (1984). Toward an integrative approach to the study of stress. Journal of Personality and Social Psychology, 46, 939–949.

Folkman, S., & Lazarus, R. S. (1980). An analysis of coping in a middle-aged community sample. Journal of Health and Social Behavior, 21, 219–239.

Folkman, S., & Lazarus, R. S. (1985). If it changes it must be a process: Study of emotion and coping during three stages of a college examination. Journal of Personality and Social Psychology, 48, 150–170.

Folkman, S., & Lazarus, R. S. (1988a). Coping as a mediator of emotion. Journal of Personality and Social Psychology, 54, 466–475.

Folkman, S., & Lazarus, R. S. (1988b). The relationship between coping and emotion: Implications for theory and research. Social Science in Medicine, 26, 309–317.

Folkman, S., Lazarus, R. S., Dunkel-Schetter, C., DeLongis, A., & Gruen, R. J. (1986). The dynamics of a stressful encounter. Cognitive appraisal, coping, and encounter outcomes. Journal of Personality and Social Psychology, 50, 992–1003.

Freedman, J. L., Wallington, S. A., & Bless, E. (1967). Compliance without pressure: The effect of guilt. Journal of Personality and Social Psychology, 7, 117–124.

Fridlund, A. J. (in press). Evolution and human facial action in reflex, emotion, and paralanguage. In P. Ackles, J. R. Jennings, & M. G. H. Coles (Eds.), Advances in psychophysiology (Vol. 4). Greenwich, CT: JAI Press.

Frijda, N. H. (1986). The emotions. New York: Cambridge University Press.

Frijda, N. H. (1987). Emotion, cognitive structure, and action tendency. Cognition and Emotion, 1, 115–143.

Frois-Wittmann, J. (1930). The judgment of facial expression. Journal of Experimental Psychology, 13, 113–151.

Ganellen, R. J., & Blaney, P. H. (1984). Hardiness and social support as moderators of the effects

of life stress. Journal of Personality and Social Psychology, 47, 156–163.

Hammen, C. L., Marks, T., Mayol, A., & DeMayo, A. R. (1985). Depressive self-schemas, life stress, and vulnerability to depression. Journal of Abnormal Psychology, 94, 308–319.

Hastorf, A. H., & Cantril, H. (1954). They saw a game: A case study. Journal of Abnormal and Social Psychology, 49, 129–134.

Heider, F. (1958). The psychology of interpersonal relations. New York: John Wiley & Sons.

Higgins, E. T. (1987). Self-discrepancy: A theory relating self and affect. Psychological Review, 94, 319–340.

Holahan, C. J., & Moos, R. H. (1985). Life stress and health: Personality, coping, and family support in stress resistance. Journal of Personality and Social Psychology, 49, 739–747.

Izard, C. E. (1971). The face of emotion. New York: Appleton-Century-Crofts.

Izard, C. E. (1977). Human emotions. New York: Plenum Press.

James, W. (1950). The principles of psychology (Vol. 1). New York: Dover. (Original work published 1890)

Janoff-Bulman, R., & Brickman, P. (1982). Expectations and what people learn from failure. In N. T. Feather (Ed.), Expectations and action: Expectancy-value models in psychology (pp. 207–272). Hillsdale, NJ: Lawrence Erlbaum Associates.

Janoff-Bulman, R., & Timko, C. (1987). Coping with traumatic events: The role of denial in light of people's assumptive worlds. In C. R. Snyder & C. E. Ford (Eds.), Coping with negative life events: Clinical and social psychological perspectives (pp. 135–159). New York: Plenum Press.

Jones, E. E. (1986). Interpreting interpersonal behavior: The effects of expectancies. Science, 234, 41–46.

Jones, E. E., Kanouse, D. E., Kelley, H. H., Nisbett, R. E., Valins, S., & Weiner, B. (Eds.). (1972). Attribution: Perceiving the causes of behavior. Morristown, NJ: General Learning Press.

Kasl, S. V., Evans, A. S., & Niederman, J. C. (1979). Psychosocial risk factors in the development of infectious mononucleosis. Psychosomatic Medicine, 41, 445–466.

Kilpatrick, D. G. (1972). Differential responsiveness of two electrodermal indices to psychological stress and performance of a complex cognitive task. *Psychophysiology, 9*, 218–226.

Klinger, E. (1975). Consequences of commitment to and disengagement from incentives. *Psychological Review, 82*, 1–25.

Lacey, J. I., & Lacey, B. C. (1958). Verification and extension of the principle of autonomic response-stereotypy. *American Journal of Psychology, 71*, 50–73.

Larsen, R. J., Diener, E., & Emmons, R. A. (1986). Affect intensity and reactions to daily life events. *Journal of Personality and Social Psychology, 51*, 803–814.

Lazarus, R. S. (1966). *Psychological stress and the coping process.* New York: McGraw-Hill.

Lazarus, R. S. (1968). Emotions and adaptation: Conceptual and empirical relations. In W. J. Arnold (Ed.), *Nebraska Symposium on Motivation, 1968* (pp. 175–266). Lincoln: University of Nebraska Press.

Lazarus, R. S. (1982). Thoughts on the relations between emotion and cognition. *American Psychologist, 37*, 1019–1024.

Lazarus, R. S. (1983). The costs and benefits of denial. In S. Breznitz (Ed.), *The denial of stress* (pp. 1–30). New York: International Universities Press.

Lazarus, R. S. (1984). On the primacy of cognition. *American Psychologist, 39*, 124–129.

Lazarus, R. S. (in press-a). Constructs of the mind in adaptation. In N. Stein, B. Leventhal, & T. Trabasso (Eds.), *Psychological and biological approaches to emotion.* Hillsdale, NJ: Lawrence Erlbaum Associates.

Lazarus, R. S. (in press-b). Theory-based stress measurement. *Psychological Inquiry.*

Lazarus, R. S., Averill, J. R., & Opton, J. R., Jr. (1970). Toward a cognitive theory of emotion. In M. B. Arnold (Ed.), *Feelings and Emotions: The Loyola symposium* (pp. 207–232). New York: Academic Press.

Lazarus, R. S., & Folkman, S. (1984). *Stress, appraisal, and coping.* New York: Springer.

Lazarus, R. S., Kanner, A. D., & Folkman, S. (1980). Emotions: A cognitive-phenomenological analysis. In R. Plutchik & H. Kellerman (Eds.), *Emotion: Theory, research, and experience: Vol. 1. Theories of emotion* (pp. 189–217). New York: Academic Press.

Lazarus, R. S., & Launier, R. (1978). Stress-related transactions between person and environment. In L. A. Pervin (Ed.), *Perspectives in interactional psychology* (pp. 287–327). New York: Plenum Press.

Lazarus, R. S., & Smith, C. A. (1988). Knowledge and appraisal in the cognition-emotion relationship. *Cognition and Emotion, 2*, 281–300.

Leeper, R. W. (1948). A motivational theory of emotion to replace "emotion as disorganized response." *Psychological Review, 55*, 5–21.

Leeper, R. W. (1965). Some needed developments in the motivational theory of emotions. In D. Levine (Ed.), *Nebraska symposium on motivation, 1965* (pp. 25–122). Lincoln: University of Nebraska Press.

Levenson, R. W. (1988). Emotion and the autonomic nervous system: A prospectus for research on autonomic specificity. In H. L. Wagner (Ed.), *Social psychophysiology and emotion: Theory and clinical applications* (pp. 17–42). New York: John Wiley & Sons.

Leventhal, H. (1980). Toward a comprehensive theory of emotion. In L. Berkowitz (Ed.), *Advances in experimental social psychology* (Vol. 13, pp. 139–207). New York: Academic Press.

Leventhal, H. (1984). A perceptual motor theory of emotion. In K. R. Scherer & P. Ekman (Eds.), *Approaches to emotion* (pp. 271–291). Hillsdale, NJ: Lawrence Erlbaum Associates.

Leventhal, H., & Scherer, K. R. (1987). The relationship of emotion to cognition: A functional approach to a semantic controversy. *Cognition & Emotion, 1*, 3–28.

Lewin, K. (1936). *Principles of topological psychology.* New York: McGraw-Hill.

Lindsley, D. B. (1951). Emotions. In S. S. Stevens (Ed.), *Handbook of experimental psychology* (pp. 473–516). New York: John Wiley & Sons.

Little, B. R. (1983). Personal projects: A rationale and method for investigation. *Environment and Behavior, 15*, 273–309.

Markus, H. (1977). Self-schemata and processing information about the self. *Journal of Personality and Social Psychology, 35*, 63–78.

Markus, H., & Nurius, P. (1986). Possible selves. *American Psychologist, 41*, 954–969.

McCrae, R. R. (1984). Situational determinants of coping responses: Loss, threat, and challenge. *Journal of Personality and Social Psychology, 46*, 919–928.

Nisbett, R., & Ross, L. (1980). *Human inference:*

Strategies and shortcomings of social judgment. Englewood Cliffs, NJ: Prentice-Hall.

Ortony, A., Clore, G. L., & Foss, M. A. (1987). The referential structure of the affective lexicon. *Cognitive Science, 11*, 341–364.

Palys, T. S., & Little, B. R. (1983). Perceived life satisfaction and the organization of personal project systems. *Journal of Personality and Social Psychology, 44*, 1221–1230.

Pastore, N. (1952). The role of arbitrariness in the frustration-hypothesis. *Journal of Abnormal and Social Psychology, 47*, 728–731.

Plutchik, R. (1980). *Emotion: A psychoevolutionary synthesis*. New York: Harper & Row.

Riskind, J. H. (1984). They stoop to conquer: Guiding and self-regulatory functions of physical posture after success and failure. *Journal of Personality and Social Psychology, 47*, 479–493.

Roseman, I. J. (1984). Cognitive determinants of emotion: A structural theory. In P. Shaver (Ed.), *Review of personality and social psychology: Vol. 5. Emotions, relationships, and health* (pp. 11–36). Beverly Hills, CA: Sage Publications.

Rosenberg, M. (1979). *Conceiving the self*. New York: Basic Books.

Ross, L. (1977). The intuitive psychologist and his shortcomings: Distortions in the attribution process. In L. Berkowitz (Ed.), *Advances in experimental social psychology* (Vol. 10, pp. 173–220). New York: Academic Press.

Ross, L. (1987). The problem of construal in social inference and social psychology. In N. E. Grunberg, R. E. Nisbett, J. Rodin, & J. E. Singer (Eds.), *A distinctive approach to psychological research: The influence of Stanley Schachter* (pp. 118–150). Hillsdale, NJ: Lawrence Erlbaum Associates.

Sarason, I. G. (1984). Stress, anxiety, and cognitive interference: Reactions to tests. *Journal of Personality and Social Psychology, 46*, 929–938.

Schachter, S., & Singer, J. E. (1962). Cognitive, social, and physiological determinants of emotional state. *Psychological Review, 69*, 379–399.

Scheier, M. F., & Carver, C. S. (1987). Dispositional optimism and physical well-being: The influenced of generalized outcome expectancies on health. *Journal of Personality, 55*, 169–210.

Scheier, M. F., Weintraub, J. K., & Carver, C. S. (1986). Coping with stress: Divergent strategies of optimists and pessimists. *Journal of Personality and Social Psychology, 51*, 1257–1264.

Scherer, K. R. (1982). Emotion as process: Function, origin and regulation. *Social Science Information, 21*, 555–570.

Scherer, K. R. (1984a). Emotion as a multicomponent process: A model with some cross-cultural data. In P. Shaver (Ed.), *Review of personality and social psychology: Vol. 5, Emotions, relationships, and health* (pp. 37–63). Beverly Hills, CA: Sage Publications.

Scherer, K. R. (1984b). On the nature and function of emotion: A component process approach. In K. R. Scherer & P. Ekman (Eds.), *Approaches to emotion* (pp. 293–317). Hillsdale, NJ: Lawrence Erlbaum Associates.

Scherer, K. R. (1986). Vocal affect expression: A review and a model for future research. *Psychological Bulletin, 99*, 143–165.

Scherer, K. R., & Ekman, P. (Eds.). (1984). *Approaches to emotion*. Hillsdale, NJ: Lawrence Erlbaum Associates.

Scherer, K. R., Wallbott, H. G., & Summerfield, A. B. (Eds.). (1986). *Experiencing emotion: A cross-cultural study*. New York: Cambridge University Press.

Schroeder, D. H., & Costa, P. T., Jr. (1984). Influence of life event stress on physical illness: Substantive effects or methodological flaws? *Journal of Personality and Social Psychology, 46*, 853–863.

Schwartz, G. E., Weinberger, D. A., & Singer, J. A. (1981). Cardiovascular differentation of happiness, sadness, anger, and fear following imagery and exercise. *Psychosomatic Medicine, 43*, 343–363.

Selye, H. (1974). *Stress without distress*. Philadelphia: J. B. Lippincott.

Selye, H. (1976). *The stress of life* (rev. ed.). New York: McGraw-Hill.

Shaver, K. G. (1985). *The attribution of blame: Causality, responsibility, and blameworthiness*. New York: Springer-Verlag.

Shaver, P., Schwartz, J., Kirson, D., & O'Connor, C. (1987). Emotion knowledge: Further exploration of a prototype approach. *Journal of Personality and Social Psychology, 52*, 1061–1086.

Smith, C. A. (1987). The informational structure of the facial expression of emotion. *Dissertation Abstracts International, 47*, 4002B. (University Microfilms No. 87-00,820)

Smith, C. A. (1989). Dimensions of appraisal and physiological response in emotion. *Journal of Personality and Social Psychology, 56,* 339–353.

Smith, C. A., & Ellsworth, P. C. (1985). Patterns of cognitive appraisal in emotion. *Journal of Personality and Social Psychology, 48,* 813–838.

Smith, C. A., & Ellsworth, P. C. (1987). Patterns of appraisal and emotion related to taking an exam. *Journal of Personality and Social Psychology, 52,* 475–488.

Smith, C. A., & Lazarus, R. S. (in press). Emotion and adaptation. In L. A. Pervin (Ed.), *Handbook of personality: Theory and research.* New York: Guilford Press.

Smith, C. A., Lazarus, R. S., & Novacek, J. *Appraisal components, relational themes, and emotion.* Manuscript in preparation. Vanderbilt University, Nashville, TN.

Snyder, C. R. (1989). Reality negotiation: From excuses to hope and beyond. *Journal of Social and Clinical Psychology, 8,* 130–157.

Snyder, C. R., & Higgins, R. L. (1988). Excuses: Their effective role in the negotiation of reality. *Psychological Bulletin, 104,* 23–35.

Snyder, C. R., & Smith, T. W. (1982). Symptoms as self-handicapping strategies: The virtues of old wine in a new bottle. In G. Weary & H. L. Mirels (Eds.), *Integration of clinical and social psychology* (pp. 104–127). New York: Oxford University Press.

Snyder, M. (1984). When belief creates reality. In L. Berkowitz (Ed.), *Advances in Experimental Social Psychology* (Vol. 18, pp. 247–305). New York: Academic Press.

Stone, A. A., & Neale, J. M. (1984). New measure of daily coping: Development and preliminary results. *Journal of Personality and Social Psychology, 46,* 892–906.

Strauman, T. J., & Higgins, E. T. (1987). Automatic activation of self-discrepancies and emotional syndromes: When cognitive structures influence affect. *Journal of Personality and Social Psychology, 53,* 1004–1014.

Strentz, T., & Auerbach, S. M. (1988). Adjustment to the stress of simulated captivity: Effects of emotion-focused versus problem-focused preparation on hostages differing in locus of control. *Journal of Personality and Social Psychology, 55,* 652–660.

Taylor, S. E. (1983). Adjustment to threatening events: A theory of cognitive adaptation. *American Psychologist, 11,* 1161–1173.

Taylor, S. E., & Brown, J. D. (1988). Illusion and well-being: A social psychological perspective on mental health. *Psychological Bulletin, 103,* 193–210.

Tomkins, S. S. (1962). *Affect, imagery, consciousness: Vol. 1. The positive affects.* New York: Springer-Verlag.

Tomkins, S. S. (1963). *Affect, imagery, consciousness: Vol. 2. The negative affects.* New York: Springer-Verlag.

Van Hook, E., & Higgins, E. T. (1988). Self-related problems beyond the self-concept: Motivational consequences of discrepant self-guides. *Journal of Personality and Social Psychology, 55,* 625–633.

Vogel, W., Raymond, S., & Lazarus, R. S. (1959). Intrinsic motivation and psychological stress. *Journal of Abnormal and Social Psychology, 58,* 225–233.

Wallington, S. A. (1973). Consequences of transgression: Self-punishment and depression. *Journal of Personality and Social Psychology, 28,* 1–7.

Weiner, B. (1985). An attributional theory of achievement motivation and emotion. *Psychological Review, 92,* 548–573.

Weiner, B., Amirkhan, J., Folkes, V. S., & Verette, J. A. (1987). An attributional analysis of excuse giving: Studies of a naive theory of emotion. *Journal of Personality and Social Psychology, 52,* 316–324.

Weiner, B., Graham, S., & Chandler, C. (1982). Pity, anger, and guilt: An attributional analysis. *Personality and Social Psychology Bulletin, 8,* 226–232.

Wicklund, R. A., & Brehm, J. W. (1976). *Perspectives on cognitive dissonance.* Hillsdale, NJ: Lawrence Erlbaum Associates.

Winton, W. M., Putnam, L. E., & Krauss, R. M. (1984). Facial and autonomic manifestations of the dimensional structure of emotions. *Journal of Experimental Social Psychology, 20,* 196–216.

CHAPTER 8

SELF-AWARENESS AND PSYCHOLOGICAL DYSFUNCTION

Tom Pyszczynski
James C. Hamilton
Jeff Greenberg
Susan E. Becker

All persons chronically diseased are egotists, whether the disease be of the mind or body; whether it be sin, sorrow, or merely the more tolerable calamity of some endless pain, or mischief among the chords of mortal life. Such individuals are made acutely conscious of the self by the torture in which it dwells. (Hawthorne, 1843/ 1946, p. 255)

Over the last several years, theorists and researchers have begun to suggest that the simple act of directing attention toward the self may have implications for one's psychological well-being. Drawing on basic theory and research on self-focused attention (e.g., Carver & Scheier, 1981; Duval & Wicklund, 1972; Hull & Levy, 1979), self-attentional analyses of alcoholism (Hull, 1981, 1987), anxiety-related problems (Carver & Scheier, 1981; Schlenker & Leary, 1982), paranoia (Fenigstein, 1984), and depression (Lewinsohn, Hoberman, Teri, & Hautzinger, 1985; Pyszczynski & Greenberg, 1985, 1987a, 1987b; Smith & Greenberg, 1981) have been offered. The purpose of this chapter is to discuss the role of self-attentional processes in psychological disorder. We be-gin with a brief overview of basic theory and research on self-focused attention and then review the existing literature on applications of self-awareness theory to psychological disturbance.

BASIC SELF-AWARENESS THEORY

Although self-awareness theory has its roots in the symbolic interactionist theories of Mead (1934) and Shibutani (1961), contemporary interest in these issues was sparked by Duval and Wicklund's (1972) *Theory of Objective Self-Awareness*. This initial work stimulated a great deal of research, most of which has been generally supportive of the theory. Over the years, a number of refinements, revisions, and alternative models also have been offered (e.g., Buss, 1980; Carver, 1979; Carver & Scheier, 1981; Hull & Levy, 1979; Wicklund, 1975). In the following paragraphs we briefly review the central points of the most influential theoretical approaches. We then turn to a discussion of the evidence concerning the various consequences of the self-focused state.

Theories of Self-Awareness Processes

According to Duval and Wicklund, conscious attention can be directed either externally toward the environment or internally toward the self. Focusing attention of the self sets off a self-evaluative process in which one's current state, on whatever dimension is currently most salient, is compared with the most salient standard for that dimension. Exceeding the standard produces positive affect and a tendency to maintain the self-focused state. Falling short of the standard produces negative affect, which instigates efforts to either escape the self-focused state or reduce the discrepancy between current state and standard. Duval and Wicklund's self-awareness theory is clearly a motivational, drive-reduction analysis. Self-focus influences behavior by virtue of the affect that awareness of discrepancies between self and standards produce.

While adopting many of the central propositions of self-awareness theory, Carver and Scheier (1981; Carver, 1979) embedded their analysis of self-attentional processes within a more general cybernetic model of the self-regulatory process. From their perspective, self-focus is part of a self-regulatory negative feedback loop that functions to keep the organism "on-track" in its pursuit of various goals. Consistent with Duval and Wicklund, their model posits that self-focus instigates a comparison with standards, and that detection of a negative discrepancy instigates behavior aimed at reducing that discrepancy. From their perspective, however, this discrepancy-reducing behavior is not driven by affect resulting from awareness of the discrepancy; rather, they view discrepancy reduction in response to detection of discrepancies as an inherent feature of all self-regulating systems. They add that disruptions of discrepancy-reducing behavior lead to an assessment of the likelihood of the discrepancy ever being reduced. If the probability of successful discrepancy reduction is judged to be high, one persists in one's discrepancy-reducing behavior. However, if the probability of successful discrepancy reduction is low, one experiences negative affect, withdraws from the feedback loop, disengages from the goal, and diverts attention from the self.

A more radical divergence from the original self-awareness formulation was taken by Hull and Levy (1979) in their schema activation model of self-attentional processes. They argued that the only invariant consequence of self-focused attention is an increase in the accessibility of schematically organized self-referent information. Thus, the comparison of current state with standard is not a normal consequence of self-focused attention and occurs only under certain circumscribed conditions. This notion also was adopted by Carver and Scheier (1981). They posited that self-focus leads to a comparison with standards only if a behavioral standard is currently salient. If no such standard is salient, self-focus simply activates the self-schema and increases the accessibility of self-referent information.

At this point, there is simply not enough research on the key theoretical points that distinguish the three major approaches to provide an empirical justification for preference among them. Each theory has its own range of convenience in explaining what is currently known about self-attentional phenomena. In recent years, the emphasis of research on self-attentional processes has shifted from the basic theoretical issues to analyses of the role of self-focus in other psychological phenomena. In our opinion, the Carver and Scheier framework is particularly useful because it puts self-attentional processes in the broader context of a system through which behavior is regulated. Thus, although we do not agree with all aspects of their analysis, we adopt their self-regulatory framework in our analyses of pathological behavior.

Consequences of Self-Focused Attention

Comparison with Standards

The cornerstone of both the original objective self-awareness formulation and the later self-regulatory approach is that, at least when a behavioral standard is salient, self-focused attention leads people to compare themselves with that standard. Although this is a central assumption that is extremely useful in accounting for other findings, there is little research that has investigated it directly. This is probably due to the fact that the comparison with standard is an internal event that is rather difficult to assess. Scheier and Carver (1980), however, have provided indirect evidence supportive of this proposition by showing that self-focus leads to increases in the seeking of information needed to evaluate one's performance. More specifically, they found that both private self-consciousness (the dispositional tendency to focus on private aspects of self) and confrontation with one's mirror image led to more frequent inspection of a drawing that subjects were attempting to copy. In conceptual replications of these effects, they demonstrated that high levels of public self-consciousness (the dispositional tendency to focus on public aspects of self) are associated with a tendency to seek social comparison to facilitate self-evaluation of performance and that the presence of either a mirror or an audience leads subjects to choose problems for an upcoming test for which norms are available. In sum, the available evidence suggests that self-focus does indeed increase one's tendency to access behavioral standards useful for self-regulation.

Discrepancy Reduction

A wide variety of studies have supported the general notion that self-focus encourages discrepancy reduction. Research has shown that self-awareness encourages conformity to salient social norms (e.g., Diener & Srull, 1979), except when such norms violate important personal standards (e.g., Froming, Walker, & Lopyan, 1982; Gibbons & Wright, 1983). Self-awareness also has been shown to encourage attitude-consistent behavior. In fact, a number of studies have shown that attitudes guide behavior only when individuals are relatively high in self-awareness (see, e.g., Carver, 1975; Gibbons, 1983). Additionally, in a third line of research it has been shown that self-awareness does encourage moral behavior (see, e.g., Diener & Wallbom, 1976). Finally, research also has revealed that self-awareness encourages accurate self-reports of characteristics and behavior (e.g., Pryor, Gibbons, Wicklund, Fazio, & Hood, 1977). All of this research can be interpreted as evidence of discrepancy reduction under conditions of heightened self-focus. In each case, the influence of salient standards of behavior, whether derived from social norms, personal attitudes, or moral principles, is increased by heightened self-awareness.

In all of these studies, it was relatively easy for subjects to bring their behavior in line with salient standards. Carver and Scheier (1981) proposed that when the perceived probability of minimizing a discrepancy is relatively high, discrepancy reduction is the preferred response to the self-focused state. When the perceived probability of minimizing a discrepancy is low, however, they suggested that withdrawal from self-focus will be preferred.

Support for this mediating role of outcome expectancies has been obtained in studies in which the expectancy that one will be able to perform the requisite discrepancy-reducing behavior is varied (e.g., Carver & Blaney, 1977; Carver, Blaney, & Scheier, 1979). As predicted, when such expectancies are relatively favorable, discrepancy-reducing behavior occurs. When outcome expectancies are unfavorable, however, such behavior is not attempted; instead, self-focus appears to encourage either physical or mental withdrawal from the goal in question.

Avoidance of the Self-Focused State

Some of the earliest studies of self-awareness processes were tests of the hypothesis that self-focus is actively avoided when a negative discrepancy between current and desired state exists. Duval, Wicklund, and Fine (1972) provided initial support for this proposition by showing that subjects were quicker to leave a room after a failure experience if remaining in the room would have forced them to confront self-focus enhancing stimuli (a mirror and a videotape camera). Gibbons and Wicklund (1976) demonstrated that male subjects spent less time listening to a tape recording of their own voices if they had previously received a negative evaluation from an attractive female. Greenberg and Musham (1981) extended these findings by showing that not only do subjects who have engaged in counterattitudinal behavior avoid exposure to a mirror, but also that subjects who have engaged in proattitudinal behavior seek exposure to a mirror. Steenbarger and Aderman (1979) demonstrated an important limiting condition for self-focus avoidance effects. They found that self-focus is avoided after failure only if subjects perceive the discrepancy as relatively irreducible. After receiving failure feedback on a speech they had given, only those subjects who were led to believe that speaking patterns are stable for life avoided self-focus; subjects who were led to believe that speech patterns could be changed through practice neither avoided self-focus nor showed signs that they found self-focus to be aversive. These findings are generally consistent with Carver and Scheier's position that self-focus is avoided only when one perceives a low probability of successfully reducing a negative discrepancy.

An apparent contradiction to the above pattern of findings was reported by Greenberg and Pyszczynski (1986). Because the self-focusing tendencies of depressed persons have consistently been shown to differ from those of nondepressed persons, only the findings for nondepressed subjects will be discussed here. In the first of two studies, subjects were induced to either succeed or fail a supposedly well-respected test of verbal abilities. They were then asked to fill out the Exner (1973) Self-focus Sentence Completions, a measure that has previously been used successfully to assess extent of self-focus. Contrary to prior findings, subjects tended to exhibit higher levels of self-focus after failure than after success. The major difference between this and previous studies appeared to be that whereas the sentence completions used by Greenberg and Pyszczynski assessed relatively spontaneous self-referent thought, previous studies had assessed avoidance of self-focus–enhancing stimuli, such as mirrors, cameras, and tape recordings of subjects' voices. This led Greenberg and Pyszczynski to speculate that, because of the adaptive utility of self-focus in facilitating discrepancy reduction, the initial response to a detection of a discrepancy may be an increase in one's level of self-focus. Although the initial response may be a spontaneous increase in self-focus, subjects may find self-focus–enhancing stimuli aversive in such situations because they increase an already elevated level of self-focus beyond a tolerable and useful level. If this were the case, subjects' spontaneous self-focusing patterns would be expected to resemble those found in studies of mirror avoidance after the adaptive value of self-focus had diminished. Consistent with this reasoning, a second study demonstrated that although spontaneous self-focus immediately after outcome feedback was higher after failure than after success, after a brief delay and distraction this pattern was reversed to resemble that typically found in studies of mirror avoidance.

Accessibility of Self-Referent Information

Hull and Levy (1979) have argued that the one invariant effort of self-awareness manipulations is an increase in the accessibility of self-referent information or an activation of the self-schema (cf. Carver & Scheier, 1981). A broad range of findings support this proposition. For example, Hull and Levy (1979) have shown that private self-consciousness is associated with enhanced recall of words previously rated for self-descriptiveness but not for words for which other types of judgments

had been made. Geller and Shaver (1976) have shown that self-focus increases interference on a Stroop color-word task for self-relevant but not self-irrelevant words. Turner has shown that private self-consciousness is associated with more extensive self-descriptions (1978a) and faster reaction times when judging the self-descriptiveness of trait adjectives (1978b). Carver and Scheier (1978) have shown that both dispositional and situationally induced self-focus increases the tendency to fill in sentence completion forms with self-relevant information. Also consistent with this increased self-access hypothesis is a series of studies demonstrating that heightened self-awareness increases self-report accuracy regarding attitudes, behavior, and somatic symptoms (e.g., Franzoi, 1983; Gibbons, Carver, Scheier, & Hormuth, 1979; Pryor et al., 1977). In general, evidence from a variety of converging sources supports the proposition that self-focus increases one's access to internal and self-referent sources of information.

Intensification of Affect

It also has been suggested that self-focus can intensify existing affective states, relatively independent of the perception of discrepancies. To the extent that self-focus increases the accessibility of internal sources of information, one should be especially cognizant of any bodily signs of emotion when one is self-focused. To the extent that affective states are partially determined by the perception of internal bodily changes (cf. Schachter, 1964), such increased awareness of bodily state would be expected to increase the subjective intensity of one's affective state. Consistent with this reasoning, Scheier (1976) demonstrated that self-focus increased both reports of anger and subsequent aggression in subjects who had previously been induced to anger. Scheier and Carver (1977) demonstrated that both mirror exposure and high levels of private self-consciousness tended to increase the attractiveness ratings that male subjects gave to photographs of nude females; high private self-consciousness also was associated with high ratings of revulsion to pictures of atrocities. They also demonstrated that both mirror exposure and private self-consciousness increased self-reports of depressed affect after a Velton (1968) mood induction. Carver et al. (1979) reported similar effects of self-focus on self-reported anxiety among snake-phobic subjects attempting to approach and touch a large snake. Although the evidence that self-awareness amplifies negative affect is fairly consistent (e.g., Gibbons, Smith, Ingram, Pearce, Brehm, & Schroeder, 1985; Scheier, Carver, & Gibbons, 1981), the evidence for amplification of positive affect is actually rather weak (e.g., Brockner, Hjelle, & Plant, 1985; Scheier & Carver, 1977).

Internality of Attribution

Duval and Wicklund (1972) proposed that self-awareness should encourage internal attributions for one's behavior. As cognitive and attribution research has demonstrated, the greater the salience or availability of a stimulus, the greater the tendency to use it in drawing inferences (e.g., Smith & Miller, 1979; Tversky & Kahneman, 1973). Given that the self is salient when individuals are self-aware, internal attributions for behavior and outcomes should therefore be particularly likely when in this state. A wide variety of studies have supported this hypothesis (e.g., Duval & Wicklund, 1973; Fenigstein & Levine, 1984; Greenberg, Pyszczynski, Kelly, Burling, Byler, & Tibbs, 1989). Although a few studies have failed to support this hypothesis, they have tended to be studies in which self-esteem and/or self-presentational concerns were likely to have been especially great (e.g., Federoff & Harvey, 1976; Gibbons et al., 1985).

SELF-AWARENESS AND SELF-REGULATION

As is evident from the preceding sections, self-focused attention appears to be implicated in a wide variety of psychologically significant processes. The effects of self-focus cut across traditional disciplinary boundaries of cognition, memory, affect, and motivation. The ubiquitous nature of self-focus effects is consistent with Carver and Scheier's claim that self-focus is a critical element of the human self-regulatory system. Indeed, all of the effects of self-focus that have been demonstrated in the literature may serve an adaptive self-regulatory function. All of these effects are useful in preparing the individual to alter his or her behavior to bring it closer in line with his or her standards.

Although the self-regulatory utility of comparing current state with standards and engaging in behavior aimed at reducing discrepancies is clear and widely agreed upon, the roles that other effects of self-focus play in adaptive self-regulation may be less obvious. Nonetheless, intensification of affect, increased internality of attributions, increased accessibility of self-referent information, and increased accuracy of self-perception can all be useful in preparing the individual to bring his or her current state in closer line with his or her standards. An increased tendency to take responsibility for one's outcomes facilitates future goal-directed strivings because, as many theorists have suggested (e.g., Abramson, Seligman, & Teasdale, 1978; Weiner, Frieze, Kukla, Reed, Rest, & Rosenbaum, 1971), taking responsibility for outcomes is a first step in the belief that future outcomes can be affected. Likewise, an intensification of emotional states also can be viewed as serving an adaptive self-regulatory function. To the extent that the affective consequences of behavior play a central role in motivating future behavior (an assumption common to most theories of motivation), the intensification of affect can be seen as providing impetus to discrepancy-reducing behavior. Similarly, increased access to self-referent information is useful because it enables the individual to make better choices about the various courses of action that could be chosen to bring about the reduction of the discrepancy. The related increase in the accuracy of self-perception is likely to further facilitate the individual's choices by providing a more realistic assessment of what one can and cannot accomplish. Given that all of these various effects can serve an adaptive self-regulatory function, it is reasonable to argue that the tendency to focus attention on the self is motivated by self-regulatory needs.

There are, of course, other explanations available for each of these effects of self-awareness. For example, it is generally assumed that self-focus affects attributions by increasing the salience of self as a potential cause of a given effect. Similarly, self-focus is usually seen as increasing the intensity of emotional states by increasing people's awareness of their internal bodily sensations. These explanations are attempts to explain how self-focus produces its various effects. Our claim that all of these effects serve a self-regulatory function is in no way inconsistent with these process-level explanations. Rather, we are attempting to explain what all of these different consequences of the self-focused state have in common and what utility these consequences have for the individual. Thus, when disruptions in normal self-regulatory functioning occur, the individual increases his or her level of self-focus because of all the useful effects that self-focus produces. Accounting for all of these effects within one framework demonstrates the power and parsimony of the self-regulatory approach.

SELF-AWARENESS AND PSYCHOLOGICAL DISORDERS

If self-focus plays a central role in adaptive self-regulation, it seems likely that it also would play a role in cases in which the self-regulatory system goes awry. Consistent with many psychological approaches to psychopathology, we assume that psychological disturbances reflect the operation of normally adaptive psychological processes in situations where they are no longer adaptive. More specifically, we suggest that most psychopathologies can be profitably viewed as resulting from the inappropriate application of normally adaptive self-regulatory strategies.

There are many ways in which self-focused attention could contribute to psychological disturbances. Variations in consistency of behavior with internal and external standards, self-critical thinking, intensity of affect, responsibility taken for behavior and outcomes, accessibility of self-referent information, and accuracy of self-perception can be seen as differentiating so-called normal functioning from a variety of different psychopathologies. Different psychopathologies are characterized by different patterns of variability on the above dimensions. Given that self-focus has been shown to influence all of these dimensions, it seems reasonable to suspect that self-focus may play some role in pathologies that are characterized by divergence from the norm on these dimensions.

In advancing self-awareness analyses of various specific psychological disorders, it is useful to consider several key ways in which self-attention may be involved. Individuals are likely to differ in terms of the overall extent to which they are self-focused, the conditions under which they engage in high and low levels of self-focus, the particular standards that are brought into play when they are in the self-focused state, and the contextual factors that determine what specific effects their self-attentional patterns produce. Thus, it may be possible to characterize a particular self-focusing pattern specific to a given disorder. This may be

useful in providing an explanation of the process through which various characteristics or "symptoms" of the disorder are produced. However, this would be only the beginning of a complete self-regulatory analysis of the disorder in question.

Once the particular self-focusing pattern is identified, one must ask how that particular pattern is produced. If a disorder is characterized by chronically high levels of self-focus, one must ask what would produce such a pattern. We suspect that in most cases, answers to these questions will involve an analysis of how the individual in question derives his or her sense of self-esteem and consequent emotional security (for a discussion, see Greenberg, Pyszczynski, & Solomon, 1986; or Solomon, Greenberg, & Pyszczynski, in press and this volume) and how that person's current life circumstances are thwarting his or her efforts in that direction. Ernest Becker succinctly summed this up:

> If you are a psychiatrist or social worker, and want to understand what is driving your patient, ask yourself simply how he thinks about himself as a hero, what constitutes the framework of reference for his heroic strivings — or better, for the clinical case, why he does *not* feel heroic in his life. (1971, p. 77)

We are suggesting, then, that it is probably not possible or fruitful to develop a general theory of the role of self-attentional processes in psychological disturbance. Although self-attentional analyses of particular disorders may share several common features, the specific mechanisms through which the distinct features of specific disorders are produced are likely to be different. In other words, abnormal patterns of self-focused attention can contribute to psychological problems but are unlikely to be the root cause of any particular disorder.

Our discussion of the role of self-attentional processes in psychological disorders will be focused largely on three interrelated problems: depression, anxiety, and alcohol abuse. We chose these three problems for several reasons. First, these are the areas in which most of the theoretical and empirical work has been undertaken. Second, these are three very common problems that often have effects on physical health and that are likely to be experienced by many individuals at some point during their lives. More importantly, these are three very basic problems that are likely to be involved in other more specific pathologies. Finally, these three problems are highly interrelated; depression, anxiety, and substance abuse often go hand in hand. After discussing these three major problems, we will briefly discuss the role of self-awareness in other problems.

Depression

Of the various psychological disturbances to which self-attentional analyses have been applied, the most thoroughly developed and researched is probably that of depression. Smith and Greenberg (1981) were the first to point out a series of parallels between the behavior and characteristics of depressed persons under normal conditions and those of subjects in laboratory experiments under conditions of self-focused attention. They noted that both depressed persons and self-focused nondepressed persons exhibit an increase in self-evaluative tendencies and lowered self-esteem, intensified negative affect, an increased tendency to make internal attributions for negative outcomes, particularly accurate self-reports, and an increased tendency to withdraw from tasks after initial failure. Smith and Greenberg reported a small but significant correlation between depression and private self-consciousness, the dispositional tendency to be self-focused. This finding has subsequently been replicated with different measures of both depression and self-focus (e.g., Ingram & Smith, 1984; Smith, Ingram, & Roth, 1985) and in a sample of clinically depressed persons (Ingram, Lumry, Cruet, & Seiber, 1987). Based on these findings, it seems fairly clear that depressed people tend to be chronically high in self-focused attention.

A series of experiments probing the conditions under which depressed people are especially likely to focus attention on themselves suggests an exception to this general tendency. Pyszczynski and Greenberg (1985, 1986; Greenberg & Pyszczynski, 1986) have shown that depressed people exhibit a unique "depressive self-focusing style" in which they engage in high levels of self-focus after failure but actively avoid self-focus after success. This depressive self-focusing style has been demonstrated in studies using both indirect measures of reactions to self-focus enhancing stimuli, such as mirrors, and more direct thought-listing measures of the content of spontaneous thought. Combining these findings with the correlational findings reviewed above, it appears that depressed people

are generally highly self focused, but avoid self-focus after positive outcomes.

Based on these initial findings, Pyszczynski and Greenberg (1987a, 1987b) proposed a self-regulatory perseveration theory of reactive depression (for a related, but somewhat different perspective, see Lewinsohn et al., 1985). According to the theory, depression occurs when one is unable or unwilling to exit a self-regulatory cycle in which successful discrepancy reduction is unlikely. Recall that Carver and Scheier posited that if the individual determines that successful discrepancy reduction is unlikely, he or she will withdraw from the cycle, disengage from the goal or standard, and divert attention away from the self. According to self-regulatory perseveration theory, high levels of investment in a goal and a scarcity of alternative sources of what the goal provides make it difficult to disengage from the cycle. Thus, a person who loses a central source of self-esteem and has few alternative sources of self-esteem available will experience difficulty exiting a self-regulatory cycle focused on the lost source of self-worth. He or she will essentially become "trapped" in a self-regulatory cycle focused on an irreducible negative discrepancy. The high level of self-focus inherent in such self-regulatory perseveration sets a series of processes in motion that ultimately culminate in a state of depression.

As we suggested earlier, the function of self-focused attention is to instigate processes that are useful in staying on track in pursuit of one's goals. Thus, after a loss of a central source of self-esteem, self-focus would normally be increased (cf. Greenberg & Pyszczynski, 1986). Note that this is somewhat of a departure from other theories of self-awareness processes. Pyszczynski and Greenberg argue that because attention constantly shifts between the self and environment, individuals are generally sufficiently self-focused to detect major discrepancies between current and desired states. When such a discrepancy is detected, self-focus is increased to enable one to better deal with the discrepancy. This increased self-focus leads to increased awareness of the discrepancy, intensification of affect, increased responsibility being taken for the outcome, increased access to self-referent information, and increased accuracy of self-perception. To the extent that instrumental responses are available that are likely to be successful in reducing the discrepancy, these consequences of self-focus are all highly adaptive. However, if there is nothing that can be done to close the gap between current and desired states, the elevated level of self-focus produces a variety of characteristics commonly associated with depression. The individual essentially "spins his or her wheels" in pursuit of an unattainable goal.

According to the theory, this self-regulatory perseveration is likely to lead to (a) an intensification of negative affect, resulting from both the virtually constant confrontation with the discrepancy and the increased sensitivity to internal states; (b) an increased tendency to blame oneself for the discrepancy; (c) a loss of self-esteem, resulting from the confrontation with the discrepancy, the increased tendency to blame oneself for the discrepancy, and the likely disruptions in other areas of one's life; (d) particularly accurate self-perceptions; and (e) decrements in motivation and performance in other domains. Persistent focus on an irreducible negative discrepancy is seen as the proximal cause of many of the common symptoms of depression. Eventually a depressive self-focusing style emerges, in which the depressed individual is chronically self-focused, persists in high levels of self-focus after negative outcomes, and avoids self-focus after positive outcomes. This depressive self-focusing style then maintains and exacerbates the depression.

Although additional research is needed, the available evidence is consistent with the proposition that many of the characteristics commonly associated with depression are mediated by an elevated level of self-focused attention. Gibbons et al. (1985) demonstrated a significant increase in negative affect and a marginal decrease in positive affect as a result of exposing depressed subjects to a mirror; these subjects were also more accurate in their reports of number of hospitalizations and duration of their problems. Strack, Blaney, Ganellen, and Coyne (1985) found that encouraging depressed subjects to concentrate on the task at hand facilitated their performance. Presumably these instructions discouraged subjects from excessive self-referent thought.

A series of more recent studies have provided more direct evidence for the mediational role of self-focus in depressive symptomatology by showing that depression-related characteristics are reduced or eliminated when depressed persons are prevented from focusing internally. Pyszczynski, Holt, and Greenberg (1987) found that pessimism concerning the future was greatly reduced when depressed subjects were induced to focus externally. Pyszczynski, Hamilton, Herring, and Greenberg (1989) demonstrated that the negative bias in autobiographical recall commonly found among the depressed is eliminated by an external focus induction; a second study replicated this effect and demonstrated that it does not generalize to recall for events that happened to others. Also consistent with the theory are a series of studies investigating the effect of distraction on depressive thought and affect in clinically depressed patients (Fennell & Teasdale, 1984; Fennell, Teasdale, Jones, & Damle, 1987; Teasdale & Rezin, 1978). These studies have consistently shown that inducing depressed patients to focus their attention on a series of slides of outdoor scenes reduces both the frequency of depressive thought and the extent of depressive affect. These effects were confined largely to those patients categorized as nonendogenous on the basis of the Newcastle Diagnosis Scale (Carney, Roth, & Garside, 1965), leading Fennell et al. (1987) to suggest that the processes through which depressive symptoms are produced in endogenous patients may be substantially different from those involved in nonendogenous patients.

Greenberg et al. (1989) tested the hypothesis that the depressive self-focusing style mediates differences between depressed and nondepressed persons in the attributions they make for performance outcomes. Previous research has shown that whereas nondepressed subjects exhibit a robust self-serving attributional bias, making more internal attributions for successes than for failures, depressed subjects do not exhibit such a bias (e.g., Kuiper, 1978; Rizley, 1978). Greenberg et al. (1989) induced depressed and nondepressed subjects to either succeed or fail a supposedly well-respected test of verbal ability and then complete a story-writing task that directed their attention either internally or externally. When forced to focus their attention as nondepressed persons typically do (self-focus after success and external focus after failure), both nondepressed and depressed subjects exhibited a strong self-serving bias; however, when forced to focus their attention as depressed persons typically do, neither nondepressed nor depressed subjects exhibited a self-serving bias. In other words, depression-related differences in attributions for performance outcomes were eliminated when attentional focus was controlled.

In sum, the available evidence has consistently shown that the self-focusing tendencies of depressed people are substantially different from those of nondepressed people. Depressed individuals are chronically high in self-focus, but avoid self-focus after positive outcomes. It also has been shown that this high level of self-focus at least partially mediates many of the maladaptive characteristics typically associated with depression. These latter studies suggest that interventions aimed at altering depressed people's self-focusing tendencies may be a useful avenue in the treatment of depression. Although external focus clearly alleviates certain symptoms in mildly depressed individuals, a number of questions have yet to be addressed. For example, would external focus alleviate symptoms in more severely depressed individuals? And, even if it did, how could depressed individuals be encouraged to focus externally over an extended period of time? Research on such issues is clearly needed.

Anxiety

Analyses of specific anxiety-related problems have often invoked the concept of self-awareness or self-preoccupation. For example, theories of test anxiety (e.g., Sarason, 1975; Wine, 1979, 1980) posit that this state is characterized by unusually high levels of self-focused attention. Consistent with this proposition, research has shown that highly test-anxious individuals report more self-referent and self-evaluative thinking while taking tests than do low test-anxious individuals (e.g., Ganzer, 1968; Mandler & Watson, 1966; Marlett & Watson, 1968); this relationship appears particularly pronounced when the test is given under highly evaluative or stressful conditions (Deffenbacher, 1978). These theories assume that performance decrements due to test anxiety result from these self-referent thoughts decreasing the attentional capacity available for task-relevant thoughts. Consistent with this reasoning, research has shown that distraction impairs performance on challenging tasks (e.g., Sanders, 1981). However, theories of test anxiety have not taken into account the broader consequences of self-focused attention posited by self-awareness theories.

One of Duval and Wicklund's (1972) initial assumptions was that self-awareness is an aversive, tension-filled state because it inevitably leads to an awareness of one's shortcomings. Wicklund (1975) later modified this position, allowing for the possibility that self-awareness can produce positive affect when one is currently meeting or exceeding one's standards. He argued, however,

that because of a tendency to constantly revise one's standards upwards after success, such instances are relatively rare. From this perspective, self-awareness is, in most instances, associated with negative, tension-filled emotions, which is only a small step away from viewing this negative emotional state as anxiety.

A different mechanism through which self-awareness can affect anxiety is suggested by the research showing that self-focus increases one's awareness of internal states (e.g., Scheier & Carver, 1977). Self-awareness should increase one's awareness of bodily signs of anxiety and thus intensify the subjective experience of anxiety. Consistent with this notion are studies showing that self-focus intensifies negative affect in response to pictures of atrocities (Scheier & Carver, 1977), and anxiety in response to a snake (Carver et al., 1979).

Carver and Scheier's (1981) analysis of the effect of anxiety on self-regulatory processes builds on this finding. They argue that the heightened awareness of anxiety produced by self-focus increases the likelihood that discrepancy-reducing behavior will be disrupted. From their perspective, the effect of this disruption depends on the individual's perception of the likelihood that the discrepancy can be successfully reduced. When the likelihood of successful discrepancy reduction is high, self-focus increases the tendency to persist at the task at hand and improves performance. When the likelihood of successful discrepancy reduction is low, however, self-focus encourages withdrawal from the task and leads to poorer performance. Recall that, according to Carver and Scheier (1981), the detection of a negative discrepancy does not, in and of itself, generate affect. Rather, they argue that negative affect is produced when one perceives a negative discrepancy as unlikely to be successfully reduced. Thus, within Carver and Scheier's model, self-focus affects the experiences of anxiety in two ways: (a) self-focus intensifies the experience of any emotional state, and (b) when self-focused, the perception that a negative discrepancy is unlikely to be reduced can cause anxiety.

The available research is generally consistent with their analysis of the effects of anxiety on persistence and withdrawal from tasks. Scheier, Carver, and Gibbons (1981) found that self-focus increases the tendency of highly fearful subjects to withdraw from approaching a feared object (a snake or electric shock). Carver et al. (1979) demonstrated that self-focus leads subjects who doubt their ability to successfully complete an anxiety-producing task to withdraw earlier from that task. Carver, Peterson, Follansbee, and Scheier (1983) showed that highly test-anxious people withdraw from a task earlier than low test-anxious people when self-focused but not when externally focused. Slapion and Carver (1981) reported that self-focus actually facilitated the performance of highly test-anxious subjects on a relatively easy and nonthreatening test. In interpreting this finding, they assumed that because of the easiness of the task, subjects generally had favorable outcome expectancies. To the extent that this is true (unfortunately, expectancies were not directly assessed), this finding supports the contention that outcome expectancy mediates the effects of anxiety and self-focus on task persistence. Self-focus can lead to either intensified efforts or earlier withdrawal, depending on one's expectancies.

Pyszczynski and Greenberg's (1987a, 1987b) self-regulatory perseveration theory suggests yet another way in which anxiety and self-awareness may be related. Self-regulatory perseveration theory posits that depression occurs when an individual persists in focusing attention on an undesirable self-relevant event that has already occurred and is unlikely to be corrected. We suggest that anxiety occurs when an individual focuses attention on an undesirable event that has not yet occurred but is perceived as likely to occur in the future. This idea goes back at least as far as Freud (1926), who conceptualized anxiety as a danger signal. Beck, Brown, Steer, Eidelson, and Riskind (1987) and Tellegen (1985) also conceptualized the distinction between depression and anxiety as depending on whether an aversive event has already happened or is expected in the future. Of course, for Freud the danger resulted from internal conflict, whereas contemporary analyses focus on external threats. From a self-regulatory perseveration perspective, anxiety-related problems are likely when an individual becomes highly self-focused on an aversive event that he or she fears may happen in the future.

Recall that self-regulatory perseveration theory posits that the detection of a discrepancy between current and desired states leads to an increase in extent of self-focus. Carrying this analysis further, it may be that an increase in self-focus also is stimulated by the expectation of an aversive event because self-focus may facilitate attempts to avert the feared outcome. However, an increase in self-focus in response to the expectation of a future aversive event also is likely to increase anxiety. Focusing attention on a feared future event is adaptive insofar as the anxiety that it creates motivates the individual to take action to ensure that the feared event does not occur.

Focusing attention on a feared future event becomes maladaptive, however, when the event cannot be avoided, when the individual has doubts about his or her ability to avoid it, or when the anxiety becomes so intense that it interferes with the execution of goal-directed behavior. In the first case, the increased anxiety that continued self-focus is likely to create cannot be channeled into effective action because no such action is possible. In the second case, the increased anxiety that self-focus is likely to produce, coupled with low efficacy expectations, encourages a premature withdrawal from the goal and disengagement of the self-regulatory cycle. In the final case, either an individual propensity to experience anxiety or a situation laden with anxiety-provoking cues may lead to an overload of anxiety that interferes with the individual's ability to concentrate on the task at hand. As research has shown (e.g., Baumeister, Hamilton, & Tice, 1985), high levels of anxiety can inhibit successful performance on a variety of tasks. Although an increase in self-focus in response to the expectation of an aversive event may sometimes facilitate efforts to avoid the event, in other cases it is clearly maladaptive.

This analysis raises the issue of the close relationship often observed between depression and anxiety (e.g., Gotlib, 1984; Hollon & Kendall, 1980). Because of the high correlation typically found between measures of anxiety and depression, some researchers have voiced concerns about the discriminant validity of research in these areas. We suggest, however, that these high correlations exist, not because of flaws in the scales used to assess these disorders, but because these problems are, in fact, closely related. Given the above analysis, depressed people who have experienced a recent loss of a central source of self-worth are likely to experience anxiety when they consider the implications of the precipitating event for their futures. Similarly, people who are anxious about an upcoming event may experience depression if they become convinced that the aversive event is a foregone conclusion. We suspect that both of these types of thinking are fairly common among people faced with discrepancies of the sorts expected to produce anxiety and depression. Given these considerations, it is probably fruitless to attempt to develop measures of anxiety and depression that are completely uncorrelated with each other. Nonetheless, researchers need to be aware of the relatedness of these two sets of problems.

All of the perspectives discussed thus far are concerned with relatively circumscribed cases of anxiety about specific life events, such as the outcome of a test or social encounter. Anxiety is viewed as resulting from the simple awareness of a discrepancy between current and desired state, the perception that there is a low probability that the discrepancy will be reduced in the future, or the awareness of a possible discrepancy arising in the future. Self-awareness also is seen as exacerbating existing feelings of anxiety.

Many clinical observers and theorists have suggested, however, that these circumscribed sources of anxiety ultimately derive from some very basic sources of concern, such as death, sexuality, and life itself (e.g., Becker, 1973; Freud, 1926; Rank, 1959). In other words, anxiety about specific life events is seen as reflecting some more basic, and largely unconscious, sources of concern. Interestingly, clinically oriented analyses of anxiety have tended to focus on either specific, circumscribed problems of living or more global existential problems, but have rarely attempted to explain how these two types of anxiety might be related. We suggest that a synthesis of self-awareness theory and the recently formulated terror management theory (Greenberg et al., 1986; Solomon, Greenberg, & Pyszczynski, in press; this volume) may provide a vehicle for understanding the relationship between anxiety stemming from deep sources and that stemming from specific life concerns.

To approach this issue, we must first ask the question, *why* does self-awareness lead to a comparison with standards and other self-evaluative activities? This relationship between self-awareness and self-evaluation is taken as an unexplained postulate both by Duval and Wicklund (1972) and Carver and Scheier (1981). Terror management theory suggests a possible answer to this question. In the following paragraphs we present a brief summary of the theory and how it can contribute to an understanding of the relationship between self-awareness and anxiety (for a more thorough discussion of this relationship, see Pyszczynski, Greenberg, Solomon, & Hamilton, in press).

Based on the work of Ernest Becker (1971, 1973), terror management theory proposes that the human capacity for self-awareness creates the potential for paralyzing terror concerning our vulnerability and ultimate mortality. A cultural anxiety buffer evolved to help assuage the terror that self-awareness engenders. This cultural anxiety buffer consists of a set of beliefs about reality, a set of standards of value associated with those beliefs, and the perception that one's behavior and characteristics meet those standards of value. From the perspective of terror management theory, the individual is protected from the anxiety that self-awareness creates by accepting and living up to the standards of value espoused by the culture to which the individual subscribes.

This anxiety-buffering function of meeting cultural standards of value may help explain why people compare themselves with standards when they become self-aware. If meeting one's standards provides immunity from anxiety resulting from self-awareness, then self-awareness would be expected to instigate processes aimed at ensuring that these standards are met. Comparison of oneself with whatever standard of value is currently most salient and then engaging in behavior to bring oneself in line with that standard would thus be an effective way of bolstering the anxiety buffer when confronted with a source of anxiety. Research clearly shows that self-awareness does, in fact, lead individuals to bring their behavior in line with their standards (e.g., Carver, 1975). This analysis also suggests that, when self-aware, individuals will be especially motivated to defend self-esteem. Indeed, research has shown that self-awareness increases the use of a variety of self-esteem maintenance strategies (e.g., Federoff & Harvey, 1976; Kernis, Zuckerman, Cohen, & Spadofora, 1982).

This analysis implies that one of the most important superordinate functions of self-awareness processes is to keep anxiety at a minimum. Carver and Scheier's (1981) concept of a hierarchy of standards can be profitably applied here to shed light on how the self operates to control anxiety. They suggest that behavioral standards are hierarchically organized, from the very concrete to the very abstract. As one moves up the hierarchy to increasingly abstract levels, the standard at any given level becomes the criterion behavior at the next highest level. Thus, the goal of getting an "A" on a psychology exam toward which a student's studying behavior is oriented becomes the criterion behavior through which he or she achieves the next highest level standard of getting a good grade in his or her psychology course. Getting a good grade in his or her psychology course becomes the criterion behavior through which he or she meets the next highest standard of maintaining a high grade point average, and so on up the hierarchy.

As Carver and Scheier have suggested, near the top of this hierarchy is the superordinate goal of maintaining a positive self-image. The higher up in the hierarchy one moves, the greater the variety of pathways through which a goal can be met. Thus, subordinate to the general goal of maintaining a positive self-image are the many specific life goals through which a positive self-image is achieved and maintained.

We suggest that superordinate to the goal of maintaining a positive self-image are the goals of maintaining faith in the validity of the standards of value through which self-esteem is attained and faith in the cultural worldview from which the standards of value are derived. Above that is the goal of managing the terror associated with awareness of our vulnerability and mortality. In other words, deep existential concerns are represented near the very top of the hierarchy. By meeting standards subordinate to the goal of terror management, the individual is able to avoid direct confrontation with the basic existential dilemma. Conceptualizing different sources of anxiety at varying levels of a self-regulatory hierarchy illuminates the relationship between the various sources and how deep sources of anxiety may motivate behavior oriented toward more circumscribed sources.

The vast majority of one's conscious attention is focused on the intermediate levels of the hierarchy at which one's specific life goals are represented. Thus, rather than thinking a great deal about one's ultimate value as a person, people tend to think about whether they will pass a specific test, get along with a particular other, or be hired for a particular job. As both Carver and Scheier (1981) and Vallacher and Wegner (1985) have suggested, a disruption at any given level of the hierarchy leads to a shifting of attention toward lower levels of abstraction. Thus, failing a test might lead a student to reconsider his or her approach to studying. We suggest, however, that if attempts to meet the standard continue to be unsuccessful, attention shifts upward in the hierarchy and the individual begins to question his or her value on superordinate standards. Thus, continued failure in a course may initially lead to questioning one's academic ability. Perseverated

focus on this problem may eventually lead to questioning one's value as a person. An individual who either lacks alternative pathways to self-worth or experiences discrepancies in a large proportion of these pathways may question the standards of value through which self-esteem is derived and, ultimately, the conception of reality that gives rise to those standards. Thus, a severe threat to self-esteem can shake the very foundation of psychological equanimity (cf. Snyder, 1989).

This analysis implies that, although the potential for experiencing deeply rooted anxiety is present whenever one is self-aware, it is generally short-circuited by attempting to meet standards relatively low in the hierarchy. However, failures at a subordinate level can reverberate up the hierarchy. Failing an exam is certain to create anxiety about one's chances of passing the course, is likely to create anxiety about one's ability to maintain a high grade point average, and may even create anxiety about one's general academic ability. In some cases, conscious thoughts about one's value as a person are also likely to surface. This reverberation up the hierarchy also is affected by the distance from the initial standard increases. Reverberation up the hierarchy is also affected by the extent of differentiation in the hierarchy. The more alternative means of meeting the standard the person has access to, the less continued failure to meet any one standard will reverberate up the hierarchy. A useful analogy may be to view sources of self-worth as pillars on which self-esteem is mounted. The more support one has, the less likely it is that damage to any one pillar will threaten the integrity of the structure (cf. Linville, 1985). This approach suggests that although one's conscious attention may be focused on a specific goal at a relatively low level of abstraction, this goal is likely to be subservient to the meeting of deeper needs that often lie outside of the person's awareness.

One interesting implication of this theory is that individuals experiencing "free-floating" or existential anxiety may be suffering from the consequence of persistent low-level threats that have reverberated up the hierarchy. Thus, rather than focusing on the existential matters per se, these individuals may simply need to shore up the lower level pillars that support their self-esteem. This should allow the individual to imbed him or herself back within the security of the cultural anxiety-buffer and thereby end the confrontation with the existential dilemma. Interestingly, Yalom

(1980) suggested that the opposite strategy also may sometimes be necessary. Sometimes it may be useful to encourage confrontation with higher level concerns in individuals consciously attending to lower level concerns. Realizing that there are a wide variety of different lower level goals may help one achieve the higher level goals. The only way to come to this realization is to become aware of those higher level goals; then one can seek more fruitful paths to achieve them.

This analysis also may help explain the prevalence of anxiety in depressed individuals. According to self-regulatory perseveration theory, depression is instigated when one is both unable to reduce a centrally important negative discrepancy and unwilling to exit a self-regulatory cycle focused on this problem. The present model suggests that this perseverated focus on an irreducible negative discrepancy will eventually shift attention upward in the hierarchy. Thus, depressed individuals are likely to experience anxiety not just about their self-worth but also about the meaning of life (i.e., the validity of the cultural worldview) and mortality itself. Of course, clinical observations are highly consistent with this analysis; despair and thoughts of death are very common characteristics of depressive thought (American Psychiatric Association, 1987 [*Diagnostic and Statistical Manual of Mental Disorders*, 3rd ed., rev. (DSM-III-R)]).

Understanding the dynamic operation of this putative hierarchy may facilitate the successful application of self-regulation theories to other psychological disorders. For example, it is possible that disorders such as hypochondriasis, somatization disorder, or obsessive-compulsive disorder, all of which are characterized by low-level goal-directed behavior, may reflect the use of lower order goals as a means of avoiding awareness of higher order discrepancies. Similarly, disorders characterized by overgeneralized negative thoughts about the self, such as depression, may be caused by or may indicate a tendency to respond to failure at lower level activities (failing a test) by focusing attention on the higher order goals (being successful) from which the lower ones are derived. Such a tendency may be related to the complexity of an individual's goal hierarchy (cf. Linville, 1985, 1987). A clearer understanding of how the goal hierarchy operates may enhance the utility of self-regulation theories for understanding these important clinical phenomena.

Alcohol Intoxication and Abuse

Clinical observations suggest that alcohol intoxication is often associated with the occurrence of negative life events (e.g., Marlatt & Gordon, 1979). It is also likely that alcohol use reduces negative affect resulting from the occurrence or anticipation of negative life events (cf. Russell & Mehrabian, 1975). Indeed, abuse of alcohol is especially common among individuals experiencing depression or anxiety-related problems (Chambless, Cherney, Caputo, & Rheinstein, 1987; Lutz & Snow, 1985). Given the important role that self-awareness appears to play in depression and anxiety, it seems likely that self-awareness also is involved in the use and abuse of alcohol. Indeed, Hull and his associates have suggested just that (Hull, 1981, 1987; Hull & Young, 1983).

Hull (1981) noted that the circumstances that precipitate alcohol abuse are those in which people ordinarily attempt to avoid or escape self-awareness. Specifically, alcohol abuse is likely when one has fallen short of an important ego-relevant standard and is unlikely to be able to reduce that discrepancy in the near future. Furthermore, the affective consequences of alcohol intoxication are similar to those resulting from reductions in self-awareness. These observations led Hull (1987) to suggest that alcohol reduces self-awareness "by inhibiting higher order cognitive processes related to the encoding of information in terms of its self-relevance" (p. 275).

In support of this position, Hull, Levenson, Young, and Sher (1983) found that alcohol-intoxicated subjects exhibited significantly lower levels of self-awareness than did nonintoxicated subjects. Hull, Levenson, and Young (1981) found that although unintoxicated, highly self-conscious subjects exhibited especially high levels of anxiety, no such relationship between self-awareness and anxiety was found among intoxicated subjects. Alcohol presumably reduced anxiety among highly self-conscious subjects by reducing their levels of self-awareness. Hull and Young (1983) supported these notions by showing that whereas subjects high in self-consciousness who received failure feedback on a supposed intelligence test consumed especially large amounts of alcohol in a supposed wine-tasting study, the wine consumption of subjects low in self-consciousness was not affected by failure. Finally, Hull, Young, and Jouriles (1986) demonstrated that among highly self-conscious subjects who had completed an alcohol rehabilitation program, those who experienced predominantly negative life events following detoxification had the highest relapse rate, whereas those who experienced mostly positive life events had the lowest relapse rates. Subjects low in self-consciousness showed intermediate rates of relapse that were not associated with negativity of life events. These results suggest that Hull's model is applicable not only to moderate alcohol use among college students, but to clinically significant alcohol abuse as well.

Taken together, the studies reported by Hull and his colleagues provide compelling evidence that the avoidance of self-awareness represents an important cause of alcohol use and abuse. Moreover, the studies by Hull and Young (1983) and by Hull et al. (1981) indicate that a high level of self-awareness does not in and of itself lead to alcohol use. Rather, alcohol use is predicted by the combination of high self-awareness and the occurrence of events that hold negative implications for the self. These findings support the view we propose in this paper; namely, that psychopathology is not simply a function of self-awareness per se, but is a function of the operation of self-awareness in the broader context of self-regulation.

Hull's work on the self-awareness–reducing properties of alcohol may have broader implications for understanding the role of self-awareness in psychopathology. If alcohol reduces self-awareness, one might argue that disorders for which alcohol abuse is an associated feature may be disorders in which high levels of self-awareness play a role. Accordingly, alcohol use should be associated with disorders characterized by negative outcomes, painful emotions, and negative self-evaluations. Thus one would expect affective disorders, anxiety disorders, and certain personality disorders to show a greater coincidence with alcoholism than disorders such as schizophrenia and other psychotic disorders in which negative affect and self-evaluation problems are less prominent. Consistent with this reasoning, research has shown a high coincidence of alcoholism with depression, anxiety disorders, and antisocial personality (Chambless et al., 1987; Lutz & Snow, 1985; Peace & Mellsop, 1987; Whitters, Cadoret, & McCalley, 1987; Wilson, 1988). In contrast, studies reviewed by Peace and Mellsop (1987) suggest a low rate of coincidence between schizophrenic and other psychotic disorders with alcoholism. To the extent that alcohol abuse covaries with these disorders, self-awareness is likely to play some role in its etiology or maintenance.

Other Clinical Phenomena Related to Self-Awareness

Although the bulk of the available research has been focused on the role of self-awareness in depression, anxiety, and alcohol abuse, there have recently been several attempts to apply self-awareness analyses to other problems. Both empirical and theoretical work on these other disorders undoubtedly will become more prominent in the years to come. We now briefly review the work emerging on other disorders and psychological problems.

Paranoid Ideation

Fenigstein (1984) suggested that self-awareness may lead individuals to see themselves as the targets of others' behavior. In two studies, he told students that one particular student, whom he did not name, had done particularly well or particularly poorly on a recent examination. When asked to estimate the probability that the exam was theirs, subjects high in self-consciousness were especially likely to overestimate this likelihood. Fenigstein interpreted these findings by suggesting that self-awareness increases the tendency to perceive the behavior of others as relating to the self by increasing the salience of the self as an object in the social environment. The tendency to believe that one is being observed, talked about, laughed at, or plotted against, which occurs in a number of psychological disorders, may be similar to the phenomena demonstrated in these studies. Although it is unlikely that high levels of self-awareness play an important role in paranoid schizophrenia or delusional (previously termed paranoid) disorder, it may be that high self-awareness does contribute to disorders such as paranoid, borderline, avoidant, and narcissistic personality disorders, and social phobias, all of which are associated with fears of disapproval or harm from others. However, regardless of whether one fears embarrassment, rejection, or harm, it is likely that the tendency to see oneself as the object of others' behavior will exacerbate these fears and increase the extent to which they interfere with social and occupational functioning.

Aggression

Antisocial aggression is undoubtedly among the most serious problems faced by any society. Excessive aggression also is commonly associated with several types of psychological disorders, including psychotic disorders, intermittent explosive disorder, and antisocial and borderline personality disorders.

Research on the relationship between self-awareness and aggression suggests that self-awareness generally increases the correspondence between behavior and salient standards regarding aggression. For example, Scheier, Fenigstein, and Buss (1974) reported that self-awareness was associated with reduced aggression by male subjects against a female confederate. The authors argued that cultural prescriptions exist against acting aggressively toward women, and that increased self-awareness brought subjects' behavior in line with this standard. In a similar study (Carver, 1974), self-awareness was associated with increased aggression if the use of punishing electric shocks was presented as an effective means of improving the performance of a confederate on a concept-formation task. These studies indicate that self-awareness in and of itself neither increases nor decreases aggression. Rather, self-awareness increases the correspondence between salient standards concerning aggression and aggressive behavior.

Decreased self-awareness, on the other hand, is more generally linked to increases in aggressive behavior. According to the cybernetic model, self-awareness increases the tendency for behavior to be guided by higher order goals. For most people in most circumstances, aggressive behavior is inconsistent with the pursuit of higher order standards. For example, a person whose higher order goal is to "succeed in one's career" would be unlikely to act aggressively toward his or her boss because such behavior would probably increase discrepancies between current conditions and standards. However, in the absence of self-awareness, the internal standards that usually inhibit aggressive behavior have less influence on behavior, and thus decreased self-awareness is likely to increase aggression. Support for the notion that decreased self-awareness can increase aggression can be found in the deindividuation literature. According to Diener (1979), emersion in a group reduces self-awareness and, consequently, disinhibits aggressive impulses. Also supportive of this notion is the fact that alcohol use, which de-

creases self-awareness, increases aggression (Taylor & Gammon, 1975).

Health-Related Behaviors

The notion that self-awareness leads to greater awareness of physical symptoms has been supported in a series of studies by Pennebaker and Lightner (1980). In these studies, subjects who exercised in an unstimulating environment experienced and acted on fatigue symptoms sooner than subjects who exercised in a stimulating environment that presumably distracted attention away from bodily sensation. This symptom perception effect closely parallels those studies (reviewed earlier) that demonstrate that self-awareness leads to intensified perceptions of emotions. The relationship between self-focused attention and the perception of physical symptoms have led investigators to suspect that self-awareness plays an important role in the regulation of health-related behavior.

Carver and Scheier (1982) have suggested that their self-regulatory theory may be usefully applied to understanding people's effectiveness in maintaining their health. In this regard, Mullen and Suls (1982) have shown that highly self-aware individuals reported fewer illnesses in the face of stressful life events than did subjects who were less self-aware. Mullen and Suls suggest that highly self-aware subjects are both more attentive to physiological signs of stress and more motivated to reduce the negative effects of stress than are low self-aware subjects. A related finding suggests that increased levels of self-awareness may inhibit superfluous eating behavior under certain circumstances (Polivy, Herman, Hackett, & Kuleshnyk, 1986). However, Carver and Scheier (1982) point out that a focus on physical symptoms may lead to misregulation of health behavior in certain circumstances. For example, the proper regulation of hypertension involves adherence to a regimen of maintenance medication. Because medication must ideally be taken even in the absence of hypertension symptoms, using the presence or absence of symptoms to guide medication use can lead to less than optimal health behavior.

SUMMARY AND CONCLUSIONS

From the theory and research reviewed in this chapter it is clear that there is not a simple linear relationship between self-awareness and psychopathology. Disorders such as depression appear to result from excessive self-awareness, while research on aggression and impulsivity suggests that these problems may reflect a lack of self-awareness. The various roles that self-awareness processes might play in psychopathology are probably best understood within the broader context of self-regulation in general. For example, high self-awareness may promote a resistance to stress-related illness because the stress-producing discrepancies can be reduced effectively through active self-regulatory activities. In contrast, the discrepancies experienced by depressed people may for a variety of reasons be irreducible, and consequently, self-awareness leads only to painful perseveration and the experience of discrepancy-related negative mood. It is doubtful that the essence of any psychological disorder is too much or too little self-awareness. More likely, psychological disorders reflect the interaction of self-awareness and factors such as the absence of effective strategies for attaining goals, unrealistic expectations surrounding goal attainment, or an inhospitable social environment that interferes with one's ability to satisfy one's goals and needs.

REFERENCES

Abramson, L. Y., Seligman, M. E. P., & Teasdale, J. D. (1978). Learned helplessness in humans: Critique and reformulation. *Journal of Abnormal Psychology, 87*, 49–74.

American Psychiatric Association. (1987). Diagnostic and statistical manual of mental disorders (3rd ed., rev.). Washington, DC: Author.

Baumeister, R. F., Hamilton, J. C., & Tice, D. M. (1985). Public versus private expectancy of success—Confidence booster or performance pressure. *Journal of Personality and Social Psychology, 48*, 1447–1457.

Beck, A. T., Brown, G., Steer, R. A., Eidelson, J. I., & Riskind, J. R. (1987). Differentiating anxiety and depression: A test of the cognitive content-specificity hypothesis. *Journal of Abnormal Psychology, 96*, 179–183.

Becker, E. (1971). *The birth and death of meaning*. New York: Free Press.

Becker, E. (1973). *The denial of death*. New York: Free Press.

Brockner, J., Hjelle, L., & Plant, R. W. (1985). Self-focused attention, self-esteem, and the experience of state-depression. *Journal of Personality, 52*, 425–434.

Buss, A. H. (1980). *Self-consciousness and social anxiety*. San Francisco: W. H. Freeman.

Carney, M. W., Roth, M., & Garside, R. F. (1965). The diagnosis of depressive syndromes and the prediction of ECT response. *British Journal of Psychiatry, 111*, 659–674.

Carver, C. S. (1974). Facilitation of physical aggression through objective self-awareness. *Journal of Personality and Social Psychology, 10*, 365–370.

Carver, C. S. (1975). Physical aggression as a function of objective self-awareness. *Journal of Personality and Social Psychology, 11*, 510–519.

Carver, C. S. (1979). A cybernetic model of self-attention processes. *Journal of Personality and Social Psychology, 37*, 1251–1281.

Carver, C. S., & Blaney, P. H. (1977). Perceived arousal, focus of attention, and avoidance behavior. *Journal of Abnormal Psychology, 86*, 154–162.

Carver, C. S., Blaney, P. H., & Scheier, M. F. (1979). Reassertion and giving up: The interactive role of self-directed attention and outcome expectancy. *Journal of Personality and Social Psychology, 37*, 1859–1870.

Carver, C. S., Peterson, L. M., Follansbee, D. J., & Scheier, M. F. (1983). Effects of self-directed attention among persons high and low in test anxiety. *Cognitive Therapy and Research, 7*, 333–354.

Carver, C. S., & Scheier, M. F. (1978). Self-focusing effects of dispositional self-consciousness, mirror presence, and audience presence. *Journal of Personality and Social Psychology, 36*, 324–332.

Carver, C. S., & Scheier, M. F. (1981). *Attention and self-regulation*. New York: Springer-Verlag.

Carver, C. S., & Scheier, M. F. (1982). *Attention and self-regulation: A control theory approach to human behavior*. New York: Springer-Verlag.

Chambless, D. L., Cherney, J., Caputo, G., & Rheinstein, B. J. (1987). Anxiety disorders and alcoholism: A study with inpatient alcoholics. *Journal of Anxiety Disorders, 1*, 29–40.

Deffebbacher, J. L. (1978). Worry, emotionality, and task-generated interference in test-anxiety: An empirical test of attentional theory. *Journal of Educational Psychology, 70*, 248–254.

Diener, E. (1979). Deindividuation, self-awareness, and disinhibition. *Journal of Personality and Social Psychology, 37*, 1160–1171.

Diener, E., & Srull, T. K. (1979). Self-awareness, psychological perspective, and the self-reinforcement in relation to personal and social standards. *Journal of Personality and Social Psychology, 37*, 413–423.

Diener, E., & Wallbom, M. (1976). Effects of self-awareness on anti-normative behavior. *Journal of Research in Personality, 10*, 107–111.

Duval, S., & Wicklund, R. (1972). *A theory of objective self-awareness*. New York: Academic Press.

Duval, S., & Wicklund, R. (1973). Effects of objective self-awareness on attributions of causality. *Journal of Experimental Social Psychology, 9*, 17–31.

Duval, S., Wicklund, R. A., & Fine, R. L. (1972). Avoidance of objective self-awareness under conditions of high and low intra-self discrepancy. In S. Duval & R. A. Wicklund (Eds.), *A theory of objective self-awareness*. New York: Academic Press.

Exner, J. E. (1973). The self-focus sentence completion: A study of egocentricity. *Journal of Personality Assessment, 37*, 437–455.

Federoff, N. A., & Harvey, J. H. (1976). Focus of attention, self-esteem, and attribution of causality. *Journal of Research in Personality, 10*, 336–345.

Fenigstein, A. (1984). Self-consciousness and the over-perception of self as target. *Journal of Personality and Social Psychology, 47*, 860–870.

Fenigstein, A., & Levine, M. P. (1984). Self-attention, concept activation and the causal self. *Journal of Experimental Social Psychology, 20*, 231–245.

Fennell, M. J., & Teasdale, J. D. (1984). Effects of distraction on thinking and affect in depressed patients. *British Journal of Clinical Psychology, 23*, 65–66.

Fennell, M. J., Teasdale, J. D., Jones, S., & Damle, A. (1987). Distraction in neurotic and endogenous depression: An investigation of negative thinking in major depressive disorder. *Psychological Medicine, 17*, 441–452.

Franzoi, S. L. (1983). Self-concept differences as a function of private self-consciousness and social anxiety. *Journal of Research in Personality, 17*, 275–287.

Freud, S. (1926). *The problem of anxiety*. New York: W. W. Norton.

Froming, W. E., Walker, G. R., & Lopyan, K. I. (1982). Public and private self-awareness: When personal attitudes conflict with societal expectations. *Journal of Experimental Psychology, 18*, 476–487.

Ganzer, V. J. (1968). Effects of audience presence and test anxiety on learning and retention in a serial learning situation. *Journal of Personality and Social Psychology, 8*, 194–199.

Geller, V., & Shaver, P. (1976). Cognitive consequences of self-awareness. *Journal of Experimental Social Psychology, 12*, 99–108.

Gibbons, F. X. (1983). Self-attention and self-report: The "veridicality" hypothesis. *Journal of Personality, 51*, 517–542.

Gibbons, F. X., Carver, C. S., Scheier, M. F., & Hormuth, S. E. (1979). Self-focused attention and the placebo effect: Fooling some of the people some of the time. *Journal of Experimental Social Psychology, 15*, 263–274.

Gibbons, F. X., Smith, T. W., Ingram, R. E., Pearce, K., Brehm, S. S., & Schroeder, D. (1985). Self-awareness and self-confrontation: Effects of self-focused attention on members of a clinical population. *Journal of Personality and Social Psychology, 48*, 662–675.

Gibbons, F. X., & Wicklund, R. (1976). Selective exposure to self. *Journal of Research in Personality, 10*, 98–106.

Gibbons, F. X., & Wright, R. A. Self-focused attention and reactions to conflicting standards. *Journal of Research in Personality, 17*, 263–273.

Gotlib, I. H. (1984). Depression and general psychopathology in university students. *Journal of Abnormal Psychology, 93*, 19–30.

Greenberg, J., & Musham, C. (1981). Avoiding and seeking self-focused attention. *Journal of Research in Personality, 15*, 191–200.

Greenberg, J., & Pyszczynski, T. (1986). Persistent high self-focus after failure and low self-focus after success: The depressive self-focusing style. *Journal of Personality and Social Psychology, 50*, 1039–1044.

Greenberg, J., Pyszczynski, T., Kelly, C., Burling, J., Byler, E., & Tibbs, K. (1989). *Depression, self-focus, and the self-serving attributional bias*. Unpublished manuscript, University of Arizona, Tucson.

Greenberg, J., Pyszczynski, T., & Solomon, S. (1986). The causes and consequences of a need for self-esteem: A terror management theory. In R. F. Baumeister (Ed.), *Public self and private self*. New York: Springer-Verlag.

Hawthorne, N. (1946). Egotism; or the bosom

serpent. In N. Arrin (Ed.), *Hawthorne's short stories*. New York: Random House. (Original work published 1843)

Hollon, S. D., & Kendall, P. C. (1980). Cognitive self-statements in depression: Development of an automatic thoughts questionnaire. *Cognitive Therapy and Research, 4*, 383–395.

Hull, J. G. (1981). A self-awareness model of the causes and effects of alcohol consumption. *Journal of Abnormal Psychology, 90*, 586–600.

Hull, J. G. (1987). Self-awareness model. In H. T. Blane & K. E. Leonard (Eds.), *Psychological theories of drinking and alcoholism*. New York: Guilford Press.

Hull, J. G., Levenson, R. W., & Young, R. D. (1981). *The effects of social anxiety, private self-consciousness, public self-consciousness, and alcohol consumption in response to a social stressor*. Unpublished manuscript, Indiana University, Bloomington.

Hull, J. G., Levenson, R. W., Young, R. D., & Sher, K. J. (1983). Self-awareness–reducing effects of alcohol consumption. *Journal of Personality and Social Psychology, 44*, 461–473.

Hull, J. G., & Levy, A. S. (1979). The organizational functioning of the self: An alternative to the Duval and Wicklund model of self-awareness. *Journal of Personality and Social Psychology, 37*, 756–768.

Hull, J. G., & Young, R. D. (1983). Self-consciousness, self-esteem and success-failure as determinants of alcohol consumption in male social drinkers. *Journal of Personality and Social Psychology, 44*, 1097–1109.

Hull, J. G., Young, R. D., & Jouriles, E. (1986). Applications of the self-awareness model of alcohol consumption: Predicting patterns of use and abuse. *Journal of Personality and Social Psychology, 51*, 790–796.

Ingram, R. E., Lumry, A. B., Cruet, D., & Sieber, W. (1987). Attentional processes in depressive disorders. *Cognitive Therapy and Research, 11*, 351–360.

Ingram, R. E., & Smith, T. S. (1984). Depression and internal versus external locus of attention. *Cognitive Therapy and Research, 8*, 139–152.

Kernis, M. H., Zuckerman, M., Cohen, A., & Spadofora, S. (1982). Persistence following failure: The interactive role of self-awareness and attributional bias for negative expectancies. *Journal of Personality and Social Psychology, 43*, 1184–1191.

Kuiper, N. A. (1978). Depression and causal attributions for success and failure. *Journal of Personality and Social Psychology, 36*, 236–246.

Lewinsohn, P. M., Hoberman, H., Teri, L., & Hautzinger, M. (1985). An integrative theory of depression. In S. Reiss & R. Bootzin (Eds.), *Theoretical issues in behavior therapy*. New York: Academic Press.

Linville, P. W. (1985). Self-complexity and affective extremity—don't put all your eggs in one cognitive basket. *Social Cognition, 3*, 94–120.

Linville, P. W. (1987). Self-complexity as a cognitive buffer against stress-related illness and depression. *Journal of Personality and Social Psychology, 54*, 663–676.

Lutz, D. J., & Snow, P. A. (1985). Understanding the role of depression in the alcoholic. *Clinical Psychology, 5*, 535–551.

Mandler, G., & Watson, D. L. (1966). Anxiety and the interruption of behavior. In C. D. Spielberger (Ed.), *Anxiety and behavior*. New York: Academic Press.

Marlatt, G. A., & Gordon, J. R. (1979). Determinants of relapse: Implications for the maintenance of behavior change. In D. Davidson (Ed.), *Behavioral medicine: Changing health lifestyles*. New York: Brunner/Mazel.

Marlett, N. J., & Watson, D. (1968). Test anxiety and immediate or delayed feedback in a test-like avoidance task. *Journal of Personality and Social Psychology, 8*, 200–203.

Mead, G. H. (1934). *Mind, self, and society from the standpoint of a social behaviorist*. Chicago: University of Chicago Press.

Mullen, B., & Suls, J. (1982). Know thyself: Stressful life changes and the ameliorative effect of private self-consciousness. *Journal of Experimental Social Psychology, 18*, 43–55.

Peace, K., & Mellsop, G. (1987). Alcoholism and psychiatric disorder. *Australian and New Zealand Journal of Psychiatry, 21*, 94–101.

Pennebaker, J. W., & Lightner, J. M. (1980). Competition of internal and external information in an exercise situation. *Journal of Personality and Social Psychology, 39*, 165–174.

Polivy, J., Herman, C. P., Hackett, R., & Kuleshnyk, I. (1986). The effects of self-attention and public attention on eating in restrained and unrestrained subjects. *Journal of Personality and Social Psychology, 50*, 1253–1260.

Pryor, J. B., Gibbons, F. X., Wicklund, R. A., Fazio, R. H., & Hood, R. (1977). Self-focused attention and self-report validity. *Journal of Personality, 45*, 513–527.

Pyszczynski, T., & Greenberg, J. (1985). Depression and preference for self-focusing stimuli following success and failure. *Journal of Personality and Social Psychology, 49*, 1066–1075.

Pyszczynski, T., & Greenberg, J. (1986). Evidence for a depressive self-focusing style. *Journal of Research in Personality, 20*, 95–106.

Pyszczynski, T., & Greenberg, J. (1987a). Self-regulatory perseveration and the depressive self-focusing style: A self-awareness theory of reactive depression. *Psychological Bulletin, 102*, 1–17.

Pyszczynski, T., & Greenberg, J. (1987b). Depression, self-focused attention, and self-regulatory perseveration. In C. R. Snyder & C. E. Ford (Eds.), *Coping with negative life events: Clinical and social psychological perspectives.* New York: Plenum Press.

Pyszczynski, T., Greenberg, J., Solomon, S., & Hamilton, J. (in press). A terror management analysis of self-awareness processes: The hierarchy of terror. *Anxiety Research.*

Pyszczynski, T., Hamilton, J., Herring, F., & Greenberg, J. (1989). Depression, self-focused attention and the negative memory bias. *Journal of Personality and Social Psychology, 57*, 351–357.

Pyszczynski, T., Holt, K., & Greenberg, J. (1987). Depression, self-focused attention and expectancies for future positive and negative events for self and others. *Journal of Personality and Social Psychology, 52*, 994–1001.

Rank, O. (1959). *The myth of the birth of the hero, and other writings.* New York: Vintage Books.

Rizley, R. (1978). Depression and distortion in the attribution of causality. *Journal of Abnormal Psychology, 87*, 32–48.

Russell, J. A., & Mehrabian, A. (1975). The mediating role of emotions in alcohol use. *Journal of Studies on Alcohol, 36*, 1508–1536.

Sanders, G. S. (1981). Driven by distraction: An integrative review of social facilitation theory and research. *Journal of Experimental Social Psychology, 17*, 227–251.

Sarason, I. (1975). Test anxiety and the self-disclosing coping model. *Journal of Consulting and Clinical Psychology, 43*, 148–153.

Schachter, S. (1964). The interaction of cognitive and physiological determinants of emotional state. In L. Berkowitz (Ed.), *Advances in experimental social psychology.* New York: Academic Press.

Scheier, M. F. (1976). Self-awareness, self-consciousness and angry aggression. *Journal of Personality, 44*, 627–644.

Scheier, M. F., & Carver, C. (1977). Self-focused attention and the experience of emotion: Attraction, repulsion, elation, and depression. *Journal of Personality and Social Psychology, 35*, 625–636.

Scheier, M. F., & Carver, C. S. (1980). Individual differences in self-concept and self-process. In D. M. Wegner & R. R. Vallacher (Eds.), *The self in social psychology.* New York: Oxford University Press.

Scheier, M. F., Carver, C. S., & Gibbons, F. X. (1981). Self-focused attention and reactions to fear. *Journal of Research in Personality, 15*, 1–15.

Scheier, M. F., Fenigstein, A., & Buss, A. H. (1974). Self-awareness and physical aggression. *Journal of Experimental Social Psychology, 10*, 264–273.

Schlenker, B. R., & Leary, M. R. (1982). Social anxiety and self-presentation: A conceptualization and model. *Psychological Bulletin, 92*, 641–669.

Shibutani, T. (1961). *Society and Personality: An interactionist approach to social psychology.* Englewood Cliffs, NJ: Prentice-Hall.

Slapion, M. J., & Carver, C. S. (1981). Self-directed attention and facilitation of intellectual performance among persons high in test anxiety. *Cognitive Therapy and Research, 5*, 115–121.

Smith, E. R., & Miller, F. D. (1979). Attributional information processing: A reaction time model of causal subtraction. *Journal of Personality and Social Psychology, 37*, 1723–1731.

Smith, T. W., & Greenberg, J. (1981). Depression and self-focused attention. *Motivation and Emotion, 5*, 323–331.

Smith, T. W., Ingram, R. E., & Roth, D. L. (1985). Self-focused attention and depression: Self-evaluation, affect, and life stress. *Motivation and Emotion, 9*, 323–331.

Snyder, C. R. (1989). Reality negotiation: From excuses to hope and beyond. *Journal of Social and Clinical Psychology, 8*, 130–157.

Solomon, S., Greenberg, J., & Pyszczynski, T. (in press). A terror management theory of self-esteem and its role in social behavior. In M. Zanna (Ed.), *Advances in experimental social psychology*. New York: Academic Press.

Steenbarger, B. N., & Aderman, D. (1979). Objective self-awareness as a nonaversive state: Effect of anticipating discrepancy reduction. *Journal of Personality, 47*, 330–334.

Strack, S., Blaney, P. H., Ganellen, R. J., & Coyne, J. C. (1985). Pessimistic self-preoccupation, performance deficits, and depression. *Journal of Personality and Social Psychology, 49*, 1076–1085.

Taylor, S. E., & Gammon, C. B. (1975). Effects of type and dose of alcohol on human physical aggression. *Journal of Personality and Social Psychology, 32*, 169–175.

Teasdale, J. D., & Rezin, V. (1978). The effects of reducing frequency of negative thoughts on the mood of depressed patients: Tests of a cognitive model of depression. *British Journal of Social and Clinical Psychology, 17*, 65–74.

Tellegen, A. (1985). Structures of mood and personality and their relevance to assessing anxiety, with an emphasis on self-report. In A. H. Tuma & J. D. Maser (Eds.), *Anxiety and the anxiety disorders* (pp. 681–706). Hillsdale, NJ: Lawrence Erlbaum Associates.

Turner, R. G. (1978a). Effects of differential request procedures and self-consciousness on trait attributions. *Journal of Research in Personality, 12*, 431–438.

Turner, R. G. (1978b). Self-consciousness and speed of processing of self-relevant information. *Personality and Social Psychology Bulletin, 4*, 456–460.

Tversky, & Kahneman. (1973). Availability: A heuristic for judging frequency and probability. *Cognitive Psychology, 5*, 207–232.

Vallacher, R. R., & Wegner, D. M. (1985). *A theory of action identification*. Hillsdale, NJ: Lawrence Erlbaum Associates.

Velton, E. (1968). A laboratory task for induction of mood states. *Behavior Research and Therapy, 6*, 473–482.

Weiner, B., Frieze, I., Kukla, A., Reed, L., Rest, B., & Rosenbaum, R. (1971). *Perceiving the causes of success and failure*. Morristown, NJ: General Learning Press.

Whitters, A. C., Cadoret, R. J., & McCalley, M. K. (1987). Further evidence for heterogeneity in anti-social alcoholics. *Comprehensive Psychology, 28*, 513–519.

Wicklund, R. (1975). Objective self-awareness. In L. Berkowitz (Ed.), *Advances in experimental social psychology* (Vol. 8). New York: Academic Press.

Wilson, G. T. (1988). Alcohol and anxiety. *Behavior Research and Therapy, 26*, 369–381.

Wine, J. D. (1979). Test anxiety and direction of attention. *Psychological Bulletin, 76*, 92–104.

Wine, J. D. (1980). Cognitive-attentional theory of test anxiety. In I. G. Sarason (Ed.), *Test anxiety: Theory, research, and applications*. Hillsdale, NJ: Lawrence Erlbaum Associates.

Yalom, I. D. (1980). *Existential psychotherapy*. New York: Basic Books.

CHAPTER 9

ACCURACY AND BIAS IN SELF-KNOWLEDGE

Jonathon D. Brown

Life is the art of being well-deceived; and in order that the deception may succeed it must be habitual and uninterrupted. (William Hazlitt, 1817)

Hazlitt's prescription for happiness notwithstanding, most observers of human nature have maintained that a reliance on deception negatively affects well-being. Indeed, many theorists have regarded the ability to view the self and the world accurately as the sine qua non of psychological health. However intuitive and venerable this notion might be, a good deal of the recent research has failed to support the view that psychological well-being is characterized by the complete absence of distortion. Instead, accumulating evidence indicates that nearly all individuals, and particularly those who score highest on measures of psychological adjustment, exhibit a pervasive tendency to view the self and their world in a more positive way than can realistically be justified (Lazarus, 1983; Sackeim, 1983; Taylor & Brown, 1988). Moreover, rather than undermining health, these *illusions*, as they have been referred to else-where (Taylor & Brown, 1988), appear to contribute to effective functioning, and also to foster well-being.

In this chapter, the self-enhancing nature of individuals' self-peceptions and the role that these perceptions play in promoting health will be considered. To begin, the structure and nature of the self-concept will be outlined. A number of theoretical perspectives that have emphasized the need for accurate self-knowledge will then be critically reviewed. Subsequently, the evidence that pertains to the illusory nature of individuals' self-conceptions will be presented, and the relation between self-enhancing illusions and adjustment will be discussed. Next, a number of mechanisms, both intrapersonal and social in origin, that enable individuals to maintain self-enhancing illusions will be considered. Finally, some additional issues, including the relation between illusions and defense mechanisms, and the practical implications of the present analysis will be explored.

THE SELF

As it is used in this chapter, the term "the self" refers to a cognitive structure that incorporates all of the ways in which a person characteristically answers the question, "Who am I?" This usage corresponds to what James (1890) referred to as the self-as-known, or the "me." Throughout this paper, however, the self also is viewed as being actively involved in the processing of personal information. Thus, here the self is also taken to include self-as-knower, or the "I" in James's scheme. These dual aspects of the self are joined in what Markus (1977; Markus & Wurf, 1987) has labeled self-schemata.

An individual's answers to "Who am I?" typically fall into three broad categories (Gordon, 1968; Rosenberg, 1979). First, there are one's physical attributes (e.g., "I am a man"). Second, there are one's *social identities*. These identities are usually expressed as nouns and include the various formal and informal social roles that individuals occupy. They may refer to either ascribed (e.g., "I am a son") or attained (e.g., "I am a professor") roles or statuses. Finally, there are aspects of identity that are more individualistic in nature. These *personal identities* tend to be adjectival and include (a) one's perceived traits and dispositions (e.g., "I am impatient"); (b) one's presumed talents and abilities (e.g., "I am athletic"); and (c) one's attitudes, values, and interests (e.g., "I am an ardent environmentalist"). Together, physical characteristics and social and personal identities comprise the content of the self, or the self-concept.

When defined in this manner the self can be said to reflect individuals' subjective perceptions of who they are and of what they are like. These perceptions may or may not coincide with some objective measure. That is, a person's picture of the self (i.e., the self-concept) may or may not correspond closely to the "actual" self (i.e., the self as defined by some consensual or normative criteria). This is particularly true with respect to one's personal identities. That is, although there is generally little dispute regarding one's physical characteristics and social identities, one's personal identities are more open to interpretation. A student who earns high grades in her classes may nonetheless view herself as unintelligent and inadequate. Alternatively, an individual who conceives of himself as genteel and refined may actually be regarded by others as boorish and crude.

Given these possibilities, one may ask, What is the proper relation between the perceived self and the actual self? In particular, do well-adjusted, emotionally healthy individuals possess views of the self that closely parallel the actual self? Before turning to an empirical examination of this issue, it will be useful to first consider various theoretical perspectives on the matter. As will be seen, although they differ in many important respects, these perspectives share a common element: they all agree that individuals ought to and/or need to possess views of the self that are largely accurate and free of distortion.

Accuracy and Self-Knowledge

For centuries, philosophers, theologians, sages, and poets have enjoined us to look beneath the shroud of illusion and confront the self as it actually is. This injunction is embodied in the ancient dictum, "Know thyself," which has been attributed to Plato, Pythagoras, and Socrates, among others (see Gergen, 1971). The search for accurate self-knowledge appears to be encouraged for two reasons. First, self-understanding is championed on moral grounds. This perspective, which was initially advocated by early theologians and was later taken up by the existentialist philosophers (e.g., Nietzsche, Kierkegaard, Sartre), holds that individuals have an obligation to come to terms with their true nature; those who evade self-understanding are considered weak and cowardly and are perceived as living a depraved or purposeless existence (cf. Martin, 1985).

A second reason why individuals are urged to acquire veridical self-knowledge is for functional purposes. According to this view, successful commerce with the world requires a healthy measure of self-understanding. Indeed, legend has it that the need to "know thyself" was viewed with such supreme importance that this statement was inscribed on the Delphic oracle, a place where Kings allegedly came for guidance in matters of law, war, and the like.

In more recent years, the belief that accurate self-knowledge is essential for effective functioning has been embraced by psychiatrists, and personality and clinical psychologists. Somewhat paradoxically, with all of its emphasis on irrationality and distortion, Freudian theory represents one such view. Freud (1915/1957) believed that in their efforts to accommodate unacceptable instinctual impulses to the inexorable demands of the external world, individuals engage in self-deception in which their feelings, wishes, and desires are distorted or denied. The inevitable consequence of this self-deception is psychopathology. Consequently, the goal of psychoanalysis is to minimize distortion and reduce self-deception. Although Freud was never particularly sanguine about the possibility that individuals could achieve accurate self-knowledge, he was adamant in his belief that the price of self-deception was neurosis (see Sackeim, 1983, for a further discussion of these issues).

Other theorists also have endorsed the principle that psychological health depends on accurate self-knowledge. Jahoda (1958), for example, defined the mentally healthy person as one who is capable of perceiving the self as it actually is, without distorting one's perceptions to fit one's wishes. Similarly, Maslow (1950) wrote that healthy individuals are able to accept themselves and their own nature, with all of its discrepancies from their ideal image. Other psychologists (e.g., Allport, 1943; Erikson, 1950; Fromm, 1955; Haan, 1977; Menninger, 1963; Rogers, 1951) also have proposed that emotional well-being and accurate self-perception go hand in hand. Many of the so-called insight therapies these theorists helped develop are based on the principle that lasting therapeutic change can be achieved only when individuals come to view the self as it actually is.

In sum, though not the only view of mental health (e.g., Becker, 1973; Rank, 1936), many prominent theorists from the fields of psychiatry and personality and clinical psychology have asserted that the capacity to perceive the self, and the self's ability to act on the environment, without distortion are essential requirements for effective functioning. In some respects it is easy to see how such a perspective developed. Psychiatrists and clinical psychologists most often study abnormal behavior. Thus, the data base on which this view of mental health rests is comprised of individuals who experience a variety of pathologies. Some of these individuals suffer from severe psychoses, such as manic depression, schizophrenia, and the like. These conditions may be characterized by views of the self that are wholly without foundation in reality. For example, in the midst of a manic episode, an individual may believe that he has the power of a Napolean or the charms of a Valentino. These beliefs provide compelling evidence that distorted views of the self can be unhealthy. It is tempting, therefore, to conclude that accurate perceptions of the self must be necessary for normal functioning. However, the logic underlying this inference process is faulty: The fact that mental illness is sometimes characterized by gross distortions of the self does not necessarily mean that mental health is characterized by the absence of distortion.

The broader issue here is that the study of abnormal behavior may not provide the best perspective on what normal behavior is like (cf. Baumeister, 1989; Snyder, 1989). Indeed, it seems arguable that if one wants to know what normal behavior is like, one ought to study normal individuals (i.e., individuals who are free from psychopathology). For the most part, this is the domain of social and health psychologists. Thus, one can ask, What does research in these disciplines reveal regarding the relation between the perceived self and the actual self?

Although still incomplete in some respects, the portrait that emerges from decades of research in these and allied fields is not one that stresses the absolute accuracy of self-perceptions. Instead, normal individuals appear to consistently bias their self-perceptions in a self-enhancing direction (Taylor & Brown, 1988). Three such tendencies are particularly evident: (a) individuals harbor unrealistically positive views of the self; (b) individuals exaggerate their ability to control environmental events, including events that are objectively uncontrollable; and (c) individuals are overly optimistic in that their beliefs about their future are brighter than can realistically be justified. In the sections that follow, the evidence pertaining to each of these illusions is reviewed.

Self-Enhancing Illusions

Unrealistically Positive Views of the Self

As previously noted, traditional conceptions of mental health maintain that well-adjusted individuals are aware of, and accepting of, both the positive and negative aspects of self. In contrast to this assertion, evidence indicates that most individuals conceive of the self in terms that are overwhelmingly more positive than negative. That is, nearly all individuals believe that they possess far more positively valued than negatively valued characteristics (Brown, 1986; Brown & Gallagher, 1990; Dunning, Meyerowitz, & Holzberg, 1989).

By itself, this imbalance does not provide evidence that such views are unrealistic or illusory.

After all, most individuals may possess more positive than negative qualities. Evidence for the illusory nature of such beliefs does exist, however. First, nearly all individuals show a pervasive tendency to see the self as "better" than others. They judge positive attributes to be more descriptive of the self than of the average person, but see negative attributes as less descriptive of the self than of the average person (Brown, 1986; Brown & Gallagher, 1990; Dunning et al., 1989). Moreover, far from being limited in scope, this self-other bias (Brown, 1986) has been documented for a wide range of traits and abilities (Alicke, 1985; Dunning et al., 1989). Insofar as it is logically impossible for most people to be better than the average person, these highly skewed, positive views of the self provide evidence for their unrealistic and illusory nature.

The overly positive manner in which individuals view the self also extends to appraisals of their friends and intimates. Specifically, although the tendency to see the self as better than others is attenuated when the others being evaluated are close friends or relatives, there exists a corresponding tendency for individuals to see their companions as better than average (Brown, 1986). Moreover, these effects at the individual level also occur at the group level. Even under the most minimal of social conditions, there is a pervasive tendency for individuals to see their own group as better than other groups (Brown, Collins, & Schmidt, 1988; for a review, see Tajfel & Turner, 1986). Thus, although research also demonstrates a general positivity bias in person-perception (Sears, 1983), individuals are inclined to appraise their friends, family, and own group members in far more positive and less negative terms than they appraise most other people. Again, because it is logically impossible for most people's associates to be better than average, this tendency may be regarded as illusory.

A second source of evidence pertaining to the illusory nature of positive self-perceptions comes from investigations that have compared self-ratings with judgments made by observers. Lewinsohn, Mischel, Chaplin, and Barton (1980) had observers watch subjects complete a group interaction task. Observers then rated each subject along a number of personality dimensions (e.g., friendly, warm, assertive); subjects also rated themselves along each of the attributes. The results showed that self-ratings were significantly more positive than were the observers' ratings. In

other words, individuals saw themselves in more flattering terms than they were seen by others (see also Gotlib & Meltzer, 1987).

In sum, the perception of self that most individuals hold is not as well balanced as traditional models of mental health suggest. Rather than being attentive to both the favorable and unfavorable aspects of self, normal individuals appear to be very cognizant of their strengths and assets and considerably less aware of their weaknesses and faults. Evidence that these flattering self-portrayals are illusory comes from studies that have found that (a) most individuals see themselves (and their intimates) as better than the average person, and (b) most individuals see themselves as better than they are seen by others (Taylor & Brown, 1988).

Illusions of Control

Illusory beliefs regarding the positivity of the self are accompanied by a second illusion; namely, an exaggerated belief in one's ability to control the environment. Several lines of research from the areas of human learning, social, and clinical psychology suggest that individuals often believe that they can control events, even when the events are entirely determined by chance (for a review, see Abramson & Alloy, 1980). Moreover, this illusion of control (Langer, 1975) is particularly evident when desirable outcomes are obtained (Alloy & Abramson, 1979; Greenwald, 1980). Thus, although accurate knowledge of the relation between one's actions and environmental outcomes would seem to be essential for effective functioning, a good deal of evidence suggests that people overestimate the degree to which their actions produce environmental events, especially when these events are positive in valence.

Unrealistic Optimism

The belief that one is good and that one can control events gives rise to a third self-enhancing illusion. This illusion may be termed unrealistic optimism. Simply put, most people believe that their future will be brighter than base rate data can justify. People estimate the likelihood that they will experience a wide variety of pleasant events, such as liking their first job, getting a good salary, or having a gifted child, as higher than those of their peers (Weinstein, 1980). Conversely, when asked their chances of experiencing a wide variety of negative events, including having an automobile accident (Robertson, 1977), being a crime victim (Perloff & Fetzer, 1986), having trouble finding a job (Weinstein, 1980), or becoming ill (Perloff & Fetzer, 1986; Weinstein, 1982) or depressed (Kuiper & MacDonald, 1982), most people believe that they are less likely than their peers to experience such negative events. Insofar as everyone's future cannot logically be rosier than average, the extreme optimism individuals display appears to be illusory.

It should be noted that beliefs in personal control and perceptions of the future need not always involve self-referent cognitions. However, many times they do. For example, with respect to perceptions of control, many theorists have argued that a sense of agency is integral to the self-concept (White, 1959). When subjects overestimate their control over objectively uncontrollable outcomes, they seem tacitly to be saying, "I am efficacious." Similarly, although beliefs about the future do not always center around the self, Markus and Nurius' (1986) work on possible selves suggests that individuals' notions of the future are often wedded to their thoughts about the self. For these reasons, then, like overly positive views of the self, illusions of control and unrealistic optimism are treated as self-referent cognitions in the present paper.

Self-Enhancing Illusions and Psychological Adjustment

The previous discussion documents that most individuals harbor unrealistically positive views of the self, their ability to control events in their lives, and their future. These findings seem to be at odds with the claim that accurate self-perceptions are necessary for effective functioning. However, evidence relating illusions to adjustment has yet to be presented. If, for instance, the illusions documented above were found to be more prevalent among individuals who are psychologically distressed than among those who score high on measures of psychological adjustment, traditional notions of mental health would be upheld.

Illusions and Depression

A useful point of departure for addressing this issue is to examine the relation between illusions and the depressive disorders. Although not the only form of psychopathology, depression is far and away the most common. According to some estimates, depression accounts for 75% of all psychiatric hospitalizations and at any given time, 15% of the adult population suffers from depressive symptoms (cited in Abramson & Martin, 1981). If self-enhancing illusions are detrimental to psychological health, they should be positively linked to depression.

In fact, an examination of the association between illusions and depression suggests that just the opposite is true. A good deal of research subsumed under the rubric of "depressive realism" has found that self-enhancing illusions are relatively absent among depressed people (Alloy & Abramson, 1988). Specifically, compared with nondepressed people, those who are moderately or severely depressed (a) are relatively more attentive to the self's positive and negative qualities (Kuiper & MacDonald, 1982); (b) display greater congruence between self-evaluations and evaluations of others (Ahrens, Zeiss, & Kanfer, 1988; Kuiper & MacDonald, 1982); and (c) offer self-appraisals that coincide more with those of objective observers (e.g., Lewinsohn et al., 1980). Additionally, they are less likely to fall prey to an illusion of control (Alloy & Abramson, 1979; Golin, Terrell, & Johnson, 1977; Golin, Terrell, Weitz, & Drost, 1979) and are less apt to display unrealistic optimism about the future (Alloy & Ahrens, 1987; Pyszczynski, Holt, & Greenberg, 1987). In short, relative to nondepressed people, depressives tend to show more balanced and/or accurate perceptions of the self, the degree to which their responses control environmental outcomes, and their future. These findings, which are somewhat inconsistent with traditional cognitive models of depression (e.g., Beck's [1967] notion of the negative cognitive triad), pose a challenge to the claim that accurate self-knowledge is linked to psychological health.

Other areas of research offer additional evidence that accurate self-views may be linked to depression and other forms of psychological distress (i.e., neuroticism, anxiety, low self-esteem). The Self-Deception Questionnaire (Sackeim & Gur, 1979) measures the degree to which individuals typically deny psychologically threatening but universally true statements (e.g., "Do you ever feel guilty?"). High scores on this scale have been found to be negatively related to depression and neuroticism (Roth & Ingram, 1985; Sackeim, 1983). The fact that individuals who are most prone to engage in self-deception also score lowest on some measures of psychopathology further suggests that accurate self-knowledge may not be essential for mental health.

Conceptually similar findings come from research on the correlates of private self-consciousness (Fenigstein, Scheier, & Buss, 1975). Private self-consciousness refers to the degree to which a person characteristically attends to the private, covert aspects of the self (e.g., "I'm always trying to figure myself out"). People who are high in private self-consciousness (i.e., those who are generally attentive to these aspects of the self) have been shown to possess more detailed and accurate self-knowledge than those who are low in private self-consciousness (Franzoi, 1983; Turner, 1978). Research also has found that private self-consciousness is positively related to depression (Ingram & Smith, 1984; Smith & Greenberg, 1981; Smith, Ingram, & Roth, 1985). In other words, those who "know" themselves best score highest on measures of affective distress.

In sum, self-enhancing illusions are more characteristic of psychologically healthy individuals (i.e., those who are nondepressed, low in neuroticism) than they are of individuals who are less well adjusted. In some cases, the absence of self-enhancing illusions on the part of distressed individuals may reflect undue pessimism and self-deprecation. Nonetheless, there is scant evidence that psychologically healthy individuals are less biased or more accurate in their self-perceptions than are those who suffer from some of the most common forms of psychological distress. Consequently, there is little evidence that evenhanded and realistic perceptions of self are essential for mental health.

Illusions and Achievement

Although emotional well-being is certainly an important component of mental health, it is not the only element of psychological adjustment. Another important constituent of adjustment is the capacity for creative and productive work. Interestingly, illusions also have been linked to success in the achievement domain. A number of studies have shown that individuals who approach intellectual or creative tasks with a belief in their ability, an attitude that such tasks can be mastered, and a high expectancy of success perform better than do those who display an absence of these tendencies (e.g., Bandura & Schunk, 1981; Baumeister, Hamilton, & Tice, 1985; Feather, 1966). Moreover, these effects occur even when objective assessments of ability indicate that those

who exhibit positive self-relevant cognitions are no more able than are those who display an absence of such tendencies (Dweck & Leggett, 1988). Thus, under some conditions, the belief that one can succeed is a better predictor of success than is actual ability level.

The positive relation between illusions and achievement appears to be most evident for tasks of moderate or high difficulty and is mediated by several factors. First, individuals with high self-perceptions of ability adopt more efficient problem-solving strategies than do those who harbor doubts about their ability to succeed (Bandura, 1989; Dweck & Leggett, 1988). Second, whereas individuals who are confident in their abilities are able to keep their attention focused on the task at hand, the attention of those with low self-perceptions of ability tends to wander toward task-irrelevant cognitions that serve to undermine performance (Sarason, 1975). Third, individuals with positive self-views and a belief in their abilities tend to work harder and persist longer at difficult tasks than do those with negative self-views; consequently, they perform better, particularly after prior failure (Bandura, 1989; Felson, 1984; Shrauger & Sorman, 1977). Because nearly all important goals in life entail periodic setbacks and thus require that obstacles to goal attainment be surmounted, it follows that individuals with positive self-views will reach higher levels of achievement in the real world. Although the evidence here is sparse, an investigation by Mortimer and Lorence (1979) supports this conjecture (see also Bachman & O'Malley, 1977). Finally, it is important to note that perseverance can sometimes be maladaptive, as when one endlessly persists at a task that is truly intractable (Janoff-Bulman & Brickman, 1982). Here again, however, the advantage may lie with those who possess positive views of the self. Individuals with positive self-conceptions appear to be most sensitive to the conditions under which persistence will and will not pay dividends (Janoff-Bulman & Brickman, 1982; McFarlin, 1985; Sandelands, Brockner, & Glynn, 1988; [see also Baumeister & Tice, 1985; McFarlin, Baumeister, & Blascovich, 1984]).

The associations between illusions and achievement are particularly interesting because they contradict the widespread belief that individuals need to know their true ability level in order to maximize their outcomes in life. Although drastically overestimating one's ability can certainly beget disappointment and failure, performance does not solely (or even predominantly) depend on ability. Instead, achievement-outcomes typically depend on a host of other factors, including the particular strategies one uses, and how hard and how long one tries. As just noted, beliefs in one's ability have been shown to be positively related to all of these factors. That is, in achievement-related situations, high self-perceptions of ability are linked to the use of more effective strategies and to greater motivation and persistence (Bandura, 1989). Although the presence of these factors does not guarantee that success will be realized, their existence almost assuredly results in a higher level of goal attainment than would be possible in their absence. Thus, positive perceptions of one's ability, even if somewhat illusory, may actually enable individuals to maximize their likelihood of attaining important goals.

Summary

In this section the link between self-enhancing illusions and psychological adjustment has been reviewed. In some cases further research is needed. But the bulk of the evidence indicates that self-enhancing illusions are associated with superior psychological functioning. Individuals who possess positive views of the self, a steadfast belief in their ability to control events, and a positive view of the future are less apt to be depressed than are those who fail to exhibit such beliefs. They also are more apt to succeed at achievement-related activities. Thus, far from undermining psychological health, the evidence suggests that self-enhancing illusions are positively related to well-being and adjustment.

MAINTAINING ILLUSIONS

As we have documented the prevalence of self-enhancing illusions and considered their relation to psychological health, many readers may well be wondering at this point how individuals are able to harbor illusions with apparent impunity. Even in the most benign of worlds, it would seem that people would occasionally have to put their self-enhancing beliefs to a test. In other words, doesn't reality intrude on one's private musings, at least from time to time?

At the risk of being glib, the first answer to this question is "it depends." More specifically, it depends on how we define reality. In his analysis of this issue, Watzlawick (1976) distinguished between two aspects of the term. The first may be

called *perceptive reality*; this facet refers to the sensory perception of the objective and tangible property of objects and events. The second may be called *interpretive reality*; this facet refers to the subjective meaning individuals ascribe to these objects and events. The critical difference between these terms is their relative verifiability. Although our perceptions of physical reality generally are subject to confirmation, our interpretations of reality remain very much in the realm of subjectivity. To illustrate, whether I am writing a paragraph can be verified with relative ease; whether I am writing an exceptionally insightful paragraph, however, is very much open to interpretation. Thus, when speaking of the inevitable intrusion of reality, one must distinguish between perceptive reality and interpretive reality. Whereas individuals are constrained in their perceptions of physical reality, they are relatively free to construct their own interpretive reality.

For the most part, the illusions we have considered involve matters of interpretive reality, not ones of perceptive reality. Notions of how compassionate, kind, and courageous we are, for example, are not subject to verification. Objective measures of compassion do not exist; standardized tests of kindness await development. Nor can one simply refer to a class of behaviors to define a person's standing on attributes like these. For some, race car driving may represent the essence of courage; for others, it constitutes the epitome of foolishness and immaturity. Neither of these interpretations can be considered inaccurate because there is no absolute standard of accuracy against which they can be measured. Given the inherently subjective nature of traits such as these, individuals have more or less free rein to define their standing on many, if not most, personal attributes (Dunning et al., 1989). In a large sense, then, the indeterminate nature of social reality promotes the use of self-enhancing illusions.

One implication of the preceding analysis is that self-enhancing illusions ought to be more evident for relatively ambiguous attributes than for attributes that are more easily subject to verification. An investigation by Felson (1981) supports this conjecture. Felson had college football players rate themselves on a number of attributes relevant to performance in football; the players' coaches also evaluated the players along these dimensions. Some of the abilities (e.g., speed, size) were considered relatively unambiguous and verifiable insofar as clear standards exist for assessing one's standing on these attributes (speed can be measured, for instance). The remaining abilities (e.g., mental toughness, football sense) were deemed to be more ambiguous and subjective in nature insofar as one's standing on these measures cannot easily be determined. The prediction was that the player's estimates would be more likely to exceed the coaches' on the ambiguous attributes than on the unambiguous attributes. This prediction was confirmed (see also Dunning et al., 1989). Thus, people's self-appraisals may remain relatively close to the "data" with respect to attributes that are easily subject to verification, while their most aggrandizing self-assessments are reserved for attributes that are more subjective in nature.

But what about those attributes that are capable of objective verification? How, for example, are the majority of people able to cling to the belief that they are above average in intelligence when standardized test scores and the like seem readily available to potentially convince them otherwise? Research suggests that individuals are able to sustain favorable self-perceptions like these by closely adhering to three general strategies. These involve (a) behavioral strategies that minimize the likelihood that negative self-relevant feedback will be encountered; (b) cognitive strategies that lessen the probability that negative feedback, when encountered, will be registered or perceived as implicating the self; and (c) "damage control" strategies that reduce the chances that negative feedback, when encountered and acknowledged, will impact negatively on overall feelings of self-worth. The nature of these strategies is explored in the ensuing sections.

Behavioral Strategies for Avoiding Negative Feedback

The first class of strategies to be discussed comprises behavioral attempts to ensure exposure to negative feedback will be minimal. This goal can be achieved either (a) by selective exposure to positive feedback or (b) by taking active efforts to ensure that the causes of negative outcomes are ambiguous.

Selective Exposure to Favorable Feedback

One way individuals would be able to sustain their self-enhancing beliefs would be to arrange matters so that negative self-relevant feedback is never encountered. However, completely insulat-

ing oneself from receiving negative feedback is doomed to be maladaptive. An individual who remained entirely oblivious to his lack of ability in some domain would be condemned to experience repeated failure in that aspect of life. A more modest, but infinitely more adaptive, strategy would be to approach positive self-relevant information more vigorously than negative self-relevant information. In this manner, the preponderance of the feedback one received would be positive, but negative feedback, though not actively sought, would still be encountered from time to time.

Evidence supporting just such a biased pattern of information-seeking behavior has been uncovered (e.g., Brown, in press; Frey & Stahlberg, 1986; Pyszczynski, Greenberg, & LaPrelle, 1985). For example, Brown (in press; Study 1) first gave subjects success, failure, or no feedback on a pretest. Subsequently, they were given the opportunity to learn more about their ability level by choosing to work on one of two tests during the second part of the experiment. One of the tests allegedly provided subjects with immediate performance feedback, whereas feedback was allegedly unavailable for a second task. The prediction was that individuals would seek self-relevant feedback less actively when they expected to receive unfavorable as opposed to favorable information. As anticipated, the tendency to choose the test yielding performance feedback was significantly less pronounced among subjects who anticipated finding out that their ability was low (i.e., those who had experienced prior failure) than among those who expected to succeed. In a subsequent study, this ambivalence toward gaining negative information concerning one's abilities was not found to depend on differential perceptions of test validity or negative mood states. Nor did this information-seeking strategy merely represent a desire to maintain a public image of competency in the eyes of others: Further investigation found that this tendency was more prevalent under private conditions than under public conditions. Collectively, the findings suggest that individuals may actively approach feedback about their abilities when they expect it to be positive but largely refrain from seeking feedback about their abilities when they expect it to be negative. This pattern of information-seeking ensures that most of the information they receive about their abilities will be favorable.

At first blush, these findings seem inconsistent with prior research regarding self-evaluation of abilities in achievement settings. Several investigations have found that when subjects are offered a choice between tasks that vary in their informational value, most subjects choose tasks that provide them with the most ability-relevant information (for a review, see Trope, 1986). These findings have been interpreted to indicate that individuals seek information about their abilities without regard to whether this information is apt to be positive or negative (Trope, 1986). However, most prior studies have not given sufficient attention to the fact that the vast majority of subjects believe that they have high ability, and thus expect to succeed at the target task. Consequently, like those subjects who recently experienced success in the Brown (in press) studies, the preference they have shown for tasks of high informational value is easily understood as representing a desire to confirm an image of competency and gain additional favorable information about the self.

Two additional points about selective exposure to positive feedback are worth noting. First, avoidance of negative feedback is not always obvious or deliberate (Greenwald, 1988). Oftentimes individuals may believe that they possess some ability or talent but are not sure. They can evade finding out whether the ability is truly present or not by avoiding situations that call for its display (Shrauger, 1982). For instance, suppose that in the privacy of his mind (or shower) an individual believes that his singing voice is second only to Sinatra's. By judiciously avoiding situations that call for public singing, he would never have to put this belief to a test. As a result, he would forever be free to cling to the belief that he is a spellbinding vocalist.

Second, it is important to acknowledge that individuals do often seek out purely diagnostic feedback on aspects of the self that are modifiable. Many of us routinely send our manuscripts to others for comments, or ask our colleagues for help in polishing a talk before delivering an important colloquium. Although, to some extent, this practice probably stems from an expectation that the remarks we receive will be favorable, it also reflects a genuine desire to improve the quality of our work. But seeking feedback about the products of one's ability is not the same as seeking feedback about one's ability per se. Whereas one's work is subject to modification and improvement, one's abilities are relatively fixed. Consequently, though we may ask for feedback on what we have produced, few of us ever ask our colleagues to tell us whether they truly think we possess the intellec-

tual ability to make a contribution to the field, whether we have any innate ability as a writer, and so forth.

Self-Handicapping Strategies

Of course, individuals do not always avoid diagnostic situations; nor can they. A student who is doing poorly in a course, for example, typically does not have the luxury of choosing whether or not to take the final exam if the class is one that is required for his major. Although in such situations a negative outcome may be inevitable, individuals may be able to control the degree to which the negative outcome implicates central aspects of the self. They may do so, according to Berglas and Jones (1978), by engaging in *self-handicapping strategies*. Interestingly, these strategies entail erecting self-induced barriers to performance in order to ambiguate the cause of an anticipated negative outcome. The student who fears that his test performance will be less than exemplary may sabotage his performance by not studying for the impending exam. If he receives the poor grade he expects, lack of effort provides a ready cause of failure; the extent to which the negative outcome reveals low ability is therefore obfuscated. Moreover, if by chance he should succeed, lack of effort provides persuasive evidence of high ability. After all, who but a veritable genius could succeed when saddled with the impediment of insufficient preparation?

To test whether individuals engage in self-handicapping behaviors when failure is anticipated, Berglas and Jones (1978) first led some male subjects to believe that they were likely to succeed on an upcoming test; others were given sufficient reason to believe that future success was unlikely. All subjects were then told that the second part of the experiment involved testing the effects of two new drugs on test performance. One of the drugs purportedly facilitated test performance, the other supposedly impaired performance. The subjects were then given a choice as to which drug they wished to ingest. Consistent with the notion that individuals will take active efforts to sabotage their performance when future success is improbable, subjects who believed that success was unlikely were most apt to select the performance-inhibiting drug. These findings suggest that in at least some situations where negative feedback is unavoidable, individuals actively ensure that failure does not implicate valued aspects of the self (i.e., low ability). In this manner, they are able to cling to an image of competency even when negative outcomes are encountered.

Extensions to Social Behavior

Thus far, only intrapersonal information-seeking strategies have been discussed. However, each of the tendencies reviewed above has parallels in the interpersonal domain. With respect to selective exposure to favorable feedback, research indicates that individuals gravitate toward social relationships in which their interaction partners view them in a manner that is consistent with how they see themselves (Swann, 1987). Because most people have positive self-views, most choose to associate with others who also view them positively. This ensures that most of the interpersonal feedback that they receive will be favorable (cf. Rosenberg, 1979). Even in situations where people must interact with others who hold views of them that are discrepant from their own, they may be able to orchestrate the interaction so that their partners are virtually forced to confirm their self-views (Swann & Hill, 1982). Again, because most people hold favorable views of the self, these constraining interaction strategies mean that predominantly positive feedback about the self will be encountered. Finally, self-handicapping strategies are relevant to the affiliative domain. A suitor who fears rejection may wait until the last minute to call his intended for a date. If his advances meet with the rejection he anticipates, he can attribute the negative outcome to his failure to call early enough, rather than to more central aspects of the self (e.g., an obnoxious personality). Other social factors that are not specifically related to information-seeking patterns also maximize the likelihood that individuals receive mostly positive feedback from their interaction partners. For instance, although people are generally reluctant to give interpersonal feedback, they are especially disinclined to do so when feedback is negative (e.g., Blumberg, 1972; Tesser & Rosen, 1975). Normative standards like these ensure that most of the feedback we receive from others is favorable.

Cognitive Strategies for Coping with Negative Feedback

Direct avoidance of negative feedback and self-handicapping strategies may be considered proactive behavioral tactics that individuals deploy to lessen the likelihood that negative feedback about the self will be encountered. However, because these strategies are used only when negative feedback is anticipated, they do not guarantee that self-deflating feedback can be evaded entirely. Oftentimes negative feedback is unexpected, as when one anticipates victory but tastes defeat. Under such conditions, do individuals passively resign themselves to receiving negative feedback?

Clearly not! Instead, they rely on a series of cognitive strategies to either color the feedback they receive or, at the very least, cushion the adverse impact of negative feedback. These strategies involve selectivity in how individuals interpret, attend to, remember, and explain evaluative feedback. The evidence relating to each of these tendencies is briefly summarized below.

Selective Interpretation

In many evaluative situations the feedback one receives is somewhat ambiguous. Suppose, after a good night kiss on the doorstep, one's date remarks, "Well, I can say in all honesty that I've never been kissed like *that* before." Whether this is the grandest of compliments or a monumental put-down is not entirely clear. Given this latitude, individuals are free to interpret ambiguous feedback in a benign manner if they are so inclined. An investigation by Dykman and Volpicelli (1983) suggests that many individuals are so inclined. On each of 40 trials, these researchers gave subjects either success, failure, or ambiguous feedback regarding their task performance. Through the course of the experiment, nondepressed subjects increasingly came to interpret ambiguous feedback as positive feedback. Interestingly, this bias was not present among depressed subjects.

Selective Attention

Even in situations where the feedback one receives is relatively unambiguous, there generally exists a mixture of good news and bad news. For example, even manuscripts that meet with rejection typically come back with reviews that include perfunctory plaudits regarding the paper's organization or writing style and obligatory remarks concerning the potential for publication in another journal. By selectively attending to these favorable comments, individuals can cognitively "snatch victory from the jaws of defeat."

Somewhat surprisingly, there is little evidence directly testing whether individuals selectively attend to positive feedback (but see Mischel, Ebbesen, & Zeiss, 1973; Roth & Rehm, 1980, for exceptions). There is, however, a good deal of evidence that individuals selectively attend to information that is congruent with their expectations (for a review, see Fiske & Taylor, 1984), and this includes expectancies that implicate the self (Swann & Read, 1981). Considering that most people have positive self-views and expect positive outcomes, these general findings suggest that most people selectively attend to positive self-relevant information.

Selective Memory

In addition to biases in interpretation and attention, individuals also can influence the nature of the feedback they receive by differentially recalling performance feedback. If after giving a presentation one remembers all of the compliments one received but few of the criticisms, one might easily conclude that the presentation was a resounding success (Gilbert & Cooper, 1985). In line with this notion, research indicates that most people, and particularly those who are nondepressed or high in self-esteem, exhibit better memory for positive feedback than for negative feedback (Johnson, Petzel, Hartney, & Morgan, 1983; Mischel, Ebbesen, & Zeiss, 1976; for a review, see Greenwald, 1980).

Selective Attributions

A final strategy for limiting negative feedback is to acknowledge its existence but deny its implications. One of the most reliable findings in social psychology over the last 20 years has been a pervasive tendency on the part of most individuals to accept greater personal responsibility for success than for failure (for reviews, see Snyder, Higgins, & Stucky, 1983; Taylor & Brown, 1988; Zuckerman, 1979). In particular, whereas positive outcomes are typically attributed to stable, central aspects of the self (e.g., "I received a high test grade because I am smart"), negative outcomes tend to be attributed to external factors (e.g., "I received a low test grade because the test was unclear") or, at the very least, less stable and/or central aspects of the self (e.g., "I received a low test grade because I studied the wrong material"). By admitting that only positive outcomes are due to one's traits, abilities, and/or dispositions, individuals are able to hold onto their self-enhancing beliefs even when confronted with failure.

How are such self-enhancing explanations for events derived? As noted elsewhere (Kunda, 1987; Pyszczynski & Greenberg, 1987), one possibility is that individuals bypass all semblance of logical information processing and decide on a cause that "feels good." However, such a process would be problematic for at least two reasons. First, most individuals like to think of themselves as being rational, thoughtful, and usually quite logical. To completely disregard all rules of logic when making causal judgments would threaten this image. Moreover, explanations for events that are wholly without logical underpinnings would seemingly be easily discredited and vulnerable to disconfirmation. For these reasons, then, it is unlikely that self-enhancing causal explanations for events are reached in a careless, haphazard way.

Instead, self-serving attributions are apt to be generated by a process that, at least to the attributor, seems logical. One attempt to specify how this process might proceed has been offered by Pyszczynski and Greenberg (1987). Their model begins by assuming a general sequence of the attribution process of the following form. After an event occurs, a plausible causal hypothesis is generated. Inference rules needed for testing the hypothesis are then settled on. Subsequently, data relevant to testing the hypothesis are gathered, and the validity of the data evaluated. Finally, the data are weighted and integrated and a final causal judgment is reached.

Pyszczynski and Greenberg (1987) assume that a desire to reach a self-enhancing conclusion can potentially exert an important influence at each of these steps. To illustrate, reconsider the student who has done poorly on an important exam. Initially, the student may generate a self-serving causal hypothesis (cf. Kunda, 1987). She may decide that the poor performance was probably due to ambiguous test questions rather than to her own lack of ability. At this point, she might settle on an inference rule that is especially congenial to her self-serving hypothesis. Perhaps she concludes that in order to properly test her hypothesis, she need only determine whether some of her fellow students also found the questions to be lacking in clarity. When gathering data relevant to testing this proposition, she might then be prone to sample from the population in such a way that her hypothesis is apt to be supported. For example, she might query only students who did at least as poorly, if not worse, on the exam as she did (Pyszczynski et al., 1985). If these students also found the test questions to be vague and equivocal, her hypothesis would seemingly have received support. In the event that any evidence inconsistent with the hypothesis is encountered, it can be dismissed as invalid or, at the very least, less relevant. For instance, if another student who did poorly did not find the questions confusing, the attributor may dismiss that student's perceptions as atypical and aberrant (e.g., "He's so out of it, he probably didn't even read the questions!"). By adhering to such a strategy, the attributor is able to cling to the belief that her conclusion regarding the causal role of the ambiguous test questions is fully justified on the basis of the available evidence. The fact that this process violates the dictates of formal logic and deviates from normatively correct rules of hypothesis-testing is apt to be of little concern; phenomenologically, the process is likely to be perceived as logical, thorough, and appropriate. Thus, it enables the attributor to maintain an illusion of objectivity while ensuring that only self-serving conclusions are reached.

A final word before concluding this discussion. For a number of years, there has been a debate over the mechanisms that underlie self-serving causal judgments (for reviews of this debate, see Brown & Rogers, 1990; Markus & Zajonc, 1985; Tetlock & Levi, 1982). Proponents of the motivational view (e.g., Pyszczynski & Greenberg, 1987; Zuckerman, 1979) assert that self-serving attributions and excuses are driven by a desire to perceive the self as good and efficacious. That is, the motivational perspective assumes that self-serving attributions are reached in order to defend, maintain, and promote high self-esteem. More cognitively-oriented theorists (Miller & Ross, 1975; Nisbett & Ross, 1980) have argued that recourse to motivational factors is unnecessary. These theorists argue that the self-serving attributional pattern can be accounted for entirely in terms of logical information-processing assumptions. After all, if one believes that one has the ability to succeed but fails, it is not entirely illogical to assume that failure must have been due to some factor other than one's ability.

In the present view, research attempting to distinguish these two positions has clearly supported the motivational perspective (e.g., Brown & Rogers, 1990; Fries & Frey, 1980; Gollwitzer, Earle, & Stephan, 1982). But whatever the ultimate source of this bias turns out to be, the critical point for the present discussion is that the tendency to deny that failure implicates low ability enables individuals to maintain the belief that they are competent even when negative feedback is encountered. In other words, the cognitive consequences of self-serving attributions are absolutely clear, even if their antecedents remain the source of some debate.

Strategies for Minimizing the Impact of Negative Feedback

Even the most exhaustive efforts to steer clear of negative feedback and avoid accepting responsibility for negative outcomes will not completely insulate individuals from unfavorable feedback. For some, years of struggling with even the most basic of household repairs provide compelling evidence that they lack mechanical ability. To simply deny the implications of such facts would be to experience repeated failure in that domain.

Under such conditions, individuals are apt to develop "acknowledged pockets of incompetence" (Taylor & Brown, 1988). That is, they readily admit to possessing the limitation in question, to the point where they may even exaggerate the extent of their deficiency. At the same time, however, most are able to do so in a manner that ensures that the damage to their overall sense of self-worth will be minimal. They accomplish this in part by calling on a host of reserve strategies that serve to maintain self-esteem. Five of these "damage-control" strategies are (a) selective importance, (b) selective consensus, (c) downward social comparison, (d) basking in reflected glory, and (e) compensatory self-enhancement.

Selective Importance

One way individuals can minimize the impact of an acknowledged limitation is by trivializing its importance. In support of this conjecture, substantial positive correlations have been found between an individual's perceived standing on an attribute and the perceived importance of that attribute (e.g., Rosenberg, 1979). Those who believe that they are intellectually gifted but inept in social situations tend to believe that intellectual ability is of greater importance than sociability. The reverse holds true for those who believe they perform better in social situations than in intellectual settings. To some extent, the tendency to see one's positive qualities as more important than one's negative qualities is quite logical. The individual who makes her living as an athlete may reasonably believe that coordination and strength are more important than are analytical and reasoning ability.

However, recent experimental research has documented the illusory nature of these beliefs. Gallagher and Brown (1989) first gave subjects information about a novel ability that purportedly measured flexibility in mental transformations.

Based on their alleged performance on a test, some subjects were told that they had scored high in the ability and others were told that they had scored low in the ability. Consistent with the notion that individuals belittle the importance of things that they are deficient at, those given failure feedback subsequently judged the ability to be less important than did those who received success feedback (see also Johnson et al., 1983). By derogating the importance of the qualities that they believe they lack, individuals are able to accept a limitation and still ensure that its negative impact on the self is minimal.

Selective Consensus

A closely related strategy to the one documented above is a tendency to exaggerate the percentage of individuals who share one's limitation. Campbell (1986) found that although subjects underestimated consensus for their perceived abilities (e.g., few people can solve crossword puzzles as quickly as I can), they overestimated consensus for their perceived deficiencies (e.g., many people also have trouble with math). Viewing one's shortcomings as common allows the negative impact of an accepted liability to be softened (see also Snyder et al., 1983; Marks, 1984).

Downward Social Comparison

Another tactic for dealing with negative feedback involves downward social comparison (Brickman & Bulman, 1977; Wills, 1981). This strategy involves comparing oneself with those who are relatively disadvantaged on some dimension. A student who receives a "D" in a course can console himself by comparing with those who failed the class. By focusing on those who are worse off than the self, one's own situation looks good in comparison. Recent research suggests that downward social comparison may be a particularly prevalent and adaptive strategy for coping with victimizing events. In a study of breast cancer patients, Wood, Taylor, and Lichtman (1985) found that the majority of women compared their condition with worse off others. Moreover, those who did so scored higher on measures of psychological adjustment. These findings suggest that downward social comparisons may be a ubiquitous and powerful strategy for maintaining self-worth following negative events.

Basking in Reflected Glory

Another strategy for dealing with negative feedback is in a sense the converse of downward comparison. Instead of comparing with those who are relatively disadvantaged on some dimension, one can attempt to augment self-worth after failure by emphasizing one's association with those who are relatively advantaged on some dimension. Cialdini and his associates have termed such a strategy basking in reflected glory (Cialdini, Borden, Thorne, Walker, Freeman, & Sloan, 1976; Cialdini & Richardson, 1980). In their research they found that students were more likely to use the pronoun *we* when discussing a football game their university team had won than when talking about a game their team had lost. Moreover, this tendency was most apparent after subjects had first experienced a personal failure. Emphasizing one's association with successful others appears to represent an additional method for minimizing the damage that failure causes to overall feelings of self-worth (see Tesser, 1988, for related research).

Compensatory Self-Enhancement

A final strategy that may be used to offset negative feedback regarding one aspect of the self is to exaggerate one's worth in other aspects of the self (Baumeister & Jones, 1978). An individual who has recently been rebuffed by his lover, for example, may try to counter this blow to self-worth by overemphasizing his ability in the athletic domain. In a test whether individuals engage in such compensatory self-enhancement tactics, Brown, Smart, and Gallagher (1990) first gave subjects positive or negative feedback on an alleged test of their intellectual ability. Subsequently, in an ostensibly unrelated experiment, subjects rated the degree to which a series of trait adjectives described them. Half of the attributes referred to qualities relevant to the achievement domain (e.g., smart, competent, etc.), the other half were interpersonal in nature (e.g., sincere, loyal, etc.). As predicted, although subjects' ratings of their achievement-related abilities were less favorable after failure than after success, their ratings of their interpersonal attributes were more favorable after failure than after success. Thus, subjects appeared to compensate for failure in the achievement domain by exaggerating their worth in the affiliative domain (see Steele, 1988, for related research).

Summary

A host of mechanisms that allow individuals to preserve their illusory self-conceptions have been explored in this section. Some of these strategies are designed to ensure that individuals receive predominantly positive feedback in their lives; others are designed to minimize the degree to which negative feedback implicates central aspects of the self; others represent attempts to preserve and restore self-esteem in the event that negative self-relevant feedback is encountered and acknowledged. Together, they furnish individuals with an impressive array of weapons for staving off attacks on self-worth. (This discussion is not meant to be exhaustive. Other strategies for promoting self-worth related to those discussed above have been documented by Lewicki (1983, 1984), Wicklund and Gollwitzer (1982), and Conway and Ross (1984), among others.)

RELATED ISSUES

The preceding sections have documented the prevalence of self-enhancing illusions, their association with psychological adjustment and performance in achievement-related situations, and the means by which they are maintained. In the next section of this paper, consideration is given to some related issues.

Illusions and Mechanisms of Defense

As noted elsewhere (Snyder, 1985, 1988), illusions and the strategies that give rise to them are reminiscent of the psychoanalytic mechanisms of defense. Most notably, they both serve to protect an individual's sense of self-worth (cf. Hilgard, 1949). At the same time, however, there exist some important differences between these constructs. The first concerns their motivational bases. As conceived by Freud (1915/1957), defense mechanisms were presumed to be motivated solely by a desire to avoid pain and ward off anxiety from internal threats. Later on, more ego-oriented theorists expanded Freud's idea by postulating that defense mechanisms also served to protect the individual from threats that originated in the external world (see Ansbacher & Ansbacher, 1967). Despite this extension, defense mechanisms were still presumed to be invoked only in response to a perceived threat. Hence, the name *defense*. In contrast, self-enhancing illusions appear to be in service of both esteem enhancement and esteem protection. In other words, self-enhancing illusions may often be offensive, rather than solely defensive, in nature (see Sackeim, 1983, for an elaboration of this point).

A second important difference between defense mechanisms and self-enhancing illusions concerns

the role of the unconscious. According to psychoanalytic theory, defense mechanisms must occur outside of conscious awareness in order to be effective. This does not appear to be so for illusions. That is, in order to "work," illusions need not necessarily be restricted from awareness. For example, an individual may be fully cognizant of the fact that he will feel better about his tennis playing ability if he habitually plays with people whom he is likely to beat. The effectiveness of the illusion is not necessarily vitiated by an awareness of these facts.

In a related vein, self-enhancing illusions do not necessarily involve self-deception. According to most treatments of this issue, individuals are engaging in self-deception when they simultaneously hold two contradictory self-relevant beliefs: a positive belief that is fully conscious and a conflicting negative belief that is at least partly unconscious (Sackeim, 1983, 1988). Evidence of self-deception thus requires that at some less conscious level, individuals know that their beliefs are fanciful.

This does not appear to be the case with self-enhancing illusions. As indicated earlier, most illusions concern an individual's interpretation or construction of reality. Because reality can be construed in multiple ways, individuals are able to harbor most self-enhancing illusions without "resorting" to self-deception. Social attributes, for instance, are so amorphous that individuals can define them in nearly any way they choose. To see oneself as extremely sincere, for example, does not require self-deception (i.e., that at some level one doubts one's sincerity); it only requires an idiosyncratic definition of sincerity that emphasizes one's own perceived virtues (Dunning et al., 1989). Moreover, this is true even for attributes that are not social in nature. Some people (usually those who are agile and quick) define athletic ability in terms of balance and speed; others (who are usually brawny and thick) define athletic ability in terms of power and strength. Who's to say who's right? Hence, if both think that they are more athletic than the other, there is no reason to assume that any sort of deception is occurring.

Another related difference between defense mechanisms and illusions concerns the amount of distortion. Defense mechanisms may sometimes entail significant misrepresentations of physical reality. In extreme cases of repression, for example, an individual may entirely block out a threatening experience because it is too painful to acknowledge. Illusions, in contrast, typically do not involve major distortions of reality. Rather, they entail important variations in how reality is interpreted or represented. A woman who is suffering through a divorce, for example, may comfort herself in a number of ways. She could belittle the importance of marriage as a life-style, remind herself of the number of other couples who have separated due to marital difficulties, compare herself with those who are helplessly trapped in unhappy marriages, and so on. All of these strategies are likely to make her feel better, but none involve a major distortion of reality.

A final distinction worth noting between defense mechanisms and illusions concerns the degree to which each is responsive to environmental feedback. Whereas defense mechanisms tend to be held more rigidly as threats to the self increase, illusions are relatively responsive to threat (Taylor, 1988). For instance, earlier it was noted that rather than denying the implications of pervasive negative feedback in some domain of life, individuals accept the limitation but compensate by exaggerating their worth in other respects of life (Brown et al., 1990; Taylor, Collins, Skokan, & Aspinwall, 1989). These findings suggest that illusions are more flexible and accommodating to the environment than are the defense mechanisms.

Potential Risks

A complete account of illusions must include a consideration of their potential liabilities. To be sure, self-enhancing illusions involve some inherent risks. Overly positive views of the self may lead individuals to pursue goals that are beyond their capabilities; an exaggerated sense of control may lead people to blame themselves for negative outcomes that were truly not within their control; excessive optimism may lead individuals to underestimate their susceptibility to some diseases, thereby limiting the likelihood that they will take appropriate preventive measures. Thus, associated with each of the illusions considered above is an attendant set of risks.

The extent to which these potential risks mitigate the effectiveness of illusions, however, is unclear. Because they are positively related to psychological adjustment and performance outcomes, whatever limitations inherent in illusions appear to be outweighed by the benefits they provide. One possible explanation for this fact has been offered by Taylor and Brown (1988). These theorists speculated that the negative aspects of illusions may cancel out one another. For instance, although unrealistic optimism may diminish the chances that individuals will initiate proper health behaviors, a strong sense of mastery and the belief that one can control events may lead them to assiduously maintain proper health habits once they are begun (cf. Bandura, 1988). In this manner, illusions may operate in a sort of "checks and balances" fashion that ensures that their potential liabilities do not exceed their advantages. However, there is currently a paucity of research on this matter, and investigations regarding the potential liabilities of illusions represent an important topic for future research.

Implications for Psychotherapy

Assuming that the limitations of illusions are minimal, or at least manageable, the present analysis would seemingly have important implications for psychotherapy. As indicated earlier, many, though not all, approaches to psychotherapy stress that therapeutic change requires the acquisition of accurate self-knowledge. For instance, therapies developed by humanistic psychologists (e.g., Perls, 1973; Rogers, 1951) encourage individuals to "get in touch with their true selves"; many cognitive-behavioral therapies (e.g., Beck, 1967) urge individuals to carefully monitor their self-relevant thoughts, in the hope that distorted patterns of thinking can be corrected (i.e., made to be more realistic); finally, even psychoanalysis is based on the notion that treatment should involve a search for truth. Thus, although different in many ways, the tie binding these approaches is that accurate self-knowledge will help ameliorate individuals' distress.

The research reviewed in this paper suggests that this assumption may be unfounded. As we have seen, at least with respect to the most common psychological disorder (i.e., depression), accurate self-understanding appears to be negatively related to adjustment. This admits the possibility that rather than encouraging individuals to gain unbiased self-knowledge, greater therapeutic progress might be achieved by encouraging individuals to acquire self-enhancing illusions (Alloy & Abramson, 1988).

How might such an intervention proceed? A useful starting point might be to train clients in the strategies normal individuals use for enhancing self-worth. Interestingly, these strategies tend to be less evident among individuals who are psychologically distressed (i.e., depressed, anxious, or low in self-esteem). For example, compared with normals, distressed individuals are less likely to (a) interpret ambiguous feedback to be positive feedback (Dykman & Volpicelli, 1983); (b) selectively attend to and remember positive self-relevant feedback over negative self-relevant feedback (Nelson & Craighead, 1977; Johnson et al., 1983); (c) attribute positive outcomes to the self but deny responsibility for negative outcomes (Campbell & Fairey, 1985; Kuiper, 1978); (d) judge their positive attributes to be more important than their deficiencies (Wenzlaff & Grozier, 1988); (e) view their assets as unique but their liabilities as commonly shared by others (Campbell, 1986); and (f) show compensatory self-enhancement following failure (Baumeister, 1982; Brown et al., 1990). In short, like the illusions they give rise to, strategies for promoting self-worth are relatively absent among distressed individuals. By exposing clients to these strategies and encouraging their judicious use, therapists might be able to help their clients experience improvements in symptomatology (cf. Sackeim, 1983; Shrauger, 1982).

Of course, before such interventions can be implemented on anything more than an experimental basis, more evidence pertaining to the causal role of illusions in promoting mental health needs to be amassed. To date, most of the research regarding illusions and adjustment is correlational. However, some experimental evidence linking illusions to emotional well-being does exist. For instance, McFarland and Ross (1982) found that leading subjects to make self-serving attributions resulted in greater positive affect after success and lower negative affect after failure. There is also evidence that encouraging subjects to focus on their likely success at an upcoming task actually improves task performance (Campbell & Fairey, 1985). These are just a few of the ways that self-enhancing illusions might promote emotional health and psychological well-being (for additional evidence, see Snyder & Higgins, 1988; Taylor & Brown, 1988). If future research continues to document causal relations between illusions and adjustment, treatment regimens based on encouraging illusory thinking would seem to represent a viable therapeutic intervention.

NEED FOR ACCURATE SELF-KNOWLEDGE

To conclude, it is appropriate to reconsider the question that was posed earlier in this paper: what is the proper relation between an individual's picture of the self and the "actual" self? Although theorists from a variety of disciplines have asserted that individuals ought to, and need to, possess accurate and realistic self-perceptions, the present review suggests that most individuals possess views of the self that are more favorable than can realistically be justified, and that this tendency is associated with, and may contribute to, psychological adjustment and superior functioning. Thus, setting aside issues of morality, the answer to this question seems to be that the *proper* relation is one in which one's picture of the self is brighter, more colorful, and more beautiful than the "actual" self.

An appropriate analogy can perhaps be drawn between self-enhancing illusions and the new magnetic levitation vehicles that are currently being developed for use in Japan, France, and West Germany. These passenger trains are capable of achieving speeds of up to 300 miles per hour by riding an electromagnetic current that raises them just slightly above the rails. The trick is in keeping the train just the right distance off the ground; rising too high causes the train to gyrate and crash; riding too close to the ground causes the train to grind to a halt.

In a similar vein, self-enhancing illusions are probably most effective when they are only slightly more positive than can realistically be justified (Baumeister, 1989). Being too grandiose in one's thinking can have serious consequences, as the destructive delusions of grandeur that can accompany manic depressive illness illustrate. But being too modest in one's self-appraisals can also be debilitating, as research on depressive realism attests (Alloy & Abramson, 1988). Thus, much like the new passenger trains under development, individuals' self-appraisals appear to be most effective when they rise slightly above the ground.

REFERENCES

Abramson, L. Y., & Alloy, L. B. (1980). Judgment of contingency: Errors and their implications. In A. Baum & J. E. Singer (Eds.), *Advances in environmental psychology* (Vol. 2, pp. 111–130). Hillsdale, NJ: Lawrence Erlbaum Associates.

Abramson, L. Y., & Martin, D. J. (1981). Depression and the causal inference process. In J. H. Harvey, W. Ickes, & R. F. Kidd (Eds.), *New directions in attribution research* (Vol. 3, pp. 117–168). Hillsdale, NJ: Lawrence Erlbaum Associates.

Ahrens, A. J., Zeiss, A. M., & Kanfer, R. (1988). Dysphoric deficits in interpersonal standards, self-efficacy, and social comparison. *Cognitive Therapy and Research, 12*, 53–67.

Alicke, M. D. (1985). Global self-evaluation as determined by the desirability and controllability of trait adjectives. *Journal of Personality and Social Psychology, 49*, 1621–1630.

Alloy, L. B., & Abramson, L. Y. (1979). Judgments of contingency in depressed and nondepressed students: Sadder but wiser? *Journal of Experimental Psychology: General, 108*, 441–485.

Alloy, L. B., & Abramson, L. Y. (1988). Depressive realism: Four theoretical perspectives. In L. B. Alloy (Ed.), *Cognitive processes in depression* (pp. 223–265). New York: Guilford Press.

Alloy, L. B., & Ahrens, A. H. (1987). Depression and pessimism for the future: Biased use of statistically relevant information in predictions for self versus others. *Journal of Personality and Social Psychology, 52*, 366–378.

Allport, G. W. (1943). *Becoming: Basic considerations for a psychology of personality*. New Haven, CT: Yale University Press.

Ansbacher, H. L., & Ansbacher, R. R. (Eds.). (1967). *The individual psychology of Alfred Adler*. New York: Harper & Row. (Originally published by Basic Books, New York, 1956)

Bachman, J. G., & O'Malley, P. M. (1977). Self-esteem in young men: A longitudinal analysis of the impact of education and occupational attainment. *Journal of Personality and Social Psychology, 35*, 365–380.

Bandura, A. (1988). Self-efficacy mechanism in physiological activation and health-promoting behavior. In J. Madden IV, S. Mathysse, & J. Barchas (Eds.), *Adaptation, learning, and affect*. New York: Raven Press.

Bandura, A. (1989). Self-regulation of motivation and action through internal standards and goal systems. In L. Pervin (Ed.), *Goal concepts in personality and social psychology* (pp. 19–86). Hillsdale, NJ: Lawrence Erlbaum Associates.

Bandura, A., & Schunk, D. H. (1981). Cultivating competence, self-efficacy, and interest through proximal self-motivation. *Journal of Personality and Social Psychology, 41*, 586–598.

Baumeister, R. F. (1982). Self-esteem, self-presentation, and future interaction: A dilemma of reputation. *Journal of Personality, 50*, 29–45.

Baumeister, R. F. (1989). The optimal margin of illusion. *Journal of Social and Clinical Psychology, 8*, 176–189.

Baumeister, R. F., Hamilton, J. C., & Tice, D. M. (1985). Public versus private expectancy of success: Confidence booster or performance pressure? *Journal of Personality and Social Psychology, 48*, 1447–1457.

Baumeister, R. F., & Jones, E. E. (1978). When self-presentation is constrained by the target's knowledge: Consistency and compensation. *Journal of Personality and Social Psychology, 36*, 608–618.

Baumeister, R. F., & Tice, D. M. (1985). Self-esteem and responses to success and failure: Subsequent performance and intrinsic motivation. *Journal of Personality, 53*, 450–467.

Beck, A. T. (1967). *Depression: Clinical, experimental, and theoretical aspects*. New York: Harper & Row.

Becker, E. (1973). *The denial of death*. New York: Free Press.

Berglas, S., & Jones, E. E. (1978). Drug choice as a self-handicapping strategy in response to noncontingent success. *Journal of Personality and Social Psychology, 36*, 405–417.

Blumberg, H. H. (1972). Communication of interpersonal evaluations. *Journal of Personality and Social Psychology, 23*, 157–162.

Brickman, P., & Bulman, R. J. (1977). Pleasure and pain in social comparison. In J. Suls & R. Miller (Eds.), *Social comparison processes: Theoretical and empirical perspectives* (pp. 149–186). Washington, DC: Hemisphere.

Brown, J. D. (1986). Evaluations of self and others: Self-enhancement biases in social judgments. *Social Cognition, 4*, 353–376.

Brown, J. D. (in press). Evaluating one's abilities: Short cuts and stumbling blocks on the road to self-knowledge. *Journal of Experimental Social Psychology*.

Brown, J. D., Collins, R. L., & Schmidt, G. W. (1988). Self-esteem and direct versus indirect forms of self-enhancement. *Journal of Personality and Social Psychology, 55*, 445–453.

Brown, J. D., & Gallagher, F. M. (1990). *Motivational bases of self-enhancing social evaluations*. Manuscript in preparation.

Brown, J. D., & Rogers, R. J. (1990). *Physiological arousal as a mediator of self-serving attributions*. Manuscript submitted for publication.

Brown, J. D., Smart, S. A., & Gallagher, F. M. (1990). *Keeping one's head above water: Compensatory self-enhancement strategies following failure.* Manuscript in preparation.

Campbell, J. D. (1986). Similarity and uniqueness: The effects of attribute type, relevance, and individual differences in self-esteem and depression. *Journal of Personality and Social Psychology, 50*, 281–294.

Campbell, J. D., & Fairey, P. J. (1985). Effects of self-esteem, hypothetical explanations, and verbalization of expectancies on future performance. *Journal of Personality and Social Psychology, 48*, 1097–1111.

Cialdini, R. B., Borden, R. J., Thorne, A., Walker, M. R., Freeman, S., & Sloan, L. R. (1976). Basking in reflected glory: Three (football) field studies. *Journal of Personality and Social Psychology, 34*, 366–375.

Cialdini, R. B., & Richardson, K. D. (1980). Two indirect tactics of image management: Basking and blasting. *Journal of Personality and Social Psychology, 39*, 406–415.

Conway, M., & Ross, M. (1984). Getting what you want by revising what you had. *Journal of Personality and Social Psychology, 47*, 738–748.

Dunning, D., Meyerowitz, J. A., & Holzberg, A. (1989). Ambiguity and self-evaluation: The role of idiosyncratic definitions in self-serving assessments of ability. *Journal of Personality and Social Psychology, 57*, 1082–1090.

Dweck, C. S., & Leggett, E. L. (1988). A social-cognitive approach to personality and motivation. *Psychological Review, 95*, 256–273.

Dykman, B. M., & Volpicelli, J. R. (1983). Depression and negative processing of evaluative feedback. *Cognitive Therapy and Research, 7*, 485–498.

Erikson, E. H. (1950). *Childhood and society* (2nd ed.). New York: W. W. Norton.

Feather, N. T. (1966). Effects of prior success and failure on expectations of success and subsequent performance. *Journal of Personality and Social Psychology, 3*, 287–298.

Felson, R. B. (1981). Ambiguity and bias in the self-concept. *Social Psychology Quarterly, 44*, 64–69.

Felson, R. B. (1984). The effect of self-appraisals of ability on academic performance. *Journal of Personality and Social Psychology, 47*, 944–952.

Fenigstein, A., Scheier, M. F., & Buss, A. H. (1975). Public and private self-consciousness:

Assessment and theory. *Journal of Consulting and Clinical Psychology, 43*, 522–528.

Fiske, S. T., & Taylor, S. E. (1984). *Social cognition*. Reading, MA: Addison-Wesley.

Franzoi, S. L. (1983). Self-concept differences as a function of private self-consciousness and social anxiety. *Journal of Research in Personality, 17*, 272–287.

Freud, S. (1957). Repression. In J. Strachey (Ed. and Trans.), *The standard edition of the complete psychological works of Sigmund Freud* (Vol. 14, pp. 143–158). London: Hogarth Press. (Original work published 1915)

Frey, D., & Stahlberg, D. (1986). Selection of information after receiving more or less reliable self-threatening information. *Personality and Social Psychology Bulletin, 12*, 434–441.

Fries, A., & Frey, D. (1980). Misattribution of arousal and the effects of self-threatening information. *Journal of Experimental Social Psychology, 16*, 405–416.

Fromm, E. (1955). *The sane society*. New York: Holt, Rinehart & Winston.

Gallagher, F. M., & Brown, J. D. (1989). *Selective importance of an attribute following success and failure.* Unpublished data. Southern Methodist University, Dallas, TX.

Gergen, K. J. (1971). *The concept of self.* New York: Holt, Rinehart, & Winston.

Gilbert, D. T., & Cooper, J. (1985). Social psychological strategies of self-deception. In M. W. Martin (Ed.), *Self-deception and self-understanding: New essays in philosophy and psychology* (pp. 75–93). Lawrence: University of Kansas Press.

Golin, S., Terrell, T., & Johnson, B. (1977). Depression and the illusion of control. *Journal of Abnormal Psychology, 86*, 440–442.

Golin, S., Terrell, T., Weitz, J., & Drost, P. L. (1979). The illusion of control among depressed patients. *Journal of Abnormal Psychology, 88*, 454–457.

Gollwitzer, P. M., Earle, W. B., & Stephan, W. G. (1982). Affect as a determinant of egotism: Residual excitation and performance attributions. *Journal of Personality and Social Psychology, 43*, 702–709.

Gordon, C. (1968). Self-conceptions: Configurations of content. In C. Gordon & K. J. Gergen (Eds.), *The self in social interaction* (pp. 115–136). New York: John Wiley & Sons.

Gotlib, I. H., & Meltzer, S. J. (1987). Depression and the perception of social skill in dyadic interaction. *Cognitive Therapy and Research, 11*, 41–54.

Greenwald, A. G. (1980). The totalitarian ego: Fabrication and revision of personal history. *American Psychologist, 35*, 603–618.

Greenwald, A. G. (1988). Self-knowledge and self-deception. In J. S. Lockard & D. L. Paulhus (Eds.), *Self-deception: An adaptive mechanism?* (pp. 113–131). Englewood Cliffs, NJ: Prentice-Hall.

Haan, N. (1977). *Coping and defending: Processes of self-environment organization*. New York: Academic Press.

Hilgard, E. R. (1949). Human motives and the concept of the self. *American Psychologist, 4*, 374–382.

Ingram, R. E., & Smith, T. W. (1984). Depression and internal versus external focus of attention. *Cognitive Therapy and Research, 8*, 139–151.

Jahoda, M. (1958). *Current concepts of positive mental health*. New York: Basic Books.

James, W. (1890). *The principles of psychology* (Vol. 1). New York: Holt.

Janoff-Bulman, R., & Brickman, P. (1982). Expectations and what people learn from failure. In N. T. Feather (Ed.), *Expectations and action: Expectancy-value models in psychology* (pp. 207–272). Hillsdale, NJ: Lawrence Erlbaum Associates.

Johnson, J. E., Petzel, T. P., Hartney, L. M., & Morgan, R. A. (1983). Recall and importance ratings of completed and uncompleted tasks as a function of depression. *Cognitive Therapy and Research, 7*, 51–56.

Kuiper, N. A. (1978). Depression and causal attributions for success and failure. *Journal of Personality and Social Psychology, 36*, 236–246.

Kuiper, N. A., & MacDonald, M. R. (1982). Self and other perception in mild depressives. *Social Cognition, 1*, 233–239.

Kunda, Z. (1987). Motivated inference: Self-serving generation and evaluation of causal theories. *Journal of Personality and Social Psychology, 53*, 636–647.

Langer, E. J. (1975). The illusion of control. *Journal of Personality and Social Psychology, 32*, 311–328.

Lazarus, R. S. (1983). The costs and benefits of denial. In S. Breznitz (Ed.), *Denial of stress* (pp. 1–30). New York: International Universities Press.

Lewicki, P. (1983). Self-image bias in person perception. *Journal of Personality and Social Psychology, 45*, 384–393.

Lewicki, P. (1984). Self-schema and social information processing. *Journal of Personality and Social Psychology, 47*, 1177–1190.

Lewinsohn, P. M., Mischel, W., Chaplin, W., & Barton, R. (1980). Social competence and depression: The role of illusory self-perceptions. *Journal of Abnormal Psychology, 89*, 203–212.

McFarland, C., & Ross, M. (1982). The impact of causal attributions on affective reactions to success and failure. *Journal of Personality and Social Psychology, 43*, 937–946.

Marks, G. (1984). Thinking one's abilities are unique and one's opinions are common. *Personality and Social Psychological Bulletin, 10*, 203–208.

Markus, H. (1977). Self-schemata and processing information about the self. *Journal of Personality and Social Psychology, 35*, 63–78.

Markus, H., & Nurius, P. (1986). Possible selves. *American Psychologist, 41*, 954–969.

Markus, M., & Wurf, E. (1987). The dynamic self-concept: A social psychological perspective. *Annual Review of Psychology, 38*, 299–337.

Markus, H., & Zajonc, R. B. (1985). The cognitive perspective in social psychology. In G. Lindzey & E. Aronson (Eds.), *The handbook of social psychology* (3rd ed., Vol. 1, pp. 137–230). New York: Random House.

Martin, M. W. (Ed.). (1985). *Self-deception and self-understanding: New essays in philosophy and psychology*. Lawrence: University of Kansas Press.

Maslow, A. H. (1950). Self-actualizing people: A study of psychological health. *Personality*, Symposium No. 1, 11–34.

McFarlin, D. B. (1985). Persistence in the face of failure: The impact of self-esteem and contingency information. *Personality and Social Psychology Bulletin, 11*, 153–163.

McFarlin, D. B., Baumeister, R. F., & Blascovich, J. (1984). On knowing when to quit: Task failure, self-esteem, advice, and nonproductive assistance. *Journal of Personality, 52*, 138–155.

Menninger, K. A. (1963). *The vital balance*. New York: Viking.

Miller, D. T., & Ross, M. (1975). Self-serving biases in the attribution of causality: Fact or fiction? *Psychological Bulletin, 82*, 213–235.

Mischel, W., Ebbesen, E. B., & Zeiss, A. R. (1973). Selective attention to the self: Situational and dispositional determinants. *Journal of Personality and Social Psychology, 27*, 129–142.

Mischel, W., Ebbesen, E. B., & Zeiss, A. R. (1976). Determinants of selective memory about the self. *Journal of Consulting and Clinical Psychology, 44*, 92–103.

Mortimer, J. L., & Lorence, J. (1979). Occupational experience and the self-concept: A longitudinal study. *Social Psychology Quarterly, 42*, 307–323.

Nelson, R. E., & Craighead, W. E. (1977). Selective recall of positive and negative feedback, self-control behavior, and depression. *Journal of Abnormal Psychology, 86*, 379–388.

Nisbett, R. E., & Ross, L. (1980). *Human inference: Strategies and shortcomings of social judgment.* Englewood Cliffs, NJ: Prentice-Hall.

Perloff, L. S., & Fetzer, B. K. (1986). Self-other judgments and perceived vulnerability of victimization. *Journal of Personality and Social Psychology, 50*, 502–510.

Perls, F. S. (1973). *The gestalt approach to therapy.* Palo Alto, CA: Science and Behavior Books.

Pyszczynski, T., & Greenberg, J. (1987). Toward an integration of cognitive and motivational perspectives on social inference: A biased hypothesis-testing model. In L. Berkowitz (Ed.), *Advances in experimental social psychology* (Vol. 20, pp. 297–340). New York: Academic Press.

Pyszczynski, T., Greenberg, J., & LaPrelle, J. (1985). Social comparison after success and failure: Biased search for information consistent with a self-serving conclusion. *Journal of Experimental Social Psychology, 21*, 195–211.

Pyszczynski, T., Holt, K., & Greenberg, J. (1987). Depression, self-focused attention, and expectancies for positive and negative future life events for self and others. *Journal of Personality and Social Psychology, 52*, 994–1001.

Rank, O. (1936). *Will therapy and truth and reality.* New York: Knopf.

Robertson, L. S. (1977). Car crashes: Perceived vulnerability and willingness to pay for crash protection. *Journal of Community Health, 3*, 136–141.

Rogers, C. R. (1951). *Client-centered therapy: Its current practice, implications, and theory.* Boston: Houghton Mifflin.

Rosenberg, M. (1979). *Conceiving the self.* New York: Basic Books.

Roth, D. L., & Ingram, R. E. (1985). Factors in the Self-Deception Questionnaire: Associations with depression. *Journal of Personality and Social Psychology, 48*, 243–251.

Roth, D., & Rehm, L. P. (1980). Relationships among self-monitoring processes, memory, and depression. *Cognitive Therapy and Research, 2*, 149–157.

Sackeim, H. A. (1983). Self-deception, self-esteem, and depression: The adaptive value of lying to oneself. In J. Masling (Ed.), *Empirical studies of psychoanalytical theories* (Vol. 1, pp. 101–157). Hillsdale, NJ: Analytic Press.

Sackeim, H. A. (1988). Self-deception: A synthesis. In J. S. Lockard & D. L. Paulhus (Eds.), *Self-deception: An adaptive mechanism?* (pp. 146–163). Englewood Cliffs, NJ: Prentice-Hall.

Sackeim, H. A., & Gur, R. C. (1979). Self-deception, other-deception, and self-reported psychopathology. *Journal of Consulting and Clinical Psychology, 47*, 213–215.

Sandelands, L. E., Brockner, J., & Glynn, M. A. (1988). If at first you don't succeed, try, try again: Effects of persistence-performance contingencies, ego-involvement, and self-esteem in task persistence. *Journal of Applied Psychology, 73*, 208–216.

Sarason, I. G. (1975). Anxiety and self-preoccupation. In I. G. Sarason & C. D. Spielberger (Eds.), *Stress and anxiety* (Vol. 2, pp. 27–44). Washington, DC: Hemisphere.

Sears, D. O. (1983). The person-positivity bias. *Journal of Personality and Social Psychology, 44*, 233–250.

Shrauger, J. S. (1982). Selection and processing of self-evaluative information: Experimental evidence and clinical implications. In G. Weary & H. L. Mirels (Eds.), *Integrations of clinical and social psychology* (pp. 128–153). New York: Oxford University Press.

Shrauger, J. S., & Sorman, P. B. (1977). Self-evaluations, initial success and failure, and improvement as determinants of persistence. *Journal of Consulting and Clinical Psychology, 45*, 784–795.

Smith, T. W., & Greenberg, J. (1981). Depression and self-focused attention. *Motivation and Emotion, 5*, 323–331.

Smith, T. W., Ingram, R. E., & Roth, D. L. (1985). Self-focused attention and depression: Self-evaluation, affect, and life stress. *Motivation and Emotion, 9*, 381–389.

Snyder, C. R. (1985). Collaborative companions: The relationship of self-deception and excuse making. In M. W. Martin (Ed.), *Self-deception and self-understanding: New essays in philosophy and psychology* (pp. 35–51). Lawrence: University of Kansas Press.

Snyder, C. R. (1988). From defenses to self-protection: An evolutionary perspective. *Journal of Social and Clinical Psychology, 6*, 155–158.

Snyder, C. R. (1989). Reality negotiation: From excuses to hope and beyond. *Journal of Social and Clinical Psychology, 8*, 130–157.

Snyder, C. R., Higgins, R. L., (1988). Excuses: Their effective role in the negotiation of reality. *Psychological Bulletin, 104*, 23–35.

Snyder, C. R., Higgins, R. L., & Stucky, R. J. (1983). *Excuses: Masquerades in search of grace.* New York: Wiley-Interscience.

Steele, C. M. (1988). The psychology of self-affirmation: Sustaining the integrity of the self. In L. Berkowitz (Ed.), *Advances in experimental social psychology* (Vol. 21, pp. 261–302). New York: Academic Press.

Swann, W. B., Jr. (1987). Identity negotiation: Where two roads meet. *Journal of Personality and Social Psychology, 53*, 1038–1051.

Swann, W. B., Jr., & Hill, C. A. (1982). When our identities are mistaken: Reaffirming self-conceptions through social interaction. *Journal of Personality and Social Psychology, 43*, 59–66.

Swann, W. B., Jr., & Read, S. J. (1981). Self-verification processes: How we sustain our self-conceptions. *Journal of Experimental Social Psychology, 17*, 351–370.

Tajfel, H., & Turner, J. C. (1986). The social identity theory of intergroup behavior. In S. Worchel & W. Austin (Eds.), *Psychology of intergroup relations* (pp. 7–24). Chicago: Nelson-Hall.

Taylor, S. E. (1988). *The healthy mind.* New York: Basic Books.

Taylor, S. E., & Brown, J. D. (1988). Illusion and well-being: A social psychological perspective on mental health. *Psychological Bulletin, 103*, 193–210.

Taylor, S. E., Collins, R. L., Shokan, L. A., & Aspinwall, L. G. (1989). Maintaining positive illusions in the face of negative information: Getting the facts without letting them get to you. *Journal of Social and Clinical Psychology, 8*, 114–129.

Tesser, A. (1988). Toward a self-evaluation maintenance model of social behavior. In L. Berkowitz (Ed.), *Advances in experimental social psychology* (Vol. 21, pp. 181–227). New York: Academic Press.

Tesser, A., & Rosen, S. (1975). The reluctance to transmit bad news. In L. Berkowitz (Ed.), *Advances in experimental social psychology* (Vol. 8, pp. 193–232). New York: Academic Press.

Tetlock, P. E., & Levi, A. (1982). Attribution bias: On the inconclusiveness of the cognition-motivation debate. *Journal of Experimental Social Psychology, 18*, 68–88.

Trope, Y. (1986). Self-enhancement, self-assessment, and achievement behavior. In R. M. Sorrentino, & E. T. Higgins (Eds.), *Handbook of motivation and cognition* (pp. 350–378). New York: Guilford Press.

Turner, R. G. (1978). Effects of differential request procedures and self-consciousness on trait attributions. *Journal of Research in Personality, 12*, 431–438.

Watzlawick, P. (1976). *How real is real?* New York: Random House.

Weinstein, N. D. (1980). Unrealistic optimism about future life events. *Journal of Personality and Social Psychology, 39*, 806–820.

Weinstein, N. D. (1982). Unrealistic optimism about susceptibility to health problems. *Journal of Behavioral Medicine, 5*, 441–460.

Wenzlaff, R. M., & Grozier, S. A. (1988). Depression and the magnification of failure. *Journal of Abnormal Psychology, 97*, 90–93.

White, R. W. (1959). Motivation reconsidered: The concept of competence. *Psychological Review, 66*, 297–335.

Wicklund, R. A, & Gollwitzer, P. M. (1982). *Symbolic self-completion.* Hillsdale, NJ: Lawrence Erlbaum Associates.

Wills, T. A. (1981). Downward comparison principles in social psychology. *Psychological Bulletin, 90*, 245–271.

Wood, J. V., Taylor, S. E., & Lichtman, R. R. (1985). Social comparison and adjustment to breast cancer. *Journal of Personality and Social Psychology, 49*, 1169–1183.

Zuckerman, M. (1979). Attribution of success and failure revisited, or: The motivational bias is alive and well in attribution theory. *Journal of Personality, 47*, 245–287.

CHAPTER 10

GENDER ROLES AND HEALTH

Karina Davidson-Katz

In Western society today, women report more physical illness, more psychological distress, and more psychiatric symptoms than do men. Yet women live longer than men. Most of us assume that these sex differences exist across times and cultures, and have biological causes.

But are these assumptions warranted? The sex difference in mortality is greater or lesser, or even reversed, depending on what culture is examined (Waldron, 1982). The sex difference in illness reports changes size with the method of data collection (Nathanson, 1978). The extent of the sex difference in psychological distress fluctuates with this century's progression (Kessler & McRae, 1981). Finally, whether there is a sex difference in psychiatric symptomatology depends on environmental factors such as education (Jenkins, 1985). Thus, contrary to our assumptions, it appears that sex differences in morbidity and mortality are not determined exclusively by biology.

Even when a sex difference is consistently found — as in the case of depression — biology alone cannot provide a complete explanation (Nolen-Hoeksema, 1987). To fully explain sex differences in health, one needs to seek more than just biological determinants; one also must ask what psychological variables both differentiate women and men and predict good health outcomes. One such variable that is being investigated is the gender role adopted by the individual (Maccoby & Jacklin, 1974).

What is a gender role? The term has been used to refer to attributes, preferences, characteristics, stereotypes, expectations, and behaviors. This kind of multifaceted definition does not lend itself well to the investigation of gender roles and outcome variables. Thus, more precise and specific definitions of terms are in order.

Widom (1984) suggested dividing the study of sex differences into biological, psychological, and social components. Sex differences examined at the biological level will be referred to here simply by the term *sex*. Next, sex differences can be investigated at a psychological level; individual differences in characteristics, behaviors, preferences,

This chapter was written while the author was supported by a fellowship grant from the Canadian Social Sciences and Humanities Research Council Grant No. 453-88-0065.

and self-concept are then the variables of interest. The psychological category of sex differences will be referred to here as *gender roles. Masculinity* refers to the psychological characteristics associated with males' gender role; *femininity* to the psychological characteristics associated with females' gender role. When theorists intend to refer only to one component of a gender role, such as expressive behavior, the element of interest will be separately named. This separation should help the reader avoid invoking all connotations of the term *gender role* when only one part is under investigation. Finally, sex differences can be examined at a social or cultural level. Shared beliefs about what constitute appropriate behaviors, characteristics, abilities, and preferences for each sex will be called *gender role stereotypes.*

These three divisions of sex differences are not entirely independent of one another; gender role stereotypes in conjunction with one's sex likely influence the gender role that one eventually adopts. For example, being female may not directly cause passivity and emotional expressivity, but it may do so indirectly by activating a socialization process in which a girl internalizes the gender role stereotype of her culture—passivity and expressivity, in this example.

Distinguishing among the various meanings hidden in prior uses of the term *gender roles* allows one to examine separately biological, social, and psychological theories. This chapter will review primarily the last set of theories.

Although most of the current psychological and social theories linking gender roles and health have received some empirical support, none of them adequately explains how gender roles cause good (or poor) health. I will begin my discussion by presenting the various gender role theories. Then I will highlight the limitations of these theories by analyzing the difficulties with current research. Next, I will describe two new research directions that may allow us to explore the causal relationship between sex-differentiating personality variables and health. Finally, I will present some of the evidence produced so far by researchers who have pursued these new avenues.

EVOLUTION OF GENDER ROLE THEORY

Traditional Theories

The view prevalent prior to 1960 was that good health outcomes are linked with sex-appropriate gender role affiliation (Spence & Helmreich, 1978). Early gender role theorists contended that assuming the gender role appropriate to one's biological sex carries psychological, social, and evolutionary benefits. Adoption of a biologically inappropriate gender role was thought to be the result of intrapsychic conflict or improper socialization and to cause distress and pathology in both the individual and society.

One of the major assumptions of these early gender role theorists was that masculinity and femininity are polar opposites; the more you possessed attributes of the other gender role, the less you possessed attributes of the other gender role. Early scales that measured gender role affiliation tended to reflect this assumption (Constantinople, 1973).

Although a few early theorists proposed that masculine and feminine attributes—particularly expressiveness and agency—may not be polar opposites (Bakan, 1966), no serious interest in the relationship between masculinity and femininity occurred until the 1970s.

Bem's Theories of Androgyny

In 1974, Bem offered an alternative hypothesis concerning the relationship between good psychological health and gender roles. She also introduced a new measure of gender role affiliation—the Bem Sex Role Inventory (BSRI). Bem suggested that those individuals scoring either high in both masculine and feminine gender role affiliation or low in both (called *androgynous*) are better off than those scoring high only in the gender role associated with their biological sex (called *sex-typed*). She suggested that the ability to perform both masculine and feminine behaviors is healthy, regardless of one's sex. Androgynous individuals, according to Bem, "might be *both* masculine and feminine, *both* assertive and yielding, *both* instrumental and expressive—depending on the situational appropriateness of these various behaviors" (p. 155).

Although this theoretical formulation of androgyny and its relationship to psychological health may seem straightforward, it is not. As critics later suggested, there are a number of hidden assumptions and logical problems with Bem's original theory.

For example, although Bem was clear in stating that androgynous individuals should have better health than others, she was not definite about how or why this relationship operates. Other theorists presumed Bem proposed that since androgynous individuals have both masculine and feminine behaviors in their repertoire, they can respond to stressors with the most adaptive coping behavior. Hidden within this interpretation is an important assumption; namely, that the androgynous person can identify the behavior that is most appropriate in any situation. That is, it is not simply the possession of masculine and feminine attributes that leads to good health, but also the ability to use the attributes judiciously. For example, faced with a friend whose spouse has died suddenly, a stereotypical masculine response might be to offer help with the funeral arrangements. A stereotypical feminine response might be to offer sympathy and attention to the bereaved friend. Bem would have to say that the androgynous individual could not only provide both kinds of assistance but also select the kind that would be most helpful at a given moment.

It should be noted once more that Bem did not explicitly state this assumption about the ability to select the right behavior; she merely implied it when she stated that androgynous individuals use masculine and feminine attributes "depending on the situational appropriateness of these various behaviors" (p. 155). The theory implicit in these comments has been labeled the *emergent properties* theory of androgyny, because it suggests that when masculine and feminine traits are both present, new qualities, over and above the masculine and feminine qualities, emerge (Hall & Taylor, 1985). These new qualities are flexibility and adaptability.

It is possible that Bem meant only that the simple presence of both types of attributes is better than possessing one set of attributes; this theory is different from the emergent properties theory and has different implications for the relationship between androgyny and health. This variation of the androgyny theory had been labeled the *main effects* theory (Taylor & Hall, 1982). Most researchers, however, understood Bem to imply the emergent properties theoretical assumptions, and some of Bem's later articles (e.g., Bem, 1975) more explicitly stated the assumptions necessary for the emergent properties theory.

Bem (1974) also stated that the key to androgyny is the balance of reported masculine and feminine attributes, regardless of their number. In other words, people with no gender role–related attributes and persons with many attributes of both gender roles were grouped together under the rubric *androgyny*. The implication was that they

are equally better off than sex-typed individuals because their choice of behavior is not restricted by gender role stereotypes. This way of conceptualizing androgyny has been labeled the *balance* theory of androgyny (Taylor & Hall, 1982).

If it appears that there are as many as three different theories of androgyny that may have been forwarded in the Bem (1974) article, with three different implications about who is healthy, this is indeed the case.

Despite the untested (and often unstated) theoretical assumptions inherent in the proposed relationships between gender roles and health, claims that androgyny is an index of psychological health were quickly accepted; therapy that widened a client's behavioral repertoire to include both masculine and feminine behaviors came to be considered desirable (Gilbert, 1981). Those who scored high only on the scale associated with their biological sex were called "restricted" and "psychologically inferior" to the androgynous types (Kaplan & Bean, 1976).

However, there was also criticism of Bem's original theory and measurement of gender roles. Spence, Helmreich, and Stapp in 1973 introduced their own measure of gender roles, the Personal Attributes Questionnaire (PAQ). While presenting their own measure, they pointed out that Bem's measurement of androgyny captured a heterogeneous group of individuals. In contrast, Spence and her colleagues classified their subjects as above or below the median on the two gender role dimensions and thus created four types of gender roles: masculine (high on masculinity and low on femininity), feminine (high on femininity and low on masculinity), androgynous (high on both scales), and undifferentiated (low on both scales). They found that both masculinity and femininity had main effects on a measure of self-esteem, and the effects were additive, so that high masculine, high feminine scorers had the highest self-esteem. Thus, individuals whom Bem would have included in the androgynous category (specifically, those who scored low on both scales) had significantly lower self-esteem than the androgynous individuals who scored high on both scales.

Although some have seen this revision as merely a difference in scoring systems, Taylor and Hall (1982) pointed out that it implies a different theory of androgyny; with this scoring change the balance theory of androgyny is discarded in favor of the main effects theory.

Bem initially saw this new scoring procedure as competing with her own (Bem & Lenney, 1976), but she eventually revised her criteria for androgyny so that the category included only those who scored high in both masculine and feminine attributes; those individuals low in both were no longer considered androgynous (Bem, 1977). In accepting this revision to her scoring scheme, in effect, Bem was changing her theory from the balance to the main effects theory of androgyny.

Testing Theories of Androgyny

Taylor and Hall (1982), in their excellent disentanglement of the various theories of androgyny, pointed out that the balance and main effects theories can be tested against each other and do not require completely different methodologies as originally thought. They suggest entering masculinity scores (M), femininity scores (F), and their interaction (M*F) into a two-way analysis of variance (ANOVA). The balance theory would be supported by a significant interaction term in a two-way ANOVA, whereas the main effects theory would be supported by two significant main effects in a two-way ANOVA. According to Hall and Taylor (1985) all three effects (i.e., each of the M, F, and M*F terms) must be significant for the emergent properties theory of androgyny to be supported. In this way, different conceptions of androgyny can be tested against each other with the same data.

Hall and Taylor (1985) went on to point out some theoretical confusion that theorists have generated in setting up tests of the three androgyny theories. Hall and Taylor believe that many investigators forwarding the main effects theory have really been discussing the emergent properties theory. That is, main effects theorists have been postulating that special benefits accrue to individuals who score high on both the masculinity and femininity scales, but they have tested this claim with analyses appropriate for the additive effects model. Thus, there is a history in gender role research of explaining or forwarding one theory of androgyny, and testing another. This practice has added conceptual as well as methodological confusion to the entire area.

Even though the three theories of androgyny can be tested against one another as described, most researchers have preferred to follow Bem's (1977) lead and test only the main effects theory of androgyny. Hence, they do not offer the information that would be necessary for the other theoretical formulations to be assessed. For this reason, I will examine primarily the main effects theory; the few studies that do explicitly test the three theories against one another will be noted.

GENDER ROLES AND PSYCHOLOGICAL HEALTH

Extensive research on gender roles has produced little evidence that androgyny is advantageous to psychological health (Pedhazur & Tetenbaum, 1979; Taylor & Hall, 1982). In this research, psychological health has been measured by a number of indexes, including overall adjustment, ego strength, self-esteem, psychiatric symptoms, depressive symptoms, and level of anxiety. Sufficient research has been conducted on the relationship between psychological health and gender roles to have allowed for four meta-analytic reviews of the literature.

Bassoff and Glass (1982) analyzed 26 studies and found a small, significant relationship between masculinity and psychological health, the latter measured with self-esteem and depression scales. No significant relationship between femininity and health was found. Thus, the main effects theory of androgyny was not supported; support would only have been shown if both the masculine and feminine scales were significantly associated with psychological health.

In a second meta-analysis, Taylor and Hall (1982) concluded that there was not much support for either the balance or the main effects androgyny theories, whereas there was support for a masculinity effect across a number of psychological health measures. Hall and Taylor (1985) pointed out that if there is no support for either the balance or the main effects theory, there is clearly no support for the emergent properties theory (which requires support for both of the others).

Whitley (1983) performed a meta-analysis of 35 studies investigating the relationship between self-esteem and gender roles. Although he found weak support for both the main effects and balance theories of androgyny, he pointed out that androgyny, as defined by either theory, accounted for only 1% of the variance in self-esteem; masculinity alone explained approximately 27% of the variance.

In a subsequent meta-analysis, Whitley (1984) explicitly tested the three androgyny theories (balance, main effects, and emergent properties) against one another. He found that none of the three variations of the androgyny hypothesis was supported; once again, only the masculinity scale predicted meaningfully to psychological health.

Meta-analyses are not always considered legitimate summaries of findings because they treat crude, uncontrolled studies and sophisticated, carefully planned studies as equals (Searles, 1985). But even individual studies that are methodologically sound and theoretically rigorous have not offered support for any of the androgyny hypotheses.

For example, Nezu, Nezu, and Peterson (1986) examined the moderating influence of gender roles and family support on the relationship between negative life stress and depressive symptomatology. They found that the more masculine one was, the lower the reported depression under high levels of stress. Femininity (and the interaction between masculinity and femininity) was not significantly related to depression.

Using a longitudinal design, Roos and Cohen (1987) examined the buffering effects of social support and gender roles on the relationship between life stress and trait anxiety and depression. They measured all variables cross-sectionally and then measured all variables but gender role orientation 8 weeks later. They found, with both the cross-sectional and the longitudinal data, that masculinity was a significant buffer of negative life events, whereas femininity was not. To the author's surprise, however, the interaction between masculinity and femininity (in this case, androgyny as defined by the balance theory) was also a significant buffer of stress when mood was measured 8 weeks later.

GENDER ROLES AND PHYSICAL HEALTH

There has been relatively little research into the nature of the relationship between gender roles and physical health. One reason for this is that gender role theorists usually do not explicitly state that gender roles should be related to physical health. A second reason for this dearth of relevant research has been the difficulty in defining optimal physical health. In the studies that will be briefly reviewed here, three indexes of physical health were used: self-perceived health status, use of medical resources, and physiological reactivity to stress.

Olds and Shaver (1980) found that high scorers on the femininity dimension reported significantly higher numbers of physical symptoms than all others. Consistent with this result was Hatzenbuehler and Joe's (1981) finding that masculine males reported fewer health problems than other males, as well as Wech's (1983) finding that masculine sex-type females reported significantly fewer health problems than feminine females. But it is unclear from such findings whether masculine types are healthier or just more reluctant to admit to physical frailties (Meinecke, 1981). The only study to find androgynous individuals (as defined by the main effects theory) reporting better health than their masculine peers was a study by Downey (1984), which had middle-aged males as its subjects.

Another index of physical health that has been measured is (infrequent) use of physician services. Marcus and Siegel (1982) found that high scorers on the masculine dimension made less use of medical resources than other gender role types.

Finally, some researchers have used cardiovascular and other physiological responses to lab stressors as health indexes, because greater reactivity has been associated with greater vulnerability to long-term health problems. Some prospective studies have supported this hypothesis, particularly when cardiovascular reactivity and later cardiac problems are examined. There is also some evidence that there is a link between short-term reactivity and certain personality variables (Krantz & Manuck, 1984; Julius, Weder, & Hinderliter, 1986).

Many psychological variables have been examined as possible causal agents of hyperreactivity to lab stressors, but gender roles have rarely been included. Myrsten, Lundberg, Frankenhaeuser, Ryan, Dolpin, and Cullen (1984) measured the gender role of their subjects and then recorded blood pressure and electrocardiograph (ECG) responses to an achievement stress and an orthostatic stress (which involves placing subjects on a horizontal tilt-table and then tilting them feet downward by 45 degrees). They found that there was no significant sex effect on the "stressed" blood pressure, but that there was a significant sex–times–gender role interaction. Post hoc analyses of their results indicated that among males, feminine types had the lowest blood pressure during the stressors, whereas among the females the undifferentiated types had significantly lower blood pressure than the other females.

Although there have been no other direct examinations of gender roles and reactivity, Frankenhaeuser and her colleagues have done some indirect work in this area. Looking at neuroendo-crine responses to an achievement stressor, Fran-kenhaeuser, Lundberg, and Forsman (1980) found that males were far more reactive than females. In subsequent work employing similar measures, Frankenhaeuser (1982) split her females into tradi-tionally employed and nontraditionally employed. Results indicated that the latter group was not significantly different from the males in reactivity to achievement demands; of the females, only the traditionally employed group was significantly less reactive than the males.

Other researchers have examined the effects of gender role–related interests on levels of epineph-rine secretion; high levels over a long period are thought to contribute to cardiovascular disease (Polefrone & Manuck, 1987). Girls showing the smallest elevations in urinary epinephrine during an exam were more oriented toward a traditional feminine role than were girls showing higher eleva-tions (Rauste-von Wright, von Wright, & Fran-kenhaeuser, 1981). During an achievement task, female undergraduates who had masculine aca-demic interests were closer to males in level of urinary epinephrine excretion than were females who did not have masculine academic interests (Collins & Frankenhaeuser, 1978).

Thus, there have been few tests of any androgy-ny hypothesis in the area of physical health. When self-report measures of health have been used, none of the androgyny hypotheses have been sup-ported; only masculinity appears to predict good health. In the area of short-term reactivity, there is a (very tentative) suggestion that higher scores on the masculinity dimension predict greater reactiv-ity, which in turn is associated with greater vulner-ability to long-term health problems. In all but one of the reactivity studies, gender roles were not measured with the usual measures—instead, vari-ables such as masculine academic interests were used. So although these results are thought pro-voking, conclusions about gender roles and reac-tivity should await further investigation (Pole-frone & Manuck, 1987).

MASCULINITY THEORY OF HEALTH

In response to the above findings, a fifth theory has been proposed. According to this theory, called the masculinity theory, the higher one's masculinity gender role score, the better off physi-cally and psychologically one will be, regardless of one's sex or femininity score (Antill & Cun-

ningham, 1979; Silvern & Ryan, 1979). Some the-orists have proposed that masculinity is even more beneficial for females than it is for males (Jones, Chernovetz, & Hansson, 1978).

These findings also have suggested to some in-vestigators that increasing masculinity would be an appropriate and desirable goal of psychother-apy (Vogel, 1979). Given the psychometric, meth-odological, and theoretical weaknesses of the research performed to date, however, such a con-clusion seems premature at best. These weak-nesses will be outlined in detail in the follow-ing section.

LIMITATIONS OF GENDER ROLE RESEARCH

Correlational Nature of the Research

Plaguing the entire investigation of the rela-tionship between gender roles and health is the problem that almost all studies have been corre-lational in nature. For example, shared methodol-ogy could in fact be responsible for the previously noted relationship between masculinity and health. There are two possible ways of minimizing potential artifactual findings of correlational de-signs: randomizing assignment to conditions or using more sophisticated research designs. Gender role assignment is obviously impossible to ran-domize, but very little effort has been made to improve correlational designs by implementing prospective or longitudinal data collection.

As mentioned earlier, Roos and Cohen (1987) conducted one of the few studies in which longitu-dinal data were collected on gender roles and psy-chological health. In support of the masculinity hypothesis, the investigators found that masculin-ity was the only significant buffer between life stress and mood disturbance when all measures were obtained at the same time. However, when the longitudinal data were examined, the balance theory of androgyny was supported. That is, mas-culine and feminine subjects became more de-pressed in response to high life stress than did androgynous and undifferentiated subjects.

Even though these findings suggest that there may be some support for the balance theory when measurement artifact is minimized, all correla-tional studies, including longitudinal ones, are vulnerable to alternative causal explanations. These findings do, nevertheless, allow us to question the support for the recent, empirically derived masculinity theory.

Social Desirability Confound

A second criticism about gender role research has concerned a possible social desirability confound, or the tendency to endorse the socially approved answer rather than the socially disapproved one. With the self-report instruments typically used to assess gender role identification, it is clear that there is the potential for social desirability to play a large role in gender role assignment.

Bem (1974) employed two different methods to ensure that her measure was not simply tapping social desirability. She first had students rate each item for its social desirability for the appropriate sex. Bem reported that the average social desirability ratings of her sex-appropriate traits were not significantly different: her masculine items for males were as socially desirable as her feminine items for females.

Second, in the original gender role scale Bem included a set of "neutral" socially desirable items, to ensure that high masculine, high feminine individuals were not simply endorsing socially desirable items. With these two methods in place, Bem declared that her gender role measure was not greatly influenced by social desirability.

Pedhazur and Tetenbaum (1979) attempted to replicate Bem's findings concerning the (lack of) influence of social desirability on gender role assignment and discovered two problems. First, some of the feminine items were actually socially undesirable with their sample of subjects—a finding also reported by Silvern and Ryan (1979). These two studies suggest that there are sample-to-sample fluctuations in the relative social desirability of the M and F scales.

Next, Pedhazur and Tetenbaum asked their subjects to rate the social desirability of the items for an adult of unspecified gender and found that the feminine traits dropped considerably in social desirability. One might argue that when no gender is announced, subjects assume that the adult is a male; however, the work by Broverman, Broverman, Clarkson, Rosenkrantz, and Vogel (1970) suggested that there are other influences to consider. They found that mental health professionals rated certain traits as mentally healthy for women, others as mentally healthy for men, and that these resulting stereotypes mapped quite well onto their stereotypes of mentally unhealthy and mentally healthy adults, respectively. That is, "healthy" adults (with no sex specified) have masculine traits, and "unhealthy" adults (again, with no sex specified) have feminine traits. This finding suggests that it is unhealthy, or socially undesirable, to be viewed as feminine.

Whitley (1983) also raised the question about shared variance between gender role scales and social desirability. He noted that the M and F scales of both the BSRI and the PAQ ask subjects to rate the degree to which they have socially desirable—but not socially undesirable—traits. He also pointed out that most self-esteem measures ask subjects to do exactly the same thing: to endorse a number of socially desirable items. Thus, it is not surprising that masculine items (which are more socially desirable) correlate significantly with self-esteem items (which are also socially desirable). What is not clear is whether this relationship is due to the causal influence of masculinity on self-esteem or to some third variable, such as social desirability, which is likely to be associated with higher scores on both masculinity and self-esteem.

If social desirability is related to masculinity, then the relative influences of the two overlapping constructs in determining self-esteem must be ascertained. Is it masculinity per se or the part of masculinity that overlaps with social desirability that is responsible for the increase in reported well-being? A revised gender role measure that could isolate the effects of social desirability and gender roles would help disentangle this knot.

In order to redress the possible social desirability confound in the PAQ, Spence, Helmreich, and Holahan (1979) extended their measure (hereafter called EPAQ) to include one scale of socially undesirable masculinity items and two scales of socially undesirable femininity items. By using such a scale, in which endorsement of both socially desirable and socially undesirable items determines gender role assignment, one can discover whether it is simply the endorsement of any masculine items (regardless of their social desirability level) that is related to self-esteem or whether only socially desirable masculine items predict high self-esteem.

It should be noted that Spence and her associates also created a fifth scale when analyzing the factor structure of their new gender role measure. The items on this new scale were bipolar; the ideal man fell on one side of the scale and the ideal woman fell on the other. The possible meaning of this new scale will be discussed below.

Use of Masculine-Dependent Measures

A third criticism about gender role research is that the benefits of masculine traits are more behaviorally anchored and thus more likely to be studied than the benefits of feminine traits, which are more relational (Hall & Halberstadt, 1980). If many of the outcome measures in previous studies were from the masculine domain, then it is not surprising that masculinity was significantly related to them.

Indeed, one could argue that much of the previous research cited concerning the gender roles–health links has instead tested the construct validity of the masculinity scales. Even such constructs as self-esteem and locus of control (for achievement) can be viewed as more masculine than, for example, empathy or emotional expressivity.

Taylor and Hall (1982) point out that in order to test whether or not androgyny is related to health, one should have outcome measures that are not sex typed or from one gender role domain. For example, evidence that androgynous individuals (as defined by the emergent properties theory) are superior to all others on non–sex-typed outcome measures would be considered support for an androgyny hypothesis. However, evidence that androgynous and feminine individuals are superior to others on female-typed outcome measures is simply construct validation of the femininity scale; similarly, evidence that androgynous and masculine individuals are superior to others on male-typed outcome measures is again only construct validation of the masculinity scale.

In one of the studies that examined a clearly nonmasculine dependent measure (marital satisfaction), Antill (1983) found that subjects' femininity was significantly related to their own increased marital satisfaction. In addition, they found that partners who had a feminine partner (regardless of the sex of that partner) were significantly happier than partners who had other types of partners. Similarly, femininity was positively and meaningfully related to a number of female-typed outcome measures in a meta-analysis of such studies (Taylor & Hall, 1982). Although these are not a substantive test of a gender roles–health relationship—they are again construct validity studies—they do suggest that there may be some benefits accruing to those who are feminine.

Perhaps these benefits are not being studied because the feminine outcome measures are less amenable to measurement.

Multidimensionality of the Bem Sex Role Inventory

As mentioned earlier, the most popular instrument for determining gender role is the BSRI. There are two assumptions about Bem's scale that need to be discussed.

The first assumption is that masculine and feminine gender roles are independent; individuals can have both, neither, or some combination of the two. Bem has been quite clear on this point, stating that her scale was designed to measure the two gender roles as independent dimensions (Bem, 1974). In factor analytic terms, this means that two orthogonal factors are hypothesized.

The underlying factor structure of the BSRI has been found to deviate substantially from the factor structure proposed by Bem. Pedhazur and Tetenbaum (1979) conducted a study in which they asked students to rate the average man and woman with the BSRI items, using the same instructions Bem (1974) had employed. They then gave the scale to a second sample and asked this new sample to rate themselves (and not stereotypes) using the BSRI. Comparison of factor analyses of these two studies revealed clearly different factor structures, neither of which had two factors. Thus, the assumption that the BSRI consists of only two orthogonal factors was not supported.

Wilson and Cook (1984) examined the concurrent validity of four popular gender role instruments, including the BSRI and the EPAQ. When examining the factor structure of the BSRI, they found 10 factors with eigenvalues exceeding 1. Only the EPAQ had the theorized number of factors—5. This finding also supports the contention that the BSRI does not measure two orthogonal dimensions.

A second assumption underlying Bem's measure is that both the M and F scale are unidimensional. That is, feminine traits such as affectionate and warm should correlate positively with each other as well as with other feminine traits such as innocence and yielding. If this assumption is correct, then the various items belonging to one gender role should load on only one factor.

Again, however, factor analyses reveal that neither the M nor the F scale assesses a unidimensional cluster of attributes. Wilson and Cook

(1984) reported that the BSRI M scale yields four factors with eigenvalues above 1, and the BSRI F scale yields five factors; only the EPAQ M and F scales yields one factor each. It appears then that the BSRI M and F scales are neither orthogonal nor unidimensional.

It is interesting to note that the BSRI item *masculine* itself does not load on the same factors as the items from the BSRI M scale; nor does the BSRI item *feminine* load on the same factors as the items in the BSRI F scale (Pedhazur & Tetenbaum, 1979). Instead, these two items load on a single (distinct) factor in a bipolar fashion. What, then, are the M and F scales measuring?

Predictive Validity of the Bem Sex Role Inventory

Spence and Helmreich (1978) pointed out that many gender role theorists make the questionable assumption that there is a high correlation between gender roles (i.e., self-ascribed traits) and behaviors. In so doing, they raised a serious concern about the predictive validity of the BSRI. Whitley (1988) conducted a multitrait-multimethod analysis of masculinity, femininity, and self-esteem to explore the predictive validity of masculinity and femininity. He collected (self-reported) trait and behavior measures of all three variables and found that masculine trait measures and self-esteem overlapped to such an extent that the two were indistinguishable. In fact, masculine trait measures were more related to self-esteem than they were to measures of masculine behavior. Given this finding, it is not surprising that masculine gender role scores predict to self-esteem; the problem is that masculinity gender role scores may not predict to masculine behavior.

LIMITATIONS OF GENDER ROLE THEORY

Given the factorial complexity of masculine and feminine gender role measures and the lack of extensive validity testing, one must ask what is being measured when one obtains a gender role score for an individual.

As previously mentioned, the term *gender role* has many meanings. It can encompass any personality traits, behaviors, preferences, occupational categories, or social positions that are associated with one sex more than the other. Psychologists who theorize about gender roles are typically concerned with personality traits and behaviors, rather than the panoply of variables associated with one sex more than the other.

But what if the constellation of personality traits and behaviors said to be associated with a gender role change as a result of whom you ask and when you ask? An operational definition of a construct that fluctuates according to culture and time should be disquieting to investigators.

What then do theorists mean when they say that someone is masculine or that someone else is feminine? Spence (1985) posed this question and arrived at the unsettling conclusion that, historically, theorists have measured (and therefore appear to have meant) simply those attributes that differentiate the sexes. If sex differences are defined in this way, even height can be considered an indicator of gender role, because men are generally taller than women. Clearly, contemporary gender role theorists thought that they were successfully limiting the range of the term by not using all sex-differentiating qualities as indicators of a gender role. However, this restriction has not led as hoped to a less ambiguous concept. What is still sorely lacking is an explanation of what the terms *masculinity* and *femininity* denote.

If gender role researchers were to limit their conclusions to such statements as "These particular sex-differentiating items are related to this health outcome measure," then the unspoken assumptions and connotations that cleave to the concepts of masculinity and femininity could be avoided. However, gender role theorists typically believe that they are measuring more than simply sex-differentiating traits. Often they propose that they are examining the amount or degree of gender role affiliation the individual possesses, or how sex typed the individual is. Thus, they claim to be measuring more than how much of certain sex-differentiating traits an individual possesses.

Although gender role theorists have not defined masculinity and femininity without ambiguity, lay individuals in our society (who use the terms so frequently) may be able to do so. Myers and Gonda (1982) asked 747 community residents and 233 college students to tell them what the terms *masculine* and *feminine* mean, using an open-ended response format. The authors were able to code the responses into four broad categories: personality or behavioral characteristics, gender (sex) reference, physical reference, and societal or biological reference. Gender and physical characteristics were given more frequently than personality and behavioral characteristics. In fact, Myers and Gonda noted that only 10% of the community responses and 14% of the college responses reflected the item content of the BSRI. They also noted that there was no consensus among subjects about what the terms specifically mean.

It is commonly assumed in Western society that females are more inclined to have an expressive, communal orientation, whereas males are more apt to have an instrumental, assertive orientation. In fact, the EPAQ, and to some extent the BSRI, appear to measure these two factors, rather than global masculinity and femininity. (The actual items *masculinity* and *femininity*, it will be recalled, load on another, bipolar factor.) Psychometric and theoretical analyses thus indicate that current gender role measures actually tap (at best) an expressive, communal orientation and an instrumental, assertive orientation. The EPAQ accomplishes this task more successfully than does the BSRI, which appears to tap many other factors as well.

All the other traits and behaviors that are thought to differentiate the sexes in Western society have not yet been reliably identified and measured, and so cannot (yet) be discussed. Therefore, rather than referring to the two factors assessed by gender role measures as masculine and feminine (terms that imply so much more than gender role instruments assess), I will henceforth call the two factors *emotional orientation* and *instrumental orientation*. Both orientations have been linked to health, although each has its own costs and benefits.

NEW RESEARCH DIRECTIONS

According to the work of Myers and Gonda (1982), we all have idiosyncratic concepts of what constitutes a gender role. A promising direction for the field of gender role theory, therefore, would be to measure individuals' definition of masculinity or femininity, and then see how close they feel they are to that concept. Baldwin, Critelli, Stevens, and Russell (1986) constructed a measure of gender role identification (the Sex-Rep) that measures the extent of an individual's identification with his or her personal definition of masculinity or femininity. They noted that the BSRI and Sex-Rep are nonredundant because the latter measures affiliation with personal gender role constructs and the former measures conformity to cultural stereotypes. Use of this new mea-

sure may improve the ability of researchers to study the relationship between gender role identification and health, if that is their goal.

A second research direction that seems promising for gender role theorists consists of the examination of sex-differentiating personality traits. It appears that sex-differentiating traits do not form one cluster or category, and indeed factor analyses (e.g., Wilson & Cook, 1984) confirm that personality traits that discriminate between the sexes are multidimensional. It seems reasonable, then, not to study any and all sex-differentiating personality traits and behaviors, but rather to choose as candidates for study those variables that are thought to cause some outcome of interest—in the present case, good health. For example, although applying makeup may be a behavior that differentiates the sexes, it is not a likely candidate for study because it is not regarded a determinant of health. On the other hand, emotional expressivity has been linked to health and also has been found to differentiate the sexes.

It is also important to examine how individuals internalize certain sex-differentiated personality traits; internalization can be considered in two ways. First, Spence (1985) believes that gender identity may be the mechanism through which individuals internalize certain attributes. Gender identity, or the acceptance of one's maleness or femaleness, is established very early in life.

> Gender identity . . . is thus a primitive, unarticulated concept of self, initially laid down at an essentially preverbal stage of development and maintained at an unverbalized level. As such, a person's sense of masculinity or femininity is ineffable—incapable of being put into words. (Spence, 1985, p. 80)

Spence proceeded to explain that while gender identity is being established, individuals may adopt sex-congruent attributes to confirm their sense of gender identity. As individuals age, however, their sense of what constitutes masculine and feminine becomes increasingly complex and is shaped by their particular environment and abilities. Developed in this way, a person's sense of masculinity or femininity is not universally tied to a consistent and limited set of traits or behaviors, but rather to a multidimensional and uniquely constructed constellation of attributes. This would explain why the meanings of masculinity and femininity are so difficult to capture.

An alternative way of understanding how the

sexes adopt different personality traits is to examine the socialization patterns or reinforcement contingencies of boys and girls for various behaviors and personality styles. Although Spence's gender-identity approach is fascinating, socialization patterns for specific attributes are more easily investigated. (Ultimately, work on Spence's theory of preverbal gender identity will likely be fruitful, but measurement of such constructs will require some ingenuity.)

Thus, the second direction that gender role theory could move in would be to study specific variables that (a) cause a particular outcome, (b) differentiate men and women, and (c) are differentially reinforced in boys and girls. This direction may provide a useful framework for understanding why modern-day American men report fewer physical and psychological symptoms and die earlier than modern-day American women. In order to elucidate this research direction, three promising personality variables will be examined for evidence of (a) their relationship to health, (b) differentiation between men and women, and (c) different socialization patterns.

SEX-DIFFERENTIATING VARIABLES AND HEALTH

Emotional Orientation

Both expressing one's feelings and being aware of one's emotions have been found to be linked to good health. Although the expression and awareness of emotion are probably related, and together may be considered as a general emotional orientation, they will be discussed separately.

The relationship between emotional expressivity and physiological reactivity has been investigated. Notarius and Levenson (1979), for example, coded the overall facial expressivity of subjects as well as recording heart rates, respiration rates, and galvanic skin responses during a stressful situation. They found that the greater the facial expressive tendency, the less the physiological reactivity (in the form of heart and respiration rate). Thus, those individuals who expressed their emotions during the stressor actually responded less severely on the physiological level than those who expressed less emotion. Additionally, Notarius and Levenson coded expressivity during a second stressful situation and demonstrated that the tendency to inhibit or express emotions was relatively stable.

Although other researchers have not found the inverse relationship between facial expressivity and reactivity (Laird, 1974; Lanzetta, Cartwright-Smith, & Kleck, 1976), many other studies have, even when employing different stressful tasks, different measures of emotional expressivity, and different indices of physiological reactivity (Buck, Miller, & Caul, 1974; Buck, Savin, Miller, & Caul, 1972; Lanzetta & Kleck, 1970).

The inverse relationship found between emotional expressivity and physiological reactivity shows support for the *discharge theory* of emotion. According to this model, when emotional reactions are aroused they must be discharged, either directly through overt expressions or indirectly through physiological reactivity. There are implications about long-term physical health from the discharge theory of emotion; expressing emotions is thought to be related to decreased physiological reactivity, which in turn is thought to be related to good health. Additionally, inhibiting the expression of emotion will have a deleterious effect on long-term health.

The second facet of an emotional orientation, the experience of emotion, may be associated with decreased psychological health. Watson and Clark (1984), in an extensive, integrative review of past studies, suggested that the disposition to experience and report negative emotion is associated with poor psychological health, even in the absence of overt stress.

Watson and Clark (1984) reviewed many diverse personality scales and demonstrated that a large number of popular tests alleging to measure anxiety, depression, neuroticism, and defensive style all are highly intercorrelated (p. 467). They concluded from this analysis that in fact these measures tap a general disposition to experience negative affect (NA). They then reviewed past research findings and reinterpreted the findings with this new, integrative construct in mind.

For example, White and Wilkins (1973) asked subjects to identify the mood expressed in ambiguous slides while false physiological feedback was being given. High NA individuals interpreted the moods of slides faster than low NA subjects, particularly when high arousal physiological feedback was provided. Watson and Clark (1984) deducted from this finding that high NA individuals are more eager to identify their emotions, whereas low NA individuals are, if anything, reluctant to do so.

Thus it appears that expressing one's emotions

decreases one's physical health risks, but focusing on one's emotions increases one's psychological health risks. Before we accept this puzzling conclusion, however, we must examine some crucial distinctions between the two sets of results.

One difference between the two general areas of emotion research is that Notarius and Levenson (1979) measured overall emotion, not positive and negative emotions separately, whereas Watson and Clark (1984) concentrated on negative emotion. The facial expressivity in Notarius and Levenson's study, however, was measured during exposure to an industrial accident film and threat of shock. Consequently, it is unlikely that many of the expressions could have been positive. Therefore, the data in both these studies largely consists of negative emotion. Further studies will be needed if we are to examine the effects both of focusing on and of expressing positive affect.

It is also important to note that Notarius and Levenson measured expressivity in response to a stressful task, whereas Watson and Clark addressed a more pervasive tendency to focus on and experience negative affect. The expression of negative emotion in stressful circumstances may be more of a coping style, whereas constant rumination about negative emotion may be more of a pervasive trait or personality style.

The next step is to examine the evidence that men and women differ in their experience and expression of emotion. Allen and Haccoun (1976), while examining variables that influence emotional expressivity, found that women express more emotions than men—particularly fear and sadness. From their other findings, the authors speculate that for females, emotion—particularly fear and sadness—may have a relatively important communicative function: eliciting help.

Brody (1985) also noted pervasive sex differences in emotional expression. She reviewed developmental research on sex differences in expressivity and reported that as boys grow older they decrease in their overall expressiveness, whereas girls decrease in the expression of only a few emotions, notably anger. She concluded that males and females are subject to different social pressures and sanctions concerning the expression and experience of emotions. She also has noted that females may be less subject to social constraints about emotional expression in experimental situations—that is, under stress—than are men.

Although we could speculate that a person must be aware of or experience negative emotions before expressing them—that one cannot have the benefits of the coping style without the costs of the personality style—Watson and Clark (1984) provide evidence that there are individuals who can be aware of and express their negative emotions when stressed, though they are not constantly aware of negative emotion in the absence of stress.

Unfortunately, it may be that individuals currently are socialized to have either both attributes—a constant awareness and an expression of negative emotion—or neither. Thus, it may be that society currently socializes females to focus on their negative emotions generally (i.e., as a personality style) and to express their negative emotions as a coping response, to elicit help. Men, on the other hand, may be socialized to not dwell on their negative emotions generally and also to not express them in response to stress.

If further investigation should support the above conjectures, then emotionality may turn out to be useful in explaining why women differ from men in terms of psychological and physical distress. Constant awareness of negative emotion as a personality style may have deleterious effects on one's psychological health, whereas expression of negative emotion as a response to stress may be beneficial to one's physical health; clearly this sex-differentiating personality variable warrants closer scrutiny.

Locus of Control

Locus of control—the attribution of control over events to oneself (internal locus) or to focus outside oneself (external locus)—also has been linked to both physical and psychological health. For example, Cohen and Edwards (1989) reviewed numerous personality characteristics that may act as buffers against stress and concluded that an internal locus of control is one of the few clearly demonstrated stress buffers for psychological health. Consistent with this result, in a longitudinal study Reid and Ziegler (1981) found that internals (in this case, those individuals who had a sense of personal control over the occurrence of desired events) had better physical health and physical ability to do everyday tasks than externals 5 years later. The relationship between locus of control and health is not simple; variables such as level of social support may affect the type of relationship that is found (Lefcourt, Martin, & Saleh, 1984).

In addition, men and women sometimes appear to differ in their levels of perceived control. Doherty and Baldwin (1985) examined longitudinal data from four large national probability samples and found that during the 1960s there were not any large sex differences in locus of control. However, by the mid-1970s women had become more external in their control orientation, whereas men's orientations remained the same. Pearlin and Schooler (1978) also found that women had less of a sense of mastery than men and suggested that the source of this difference may be different socialization patterns.

In their classic text on sex differences, Maccoby and Jacklin (1974) found a consistent sex difference in child-rearing practices: the actions of boys more often had greater consequences than did the actions of girls. That is, both rewards and punishments were contingent upon boys' behaviors. Girls, on the other hand, were less likely to suffer consequences, and so may have had less opportunity to develop a sense of the connection between their behavior and subsequent events.

In sum, society may reinforce women in such a way that they develop an external locus of control, and this personality variable in turn may decrease both their physical and their psychological health.

Problem Recognition

The link between problem recognition and health outcomes has been investigated and debated extensively. Often the debate has focused on accurate problem recognition, or stress appraisal. Lazarus (1983) indicated that the question posed usually receives an either/or answer; either an accurate appraisal is said to be a mark of mental health, or it is not. In fact, Lazarus suggested, whether accurate reality testing is costly or beneficial may depend on the context in which it occurs.

One conclusion Lazarus drew from the research he reviewed was that failure to recognize that there is a health problem (i.e., denial) when direct action could change the outcome leads to poor health outcomes. For example, denying that one is having a heart attack is likely to lead to more severe complications than would awareness and recognition of the attack.

Evidence to support Lazarus' speculation comes from Weinstein (1982), who asked students how interested they were in doing more to reduce their own risk for each of 41 health problems. Students also were asked to rate their own worry

about each health problem and their perceived risk for each problem compared with other, similar students. The health problems ranged from minor illnesses such as headaches to life-threatening ones such as cancer. The results suggested that unrealistic optimism (i.e., consistently rating one's chance of experiencing a health problem as below average) was related to less worry, and where there is less worry, there is less interest in performing actions to reduce health risks.

On the other hand, when direct action cannot change the outcome, denial should not be destructive and may even have some psychological value. Lazarus (1983) noted that some types of denial (namely partial denial, or illusions) may in fact be beneficial for one's mental health. In reviewing research on this topic, Taylor and Brown (1988) found that some illusions about one's control and self-worth may indeed promote psychological health.

Lazarus (1983) also pointed out that a time perspective may be necessary in order to accurately weigh the costs and benefits of denial. Denial may very well be adaptive during the early stages of a stressful encounter but maladaptive at the later stages. Hofer, Wolff, Friedman, and Mason (1972) studied the grief process among parents of children who were dying of leukemia. At an earlier contact, levels of corticosteroids—which indicate level of physiological distress—were measured for the parents. Initially, denying parents had lower levels of corticosteroids (less physiological distress) than did nondenying parents, who had elevated levels. Many months later, this pattern reversed, and the denying parents had higher levels of corticosteroids than did the nondenying parents. Although this finding has not yet been replicated, it implies that denial may help one through the crisis, but also may have (physical) costs down the road.

Do men and women differ in their problem recognition or stress appraisal? Shaw (1982) found (unexpectedly) that college men reported significantly fewer stressful life events than did college women. Folkman and Lazarus (1980) found that men and women in the larger community reported different sources of stress. Specifically, women reported significantly more health-related stressful episodes than did men. It also may be that the difference found by Shaw (1982) reflects a difference in reporting health-related events, but the type of stressful life event was not reported in his study.

Kessler, Brown, and Broman (1981) analyzed

sex differences in psychiatric help-seeking in four large surveys. Again, women were more likely to have reported a serious life problem (concerning personal, emotional, behavioral, or mental problems) within the last year than were men. Consistent with other epidemiological surveys, they found that women were more likely to have sought psychiatric help. They also found, however, that women were more ready than men to translate a given level of nonspecific distress into a conscious recognition that there was a problem. Once a problem was recognized, men and women were equally likely to seek professional help. Thus, it was a difference in the interpretation of distress as a sign of an emotional problem (i.e., problem recognition) that accounted for the sex difference in seeking psychiatric help.

Lazarus and DeLongis (1983) pointed out that the impact of some stressors "may be obscured by culturally imposed values and constraints and hence be considered unimportant or even go unacknowledged by the person experiencing [the stressors]" (p. 247). One could hypothesize, then, that men are socialized differently from women in terms of general problem recognition, and that recognition of health problems may be particularly different for men and women. Mechanic (1964) has asserted that boys and girls are taught to interpret physical symptoms differently and to react differently when feeling ill. Also, sex differences in physical-symptom acknowledgment and response increase as children get older (Mechanic, 1964).

Thus, an intriguing picture about sex differences, health-problem acknowledgment, and health begins to emerge. There is some evidence that problem recognition is related to health — positively for controllable stressors and negatively for uncontrollable stressors (although further longitudinal studies may suggest otherwise). Health problems are quite often (although not always) controllable, and it is with health problems that sex differences emerge most clearly. Finally, there is some evidence that girls are taught to recognize and respond to physical and psychological problems differently from boys. So it may be that women, by recognizing health problems more readily than men, take more appropriate health-producing action in the face of threats to health.

SUMMARY

Five major hypotheses about the relationship between gender roles and health have been advanced. First, the traditional hypothesis was that sex-appropriate gender roles promote the best health. Second, the balance theory of androgyny predicted that those who possess equal numbers of masculine and feminine attributes will be the healthiest. Third, the main effects androgyny hypothesis suggested that those individuals high in both masculine and feminine attributes will have the additive beneficial effects of both gender roles and so be better off than those who have access to the attributes of only one gender role. Fourth, the emergent properties theory of androgyny suggested that individuals who score high on both the masculine and feminine scales will be in the position to cope with stress most adaptively because they have both a larger coping repertoire and the flexibility to select appropriate coping strategies. Finally, the masculinity hypothesis proposed that the more masculine one is, the healthier one will be. Although there are findings to support each theory, the masculinity hypothesis has garnered the most support across a number of health indexes.

However, limitations to both the research and the theory were noted. Of most importance is the lack of construct validity for the most popular gender role measure, the BSRI. Factor analyses suggest that the masculinity and femininity scales assess, at best, instrumental and emotional orientations, respectively. It is difficult to continue within a theoretical framework when the scales available do not measure what is expected.

Two new research directions were discussed that could help to advance the investigation of sex differences in psychological and physical health. First, one could collect idiographic gender role definitions, as well as subject's conformity with these personally defined gender role definitions. Subsequently, one could examine the relationship between gender role conformity and health. Gender role researchers believed that they were assessing gender role conformity when measuring deviations from gender role stereotypes. Recent evidence, however, suggests otherwise.

When considering gender role attributes that differentiate the sexes, not every possible attribute should be evaluated. Rather, gender role researchers should study specific variables that (a) cause a particular health outcome, (b) differentiate men and women, and (c) are differentially reinforced in boys and girls.

Three personality variables and their relationship to health were examined: emotional orientation, locus of control, and problem recognition. Although it is tempting to equate an emotional orientation with the outmoded femininity scale, and locus of control with the outmoded masculinity scale, this would be unwise, given the factorial complexity of the two gender role scales. It is probably easier to simply measure the variables that appear to be related to health and then study how (and why) they differ between the sexes.

Finally, it should be noted that understanding sex differences in problem recognition may be pivotal for understanding sex differences in morbidity and mortality. It may be that women are socialized to recognize and respond to health issues more readily than men do, and that this accounts for both the increased health complaints and the longer lives of American women.

REFERENCES

Allen, J. G., & Haccoun, D. M. (1976). Sex differences in emotionality: A multidimensional approach. *Human Relations, 29*, 711–722.

Antill, J. K. (1983). Sex role complementarity versus similarity in married couples. *Journal of Personality and Social Psychology, 45*, 145–155.

Antill, J. K., & Cunningham, J. D. (1979). Self-esteem as a function of masculinity in both sexes. *Journal of Consulting and Clinical Psychology, 47*, 783–785.

Bakan, D. (1966). *The duality of human existence*. Chicago: Rand McNally.

Baldwin, A. C., Critelli, J. W., Stevens, L. C., & Russell, S. (1986). Androgyny and sex role measurement: A personal construct approach. *Journal of Personality and Social Psychology, 51*, 1081–1088.

Bassoff, E. S., & Glass, G. V. (1982). The relationship between sex roles and mental health: A meta-analysis of twenty-six studies. *Counseling Psychologist, 10*, 105–112.

Bem, S. L. (1974). The measurement of psychological androgyny. *Journal of Consulting and Clinical Psychology, 42*, 155–162.

Bem, S. L. (1975). Sex role adaptability: One consequence of psychological androgyny. *Journal of Personality and Social Psychology, 31*, 634–643.

Bem, S. L. (1977). On the utility of alternate procedures for assessing psychological androgyny. *Journal of Consulting and Clinical Psychology, 45*, 196–205.

Bem, S. L., & Lenney, E. (1976). Sex-typing and the avoidance of cross-sex behavior. *Journal of Personality and Social Psychology, 33*, 48–54.

Brody, L. R. (1985). Gender differences in emotional development: A review of theories and research. *Journal of Personality, 53*, 102–149.

Broverman, I. K., Broverman, D. M., Clarkson, F. E., Rosenkrantz, P. S., & Vogel, S. R. (1970). Sex-role stereotypes and clinical judgements of mental health. *Journal of Consulting and Clinical Psychology, 34*, 1–7.

Buck, R. W., Miller, R. E., & Caul, W. F. (1974). Sex, personality, and physiological variables in the communication of affect via facial expression. *Journal of Personality and Social Psychology, 30*, 587–596.

Buck, R. W., Savin, V. J., Miller, R. E., & Caul, W. F. (1972). Communication of affect through facial expressions in humans. *Journal of Personality and Social Psychology, 23*, 362–371.

Cohen, S., & Edwards, J. R. (1989). Personality characteristics as moderators of the relationship between stress and disorder. In R. W. Neufeld (Ed.), *Advances in the investigation of psychological stress*. New York: John Wiley & Sons.

Collins, A., & Frankenhaeuser, M. (1978). Stress responses in male and female engineering students. *Journal of Human Stress, 4*, 43–48.

Constantinople, A. (1973). Masculinity-femininity: An exception to the famous dictum? *Psychological Bulletin, 80*, 389–407.

Doherty, W. J., & Baldwin, C. (1985). Shifts and stability in locus of control during the 1970s: Divergence of the sexes. *Journal of Personality and Social Psychology, 48*, 1048–1053.

Downey, A. M. (1984). The relationship of sex-role orientation to self-perceived health status in middle-aged males. *Sex Roles, 11*, 211–225.

Folkman, S., & Lazarus, R. (1980). An analysis of coping in a middle aged community sample. *Journal of Health and Social Behavior, 21*, 219–239.

Frankenhaeuser, M. (1982). Challenge-control interaction as reflected in sympathetic-adrenal and pituitary-adrenal activity: Comparison between the sexes. *Scandinavian Journal of Psychology*, (Suppl. 1), 158–164.

Frankenhaeuser, M., Lundberg, U., & Forsman, L. (1980). Dissociation between sympathetic-adrenal and pituitary-adrenal responses to an achievement situation characterized by high controllability: Comparison between Type A and Type B males and females. *Biological Psychology, 10*, 79–91.

Gilbert, L. A. (1981). Toward mental health: The

benefits of psychological androgyny. *Professional Psychology, 12,* 29–38.

Hall, J. A., & Halberstadt, A. G. (1980). Masculinity and femininity in children: Development of the children's personal attributes questionnaire. *Developmental Psychology, 16,* 270–280.

Hall, J. A., & Taylor, M. C. (1985). Psychological androgyny and the masculinity × femininity interaction. *Journal of Personality and Social Psychology, 49,* 429–435.

Hatzenbuehler, L. C., & Joe, V. C. (1981). Stress and androgyny: A preliminary study. *Psychological Reports, 48,* 327–332.

Hofer, M. A., Wolff, E. T., Friedman, S. B., & Mason, J. W. A. (1972). A psychoendocrine study of bereavement, Parts I and II. *Psychosomatic Medicine, 34,* 481–504.

Jenkins, R. (1985). *Sex differences in minor psychiatric morbidity* (Psychological Medicine Monograph Supplement No. 7). Cambridge: Cambridge University Press.

Jones, W. H., Chernovetz, M. E., & Hansson, R. O. (1978). The enigma of androgyny: Differential implications for males and females? *Journal of Consulting and Clinical Psychology, 46,* 298–313.

Julius, S., Weder, A. B., & Hinderliter, A. L. (1986). Does behaviorally induced blood pressure variability lead to hypertension? In K. A. Matthews, S. M. Weiss, B. Falkner, S. B. Manuck, & R. B. Williams, Jr. (Eds.), *Handbook of stress reactivity & cardiovascular disease* (pp. 71–82). New York: John Wiley & Sons.

Kaplan, A. G., & Bean, J. P. (1976). *Beyond sex-role stereotypes: Readings toward a psychology of androgyny.* Boston: Little, Brown.

Kessler, R. C., Brown, R. L., & Broman, C. L. (1981). Sex differences in psychiatric help-seeking: Evidence from four large-scale surveys. *Journal of Health and Social Behavior, 22,* 49–64.

Kessler, R. C., & McRae, J. (1981). Trends in the relationship between sex and psychological distress: 1957–1976. *American Sociological Review, 46,* 443–452.

Krantz, D. S., & Manuck, S. B. (1984). Acute psychophysiologic reactivity and risk of cardiovascular disease: A review and methodological critique. *Psychological Bulletin, 96,* 435–464.

Laird, J. D. (1974). Self-attribution of emotion: The effects of expressive behavior on the quality of emotional experience. *Journal of Personality and Social Psychology, 29,* 475–486.

Lanzetta, J. T., Cartwright-Smith, J., & Kleck, R. E. (1976). Effects of nonverbal dissimulation on emotional experience and autonomic arousal. *Journal of Personality and Social Psychology, 33,* 354–370.

Lanzetta, J. T., & Kleck, R. E. (1970). Encoding and decoding of nonverbal affect in humans. *Journal of Personality and Social Psychology, 16,* 12–19.

Lazarus, R. S. (1983). The costs and benefits of denial. In S. Breznitz (Ed.), *Denial of stress* (pp. 1–30). New York: International Universities Press.

Lazarus, R. S., & DeLongis, A. (1983). Psychological stress and coping in aging. *American Psychologist, 38,* 245–254.

Lefcourt, H. M., Martin, R. A., & Saleh, W. E. (1984). Locus of control and social support: Interactive moderators of stress. *Journal of Personality and Social Psychology, 47,* 378–389.

Maccoby, E. E., & Jacklin, C. N. (1974). *The psychology of sex differences.* Stanford: Stanford University Press.

Marcus, A. C., & Siegel, J. M. (1982). Sex differences in the use of physician services: A preliminary test of the fixed role hypothesis. *Journal of Health and Social Behavior, 23,* 186–197.

Mechanic, D. (1964). The influence of mothers on their children's health attitudes and behaviors. *Pediatrics, 33,* 444–453.

Meinecke, C. E. (1981, December). Socialized to die younger? Hypermasculinity and men's health. *The Personnel and Guidance Journal,* pp. 241–245.

Myers, A. M., & Gonda, G. (1982). Empirical validation of the Bem sex-role inventory. *Journal of Personality and Social Psychology, 43,* 304–318.

Myrsten, A. L., Lundberg, U., Frankenhaeuser, M., Ryan, G., Dolphin, C., & Cullen, J. (1984). Sex-role orientation as related to psychological and physiological responses during achievement and orthostatic stress. *Motivation and Emotion, 8,* 243–258.

Nathanson, C. A. (1978). Sex roles as variables in the interpretation of morbidity data: A methodological critique. *International Journal of Epidemiology, 7,* 253–262.

Nezu, A. M., Nezu, C. M., & Peterson, M. A. (1986). Negative life stress, social support, and depressive symptoms: Sex roles as a moderator variable. *Journal of Social Behavior and Personality, 1*, 599–609.

Nolen-Hoeksema, S. (1987). Sex differences in unipolar depression: Evidence and theory. *Psychological Bulletin, 101*, 259–282.

Notarius, C. I., & Levenson, R. W. (1979). Expressive tendencies and physiological response to stress. *Journal of Personality and Social Psychology, 37*, 1204–1210.

Olds, D. E., & Shaver, P. (1980). Masculinity, femininity, academic performance, and health: Further evidence concerning the androgyny controversy. *Journal of Personality, 48*, 323–341.

Pearlin, L. I., & Schooler, C. (1978). The structure of coping. *Journal of Health and Social Behavior, 19*, 2–21.

Pedhazur, E. J., & Tetenbaum, T. J. (1979). Bem sex role inventory: A theoretical and methodological critique. *Journal of Personality and Social Psychology, 37*, 996–1016.

Polefrone, J. M., & Manuck, S. B. (1987). Gender differences in cardiovascular and neuroendocrine response to stressors. In R. C. Barnett, L. Biener, & G. K. Baruch (Eds.), *Gender and stress* (pp. 13–38). New York: The Free Press.

Rauste-von Wright, M., von Wright, J., & Frankenhaeuser, M. (1981). Relationships between sex-related psychological characteristics during adolescence and catecholamine excretion during achievement stress. *Psychophysiology, 18*, 362–370.

Reid, D. W., & Ziegler, M. (1981). *The desired control measure and adjustment among the elderly.* Paper presented at the joint meeting of the Gerontological Society of America and the Canadian Association of Gerontology, Toronto, Canada.

Roos, P. E., & Cohen, L. H. (1987). Sex roles and social support as moderators of life stress adjustment. *Journal of Personality and Social Psychology, 52*, 576–585.

Searles, J. S. (1985). A methodological and empirical critique of psychotherapy outcome meta-analysis. *Behaviour Research and Therapy, 23*, 453–463.

Shaw, J. S. (1982). Psychological androgyny and stressful life events. *Journal of Personality and Social Psychology, 43*, 145–153.

Silvern, L. E., & Ryan, V. L. (1979). Self-rated adjustment and sex-typing on the Bem sex-role inventory: Is masculinity the primary predictor of adjustment? *Sex Roles, 5*, 739–763.

Spence, J. T. (1985). Gender identity and its impli-

cations for the concepts of masculinity and femininity. In T. B. Sonderegger (Ed.), *Nebraska symposium on motivation 1984: The psychology of gender* (pp. 179–226). Lincoln: University of Nebraska.

Spence, J. T., & Helmreich, R. L. (1978). *Masculinity and femininity: Their psychological dimensions, correlates, and antecedents.* Austin: University of Texas Press.

Spence, J. T., Helmreich, R. L., & Holahan, C. K. (1979). Negative and positive components of psychological masculinity and femininity and their relationships to self-reports of neurotic and acting out behaviors. *Journal of Personality and Social Psychology, 37*, 1673–1682.

Spence, J. T., Helmreich, R., & Stapp, J. (1973). A short version of the attitudes toward women scale (AWS). *Bulletin for the Psychonomic Society, 2*, 219–220.

Taylor, M. C., & Hall, J. A. (1982). Psychological androgyny: Theories, methods, and conclusions. *Psychological Bulletin, 92*, 347–366.

Taylor, S. E., & Brown, J. D. (1988). Illusion and well-being: A social psychological perspective on mental health. *Psychological Bulletin, 103*, 193–210.

Vogel, S. (1979). Applications of androgyny to the theory and practice of psychotherapy. *Psychology of Women Quarterly, 3*, 255–258.

Waldron, I. (1982). An analysis of causes of sex differences in mortality and morbidity. In W. R. Grove & G. R. Carpenter (Eds.), *The fundamental connection between nature and nurture* (pp. 69–116). Lexington, KY: Lexington Books, D. C. Heath.

Watson, D., & Clark, L. E. (1984). Negative affectivity: The disposition to experience aversive emotional states. *Psychological Bulletin, 96*, 465–490.

Wech, B. A. (1983). Sex-role orientation, stress, and subsequent health status demonstrated by two scoring procedures for BEM's scale. *Psychological Reports, 52*, 69–70.

Weinstein, N. D. (1982). Unrealistic optimism about susceptibility to health problems. *Journal of Behavioral Medicine, 5*, 441–460.

White, M. C., & Wilkins, W. (1973). Bogus physiological feedback and response thresholds of repressors and sensitizers. *Journal of Research in Personality, 7*, 78–87.

Whitley, B. E. (1983). Sex role orientation and self-esteem: A critical meta-analytic review.

Journal of Personality and Social Psychology, *44,* 765–778.

Whitley, B. E. (1984). Sex-role orientation and psychological well-being: Two meta-analyses. *Sex Roles, 12,* 207–225.

Whitley, B. E., Jr. (1988). Masculinity, femininity, and self-esteem: A multitrait-multimethod analysis. *Sex Roles, 18,* 419–431.

Widom, C. S. (1984). Sex roles and psychopathology. In C. S. Widom (Ed.), *Sex roles and psychopathology* (pp. 3–17). New York: Plenum Press.

Wilson, F. R., & Cook, E. P. (1984). Concurrent validity of four androgyny instruments. *Sex Roles, 11,* 813–837.

CHAPTER 11

CURRENT ISSUES IN TYPE A BEHAVIOR, CORONARY PRONENESS, AND CORONARY HEART DISEASE

Frederick Rhodewalt
Timothy W. Smith

It has been almost 30 years since cardiologists Meyer Friedman and Ray Rosenman first introduced their description of the Type A behavior pattern (TABP; Friedman & Rosenman, 1959). Based on observations gleaned from their medical practice, Friedman and Rosenman suggested that the tendency to exhibit ambition, time urgency, extreme competitiveness, easily evoked hostility, explosive vocal stylistics, and rapid motoric mannerisms placed one at risk for premature coronary heart disease (CHD). Specifically, they defined the TABP as "an action emotion complex that can be observed in any person *aggressively* involved in a *chronic, incessant* struggle to achieve more and more in less and less time, and if required to do so, against the opposing efforts of other things and other persons" (Friedman & Rosenman, 1974, p. 84). According to Friedman and Rosenman, the Type A action-emotion complex is best thought of as a person-environment interaction in that the behaviors are observed only among predisposed persons (i.e., Type A) in challenging environments.

In the ensuing three decades, the TABP has been the focal point of a massive research effort to understand biobehaviorally mediated risk for CHD. In general, this research has contributed much to our broadened understanding of biopsychosocial models of personality and disease. However, enthusiasm for the TABP has waxed and waned with the accumulation of additional epidemiological evidence. As of 1981, the available evidence led the American Heart Association to conclude that the TABP was an independent risk factor for CHD (Review Panel, 1981). Since that time there have been several failures to replicate the earlier Type A–CHD association (e.g., Case, Heller, Case, Moss, & Multicenter Postinfarction Research Group, 1985; Shekelle, Gale, & Norusis, 1985; Shekelle, Hulley, et al., 1985). Recent reviews, both qualitative (Haynes & Matthews, 1988; Matthews & Haynes, 1986) and quantitative (Booth-Kewley & Friedman, 1987; Matthews, 1988), support the conclusion that Type A behavior as indexed by the Structured Interview (SI; Rosenman, 1978) is a reliable predictor of CHD, but that Type A behavior as measured by the Jenkins Activity Survey (JAS; Jenkins, Zyzanski,

& Rosenman, 1971), the most frequently used self-report measure of Type A, is not. Moreover, this conclusion is qualified by the fact that the SI does not predict CHD risk in populations with elevated levels of CHD risk factors (i.e., plasma cholesterol, hypertension, smoking) or previous myocardial infarction (MI; Matthews, 1988).

The above findings have led some to suggest that Type A behavior should be abandoned in favor of a search for the more "toxic" components of coronary-prone behavior such as hostility (Dembroski & Costa, 1988). However, acceptance of this recommendation should be tempered, perhaps, by recent evidence indicating that treatments intended to modify global Type A behavior lead to significant reductions in recurrent MIs among CHD patients (Friedman et al., 1986). Although the Type A modification findings suggest that some sort of TABP-CHD link is still viable, the recent spate of negative epidemiological findings raise fundamental questions about Friedman and Rosenman's original Type A hypothesis and have forced researchers to reconsider and revise their views of behavioral risk for CHD.

The present chapter will survey the central issues facing investigators in the Type A area. Research on TABP is far too vast to cover thoroughly in one chapter. Thus, we will briefly summarize each area and direct the reader to the most up-to-date reviews on the topic. We begin by discussing issues around assessment of TABP, the potential linkages of behavior to CHD, and the related issue of the search for the toxic behavioral element. After this survey we will turn to the main topic of the chapter. Because Type A intervention appears to hold promise in the treatment of CHD, we will focus at some length on psychological processes and motives thought to underlie Type A behavior and relate these models to attempts at Type A modification. The chapter concludes with a discussion of the lessons provided by research on Type A and CHD for general models of personality and disease.

ASSESSMENT OF TYPE A AND CORONARY PRONENESS

The reliable and valid assessment of the TABP has been a major obstacle limiting the study of individual differences in behavioral risk for CHD. At present, the failure to obtain consistent patterns of association between the various measures of the TABP and physiological mediators and

clinical endpoints of CHD indicates that the measurement issue is far from resolved. Three Type A assessment devices, the SI, the JAS, and the Framingham Type A Scale (FTAS; Haynes, Feinleib, & Kannel, 1980) have received the preponderance of research attention and are considered here.

The Structured Interview

Believing that Type As lack insight into their behavior, Friedman and Rosenman developed the SI to assess the behavior pattern (Rosenman, 1978). The SI is an orally administered interview in which respondents are asked a series of questions about their style of responding to situations that elicit impatience, competitiveness, and hostility. The questions are asked in such a manner as to elicit speech characteristics and behaviors thought to be indicative of Type A. In scoring the SI, particular attention is given to speech stylistics, behavioral mannerisms, and, to a lesser extent, self-reports of behavior. The scoring scheme results in individuals being categorized as either A1 (fully developed Type A), A2 (incompletely developed Type A), X (a combination of Type A and Type B characteristics), B3 (incompletely developed Type B), or B4 (fully developed Type B).

As noted previously, the SI appears to be the measure of TABP most clearly related to the development of CHD in population-based studies (Haynes & Matthews, 1988; Matthews, 1988; Matthews & Haynes, 1986). The SI is also the most reliable Type A predictor of cardiovascular reactivity, a presumed mediator of the association between behavior and CHD (Houston, 1988). In contrast, the findings have been mixed in studies examining coronary artery disease (CAD) via angiography. While there are approximately a half dozen investigations finding a positive association, roughly as many studies find no relationship between SI Type A and extent of artery disease (i.e., Matthews, 1988). These contradictory findings may reflect limitations of cross-sectional angiographic studies rather than the invalidity of the SI (Haynes & Matthews, 1988; Matthews, 1988).

Nonetheless, there are several reasons for concern about the reliability and validity of the SI. Although the SI was initially thought to possess acceptable reliability (Dembroski, 1978), Scherwitz (1989) has questioned this assumption with evidence that SI administration procedures have evolved over the years such that earlier tests of reliability and validity may no longer be meaningful. This contention is supported by the fact that although SI Type A was normally distributed in the Western Collaborative Group Study (WCGS; Rosenman, Brand, Jenkins, Friedman, Straus, & Wurm, 1975), the population on which it was first validated, the proportion of Type A is higher in many of the more recent epidemiological studies. This suggests that the proportion of Type As in the population is increasing, changes in the administration of the SI over time have artifactually produced increased estimates of the prevalence of Type A, or some other selection factor such as differential referral of Type As and Type Bs leads to overrepresentation of Type As in research populations. Any of these possibilities make epidemiological data difficult to interpret.

Interpretive ambiguities are all the more a problem in studies of at risk populations. The high proportion of Type As may restrict the range of scores and, thus, the study's sensitivity to detect relationships between TABP and CHD endpoints. Or, Type As' and Bs' admission into any study may be based on different decisions that are, in turn, differentially related to CHD. For example, Type As and Bs might differ in the criterion used for referral into the studies and thus be evaluated at systematically different stages in the disease process (Matthews & Haynes, 1986). In brief, the shifting proportions of Type As in different epidemiological investigations raise concerns about the SI as a measure of the TABP and the resulting ability to estimate TABP-CHD relationships accurately.

A recently recognized concern with the SI is that the manner in which it is administered appears to be a critical determinant of its predictive validity. Scherwitz (1988) reanalyzed the Multiple Risk Factor Intervention Trial data (MRFIT; Shekelle, Hulley et al., 1985) that initially found no relationship between SI Type A and CHD mortality. In his reanalysis, Scherwitz compared Type A assessments made by interviewers who employed a more relaxed, slower paced interview style with those who used a challenging, faster paced interview style. Type A classifications generated by the former were more predictive of CHD than classifications generated by the latter (Scherwitz, Graham, Grandits, & Billings, 1987).

Finally, the SI may not measure the global TABP as originally conceived by Friedman and Rosenman (Matthews, 1982). With the exceptions of vocal stylistics and hostility, it is clear that global Type A versus B ratings from the SI do not reflect several characteristics contained in the definition of Type A behavior. As Scherwitz (1989) noted, the validity of the SI as an assessment tool rests on the conceptual clarity of the hypothesized underlying construct. Thus, as psychometric development of TABP assessment instruments continues, greater attention should be paid to the psychosocial and behavioral processes hypothesized to underlie CHD risk. This important trend is already apparent in discussions of assessments of hostility (Costa, McCrae, & Dembroski, 1989; Siegman, 1989).

The Jenkins Activity Survey

The JAS was developed midway through the WCGS as a self-report measure of the TABP (Jenkins et al., 1971). The JAS (Form C) contains 52 questions similar to the SI. A discriminant function analysis was conducted using JAS item responses to predict SI classifications in the WCGS. The Type A subscale of the JAS is comprised of 21 items and is scored using optimal discriminant function weights. However, given that they are intended to be alternative assessments of a single construct, concordance rates between the JAS and simple SI A-B categories are in the alarmingly low 60% to 70% range (chance being 50% [MacDougall, Dembroski, & Musante, 1979; Matthews, Krantz, Dembroski, & MacDougall, 1982]). Thus, it appears that the SI and JAS are measuring different things. This observation is borne out by epidemiological and laboratory findings. With the notable exception of the WCGS, the JAS has not been reliably associated with CHD or angiographic findings (Matthews & Haynes, 1986). Further, the JAS is not related to cardiovascular reactivity as consistently as the SI (Houston, 1988). At the same time, however, the JAS has been found to be related to many behavioral and cognitive features of earlier definitions of the TABP (Glass, 1977; Matthews, 1982).

It is noteworthy that many of the epidemiological investigations that produce null findings with the JAS are troubled by methodological and interpretive flaws. In addition, it is likely that because the JAS scoring procedure was derived to predict SI classifications and not CHD outcomes, it has obscured the ability of the JAS to predict CHD. That is, the SI is a significant but imperfect correlate of CHD and the JAS is an imperfect correlate of the SI. Nonetheless, while a reexamination of the JAS's predictive validity might be warranted, at this point the JAS should not be considered a valid measure of CHD risk (Dembroski & Costa, 1988).

The Framingham Type A Scale

The FTAS is a 10-item scale derived from a 300-item questionnaire administered in the Framingham Heart Study (Haynes & Feinleib, 1982). The predictive validity of the FTAS is largely limited to the Framingham Heart Study in which it predicted CHD endpoints associated with angina. For example, the FTAS did not predict MI in the absence of angina. This unique pattern of CHD endpoints, when considered with information about the construct validity of the scale, raises important questions about the interpretation of the FTAS as a measure of the TABP. The FTAS is unique among TABP assessments in that it is associated with neuroticism and somatic complaints in healthy samples (r_s = .26 to .42 [Smith, Houston, & Zurawski, 1983; Smith & O'Keefe, 1985; Smith, O'Keefe, & Allred, 1989]). Measures of neuroticism also predict development of angina but not MI (French-Belgian Collaborative Group, Wilhelmsen, Wedel, & Pennert, 1982; Hagman, 1987; Medalie & Goldbourt, 1976; Otsfeld, Lebovitis, Shekelle, & Paul, 1964). Further, neuroticism is associated with persistent angina-like chest pain complaints in the absence of underlying CAD (Bass & Wade, 1984; Costa, Fleg, McCrae, & Lakatta, 1982; Roll & Theorell, 1984; Schocken, Greene, Worden, Harrison, & Spielberger, 1987; Wielgosz, Fletcher, McCants, McKinnis, Haney, & Williams, 1984). Thus, it is possible that the results from the Framingham study reflect an association between neuroticism and the tendency to complain of anginalike chest pain, rather than an association between TABP and CHD (Costa, 1986; Smith et al., 1989). At the very least, it is clear that the FTAS assesses a different dimension than that tapped by either the JAS or SI.

Current Developments in the Assessment of Coronary Proneness

Given the apparent difficulties with global Type A as a predictor of CHD, researchers have turned their attention to the components of TABP in an attempt to identify the toxic element of the behavior pattern. This strategy acknowledges that TABP is a multidimensional individual difference

and that, perhaps, only some components are associated with risk for CHD (see Chesney, Hecker, and Black, 1988, and Dembroski & Czajkowski, 1989, for reviews). In the first such attempt, Matthews, Glass, Rosenman, and Bortner (1977) compared new CHD cases to disease-free, matched control participants from the WCGS on a variety of characteristics derived from the SI. Among the characteristics that discriminated cases from controls were the potential for hostility, outward expression of anger, competitiveness, the frequent experience of anger, vigorous response style, and explosiveness of speech. In another reanalysis of the WCGS data, Chesney, Hecker, and Black (1988) rated 12 separate components of the original global TABP. Hostility was the strongest of five significant predictors of CHD in univariate analyses and the only significant predictor in multivariate analyses considering all TABP characteristics simultaneously.

Dembroski (1978) has developed a coding system for rescoring the SI for what he terms potential for hostility. The scoring protocol considers separately (a) self-reports of displays of anger, irritation, annoyance, and resentment; (b) the intensity of response; and (c) the degree of antagonism in the interview interaction. Dembroski and his colleagues have demonstrated positive associations between overall potential for hostility or its elements and both CAD and CHD, even in reanalyses of SIs from studies in which SI-global Type A failed to predict such relationships (Dembroski & Costa, 1987; Dembroski & Czajkowski, 1989).

Independent evidence for the nomination of hostility as the toxic element in behavioral risk for CHD comes from studies employing the Cook-Medley Hostility (Ho) Scale (1954), a self-report measure of hostility derived from the MMPI. Not only does the Cook-Medley predict CAD (Williams, Haney, Lee, Kong, Blumenthal, & Whalen, 1980) and CHD (Barefoot, Dahlstrom, & Williams, 1983), but it appears to predict mortality from all causes (Barefoot, Dodge, Dahlstrom, & Williams, 1989; Shekelle, Gale, Ostfeld, & Paul, 1983). Three failures to replicate this association between Ho scores and CHD risk have been reported (Hearn, Murray, & Luepke, 1988; Leon, Finn, Murray, & Bailey, 1988; McCranie, Watkins, Brandsima, & Sisson, 1986). However, methodological factors may account for some of the inconsistency (Williams, 1987), and a similar self-report scale has been found to predict mortality in two other prospective studies (Barefoot, Siegler,

Nowlin, Peterson, Haney, & Williams, 1987; Ostfeld et al., 1964). Although the Ho scale has been found to be related to self-reported and behaviorally rated overt hostility (Barefoot et al., 1989; Smith & Frohm, 1985; Smith, Sanders, & Alexander, 1988), it is more closely associated with measures of anger proneness, resentment, mistrust, and suspicion (Smith & Frohm, 1985; Smith et al., 1989; Pope, Smith, & Rhodewalt, 1989).

The Cook-Medley scale and Potential for Hostility are correlated (Dembroski, MacDougall, Williams, Haney, & Blumenthal, 1985), but the former primarily reflects covert or experiential aspects of hostility while the latter primarily reflects the overt expression of hostility. Recently, Siegman (1989) argued that these two aspects of hostility may not be equally related to CHD. At least some evidence suggests that more overt, experiential aspects of hostility are better predictors of CAD severity in angiography populations. However, both forms are conceivably linked to CHD. If, as Dembroski and Czanjkowski (1989) suggest, it is the overt expression of hostility and its attendant interpersonal difficulties that increase the risk for CHD, then potential for hostility is, in all likelihood, assessing a toxic aspect of hostility. However, it is also plausible that mistrust and resentment of others leads one to be chronically hypervigilant, a cardiologically taxing condition (Williams, 1989). In addition, the individual who harbors negative beliefs and expectancies about others also should experience a higher frequency of conflictive interactions with an associated increase in physiological arousal (Smith & Pope, 1990).

Work is also in progress that examines the relation of more general dimensions of personality to CHD outcomes. For example, Costa et al. (1989) argue that hostility toward others can be viewed as an aspect of the more basic personality dimension of agreeableness-antagonism. According to their reasoning, it is chronically irritable, impatient, antagonistic individuals who experience repeated episodes of autonomic arousal and, consequently, are at risk for CHD. This research is preliminary but offers promise for behavioral risk for CHD from a broad individual difference perspective.

In sum, 30 years of research indicates that attributes of certain individuals place them at risk for CHD. However, at present it is not clear precisely which characteristic or set of characteristics is the causal agent. The SI is capturing some attribute, perhaps a potential for hostility or even antagonism, that predicts CHD. It is equally clear that the JAS does not reliably predict CHD. Yet certain aspects of JAS Type A would appear to reflect stress-exacerbating appraisal processes and stressful coping responses. Perhaps, as we note elsewhere (Smith, 1989; Smith & Anderson, 1986; Smith & Rhodewalt, 1986), the JAS may indirectly increase CHD risk by its association with the tendency to create stressful environments. Perhaps it is JAS in combination with an additional individual difference (i.e., a hyperreactive cardiovascular system [Musante, MacDougall, Dembroski, & Van Horen, 1983]) or hypervigilance (Rhodewalt & O'Keeffe, 1986; Williams, 1979) that synergistically elevates CHD risk. In this regard, we endorse Costa, McCrae, and Dembroski's (1989) suggestion that the search for coronary-prone behavior might do well to move beyond the Type A construct.

MEDIATING LINK BETWEEN TYPE A BEHAVIOR AND CORONARY HEART DISEASE

The TABP→Reactivity Hypothesis

The clinical manifestations of CHD result from coronary artery disease (CAD), the thickening of the walls of the coronary arteries known as atherosclerosis. CAD leads to reduced or blocked blood supply to the heart, resulting in angina pectoris (chest pain stemming from insufficient blood flow to the heart), myocardial infarction (death of heart muscle tissue), and sudden coronary death.

A central issue in research on the TABP has been specification of the mechanisms through which behavior contributes to CHD. The presumed culprits are thought to be Type As' excessive cardiovascular and neuroendocrine responses to appropriately challenging or stressful situations. It is the magnitude of change from baseline, or reactivity, and not resting or chronic differences between Type As and Bs that is thought to accelerate CAD. Accumulating evidence indicates that activity of the sympathetic-adrenomedullary system and its concomitant increases in blood pressure, heart rate, myocardial oxygen demand, and elevations in circulating epinephrine, norepinephrine, and free fatty acids hastens CAD and probably precipitates acute CHD events (see Krantz, Glass, Schaeffer, & Davia, 1982, for a review), although this conclusion is still controversial (Krantz & Manuck, 1984). There is also evidence, albeit sparse, that Type As, compared with Type Bs, display greater pituitary-adrenocortical reactivity, another mechanism implicated in the etiology of CHD (Williams, Lane, Kuhn, Melosh, White, & Schanberg, 1982; Henry, 1983).

Laboratory evidence for the Type A-reactivity hypothesis is fairly consistent for SI-defined Type A but less so for JAS-defined Type A (see Contrada & Krantz, 1988; Houston, 1988; and Wright, Contrada, & Glass, 1985, for reviews). While not differing in resting levels, Type As respond to environmental challenge, social competition, and threats to self-esteem with larger increases in blood pressure than do Type Bs (Dembroski, MacDougall, Herd, & Shields, 1979; Glass et al., 1980; Pittner & Houston, 1980; van Schijndel, De Mey, & Naring, 1984). For example, Glass et al. (1980) demonstrated both elevated cardiovascular (systolic blood pressure, [SBP]) and neuroendocrine (plasma epinephrine) reactivity in Type As who were playing a competitive game while being harassed by their opponent compared with harassed Type Bs and nonharassed Type As and Bs.

In sum, researchers concluded that Type As are most physiologically reactive in situations that elicit active, effortful coping or anger arousal (Contrada & Krantz, 1988). This conclusion is complemented by Obrists' (1981) work that indicates that active coping is accompanied by the greatest sympathetically mediated cardiovascular reactivity. It is noteworthy that Type A-B differences in reactivity are most pronounced in situations that are moderately as opposed to extremely challenging, difficult, or of moderate incentive value. Type As and Bs appear to be equally reactive to highly challenging or stressful situations. It is also of interest that Type As experience heightened cardiovascular arousal in anticipation of difficult or challenging tasks (Gastorf, 1981).

An important test of the Type A-challenge-reactivity-CHD hypothesis would be provided by examinations of Type A reactivity in naturalistic settings. Unfortunately, few such tests have been conducted and those that do exist have produced somewhat inconsistent findings (Contrada & Krantz, 1988). Interpretive problems with these field studies have been compounded by their failure to translate models of Type A-reactivity into meaningful experimental designs (Matthews, 1982; Rhodewalt, Hayes, Chemers, & Wysocki, 1984; Smith & Rhodewalt, 1986; Smith, 1989). Although conceptual models of the TABP empha-size the interaction between the individual difference dimension and appropriate situational variables such as challenge or demand, many investigations simply report the presence or absence of Type A-B main effects on cardiovascular or biochemical responses. Epidemiological studies linking TABP to CHD endpoints are clear examples of this "main effect" approach to TABP.

A faithful translation of the laboratory TABP by challenge interactions on reactivity would involve assessment of level of challenge in the field, TABP, and degree of reactivity. Studies meeting these requirements do not exist (Ganster, Syme, & Mayes, 1989); however, there is evidence that such an interactive approach might be useful. For example, studies do show that Type As respond to high levels of perceived job stress with greater reports of psychological and physical symptoms than do Type Bs (Rhodewalt et al., 1984). Perceptions of challenge in the workplace (i.e., reduced control [Rhodewalt, Sansone, Hill, Chemers, & Wysocki, 1988], role ambiguity [Howard, Cunningham, Rechnitzer, 1986], or low autonomy and peer cohesiveness [Chesney, Sevelius, Black, Ward, Swan, & Rosenman, 1981]) lead to reports of higher job stress (Rhodewalt, Strube, Hill, & Sansone, 1988) and job dissatisfaction (Howard et al., 1986) in Type As than in Type Bs. Moreover, perceived job demand by TABP interactions have been found on cardiovascular outcomes such as systolic and diastolic blood pressure (Chesney, Eagleston, & Rosenman, 1981; Howard et al., 1986).

The studies described above are quite limited in the conclusions they permit. Studies are needed that examine Type A-B differences in cardiovascular reactivity to objective job demands. Taken together, however, the research described above suggests that such field studies would further our understanding of behavioral risk for CHD.

The Reactivity→TABP Hypothesis

An alternative approach to the Type A-reactivity relationship has been proposed by Krantz and his colleagues (Contrada & Krantz, 1988; Krantz, Arabian, Davia, & Parker, 1982; Krantz & Durel, 1983). This model is based on findings from patients undergoing coronary artery bypass surgery. Compared with Type B patients, Type A patients exhibit elevated SPB while under general anesthesia. Additionally, beta-adrenergic blocking agents, medications that dampen cardiovascular reactivity, also mute Type A speech stylistics and potential for hostility (Krantz, Durel, Davia, Shaffer, Arabian, Dembroski, & MacDougall, 1982). Krantz argues that Type A behavior may be a correlate of a biological predisposition to exaggerated cardiovascular reactivity rather than its cause. Thus, Type As learn to become behaviorally reactive to challenge and demand, in part because they experience exaggerated physiological arousal to such events. Although this is a plausible and provocative hypothesis, available data are not completely consistent (Contrada, Krantz, & Hill, 1988). For example, Kornfield, Kahn, Frank, Heller, Freeman, and Keller-Epstein (1985) found that SI-Type A was unrelated to intraoperative SBP among patients undergoing general surgery who had no history of CHD. Internal analyses did reveal, however, that SI-Type A was associated with intraoperative SBP among the small number of patients who had a positive family history of CHD.

Evidence for the heritability of Type A would provide further support for the somatopsychic model of Type A. While a global Type A does not evidence significant heritability (Rahe, Hervig, & Rosenman, 1978), the Type A components of explosive speech stylistics and potential for hostility do appear to reflect significant heritability quotients (Matthews, Rosenman, Dembroski, Harris, & MacDougall, 1984). Moreover, cardiovascular hyperresponsiveness to stress also may be heritable (Rose, Grim, & Miller, 1984; Smith et al., 1987). It appears that the biological contributions to Type A behavior and CHD risk merit further study; however, at present the data are too limited to permit any conclusions.

One implication of the biological approach to TABP might be that the behaviors are little more than epiphenomena with no direct relation to CHD. Such a conclusion is, at minimum, premature and, if accepted, could limit further understanding of biobehavioral pathways to CHD (Smith, 1989; Smith & Anderson, 1986). This point is illustrated by animal research on CAD (Manuck, Muldoon, Kaplan, Adams, & Polefrone, 1989). These investigators placed cynomologus monkeys fed an atherogenic diet into stable or unstable social environments. Two individual difference measures, heart rate reactivity to a capture stressor and social dominance, also were obtained. Autopsy data indicate that socially dominant male animals in an unstable social environment exhibited significantly greater CAD than did socially submissive animals in an unstable environment or both types of animals in a stable environment. Monkeys exhibiting greater heart rate reactivity also had more advanced CAD than their low reactivity counterparts. However, heart rate reactivity was not related to social dominance. Thus, simple individual differences in reactivity could not explain the interactive effect of social dominance and situational stress on CAD, even though subsequent research has indicated that this interactive effect is mediated by beta-andrenergic, sympathetic nervous system activity (Kaplan, Manuck, & Clarkson, 1987).

Type A→Reactivity: Additional Considerations

Although research available to date is not definitive, it does support the hypothesis that repeated episodes of cardiovascular and neuroendocrine arousal contribute to CHD (Manuck & Krantz, 1984). Individual differences, particularly TABP and its components, have been at the center of this research effort. Although precisely which element of Type A is related to reactivity and disease is an open question, the individual difference approach to CHD risk is still viable. However, as we have noted elsewhere (Smith, 1989; Smith & Anderson, 1986; Smith & Rhodewalt, 1986), basic conceptual issues guiding the study of individual differences in cardiovascular reactivity may restrict our full understanding of the ways in which individual differences in reactivity link TABP to disease.

Specifically, our concern is the ways in which individual difference variables are examined with regard to cardiovascular reactivity. One of two approaches is typically taken (Manuck & Krantz, 1984). Reactivity is often treated as a trait that is triggered by a pervasive set of daily events and produces a chronically elevated steady state of cardiovascular arousal in Type A individuals, which in turn places them at greater risk than Type Bs for CHD. Alternatively, reactivity is viewed as an attribute of the person who statically interacts with certain eliciting situations to produce greater increases in reactivity in Type As than in Type Bs confronted with the same situation. It is the relative increase in magnitude of reactivity that places the Type A at added risk for CHD. The focus in this latter model is on differences in reactivity between Type As and Bs in specified equivalent situations.

Both the trait and static interaction models of individual difference in cardiovascular reactivity have the potential to obscure the complex relationships between people and their environments conveyed in most recent approaches to personality (Cantor & Kihlstrom, 1987). Rather than statically interacting with situations, person characteristics can actively produce differences in situations. Individuals modify situations through their cognitions and behavior and, in turn, situations selectively elicit and reinforce certain cognitions and behaviors. Rather than simply possessing a set of stressful and cardiovascularly taxing coping responses, Type As may actually create many of the situations to which they are responding with exaggerated reactivity.

A transactional approach such as we are advocating appears to be warranted by an extensive body of recent research that collectively indicates TABP is related to a variety of stress-engendering social and cognitive processes (reviewed in Smith & Anderson, 1986; Smith & Rhodewalt, 1986). Through their choice of situations (Feather & Volkmer, 1988; Ortega & Pepal, 1984), appraisals of situations (Carver, 1980; Rhodewalt & Comer, 1982; Rhodewalt & Davison, 1983; Smith & Brehm, 1981a), social interactions (Van Egeren, 1979a,b; Van Egeren, Sniderman, & Roggelin, 1982), and self-appraisals (Cooney & Zeichner, 1985; O'Keeffe & Smith, 1988), Type As operate on their environments in ways that should increase the frequency, duration and intensity of stressors, and, presumably, episodes of cardiovascular reactivity. The stress-engendering aspect of Type A behavior and its relation to cardiovascular reactivity is clearly illustrated in a study by Ortega and Pepal (1984). Compared with Type Bs, Type A subjects selected higher levels of task difficulty and exhibited higher levels of cardiovascular arousal when working on such tasks.

Differences between Type As and Type Bs in coping behaviors are also consistent with the view of TABP as stress-engendering behavior. Compared with Type Bs, Type As prefer to work alone when under stress (Dembroski & MacDougal, 1978), have difficulty delegating work load (Strube & Werner, 1985), suppress or deny fatigue (Carver, Coleman, & Glass, 1976), and engage in active, problem-focused coping (Rhodewalt & Agustsdottir, 1984; Smith & Brehm, 1981b). All of these responses should increase the duration and, perhaps, intensity of exposure to reactivity-arousing situations.

The transactional model of TABP and reactivity, although as yet untested, has several implications for future research. First, as noted previously, the SI is a better predictor of cardiovascular reactivity and CHD than the JAS. However, the JAS has been most closely associated with stress-engendering behavior. Tests of SI-TABP as a correlate of a challenge-and-demand–engendering style, for the most part, have not been undertaken. It is possible, however, that different TABP assessment instruments vary in the degree to which they measure reactivity versus tendencies to create stressful situations. As has been suggested elsewhere, the best prediction of behavioral risk for CHD may be gained from a combination of independent predictors of reactivity and challenge-and-demand–engendering style (Musante et al., 1983; Smith, 1989; Smith & Anderson, 1986; Smith & Rhodewalt, 1986).

Second, if future research confirms that hostility or antagonism and not other components of the TABP are the sole toxic elements, the transactional model will still be a useful framework in which to study behavior, reactivity, and CHD risk (Smith, 1989; Smith & Frohm, 1985; Smith & Rhodewalt, 1986). As with global Type A, physiological reactivity is the presumed mediator between hostile behavior and disease (Williams, Barefoot, & Shekelle, 1985). Thus, hostile persons, through their cognitions, affective reactions, and behaviors, create more frequent, intense, and longer lasting interpersonal stresses, and experience concomitant episodes of arousal (Smith & Pope, 1990).

Although limited, recent research with the Cook-Medley Scale is consistent with this interpretation. Highly cynical, hostile people report more interpersonal stress and conflict in their families, marriages, and jobs than do low hostile individuals (Smith & Frohm, 1985; Smith, Pope, Sanders, Allred, & O'Keeffe, 1988). High scores on the Ho scale are also associated with increased levels of antagonism, anger, and blame during discussions of marital conflicts (Smith et al., 1988). Further, highly hostile individuals, compared with their less hostile counterparts, displayed more aggression, reported more anger, and viewed their interaction partner more negatively when playing a mixed-motive game (Pope et al., 1989). Finally, compared with less hostile individuals, highly cynical, hostile people evidence greater increases in blood pressure during exposure to interpersonal stressors (Hardy & Smith, 1988; Smith & Allred,

1989; Suarez, Williams, & McCrae, 1988). It is equally plausible that the impatience and irritability associated with potential for hostility also has interpersonal consequences in terms of stressful, conflictive interactions. These findings highlight the potential relevance of the transactional approach to the study of hostility and CHD risk (Smith & Pope, 1990).

TABP → Health Behavior → Disease

In addition to differences in the creation of, or responses to, demanding situations, Type As and Bs differ on several other health-relevant dimensions that could place them at differential risk for CHD as well as for other health difficulties.

Type As are more likely than Type Bs to use denial and suppression when coping with a stressor (Carver, Coleman, & Glass, 1976; Gentry, Oude-Weme, Musch, & Hall, 1981; Pittner & Houston, 1980; Pittner, Houston, & Spiridigliozzi, 1983). Coping with denial is particularly prevalent among Type As when they are engaged in a task. For example, Type As who expected to continue working on an aversive task reported less fatigue and fewer symptoms than Type As who believed they had completed the task and Type Bs regardless of task involvement (Weidner & Matthews, 1978; see also Stern, Harris, & Elverum, 1981). Similarly, Schlegel, Wellwood, Copps, Gruchow, and Sharratt (1980) asked Type A and B postinfarct patients to report daily levels of challenge and MI-related symptoms such as chest pain. In addition, neuroendocrine measures constituted a physiological index of challenge. For both self-report and physiological measures of challenge, Type As reported fewer symptoms on high challenge days than on low challenge days. In contrast, Type Bs reported more symptoms with greater challenge.

Taken together, these findings indicate that Type As, particularly when they are engaged in an involving or challenging task, deny or fail to notice physical symptoms of fatigue and illness. Such denial can cause delay in seeking treatment and, in the case of MI, delay can lead to a more severe infarction and death (Matthews, Kuller, Siegal, Thompson, & Varat, 1983). More generally, Type As' tendency to ignore symptoms and signs of distress may prolong their contact with stressful environments and delay or interfere with their seeking care and assistance.

Type As and Bs also differ in the way they respond to medical treatment. Type As are more sensitive to threats to behavioral freedom than are Type Bs (Glass, 1977) and respond to such threats with active and often demand-engendering attempts to reassert control. Studies indicate that, relative to Type Bs, Type As are more likely to perceive coercive intent (Carver, 1980) and respond with "reactance" (Wicklund & Brehm, 1976) or efforts to reacquire the threatened behavior (Rhodewalt & Comer, 1982; Rhodewalt & Davison, 1983; Snyder & Frankel, 1975).

Rhodewalt and his colleagues (Rhodewalt & Fairfield, 1990; Rhodewalt & Marcroft, 1988; Rhodewalt & Strube, 1985) have argued that to the extent that aspects of the health-care setting threaten one's behavioral freedom, Type As should be likely to display reactance-motivated noncompliance with treatment (see also Taylor, 1979). In two demonstrations, JAS-defined TABP was significantly associated with noncompliance (Rhodewalt & Marcroft, 1988; Rhodewalt & Strube, 1985). Moreover, medically noncompliant Type As reported greater self-blame for the health problem, were angrier about it, and thought of it more as an entity to be fought than did compliant Type As and Bs (all responses thought to be characteristic of reactance).

Because studies also found many Type As to be compliant, the model requires additional refinement. Nonetheless, available data suggest that treatment noncompliance motivated by reactance is an alternative pathway through which Type A behavior affects health status. This observation takes on added significance when one considers the kinds of life-style changes prescribed to MI patients in order to reduce the risk of recurrent MI. Type A patients are more likely to construe such recommendations as threats to their behavioral freedom. They should then be more apt to continue unhealthy behaviors such as smoking or excessive work load and, consequently, increase the risk for recurrent MI. This speculation suggests that those providing cardiac rehabilitation should be sensitive to the control dynamics of the treatment regimen.

To summarize, the TABP-cardiovascular reactivity hypothesis has received the most attention and appears to be the most viable direct path between individual attributes and behaviors and CHD risk. Regardless of what component of the TABP turns out to be most toxic, exaggerated and frequent episodes of reactivity are likely to be the mediating link to accelerated CAD and increased risk of CHD. Other aspects of the TABP also may contribute to CHD risk. Type As' selective attention to symptoms and response to illness and treatment may indirectly contribute to increased risk for CHD.

THE PSYCHOLOGY OF TABP

A key question guiding much research on the TABP asks, Why do Type As behave as they do? This question becomes all the more important in the context of recent attempts to modify TABP in order to reduce CHD risk (Friedman et al., 1986; Gill et al., 1985). A thorough understanding of the psychological dynamics underlying TABP will permit the identification of critical cognitions, motivations, and behaviors as targets for intervention.

While Friedman and Rosenman provided a detailed description of the TABP, they were less specific about the developmental antecedents or psychological underpinnings of the behavioral syndrome. Friedman and Rosenman (1974) conjectured that feelings of insecurity and concerns about personal worth were at the core of the TABP. They suggested that these concerns probably went back to the Type A individual's childhood experiences. Accordingly, the Type A's excessive strivings and persistent struggles were attempts to acquire symbols of recognition and worth. After 15 years of research on the psychology of the TABP, researchers are just now beginning to substantiate Friedman and Rosenman's observations.

TABP and Control Threat

David Glass was the first to investigate systematically a psychological account of the TABP. In a seminal monograph, Glass (1977) depicted the TABP as a set of coping responses elicited by perceived threats to control. According to Glass, the Type A behaviors of time urgency, achievement striving, competitiveness, aggressiveness, and hostility could all be considered control mastery behaviors that permit the Type A to reassert or maintain control in challenging situations. Repeated performance of these control mastery behaviors elicits cardiovascular and neuroendocrine arousal, and ultimately places Type As at elevated risk for CHD.

More than a decade of theory and research has elaborated on Glass' original formulation. While the emerging perspectives to some degree share the assumption that the TABP is an active coping response to threat, they differ in their explanations for why this reactivity occurs. Collectively, the theory and research implicate a variety of self-evaluative and self-regulatory processes as central to the psychology of TABP.

TABP, Self-Involvement, and Identity

Scherwitz and colleagues (Scherwitz, Berton, & Leventhal, 1978; Scherwitz & Canick, 1988) proposed that Type As are more self-involved than Type Bs and that it is self-involvement that underlies CHD risk. This conclusion is based on the observation that SI-defined Type As respond to the SI with frequent self-references (the use of the personal pronouns I, me, my, mine). JAS-defined Type A is also associated with greater self-referencing (Rhodewalt, 1984). More important, Scherwitz, Berton, and Leventhal (1977, 1978) found that highly self-referencing Type As also displayed elevated systolic and diastolic blood pressure during the SI compared with low self-referencing Type As and highly and low self-referencing Type Bs (Scherwitz et al., 1977, 1978). Self-referencing is related to CAD severity (Scherwitz et al., 1983) and prospectively related to CHD, death from CHD (Scherwitz et al., 1987), and recurrent CHD (Powell & Thoresen, 1985). Self-referencing, then, particularly in interaction with extreme Type A behavior, appears to place one at risk for CHD (see Krantz, 1984, for an exception).

Initially, Scherwitz and colleagues (Scherwitz et al., 1978, 1983) suggested that Type A self-referencing reflected a greater degree of objective self-awareness or self-focused attention (Carver & Scheier, 1981). As such, Type As were more likely to compare performance outcomes with internal standards. Because most individuals and Type As in particular tend to hold high internal standards (cf. O'Keeffe & Smith, 1988), the comparison process typically results in a large discrepancy between current performance and internal standards and subsequent effortful attempts to reduce the discrepancy. Although quite plausible, the chronic self-awareness hypothesis is not supported by the fact that in males TABP is unrelated to trait self-consciousness as indexed by the Private Self-Consciousness Scale (it is weakly related in women; Smith & Brehm, 1981b). In addition, self-referencing, at least in JAS Type As, appears to be a function of self-attributional statements and not an indicator of more general self-salience in thought (Rhodewalt, 1984).

More recently, Scherwitz and Canick (1988) proposed that self-referencing is prominent in those with a fragile or vulnerable identity. Perhaps because of a lack of clear identity, Type As are constantly engaged in a chronic struggle to "shore up" their identity images. Self-referencing is thought to be in the service of maintaining and repairing desired, weakly held identities.

Scherwitz and Canick drew the parallels between self-referencers and narcissism and speculated that individuals with easily threatened identities may use hostility as a coping mechanism to ward off such threats. This speculation is supported by the reported association between frequency of self-referencing and potential for hostility (Dembroski, reported in Scherwitz & Canick, 1988). Although as yet untested, pursuing the relations among identity process, TABP, and CHD risk appears to be a potentially fruitful avenue.

TABP and Cognitive Social Learning

An alternative perspective was offered by Price (1982), who contended that the TABP is the result of cognitive social learning processes occurring in a context of social and cultural imperatives. At the core of her model is the assumption that Western society promotes the beliefs that one must constantly prove oneself and that resources are in short supply. Related to these beliefs are fears of insufficient self-worth, that self-worth is not constant and must always be demonstrated, and that insufficient resources are available. These beliefs, according to Price, form the cognitive basis of TABP and underpin the psychological and interpersonal characteristics of ambition and competitiveness. TABP, in this view, reflects a chronic striving for approval and material gain in order to prove one's self-worth. At the interpersonal level, attempting to prove oneself while coacting with hard-driving people engenders competitiveness. Competitiveness, in turn, triggers overt aggressiveness, easily aroused impatience, irritability, and hostility. Finally, while noting positive and negative, short- and long-term consequences of TABP, Price argued that, overall, the behavior pattern is sustained because the underlying beliefs guide the interpretation of positive and negative outcomes in a self-confirmatory fashion.

As noted previously, cognitive self-regulatory processes have been tied to TABP. Type As set higher goals for performance (Grimm & Yarnold, 1984; O'Keeffe & Smith, 1988), are chronically self-critical (O'Keeffe & Smith, 1988), and attend more to negative feedback than do Type Bs (Cooney & Zeichner, 1985). Further, Type A-B differences in satisfaction with performance are greatest when performance standards are ambiguous and disappear when performance standards are clear (O'Keeffe & Smith, 1988). As O'Keeffe and Smith noted, the pattern of Type A high standards and self-criticism are characteristic of cognitive social learning explanations for competitive, hard-driving, and achievement-oriented behavior (Carver & Scheier, 1981; Mischel, 1973). However, the predicted self-regulatory correlates are much more closely related to the TABP as defined by the JAS than by the SI (O'Keeffe & Smith, 1988).

In sum, Price's social cognitive model of Type A is supported by studies of Type A self-regulatory processes. However, evidence of the proposed underlying cognitive set of beliefs and values is lacking. Burke (1984a, 1984b) reported small associations between TABP and measures of the beliefs described by Price, although the meaning of these findings is unclear because Price contended that Type As have little insight into these beliefs.

TABP and Self-Appraisal

Strube (1985) provided yet a different perspective on the psychology of the TABP. He suggested that Type As place a high value on the attainment and accurate assessment of success and productivity. In situations that create uncertainty about their ability, Type As, compared with Type Bs, respond with greater attempts to generate diagnostic feedback. In Strube's view, the TABP is a set of coping behaviors designed to acquire uncertainty-reducing, self-evaluative information. Strube reinterpreted much of the laboratory research on the TABP and responses to uncontrollability as evidence for Type As' exaggerated attempts to reduce uncertainty. In direct tests of the self-appraisal model, Strube and his colleagues (Strube & Boland, 1986; Strube, Boland, Manfredo, & Al-Falaij, 1987) demonstrated that compared with Type Bs, JAS-defined Type As made uncertain about an ability will select performance settings and work harder and longer in order to obtain uncertainty-reducing feedback.

Although Strube's model is provocative and ex-

isting data are largely congruent with his conclusions, the basic premise that Type As strive for
accurate self-evaluation may be called into
question. Rather, it seems that Type As strive for
feedback and appraise such feedback in ways that
substantiate their sense of self-worth and self-efficacy. For instance, Type As' self-attributions appear to be in the service of enhanced self-efficacy
or control motives rather than for the purpose of
accurate self-appraisal (Rhodewalt, Strube, Hill,
& Sansone, 1988).

It is also noteworthy that although the findings
of Strube and Boland (1986) and Strube et al.
(1987) are consistent with self-appraisal predictions, they are also open to alternative interpretations. Specifically, in each study, attempts to make
subjects uncertain about their abilities also may
have threatened their control or challenged their
self-worth. Seeking diagnostic feedback or persisting at a task may not have been behaviors
aimed at obtaining accurate self-assessments so
much as behaviors aimed at reasserting control or
self-worth. The studies do not permit one to distinguish clearly which motives were operating. It
is quite possible that the Type A-B differences in
self-evaluative behaviors, taken as evidence for the
self-appraisal model are, in fact, behaviors motivated by concerns about self-worth and identity
(e.g., Price, 1982; Scherwitz & Canick, 1988).

TABP and Antagonism

Recently, Costa et al. (1989) proposed that the
TABP component of potential for hostility is a
correlate of the more basic personality dimension
of agreeableness-antagonism. At this point the research is more descriptive than explanatory. However, antagonistic people are described as "self-
centered, concerned with their own status, gain,
or amusement. They are willing to fight for their
goals and they view others as either hostile com-
petitors seeking the same selfish ends or as con-
temptible fools" (Costa et al., 1989, p. 51). It is
striking that antagonism also may be a manifestation of underlying concerns about identity and
self-worth. Of course this conjecture, as well as
the linking of antagonism with CHD outcomes,
must await further research.

TABP and Developmental Perspectives

A theme that emerges across the theoretical
statements about Type A people is that the TABP

is motivated by concerns about the self-system.
This conclusion is complemented by work addressing the developmental antecedents of adult
behavior (Matthews & Siegel, 1982, 1983; Matthews & Woodall, 1988; Thoresen & Pattillo,
1988). Parent-child interactions and cognitive social learning processes are thought to contribute
to TABP. For example, Matthews and Siegel
(1982) proposed that during their developmental
history, Type As' parents taught them to value performance and productivity but failed to provide
clear performance standards. The consequence of
these child-rearing practices is a child, and eventually an adult, who is chronically striving for
poorly defined goals.

In a recent review of the literature on TABP and
children, Thoresen and Pattillo (1988) also point
to child-rearing practices and the development of
self-regulatory behaviors in Type A children. They
add to this discussion intriguing speculations
about the relation of early attachment behavior
and development of TABP. Borrowing from the
infant attachment literature (Bowlby, 1982),
Thoresen and Pattillo posited that 12- to 18-
month-old infants who exhibit avoidant behavior
when reunited with their mothers after a brief separation are likely to display TABP later in life.
Specifically, children who were avoidant as infants
were found 7 years later to be more hostile and
easily angered (Sroufe, 1986).

Early infant attachment behavior is thought to
reflect inner cognitive representations of reality
that serve to guide expectations and explanations
for future outcomes. Thus, Thoresen and Pattillo
suggested that the underlying social cognitive
schema of the Type A develops, in part, from the
early experiences of the insecure-avoidant infant.

Like Scherwitz and Canick (1988), Thoresen
and Pattillo also drew parallels between TABP
and the literature on narcissistic personalities. It is
striking that narcissists respond to threats to self-
esteem with intense anger and hostility toward
others. Thoresen and Pattillo also cited similarities between child-rearing practices implicated in
the development of narcissism and the TABP. The
parents of narcissists are believed to be inconsistent in meting out affection, highly competitive
and critical, quick to anger, and eager to bask in
the reflected accomplishments of their children
(Miller, 1981).

Before proceeding to evidence pertinent to the
development of the TABP, we should note that
TABP can be assessed reliably in children as

young as 4 or 5 years of age (Corrigan & Moskowitz, 1983; Matthews & Angulo, 1980; Murray, Bruhn, & Bunce, 1983). However, several assessment instruments have been developed with only moderate convergent validity (for a review, see Thoresen & Pattillo, 1988). Thus, it is a concern that, as in the case of adults, the various modes of Type A assessment for children and adolescents are not measuring identical Type A characteristics. Therefore, additional psychometric development is in order. These assessment difficulties notwithstanding, there are findings indicating that Type A assessments in childhood predict individual differences in the TABP in adolescence and early adulthood (Steinberg, 1986; Visintainer & Matthews, 1987).

A group of investigations implicate parent behaviors in the development of the TABP and are consistent with a cognitive social learning interpretation. Mothers of Type A children give fewer positive evaluations to their child, encourage effort, and are more often rejecting than the mothers of Type B children (Matthews, 1977). Parents of Type A children are also more indiscriminate in their administration of both encouragement and criticism (Bracke, reported in Thoresen & Pattillo, 1988).

Perhaps most important is the finding that mothers of Type A children, particularly non-Type A mothers, are more likely to provide unclear or ambiguous performance standards for their children (Matthews, 1977). This practice no doubt contributes to the Type A child's preference to compare socially with superior others and to make negative self-statements and attributions, particularly under conditions of challenge and ambiguous performance standards (Matthews & Volkin, 1981; Murray, Matthews, Blake, Prineas, & Gillum, 1986).

To summarize the theoretical perspectives of TABP, a picture of the Type A individual is developing that is more firmly tied to current cognitive social learning theories of individual differences (Cantor & Kihlstrom, 1987). Although still undocumented, current researchers are suggesting that either overly rigid or poorly formed self-conceptions make Type As sensitive to self-evaluative threats and motivate them to operate on their social environments to obtain feedback and symbols of their self-worth. The available developmental evidence is consistent with the view that child-rearing practices, particularly but not exclusively those of the mother, foster different self-regulatory strategies that could account for adult TABP. However, as with other areas of TABP investigation, issues concerning the valid and reliable assessment of coronary-proneness are limiting progress. It is clear that life-span studies of CHD risk, including multiple means of TABP assessment and employing transactional or at least interactionist methodologies, are required to understand fully the complex relationships among familial factors, individual differences, social interactions, environment, and CHD. Further, many psychological approaches to the development and maintenance of the TABP have focused on the global pattern rather than on the more specific and toxic element of hostility. More specific — or perhaps different — approaches may be necessary as the focus of Type A research shifts.

TABP, INTERVENTION, AND REDUCED RISK FOR CHD

A justification for the need to understand any disease risk factor is the presumption that such knowledge will permit the development of risk-reduction interventions. Such has been the case with the TABP. In fact, interest in the TABP has been sustained in part because of recent reports of successful TABP modification and concomitant reductions in CHD risk (Friedman et al., 1986; Gill et al., 1985). These recent, broad-based intervention trials were preceded by a group of small-sample, narrow-focused, relatively brief duration intervention studies. Although these studies suggested that modification of the TABP might be viable, they were generally burdened with conceptual and methodological shortcomings that made them of limited value. Reviews of this earlier work may be found in Chesney, Eagleston, and Rosenman (1981), Haaga (1987), and Nunes, Frank, and Kornfeld (1987) and will not be discussed here.

The Recurrent Coronary Prevention Project under the direction of Meyer Friedman (RCPP; Friedman et al., 1982) was a 5-year clinical intervention trial with 1,035 postinfarct patients. The RCPP attempted to modify the TABP, document its alteration, and evaluate reductions in the TABP against "hard" clinical endpoints of CHD, specifically recurrent MI and coronary death. RCPP participants were individuals who had suffered a documented MI 6 or more months previous to the study. Both self-reports and video-taped structured interviews (VSI) were used to assess the TABP and these measures revealed that approximately 97% of the participants exhibited moderate to extreme Type A behavior. Participants were randomly assigned to either a cardiac counseling group who received information about diagnosis and treatment of CHD, along with counseling to enhance adherence to dietary, exercise, and drug regimens, or a cardiac counseling plus TABP modification group. There was also a control group from whom only intake and outcome measures were obtained.

The TABP modification group received broad-based group therapy designed to teach them relaxation techniques and ways of modifying their Type A cognitions, behaviors, and affective responses (see Powell & Thoresen, 1987, for a detailed description of TABP group therapy). Modification of the TABP included instruction of self-observation and assessment, and restructuring of the environment. Participants were taught to modify Type A assumptions, attitudes, and beliefs, and to acquire new realistic values, beliefs, and internal standards. They were taught self-management through observation and role-plays of Type B behavior. Finally, they were encouraged to invest in "things worth being" such as the renewal of old friendships, the acquisition of new hobbies, and the substitution of assertiveness for hostility.

Several follow-up reports of the effectiveness of the modification attempt are now available and the results are quite striking. At the end of 4.5 years, patients receiving Type A and cardiac counseling had a significantly lower level of recurrent CHD (12.9%) than did patients receiving only cardiac counseling (21.2%; Friedman et al., 1986). In addition, both self-report and VSI data revealed significantly greater reductions in the TABP in the Type A modification group compared with the cardiac counseling group. At the end of 4.5 years, 35.1% of the TABP modification group had shown at least a 1 standard deviation [SD] decline in both self-reported and VSI Type A scores compared with only 9.8% of the cardiac counseling group ($p < .0001$; Friedman et al., 1986). More importantly, regardless of the treatment group, those patients who showed a clear reduction in the TABP suffered only one-fourth the CHD recurrences as those who failed to show a change. Participants who displayed only some reduction in Type A scores had CHD recurrence rates between the clear reduction and no reduction groups, indicating a nonsignificant trend toward

a dose-response relationship (Powell, Friedman, Thoresen, Gill, & Ulmer, 1984).

Gill et al. (1985) employed the RCPP's Type A modification program with a group of healthy Type A participants (officer-students at the U.S. Army War College [USAWC]). At the end of the 9-month treatment program, over 40% of the Type A modification group showed a significant reduction in TABP scores compared with 9% of no-treatment controls. Moreover, significant reductions in Type A scores were associated with significantly lower serum cholesterol levels.

The two intervention studies reported above provide fairly compelling evidence that the TABP can be modified and that such changes are associated with reduction in CHD risk. However, as Price (1988) noted, these studies leave many unanswered questions. After successful replication of these treatment effects, studies are needed to evaluate the duration of reductions in Type A behavior and the long-term risk reductions associated with such changes (Price, 1988).

A related concern has to do with the length of treatment necessary to produce meaningful alterations in the TABP. Counseling in the RCPP continued throughout the study; biweekly for the initial 3 months, monthly for the next 3 months, and bimonthly for the remainder of the study (a total of 33 sessions). Friedman et al. (1986) noted that although the effect of Type A treatment on decline in TABP is continuous over the 4.5 years, the greatest decline is observed after the first year. Treatment in the USAWC study lasted for 9 months (21 counseling sessions). Gill et al. (1985) reported that 44% of the TABP counseling subjects displayed marked or some reduction in Type A scores compared with 8.9% for controls at 8 months.

Collectively, the findings from these intervention trials indicate that statistically reliable reductions in Type A behavior can be obtained after as little as 8 months of counseling and maintained with continued counseling for up to 4.5 years. They also reveal that for many Type As the interventions do not produce marked reductions (-1 SD) in Type A behavior (65% in the RCPP, including those who dropped out of treatment, and 58% in the USAWC sample). There are two important implications in these data. First, 42.7% of the RCPP TABP counseling participants dropped out of treatment. To the extent that treatment is beneficial, then attention should be directed toward promoting participation and adherence to therapeutic recommendations. Treatment endeavors should be cognizant of the potential threats to control and self-esteem inherent in broad-based life-style interventions, threats to which the Type A is likely to be particularly sensitive and reactant (Rhodewalt & Fairfield, 1990; see also Krantz & Schulz, 1980). Thus, TABP modification procedures are likely to be more effective if they permit the individual to maintain a sense of self-efficacy and worth.

In addition, as Price (1988) suggested, new treatment approaches based on recent developments in the conceptual models of the TABP need to be tested and compared with current treatments. If only certain components of the TABP such as hostility are toxic, then focused interventions targeted at hostility or the self-concept might be more effective than attempting to modify the global TABP. Several interventions have been found effective in reducing anger and hostility (Hazuleus & Deffenbacher, 1986; Moon & Eisler, 1983; Novaco, 1975; for a review see Biaggio, 1987). Narrowly focused interventions may also be less threatening to the Type A individual.

These are only a few of the issues facing those interested in reducing CHD risk through modification of behavioral risk factors. The reader is directed to recent, more extensive reviews of the conceptual, methodological, logistical, and ethical concerns facing intervention researchers (Levenkron & Moore, 1988; Price, 1988). In sum, large-scale, long-duration intervention studies are needed to address the many questions remaining. Future intervention trials will be useful not only for their applied significance, but for the opportunity they provide to test basic theoretical questions. Finally, one need always keep in mind that CHD is a multidetermined outcome and that reduction of other risk factors is desirable, particularly in Type As who are resistant to behavioral change.

CURRENT STATUS AND REFLECTIONS

This chapter has attempted the daunting task of summarizing 30 years of theory and research on the TABP as a behavioral risk for CHD. We have sought to evaluate the current status of the Type A hypothesis and clarify unresolved issues for future research. At present, the consensus is that some but not all of the loose constellation of attributes defining the TABP place Type A individuals at

elevated risk for CHD. The most likely culprit in the array is hostility. This elevated risk most likely occurs through the contribution of frequent, exaggerated episodes of cardiovascular and neuroendocrine reactivity to CAD. This general conclusion is qualified by the method of assessing the TABP and its components and by the populations studied. Further, research indicates that a set of self-conceptions and self-regulatory behaviors, probably acquired through social learning experiences beginning in early childhood, form the psychological foundation for much of the TABP. Moreover, successful modification of the TABP is associated with reduced risk for recurrent CHD.

The above statement about the current status of the TABP is a global summary based on active areas of research. Thus, current conclusions will be confirmed or revised through continued research on assessment of risk, biobehavioral pathways to disease, underlying developmental, social, and psychological processes associated with behavioral risk, and the efficacy of clinical intervention.

Despite the eventual judgment about the importance of the TABP in the development of CHD, research on the TABP provides valuable lessons for those concerned with models of personality and disease and their clinical applications. That is, 30 years of research on psychosocial and behavioral risks for CHD serve as the prototype for individual difference approaches to health outcomes such as cancer (Greer & Watson, 1985). Investigators in these fields will benefit by examples from research on the TABP.

What are those lessons? First, research on the TABP and CHD illustrates the complexity of studying personality and disease relationships. Epidemiological evidence is often not as informative as it might be. Epidemiological studies as well as intervention trials are costly, labor intensive, and time consuming. Such studies of risk and intervention will be more useful if greater attention is given to the testing of underlying theory. Epidemiological investigations and clinical intervention trials will be most useful if preceded by thoughtful development of conceptual models and careful psychometric development of assessment devices. Then, the conceptual models must be faithfully translated into epidemiological designs. For example, there is a vast discrepancy between models of the TABP-CHD association and epidemiological studies of those models. As noted previously, the models suggest that Type As in certain situations display exaggerated reactivity and are ultimately at increased risk. Yet, situational factors are rarely assessed, and the conceptually more precise interactional effect cannot be tested. The default test of the Type A main effect is not the most theoretically relevant and may be less sensitive.

An additional interpretive difficulty is present in many studies of the TABP and CHD risk. Most conceptual models of TABP propose that the behavioral risk contributes to CHD by accelerating CAD. Frequent, exaggerated cardiovascular and neuroendocrine responses are thought to mediate the disease process. Often, epidemiological investigators confuse independent and mediating variables and seek to find an independent relationship between TABP and CHD while controlling for serum cholesterol or blood pressure, variables reflecting or at least related to the presumed mediator.

The same concern holds for the TABP and other risk factors as well. To illustrate, if the relationship between TABP and CHD holds only before controlling for cigarette smoking, then the typical conclusion is that TABP is not an independent risk factor for CHD above the risk accrued from smoking. This is true, but it begs the important question of why the TABP might be associated with smoking.

At the same time, we encourage investigators to consider null findings carefully. Early Type A research appears to be limited by a confirmatory bias that prohibited the critical evaluation of the Type A construct, and thus, encouraged investigators to invest research resources into areas with limited potential for advancing our understanding of behavioral risk for CHD (Booth-Kewley & Friedman, 1987).

In sum, there have been many false starts and dead ends encountered along the way and there are many questions as yet unanswered. However, the cumulative result of the vast literature on the TABP is an emerging understanding of the basic mechanisms that define coronary-prone behavior.

REFERENCES

Barefoot, J., Dahlstrom, W. G., & Williams, R. B. (1983). Hostility and CHD incidence, and total mortality: A 25 year follow-up study of 225 physicians. *Psychosomatic Medicine, 45*, 59–64.

Barefoot, J., Dodge, K. A., Dahlstrom, W. G., & Williams R. B. (1989). The Cook-Medley Hostility Scale: Item content and ability to predict survival. *Psychosomatic Medicine, 51*, 46–57.

Barefoot, J., Siegler, I. C., Nowlin, J. B., Peterson, B., Haney, T. L., & Williams, R. B. (1987). Suspiciousness, health, and mortality: A follow-up study of 500 older adults. *Psychosomatic Medicine, 49*, 450–457.

Bass, C., & Wade, C. (1984). Chest pain with normal coronary arteries: A comparative study of psychiatric and social morbidity. *Psychosomatic Medicine, 14*, 51–61.

Biaggio, M. K. (1987). Therapeutic management of anger. *Clinical Psychology Review, 7*, 663–675.

Booth-Kewley, S., & Friedman, H. S. (1987). Psychological predictors of heart disease: A quantitative review. *Psychological Bulletin, 101*, 343–362.

Bowlby, J. (1982). *Attachment and loss: Vol. 1. Attachment* (2nd ed.). New York: Basic Books.

Burke, R. J. (1984a). Beliefs and fears underlying Type A behaviour. *Psychological Reports, 54*, 655–662.

Burke, R. J. (1984b). Beliefs and fears underlying Type A behaviour: What makes Sammy run so fast and aggressively. *Journal of Human Stress, 10*, 174–182.

Cantor, N., & Kihlstrom, J. F. (1987). *Personality and social intelligence*. New York: Prentice-Hall.

Carver, C. S. (1980). Perceived coercion, resistance to persuasion, and the Type A behavior pattern. *Journal of Research in Personality, 14*, 467–481.

Carver, C. S., Coleman, A. E., & Glass, D. C. (1976). The coronary-prone behavior pattern and the suppression of fatigue on a treadmill test. *Journal of Personality and Social Psychology, 33*, 460–466.

Carver, C. S., & Scheier, M. F. (1981). *Attention and self-regulation*. New York: Springer-Verlag.

Case, R. B., Heller, S. S., Case, N. B., Moss, A. J., & Multicenter Postinfarction Research Group. (1985). Type A behavior and survival after acute myocardial infarction. *The New England Journal of Medicine, 312*, 737–741.

Chesney, M. A., Eagleston, J. R., & Rosenman, R. H. (1981). Type A behavior: Assessment and intervention. In C. K. Prokop & L. A. Bradley (Eds.), *Medical Psychology: Contributions to behavioral medicine* (pp. 19–36). New York: Academic Press.

Chesney, M. A., Hecker, M. H. L., & Black, G. W. (1988). Coronary-prone components of Type A behavior in the WCGS: A new methodology. In B. K. Houston & C. R. Snyder (Eds.), *Type A behavior pattern: Research, theory, and intervention* (pp. 168–188). New York: John Wiley & Sons.

Chesney, M. A., Sevelius, G., Black, G. W., Ward, M. M., Swan, G. E., Rosenman, R. H. (1981). Work environment, Type A behavior, and coronary heart disease risk factors. *Journal of Occupational Medicine, 23*, 551–555.

Contrada, R. J., & Krantz, D. S. (1988). Stress, reactivity, and Type A behavior: Current status and future directions. *Annals of Behavioral Medicine, 10*, 64–70.

Contrada, R. J., Krantz, D. S., & Hill, R. (1988). In B. K. Houston & C. R. Snyder (Eds.), *Type A behavior pattern: Research, theory, and intervention*. New York: John Wiley & Sons.

Cook, W., & Medley, D. (1954). Proposed hostility and pharisaic scales for the MMPI. *Journal of Applied Psychology, 238*, 414–418.

Cooney, J. L., & Zeichner, A. (1985). Selective attention to negative feedback in Type A and Type B individuals. *Journal of Abnormal Psychology, 91*, 110–112.

Corrigan, S. A., & Moskowitz, D. S. (1983). Type A behavior in preschool children: Construct validation evidence for the MYTH. *Child Development, 54*, 1513–1521.

Costa, P. (1986). Is neuroticism a risk factor for CAD? Is Type A a measure of neuroticism? In T. Schmidt, T. M. Dembroski, & G. Blumchen (Eds.), *Biological and psychological factors in cardiovascular disease* (pp. 85–95). New York: Springer-Verlag.

Costa, P., Fleg, J. L., McCrae, R. R., & Lakatta, E. G. (1982). Neuroticism, coronary artery disease, and chest pain complaints: Cross-sectional and longitudinal studies. *Experimental Aging Research, 8*, 37–44.

Costa, P., McCrae, R. R., & Dembroski, T. (1989). Agreeableness versus antagonism: Explication of a potential risk factor for CHD. In A. Siegman & T. Dembroski (Eds.), *In search of coronary-prone behavior: Beyond Type A* (pp. 41–64). Hillsdale, NJ: Lawrence Erlbaum Associates.

Dembroski, T. M. (1978). Reliability and validity of procedures used to assess coronary-prone behavior. In T. M. Dembroski, S. M. Weiss, J. L. Shields, S. G. Haynes, & M. Feinleib (Eds.), *Coronary-prone behavior*. New York: Springer-Verlag.

Dembroski, T. M., & Costa, P. (1987). Coronary-prone behavior: Components of the Type A behavior pattern and hostility. *Journal of Personality, 55*, 211–235.

Dembroski, T. M., & Costa, P. (1988). Assessment of coronary-prone behavior: A current overview. *Annals of Behavioral Medicine, 10*, 60–63.

Dembroski, T. M., & Czjakowski, S. M. (1989). Historical and current developments in coronary-prone behavior. In A. Siegman & T. Dembroski (Eds.), *In search of coronary-prone behavior: Beyond Type A* (pp. 21–39). Hillsdale, NJ: Lawrence Erlbaum Associates.

Dembroski, T. M., & MacDougall, J. M. (1978). Stress effects on affiliation preferences among subjects possessing the Type A coronary-prone behavior pattern. *Journal of Personality and Social Psychology, 36*, 23–33.

Dembroski, T., MacDougall, J., Herd, J., & Shields, J. (1979). Effects of level of challenge on pressor and heart rate responses in Type A and B subjects. *Journal of Applied Social Psychology, 9*, 209–228.

Dembroski, T. M., MacDougall, J. M., Williams, R. B., Haney, T. L., & Blumenthal, J. A. (1985). Components of Type A, hostility, and anger-in: Relationships to angiographic findings. *Psychosomatic Medicine, 47*, 219–233.

Feather, N. T., & Volkmer, R. E. (1988). Preference for situations involving effort, time pressure, and feedback in Type A behavior, locus of control, and test anxiety. *Journal of Personality and Social Psychology, 55*, 266–271.

French-Belgian Collaborative Group. (1982). Ischemic heart disease and psychological patterns: Prevalence and incidence studies in Belgium and France. *Advances in Cardiology, 29*, 25–31.

Friedman, M., & Rosenman, R. H. (1959). Association of specific overt behavior pattern with blood and cardiovascular findings. *Journal of American Medical Association, 169*, 1286–1296.

Friedman, M., & Rosenman, R. H. (1974). *Type A behavior and your heart*. New York: Alfred A. Knopf.

Friedman, M., Thoresen, C. E., Gill, J. J., Ulmer, D., Powell, L. H., Price, V. A., Brown, B., Thompson, L., Rabin, D. D., Breal, W. S., Bourg, E., Levy, R., & Dixon, T. (1986). Alteration of Type A behavior and its effect on recurrences in post-myocardial infarction patients: Summary results of the recurrent coronary prevention project. *American Heart Journal, 112,* 653–665.

Friedman, M., Thoresen, C. E., Gill, J. J., Ulmer, D., Thompson, L., Powell, L. H., Price, V., Elek, S. R., Rabin, D. D., Breall, W., Piaget, G., Dixon, T., Bourg, E., Levy, R. A., & Tasto, D. L. (1982). Feasibility of altering Type A behavior pattern. Recurrent coronary prevention study: Methods, baseline results, and preliminary findings. *Circulation, 66,* 83–92.

Ganster, D. C., Syme, W. E., & Mayes, B. T. (1989). Type A behavior in the work setting: A review and some new data. In A. Siegman & T. Dembroski (Eds.), *In search of coronary-prone behavior: Beyond Type A* (pp. 169–194). Hillsdale, NJ: Lawrence Erlbaum Associates.

Gastorf, J. W. (1981). Physiologic reaction of Type As to objective and subjective challenge. *Journal of Human Stress, 7,* 16–20.

Gentry, W. D., Oude-Weme, J. D., Musch, F., & Hall, R. P. (1981). Differences in Type A and B behavior in response to acute myocardial infarction. *Heart and Lung, 10,* 1101–1105.

Gill, J. J., Price, V. A., Friedman, M., Thoresen, C. E., Powell, L. H., Ulmer, D., Brown, B., & Drews, F. R. (1985). Reduction of Type A behavior in healthy middle-aged American military officers. *American Heart Journal, 110,* 503–514.

Glass, D. C. (1977). *Behavior patterns, stress, and coronary disease.* Hillsdale, NJ: Lawrence Erlbaum Associates.

Glass, D. C., Karkof, L. R., Contrada, R. J., Hilton, W. F., Kehoe, K., Mannucci, E. G., Collins, C., Snow, B., & Elting, E. (1980). Effect of harassment and competition upon cardiovascular and plasma catecholamine responses in Type A and B individuals. *Psychophysiology, 17,* 453–463.

Greer, S., & Watson, M. (1985). Towards a psychobiological model of cancer: Psychological considerations. *Social Science and Medicine, 20,* 773–777.

Grimm, L., & Yarnold, P. (1984). Performance standards and the Type A behavior pattern. *Cognitive Therapy and Research, 8,* 59–66.

Haaga, D. A. (1987). Treatment of the Type A behavior pattern. *Clinical Psychology Review, 7,* 557–574.

Hagman, M., Wilhelmsen, L., Wedel, H., & Pennert, K. (1987). Risk factors for angina pectoris in a population of Swedish men. *Journal of Chronic Diseases, 40,* 265–275.

Hardy, J. D., & Smith, T. W. (1988). Cynical hostility and vulnerability to disease: Social support, life stress, and physiological response to conflict. *Health Psychology, 7,* 447–459.

Haynes, S. G., & Feinleib, M. (1982). Type A behavior and the incidence of coronary heart disease in the Framingham heart study. *Advances in Cardiology, 29,* 85–95.

Haynes, S. B., Feinleib, M., & Kannel, W. B. (1980). The relationship of psychosocial factors to coronary heart disease in the Framingham study: III. Eight year incidence of coronary heart disease. *American Journal of Epidemiology, 111,* 37–58.

Haynes, S. B., & Matthews, K. A. (1988). The association of Type A behavior with cardiovascular disease: Update and critical review. In B. K. Houston & C. R. Snyder (Eds.), *Type A behavior pattern: Research, theory, and intervention* (pp. 51–82). New York: John Wiley & Sons.

Hazaleus, S. L., & Deffenbacher, J. L. (1986). Relaxation and cognitive treatment of anger. *Journal of Consulting and Clinical Psychology, 54,* 222–226.

Hearn, M. D., Murray, D. M., & Luepke, R. V. (1988). Hostility, coronary heart disease, and total mortality: A 33 year follow-up study of university students. *Proceedings of the Society of Behavioral Medicine.* Boston: MA, April 27–30, p. 129.

Henry, J. P. (1983). Coronary heart disease and the arousal of the adrenal cortical axis. In T. Dembroski & T. Schmidt (Eds.), *Biobehavioral basis of coronary heart disease.* Basel, Switzerland: Krager.

Houston, B. K. (1988). Cardiovascular and neuroendocrine reactivity, global Type A, and components of Type A behavior. In B. K. Houston & C. R. Snyder (Eds.), *Type A behavior pattern: Research, theory, and intervention* (pp. 212–253). New York: John Wiley & Sons.

Howard, J. H., Cunningham, D. A., & Rechnitzer, P. A. (1986). Role ambiguity, Type A behavior, and job satisfaction: Moderating effects on cardiovascular and biochemical responses associated with coronary risk. *Journal of Applied Psychology, 71,* 95–101.

Jenkins, C. D., Zyzanski, S., & Rosenman, R. (1971). Progress toward validation of a computer-scored test for the Type A coronary-prone behavior pattern. *Psychosomatic Medicine, 33*, 193–202.

Kaplan, J. R., Manuck, S. B., & Clarkson, T. B. (1987). The influence of heart rate on coronary artery atherosclerosis. *Journal of Cardiovascular Pharmacology, 10*(Suppl. 2), 112–115.

Kornfeld, D. S., Kahn, J. P., Frank, K. A., Heller, S., Freeman, P., & Keller-Epstein, W. (1985). Type A behavior and blood pressure during general surgery. *Psychosomatic Medicine, 47*, 214–241.

Krantz, D. S. (1984). [Letter to the editor]. *Psychosomatic Medicine, 46*, 67–68.

Krantz, D. S., Arabian, J. M., Davia, J., & Parker, J. (1982). Type A behavior and coronary bypass surgery: Intraoperative blood pressure and perioperative complications. *Psychosomatic Medicine, 44*, 273–284.

Krantz, D. S., & Durel, L. A. (1983). Psychobiological substrates of the Type A behavior pattern. *Health Psychology, 2*, 393–411.

Krantz, D. S., Durel, L. A., Davia, J. E., Shaffer, R., Arabian, J. M., Dembroski, T. M., & MacDougall, J. M. (1982). Propranolol medication among coronary patients: Relationship to Type A behavior pattern and cardiovascular response. *Journal of Human Stress, 8*, 4–12.

Krantz, D. S., Glass, D. C., Schaeffer, M., & Davia, J. (1982). Behavior patterns and coronary disease: A critical evaluation. In J. Cacioppo & R. Petty (Eds.), *Focus on cardiovascular psychopathology*. New York: Guilford Press.

Krantz, D. S., & Manuck, S. B. (1984). Acute psychophysiologic reactivity and risk of cardiovascular disease: A review and methodological critique. *Psychological Bulletin, 96*, 435–464.

Krantz, D. S., & Schulz, R. (1980). A mode of life crisis, control, and health outcomes: Cardiac rehabilitation and relocation of the elderly. In A. Baum & J. Singer (Eds.), *Advances in Environmental Psychology* (Vol. 1, pp. 23–57). Hillsdale, NJ: Lawrence Erlbaum Associates.

Leon, G. R., Finn, S. E., Murray, D., & Bailey, J. M. (1988). The inability to predict cardiovascular disease from hostility scores or MMPI items related to Type A behavior. *Journal of Consulting and Clinical Psychology, 56*, 597–600.

Levenkron, J. C., & Moore, L. G. (1988). The Type A behavior pattern: Issues for intervention research. *Annals of Behavioral Medicine, 10*, 78–83.

MacDougall, J. M., Dembroski, T. M., & Musante, L. (1979). The structured interview and questionnaire measures of coronary-prone behavior in male and female college students. *Journal of Behavior Medicine, 2*, 71–83.

Manuck, S. B., & Krantz, D. S. (1984). Psychophysiologic reactivity in coronary heart disease. *Behavioral Medicine Update, 6*, 11–33.

Manuck, S. B., Muldoon, M. F., Kaplan, J. R., Adams, M. R., & Polefrone, J. M. (1989). Coronary atherosclerosis and cardiac response to stress in cynomolgus monkeys. In A. W. Siegman & T. M. Dembroski (Eds.), *In search of coronary-prone behavior: Beyond Type A* (pp. 207–227). Hillsdale, NJ: Lawrence Erlbaum Associates.

Matthews, K. A. (1977). Caregiver-child interactions and the Type A coronary-prone behavior pattern. *Child Development, 42*, 1752–1756.

Matthews, K. A. (1982). Psychological perspectives on the Type A behavior pattern. *Psychological Bulletin, 91*, 293–323.

Matthews, K. A. (1988). CHD and Type A behaviors: Update on and alternative to the Booth-Kewley and Friedman quantitative review. *Psychological Bulletin, 104*, 373–380.

Matthews, K. A., & Angulo, J. (1980). Measurement of the Type A behavior pattern in children: Assessment of children's competitiveness, impatience-anger, and aggression. *Child Development, 51*, 466–475.

Matthews, K. A., Glass, D., Rosenman, R. H., & Bortner, R. (1977). Competitive drive, pattern A, and coronary heart disease: A further analysis of some data from the Western collaborative group. *Journal of Chronic Diseases, 30*, 489–498.

Matthews, K. A., & Haynes, S. G. (1986). Type A behavior pattern and coronary risk: Update and critical evaluation. *American Journal of Epidemiology, 123*, 923–960.

Matthews, K. A., Krantz, D. S., Dembroski, T. M., & MacDougall, J. M. (1982). The unique and common variance in the structured interview and Jenkins activity survey measures of the Type A behavior pattern. *Journal of Personality and Social Psychology, 42*, 303–313.

Matthews, K. A., Kuller, L. H., Siegal, J. M., Thompson, M., & Varat, M. (1983). Determinants of decisions to seek treatment by patients with acute myocardial infarction symptoms.

Journal of Personality and Social Psychology, *44*, 1144–1156.

Matthews, K. A., Rosenman, R. H., Dembroski, T. M., Harris, E., & MacDougall, J. M. (1984). Familial resemblances in components of Type A behavior pattern: A reanalysis of the California twin study. *Psychosomatic Medicine, 46,* 512–522.

Matthews, K. A., & Siegel, J. M. (1982). Type A behavior pattern in children and adolescents. In A. Baum & J. E. Singer (Eds.), *Handbook of psychology and health* (Vol. 2, pp. 99–118). Hillsdale, NJ: Lawrence Erlbaum Associates.

Matthews, K. A., & Siegel, J. M. (1983). Type A behaviors for children, social comparison, and standards for self-evaluation. *Developmental Psychology, 19,* 135–140.

Matthews, K. A., & Volkin, J. A. (1981). Efforts to excel and the Type A behavior pattern in children. *Child Development, 52,* 1283–1289.

Matthews, K. A., & Woodall, K. (1988). Childhood origins of overt Type A behavior and cardiovascular reactivity to behavioral stressors. *Annals of Behavioral Medicine, 10,* 71–77.

McCranie, E. W., Watkins, L. O., Brandsma, J. M., & Sisson, B. D. (1986). Hostility, coronary heart disease (CHD), incidence, and total mortality: Lack of association in a 25-year follow-up study of 478 physicians. *Journal of Behavioral Medicine, 9,* 119–125.

Medalie, J. H., & Goldbourt, U. (1976). Angina pectoris among 10,000 men. II. Psychosocial and other risk factors as evidenced by multivariate analysis of a five-year incidence study. *American Journal of Medicine, 60,* 910–920.

Miller, A. (1981). *Prisoners of childhood.* New York: Basic Books.

Mischel, W. (1973). Toward a cognitive social learning reconceptualization of personality. *Psychological Review, 80,* 252–283.

Moon, J. R., & Eisler, R. M. (1983). Anger control: An experimental comparison of three behavioral treatments. *Behavior Therapy, 14,* 493–505.

Murray, D. M., Matthews, K. A., Blake, S. M., Prineas, R. J., & Gillum, R. F. (1986). Type A behavior in children: Demographic, behavioral, and physiological correlates. *Health Psychology, 5,* 159–169.

Murray, L. H., Bruhn, J. G., & Bunce, H. (1983). Assessment of Type A behavior pattern in preschoolers. *Journal of Human Stress, 9,* 32–39.

Musante, L., MacDougall, J. M., Dembroski, T.

M., & Van Horen, A. E. (1983). Component analysis of the Type A coronary-prone behavior pattern in male and female college students. *Journal of Personality and Social Psychology, 45,* 1104–1117.

Novaco, R. (1975). *Anger control: The development and evaluation of an experimental treatment.* Lexington, MA: D. C. Heath.

Nunes, E. V., Frank, K. A., & Kornfeld, D. S. (1987). Psychologic treatment for the Type A behavior pattern and for coronary heart disease: A meta-analysis of the literature. *Psychosomatic Medicine, 48,* 159–173.

Obrist, P. A. (1981). *Cardiovascular psychophysiology.* New York: Plenum Press.

O'Keeffe, J. L., & Smith, T. W. (1988). Self-regulation and Type A behavior. *Journal of Research in Personality, 22,* 232–251.

Ortega, D., & Pepal, J. (1984). Challenge seeking and the Type A coronary-prone behavior pattern. *Journal of Personality and Social Psychology, 46,* 1328–1334.

Ostfeld, A. M., Lebovits, B. Z., Shekelle, R. B., & Paul, O. (1964). A prospective study of the relationship between personality and coronary heart disease. *Journal of Chronic Diseases, 17,* 265–276.

Pittner, M., & Houston, B. K. (1980). Response to stress, cognitive coping strategies, and the Type A behavior pattern. *Journal of Personality and Social Psychology, 39,* 147–157.

Pittner, M. S., Houston, B. K., & Spiridigliozzi, G. (1983). Control over stress, Type A behavior pattern, and response to stress. *Journal of Personality and Social Psychology, 44,* 627–637.

Pope, M. K., Smith, T. W., & Rhodewalt, F. (1989). *Cognitive, behavioral, and affective correlates of the Cook and Medley Ho Scale.* Unpublished manuscript, University of Utah.

Powell, L. H., Friedman, M., Thoresen, C. E., Gill, J. J., & Ulmer, D. (1984). Can the Type A behavior pattern be altered after myocardial infarction? A second year report from the recurrent coronary prevention project. *Psychosomatic Medicine, 46,* 293–313.

Powell, L., & Thoresen, C. (1985). Behavioral and physiologic determinants of long-term prognosis after myocardial infarction. *Journal of Chronic Disability, 38,* 253–263.

Powell, L., & Thoresen, C. E. (1987). Modifying the Type A behavior pattern: A small group treatment approach. In J. A. Blumenthal & D. McKee (Eds.), *Applications in behavioral* medicine and health psychology: A clinicians source book (pp. 171–207). Sarasota, FL: Professional Resource Exchange.

Price, V. A. (1982). *The Type A behavior pattern: A model for research and practice*. Orlando, FL: Academic Press.

Price, V. A. (1988). Research and clinical issues in treating Type A behavior. In B. K. Houston & C. R. Snyder (Eds.), *Type A behavior pattern: Research, theory, and intervention* (pp. 275–311). New York: John Wiley & Sons.

Rahe, R. H., Hervig, L., & Rosenman, R. H. (1978). The heritability of Type A behavior. *Psychosomatic Medicine, 40*, 478–486.

Review Panel: Coronary-prone behavior and coronary heart disease. (1981). Coronary-prone behavior and coronary heart disease: A critical review. *Circulation, 63*, 1199–1215.

Rhodewalt, F. (1984). Self-attribution, self-involvement, and the Type A coronary-prone behavior pattern. *Journal of Personality and Social Psychology, 47*, 662–670.

Rhodewalt, F., & Agustsdottir, S. (1984). On the relationship of hardiness to the Type A behavior pattern: Perception of life events versus coping with life events. *Journal of Research in Personality, 18*, 212–223.

Rhodewalt, F., & Comer, R. J. (1982). Coronary-prone behavior and reactance: The attractiveness of an eliminated choice. *Personality and Social Psychology Bulletin, 8*, 152–158.

Rhodewalt, F., & Davison, J. (1983). Reactance and the Type A coronary-prone behavior pattern: The role of self-attribution in response to reduced behavioral freedom. *Journal of Personality and Social Psychology, 44*, 220–228.

Rhodewalt, F., & Fairfield, M. L. (1990). An alternative approach to Type A behavior and health: Psychological reactance and medical noncompliance. *Journal of Social Behavior and Personality* (Special Issue), *5*, 323–342.

Rhodewalt, F., Hayes, R. B., Chemers, M. M., & Wysocki, J. (1984). Type A behavior, perceived stress, and illness: A person-situation analysis. *Personality and Social Psychology Bulletin, 10*, 149–159.

Rhodewalt, F., & Marcroft, M. (1988). Type A behavior and diabetic control: Implications of psychological reactance for health outcomes. *Journal of Applied Social Psychology, 18*, 139–159.

Rhodewalt, F., & O'Keeffe, J. (1986). Type A behavior, field dependence, and hypervigilance: Toward increased Type A specificity. *Motivation and Emotion, 10*, 105–114.

Rhodewalt, F., Sansone, C., Hill, C. A., Chemers, M. M., & Wysocki, J. (1988). *Stress and distress as a function of (JAS) Type A behavior and control over the work environment*. Unpublished manuscript, University of Utah.

Rhodewalt, F., & Strube, M. (1985). A self-attribution reactance model of recovery from injury in Type A individuals. *Journal of Applied Social Psychology, 15*, 330–344.

Rhodewalt, F., Strube, M., Hill, C. A., & Sansone, C. (1988). Strategic self-attribution and Type A behavior. *Journal of Research in Personality, 22*, 60–74.

Roll, M., & Theorell, T. (1987). Acute chest pain without obvious organic cause before age 40 — personality and life events. *Journal of Psychosomatic Research, 31*, 215–221.

Rose, R. J., Grim, C. J., & Miller, J. Z. (1984). Familial influences on cardiovascular stress reactivity: Studies of normotensive twins. *Behavioral Medicine Update, 6*, 21–24.

Rosenman, R. H. (1978). The interview method of assessment of the coronary-prone behavior pattern. In T. M. Dembroski, S. M. Weiss, J. L. Shields, S. G. Haynes, & M. Feinleib (Eds.), *Coronary-prone behavior*. New York: Springer-Verlag.

Rosenman, R. H., Brand, R. J., Jenkins, C. D., Friedman, M., Straus, R., & Wurm, M. (1975). Coronary heart disease in the western collaborative group study: Final follow-up of 8½ years. *Journal of the American Heart Association, 233*, 872–877.

Scherwitz, L. (1988). Interviewer behaviors in the western collaborative group study and the multiple risk factor intervention trial. In B. K. Houston & C. R. Snyder (Eds.), *Type A behavior pattern: Theory, research, and intervention* (pp. 32–50). New York: John Wiley & Sons.

Scherwitz, L. (1989). Type A behavior assessment in the structured interview: Review, critic, and recommendations. In A. Siegman & T. Dembroski (Eds.), *In search of coronary-prone behavior: Beyond Type A* (pp. 117–148). Hillsdale, NJ: Lawrence Erlbaum Associates.

Scherwitz, L., Berton, K., & Leventhal, H. (1977). Type A assessment and interaction in the behavior pattern interview. *Psychosomatic Medicine, 39*, 229–240.

Scherwitz, L., Berton, K., & Leventhal, H. (1978). Type A behavior, self-involvement, and cardiovascular response. *Psychosomatic Medicine, 40*, 593–609.

Scherwitz, L., & Canick, J. D. (1988). Self-reference and coronary heart disease risk. In B. K. Houston & C. R. Snyder (Eds.), *Type A behavior pattern: Research, theory, and intervention* (pp. 146–167). New York: John Wiley & Sons.

Scherwitz, L., Graham, L., Grandits, G., & Billings, J. (1987, March). *Interviewer style and CHD predictiveness in the multiple risks factor intervention trial.* Paper presented at the annual meeting of the Society of Behavioral Medicine, New Orleans.

Scherwitz, L., McKalvain, R., Laman, C., Patterson, J., Dutton, L., Yusim, S., Lester, J., Kraft, I., Rochelle, D., & Leachman, R. (1983). Type A behavior, self-involvement, and coronary atherosclerosis. *Psychosomatic Medicine, 45*, 47–57.

Schlegel, R. P., Wellwood, J. K., Copps, B. E., Gruchow, W. H., & Sharratt, M. T. (1980). The relationship between perceived challenge and daily symptom reporting in Type A versus Type B postinfarct patients. *Journal of Behavioral Medicine, 3*, 191–204.

Schoken, D. D., Greene, A. F., Worden, T. J., Harrison, E. F., & Spielberger, C. D. (1987). Effects of age and gender on the relationship between anxiety and coronary artery disease. *Psychosomatic Medicine, 49*, 118–126.

Siegman, A. W. (1989). The role of hostility, neuroticism, and speech style in coronary artery disease. In A. W. Siegman & T. M. Dembroski (Eds.), *In search of coronary-prone behavior: Beyond Type A* (pp. 65–89). Hillsdale, NJ: Lawrence Erlbaum Associates.

Shekelle, R. B., Gale, M., & Norusis, M. (1985). Type A score (Jenkins activity survey) and risk of recurrent coronary heart disease in the aspirin myocardial infarction study. *American Journal of Cardiology, 56*, 221–225.

Shekelle, R. B., Gale, M., Ostfeld, A. M., & Paul, O. (1983). Hostility, risk of coronary heart disease, and mortality. *Psychosomatic Medicine, 45*, 219–228.

Shekelle, R. B., Hulley, S. B., Neaton, J. D., Billings, J. H., Borhani, N. O., Gerace, T. A., Jacobs, D. R., Lasser, N. L., Mittlemark, M. B., & Stamler, J. for the Multiple Risk Factor Intervention Group (1985). The MRFIT behavior pattern study, Type A behavior and incidence of coronary heart disease. *American Journal of Epidemiology, 122*, 559–570.

Smith, T. W. (1989). Interactions, transactions, and the Type A behavior pattern: Additional avenues in the search for coronary-prone behavior. In A. Siegman & T. Dembroski (Eds.), *In search of coronary-prone behavior: Beyond Type A* (pp. 91–116). Hillsdale, NJ: Lawrence Erlbaum Associates.

Smith, T. W., & Allred, K. D. (1989). Blood pressure response during social interaction in high and low cynically hostile males. *Journal of Behavioral Medicine, 11*, 145–153.

Smith, T. W., & Anderson, N. B. (1986). Models of personality and disease: An interactional approach to Type A behavior and disease. *Journal of Personality and Social Psychology, 50*, 1166–1173.

Smith, T. W., & Brehm, S. S. (1981a). Person perception and the Type A coronary-prone behavior pattern. *Journal of Personality and Social Psychology, 40*, 1137–1149.

Smith, T. W., & Brehm, S. S. (1981b). Cognitive correlates of the Type A coronary-prone behavior pattern. *Motivation and Emotion, 5*, 215–223.

Smith, T. W., & Frohm, K. D. (1985). What's so unhealthy about hostility? Construct validity and psychosocial correlates of the Cook-Medley Ho Scale. *Health Psychology, 4*, 503–520.

Smith, T. W., Houston, B. K., & Zurawski, R. M. (1983). The Framingham Type A scale and anxiety, irrational beliefs, and self-control. *Journal of Human Stress, 9*, 32–37.

Smith, T. W., & O'Keeffe, J. L. (1985). The inequivalence of self-reports of Type A behavior: Differential relationships of the Jenkins Activity Survey and Framingham Scale with affect, stress, and control. *Motivation and Emotion, 9*, 299–311.

Smith, T. W., O'Keeffe, J. L., & Allred, K. D. (1989). Neuroticism, symptom reports, and Type A behavior: Interpretive cautions for the Framingham scale. *Journal of Behavioral Medicine, 12*, 1–9.

Smith, T. W., & Pope, M. K. (1990). Cynical hostility as a health risk: Current status and future directions. *Journal of Social Behavior and Health* (Special Issue), *5*, 77–88.

Smith, T. W., Pope, M. K., Sanders, J. D., Allred, K. D., & O'Keeffe, J. L. (1988). Cynical hostility at home and work. *Journal of Research in Personality, 22*, 525–548.

Smith, T. W., & Rhodewalt, F. (1986). On states, traits, and processes: A transactional alternative to the individual difference assumptions in Type A behavior and physiological reactivity. *Journal of Research in Personality, 20*, 229–251.

Smith, T. W., Sanders, J. D., & Alexander, J. F. (1988, August). *Cynical hostility in marital interactions.* Paper presented at the American Psychological Association annual meeting, Atlanta.

Smith, T. W., Turner, C. W., Ford, M. H., Hunt, S. C., Barlow, G. K., Stults, B. M., & Williams, R. R. et al. (1987). Blood pressure reactivity in adult male twins. *Health Psychology, 6*, 209–220.

Snyder, M. L., & Frankel, A. (1975). *Reactance and the Type A.* Unpublished manuscript, Dartmouth College, Hanover, NH.

Sroufe, L. A. (1986). *The role of infant-caregiver attachment in development.* Unpublished manuscript, Department of Psychology, University of Minnesota, Minneapolis.

Steinberg, L. (1986). Stability (and instability) of Type A behavior from children to young adulthood. *Developmental Psychology, 22*, 393–402.

Stern, G. S., Harris, J. R., & Elverum, J. (1981). Attention to important versus trivial tasks and salience of fatigue-related symptoms for coronary-prone individuals. *Journal of Research in Personality, 15*, 467–474.

Strube, M. (1985). A self-appraisal model of the Type A behavior pattern. In R. Hogan & W. H. Jones (Eds.), *Perspectives in personality* (Vol. 2, pp. 201–250). Greenwich, CT: JAI Press.

Strube, M. J., & Boland, S. M. (1986). Post-performance attributions and task persistence among Type A and B individuals: A clarification. *Journal of Personality and Social Psychology, 50*, 413–420.

Strube, M. J., Boland, S. M., Manfredo, P. A., & Al-Falaij, A. (1987). Type A behavior pattern and the self-evaluation of abilities: Empirical tests of the self-appraisal model. *Journal of Personality and Social Psychology, 52*, 956–974.

Strube, M. J., & Werner, C. M. (1985). Relinquishment of control and the Type A behavior pattern. *Journal of Personality and Social Psychology, 48*, 688–701.

Suarez, E., Williams, R. B., & McRea, A. (1988). *High Cook-Medley scores predict cardiovascular reactivity but only during harassment.* Pa-

per presented at the American Psychological Association annual meeting, Atlanta.

Taylor, S. E. (1979). Hospital patient behavior: Reactance, helplessness, or control. *Journal of Social Issues, 35*, 156–184.

Thoresen, C. E., & Pattillo, J. R. (1988). Exploring the Type A behavior pattern in children and adolescents. In B. K. Houston & C. R. Snyder (Eds.), *Type A behavior pattern: Research, theory, and intervention* (pp. 98–145). New York: John Wiley & Sons.

Van Egeren, L. F. (1979a). Social interactions, communications, and the coronary-prone behavior pattern: A psychophysiological study. *Psychosomatic Medicine, 41*, 2–18.

Van Egeren, L. F. (1979b). Cardiovascular changes during a social competition in a mixed motive game. *Journal of Personality and Social Psychology, 37*, 858–864.

Van Egeren, L. F., Sniderman, L. D., & Roggelin, M. S. (1982). Competitive two-person interactions of Type A and Type B individuals. *Journal of Behavioral Medicine, 5*, 55–66.

van Schijndel, M., De Mey, H., & Naring, G. (1984). Effects of behavioral control and Type A behavior on cardiovascular responses. *Psychophysiology, 21*, 501–509.

Visintainer, P. F., & Matthews, K. A. (1987). Stability of overt Type A behaviors in children: Results from a two- and five-year longitudinal study. *Child Development, 58*, 1586–1591.

Weidner, G., & Matthews, K. A. (1978). Reported physical symptoms elicited by unpredictable events and the Type A coronary-prone behavior pattern. *Journal of Personality and Social Psychology, 36*, 1213–1220.

Wicklund, R., & Brehm, J. W. (1976). *Perspectives on cognitive dissonance.* Hillsdale, NJ: Lawrence Erlbaum Associates.

Wielgosz, A. T., Fletcher, R. H., McCants, C. B., McKinnis, R. A., Haney, T. L., & Williams, R. B. (1984). Unimproved chest pain in patients with minimal or no coronary disease: A behavioral phenomenon. *American Heart Journal, 108*, 67–72.

Williams, R. B. (1979). Physiological mechanisms underlying the association between psychosocial factors and coronary disease. In W. D. Gentry & R. B. Williams (Eds.), *Psychological aspects of myocardial infarction and coronary care* (2nd ed.). St. Louis: Mosby.

Williams, R. B. (1987). Psychological factors in coronary artery disease: Epidemiological evidence. *Circulation, 76*(Suppl. I), I177–I183.

Williams, R. B. (1989). Biological mechanisms mediating the relationship between behavior and coronary heart disease. In A. Siegman & T. Dembroski (Eds.), *In search of coronary-prone behavior: Beyond Type A* (pp. 195–206). Hillsdale, NJ: Lawrence Erlbaum Associates.

Williams, R. B., Barefoot, J. C., & Shekelle, R. B. (1985). The health consequences of hostility. In M. Chesney & R. H. Rosenman (Eds.), *Anger and hostility in cardiovascular and behavioral disorders* (pp. 173–185). Washington, DC: Hemisphere.

Williams, R. B., Haney, T. L., Lee, K. L., Kong, Y., Blumenthal, J., & Whalen, R. (1980). Type A behavior, hostility, and coronary atherosclerosis. *Psychosomatic Medicine, 242*, 539–549.

Williams, R. B., Lane, J. D., Kuhn, C. M., Melosh, W., White, A. D., & Schanberg, S. M. (1982). Type A behavior and elevated physiological and neuroendocrine responses to cognitive tasks. *Science, 218*, 483–485.

Wright, R. A., Contrada, R., & Glass, D. C. (1985). Psychophysiologic correlates of Type A behavior. In E. D. Katkin & S. B. Manuck (Eds.), *Advances in Behavioral Medicine* (Vol. 1, pp. 39–88). Greenwich, CT: JAI Press.

CHAPTER 12

GENERAL AFFECTIVE DISPOSITIONS IN PHYSICAL AND PSYCHOLOGICAL HEALTH

Lee Anna Clark
David Watson

Several years ago, we reviewed the literatures relating "a number of apparently diverse personality scales — variously called trait anxiety, neuroticism, ego strength, general maladjustment, repression-sensitization, and social desirability" (Watson & Clark, 1984, p. 465) and concluded that these dimensions all represented facets of a broad underlying construct, which we termed *negative affectivity* (NA), following Tellegen (1982). Since then, a remarkable number of articles have been published that support and extend our view of NA as a stable and pervasive mood-dispositional dimension. In this chapter, we will discuss developments that have taken place in the intervening years. We will first summarize the key points of our original presentation for readers unfamiliar with this work. We will then discuss, from both substantive and methodological viewpoints, research that further documents the breadth and stability of the NA construct, including studies that have investigated its genetic etiology. Some of this work suggests that the influence of NA is even more pervasive than we had originally envisioned. Other studies indicate that NA may act as a confound

(an underlying "third variable") leading to spurious correlations between variables previously thought to be more causally related to one another.

As we will see, the NA construct has important and broad implications for health. However, despite the pervasiveness of NA, a single dimension certainly cannot account for all health-related phenomena. Among other things, the importance of a second broad dimension, *positive affectivity* (PA), has become increasingly apparent. Positive Affectivity forms the core of *extraversion*, with components of well-being, energy, social dominance, affiliation, and perhaps achievement motivation and adventurousness (Watson & Clark, in press). It is noteworthy that, as regards health, NA has been shown to be related primarily to indices of poor physical and psychological health. Similarly, the low end of the PA dimension has been related to several indices of poor functioning. However, it is significant that when measures of positive health are considered, the PA dimension appears to play the more important role. Thus, we will also discuss research developments that regard the distinctive and complementary dimension of PA. Finally, we will place NA and PA in the context of a larger, three-factor model that is emerging at the interface of research in emotion, personality, psychiatry, and neurophysiology, and discuss directions for future research.

NEGATIVE AFFECTIVITY AS A "MOOD-DISPOSITIONAL" DIMENSION

We take no credit for "discovering" the basic phenomenon of NA. Earlier writers such as Eysenck, Block, Guilford, and Cattell all recognized the importance of this major personality dimension. What we have contributed to the field is conceptual — an interpretation of the NA construct as fundamentally an emotion-based trait. As such it can be linked to research into emotional states, emotional disturbance, and factors that affect both inter- and intra-individual variation in emotional experience. Further, although emotion-centered, the interplay between affect and cognition is critical to a full understanding of the NA construct.

Central Features

The single most important feature of NA is the pervasive tendency to experience a wide variety of negative and upsetting emotions. Distressed mood states such as anxiety, tension or jitteriness, and worry are central, but anger, frustration, hostility, contempt, disgust, guilt, worthlessness, dissatisfaction, feelings of rejection, sadness, loneliness, discomfort, irritability, and so forth also are frequently experienced by high NA individuals, even in the absence of obvious stressors (see Watson & Clark, 1984, Tables 5–7; Watson & Tellegen, 1985).

Closely associated with these emotional experiences is a negative self-concept and a propensity to self-criticalness (see Watson & Clark, 1984, Table 3). People high in NA tend to be dissatisfied with themselves and describe themselves unfavorably. They are also likely to be more introspective than low NA individuals, and tend to dwell particularly on their mistakes and failings (Block, 1965). There is also evidence that this negative bias is not limited to the self, but extends to encompass a more negative worldview. For example, high NA individuals interpret ambiguous stimuli more negatively (Goodstein, 1954; Phares, 1961), and rate their peers less favorably (Bass & Fielder,

1961; Kaplan, 1968). They are also more likely than those low in NA to view people (especially themselves) as victims of negative events (Crocker, Alloy, & Kayne, 1988).

Distinctive Characteristics

In addition to these substantive features, it is important to recognize several distinctive characteristics of the NA construct. First, NA is simultaneously a very broad and yet cohesive dimension. Although it manifests itself in such diverse areas as emotions, cognitions, social attitudes, self- and worldview, and behavioral adjustment, it nonetheless is a unitary concept. Measures of the various components of NA are intercorrelated to the point that a strong general factor almost inevitably emerges in factor analytic studies, and any self-report instrument with an evaluative component will almost invariably be correlated with measures of NA.

Second, as a mood-based disposition NA exhibits an unusual combination of stability and change. In the short run (up to 6 months), NA is highly stable, with average retest coefficients around .80. However, over periods of 1 to 5 years, stability falls to about .60 (Watson & Clark, 1984, Table 2). Yet, it is noteworthy that long-term stabilities (over 20 years) are only slightly less, averaging around .50 (Schuerger, Zarrella, & Hotz, 1989). A recent meta-analysis also suggests that NA exhibits somewhat less stability than extraversion/PA: Over all time frames the average retest coefficient was .64 for anxiety/NA compared with .72 for extraversion/PA (Schuerger et al., 1989). Although genetics undoubtedly play a role in the long-term stabilities of these and other personality traits, the major factors inducing changes on these dimensions are still unknown.

Third, the negative emotions regularly experienced by those high in NA are not simply strong reactions to stressful situations. Although high NA individuals do report more state (i.e., transient, short-term) negative affect in such situations, they do not report greater increases in state NA when exposed to stressors. Rather, those high in trait NA consistently report higher levels of state NA across all types of situations, both stressful and nonstressful (Watson & Clark, 1984, Tables 6 & 7). This suggests a higher basal level of negative emotional experience rather than a greater reactivity. It is likely that this not only reflects an endogenous (i.e., biological) propensity, but also a psychological bias toward interpreting objectively nonthreatening situations as stressful, although the etiologies of these tendencies are unclear.

The strong and consistent relation between trait and state measures of NA is one of the primary arguments supporting our interpretation of the NA construct as mood dispositional. It is important to note that this relation is observed not only when trait and state NA are measured simultaneously, but even with time lapses of up to 10 years (Costa & McCrae, 1980; Aldwin, Levenson, Sprio, & Bossé, 1989). This, of course, follows logically from the previous two characteristics. Given that trait NA is relatively stable and consistently related to average state NA levels, it is not surprising that we observe a certain stability in the state-trait—and even in the state-state—relation.

Finally, it is important to emphasize that NA is based primarily in subjective experience. Although a number of objective correlates have been established, the "power" of NA lies in the inescapability of the individual's phenomenological world. The pervasiveness of NA results from the consistent ways in which high or low NA persons experience, interpret, and reflect on themselves and the world around them.

Summary of Recent Developments

In 1984 we sought to reveal the core of the NA construct, to sharpen our understanding of its most central features, and to highlight areas in which further research was needed. Since that time, two major trends have emerged in research on the NA construct. One type of research has investigated the many convergent correlations of NA (although not always under the NA label). For example, a large number of studies have documented the role of NA in marital and job satisfaction, in attributional and coping style, and in perceptions of social support, daily hassles, stress, physical symptoms, and so forth. This research has led to an awareness that some observed correlations may stem from an underlying component (i.e., NA) common to the two variables. That is, if two apparently distinct constructs both contain a self-evaluative element, high NA individuals will tend to rate themselves negatively on both dimensions—and low NA persons will not—because of the pervasive negative cognitive set associated with NA. The influence of this set will thus lead to the variables being at least moderately correlated.

However, in terms of the true relation between the variables (i.e., if they were both objectively defined, with the common NA element removed), the observed correlation would be spuriously high. Nevertheless, such correlations also help to reveal the range of phenomena affected by NA.

The second line of research has been concerned primarily with differentiating NA from its companion dimension, PA. These studies have served the twofold purpose of (a) demonstrating that NA is not simply a generalized good versus bad response bias, but is specifically oriented toward negativity; and (b) examining the specific convergent correlates of PA in order to understand this distinct and complementary dimension more fully. Together, these two research strategies have clarified those areas in which NA and PA, respectively, play a more central role, and also have revealed domains in which both dimensions are important. We will discuss each of these broad research trends in turn, and then direct our attention toward more comprehensive models of emotional experience that integrate findings from the biological, intrapsychic, and interpersonal domains.

FURTHER DELINEATION OF THE NA CONSTRUCT

The Pervasiveness of NA

NA and Diverse Affective States and Traits: A Hierarchical Model

At the level of state emotions, there has been significant debate between the "discrete emotions" theorists (e.g., Izard, 1972) and those who view emotions in terms of two or three broad dimensions. Watson and Tellegen (1985), however, have suggested that the two positions can be reconciled with the adoption of a hierarchical model, in which Positive and Negative Affect represents higher order dimensions comprised of several lower order, more specific emotions, such as Interest and Enjoyment (PA) or Anger and Fear (NA). In addition, some discrete emotions (e.g., Surprise, Sadness) may load significantly on both factors. A similar structure appears to apply at the level of affective traits, although this has not been as well documented as for affective states. One difficulty in reviewing this area is that researchers do not always indicate clearly the time frame of their measures, so it is not always known whether they are assessing affective traits, mood states, or something in between, such as subjects' affect over the past week or 6 months.

Support for the overlap among negative emotions (both state and trait) has been abundant. Gotlib (1984) reviewed a large number of studies and presented data suggesting the presence of a broad general factor underlying many common measures related to psychopathology, such as depression, anxiety, fear, loneliness, and even (un)assertiveness. Similar results have been obtained with other sets of measures that only partially overlap with Gotlib's (e.g., Nezu, Nezu, & Nezu, 1986; Tanaka-Matsumi & Kameoka, 1986). Similarly, evidence for a large NA or Neuroticism factor in the personality literature is ubiquitous, and actually dates back a number of years (e.g., Comrey & Duffy, 1968; Comrey, Jamison, & King, 1968; Noller, Law, & Comrey, 1987; Zuckerman, Kuhlman, & Camac, 1988). Scales that load on this higher order dimension carry such diverse names as Inferiority, Pessimism, Tense-Relaxed, Emotionally (Un)Stable, Apprehensive, Anger/Hostility, and Emotionality.

Although most of these studies are student based, the findings have been replicated in other populations as well, including community-residing married individuals (Folkman & Lazarus, 1986; Schaefer & Burnett, 1987), factory workers (Siegel, 1986), children and adolescents (e.g., Bernstein, Garfinkel, & Hoberman, 1989; Eason, Finch, Brasted, & Saylor, 1985; Rowlinson & Felner, 1988), and psychiatric populations (see Clark & Watson, in press, for a review of this literature focusing particularly on anxiety and depression). Nor have the data been limited to strictly correlational studies. For example, "depressive" mood inductions yielded increases on all three subscales — depression, anxiety, and hostility — of the Multiple Affect Adjective Check List (MAACL) (Finman & Berkowitz, 1989). In his review, Gotlib (1984) also noted a number of studies that demonstrated generalized affective improvement as a result of therapies targeted at more specific deficits.

However, these studies provide only half the picture. The relations among specific affect scales are rarely so high as to suggest that the measures are interchangeable. Rather, consistent with a hierarchical model, they typically range from .40 to .60, suggesting that there is some degree of lower order specificity not accounted for by the higher order construct. Further, differentiation among measures with a common NA component may be increased under at least three conditions.

1. When highly specific affects are assessed, intercorrelations among them are decreased. For example, Clark and Watson (in press) present data showing that when the measurement of anxiety focuses on its perceived physiological component (i.e., jumpy, shaky, easily rattled), it is less highly correlated with both depression and more general NA measures. Measures of harm-avoidance (i.e., physical danger anxiety or timidity) are also somewhat distinct from general NA (Tellegen, 1985; Zuckerman et al., 1988). Similarly, specific hostility or aggression scales can show a reasonable convergent/discriminant pattern in relation to measures of depression and anxiety (e.g., Smith & Frohm, 1985; Zuckerman et al., 1988).

2. When the affective component is reduced relative to the total scale content (e.g., the measures focus on cognitions, life events, interpersonal relationships, etc., rather than on mood per se), discrimination is increased. Given that NA is primarily mood based, this is not surprising. Nevertheless, the NA component of overtly nonaffective measures is by no means inconsequential. This point will be discussed subsequently.

3. When observer ratings are used rather than self-report, NA-based scales tend to be less highly correlated. This is, of course, consistent with the primarily subjective nature of NA, but it must also be emphasized that it is a relative statement. For example, correlations between clinician-rated Hamilton Depression and Anxiety scales average about .70 (Clark & Watson, in press). Moreover, substantial overlap among patients remains, even using the rescored Hamilton scales (revised to improve discrimination). Beck, Brown, Steer, Eidelson, and Riskind (1987) examined over 600 patients diagnosed with either an anxiety or a depressive disorder, and found that only about one half had Hamilton scores that were different in the direction consistent with their diagnosis by .5 standard deviations or more.

Furthermore, even when greater differentiation by observers is found, its meaning warrants careful examination. For example, Saylor, Finch, Baskin, Furey, and Kelly (1984) found a better convergent/discriminant pattern among their peer and teacher ratings of depression and anger than in self-report. However, an inspection of the measures reveals that the self-report measures were mood based, whereas the observers rated aggressive, acting-out behaviors for the anger measure, and behaviors such as playing alone or sleeping in class for depression. Consequently, neither the difference in the convergent/discriminant patterns nor the poor self-observer correlations are surprising, because rather different variables were assessed with the two methods. This type of measurement discrepancy is quite common, and needs to be more widely acknowledged, rather than using the resulting inconsistency to denigrate either type of rating as unreliable or invalid.

NA and Nonmood Variables: Methodological Issues

Before reviewing the various substantive areas that have been related to NA (e.g., coping, hardiness, optimism), it is worthwhile to note certain methodological issues that they share. Most striking is a common historical pattern, beginning with the hypothesis that a given variable is related to either physical or to psychological health. Typically, early research in an area would establish that, indeed, the variable of interest was related to poorer health, but at a rather low level. Researchers would then argue that this low level of relation was due to the fact that the hypothesized predictor was measured nomothetically, whereas individuals make widely varying interpretations of the same events, social structures, or situations. Moreover, it was argued, they also possess different personality traits or coping skills for dealing with the vicissitudes of life, and because objective measures did not take these sources of variance into account, the hypothesized relation was attenuated. In response, researchers usually adopted one of two strategies in order to clarify the relation of interest.

One strategy was to measure subjects' perceptions of the variable(s) directly. For example, ratings of the stressfulness of an event were obtained rather than a simple report on their occurrence, or perceived social support was assessed rather than descriptions of social networks. Similarly, for the dependent variable self-reported symptoms were commonly substituted for physician or clinician ratings. The result was typically a dramatic increase in the level of observed relation between the variable of interest and the physical or psychological health measure. However, it was quickly recognized that embedded in these conceptual revisions was a potential confound. If individuals posed a generalized self- or worldview, their pervasive interpretive/perceptual stance would result in a correlation between any subjectively rated variables. As we shall see, a number of researchers in diverse areas have conceptualized this underlying variable as NA or some highly related variable,

such as neuroticism or maladaptive distress (e.g., Allred & Smith, 1989; Cohen & Wills, 1985; Costa & McCrae, 1987; Depue & Monroe, 1986; Dohrenwend & Shrout, 1985; Rhodewalt & Zone, 1989).

A second strategy has been to measure the mediating personality trait or cognitive/behavioral style independently, entering it into the equation as a moderator variable. This strategy has generally met with less overt success, unless implemented together with the use of self-perception measures (e.g., Schmied & Lawler, 1986). In this case the hypothetically intervening trait often has been shown to be correlated directly with the variables of interest (due to the shared NA component) rather than exerting an interactive or buffering effect (e.g., Allred & Smith, 1989; Brewin, 1985; Funk & Houston, 1987).

In sum, these strategies have led to the hoped-for higher correlations, but at a cost. To the extent that we can show our "independent" and "dependent" variables to be confounded by NA, we have expanded our understanding of the NA construct, but have not learned much about the real consequences of objectively rated stressors, social support, coping strategies, and so forth, or about the antecedents of actual physical or mental health. Because it appears unlikely that any single factor will be discovered that will account for a large percentage of the variance in objective health measures, future research that avoids these pitfalls will probably yield more modest empirical findings, but will nevertheless represent a more significant conceptual advance.

NA and Nonmood Variables: Substantive Issues

The following reviews are not intended to be exhaustive, either in terms of the areas covered, or in the coverage of each area. Rather, they are meant to illustrate the range and diversity of health research that is relevant to the NA concept. Although most of the variables we will examine have been related to measures of both physical and mental health, most research in a given area has focused on one arena or the other. Of course, the relation of these two types of health is itself a major topic. As a purely practical strategy, we will first discuss the relation of physical and mental health, then review variables that have been proposed as especially relevant to physical health, followed by those that have been researched primarily in relation to mental health.

226					HANDBOOK OF SOCIAL AND CLINICAL PSYCHOLOGY

NA in relation to physical and mental health. In the minds of many, high NA is synonymous with psychopathology. Although this is an oversimplification, it contains more than a kernel of truth. Most NA-type measures are labeled in psychopathological terms (e.g., anxiety, depression, neuroticism, psychasthenia, dysfunctional attitudes, symptom checklists, etc.), and an item inspection of those that bear more wholesome-sounding labels (e.g., ego resiliency, social desirability) suggests that their authors intended these positive qualities to be inferred from the lack of negative ones. It is important to emphasize, however, that whereas most psychiatric patients score high on measures of NA (the exceptions tend to be psychopathic or manic in character), not all who score high on NA measures are patients. The dimension is one of subjective distress, not overt adjustment, and many individuals continue to function despite their internal misery. Conversely, low NA individuals have not been widely studied, but this group probably includes defensive people who will not acknowledge personal failings even to themselves, and people with certain types of personality disorders (e.g., narcissistic, histrionic) who are more likely to make others miserable than to report personal distress themselves. Nevertheless, NA scales are widely used as measures of psychopathology, and because reasonably strong convergent relations have consistently been demonstrated between NA measures and diverse clinical ratings of psychopathology, we will follow that tradition here.

The relation of self-reported symptom measures, objective health measures, and NA is more complex. Because Watson and Pennebaker (1989) have recently reviewed this extensive literature, we shall only summarize their findings here. Self-report health complaint scales typically ask subjects to rate the frequency or intensity of a number of common physical symptoms and complaints. Considerable research validating these scales against objective criteria such as medical records has yielded encouraging data, leading to widespread use of self-report measures in health research. However, while statistically significant, the convergence between self-reports of illness and more objective indices is generally modest. Thus, when a correlation is found between stress or optimism and self-rated illness, for example, it may not be warranted to infer a relation between these variables and actual health status.

Moreover, other evidence suggests that these self-reports contain a strong subjective component, which is clearly identifiable as NA based. In fact, the level of relation is sufficiently strong that Watson and Pennebaker (1989) have proposed extending the NA construct to include not only negative moods and psychological distress, but physiologically expressed distress as well. However, as regards actual health status, this subjective, NA-related component appears to represent largely invalid variance. That is, intermediate or longer term health and health-related measures (e.g., immune system functioning, serum blood counts, heart attacks, disease incidence rates, mortality rates, health behaviors, etc.) show nonsignificant or inconsistent relations with NA. Clarifying the inconsistencies will be an important area for future research. At the same time, these results suggest that we must reexamine studies investigating the antecedents or correlates of health. If the predictor variables themselves contain an NA component (and we will show that many do), their correlation with self-reported health may be most parsimoniously explained by this shared variance. That is, such measures may represent facets of Watson and Pennebaker's (1989) proposed dimension of somatopsychic distress.

Life stress and daily hassles. The relation between health and life stress/daily hassles is one of the most hotly debated topics in health psychology, and the question of whether stress measures (especially the widely used Daily Hassles Scale; Kanner, Coyne, Schaefer, & Lazarus, 1981) is confounded with pathology has been a particular concern. In essence, B. P. Dohrenwend and colleagues (e.g., Dohrenwend & Shrout, 1985; Dohrenwend, Dohrenwend, Dodson, & Shrout, 1984) have argued that because many hassles/stress items can themselves be viewed as symptoms of pathology, correlations between hassles and disorder are attributable to this overlap. Lazarus and colleagues (e.g., Delongis, Folkman, & Lazarus, 1988; Lazarus, Delongis, Folkman, & Gruen, 1985) have responded that specific item content is less important than the more general process of appraising the situation as stressful.

Viewed within the larger context of the NA construct, however, the two positions appear more complementary than contradictory. The chronic disturbances associated with high NA are themselves hassles and surely generate considerable stress; further, high NA people do appear to be predisposed to view life's microstresses as hassles

(Depue & Monroe, 1986). Because the essence of NA is a propensity to experience negative emotions and to view the world and oneself through this negative lens, the particular field of expression is less important than the pervasive negativity itself. Just as psychological and physical complaints form a common dimension of somatopsychic distress, perceived stress and daily hassles are further content areas that fall under the broad influence of NA. Depue and Monroe (1986) speculate that the breadth of this dimension may stem from a "general susceptibility to medical and psychological disorders, . . . a heightened [biological] vulnerability to the development of several conditions over a lifetime" (p. 48).

This synthetic view has several implications, each of which is supported by data. First, if item content is less important than generalized negative emotional experience, then negative affect should be correlated equally with physical symptom and stress measures, which in turn should themselves be correlated. In support of this point, Watson and Pennebaker (1989) report that the average intercorrelation between NA and three physical symptom measures was .43, whereas NA's correlation with the Hassles Frequency scale was .42. Hassles and physical symptoms were also significantly correlated (range = .31 to .36). Rowlinson and Felner (1988) reported even stronger data on this point in a sample of 682 adolescents. They found intercorrelations ranging only from .50 to .56 among a composite NA measure, a physical symptom measure, and hassles. Thus, in both data sets these three conceptually distinct domains are all intercorrelated, suggesting they share a common core, which we would argue is the NA dimension.

A second implication of this view is that the correlations between stress and physical symptoms or NA should not be strongly affected by whether or not the stress scale contains specifically pathological content. As a test of this notion, Rowlinson and Felner (1988) divided the hassles by whether they were symptomatic or nonsymptomatic of psychological disorder, and by whether they were controllable or not. They then correlated each of these hassles subscales with an NA measure, a physical symptom measure, and a life events checklist. The results strongly confirmed our second implication: The hassles subscales were all highly intercorrelated (.70 or higher), and their correlational patterns with the other measures were virtually identical. To those

accustomed to thinking in terms of substantive relations between distinct content domains, these findings may be disconcerting because they appear to undermine our ability to study the mutual causal influences among mood, stress, and health. However, if we accept the pervasiveness and power of emotionality in determining individual responses, we are then in a position to grapple with the issue of how emotions "homogenize" subjective experience, and to go beyond self-report in measuring the antecedents, moderators, and consequences of this experience.

This brings us to a third implication. If specific item content is secondary to the emotional/evaluative component of self-report scales, then we should expect to find other domains that overlap in a similar way with NA, stress, and somatic distress. Several subsequent topics to be discussed provide good evidence for the existence of such domains. The reader is also referred to Depue and Monroe (1986) for further discussion of the problem of chronic disturbance in conceptualizing and measuring life stress.

Finally, if NA, stress, and reported health all share a common base, then they should show similar levels of stability over time. In a longitudinal study of 75 community couples, in which hassles, physical complaints, and mood were assessed every 4 days for 6 months, autocorrelations of .77, .61, and .50 were reported, respectively (Delongis et al., 1988). The fact that the level of daily hassles and reported symptoms exhibit such a high degree of stability (even higher than mood in this case) supports the notion that these measures are tapping a strong underlying disposition, such as NA.

Hardiness. Of the various areas that we are considering, hardiness (Kobasa, 1979) has perhaps been subjected to the greatest criticism. Among the chief concerns have been (a) the multidimensional nature of the hardiness concept; (b) the fact that the proposed substructure of *challenge, commitment*, and *control* is not reflected in the empirical relations among the component scales; and (c) that the subscales have dissimilar correlational patterns with other variables in the model (e.g., Funk & Houston, 1987; Hull, VanTreuren, & Virnelli, 1987; Schmied & Lawler, 1986). Another frequently cited problem is that certain aspects of the hardiness concept must be inferred from measures assessing opposite characteristics; for example, measures of commitment are actually scales tapping *alienation* from *self* and *work*

(Allred & Smith, 1989; Funk & Houston, 1987). Despite these methodological problems, however, most studies have found that hardiness is moderately correlated with self-reported health, as predicted by the hardiness theory. An exception is Schmied and Lawler (1986) who found no hardiness-illness correlation, for reasons that are unclear.

More problematic for the hardiness concept is its overlap with NA. Descriptions of the nonhardy individual are congruent with those for high NA: alienated, helpless, threatened, passive, and avoidant (Kobasa, Maddi, & Kahn, 1982). Moreover, correlations of various measures of NA with hardiness ranging from .30 to .40 have been reported (similar to the level of association among NA, stress, and physical health), with the Alienation and Powerlessness subscales tending to be the most strongly related (Allred & Smith, 1989; Funk & Houston, 1987; Hull et al., 1987; Rhodewalt & Zone, 1989; Schmied & Lawler, 1986). Moreover, when NA is partialled out of the hardiness-health relation, the two variables are no longer related (Funk & Houston, 1987; Rhodewalt & Zone, 1989). This suggests that hardiness is related to health complaint scales primarily through their shared NA component.

Data regarding the hardiness-stress relation also suggest that hardiness overlaps with NA. Hardiness has been proposed to affect illness primarily via its effects on the appraisal of potentially stressful life events (e.g., Kobasa, 1979; Kobasa et al., 1982). That is, nonhardy subjects are expected to perceive the same events as more stressful, thus leading to higher levels of illness. Clearly, our NA-based model would make this same prediction. Data reported by Rhodewalt and Zone (1989) address this issue. Their women subjects reported the same number and type of stressful events regardless of their hardiness score. (This is the usual, although not universal, finding. Schmied and Lawler, 1986, for example, reported a .39 correlation between number of stressful life events and hardiness.) However, women low in hardiness rated the events as more undesirable, less controllable, and more difficult to adjust to.

How then do we choose between these models? Three factors argue for an NA-based interpretation of the data. First, although both make similar predictions regarding relations among hardiness/NA, stress, and health, the NA-based model is the more parsimonious. Rather than hypothesizing buffering effects, the NA model simply suggests that trait NA (low hardiness), the experience of negative life events, and illness reports are all a function of a common underlying dimension. Second, the data suggest that NA measures may capture more of the relevant variance. That is, stressful life events remain correlated with illness when hardiness is partialled out, but not when the effect of NA is removed (Rhodewalt & Zone, 1989). A final and related point is that a number of conceptual and measurement problems remain unresolved for hardiness. Given the available evidence, it seems at the least, that significant aspects of the hardiness concept may be fruitfully viewed as falling within the NA domain. Let us add, however, that the original conceptualization of hardiness (although not its measurement) bears a strong resemblance to PA, and hardiness researchers may wish to consider developing measures of the positive end of the dimension along these lines.

Optimism/pessimism. Of all the constructs that we are considering, optimism/pessimism is perhaps the one most clearly synonymous with NA. Certainly the two constructs overlap conceptually. Optimism/pessimism has been operationalized in terms of general positive versus negative expectations (Scheier & Carver, 1985), and people with negative expectations (pessimists) are expected to focus on these expectancies and on the distress associated with them (Scheier, Weintraub, & Carver, 1986). This view of optimism/pessimism clearly represents it as an important facet of NA.

The two constructs also overlap psychometrically. In our original paper, we noted a correlation of −.87 between clinical ratings of optimism and an NA measure (Eriksen & Davids, 1955). Similarly, in introducing their optimism measure—the Life Orientation Test (LOT)—Scheier and Carver (1985) reported correlations of around |.50| with measures of depression, perceived stress, hopelessness, and self-esteem. Authors of the Generalized Expectancy for Success Scale (GESS; Fibel & Hale, 1978)—a measure conceptually similar to the LOT—also reported correlations ranging from .20 to .74 ($M = .46$) with measures of depression, anxiety, suicidal ideation, and hopelessness. Additionally, significant correlations with hardiness have been reported (Hull et al., 1987). In a thorough examination of the convergent/discriminant validity of measures of optimism and NA, Smith, Pope, Rhodewalt, and Poulton (1989) concluded that, as currently assessed, optimism was "difficult if not impossible to distinguish" from NA (p. 645).

As was the case with hardiness, predictions regarding the relation of optimism with health have been supported (e.g., Carver & Gaines, 1987; Scheier & Carver, 1985, 1987). However, these coefficients again most likely reflect a common NA component. Smith et al. (1989) reported that optimism-symptom report correlations disappeared (or, in one case, reversed direction) when NA was partialled out. However, the opposite was not true; that is, NA-symptom correlations remained significant even when the effects of both the LOT and GESS were removed. They hypothesized that this pattern emerged because the optimism scales were weaker measures of the general NA trait than were more traditional measures of the construct.

It is important to emphasize that identifying optimism as an aspect of NA in no way implies that optimism research is somehow invalid or unimportant. On the contrary, it was precisely through this process of identifying nominally diverse but psychometrically equivalent scales that we elaborated the NA dimension in the first place. Thus, the recognition that optimism is another facet of NA permits us to integrate optimism research into our understanding of this important and pervasive construct. We should also point out that optimism has been conceptualized as positive versus negative expectations, whereas it has been shown in such diverse realms as major and minor life events, self-statements and attributions, and mood and arousal states that positive and negative phenomena are rarely opposites and are in fact frequently unrelated. Thus, it might prove fruitful for research on optimism if separate measures of negative and positive expectations were developed. We predict that they would show a convergent/discriminant pattern with NA and PA, respectively.

Coping. Although both hardiness and optimism are believed to mediate health outcomes, the hypothesized mechanisms differ. As mentioned earlier, hardiness is thought to operate through differential appraisal of stressful events, and we have shown how this is consistent with an NA-based interpretation of hardiness. Optimism, however, has been hypothesized to affect health through differential responses to stress. Specifically, optimists are expected to cope more persistently and effectively, whereas pessimists may exhibit behavioral withdrawal, and/or focus on expressing their feelings in response to stress (Scheier et al., 1986).

The predictions for pessimists are quite compatible with those that would be made for high NA individuals. For example, we mentioned earlier that high NA individuals are more introspective and ruminative than those low in NA. Moreover, behavioral withdrawal may reflect feelings of helplessness associated with depression, which has been shown to have a strong NA component (Watson, Clark, & Carey, 1988). A finding of positive behavioral consequences for low NA, on the other hand, would extend our view of the NA construct.

The available data, however, provide mixed support for these predictions. First, the reported correlations between various measures of coping and optimism/NA are more variable and generally lower (typically ranging from .15 to .30) than any of the other intercorrelations we have been considering (e.g., Parkes, 1986; Scheier et al., 1986). However, one study that used a measure of psychological symptoms as the NA scale found somewhat higher correlations—up to .50, with an average around .30 (Folkman, Lazarus, Gruen, & Delongis, 1986). Second, although the results have been somewhat inconsistent across studies, optimism/NA appears to be more strongly related to what have variously been called avoidance or emotion-based coping strategies than to approach or problem-focused strategies (Folkman et al., 1986; Holahan & Moos, 1985; Scheier & Carver, 1985). These findings support the idea that NA is primarily mood based rather than being a behavioral dimension, although it is certainly not devoid of behavioral consequences. As we suggested earlier, however, stronger support for the predictions of the optimism model might be obtained if positive and negative expectations were assessed separately. We will present data later in support of this notion.

Attributional style and pathogenic cognitions. The literature on attributional style and its relation to depression in particular, and to NA more generally, is enormous. A full review is obviously beyond our scope, so we will highlight only a few points suggesting that (a) the so-called depressive attributional style (i.e., the tendency to make stable, internal, and global attribution about negative events) is not specific to depression but is more generally related to negative affective states; and (b) this attributional style is better viewed as a facet of depression/NA rather than as a separate causal variable as originally proposed (Abramson, Seligman, & Teasdale, 1978).

Until recently, research into "depressive" attributions has focused solely on convergent validity; that is, on testing the basic hypothesis that certain types of attributions are more frequent in depressives than in normals. Most studies have provided support for this basic hypothesis (for reviews see Coyne & Gotlib, 1983; Sweeney, Anderson, & Bailey, 1986). However, data regarding the ability of attributional measures to discriminate among various types of patient groups has been quite mixed, and varies in part as a function of the specific measure used (see Heimberg, Klosko, Dodge, Becker, & Barlow, 1989; Hollon, Kendall, & Lumry, 1986). In particular, the ability of attributional style to differentiate anxious and depressed patient groups is generally quite low, unless specific attention has been paid to the issue of discrimination.

For example, Heimberg et al. (1989) compared patients who had either depression (dysthymia) or one of several anxiety diagnoses (agoraphobia, panic, or social phobia) on the Attributional Style Questionnaire (ASQ; Peterson, Semmel, von-Baeyer, Abramson, Metalsky, & Seligman, 1982). Patient scores were all higher (i.e., in the supposedly depressive direction) than those of a normal control group, but did not differ among each other. That is, nondepressed but anxious patients exhibited the same global attributional style that has theoretically been associated with depression. This suggests that the style may be more diffusely related to NA and not specific to depression. This is not surprising, of course, because depression itself has been shown to be highly saturated with NA (Watson, Clark, & Carey, 1988; Watson, Clark, & Tellegen, 1988). This conclusion is further supported by the strong correlations found among measures of attributional style, depression, other NA scales, and health complaints (Hollon et al., 1986; Nezu et al., 1986).

Similarly, Snyder and Higgins (1988) have presented evidence indicating that the classical negative attributional style is the obverse of the prototypic excuse-making pattern, which is broadly related to self-esteem maintenance, as well as to lower levels of negative affect/anxiety and depression. In this context, it is also noteworthy that some of the original researchers in the attributional domain now refer instead to "pessimistic explanatory style," and have reported a significant long-term relation with physical health ratings (Peterson, Seligman, & Vaillant, 1988).

Recent research into pathogenic cognitions has focused specifically on differentiating the types of self-statements/attributions that are made by depressed versus anxious patients (e.g., Beck et al., 1987; Greenberg & Beck, 1989). As was discussed earlier with regard to mood and syndromal measures of depression and anxiety, these studies have demonstrated that by paying particular attention to discriminant validity, correlations between types of specific negative cognitions can be reduced, but rarely below .40. In other words, a strong general factor inevitably emerges.

Although an empirical association has been established between attributional style and depression/NA, the causal model hypothesized to underlie this relation (i.e., that in the face of a stressful event, those with a depressive attributional style are more likely to become depressed) has met with much less success (see Brewin, 1985, for a comprehensive review). One difficulty with the model is that the necessity of a precipitating event has not been demonstrated, in part because it is hard to rule out alternative explanations. However, several corollary hypotheses that make fewer assumptions and do not require the presence of a stressful event have been well supported (Brewin, 1985). A second, more serious problem is that depressive attributions, while exhibiting a certain traitlike stability, also appear to fluctuate with depressed mood, and may follow rather than precede the onset of depression. For example, Hollon et al. (1986) reported that remitted bipolar and unipolar depressives both scored the same as normal controls on the Automatic Thoughts Questionnaire (ATQ; Hollon & Kendall, 1980). Further, if initial depression scores are controlled, cognitive attribution measures are no longer able to predict subsequent depression (Peterson, Schwartz, & Seligman, 1981). Thus, such cognitions appear to represent a symptom of depression rather than a causal factor.

Taken together, the data suggest that attributional style and related cognitive factors are neither specific to, nor causal factors in, depression. Having said this, we must emphasize that we do not reject the more dynamic view that negative moods and cognitions are mutually reinforcing in a kind of progressive negative cycle. We do, however, feel that affective experience represents the center of the process. Brewin (1985) concluded that attributions were more directly related to depressed mood than the original model hypothesized, and "may reflect a positive or negative coping style" (p. 308). We would go one step further and suggest that this style represents an important cognitive facet of the larger affective dimension of NA. Similarly, Carver (1989) has suggested that the components of attributional style may each be imperfect manifestations of a latent variable — he proposes optimism/pessimism — that actually underlies its behavioral effects.

Finally, it should be noted that not all of the research into negative cognitions has focused on causal attributions. For example, Emmons and King (1988) investigated individuals' stated personal strivings (goals), and derived several experience sampling-based measures of rumination, ambivalence, and conflict related to these strivings. They then correlated these measures with state and trait NA and PA scales and symptom ratings, and found that all four indices were related to the NA and symptom scales, but none was correlated with the PA scales.

Social support and loneliness. Like hardiness, social support was conceived originally as a buffer against stress; specifically, as protecting people from the adverse physical and psychological effects of negative life events. Thus, under high stress conditions, individuals with adequate social support were hypothesized to have fewer health problems than those without such support. A large number of studies relevant to this hypothesis were reviewed by Cohen and Wills (1985) who concluded that evidence for a buffering effect appeared only if the perceived availability of social support was assessed. That is, little evidence for a buffering effect was provided if social support was measured strictly in terms of the presence and extent of a subject's social network.

Data such as these are consistent with the widely accepted notion that social support is primarily a subjective state rather than an objective circumstance (Heller, Swindle, & Dusenbury, 1986; Thoits, 1985; Turner, Frankel, & Levin, 1983). Sarason, Sarason, and Shearin (1986) also have provided evidence that social support is itself an individual differences variable, with properties of stability and cross-situational consistency similar to those of more traditional trait measures. For example, 3-year stability coefficients for the number of, and satisfaction with, social contacts were .67 and .55, respectively, which represent a degree of stability typical of NA measures.

Moreover, other data suggest that perceptions of current social support are relatively consistent, regardless of who is providing the support (Ruehlman & Wolchik, 1988). Further, Sarason et al. (1986) found that subjects' retrospective ratings of childhood relationships with their parents were significantly correlated with current number of social contacts and satisfaction with current relationships. Thus, recollections of childhood relationships were more or less congruent with interpersonal experiences as young adults.

In addition to having traitlike properties, social support measures have been shown to be negatively correlated with NA (Sarason et al., 1986; Vinokur, Schul, & Caplan, 1987). (And, not surprisingly, social conflict measures and NA are positively correlated; Cohen & Wills, 1985.) Furthermore, social support is negatively related to loneliness (Sarason et al., 1986; Stokes, 1985), which itself has been shown to correlate with a number of other NA measures (Gotlib, 1984; Stokes, 1985). Although these correlations are by no means so high as to suggest that loneliness, low social support, and NA are indistinguishable constructs, they do indicate that negative affective tone broadly influences ratings of diverse content relevant to subjectively perceived experience in interpersonal relations.

Beyond this, however, NA and social support appear to be related in at least one additional way. As mentioned earlier, Cohen and Wills (1985) found a buffering effect for social support only when support perceptions were targeted. However, when structural measures were used to assess social support, they found that social support and pathology were directly related — that is, individuals reporting few social contacts also reported more pathology, regardless of stress level. This is congruent with the fact that low levels of social support are often taken as symptoms of psychological disorders, as well as contributing to them (American Psychiatric Association, 1987). In an insightful discussion of what they term the "person-environment covariance problem," Depue and Monroe (1986) addressed this issue of how personality variables can effect social support. They noted that "the association between events, social support, and chronic disorder is not unidirectional, flowing from input variables to disorder" (p. 43). That is, disorder (either physical or psychological) can generate low levels of social support as well as stem from them (Dohrenwend et al., 1984; Monroe & Steiner, 1986).

Another important finding of the Cohen and Wills (1985) review was that evidence for the effect of social support was most clear when the outcome measure was self-reported psychological distress; that is, NA. Social support was less clearly related to self-reported physical symptoms, and was completely unrelated to objectively assessed health problems. Altogether these results strongly suggest that the assessment of social support cannot be divorced from the measurement of individual differences in NA. Not only may social support help buffer against the experience of physical and psychological distress (including loneliness) in the face of multiple life changes, but conversely, NA may play an important role both in general perceptions of social support and in the creation and maintenance of social networks.

Marital, job, and life satisfaction. At this point in our review, it will not surprise the reader to learn that measures of subjective satisfaction with various life domains are each correlated with measures of NA. Moreover, they are themselves intercorrelated, most likely because of their overlapping NA component. Both job and marital satisfaction have been shown to be important facets of a more general life satisfaction (Diener, 1984; Schaefer & Burnett, 1987). Life satisfaction is a significant predictor of job satisfaction even when major demographic and job design variables are controlled, and job satisfaction, in turn, has been found to predict later life satisfaction in retirement (Schmitt & Pulakos, 1985). Similarly, "marriage and family satisfaction is one of the most important predictors of subjective well-being" (Diener, 1984, p. 556).

Both marital and job satisfaction exhibit a traitlike degree of stability and/or cross-situational consistency. For example, Schaefer and Burnett (1987) reported a 3-year stability coefficient of .56 for marital satisfaction (compared with .72 for their composite NA measure). Various facets of job satisfaction have been found to be reasonably stable over time periods ranging from 16 months (Schneider & Dachler, 1978) to 5 years (Staw & Ross, 1985). Moreover, Staw and Ross (1985) demonstrated consistent employee attitudes even when workers had changed employers and/or occupations.

Various measures of satisfaction also show similar levels of association with NA (Brief, Burke, George, Robinson, & Webster, 1988), and NA-related variables such as hassles (Zika & Chamberlain, 1987), and self-esteem, a core characteristic of (low) NA (Diener, 1984). Moreover, these relations can be observed both concurrently and pro-

spectively. For example, Watson and Keltner (1989) found that NA was significantly correlated with certain facets of job satisfaction assessed both concurrently and an average of over 2 years later. Similarly, Schaefer and Burnett (1987) reported a −.50 correlation between NA and marital satisfaction when measured simultaneously, which dropped only to −.44 with a 3-year lag. Thus, the lagged relation between NA and marital satisfaction was only slightly less than the stability of marital satisfaction itself (.56). In this regard, the results of a study by Staw, Bell, and Clausen (1986) are especially impressive. They found that an affective disposition scale assessed in adolescence was a significant predictor of job satisfaction nearly 50 years later, even after controlling for objective differences in job conditions.

Relations between marital satisfaction and depressive symptoms also have been well documented, using both cross-sectional and longitudinal designs (e.g., Ilfeld, 1977; Monroe, Bromet, Connell, & Steiner, 1986). As with social support, it is likely that the observed correlations between NA and various domains of life satisfaction reflect both the broad influence of the NA dimension in subjective experience, and also the fact that some of the core characteristics of high NA itself contribute, in a causal sense, to difficulties in marital, job, and other life situations. Conversely, it also seems plausible that substantial levels of prolonged marital and/or job difficulties may lead to higher NA levels (Watson & Keltner, 1989).

Summary. We have reviewed a number of interrelated substantive areas broadly in the domain of physical and psychological health, and have presented extensive evidence to suggest that—although originally proposed as conceptually distinct—these constructs actually share a good deal of common variance. We have interpreted this overlap as reflecting NA: a pervasive tendency to report negative emotional states and to interpret experiences with a negativistic bias. We have shown not only that NA markers are significantly correlated with measures of these diverse constructs, but also that this shared NA component accounts for most of the observed cross-domain correlations. That is, when this inexorable nonspecific emotional/evaluative component of self-report scales is controlled, correlations among other variables are eliminated or substantially reduced.

Thus, the data indicate that the NA component

of self-report scales is sufficiently strong that it emerges regardless of the substantive domain, and that the general affective tone of assessed material is as important (or more important) than the specific item content. We emphasize that we are not thereby implying that social support, hardiness, and coping are all simply measures of NA, that they are all the same thing, or that it is fruitless to distinguish among pessimistic attributions, health complaints, and stress. Rather, what we wish to convey is that underlying these seemingly diverse phenomena is a very powerful dimension of individual differences that binds them to one another in ways that are both simple and obvious, subtle and complex. This situation frustrates simplistic efforts to study the relations among diverse constructs; nevertheless, if we are to progress in our understanding of how behaviors, cognitions, interpersonal relations, and exogenous environmental variables influence health, we must first grapple with the broad influence of this mood-based disposition.

Just as we did not "discover" NA, neither are we the first or only ones to struggle with the implications of its pervasiveness. We have already mentioned several reviews and factor analytic studies that reached similar conclusions regarding the diversity of measures tapping this broad dimension. In this context, we wish to state that, although labels are important insofar as they attempt to convey the essence of a construct, higher-order dimensions such as we are discussing here will never be adequately captured by a single term. We have chosen to call the construct Negative Affectivity because we believe its core is affective, but it is ultimately more important that psychologists recognize the existence and nature of this complex but ultimately homogeneous disposition than agree with its label.

Stability, Change, and the Genetic Basis of NA

One of the unsolved puzzles of the NA dimension is that it exhibits a fair degree of long-term stability, but also may show significant change over periods of 1 to 5 years. We have previously speculated that this may stem, at least in part, from the fact that NA is a mood-based trait. To the extent that transient mood variations affect trait scores, the result will be instability; in contrast, to the extent that individuals possess a typical mood level around which they fluctuate, stability will be evidenced. Further, some of the

instability undoubtedly reflects true change on the dimension due to strong internal and/or external forces. For example, major life crises (e.g., a death in the family, unexpected and/or prolonged unemployment, divorce), devastating natural disasters, or, on the positive side, psychotherapy, may have the power to alter a person's characteristic temperament for a period of time or more permanently. However, because such extreme events occur relatively infrequently, large-sample statistics indicate a good deal of stability. To test these hypotheses, it will be necessary to collect systematic data on many individuals on both state and trait NA over relatively long periods of time.

In this regard, collection of naturalistic data in large community samples will be important, but it is also difficult and time consuming. Therefore, it also may prove fruitful to study groups that would be expected to show broad temperamental changes in a somewhat shorter time frame (e.g., therapy patients). In this context it is noteworthy that Schuerger et al. (1989) found the NA levels of patients or prisoners to be less stable than those of normal subjects. Additionally, some studies have found greater stability with increasing age (Helson & Moane, 1987; Schuerger et al., 1989). Others, however, have not found any age-related effects (Costa, McCrae, & Arenberg, 1980; Finn, 1986), so this issue requires further consideration.

Investigation of various methodological factors that influence stability also is warranted. Observations of NA's stability, or lack thereof, have not been based on a single, common scale, but on a multitude of measures, and average stability levels mask marked discrepancies across studies that may be measurement based. For example, as mentioned earlier, Schuerger et al.'s (1989) meta-analyses of measures of anxiety/adjustment yielded a mean 1- to 5-year retest correlation of about .60, whereas 6-year stabilities as high as .83, and 12-year stabilities of .70+, have been reported for several NA/neuroticism scales not included in the meta-analyses (Costa & McCrae, 1988; Costa et al., 1980). Inconsistencies of this magnitude suggest that the measures and methods used to determine stability deserve close scrutiny.

Given that NA is a broad-band dimension, scales designed to assess the trait vary considerably in their core characteristics. For example, some NA measures feature primarily affect, whereas others focus on more cognitive characteristics such as negative self-view; moreover, some are largely pathological in nature, whereas others assess more normal range NA variation. NA scales also vary in their item homogeneity. As a consequence of these content differences, two NA scales could have notably different stabilities despite being highly correlated at a given point in time. Systematic longitudinal study of diverse NA scales will be needed to clarify whether the observed variations in stability are due to the differential stabilities of the various facets of the construct, or to other psychometric properties of the scales used.

In sum, our knowledge of the many factors that contribute to the observed degree of stability and change in NA levels is still rudimentary. Further, as we document in the next section, genetic factors most certainly play an important etiological role, so a full understanding will require not only more careful descriptive work, but also will involve research into brain-behavior relations.

Heritability of NA. A number of large-scale studies investigating genetic factors in personality have recently been completed and have yielded remarkably convergent results despite their different methodologies. For example, Rose and colleagues (Rose, 1988; Rose, Koskenvuo, Kaprio, Sarna, & Langinvainio, 1988) studied monozygotic and dyzygotic twins, whereas Loehlin, Willerman, and Horn (1987) used an adoption design. At least two studies (Pedersen, Plomin, McClearn, & Friberg, 1988; Tellegen, Lykken, Bouchard, Wilcox, Segal, & Rich, 1988) have combined these methods, examining monozygotic and dyzygotic twins raised either separately or apart. Fortunately for comparative purposes, measures of NA (neuroticism), and PA (extraversion) have been included in all recent genetic studies of personality, and the researchers have consistently concluded that there is significant genetic variation in these dimensions. Although the precise estimates of heritability have varied, it is generally agreed that the heritability of NA falls between .30 and .55, whereas that of PA falls more narrowly between about .35 and .50 (Pedersen et al., 1989; Rose, 1988; Tellegen et al., 1988).

Another consistent, and in some ways more disconcerting, conclusion of these studies is that the common familial (i.e., environmental) influence on personality is near zero for NA, and roughly half the size of the genetic component for PA (approximately 20%). This means that about half of the observed variability in these personality traits remains unexplained. Some of this residual variance is undoubtedly error, leading Tellegen et al.

(1988) to estimate that only 15% to 30% of the trait variance can be attributed to unshared or unique environmental variation that is psychologically meaningful. These data challenge psychologists to identify any systematic exogenous factors that are operating in what are apparently highly individualized environments. If such factors can be isolated, they may ultimately solve the puzzle of what variables produce instability in NA levels.

THE TWO-FACTOR MODEL

We have concentrated this chapter on the NA dimension, updating and expanding our earlier work. Despite the fact that we remain impressed with the pervasiveness of this disposition, however, it has become increasingly clear that NA alone fails to capture significant aspects of both physical and mental health. In both the mood and personality literatures, a second major factor—state/trait PA, which is traditionally called extraversion—inevitably emerges as a separate and indispensable dimension. We view PA, like NA, as a mood-based disposition that has broad implications for behavior, cognitive processes, and interpersonal relations.

Despite its opposite-sounding name, it is important to note that PA is distinct from NA, not only psychometrically, but also in terms of the external variables with which it correlates. For example, PA—but not NA—is consistently related to current levels of social activity (Clark & Watson, 1988, 1989; Watson, 1988; Watson & Clark, in press), whereas PA is largely unrelated to health complaints and daily hassles, both of which, as we have seen, have strong NA components (Watson, 1988; Watson & Pennebaker, 1989). In the next section, we will recap the main features of PA, which we have set forth elsewhere (Watson & Clark, in press), and then discuss a few areas in which PA appears to have its major influence on health.

Central Features

Like NA, PA is a broad, higher order disposition that is composed of several primary traits. In addition to its core positive mood component, trait PA has at least five additional facets: Energy, Affiliation, Ascendance, Venturesomeness, and Ambition. The (lower order) PA component itself represents interindividual variation in the frequency and intensity of positive mood experiences. Individuals high in this facet are joyful, enthusiastic, and—it is interesting to note—optimistic about the future. Energy—which includes feelings of active mental alertness and of wholehearted interest, as well as perceived health and vigor—is the other facet most highly related to positive mood. Affiliation and Ascendance, on the other hand, are most closely identified with the traditional view of extraversion, and reflect differences in sociability, interpersonal warmth, social dominance, and exhibitionism. Venturesomeness represents tendencies toward boldness and excitement-seeking, whereas Ambition reflects individual differences in mastery-seeking and perseverance.

The pattern of intercorrelations among these primary traits provides a strong argument for viewing PA as the core underlying component (Watson & Clark, in press). Specifically, they all tend to be more highly related to PA than to each other. Furthermore, they are all significantly correlated with measures of state PA (Costa & McCrae, 1984; Watson & Clark, in press). For example, in a sample of 528 undergraduates, the correlation of state PA with Goldberg's (cited in McCrae & Costa, 1985) higher order PA scale (which he terms *surgency*, following Cattell) was .61, while the correlations of the individual facets with state PA averaged about .37, ranging from .58 (unenergetic vs. energetic) to .25 (humble vs. proud). In contrast, the average correlation of the facets with state NA was −.14 (Watson & Clark, in press).

PA and Affective Disorder

Studies of affective disorder have yielded compelling data regarding the important role that PA plays in mental health. Two lines of research are of particular interest. The first involves the differentiation of depression from other NA-related phenomena, particularly anxiety. In the previous section, we frequently treated depression as a facet of NA. From a strictly convergent viewpoint, this is irrefutable. Measures of the depressive syndrome correlate highly with anxiety and other NA scales (e.g., Clark, 1989; Clark & Watson, in press; Gotlib, 1984; Nezu et al., 1986), and specific depressive symptoms and diagnoses have as strong an NA component as do anxiety symptoms and diagnoses (Watson, Clark, & Carey, 1988). However, when both NA and PA are considered, it becomes possible to distinguish depression from other NA phenomena because depression has an additional (low) PA component. That is, PA is (negatively) correlated with depression measures (Blumberg & Izard, 1986; Tellegen, 1985; Watson, Clark, & Tellegen, 1988), and also with depressive symptoms and diagnoses (Bouman & Luteijn, 1986; Hall, 1977; Watson, Clark, & Carey, 1988), whereas anxiety measures, symptoms, and diagnoses are essentially uncorrelated with PA (Hall, 1977; Tellegen, 1985; Watson, Clark, & Carey, 1988).

In a test of the "cognitive specifity" hypothesis, Greenberg and Beck (1989) reported that depressed and anxious patients responded similarly to material that was theoretically anxiety related, whereas only depressed patients showed the expected effect for depression-related material. If we assume that the anxiety materials were largely NA based, whereas the "depression" materials were strongly PA oriented, these data are congruent with the above view. That is, both anxious and depressed patients frequently exhibit negative thoughts, but "low PA cognitions" are common only in depressed patients.

A second, related area of research on PA and affective disorder has been pursued by Depue and colleagues, who have provided data suggesting that the various components of the higher order PA dimension (outlined earlier) covary systematically in bipolar disorder (Depue, Krauss, & Spoont, 1987). That is, in manic states one observes not only elevated mood, but also heightened energy, hyperactivity, increased social interest, exhibitionism, excitement-seeking, inflated ambition, and so forth, whereas depression is characterized by low mood and energy, decreased activity and interest, social withdrawal, avoidance of stimulation, and feelings of worthlessness. This bipolar dimension, which Depue terms *behavioral engagement* (BE), has been identified in normal as well as clinical populations (Depue et al., 1987; Depue, Krauss, Spoont, & Arbisi, 1989).

The conceptual links between Depue's BE dimension and PA/Extraversion are quite clear, and empirical evidence supporting their relation is being amassed. For example, we have found state and/or trait PA to be related to several of the behavioral components of BE, including hedonia (e.g., heightened interest in social activity, sex, food), (decreased) sleep, and increased activity (e.g., exercise) (Clark & Watson, 1988, 1989; Watson, 1988; Watson & Clark, in press). Furthermore, Depue and colleagues are now involved in an extensive analysis of the personality dimensions related to the BE construct, including PA/ Extraversion. Direct confirmation of this relation will provide further evidence of the importance of the PA dimension for mental health.

PA, Health, and Health-Related Variables

In our examination of the various correlates of NA, we noted several health-related variables that appeared to have an additional PA component, which we will now examine more closely. First, the descriptive conceptualizations of both hardiness and optimism have strong PA features, and it is unfortunate that the measures developed to assess these constructs have not focused more on these positive emotional aspects. However, some data suggest that the standard (composite) hardiness scale may already contain a significant PA component. Allred and Smith (1989) compared the self-statements of hardy and nonhardy individuals who had been assigned to a high- or low-stress condition. As expected, a main effect for hardiness was found for negative self-statements, which disappeared when NA was controlled. However, a significant interaction was found for positive self-statements that was not a function of NA. Both groups were similar under low stress conditions, but under high stress conditions, nonhardy subjects made fewer positive self-statements, even when NA was controlled. This type of effect is seldom if ever found when pure NA markers are studied in relation to positive behaviors. These data therefore suggest that hardiness includes a PA component as well.

In our discussion of NA and coping, we reported findings that supported the notion of NA as primarily a mood-based rather than a behavioral dimension. In contrast, although PA is also a mood-centered disposition, it appears to have stronger associations with behavior in general and with positive behaviors in particular (Clark & Watson, 1988, 1989). Thus, the positive coping style hypothesized for optimists may actually be characteristic of the high PA person rather than the low NA person. To test this notion, it would be necessary to develop optimism measures that focused specifically on positive expectations, as was discussed earlier. McCrae and Costa (1986) specifically studied coping in an NA/PA framework, and presented data relevant to this issue. In two studies, they obtained measures of trait and state NA and PA, as well as ratings regarding the use of 27 specific coping strategies. They found that a greater number of strategies were reliably related to trait NA than to trait PA (30% vs. 15%), but that the coping strategies typically used by high NA individuals also were rated the least effective. In contrast, those that were associated with trait PA tended to be among the most effective. Moreover, subjects' use of "neurotic" and "mature" coping strategies were differentially correlated with state NA and PA, respectively. Finally, when trait NA and PA were partialled out of these relations, neurotic coping was no longer associated with state NA, but mature coping remained significantly correlated with state PA. This suggests that the distress associated with neurotic coping is largely a function of the high NA personality trait, but that positive mood may be independently influenced both by trait PA and by the use of effective coping strategies. These results are generally consistent with the optimism model, but to support that model directly, the findings would need to be replicated using a measure of positive expectations.

Given the strong relation that has been found between PA and social activity (mentioned earlier), it seems that PA also should be relevant to social support. Indeed, theoretical writings in the area have not neglected PA-related aspects of social support. For example, Thoits (1985) noted that perceived support should influence self-evaluations of "lovability, importance, and competence" (p. 58), all of which are positive, PA-relevant qualities (see also Heller et al., 1986). Because the support literature has focused primarily on indices of ill health and psychopathology as outcome measures, however, the positive affective component of social support has not been widely assessed or studied.

Nevertheless, existing data, while preliminary, suggest that it may indeed be fruitful to examine the PA component of social support. First, extraversion has been shown to correlate positively with social support variables and negatively with loneliness (Stokes, 1985). Further, results from a few studies that have examined positive outcomes, and/or have assessed the positive and negative aspects of interpersonal relations separately, suggest the utility of these distinctions. For example, Rook (1984) found that measures specifically tapping positive emotional support (e.g., encouragement) were related to an index of well-being, whereas those assessing purely instrumental support were not.

In a study of personal projects that obtained separate measures of perceived support and hindrance (Ruehlman & Wolchik, 1988), only hindrance was correlated with a distress (i.e., NA) scale, whereas a well-being (i.e., PA) measure was equally related to both hindrance (negatively) and support (positively). Unfortunately, the distress and well-being scales used were significantly correlated with one another, and so were not pure measures of the NA and PA constructs; otherwise, an even stronger convergent/discriminant pattern might have emerged. When ratings of the projects themselves were factor analyzed, separate factors of mastery (absorbing, enjoyable; i.e., PA-related) and strain (difficulty, stress; i.e., NA-related) were obtained. These factors also showed a weak convergent/discriminant pattern with the well-being and distress scales, respectively.

In sum, social support is a promising area for investigation of the individual and combined relations of NA and PA to health. Because social interactions can have both positive and negative aspects, it will be particularly important to assess these qualities separately. Similarly, we would expect the clearest results if positive and negative health outcomes also were distinguished from one another.

Finally, we cited a number of studies earlier showing that NA is a significant correlate of subjective well-being or life satisfaction, as well as its various subareas, such as job or marital satisfaction. However, well-being is conceptualized as more than the mere absence of distress; that is, it is intended to be primarily a positively valenced construct (Diener, 1984) and should therefore be strongly PA related. Indeed, considerable work suggests that life satisfaction is a complex entity, resulting from a subjective averaging of the individual's positive and negative affective experiences (Andrews & Withey, 1976).

In simple, global assessments of satisfaction, however, positive and negative responses are confounded, so that the results of research using single-dimension scales of satisfaction (and depression) are ambiguous as to whether the findings are due primarily to NA, PA, or to some combination of these dispositions. For example, prospective studies examining the premorbid personalities of cancer patients have yielded mixed results (Watson & Pennebaker, 1989). When relatively pure NA markers have been used to assess premorbid personality, the results have been negative. However, when affectively complex constructs—such as life satisfaction and depression—were assessed premorbidly, positive associations with cancer were found in some, but not all, cases. On the basis of these data, we suggest that it is the PA component of these latter constructs that is actually associated with the development of cancer. However, without confirmation from studies using clear NA and PA markers, this conclusion remains speculative.

Two studies of job satisfaction illustrate how the separate effects of NA and PA can be disentangled through multivariate assessment. First, Brief and Roberson (1989) found significant correlations between several indices of job satisfaction and measures of both state NA and PA, with the PA-satisfaction correlations slightly higher in every case. Using a prospective design, Watson and Keltner (1989) assessed trait NA and PA approximately 2 years before obtaining both multidimensional and general measures of job satisfaction; trait affect also was reassessed at this point. When measured concurrently, NA was somewhat more highly related to the various facets of job satisfaction, but in the prospective analyses PA appeared equally important. Moreover, NA and PA tended to be correlated with different facets of job satisfaction. Finally, it is noteworthy that the general job satisfaction measure was more highly related to PA than to NA, both concurrently and prospectively.

In this section, we have illustrated that it is necessary to go beyond NA and include a second mood-dispositional dimension—PA—in health research. In the last section, we will describe briefly how biobehavioral theorists are trying to link these dimensions with an emerging understanding of neuropsychological functioning. Finally, we will raise what we feel are some important questions that future researchers in this area should address.

TOWARD A COMPREHENSIVE MODEL OF EMOTIONALITY

A full discussion of the larger context in which the NA and PA dimensions exist must be reserved for another time and place. However, we would be remiss if we did not mention the rich tradition within which these constructs have developed and continue to evolve. We have already noted the link between NA and PA (which derive from Tellegen's work on mood and personality) and the Eysenckian dimensions of Neuroticism and Extraversion, respectively. Each of these models also contains a third higher order dimension, Constraint and Psychoticism (which are oppositely keyed from one another), respectively. Tellegen (1985) has described this dimension as "an affect-relevant indicator of a person's 'preparedness' to respond to a range of emotion-related circumstances . . . with either caution, timidity, and respect or with recklessness, boldness, and defiance" (p. 697). Additionally, Gray (1971, 1985) has proposed a psychobiological model comprising three fundamental emotional systems that can be interpreted fairly directly as NA, PA, and Constraint (Tellegen, 1985). Finally, building on the work of these writers, Cloninger (1986, 1987a, 1987b) has outlined a three-factor biopsychosocial model for linking personality with psychopathology.

Although these dimensions are generally viewed as attempts to represent "real" entities, and not simply convenient psychometric fictions, research establishing their biological bases is still in its infancy. However, several directions appear promising. Based primarily on animal research, but also on investigations of the drug effects in human beings, Gray (1971, 1985) has linked NA (his Behavioral Inhibition System; BIS) with noradrenergic and serotonergic impulses to the septohippocampal system under conditions of stress. Cloninger's model appears highly congruent with regard to this system (although his scale is tipped toward measuring NA vs. PA, rather than high vs. low NA per se). However, there are more significant inconsistencies between the two models' views of PA and Constraint.

To understand these discrepancies, a brief review of the historical confusion between these dimensions will be helpful (see Watson & Clark, in press, for a fuller discussion). As we noted earlier, the higher order PA/Extraversion dimension contains a number of facets that are themselves only moderately correlated. Eysenck's original conception of Extraversion also contained a strong Impulsivity component, and his revised scale still taps this facet to a greater degree than other PA/Extraversion scales (Watson & Clark, in press). Although Impulsivity is now generally recognized to form part of the higher order Constraint dimension, the influence of this view lingers on. For example, both Gray and Cloninger propose the existence of a Behavioral Activating System (BAS), which they describe similarly as involving appetitive approach or approach learning, and also active avoidance or skilled escape behavior. However, they view the stimuli that activate this

system, the relevant brain systems, and the corresponding personality dimensions differently, paralleling the current versus Eysenckian view of PA/Extraversion.

Specifically, Gray's model of the BAS appears to be largely congruent with current conceptualizations of PA/Extraversion, and his remaining third dimension ("Flight/Fight") can be linked with Constraint/Psychoticism (Gray, 1971; Tellegen, 1985). In contrast, Cloninger partially follows the old Eysenckian model, combining two components of PA/Extraversion—Positive Mood (specifically, feelings of excitement, interest, and enthusiasm) and Ascendance—with Impulsivity into a dimension he terms *novelty seeking* (Cloninger, 1987b). He then combines the Extraversion components of Sociability and Ambition into a third dimension, which he terms *reward dependence*. The neural substrates he proposes for these dimensions are also a blend of those put forth for PA and Constraint by Gray. Cloninger (1987a) has argued for his model on the general grounds that "underlying genetic variation does not correspond well to observed behavioral variation" (p. 413). However, no one expects brain-behavior associations to be simple, and the existing data do not clearly support or refute any particular model.

While these models have focused primarily on limbic system activity, Fox and Davidson (1984) have proposed a model of cortical hemispheric asymmetry. They conceptualize positive and negative affective states as representing approach and withdrawal tendencies, respectively, and link them with left and right frontal lobe processing. Leventhal and Tomarken (1986) review extensive evidence supporting the lateralization of emotional states, but also note the existence of competing models (e.g., Tucker & Williamson, 1984). In any case, all existing models (regarding both limbic and cortical systems) are still quite skeletal, and current links between mood-dispositions and brain represent informed speculations rather than empirically based conclusions.

Directions for Future Research

Although these discussions of brain-behavior relations may appear to take us far afield of our original topic, this research may eventually yield some exciting breakthroughs in our understanding of the psychological correlates and determinants of health. By linking personality/health research with work in neuroscience, we have the opportunity to make major advances in our basic understanding of emotional distress and well-being. In a recent recognition of the importance of such research, the National Advisory Mental Health Council (NAMHC) identified 50 important questions for neuroscience to answer in the decade ahead, and a significant number involved the role of emotions or stress in physical or mental health (NAMHC, 1988). To cite but one, "What are the detailed neuronal systems mediating basic drives and experiences such as pain, pleasure, attention, and emotions?" (p. vii).

To this type of broad question, we would append more specific — but no less fundamental — questions such as, "Why, from a neurological perspective, is the NA dimension so broad and pervasive?" And "Why do these marked individual differences in the tendency to experience positive and negative emotions exist at all; for example, evolutionarily speaking, are varying levels of the dimensions differentially adaptive?" Future research in neuroscience will need to resolve the inconsistencies between contrasting views of cortical involvement in emotional behavior, and to develop more comprehensive models that integrate both cortical and limbic inputs. The knowledge that half of the (phenotypic) variation stemming from these neural structures/processes is genetically based may help to guide these inquiries. Conversely, advances in neuropsychology will inform investigations into the basic question of what, specifically, is inherited.

We wish to stress that we are not making the reductionistic argument that our understanding of psychological phenomena is complete only when we have grasped the underlying biological mechanisms. Rather we believe that biological and psychological perspectives can be mutually enhancing. Theoretically and empirically sound behavioral/descriptive work is as critically important to biological approaches as vice versa. Thus, it also will be important to pursue answers to unresolved issues at the social, behavioral, and phenomenological levels. For example, much psychometric work needs to be done to clarify relations among the various personality traits hypothesized to be associated with, or modifiers of, stress. We have suggested that many have a large NA component, but what of the remaining unexplained variance? For example, can measures of hardiness or optimism be developed that better reflect the PA component in their respective conceptualizations?

Another important issue involves further examination of relations among subjective and objective measures of various phenomena. For example, how can we separate the contributions of NA and actual health status and so enhance our understanding of physical symptom reports? How do social network variables interact with personality (both NA and PA) to produce perceived social support, and further, how does personality affect actual social networks? Finally, does the third major higher order dimension, Constraint, play a role in either physical or mental health? For example, to the extent that this disposition represents individual differences in behavioral and affective regulation, it may be relevant to life-style diseases, such as obesity and perhaps substance abuse, that require conscious or habitual self-control, or to personality disorders, in which dysregulation appears to be a major symptom dimension.

In conclusion, let us note that the theme of separate systems regulating approach (PA) and withdrawal/avoidance (NA) is common to several models, both neurological and psychological, and thus represents a potentially important avenue for integration. Gray (and by extension, Tellegen), Cloninger, Depue and colleagues, and Fox and Davidson all utilize the concepts of approach and avoidance in their models. Coping mechanisms also were categorized into approach and withdrawal/avoidance strategies, and optimists/pessimists are hypothesized to use these strategies differentially. Support systems also no doubt depend heavily on individual differences in social approach and withdrawal tendencies. In this context, it is interesting to recall that approach and avoidance were central concepts in the early work of Dollard and Miller (1950), examining relations between personality and psychopathology. Furthermore, Tellegen (1985) has suggested that "the real psychoanalytic model incorporates two basic affect-signal systems," one of which "controls avoidance of distress" (anxiety/NA), the other of which "controls the procurement of satisfaction" (approach/PA) (p. 701). Clearly, we have a long way to go in our understanding and integration of these diverse theoretical models and empirical phenomena, but it is just as clear that great strides are being made toward a comprehensive biopsychosocial model of the major dimensions of emotionality.

REFERENCES

Abramson, L. Y., Seligman, M. E. P., & Teasdale, J. D. (1978). Learned helplessness in humans: Critique and reformulation. *Journal of Abnormal Psychology, 87*, 49–74.

Aldwin, C. M., Levenson, M. R., Sprio, A. III, Bossé, R. (1989). Does emotionality predict stress? Findings from the Normative Aging Study. *Journal of Personality and Social Psychology, 56*, 618–624.

Allred, K. D., & Smith, T. W. (1989). The hardy personality: Cognitive and physiological responses to evaluative threat. *Journal of Personality and Social Psychology, 56*, 257–266.

American Psychiatric Association. (1987). Diagnostic and statistical manual (3rd ed., revised). Washington, DC: Author.

Andrews, F. M., & Withey, S. B. (1976). *Social indicators of well-being: America's perception of life quality*. New York: Plenum Press.

Bass, A. R., & Fielder, F. E. (1961). Interpersonal perception scores and their components as predictors of personality adjustment. *Journal of Abnormal and Social Psychology, 62*, 442–445.

Beck, A. T., Brown, G., Steer, R. A., Eidelson, J. I., & Riskind, J. H. (1987). Differentiating anxiety from depression: A test of the content-specificity hypothesis. *Journal of Abnormal Psychology, 96*, 179–183.

Bernstein, G. A., Garfinkel, B. D., & Hoberman, H. M. (1989). Self-reported anxiety in adolescents. *American Journal of Psychiatry, 146*, 384–386.

Block, J. (1965). *The challenge of response sets: Unconfounding meaning, acquiescence, and social desirability in the MMPI*. New York: Appleton-Century-Crofts.

Blumberg, S. H., & Izard, C. E. (1986). Discriminating patterns of emotions in 10- and 11-year-old children's anxiety and depression. *Journal of Personality and Social Psychology, 51*, 852–857.

Bouman, T. K., & Luteijn, F. (1986). Relations between the Pleasant Events Schedule, depression, and other aspect of psychopathology. *Journal of Abnormal Psychology, 95*, 373–377.

Brewin, C. R. (1985). Depression and causal attributions: What is their relation? *Psychological Bulletin, 98*, 297–309.

Brief, A. P., Burke, M. J., George, J. M., Robinson, B. S., & Webster, J. (1988). Should negative affectivity remain an unmeasured variable in the study of job stress? *Journal of Applied Psychology, 73*, 193–198.

Brief, A. P., & Roberson, L. (1989). Job attitude organization: An exploratory study. *Journal of Applied Social Psychology, 19*, 717–727.

Carver, C. S. (1989). How should multifaceted personality constructs be tested? Issues illustrated by self-monitoring, attributional style, and hardiness. *Journal of Personality and Social Psychology, 56*, 577–585.

Carver, C. S., & Gaines, J. G. (1987). Optimism, pessimism, and postpartum depression. *Cognitive Therapy and Research, 11*, 449–462.

Clark, L. A. (1989). The anxiety and depressive disorders: Descriptive psychopathology and differential diagnosis. In P. C. Kendall & D. Watson (Eds.), *Anxiety and depression: Distinctive and overlapping features* (pp. 83–129). New York: Academic Press.

Clark, L. A., & Watson, D. B. (1988). Mood and the mundane: Relations between daily life events and self-reported mood. *Journal of Personality and Social Psychology, 54*, 296–308.

Clark, L. A., & Watson, D. B. (1989). *Predicting momentary mood from ordinary life events and personality*. Manuscript submitted for publication.

Clark, L. A., & Watson, D. B. (in press). Theoretical and empirical issues in differentiating depression from anxiety. In J. Becker & A. Kleinman (Eds.), *Advances in mood disorders: Vol. 1. Psychological Aspects*. Hillsdale, NJ: Lawrence Erlbaum Associates.

Cloninger, C. R. (1986). A unified biosocial theory of personality and its role in the development of anxiety states. *Psychiatric Developments, 3*, 167–226.

Cloninger, C. R. (1987a). Neurogenic adaptive mechanisms in alcoholism. *Science, 236*, 410–416.

Cloninger, C. R. (1987b). A systematic method for clinical description and classification of personality variants: A proposal. *Archives of General Psychiatry, 44*, 573–588.

Cohen, S., & Wills, T. A. (1985). Stress, social support, and the buffering hypothesis. *Psychological Bulletin, 98*, 310–357.

Comrey, A. L., & Duffy, K. E. (1968). Cattell and Eysenck factors scores related to Comrey personality factors. *Multivariate Behavioral Research, 3*, 379–392.

Comrey, A. L., Jamison, K., & King, N. (1968). Integration of two personality factor systems. *Multivariate Behavioral Research, 3*, 147–159.

Costa, P. T., Jr., & McCrae, R. R. (1980). Influence of extraversion and neuroticism on subjective well-being: Happy and unhappy people. *Journal of Personality and Social Psychology, 38*, 668–678.

Costa, P. T., Jr., & McCrae, R. R. (1984). Personality as a lifelong determinant of well-being. In C. Z. Malatesta & C. E. Izard (Eds.), *Emotion in adult development* (pp. 141–159). Beverly Hills, CA: Sage Publications.

Costa, P. T., Jr., & McCrae, R. R. (1987). Neuroticism, somatic complaints, and disease: Is the bark worse than the bite? *Journal of Personality, 55*, 299–316.

Costa, P. T., Jr., & McCrae, R. R. (1988). Personality in adulthood: A 6-year longitudinal study of self-ratings and spouse ratings on the NEO Personality Inventory. *Journal of Personality and Social Psychology, 54*, 853–863.

Costa, P. T., Jr., McCrae, R. R., & Arenberg, D. (1980). Enduring dispositions in adult males. *Journal of Personality and Social Psychology, 38*, 793–800.

Coyne, J. C., & Gotlib, I. H. (1983). The role of cognition in depression: A critical appraisal. *Psychological Bulletin, 94*, 472–505.

Crocker, J., Alloy, L. B., & Kayne, N. T. (1988). Attributional style, depression, and perceptions of consensus for events. *Journal of Personality and Social Psychology, 54*, 840–846.

Delongis, A., Folkman, S., & Lazarus, R. (1988). The impact of daily stress on health and mood: Psychological and social resources as mediators. *Journal of Personality and Social Psychology, 54*, 486–495.

Depue, R. A., Krauss, S., & Spoont, M. R. (1987). A two-dimensional threshold model of seasonal bipolar affective disorder. In D. Magnusson & A. Ohrman (Eds.), *Psychopathology: An interactional perspective* (pp. 95–123). New York: Academic Press.

Depue, R. A., Krauss, S., Spoont, M. R., & Arbisi, P. (1989). General Behavior Inventory identification of unipolar and bipolar affective conditions in a nonclinical university population. *Journal of Abnormal Psychology, 98*, 117–126.

Depue, R. A., & Monroe, S. M. (1986). Conceptualization and measurement of human disorder in life stress research: The problem of chronic disturbance. *Psychological Bulletin, 99*, 36–51.

Diener, E. (1984). Subjective well-being. *Psychological Bulletin, 95*, 542–575.

Dohrenwend, B. P., & Shrout, P. E. (1985). "Hassles" in the conceptualization and measurement of life stress variables. *American Psychologist, 40*, 780–785.

Dohrenwend, B. S., Dohrenwend, B. P., Dodson, M., & Shrout, P. E. (1984). Symptoms, hassles, social supports, and life events: Problem of confounded measures. *Journal of Abnormal Psychology, 93*, 222–230.

Dollard, J., & Miller, N. E. (1950). *Personality and psychotherapy: An analysis in terms of learning, thinking, and culture.* New York: McGraw-Hill.

Eason, L., Finch, A. J., Brasted, W., & Saylor, C. F. (1985). The assessment of depression and anxiety in hospitalized pediatric patients. *Child Psychiatry and Human Development, 16*, 57–64.

Emmons, R. A., & King, L. A. (1988). Conflict among personal strivings: Immediate and long-term implications for psychological and physical well-being. *Journal of Personality and Social Psychology, 54*, 1040–1048.

Eriksen, C. W., & Davids, A. (1955). The meaning and clinical validity of the Taylor Anxiety Scale and the Hysteria-Psychasthenia scales from the MMPI. *Journal of Abnormal and Social Psychology, 50*, 135–137.

Fibel, B., & Hale, W. D. (1978). The Generalized Expectancy for Success Scale—A new measure. *Journal of Consulting and Clinical Psychology, 46*, 924–931.

Finman, R., & Berkowitz, L. (1989). Some factors influencing the effect of depressed mood on anger and overt hostility toward another. *Journal of Research in Personality, 23*, 70–84.

Finn, S. E. (1986). Stability of personality self-ratings over 30 years: Evidence for an age/cohort interaction. *Journal of Personality and Social Psychology, 50*, 813–818.

Folkman, S., & Lazarus, R. S. (1986). Stress process and depressive symptomatology. *Journal of Abnormal Psychology, 95*, 107–113.

Folkman, S., Lazarus, R. S., Gruen, R. J., & Delongis, A. (1986). Appraisal, coping, health status, and psychological symptoms. *Journal of Personality and Social Psychology, 50*, 571–579.

Fox, N. A., & Davidson, R. J. (1984). Hemispheric substrates of affect: A developmental model. In N. A. Fox & R. J. Davidson (Eds.), *The psychology of affective development* (pp. 353–381). Hillsdale, NJ: Lawrence Erlbaum Associates.

Funk, S. C., & Houston, B. K. (1987). A critical

analysis of the hardiness scales' validity and utility. *Journal of Personality and Social Psychology, 53*, 572–578.

Goodstein, L. D. (1954). Interrelationships among several measures of anxiety and hostility. *Journal of Consulting Psychology, 18*, 35–39.

Gotlib, I. H. (1984). Depression and general psychopathology in university students. *Journal of Abnormal Psychology, 93*, 19–30.

Gray, J. A. (1971). Causal theories of personality and how to test them. In J. R. Royce (Ed.), *Multivariate analysis and psychological theory* (pp. 409–463). New York: Academic Press.

Gray, J. A. (1985). Issues in the neuropsychological study of anxiety. In A. H. Tuma & J. D. Maser (Eds.), *Anxiety and the anxiety disorders* (pp. 5–26). Hillsdale, NJ: Lawrence Erlbaum Associates.

Greenberg, M. S., & Beck, A. T. (1989). Depression vs. anxiety: A test of the content-specificity hypothesis. *Journal of Abnormal Psychology, 98*, 9–13.

Hall, C. A. (1977). *Differential relationships of pleasure and distress with depression and anxiety over a past, present, and future time framework*. Unpublished doctoral dissertation, University of Minnesota, Minneapolis.

Heimberg, R. G., Klosko, J. S., Dodge, C. S., Becker, R. E., & Barlow, D. H. (1989). Anxiety disorders, depression, and attributional style: A further test of the specificity of depressive attributions. *Cognitive Therapy and Research, 13*, 21–36.

Heller, K., Swindle, R. W., Jr., & Dusenbury, L. (1986). Component social support processes: Comments and integration. *Journal of Clinical and Consulting Psychology, 54*, 466–470.

Helson, R., & Moane, G. (1987). Personality change in women from college to midlife. *Journal of Personality and Social Psychology, 53*, 176–186.

Holahan, C. J., & Moos, R. H. (1985). Life stress and health: Personality, coping, and family support in stress resistance. *Journal of Personality and Social Psychology, 49*, 739–747.

Hollon, S. D., & Kendall, P. C. (1980). Cognitive self-statements in depression: Development of an automatic thoughts questionnaire. *Cognitive Therapy and Research, 4*, 383–395.

Hollon, S. D., Kendall, P. C., & Lumry, A. (1986). Specificity of depressotypic cognitions in clinical depression. *Journal of Abnormal Psychology, 95*, 52–59.

Hull, J. G., VanTreuren, R. R., & Virnelli, S. (1987). Hardiness and health: A critique and alternative approach. *Journal of Personality and Social Psychology, 53*, 518–530.

Ilfeld, F. W. (1977). Current social stressors and symptoms of depression. *American Journal of Psychiatry, 134*, 161–166.

Izard, C. E. (1972). *Patterns of emotions: A new analysis of anxiety and depression*. New York: Academic Press.

Kanner, A. D., Coyne, J. C., Schaefer, C., & Lazarus, R. S. (1981). Comparison of two modes of stress measurement: Daily hassles and uplifts versus major life events. *Journal of Behavioral Medicine, 1*, 1–39.

Kaplan, M. F. (1968). Elicitation of information and response biases of repressors and sensitizers, and neutrals in behavior prediction. *Journal of Personality, 36*, 84–91.

Kobasa, S. C. (1979). Stressful life events, personality, and health: An inquiry into hardiness. *Journal of Personality and Social Psychology, 37*, 1–11.

Kobasa, S. C., Maddi, S. R., & Kahn, S. (1982). Hardiness and health: A prospective study. *Journal of Personality and Social Psychology, 42*, 168–177.

Lazarus, R. S., Delongis, A., Folkman, S., & Gruen, R. (1985). Stress and adaptational outcomes. *American Psychologist, 40*, 770–779.

Leventhal, H., & Tomarken, A. J. (1986). Emotion: Today's problems. *Annual Review of Psychology, 37*, 565–610.

Loehlin, J. C., Willerman, L., & Horn, J. M. (1987). Personality resemblance in adoptive families: A 10-year followup. *Journal of Personality and Social Psychology, 53*, 961–969.

McCrae, R. R., & Costa, P. T., Jr. (1985). Updating Norman's "Adequate Taxonomy": Intelligence and personality dimensions in natural language and in questionnaires. *Journal of Personality and Social Psychology, 49*, 710–721.

McCrae, R. R., & Costa, P. T., Jr. (1986). Personality coping, and coping effectiveness in an adult sample. *Journal of Personality, 56*, 385–405.

Monroe, S. M., Bromet, E. J., Connell, M. M., & Steiner, S. C. (1986). Social support, life events, and depressive symptoms: A 1-year prospective study. *Journal of Consulting and Clinical Psychology, 54*, 424–431.

Monroe, S. M., & Steiner, S. C. (1986). Social

support and psychopathology: Interrelations with preexisting disorder, stress, and personality. *Journal of Abnormal Psychology, 95,* 29–39.

National Advisory Mental Health Council. (1988). *Approaching the 21st century: Opportunities for NIMH neuroscience research.* Rockville, MD: U.S. Department of Health and Human Services.

Nezu, A. M., Nezu, C. M., & Nezu, V. A. (1986). Depression, general distress, and causal attributions among university students. *Journal of Abnormal Psychology, 95,* 184–186.

Noller, P., Law, H., & Comrey, A. L. (1987). Cattell, Comrey, and Eysenck personality factors compared: More evidence for the five robust factors? *Journal of Personality and Social Psychology, 53,* 775–782.

Parkes, K. R. (1986). Coping in stressful episodes: The role of individual differences, environmental factors, and situational characteristics. *Journal of Personality and Social Psychology, 51,* 1277–1292.

Pedersen, N. L., Plomin, R., McClearn, G. E., & Friberg, L. (1988). Neuroticism, extraversion, and related traits in adult twins reared apart and reared together. *Journal of Personality and Social Psychology, 55,* 950–957.

Peterson, C., Schwartz, S. M., & Seligman, M. E. P. (1981). Self-blame and depressive symptoms. *Journal of Personality and Social Psychology, 41,* 253–259.

Peterson, C., Seligman, M. E. P., & Vaillant, G. (1988). Pessimistic explanatory style is a risk factor for physical illness: A 35-year longitudinal study. *Journal of Personality and Social Psychology, 55,* 23–27.

Peterson, C., Semmel, A., vonBaeyer, C., Abramson, L. Y., Metalsky, G. I., & Seligman, M. E. P. (1982). The attributional style questionnaire. *Cognitive Therapy and Research, 6,* 287–300.

Phares, E. J. (1961). TAT performance as a function of anxiety and coping-avoiding behavior. *Journal of Consulting Psychology, 25,* 257–259.

Rhodewalt, F., & Zone, J. (1989). Appraisal of life change, depression, and illness in hardy and nonhardy women. *Journal of Personality and Social Psychology, 56,* 81–88.

Rook, K. S. (1984). The negative side of social integration: Impact on psychological well-being. *Journal of Personality and Social Psychology, 46,* 1097–1108.

Rose, R. J. (1988). Genetic and environmental variance in content dimensions of the MMPI. *Journal of Personality and Social Psychology, 55,* 302–311.

Rose, R. J., Koskenvuo, M., Kaprio, J., Sarna, S., & Langinvainio, H. (1988). Shared genes, shared experiences, and similarity of personality: Data from 14,288 adult Finnish co-twins. *Journal of Personality and Social Psychology, 54,* 161–171.

Rowlinson, R. T., & Felner, R. D. (1988). Major life events, hassles, and adaptation in adolescence: Confounding in the conceptualization and measurement of life stress and adjustment revisited. *Journal of Personality and Social Psychology, 55,* 432–444.

Ruehlman, L. S., & Wolchik, S. A. (1988). Personal goals and interpersonal support and hindrance as factors in psychological distress and well-being. *Journal of Personality and Social Psychology, 55,* 293–301.

Sarason, I. G., Sarason, B. R., & Shearin, E. N. (1986). Social support as an individual difference variable: Its stability, origins, and relational aspects. *Journal of Personality and Social Psychology, 50,* 845–855.

Saylor, C. F., Finch, A. J., Baskin, C. H., Furey, W., & Kelly, M. M. (1984). Construct validity for measures of childhood depression: Application of multitrait-multimethod methodology. *Journal of Consulting and Clinical Psychology, 52,* 977–985.

Schaefer, E. S., & Burnett, C. K. (1987). Stability and predictability of quality of women's marital relationships and demoralization. *Journal of Personality and Social Psychology, 53,* 1129–1136.

Scheier, M. F., & Carver, C. S. (1985). Optimism, coping, and health: Assessment and implications of generalized outcome expectancies. *Health Psychology, 4,* 219–247.

Scheier, M. F., & Carver, C. S. (1987). Dispositional optimism and physical well-being: The influence of generalized outcome expectancies. *Journal of Personality, 55,* 169–210.

Scheier, M. F., Weintraub, J. K., & Carver, C. S. (1986). Coping with stress: Divergent strategies of optimists and pessimists. *Journal of Personality and Social Psychology, 51,* 1257–1264.

Schmied, L. A., & Lawler, K. A. (1986). Hardiness, Type A behavior, and the stress-illness relation in working women. *Journal of Personality and Social Psychology, 51,* 1218–1223.

Schmitt, N., & Pulakos, E. D. (1985). Predicting job satisfaction from life satisfaction: Is there a general satisfaction factor? *International Journal of Psychology, 20*, 155–167.

Schneider, B., & Dachler, H. P. (1978). A note on the stability of the Job Descriptive Index. *Journal of Applied Psychology, 63*, 650–653.

Schuerger, J. M., Zarrella, K. L., & Hotz, A. S. (1989). Factors that influence the temporal stability of personality by questionnaire. *Journal of Personality and Social Psychology, 56*, 777–783.

Siegel, J. M. (1986). The multidimensional anger inventory. *Journal of Personality and Social Psychology, 51*, 191–200.

Smith, T. W., & Frohm, K. B. (1985). What's so unhealthy about hostility? Construct validity and psychosocial correlates of the Cook and Medley Ho scale. *Health Psychology, 4*, 503–520.

Smith, T. W., Pope, M. K., Rhodewalt, F., & Poulton, J. L. (1989). Optimism, neuroticism, coping, and symptom reports: An alternative interpretation of the Life Orientation Test. *Journal of Personality and Social Psychology, 56*, 640–648.

Snyder, C. R., & Higgins, R. L. (1988). Excuses: Their effective role in the negotiation of reality. *Psychological Bulletin, 104*, 23–35.

Staw, B. M., Bell, N. E., & Clausen, J. A. (1986). The dispositional approach to job attitudes: A lifetime longitudinal test. *Administrative Science Quarterly, 31*, 56–77.

Staw, B. M., & Ross, J. (1985). Stability in the midst of change: A dispositional approach to job attitudes. *Journal of Applied Psychology, 70*, 469–480.

Stokes, J. P. (1985). The relation of social network and individual difference variables to loneliness. *Journal of Personality and Social Psychology, 48*, 981–990.

Sweeney, P. D., Anderson, K., & Bailey, S. (1986). Attributional style in depression: A meta-analytic review. *Journal of Personality and Social Psychology, 50*, 974–991.

Tanaka-Matsumi, J., & Kameoka, V. A. (1986). Reliabilities and concurrent validities of popular self-report measures of depression, anxiety, and social desirability. *Journal of Consulting and Clinical Psychology, 54*, 328–333.

Tellegen, A. (1982). *Brief manual for the Differential Personality Questionnaire.* Unpublished manuscript, University of Minnesota, Minneapolis.

Tellegen, A. (1985). Structures of mood and personality and their relevance to assessing anxiety, with an emphasis on self-report. In A. H. Tuma & J. D. Maser (Eds.), *Anxiety and the anxiety disorders* (pp. 681–706). Hillsdale, NJ: Lawrence Erlbaum Associates.

Tellegen, A., Lykken, D. T., Bouchard, T. J., Jr., Wilcox, K. J., Segal, N. L., & Rich, S. (1988). Personality similarity in twins reared apart and together. *Journal of Personality and Social Psychology, 54*, 1031–1039.

Thoits, P. A. (1985). Social support and psychological well-being: Theoretical possibilities. In I. G. Sarason & B. R. Sarason (Eds.), *Social support: Theory, research and applications* (pp. 51–72). The Hague, The Netherlands: Martinus, Nijhof.

Tucker, D. M., & Williamson, P. A. (1984). Asymmetric neural control in human self-regulation. *Psychological Review, 80*, 352–373.

Turner, R. J., Frankel, B. G., & Levin, D. M. (1983). Social support: Conceptualization, measurement, and implications for mental health. In J. Greeley (Ed.), *Research in community and mental health* (Vol. 3, pp. 67–111). Greenwich, CT: JAI Press.

Vinokur, A., Schul, Y., & Caplan, R. (1987). Determinants of perceived social support: Interpersonal transactions, personal outlook, and transient affective state. *Journal of Personality and Social Psychology, 53*, 1137–1145.

Watson, D. (1988). Intraindividual and interindividual analyses of positive and negative affect: Their relation to health complaints, perceived stress, and daily activities. *Journal of Personality and Social Psychology, 54*, 1020–1030.

Watson, D., & Clark, L. A. (1984). Negative affectivity: The disposition to experience aversive emotional states. *Psychological Bulletin, 96*, 465–490.

Watson, D., & Clark, L. A. (in press). Extraversion and its positive emotional core. In S. Briggs, W. Jones, & R. Hogan (Eds.), *Handbook of personality psychology.* New York: Academic Press.

Watson, D., Clark, L. A., & Carey, G. (1988). Positive and negative affect and their relation to anxiety and depressive disorders. *Journal of Abnormal Psychology, 97*, 346–353.

Watson, D., Clark, L. A., & Tellegen, A. (1988). Development and validation of brief measures of positive and negative affect: The PANAS scales. *Journal of Personality and Social Psychology, 54*, 1063–1070.

Watson, D., & Keltner, A. C. (1989). *General factors of affective temperament and their relation to job satisfaction over time*. Unpublished manuscript, Southern Methodist University, Dallas, TX.

Watson, D., & Pennebaker, J. W. (1989). Health complaints, stress, and distress: Exploring the central role of negative affectivity. *Psychological Review, 96*, 234–254.

Watson, D., & Tellegen, A. (1985). Toward a con-

sensual structure of mood. *Psychological Bulletin, 98*, 219–235.

Zika, S., & Chamberlain, K. (1987). Relation of hassles and personality to subjective well-being. *Journal of Personality and Social Psychology, 53*, 155–162.

Zuckerman, M., Kuhlman, D. M., & Camac, C. (1988). What lies beyond E and N? Factor analyses of scales believed to measure basic dimensions of personality. *Journal of Personality and Social Psychology, 54*, 96–107.

CHAPTER 13

LOCUS OF CONTROL AND HEALTH

Herbert M. Lefcourt
Karina Davidson-Katz

The locus of control construct has occupied a prominent position in the personality literature for more than two decades. Since the publication of the first article describing the construct (Rotter, Seeman, & Liverant, 1962) the number of research reports concerned with locus of control had become so voluminous by 1975 that *Current Digest*, the abstracting journal, concluded that the locus of control construct had come to be the central preoccupation in personality research. At least four articles pertaining to locus of control have become citation classics (Lefcourt, 1966; Nowicki & Strickland, 1973; Rotter, 1966; Strickland, 1965). Despite the passage of time, interest in the construct persists.

Although some of the recent research studies concerning control expectancies retain the same personality focus that characterized the earlier social learning–derived investigations, there is also much research examining control-related phenom-ena that departs from that perspective. For example, there are a number of studies in which the impact of situations varying in controllability have been examined. In addition, other studies have employed measures of efficacy, mastery, helplessness, and perceived control. What all of these constructs and phenomena have in common is a concern for the manner in which individuals regard their personal experiences, and whether they perceive themselves to be capable of dealing with their circumstances or not. When persons are said to have an internal locus of control, a heightened sense of mastery or competence, and feelings of efficacy, it is assumed that they will respond more actively and effectively in a range of tasks and situations than would people characterized as external, helpless, or incompetent.

Within the last two decades there has been an increasing interest in understanding the processes involved in becoming ill, and in coping with ill-

This chapter was written while the senior author was supported by a research grant from the Canadian Social Sciences and Humanities Research Council Grant Nos. 410-87-0255 and 410-89-0926 and the second author held a fellowship from the same agency.

nesses once they have occurred. Through the growth of the disciplines of behavioral medicine and health psychology, as well as the practice of holistic medicine, there has been increasingly greater interest in the effects of different life-styles upon health and the development of both mental and physical illness. It seems inevitable now that control-related beliefs would have eventually become regarded as relevant to health and illness, given the presumed relationship of control beliefs to life-styles. If internals are regarded as better information-seekers and more effective learners than externals, then one might easily presume that if there were reason to become concerned about health, internals would make themselves better informed about preventive measures and consequently retain their health longer than externals.

Among the early investigations conducted with the locus of control construct, there was only one that directly pertained to health-related issues. This study (Seeman & Evans, 1962) indicated that tuberculosis patients who were classified as internals, from a 12-item measure of powerlessness, knew more about tuberculosis than did those classified as externals, with knowledge having been assessed by hospital staff ratings and from inquiries made of the patients themselves. Given that a patient's knowledge about his or her medical disorder may influence the ways in which an illness is responded to, this finding was very promising for the possible connections between control beliefs and health-related issues.

In the years subsequent to this early report there has been much research conducted that bears on the relationship between locus of control and health-related attitudes and behaviors. There are locus of control scales specifically pertaining to health (Wallston & Wallston, 1981) as well as to specific illnesses (Saltzer, 1981), and there have been monographs (Wallston & Wallston, 1978) and review articles (Strickland, 1978, 1979) describing the fairly extensive literature linking control beliefs with health-related phenomena.

In her review of the control and health literature, Strickland (1978) contended that "the I-E variable is only one of a number of complex factors that may converge to predict health attitudes and behaviors. The amount of variance for which I-E accounts is probably quite small in many, if not most, situations. For example, whether persons present themselves to a physician's office for relief of symptoms may be much more a function of severity of symptoms, the individual's financial

condition, and/or the availability of health care than the person's beliefs about control of reinforcement" (p. 1204).

Despite these qualms, Strickland concluded that "the bulk of research is consistent in implying that when faced with health problems, internal individuals do appear to engage in more generally adaptive responses than do externals. These range from engagement in preventive and precautionary health measures through appropriate remedial strategies when disease or disorder occurs" (p. 1205).

In this review of the control-health literature, Strickland expressed both the cautions necessary in the consideration of this linkage as well as the reasons for optimism in assuming a meaningful connection between health and control-related beliefs. In a very recent review of the literature concerned with stress, personality moderators of stress, and disorder, Cohen and Edwards (1988) contended that locus of control was one of the few variables that has been found to operate as a stress buffer with any reliability, thus playing some role in mitigating the development of stress-related illnesses. This assertion also was made with reservations. Most notably, Cohen and Edwards (1988) argued that most investigators exploring the efficacy of personality moderators of stress have assumed that persons exemplifying particular characteristics such as internality would succeed in their encounters with stressful events because they are more likely to cope appropriately with their personal crises. However, as these authors noted, this assumption has rarely been put to empirical test. Consequently, they advocate the study of the relationships among stress appraisal, coping activity, style, or effort with the various stress-moderating personality variables that they reviewed in their chapter.

In this chapter, we will attempt to review the three literatures that focus on the relationship between control beliefs and coping styles that may help to account for resilience in the face of stress: (a) the evidence concerning locus of control as a stress-moderator, (b) the specific ways in which locus of control has been used to predict the onset of illnesses, and (c) the way in which people cope with illnesses once they have occurred.

LOCUS OF CONTROL AND STRESS-RELATED ILLNESSES

Cohen and Edwards (1988) have suggested that there are two points in the pathway from stress to illness at which personality characteristics may operate as buffers, deterring the sequence of events that could result in health disorders. These are during the initial phase of stress appraisal and at the subsequent appraisal period occurring after events have been construed as stressful. These appraisal processes are the same as those that Lazarus and Folkman (1984) have called primary and secondary appraisal. Primary appraisal concerns whether a person interprets events as potentially stressful in the first place. For some people, for example, being closely evaluated for some skill or talent may be regarded as terribly stressful, while for others, this kind of situation may be interpreted as challenging rather than threatening.

Personality characteristics such as locus of control could be expected to be related to this initial appraisal process, with externals, or those who characteristically regard themselves as unable to effect important events, being more likely to perceive challenging situations as threatening to their well-being. Subsequent to the appraisal of stress, a self-assessment or secondary appraisal is said to occur when individuals estimate their resources and capacities for coping with the particular stressful events that they are about to experience. At this point too, one might anticipate that locus of control could be a useful variable for predicting the responses to events acknowledged as being stressful. It could be anticipated that externality or helplessness would be associated with the belief that one did not have adequate resources for coping with the stressful events being experienced. Given these facts, potentially stressful experiences would seem to have greater portents for externals than they might for internals, and one might expect to find more signs of distress from the former than the latter.

Within the models linking stress with illness, the appraisal of events as being stressful, followed by the self-appraisal that one is not capable of dealing with those stressors, is thought to result in dysphoric mood states that are in turn viewed as prodromal to the development of illness. The assumption that dysphoria could result in illness has received support in recent research, implicating immunological processes that ordinarily protect organisms from debilitating illnesses. Jemmott and his colleagues (Jemmott, 1985; Jemmott, Hellman, McClelland, Locke, Kraus, Williams, & Valeri, 1988; Jemmott & Magloire, 1988) have found that when people are stressed in need areas that are of importance to them, certain changes in

immune system functioning become evident; for example, declines in the concentrations of secretory immunoglobulin A (S-IgA) and natural killer cell activity. Such declines are associated with increased vulnerability to upper respiratory infection and unchecked growth of neoplasms, respectively. Kiecolt-Glaser and her colleagues (Kiecolt-Glaser & Glaser, 1988a, 1988b; Kiecolt-Glaser, Fisher, Ogrocki, Stout, Speicher, & Glaser, 1987; Kiecolt-Glaser, Glaser, Dyer, Shuttleworth, Ogrocki, & Speicher, 1987; Kiecolt-Glaser, Kennedy, Malkoff, Fisher, Speicher, & Glaser, 1988) likewise have found deficient immune system functioning on a host of indexes to be associated with depression, loneliness, and with the distress that accompanies separation and divorce. Similar immune system malfunctioning is found during the stressful periods of examination in medical school. Stone, Cox, Valdimarsdottir, Jandorf, and Neale (1987) have similarly found concentrations of S-IgA to vary with moods recorded in daily diaries. Antibody responses have been found to be lower on days when subjects have reported high negative mood states. Finally, Dillon, Minchoff, and Baker (1985), Martin and Dobbin (1988), and Lefcourt, Davidson-Katz, and Kueneman (in press) have reasoned that if immune system suppression accompanies dysphoric affects, then positive feelings associated with the expression of humor should result in increased immune system activity. As had been predicted, laughter and predilections toward humor were associated with increased concentrations of S-IgA in these investigations. From these studies it is possible to surmise that the linkage between affect states and illnesses that had been assumed in the stress literature is becoming substantiated in the more molecular immunology research. This link between affect and immunological functioning then accounts for vulnerability to illness.

At this point, we will turn our attention to the question of whether there is any empirical evidence indicating that locus of control is associated with the manner in which individuals cope with stressful events.

LOCUS OF CONTROL, COPING PROCESSES, AND APPRAISAL OF THREAT

Among the earliest findings that were reported with the locus of control construct were those indicating that persons with more internal control expectancies seemed to be more alert and attentive to information that had relevance for their well-being. Seeman and Evans (1962), as noted earlier, were able to predict the amount of knowledge that tuberculosis patients had about their own threatening disease. Externally oriented tuberculosis patients were found to know less about tuberculosis than internals on both a direct and an indirect (staff rating) measure of same. The results of this study indicated that internals avail themselves of information even if it has negative connotations for themselves. Externals, on the other hand, seemed to have been less concerned with the gathering of information that would have allowed them to more accurately appraise the level of potential threat that was inherent in their circumstances. If there were some actions that could, in fact, affect the course of that disease, externals, as a consequence of their failure to attend to relevant information, presumably would have been less likely to discover the corrective or beneficial behaviors than would internals.

For example, early research with locus of control also had indicated that externals were more likely to smoke and less likely to give up the smoking habit than were internals (James, Woodruff, & Werner, 1965; Straits & Sechrest, 1963). Later investigations replicated these findings (Coan, 1973; Mlott & Mlott, 1975; Steffy, Meichenbaum, & Best, 1970; Williams, 1973), though a few studies failed to confirm this linkage between smoking and externality (Danaher, 1977; Lichtenstein & Keutzer, 1967).

On balance, it would seem that externals were less likely than internals to respond adaptively to threatening evidence. This difference could be said to reflect a failure in the primary appraisal process, that externals were less likely to assimilate information attesting to the fact that smoking is injurious to health (threatening). Consequently, they failed to engage in problem-solving behavior that would involve an alteration of life habits.

It also is arguable, however, that the failure of people to quit smoking despite information about its negative effects may be more reflective of secondary appraisals. When individuals assess their capabilities for dealing with stressful events it is assumed that they will engage in problem-focused coping if they feel equal to the challenges inherent in those stressful situations. However, if the demands of that stressful situation are perceived as being beyond their ability to deal with them, it is assumed that people will engage in emotion-fo-cused coping, whereby affective arousal is muted by various defensive maneuvers. Emotion-focused coping devices such as denial, which one would expect from more fatalistic people who are prone to belittle their coping capacities, may account for the failure to quit smoking more readily than the failure to perceive the dangers involved in smoking.

Seeman found corroboration for his previous findings with tuberculosis patients in a second study that was conducted with reformatory inmates (Seeman, 1963). In this study the focus was on the gathering of information pertaining to parole. Seeman found that people who denied that they were powerless (internals) were more accurate in their recollection of information concerning the attainment of parole, but not in their recall of information related to reformatory life that was of less personal relevance. His results led him to conclude that an individual's sense of powerlessness governs his or her attention and information-acquisition processes. This connection between beliefs about control and information assimilation that would be prodromal to the appraisal of threat has been supported by the findings of several other research investigators.

In our own laboratory, we have explored the attention processes of people varying in their beliefs about control as they underwent mildly stressful experiences. In each of several tasks we "double crossed" our subjects by misleading them as to the purpose and meaning of what they were doing. For example, in one study (Lefcourt, Gronnerud, & McDonald, 1973) our subjects had undergone a series of very boring verbal tasks and believed that we were interested primarily in developing some arcane measures of verbal facility. The last task, however, proved to be revelatory insofar as our ostensible purposes were concerned. The task was a word association test that began innocently enough but became progressively more focused on sexual content. The provocative words (rubber, bust, snatch, etc.) were all double entendres so that the underlying substance and meaning of the task and the consequent suspicion about our intentions could justifiably be allayed for a while until so many double entendres had been presented that it would have required massive denial to remain unaware of the sexual content and to our possible duplicity. From an observation room adjacent to the room in which the subject was seated we had recorded their facial expressions on videotape as they performed on the test.

In that study we found a range of evidence attesting to the fact that internals were the quickest to "catch on"; that is, to note that "something was amiss," and then they were the quickest to act on that observation. Their response times to the double entendres increased earlier in the sequence of words administered than they did for externals indicating that internals had become "aware" sooner than had externals. In addition, their eye movements, laughter, and subsequent joking indicated that they surely knew "something was up" and that they were not intimidated by their discovery. Externals, by contrast, were slow to "catch on" and less given to expressions of mirth in the process (Lefcourt, Sordoni, & Sordoni, 1974).

We have found confirmation of these data in other "double cross" research studies. Internals have generally been quicker than externals to note the circumstances and contextual cues that help to reveal the secret meanings of the experiments in which they have been engaged. Consequently, they have been found to be less embarrassed or surprised by these experimental situations when the purposes of the experiments have become more explicit. In one such study where subjects were presented with their own photograph at the end of a series of photographs of rather disreputable looking persons whose crimes they were attempting to deduce from appearances (the photographs were described as police mug shots), internals often rebounded with humorous retorts whereas externals appeared to be offended, and in some cases, angry (Lefcourt & Martin, 1986). For example, one internal subject leered at the female experimenter and, after a long pause, exclaimed loudly, "He's a rapist," and subsequently dissolved in laughter.

In laboratory situations, then, evidence has indicated that internals are more apt to be aware of changing circumstances, a necessary precondition of stress appraisal. However, this is not to say that they necessarily come to regard those circumstances as threatening. As has been noted in several studies, externals more often regard their experiences as stressful than do internals. Given that internals seem to be more aware of changes in their circumstances yet may be less threatened, it is possible that we are observing the effects of secondary appraisals, the judgments individuals make as to whether they can do something that will alter the threatening circumstances that they are encountering. At this point we may ask whether internals are better equipped to deal with poten-

tially stressful experiences than are externals, such that they are less potentially disarmed by them.

In a suggestive field study, Anderson (1977) examined the responses of businessmen to a flood that occurred in 1972 that all but wiped out the commercial enterprises in a small Pennsylvania community following Hurricane Agnes. Anderson studied the business performance of 90 men over a 3½-year period following that flood. The businessmen were assessed for locus of control beliefs, perceived stress, coping behaviors, and organizational performance. With coping behavior classified as problem-solving versus emotion-focused, externals were found to have used fewer problem-solving coping methods and more emotion-directed coping devices (withdrawal, hostility, etc.) than internals. In addition, externals were more likely to have perceived their circumstances as being highly stressful than were internals. Organizational performance was assessed by credit ratings of their businesses after the 3½-year period had ended. The author concluded that "the task-oriented coping behaviors of internals are apparently associated with a more successful solution of the problems created by the stressful event, since the performance of the internals' organizations is higher" (p. 450).

In three other field studies concerned with natural disasters that were conducted by social geographers, further evidence has been obtained to suggest that internals are both more aware of potential dangers and more planful in their response to them. Sims and Baumann (1972) in a study that examined responses to tornadoes found that in communities where beliefs about control were more modally internal (rural Illinois), people were more apt to behave appropriately to that threat — listening to the radio and staying in their basements — than were those who lived in an area where externality was more common (rural Alabama). People in Alabama were more likely to have gone outside to see if and when the suspected tornado was coming their way. Consequently, there were more serious accidents in Alabama than there were in Illinois. A few years later, two studies, one conducted in Canada and the other in New Zealand, offered some corroborative evidence linking locus of control to the responses made to natural disasters. In the former, Simpson-Housley, Lipinski, and Trithardt (1978) reported that internals were more knowledgeable about the potential dangers of flooding river plains around Lumsden, Saskatchewan, than were externals.

Also, there was a tendency for internals to live in residences that were farther away from the flood-plain than were those of externals. In the New Zealand study, Simpson-Housley and Bradshaw (1978) reported analogous data concerning earth-quake hazards in a suburb of Wellington where there are two active geological faults in the sub-structure of that city. Residents were queried about their perceptions of earthquake hazards. Internals were more frequently found to have taken preventive measures to help withstand the threat of earthquakes, thereby indicating a height-ened awareness of the potential danger. Externals, on the other hand, were found more ready to take reparative measures after the occurrence of earth-quakes. In other words, either externals were fail-ing to consider the danger of earthquakes before they actually occurred or were engaging in emo-tion-focused coping, denying the threat until after the crisis. In essence, externals could be said to have been operating in an "out of sight, out of mind" style. Internals were also found to expect more disruption from an experience with earth-quakes than were externals. These more accurate primary appraisals may, in turn, help to account for their greater preparedness.

Though the methods used in these three studies of natural disasters were overly simple in compari-son with those routinely used by psychological in-vestigators (use of single-item scales, simple t tests, etc.), the consistency of the findings encour-ages us to believe that internals are more ready to perceive potential threats and are more prepared to take some kind of action to help ward off the effects of those stressors whether they be torna-does, floods, or earthquakes. It is reasonable to predict that fatalistic people would be found living in hazardous areas more often than would people who readily assume responsibility for themselves, and that externals would engage in more emotion-focused than problem-solving coping in order to continue living in such perilous circumstances.

A number of investigations, in addition to these field studies, have found evidence to the effect that internals are more apt to engage in problem-solving coping processes than are externals, and that externals are more likely to engage in emo-tion-focused coping than are internals (Silver & Auerbach, 1986; Silver, Auerbach, Vishniavsky, & Kaplowitz, 1986; Strickland, 1978). In a dramatic 4-day simulation of a hostage-taking incident, Strentz and Auerbach (1988) found that external airline employees were most distressed in the con-dition where they had been taught problem-solv-ing coping methods as opposed to either a control condition or one in which they had been taught emotion-focused coping strategies. On the other hand, externals did not differ from internals when they had been taught emotion-focused coping procedures or when they were in the control condi-tion. Thus, while internals benefited as much as externals from emotion-focused coping, the latter were not as able to benefit from their exposure to problem-focused coping. A problem-solving cop-ing style seems to be more comfortably adopted by internals.

Recently, Solomon, Mikulincer, and Avitzur (1988) have found some corroborative evidence linking the stress of war, locus of control, coping styles, and posttraumatic-stress disorders. With a sample of 262 Israeli soldiers who had fought in the 1982 Lebanon war, locus of control (scored in a positive direction) was found to be negatively correlated with the intensity of posttraumatic stress disorders at both 2 and 3 years after the war ($rs = -.38$ and $-.29$, respectively). Veterans of that war who were external with regard to locus of control, then, were more apt than internals to suf-fer from stress disorders. Coping style was related to locus of control as well, with externals employ-ing more emotion-focused coping than internals. In turn, emotion-focused coping was positively related to the intensity of posttraumatic stress dis-orders and, in a regression analysis proved to be the most potent variable for predicting that disor-der. These findings bear similarity to those of An-derson (1977), implicating both beliefs about con-trol and coping style in the responses made to traumatic events.

In another study assessing the stressful impact of participation in the Lebanese war, Hobfoll, London, and Orr (1988) found that Pearlin and Schooler's (1978) Mastery Scale, which bears sim-ilarity to measures of locus of control, was nega-tively related to anger and anxiety in samples of Israeli male and female university students. Those whose scores indicated that they believed that they could be effective or "masterful" in dealing with their life problems were less apt to be angry or anxious. However, there was no interaction found between the war-related stressful event measure and the mastery scale, which led the authors to question the stress moderator role of feelings of mastery. It is interesting to note in this study, though, that war-related stressful events did not produce a main effect on anxiety or anger in and of itself. This scale, which queried subjects' closeness to the war, did not actually assess experienced stresses of war. Rather, questions focused on whether or not subjects had to serve in the war at all or were close to those who did serve and whether anyone to whom they were close had been injured or died in that war. But the actual experiences of the subjects themselves were not assessed by this scale as they are in the more conventional measures of stress. This may help to account for its failure to produce main effects or interactions in the prediction of anxiety or anger.

From these studies and others concerned with stress experienced in medical education (Kilpatrick, Dubin, & Marcotte, 1974), in commuting to work (Novaco, Stokols, Campbell, & Stokols, 1979), in adapting to Marine Corps training (Cook, Novaco, & Sarason, 1980), and in caring for sick children (Hobfoll & Lerman, 1988), beliefs about control and mastery have been found to play a significant role in predicting the kinds of responses that people make to those stressors, although the results have not always been strong, clear, and free of enigma.

Returning to our earlier discussion of awareness and/or cognitive alertness as components of primary appraisal, we have conducted several experiments in our labs that bear on people's awareness or sensitivity to each other during social interactions. We have examined the ways in which people attend to each other during protracted conversations that could have become stressful if the social interchanges were not handled competently. In one such study (Lefcourt, Martin, Fick, & Saleh, 1985), we observed same-sex strangers discussing how they had dealt with their feelings while watching "Subincision," a film that Lazarus (1966) had used as a stressor for his laboratory studies of stress. In this anthropological film, Australian aborigines were observed during a rite of passage in which young boys suffered ritualized genital mutilation. The film is generally regarded as gruesome to watch and quite easily elicits emotion-focused coping. Consequently, we believed that subjects would share their feelings with another easily. In talking to a stranger about one's personal responses to an aversive presentation that contains elements of sex, blood, repulsion, and violence, however, a person needs to carefully gauge his or her partner's responses to his or her own disclosures during a discussion to avoid embarrassing the other person or becoming embarrassed oneself; otherwise the conversation could degenerate into unpleasantness or a sullen silence. Therefore, close attention and sensitivity to one's partner should facilitate better communication. The listening behavior or attentiveness of subjects in one sample were rated globally; in a second sample, subjects were rated on several components of social competence that reflected on attention. The latter consisted of time spent talking, length of utterances, eye contact when listening and talking, nonverbal affirmations and encouragements, silences, and so forth.

In both studies, those who had scored as internals with regard to affiliation were found to have displayed more active listening and responsiveness than had externals for affiliation. This measure, the locus of control for affiliation scale, derives from the Multidimensional-Multiattributional Causality Scale (Lefcourt, von Baeyer, Ware, & Cox, 1979), which also contains a locus of control scale for achievement. As a point of interest, the achievement locus of control scale was much less related to the social criteria than was the affiliation locus of control scale. Thus, attentiveness and sensitivity to one's partner's responses, which should alert one to potential sources of discomfort in the interaction, has been found to be associated with an internal locus of control.

In a subsequent study conducted with married couples that concerned locus of control and coping processes (Miller, Lefcourt, Holmes, Ware, & Saleh, 1986), 88 married couples were videotaped as they attempted to deal with conflicts that are fairly common sources of marital discord. The research was originally undertaken in the hope that we might be able to uncover some of the reasons for the high rate of divorce that characterizes contemporary North American life. We had hypothesized that individuals who believed that their spouse's behaviors were mysterious (unpredictable) and uncontrollable would be less attentive to their partners and therefore less aware of potential problems that could surface between them than would people who believed that their actions played a significant role in shaping their spouse's behaviors. In turn, we anticipated that those who believed that they could affect their partners would be more able to cope with quandaries as they arose, given their earlier and greater awareness of emerging difficulties. To assess these beliefs we had developed a Marital Locus of Control Scale (Miller, Lefcourt, & Ware, 1983) for which we had found reliability and some preliminary evidence of validity.

Couples were asked to improvise responses to three conflict situations that had been previously constructed by Gottman (1979). Whereas the conflict situations were like a set of standardized tasks with explicit role descriptions, participants were asked to add their own personal information to the role enactment that would individualize the situations, thus increasing their potential involvement in them. The three situations consisted of (a) an "in-law problem" wherein the husband believed that plans had been made to spend Christmas with his family, but his wife had not regarded the plans as finalized and had reservations about the visit; (b) a "money problem" wherein the wife had spent money on clothing that had been considered as part of their long-range savings program; and (c) a "communication problem" wherein a tired wife wanted some time to herself while her husband desired conversation and closeness after returning home from work.

Throughout the enactments of each role, the interactions were videotaped and were later rated for "engagement" and "problem-solving effectiveness," the latter being composed of "solution quality" and "solution satisfaction." Engagement consisted of ratings of an individual's tendency to become involved in conflict in an open, direct, and persistent way. Solution quality was rated by observers whereas solution satisfaction was derived from spouses' ratings. Solutions were judged as more successful when the points of view of both spouses were understood and taken into account in devising some resolution of the problem. If feelings were still ruffled and not addressed by the solution, the quality of the solution would have been adjudged as being less than adequate. Engagement was regarded as a sine qua non of solution quality and satisfaction. Independent raters were used to rate each set of variables so as to preclude rating generalizations.

The rated behaviors and solutions of the couples were correlated with one another as we had hypothesized. Engagement did seem to be a precondition of solution quality and satisfaction, and the latter two were strongly related to one another. Most importantly, locus of control for marital satisfaction was related to all three in the expected directions and, in turn, all of these variables were related to an independent measure of marital satisfaction that husbands and wives had completed separately.

In this study we were able to observe the actual coping behavior of spouses faced with conflicts within their marriages. The veridicality of the role enactments was obvious in the involvement that was evident and in the commentary of the couples at the end of the experiment. These are very real situations for married couples as Gottman (1979) has argued. Our subjects' coping behaviors, then, were quite meaningful, especially because they were related to their self-ratings of marital satisfaction. In this situation, we were able to observe couples appraising each other's feelings to ascertain how serious a problem they were encountering. Our findings attest to the fact that internals are more apt to be observant than are externals, and are better able to resolve difficulties when they are unearthed. Internals proved to be more ready than externals to perceive and encounter potential conflicts with problem-focused coping, working to understand and alter conditions that were sources of grievance for their spouses.

One other study reported by Parkes (1984) helped to reveal the relationship between control beliefs and coping behaviors. Parkes had nursing students recall some specific stressful experiences that had occurred during their training. Internals were found to have coped more actively when they had encountered stressors that were perceived as controllable than had externals. On the other hand, suppression, an example of emotion-focused coping, was most prevalent among externals and least evident among internals in controllable situations. Internals exhibited suppression primarily in response to stresses adjudged as simply necessary to accept.

What was revealed in Parkes' study is that internals respond more appropriately to their stressful experiences, coping in accord with the perceived controllability of events. Externals, by contrast, seemed prepared to behave inappropriately, manifesting avoidance behavior and less active coping when action to change the situation seemed most called for.

From most of the research concerned with coping processes it would seem that internality is associated with greater attentiveness to potential threats and more active problem-solving behavior. Failure to take heed of impending threats and emotion-focused coping, on the other hand, seem to be more common among people classified as external with regard to locus of control. Therefore, if stressors are potentially controllable, internals would seem to be in a better position than externals to modify their impacts, perceiving imminent threats earlier than externals, and coping more actively in the attempt to alter the threatening circumstances.

It could be hypothesized as well, however, that externals would adapt more readily in uncontrollable circumstances than would internals, given externals' greater penchant to engage in emotion-focused coping. Reid (1984) in fact, has, discussed this likelihood, arguing that the acceptance of one's helplessness in uncontrollable circumstances, without undue and unsuccessful problem-solving coping, may be the best first step for coming to terms with uncontrollable disorders. Nevertheless, Reid also speaks of "participatory control," a sharing of control with professionals, as a necessary later stage of coping with the uncontrollable. Additionally, though several studies have indicated that internals are more apt to engage in problem-solving coping than externals, and that the latter more commonly engage in emotion-focused coping, internals have not been found to be unable to engage in emotion-focused coping. As Strentz and Auerbach (1988) have noted, externals seem uncomfortable and have difficulty adopting problem-solving methods for dealing with stress. Thus, it is possible that internals have greater versatility in their coping behavior than externals, and that the latter have a more singular style of dealing with problems that is characteristically emotion focused.

In the following section we will review the literature explicitly concerned with the moderator role of locus of control. Here, we will examine the findings concerned with the affective states that victims of stress experience. If an internal locus of control does bode well for the way in which stressors are handled, then the mood states of people undergoing stress should differ in accord with control orientations.

LOCUS OF CONTROL AS A STRESS MODERATOR

Much research concerning stress has made use of survey devices such as the Social Readjustment Scale (Holmes and Rahe, 1967) or more recent scales such as the Life Experiences Survey (Sarason, Johnson, & Siegel, 1978); and in studying the role of control beliefs some investigators have used published forms of locus of control scales while others have simply queried their subjects as to the controllability of the life experiences that they have acknowledged on surveys of stressful events. For example, researchers such as Hu-

saini and Neff (1980) and McFarlane, Norman, Streiner, Roy, and Scott (1980) have found personal judgments of the controllability of experienced events predictive of psychiatric symptomatology and subjective strain. That is, events regarded by a subject as having been uncontrollable were found to be associated with greater strain and disturbance than were events that subjects deemed controllable.

On the other hand, Manuck, Hinrichsen, and Ross (1975a, 1975b), using independent measures of stress and locus of control, found that externals did not differ from internals with regard to anxiety or help-seeking after having experienced stressful events. In the absence of stressful experiences, however, externals had higher anxiety scores and sought help more than their internal peers. In other words, externals seemed to be characteristically anxious and help-seeking whether they were undergoing stressful experiences or not. Internals, however, who were customarily less anxious than externals, became as distressed as externals only when they encountered stressful events.

In contrast, other investigators such as Johnson and Sarason (1978) and Kobasa (1979) found some evidence suggesting that locus of control operated as a stress buffer. In these investigations externals have shown stronger relationships between stress and depression, anxiety, and illness than have internals. The affective responses of internals have seemed less predictable than those of externals from measures of stressful experiences. Along with scales assessing what she has referred to as commitment and challenge, Kobasa (1979) considers control to be a major component of hardiness, a construct indicating buoyance and resilience during encounters with stress. More recent investigations have replicated some of Kobasa's findings, though some investigators (Hull, Van Treuren, & Virnelli, 1987) have found support only for the control and commitment components, and have argued that their effects are primarily direct, in that feelings of helplessness or a lack of control and an absence of commitments are psychologically stressful in and of themselves. Any interactive effects that would be indicative of stress-buffering are seen as secondary and likely to be observed only in particular situations.

Both Sandler and Lakey (1982) and Lefcourt, Martin, and Saleh (1984), have found higher order interactions between stressful events, locus of control, and social support in the prediction of mood disturbances. In each study internals who had a high degree of social support proved to be more resilient in the face of stress than internals with less social support or externals with or without social support. In both of these investigations there was little direct support for control as a singular moderator of stress, a finding that has also been reported by Nelson and Cohen (1983). It was only in interaction with social support that control was found to ameliorate the effects of stress in these studies. Similar findings have more recently been reported by Hobfoll and Lerman (1988), who found that mothers of seriously ill children who were high in their sense of mastery and enjoyed general social support or good intimacy with a friend were the least emotionally distressed during their travail. However, in this study the sense of mastery also produced a significant main effect. A high sense of mastery was associated with less emotional distress in general.

In an investigation from our own labs (Lefcourt, Miller, Ware, & Sherk, 1981), further clarifications, as well as complications, were uncovered. In this study we had used two different life event measures, the Coddington Life Events Scale (Coddington, 1972), which assesses the occurrence of stressful experiences in each of four stages of development, from early childhood through the high school years, and Sarason's Life Experiences Survey (Sarason et al., 1978), which assesses stressful experiences within the preceding year. In addition, we used four different locus of control scales in an attempt to predict mood scores that were to be obtained over a period of several weeks. Repeated testing of moods allowed us to closely monitor the main and interactive or stress-buffering effects of control. What we found in three successive studies was that externals tended to be dysphoric generally, whereas internals only showed indications of mood disturbance when undergoing current or recent stress, as was measured by Sarason's Life Experiences Survey. However, when the stressful events measured by the Coddington scale did not immediately precede the period during which moods were being assessed, the results looked more supportive of the moderator effect model.

When the stressful life events (assessed by the Coddington scale) had occurred some 3 to 5 years before the mood assessment period, we found that the current mood states of internals were less likely to be correlated with them, whereas among externals those same relationships were highly sig-

nificant. These data led us to conjecture that while everyone may show immediate affective responses to stressful experiences, internals are more apt to recover given the passage of time. In turn, we guessed that the greater propensity of internals to become involved in their pursuit of current goals and satisfactions—to be problem-solving focused—would serve to hasten the decay of effects deriving from those earlier events. The more passive, emotion-focused coping that characterizes externals, on the other hand, should lead to less coping with and less acceptance of prior stressful experiences so that these aversive events have a more enduring impact on externals than on internals.

Caldwell, Pearson, and Chin (1987) have also found evidence to the effect that locus of control operates as a stress moderator, but only in interaction with other variables such as gender and social support. They found no support for a straightforward and simple interaction between locus of control and stress in predicting depression or maladjustment. Only among males did locus of control have an impact on symptom formation such that internal males were more apt to develop psychosomatic health symptoms under stress whereas external males were more likely to become depressed under such circumstances. Females showed no such effects as a function of locus of control, though they did vary in their responses in accord with social support. These findings are similar to those reported by Hunsley (1981), as described in Lefcourt (1982). In that study, locus of control did not affect either the level or reactivity of moods following stress among females. Males, on the other hand, showed strong locus of control effects, with externals reporting deflated mood levels following stress in contrast to internals who seemed to be less marked by their stressful experiences.

Most recently, Lakey (1988) found evidence to the effect that locus of control strongly moderated the effect of life stresses in a prospective study with both male and female university students. With dysphoria measured by the Beck Depression Inventory (Beck, Ward, Mendelson, Mock, & Erbaugh, 1961) and the Zung Depression Scale (Zung, 1965) at two initial points in time, and the Beck inventory used as the dependent measure some 2 months later, locus of control measured by the Mirels personal control factor (Mirels, 1970) of Rotter's Internal-External Control Scale (Rotter, 1966) was found to interact with a measure of life stress in predicting dysphoria after prior measures of dysphoria and all other main effects and interactions had been partialled out. Using a tripartite division, internals were found to show no change in depression with the experience of stressful events, whereas externals and those scoring intermediate on the locus of control scale exhibited marked increases in depression following stressful events.

The ultimate conclusion to be drawn from these data is that while locus of control does obviously play some role in determining responses to stressful experiences, it does not always do so in a simple, reliable, and straightforward way. This may derive from certain inadequacies in research employing self-report measures that complicate the study of moderator effects. There is little doubt that externality is associated with negative affects such as depression. A recent meta-analysis of the locus of control-depression linkage (Benassi, Sweeney, & Dufour, 1988) affirms that locus of control orientation and degree of depression are significantly related, that the relationship is moderately strong, and that it has been consistent across studies even when control expectancies concern failures and successes separately. Thus, we can be assured that externality is associated with depressive affect. What is uncertain is whether an internal locus of control and its associated coping characteristics reliably minimize the depressive effects that can result from specific stressful experiences.

The uncertainty concerning the linkage between stress, locus of control, and the dysphoric affects derives largely from those studies wherein stress has been assessed by aggregate life event measures. When life event scales have been used in stress research, sex of subjects, access to social supports, and beliefs about control often seem to interact in complex and not always consistent ways that determine whether or not these variables will have a stress-moderating effect. In addition, we have found evidence that the temporal proximity of experienced life events to the time period during which assessment of moods is obtained can make a considerable difference with regard to whether locus of control is found to have stress-moderating properties.

Given the fact that negative affects are associated with illnesses and with the immune system functioning that would make an individual more susceptible to illness, the reliable relationship between locus of control and mood states would indicate that locus of control is meaningfully related to health and illness. If, in addition, locus of control was eventually found to be a more reliable moderator of the relationship between stress and mood disturbance, then it would be fair to say that locus of control is a major determinant of the illness effects of stress. At the present time, however, we can assert with confidence only that people who do not believe that they can influence the events that are important to them are likely to suffer with dysphoric affect; and, in turn, that such negative affects are often associated with the development of illness.

In the subsequent section we will turn our attention to the literature concerned with beliefs about control and the experience of illness.

CONTROL BELIEFS AND ILLNESS

Following their earlier work linking locus of control beliefs to information-gathering pertinent to illness, Seeman and Seeman (1983) conducted an extensive survey with close to a thousand adults in the Los Angeles area concerning health-related behavior. Subjects were assessed at two points of time a year apart. Among the predictor variables were abbreviated versions of the Health Locus of Control Scales (Wallston & Wallston, 1981) and a measure of the motivation for or degree of concern about health. The criteria concerning health comprised preventive health measures (diet, exercise, alcohol moderation), avoidance of smoking, health knowledge, as well as incidents of acute and chronic illnesses. The sense of internal control was found to be positively associated with the practice of preventive health measures, the attempt to avoid the harm involved in smoking, knowledge about medical treatment for cancer, self-ratings of health status, less reports of chronic and acute illness, a more vigorous management style with respect to illness, and less dependence on physicians.

Though some of the results in this study were only noteworthy if the subjects were very concerned about health, the overall findings clearly implicate control beliefs in the maintenance of health. Internals behave in ways that would seem more beneficial for maintaining their health and were in fact healthier in the year of the survey than were externals. These findings compliment previous evidence concerning preventive health behavior. As noted earlier, the larger number of studies indicate that internals avoid smoking

(Strickland, 1978). In addition, internals who value their health have been found to be more informed about disease and health maintenance than externals (Wallston, Maides, & Wallston, 1976; Wallston, Wallston, Kaplan, & Maides, 1976); to use seat belts while riding in cars more often than externals (Williams, 1972); and to be more positive about physical exercise and cardiovascular fitness, and more likely to engage in voluntary exercise than externals (Sonstoem & Walker, 1973).

It would seem then, that an internal locus of control augurs well for health in that people who perceive themselves as determiners of their own experiences are more apt to know what the ramifications of their health behaviors are likely to be. Armed with such knowledge, they are also more likely than externals to take preventative actions to maintain their health status. Another set of investigations in the literature concerning health and control beliefs concerns the ways in which people come to terms with illnesses once they have occurred.

Among such studies there is one exemplary investigation that has explored the ways in which patients undergoing myocardial infarctions have dealt with their life-threatening experiences. Cromwell, Butterfield, Brayfield, and Curry (1977) were able to examine the behavioral and physiological correlates of locus of control as patients came to terms with myocardial infarctions within an intensive care unit. Patients who were classified as internal from Rotter's Internal-External Locus of Control Scale (Rotter, 1966) were rated by the professional staff as being more cooperative and less depressed than were externals throughout their stay in the intensive care unit. On three highly intercorrelated physiological measures (sedimentation rates, serum glutamic oxaloacetic transaminase levels, and lactate dehydrogenase levels), externals were found to have worse prognoses than internals. Additionally, externals had higher peak temperatures during intensive care and remained longer in the unit, and in the hospital, than did internals.

Though these data may be interpreted in different ways, one tempting hypothesis is that internals simply behave in a manner that does not aggravate their fragile conditions. Rather than becoming distressed, with all of the personal and physiological consequences of distress, in this study internals evinced greater cooperation and less depression than externals, possibly reflecting their more active participation and greater hope in the struggle for survival. It is plausible that responses to life-endangering threats such as myocardial infarctions may be at least partially determined by personality characteristics such as locus of control.

Similar findings attesting to the positive effects of internality during treatment for life-threatening conditions have been reported by Poll and Kaplan De-Nour (1980). Among 40 patients on chronic hemodialysis, locus of control was found to be related to compliance with prescribed diets, acceptance of the disability, and involvement in vocational rehabilitation. In each case, it was the more internal subjects who displayed the more favorable responses to their chronic conditions and treatment. Since failure to comply with procedures prescribed for renal failure may result in death, these findings led the authors to assert that externality "is not adaptive in terms of adjustment to chronic disease."

In another study concerned with renal failure (Devins, Binik, Gorman, Dattel, McCloskey, Oscar, & Briggs, 1982), patients who were undergoing dialysis or had had a kidney transplant were found to be more depressed and to have lower self-esteem and greater feelings of helplessness if they were more external on locus of control measures, and felt less efficacious about their lives in general. Given the negative implications of depression for health, such an adaptation to renal disorder may have compounded the difficulties experienced with it.

Among the diseases that humans are heir to, cancer is probably the one that can most easily arouse anxiety and depression among potential victims of the disease. Marks, Richardson, Graham, and Levine (1986) have found evidence in support of support of earlier findings by Taylor, Lichtman, and Wood (1984) attesting to the role of control beliefs in the adjustment to cancer diagnosis and treatment. Taylor et al. (1984) had found that breast cancer patients who believed that their illness could be controlled through some efforts of their own or their physicians adjusted better than fatalistic patients both in the short and long term. Their measure of adjustment was quite elaborate, consisting of physicians' and interviewers' scores on the Global Adjustment to Illness Scale (GAIS; Derogatis, 1975), the patients' self-ratings of adjustment, the patients' summed reports of current psychological distress, the Campbell, Converse, and Rogers (1976) Index of

Well-Being, and the total mood disturbance scores from the Profile of Mood States (POMS; McNair, Lorr, & Droppleman, 1971). These scores were combined with weightings derived from factor loadings and standardized for each subject. With this elaborate and reliable index of adjustment, Taylor et al. (1984) found that patients who believed that they and/or others such as the physician could exert some control over the course of the cancer proved to be better adjusted to their travails than were those who disbelieved in such control. These findings were unchanged when prognosis or severity of cancer and socioeconomic status were controlled for.

Whereas Taylor et al. (1984) had used an entirely female sample, most members of which had undergone some surgery for breast cancer, Marks et al. (1986) examined the adjustment of both men and women who had just been found to have hemotologic malignancies that ranged in severity from relatively indolent diseases (chronic leukemias, Hodgkin's disease, and small cleaved lymphoma) to highly aggressive tumors (acute leukemias, convoluted T lymphoma, small noncleaved lymphoma). Since Taylor's subjects had, for the most part, already undergone surgery, their views of treatment efficacy and beliefs about recovery could have been shaped to a degree by their immediate experience. The subjects in the study by Marks et al., on the other hand, were novices with regard to cancer and, thus, less likely to have experience-derived feelings and beliefs about treatment.

Marks et al. used measures of control beliefs similar to those that Taylor et al. had used, combining items from the Wallstons' Multidimensional Health Locus of Control (Wallston & Wallston, 1981) and Rotter's I-E scale (Rotter, 1966) to construct measures of personal control, physician control, and chance control of the disease. With actual and perceived severity of the cancer as the first variables entered into regression equations predicting depression (as measured by the Zung Depression Scale [Zung, 1965]), highly significant interactions were found both for personal control and expectancies of treatment efficacy. As the authors had predicted, it was those who disavowed personal control and who had low expectancies regarding treatment efficacy who exhibited the strongest relationships between perceived severity and depression. The results with actual or diagnosis-derived severity ratings were not even related to depression.

From these two studies, it would seem that perceived control plays a significant role in predicting the affective responses accompanying diagnosis and treatment of cancer. Because dysphoria has negative implications for immune system functioning, it is possible that cancers, which are often said to derive from malfunctioning immune system operations in the first place, may prove to be more resistant to treatment when patients become depressed. Thus, feelings of helplessness or a lack of personal control may have decided negative consequences in the treatment of this disease.

There have been a number of other studies dealing with the responses to a host of physical disorders and diseases in which beliefs about control have been found to have prognostic consequences. For example, Shadish, Hickman, and Arrick (1981) found that although all of the patients in their sample exhibited emotional distress in the year immediately following incapacitating spinal injuries, those who were more internal on each of the three factors (internality, powerful others, and chance) in Levenson's (1981) measure of locus of control were eventually better able to recover their emotional equilibrium. Though adjustment was associated with internality within the year following injury, there was an interaction as well suggesting that after the first year following the injury, externals continued to report high levels of distress while internals decreased in their reported dysphoria. Thus, recovery seemed to have occurred more readily among persons who customarily assumed responsibility for their own experiences.

In a study concerning adaptation to recurring genital herpes infections by men and women, Silver et al. (1986) found that their subjects were emotionally distraught, compared with the general population, as measured by an index of "general emotional dysfunction" derived from the Symptom Check List 90 (SCL-90; Derogatis, 1977). Despite their generally elevated distress, subjects who scored in an external direction on Rotter's I-E scale (Rotter, 1966) and engaged in more emotion-focused coping were found to report greater emotional dysfunction than internals and those less prone to emotion-focused coping strategies. In addition, when all predictor variables were entered into stepwise regression analyses predicting each of four characteristics of herpes symptomatology (recurrences, duration, pain, and bother), an external locus of control and wishful thinking (emotion-focused coping) were both found to be strong predictors of recurrences and the bother of recurrences. On the other hand, neither were related to the duration or pain of the recurring episodes and there were no relationships between a life stress measure and any of the dependent measures among these subjects.

Auerbach and his colleagues (Auerbach, Kendall, Cuttler, & Levitt, 1976; Auerbach, Martelli, & Mercuri, 1983) examined the role of control beliefs in the adjustment of patients to dental surgery in two studies. In each study, patients were exposed to information that was either immediately relevant to the kind of surgery that they were to undergo, or to information about the dental clinic that was at best a palliative, assuring patients that the clinic was a reputable institution. Since internals are more prone to engage in problem-solving types of coping and less in emotion-focused coping, it was assumed that they would react more positively to information that would inform them about what they were about to experience than they would to the more soporific presentation, which contained little useful information. In contrast, externals were expected to prefer the distracting to the informative presentation. Patients completed the State Anxiety Inventory (Spielberger, Gorsuch, & Lushene, 1970) four times, thrice prior to surgery and once postextraction. Additionally, the oral surgeons rated each patient's adjustment on four items, the response to anesthesia, anxiety displayed during surgery, cooperation, and verbal admissions of pain.

In the first study reported (Auerbach et al., 1976), locus of control produced significant interactions with the type of information provided in the prediction of state anxiety scores and with surgeons' ratings of adjustment. Though the authors were not able to unravel the source of interaction in the state anxiety analysis, internals who had received the information relevant to surgery seemed to differ from each of the other three groups (internals with distracting information and externals in both conditions). In the two periods immediately before surgery, internals with relevant preparatory information reported more anxiety than other subjects. However, immediately after surgery, these same subjects showed the greatest decline in anxiety, scoring even lower than the other three groups.

Even more significant were the surgeons' adjustment ratings. Internals who had viewed the surgery-relevant presentation exhibited much better adjustment to surgery than internals who had received the distracting presentation, and the exact reverse was the case for externals. These findings bear similarity to those obtained with regard to coping strategies. As Strentz and Auerbach (1988) have noted, internals more readily learn problem-solving coping strategies whereas externals seem to have difficulty accepting such training and seem to be more facile at adopting emotion-focused coping strategies. This preference among internals for information that can allow for greater problem-solving coping has been noted elsewhere as well (Anderson, 1977; Seeman, 1963; Seeman & Evans, 1962).

Following this successful demonstration of the role that locus of control can occupy in confrontation with medical stressors, Auerbach et al. (1983) failed to replicate their earlier findings in a subsequent study. Certain differences between these investigations, however, may have limited the likelihood of replication. For one, the sample in the second study consisted of only 40 subjects, compared with 63 in the first. In addition to the smaller number of subjects there were also more conditions in the second study. The relevant versus irrelevant conditions were further subdivided by the affective tone with which the information was provided (warm vs. cold) such that the number of subjects per cell was reduced, the cell sizes varied, and the original relevant versus irrelevant conditions were diluted. Nevertheless, a measure of receptiveness for information in treatment situations (Krantz, Baum, & Wideman, 1980) did interact with information conditions in the same manner as locus of control had in the earlier study in predicting adjustment to surgery.

Finally, in the well-known research studies reported by Langer and Rodin (1976) and Rodin and Langer (1977), the elderly residents of a nursing home who had been encouraged to take a more responsible stance toward their own well-being were found to have become more socially and physically active, reported feeling happier, and were more alert than those who had received the impression that the staff was there to take care of them and that they were to be passive recipients of attention and care. Most important for this article is that in the follow-up investigation (Rodin & Langer, 1977) 18 months later, not only did the behavioral differences persist, but mortality rates were higher among the passive group (30%) than among those for whom self-responsibility was emphasized (15%). These findings suggested that both psychological and physical well-being are associated with feelings of control or responsibility.

These studies by Rodin and Langer, though fascinating, would not be as encouraging for the hypothesized linkage between control and health if there were not other substantial investigations that replicated some of their results. Reid and his colleagues (Reid & Ziegler, 1981a, 1981b; Ziegler & Reid, 1979) devised a scale entitled Locus of Desired Control, which focuses on everyday events that had been described as contributing to happiness in an extensive survey of elderly adults. These survey findings had been content analyzed until a number of valued satisfactions had been identified. The resulting questionnaire consisted of 35 items that measured the desire for certain occurrences or circumstances such as privacy, and a parallel set of 35 items that pertained to expectancies for being personally capable of obtaining those satisfactions. The scores on the desire and expectancy sets of items were then multiplied to create a composite measure wherein the highest scores reflected both strong desires and high expectancies of control for the set of satisfactions, and the lowest scores reflected little desire and low expectancies of control. In research with this measure, the expectancy for control part of the scale accounted for most of the results that have been obtained.

In a set of nine studies, Reid and Ziegler (1981b) found substantial evidence to the effect that people who feel in control of desired events are rated and claim to have a greater sense of well-being or better psychological adjustment. As well, functional health (physical ability to accomplish everyday tasks) was positively related and decreasing physical health was negatively related to the Desired Control Scale among an aggregate of 122 elderly persons. Of most interest, however, are the cross-lagged correlations that were obtained in four studies with 6-, 12-, or 18-month intervals and in one set of longitudinal data from a 5-year period for a sample of 122 subjects. In each of the shorter-time interval correlation sets where there was a sufficient number of subjects in the sample, lower desired control scores were associated with declining physical health. In every case, the more external or helpless people felt about attaining valued satisfactions at time one, the poorer was their physical health at a point 6, 12, or 18 months later. The cross-lagged correlations between desired control at point one and adjustment and physical health 5 years later were marked. Life satisfaction (.43), negative physical health ($-.35$), and functional health (.32) were each significantly

related to desired control at the .001 probability level. Those who believed that they could influence the occurrences of desired satisfactions were happier and healthier than persons who had expressed helplessness about being able to secure desired pleasures 5 years earlier.

Finally, Reid and Ziegler found evidence to the effect that when they compared those 61 persons who had died during the 5-year period with those who were still alive (the 122 subjects in the longitudinal study), their mean desired control scores differed significantly at the .002 probability level. Survivors had had significantly higher initial desired control scores than had those who had died. Thus, both illness and incidents of death seemed to be more prevalent among those who have felt incapable of effecting the occurrence of desired experiences.

The relationship between control beliefs and mortality is initially bound to elicit skepticism. However, there are other studies that corroborate these data. For example, Botwinick, West, and Storandt (1978) found that a simple one-item measure of self-rated control allowed for a prediction of mortality among the elderly. Similarly, Ferrara (1963) reported that people who believed that it was their own choice to enter a home for the aged, and therefore an event reflecting the exercise of personal control, lived significantly longer than those who felt that they had been coerced into entering the home.

These findings linking control beliefs and/or circumstances promoting control beliefs with illness and mortality help to underline similar assertions that have been made by authors concerned with locus of control as a personality characteristic (Lefcourt, 1982) and helplessness as a psychological state (Seligman, 1975). Feeling able to determine the kinds of experiences one is likely to have seems to be life enhancing, whereas the belief that one is no longer or never has been able to influence the directions in one's life seems to be debilitating, leading to a loss of vitality, and perhaps life itself.

CONCLUSIONS

This review has not been exhaustive. However, though there are more studies than those discussed in this chapter that bear on the relationship between feelings of control and health, the investigations included were those that seemed to have presented the clearest results; and the findings that were discussed in these are quite encouraging. Though behavioral medicine or health psychology are young interests, there does seem to be enough in the way of substantial information for us to pursue further research and to draw tentative conclusions.

As should be evident, many of the studies discussed in this chapter define beliefs about control in different ways: some through situational manipulations, others through a variety of measuring devices, and yet others with a variety of names and theoretical underpinnings. With regard to the latter, diversity of construct names and descriptions, it is the impression of these writers that more is to be gained by ignoring the seeming differences and concentrating on the convergent results that have been reported with cognate variables. Although not wishing to dwell on the subject, it would seem commonsensical to expect that someone who believes that he or she is highly efficacious with regard to a number of tasks (efficacy) will be more likely to believe that outcomes and actions are generally related to one another (locus of control or perceived contingency). If they were not related, why should one engage in effort from which efficacy feelings would derive? Likewise, beliefs about contingency and perceived control would have to be related to one another. One cannot perceive that he or she is able to accomplish something unless outcomes are perceived to be contingent on efforts; and finally, there is evidence to the effect that causal attributions (post-hoc causal explanations) are related to customary ways of perceiving causality (locus of control) if subjects are given enough time to draw conclusions about their performance outcomes (Lefcourt, Hogg, Struthers, & Holmes, 1975). Therefore, it is our presumption that the studies we have discussed concern similar constructs, ones that deal with our beliefs that we can exert some influence on our experiences or, in contrast, with our beliefs that there is nothing that we can do to alter the circumstances of our existence.

Given these assertions, what may we conclude from the literature reviewed in this chapter? First of all, life stressors that occur to us all do have an impact on our health. Illness is often found among those who have endured stressful experiences. However, there are some people who seem to be more resilient in the face of certain stressors that leave others dysphoric and ailing. When trying to account for these differences, attention is turned to characteristics of the person undergoing stress that have implications for the ways in which that person copes with his or her difficulties. We have focused on beliefs or perceptions of control as one such characteristic that has ramifications for stress management. In our literature review we have found evidence to suggest that people who are characterized as internals are more attentive to events occurring around them and therefore more ready to perceive potential threats or challenges than are those characterized as externals. Secondly, there is some evidence to suggest that internals are more apt to construe threatening events as challenges rather than as reasons for despair, as would be more common among fatalistic persons.

Subsequent to the appraisal of stress, evidence has accrued suggesting that internals are more likely to cope with stress by trying to solve the problems inherent in the threatening situation. By contrast, fatalistic individuals seem more ready to direct their attention to their own emotional responses rather than to the threats themselves. Thus, defensive maneuvering, which mutes the thoughts and affects associated with threatening experiences, is more readily apparent among externals. On the other hand, internals seem able to resort to emotion-focused coping when circumstances seem to offer little opportunity for remediation. Externals, however, do not seem to be quite as flexible, in that they do not shift as easily to problem-solving coping when the situations would seem to call for such an approach. Therefore, it would seem as if internals, or those who feel effective and competent in managing their affairs, are better able to flexibly respond to stressful experiences.

In turn, the coping styles associated with internality seem to result in less dysphoria following the advent of stressful events than the coping styles characteristic of externals. Externality is reliably related to depression and anxiety, and internality to vigor, humor, and life satisfaction. These affective states have recently been found to have implications for illness, with dysphoria being associated with the onset of maladies; and most recently, evidence has been accruing that suggests that dysphoric affects lead to the suppression of immunological functioning which, in turn, leaves the person more vulnerable to various internal and external sources of illness and disease. In contrast, the more positive affects associated with internality seem to facilitate the functioning of the immune system, so that internals would possibly be better protected against the onslaught of sicknesses.

Though evidence in support of these linkages between stress-control-dysphoria-immune system functioning-illness are to be found in the literature, as with most such literature, there is much room for clarification and substantiation. However, there is much reason to be encouraged and to continue investigation at each point of the linkages that we have presented.

REFERENCES

Anderson, C. R. (1977). Locus of control, coping behaviors and performance in a stress setting: A longitudinal study. *Journal of Applied Psychology, 62,* 446–451.

Auerbach, S. M., Kendall, P. C., Cuttler, H. F., & Levitt, N. R. (1976). Anxiety, locus of control, type of preparatory information, and adjustment to dental surgery. *Journal of Consulting and Clinical Psychology, 44,* 809–818.

Auerbach, S. M., Martelli, M. F., & Mercuri, L. G. (1983). Anxiety, information, interpersonal impacts, and adjustment to a stressful health care situation. *Journal of Personality and Social Psychology, 44,* 1284–1296.

Beck, A. T., Ward, C. H., Mendelson, M., Mock, J. E., & Erbaugh, J. K. (1961). An inventory for measuring depression. *Archives for General Psychiatry, 4,* 561–571.

Benassi, V. A., Sweeney, P. D., & Dufour, C. L. (1988). Is there a relationship between locus of control orientation and depression? *Journal of Abnormal Psychology, 97,* 357–367.

Botwinick, J., West, R., & Storandt, M. (1978). Predicting death from behavioral test performance. *Journal of Gerontology, 33,* 755–762.

Caldwell, R. A., Pearson, J. L., & Chin, R. J. (1987). The stress moderating effects of social support in the context of gender and locus of control. *Personality and Social Psychology Bulletin, 13,* 5–17.

Campbell, A., Converse, P., & Rodgers, W. L. (1976). *The quality of American life: Perceptions, evaluations and satisfactions.* New York: Sage Publications.

Coan, R. W. (1973). Personality variables associated with cigarette smoking. *Journal of Personality and Social Psychology, 26,* 86–104.

Coddington, R. D. (1972). The significance of life events as etiologic factors in the diseases of children. *Journal of Psychosomatic Research, 16,* 7–18.

Cohen, S., & Edwards, J. R. (1988). Personality characteristics as moderators of the relationship between stress and disorder. In R. W. J. Neufeld (Ed.), *Advances in the Investigation of Psychological Stress.* New York: John Wiley & Sons.

Cook, T. M., Novaco, R. W., & Sarason, I. G. (1980). *Generalized expectancy, life experience, and adaptation to Marine Corps recruit training* (Ar-002). Seattle, WA: University of Washington.

Cromwell, R. L., Butterfield, E. C., Brayfield, F. M., & Curry, J. J. (1977). *Acute myocardial infarction.* St. Louis: C. V. Mosby.

Danaher, B. G. (1977). Rapid smoking and self-control in the modification of smoking behavior. *Journal of Consulting and Clinical Psychology, 45,* 1068–1075.

Derogatis, L. R. (1975). *The global adjustment to illness scale (GAIS).* Baltimore, MD: Clinical Psychometric Research.

Derogatis, L. R. (1977). The SCL-90-Revised (Symptom Check List), Manual 1. Baltimore, MD: Johns Hopkins University School of Medicine.

Devins, G. M., Binik, Y. M., Gorman, P., Dattel, M., McCloskey, B., Oscar, G., & Briggs, J. (1982). Perceived self-efficacy, outcome expectancies, and negative mood states in end-stage renal diseases. *Journal of Abnormal Psychology, 91,* 241–244.

Dillon, K. M., Minchoff, B., & Baker, K. H. (1985). Positive emotional states and enhancement of the immune system. *International Journal of Psychiatry in Medicine, 15,* 13–18.

Ferrara, N. A. (1963). Freedom of choice. *Social Work, 8,* 104–106.

Gottman, J. M. (1979). *Marital Interaction: Experimental Investigations.* New York: Academic Press.

Hobfoll, S. E., & Lerman, M. (1988). Personal relationships, personal attributes, and stress resistance: Mothers' reactions to their child's illness. *American Journal of Community Psychology, 16,* 565–589.

Hobfoll, S. E., London, P., & Orr, E. (1988). Mastery, intimacy, and stress resistance during war. *Journal of Community Psychology, 16,* 317–330.

Holmes, T. H., & Rahe, R. H. (1967). The social readjustment scale. *Journal of Psychosomatic Research, 11,* 213–218.

Hull, J. G., Van Treuren, R. R., & Virnelli, S. (1987). Hardiness and health: A critique and alternative approach. *Journal of Personality and Social Psychology, 53*, 518–530.

Hunsley, J. (1981). *Stressful life events and moods: Moderating effects of locus of control and coping styles.* Unpublished honor's thesis, University of Waterloo, Ontario.

Husaini, B. A., & Neff, J. A. (1980). Characteristics of life events and psychiatric impairment in rural communities. *Journal of Nervous and Mental Disease, 168*, 159–166.

James, W. H., Woodruff, A. B., & Werner, W. (1965). Effect of internal and external control upon changes in smoking behavior. *Journal of Consulting Psychology, 29*, 184–186.

Jemmott, J. B. (1985). Psychoneuroimmunology: The new frontier. *American Behavioral Scientist, 28*, 497–509.

Jemmott, J. B., Hellman, C., McClelland, D. C., Locke, S. E., Kraus, L., Williams, R. M., & Valeri, C. R. (1988). *Motivational syndromes associated with natural killer cell activity and illness.* Manuscript submitted for publication, Princeton University, New Jersey.

Jemmott, J. B., & Magloire, K. (1988). Academic stress, social support, and secretory immunoglobulin A. *Journal of Personality and Social Psychology, 55*, 803–810.

Johnson, J. H., & Sarason, I. G. (1978). Life stress, depression and anxiety: Internal-external control as a moderator variable. *Journal of Psychosomatic Research, 22*, 205–208.

Kiecolt-Glaser, J. K., & Glaser, R. (1988a). Immunological competence. In E. A. Blechman & K. D. Brownell (Eds.), *Handbook of Behavioral Medicine for Women.* Elmsford, NY: Pergamon Press.

Kiecolt-Glaser, J. K., & Glaser, R. (1988b). Behavioral influences on immune function: Evidence for the interplay between stress and health. In T. M. Field, P. M. McCabe, & N. Schneiderman (Eds.), *Stress and coping across development.* Hillsdale, NJ: Lawrence Erlbaum Associates.

Kiecolt-Glaser, J. K., Fisher, L., Ogrocki, P., Stout, J. C., Speicher, C. E., & Glaser, R. (1987). Marital quality, marital disruption, and immune function. *Psychosomatic Medicine, 49*, 13–34.

Kiecolt-Glaser, J. K., Glaser, R., Dyer, C., Shuttleworth, E., Ogrocki, P., & Speicher, C. E. (1987). Chronic stress and immunity in family caregivers of Alzheimer's Disease victims. *Psychosomatic Medicine, 49*, 523–535.

Kiecolt-Glaser, J. K., Kennedy, S., Malkoff, S.,

Fisher, L., Speicher, C. E., & Glaser, R. (1988). *Psychosomatic Medicine, 50*, 213–229.

Kilpatrick, D. G., Dubin, W. R., & Marcotte, D. B. (1974). Personality, stress of the medical education process, and changes in affective mood state. *Psychological Reports, 34*, 1215–1223.

Kobasa, S. C. (1979). Stressful life events, personality, and health: An inquiry into hardiness. *Journal of Personality and Social Psychology, 37*, 1–11.

Krantz, D. S., Baum, A., & Wideman, M. (1980). Assessment of preferences for self-treatment and information in health care. *Journal of Personality and Social Psychology, 39*, 977–990.

Lakey, B. (1988). Self-esteem, control beliefs and cognitive problem solving skill as risk factors in the development of subsequent dysphoria. *Cognitive Therapy and Research, 12*, 409–420.

Langer, E. J., & Rodin, J. (1976). The effects of choice and enhanced personal responsibility for the aged: A field experiment in an institutional setting. *Journal of Personality and Social Psychology, 34*, 191–198.

Lazarus, R. S. (1966). *Psychological stress and the coping process.* New York: McGraw-Hill.

Lazarus, R. S., & Folkman, S. (1984). *Stress, appraisal, and coping.* New York: Springer-Verlag.

Lefcourt, H. M. (1966). Internal-external control of reinforcement: A review. *Psychological Bulletin, 65*, 206–220.

Lefcourt, H. M. (1982). *Locus of control: Current trends in theory and research* (2nd ed.). Hillsdale, NJ: Lawrence Erlbaum Associates.

Lefcourt, H. M., Davidson-Katz, K., & Kueneman, K. (in press). Humor and immune system functioning. *Humor: International Journal of Humor Research.*

Lefcourt, H. M., Gronnerud, P., & McDonald, P. (1973). Cognitive activity and hypothesis formation during a double entendre word association test as a function of locus of control and field dependence. *Canadian Journal of Behavioral Science, 5*, 161–173.

Lefcourt, H. M., Hogg, E., Struthers, S., & Holmes, C. (1975). Causal attributions as a function of locus of control, initial confidence, and performance outcomes. *Journal of Personality and Social Psychology, 32*, 391–397.

Lefcourt, H. M., & Martin, R. A. (1986). *Humor and stress: Antidote to adversity.* New York: Springer-Verlag.

Lefcourt, H. M., Martin, R. A., Fick, C., & Saleh, W. E. (1985). Locus of control for affiliation and behavior in social interactions. *Journal of Personality and Social Psychology, 48,* 755–759.

Lefcourt, H. M., Martin, R. A., & Saleh, W. E. (1984). Locus of control and social support: Interactive moderators of stress. *Journal of Personality and Social Psychology, 47,* 378–389.

Lefcourt, H. M., Miller, R. S., Ware, E. E., & Sherk, D. (1981). Locus of control as a modifier of the relationship between stress and moods. *Journal of Personality and Social Psychology, 41,* 357–369.

Lefcourt, H. M., Sordoni, C., & Sordoni, C. (1974). Locus of control, field dependence and the expression of humor. *Journal of Personality, 42,* 130–143.

Lefcourt, H. M., VonBaeyer, C. L., Ware, E. E., & Cox, D. J. (1979). The multidimensional-multiattributional causality scale: The development of a goal specific locus of control scale. *Canadian Journal of Behavioral Science, 11,* 286–304.

Levenson, H. (1981). Differentiating among internality, powerful others, and chance. In H. M. Lefcourt (Ed.), *Research with the locus of control construct* Vol. 1 (pp. 15–63). New York: Academic Press.

Lichtenstein, E., & Keutzer, C. S. (1967). Further normative and correlational data on the internal-external (I-E) control of reinforcement scale. *Psychological Reports, 21,* 1014–1016.

Manuck, S. B., Hinrichsen, J. J., & Ross, E. O. (1975a). Life stress, locus of control, and state and trait anxiety. *Psychological Reports, 36,* 413–414.

Manuck, S. B., Hinrichsen, J. J., & Ross, E. O. (1975b). Life stress, locus of control and treatment-seeking. *Psychological Reports, 37,* 589–590.

Marks, G., Richardson, J. L., Graham, J. W., & Levine, A. (1986). The role of health locus of control beliefs and expectations of treatment efficacy in adjustment to cancer. *Journal of Personality and Social Psychology, 51,* 443–450.

Martin, R. A., & Dobbin, J. P. (1988). Sense of humor, hassles, and immunoglobulin A: Evidence for a stress-moderating effect of humor. *International Journal of Psychiatry in Medicine, 18,* 93–106.

McFarlane, A. H., Norman, G. R., Streiner, D. L., Roy, R., & Scott, D. J. (1980). A longitudinal study of the influence of the psychological environment on health status: A preliminary report. *Journal of Health and Social Behavior, 21,* 124–133.

McNair, D. M., Lorr, M., & Droppleman, L. F. (1971). *The profile of mood states.* San Diego, CA: EDITS.

Miller, P. C., Lefcourt, H. M., Holmes, J. G., Ware, E. E., & Saleh, W. E. (1986). Marital locus of control and marital problem solving. *Journal of Personality and Social Psychology, 51,* 161–169.

Miller, P. C., Lefcourt, H. M., & Ware, E. E. (1983). The construction and development of the Miller marital locus of control scale. *Canadian Journal of Behavioral Science, 15,* 266–279.

Mirels, H. L. (1970). Dimensions of internal versus external control. *Journal of Consulting and Clinical Psychology, 34,* 226–228.

Mlott, S. R., & Mlott, Y. D. (1975). Dogmatism and locus of control in individuals who smoke, stopped smoking, and never smoked. *Journal of Community Psychology, 3,* 53–57.

Nelson, D. W., & Cohen, L. H. (1983). Locus of control and control perceptions and the relationship between life stress and psychological disorder. *American Journal of Community Psychology, 11,* 705–722.

Novaco, R. W., Stokols, D., Campbell, J., & Stokols, J. (1979). Transportation, stress, and community psychology. *American Journal of Community Psychology, 7,* 361–380.

Nowicki, S., & Strickland, B. R. (1973). A locus of control scale for children. *Journal of Consulting and Clinical Psychology, 40,* 148–154.

Parkes, K. R. (1984). Locus of control, cognitive appraisal and coping in stressful episodes. *Journal of Personality and Social Psychology, 46,* 655–668.

Pearlin, L. I., & Schooler, C. (1978). The structure of coping. *Journal of Health and Social Behavior, 19,* 2–22.

Poll, I. B., & Kaplan De-Nour, A. (1980). Locus of control and adjustment to chronic hemodialysis. *Psychological Medicine, 10,* 153–157.

Reid, D. W. (1984). Participatory control and the chronic-illness adjustment process. In H. M. Lefcourt (Ed.), *Research with the locus of control construct* (Vol. 3, pp. 361–389). New York: Academic Press.

Reid, D. W., & Ziegler, M. (1981a). *Longitudinal studies of desired control and adjustment among the elderly.* Paper presented at the joint meeting of the Gerontological Society of America and the Canadian Association of Gerontology, Toronto.

Reid, D. W., & Ziegler, M. (1981b). The desired control measure and adjustment among the elderly. In H. M. Lefcourt (Ed.), *Research with the locus of control construct* (Vol. 1, pp. 127–159). New York: Academic Press.

Rodin, J., & Langer, E. J. (1977). Long-term effects of a control-relevant intervention with institutionalized aged. *Journal of Personality and Social Psychology, 35*, 897–902.

Rotter, J. B. (1966). Generalized expectancies for internal versus external control of reinforcement. *Psychological Monographs, 80*, (whole No. 609).

Rotter, J. B., Seeman, M., & Liverant, S. (1962). Internal versus external control of reinforcement: A major variable in behavior theory. In N. F. Washburne (Ed.), *Decisions, values and groups* (Vol. 2). Oxford: Pergamon Press.

Saltzer, E. B. (1981). Cognitive moderators of the relationship between behavioral intentions and behavior. *Journal of Personality and Social Psychology, 41*, 260–271.

Sandler, I. N., & Lakey, B. (1982). Locus of control as a stress moderator: The role of control perceptions and social support. *American Journal of Community Psychology, 10*, 65–80.

Sarason, I. G., Johnson, J. H., & Siegel, J. M. (1978). Assessing the impact of life changes: Development of the life experiences survey. *Journal of Consulting and Clinical Psychology, 46*, 932–946.

Seeman, M. (1963). Alienation and social learning in a reformatory. *American Journal of Sociology, 69*, 270–284.

Seeman, M., & Evans, J. W. (1962). Alienation and learning in a hospital setting. *American Sociological Review, 27*, 772–783.

Seeman, M., & Seeman, T. E. (1983). Health behavior and personal autonomy: A longitudinal study of the sense of control in illness. *Journal of Health and Social Behavior, 24*, 144–160.

Seligman, M. E. P. (1975). *Helplessness*. San Francisco: W. H. Freeman.

Shadish, W. R., Hickman, D., & Arrick, M. C. (1981). Psychological problems of spinal cord injury patients: Emotional distress as a function of time and locus of control. *Journal of Consulting and Clinical Psychology, 49*, 297.

Silver, P., & Auerbach, S. M. (1986). *Locus of control and coping processes*. Unpublished raw data.

Silver, P., Auerbach, S. M., Vishniavsky, N., & Kaplowitz, L. G. (1986). Psychological factors in recurrent genital herpes infection: Stress, coping style, social support, emotional dysfunction, and symptom recurrence. *Journal of Psychosomatic Research, 30*, 163–171.

Sims, J., & Baumann, D. (1972). The tornado threat and coping styles of the north and south. *Science, 176*, 1386–1392.

Simpson-Housley, P., & Bradshaw, P. (1978). Personality and the perception of earthquake hazard. *Australian Geographical Studies, 16*, 65–72.

Simpson-Housley, P., Lipinski, G., & Trithardt, E. (1978). The flood hazard at Lumsden, Saskatchewan: Residents' cognitive awareness and personality. *Prairie Forum, 3*, 175–188.

Solomon, Z., Mikulincer, M., & Avitzur, E. (1988). Coping, locus of control, social support, and combat-related posttraumatic stress disorder: A prospective study. *Journal of Personality and Social Psychology, 55*, 279–285.

Sonstroem, R. J., & Walker, M. I. (1973). Relation of attitudes and locus of control to exercise and physical fitness. *Perceptual and Motor Skills, 36*, 1031–1034.

Spielberger, C. D., Gorsuch, R. L., & Lushene, R. E. (1970). *Manual for the state-trait anxiety inventory*. Palo Alto, CA: Consulting Psychologists Press.

Steffy, R. A., Meichenbaum, D., & Best, J. A. (1970). Aversive and cognitive factors in the modification of smoking behavior. *Behavior Research and Therapy, 8*, 115–125.

Stone, A. A., Cox, D. S., Valdimarsdottir, H., Jandorf, J., & Neale, J. M. (1987). Evidence that secretory IgA is associated with daily mood. *Journal of Personality and Social Psychology, 52*, 988–993.

Straits, B. C., & Sechrest, L. (1963). Further support of some findings about characteristics of smokers and non-smokers. *Journal of Consulting Psychology, 27*, 282.

Strentz, T., & Auerbach, S. M. (1988). Adjustment to the stress of simulated captivity: Effects of emotion-focused versus problem-focused preparation on hostages differing in locus of control. *Journal of Personality and Social Psychology, 55*, 652–660.

Strickland, B. R. (1965). The prediction of social action from a dimension of internal-external control. *Journal of Social Psychology, 66,* 353–358.

Strickland, B. R. (1978). Internal-external expectancies and health-related behavior. *Journal of Consulting and Clinical Psychology, 46,* 1192–1211.

Strickland, B. R. (1979). Internal and external expectancies and cardiovascular functioning. In L. C. Perlmuter & R. A. Monty (Eds.), *Choice and perceived control.* Hillsdale, NJ: Lawrence Erlbaum Associates.

Taylor, S. E., Lichtman, R. R., & Wood, J. V. (1984). Attributions, beliefs about control, and adjustment to breast cancer. *Journal of Personality and Social Psychology, 46,* 489–502.

Wallston, K. A., Maides, S. A., & Wallston, B. S. (1976). Health-related information seeking as a function of health related locus of control and health value. *Journal of Research in Personality, 10,* 215–222.

Wallston, K. A., & Wallston, B. S. (Eds.). (1978). Health locus of control. *Health Education Monographs, 6,* (whole issue).

Wallston, K. A., & Wallston, B. S. (1981). Health locus of control scales. In H. M. Lefcourt (Ed.), *Research with the Locus of Control Construct* (Vol. 1, pp. 189–239). New York: Academic Press.

Wallston, B. S., Wallston, K. A., Kaplan, G. D., & Maides, S. A. (1976). Development and validation of the health locus of control (HLC) scale. *Journal of Consulting and Clinical Psychology, 44,* 580–585.

Williams, A. F. (1972). Factors associated with seat belt use in families. *Journal of Safety Research, 4,* 133–138.

Williams, A. F. (1973). Personality and other characteristics associated with cigarette smoking among young teenagers. *Journal of Health and Social Behavior, 14,* 374–380.

Ziegler, M., & Reid, D. W. (1979). Correlates of locus of desired control in two samples of elderly persons: Community residents and hospitalized patients. *Journal of Consulting and Clinical Psychology, 47,* 977–979.

Zung, W. K. (1965). A self-rating depression scale. *Archives of General Psychiatry, 12,* 63–70.

CHAPTER 14

EXPLANATORY STYLE, HELPLESSNESS, AND DEPRESSION

Melanie O. Burns
Martin E. P. Seligman

In the past several decades there has been a proliferation of research on the role of cognitive factors in the development of both depressive affect and diagnosable major depressive episodes (Coyne & Gotlib, 1983). One particular focus of research has been the reformulated learned helplessness model of depression (Abramson, Seligman, & Teasdale, 1978), which analyzes the role of explanations — or attributions — for bad events in the etiology of depression. This chapter reviews research on the reformulated learned helplessness model of depression. We begin with a discussion of original helplessness theory, and continue by describing the reformulated learned helplessness model. We then discuss data that support the reformulated model, and data that are inconsistent with the model. We conclude this chapter by posing several questions about the nature of the relationship between explanations, helplessness, and depression, and by suggesting answers to those questions and directions for future research.

THE ORIGINAL LEARNED HELPLESSNESS MODEL OF DEPRESSION

The reformulated learned helplessness model of depression is based on earlier helplessness research with a variety of organisms (Maier & Seligman, 1976). Results from this research indicate that when organisms are exposed to uncontrollable negative events they often react with a characteristic passivity, and demonstrate subsequent cognitive, behavioral, and emotional deficits that are similar to the symptoms of depression. For example, a typical helplessness experiment (Seligman & Maier, 1967) used three groups of dogs. One group of dogs was shocked in a harness, but they could turn off the shock by pressing a panel with their noses. A second group of dogs was yoked to the first group so that they received equal amounts of shock, but had no control over shock termination. A third group, the control group, received no shock. Dogs in all groups were then

tested in a two-way shuttle box. Although jump-
ing the partition in the shuttle box would have
quickly terminated shock for all groups of dogs,
the dogs who had been unable to control shock
termination became helpless and tended not to
jump the partition, but instead passively tolerated
the shock.

What is the basis for this apparent helplessness?
Central to the effect appears to be the lack of
control over shock termination in the yoked dogs.
In fact, the animals appear to have learned that
their responses do not control outcomes, and to
expect that future responses and outcomes will be
noncontingent. When their initial responses are
ineffective in controlling shock, the dogs become
passive and helpless, eventually failing to learn
new contingencies between responses in their repertoire and outcomes.

Seligman proposed the phenomenon of helplessness as a model for human depression (Miller
& Seligman, 1975; Seligman, 1975). The helpless
dogs appeared to demonstrate many of the same
cognitive, motivational, and affective symptoms
as the depressed human. For example, helpless
dogs behaved as though they expected outcomes
to be uncontrollable. This behavior is similar to
the apparent expectations of depressed people—
they often report feeling hopeless about change
for the better and unable to cope with problems in
the present. Similarly, depressed individuals often
appear unmotivated and show lower levels of response initiation. Finally, the helpless dogs tended
to huddle, whimpering, in a corner of the shuttle-
box, a possible animal equivalent of the crying,
pervasive sadness, and anhedonia reported by depressives.

However, one problem with the original helplessness theory of depression was its failure to
mark boundary conditions, especially when human subjects were involved (Seligman & Nolen-
Hoeksema, 1987). For example, research that attempted to demonstrate helplessness in humans by
using unsolvable anagrams or inescapable noise
sometimes demonstrated the opposite effect: a facilitation of performance through increased activity and attempts at mastery (Roth, 1980). While
some individuals became helpless, others appeared to be quite resistant to helplessness deficits. In addition, the original theory could not
explain why depressed individuals often blame
themselves for bad events, especially when those
events are clearly not their fault. Finally, the original theory could not predict the chronicity and

generality of depressive reactions to bad events.
Why do some individuals experience transient and
specific affective reactions to a negative event
whereas others slide into a major depressive episode when confronted with the same type of
event?

THE REFORMULATED MODEL

The reformulated learned helplessness model of
depression (Abramson et al., 1978) suggested that
individual differences in a cognitive variable—the
way people characteristically explain bad events—
might account for these individual differences in
depressive tendencies in response to bad events.
According to the reformulated model, when people experience an aversive event they often ask why
the event occurred. The reasons they give for bad
events can then be analyzed along three theoretically orthogonal dimensions: internal-external,
stable-unstable, and global-specific. The model
predicts that individuals who characteristically
produce internal, stable, and global explanations
for bad events are more likely to become depressed
in response to a bad event than individuals who
make external, unstable, and specific explanations.

The model assigns a particular role to each attributional dimension in producing depression
and helplessness deficits. First, if an individual
believes that something about him or her caused
a bad event (an internal explanation such as,
"It's my fault"), he or she will experience self-esteem deficits in response to bad events. Second,
an explanation invoking causes that persist over
time (a stable explanation such as, "This always
happens") may be responsible for the chronicity
of depressive deficits. Finally, if an individual believes that the cause will affect many aspects of his
or her life (a global explanation such as, "Everything's a mess"), helplessness deficits may become
generalized. Individuals who characteristically
make internal, stable, and global explanations
about negative events (for example, "I always mess
up everything") can be said to have a pessimistic
explanatory style and, according to the Abramson
et al. (1978) model, will be at risk for development
of the cognitive, motivational, and affective deficits that are characteristic of a depressive episode
whenever they confront an important negative
event. In contrast, individuals who make external,
unstable, and specific explanations about bad

events are less likely to experience loss of self-esteem and more likely to respond with a transient and circumscribed affective reaction to that event.

Note that this model makes several testable predictions. First, the model suggests that individuals have a characteristic way of explaining bad events. In other words, there may be stable individual differences in the types of explanations that individuals tend to make for good and bad events, and at least some cross-situational consistency in explanatory style. Second, the model predicts that individuals with a pessimistic explanatory style will be more likely than individuals with an optimistic explanatory style to become depressed following bad events, particularly when those events are very important to the individual concerned. Finally, the model posits a specific association between a pessimistic explanatory style and the deficits associated with helplessness and depression. Pessimists are hypothesized to be at increased risk for symptoms of depression and helplessness when confronted with bad events, but not necessarily at greater risk for other psychological problems.

MEASUREMENT OF EXPLANATORY STYLE

Researchers have employed diverse methods of assessing explanatory style. For example, some investigators have measured solely internal and external attributions (Parry & Brewin, 1988) or have asked individuals to report recent stressful events and to rate them along attributional lines (e.g., Cochran & Hammen, 1985; Cutrona, Russell, & Jones, 1984; Miller, Klee, & Norman, 1982). However, these approaches often either fail to provide all the necessary measures to fully test the reformulated model or are frequently of unreported and possibly low reliability, especially if only one or two events are utilized in determining explanatory style (Peterson, Villanova, & Raps, 1985). In contrast, the two most commonly used techniques for measuring explanatory style appear to have achieved adequate reliability and validity.

The Attributional Style Questionnaire

One way to measure explanatory style is with the Attributional Style Questionnaire (ASQ; Peterson, Semmel, von Baeyer, Abramson, Metalsky, & Seligman, 1982). This questionnaire asks individuals to imagine that a hypothetical event has happened to them, to provide a cause for each

event, and to rate each cause on a scale of 1 to 7 for internality, stability, and globality. Subjects' scores on each dimension for good and bad events can then be summed in order to yield a composite measure of explanatory style for negative and positive events. Reliabilities for the composite on the ASQ have proven to be modest but usually adequate: in the range of .30 to .70. In addition, Peterson and Villanova (1988) have developed an expanded version of the ASQ that utilizes only negative events, and for which reliabilities have proved quite satisfactory: in the range of .66 to .88.

A similar instrument, the Children's Attributional Style Questionnaire (CASQ; Seligman, Peterson, Kaslow, Tanenbaum, Alloy, & Abramson, 1984) has been developed in order to study explanatory style in children. The CASQ is a forced choice version of the ASQ, and yields scores on the same three dimensions as the ASQ, as well as composite scores for negative and positive events. Reliabilities of composite scores on the CASQ tend to be modest: in the range of .50 to .73.

Content Analysis of Verbatim Explanations

The second technique for measuring explanatory style is the Content Analysis of Verbatim Explanations (CAVE; Peterson, Luborsky, & Seligman, 1983). This approach uses independent trained judges to rate verbatim causal statements extracted from spoken or written material on a scale of 1 to 7 for the same three dimensions. The CAVE technique has demonstrated high interrater reliability, and adequate intrasubject consistency (Burns & Seligman, 1989; Peterson et al., 1983). Ratings derived from the CAVE also correlate significantly with ratings on the ASQ (Peterson, Bettes, & Seligman, 1985), although these correlations tend to be modest: in the range of .30 (Peterson & Seligman, 1984; Peterson & Villanova, 1988).

Using the ASQ, the CASQ, and the CAVE techniques, it is possible to examine the predictions of the reformulated learned helplessness theory of depression. Results from several lines of research converge in demonstrating that explanatory style for negative events may be a stable individual difference, and that a pessimistic explanatory style is a risk factor for subsequent depression. In addition, several studies provide some evidence that explanatory style is specifically associated with development of the cognitive, motivational, and affective deficits associated with helplessness and depression. We will examine each of these issues separately.

IS EXPLANATORY STYLE A TRAIT?

Can explanatory style be considered a personality "trait?" There are three criteria against which to judge the "traitness" of explanatory style: stability across time, consistency across domains, and intrasubject consistency.

The Stability of Explanatory Style

Evidence from several studies suggests that explanatory style, at least for negative events, is a stable individual difference, and in fact may be considered a trait. For example, studies using undergraduates' responses to the ASQ have obtained stability coefficients for attributions about negative events in the range of .50 to .70 over a 1-month period (Peterson et al., 1982). Similarly, Eaves and Rush (1984) found some evidence for stability of explanatory style in depressed patients. They studied patients while depressed (Time 1) and after symptoms of depression had remitted (Time 2). The mean explanatory style of the depressives did not change significantly upon remission, and continued to be more pessimistic than the explanations made by controls.

More evidence for stability comes from two studies that used the CAVE technique to analyze explanatory style over longer time periods. Seligman and Elder (1985) assessed explanatory style in the sample of 28 women from the Berkeley-Oakland growth study. Content analysis of oral interviews conducted 27 years apart revealed significant stability for explanatory style for negative events over the time period analyzed ($r = .38$) and no stability of explanatory style for positive events. Similarly, Burns and Seligman (1989) analyzed explanatory style across the adult lifespan. Thirty subjects whose average age was 72 years responded to questions about their current life and provided diaries or letters written an average of 52 years earlier. Event-explanation units were extracted from these two sources and randomized so that raters were not able to identify units as belonging to a particular subject. A content analysis of explanatory style derived from these two sources revealed that explanatory style for negative events was relatively stable throughout adult

life ($r = .54$, $p < .002$). However, there appeared to be no stability of explanatory style for positive events between the same two time periods. These results suggest that people have a characteristic way of explaining negative events.

Consistency of Explanatory Style

What about the second and third criteria, consistency across domains and intrasubject consistency? Some researchers have suggested that individuals do not actually have a characteristic style for explaining diverse negative events (Cutrona et al., 1984). However, studies that have reported inconsistency have often done so on the basis of only two or three attributions (e.g., Cutrona et al., 1984; Miller et al., 1982), and sometimes have interpreted coefficient alphas in the .50 range as indicative of inconsistency. Because current psychometric theory (Nunnally, 1978) indicates that more than two instances of a particular trait might be needed in order to uncover evidence of intrasubject consistency, it might be useful to examine evidence from studies that have analyzed explanations about larger numbers of events. In addition, while coefficients in the .50 range obviously do not indicate perfect consistency, they nonetheless provide some evidence of a tendency toward a moderately consistent individual explanatory style.

Studies that asked for explanations about five or more events have typically uncovered moderate consistency in the way individuals explain negative events from different domains. For example, Peterson et al. (1982) reported correlations in the range of .23 to .59 between achievement events and affiliative events on the ASQ. Surprisingly strong evidence for consistency was also reported by Anderson, Jennings, and Arnoult (1988) based on attributions derived from a different instrument, Anderson's Attributional Style Assessment Test. These investigators tested 413 subjects on ratings of interpersonal failures and noninterpersonal failures. After correcting for attenuation, the two attributional domains were correlated at the .91 level.

Further evidence for consistency across domains and within a given individual comes from an examination of coefficient alphas for negative events on the ASQ. These alphas typically are reported to be in the range of .30 to .70 (Cutrona et al., 1984; Peterson et al., 1982; Seligman, Abramson, Semmel, & von Baeyer, 1979; Zautra,

Guenther, & Chartier, 1985). Furthermore, the expanded version of the ASQ (Peterson & Villanova, 1988), on which subjects are asked to make attributions for 24 negative events, yields acceptable consistency: .66 for the internal dimension, .85 for the stable dimension, and .88 for the global dimension.

Finally, there is some evidence that scores on the ASQ tend to be significantly correlated with explanations for actual negative events. For example, Zautra et al. (1985) studied 131 subjects and reported that these subjects' attributional ratings of 14 real negative events correlated .55 with their ratings of hypothetical negative events on the ASQ. And Peterson and Villanova (1988) reported significant correlations between attributional ratings of actual bad events and ratings derived from their expanded ASQ. Taken together, these studies demonstrate that explanatory style is moderately consistent within individuals and across situations, and suggest that explanatory style satisfies the criteria for being considered a trait.

Evidence for Changes in Explanatory Style

Although results from numerous research projects utilizing diverse measures of explanatory style converge in providing evidence that individuals have a characteristic way of explaining bad events, we must qualify this finding based on reports that explanatory style sometimes changes as symptoms of depression remit (Persons & Rao, 1985; Seligman, Castellon, Cacciola, Schulman, Luborsky, Ollove, & Downing, 1988). For example, Seligman et al. (1988) compared the pretreatment explanatory styles of 31 depressed individuals with measures of their explanatory style after treatment with cognitive therapy. Results indicated a significant difference in composite explanatory styles between the two times. As symptoms of depression lessened during the course of cognitive therapy, individuals became less pessimistic in their explanations for negative events. This finding initially appears to contradict our claim that explanatory style may be a trait. How might we reconcile this contradictory evidence?

One possibility is that cognitive therapy can change explanatory style (Seligman et al., 1988). According to this reasoning, explanatory style would remain stable in the absence of exposure to the specific techniques of cognitive therapy. However, as a result of involvement in cognitive ther-apy, individuals might learn to be less pessimistic in explaining negative events.

Some support for this hypothesis was obtained in a study by DeRubeis, Evans, Hollon, Garvey, Grove, and Tuason (1988). These researchers randomly assigned 106 unipolar depressed patients to a 12-week course of one of three active treatments. Patients were treated with cognitive therapy alone, imipramine pharmacotherapy alone, or combined cognitive and imipramine therapy. All patients completed the ASQ and several other cognitive measures. Interestingly, although patients treated solely with imipramine improved about as much as patients treated with cognitive therapy, only the patients treated with cognitive therapy demonstrated marked changes for the better in their explanatory styles for negative events. There was no significant change in ASQ scores in patients treated solely with pharmacotherapy. Thus, this study provided some support for the stability of explanatory style in the absence of techniques designed specifically to change an individual's style.

These results also are consistent with the stability of explanatory style reported by Eaves and Rush (1984) in a sample of depressed patients over a course of therapy in which none of them were treated with cognitive therapy. Because these patients were not exposed to some of the reattribution training procedures often used in cognitive therapy, they would have been less likely to have changed their explanatory style. Further research is needed to determine the stability of explanatory style across diverse populations and circumstances. However, current research results appear to demonstrate that for many individuals, explanatory style is relatively stable throughout adult life, and that in the absence of the reattribution training provided by cognitive therapy, explanatory style may be a relatively enduring risk factor for symptoms of depression and helplessness.

RELATIONSHIP BETWEEN EXPLANATORY STYLE AND DEPRESSION

Cross-Sectional Studies

Numerous studies have looked for a concurrent association between explanatory style and depression using demographically diverse samples and varied instruments. It is not our intention to cite every published report in this chapter. Rather, we will examine evidence from several typical studies, then broadly summarize what appear to be basic findings about the relationship between explanatory style and depression. We will focus mainly on explanatory style for negative events, because this association has been the most widely researched and is most central to the predictions of the reformulated learned helplessness theory.

In an early investigation of the reformulated theory, Seligman et al. (1979) administered the ASQ and the short form of the Beck Depression Inventory (BDI, Beck & Beck, 1972) to a sample of 143 students at the University of Pennsylvania. The composite explanatory style for negative events was significantly correlated ($r = .48$) with depression as measured by the BDI. Similar results were obtained in a study of the ASQ scores of depressed patients and nondepressed patient controls (Raps, Peterson, Reinhard, Abramson, & Seligman, 1982). Patients with a diagnosis of primary affective disorder were more internal, stable, and global in their explanations for bad events than were psychiatric patients with diagnoses of schizophrenia or nondepressed medical patients. These results provide evidence in support of the reformulated learned helplessness theory by demonstrating a relationship between a pessimistic explanatory style and depression in two quite different samples of adults.

Studies of a dissimilar population — depressed children — have revealed a similar relationship between explanatory style and depressive symptoms (Kaslow, Rehm, & Siegel, 1984; McCauley, Mitchell, Burke, & Moss, 1988; Nolen-Hoeksema, Girgus, & Seligman, 1986; Seligman et al., 1984). For example, Nolen-Hoeksema et al. (1986) studied 168 children from New Jersey elementary schools. These children completed the CASQ and the Children's Depression Inventory (CDI; Kovacs, 1980) five times over a 1-year period. As predicted, a pessimistic explanatory style was associated with higher concurrent levels of depression. Moreover, depressive explanatory style for bad events measured at Time 1 was significantly correlated with depression 3 months to 1 year later, even when Time 1 CDI scores were partialled out of the prediction.

The studies described above demonstrate a clear association between a pessimistic explanatory style and depression. Has research from other labs converged with these results? In general, the answer appears to be yes. Although an early review of cross-sectional data on the relationship be-

tween explanatory style and depression reported several negative findings and suggested equivocal support for the hypothesized relationship between depression and explanatory style (Coyne & Gotlib, 1983), recent reviews provide stronger evidence for the existence of a relationship of moderate size between explanatory style and scores on measures of depression such as the BDI (Beck, Ward, Mendelson, Mock, & Erbaugh, 1961). For example, a recent meta-analysis (Sweeney, Anderson, & Bailey, 1986) examined results of 104 studies based on a total of 15,000 subjects. Correcting for attenuation due to reliabilities of the instruments used, they reported an average correlation of .44 between composite explanatory style for negative events and depression. Effect sizes of the underlying internal, stable, and global dimensions were slightly smaller in magnitude, ranging from .34 to .37. In addition, mediator analyses demonstrated that there was a significant relationship between internal, stable, global, and composite dimensions of explanatory style and depression regardless of type of subject (college student or psychiatric depressive), type of outcome about which explanations were made (hypothetical or real), and many of the other mediators tested.

How might we explain findings by some researchers of a lack of association between some dimensions of explanatory style and depression? A recent power analysis (Robins, 1988) suggests one answer. Robins (1988) demonstrated that only five of the numerous published studies he analyzed had a probability of at least .80 of detecting a small to medium relationship between the underlying dimensions of explanatory style and depression. In fact, five of those high-power studies revealed an association between the stable and global dimensions of explanatory style for negative events and depression. In contrast, results of low-power studies were almost evenly divided in reporting confirming or disconfirming evidence for the hypothesized association between stable and global dimensions of explanatory style and depression. Robins' (1988) results highlight the fact that nonsignificant findings are more likely in low-power investigations, and raise the possibility that studies that report a lack of association between explanatory style and depression may merely have had insufficient power to detect a significant correlation. Robins' (1988) study also suggests that investigators in this field need to pay close attention to the power of their research designs. For example, researchers may need to increase their sample sizes and use instruments of demonstrated acceptable reliability, such as the expanded ASQ developed by Peterson and Villanova (1988), in order to reveal a significant relationship between explanatory style and depression.

Evidence for an Interaction Between Explanatory Style and Negative Life Events

We have described results of cross-sectional studies that establish the existence of a concurrent relationship between explanatory style and depression. The more critical question for the model is whether explanatory style and negative events interact to predict depression. As noted by several researchers (Alloy, Abramson, Metalsky, & Hartlage, 1988; Seligman & Nolen-Hoeksema, 1987), the reformulated learned helplessness model specifies that explanatory style is merely a risk factor for subsequent depression. In other words, a pessimistic explanatory style is neither necessary nor sufficient for the development of depression. The pessimistic explanatory style is not necessary because there may be other risk factors for depression; for example, neurochemical imbalances. The pessimistic explanatory style is not sufficient because individuals with a pessimistic explanatory style are at increased risk for depression only when confronting negative life events. In the absence of negative events these pessimists will be no more likely than optimists to experience depression.

What then is the evidence for the existence of this interaction?

Experiments of Nature

One way to answer this question is to analyze the results of experiments of nature. Because it is not possible to expose human subjects to important aversive outcomes, we can study their reactions to naturally occurring aversive events. One such aversive event for college students is the midterm examination.

Several researchers have studied college students before and after their midterm exams (Follete & Jacobson, 1987; Metalsky, Abramson, Seligman, Semmel, & Peterson, 1982; Metalsky, Halberstadt, & Abramson, 1987). The helplessness reformulation predicts that students who explain bad events — for example, failure on an exam — in terms of internal, stable, and global factors will be likely to react with depressive affect

in response to the bad event. Upon learning that they have received a bad grade in the midterm, these pessimists would be more likely to become depressed than students who receive an equally bad grade but explain bad events by invoking external, unstable, and specific factors.

The results of the Metalsky et al. (1982, 1987) studies tend to support the prediction. For example, in the Metalsky et al. (1982) study, undergraduates completed the ASQ and the Multiple Affect Adjective Check List (MAACL; Zuckerman & Lubin, 1965) in class several days before they took their midterm. They also were asked to indicate with what grades they would be happy or unhappy. After the midterm students again completed the MAACL. Internality and globality for bad events predicted increases in depressed mood for those students receiving low grades but not for students receiving high grades.

The Metalsky et al. (1987) study modified the original procedure in order to perform a more fine-grained analysis of the interaction. Two changes are noteworthy. First, students completed the MAACL at several times shortly after the midterm in order to assess the temporal parameters of any affective response to a bad grade. Second, students completed an expanded ASQ utilizing twice as many negative events in both the achievement and interpersonal domains, and focusing only on the relation between depressed affect and the dimensions of stability and globality of bad events. Results from the Metalsky et al. (1987) study indicated that students' moods immediately following their grades were predicted solely by the outcomes themselves, such that regardless of their explanatory styles (which in this study were a composite of stability and globality scores for bad events), getting a poor grade on the exam was associated with transient depressive affect. However, students' enduring affective reactions conformed to the predictions of the model. Explanatory style was a significant predictor of depressed mood several days after receiving a bad grade. This interaction indicates that in the group of students who had done poorly on the exam, explanatory style was associated with enduring depressed affect, whereas there was no relationship between explanatory style and mood in the group of students who had done well on the exam.

Similar to the Metalsky et al. (1987) study, Follete and Jacobson (1987) found no significant relationship between explanatory style and depressed affect measured at the same time students were informed that they had done poorly on their exam. However, Follete and Jacobson (1987) apparently did not measure affective distress several days after the exam, so it is not clear whether overall results of this study provide evidence that is consistent or inconsistent with the reformulated learned helplessness model of depression.

Studies of children (Nolen-Hoeksema et al., 1986), prisoners (Peterson & Seligman, 1984), and women after childbirth (Cutrona, 1983) also have demonstrated the hypothesized interaction between life events and explanatory style in the prediction of depressed affect. Thus, evidence based on different samples converges in demonstrating support for the reformulated model. Based on this research, a pessimistic explanatory style appears to increase the likelihood of an enduring depressive reaction in response to bad events.

Despite convergent evidence, by themselves these studies do not provide a definitive test of the predictions of the reformulated model. The number of studies that specifically test the diathesis-stress component of the reformulated theory is still very small. As noted by Alloy et al. (1988) and Brewin (1985), an adequate test of the basic postulates of the reformulated learned helplessness theory of depression would necessitate future research with a clearer focus on the interactive component of the theory. Although several studies appear to support the existence of the interaction, more research is needed in order to assess the robustness and generality of these findings. In addition, it could be useful to systematically examine how differences in the type of bad events, or the frequency and quantity of events might interact with explanatory style to produce different outcomes. It also should be noted that not all studies that have tested the interactive component of the theory have found evidence of an interaction. For example, Hammen, Adrian, and Hiroto (1988) reported that depression in children at Time 2 was predicted by symptom levels measured at Time 1 and by stressful life events, but not by attributions or the interaction between explanatory style and life events. It is as yet unclear what factors (other than chance) might account for positive results in one study and negative results in another. Finally, studies that depend on experiments of nature can be criticized on several grounds. For example, we are unable to exert experimental control over bad events, and we cannot rule out potential confounds in interpreting obtained results (Seligman & Nolen-Hoeksema, 1987).

Experimental Studies

Although laboratory procedures do not have the ecological validity that is a major strength of an experiment of nature, laboratory work permits experimental control over the presentation of bad events and subsequent examination of systematic differences in subjects' responses. Two basic approaches have been used to study explanatory style and depressed affect in the lab. The first approach is to classify individuals based on their characteristic explanatory styles and look for variations in their responses to good and bad events. The second approach is to attempt to manipulate individuals' explanations for a bad event and look for subsequent changes in performance or mood.

Results of an experiment by Sacks and Bugental (1987) provide evidence that composite scores on the ASQ interact with negative events to predict subsequent depression. In this study, undergraduates were first tested on the ASQ, then exposed to an experimentally rigged social failure or success. When exposed to social failure, subjects with a pessimistic explanatory style became more depressed than optimistic subjects or both pessimists and optimists who were exposed to social success.

In addition, results of several laboratory investigations of explanatory style have provided some evidence in support of the idea that each attributional dimension may mediate a qualitatively distinct class of responses to a bad event. For example, in an examination of the role of the internal-external dimension of explanatory style, subjects induced to make more internal explanations for a bad event tended to exhibit more loss of self-esteem than a group making external explanations (Abramson, 1979). Similar results were obtained by Mikulincer (1986, 1988). In one study (Mikulincer, 1988), subjects were divided into three groups—internal, nondefined, and external attributors—on the basis of their explanatory style for bad events. Mikulincer (1988) then exposed these subjects to either one unsolvable problem, four unsolvable problems, or no unsolvable problems. Following exposure to four unsolvable problems, individuals with an internal explanatory style demonstrated poorer performance on a test task and stronger feelings of incompetence than individuals with an external explanatory style. These studies thus provide preliminary evidence for the hypothesized relationship between internal explanations for a bad event and subsequent self-esteem deficits.

Several studies also have examined the stable-unstable and global-specific dimensions of explanatory style. Consistent with the reformulated learned helplessness theory, Peterson and Seligman (1981) found that subjects induced to explain an uncontrollable event in stable instead of unstable terms exhibited helplessness deficits for a longer time period. And studies that have examined the hypothesized relationship between global explanations and the generality of depressive deficits have demonstrated that subjects who make global explanations for bad events tend to generalize helplessness deficits from the experimental task to a new task (Alloy, Peterson, Abramson, & Seligman, 1984; Mikulincer, 1986; Pasahow, 1980). In contrast, subjects in these studies who made specific attributions for failure demonstrated little generalization of performance deficits.

Are the Three Dimensions of Explanatory Style Orthogonal?

In addition to assigning a particular role to each attributional dimension, the reformulated model described the three dimensions of explanatory style as theoretically orthogonal. However, while it may be useful to conceptualize the three dimensions as theoretically distinct, there is currently good evidence that ratings on each dimension are probably not orthogonal, but instead are at least moderately correlated (e.g., Peterson et al., 1982; Peterson & Villanova, 1988). Moreover, several experimental studies have demonstrated interactions between the three dimensions. These interactions suggest that lowered self-esteem, chronicity of deficits, and generalization of deficits after exposure to negative events may be a function of elevated scores on all three dimensions, rather than each type of deficit being uniquely attributable to an elevated score on just one. For example, Mikulincer (1986) demonstrated that, compared with individuals who scored high on only one attributional dimension, individuals who made both global and stable attributions or both global and internal attributions for failure exhibited more generalization of performance deficits to a new task.

Brewin and Shapiro (1985) also described an interaction between the three dimensions of explanatory style. In the initial phase of the Brewin and Shapiro (1985) study, all subjects were exposed to four unsolvable problems and asked to make attributional ratings for their failure on this task. The second phase involved an assessment of subjects' subsequent performance on a test task using

20 anagrams. Finally, all subjects were told that the experimenter had manipulated their initial failures, a procedure designed to induce subjects who had initially made internal and global attributions to reattribute their failure to external and specific causes. After this reattribution manipulation, subjects were asked to solve 10 additional anagrams. Results indicated that this manipulation selectively improved the performance of subjects who had initially made internal and stable, or internal and global, attributions for their failure.

Summary of Evidence for the Hypothesized Interaction

Taken together, results of experiments of nature and work in the lab provide support for the diathesis-stress component of the reformulated learned helplessness model. Based on current research, we can conclude that a maladaptive explanatory style interacts with negative life events to predict helplessness and depressive deficits. Based on current research, we also can conclude that individuals who make internal, stable, and global explanations for negative events are at risk for the lowered self-esteem, enduring affective reactions, and generalized performance deficits that are predicted by the reformulated model. And while there is some evidence for the role of each underlying dimension in producing specific depressive deficits, there is also evidence that the dimensions of explanatory style may interact to increase vulnerability to depression.

PESSIMISTIC EXPLANATORY STYLE

The reformulated learned helplessness model of depression predicts that individuals with a maladaptive explanatory style will be at increased risk for depression and helplessness when confronting important negative life events. Part of the strength of this prediction stems from its specificity to helplessness and depression. The model is most useful if it clearly specifies who will tend to experience problems, under what circumstances the problems will occur, and what the exact nature of the problems we would expect to observe will be. Thus, based on the model, we would expect research results to reveal a clear link between a pessimistic explanatory style and depression or helplessness, but little or no link between a pessimistic explanatory style and psychopathology in general. This, of course, amounts in part to a question about the discriminant validity of the construct (Campbell & Fiske, 1959).

Explanatory Style and Anxiety

We will examine the issue of discriminant validity by first looking at evidence from several studies that have compared explanatory styles of individuals diagnosed as depressed and individuals diagnosed as primarily anxious. Despite the fact that there is often a great deal of overlap between symptoms of anxiety and symptoms of depression (Lipman, 1982), these symptoms are classified by the *Diagnostic and Statistical Manual of Mental Disorders* (DSM-III-R; American Psychiatric Association, 1987) into clinically distinct syndromes. In addition, anxiety and depression are theoretically distinguishable (Garber, Miller, & Abramson, 1980). Although many actual situations involve aversive stimuli that are perceived as both unpredictable and uncontrollable, the unpredictability and uncontrollabilty of events can be dissociated in the lab to reveal corresponding differences in behavior and motivation. In theory, subjects exposed solely to unpredictable aversive stimuli should demonstrate anxiety and increased motivation (Miller, 1981), whereas subjects exposed to uncontrollable aversive events should demonstrate mainly depressed affect and decreases in motivation (see Garber et al., 1980, for a more complete discussion of this distinction). Because the reformulated learned helplessness model suggests that it is primarily the expectation that important outcomes will be uncontrollable that leads to symptoms of helplessness and depression, the model predicts a stronger association between a pessimistic explanatory style and depression than between a pessimistic explanatory style and anxiety.

A recent comparison of explanatory styles of depressed and anxious outpatients (Riskind, Castellon, & Beck, 1989) provides some evidence in support of this prediction. Riskind et al. (1989) used the CAVE technique to analyze the thought diaries of 12 depressed and 12 anxious outpatients. A discriminant function analysis based on explanatory style for negative events correctly classified 92% of the depressed patients and 58% of the anxious patients. Because anxiety was classified at a level no different than chance, results of this study suggest that depression, but not anxiety, is associated with a characteristic explanatory style.

Other investigators have reached similar conclusions. Heimberg, Vermilyea, Dodge, Becker, and Barlow (1987) compared scores on the ASQ for individuals diagnosed by structured clinical interview as dysthymic patients, anxiety disorder patients, and normal controls. They also administered the BDI to all subjects in the study, and classified both anxious and dysthymic groups by level of depression reported on the BDI. Results tended to support the reformulated model. Dysthymic subjects demonstrated a pessimistic explanatory style for negative events, and anxious subjects demonstrated a pessimistic explanatory style only if they were also at least moderately depressed. The composite explanatory styles of patients suffering only from symptoms of anxiety were not significantly different from the explanatory style of the normal controls.

The results of these two studies provide some evidence that depression is associated with a characteristic explanatory style whereas anxiety is not. However, not all studies have supported this aspect of the model. For example, Ganellen (1988) administered the ASQ to 50 anxiety disorder patients, many of whom were also depressed. His results indicated that anxiety symptom severity and depression symptom severity were both positively and significantly correlated with explanatory style for negative events. Consistent with the model, anxiety was uncorrelated with ASQ scores when depression was partialled out. However, less consistent with the model, depression was uncorrelated with ASQ scores when anxiety was partialled out. One reason for these results may be the reported high correlation in this sample between symptoms of depression and symptoms of anxiety, leaving little unique variance for either. However, because the study did not include patients diagnosed as primarily depressed it is difficult to resolve this issue.

A recent study by Heimberg, Klosko, Dodge, Shadick, Becker, and Barlow (1989) also revealed a significant assocation between a pessimistic explanatory style and social phobia. These researchers compare the explanatory styles of dysthymic patients with those of individuals suffering from agoraphobia, social phobia, or panic disorder. Surprisingly, although the patients diagnosed as social phobics were significantly less depressed than the dysthymic patients, they obtained similar scores on the composite ASQ for negative events. Furthermore, in an analysis of covariance that controlled for subjects' scores on the BDI, a diagnosis of social phobia was still significantly associated with a maladaptive explanatory style.

In summary, explanatory style appears to have demonstrated some discriminant validity in several comparisons of depressed and anxious individuals. However, current evidence is mixed, and the number of studies that have focussed on this issue is still quite small. In particular, current research suggests that some anxious individuals, especially those individuals suffering from social phobia, may be nearly as pessimistic as depressed individuals in their explanations for negative events. Further research will be needed before we can resolve the theoretical questions raised by these findings.

Explanatory Style and Other Psychological Problems

While it seems clear that explanatory style is probably unrelated to the development of psychoses or disorders such as schizophrenia (Raps et al., 1982), explanatory style has been found to be associated with a number of psychological problems other than depression. These include reports of an association between a pessimistic explanatory style and loneliness (Anderson et al., 1988), and reports of associations between a pessimistic explanatory style and general distress (Nezu, Nezu, & Nezu, 1986; Zautra et al., 1985).

There are several possible interpretations of these results. First, depression is probably not a unitary entity (Abramson, Metalsky, & Alloy, 1989; Alloy et al., 1988; Watson & Clark, 1984). Rather, by current diagnostic criteria, such as those recommended in DSM-III-R, depression may be conceptualized as a syndrome composed of diverse symptoms, none of which is necessary or sufficient for a diagnosis of depressive disorder. Because several studies have reported positive zero-order correlations between measures of depression and measures of loneliness and general distress (e.g., Anderson, Horowitz, & French, 1983; Gotlib, 1984; Nezu et al., 1986), it is possible that explanatory style is indirectly related to variables such as loneliness via the relationship of loneliness to the syndrome of depression. If this interpretation were correct, partialling depression out of the correlation between explanatory style and variables such as loneliness would result in a nonsignificant relationship between explanatory style and loneliness. However, the studies cited did not report the partial correlations that would be necessary to test this hypothesis.

The above interpretation of the relationship between explanatory style and problems other than depression does not particularly challenge the claim that explanatory style should be specifically related to depression and helplessness. However, a second type of interpretation is possible; namely, that explanatory style is actually directly related to the development of loneliness and other psychological problems through as yet unspecified mechanisms. Can the reformulated learned helplessness model handle data that suggest that explanatory style may function as a predictor of psychological problems other than depression? We believe that the reformulated learned helplessness model can accommodate these data, and accommodate them without a serious loss of specificity. We will elaborate on this issue at the end of the following discussion.

DISCUSSION AND SUGGESTIONS FOR FUTURE RESEARCH

Explanatory Style—A New Trait?

We have provided evidence that explanatory style can be conceptualized as a personality trait. Research suggests that explanatory style for negative events demonstrates some cross-situational consistency and moderate stability over the adult lifespan. The stability of explanatory style compares favorably with stabilities reported for many traditional personality constructs. For example, Conley (1984) reported correlations in the range of .30 to .40 for variables such as neurotic tendency and introversion over a period of 45 years. Similarly, Leon, Gillum, Gillum, and Gouze (1979) analyzed the stability over a 30-year period of scores on 13 scales of the Minnesota Multiphasic Personality Inventory (MMPI) and reported correlations ranging from .28 for hypochondriasis to .74 for introversion.

The suggestion that explanatory style may be a trait inevitably leads to a question about what kind of trait it might be. We wonder about the relationship between explanatory style and personality constructs such as neuroticism and introversion. An understanding of a personality variable usually develops gradually over years of research on the convergent and discriminant validity of components of the construct. However, research on the convergent and discriminant validity of explanatory style is still in its infancy, and much work remains to be done.

Recent research on the constructs of negative affectivity (NA) and positive affectivity (PA; Watson & Clark, 1984; see also their chapter in this volume) may be of relevance to questions about explanatory style as a personality trait. Watson and Clark (1984) have suggested that constructs such as neuroticism might be subsumed by the more general construct of negative affectivity. Moreover, they report that negative affectivity seems to be more clearly and specifically associated with anxiety than with depression (Watson, Clark, & Carey, 1988). While depressed individuals are often high in NA, their research suggests that depressed individuals are also low in PA and that depression may be a complex and multidimensional psychological state. Thus, we do not believe that explanatory style is merely another way to measure neuroticism or negative affectivity. Results of studies that have reported significant associations between explanatory style and depression, but not between explanatory style and anxiety, suggest that explanatory style measures something other than neuroticism. However, a satisfactory resolution of this issue awaits further research.

A more interesting possibility is that explanatory style measures an entirely new aspect of personality. In theory, event-explanation units are examples of causal reasoning and may reflect actual processes by which individuals interpret their lives or negotiate reality (e.g., Higgins & Snyder, this volume; Snyder, 1989; Snyder & Higgins, 1988). Investigations of the relationship between event-explanation units and causal versus noncausal reasoning are currently underway (Stearns, 1989), and we soon hope to be able to answer more fully some of these questions.

The Role of Explanatory Style in the Onset, Maintenance, and Relapse of Symptoms of Depression

Several recent studies have examined the interaction between explanatory style and negative events. Consistent with the reformulated learned helplessness model, results from these studies suggest that a pessimistic explanatory style may increase the risk of experiencing depressive deficits in response to bad events. However, as noted by Brewin (1985) the reformulated learned helplessness model is primarily a vulnerability model of depression. The model specfies who is at risk for development of symptoms of depression, and in-

dicates that the chronicity of those symptoms is determined mainly by the stability of the explanation for the event that was originally related to onset of depressive deficits. According to the reformulated model, the more stable the original causal explanation, the greater the duration of the episode of depression.

The reformulated learned helplessness model's focus on factors that increase vulnerability to the onset of symptoms of depression has been empirically useful. However, recent research suggests that the scope of the theory may be too narrow. In other words, explanatory style may be related not only to the initiation of an episode of depression, but to the maintenance of depressive symptoms and relapse as well. For example, the results of research by Seligman, Kamen, and Nolen-Hoeksema (1988) on patients involved in therapy for depression demonstrated a significant positive correlation between change in explanatory style and change in symptoms of depression. The more an individual's explanatory style improved, the more their depression improved. The change in the composite ASQ score for negative events was correlated .65 ($p < .0001$) with the change in depressive symptoms as measured by the BDI, and .52 with the change in clinician-rated measures of depression. Several interpretations of this finding are possible, but one plausible interpretion suggests a role for explanatory style in the maintenance of at least some depressive symptoms. As explanatory style changes for the better, depressive symptoms are no longer maintained, and symptoms of depression remit.

The impact of individual differences in explanatory style on potential for relapse was explored in a 2-year follow-up of 44 patients treated with either pharmacotherapy or cognitive therapy for depression (Evans et al., 1988). Results of the initial phase of treatment for both groups of patients were reported by DeRubeis et al. (1988) and were discussed briefly earlier in this chapter. Recall that while patients in both the pharmacotherapy and the cognitive therapy groups demonstrated posttreatment remission of symptoms of depression, only the patients treated with cognitive therapy demonstrated corresponding improvement in their scores on the ASQ. Interestingly, patients treated with medication relapsed at twice the rate of the cognitive therapy patients. Furthermore, there was some evidence that explanatory style mediated the likelihood of relapse. Across both groups, posttreatment ASQ scores were a significant predictor of time to subsequent relapse, even when posttreatment depression scores were partialled out.

These results must be replicated before we can draw firm conclusions. However, evidence is accumulating that explanatory style may affect the entire course of depressive illness, increasing an individual's risk of development of depression, acting to maintain symptoms of depression, and promoting an eventual recurrence of symptoms. Like an insidious virus, the effects of a pessimistic explanatory style may lie dormant in afflicted individuals, increasing the likelihood of an outbreak of symptoms, and maintaining those symptoms once they occur. Furthermore, the research is consistent with the possibility that antidepressant medication may provide only symptomatic relief in depressed individuals, whereas cognitive therapy may act in a curative fashion on at least one of the causes of depression — an individual's pessimistic explanatory style.

From a clinical perspective, it could be useful to determine if explanatory style is actually involved in the entire course of a depressive episode. For example, if a pessimistic explanatory style is involved in the maintenance of depression and increases the likelihood of subsequent relapse, then scores on the ASQ might provide a cognitive marker of the efficacy of any treatment for depression and of an individual's risk for subsequent relapse.

An Analysis of the Issue of Specificity

We have reviewed evidence from several studies that suggests that explanatory style predicts depression better than it predicts anxiety. However, other studies have suggested that explanatory style may be associated with symptoms of anxiety, loneliness, and indices of general psychological distress. In addition, explanatory style appears to predict outcomes as diverse as quitting a job, health and illness throughout the adult lifespan, and pathological gambling. In one study, life insurance sales agents with a relatively pessimistic explanatory style were less productive and more likely to quit their jobs than were the more optimistic sales agents (Seligman & Schulman, 1986). In another study, Peterson, Seligman, and Vaillant (1988) analyzed the explanatory styles of 99 graduates of the Harvard classes of 1942–1945. Pessimistic explanatory style predicted poorer

health in these individuals 20 to 35 years later, even after controlling for earlier physical health. Finally, McCormick and Taber (1988) demonstrated greater relapse to gambling after treatment in individuals with a pessimistic explanatory style.

These findings suggest that explanatory style can predict a rather diverse set of variables, ranging from increased likelihood of quitting a job, through loneliness and depression, to disease and perhaps death. The research indicates an association between explanatory style and a broad range of outcomes, yet earlier in the chapter we claimed that this diversity fails to significantly compromise the specificity of explanatory style. We now review the reasoning behind this claim.

As noted earlier in the chapter, there are several possible interpretations of these findings. The first interpretation is the easiest for the reformulated learned helplessness theory to accommodate. This interpretation suggests that the relationship between explanatory style and diverse psychological problems is generally mediated by the effects of depression. For example, the relationship between explanatory style and health in the Peterson et al. (1988) study could have been caused by the following sequence of events. First, as documented in this chapter, individuals with a poor explanatory style are more likely to become depressed. Depression may then have a number of health consequences (see Peterson & Seligman, 1987, for a discussion of this issue). One consequence might be that changes in appetite, feelings of hopelessness, and lowered response initiation would lead to poorer nutrition, fewer doctor visits, and less vigilant health care, making the depressed individual more susceptible to health problems. Alternatively, exposure to uncontrollable events, and feelings of depression and anxiety, may lead directly to higher production of corticosteroid and endogenous opioids, with resultant lowered immunocompetence (see Sklar & Anisman, 1981; Jemmott & Locke, 1984, for reviews of this literature). By either account, explanatory style specifically predicts only those symptoms characteristic of depression. Depression, in turn, may be associated with the development of diverse psychological and physiological problems.

A second possibility is that explanatory style is directly related to outcomes such as loneliness and disease through the relationship between explanatory style and helplessness. Recall that the reformulated learned helplessness theory not only suggests an association between explanatory style and depression, but also proposes an association between a pessimistic explanatory style and helplessness. And although helplessness is a syndrome characterized by cognitive, motivational, and affective deficits that are similar to the symptoms exhibited by depressed individuals, the deficits associated with helplessness are not necessarily identical to the deficits associated with depression. Rather, the syndrome of helplessness and the syndrome of depression might be regarded as overlapping constructs that share many, but not all, elements.

Because the reformulated model suggests that explanatory style is directly related to helplessness, and symptoms of helplessness are not necessarily identical to symptoms of depression, we might sometimes find helplessness deficits in individuals who demonstrate few depressive deficits. While this interpretation does not seriously compromise the specificity of the model, because the reformulated learned helplessness theory was developed as a model of both helplessness and depression, it creates a major practical problem. Namely, although we can easily describe and predict depressive deficits by using reasonably well defined and researched diagnostic criteria, there is less research and no clearly described diagnostic category that specifically predicts the kinds of deficits to be expected in the related category of human helplessness. We expect current research on the relationship between explanatory style and diverse psychological problems to provide an empirical base that will support theoretical development of this issue.

A third possible interpretation of the relationship between explanatory style and diverse psychological problems would be that explanatory style is related to various problems either by mechanisms other than those specified by the helplessness theory, or in a superficial and epiphenomenal fashion. We believe that the evidence presented in this chapter, much of which conforms to the specific predictions of the reformulated learned helplessness model, renders this last possibility implausible. However, because theories can be disproved but not proved, the merits of this last interpretation await future critical tests of the reformulated learned helplessness model.

CONCLUSIONS

We have presented evidence that explanatory style may be a personality trait and that a pessi-

mistic explanatory style increases the risk of development of symptoms of depression in response to bad events. We also have suggested that explanatory style may predict other psychological problems in which the cognitive, behavioral, and affective symptoms characteristic of helplessness play a role. It is possible that the tendency to become helpless—to give up—when confronting bad events is associated with human dysfunction in a number of domains, and it remains for future research to establish the mechanism that links a pessimistic explanatory style to diverse outcomes.

A final question involves the role of other variables in the development of depression and helplessness. While there is good evidence that having a pessimistic explanatory style is an important risk factor for depression, it seems likely that other cognitive variables also play a role. For example, preattributional variables such as consensus or consistency (Brewin & Furnham, 1986), and individual differences in rumination (Zullow, 1984; Zullow, Oettingen, Peterson, & Seligman, 1988) or off-task cognitions (Mikulincer, 1989; Mikulincer & Nizan, 1988) may have important additive effects in the etiology and maintenance of a depressive episode. Researchers are slowly piecing together a complete model of cognitive factors that influence the course of depression.

REFERENCES

Abramson, L. Y. (1979). *Universal versus personal helplessness: An experimental test of the reformulated theory of learned helplessness and depression*. Unpublished doctoral dissertation, University of Pennsylvania, Philadelphia.

Abramson, L. Y., Metalsky, G. I., & Alloy, L. B. (1989). Hopelessness depression: A theory-based subtype of depression. *Psychological Review, 96*, 358–372.

Abramson, L. Y., Seligman, M. E. P., & Teasdale, J. (1978). Learned helplessness in humans: Critique and reformulation. *Journal of Abnormal Psychology, 87*, 32–48.

Alloy, L. B., Abramson, L. Y., Metalsky, G. I., & Hartlage, S. (1988). The hopelessness theory of depression: Attributional aspects. *British Journal of Clinical Psychology, 27*, 5–21.

Alloy, L. B., Peterson, C., Abramson, L. Y., & Seligman, M. E. P. (1984). Attributional style and the generality of learned helplessness. *Journal of Personality and Social Psychology, 46*, 681–687.

American Psychiatric Association. (1987). *Diagnostic and Statistical Manual of Mental Disorders* (3rd ed., rev.). Washington, DC. Author.

Anderson, C. A., Horowitz, L. M., & French, R. D. (1983). Attributional style of lonely and depressed people. *Journal of Personality and Social Psychology, 45*, 127–136.

Anderson, C. A., Jennings, D. L., & Arnoult, L. H. (1988). Validity and utility of the attributional style construct at a moderate level of specificity. *Journal of Personality and Social Psychology, 55*, 979–990.

Beck, A. T., & Beck, R. W. (1972). Screening depressed patients in family practice: A rapid technique. *Postgraduate Medicine, 52*, 81–85.

Beck, A. T., Ward, C. H., Mendelson, M., Mock, J. E., & Erbaugh, J. (1961). An inventory for measuring depression. *Archives of General Psychiatry, 4*, 561–571.

Brewin, C. R. (1985). Depression and causal attributions: What is their relation? *Psychological Bulletin, 98*, 297–309.

Brewin, C. R., & Furnham, A. (1986). Attributional versus preattributional variables in self-esteem and depression: A comparison and test of learned helplessness theory. *Journal of Personality and Social Psychology, 50*, 1013–1020.

Brewin, C. R., & Shapiro, D. A. (1985). Selective impact of reattribution of failure on task performance. *British Journal of Social Psychology, 24*, 37–46.

Burns, M. O., & Seligman, M. E. P. (1989). Explanatory style across the life span: Evidence for stability over 52 years. *Journal of Personality and Social Psychology, 56*, 471–477.

Campbell, D. T., & Fiske, D. W. (1959). Convergent and discriminant validity by the multitrait-multimethod matrix. *Psychological Bulletin, 56*, 81–104.

Cochran, S. D., & Hammen, C. L. (1985). Perceptions of stressful life events and depression: A test of attributional models. *Journal of Personality and Social Psychology, 48*, 1562–1571.

Conley, J. J. (1984). Longitudinal consistency of adult personality: Self-reported psychological characteristics across 45 years. *Journal of Personality and Social Psychology, 47*, 1325–1333.

Coyne, J. C., & Gotlib, I. H. (1983). The role of cognition in depression: A critical appraisal. *Psychological Bulletin, 94*, 472–505.

Cutrona, C. E. (1983). Causal attributions and perinatal depression. *Journal of Abnormal Psychology, 92*, 161–172.

Cutrona, C. E., Russell, D., & Jones, R. D. (1984). Cross-situational consistency in causal attributions: Does attributional style exist? *Journal of Personality and Social Psychology, 47*, 1043–1058.

DeRubeis, R. J., Evans, M. D., Hollon, S. D., Garvey, M. J., Grove, W. M., & Tuason, V. B. (1988). *Active components and mediating mechanisms in cognitive therapy, pharmacotherapy, and combined cognitive-pharmacotherapy for depression: III. Processes of change in the CPT project.* Manuscript submitted for publication.

Eaves, G., & Rush, A. J. (1984). Cognitive patterns in symptomatic and remitted unipolar major depression. *Journal of Abnormal Psychology, 93*, 31–40.

Evans, M. D., Hollon, S. J., DeRubeis, R. J., Piasecki, J. M., Grove, W. M., Garvey, M. J., & Tuason, V. B. (1988). Differential relapse following cognitive therapy, pharmacotherapy, and combined cognitive-pharmacotherapy for depression: IV. A two-year follow-up of the CPT project. Manuscript submitted for publication.

Follette, V. M., & Jacobson, N. S. (1987). Importance of attributions as a predictor of how people cope with failure. *Journal of Personality and Social Psychology, 52*, 1205–1211.

Ganellen, R. J. (1988). Specificity of attributions and overgeneralization in depression and anxiety. *Journal of Abnormal Psychology, 97*, 83–86.

Garber, J., Miller, S. M., & Abramson, L. Y. (1980). On the distinction between anxiety and depression: Perceived control, certainty, and probability of goal attainment. In J. Garber & M. E. P. Seligman (Eds.), *Human helplessness: Theory and applications* (pp. 131–169). New York: Academic Press.

Gotlib, I. H. (1984). Depression and general psychopathology in university students. *Journal of Abnormal Psychology, 93*, 19–30.

Hammen, C., Adrian, C., & Hiroto, D. (1988). A longitudinal test of the attributional vulnerability model in children at risk for depression. *British Journal of Clinical Psychology, 27*, 37–46.

Heimberg, R. G., Klosko, J. S., Dodge, C. S., Shadick, R., Becker, R. E., & Barlow, D. H. (1989). Anxiety disorders, depression, and attributional style: A further test of the specificity of depressive attributions. *Cognitive Therapy and Research, 13*, 21–36.

Heimberg, R. C., Vermilyea, J. A., Dodge, C. S., Becker, R. E., & Barlow, D. H. (1987). Attributional style, depression, and anxiety: An evaluation of the specificity of depressive attributions. *Cognitive Therapy and Research, 11*, 537–550.

Jemmott, J. B., & Locke, S. E. (1984). Psychosocial factors, immunologic mediation, and human susceptibility to infectious diseases: How much do we know? *Psychological Bulletin, 95*, 78–108.

Kaslow, N. J., Rehm, L. P., & Siegel, A. W. (1984). Social-cognitive and cognitive correlates of depression in children. *Journal of Abnormal Child Psychology, 12*, 605–620.

Kovacs, M. (1980). Rating scales to assess depression in school-aged children. *Acta Paedopsychiatria, 46*, 305–315.

Leon, G. R., Gillum, B., Gillum, R., & Gouze, M. (1979). Personality stability and change over a 30 year period—Middle age to old age. *Journal of Consulting and Clinical Psychology, 47*, 517–524.

Lipman, R. S. (1982). Differentiating anxiety and depression in anxiety disorders: Use of rating scales. *Psychopharmacology Bulletin, 18*, 69–77.

Maier, S. F., & Seligman, M. E. P. (1976). Learned helplessness: Theory and evidence. *Journal of Experimental Psychology: General, 105*, 3–46.

McCauley, E., Mitchell, J. R., Burke, P., & Moss, S. (1988). Cognitive attributes of depression in children and adolescents. *Journal of Consulting and Clinical Psychology, 56*, 903–908.

McCormick, R. A., & Taber, J. I. (1988). Attributional style in pathological gamblers in treatment. *Journal of Abnormal Psychology, 97*, 368–370.

Metalsky, G. I., Abramson, L. Y., Seligman, M. E. P., Semmel, A., & Peterson, C. (1982). Attributional styles and life events in the classroom: Vulnerability and invulnerability to depressive mood reactions. *Journal of Personality and Social Psychology, 43*, 612–617.

Metalsky, G. I., Halberstadt, L. J., & Abramson, L. Y. (1987). Vulnerability to depressive mood reactions: Toward a more powerful test of the diathesis-stress and causal mediation components of the reformulated theory of depression. *Journal of Personality and Social Psychology, 52*, 386–393.

Mikulincer, M. (1986). Attributional processes in the learned helplessness paradigm: Behavioral effects of global attributions. *Journal of Personality and Social Psychology, 51*, 1248–1256.

Mikulincer, M. (1988). Reactance and helplessness following exposure to unsolvable problems: The effects of attributional style. *Journal of Personality and Social Psychology, 54*, 679–686.

Mikulincer, M. (1989). Cognitive interference and learned helplessness: The effects of off-task cognitions on performance following unsolvable problems. *Journal of Personality and Social Psychology, 57*, 129–135.

Mikulincer, M., & Nizan, B. (1988). Causal attribution, cognitive interference, and generalization of learned helplessness. *Journal of Personality and Social Psychology, 55*, 470–478.

Miller, I. W., Klee, S. H., & Norman, W. H. (1982). Depressed and nondepressed inpatients' cognitions of hypothetical events, experimental tasks, stressful life events. *Journal of Abnormal Psychology, 91*, 78–81.

Miller, S. M. (1981). Predictability and human stress: Toward a clarification of evidence and theory. *Advances in Experimental Social Psychology, 14*, 203–256.

Miller, W. R., & Seligman, M. E. P. (1975). Depression and learned helplessness in man. *Journal of Abnormal Psychology, 84*, 228–238.

Nezu, A. M., Nezu, C. M., & Nezu, V. A. (1986). Depression, general distress, and causal attributions among university students. *Journal of Abnormal Psychology, 95*, 184–186.

Nolen-Hoeksema, S., Girgus, J. S., & Seligman, M. E. P. (1986). Learned helplessness in children: A longitudinal study of depression, achievement, and explanatory style. *Journal of Personality and Social Psychology, 51*, 435–442.

Nunnally, J. (1978). *Psychometric theory* (2nd ed.). New York: McGraw-Hill.

Parry, G., & Brewin, C. R. (1988). Cognitive style and depression: Symptom-related, event-related, or independent provoking factor? *British Journal of Clinical Psychology, 27*, 23–35.

Pasahow, R. J. (1980). The relation between an attributional dimension and learned helplessness. *Journal of Abnormal Psychology, 89*, 358–367.

Persons, J. B., & Rao, P. A. (1985). Longitudinal

study of cognitions, life events, and depression in psychiatric inpatients. *Journal of Abnormal Psychology, 94*, 51–63.

Peterson, C., Bettes, B. A., & Seligman, M. E. P. (1985). Depressive symptoms and unprompted causal attributions: Content analysis. *Behavior Research and Therapy, 23*, 379–382.

Peterson, C., Luborsky, L., & Seligman, M. E. P. (1983). Attributions and depressive mood shifts: A case study using the symptom-context method. *Journal of Abnormal Psychology, 92*, 96–103.

Peterson, C., & Seligman, M. E. P. (1981). Helplessness and attributional style in depression. *Tidskrift for Norsk Psykologforening, 18*, 3–18.

Peterson, C., & Seligman, M. E. P. (1984). Causal explanations as a risk factor for depression: Theory and evidence. *Psychological Review, 91*, 347–374.

Peterson, C., & Seligman, M. E. P. (1987). Explanatory style and illness. *Journal of Personality, 55*, 237–265.

Peterson, C., Seligman, M. E. P., & Vaillant, G. (1988). Pessimistic explanatory style is a risk factor for physical illness: A thirty-five-year longitudinal study. *Journal of Personality and Social Psychology, 55*, 23–27.

Peterson, C., Semmel, A., von Baeyer, C., Abramson, L. Y., Metalsky, G. I., & Seligman, M. E. P. (1982). The attributional style questionnaire. *Cognitive Therapy and Research, 6*, 287–300.

Peterson C., & Villanova, P. (1988). An expanded attributional style questionnaire. *Journal of Abnormal Psychology, 97*, 87–89.

Peterson, C., Villanova, P., & Raps, C. S. (1985). Depression and attributions: Factors responsible for inconsistent results in the published literature. *Journal of Abnormal Psychology, 94*, 165–168.

Raps, C. S., Peterson, C., Reinhard, K. E., Abramson, L. Y., & Seligman, M. E. P. (1982). Attributional style among depressed patients. *Journal of Abnormal Psychology, 91*, 102–108.

Riskind, J. H., Castellon, C. S., & Beck, A. T. (1989). Spontaneous causal explanations in unipolar depression and generalized anxiety: Content analysis of dysfunctional-thought diaries. *Cognitive Therapy and Research, 13*, 97–108.

Robins, C. J. (1988). Attributions and depression: Why is the literature so inconsistent? *Journal of Personality and Social Psychology, 54*, 880–889.

Roth, S. (1980). A revised model of learned helplessness in humans. *Journal of Personality, 48*, 103–133.

Sacks, C. H., & Bugental, D. B. (1987). Attributions as moderators of affective and behavioral responses to social failure. *Journal of Personality and Social Psychology, 53*, 939–947.

Seligman, M. E. P. (1975). *Helplessness: On depression, development, and death*. San Francisco: W. H. Freeman.

Seligman, M. E. P., Abramson, L. Y., Semmel, A., & von Baeyer, C. (1979). Depressive attributional style. *Journal of Abnormal Psychology, 88*, 242–247.

Seligman, M. E. P., Castellon, C., Cacciola, J., Schulman, P., Luborsky, L., Ollove, M., & Downing, R. (1988). Explanatory style change during cognitive therapy for unipolar depression. *Journal of Abnormal Psychology, 97*, 13–18.

Seligman, M. E. P., & Elder, G. (1985). Learned helplessness and life span development. In A. Sorenson, F. Weinert, & L. Sherrod (Eds.), *Human development and the life course: Multidisciplinary perspectives* (pp. 377–427). Hillsdale, NJ: Lawrence Erlbaum Associates.

Seligman, M. E. P., Kamen, L. P., & Nolen-Hoeksema, S. (1988). Explanatory style across the lifespan: Achievement and health. In R. M. Lerner, E. M. Hetherington, & M. Perlmutter (Eds.), *Child development in lifespan perspective* (pp. 91–114). Hillsdale, NJ: Lawrence Erlbaum Associates.

Seligman, M. E. P., & Maier, S. F. (1967). Failure to escape traumatic shock. *Journal of Experimental Psychology, 74*, 1–9.

Seligman, M. E. P., & Nolen-Hoeksema, S. (1987). Explanatory style and depression. In *Psychopathology, an interactional perspective* (pp. 125–139). New York: Academic Press.

Seligman, M. E. P., Peterson, C., Kaslow, N. J., Tanenbaum, R. L., Alloy, L. B., & Abramson, L. Y. (1984). Attributional style and depressive symptoms among children. *Journal of Abnormal Psychology, 93*, 235–238.

Seligman, M. E. P., & Schulman, P. (1986). Explanatory style as a predictor of productivity and quitting among life insurance sales agents. *Journal of Personality and Social Psychology, 50*, 832–838.

Sklar, L. S., & Anisman, H. (1981). Stress and cancer. *Psychological Bulletin, 89*, 369–406.

Snyder, C. R. (1989). Reality negotiation: From excuses to hope and beyond. *Journal of Social and Clinical Psychology, 8*, 130–157.

Snyder, C. R., & Higgins, R. L. (1988). Excuses: Their effective role in the negotiation of reality. *Psychological Bulletin, 104*, 23–35.

Stearns, D. (1989). Unpublished data, University of Pennsylvania, Philadelphia.

Sweeney, P. D., Anderson, A., & Bailey, S. (1986). Attributional style in depression: A meta-analytic review. *Journal of Personality and Social Psychology, 50*, 974–991.

Watson, D., & Clark, L. A. (1984). Negative affectivity: The disposition to experience aversive emotional states. *Psychological Bulletin, 96*, 465–490.

Watson, D., Clark, L. A., & Carey, G. (1988). Positive and negative affectivity and their relation to depression and anxiety disorders. *Journal of Abnormal Psychology, 97*, 346–353.

Zautra, A. J., Guenther, R. T., & Chartier, G. M. (1985). Attributions for real and hypothetical events: Their relation to self-esteem and depression. *Journal of Abnormal Psychology, 94*, 530–540.

Zuckerman, M., & Lubin, B. (1965). *Manual for the multiple affect adjective check list*. San Diego, CA: Educational and Industrial Testing Service.

Zullow, H. M. (1984). *The interaction of rumination and explanatory style in depression*. Unpublished manuscript, University of Pennsylvania, Philadelphia.

Zullow, H. M., Oettingen, G., Peterson, C., & Seligman, M. E. P. (1988). Pessimistic explanatory style in the historical record: CAVing LBJ, presidential candidates, and East versus West Berlin. *American Psychologist, 43*, 673–682.

CHAPTER 15

HOPE AND HEALTH

C. R. Snyder
Lori M. Irving
John R. Anderson

"*Modo liceat vivere, est spes* (While there's life, there's hope)"
— Terence (190–159 BC), *Andria* [*The Lady of Andros*], line 981

HOPE ACROSS TIME

Historical viewpoints on hope are best collectively characterized as being strongly ambivalent. These views are "strong" in that writers agree that hope is important, but the ambivalence stems from disagreement about whether hope is good or bad. Perhaps the most famous historical touchstone involves the myth of Pandora. Zeus, who was angry with Prometheus for stealing fire from the Gods, sent Pandora to earth with a box filled mostly with evil creatures. Knowing that Pandora would ignore his instructions to keep the box unopened, Zeus extracted his revenge as Pandora unleashed all but one of the creatures before she replaced the lid. That creature was hope. The myth of Pandora proclaims hope to be the great consolation that makes human cares and troubles seem bearable (Smith, 1983).

Spanning the centuries, Pandora's consolatory creature has been treated as both a blessing and a curse. Writers such as Sophocles and Nietzsche denounced hope as an evil force responsible for prolonging human torment. Saint Paul and Martin Luther, on the other hand, felt that hope should be placed alongside love as the essence of what is good and truthful in life. Rather than advocating either of these positions, Tillich (1965) more recently attempted to reconcile them, stating, "Hope is easy for the foolish, but hard for the wise. Everybody can lose himself into foolish hope, but genuine hope is something rare and great" (p. 17). Modern writers have shared this view of foolish hope as bad and genuine hope as good, but remain uncertain as to how one distinguishes between the two. Actually, no one is quite sure whether such a distinction can be made. Part of the problem has to do with the possibility that even hope that appears foolish has the potential for bringing about positive outcomes. For example, many would label hope associated with the healings of snake oil salesmen and revivalist preachers as "false hope"; yet, the occasional success of such cures is documented (see Frank, 1973, for a review).

Proponents of holistic medicine have no trouble accepting "hope cures" as genuine because they do not make a distinction between mental and bodily states. The traditional medical community, however, is rooted in Cartesian dualism, and tends to regard all nonphysical cures as the stock-in-trade of the quack. Large segments of the medical community still refer to hope cures as placebos, implying that they are ingenuine and as such must be distinguished from the effects of legitimate forms of treatment. A growing list of physicians (e.g., Ader, 1981; Frank, 1968, 1973, 1975; Locke & Colligan, 1986; Menninger, 1959; Pelletier, 1979; Siegel, 1986; Simonton, Matthews-Simonton, & Creighton 1978), however, have argued that hope and positive emotions are integral to all forms of healing and therefore should be enhanced to facilitate more traditional forms of treatment.

From the late 1950s to the 1960s, a number of psychiatrists (e.g., Frank, 1968; Frankl, 1963; Melges & Bowlby, 1969; Menninger 1959; Schachtel, 1959) and psychologists (e.g., Cantril, 1964; Farber, 1968; Mowrer, 1960; Stotland, 1969) addressed the topic of hope in a more formal, scientific manner. While the emphases of these authors differed, they all agreed that hope was a psychological construct worthy of investigation; moreover, these writers shared a definitional perspective in which hope was described as a *positive expectation for goal attainment*. Although the efforts of these early authors seemed promising, their work did not capture the interest of the wider scientific community. This disinterest may have stemmed from investigators' concerns about operationalization, credibility, and the impact that acceptance of psychological processes such as hope might have on the status of their own, unique methods of treatment (Frank, 1968).

Interest in hope, as well as positive emotions, was renewed in the mid-1970s as a result of psychological research and writings related to stress, coping, and illness. Research in this area suggested that negative thoughts and emotions contribute to the development of illness, stifle efforts to cope, interfere with social support, and generally impede medical recovery (see Cohen, 1979; Cohen & Lazarus, 1979, for reviews). Several writers (Cousins, 1976; Frank, 1975; Mason, Clark, Reeves, & Wagner, 1969; Simonton et al., 1978) reasoned that if negative thoughts and emotions could impede recovery, then positive processes

such as hope might promote it. Such reasoning has been supported by empirical work suggesting that enhanced positive self-evaluations and perceptions of control or mastery promote psychological and physical well-being (see Snyder, 1989; Taylor, 1989; Taylor & Brown, 1988, for reviews). (The writings of Norman Vincent Peale [e.g., Peale, 1956] since the 1950s have received widespread popular attention. It was Peale who put the phrase "the power of positive thinking" into the public consciousness.)

The increasing attention paid to positive cognitive and emotional motivational states has led several investigators to develop specific theoretical viewpoints. This chapter reviews theory and research related to a particular positive process—hope—as it relates to health-relevant outcomes. Particular attention is paid to a recent definition of hope posited by Snyder and his colleagues (Snyder, 1989; Snyder et al., 1989), including a discussion of how it differs from other similar conceptualizations. Mechanisms through which hope and other related positive processes may confer their beneficial effects, as well as suggestions for future research, also are presented.

DEFINING HOPE

How is hope defined? And how does the present view of hope differ from previous definitions? Beginning answers to these questions emerge in a story illustrating hope's import in matters of life and death.

Mr. Wright, one of psychologist Bruno Klopfer's clients, was diagnosed with an untreatable cancer that had spread throughout his body. Despite his state of health, Mr. Wright's will to live was strong. He begged to be administered a promising experimental drug named Krebiozen that was currently being given to patients with prognoses more favorable than his own. In response to Mr. Wright's pleas, doctors agreed to give him one injection of the drug. Mr. Wright evidenced fantastic improvement within several days. After 10 days of continued treatment, practically all signs of his disease were gone. Two months later, when conflicting reports of Krebiozen's efficacy began to appear, Mr. Wright's health deteriorated and he relapsed to his original state. Observing his client's timely recovery and relapse, Klopfer decided to see if he could, through the use of a placebo, induce another recovery. After reassuring him that Krebiozen was an effective treatment but that early shipments of the drug had been made ineffective by improper storage, Mr. Wright was administered a "new" shipment of the drug (actually water). To Klopfer's amazement, Mr. Wright responded more dramatically to the placebo than he had to his initial treatment. After 2 symptom-free months, the American Medical Association announced that Krebiozen was indeed worthless in the treatment of cancer. " . . . Within a few days of this report Mr. Wright was readmitted to the hospital in extremis; his faith was now gone, his last hope vanished, and he succumbed in less than two days" (Klopfer, 1957, p. 339). Although there were objective indices taken of the actual progression of the cancer (e.g., radiographs), one obviously cannot infer causality from the apparent correlation between Mr. Wright's states of inflated or deflated hope and his cancer. With this caveat in mind, however, we nevertheless will return to this example later in order to illustrate the components of the hoping process.

Most writers (Cantril, 1964; Erickson, Post, & Paige, 1975; Farber, 1968; Frank, 1968; Frankl, 1963; French, 1952; Gottschalk, 1974; Lewin, 1938; Melges & Bowlby, 1969; Menninger, 1959; Mowrer, 1960; Schachtel, 1959; Stotland, 1969) who have speculated about the composition of the hope process have postulated that it is a unidimensional construct involving an overall perception that goals can be met. According to this view, individuals' behavior can be explained by looking at their expectancies for goal attainment. Individuals exhibiting favorable expectancies are likely to be mentally and physically healthy. Somatic disturbance and psychopathology, on the other hand, are portrayed as being the mark of exceptionally low expectancies for goal attainment (Erickson et al., 1975; Gottschalk, 1974; Melges & Bowlby, 1969).

While these earlier conceptualizations of hope assumed that human beings were goal-directed creatures, they generally did not attempt to explain the means by which goals were pursued. Rather, these earlier views of hope reflected expectancy or value-based theories of behavior, which focus on " . . . what an individual wants or desires rather than what he or she necessarily needs to survive or be healthy" (Lee, Locke, & Latham, 1989, p. 294). While value-based theories are empirically superior to their need-based predecessors in that goals related to the values are generally specified, the predictive power of these theories is weakened by a lack of attention to the strategies individuals use to meet goals (Lee et al., 1989). As such, value-based definitions of hope may tap positive expectations that are based on the somewhat magical belief that "wishing can make it so." In Mr. Wright's case, this perspective suggests that his "will to live," or positive expectation for survival alone, should have succeeded in keeping him alive.

In an expansion of earlier views, Snyder et al.'s (1989) recent analysis of hope draws on goal-setting theory (Lee et al., 1989; Pervin, 1989) in order to emphasize both the individual's desires and the strategies by which those desires are met. In accord with the tenets of goal-setting theory, Snyder and his colleagues (Snyder, 1989; Snyder et al., 1989) propose that there are two major, interrelated ingredients to the hope process. First, it is hypothesized that the hope process is fueled by a sense of successful goal-directed determination (the agency component); second, hope involves a successful sense of planning to meet one's goals (the pathways component). More specifically, hope is defined as a positive motivational state that is based on an interactively derived sense of successful (a) agency (goal-directed energy), and (b) pathways (planning to meet goals).

Although this overall definition of hope emphasizes cognitive factors pertaining to goal-related behaviors, the agency component captures a sense of personal energy and determination and as such may have more emotional manifestations than the pathways component.

Applied to the case of Mr. Wright, this view distinguishes Mr. Wright's will to live (agency) from the ways through which he remained alive (pathways). Mr. Wright's will to live was strong enough to send him searching for possible viable treatment strategies (even in the context of the initial feedback that his cancer was untreatable). The discovery of Krebiozen provided a pathway for Mr. Wright in his goal to fight cancer; in turn, his will to live was enhanced. Thus, one can see how hope's agency and pathways components interacted for Mr. Wright; moreover, this interplay of the components of hope was correlated with improvement in the reported symptoms of Mr. Wright's disease. When his chosen pathway was questioned, however, Mr. Wright's hope withered, and he died shortly thereafter.

Discussion of the present definition of hope would be incomplete without mention of two other recent conceptualizations of this process. In this vein, the most recognized previous measure was developed by Beck and his colleagues (Beck, Weissman, Lester, & Trexler, 1974). Following Stotland's (1969) view of hope as generalized positive expectations about oneself and future outcomes, Beck et al. (1974) theorized a mirrored motive of hopelessness, comprised of negative generalized expectancies about oneself and future outcomes. This Beck et al. conceptualization obviously taps the more negative side of this construct, and as such it has been employed to predict pathological sequelae of hopelessness (e.g., suicide; Beck, Steer, Kovacs, & Garrison, 1985). Generally, the Hopelessness Scale appears to be derived from a medical model (i.e., emphasis on deficiencies or problems in people) rather than a health psychology framework. In comparing the Hopelessness Scale with the Hope Scale, therefore, it should be noted that the latter measurement device evolved out of a health psychology tradition. A second distinction is that the Hopelessness Scale emphasizes a loss of motivation (a giving up response) and the emotional state of the respondent, whereas the Hope Scale emphasizes a cognitive set involving goal-directed behavior with less reference to emotionality.

More recently, Staats and her colleague (Staats, 1987, 1989; Staats & Stassen, 1986) presented hope as a multidimensional construct consisting of cognitive and affective components. These authors have developed individual difference measures of both the affective and cognitive components of hope, based on their belief that "hope refers to future referenced events that are wished for, have positive affect and have some cognitively perceived probability of occurrence" (Staats, 1989, p. 366). Staats' (1987) Expected Balance Scale (EBS) stresses the affective component of hope, which is the difference between expected positive and expected negative affect. The Hope Index stresses the cognitive component of hope, which is defined as the interaction between wishes and expectations (Staats & Stassen, 1986); it taps specific desired circumstances (e.g., "To have good health," or "Understanding by my family").

While Staats and her colleague and Snyder et al. (1989) both view hope as a multidimensional construct, the dimensions described by these authors are different. Hope as defined by Snyder et al. is related to positive affect, but is not synonymous with happiness or contentment. Rather, Snyder et al.'s construct of hope is centered around goal-directed agency and planning. The

EBS (Staats, 1987) is a measure of expected positive affect or happiness, without reference to goal-directed behavior. With its emphasis on expectations, Staats and Stassen's (1986) Hope Index seems to bear greater resemblance to hope as defined by Snyder et al. (1989). However, the Hope Index focuses on wishes and expectations, and ignores strategies by which they are met, hearkening back to earlier, value-based definitions of hope. Thus, Staats and Stassen's construct of hope is similar in name but not in content to the model and measure presented by Snyder et al.

HOPE AND RELATED INDIVIDUAL DIFFERENCES CONSTRUCTS

Hope as defined by Snyder and his colleagues is conceptually related to other constructs emphasizing the importance of individuals' expectancies in mediating goal-directed behavior. In this vein, hope is related to optimism as defined by Scheier and Carver (1985), self-efficacy as outlined by Bandura (1977, 1982, 1986), helplessness as described by Abramson, Seligman, and Teasdale's (1978) attributional revised model, and resourcefulness as developed by Rosenbaum (1980a, 1980b). The construct of psychological hardiness as developed by Kobasa (1979; Kobasi, Maddi, & Kahn, 1982) will not be addressed in this section because it does not lend itself readily to an expectancy analysis; moreover, the conceptualization, components, and underlying explanatory mechanisms of hardiness have been questioned in recent critical analyses (see Carver, 1989; Funk & Houston, 1987; Hull, Van Treuren, & Virnelli, 1987).

While these constructs share an emphasis on expectancies in explaining goal-directed behavior, their interpretations of the processes by which such expectancies operate differ. Similarities and distinctions between hope and these related constructs are outlined in the following discussion.

Optimism

According to Scheier and Carver, optimism refers to a generalized expectancy that good things will happen (1985).

This definition bears a strong similarity to one employed earlier. In this regard, Fibel and Hale (1978) developed the Generalized Expectancy for Success Scale, which they defined as "the expectancy held by an individual that in most situations he/she will be able to attain desired goals" (p. 924). It should be noted that Fibel and Hale evolved their scale from the more general context of Rotter's social learning theory (Rotter, 1954), which emphasized the importance of generalized expectancies (see Lefcourt chapter in this volume for a discussion of another measure—locus of control—that is derived from Rotter's generalized expectancies notion).

This construct is similar to Snyder et al.'s in a number of respects. Both hope and optimism focus on general rather than specific expectancies, and thus have their greatest applicability to problems that are general, novel, ongoing, or multiply determined. When explaining behavior involving specific outcome expectancies, authors of both constructs agree that addressing those specific outcomes may be of greater relevance (e.g., using an index of test anxiety to identify potentially test-anxious student). With their emphasis on general expectancies, hope and optimism are both construed as stable personality traits rather than situation-specific states. Finally, both of these constructs were designed as part of an effort to understand individual differences in goal-directed behavior.

While hope and optimism share an emphasis on the importance of generalized expectancies in predicting goal-directed behavior, they differ in their understanding of how these expectancies operate in this prediction. Scheier and Carver (1985) argued that outcome expectancies (generalized beliefs about the likelihood that a desired outcome will occur) are the most important predictors of goal-directed behavior. Scheier and Carver place little importance, however, on the bases from which these outcome expectancies are derived. In other words, an optimist's anticipation of success could be based on an expectation with little basis in reality (i.e., possessing a rabbit's foot, wishing on a star). Hope, on the other hand, is conceptualized as an iterative process between an efficacy expectancy (a self-belief based on past experience that one can achieve one's goals [i.e., agency]), and an outcome expectancy (the perception of one or more strategies that can be implemented in order to achieve one's goals [i.e., pathways]). In this latter vein, a high-hope person would not be likely to rely exclusively on luck or superstition as a means by which to achieve a goal.

Comparing the models of hope and optimism,

we are reminded of the previous discussion of value-based versus goal-setting approaches to hope. Proponents of value-based theories conceptualized hope as a unidimensional construct involving an overall perception that goals will be met. This is strikingly similar to Scheier and Carver's (1985) view of optimism as a generalized expectancy that good things will happen. Thus, while both hope and optimism are attempts at predicting goal-directed behavior, Carver and Scheier's construct of optimism bears greater resemblance to earlier, value-based views of hope (Cantril, 1964; Erickson et al., 1975; Farber, 1968; Frank, 1968; Frankl, 1963; French, 1952; Gottschalk, 1974; Lewin, 1938; Melges & Bowlby, 1969; Menninger, 1959; Mowrer, 1960; Schachtel, 1959; Stotland, 1969) than to the goal-directed view on which Snyder et al.'s construct is based. As with these earlier views, Scheier and Carver's emphasis on optimists' expectation for good outcome without reference to strategies for achieving such outcomes may limit their model's predictive power.

In fairness to the work of Scheier and Carver, it has been reported in two studies (Scheier, Weintrab, & Carver, 1986) that optimism has correlated positively ($r = .17$, $p < .01$; $r = .14$, $p < .05$) with problem-focused coping as measured by the Ways of Coping Checklist (Folkman & Lazarus, 1980). In this vein, the generalized positive outcome expectancies that are tapped by optimism should at times be accompanied by a sense that one has the appropriate pathways. The magnitudes of the aforementioned correlations suggest, however, that the problem-solving pathways often do not accompany the optimism.

Self-Efficacy

Bandura's theory of self-efficacy (1977, 1982, 1986; see Maddux in this volume), like those of hope and optimism, distinguishes (self-) efficacy expectancies from outcome expectancies in understanding goal-directed behavior. Bandura defines outcome expectancy as a belief that a particular behavior will produce a particular outcome, and efficacy expectancy as the degree of confidence that an individual has in his or her ability to perform a given behavior that will lead to the desired outcome. Unlike theories of hope and optimism, self-efficacy theory views expectancies based on personal efficacy as the most powerful predictors of behavior.

According to Bandura, judgments of self-efficacy are derived from assessments of how well one will perform a particular task in a particular setting. This differs from both Scheier and Carver (1985) and Snyder et al.'s (1989) view that expectancies can operate at many different levels of specificity (ranging from very specific to very general). Specific expectancy models such as self-efficacy theory should be most effective in predicting behavior in distinctive situations. In situations involving generalized expectancies, however, generalized expectancy models such as hope and optimism are likely to be better predictors of behavior.

Both Scheier and Carver (1987) and Snyder et al. are critical of Bandura's reliance on self-efficacy expectancies in understanding goal-directed behavior. According to Scheier and Carver (1987), Bandura's reliance on efficacy rather than outcome expectancies excludes outcomes based on forces beyond the control of the individual (religious faith, luck, interventions from powerful others, etc.), thus ignoring an entire class of goal-directed behavior. Snyder et al. believe that Bandura's focus on efficacy expectancies, as with Scheier and Carver's focus on outcome expectancies, fails to acknowledge that goal-directed behavior is typically a sum of their reciprocal interactions.

Helplessness

The revised attributional model of helplessness also relies on the use of expectancies in explaining human behavior (Abramson et al., 1978; Miller & Norman, 1979; Roth, 1980; Weiner & Litman-Adizes, 1980; see also Burns & Seligman, in this volume). According to Abramson et al. (1978), attributions for good and bad outcomes have an effect on outcome expectancies, which, in turn, affect the decision to engage in behavior. Outcome expectancies can be described in terms of three attributional dimensions: locus of control (internal or external), stability (stable or variable), and generality (specific or global). Within this model, a style of attributing bad outcomes to internal, stable, global factors manifests itself in feelings of helplessness, thereby making an individual more likely to refrain from engaging in behaviors.

An underlying emphasis on outcome expectancies as the final determinants of behavior makes Abramson et al.'s view of helplessness similar to Scheier and Carver's concept of optimism. Despite their emphasis on outcome expectancies, however, Abramson et al. focus on attributions in their discussions. Thus, while helplessness theory relies heavily on outcome expectancies, Abramson et al. generally do not measure or discuss them (Scheier & Carver, 1987).

Resourcefulness

Within the general framework of understanding the self-regulatory behaviors whereby people generate and sustain goal-directed behavior (see Kanfer, 1980; Kanfer & Hagerman, 1981), Rosenbaum (1980a) developed an individual differences measure of resourcefulness. The Self-Control Schedule (Rosenbaum, 1980a) assesses "tendencies to apply self-control methods to the solution of behavioral problems" (Rosenbaum & Palmon, 1984, p. 246). In particular, this scale taps four content areas related to the individual's self-regulatory skills: (a) belief in one's ability to self-regulate cognition and feelings, (b) use of cognition to cope with physical and emotional responses, (c) delaying of immediate gratification, and (d) application of problem-solving strategies.

Although Rosenbaum and his colleagues have not conceptualized their construct in terms of expectancies, their discussion of problem-solving and coping strategies (e.g., content areas b and d above) appears similar to the concept of outcome expectancy; moreover, belief in one's ability to self-regulate cognition and feelings (which Rosenbaum initially described as "perceived self-efficacy" [1980a]), is similar to the concept of efficacy expectancy. Given the emphasis on tapping "tendencies to apply self-control methods to the solution of behavioral problems," however, the resourcefulness construct appears to stress outcome over self-efficacy expectancies. Nevertheless, self-efficacy expectancies are part of this construct and, as such, relative to the previously described optimism, efficacy, and helplessness models, it bears greater similarity to the present model of hope. Likewise, the resourcefulness and hope constructs were both developed from the underlying premise that goal-directed cognitions are important in understanding human motivation. The measure of resourcefulness, however, includes concepts other than those related to goal-directed behavior (e.g., delay of gratification). Furthermore, there is no explication of how the various components of resourcefulness interact or contribute to the overall motivational state.

HOPE SCALE DEVELOPMENT

On the basis of the theoretical model of hope described in this chapter, Harris (1988) constructed an initial version of an individual differences measure of hope. In the first stage of scale development, 45 hope-relevant items were condensed into a reasonably concise and psychometrically sound 14-item index. The original 45 items were reduced by discarding those items that did not evidence high item-remainder coefficients. Seven items tapping goal-directed agency (e.g., "I energetically pursue my goals") and seven items tapping pathways to meet goals (e.g., "I can think of many ways to get out of a jam") were retained in this version of the scale. Four filler items were then added. This initial 14-item version (18 items including the fillers) of the Hope Scale had individual item-remainder coefficients ranging from .31 to .53, and an overall alpha of .71. The 3-week test-retest coefficient for the initial version of the Hope Scale was .86.

In a subsequent stage of scale development, Snyder et al. (1989) shortened the original version of the Hope Scale while retaining both the agency and pathways subcomponents. This later version of the Hope Scale contains eight hope items (four agency and four pathways) and four filler items. Item-remainder coefficients for this version of the scale have ranged from .29 to .53, and the alpha has ranged from .74 to .78 across four separate samples. The test-retest coefficients (8 to 10 weeks) for this version of the scale have ranged from .73 to .82 in three separate samples. In factor analyses (with oblique rotations) of the revised version of the Hope Scale, the four agency items were found to load on one factor, while the four pathways items loaded on a second factor. Thus, the Hope Scale appears to meet the psychometric standards for internal reliability, while also tapping the theorized agency and pathways components.

In an interview study with Lawrence, Kansas, residents, Langelle (1989) explored whether Hope Scale scores were predictive of actual agency and pathways cognitions and behaviors in six life arenas. Results provided strong support for the initial hypothesis that higher hope persons would report more agency and a greater number of pathways in the goal-directed activities of their lives. In order to provide a further test of whether Hope Scale scores predicted actual goal-directed behavior, high- and low-hope college students were asked to imagine themselves in a situation in which they either did or did not face an obstacle to reaching their goal of obtaining a particular course grade (Yoshinobu, 1989). As predicted, the high-hope students produced more responses related to agency and pathways behaviors than the low-hope students. More interestingly, these effects were greatest when an obstacle was introduced. That is, the agency and pathways manifestations of hope were most apparent for the higher hope persons when they faced a problematic situation. A similar point has emerged in research with Rosenbaum's (1980a) measure of resourcefulness in that the hypothesized problem-solving responses are especially elicited under stressful circumstances (Rosenbaum & Ben-Ari, 1985; Rosenbaum & Jaffe, 1983).

To examine the convergent and discriminant validity of the Hope Scale, both the original 14-item and revised 8-item versions were correlated with other individual difference scales. The results reported in the next three paragraphs for the 14- and 8-item versions of the Hope Scale are taken from studies by Harris (1988) and Gibb (1989). With regard to convergent validity, the original 14-item and the revised 8-item scales correlated in the predicted negative direction with the Hopelessness Scale of Beck et al. (1974) ($rs = -.29$ and $-.51$, respectively), and in the predicted positive direction with Scheier and Carver's (1985) measure of optimism ($rs = .65$ and $.60$, respectively). As an index of a positive cognitive set, the Hope Scale was expected to exhibit positive correlations with scales designed to measure positive emotions or attitudes, and negative correlations with scales designed to measure negative emotions or attitudes. As predicted, both the 14- and 8-item Hope Scales were positively correlated with Rosenberg's Self-Esteem Scale (Rosenberg, 1965) ($rs = .56$ and $.58$, respectively). Conversely, the 14- and 8-item versions of the Hope Scale were negatively correlated with trait anxiety ($rs = -.46$ and $-.56$) as measured by the trait form of the State-Trait Anxiety Inventory (STAI: Spielberger, Gorsuch, & Luchene, 1970).

Further convergent validation correlational studies were conducted in order to examine theoretically predicted relationships between hope and (a) desire for control, and (b) problem-solving. The importance of goals and goal-directed behavior in the present definition of hope suggests that it would be related to individuals' perception of their ability to control various outcomes. Therefore, people with higher hope would be expected to evidence greater desire to control the events in their lives and to believe that they have the ability to successfully solve problems they encounter. Consistent with this reasoning, both the 14- and 8-item versions of the Hope Scales were positively correlated with the Desirability of Control Scale (Burger & Cooper, 1979) (rs = .45 and .54, respectively), and with enhanced perceptions of problem-solving ability (rs = .51 and .62) as measured by the Problem-Solving Inventory (Heppner & Petersen, 1982).

In order to establish the discriminant validity of the Hope Scale, it was predicted that scores should not exhibit strong relationships with selected self-report measures. For example, there is no theoretical reason to predict a relationship between self-consciousness and hope. In this vein, self-consciousness as measured by the Self-Consciousness Scale (Fenigstein, Scheier, & Buss, 1975) did not correlate strongly with the 14- and 8-item versions of the Hope Scale (rs = −.11 and −.18, respectively). The more usual indexes against which a new individual differences measure must demonstrate discriminate validity involve social desirability or unrealistically positive self-presentation. In other words, a traditional viewpoint has been that responses on a new self-report scale should not be explicable in terms of favorable self-presentational response styles. Related to this point, higher scores on both the 14- and 8-item versions of the Hope Scale have exhibited small, positive correlations with tendencies to endorse unrealistically positive statements about oneself as measured by the Marlowe-Crowne Social Desirability Scale (Crowne & Marlowe, 1960) (rs = .20 and .30, respectively), and the Self-Presentation Scale (Roth, Harris, & Snyder, 1988; Roth, Snyder, & Pace, 1986) (rs = .26 and .28, respectively).

Because recent work has suggested that negative affect is an underlying variable that explains other motivational variables (e.g., Costa & McCrae, 1987; Clark & Watson, in this volume; Holroyd & Coyne, 1987; Watson & Pennebaker, 1989), and because a recent empirical test of this rival hypothesis revealed that Scheier and Carver's Life Orientation Test of optimism was indistinguishable from measures of neuroticism/negative affectivity (Smith, Pope, Rhodewalt, & Poulton, 1989), one additional study was performed to test the discriminant validity of the Hope Scale relative to measures of negative affectivity. In this latter vein, the relationships of Hope Scale responses to par-

ticular coping responses were examined by partialling out the shared variance related to negative affect. Results showed that the predicted positive correlations of Hope Scales scores with the problem-focused coping, seeking of social support, and focusing on the positive subscales of the Ways of Coping Scale (Folkman & Lazarus, 1980, 1985) remained significant and basically unaltered when the shared variance as related to negative affect (see the STAI in Spielberger et al., 1970, and the Taylor Manifest Anxiety Scale in Taylor, 1953) was removed. Thus, even though hope is theoretically and practically related to less negative affectivity, Hope Scale scores are distinguishable from negative affect.

Data regarding the Hope Scale's convergent validity suggest that, as predicted, the scale is related to the presence of adaptive, positive emotions and attitudes and the relative absence of potentially maladaptive, negative emotions and attitudes. In addition, Hope Scale scores evidence discriminant validity relative to selected other individual differences measures.

HOPE AND HEALTH-RELEVANT OUTCOMES

Hope's relationship to health-relevant outcomes can be studied on a number of levels, including (a) the appraisal process related to hope level and goal-setting, (b) problem-solving, (c) health symptom reporting, and (d) objective health status. This section reviews research focusing on these various levels of analysis in investigating the relationship between hope and health.

Hope, Appraisal, and Goal-Setting

In the 1960s, many researchers (see Lazarus, 1966, 1968; Lazarus, Averill, & Opton, 1970, for reviews) studied the relationship between cognition and stress. They found that the degree of stress associated with any particular event was a function of how that event was perceived by the individual (i.e., appraised). For example, faced with identical situations, one person may respond with anger, another with depression, another with anxiety, and another with the excitement of feeling challenged. According to Lazarus and Launier (1978), person-based factors and situation-based factors affect the appraisal process by influencing whether particular events signal threat, challenge, loss, or pain. As an individual difference variable, hope and its relationship to health-relevant outcomes can be conceptualized as a person-based factor in the process of appraisal.

Properties of stressors that appear to be related to the appraisal of situations as stressful include novelty, predictability, probability of occurrence, imminence, duration, uncertainty about the timing of occurrence, and the timing in relation to the life cycle of the stressor (see Lazarus & Folkman, 1984, for a review). Person factors, such as dispositional differences in hopefulness, are likely to have their greatest influence on the appraisal process when environmental conditions are not clearly defined (Archer, 1979; Lazarus, Erikson, & Fonda, 1951). Conversely, if a group of individuals are aware of the type of stressful event that is going to occur, the likelihood of its occurrence, when it will happen, and how long it will last, the role of individual differences in appraisal and subsequent coping should be minimized.

An individual's belief system appears to play a prominent role in the process of appraisal of ambiguous situations (Lazarus & Folkman, 1984). Beliefs in this sense refer to cognitive configurations or schemas about reality. They serve as a perceptual set. In appraisal, beliefs determine what is considered to be the fact of how things are in the environment. They also shape the meaning of such "facts." Beliefs about hope seem particularly relevant to appraisals of stress because they pertain to whether things will eventually work out in the end. Such beliefs also are likely to affect the perception of a potentially stressful encounter as a challenge or a threat (Folkman & Lazarus, 1985).

Bem's (1970) work provides a useful framework for understanding the role of beliefs in the appraisal process. Bem distinguishes between primitive and higher order beliefs. Primitive beliefs are based on widely held premises about the nature of the universe. They generally are not open to question (e.g., object permanence, object constancy, belief in the Piagetian principle of conservation, etc.). Higher order beliefs come about as a result of inductive reasoning based on specific experiences. With repeated experience of a particular kind, higher order beliefs can develop into primitive beliefs that are generally sustained without reference to specific evidence. In ambiguous situations, such beliefs hold sway.

Stotland (1969) argued that many people develop higher order beliefs that their goals will be achieved. For certain hopeful individuals who encounter repeated success, these higher order beliefs about goal attainment come to have an increasingly wider range of applicability. Eventually, separate higher order beliefs related to hope may merge into a primitive belief system about goal attainment. When faced with ambiguous situations, hopeful people are thought to invoke broad-based, primitive beliefs that their goals will be achieved. These beliefs are likely to influence them to appraise the ongoing flow of events in generally positive terms.

High hope individuals' appraisal of situations in generally positive terms may be related to their assessment of stressful situations as challenging rather than threatening. Hopeful people may be more likely to engage in what Lazarus and his colleagues refer to as "challenge" appraisal. According to Lazarus and Launier (1978), some individuals can be characterized by a style of thinking that disposes them to view potentially stressful situations in terms of challenge rather than threat (Folkman & Lazarus, 1985; Lazarus & Folkman, 1984; Lazarus & Launier, 1978; McCrae, 1984). The distinction between challenge and threat appraisals was summarized by Lazarus and Launier (1978) as follows: "The difference seems to be a matter of positive versus negative tone, that is whether one emphasizes in the appraisal the potential harm in the transaction (threat), or the difficult-to-attain, possibly risky, but positive mastery or gain (challenge)" (p. 304).

Lazarus and Launier (1978) argue that challenge and threat appraisal lead to different kinds of coping behavior. This argument was supported by McCrae (1984), who found that appraisals of threat were associated with the use of faith, fatalism, and wishful thinking—all mechanisms of coping designed to reduce anxiety by reconstruing the event or its likely outcome. Challenge appraisals, on the other hand, were associated with more vigorous and diverse coping strategies such as rational action, perseverance, positive thinking, intellectual denial, restraint, self-adaptation, drawing strength from adversity, and humor.

A subsequent study by Folkman and Lazarus (1985) investigated the relationship between appraisal and coping with a prospective design in which appraisals were assessed before an upcoming stressful event (i.e., a midterm exam). They found that threat appraisals were associated with wishful thinking and attempts to garner social support. Challenge appraisals, on the other hand, were associated with problem-focused coping and self-isolation (e.g., "avoid being with people"). Results suggest that those who view situations as challenging tend to focus on rational planning and action.

In a 1988 dissertation, Anderson hypothesized that individuals with high as compared with lower levels of hope as measured by the Hope Scale would be more likely to view personal goals in positive and challenging terms, focusing on the potential for gain. Hypotheses were tested by assessing threat and challenge cognitions and emotions pertaining to 1-month and 6-month goals formulated by subjects who were classified in terms of their level of hope (high, medium, and low). Goals were set by subjects in each of four life domains (work and school, primary family life, intimate relationships, and personal changes and development).

High hope subjects were found to focus more of their attention on the consequences of success and to estimate a greater probability of success than subjects in the low hope group. These findings occurred for both 1-month and 6-month goals. By expecting success and focusing on its consequences, individuals with high hope may actually improve their chances of success by promoting positive affective states that are associated with a greater degree of behavioral persistence and organized action (French, 1952; Greenwald, 1980; Lewinsohn, Mischel, Chaplin, & Barton, 1980; Stotland, 1969; Taylor, 1983).

Support for the relationship between affective states, dispositional hopefulness, and goal-striving also has been provided by Anderson (1988). The author assessed positive and negative feelings in subjects as they visualized striving toward 1-month and 6-month goals. Higher levels of dispositional hopefulness as measured by the Hope Scale were associated with more positive feelings about goals. At the same time, hopefulness was largely unrelated to negative feelings about goals.

Cognitive theory of emotion asserts that the quality and intensity of any emotion is generated by its own particular appraisal (Beck, 1971; Ellis, 1962; Lazarus, Kanner, & Folkman, 1980; Lazarus & Launier, 1978; Weiner, Graham, & Chandler, 1982). For example, an appraisal of challenge might evoke eagerness or excitement whereas an appraisal of threat might evoke foreboding or worry. Based on these cognitive assumptions, the findings of Anderson (1988) suggest that appraisals made by individuals who differ in level of dispositional hopefulness do not

fall along a simple continuum with positive appraisals of high-hope individuals at one end and negative appraisals of low-hope individuals at the other. As far as the present construct of hope as it relates to goal-setting is concerned, what appears to matter most is the amount of positive rather than negative feelings connected with appraisals. This distinction has significant implications for how hope is conceptualized.

Hope's association with appraisals producing positive feelings and its lack of association with appraisals producing negative feelings suggests an orientation of energy, eagerness, and vibrancy that should not be defined solely in terms of a lack of negativism. Thus, one cannot fully appreciate the concept of hope by speaking in terms of an "absence of negativism." Obviously, many previous researchers have focused on constructs involving pathological rather than healthy processes. As such, scales measuring depression (Beck, 1967) and hopelessness (Beck et al., 1974) may have a restricted or different range of measurement because of their emphasis on negative or pathological conditions. According to Beck and his colleagues, for example, hopelessness is derived from the activation of specific cognitive schemas that produce intensely negative feelings. However, the findings of Anderson (1988) indicate that negative feelings do not fully capture the present conceptualization of hope as it relates to goal-setting. Rather, hopefulness may refer to cognitive style that cannot be explained only in terms of the absence of depression or negative affect.

Hope and Problem-Solving

The tendency of individuals with high hope to experience positive affect when considering their goals has potential implications for the manner in which they approach problem-solving. Isen, Daubman, and Norwicki (1987) conducted four experiments in which positive affect improved performance on tasks that are generally regarded as requiring creative ingenuity: Duncker's (1945) candle task, and Mednick, Mednick, and Mednick's (1964) Remote Associates Test. The authors argue that positive appraisals may promote creative problem-solving by fostering a complex cognitive context. That is, positive appraisals may facilitate either seeing more aspects of objects or concepts, or seeing objects or concepts more fully, including their potential for combination with other objects or concepts related to the problem at hand.

Given the findings of Isen et al. (1987), it follows that hopeful people may be more successful in accomplishing their goals because of their tendency to make appraisals that produce positive affect, which, in turn, creates a complex cognitive context. A complex context in hopeful people might arise from the fact that positive feelings facilitate access to positive material in memory (e.g., Isen, Shalker, Clark, & Karp, 1978; Teasdale & Fogarty, 1979), and positive material in memory is more extensive and diverse than other material (e.g., Boucher & Osgood, 1969). Complexity of context has been specifically related to originality of word associations (Cramer, 1968) and to a relaxing or broadening of focus of attention (Martindale, 1981). Furthermore, Isen et al. (1987) argue that the presence of a complex cognitive context may cause many features of items and problems to become salient, so that more possibilities for solution can be seen. Thus, the fact that higher hope persons perceive themselves as being better at problem-solving, as we have discussed previously in this chapter (e.g., Gibb, 1989), may be related to an affectively positive and cognitively complex appraisal process.

Hope, Life Stress, and Reported Health Symptoms

Until now, we have been discussing mediators (e.g., challenge appraisals and problem-solving) of the relationship between hope and health-relevant outcomes. This relationship also can be addressed in studies of hope, life stress, and symptom reporting.

The impact of common stressors on health has been documented in a substantial body of research that demonstrates that events such as loss of work, divorce, or birth of a child affect the incidence of physical illness (e.g., Dohrenwend & Dohrenwend, 1974; Mechanic, 1974; Sarason, Johnson, & Siegel, 1978) and emotional disturbance (e.g., Dekker & Webb, 1974; Markush & Favero, 1974; Warheit, 1979). Although numerous clinical studies have found that lack or loss of hope is related to the onset of disease (Schmale, 1958), fatal illness (Green, Young, & Swisher, 1956; Kübler-Ross, 1969; LeShan, 1961), suicide (Beck et al., 1985; Farber, 1968), and depression (Beck, Ruch, Shaw, & Emery, 1979), only two studies (Anderson, 1988; Scheier & Carver, 1985)

have focused specifically on the relationship between positive cognitive sets, stress, and health symptoms.

Scheier and Carver (1985) used their measure of optimism (the LOT) to study a group of college students during the final 4 weeks of an academic semester. Subjects completed the LOT and a physical symptom checklist at the outset of the study and 4 weeks later. Optimism was negatively associated with symptom-reporting at both assessment periods. Additionally, persons who reported being optimistic at the start of the study reported fewer symptoms 4 weeks later. The relationship between optimism and symptom-reporting remained significant even after the association between optimism and symptom-reporting at the time of the initial assessment was partialled out. The authors appropriately interpreted their results with caution. They pointed out that optimism may have had an effect on the level of symptoms reported, but not on the level of symptoms experienced. Rather than experiencing better health, optimists may tend to "put a happy face" on underlying physical states.

Reverse causality is another reason to interpret Scheier and Carver's (1985) findings with caution. Does physical well-being lead to optimism over time, or does an optimistic outlook lead to reports of heightened physical well-being? Scheier and Carver found that variations in health did not seem to lead to changes in optimism over time. However, the health index used in their study assessed minor physical symptoms, and it remains uncertain as to whether more extreme variations in health might produce similar effects. The onset of major health problems might induce changes in one's level of optimism, whereas variations in minor physical symptoms may not.

In a similar prospective design, Anderson (1988) investigated the ability of hope and optimism to moderate the impact of stressful life events on mental and physical symptom reports. Initially, subjects completed questionnaires assessing individual differences in hope, optimism and stressful life events. Ten weeks later, subjects completed mental and physical health symptom checklists. In a stepwise multiple regression analysis, mental and physical symptoms were regressed on stressful life events followed by the variables of hope and optimism. The unique contributions of hope and optimism were assessed by altering their order of entry in the regression equation.

As expected, life stress was positively related to

increasing reports of physical symptoms. Hope and optimism, however, were negligibly related to physical symptom-reporting, contributing little beyond that of life stress alone. The author speculated that the college sample may have been too young and healthy for hope or optimism to play a coping role in physical health. Anderson argued that hope and optimism may play greater roles in older samples exhibiting greater variation in physical health symptoms in response to stress.

Hope and optimism evidenced stronger relationships with reports of mental than physical health symptoms. Both hope and optimism accounted for a significant amount of the variation in mental health symptoms above and beyond life stress alone. Contrary to predictions, however, neither hope nor optimism were found to serve as moderators between life stress and mental health symptoms. In other words, subjects with higher levels of stress experienced more mental health symptoms regardless of their level of dispositional hope or optimism. The author suggested that hope and optimism may operate as moderators only in cases where an individual experiences relatively high levels of negative life stress.

In additional multiple regression analyses, Anderson (1988) attempted to determine the significance of the relative contributions of hope, optimism, and locus of control in predicting mental health symptoms. Results revealed that neither optimism nor locus of control (Rotter, 1966) scores significantly enhanced the prediction of mental health symptoms beyond the level of prediction obtained by life stress and hope scores. Results also showed that hope scores significantly enhanced the prediction of mental health symptoms beyond the level of prediction obtained by life stress and optimism or life stress and locus of control scores. Additionally, Anderson found that hope scores significantly enhanced prediction of mental health symptoms beyond the level of prediction achieved by optimism scores, locus of control scores, and the combination of optimism and locus of control scores. Thus, hope as measured by the Hope Scale appears to explain variance in mental health symptoms that cannot be explained by life stress, optimism, or locus of control.

Hope and Objective Health

Most studies addressing the relationship between positive emotional states and health have relied on subjective symptom reports and relatively "well" college populations. Subjective symptom reports have been criticized, however, on the grounds that they exhibit negligible correlations with indices of objective health status (Costa & McCrae, 1985, 1987). The minimal variation observed in college populations' symptom reports, as well as the restricted generalizability of their data, also limit their utility. The more valid, direct way of assessing hope's relationship to health-relevant outcomes is through studies of the objective health status of mentally or physically ill populations.

Objective Mental Health

In 1969, Melges and Bowlby suggested that hopelessness, "a feeling that the future holds little promise," plays an important role in many psychopathological conditions. Melges and Bowlby went on to describe distinct types of hopelessness associated with depressive and sociopathic disturbances. While not backed by empirical data, their theoretical argument did provide a valuable source of hypotheses for others' research in this area (Gottschalk, 1974; Obayuwana, Collins, Carter, Rao, Mathur, & Wilson, 1982).

In studies comparing nonpatient adults with acute schizophrenics (Gottschalk, 1974), general psychiatric populations (Erickson et al., 1975; Obayuwana et al., 1982), and outpatient crisis center clients (Gottschalk, 1974), hope (measured in various ways) was found to be inversely related to psychiatric morbidity. While Erickson et al. (1975) did not find hopefulness to significantly distinguish patients with different diagnoses, Obayuwana et al. (1982) did find patients attempting suicide to evidence lower levels of hope than nonsuicidal depressed patients. These latter authors concluded that hopelessness may be more important than depression in determining the severity of a patient's suicidal intent (see also Beck et al., 1985).

Two of these studies (Erickson et al., 1975; Gottschalk, 1974) examined the relationship between hope and treatment for psychiatric disturbance. Among crisis center clients, pretreatment levels of hope were found to be significant predictors of patient improvement, as well as being inversely related to psychiatric morbidity among clients receiving treatment (Gottschalk, 1974). Among acute schizophrenics, levels of hope improved significantly after receiving the drug thioridazine. In addition, the greater schizophrenics' predrug hope scores, the greater the drop in their postthioridazine depression scores. Erickson et al. (1975) found that the pretreatment levels of hope among psychiatric patients at a Veterans' Administration hospital improved following treatment. Patients' posttreatment levels of hope were similar to those found in a college student population.

These studies provide important evidence of hope's facilitative role in mental health, but are limited by their often ambiguous definitions and measurements of hope (e.g., Gottschalk measures hope via a content analysis of a 5-minute speech sample, and defines hope as "measure of optimism that a favorable outcome is likely to occur, not only in one's personal earthly activities but also in cosmic phenomena and even in spiritual or imaginary events" [p. 779]; Obayuwana et al. define hope as " . . . the state of mind which results from the positive outcome of ego strength, perceived family support, religion, education, and economic assets" [p. 761]). These studies also suffer from a lack of statistical and methodological rigor. The use of a reliable, valid index of hope in these populations will increase our understanding of the beneficial effects of hope as it relates to psychological health.

Work with Scheier and Carver's optimism measure has already yielded useful results in this regard. First, optimism scores during pregnancy were related to less postpartum depression (controlling for initial levels of depression) (Carver & Gaines, 1987). Second, Strack, Carver, and Blaney (1987) found that optimism scores predicted completion of an alcohol treatment program. It also should be noted that work with Rosenbaum's (1980a) measure of resourcefulness has produced results related to indices of psychological health. For example, higher resourcefulness scores have been found to be related to (a) tolerance of laboratory-produced pain (Rosenbaum (1980b) and actual clinical pain (Courey, Feuerstein, & Bush, 1982); (b) coping with seasickness (Rosenbaum & Rolnick, 1983); (c) success at weight reduction (Smith, 1979); (d) control of nail biting (Frankel & Merbaum, 1982); and (e) improvement following cognitive behavior therapy as compared with pharmacotherapy (Simons, Lustman, Wetzel, & Murphy, 1985).

Objective Physical Health

Although the potential health benefits of positive emotions are often discussed in the health psychology literature (e.g., Cohen & Lazarus, 1979; Lazarus & Folkman, 1984), the available

research on the relationship of hope-related variables to physical health is sparse.

Scheier et al. (1990) examined the beneficial effects of dispositional optimism on the physical and psychological well-being of middle-aged men undergoing coronary artery bypass surgery. Dispositional optimism was associated with a faster rate of physical recovery during hospitalization, a faster rate of return to normal life activities after discharge, and reports of better quality of life 6 months after surgery. While this study provides support for the beneficial impact that dispositional positive motivational states can have on health, in the future it also will be important to assess the interaction between individual differences in motivation (e.g., hope, optimism) and treatment interventions. Such person-by-treatment interactions may yield useful benefits for various physical problems.

HOPE FOR THE FUTURE

Individual differences in hope may operate in a variety of arenas related to physical and psychological well-being. In this section, we briefly explore one example from each of these arenas. In regard to a physical issue, the role of hope in cancer will be examined; in regard to a psychological issue, the role of hope in psychotherapy will be discussed.

Hope and Cancer

Cancer is perceived by the population at large to be a "hopeless" disease. For many, cancer is synonymous with death. This ominous reputation stems in part from the public's lack of knowledge about the nature of cancer. Seen as a uniform, fatal disease, cancer is in reality a host of diseases, each with a somewhat different etiology, course, treatment, and prognosis. Improvements in cancer detection and treatment have increased the odds of surviving it, and current statistics suggest that approximately 50% of all serious cancers can be cured (Bloch & Bloch, 1985). Cancer's frightening reputation persists, however, despite such statistics.

Researchers' tendency to focus on pathological emotional aspects of cancer may be another reason for its continued unsavory reputation. Investigators steeped in medical or psychoanalytic traditions have relied on negative constructs in understanding how individuals cope with and respond to their disease. References to constructs such as hopelessness, repression, and denial are much more common in the cancer literature than are references to positive motivational states such as hope.

Dissatisfied with the negative bias of existing literature, a number of individuals have written books and instigated treatment and support programs that focus on the role of positive motives and emotions in cancer recovery and prevention (Bloch & Bloch, 1981, 1985; Siegel, 1986; Simonton et al., 1978). While research scientists have criticized these writers for going beyond the available data in describing the facilitative role of positive mental states in cancer, their impact on research and writing in this field cannot be denied.

According to Levy (1983), emotional factors such as hope may play one of two roles in the process of carcinogenesis: the role of an independent variable contributing to the progression of tumor growth, or the role of a dependent variable resulting from the disease of cancer or from aggressive cancer treatment. To date, the focus of research generally has been on emotions rather than hope per se. In this vein, emotion's role as an independent variable has been addressed in longitudinal and other prospective studies linking certain personality characteristics or types with the occurrence of cancer (Eysenck, 1988; Grossarth-Maticek, Bastiaans, & Kanazir, 1985; Kissen, 1967; LeShan, 1961; Persky, Kempthorne-Rawson, & Shekelle, 1987; Shaffer, Graves, Swank, & Pearson, 1987). Emotional states have been assessed as dependent, postdiagnostic variables in studies of emotional reactions and coping strategies evidenced among cancer patients (Derogatis, Abeloff, Melisaratos, 1979; Eysenck, 1988; Jensen, 1987; Marks, Richardson, Graham, & Levine, 1986; Meyerowitz, 1983; Orr, 1986; Pettingale, 1984; Taylor, Lichtman, & Wood, 1984; Timko & Janoff-Bulman, 1985; Zemore & Shepel, 1987). In turn, these postdiagnostic variables have been used as predictors of patients' psychological and physical adjustment to cancer.

Longitudinal and other prospective studies suggest that suppression of emotion (Eysenck, 1988; Grossarth-Maticek et al., 1985; Kissen, 1967; Shaffer et al., 1987), inability to cope with stress (Eysenck, 1988), and feelings of hopelessness or helplessness (Grossarth-Maticek et al., 1985; Schmale & Iker, 1966, 1971; Eysenck, 1988) are associated with later diagnoses of cancer. While

the psychometric rigor of these studies has been challenged (see Stam & Steggles, 1987, for a review), the consistency of their findings should be acknowledged.

Investigations of emotional reactions among individuals who have been diagnosed with cancer also have produced consistent results. A highly emotional, "acting out" response to a diagnosis of cancer has been associated with increased rates of survival among breast cancer patients (Derogatis et al., 1979; Pettingale, 1984). Conversely, hopelessness/helplessness, stoicism, and negative affect have been associated with continued neoplastic spread after the initial diagnosis (Jensen, 1987; Pettingale, 1984). Personality descriptions of individuals evidencing poorer rates of survival thus appear to be similar to those of individuals at greater risk for initial development of cancer (Eysenck, 1988).

Postdiagnostic coping strategies have been explored through attributional (Taylor et al., 1984; Timko & Janoff-Bulman, 1985), control (Marks et al., 1986), denial (Meyerowitz, 1983), and information seeking (Orr, 1986; Zemore & Shepel, 1987) paradigms. Taken together, these studies suggest that a realistic, hopeful assessment of the threat of disease, and a belief in one's ability to cope with the disease with the help of external sources (medical professionals, significant others, or appropriate information) are related to better social and emotional adjustment among cancer patients. Characterological self-blame, and the belief the future outcomes are out of one's control, are related to poorer adjustment.

Just as cancer is perceived as a hopeless disease, it appears that its onset and progression have become associated with a hopeless personality profile. While the findings of authors studying emotional precursors to and consequences of cancer are fascinating, their focus on psychopathological factors serves to perpetuate cancer's dark, hopeless image. Critics of these studies argue that the inclusion of personality as a risk factor will result in "victim blaming," or placing more responsibility on the shoulders of cancer patients who are already suffering a great deal (Stam & Steggles, 1987).

But the findings of these authors need not be interpreted in a psychopathological light. While currently framed in negative terms, they can be reframed positively. If hopelessness is hurtful, perhaps the inclusion of hopefulness in discussion of detection, prevention, and treatment of cancer can be helpful. The research reviewed in this chapter suggests that high hope individuals exhibit some of the same cognitive, emotional, and attitudinal attributes as do people who are successful in avoiding cancer, or who evidence greater emotional and social adjustment following a diagnosis of cancer. Finding cancer patients "guilty" of hopelessness may appropriately be labeled as victim-blaming. Encouraging them to mobilize their resources in order to identify strategies for improving the quantity or quality of their life, however, is empowering. Individual differences measures such as the Hope Scale may help in the unraveling of the person-based forces that operate in the etiology and treatment of cancer. In a similar vein, the Hope Scale may contribute to our understanding of person-based forces involved in the development and treatment of other physical illnesses.

Hope and Psychotherapy

Studies of the effectiveness of psychological treatment have focused on two components of this process: a nonspecific treatment factor (sometimes called placebo) and a specific treatment factor. Through meta-analysis, researchers have attempted to examine the relative effectiveness of nonspecific and specific treatments to no treatment control groups, as well as to each other (i.e., nonspecific vs. specific treatments) (see Landman & Dawes, 1982; Prioleau, Murdock, & Brody, 1983; Shapiro & Shapiro, 1982; Smith & Glass, 1977). Results of these meta-analyses are consistent in their finding that specific treatment produces a more favorable outcome than participation in either no treatment control or nonspecific factors groups. These results have been interpreted to mean that both the presence of generalized positive expectations for improvement (in the form of specific or nonspecific treatment) (Frank, 1973; Frank, Hoehn-Saric, Imber, Liberman, & Stone, 1978; Kazdin, 1980), and provision of a strategy for improvement (specific treatment alone) are necessary in order for psychotherapy to have its intended effect. In the context of this chapter, the parallels between this interpretation of the psychotherapy process and hope's agency and pathways components are obvious.

While appealing in its efficiency and applicability to the hope model, this interpretation of results is not without problems. Previous meta-analyses of psychotherapy's effectiveness have failed to asscertain that the nonspecific factors groups exhibited levels of positive expectations for improvement comparable with those evidenced by specific treatment groups. This failure to verify what is assumed to be a central or defining characteristic of nonspecific factors groups (i.e., a positive expectation for improvement in the absence of a treatment strategy) makes the unequivocal interpretation of results tenuous.

Responding to this criticism, Barker, Funk, and Houston (1988) conducted a meta-analysis evaluating treatment studies in which expectations for improvement between specific and nonspecific factors conditions had been shown to be comparable. Consistent with previous meta-analyses, Barker et al. found that the nonspecific factors group exhibited a significantly improved psychotherapy outcome relative to the no treatment control group; and that the treatment group exhibited significant improvement relative to the nonspecific factors group. Additionally, the magnitude of the improvement for the treatment group relative to the no treatment group was twice that exhibited by the nonspecific factors group. Using the hope model as a framework through which to interpret these results, the nonspecific factors group can be seen as reflecting hope's agency component, and the treatment group can be seen to reflect the reciprocal workings of hope's agency and pathways components. The results suggest that a sense of agency improves psychological functioning, and that the additional sense of pathways doubles this improvement.

Our point in using the hope construct to understand the psychotherapy process is not to suggest that there is only one way to engender a sense of agency or pathways in helping people. On the contrary, we believe that there are innumerable ways through which to help clients build their sense of personal efficacy (agency) and arsenal of strategies (pathways) for coping with problems. The enormous literature on psychological treatment provides a plethora of approaches, each of which may work for certain people. As such, an individual differences measure such as the Hope Scale may facilitate answers to important applied questions. For example, do high- as compared with low-hope persons handle their stressors differently? Would low-hope persons evidence particular benefits as a result of interventions aimed at both agency and pathways? How do the person variable of hope and the situation variable of treatment interact?

CONCLUSION

According to the old maxim, "Where there's a will, there's a way." Sometimes this is true, but the underlying premise of the theory and individual differences measure described in this chapter is that both components must be studied in order to discover the full meaning of the hope concept. Neither component alone may be sufficient. For example, has the reader ever experienced a strong sense of goal-directed determination (agency), only to find that a strategy (pathway) for pursuing the goal seemed lacking? Or, the pathway may be evident, but the agency may be nonexistent. Having made this case for the necessity of both components, however, it should be acknowledged that the most effective way to ignite hope may be to concentrate on one of the components. How long, for example, can the goal-energized person refrain from not finding a pathway? Similarly, a person who suddenly finds a pathway to a goal may then feel a surge of determination and energy. It is this reciprocal relationship of the will and the way that defines the essence of hoping. As such, hope is one important wellspring by which we nourish our psychological and physical health. To turn a twist on Terence's line cited at the beginning of this chapter, "While there's hope, there's life."

REFERENCES

Abramson, L. Y., Seligman, M. E. P., & Teasdale, J. D. (1978). Learned helplessness in humans: Critique and reformulation. *Journal of Abnormal Psychology, 87*, 49–74.

Ader, R. (1981). *Psychoneuroimmunology*. New York: Academic Press.

Anderson, J. R. (1988). *The role of hope in appraisal, goal-setting, expectancy, and coping*. Doctoral dissertation. University of Kansas, Lawrence, Kansas.

Archer, R. P. (1979). Relationships between locus of control, trait anxiety, and state anxiety: An interactionist perspective. *Journal of Personality, 47*, 305–316.

Bandura, A. (1977). Self-efficacy: Toward a unifying theory of behavior change. *Psychological Review, 84*, 191–215.

Bandura, A. (1982). Self-efficacy mechanism in human agency. *American Psychologist, 37*, 122–147.

Bandura, A. (1986). *Social foundations of thought and action: A social cognitive theory*. Englewood Cliffs, NJ: Prentice-Hall.

Barker, S. L., Funk, S. C., & Houston, B. K. (1988). Psychological treatment versus nonspecific factors: A meta-analysis of conditions that engender comparable expectations for improvement. *Clinical Psychology Review, 8*, 579–594.

Beck, A. T. (1967). *Depression: Clinical, experimental, and theoretical aspects*. New York: Hoebner Medical Division, Harper & Row.

Beck, A. T. (1971). Cognition, affect, and psychopathology. *Archives of General Psychiatry, 24*, 495–500.

Beck, A. T., Ruch, A. J., Shaw, B. F., & Emery, G. (1979). *Cognitive therapy of depression*. New York: Guilford Press.

Beck, A. T., Steer, R. A., Kovacs, M., & Garrison, B. (1985). Hopelessness and eventual suicide: A 10-year prospective study of patients hospitalized with suicidal ideation. *American Journal of Psychiatry, 142*, 559–563.

Beck, A. T., Weissman, A., Lester, D., & Trexler, L. (1974). The measurement of pessimism: The hopelessness scale. *Journal of Clinical and Consulting Psychology, 42*, 861–865.

Bem, D. J. (1970). *Beliefs, attitudes and human affairs*. Belmont, CA: Brooks/Cole.

Bloch, A., & Bloch, R. (1985). *Fighting cancer*. Kansas City, MO: Cancer Connection, Inc.

Bloch, R., & Bloch, A. (1981). *Cancer . . . there's hope*. Kansas City, MO: Cancer Connection, Inc.

Boucher, J., & Osgood, C. E. (1969). The Pollyanna hypothesis. *Journal of Verbal Learning and Verbal Behavior, 8*, 1–8.

Burger, J. M., & Cooper, H. M. (1979). The desirability of control. *Motivation and Emotion, 3*, 381–393.

Cantril, H. (1964). The human design. *Journal of Individual Psychology, 20*, 129–136.

Carver, C. S. (1989). How should multifaceted personality constructs be tested? Issues illustrated by self-monitoring, attributional style, and hardiness. *Journal of Personality and Social Psychology, 56*, 577–585.

Carver, C. S., & Gaines, J. G. (1987). Optimism, pessimism, and postpartum depression. *Cognitive Therapy and Research, 11*, 449–462.

Cohen, F. (1979). Personality, stress, and the development of physical illness. In G. C. Stone, F. Cohen, & N. Adler (Eds.), *Health psychology: A handbook* (pp. 77–111). San Francisco: Jossey-Bass.

Cohen, F., & Lazarus, R. S. (1979). Coping with the stresses of illness. In G. C. Stone, F. Cohen, & N. Adler (Eds.), *Health psychology: A handbook* (pp. 217–254). San Francisco: Jossey-Bass.

Costa, P. T., Jr., & McCrae, R. R. (1985). Hypochondriasis, neuroticism, and aging: When are somatic complaints unfounded? *American Psychologist, 40*, 19–28.

Costa, P. T., Jr., & McCrae, R. R. (1987). Neuroticism, somatic complaints, and disease: Is the bark worse than the bite? *Journal of Personality, 55*, 299–316.

Courey, L., Feuerstein, M., & Bush, C. (1982). Self-control and chronic headache. *Journal of Psychosomatic Research, 26*, 519–526.

Cousins, N. (1976). Anatomy of an illness (as perceived by the patient). *New England Journal of Medicine, 295*, 1458–1463.

Cramer, P. (1968). *Word association.* New York: Academic Press.

Crowne, D. P., & Marlowe, D. (1960). A new scale of social desirability independent of psychopathology. *Journal of Consulting and Clinical Psychology, 24*, 349–354.

Dekker, D., & Webb, J. (1974). Relationships of the social readjustment rating scale to psychiatric patient status, anxiety, and social desirability. *Journal of Psychosomatic Research, 18*, 125–130.

Derogatis, L. R., Abeloff, M. D., & Melisaratos, N. (1979). Psychological coping mechanisms and survival time in metastatic breast cancer. *Journal of the American Medical Association, 242*, 1504–1508.

Dohrenwend, B. S., & Dohrenwend, B. P. (1974). *Stressful life events: Their nature and effects.* New York: John Wiley & Sons.

Duncker, K. (1945). On problem solving. *Psychological Monographs, 58*, (5, Whole No. 270).

Ellis, A. (1962). *Reason and emotion in psychotherapy.* New York: Lyle Stuart.

Erickson, R. C., Post, R., & Paige, A. (1975). Hope as a psychiatric variable. *Journal of Clinical Psychology, 31*, 324–329.

Eysenck, H. J. (1988, December). Health's character. *Psychology Today*, pp. 28–35.

Farber, M. L. (1968). *Theory of suicide.* New York: Funk & Wagnall's.

Fenigstein, A., Scheier, M. F., & Buss, A. H. (1975). Public and private self-consciousness: Assessment and theory. *Journal of Consulting and Clinical Psychology, 43*, 522–527.

Fibel, B., & Hale, W. D. (1978). The generalized expectancy for success scale—A new measure. *Journal of Consulting and Clinical Psychology, 46*, 924–931.

Folkman, S., & Lazarus, R. S. (1980). An analysis of coping in a middle-aged community sample. *Journal of Health and Social Behavior, 21*, 219–239.

Folkman, S., & Lazarus, R. S. (1985). If it changes it must be a process: Study of emotion and coping during three stages of a college examination. *Journal of Personality and Social Psychology, 48*, 150–170.

Frank, J. D. (1968). The role of hope in psychotherapy. *International Journal of Psychiatry, 5*, 383–395.

Frank, J. D. (1973). *Persuasion and healing* (rev. ed.). Baltimore, MD: Johns Hopkins University Press.

Frank, J. D. (1975). The faith that heals. *The Johns Hopkins Medical Journal, 137*, 127–131.

Frank, J. D., Hoehn-Saric, R., Imber, S. D., Liberman, B. L., & Stone, A. R. (1978). *Effective ingredients of successful psychotherapy.* New York: Brunner/Mazel.

Frankel, M. J., & Merbaum, M. (1982). Effects of therapist contact and a self-control manual on nailbiting reduction. *Behavior Therapy, 13*, 125–129.

Frankl, V. (1963). *Man's search for meaning.* New York: Washington Square Press.

French, T. M. (1952). *The integration of behavior: Vol. 1. Basic postulates.* Chicago: University of Chicago Press.

Funk, S. C., & Houston, B. K. (1987). A critical analysis of the hardiness scale's validity and utility. *Journal of Personality and Social Psychology, 53*, 572–578.

Gibb, J. (1989). *The relationship of hope to problem-solving and coping.* Unpublished thesis in progress. University of Illinois, Champaign.

Gottschalk, L. A. (1974). A hope scale applicable to verbal samples. *Archives of General Psychiatry, 30*, 779–785.

Green, W. A., Jr., Young, L., & Swisher, S. N. (1956). Psychological factors and reticuloendothelial disease: II. Observations on a group of women with lymphomas and leukemia. *Psychosomatic Medicine, 18*, 284–303.

Greenwald, A. G. (1980). The totalitarian ego: Fabrication and revision of personal history. *American Psychologist, 35*, 603–618.

Grossarth-Maticek, R., Bastiaans, J., & Kanazir,

D. T. (1985). Psychosocial factors as strong predictors of mortality from cancer, ischaemic heart disease and stroke: The Yugoslav prospective study. *Journal of Psychosomatic Research, 29*, 167–176.

Harris, C. B. (1988). *Hope: Construct definition and the development of an individual differences scale*. Doctoral dissertation, University of Kansas, Lawrence, Kansas.

Heppner, P. P., & Petersen, C. H. (1982). The development and implications of a personal problem-solving inventory. *Journal of Counseling Psychology, 29*, 66–75.

Holroyd, K. A., & Coyne, J. (1987). Personality and health in the 1980s: Psychosomatic medicine revisited? *Journal of Personality, 55*, 359–375.

Hull, J. G., Van Treuren, R. R., & Virnelli, S. (1987). Hardiness and health: A critique and alternative approach. *Journal of Personality and Social Psychology, 53*, 518–530.

Isen, A. M., Daubman, K. A., & Nowicki, G. P. (1987). Positive affect facilitates creative problem-solving. *Journal of Personality and Social Psychology, 52*, 1122–1131.

Isen, A. M., Shalker, T. E., Clark, M., & Karp, L. (1978). Affect, accessibility of material in memory, and behavior: A cognitive loop? *Journal of Personality and Social Psychology, 36*, 1–12.

Jensen, M. R. (1987). Psychobiological factors predicting the course of breast cancer. *Journal of Personality, 55*, 317–342.

Kanfer, F. H. (1980). Self-management methods. In F. H. Kanfer & A. P. Goldstein (Eds.), *Helping people change* (2nd ed., pp. 334–389). Elmsford, NY: Pergamon Press.

Kanfer, F. H., & Hagerman, S. (1981). The role of self-regulation. In L. P. Rehm (Ed.), *Behavior therapy for depression: Present status and future directions* (pp. 143–179). New York: Academic Press.

Kazdin, A. E. (1980). *Research design in clinical psychology*. New York: Harper & Row.

Kissen, D. M. (1967). Psychosocial factors, personality and lung cancer. *British Journal of Medical Psychology, 40*, 29–43.

Klopfer, B. (1957). Psychological variables in human cancer. *Journal of Projective Techniques, 21*, 331–340.

Kobasa, S. C. (1979). Stressful life events, personality, and health: An inquiry into hardiness. *Journal of Personality and Social Psychology, 37*, 1–11.

Kobasa, S. C., Maddi, S. R., & Kahn, S. (1982). Hardiness and health: A prospective study. *Journal of Personality and Social Psychology, 42*, 168–177.

Kübler-Ross, E. (1969). *On death and dying*. New York: Macmillan.

Landman, J. T., & Dawes, R. M. (1982) Psychotherapy outcome: Smith and Glass' conclusions stand up under scrutiny. *American psychologist, 37*, 504–516.

Langelle, C. (1989). *Hope in a community sample*. Unpublished Masters thesis. University of Kansas, Lawrence, Kansas.

Lazarus, R. S. (1966). *Psychological stress and the coping process*. New York: MacGraw-Hill.

Lazarus, R. S. (1968). Emotions and adaptation: Conceptual and empirical relations. In W. J. Arnold (Ed.), *Nebraska symposium on motivation* (pp. 175–266). Lincoln: University of Nebraska Press.

Lazarus, R. S., Averill, J. R., & Opton, E. M., Jr. (1970). Toward a cognitive theory of emotions. In M. Arnold (Ed.), *Feelings and emotions* (pp. 207–232). New York: Academic Press.

Lazarus, R. S., Eriksen, C. W., & Fonda, C. P. (1951). Personality dynamics and auditory perceptual recognition. *Journal of Personality, 19*, 471–482.

Lazarus, R. S., & Folkman, S. (1984). *Stress, appraisal, and coping*. New York: Springer.

Lazarus, R. S., Kanner, A. D., & Folkman, S. (1980). Emotions: A cognitive-phenomenological analysis. In R. Plutchik & H. Kellerman (Eds.), *Theories of emotion* (pp. 189–217). New York: Academic Press.

Lazarus, R. S., & Launier, R. (1978). Stress-related transactions between person and environment. In L. A. Pervin & M. Lewis (Eds.), *Perspectives in interactional psychology* (pp. 287–327). New York: Plenum Press.

Lee, T. W., Locke, E. A., & Latham, G. P. (1989). Goal setting theory and job performance. In L. A. Pervin's (Ed.), *Goal concepts in personality and social psychology* (pp. 291–326). Hillsdale, NJ: Lawrence Erlbaum Associates.

LeShan, L. L. (1961). A basic psychological orientation apparently associated with malignant disease. *The Psychiatric Quarterly, 35*, 314.

Levy, S. M. (1983). Host differences in neoplastic risk: Behavioral and social contributors to disease. *Health Psychology, 2*, 21–44.

Lewin, K. (1938). The conceptual representation and measurement of psychological forces.

Contributions to Psychological Theory, 1, 1–36.

Lewinsohn, P. M., Mischel, W., Chaplin, W., & Barton, R. (1980). Social competence and depression: The role of illusory self-perceptions. *Journal of Abnormal Psychology, 89*, 203–212.

Locke, S., & Colligan, D. (1986). *The healer within: The new medicine of mind and body*. New York: Mentor Books.

Marks, G., Richardson, J. L., Graham, J. W., & Levine, A. (1986). Role of health locus of control beliefs and expectations of treatment efficacy in adjustment to cancer. *Journal of Personality and Social Psychology, 51*, 443–450.

Markush, R. E., & Favero, R. V. (1974). Epidemiologic assessment of stressful life events, depressed mood, and psychophysiological symptoms—A preliminary report. In B. S. Dohrenwend & B. P. Dohrenwend (Eds.), *Stressful life events: Their nature and effects* (pp. 171–190). New York: John Wiley & Sons.

Martindale, C. (1981). *Cognition and consciousness*. Homewood, IL: Dorsey Press.

Mason, R. C., Clark, G., Reeves, R. B., & Wagner, B. (1969). Acceptance and healing. *Journal of Religion and Health, 8*, 123–142.

McCrae, R. R. (1984). Situational determinants of coping responses: Loss, threat, and challenge. *Journal of Personality and Social Psychology, 46*, 919–928.

Mechanic, D. (1974). Discussion of research paradigms on relations between stressful life events and episodes of physical illness. In B. S. Dohrenwend & B. P. Dohrenwend (Eds.), *Stressful life events: Their nature and effects* (pp. 87–97). New York: John Wiley & Sons.

Mednick, M. T., Mednick, S. A., & Mednick, E. V. (1964). Incubation of creative performance and specific associative priming. *Journal of Abnormal and Social Psychology, 69*, 84–88.

Melges, R., & Bowlby, J. (1969). Types of hopelessness in psychopathological processes. *Archives of General Psychiatry, 20*, 690–699.

Menninger, K. (1959). The academic lecture on hope. *The American Journal of Psychiatry, 116*, 481–491.

Meyerowitz, B. E. (1983). Postmastectomy coping strategies and quality of life. *Health Psychology, 2*, 117–132.

Miller, I. H., & Norman, W. H. (1979). Learned helplessness in humans: A review and attribu-

tion theory model. *Psychological Bulletin, 86*, 93–118.

Mowrer, O. H. (1960). *The psychology of hope*. San Francisco: Jossey-Bass.

Obayuwana, A. O., Collins, J. S., Carter, A. L., Rao, M. S., Mathur, C. C., & Wilson, S. B. (1982). Hope index scale: An instrument for the objective assessment of hope. *Journal of the National Medical Association, 74*, 761–765.

Orr, E. (1986, winter). Open communication as an effective stress management method for breast cancer patients. *Journal of Human Stress*, pp. 175–185.

Peale, N. V. (1956). *The power of positive thinking*. New York: Fawcett Crest.

Pelletier, K. R. (1979). *Holistic medicine: From stress to optimum health*. New York: Delacorte Press/Seymour Lawrence.

Persky, V. W., Kempthorne-Rawson, J., & Shekelle, R. B. (1987). Personality and risk of cancer: 20-year follow-up of the Western Electric study. *Psychosomatic Medicine, 49*, 435–449.

Pervin, L. A. (Ed.). (1989). *Goal concepts in personality and social psychology*. Hillsdale, NJ: Lawrence Erlbaum Associates.

Pettingale, K. W. (1984). Coping and cancer prognosis. *Journal of Psychosomatic Research, 28*, 363–364.

Prioleau, L., Murdock, M., & Brody, N. (1983). An analysis of psychotherapy versus placebo studies. *The Behavioral and Brain Sciences, 6*, 275–310.

Rosenbaum, M. (1980a). A schedule for assessing self-control behaviors: Preliminary findings. *Behavior Therapy, 11*, 109–121.

Rosenbaum, M. (1980b). Individual differences in self-control behaviors and tolerance of painful stimulation. *Journal of Abnormal Psychology, 89*, 581–590.

Rosenbaum, M., & Ben-Ari, K. (1985). Learned helplessness and learned resourcefulness: Effects of noncontingent success and failure on individuals differing in self-control skills. *Journal of Personality and Social Psychology, 48*, 198–215.

Rosenbaum, M., & Jaffe, Y. (1983). Learned helplessness: The role of individual differences in learned resourcefulness. *British Journal of Social Psychology, 22*, 215–225.

Rosenbaum, M., & Palmon, N. (1984). Helplessness and resourcefulness in coping with epilepsy. *Journal of Consulting and Clinical Psychology, 52*, 244–253.

Rosenbaum, M., & Rolnick, A. (1983). Self-control behaviors and coping with seasickness. *Cognitive Therapy and Research, 7*, 93–98.

Rosenberg, M. (1965). *Society and adolescent self-image.* Princeton: Princeton University Press.

Roth, D. L., Harris, R. L., & Snyder, C. R. (1988). An individual differences measure of attributive and repudiative tactics of favorable self-presentation. *Journal of Social and Clinical Psychology, 6*, 159–170.

Roth, D. L., Snyder, C. R., & Pace, L. M. (1986). Dimensions of favorable self-presentation. *Journal of Personality and Social Psychology, 51*, 867–874.

Roth, S. (1980). A revised model of learned helplessness in humans. *Journal of Personality, 48*, 103–133.

Rotter, J. B. (1954). *Social learning and clinical psychology.* Englewood Cliffs, NJ: Prentice-Hall.

Rotter, J. B. (1966). Generalized expectancies for internal versus external control of reinforcement. *Psychological Monographs: General and Applied, 80* (Whole No. 609).

Sarason, I. G., Johnson, J. H., & Siegel, J. M. (1978). Assessing the impact of life changes: Development of the life experiences survey. *Journal of Consulting and Clinical Psychology, 46*, 932–946.

Schachtel, E. (1959). *Metamorphosis.* New York: Basic Books.

Scheier, M. F., & Carver, C. S. (1985). Optimism, coping, and health: Assessment and implications of generalized outcome expectancies. *Health Psychology, 4*, 219–247.

Scheier, M. F., & Carver, C. S. (1987). Dispositional optimism and physical well-being: The influence of generalized outcome expectancies on health. *Journal of Personality, 55*, 169–210.

Scheier, M. F., Matthews, K. A., Owens, J., Magovern, G. J., Lefebvre, R. C., Abbott, R. A., & Carver, C. S. (1990). Dispositional optimism and recovery from coronary artery bypass surgery: The beneficial effects of physical and psychological well-being. *Journal of Personality and Social Psychology, 57*, 1024–1040.

Scheier, M. F., Weintrab, J. K., & Carver, C. (1986). Coping with stress: Divergent strategies of optimists and pessimists. *Journal of Personality and Social Psychology, 51*, 1257–1264.

Schmale, A. H. (1958). Relationship of separation and depression to disease. *Psychosomatic Medicine, 20*, 259–277.

Schmale, A. H., & Iker, H. P. (1966). The affect of hopelessness and the development of cancer. *Psychosomatic Medicine, 28*, 714–721.

Schmale, A. H., & Iker, H. P. (1971). Hopelessness as a predictor of cervical cancer. *Social Science Medicine, 5*, 95–100.

Shaffer, J. W., Graves, P. L., Swank, R. T., & Pearson, T. A. (1987). Clustering of personality traits in youth and the subsequent development of cancer among physicians. *Journal of Behavioral Medicine, 10*, 441–447.

Shapiro, D. A., & Shapiro, D. (1982). Meta-analysis of comparative therapy outcome studies: A replication and refinement. *Psychological Bulletin, 92*, 581–604.

Siegel, B. S. (1986). *Love, medicine, and miracles.* New York: Harper & Row.

Simons, A. D., Lustman, P. J., Wetzel, R. D., & Murphy, G. E. (1985). Predicting response to cognitive therapy of depression: The role of learned resourcefulness. *Cognitive Therapy and Research, 9*, 79–89.

Simonton, O. C., Mathews-Simonton, S., & Creighton, J. L. (1978). *Getting well again.* New York: Bantam Books.

Smith, M. B. (1983). Hope and despair: Keys to the socio-psychodynamics of youth. *American Journal of Orthopsychiatry, 53*, 388–399.

Smith, M. L., & Glass, G. V. (1977). Meta-analysis of psychotherapy outcome studies. *American Psychologist, 32*, 752–760.

Smith, T. V. G. (1979). *Cognitive correlatives of response to a behavioral weight control program.* Doctoral dissertation, Queen's University, Kingston, Canada.

Smith, T. W., Pope, M. K., Rhodewalt, F., & Poulton, J. L. (1989). Optimism, neuroticism, coping and symptom reports: An alternative interpretation of the Life Orientation Test. *Journal of Personality and Social Psychology, 56*, 1–9.

Snyder, C. R. (1989). Reality negotiation: From excuses to hope and beyond. *Journal of Social and Clinical Psychology, 8*, 130–157.

Snyder, C. R., Harris, C. B., Anderson, J. R., Gibb, J., Yoshinobu, L., Langelle, C., Harney, P., Holleran, S., & Irving, L. M. (1989). *The development and validation of an individual differences measure of hope.* Paper presented at the American Psychological Association Convention, New Orleans, August.

Spielberger, C. D., Gorsuch, R. L., & Luchene, R. E. (1970). *The state-trait anxiety inven-*

tory. Palo Alto, CA: Consulting Psychologists' Press.

Staats, S. (1987). Hope: Expected positive affect in an adult sample. *Journal of Genetic Psychology, 148*, 357–364.

Staats, S. (1989). Hope: A comparison of two self-report measures for adults. *Journal of Personality Assessment, 53*, 366–375.

Staats, S., & Stassen, M. A. (1986). *The hope index: A measure of self-other-world expectations for adults.* Paper presented at the American Psychological Association Convention, Washington, DC, September.

Stam, H. J., & Steggles, S. (1987). Predicting the onset or progression of cancer from psychological characteristics: Psychometric and theoretical issues. *Journal of Psychosocial Oncology, 5*, 35–46.

Stotland, E. (1969). *The psychology of hope.* San Francisco: Jossey-Bass.

Strack, S., Carver, C. S., & Blaney, P. H. (1987). Predicting successful completion of an aftercare program following treatment for alcoholism: The role of dispositional optimism. *Journal of Personality and Social Psychology, 53*, 579–584.

Taylor, J. A. (1953). A personality scale of manifest anxiety. *Journal of Abnormal and Social Psychology, 48*, 285–290.

Taylor, S. (1983). Adjustment to threatening events: A theory of cognitive adaptation. *American Psychologist, 38*, 1161–1173.

Taylor, S. E. (1989). *Positive illusions: Creative self-deception and the healthy mind.* New York: Basic Books.

Taylor, S. E., & Brown, J. D. (1988). Illusion and well-being: A social psychological perspective on mental health. *Psychological Bulletin, 103*, 193–210.

Taylor, S. E., Lichtman, R. R., & Wood, J. V. (1984). Attributions, beliefs about control, and adjustment to breast cancer. *Journal of Personality and Social Psychology, 46*, 489–502.

Teasdale, J. D., & Fogarty, S. J. (1979). Differential effects of induced mood on the recall of pleasant and unpleasant events from episodic memory. *Journal of Abnormal Psychology, 88*, 248–257.

Tillich, P. (1965). The right to hope. *The University of Chicago Magazine, 58*, 16–22.

Timko, C., & Janoff-Bulman, R. (1985). Attributions, vulnerability, and psychological adjustment: The case of breast cancer. *Health Psychology, 4*, 521–544.

Warheit, G. J. (1979). Life events, coping, stress, and depressive symptomatology. *American Journal of Psychiatry, 136*, 502–507.

Watson, D., & Pennebaker, J. W. (1989). Health complaints, stress, and distress: Exploring the central role of negative affectivity. *Psychological Review, 96*, 233–253.

Weiner, B., Graham, S., & Chandler, C. (1982). Pity, anger, and guilt: An attributional analysis. *Personality and Social Psychology Bulletin, 8*, 226–232.

Weiner, B., & Litman-Adizes, T. (1980). An attributional, expectancy-value analysis of learned helplessness and depression. In J. Garber & M. E. P. Seligman (Eds.), *Human helplessness: Theory and applications* (pp. 35–57). New York: Academic Press.

Yoshinobu, L. R. (1989). *Construct validation of the hope scale: Agency and pathways components.* Masters thesis. University of Kansas, Lawrence, Kansas.

Zemore, R., & Shepel, L. F. (1987). Information seeking and adjustment to cancer. *Psychological Reports, 60*, 874.

PART III

ENVIRONMENT-BASED PROCESSES

CHAPTER 16

CLINICAL AND SOCIAL PERSPECTIVES ON CLOSE RELATIONSHIPS

Thomas N. Bradbury
Frank D. Fincham

In recent years much has been written about the emergence of a new field of study devoted to understanding close relationships. The flurry of activity that has accompanied this development is evidenced by the formation of new professional organizations for the study of close relationships, the establishment of a journal devoted to this topic, and the publication of numerous edited volumes. Although the potential contribution of research on close relationships to psychology is well established, the recent growth in this domain must be placed in proper perspective in order to see more clearly the steps needed for research on close relationships to be maximally informative. We therefore turn to this task before addressing the major goal of this chapter, which is to facilitate research on close relationships that integrates the perspectives of clinical and social psychology.

An essential first observation is that the field of close relationships is not new despite many claims to the contrary. Indeed, the study of close relationships began long ago and incorporated the ideas of such figures as Sullivan, Lewin, Freud, Heider, Sears, Burgess, and Terman. The more recent contributions of Cantril, Newcomb, Raush, Bell, Jackson, Patterson, Thibaut, and Kelley set the stage for the upsurge in interest witnessed in the last decade. Dispelling the belief that the study of close relationships is relatively new is important because doing so is likely to result in greater attention being devoted to earlier work, thus providing scholars in the area with a richer body of research and theory to draw on and extend.

A second observation about the field of close relationships is that it may be less cohesive than is immediately apparent. Despite numerous texts on

Preparation of this chapter was supported by a National Research Service Award from the National Institute of Mental Health and Grant 1-5-30055 from the National Science Foundation awarded to Thomas N. Bradbury, and by a Faculty Scholar Fellowship from the W. T. Grant Foundation and Grant R01 MH 44078-01 from the National Institute of Mental Health awarded to Frank D. Fincham.

close relationships, relatively few conceptual links have been forged among even seemingly related topics, and much of the work that is conducted is likely to be of immediate interest to only a small segment of the field. In this regard Hinde (1981) notes that "the literature on interpersonal relationships is scattered amongst many different disciplines. And within each discipline, it would seem that each group of investigators has been more disposed to try to tackle the complexities of interindividual relationships with their own conceptual tools than to try to specify the relations between their endeavors and those of others. This is not to say that such attempts have been lacking . . . , but it is still the case that the various paradigms and theories in the field have little coherence" (p. 19). Although this heterogeneity is an obvious strength, an unfortunate consequence of overestimating the cohesion and homogeneity of the close relationships field is that it may lead to high expectations and disenchantment with the amount of integrative research and theory that is produced. This could lead in turn to premature loss of interest in studying relationships.

A third observation is that the growth of interest in studying close relationships within psychology is in part a result of contributions from clinical psychology and social psychology, and, to a lesser degree, of work that combines these two perspectives. In fact, the study of close relationships was expected to be at the forefront of the interface between clinical and social psychology. For example, Harvey and Weary (1979) described close relationships as an "important research topic that by its very nature seems to exist at the heart of an integrated clinical-social psychology. . . . It seems evident that in the future, better progress in investigating this phenomenon and developing therapeutic procedures for this area will occur via a concerted, collaborative venture both by clinical and social psychologists" (p. 512).

However, much work remains to be done before the clinical-social interface is realized fully in the domain of close relationships. For example, a recent issue of the *Journal of Social and Clinical Psychology* (1988, *7* [1]) devoted to integrative contributions relating to close relationships included seven papers, of which none included actual clinical populations, one included a community sample of maritally distressed and nondistressed community spouses, one included actual ongoing relationships in a college community, and five in-

cluded undergraduates filling out questionnaires on their perceptions of and attitudes about relationships. Although these and similar reports typically draw from the social psychology literature and often have implications for prevention or clinical intervention, we believe that this distribution of articles may be indicative of a large gap between programmatic research on close relationships in social psychology and the systematic application of that knowledge in clinical settings. This is unfortunate insofar as narrowing the gap holds great potential not only for understanding the complexities of close relationships but also for treating individuals, couples, and families experiencing relationship problems.

The purpose of this chapter is to foster research on close relationships that combines more fully the emphases, perspectives, and methods of clinical psychology and social psychology. We believe that such an integration is most likely to come about by encouraging clinical and social researchers to combine the advantages of their respective disciplines in order to conduct research that ultimately may have application in the prevention and treatment of disturbed relationships. This strategy, which makes explicit the often overlooked fact that clinical psychology involves both research and practice, is put forth with the assumption that the interface of research (whether it be social, clinical, or otherwise) and clinical practice with regard to close relationships will be realized fully when the caliber, relevance, and consistency of research in this domain reaches a level that cannot be ignored by those who provide clinical services.

We shall attempt to accomplish our purpose by identifying a number of topics that require attention if the investigations conducted by social and clinical researchers are to influence clinical intervention. For each of these topics, the different approaches that have been taken will be discussed, representative research will be reviewed and, where appropriate, suggestions for future research will be offered. The topics discussed are intended to be heuristic rather than exhaustive. They are addressed in regard to close heterosexual relationships between adults because (a) a great deal of research in clinical and social psychology pertains to relationships of this sort, (b) it is often viewed as the prototypic close relationship, and (c) close relationships between adults are a common source of problems and hence are very likely to come to the attention of practitioners.

INTEGRATING CLINICAL AND SOCIAL RESEARCH ON CLOSE RELATIONSHIPS

If social-clinical research on close relationships is to generate a product that will have clinical utility, what should be the basic targets of inquiry? Although there are many potential targets of inquiry, at least five interrelated topics seem essential: *interaction* between relationship partners, *affective and cognitive phenomena* that occur in interactions as well as in other, noninteractional contexts, *relationship quality* and *dysfunction*, the *temporal course* of relationship events, and *psychopathology and social support*. The first of these four topics is suggested by the emphases in theoretical accounts of close relationships (e.g., Bradbury & Fincham, 1988; Gottman, 1979; Kelley et al., 1983), whereas the fifth topic is indicated by its clinical relevance and the clear association between psychopathology and relationship functioning (see Gotlib & McCabe, in press). Below we provide a selective review and critique of research on each of these topics.

Interaction

Examination of the behaviors exchanged by partners in close relationships is often viewed as important because it has the potential to ground the study of close relationships in observable and verifiable events, to allow the combination of observational data with self-report data, and to provide a descriptive background against which subsequent findings can be viewed. Two fairly distinct literatures have emerged pertaining to interaction in close relationships, involving either global retrospective judgments of behavior made by the interactants themselves or relatively specific judgments about discrete interactions made by interactants or trained coders. Each is examined in turn.

Because of their unique value for assessing individuals' subjective reactions, and in part because of the ease with which they are obtained, global self-reports of behavior in close relationships are used in a wide variety of studies in social and clinical psychology. In the past several years, for example, social psychological research has been conducted on such topics as the problem-solving responses that characterize distressed and nondistressed dating couples (e.g., "When I am unhappy with my partner, I tell her what's bothering me"

[Rusbult, Johnson, & Morrow, 1986]); the strategies that people in dating relationships use to get what they want from their partners (e.g., "I drop hints" [Falbo & Peplau, 1980]); the relation between self-disclosure and satisfaction in dating relationships (e.g., "We discuss things that I like and dislike about myself" [Franzoi, Davis, & Young, 1985]); and the contributions of relationship behaviors and the partner's perceptions of those behaviors to the partner's satisfaction with the relationship (e.g., "I never act in a selfish or egocentric way" [Davis & Oathout, 1987]). This body of research addresses an exciting array of questions and thus holds promise for uncovering important information about perceptions of behavior in relationships. However, because it is difficult to capture the subleties of this research in the present context (see Clark & Reis, 1988), our comments will be confined largely to the procedures used in these and related studies.

In contrast to this diversity of topics, a methodologically similar literature has evolved that is devoted to examining self-reports of communication behaviors and satisfaction in distressed and nondistressed married couples. In this research, spouses' reports of satisfaction are correlated with such variables as ratings of sensitivity to nonverbal cues in interaction (e.g., "Do you know the feelings of your spouse from his facial and bodily gestures?" [Navran, 1967]); the extent to which various conflict resolution behaviors reflect the spouse's interaction style (e.g., "She gets really mad and starts yelling" [Rands, Levinger, & Mellinger, 1981]); the frequency with which various statements are made in the marriage (e.g., "How often does your husband complain that you don't understand him?" [Bienvenu, 1970]); and the frequency with which spouses engage in specific verbal behaviors (e.g., "I express my appreciation verbally for things my spouse does for me" [Boyd & Roach, 1977]). In general, correlations on the order of .7 to .9 have been found between reports of behavior and relationship quality (for a review see Baucom & Adams, 1987).

As these and other studies attest, global reports of behavior can provide information that is useful both for testing hypotheses about close relationships and for informing clinical judgments in marital therapy. Although the strengths of this method should not be overlooked, it is important to emphasize that such global reports reflect perceptions of behaviors and interactions rather than veridical reports of relationship events. Because estimates of behavioral frequencies are subject to memory distortions and global evaluations of the relationship in which the behaviors occur (i.e., spouses may base their judgments of how often they argue with their partner on the perceived quality of the relationship rather than on the actual frequency of arguments), it is likely that estimated and actual rates of behaviors differ. Indeed, in a study of Robinson and Price (1980), distressed spouses reported 50% fewer positive behaviors than did trained coders watching the same interaction, and in several studies spouses have been found to agree only about half of the time on the occurrence of events in their relationship (for a review see Christensen, 1987).

Although the discrepancy between global self-reports of behavior and observational assessments is not surprising, the marked tendency to overlook the distinction between these two forms of measurement is a serious problem. For example, research involving perceptions of behavior is often discussed as though behavior was actually measured, and unwarranted inferences about overt behavior in relationships are frequently drawn. This problem is compounded when perceived frequencies of behaviors are correlated with measures of relationship quality, because the high degree of empirical dependence obtained between any such measures is inflated not only by common method variance but also by the considerable overlap in item content across measures. For example, the Marital Adjustment Test (Locke & Wallace, 1959) includes an item assessing how often the spouse confides in his or her mate, while the Primary Communication Inventory (Navran, 1967) asks, "How often do you and your spouse talk with each other about personal problems?" In such cases, significant associations at the empirical level are at least in part an artifact of the failure to make appropriate distinctions (i.e., between communication and satisfaction) at conceptual and operational levels (for a detailed discussion see Fincham & Bradbury, 1987). Because these difficulties stem more from the use of behavioral self-report measures than from the properties of the measures themselves, their resolution is straightforward: in the absence of corroborative evidence, data collected with global self-report measures of behavior should not be equated with the behavior itself, and caution should be exercised when relating such data to measures of potentially overlapping constructs.

Whereas inappropriate use of global self-reports of behavior has contributed to confusion in the literature, of far greater consequence is the failure to recognize the inherent limitations of self-report for understanding interaction. Simply stated, such measures tell us very little about the dynamic and sequential exchange of behaviors that is basic to interaction. In an attempt to achieve a closer approximation of interaction as it actually occurs, several researchers either have asked married couples to report daily on relationship events or have observed their interactions in laboratory settings. The results of this research, conducted in large part by clinical psychologists, are described below.

Efforts to study marital interaction follow directly from the rationale that an understanding of the behaviors that covary with marital satisfaction could be used "to design an intervention program that teaches couples who believe their marriages are functioning badly to interact . . . as do couples who believe their marriages are functioning well" (Gottman, 1979, p. 263). One strategy for identifying the discriminative behaviors is to ask distressed and nondistressed spouses to fill out independently a daily checklist of behaviors that occur in the marriage over the course of a few weeks (for a review see Bradbury & Fincham, 1987). Research adopting this approach reveals that, compared with nondistressed couples, distressed couples report higher rates of negative behaviors and lower rates of positive behaviors (e.g., Jacobson & Moore, 1981). By also asking spouses to make ratings of their daily satisfaction with the marriage, it has been possible to determine that negative behaviors account for more variance in daily satisfaction than do positive behaviors and that the covariation between positive and negative behaviors and daily satisfaction is greater among distressed than nondistressed couples.

Leaving aside the interesting theoretical implications of this work (e.g., that distressed spouses appear to be particularly reactive to partner behavior) and the important contributions of this technique to clinical assessment, it can be noted that the delimited 24-hour time frame used with this approach is a great improvement on the global self-report procedures reviewed above. Nevertheless, low reliability between husbands' and wives' daily ratings of relationship events, even after spouses undergo training, has been documented (see Elwood & Jacobson, 1988) and, despite numerous efforts to extract information regarding behavioral reciprocity from the daily checklists, the spouse observation paradigm affords little opportunity to examine directly the sequential character of interaction.

In contrast to this research, observational reliability and access to sequential information is maximized (albeit at the expense of ecological validity) in observational studies of interaction where each speaking turn in laboratory-based problem-solving discussions is coded by trained observers. This tradition of research, prompted by Raush, Barry, Hertel, and Swain's (1974) discontent with the many "empty facts" (p. 4) about marriage that accumulated from the use of self-report measures, has revealed that the interactions of distressed couples, compared with those of their nondistressed counterparts, are characterized by higher rates of negative behaviors (and, less consistently, by lower rates of positive behaviors), a greater likelihood of reciprocation of negative behaviors, and a greater degree of predictability between spouse behaviors. Subsequent research has shown that distressed and nondistressed couples are discriminated more powerfully on the basis of their nonverbal behaviors than on the content of their speech (for a review see Schaap, 1984).

Although there is merit to the view that social psychology is "a discipline centrally concerned with and expert in the study of human interaction" (Hendrick, 1983, p. 67), close examination of the literature reveals that within social psychology our knowledge of interaction in close relationships is often based on subjects' perceptions of behavior as assessed via global self-reports. Observational research on marital interaction has provided a much richer and more rigorous portrayal of the behaviors and patterns of behaviors that discriminate distressed and nondistressed couples; these data therefore have had far greater impact on marital therapy. It does not follow, however, that research on perceptions of behavior should be discontinued or that it is somehow inferior to the study of overt behavior. In fact, as we will discuss in the next section, several factors point clearly to the importance of examining numerous intrapersonal phenomena in close relationships, particularly in the context of interpersonal interaction. Given the significant contribution of social psychology to understanding emotional and cognitive processes in individuals, the combined study of overt and covert events may be especially propitious for the integration of

social and clinical psychology in the domain of close relationships.

Affective and Cognitive Phenomena

Considerable effort has been devoted in recent years to enriching our understanding of the relation between behavior and marital satisfaction by investigating emotional and cognitive variables that may contribute to this association. This transition has occurred for a number of reasons, including (a) data indicating that husbands and wives do not agree on the day-to-day events in their relationship and that spouses and trained coders do not agree on the events that occur in laboratory interactions, suggesting that spouses attach meaning to events in idiosyncratic ways; (b) data indicating that the nonverbal behaviors accompanying a spoken message in interaction are more effective in discriminating distressed from nondistressed couples than is the spoken message itself, suggesting that emotion in interaction may be at least as important as overt behavior; (c) low correlations between overt behavior and marital satisfaction (see Snyder, Trull, & Wills, 1987), suggesting that important aspects of interaction were being overlooked; and (d) the realization that, while behaviorally oriented marital therapy helps many couples, a significant number remain distressed after counseling (Jacobson, Follette, & Elwood, 1984), suggesting that the simple model of teaching distressed couples to behave like nondistressed couples is unduly narrow.

As a consequence of these findings, together with psychologists' increased interest in cognition, it seems quite likely that many significant advances in the study of close relationships will emerge from the examination of covert processes that elaborate on or qualify our understanding of overt behavior. This should not be taken to mean, however, that a complete understanding of overt behavior in interaction has been attained (e.g., little is known about the cross-situational consistency of marital behavior or whether behavior is predictive of changes in satisfaction) or that the study of covert processes is entirely new. Indeed, one of the earliest observational studies of marital interaction, by Raush et al. (1974), was formulated in terms of object relations schemas that serve to organize experience, a concept that some subsequent investigators sought to operationalize (e.g., Gottman, 1979). In the remainder of this section, examples of such research will be reviewed and directions for future research that take advantage of social and clinical perspectives will be identified.

Reasoning that "a complete description of communication processes must ultimately consider the perceptions and intentions that mediate partners' overt responses," Gaelick, Bodenhausen, and Wyer (1985, p. 1246) asked couples to discuss a problem in their relationship, identify six important statements that were made from a videotape of the interaction, and then rate those statements in terms of the feelings that the communicator intended to express and the recipient's reaction to those feelings. It was determined that recipients tended to reciprocate the affective tone of the messages that they perceived but that recipients were accurate only in their perception of negative messages. Further, while men viewed the absence of positive messages as an indicator of negativity, women viewed the absence of negative messages as an indicator of positivity. This pattern of results was interpreted to mean that reciprocation of negative messages is more likely than reciprocation of positive messages, that females' behavior is more critical in instigating bursts of negative affect (insofar as men may be predisposed to interpret all but positive behavior as negative), and that males' behavior is more critical in stopping such bursts (insofar as women may be predisposed to interpret all but negative behavior as positive).

These promising findings suggest that examination of perceptions of specific behaviors can add substantially to an understanding of the dynamics of interaction in close relationships. And, although overt behavior was not actually assessed, this in turn supports the need for therapeutic interventions that change not only behaviors (e.g., teaching spouses to behave more positively), but also interpretations of behaviors (e.g., teaching spouses what partner behaviors do and do not imply). This recommendation is tempered by the surprisingly few correlations that arose between ratings of messages and relationship satisfaction, however, and further speculation must await the collection of additional data.

Whereas affective elements of close relationships have been the focus of research by Gaelick et al. (1985) and several others (e.g., Berscheid, Snyder, & Omoto, 1989; Levenson & Gottman, 1985; Margolin, John, & Gleberman, 1988), attention has been devoted also to cognitive aspects of relationships, such as unrealistic relationship beliefs (e.g., Emmelkamp, Krol, Sanderman, & Ruphan,

1987), locus of control for marital outcomes (e.g., Miller, Lefcourt, Holmes, Ware, & Saleh, 1986), and judgments of equity in relationships (e.g., Hatfield, Traupmann, Sprecher, Utne, & Hay, 1985). It is interesting that examination of the most widely studied cognitive element, the attributions that partners make for relationship events, was stimulated by attribution research in social psychology (e.g., Orvis, Kelley, & Butler, 1976). The clinical implications of these studies were soon recognized and a large literature has since accumulated that documents the concurrent and predictive associations between maladaptive causal attributions (e.g., viewing the cause of negative partner behavior as internal to the partner, stable, and global) and marital distress (for reviews see Bradbury & Fincham, 1990; Harvey, 1987).

These results are important in the present context because they show that research on close relationships in clinical psychology can be extended with principles from social psychology. Recent research on marital attributions demonstrates further that examination of social principles in the clinical domain can contribute in turn to a more refined appreciation of them. For example, contrary to the current emphasis placed on causal attributions in social and clinical psychology, studies now suggest that attributions of responsibility (which involve judgments concerning the partner's intent, foresight, and harmful motivation) and attributions of blame are salient in interpersonal settings (Finchman, Beach, & Nelson, 1987). In a similar manner, whereas the failure to study the behavioral consequences of attributions in social psychology is "perhaps the single most telling criticism" of the attribution domain (Eiser, 1983, p. 162), data linking attributions to behavior in marriage aid in alleviating this shortcoming. For example, Fincham and Bradbury (1988a) have shown that a spouse's attribution for a marital difficulty correlates with the behaviors he or she exhibited while discussing that difficulty with the partner, and Fincham and Bradbury (1988b) found that manipulation of a spouse's attribution for a negative partner behavior influenced his or her subsequent behavior toward the partner in interaction.

The symbiosis between social and clinical psychology in regard to the study of attributions in close relationships has proven fruitful to date, yet we are confident that this represents only one instance of how social and clinical interests can be joined to mutual advantage. Another such promising direction would involve extrapolating Weiner's (1985) attributional model of motivation and emotion to the domain of close relationships. Adaptation of this model, which posits links between negative outcomes (e.g., failure on a test), causal attributions for those outcomes (e.g., "I am dumb"), and the consequences of those attributions for specific affective responses (e.g., decreased self-esteem, hopelessness), would be valuable because it would (a) counter the affective/cognitive dualism that is evident in research on close relationships; (b) extend research on emotion in close relationships so that it considers a variety of affects (e.g., caring, happiness, anger, sadness) rather than simply positive and negative emotions; and (c) permit generalization of the model to dyadic and clinically relevant phenomena.

Many additional topics provide fertile ground for studying affective and cognitive processes in close relationships, and growth in these areas is most likely to involve application of knowledge from social psychology to interaction between intimates. For example, little is yet known about how partners organize the stream of interaction into meaningful units (cf. Newtson, 1973), the various goals that partners seek to attain via interaction and their influence on the perception of partner behavior (cf. Swann, Pelham, & Roberts, 1987), the relation between transient and chronic affective reactions and perceptions of interaction (cf. Forgas & Bower, 1988), or the contribution of expectancies and individual differences to interaction outcomes (cf. Ickes & Tooke, 1988). An equally diverse set of issues could be identified that does not pertain directly to interaction, including memory for relationship events (cf. Messe, Buldain, & Watts, 1981) and the accounts that people offer for their continuing and terminated relationships (cf. Burnett, McGhee, & Clarke, 1988).

With the inevitable shift toward examining the diverse affective and cognitive processes that underly the association between behavior and marital satisfaction has come a significant increase in the complexity of the phenomena of interest, and in the foregoing section we have attempted to convey a few of the forms that this complexity may take. This transition from overt behavior to covert variables (especially as they are considered in the context of overt behavior) highlights the clear need for theoretical developments that will organize existing findings and guide empirical operations. One construct that is likely to be centrally important to such progress is perceptions of relationship quality and dysfunction, a topic to which we now turn.

Relationship Quality and Dysfunction

Although theoretical and empirical clarification of the links between overt behavior and covert processes would be valuable, progress of this sort will be of little clinical utility without explicit attention to the affective evaluations and judgments of relationship quality that partners make. It is evident from the two previous sections that consideration of relationship quality pervades research on close relationships. However, a clear divergence exists in how clinical and social psychologists approach this issue: relationship satisfaction among married couples is the construct of central concern in clinical research, while constructs such as trust, commitment, and especially love are of greatest interest in social psychology. We will outline below the assets and liabilities of both of these perspectives and will argue that greater integration of clinical and social research on close relationships is likely to emerge as this divergence becomes less pronounced.

The emphasis on satisfaction in clinical research on close relationships probably owes to the fact that clinical researchers became interested in marriage following the work of sociologists, who attempted to explain variance in relationship quality and stability in terms of self-reported demographic, personality, and familial variables. The many studies within the sociological tradition were criticized for being "shotgun in their approach" (Barry, 1970, p. 42) and for lacking in conceptual and methodological integrity. Clinical researchers thus reacted strongly against this approach, studying instead the contribution of overt behavior to marital discord and, in contrast, ignoring and perhaps actively avoiding articulation of the phenomenology of relationship quality and the varieties of marital satisfaction. An additional reason for this emphasis probably stems from the clinically distressed samples that were studied. That is, it is often difficult to characterize a couple in terms of, for example, their style of love when there is little love to be found and when a basic therapeutic goal is often to help spouses talk with each other without becoming hostile or disengaged.

Within the clinical tradition, marital satisfaction has come to be equated most commonly with a single dimension that is derived from responses on the Marital Adjustment Test (Locke & Wallace, 1959) or an instrument that was designed to supersede it, the dyadic Adjustment Scale (Spanier, 1976). Both instruments were developed by sociologists and include questions assessing global evaluations of how happy the respondent is with the marriage as well as questions asking the respondent about the frequency of disagreements across various topics and the outcome of those disagreements. The unidimensional view has much to offer in the way of simplicity and parsimony, and many investigators see these instruments as adequate for research and clinical screening (e.g., Gottman, 1979). Conceptualization and measurement of satisfaction have generated considerable controversy in recent years, however, with some arguing that measures must be revised by omitting any items that do not pertain directly to a global affective evaluation of the marriage (e.g., Norton, 1983) and others arguing that the multidimensional nature of marital quality must be recognized and measured accordingly (e.g., Johnson, White, Edwards, & Booth, 1986). It is not possible to do justice to the complexity of these and related arguments here, yet it is important to call attention to the diverse opinions surrounding this issue insofar as further discussion is likely as more disciplines become involved in the study of close relationships and as clinical researchers pay greater attention to covert variables.

Social psychological research on love grew out of the large literature on interpersonal attraction and, at a time when there was widespread interest in social exchange formulations of interpersonal behavior, was stimulated in part by the publication of an instrument to assess liking and loving (Rubin, 1970). Conceptual distinctions among the constituent elements of love (e.g., attachment, caring, needing, intimacy) and among types of love (e.g., companionate, passionate) were soon drawn and studied, and, although interest in the topic waned for some time, investigation of love has grown rapidly in the past several years (for reviews see Clark & Reis, 1988; Sternberg & Barnes, 1988). Whereas the clinical research literature is characterized by relatively little theory and numerous attempts to identify external correlates of relationship satisfaction, the literature pertaining to love is distinguished by relatively extensive theoretical development and efforts to differentiate among varieties of love. For example, Lee (1977) identifies passionate, game-playing, and companionate as three primary types of love, with three secondary forms deriving from combinations thereof; Sternberg (1986) identifies intimacy, passion, and decision/commitment as three components of love, the presence and absence of which serve to define eight kinds of love; Hazan and Shaver (1987) view the development of romantic love as similar to parent-child attachment and identify secure, avoidant, and anxious/ambivalent as three forms of love.

This work reflects a willingness to speculate about the range of approaches to and experiences of love in romantic relationships. Such an orientation is not limited to love, however, because attention in social psychology also has been directed to the study of trust (e.g., Rempel, Holmes, & Zanna, 1985), commitment (e.g., Kelley, 1983), envy and jealousy (e.g., Buunk & Bringle, 1987), and closeness (e.g., Berscheid, Snyder, & Omoto, 1989). In the same way that satisfaction is emphasized in clinical research because of its salience in marriage and clinical settings, the emphasis on love and related concepts may owe to their relevance to the dating couples that are typically studied in social psychological research on close relationships. Moreover, even though satisfaction is sometimes studied among dating couples, mean satisfaction scores are often very high. Assuming the validity of these self-reports, this indicates that there may be little serious dissatisfaction among dating couples who serve as subjects, which in turn means that there is very little variance in satisfaction for which to account. Thus, the relative emphasis in social psychology on such concepts as love, rather than satisfaction, is readily understood.

The thrust of our observations to this point can be examined along two dimensions, and both pertain to the relative viability of social and clinical research in applied clinical settings. First, in terms of the applied relevance of the samples that have been investigated, it is apparent that studies of married couples hold greater potential for application than do studies of dating couples. Only rarely do dating couples present for counseling, and the emphasis on varieties of love and similar concepts among such couples, while of irrefutable importance (see below), is likely to be of less interest to the clinician who is confronted routinely with the problems of married couples.

Thus, a more complete integration of social

psychology and clinical intervention in regard to close relationships is likely to occur when social psychologists collect data from married couples representing the full range of relationship quality. Apart from far-reaching conceptual advantages that such a shift would bring to the study of marriage, expansion of the social perspective in this way may help to maintain interest in the area; systematic study of interpersonal attraction, in contrast, has suffered because of "the most glaring omission, that of enduring relationships and all the vital questions . . . they encompass" (Berscheid, 1985, p. 415). In this regard we agree with McCarthy's (1981, p. 25) observation that "a diversion of some quantitative research effort away from the well-trodden paths of the white/middle-class/young/student milieu . . . might greatly extend and enliven our understanding of the diverse facets and functions of human affectional relationships." Our recommendation should not be taken to imply that research in social psychology has ignored married couples completely. It bears noting, however, that many of the studies using married couples as subjects also use dating couples, and the data from the two groups are then combined. This strategy is difficult to defend in view of the social, demographic, and interpersonal differences between these groups.

A second dimension underlying our discussion of the social and clinical approaches to relationship quality concerns the complexity and breadth of perspective taken toward the primary qualitative constructs. On the one hand, social psychologists have been successful in developing rich and interesting conceptual frameworks that lead to competing hypotheses and that encourage investigation of the full spectrum of affective, qualitative variables. On the other hand, even though these variables have not been overlooked completely by clinical researchers, the primary emphasis on accounting for variance in satisfaction stands in contrast as sterile and theoretically undeveloped. The importance of this dimension cannot be denied, yet the tacit assumption of homogeneity within distressed and nondistressed groups and the continuing reluctance to examine other pertinent qualitative dimensions of relationships seems unnecessarily restrictive (cf. Fitzpatrick, 1988; Snyder, 1979).

In this case, clinical research can gain from the strides taken within social psychology to understand such phenomena as love and trust. Although this should not be viewed as a wholesale endorsement of the prevailing research on these topics (e.g., causal questions are rarely addressed, behavioral manifestations are seldom examined, the utility of particular distinctions is unclear), greater attention to the theoretical causes and consequences of satisfaction and exploration of additional qualitative experiences in marriage is likely to prove valuable. Recent recognition of the importance of how intimacy is negotiated between spouses (e.g., Jacobson, 1989) bodes well for such a development.

We have argued that social and clinical psychologists undertake research on relationship quality in different ways, with the former emphasizing breadth in qualitative judgments among dating couples and the latter emphasizing satisfaction and dysfunction among married couples. A rapprochement between these perspectives will emerge as social researchers collect data on long-term relationships such as marriage and as clinical researchers develop theory and appreciate the diversity that underlies relationship quality. The fact that social and clinical researchers address different populations in the relationship spectrum highlights the temporal dimension of relationships, considered next.

Temporal Course

The interplay of thoughts, feelings, and behaviors in close relationships, itself highly complex, becomes even more intricate when considered along a temporal dimension. Examination of how relationships change and develop is often viewed as fundamental to their understanding, yet "the domain of relationship development is awesomely vast and incompletely charted" (Morton & Douglas, 1981, p. 3). Beyond exploring the sequential dependencies between behaviors in interaction (see "Interaction" above), relatively little attention in clinical psychology, and most of it coming only in recent years, has been devoted to how relationships evolve over time. Although a similar observation characterized social psychology a decade ago (e.g., Huston & Levinger, 1978), an increasing number of investigators are recognizing the importance of studying how relationships unfold and change. Representative research, involving longitudinal, cross-sectional, and retrospective designs, will be reviewed in this section. By way of providing a general outline for this work, studies will be discussed in terms of two research strategies that have been taken: (a) identifying the factors that distinguish continuing relationships from those that terminate (i.e., relationship stability) and (b) examining the temporal course of continuing relationships. In view of space limitations, research on transitions between relationships and on reactions to relationship dissolution will not be addressed (for a review see Harvey, Weber, Galvin, Huszti, & Granick, 1986).

In addition to testing models of relationship dissolution, identification of the factors that predict relationship stability is important because those same factors may exert effects on relationships that continue. Simpson (1987), for example, assessed in a 3-month longitudinal study a variety of factors pertaining to the functioning of dating relationships. He found that relationship instability was more characteristic of shorter, nonexclusive relationships in which there were lower levels of satisfaction and no sexual activity. Berg and McQuinn (1986), in a 4-month longitudinal study of dating couples, found that responses to measures tapping partners' global evaluations of the relationship in its early stages (e.g., lower levels of love, communication, self-disclosure) were predictive of dissolution. Studies of this sort are intuitively attractive and represent an important step forward, and continued work in this vein will help elucidate further the interpersonal processes that distinguish dissolving and continuing relationships.

Investigations also have been conducted that span longer intervals, involve long-term relationships, and assess variables that extend beyond partners' perceptions of the relationship. Kelly and Conley (1987), for example, reported on the factors that predict stability in marriage over a 50-year interval: they found that personality ratings of spouses made by their acquaintances in the 1930s were predictive of divorce likelihood through 1981. Specifically, the chance of divorce was greater among those husbands and wives who were rated by acquaintances as neurotic and among those husbands viewed as having low impulse control. As these authors noted, their findings were "strongly at variance" (p. 36) with the trend toward behavioral conceptions of marriage and highlight the significance of individual differences in close relationships. A further example, more modest in scope and using a cross-sectional design, is provided by Buunk (1987). He compared ongoing and terminated long-term relationships in which sexual affairs had occurred and found that partners in continuing relationships were less likely to view the affair as an intentional act of revenge or anger. Although causal inferences from cross-sectional data must be offered with great caution, this study supports the association between attributions and relationship quality that was described earlier and also suggests an important area for clarification in clinical cases involving extramarital affairs.

A second class of studies addressing the temporal course of relationships involves examination of changes that occur within continuing relationships. In addition to research on development in dating relationships (e.g., Fletcher, Fincham, Cramer, & Heron, 1987), investigators have turned to study factors pertinent to the transition from dating to marriage. For example, Surra, Arizzi, and Asmussen (1988) interviewed newlyweds to determine changes in commitment to their premarital relationship and the reasons for those changes. They found that reasons concerning factors external to the relationship (e.g., social networks, alternative dating partners) predicted lower satisfaction 4 years later, whereas reasons concerning internal factors (e.g., disclosure with partner, behavioral interdependence) were predictive of higher satisfaction.

Changes within the course of marriage, particularly involving variability in marital satisfaction, also have been examined. For example, in the aforementioned study by Kelly and Conley (1987), marital quality was greater over the 50-year interval to the extent that the spouses were viewed as low in neuroticism and high in impulse control; greater emotional closeness and lower levels of tension in families of origin, and fewer stressful life events, also foretold higher levels of marital satisfaction. These findings are extended by research that indicates that changes in marital satisfaction are predicted by aspects of marital interaction. Filsinger and Thoma (1988) reported that declines in satisfaction over 5 years are related to higher rates of females' interruptions and lower rates of males' positive reciprocity. A 3-year longitudinal investigation by Gottman and Krokoff (1989) revealed that the concurrent correlates of marital distress (e.g., higher rates of negative behavior and conflict engagement, lower rates of wives' positive behavior) were different from those predicting decreases in satisfaction (lower rates of husbands' negative behavior and conflict engagement, higher rates of wives' positive behavior). Additional studies are needed to integrate and clarify these findings, yet the available data indicate nonetheless that variability in satisfaction can be predicted, even over long intervals, from both intra- and interpersonal variables.

Although promising, these studies reveal little of how couples cope with particularly difficult or stressful incidents that, as the data from Kelly and Conley (1987) suggest, can accumulate to influence marital functioning over time. One particular event that has been examined to fill this lacuna, and one that appears to result in small but reliable decrements in marital quality (e.g., Belsky, Spanier, & Rovine, 1983), is the transition to parenthood. Following publication of several early studies that documented this decrement, and later research showing that the transition to parenthood was accompanied by decreases in positive marital events and increases in negative marital events, more recent investigations have been undertaken to determine why some marriages are more susceptible than others with arrival of the first child. For example, Belsky, Lang, and Huston (1986) determined that wives' evaluations of marriage were less favorable to the extent that division of labor changed more toward traditional roles after pregnancy, particularly for those who did not view themselves in sex-stereotyped ways. Research of this sort can be used to inform clinical intervention (e.g., by normalizing the transition and allowing couples to attribute their feelings to external stressors, by alerting clinicians to the sort of couples for whom the transition might be especially difficult), and it seems likely that other transitions (e.g., to the "empty nest," to retirement) will receive greater attention in the future.

Apart from highlighting basic questions that could benefit from continued study within any of several disciplines, the foregoing discussion might appear to have few immediate implications for integrating social and clinical research. We believe, however, that investigation of development in close relationships (and especially prediction of relationship stability and quality) holds considerable promise for such an integration, insofar as an understanding of predictors of relationship change afford social and clinical psychologists the ability to prevent relationship dysfunction. Although the value of traditional clinical services cannot be denied, the need for preventive interventions is supported by rising divorce rates and the impact of divorce on children, the fact that marital counseling does not always yield clinically significant change, and the fact that not all couples in need of clinical services receive them.

Gurin, Veroff, and Feld (1960), for example, estimated that less than 20% of those people identifying themselves as experiencing psychological distress sought contact with mental health professionals.

In view of this need, and given that relationship difficulties are the most common problem that people confront (Veroff, Kulka, & Douvan, 1981), it is surprising that very few steps have been taken within psychology to minimize relationship dysfunction before it comes to the attention of clinicians. Although enrichment programs have been developed in other fields, they are limited insofar as nearly all have failed to examine the impact of interventions beyond a 1-year interval (cf. Hahlweg & Markman, 1988; for a review see Bradbury & Fincham, in press). Thus, given the interest in, access to, and knowledge about young couples within social psychology, and the experience with dysfunction, intervention, and outcome research within clinical psychology, it would appear that the domain of prevention in close relationships would be a natural arena for an integration of social and clinical perspectives. Many important questions remain concerning the most appropriate approaches to prevention in this context (e.g., how to intervene, by whom, for whom, when), yet the potential benefits of addressing these questions with the combined resources of social and clinical psychologists are considerable.

Investigation of how relationships evolve over time is a complex yet essential task. We have presented a sample of research, organized around questions concerning the factors that predict whether or not relationships continue and, of those that do, the variables that predict their temporal course. The increasing prominence of research on these topics will enable researchers to achieve a more differentiated understanding of the causes of relationship change and growth that could be used by social and clinical researchers to design programs to prevent relationship dysfunction and enhance relationship quality.

Psychopathology and Social Support

Because "an unequivocal association between marital disruption and physical and emotional disorder has been demonstrated" (Bloom, Asher, & White, 1978, p. 886), psychopathology is encountered often by marital therapists and hence must be incorporated into any comprehensive framework of close relationships. However, because it necessarily implies abnormal functioning and the possibility of genetic precursors and biological remediation, psychopathology has remained largely outside the scope of social psychology in general and the study of relationships in particular. The significance of psychopathology in close relationships, on one hand, and the understandable reluctance of most close relationships researchers to broach this subject, on the other hand, would appear to hinder an integrated social and clinical exploration of psychopathology in relationships. However, recent emphasis on the interpersonal context of psychopathology suggests a convenient way out of this dilemma.

This trend and its implications for social and clinical integration with regard to close relationships is perhaps best appreciated from a historical perspective. As Goldstein (1988) observed, "in the period from the early 1950s to the late 1960s research on the family proliferated, particularly in regard to one disorder, schizophrenia. . . . However, the late 1960s to the late 1970s represents a kind of Dark Ages in research on psychopathological family conditions" (p. 283). The shift away from the family, which Goldstein attributes to conceptual and methodological limitations in family research as well as to evidence supporting the role of genetic factors and the efficacy of pharmacotherapy in psychopathology, has been challenged more recently with the realization that life events, particularly those occurring in families, are an important factor in determining how and when genetic vulnerabilities become manifested as diagnosable disorders.

As a consequence of this evolution, a large body of research is accumulating on psychopathology in marriages and families (for reviews see Jacob, 1987). With regard to schizophrenia, for example, Goldstein (1987) sought to determine whether variables characterizing family interaction involving parents and their disturbed (but not psychotic) adolescent would be predictive of the adolescent's functioning 15 years later. Measures of parental communication deviance (a traitlike variable derived from projective tests that reflects unfocused attention and vague meaning) and affective style (involving negative and guilt-inducing statements directed toward the adolescent in interaction) were indeed found to be predictive, such that lower levels on either of these variables yielded few schizophrenia-spectrum disorders whereas intermediate and higher levels on both variables yielded several such diagnoses. From

these findings, "we can assume that patterns of disordered family relationships precede the onset of schizophrenia and related disorders by a considerable period of time" (Goldstein, 1987, p. 30).

In contrast to the long history of research on the family and schizophrenia, investigators have begun only recently to examine the interplay between close relationships and affective disorders, especially depression. Moreover, because it has a later age of onset than schizophrenia, depression is studied more commonly in the context of marriages than parent-child relationships. This fact, together with the fact that affective disorders are more prevalent than schizophrenic disorders (Regier et al., 1988), suggests that any integration involving social and clinical perspectives on psychopathology in close relationships is most likely to involve depression.

Early research on depression in marriage documented consistent covariation between depression and marital dysfunction (e.g., Coleman & Miller, 1975; for a review see Gotlib & McCabe, in press); indeed, Becker (1988) has commented on the great difficulties involved in recruiting either spouses who are maritally satisfied and depressed or maritally distressed couples in which both spouses are nondepressed. Several subsequent studies have examined the interactional processes that may contribute to this association. Kowalik and Gotlib (1987), for example, determined that depressed spouses were more likely to perceive partner behaviors in interaction as less positive and more negative relative to nondepressed controls, thus implicating negative interpretive biases as an important link between depression and marital dysfunction. Attention has turned also to the causal relation between depression and marital quality. For example, Monroe, Bromet, Connell, and Steiner (1986; see also Beach & Nelson, in press) reported that higher levels of support derived from marriage and, to a lesser extent, lower rates of stressful life events were predictive of lower levels of depressive symptoms over a 1-year period in a sample of women who were initially low in depression and marital conflict.

The Goldstein (1987) and Monroe et al. (1986) studies are important to investigators of close relationships because they suggest that the quality of relationships may exert a causal influence on later psychopathology—lack of such a causal effect or one in the opposite direction could lead to diminished interest in the study of close relationships. Thus, the evolution toward studying the interpersonal context of psychopathology and the data that support this evolution serve to bring psychopathology conveniently into the relationships domain. One factor that is likely to determine the extent to which social psychologists become involved in these developments is the breadth of perspective that is taken. That is, a perspective on psychopathology that emphasizes stressful life events and/or social support is likely to gain more interest in social psychology (and other disciplines) than is a narrow focus on psychopathology per se.

Activity on a number of fronts suggests that such a movement is already occurring. For example, Rook (1987) reported a series of studies examining the relative contributions of companionship (i.e., social interaction undertaken for mutual enjoyment) and social support (i.e., social interaction undertaken for problem resolution) to loneliness, satisfaction with social relationships, and reduction of the effects of stressful events, and determined that, overall, companionship correlated more highly with psychological well-being than did social support. Other studies demonstrate that it is the quality of the marital relationship more than any other that relates to higher psychological functioning (for a review see Cobb & Jones, 1984), a finding that led Coyne and DeLongis (1986) to observe that "any strategy for increasing support might best be aimed primarily at the resolution of marital difficulties, rather than the addition of support from outside the marriage" (p. 456).

Although research of the sort conducted by Rook (1987) does not address psychopathology directly, it does demonstrate how a social psychological perspective can contribute to an understanding of the interpersonal dynamics that either promote or discourage the onset of psychopathology. Additional research from this perspective might be conducted to test models of the impact of perceptions of psychopathology on relationship quality. For example, Hooley, Richters, Weintraub, and Neale (1987) presented data to show that marriages in which one of the spouses exhibited "positive" or expressive symptoms of a psychiatric disorder (e.g., hallucinations, delusions) were higher in marital satisfaction than those marriages in which one of the spouses exhibited "negative" symptoms (e.g., social isolation, depressed affect). A social psychological perspective could be introduced in research of this sort to determine the social cognitive factors that contribute to

judgments that spouses make about their disturbed partner's symptoms. In this particular study, attributional data could be collected to test Hooley et al.'s inference that positive symptoms were attributed by spouses to factors outside the partner's control (thus leading to less blame and greater satisfaction) whereas negative symptoms were attributed to factors that the partner could control (thus leading to more blame and less satisfaction). Further instances in which social and clinical researchers can collaborate to provide a richer appreciation of psychopathology, support, and stressful events in close relationships include the process by which spouses decide to leave an abusive relationship (see Strube, 1988) and the impact that a chronic, subsyndromal tendency to experience negative affect has on relationship function (see Watson & Clark, 1984).

The growing interest in the marriages and families of psychiatric patients augurs well for an integration of social and clinical research on psychopathology and close relationships. Recent research was reviewed to demonstrate the value of studying marriages and families in this manner, and examples were given of how social psychologists could, by adopting a much broader conception of psychopathology, contribute to developments in this area. The widely held view of psychopathology as individually based and the lack of access to psychiatric populations will probably limit such contributions, yet a complete understanding of the strong and complex ties between psychopathology and close relationships is likely to emerge only with input from both perspectives.

SUMMARY AND CONCLUSION

The guiding premise of this chapter is that a complete integration of social and clinical psychology in the domain of close relationships will require, as an intermediate step, more research on close relationships that is undertaken from social and clinical perspectives. In an effort to achieve this latter goal, we identified five targets of inquiry that are likely to be essential in any comprehensive treatment of close relationships; these targets are interaction, affective and cognitive phenomena, relationship quality and dysfunction, the temporal course of relationship events, and psychopathology and social support. The rough framework provided by these constructs served not only to organize our review of existing research but also to point the way forward by clarifying important issues and by highlighting additional topics worthy of empirical attention from social and clinical investigators.

For example, we observed that (a) there is a need to recognize the limitations of global self-reports of behavior as indices of actual interaction; (b) the longstanding interest in intrapersonal phenomena among social psychologists complements and expands the current emphasis on covert processes in interaction among clinical researchers; (c) in the study of relationship quality greater attention should be paid to the varieties of qualitative experiences that people can have and that the study of dating relationships, where significant dysfunction is relatively uncommon, is likely to be of less interest clinically than the study of married couples; (d) as more is learned about the temporal course of relationships, the possibility of preventing relationship dysfunction increases, thus providing a new and important arena for both social and clinical psychologists; and (e) with the recent evolution toward examining psychopathology in the context of marriages and families, an obvious point of entry emerges for social psychologists interested in social support and stressful life events.

Our analysis, however, needs to be qualified by several observations. First, not all pertinent topics within social and clinical psychology were addressed and space limitations precluded review of contributions from other disciplines. The latter omission is in no way intended to minimize the importance of taking a multidisciplinary perspective in this domain. Second, breadth across many topics was emphasized at the expense of depth within a few of them. The present chapter is thus more like a whirlwind tour of several countries than a focused exploration of a few cities and, while both sorts of journeys have their benefits, the former holds the allure of longer, subsequent visits to places that are particularly appealing. In view of the insularity among close relationship investigators that was noted at the outset of the chapter, a whirlwind tour seemed more appropriate at this time. Finally, although we have presented some of the basic components for theoretical development, we were unable in the present context to review existing theory or to show how these components might be combined to form more encompassing frameworks. This is not meant to detract from the central role that theory should play in the investigation of close relationships or the importance of theory to continued progress in this domain.

These limitations notwithstanding, we have sought to identify a number of topics that are fundamental to understanding close relationships and to offer suggestions for how they might be approached from social and clinical vantage points. Ironically, such an analysis will be successful when the distinction between social and clinical contributions becomes blurred and attention is focused not on who does what but on the quality of theory and data that are generated and on the efficacy of interventions that are undertaken. Questions remain as to whether the integration of social and clinical psychology will produce "a genuine subspeciality in psychology or just a flash in the pan" (Leary & Miller, 1986, p. 201). We believe that the study of close relationships can be at the forefront of a viable integration and that the relevance of close relationships to psychological well-being demands such attention.

REFERENCES

Barry, W. A. (1970). Marriage research and conflict: An integrative review. *Psychological Bulletin, 73*, 41–54.

Baucom, D. H., & Adams, A. N. (1987). Assessing communication in marital interaction. In K. D. O'Leary (Ed.), *Assessment of marital discord* (pp. 139–181). Hillsdale, NJ: Lawrence Erlbaum Associates.

Beach, S. R., & Nelson, G. (in press). Pursuing research on major psychopathology from a contextual perspective: The example of depression and marital discord. In G. Brody & I. E. Sigel (Eds.), *Family research* (Vol. 2). Hillsdale, NJ: Lawrence Erlbaum Associates.

Becker, R. E. (1988). Interpersonal interaction and depression. *The Behavior Therapist, 11*, 115–118.

Belsky, J., Lang, M., & Huston, T. L. (1986). Sex typing and division of labor as determinants of marital change across the transition to parenthood. *Journal of Personality and Social Psychology, 50*, 517–522.

Belsky, J., Spanier, G. B., & Rovine, M. (1983). Stability and change in marriage across the transition to parenthood. *Journal of Marriage and the Family, 45*, 553–556.

Berg, J. H., & McQuinn, R. D. (1986). Attraction and exchange in continuing and noncontinuing dating relationships. *Journal of Personality and Social Psychology, 50*, 942–952.

Berscheid, E. (1985). Interpersonal attraction. In G. Lindzey & E. Aronson (Eds.), *The handbook of social psychology* (3rd ed., pp. 413–484). New York: Random House.

Berscheid, E., Snyder, M., & Omoto, A. M. (1989). Issues in studying close relationships: Conceptualizing and measuring closeness. *Review of Personality and Social Psychology, 10*, 63–91.

Bienvenu, M. J. (1970). Measurement of marital communication. *The Family Coordinator, 19*, 26–31.

Bloom, B. L., Asher, S. J., & White, S. W. (1978). Marital disruption as a stressor: A review and analysis. *Psychological Bulletin, 85*, 867–894.

Boyd, L. A., & Roach, A. J. (1977). Interpersonal communication skills differentiating more satisfying from less satisfying marital relationships. *Journal of Counseling Psychology, 24*, 540–542.

Bradbury, T. N., & Fincham, F. D. (1987). Assessment of affect in marriage. In K. D. O'Leary (Ed.), *Assessment of marital discord* (pp. 59–108). Hillsdale, NJ: Lawrence Erlbaum Associates.

Bradbury, T. N., & Fincham, F. D. (1988). Individual difference variables in close relationships: A contextual model of marriage as an integrative framework. *Journal of Personality and Social Psychology, 54*, 713–721.

Bradbury, T. N., & Fincham, F. D. (1990). Attributions in marriage: Review and critique. *Psychological Bulletin, 107*, 3–33.

Bradbury, T. N., & Fincham, F. D. (in press). Preventing marital dysfunction. In F. D. Fincham & T. N. Bradbury (Eds.), *The psychology of marriage*. New York: Guilford Press.

Burnett, R., McGhee, P., & Clarke, D. (Eds.). (1988). *Accounting for relationships*. London: Methuen.

Buunk, B. (1987). Conditions that promote breakups as a consequence of extradyadic involvements. *Journal of Social and Clinical Psychology, 5*, 271–284.

Buunk, B., & Bringle, R. G. (1987). Jealousy in love relationships. In D. Perlman & S. Duck (Eds.), *Intimate relationships: Development, dynamics, and deterioration* (pp. 123–147). Beverly Hills, CA: Sage Publications.

Christensen, A. (1987). Assessment of behavior. In K. D. O'Leary (Ed.), *Assessment of marital discord* (pp. 13–57). Hillsdale, NJ: Lawrence Erlbaum Associates.

Clark, M. S., & Reis, H. T. (1988). Interpersonal processes in close relationships. *Annual Review of Psychology, 39*, 609–672.

Cobb, S., & Jones, J. M. (1984). Social support, support groups, and marital relationships. In S. W. Duck (Ed.), *Personal relationships: 5. Repairing personal relationships* (pp. 47–66). New York: Academic Press.

Coleman, R. E., & Miller, A. G. (1975). The relationship between depression and marital adjustment in a clinic population: A multitrait-multimethod study. *Journal of Consulting and Clinical Psychology, 43*, 647–651.

Coyne, J. C., & DeLongis, A. (1986). Going beyond social support: The role of social relationships in adaptation. *Journal of Consulting and Clinical Psychology, 54*, 454–460.

Davis, M. H., & Oathout, H. A. (1987). Maintenance of satisfaction in romantic relationships: Empathy and relational competence. *Journal of Personality and Social Psychology, 53*, 397–410.

Eiser, J. R. (1983). From attributions to behavior. In M. Hewstone (Ed.), *Attribution theory: Social and functional extensions* (pp. 160–169). Oxford: Blackwell.

Elwood, R. W., & Jacobson, N. S. (1988). The effects of observational training on spouse agreement about events in their relationship. *Behavior Research and Therapy, 26*, 159–167.

Emmelkamp, P. M. G., Krol, B., Sanderman, S., & Ruphan, M. (1987). The assessment of relationship beliefs in a marital context. *Personality and Individual Differences, 8*, 775–780.

Falbo, T., & Peplau, L. A. (1980). Power strategies in intimate relationships. *Journal of Personality and Social Psychology, 38*, 618–628.

Filsinger, E. E., & Thoma, S. J. (1988). Behavioral antecedents of relationship stability and adjustment: A five-year longitudinal study. *Journal of Marriage and the Family, 50*, 785–795.

Fincham, F. D., Beach, S. R., & Nelson, G. (1987). Attribution processes in distressed and nondistressed couples: 3. Causal and responsibility attributions for spouse behavior. *Cognitive Therapy and Research, 11*, 71–86.

Fincham, F. D., & Bradbury, T. N. (1987). The assessment of marital quality: A reevaluation. *Journal of Marriage and the Family, 49*, 797–809.

Fincham, F. D., & Bradbury, T. N. (1988a). The impact of attributions in marriage: Empirical and conceptual foundations. *British Journal of Clinical Psychology, 27,* 77–90.

Fincham, F. D., & Bradbury, T. N. (1988b). The impact of attributions in marriage: An experimental analysis. *Journal of Social and Clinical Psychology, 7,* 147–162.

Fitzpatrick, M. A. (1988). A typological approach to marital interaction. In P. Noller & M. A. Fitzpatrick (Eds.), *Perspectives on marital interaction* (pp. 98–120). Philadelphia: Multilingual Matters.

Fletcher, G. J. O., Fincham, F. D., Cramer, L., & Heron, N. (1987). The role of attributions in the development of dating relationships. *Journal of Personality and Social Psychology, 53,* 481–489.

Forgas, J. P., & Bower, G. H. (1988). Affect in social and personal judgments. In K. Fiedler & J. Forgas (Eds.), *Affect, cognition and social behavior* (pp. 183–208). Toronto: Hogrefe.

Franzoi, S. L., Davis, M. H., & Young, R. D. (1985). The effects of private self-consciousness and perspective taking on satisfaction in close relationships. *Journal of Personality and Social Psychology, 48,* 1584–1594.

Gaelick, L., Bodenhausen, G. V., & Wyer, R. S. (1985). Emotional communication in close relationships. *Journal of Personality and Social Psychology, 49,* 1246–1265.

Goldstein, M. J. (1987). Family interaction patterns that antedate the onset of schizophrenia and related disorders. In K. Hahlweg & M. J. Goldstein (Eds.), *Understanding major mental disorder: The contribution of family interaction research* (pp. 11–32). New York: Family Process Press.

Goldstein, M. J. (1988). The family and psychopathology. *Annual Review of Psychology, 39,* 283–299.

Gotlib, I. H., & McCabe, S. B. (in press). Marriage and psychopathology. In F. D. Fincham & T. N. Bradbury (Eds.), *The psychology of marriage.* New York: Guilford Press.

Gottman, J. M. (1979). *Marital interaction: Experimental investigations.* New York: Academic Press.

Gottman, J. M., & Krokoff, L. J. (1989). Marital interaction and satisfaction: An interactional view. *Journal of Consulting and Clinical Psychology, 57,* 47–52.

Gurin, G., Veroff, J., & Feld, S. (1960). *Americans view their mental health: A nationwide survey.* New York: Basic Books.

Hahlweg, K., & Markman, H. J. (1988). Effectiveness of behavioral marital therapy: Empirical status of behavioral techniques in preventing and alleviating marital distress. *Journal of Consulting and Clinical Psychology, 56,* 440–447.

Harvey, J. H. (1987). Attributions in close relationships: Research and theoretical developments. *Journal of Social and Clinical Psychology, 5,* 420–434.

Harvey, J. H., & Weary, G. (1979). The integration of social and clinical psychology training programs. *Personality and Social Psychology Bulletin, 5,* 511–515.

Harvey, J. H., Weber, A. L., Galvin, K. S., Huszti, H. C., & Granick, N. N. (1986). Attribution and the termination of close relationships: A special focus on the account. In R. Gilmour & S. Duck (Eds.), *The emerging field of personal relationships* (pp. 189–201). Hillsdale, NJ: Lawrence Erlbaum Associates.

Hatfield, E., Traupmann, J., Sprecher, S., Utne, M., & Hay, J. (1985). Equity and intimate relations: Recent research. In W. Ickes (Ed.), *Compatible and incompatible relationships* (pp. 91–117). New York: Springer-Verlag.

Hazan, C., & Shaver, P. (1987). Romantic love conceptualized as an attachment process. *Journal of Personality and Social Psychology, 52,* 511–524.

Hendrick, C. (1983). Clinical social psychology: A birthright reclaimed. *Journal of Social and Clinical Psychology, 1,* 66–87.

Hinde, R. A. (1981). The bases of a science of interpersonal relationships. In S. Duck & R. Gilmour (Eds.), *Personal relationships: 1. Studying personal relationships* (pp. 1–22). New York: Academic Press.

Hooley, J. M., Richters, J. E., Weintraub, S., & Neale, J. M. (1987). Psychopathology and marital distress: The positive side of positive symptoms. *Journal of Abnormal Psychology, 96,* 27–33.

Huston, T. L., & Levinger, G. (1978). Interpersonal attraction and relationships. *Annual Reveiw of Psychology, 29,* 115–156.

Ickes, W., & Tooke, W. (1988). The observational method: Studying the interaction of minds and bodies. In S. W. Duck (Ed.), *Handbook of personal relationships* (pp. 79–97). New York: John Wiley & Sons.

Jacob, T. (Ed.). (1987). *Family interaction and psychopathology*. New York: Plenum Press.

Jacobson, N. S. (1989). The politics of intimacy. *The Behavior Therapist, 12*, 29–32.

Jacobson, N. S., Follette, W. C., & Elwood, R. W. (1984). Outcome research on behavioral marital therapy: A methodological and conceptual reappraisal. In K. Hahlweg & N. S. Jacobson (Eds.), *Marital interaction: Analysis and modification* (pp. 113–129). New York: Guilford Press.

Jacobson, N. S., & Moore, D. (1981). Spouses as observers of the events in their relationship. *Journal of Consulting and Clinical Psychology, 49*, 269–277.

Johnson, D. R., White, L. K., Edwards, J. N., & Booth, A. (1986). Dimensions of marital quality: Toward methodological and conceptual refinement. *Journal of Family Issues, 7*, 31–49.

Kelley, H. H. (1983). Love and commitment. In H. H. Kelley, E. Berscheid, A. Christensen, J. H. Harvey, T. L. Huston, G. Levinger, E. McClintock, L. A. Peplau, & D. R. Peterson (Eds.), *Close relationships* (pp. 265–314). New York: W. H. Freeman.

Kelley, H. H., Berscheid, E., Christensen, A., Harvey, J. H., Huston, T. L., Levinger, G., McClintock, E., Peplau, L. A., & Peterson, D. R. (1983). *Close relationships*. New York: W. H. Freeman.

Kelly, E. L., & Conley, J. J. (1987). Personality and compatibility: A prospective analysis of marital stability and marital satisfaction. *Journal of Personality and Social Psychology, 52*, 27–40.

Kowalik, D. L., & Gotlib, I. H. (1987). Depression and marital interaction: Concordance between intent and perception of communication. *Journal of Abnormal Psychology, 96*, 127–134.

Leary, M. R., & Miller, R. S. (1986). *Social psychology and dysfunctional behavior*. New York: Springer-Verlag.

Lee, J. A. (1977). A typology of styles of loving. *Personality and Social Psychology Bulletin, 3*, 173–182.

Levenson, R. W., & Gottman, J. M. (1985). Physiological and affective predictors of change in relationship satisfaction. *Journal of Personality and Social Psychology, 49*, 85–94.

Locke, H. J., & Wallace, K. M. (1959). Short marital adjustment and prediction tests: Their reliability and validity. *Marriage and Family Living, 21*, 251–255.

Margolin, G., John, R. S., & Gleberman, L. (1988). Affective responses to conflictual discussions in violent and nonviolent couples. *Journal of Consulting and Clinical Psychology, 56*, 24–43.

McCarthy, B. (1981). Studying personal relationships. In S. Duck & R. Gilmour (Eds.), *Personal relationships: 1. Studying personal relationships* (pp. 22–46). New York: Academic Press.

Messe, L. A., Buldain, R. W., & Watts, B. (1981). Recall of social events with the passage of time. *Personality and Social Psychology Bulletin, 7*, 33–38.

Miller, P. C., Lefcourt, H. M., Holmes, J. G., Ware, E. E., & Saleh, W. E. (1986). Marital locus of control and marital problem solving. *Journal of Personality and Social Psychology, 51*, 161–169.

Monroe, S. M., Bromet, E. J., Connell, M. M., & Steiner, S. C. (1986). Social support, life events, and depressive symptoms: A 1-year prospective study. *Journal of Consulting and Clinical Psychology, 54*, 424–431.

Morton, T. L., & Douglas, M. A. (1981). Growth of relationships. In S. Duck & R. Gilmour (Eds.), *Personal relationships: 2. Developing personal relationships* (pp. 3–26). New York: Academic Press.

Navran, L. (1967). Communication and adjustment in marriage. *Family Process, 6*, 173–184.

Newtson, D. (1973). Attribution and the unit of perception of ongoing behavior. *Journal of Personality and Social Psychology, 28*, 28–38.

Norton, R. (1983). Measuring marital quality: A critical look at the dependent variable. *Journal of Marriage and the Family, 45*, 141–151.

Orvis, B. R., Kelley, H. H., & Butler, D. (1976). Attributional conflict in young couples. In J. H. Harvey, W. Ickes, & R. F. Kidd (Eds.), *New directions in attribution research* (Vol. 1, pp. 353–386). Hillsdale, NJ: Lawrence Erlbaum Associates.

Rands, M., Levinger, G., & Mellinger, G. D. (1981). Patterns of conflict resolution and marital satisfaction. *Journal of Family Issues, 2*, 297–321.

Raush, H. L., Barry, W. A., Hertel, R. K., & Swain, M. A. (1974). *Communication, conflict, and marriage*. San Francisco: Jossey-Bass.

Regier, D. A., Boyd, J. H., Burke, J. D., Rae, D. S., Myers, J. K., Kramer, M., Robins, L. N., George, L. K., Karno, M., & Locke, B. Z. (1988). One-month prevalence of mental disorders in the United States. *Archives of General Psychiatry, 45*, 977–986.

Rempel, J. K., Holmes, J. G., & Zanna, M. P. (1985). Trust in close relationships. *Journal of Personality and Social Psychology, 49*, 95–112.

Robinson, E. A., & Price, M. G. (1980). Pleasurable behavior in marital interaction: An observational study. *Journal of Consulting and Clinical Psychology, 48*, 117–118.

Rook, K. S. (1987). Social support versus companionship: Effects of life stress, loneliness, and evaluation by others. *Journal of Personality and Social Psychology, 52*, 1132–1147.

Rubin, Z. (1970). Measurement of romantic love. *Journal of Personality and Social Psychology, 16*, 265–273.

Rusbult, C. E., Johnson, D. J., & Morrow, G. D. (1986). Impact of couple patterns of problem solving on distress and nondistress in dating relationships. *Journal of Personality and Social Psychology, 50*, 744–753.

Schaap, C. (1984). A comparison of the interaction of distressed and nondistressed married couples in a laboratory situation. In K. Hahlweg & N. S. Jacobson (Eds.), *Marital interaction: Analysis and modification* (pp. 133–158). New York: Guilford Press.

Simpson, J. A. (1987). The dissolution of romantic relationships: Factors involved in relationship stability and emotional distress. *Journal of Personality and Social Psychology, 53*, 683–692.

Snyder, D. K. (1979). Multidimensional assessment of marital satisfaction. *Journal of Marriage and the Family, 41*, 813–823.

Snyder, D. K., Trull, T. J., & Wills, R. M. (1987). Convergent validity of observational and self-report measures of marital interaction. *Journal of Sex and Marital Therapy, 13*, 224–236.

Spanier, G. B. (1976). Measuring dyadic adjustment: New scales for assessing the quality of marriage and similar dyads. *Journal of Marriage and the Family, 38*, 15–28.

Sternberg, R. J. (1986). A triangular theory of love. *Psychological Review, 93*, 119–135.

Sternberg, R. J., & Barnes, M. L. (Eds.). (1988). *The psychology of love*. New Haven, CT: Yale University Press.

Strube, M. J. (1988). The decision to leave an abusive relationship: Empirical evidence and theoretical issues. *Psychological Bulletin, 104*, 236–250.

Surra, C. A., Arizzi, P., & Asmussen, L. A. (1988). The association between reasons for commitment and the development and outcome of marital relationships. *Journal of Social and Personal Relationships, 5*, 47–63.

Swann, W. B., Pelham, B. W., & Roberts, D. C. (1987). Causal chunking: Memory and inference in ongoing interaction. *Journal of Personality and Social Psychology, 53*, 858–865.

Veroff, J., Kulka, R. A., & Douvan, E. (1981). *Mental health in America: Patterns of help-seeking from 1957–1976*. New York: Basic Books.

Watson, D., & Clark, L. A. (1984). Negative affectivity: The disposition to experience aversive emotional states. *Psychological Bulletin, 96*, 465–490.

Weiner, B. (1985). An attributional theory of achievement motivation and emotion. *Psychological Review, 92*, 548–573.

CHAPTER 17

AN INTERACTIONAL PERSPECTIVE ON DEPRESSION

James C. Coyne
Sue A. L. Burchill
William B. Stiles

Konrad Lorenz (1952) has recounted how he once unwittingly attracted a group of tourists during one of his imprinting experiments in a vacant lot in London. Observing him waddling through the high grass in a figure-eight pattern and quacking, the tourists had no way of knowing that he was conducting a scientific experiment and would later win a Nobel prize for his work. Given Lorenz's scraggly appearance, there seemed to be little reason to consider explanations for his odd behavior other than that it was simply an expression of some kind of psychopathology.

Like these tourists, many theorists and researchers have been so impressed with depressed persons' self-derogation, pessimism, and apparent reluctance to take even minimal initiative to remedy obviously upsetting situations that they have not bothered to consider how this behavior might be intelligible in a more inclusive context. The bulk of the literature focuses on the nature of depression and more specifically on the thinking of depressed people without even passing consideration of their predicament, their effects on others, or how others react to them. Watzlawick,

Beavin, and Jackson (1967) have anticipated how such a narrowing of the range of inquiry can result in confusion and misattribution to individuals of what is more appropriately to be viewed as features of their exchanges with their environments.

One can find ample examples of this in the depression literature. That a third of women academic physicians are clinically depressed has been discussed in terms of how some women, who are especially vulnerable to depression might be attracted to academic medicine as a career (Welner et al., 1979). Alternatively, efforts to understand the characteristic complaints of depressed people have been focused not on how their everyday lives might provide them with something about which to complain, but rather on how the thinking processes of depressed and nondepressed people differ when their success or failure on a task has been rigged by an experimenter. Undaunted by contradictory findings and past demonstrations of the inherent limitations of their methods (see Gage & Cronbach, 1955; Coyne & Gotlib, 1983), researchers continue their futile struggle for the definitive answer to the question of whether it's depressed or nondepressed people who are "realistic" (Dykman, Abramson, Alloy, & Hartlage, 1989). Of course, we cannot adequately specify subjects' thinking processes without reference to what information is generally available to them, and who appears realistic in a given experiment may largely depend on the match between the answers sustained by the subjects' everyday experiences and what the experimenter has made "realistic" by design.

Expanding the boundaries on what is considered relevant in the study of depression, an interactional perspective starts with the assumption that an understanding of depressed people requires that we know something about their ecological niches — that is, the conditions of their everyday lives, the problems they face, and how these problems may resist or even be exacerbated by how they and key people around them cope. Furthermore, whereas what depressed people think is important to how they lead their lives, it is not the only and it is often not the primary determinant of the adjustment that they achieve. Thinking and even what a person does can have only limited causal efficacy in many situations. Indeed, the apparent ineptness of depressed people's coping and intractability of their problems may well depend on unyielding features of their circumstances and the characteristic responses that they receive from others, responses that may not entirely be determined by what the depressed people do.

Adopting such a perspective entails setting a new research agenda. There is less interest in depressed people's attributions for hypothetical events or how they struggle with insolvable anagrams or bogus feedback on a laboratory task. Instead, attention is focused on how depressed people get along with key people in their lives as well as how they affect and get affected by people who do not have a history with them.

In this chapter, we will review a wide range of evidence as to the nature of the rich and reciprocal links between depressed people and their interpersonal environments. At the onset, a few cautions are in order. First, provocative though some of this evidence may be, much of it is circumstantial and suggestive, rather than indicative of the complex processes by which depressed people and those around them are influencing each other. Second, the delineation of a formal model has been limited, progressing little beyond a preliminary statement more than a decade old (Coyne, 1976a). At this point, the interactional perspective involves a broadening of the range of factors to be considered in attempts to explain depression and some tentative suggestions as to how they might be relevant, rather than a set of formal, well-delineated theoretical propositions. Nonetheless, it will be seen that existing data provide a strong impetus for further development of an interactional perspective on depression and highlight the futility of continuing to attempt to build models of depression that do not adequately take into account its interpersonal context.

In an early paper, Coyne (1976a) outlined how the behavior of depressed people and those around them might come to fit into an emergent interpersonal system — how all involved might inadvertently contribute to the perpetuation of an unsatisfactory situation. The distressed behavior of depressed people was viewed as reflecting involvement in a set of circumstances where the usual sources of security, meaning, and validation have been disrupted or have otherwise proven to be insufficient. Such circumstances are likely to be the result of stressful life changes or chronic difficulties, but they also can coevolve with depression.

Regardless of the precipitants for depression, it can be anticipated that depressed people will make demands and depend on their relationships in ways that leave others feeling depressed or annoyed themselves, pressured, or that their needs are not being met. Depressed people are thereby likely to provoke reactions that leave them feeling further insecure and even rejected. Undoubtedly, relationships differ in their ability to accommodate the distress and dysfunctional behavior characteristic of depression, as well as the overt disagreement, direct expression of negative affect, and efforts to renegotiate expectations that are likely to accompany it (Coyne, 1988a). Relationships that otherwise appear satisfactory may prove brittle when faced with such challenges.

Thus, while it is assumed that depression is likely to be preceded by stressful life circumstances and overtly problematic relationships, greater emphasis is placed on how the behavior of depressed people and those around them becomes interwoven or concatenated over time. It is conceivable, for instance, that even without the provocation of major life changes, some people are going to be chronically or intermittently needy and will test the supportiveness and patience of those around them. The outcome of this behavior may depend on how it is handled by key people and the patterning of the relationship that results. Also, some people may be inclined to be particularly obtuse, indifferent, or unfulfilling in their response to the needs of others, and whether this proves depressing to a partner may depend on the ability of the partner to cope with such behavior and how the relationship evolves. An interactional perspective does not deny the individuality of either depressed people or those who are involved with them or how each may contribute to problematic situations, but it does look to the emergent characteristics of interactions and relationships for how this individuality will be shaped and how these problems unfold.

One common feature of depressed people's interactions with others is that the obvious distress of the depressed people has the effect of engaging others, making them feel responsible, and thereby shifting the interactional burden onto them. Their distress proves aversive to others and is capable of inducing a negative mood in them. Yet, at the same time, it is also guilt inducing and inhibiting. People around depressed people may attempt to control their aversiveness by seemingly providing what is being asked, even while communicating impatience, hostility, and rejection. The subtle and overt hostility and rejection that depressed people receive validates their sense of insecurity and elicits further expression of distress, strengthening the pattern. Thus, others may become involved with depressed people in ways that unwittingly perpetuate or aggravate their problems. An interactional stalemate may be the result. Aside from the direct effects of getting caught up in such a pattern, everyone involved may find it more generally difficult to be pleasant and responsive to each other, maintain a household, deal with other problems that they face, and/or simply have the discussions necessary to renegotiate their relationship (Coyne, 1990).

More recent statements of this perspective also have acknowledged the salience of overt anger and negative outbursts in the interactions of depressed people and how these features might be related to inhibited communication at other times (Coyne, 1984; Kahn, Coyne, & Margolin, 1985). Contrary to psychoanalytic formulations of depression, depressed people have not turned all their anger inward. Particularly in their close relationships, they may at times express or receive considerable hostility. Depressed people's obvious distress and the possibility of their becoming even more distressed may serve generally to inhibit others' attempts at direct confrontation. For their part, depressed people tend to be avoidant of conflict and interpersonally sensitive, and they may therefore struggle to head off situations that could involve more criticism and rejection from others. However, despite and even because of such strategies, problems arise that cannot be so readily avoided. When it becomes necessary to face them, the interaction is burdened by the accumulation of unresolved issues and negative feelings and attitudes toward each other. The resulting exchanges are likely to be highly emotional and unproductive, strengthening the sense that problems cannot be discussed and therefore the likelihood that they will again accumulate without resolution. Thus, inhibition may beget hostile exchanges which beget more inhibition. Related to this, the Oregon Research Institute (Biglan, Hops, & Sherman, 1988) has utilized Patterson and Reid's (1970) coercion theory in conceptualizing depressive behavior as a form of aversive control. This group emphasizes how displays of depressive behavior may in the short run inhibit hostile behavior and elicit compliance from others, even though it also serves to suppress caring behavior and increase the likelihood of subsequent hostility.

Finally, Coyne (1989) has provided some hypotheses about the nature of the characteristic complaints of depressed people and the various ways in which they may be intelligible in their interactional context. He emphasized that before assuming that these complaints are prima facie evidence of cognitive distortion, it is important to explore them both as reflections of the negative experiences that depressed people accumulate and as active attempts to manage such experiences. More than simply expressing negative thoughts, depressed people's complaints may be seen as instrumental or illocutionary speech-acts (Austin, 1965). Namely, they may be a means of reducing demands, and eliciting support from others or of inhibiting them and leaving them feeling guilty. They also may be a self-manipulative or self-handicapping strategy (Snyder & Smith, 1982) in that they allow depressed people to reduce their expectations of themselves, avoid the implications of potential failures, and otherwise guard against disappointment.

Over the past decade, there have been these refinements of the interactional perspective on depression. Yet, even with such elaborations and qualifications, it still provides a rather sketchy picture of interpersonal processes in depression. Nonetheless, it can serve to organize our review of the literature, highlighting some patterns of findings that may then provide the basis for defining a research agenda for the future and the continued development of the perspective. Refinement of theory is obviously important, but we also should be sensitive to the pitfalls of its premature ossification. As well as tying together facts that might otherwise seem unrelated, theory can serve to keep crucial facts from being given the consideration that they are due. We look only at the data that fit and look only in places where we will find that kind of data. For instance, provocative findings that there is a more than 25-fold increase in the risk for depression when one is not able to talk to one's spouse (Weissman, 1987) or that spousal criticism is one of the most powerful predictors of subsequent relapse (Hooley, Orley, & Teasdale, 1986; Vaughn & Leff, 1976) warrant more attention than they are accorded by most current theories of depression. These findings are quite compatible with an interpersonal perspective and can be an important impetus to its refinement. Yet, we also should remain alert to findings whose explanation remains more elusive; for instance, that being married is associated with poorer response to antidepressant medication (Keller et al., 1984). Such findings need to be replicated, but they should not be lost from view simply because their theoretical relevance has not been established.

We will begin with survey and interview studies of life events, social support, intimacy, and depression, identifying how such research is relevant to an interactional perspective and the kinds of questions it leaves unanswered. We will next consider the unique contribution of studies of interactions between depressed people and people with whom they are not previously acquainted. Then we will consider studies of the relationships between depressed people and family members, first their spouses and then their children.

STRESS, SUPPORT, INTIMACY, AND DEPRESSION

A large body of survey research now relates measures of life events, social support, and intimacy to depressive symptoms and diagnosis. The generally accepted interpretation of this literature is that it demonstrates a role for stressful life events in the onset of depression and for positive or intimate social relationships in protecting the individual from depression both directly and by buffering the effects of stress. Yet considerable ambiguity and controversy remain. Questions have been raised as to the extent to which occurrence of life events may be the result of chronic and intermittent depressive symptoms rather than invariably the cause or precipitant; whether stress-support accounts of depression are most appropriately limited to milder forms of the disorder; and whether the referents for "life events" and "support" in the circumstances of survey respondents are distinct and what researchers have assumed them to be.

Stress

Rather consistently, measures of life events and chronic strains or difficulties have been found to be associated with depressive symptoms. Yet, it appears that some of the conditions associated with depressive symptoms are insufficient to precipitate an episode of clinical depression (Coyne & Downey, in press). Marital difficulties are associated both with depressive symptoms and clinical depression (Lewinsohn, Hoberman, & Rosenbaum, 1988), but poverty (Weissman, 1987) or having a handicapped child (Breslau & Davis, 1986) are associated with symptoms, but not an increased risk for clinical depression. Focusing on clinical depression, Paykel (1979) calculated that the risk of depression is increased by a factor of 5.6 in the 6 months following any major event he considered and a factor of 6.5 following an exit from a major social role.

Because most studies of life events and depression are retrospective in design, it is often difficult or impossible to disentangle confounds between measures of life events and depression or to identify instances in which depression brought on the events, rather than vice versa (Dohrenwend, 1974; Monroe, in press). Thus, the apparent precipitation of an episode of depression by a breakup of a relationship or the loss of a job may actually be a matter of the dysfunction associated with being depressed bringing about such events. To resolve this issue, it is necessary to go beyond the usual retrospective, checklist approach to the assessment of life events. For instance, Brown and Harris (1978) excluded chronic cases of depression and utilized in-depth analysis of extensive interview data to ensure that events did indeed precede the onset of depression and that the events were unlikely to be a consequence of depression. Even with such stringent procedures, they found that the relationship between severe life events and depression held across four different samples. For instance, in one sample of community-residing women, 53% of the new cases of diagnosable depression involved women who had had such an event of causal importance in the previous 9 months versus 19% of the women who were not cases. Yet, not all stressful life events were found to have the potential for precipitating depression, only those that had long-term threatening implications for a woman's well-being.

> The distinctive feature of the great majority of the provoking events is the experience of loss or disappointment, if this is defined broadly to include threat of or actual separation from a key figure, an unpleasant revelation about someone else, a life-threatening illness to a close relative, a major material loss of general disappointment or threat of them, and miscellaneous crises such as being made redundant after a long period of steady employment. (pp. 274–275)

Brown and Harris' (1978) strategy of focusing on events that are patently independent of any existing depression circumvents many of the criticisms of the typical study of life events and depression, and it provides a demonstration that the stress-depression link be reduced to a matter of confounds or depression-causing life events. However, it also provides an incomplete picture of the role of life events in depression, excluding many cases of depression and many instances in which life events might contribute to depression. About 40% of clinically depressed people suffer from a "double depression," with an acute depressive episode superimposed on a preexisting dysthymia (Keller & Shapiro, 1982). Whereas Brown and Harris' (1978) approach might exclude these depressed people from study, there is the possibility that the onset of the acute episode may result from the interplay of dysthymia and life events, as when a spouse threatens separation because of a person's chronic low-grade depressed mood and behavior, and this precipitates an acute episode, which leads to an actual separation. Also, an earlier study had found the single most frequent event reported by depressed women is an increase in arguments with their spouses (Paykel et al., 1969), but most recent studies exclude this event from consideration because of the difficulty in assuming its independence from depression. While allowing a stricter test of the contribution of life events to depression, this exclusion closes the question of whether such increased turmoil in close relationships may play an important role in

explaining the occurrence of depression. Thus, having established that life events that require long-term adjustment may precipitate depression, it is time that theorists and researchers explore other, more complex ways in which life events and depression may be linked. Efforts to provide a strict test of a causal role for life events may inadvertently lead to a distortion of the basic phenomena under consideration.

Over the years, there has been the persistent notion that while stress may be upsetting and demoralizing, clinical depression is an illness that cannot be explained by stress. In one version of this argument, Bebbington, Tennant, and Hurray (1981) have suggested that episodes of depression identified in people residing in the community may "have a ready explication as understandable and unmysterious responses to adversity" (p. 346), but that this would not hold for depression in psychiatric patients. Replying to this argument, Brown and Harris (1982) reviewed seven studies of depressed people in treatment and found that an average of 56% of these patients had an important or severely threatening event in the 6 months prior to the onset of their depression. They further noted that these studies did not assess the chronic life difficulties that also have been shown to be associated with depression, and suggested that this figure was therefore a low estimate of the magnitude of the stress-depression relationship in clinical populations. On the basis of these data, Brown and Harris concluded that when appropriate selection criteria are employed, depression in community and treatment samples are in fact comparable with regard to the role of stress.

An argument related to that of Bebbington et al. (1981) is that within a clinically depressed population there are two kinds of depression, one related to stress (reactive) and the other biological (endogenous), and for the latter we can afford to ignore the role of interpersonal factors. This argument is based on a misunderstanding of the nature and correlates of endogenous depression. A set of symptoms such as sleep and appetite disturbance predict a better response to antidepressant medication and electroconvulsive therapy, and endogenous depression is now defined on this basis. However, whether a precipitating stress can be identified is not relevant to diagnosing a depression as endogenous. Reactivity to changes in the environment during a depressive episode, rather than the absence of precipitating stress, has been found to predict response to biologically oriented treatment (Fowles & Gersh, 1979) and it has now replaced the lack of antecedent stress as an additional criterion for endogenicity. Further, there is evidence that endogenously depressed patients tend to have preexisting problems in their close relationships (Birchnell & Kennard, 1983), and among depressed patients the overall association between endogenous features and the presence or absence of recent life events is weak at best (Dolan, Calloway, Fonagy, De Souza, & Wakeling, 1985).

In yet another version of this argument, it also has been suggested that current diagnostic criteria for depression are overinclusive. If a sample of depressed people is selected on the basis of a demonstrable biological abnormality, then stress will be irrelevant to their depression. Some episodes of depression are associated with identifiable biological features such as nonsuppression of cortisol secretion in response to dexamethasone. Yet, among depressed persons such features are not related to whether a precipitating stress can be identified (Dolan et al., 1985). Thus, whether we consider depression in clinical populations, endogenous depression, or depression with an associated neuroendocrine abnormality, we are not precluding the importance of stressful life events for someone becoming depressed. The key question is not whether depression is to be explained in terms of the interactional context or biology, but how interactional and biological factors fit together. As yet, this question has not received the attention it deserves.

Social Support, Intimacy, and Depression

The hypothesis that having good social relationships protects against depression has been given considerable attention. Having a smaller social network, fewer close relationships, and less supportive relationships have all been shown to be related to depression (Billings & Moos, 1984; Schaefer, Coyne, & Lazarus, 1981). It also has been suggested that it is the quality of one's closest relationships that is most crucial and that the support available from other relationships does not compensate for the deficiencies of one's intimate relationships (Coyne & DeLongis, 1986).

As in the case of life events and depression, Brown and Harris' (1978) classic study gives what is perhaps the richest picture of the importance of quality of one's relationships in depression. They found that whether a woman had a confiding relationship with her spouse was a powerful mediator of the association between life events and depression. Women who lacked a confiding relationship with an intimate were three times more likely to become depressed in the face of a life event. Further, having a good intimate relationship appeared to eliminate the effects of other risk factors such as having three young children at home, being unemployed, and having lost one's mother in childhood. In subsequent analyses, Brown, Bifulco, Harris, and Bridge (1986) examined whether the difficulties in the marital relationships of depressed women could have been brought about by their affective state if they had been suffering from an insidious form of disorder. They utilized a rating based on a commonsense judgment as to whether these difficulties could be construed as contingent or probably contingent on the women's affective state, and found that only a third of the marital difficulties were rated as contingent. Two thirds of the marital difficulties involved husbands judged to be "grossly undependable."

Brown and Harris (1978) distinguished between life events as provoking agents in depression and a lack of intimacy as a vulnerability factor, with the effects of a lack of intimacy occurring in the presence of a life event. It is this aspect of their work that has been subject to the greatest criticism. Other investigators have reanalyzed the Brown and Harris (1978) data using alternative statistical techniques, and they have been able to show that the effects of lack of intimacy are independent of whether there has been a serious life event (Cleary & Kessler, 1982; Tennant & Bebbington, 1978; but see Oatley & Bolton, 1985). This reinterpretation is consistent with the robust conclusion of community surveys that a lack of social support has a direct effect on depressive symptoms and diagnosis (e.g., Andrews, Tennant, Hewson, & Valliant, 1978; Aneshensel & Stone, 1982; Costello, 1982).

Further questions have been raised as to the meaning of intimacy and social support scores and their referents in the everyday lives of survey respondents. The general assumption has been that a high score on social support or intimacy indicates that respondents have something in their lives (i.e., social support or intimacy) that low scorers lack. However, it could be that rather than indicating the presence of something positive, a high score most importantly indicates that respondents are relatively free from interactions or conditions in their relationships that might prove depressing (Coyne, Ellard, & Smith, 1990). Consistent with this notion, Roy (1978) found that women reporting an inability to confide in their husbands were but a subset of those reporting a "bad marriage," and that it was having a bad marriage that leaves women at risk for depression, and not the lack of a confiding relationship per se.

However, the most relevant and provocative data come from the Yale Epidemiologic Catchment Area Study (ECA; Weissman, 1987). In a sample of over 3,000 adults, being married and being able to talk to one's spouse apparently provided a modest reduction in the risk for depression over that associated with being single, separated, or divorced. These may be viewed as the benefits of intimacy. However, this effect was overshadowed by the negative effects of being married and indicating that one could not talk to one's spouse. The odds ratio for depression associated with being married and not being able to talk to one's spouse (i.e., the odds associated with not being able to talk to one's spouse versus the odds associated with all other conditions) was a striking 25.8 for men and 28.1 for women. Taken together, results of this study strongly suggest that most of the apparent protection from depression afforded by having a good relationship with one's spouse (i.e., spousal support or intimacy) found in other studies might better be seen as a reflection of the detrimental effects of being married but not getting along with a spouse. These findings give added credibility to arguments that not having to deal with problematic features of bad relationships may be more powerful than the purported salutory effects of good relationships.

Taken together, the kinds of studies that we have reviewed might be interpreted as suggesting that regardless of whether it is endogenous or has an associated biological abnormality, depression frequently arises in a context in which there have been losses or disappointments such that personal goals, plans, and expectations have been seriously disrupted, and more specifically when there is turmoil in close relationships. This latter association has sometimes been obscured by researchers' tendencies both to exclude relevant items from life event inventories and to interpret social support and intimacy scores primarily in terms of what good relationships provide rather than the costs of being in an unsatisfactory relationship. Being in an unsatisfactory close relationship is a powerful risk factor for depression, perhaps more so than most major life events, and is independent of the effects of life events.

Survey studies of life events, social support, and intimacy are thus consistent with an interactional perspective on depression and can lead to a sharpening of focus on the specific kinds of conditions associated with the onset of depression. Yet, these studies tell us little about why particular events befall particular people in particular contexts or the importance of how events unfold. Depression typically does not occur in single episodes, but it is a recurrent, episodic condition (Coyne & Downey, in press). At the present time, we know little about how this course reflects enduring risks or vulnerabilities of the interpersonal contexts in which depressed persons live or how recurrent depressive episodes shape these contexts. Further, as Brown and Harris (1978) noted, their study left open the question of how depressed people "get caught up in a crisis or difficulty, try to cope with it, and the resources that they have for it" (p. 293).

More basically, a social support score or an endorsement of a life event tells us little about a complex set of circumstances, and while they suggest the relevance of interactional processes to depression, they only hint at what these processes may be. In the terminology of Geerwitz (1973), an item on a life events scale such as "birth of a child" is a rather thin description. A thicker description or a closer look at the situations of two women giving birth may reveal features that make it more understandable why one gets depressed and the other does not. Addressing this question in their interview study, Brown and Harris (1978) found that for the women who became depressed, the pregnancy had given added significance to already existing problems: "pregnancy and birth . . . can bring home to a woman the disappointment and hopelessness of her position — her aspirations are made more distant or she becomes even more dependent on an uncertain relationship" (p. 141).

Although an important first step, survey studies have inherent limitations in efforts to understand interactional processes associated with depression. A richer sampling of the particulars of the lives of depressed people is needed. Brown and Harris' (1978) contextual method of interviewing represents one such solution to this problem. It involves gathering extensive background information about circumstances of respondents and then having this information rated on various dimensions by people other than the interviewers. Structured daily diaries completed by depressed people and their significant others is another. Actual sampling of interactions of depressed people and others in the home and laboratory is the method most identified with an interactional perspective, but we should be realistic about the difficulties in obtaining an adequate and representative sampling of behavior and making the fullest use of it. No single method is going to prove sufficient to generate a comprehensive view of depression.

Although encouraging of an interactional perspective on depression, the kinds of data just considered raise an important challenge as to how one can decisively test interactional hypotheses about depression. If depression often arises in the context of turmoil in close relationships, how might the emergent patterns of interaction that have been postulated be separated from the effects of such preexisting difficulties? To understand better the interactions between depressed people and the key people in their lives, it thus becomes necessary to sample interactions in which the participants do not have such a history together.

DEPRESSED PEOPLE IN INTERACTION

Studies of depressed people's interactions with strangers allow one to investigate the effects of their current behavior without the confounding effects of past interactions and background that color marital and familial interactions. Any interpersonal difficulties observed in studies of interactions with strangers cannot be attributed to the mate selection, preexisting conflict, or long-term negative attitudes of depressed people and their spouses that might explain the patterning of their enduring close relationships. Yet in the Popperian sense, the notion that depression has identifiable impact in a fleeting contact with a stranger is a "risky hypothesis"; that is, it is the kind of hypothesis that could so easily be wrong and for that very reason increases our confidence in its validity when it stands up to empirical test. Despite the intuitive notion that strangers would be less tolerant of depressed people's difficulties than would family members, several studies (e.g., Hinchliffe, Hopper, & Roberts, 1978; Weissman & Paykel, 1974) have noted that interpersonal disturbances are more pronounced within intimate relationships. A 20-minute conversation in which strangers are asked to become acquainted is socially constraining and places minimal demands on participants, and so it is quite possible that the usual difficulties of depressed people will not have

the opportunity to develop. Depressed people may be more inclined to withdraw from strangers and hide their distress than with intimates (Meyer & Hokanson, 1985). Studies of interactions with strangers can therefore serve to inform our interpretation of studies of interactions with intimates, but a lack of predicted findings should not prematurely discourage us from pursuing a potentially fruitful line of inquiry concerning the intimate relationships of depressed people. Fortunately, however, results of studies of depressed people in fleeting contacts with strangers do indeed give encouragement to development of an interactional perspective on depression.

Do Depressed People Create Negative Affect in Others?

One hypothesis that has received much attention in the literature has been that interacting with a depressed person, even for a brief period of time, can create negative mood in others. Most tests of this hypothesis have used paradigm developed by Coyne (1976b), in which college students interacted with either depressed psychiatric patients, nondepressed psychiatric patients, or nondepressed nonpsychiatric controls over the telephone. Subjects completed self-report mood checklists following the interactions. Those interacting with the depressed group experienced significantly greater negative affect themselves: anxiety and hostility, as well as depression.

Several studies have replicated Coyne's (1976b) findings, despite methodological variations. Winer, Bonner, Blaney, and Murray (1981) had subjects read transcripts describing either depressed or nondepressed persons. Strack and Coyne (1983) had subjects interact face to face with either depressed or nondepressed college students. Hammen and Peters (1978) had subjects talk over an intercom system with confederates enacting either a depressed or nondepressed role. Boswell and Murray (1981) had subjects listen to tape-recorded interviews of depressed or schizophrenic patients or staff at a psychiatric hospital and then imagine themselves interacting with these target individuals. All of these studies used self-report mood checklists and found that depressed people aroused more dysphoric emotions in others than nondepressed controls, although Boswell and Murray (1981) reported that the negative mood induction by depressed individuals was no greater than that by schizophrenic controls. However, a number of the above studies used either confederates enacting depressed roles or subjects imagining interactions with depressed people, so the ecological validity of the effect is still subject to challenge. The use of confederates helps to standardize the behavior of the "depressed" people, but it carries the risk that confederates will not accurately portray the behavior of a depressed person or that they will not accommodate the flow of interaction in a way that is similar to someone who is not enacting a role. At this point we do not know enough about the typical behavior of a depressed person in an initial encounter to assert with confidence that a script for a "depressed" confederate captures the crucial verbal and nonverbal behaviors and reactivity to the partner's response. The use of videotaped stimuli also provides some standardization of conditions, but carries the liability that the stimulus person's behavior is not contingent on the subject's behavior, and therefore there are limits to the extent to which the encounter can be construed as an interaction.

Not all of the literature has confirmed Coyne's idea about mood induction. Howes and Hokanson (1979) had subjects interact on a problem-solving task with a confederate playing a depressed, nondepressed, or physically ill role. Gotlib and Robinson (1982) studied subjects interacting with either depressed or nondepressed college students, and King and Heller (1984) utilized Coyne's original (1976a) methodology with outpatients. None of these studies found group differences in self-reported mood, although Gotlib and Robinson (1982) did find nonverbal indications of mood change, as will be discussed later. These studies highlight the remaining need to determine whether a mood induction can be obtained reliably in a fleeting encounter between a depressed person and a stranger, and if so, what the requisite conditions are for it to be observed.

How Do Others Respond to Depressed People?

Coyne (1976a) suggested that the aversive nature of interactions with depressed people often leads others to respond negatively or to avoid future interactions with these individuals. Using a questionnaire on which subjects indicated how willing they would be to interact with a target individual in the future, Coyne (1976b) found that subjects were more rejecting of depressed patients than nondepressed patients or controls. Hammen and Peters (1977, 1978), Strack and Coyne (1983),

Howes and Hokanson (1979), Winer et al. (1981), and Boswell and Murray (1981) all used essentially the same measure and found similar results, although the latter study demonstrated this trend only for male subjects. Convergently, Robbins, Strack, and Coyne (1979) found that subjects indicated that they were less willing to give positive reactions to depressed individuals, and Youngren and Lewinsohn's (1980) depressed subjects reported receiving fewer positively reinforcing responses from others. Hokanson, Sacco, Blumberg, and Landrum (1980) likewise reported that subjects communicated more extrapunitiveness (e.g., feelings of irritation) to depressed individuals than to controls. However, two studies (Gotlib & Robinson, 1982; King & Heller, 1984) used Coyne's (1976a) rejection questionnaire and found no differences in the extent to which depressed people were rejected.

In everyday situations, as opposed to laboratory analogs, rejection of depressed people may take the form of actual avoidance. Yarkin, Harvey, and Bloxom (1981) found that simply being told that someone is depressed leads to others sitting farther away before an interaction begins. Weissman and Paykel's (1974) discovery that depressed people had relatively few social contacts and limited support systems is consistent with this idea. In addition, several studies have found that depressed people are devalued and perceived as less well adjusted (e.g., Boswell & Murray, 1981; Burchill & Stiles, 1988).

Others' responses to depressed people also have been assessed through behavioral observations, including verbal codings with positive/negative evaluations of each utterance and nonverbal codings of posture, eye contact, gestures, and facial expression. Two studies suggested that others give fewer total responses, fewer positive responses, and more negative responses when interacting with depressed people (Gotlib & Robinson, 1982; Howes & Hokanson, 1979). This nonverbal indication of mood change and rejection in the Gotlib and Robinson (1982) study occurred after only 3 minutes, despite subjects not subsequently reporting less willingness to interact with depressed persons in the future. The discrepancy between self-report and behavioral measures in this study may reflect subjects' ambivalence about actually feeling annoyed when they believe they should be helpful. This interpretation is also consistent with Coyne's (1976a) contention that others respond with nongenuine support toward depressed people. Further, it could indicate that others' nonverbal reactions to depressed people are automatic and not mediated by the same kinds of conscious recognition and interpretation that would be registered in questionnaire responses.

In most of the research concerning others' reactions to depressed people, the focus has been primarily on the responses that are elicited by depressed people, and any variability or contribution by the others has been slighted. One exception is Ellard, Coyne, Showers, and Ruvulo's (1987) study of the role of others' expectancies in determining the experiences of both parties in dyadic interactions involving a depressed person. As in other research, people who expected that they were going to interact with a depressed person were negative in their evaluation of the actual interaction. Likewise, subjects who were told that the person with whom they would interact was warm and outgoing responded negatively when that person was actually depressed. Apparently, subjects reacted to the disconfirmation of their expectations. However, when subjects were told that their partner was nurturant and high in self-esteem, but uncomfortable in initial encounters, both subjects and their naive depressed partners evaluated themselves and each other positively. Ellard et al. (1987) interpreted these results in terms of this manipulation of expectations, both preparing subjects for what would follow but at the same time reducing their self-imposed responsibility for managing the interaction. Ellard et al. (1987) suggest that more emphasis be placed on what others bring to an interaction with a depressed person and the demands this puts on both parties, and we agree.

What Do Depressed People Do?

Despite some intriguing findings, it remains unclear what depressed people do in these interactions to elicit negative reactions. Depressed people's speech content and speech processes, as well as nonverbal behavior, have been assessed. It has been suggested that their negative self-statements and self-devaluations (Blumberg & Hokanson, 1983; Hokanson et al., 1980; Jacobson & Anderson, 1982), negative affective content (Gotlib & Robinson, 1982), higher level of self-disclosure (Coyne, 1976b; Jacobson & Anderson, 1982), negative facial expression and body language (Gotlib & Robinson, 1982), and nonreciprocal involvement and greater focus on self (Pyszczynski & Greenberg, 1987; Ziomek, Coyne, & Heist,

1983) contribute to the aversive nature of the interactions. However, findings concerning specific behaviors are much less consistent than the findings of the negative impact itself, and Coyne, Kahn, and Gotlib (1987) suggest that the critical behaviors of depressed people in their interactions are not yet being assessed.

Although it has been seldom done, it is important that researchers sample a wider range of interactions besides those initiated by the instructions that the participants become acquainted. Two studies creatively utilized the Prisoner's Dilemma Game for this purpose. Hokanson et al. (1980) found that in a high-power role, depressed people tend to be exploitive and uncooperative, and they communicated more self-devaluation and helplessness. This elicited uncooperativeness, extrapunitiveness, and expressions of helplessness from their partners. Low-power depressed people tended to blame their partners for their role, eliciting more friendliness and ingratiating behavior from them. In an extension of this study, Blumberg and Hokanson (1983) varied the roles played by confederates interacting with depressed and nondepressed college students. Confederates playing a critical-competitive role elicited more extrapunitiveness from depressed than from nondepressed subjects, and helpless-dependent confederates elicited more negative self-statements from depressed than from nondepressed subjects. Across confederate roles, depressed people communicated high levels of self-devaluation, sadness, helplessness, and general negative content. The interactions occurring in a Prisoners Dilemma Game are highly constrained and limited in their goal. Nonetheless, these studies provide some further insights into the behavior of depressed people and the response of others, including the observation that as well as being sad, depressed people have a capacity for being hostile, uncooperative, and extrapunitive.

Summary of Findings and Possible Hypotheses

The research surveyed earlier indicates depressed people often precipitate negative moods in others. However, there are not enough face-to-face interaction studies in the literature to consider this an established effect. The measurement of mood by checklist after imagined interactions with depressed people or interactions with confederates may not accurately reflect subtle mood induction effects that occur in actual interactions with depressed people. Gurtman (1986) also noted that the lack of significant positive correlations between mood and social rejection suggests that mood is not a crucial factor leading to rejection of depressed people. This is quite plausible, but more data are needed before accepting such an interpretation. By a similar logic, one might conclude that if a person does not contract rash after being in the woods, he was not avoiding the poison ivy. It could be that subjects reject depressed persons because of a sense that they could cause a bad mood, but subjects are still able to avoid a mood induction within the confines of brief interaction.

Overall, the accumulated research has established that strangers interact differently with depressed people than with nondepressed people and are themselves differentially affected. Furthermore, these differences are generally aversive and lead to a desire to not interact with the depressed person in the future. The rejection effects described above are quite consistent and have been found both with self-report measures and behavioral observation. Undoubtedly a number of processes are triggered in an encounter with a depressed person. Some of these may be verbally mediated and others not. One possible process is suggested by the Gotlib and Robinson (1982) study, which used face-to-face interactions of college students. As we noted, the negative behavioral responses of those interacting with depressed people occurred quickly, within the first 3 minutes of the interaction. Others' negative reactions may thus occur as an automatic emotional response that is not mediated by verbal processes. Perhaps others respond aversively with a negative "gut reaction" to the emotional cues or signals that are presented by the depressed person. It has been demonstrated that people are responsive to cues indicating anger, such that they more readily pick out an angry face in a group picture in which everybody else is happy than a happy face where everybody else is angry (Hansen & Hansen, 1988), and similar processes may be evoked by a sad or sullen face or posture. Consistent with this notion, it has been found that the severity of a patient's depression is readily reflected in an interviewing physician's nonverbal behavior (Frey, Jorns, & Daw, 1980) and that mothers briefly enacting a depressed role has a pronounced effect even on infant behavior (Cohn & Tronick, 1983).

Of course, the factors responsible for inducing a negative response in strangers might be different from those that create relationship problems over time for marriages and families. For example, the depressed person's increased self-disclosure or disclosure of intimate material may be inappropriate with strangers and lead to their being disliked by them, but the same effect might not be obtained with spouses. Or, a depressed person's display of suffering might create sympathy in strangers but be seen as yet another attempt to enact a dependent role and get others to assume responsibility when put in the context of long-term marital relationships.

Many of the effects found in the stranger studies may be exacerbated when they occur over an extended period of time. The general negativity of the depressed person's speech content, outlook, and self-absorption may create small effects in brief interactions with strangers, but they likely would be considerably more aversive when experienced daily. Convergent with this idea, Weissman and Paykel (1974) found that depressed women's greatest interpersonal disturbances were in their roles as wives and mothers.

The relationships and interactions of depressed college students and their roommates offer an intermediate position between those with strangers and those with spouses or family members. College roommates have much more extensive contact than strangers and negotiate an ongoing relationship with typical interactional styles. However, selection factors are much less important, as students are frequently assigned roommates by lottery, and their involvement is generally less intimate and interdependent than married couples'.

Roommate Studies

Two studies have indicated that the relationships of depressed college students with their roommates were more conflictful and negative than those of nondepressed students and suggested that more prolonged contact between depressed people and others does not ameliorate the effects found in interactions with strangers. Burchill and Stiles (1988) found that depressed students were rejected and disliked more, were perceived as functioning less well, and spent less time with their roommates. In addition, the roommates of depressed students came to an experimental setting in worse moods than did roommates of nondepressed students, highlighting the aversive nature of an anticipated interaction with a depressed person. However, after an interaction in which they discussed relational concerns, the moods of depressed students and their roommates actually improved, whereas the moods of nondepressed students and their roommates did not change. The positive effects of this particular interaction (likely an atypical one for depressed student-roommate dyads) may represent finally having an opportunity to directly address their relational conflicts. These students frequently remarked to the experimenter that although they recognized that the relational concerns discussed in the experiment were genuine problems, they had never attempted to address them directly. Perhaps outside of the experimental situation, these students and their roommates had avoided discussions that might have reduced their discontent with each other because of a lack of confidence that it would have been productive. By contrast, the nondepressed students and their roommates appeared to have fewer problems to tackle, and the experimental interaction was thus an innocuous one that did not affect their moods.

Hokanson and his colleagues (Howes, Hokanson, & Lowenstein, 1985; Hokanson, Lowenstein, Hedeen, & Howes, 1986) followed college roommates in a 3-month longitudinal study. Like Burchill and Stiles (1988), Howes et al. (1985) found that the roommates of depressed students were more depressed than the roommates of nondepressed students, but they also were able to show that there was an increase in depression from the first to the fifth and again to the eleventh week of rooming together. The roommates of depressed students reported that they increased their caretaking of the depressed students over time, but the depressed students themselves came to see their roommates as more distrustful and competitive (Hokanson et al., 1986). This apparent contradiction may perhaps be explained by the roommates' attempts to be supportive while simultaneously resenting the burden placed on them. Such frustration with the depressed students' inability to be helped or taken care of could lead to both members becoming angry and unhappy. Hokanson et al. (1986) also found that the depressed students were more dependent, distrustful, and self-devaluing and that the dependent behavior increased over time.

These roommate studies offer an opportunity to study more chronic effects of depressed people's relationships while still providing a control for the possible selection bias seen in marital relationships. They find that the mood induction that has been found inconsistently in studies of brief interactions occurs with students rooming with a depressed person. They also suggest that these relationships come to be characterized in negative terms and that roommates come to dislike and reject depressed people, perhaps because they resent their impossible position of trying to alleviate the depressed person's suffering. This frustration and anger may lead to blaming the depressed person, who in turn is angered by the rejection and lack of support. Both partners become stuck in a pattern of ineffective coping (see Coyne, Wortman, & Lehman [1988] for an extended account of such miscarried helping).

Effects of Intimacy on a Depressed Person's Relationships

As discussed in the preceding section, the effects of interacting with a depressed person may vary with the degree of intimacy found in the relationship. The stranger studies have shown that others respond negatively to depressed people immediately in first-time encounters. The roommate studies indicated that more extensive and long-term interactions led to the development of negative moods in roommates and relationships that were negative, rejecting, and that contained greater conflict. These findings suggest that the effects noted above likely will be more intense in marital and familial interactions, as well as being systemically more complicated. For example, the depressed student-roommate pairs in the Burchill and Stiles (1988) study developed more positive moods after only an interaction in which they discussed problematic aspects of the relationship. Marital partners placed in a similar interaction, however, would likely have unsuccessfully attempted such resolution many times previously. Their conflicts are likely to be more entrenched, complex, and less amenable to one positive interaction.

MARRIAGES AND FAMILIES OF DEPRESSED PEOPLE

A number of studies suggest that spouses corroborate depressed people's negative reports about their marriages (Coleman & Miller, 1975; Kahn et al., 1985), and so these complaints cannot be dismissed as a reflection of depressed people's general negativity or cognitive distortions as prevailing cognitive theories of depression might suggest. Yet the picture that is emerging of the marital relationships of depressed people is much more complex than can be conveyed by such global summary statements. It is becoming clear that the spouses of depressed people bring their own vulnerabilities and difficulties to the marriage, that marital interactions are quite negative during a depressive episode in ways that could be construed as depressing, and that the quality of the marriage impacts on the course of depression and the response to treatment (Coyne, 1988b).

Spouses of Depressed People

There is evidence that the spouses of depressed people have personal and family histories of psychopathology themselves and that they have heightened psychological and physical complaints during their partner's depressive episode. Furthermore, there is even evidence that some women vulnerable to depression are more likely to marry men who contribute to their becoming depressed (Quinton, Rutter, & Liddle, 1984).

Studies of assortative mating have examined the extent to which the spouses of depressed people are married to people with diagnosable psychopathology, and in one of the better designed studies, Merikangas and Spiker (1982) found that over half of spouses of affectively disturbed patients met the Research Diagnostic Criteria for a lifetime diagnosis of psychiatric illness. Most of these spouses met the criteria for affective disorder, and both the patients' and spouses' affective disturbances tend to have developed after marriage. Sex differences have been noted: women may be considerably more vulnerable to becoming depressed when living with a depressed partner than men, but this may be due in part to these women being more likely to have family histories of affective disturbance themselves. In contrast, depressed women are more likely than controls to be married to a man with an alcohol or substance abuse problem or personality disorder (see Coyne & DeLongis, 1989, for a more extensive review).

About 40% of spouses of patients currently in a depressive episode have enough symptoms to be classified as probable cases or are suitable for referral, and this contrasts with 17% of the spouses of depressed patients who are not currently in an episode (Coyne et al., 1987). Tracking the spouses of depressed patients seen in family practice, Widmar, Cadoret, and North (1980) found that they made more office visits than controls. The spouses showed a pattern of significant increases in somatic complaints leading up to the patient's diagnosis, and a decrease subsequent to it.

Several studies suggest that women's relationships with their spouses may be important mediators of the association between childhood adversity and depression in adulthood. Birchnell (1980) studied women whose mothers had died in childhood and who had a poor relationship with subsequent maternal figures and found that a good relationship with the spouse went far in compensating for this risk. Those women who had good relationships with their spouses and still became depressed did so almost a decade later than those with bad relationships. Parker and Hadzi-Pavlovic (1984) found that not only did an affectionate relationship with the spouse largely eliminate the influence of this negative childhood experience, but an unaffectionate relationship with the spouse undid the influence of a positive relationship with the father and stepmother. The spouses of women vulnerable to depression may have their own contribution to problems in the marital relationship. Quinton et al. (1984) found that poor adjustment in women raised in an institution was associated with their spouses currently having alcohol or drug problems or difficulties with the law. Furthermore, spouses' reports of their own deviance in adolescence were predictive of their wives' current adjustment.

Taken together, these studies suggest that the effects of early adverse experiences may be largely indirect and in part through the selection of the spouse. Also, taken together with the previously discussed findings of increased personality disturbance among the husbands of depressed women, it may be inferred that women whose vulnerability to depression is such that it is more critical that they maintain a positive intimate relationship also may marry men who are less able to provide it. Consistent with this, recall that Brown et al. (1986) found that depressed women with marital difficulties tended to be married to husbands who were "grossly undependable."

Depression and Marital Interaction

Not surprisingly, studies of the marital interactions of depressed people have found them to be tense, hostile, and conflictful. Kahn et al. (1985) found that there was no difference between depressed outpatients and their spouses in sadness or anger following a brief laboratory discussion, but both differed greatly from controls. The depressed people and their spouses experienced each other in the interactions as more negative, hostile, mistrusting, and detached, and less agreeable, nurturant, and affiliating. Arkowitz, Holliday, and Hutter (1982) found that husbands of outpatient depressed women did not report more general feelings of hostility than did husbands of nondepressed outpatient women or normal controls. However, following a brief laboratory interaction with their wives, they were more hostile than the control husbands who had similarly interacted with their wives. Kahn et al. (1985) also found that depressed outpatients and their spouses did not differ from each other in how they generally coped with marital conflict, but that they both differed from control couples. Depressed people and their spouses were in agreement that each was high in aggressive behavior and withdrawal and low in constructive problem-solving.

Hinchliffe, Hopper, and Roberts (1978) found that, compared with surgical controls and their spouses, interactions between depressed persons and their spouses were characterized by greater tension and negative expressiveness, more emotional outbursts, and considerable incongruence between verbal and nonverbal behavior. Interactions between depressed patients and strangers were much less negative than their interactions with their spouses, with the depressed people showing more adaptive and reciprocal behavior. The Frie Universitat Berlin group (Hautzinger, Linden, & Hoffman, 1982; Linden, Hautzinger, & Hoffmann, 1983) studied maritally distressed couples with and without a depressed partner as these couples discussed a variety of issues. Compared with the spouses in couples without a depressed partner, the partners of depressed people evaluated their partners and their relationships more negatively, and although they spoke negatively of their own well-being, they evaluated themselves more positively. They cried more often than spouses of nondepressed people. They also agreed less with their partner's statements, but they also offered more help to their partners. Depressed people made more negative self-evaluations and statements about the future, while making more positive statements about the partner and the relationship. They also agreed more often with their partners. Other studies suggest that depressed women concede more in disagreements with their husbands (Merikangas, Ranelli, & Kupfer, 1979), and that they are more likely than nondepressed women to be dominated by their husbands in decision-making (Hoover & Fitzgerald, 1981).

Researchers at the Oregon Research Institute (Biglan et al., 1985; Hops et al., 1987) have published the only studies of marital interactions of depressed people that employed sequential analysis as an analytic tool. In a problem-solving discussion, couples with a depressed woman engaged in less disclosure (excluding complaints about well-being). Further, the husbands of depressed women proposed more solutions than their wives did. In the control couples, the wives proposed more solutions. In couples with a depressed wife, the husband's facilitative behavior reduced wives' depressive behavior. In couples in which there was both marital distress and a depressed wife, the wives' depressive behavior had the effect of decreasing the husbands' subsequent aggression (expressions of sarcasm and irritation), while the husbands' aggression decreased the wives' subsequent depressive behavior. Thus, each was able to exert aversive control over the other's behavior and was able to obtain brief, though immediate respite from the other's averseness. In home observations, depressed wives' dysphoric behavior also suppressed their husbands' aggressive behavior, but it suppressed expressions of caring as well (Hops et al., 1987). Husbands' caring behavior reduced their wives' dysphoric behavior more than in couples without depression or marital distress.

Leff and Vaughn (1985) found that the majority of the spouses of depressed people were critical of them. While some of this criticism centered on their depressed partner's current symptomatic behavior, a considerable proportion of it was aimed at traits and behavior evident before the onset of the patient's depression. Such a hostile, critical environment can be the origin of a depressed person's self-complaints and hopelessness, a means of validating and expanding on existing self-criticism, and a buffer against change. Consistent with this latter possibility, experimental studies suggest that intimates who agree with a person's negative self-view can effectively insulate that person from positive experiences that might otherwise challenge this view of themselves (Swann & Predmore, 1985). Leff and Vaughn (1985) further found that the majority of depressed patients, particularly women, were fearful of loss and rejection and desirous of continual comfort and support. Yet, contextualizing this observation, Leff and Vaughn (1985) showed how depressed people may be maintained in such fears and perceptions. Namely, "few depressed patients described as chronically insecure or lacking in self-confidence were living with supportive or sympathetic spouses. . . . When this was the case, the patients were well at followup" (p. 95).

Overview

Overall, the pessimism, hopelessness, feelings of insecurity, self-complaints and lack of a sense of self-efficacy of depressed people may be more congruent with the nature of their relationships with their spouses than has generally been supposed. As can be seen, depressed people's distress and problems such as dependency, inhibition, and difficulties dealing with hostility do not occur in a vacuum, and the fit of these difficulties with the patterning of their close relationships warrants more attention. The marriages of depressed people tend to be distressing and insecure and not conducive to renegotiating expectations, to overt disagreement, or to the direct expression of negative affect. Further, rather than simply being passive and withdrawn, depressed people are often caught up in miscarried efforts to resolve their difficulties with intimates in which they are unsuccessfully confrontative as well. As Kahn et al. (1985) suggested, depressed people and their spouses may be involved in a cycle in which their unsuccessful efforts to resolve differences lead to withdrawal and avoidance and to negative affect, mistrust, and misgivings about each other. The accumulated effect of such interactions is to overwhelm the couple when they again attempt to settle specific differences, increasing their hopelessness about the possibility of improving their relationship.

Marriage, Marital Quality, and the Course and Outcome of Depression

Studies of the quality of the marriages and marital interactions of depressed people suggest the need to consider further not only how interactional factors trigger an episode of depression, but how they shape its expression, management, and consequences for both depressed people and the people around them. These influences are reflected in studies of the treatment and outcome of depression.

The finding that married patients respond less well to antidepressant medication (Keller et al., 1984) might be dismissed as an anomaly, except as that it has been found that people who have recently ended a relationship improve more than those in enduring relationships whether they receive psychotherapy for depression (Parker, Tennant, & Blignault, 1985) or were identified as depressed cases among general practice patients (Parker, Holmes, & Manicavagar, 1986) or in a community sample (Parker & Blignault, 1985). In the absense of further data, we can speculate that it may be easier to recover from the ending of a relationship than for some depressed people to renegotiate their chronically distressing relationships.

Other studies have found that marital problems predict poorer treatment outcomes. The Yale group has found that the marital problems faced by many depressed people are a negative prognostic indicator in treatment with antidepressant medication (Rounsaville, Weissman, Prusoff, & Herceg-Baron, 1979). Those patients whose marriages improve show satisfactory response to medication, but the evidence is that medication has little direct effect on the quality of depressed people's involvement in their marriages (Weissman et al., 1979). Further, 4-year follow-up assessments of depressed people with marital problems who have been treated with antidepressants suggest that they tend to continue to be vulnerable to depression and to have marital problems (Rounsaville, Prusoff, & Weissman, 1980). Courney (1984) found that depressed women with marital problems were less likely to improve in individual psychotherapy than those without problems. Although cognitive therapy has proven to be effective with depressed outpatients, Jacobson, Schmelling, Salsalusky, Follette, and Dobson (1987) found that depressed people with marital problems benefited little from it.

Two important studies suggest that the number of critical comments about a depressed patient that the spouse makes in an interview during the patient's hospitalization are predictive of posthospital relapse, independent of the patient's level of symptomatology (Hooley et al., 1986; Vaughn & Leff, 1976). In this work, criticism was defined as "a clear statement of resentment, disapproval, dislike, or rejection" (Leff & Vaughn, 1985, p. 125). In the Vaughn and Leff (1976) study, a cut-off of two critical comments by the spouse provided the best discrimination of those depressed patients who subsequently relapsed, while in the Hooley et al. (1986) study, the best discrimination was with three comments. In the latter study, none of the eight patients whose spouses were low in criticism relapsed, whereas 20 of the 31 patients whose spouses were high in criticism relapsed.

Taken together, these studies highlight the continued effects of interpersonal circumstances and specifically the marital situation beyond the instigation of a depressive episode. The findings that response to medication may be affected by marital problems point to the need to understand better the links between interpersonal circumstances and the biology of depression. Further, the finding that treatment with antidepressants may not resolve the marital problems associated with depression suggests the need to consider work with the close relationships of depressed people either as a primary treatment or an adjunct to medication. There is no incompatibility between medication and marital intervention, and for more severely depressed patients, a combination may be the approach of choice (Coyne, 1987). However, the same difficulties that suggest the need for marital intervention may limit couples with a depressed partner from seeking or benefiting from conventional conjoint therapy. Interventions may be needed that target the negative interactions and miscarried problem-solving that characterize these couples without assuming that they will be able or motivated to cooperate (Watzlawick & Coyne, 1980; for an interactional model of the treatment of depression, see Coyne, 1988a).

CHILDREN OF DEPRESSED PATIENTS

The children of depressed parents are at risk for a full range of psychological problems, academic difficulties, and physical health problems. Problems are apparent throughout infancy and early childhood (Sameroff, Barocas, & Seifer, 1985; Seifer, Sameroff, & Jones, 1981), primary school years (Fisher, Kokes, Harder, & Jones, 1980; Neale & Weintraub, 1975), and adolescence (Hirsch, Moos, & Reischl, 1985). Difficulties are apparent in self-report, as well as the reports of peers, teachers, and parents. As many as 40% to 50% of the children of a depressed parent have a diagnosable psychiatric disturbance (Cytryn, McKnew, Bartko, Lamour, & Hamovit, 1982; Decina et al., 1983; Orvachel, Walsh-Allis, & Weijai, 1988; for a review, see Downey & Coyne, in press). These children are at particular risk for affective disorder, with the children of unipolar parents having three times the rate of affective disorder and six times the rate of major depressive disorder. Some studies have found these children to have more conduct disorders, attentional disorders, and substance abuse, but these findings are not as consistent as for affective disturbance.

Links Between Parental Depression and Child Problems

It has been widely assumed that the difficulties of these children are a result of being parented by a depressed person, but the association between depression in parents and problems in children is likely to be complex. Depressed parents report that they direct even more hostility toward their children than toward their spouses, that they are less affectionate, more emotionally distant, irritable, and preoccupied, and that they experience guilt and difficulty communicating with their children (Weissman & Paykel, 1974). Observational studies also reveal hostility (Hammen, Gordon, Burge, & Adrian, 1987). Surprisingly, the influence of the sad affect of parents has not received as much attention as their hostility, but Biglan et al. (1988) showed that depressed mothers' sad affect suppressed displays of hostility from their children. Results of other studies suggest that depressed mothers use less effortful strategies in dealing with their children than nondepressed mothers. Depressed parents show lower rates of behavior, particularly the expression of positive affect, and respond slower and less contingently and consistently (Field et al., 1985; for a review, see Downey & Coyne, in press).

Depressed people thus may show many of the same difficulties with their children that they show with other adults (Libet & Lewinsohn, 1973; Youngren & Lewinsohn, 1980). Further, consistent with an interactional perspective, there is considerable evidence that the negativity and hostility between depressed parents and their older children are reciprocal (Radke-Yarrow, Cummings, Kuczynski, & Chapman, 1985; Hammen et al., 1987). Sequential analysis of interactions between depressed parents and their younger children show that they contribute equally to the maintenance of this pattern (Cohn, Campbell, Matias, & Hopkins, in press).

There is also evidence that the same contextual factors that contribute to the parents becoming depressed may be a source of their problems with their children. The children of depressed parents who score high on measures of support and low on stress have considerably fewer adjustment problems than the children of depressed parents in general (Billings & Moos, 1983). Further, the problems of the children may depend on the adjustment of the depressed person's spouse and whether there are marital problems or disruption.

Thus, the risk of child disturbance increases when both parents are disturbed (Kuyler, Rosenthal, Igel, Dunner, & Fieve, 1980; Weissman et al., 1984). Emery, Weintraub, and Neale (1982) concluded that in the absence of marital difficulties, the risk of problematic school behavior among the offspring of an affectively disturbed parent was no greater than among the offspring of normal control parents. Other studies have found that families in which there has been a divorce account for a considerable proportion of the psychological disturbance of children of depressed parents (Conners, Himmelhoch, Goyette, Ulrich, & Neil, 1979; Kuyler et al., 1980).

Depression in a parent is associated with major threats to the well-being of children, and these children are particularly at risk for depression themselves. Many of the difficulties that depressed people have with others are reflected in their parenting. Yet, as elsewhere in this review, there are suggestions of complex reciprocal processes; specifically, there are indications of the influence of the depressed parents on their children, some indications of reciprocal influences of children on their depressed parents, but also of the other parent on the relationship between depressed people and their children. We should be cautious about placing the responsibility on the depressed person for what are best seen as difficulties tied to the larger context and that may be contingent on the adjustment, behavior, or availability of the other parent as well.

OVERVIEW AND CONCLUSIONS

It seems to be true that depressed people are facing difficult and depressing circumstances, but even so, this observation is too often lost in contemporary psychological theories and studies of depression. The various literatures that we have reviewed in this chapter suggest that there are ample reasons why depressed people might complain about their circumstances, reasons that cannot be reduced to their purported depressive thinking or behavioral deficits. We started with a consideration of the circumstances in which depression arises, noting that it is often associated with loss or disappointment requiring long-term adjustment. We offered a twist on the usual interpretation of the social support and suggested that the detrimental effects of involvement in a bad close relationship may exceed the benefits of a good one. We returned to this focus on the detrimental effects of bad close relationships when we examined predictors of the course and outcome of depression.

Next, however, we reviewed studies of interactions between depressed people and strangers and then of the relationships between depressed college students and their roommates. We noted that such studies were not a substitute for consideration of what occurs in depressed people's close relationships, but that they had a unique contribution to make in terms of demonstrating that depression can engender problems between people who do not have a previous history together. Also, the mood induction that is sometimes found with brief laboratory contacts of others with depressed people apparently has its parallels in people rooming with a depressed person.

Turning to the marital relationships of depressed people, we found them to be hostile and conflictful. Living with a depressed family member can be associated with considerable distress, but we attempted to present a more complex view of depressed people's marriages, suggesting that spouses of depressed people may bring their difficulties to the relationship and that they may even contribute to depressed people's vulnerability. Data concerning treatment outcome and relapse point to the usefulness of targeting the marital relationship for intervention, whether as a primary treatment or an adjunct to medication.

Our review of the literature concerning the children of depressed people found them to be at considerable risk, particularly for depression. Depressed parents can be hostile toward their children and they use less effortful strategies in dealing with them. Their children also show considerable hostility to them. Further, many of the problems between depressed people and their children may be the result of preexisting conditions that contributed to these parents becoming depressed. The studies of the children of depressed parents highlight the need to contextualize considerations of the close relationships and to be prepared for considerable complexity.

Many of the studies that were most directly relevant to the interactional perspective were not inspired by it. For instance, the studies of children of depressed parents originally came about because of the need for a psychiatric control group in studies of the offspring of schizophrenics (see Downey & Coyne, in press, for a review of this early literature). These studies enrich our understanding of interactional aspects of depression, but it is important that research become more interactional in its conceptualization and design. An interactional perspective on depression is more than the hypothesis that depressed people are distressing and get rejected. It is a call for a different way of thinking about psychopathology, one that involves an appreciation of the rich and reciprocal links between people and their environments and of the significance of close relationships. Finally, it is important from both a theoretical and ethical point of view that we not reduce these troubled close relationships to the pure victimization of spouses and family members by depressed people or of depressed people by them, but to appreciate how everyone involved may have got caught up in difficult circumstances and how their ways of coping may perpetuate these circumstances despite intentions to the contrary.

REFERENCES

Andrews, G., Tennant, C., Hewson, D., & Valliant, G. (1978). Life stress, social support, coping style, and risk of psychological impairment. *Journal of Nervous and Mental Disease, 166*, 307–316.

Aneshensel, C. S., & Stone, J. D. (1982). Stress and depression: A test of the buffering model of social support. *Archives of General Psychiatry, 39*, 1392–1396.

Arkowitz, H., Holliday, S., & Hutter, M. (1982). *Depressed women and their husbands: A study of marital interaction and adjustment.* Paper presented at the Annual Meeting of the Association for the Advancement of Behavior Therapy, San Francisco, CA, November.

Austin, J. (1965). *How to do things with words.* New York: Oxford Press.

Bebbington, P. E., Tennant, C., & Hurray, J. (1981). Adversity and the nature of psychiatric disorder in the community. *Journal of Affective Disorders, 3*, 345–366.

Biglan, A., Hops, H., & Sherman, L. (1988). Coercive family processes and maternal depression. In R. J. McMahon & R. DeV. Peter (Eds.), *Marriages and families: Behavioral treatments and processes.* New York: Bruner/Mazel.

Biglan, A., Hops, H., Sherman, L., Friedman, L. S., Arthur, J., & Osteen, V. (1985). Problem-solving interactions of depressed women and their husbands. *Behavior Therapy, 16*, 431–451.

Billings, A. G., & Moos, R. H. (1983). Comparison of children of depressed and nondepressed parents: A social environmental perspective. *Journal of Abnormal Child Psychology, 11*, 483–486.

Billings, A. G., & Moos, R. H. (1984). Coping, stress, and social resources among adults with unipolar depression. *Journal of Personality and Social Psychology, 46*, 877–891.

Birchnell, J. (1980). Women whose mothers died in childhood: An outcome study. *Psychological Medicine, 10*, 699–713.

Birchnell, J., & Kennard, J. (1983). Does marital maladjustment lead to mental illness? *Social Psychiatry, 18*, 79–88.

Blumberg, S. R., & Hokanson, J. E. (1983). The effects of another person's response style on interpersonal behavior in depression. *Journal of Abnormal Psychology, 92*, 196–209.

Boswell, P. C., & Murray, E. J. (1981). Depression, schizophrenia, and social attraction. *Journal of Consulting and Clinical Psychology, 4*, 641–647.

Breslau, N., & Davis, G. C. (1986). Chronic stress and major depression. *Archives of General Psychiatry, 43*, 309–314.

Brown, G. W., Bifulco, A., Harris, T., & Bridge, L. (1986). Life stress, chronic subclinical symptoms and vulnerability to clinical depression. *Journal of Affective Disorders, 11*, 1–19.

Brown, G. W., & Harris, T. (Eds.). (1978). *Social origins of depression: A study of psychiatric disorder in women.* New York: Free Press.

Brown, G. W., & Harris, T. (1982). Disease, distress, and depression. *Journal of Affective Disorders, 4*, 1–8.

Burchill, S. A. L., & Stiles, W. B. (1988). Interactions of depressed college students with their roommate: Not necessarily negative. *Journal of Personality and Social Psychology, 55*, 410–419.

Cleary, P. D., & Kessler, R. C. (1982). The estimation and interpretation of modifier effects. *Journal of Health and Social Behavior, 23*, 159–168.

Cohn, J. F., Campbell, X. X., Matias, R., & Hopkins, J. (in press). Face-to-face interactions of postpartum depressed and nondepressed mother-infant pairs at two months. *Developmental Psychology.*

Cohn, J., & Tronick, E. (1983). Three-month-old infants' reaction to simulated maternal depression. *Child Development, 54*, 185–190.

Coleman, R. E., & Miller, R. E. (1975). The relationship between depression and marital maladjustment in a clinic population: A multitrait-multimethod study. *Journal of Consulting and Clinical Psychology, 43*, 647–651.

Conners, C. K., Himmelhoch, J., Goyette, C. H., Ulrich, R., & Neil, J. F. (1979). Children of parents with affective illness. *Journal of the American Academy of Child Psychiatry, 18*, 600–607.

Costello, C. G. (1982). Social factors associated with depression: A retrospective community study. *Psychological Medicine, 12*, 329–339.

Courney, R. H. (1984). The effectiveness of social workers in the management of depressed female patients in general practice. *Psychological Medicine, 14*, (Whole Monograph Supplement 6).

Coyne, J. C. (1976a). Toward an interactional description of depression. *Psychiatry, 39*, 28–40.

Coyne, J. C. (1976b). Depression and the response of others. *Journal of Abnormal Psychology, 2*, 186–193.

Coyne, J. C. (1984). Strategic therapy with married depressed persons: Agenda, themes, and interventions. *Journal of Marital and Family Therapy, 10*, 53–62.

Coyne, J. C. (1987). Depression, biology, marriage, and marital therapy. *Journal of Marital and Family Therapy, 13*, 393–407.

Coyne, J. C. (1988a). Strategic therapy. In G. Haas, I. Glick, & J. Clarkin (Eds.), *Family intervention in affective illness*. New York: Guilford Press.

Coyne, J. C. (1988b). *Depression, marriage, and the family: Implications for intervention*. Invited address at the Annual Convention of the American Psychological Association, Atlanta, GA.

Coyne, J. C. (1989). Thinking post-cognitively about depression. In A. Freeman, K. M. Simon, L. Beutler, & H. Arkowitz (Eds.), *Comprehensive handbook of cognitive therapy*. New York: Plenum Press.

Coyne, J. C. (1990). Interpersonal processes in depression. In G. I. Keitner (Ed.), *Depression and families*. Washington, DC: American Psychiatric Press.

Coyne, J. C., & DeLongis, A. (1986). Going beyond social support: The role of social relationships in adaptation. *Journal of Consulting and Clinical Psychology, 54*, 454–460.

Coyne, J. C., & DeLongis, A. (1989). The spouses of depressed persons. Unpublished manuscript.

Coyne, J. C., & Downey, G. (in press). Social factors in psychopathology. *Annual Review of Psychology*.

Coyne, J. C., Ellard, J. H., & Smith, D. A. (1990). Unsupportive relationships, interdependence, and unhelpful exchanges. In I. G. Sarason, B. R. Sarason, & G. Pierce (Eds.), *Social support: An interactional view*. New York: John Wiley & Sons.

Coyne, J. C., & Gotlib, I. H. (1983). The role of cognition in depression: a critical appraisal. *Psychological Bulletin, 94*, 472–505.

Coyne, J. C., Kahn, J., & Gotlib, I. H. (1987). Depression. In T. Jacob (Ed.), *Family interaction and psychotherapy*. New York: Plenum Press.

Coyne, J. C., Kessler, R. C., Tal, M., Turnbull, J., Wortman, C., & Greden, J. (1987). Living with a depressed person: Burden and psychological distress. *Journal of Consulting and Clinical Psychology, 55*, 347–352.

Coyne, J. C., Wortman, C., & Lehman, D. (1988). The other side of support: Emotional overinvolvement and miscarried helping. In B. Gottlieb (Ed.), *Social support: Formats, processes, and effects*. New York: Sage Publications.

Cytryn, L., McKnew, D. H., Bartko, J. J., Lamour, M., & Hamovit, J. (1982). Offspring of patients with affective disorders II. *Journal of the American Academy of Child Psychiatry, 21*, 389–391.

Decina, P., Kestenbaum, C. J., Farber, S., Kron, L., Gargan, M., Sackeim, H. A., & Fieve, R. R. (1983). Clinical and psychological assessment of children of bipolar probands. *American Journal of Psychiatry, 140*, 548–553.

Dohrenwend, B. P. (1974). Problems in defining and sampling the relevant populations of stressful life events. In B. S. Dohrenwend & B. P. Dohrenwend (Eds.), *Stressful life events: Their nature and effects*. New York: John Wiley & Sons.

Dolan, R. J., Calloway, S. P., Fonagy, P., De Souza, F. V. A., & Wakeling, A. (1985). Life events, depression, and hypothlamic-pituitary-adrenal axis function. *British Journal of Psychiatry, 147*, 429–433.

Downey, G., & Coyne, J. C. (in press). Children of depressed parents: An integrative review. *Psychological Bulletin*.

Dykman, B. M., Abramson, L. L., Alloy, L. B., & Hartlage, S. (1989). Processing of ambiguous and unambiguous feedback by depressed and nondepressed college students: Schematic biases and their implications for depressive realism. *Journal of Personality and Social Psychology, 56*, 431–445.

Ellard, J. H., Coyne, J. C., Showers, C., & Ruvulo, A. (1987). *Just shy, not depressed: The role of expectancies in interactions with depressed persons*. Paper presented at the Annual Convention of the Canadian Psychological Association, Vancouver.

Emery, R., Weintraub, S., & Neale, J. (1982). Effects of marital discord on the school behavior of children of schizophrenic, affectively disordered, and normal parents. *Journal of Abnormal Child Psychology, 16*, 215–225.

Field, T. M., Sanberg, D., Garcia, R., Vega-Lahr, N., Golstein, S., & Guy, L. (1985). Pregnancy problems, postpartum depression, and early mother-infant interactions. *Developmental Psychology, 21*, 1152–1156.

Fisher, L., Kokes, R. F., Harder, D. W., & Jones, J. E. (1980). Child competence and psychiatric risk: VI Summary and integration of findings. *Journal of Nervous and Mental Disease, 168*, 353–355.

Fowles, D. C., & Gersh, F. S. (1979). Neurotic depression: The endogenous-reactive distinction. In R. A. Depue (Ed.), *The psychobiology of depressive disorders*. New York: Academic Press.

Frey, S., Jorns, U., & Daw, W. A. (1980). A systematic description and analysis of nonverbal interaction between doctors and patients in a psychiatric interview. In S. A. Corson (Ed.), *Ethology and nonverbal communication in mental health*. Elmsford, NY: Pergamon Press.

Gage, N. L., & Cronbach, L. J. (1955). Conceptual and methodological problems in interpersonal perception. *Psychological Review, 62*, 511–522.

Geerwitz, C. (1973). *The interpretation of culture*. New York: Basic Books.

Gotlib, I. H., & Robinson, A. (1982). Responses to depressed individuals: Discrepancies between self-report and observer-rated behavior. *Journal of Abnormal Psychology, 91*, 231–240.

Gurtman, M. (1986). Depression and the response of others: Reevaluating the reevaluation. *Journal of Abnormal Psychology, 95*, 99–101.

Hammen, C., Gordon, G., Burge, D., & Adrian, C. (1987). Maternal affective disorders, illness, and stress: Risk for children's psychopathology. *American Journal of Psychiatry, 144*, 763–771.

Hammen, C. L., & Peters, S. D. (1977). Differential response to male and female depressive reactions. *Journal of Consulting and Clinical Psychology, 45*, 994–1001.

Hammen, C. L., & Peters, S. D. (1978). Interpersonal consequences of depression: Response to men and women enacting a depressed role. *Journal of Abnormal Psychology, 87*, 322–332.

Hansen, C. H., & Hansen, R. D. (1988). Finding the face in the crowd: An anger superiority effect. *Journal of Personality and Social Psychology, 54*, 917–924.

Hautzinger, M., Linden, M., & Hoffman, N. (1982). Distressed couples with and without a depressed partner: An analysis of their verbal interaction. *Journal of Behavior Therapy and Experimental Psychiatry, 13*, 307–314.

Hinchcliffe, M., Hopper, D., & Roberts, F. J. (1978). *The melancholy marriage*. New York: John Wiley & Sons.

Hirsch, B. J., Moos, R. F., & Reischl, T. M. (1985). Psychosocial adjustment of adolescent children of a depressed, arthritic, or normal parent. *Journal of Abnormal Psychology, 94*, 154–164.

Hokanson, J. E., Loewenstein, A. D., Hedeen, C., & Howes, M. J. (1986). Dysphoric college students and roommates: A study of social behaviors over a three-month period. *Personality and Social Psychology Bulletin, 12*, 311–324.

Hokanson, J. E., Sacco, W. P., Blumberg, S. R., & Landrum, G. C. (1980). Interpersonal behavior of depressive individuals in a mixed-motive game. *Journal of Abnormal Psychology, 89*, 320–332.

Hooley, J. M., Orley, J., & Teasdale, J. D. (1986). Levels of expressed emotion and relapse in depressed patients. *British Journal of Psychiatry, 148*, 642–647.

Hoover, C. F., & Fitzgerald, R. G. (1981). Dominance in the marriage of affective patients. *Journal of Nervous and Mental Disease, 169*, 624–628.

Hops, H., Biglan, A., Sherman, L., Arthur, J., Friedman, L. S., & Osteen, V. (1987). Home observations of family interactions of depressed women. *Journal of Consulting and Clinical Psychology, 55*, 341–346.

Howes, M. K., & Hokanson, J. E. (1979). Conversational and social responses to depressive interpersonal behavior. *Journal of Abnormal Psychology, 6*, 625–634.

Howes, M. J., Hokanson, J. E., & Lowenstein, D. A. (1985). The induction of depressive affect after prolonged exposure to a mildly depressed individual. *Journal of Abnormal Psychology, 49*, 1110–1113.

Jacobson, N. S., & Anderson, E. (1982). Interpersonal skills deficits and depression in college students: A sequential analysis of the timing of self-disclosure. *Behavior Therapy, 13*, 271–282.

Jacobson, N. S., Schmelling, K. B., Salsalusky, S., Follette, V., & Dobson, K. (1987). *Marital therapy as an adjunct treatment of depression*. Paper presented at the annual meeting of Association for the Advancement of Behavior Therapy, Boston.

Kahn, J., Coyne, J. C., & Margolin, G. (1985). Depression and marital conflict: The social construction of despair. *Journal of Social and Personal Relationships, 2*, 447–462.

Keller, M. B., Klerman, G. L., Lavori, P. W., Coryell, W., Endicott, J., & Taylor, J. (1984). Long-term outcome of episodes of major depression: Clinical and public health significance. *Journal of the American Medical Association, 252*, 788–792.

Keller, M. B., & Shapiro, R. W. (1982). "Double depression": Superimposition of acute depressive episodes on chronic depressive disorders. *American Journal of Psychiatry, 139*, 438–442.

King, D. A., & Heller, K. (1984). Depression and the response to others: A reevaluation. *Journal of Abnormal Psychology, 93*, 477–480.

Kuyler, P. L., Rosenthal, L., Igel, G., Dunner, D. L., & Fieve, R. R. (1980). Psychopathology among children of manic depressive patients. *Biological Psychiatry, 15*, 589–597.

Leff, J., & Vaughn, C. E. (1985). *Expressed emotion in families: Its significance for mental illness*. New York: Guilford Press.

Lewinsohn, P. M., Hoberman, H. M., & Rosenbaum, M. (1988). A prospective study of risk factors for unipolar depression. *Journal of Abnormal Psychology, 97*, 251–264.

Libet, J., & Lewinsohn, P. M. (1973). The concept of social skill with special reference to the behavior of depressed persons. *Journal of Consulting and Clinical Psychology, 40*, 304–312.

Linden, M., Hautzinger, M., & Hoffman, N. (1983). Discriminant analysis of depressive interactions. *Behavior Modification, 7*, 403–422.

Lorenz, K. Z. (1952). *King Solomon's Ring*. London: Methuen.

Merikangas, K. R., Ranelli, C. J., & Kupfer, D. J. (1979). Marital interaction in hospitalized depressed patients. *Journal of Nervous and Mental Disease, 167*, 689–695.

Merikangas, K. R., & Spiker, D. G. (1982). Assortative mating among in-patients with primary affective disorder. *Psychological Medicine, 12*, 753–764.

Meyer, B. E., & Hokanson, J. E. (1985). Situational influences on social behaviors of depression-prone individuals. *Journal of Clinical Psychology, 41*, 29–35.

Monroe, S. M. (in press). Stress and social support: Assessment issues. In P. Schneiderman, & P. Kaufman, et al. (Eds.), *Handbook of research methods in cardiovascular behavioral medicine*. New York: Plenum Press.

Neale, J. M., & Weintraub, S. (1975). Children vulnerable to psychopathology: The Stony Brook High-Risk Project. *Journal of Abnormal Child Psychology, 3*, 95–113.

Oatley, K., & Bolton, W. (1985). A social-cognitive theory of depression in reaction to recent life events. *Psychological Review, 92*, 372–388.

Orvachel, H., Walsh-Allis, G., & Weijai, Y. (1988). Psychopathology in children of parents with recurrent depression. *Journal of Abnormal Child Psychology, 148*, 686–696.

Parker, G., & Blignault, I. (1985). Psychosocial predictors of outcomes in subjects with untreated depressive disorder. *Journal of Affective Disorders, 8*, 73–81.

Parker, G., & Hadzi-Pavlovic, D. (1984). Modification of levels of depression in mother-bereaved women by prenatal and marital relationships. *Psychological Medicine, 14*, 125–135.

Parker, G., Holmes, S., & Manicavagar, V. (1986). Depression in general practice attenders: Caseness, natural history, and predictors of outcome. *Journal of Affective Disorders, 10*, 27–35.

Parker, G., Tennant, C., & Blignault, I. (1985). Predicting improvement in patients with nonendogenous depression. *British Journal of Psychiatry, 146,* 132–139.

Patterson, G. R., & Reid, J. B. (1970). Reciprocity and coercion: Two facets of social systems. In C. Neuringer & J. Michael (Eds.), *Behavior modification in clinical psychology*. New York: Appleton-Century-Crofts.

Paykel, E. S. (1979). Causal relationships between clinical depression and life events. In J. E. Barrett (Ed.), *Stress and mental disorder*. New York: Raven Press.

Paykel, E. S., Myers, J. K., Dienelt, M. N., Klerman, G. L., Lindenthal, J. A., & Pepper, M. P. (1969). Life events and depression: A controlled study. *Archives of General Psychiatry, 21,* 753–757.

Pyszczynski, T., & Greenberg, J. (1987). Self-regulatory perseveration and the depressive self-focusing style: A self-awareness theory of reactive depression. *Psychological Bulletin, 102,* 122–138.

Quinton, D., Rutter, M., & Liddle, C. (1984). Institutional rearing, parenting difficulties and marital support. *Psychological Medicine, 14,* 107–124.

Radke-Yarrow, M., Cummings, E. M., Kuczynski, L., & Chapman, M. (1985). Patterns of attachment to two- and three-year-olds in normal families and families with parental depression. *Child Development, 36,* 884–893.

Robbins, B., Strack, S., & Coyne, J. C. (1979). Willingness to provide feedback to depressed persons. *Social Behavior and Personality, 7,* 199–203.

Rounsaville, B. J., Prusoff, B. A., & Weissman, M. M. (1980). The course of marital disputes in depressed women: A 48-month follow-up study. *Comprehensive Psychiatry, 21,* 111–118.

Rounsaville, B. J., Weissman, M. M., Prusoff, B. A., & Herceg-Baron, R. L. (1979). Marital disputes and treatment outcome in depressed women. *Comprehensive Psychiatry, 20,* 483–490.

Roy, A. (1978). Risk factors and depression in Canadian women. *Journal of Affective Disorders, 3,* 69–70.

Sameroff, A. J., Barocas, R., & Seifer, R. (1985). The early development of children born to mentally ill women. In N. F. Watt, E. J. Anthony, L. C. Wynne, & J. Rolf (Eds.), *Children at risk for schizophrenia*. New York: Cambridge University Press.

Schaefer, C., Coyne, J. C., & Lazarus, R. S.

(1981). The health-related aspects of social support. *Journal of Behavioral Medicine, 4,* 381–406.

Seifer, R., Sameroff, A. J., & Jones, F. (1981). Adaptive behavior in young children of emotionally disturbed women. *Journal of Developmental Psychology, 1,* 251–276.

Snyder, C. R., & Smith, T. W. (1982). Symptoms as self-handicapping strategies: The virtue of old wine in a new bottle. In G. Weary & H. Mirels (Eds.), *Integration of clinical and social psychology*. New York: Oxford University Press.

Strack, S., & Coyne, J. C. (1983). Social confirmation of dysphoria: Shared and private reactions to depression. *Journal of Personality and Social Psychology, 44,* 806–814.

Swann, W. B., Jr., & Predmore, S. C. (1985). Intimates as agents of social support: Sources of consolation or despair? *Journal of Personality and Social Psychology, 49,* 1609–1617.

Tennant, L., & Bebbington, P. (1978). The social causation of depression. *Psychological Medicine, 8,* 565–578.

Vaughn, C. E., & Leff, J. (1976). The influence of family and social factors on the course of psychiatric illness. *British Journal of Psychiatry, 129,* 125–137.

Watzlawick, P., Beavin, J. H., & Jackson, D. D. (1967). *Pragmatics of human communication*. New York: W. W. Norton.

Watzlawick, P. W., & Coyne, J. C. (1980). Depression following stroke: Brief problem-focused family treatment. *Family Process, 19,* 13–18.

Weissman, M. M. (1987). Advances in psychiatric epidemiology: Rates and risks for depression. *American Journal of Public Health, 77,* 445–451.

Weissman, M. M., & Paykel, E. S. (1974). *The depressed woman*. Chicago: University of Chicago Press.

Weissman, M. M., Prusoff, B. A., Gammon, G. D., Merikangas, K. R., Leckman, J. F., & Kidd, K. K. (1984). Psychopathology in children (ages 6–18) of depressed and normal parents. *Journal of the American Academy of Child Psychiatry, 23,* 78–84.

Welner, A., Marten, S., Wochnik, E., Davis, M. A., Fishman, R., & Clayton, P. J. (1979). Psychiatric disorders among professional women. *Archives of General Psychiatry, 36,* 169–173.

Widmar, R. B., Cadoret, R. J., & North, C. S. (1980). Depression in family practice: Some effects in spouses and children. *Journal of Family Practice, 10,* 45–51.

Winer, D. L., Bonner, T. O., Blaney, P., & Murray, E. J. (1981). Depression and social attraction. *Motivation and Emotion, 3,* 153–166.

Yarkin, K., Harvey, J. L., & Bloxom, B. M. (1981). Cognitive sets, attribution, and social interaction. *Journal of Personality and Social Psychology, 41,* 243–252.

Youngren, M. A., & Lewinsohn, P. M. (1980). The functional relationship between depression and interpersonal behavior. *Journal of Abnormal Psychology, 89,* 333–341.

Ziomek, M., Coyne, J. C., & Heist, P. (1983). *Interactions involving depressed persons.* Presented at the Annual Convention of the American Psychological Association, Anaheim, CA.

CHAPTER 18

INTERPERSONAL ANALYSIS OF THE HELP-SEEKING PROCESS

Thomas A. Wills
Bella M. DePaulo

This chapter provides an interpersonal analysis of help-seeking. We view help-seeking behavior as a process with some complexity, involving interactions between characteristics of the help-seeker, the type of help sought, the context, and the potential helper. In this chapter we consider epidemiological evidence, suggest some theoretical issues about the nature of help-seeking, and discuss factors that could help to elucidate different types of help-seeking behavior. The aim is to provide a theoretical framework for help-seeking and to show the linkage to factors that encourage versus discourage help-seeking behavior. The focus is on the types of problems (depression, anxiety, achievement difficulties) typically confronted by mental health professionals.

The chapter begins by considering epidemiologic evidence on help-seeking. Then we present a framework of help-seeking motivation and discuss how it may apply to three kinds of predictive factors: situational, personality, and esteem maintenance. Finally, we consider implications of this formulation for social and clinical psychology.

EPIDEMIOLOGIC EVIDENCE

Correlates of help-seeking behavior have been examined in a number of epidemiological studies (for reviews see DePaulo, 1982; DePaulo, Nadler, & Fisher, 1983; Gourash, 1978; Kadushin, 1969; McKinlay, 1972; Nadler, Fisher, & DePaulo, 1983). To provide a background of evidence on help-seeking we shall discuss epidemiologic findings on sex, age, and other variables. These studies provide basic information about help-seeking as it occurs in naturalistic settings, although they do not always test specific hypotheses about processes in help-seeking.

There are two basic types of studies. A few studies have obtained direct interviews with representative samples of community residents to examine the correlates of self-reported help-seeking. Studies of clinic samples, in contrast, determine factors that differentiate treated patients from controls. Studies with community samples are preferable methodologically because they include persons who have problems but do not seek pro-

350

fessional help, thus avoiding a potential bias that may be introduced by clinic samples (Link & Dohrenwend, 1980). At the same time a number of studies are retrospective, obtaining data from subjects after help-seeking has occurred; so the effect of a predictor sometimes is not easily disentangled from the effects of the treatment experience and data on stages of help-seeking (Gross & McMullen, 1983; Wills, 1983) are not easily determined. With some exceptions (e.g., Kessler, Brown, & Bowman, 1981; Matthews, Siegel, Kuller, Thompson, & Varat, 1983), longitudinal data are rare.

Treatment Rates

A first question concerns the probability that a person with emotional distress will seek professional help. (It is presumed in these studies that the respondents sought help, but there is usually no direct evidence that the help-seeking was entirely voluntary vs. coerced by family or social institutions.) The approach in retrospective studies is to identify a subgroup of individuals with currently high psychological distress and determine what proportion of these ever have received treatment from a person in a formal helping role, such as a psychiatrist, psychologist, social worker, or counselor. Data from a variety of studies indicate that the majority of persons with distress do not seek professional treatment. Studies based on psychiatric screening scales indicate that the median treatment rate is 27% (Neugebauer, Dohrenwend, & Dohrenwend, 1980); that is, among the subgroup of persons with high distress, 73% do not receive professional help. Recent studies indicate that the phenomenon is not attributable simply to financial considerations. For example, in a study conducted in health maintenance organizations, where mental health care was available without extra cost, the 1-year treatment rate for psychological distress was 12% (Ware, Manning, Duan, Wells, & Newhouse, 1984).

While help-seeking from formal sources is relatively low, evidence on help-seeking from informal support sources (spouse, friends, family) suggests a different picture (cf. Cowen, 1982). When data on use of both formal and informal support are available, they indicate a primary reliance on informal support. For example, data from Veroff, Kulka, and Douvan (1981) indicate that for coping with "periods of unhappiness," 2% of the sample utilized formal help resources, whereas

28% used informal resources. The difference narrows somewhat for coping with specific life events or major life crises, but a 2 : 1 differential of informal : formal help is typically observed (Norcross & Prochaska, 1986; Wilcox & Birkel, 1983). A combination of help-seeking from formal and informal sources is also a common pattern; for example, Brown (1978) found that 12% of distressed persons used formal help only, 48% used informal help only, and 40% used both formal and informal help (cf. Cross, Sheehan, & Khan, 1980; McCrae, 1984; Veroff, Kulka, & Douvan, 1981). Studies with comparative data consistently find help-seeking from informal sources to be the mechanism most frequently used for coping with psychological distress (McCrae, 1984; Norcross & Prochaska, 1986; Stone & Neale, 1984; Veroff, Kulka, & Douvan, 1981). It is still unclear whether help-seeking should be classified as problem-focused or emotion-focused coping, and both positions have been expressed (see Lazarus & Folkman, 1984; Moos & Billings, 1982; Stone & Neale, 1984).

Preferred Source of Help

There are surprisingly few data on people's preferred sources of help. Scenario studies with college student samples (e.g., Christensen & Magoon, 1974; Tinsley, de St. Aubin, & Brown, 1982) report data on preferred sources and provide an estimate of the preference for help-seeking versus self-help. For personal problems the typical preference ranking is (a) friend or relative, (b) professional or paraprofessional counselor, and (c) instructor or academic advisor. These scenario studies indicate that about 49% of people preferred self-help to talking with a friend, and 66% preferred self-help to professional help. The findings were somewhat different for career decisions, where academic advisors were more likely to be consulted, but self-help was still the majority response.

Veroff, Kulka, and Douvan (1981) obtained data from a community sample on ranking of potential help sources, given different types of problems. The majority preference for coping with worries or unhappiness was informal support (from spouse or friends). For coping with persistent problems, 46% of respondents indicated they would seek some form of professional help, with the ranking of professionals being doctor (28%

of hypothetical utilization), clergy (27%), psychiatrist/psychologist (22%), and other mental health professional (17%). The data on hypothetical help-seeking were somewhat discrepant from data on actual help-seeking, which showed that 26% of respondents had ever sought help, a twofold discrepancy from the hypothetical utilization estimate of 46%. Among respondents who had sought help, the primary sources were clergy (39% of utilization), psychiatrist/psychologist (29%), doctor (21%), and other mental health professional (20%). The shift toward pastoral help was predominantly among respondents with less severe problems. Among the 10% of the sample who had ever sought help for "an impending nervous breakdown," the primary sources were doctor (52%), psychiatrist/psychologist (18%), and other mental health professional (10%). These data suggest that use of help sources depends on the severity of the problem, with a relative shift from clergy to psychologists to doctors as the problem becomes more severe.

Sex

Studies with aggregate data have shown that females appear in treatment settings in greater proportions than expected from population proportion. This is true both for medical treatment (Verbrugge, 1976) and for psychiatric treatment (Gourash, 1978). The issue is whether this indicates a higher level of morbidity, a greater tendency of females to seek help, or a greater tendency to label symptoms as requiring help.

Data from the national sample of Veroff, Kulka, and Douvan (1981) indicated some complexity. Overall there were no significant sex differences in use of formal help or in use of spouse as a confidant. For use of multiple, informal help sources there was a sex difference (59% for women compared with 50% for men), apparently because men were more likely to rely on their wives as a primary support source, whereas women engaged more friends and relatives. For use of formal help, men were more likely to use professional help for instrumental problems (work, achievement, financial), whereas women were more likely to seek professional help for interpersonal problems.

Recent studies have controlled for level of morbidity and examined different stages in the process of problem-labeling and help-seeking (Fox, 1984; Kessler, Brown, & Bowman, 1981). Retrospective questions asked whether the respondent was both-

ered in the last year by a personal problem; if so whether he or she felt the problem was of serious concern; and if so whether he or she sought professional help. Morbidity was indexed by items about current psychiatric symptoms. When morbidity level is controlled by stratifying the sample on severity of symptomatology, it is found that females are more likely to seek help at low levels of symptomatology, but males more likely to seek help at high levels. When age, marital status, and severity of symptoms are controlled, there is actually a significant male differential in help-seeking (Fox, 1984; Leaf & Bruce, 1988). Kessler et al. (1981) considered three stages of the help-seeking process, and suggested that females are more likely to define a problem as serious enough to require help; after this stage, however, there were no significant sex differences in help-seeking behavior.

Age

While there have been few studies of stratified community samples, data typically show a decline in formal help-seeking with age (Brown, 1978; Gurin, Veroff, & Feld, 1960; Veroff, Kulka, & Douvan, 1981). This is in contrast to data on age differences in mental health, which are complex and nonmonotonic but indicate increases in depression during older years (Diener, 1984; Veroff, Douvan, & Kulka, 1981). This may occur because older people are more likely to cope with problems through self-reliance (Pearlin & Schooler, 1978) or support from religious and community organizations (Veroff, Kulka, & Douvan, 1981). Data from treatment settings indicate a marked underrepresentation of elderly in mental health treatment but an overrepresentation in medical treatment settings (e.g., Fox, 1984; Schurman, Kramer, & Mitchell, 1985). It has been suggested that elderly people are more likely to attribute subjective distress to physical illness (Fox, 1984), but there have been no specific tests of this process.

Socioeconomic Status

Early data indicated a strong socioeconomic differential, with persons of higher education and income more likely to receive psychological treatment (Gurin et al., 1960; Srole, Langner, Michael, Opler, & Rennie, 1962). More recent data suggest that this effect still exists, but has been moderated by increased access to health services (Tischler,

Henesz, Myers, & Boswell, 1975). For example, data from Veroff, Kulka, and Douvan (1981) indicated that 22% of lower educated respondents sought no formal or informal help for major problems, compared with 10% for higher educated respondents. While a socioeconomic differential existed, the majority of respondents (73% to 89%) had some combination of formal and informal help. The suggestion has been made that socioeconomic effects are attributable primarily to attitudinal factors because positive attitudes toward psychotherapy are strongly related to higher socioeconomic status (Fischer, Winer, & Abramowitz, 1983; Greenley & Mechanic, 1976). Also consistent with this point is the fact that income and education are related to greater levels of subjective well-being (Diener, 1984; Veroff, Douvan, & Kulka, 1981), but also to higher rates of help-seeking.

Life Stress

Psychological distress is related to adverse life events (Lewinsohn, Hoberman, Teri, & Hautzinger, 1985), and available data indicate that negative events serve as a trigger for help-seeking behavior. Comparisons of clinic cases with controls in college populations indicate that help-seekers have experienced greater intensity of negative events, and fewer positive events, during the previous year (Goodman, Sewell, & Jampol, 1984; Greenley & Mechanic, 1976). Similarly, data on help-seeking decisions among samples of laypersons and professionals (Brown, 1978; Norcross & Prochaska, 1986) indicated that in most cases a help-seeking episode was set off by a severe negative event. In a community study, Dooley and Catalano (1984) found that a measure of recent life events was related to an index of recent help-seeking for emotional problems, either from friends and family (61% of those seeking help) or from doctors, psychotherapists, or self-help groups (39%).

It should be noted that life events also increase seeking of medical treatment (e.g., Pilisuk, Boylan, & Acredolo, 1987; Ostrove & Baum, 1983). For example, Gortmaker, Eckenrode, and Gore (1982) obtained diary data over a period of 28 days and found that the occurrence of an upsetting event on a given day doubled the probability of health care utilization on the subsequent day, even when no physical symptoms were reported. The exact mechanism in the linkage between per-

ceived stress and health care utilization, however, has not been clarified.

Social Context

Data on the relation between social networks and help-seeking are complex, and are discussed in more detail subsequently. Comparisons of clinic cases with controls typically show that people in treatment have lower support. For example, Goodman et al. (1984) obtained data on perceived social support from the Arizona Social Support Interview Schedule from 50 clinic attenders and 50 controls (nonmatched volunteers from introductory psychology classes). These data indicated that the cases (mean = 4.5 support people) scored significantly lower than the controls (mean = 6.0 support people); differences were found for several support dimensions, including instrumental support, advice and guidance, and social participation. These data, then, suggest that a deficiency in supportive relationships may contribute to emotional distress and thus lead to professional help-seeking. The case-control design, however, fails to consider people with high distress who did not seek treatment.

In data from a community sample (Brown, 1978), the level of perceived support was generally high, and among the subsample of people who had experienced negative life events, help-seekers were not strongly differentiated on most of the social support measures. People who sought professional help reported somewhat less activity and intimacy in their informal network, but these people also had a greater severity of negative life events, so there is a confound in these data. Pilisuk et al. (1987) examined the interaction of life stress and social support in predicting medical care utilization in a health maintenance organization (HMO) setting. They found that high support, indexed through marital satisfaction and availability of confidants outside the family, reduced the level of health care utilization primarily among persons who had experienced many life events; that is, this support produced a stress-buffering effect (Cohen & Wills, 1985). These data, then, suggest that low support may contribute to help-seeking because persons with lower support have increased levels of distress and less protection against the adverse effects of negative life events.

In contrast, some data indicate ways in which a large social network may facilitate help-seeking. For example, Horwitz (1977) conducted interviews with psychiatric outpatients shortly after initiation of treatment, and found that respondents had talked with an average of 4.4 members of their network before seeking professional help (2.1 for men, 6.6 for women). This represented a substantial part of the network, the proportions being .30 to .61 of the intimate network. Network members had been involved in helping define the problem, offering advice, and providing recommendations for professional help. Similarly, Cross et al. (1980) studied patients in outpatient psychiatric treatment over a 3-month period and found that the mean frequency for informal help-seeking increased from 1.3 times per week pretreatment to 2.7 times/week posttreatment. The data suggested that psychotherapy increased the utilization of informal support from friends, spouse, and family. These findings are consistent with data from Taylor, Falke, Shoptaw, & Lichtman (1986) in a study of cancer patients (predominantly female), of whom 60% were participants in self-help groups. Participants in support groups, compared with patients who were nonattenders, had more social support resources of all kinds. They had greater willingness to share cancer-related concerns with friends and spouses, were more likely to have sought help from mental health professionals, and had a higher level of participation in religious and sociocultural groups. These data thus suggest that social network members may play an active role in helping people to define problems and seek treatment when appropriate.

There is one process in which social networks may operate to restrict the type of help-seeking pursued. For example, McKinlay (1973) studied medical service utilization among a sample of low-income families in Aberdeen, Scotland. Measures of network structure were obtained, and subjects were classified as underutilizers versus utilizers of prenatal services. The data showed that underutilizers had social networks of higher density, that is, more kin-centered and with greater interconnection among network members. Similar data from a study of divorced women (Wilcox & Birkel, 1983) indicated that persons in high-density networks were less likely to seek professional help for depressive problems, and more likely to seek help from a family member. Other data suggest that larger, more diffuse networks are relevant for facilitating access to needed services (Granovetter, 1973; Henderson, Byrne, Duncan-Jones, Scott, & Adcock, 1980; Miller & Ingham,

1979). The implication is that in high-density networks there is a tendency to keep problems within the network, which in some respects may operate to reduce the use of community help resources.

To summarize, different processes are indicated by between- and within-subject designs. Social support operates to reduce psychological distress, and so may reduce the amount of help-seeking from professionals (Goodman et al., 1984; Pilisuk et al., 1987), possibly by providing an additional source of help or through a buffering effect on life stress. At the same time, several studies have shown ways in which informal networks guide troubled people toward professional help, and may augment the professional treatment process (Cross et al., 1980; Horwitz, 1977; Taylor et al., 1986). There is no necessary contradiction between these findings; if there is any general conclusion, it is that informal networks offer an additional coping resource that may be useful to distressed people in several ways.

Help-Seeking in Medical Settings

In recent years, evidence has developed concerning help-seeking for psychological distress in medical settings. While one would expect medical illness to cause some elevation of distress, the extent to which observed distress levels exceed population values has led to efforts to identify the true prevalence of psychiatric versus medical problems in primary care populations. One current explanation is that a proportion of patients visit physician and hospital practices as a means of help-seeking to deal with implicit or explicit psychological distress. For example, Tessler, Mechanic, and Dimond (1976) conducted interviews with adults enrolled in an HMO program, and medical records for 1 year subsequent to the interview were coded to index medical service utilization. Prospective analyses showed that a composite index of psychological distress (perceived stress, worry, and neuroticism) was related to greater medical utilization, with control for health status at baseline. These data suggested that some proportion of health care visits were related to mental health concerns, whether or not labeled as such by the patient.

Subsequent studies with diagnostic interviews, such as the Epidemiological Catchment Area (ECA) study, have shown that there is a high prevalence of mental disorder among patients in primary care settings and that mental health problems produce a considerable increment in medical visits (Cleary, Goldberg, Kessler, & Nycz, 1982; Kessler et al., 1987; Von Korff et al., 1987). For example, Shapiro et al. (1984) found that the average number of health provider visits in the previous 6 months was 4.6 among persons with any Diagnostic Interview Schedule (DIS) disorder compared with 2.6 in the general population, a 74% increase. The 6-month rate of hospital admissions for physical conditions was 24.7 per 100 among persons with any DIS disorder compared with 18.2 per 100 in the general population, representing a 36% increase. Of health provider visits made explicitly for mental health reasons, data showed that across sites, 41% to 63% of these visits were made to general medical practitioners. Similarly, Schurman, Kramer, and Mitchell (1985) analyzed data on visits to outpatient practitioners and found that 47% of all medical office visits resulting in a diagnosis of mental disorder were to nonpsychiatrists; these were primarily general practitioners, family practitioners, and internists. The initial visit typically had a physical symptom as the presenting complaint.

Another aspect of the ECA data is that medical service users were asked whether they had discussed emotional problems with the practitioner (Kessler et al., 1987). These questions showed that across sites, 30% of persons with a current DIS diagnosis reported talking with a practitioner about emotional problems, compared with about 15% among those without a current diagnosis. The appreciable rate among nondistressed persons is striking, but the data still indicate that the majority of persons with current mental disorder do not discuss emotional problems directly with the practitioner. What kind of treatment they do receive remains unclear.

Summary and Conclusions

The existing data are based on large and representative samples, thus provide a good source of basic findings about help-seeking behavior. Although there are some limitations on the available data base, there seems to be a sequence of help-seeking efforts. The first stage is based on conversations with informal support sources (spouse, friends, family); seeking help from clergy or general medical practitioners is the second stage; and

this may result, in the third stage, in help from a mental health specialist. The indications are that this is a pyramidal process, with the majority of help-seeking conducted within informal networks, a substantial proportion directed to medical or religious professionals, and the minority of help-seeking directed to psychologists or psychiatrists.

A second conclusion is that a stress-coping model seems useful for understanding the broad outlines of the help-seeking process. Help-seeking from both informal and formal sources clearly is primed by negative events. It is apparent that distressed people use a variety of resources, including informal support, formal help, and other nonsocial coping mechanisms, in active attempts to deal with their situations. It is less clear whether seeking of professional help is attributable to deficiencies in informal support, but it is clear that social network members can provide assistance that is complementary to professional helping efforts.

A third conclusion is that a good deal of formal help for emotional distress is provided by people who are not mental health specialists. With some variation across studies and problem types, studies show that primary-care physicians and ministers are major sources of service provision. Whether this derives from a labeling of emotional distress as a physical problem, a form of disguised help-seeking based on concerns about stigmatization, or whether distressed people perceive medical and religious professionals as more accessible than psychotherapists is not well understood at present.

Conclusions about individual differences in help-seeking tendencies are more qualified. While there is a female differential in treatment rates for both medical and psychological problems, sex differences seem to occur primarily at early stages of problem definition, not at the stage of help-seeking behavior. Socioeconomic differences, to the extent that they still exist, seem more attributable to attitudinal factors, and demographic effects are moderated by type of problem (instrumental vs. emotional). Age differences are not well understood; while elderly people are markedly underrepresented in treatment, this may occur because elderly people are more likely to define problems as physical, or to conduct help-seeking within informal community and religious sources. The only general conclusion is that help-seeking behavior is most predictable from the interaction of demographics and problem type.

THEORETICAL FRAMEWORK

For a theoretical perspective, we consider help-seeking from the standpoint of a coping mechanism. Our postulate is that evaluation of help-seeking is determined by how it is construed from a coping standpoint. In some cases, seeking help may be construed as a form of direct-action coping, used in concert with other coping mechanisms, such as information-seeking and problem-solving, which are aimed at resolution of the problem. In certain other cases the help-seeking may be dependency based, used in a context where other coping mechanisms are perceived as unavailable or ineffective, or where requests for help are part of self-presentation concerns, used as a way of eliciting sympathy from others.

Our basic prediction is that the probability of help-seeking behavior in a given situation, and the reactions of the recipient to receiving help, are determined by this aspect of the help-seeking process. Responses construed as direct action are more consistent with a positive self-image and favorable social comparisons (cf. Nelson-Le Gall, Gumerman, & Scott-Jones, 1983; Wills, 1983). In contrast, help-seeking construed as dependency based may pose a threat to a person's self-image, because it could lead to unfavorable social comparisons or continued dependency (cf. Ames, 1983a; Fisher, Nadler, & Whitcher-Alagna, 1982). In general, we expect individuals to be more likely to seek help, and to react favorably to a helping interaction, when the interaction is perceived as likely to increase competence in the long term. A corollary is that when help-seeking is linked to use of other coping mechanisms such as problem-solving, there will be greater likelihood of increased competence, so this should be perceived more favorably. There is in fact some evidence that self-change efforts that involve use of multiple coping strategies, including both social and nonsocial coping, are more effective in the long term (Perri, 1985).

The perceived distinction between the two types of help-seeking may be influenced by several factors. Distinctions may be situationally guided, influenced by situational cues that emphasize coping- versus dependency-related aspects of the help-seeking interaction. Distinctions also may be guided by dispositional factors, because personality attributes and belief systems may determine how various types of help-seeking are perceived and evaluated. The social context of help-seeking also may exert a considerable impact on how help-seeking is perceived and implemented. Finally, esteem-maintenance factors may operate to influence help-seeking perceptions and decisions. In the following sections, we consider how these factors may apply to the process of help-seeking.

SITUATIONAL FACTORS

Visibility of Help-Seeking

The act of seeking help can be an admission of inferiority, inadequacy, or dependency. It is probably for this reason that willingness to ask for help increases as the act of seeking help becomes less visible and more private (cf. Nadler & Porat, 1978; Shapiro, 1978). Often people will choose impersonal sources of help, such as self-help tapes, over the more personal touch of talking to a counselor on the telephone (Hill & Harmon, 1976). When help-seeking from impersonal sources is not an option, then help-seeking increases as the number of observers of the help request decreases (Williams & Williams, 1983).

The help request itself is not the only potentially embarrassing aspect of helping interactions. The problem or need that potentially motivates the help request can also be a source of embarrassment (Shapiro, 1983). The needy individual contemplating seeking help must weigh the embarrassment of asking for help against the prospect of continued failure or dependency (Wallston, 1976). When it is clear that potential helpers are already aware of the problem or deficiency, the probability that the needy individual will ask for help increases (Nadler & Fux, 1984). As Shapiro (1978) has demonstrated, help-seeking is especially likely to occur when the act of seeking help is private but the problem that necessitates the help is public. Although the needy may be more willing to seek help when their problems are visible to others than when they are invisible, they also may find that they are less likely to need to request help explicitly in order to obtain the desired support. This factor may help to explain the high prevalence of help-seeking within informal social networks, where network members are likely to be aware of problems, and help can be provided in a more private setting.

Controllability of the Problem

Are people more likely to be willing to ask for help if they view their problems as controllable or uncontrollable? At first blush, the evidence appears contradictory. For example, alcoholics are more willing to seek help if they believe that people have little control over whether they develop a drinking problem (Hingson, Mangione, Meyers, & Scotch, 1982). Research also indicates that helpers are more positive toward needy individuals whose problems are beyond their control than toward persons whose problems are within their control (Ickes & Kidd, 1976; Meyer & Mulherin, 1980; Wills, 1978). Thus, perceptions of the problem as uncontrollable seem to increase help-seeking. This may occur because the perception of the problem as outside one's control reduces the element of esteem-threat that deters help-seeking. The impact of this factor would in theory be most likely when previous failure has occurred.

On the other hand, research in achievement contexts indicates that students who do poorly on an exam will seek help to improve their performance on the next exam if they believe that performance is under their control; that is, they believe that they can do better if they try harder and do not blame their previous failure on uncontrollable factors such as task difficulty or teacher biases (Ames, 1983a; Ames & Lau, 1982; Testa & Major, in press). In their important statement on helping and coping, Brickman et al. (1982) posed a distinction that suggests a resolution to this puzzle — the distinction between control over the cause of the problem and control over the solution to the problem. It is the latter type of control that should predict willingness to seek certain kinds of help. Alcoholics who believe that the development of a drinking problem is not under their control are describing a belief about the origins of their problem; but students who believe that if they study harder they can do better in the future are instead making a statement about the solution to their problem. The distinction is also useful in illuminating the inclination of victims to blame themselves for their victimization, an attribution that others often find baffling. By assuming blame, victims also can assume responsibility and con-

trol, which can help them feel that they can avoid future victimization (Janoff-Bulman, Madden, & Timko, 1983). Seeking help to deal with the victimization and to learn how to avoid future victimizations might be part of the exercise of control.

In general, then, people who see the solutions to their problems as under their control may be more willing to seek the sort of help that will allow them to remedy their problems and facilitate their self-sufficiency. The distinction between control over the origin of the problem and control over the solution for the problem is also an important one for helpers to make. Brickman et al. (1982) suggest that often the most helpful perspective is one in which helpers see the origins of people's problems as beyond their control (thus justifying the rendering of aid), but the solution to problems as within their control.

The seeking and receiving of help are fraught with difficulties for people who hope eventually to be free of the need for help. The mere fact of receiving help could undermine people's independence by depriving them of opportunities to learn to succeed on their own (Skinner, 1976), or by generating self-perceptions of helplessness and inferiority (Coates, Renzaglia, & Embree, 1983; Langer & Benevento, 1978) — perceptions that also may be shared by others who view them in the recipient role (e.g., Wills, 1978). It may be possible, though, for people to seek and receive help in ways that preserve their sense of autonomy and augment their motivation to improve. For example, rather than seeking help that directly solves their problem (such as the answers to troublesome problems for students in a math class, or money for food and shelter for the impoverished), the needy might instead seek the kind of help that allows them to develop new skills so that they can then help themselves (DePaulo, Brown, & Greenberg, 1983; Nadler, in press). Gartner and Riessman (1977) argue that the potency of self-help groups stems in part from the fact that members give help as well as receive it.

Short of becoming a helper as well as a recipient of help, there are other ways that people can seek and receive help that are likely to render the aid more effective in the long run. For example, clients who are offered a choice among different types of treatment benefit more from help than do those who are not offered this type of control (Miller, 1985). A sense of control over the duration of the help also can be important (Harris, Tessler, & Potter, 1977). In fact, uncertainty about this very factor may deter many people from beginning psychotherapy and from soliciting other types of help as well.

Prior Success with the Task

Sometimes help-seeking is used strategically — for example, as a way of ingratiating (Jones, 1964; Nadler, Shapiro, & Ben-Itzhak, 1982). Other times it is used as a way of further developing and enhancing skills and talents (Fisher, Goff, Nadler, & Chinsky, 1989). More often, however, it is prompted by some perceived failure or need (e.g., Ames & Lau, 1982). Whether the experience of failure will motivate people to ask for help may depend in part on their history of successes and failures with the task. If their previous experiences were primarily positive, they may feel that future outcomes are under their control and that they need simply to redouble their efforts to succeed on their own (cf. Nadler & Fisher, 1986; Wortman & Brehm, 1975).

Prior successes, however, do not guarantee invulnerability to failure, nor do they necessarily predict reluctance to ask for help. For instance, while working on a type of problem that they have solved successfully in every prior attempt, students might notice something about it that they do not understand. This could undermine their confidence (Bandura, 1982), and motivate them to seek help. There are other subtle ways, too, that dependency can be induced in people who have a history of successes. Langer and Benevento (1978) suggest that people who are assigned a label that implies inferiority to another person (e.g., help-recipient, as opposed to helper), or who allow others to do things for them that they could have done themselves, may erroneously infer that they are incompetent. As a result, they may be likely to seek help.

Threat Appraisal

Folkman and Lazarus (1980) have described three categories of stressful life events. Challenges are events that afford opportunities for personal mastery, growth, or gain. Harms and losses are events in which damage to one's health, relationships, or self-esteem has already occurred, and threats are events in which harm or loss is anticipated, though it has not yet occurred. McCrae (1984) studied the patterns of help-seeking in re-

sponse to all three types of stressful events, and found more help-seeking by people dealing with threats and challenges than by those dealing with harms or losses. Similarly, in their study of college students' ways of coping with exams, Folkman and Lazarus (1985) found that students sought more social support before the exam (when they were experiencing threat, and perhaps challenge) than after the exam was over and the grades were posted (and any harm or loss had already occurred). There was some support-seeking after the grades were posted; this occurred primarily among the students who had done most poorly on the exam and may represent a form of social comparison behavior (Wills, 1983).

In a subsequent study, Folkman, Lazarus, Dunkel-Schetter, DeLongis, & Gruen (1986) divided threats into threats to self-esteem (e.g., appearing incompetent, losing one's self-respect or the approval of a significant other) and threats to a loved one's well-being, and found that when threat to self-esteem was high (compared with when it was low), people were especially unlikely to seek social support. Unfortunately, in most studies of coping, measures of social support mix different kinds of support, such as informational support and emotional support. The distinction between the two could be important. For example, the support sought by students prior to taking an exam may well be primarily informational; in contrast, after the exam is over and they learn that they did poorly, they may seek primarily emotional support.

Helper's Abilities

Intuitively, one might expect needy individuals to seek competent help provided by talented helpers who are especially skilled at dealing with the problem in question. In fact, there is evidence that potential help recipients value expertise in professional helpers and trustworthiness in professionals and friends (Corrigan, 1978). Further, therapists who are skilled at communicating empathy and a desire to help, and who avoid hostility and moralizing, are especially successful at influencing clients to enter and continue with treatment, and to experience successful outcomes (Miller, 1985; Wills, 1982). However, there are some data indicating that the helper's ability often is not as powerful a predictor of choice of helper, or satisfaction with help, as one might expect. In organizational settings, workers often prefer to seek help from coworkers than from higher status helpers who are more competent (Blau, 1955; Rosen, 1983). Such findings have been linked to social comparison processes, with the suggestion that people are sensitive to whether help-seeking will affect the status differential between the self and the potential helper (cf. DePaulo, 1978a; Druian & DePaulo, 1977).

Further, even when recipients have no choice of helpers and are instead assigned to a particular helper, they do not always show greater benefit from the most competent helpers. For example, in a peer tutoring study, second- and fourth-grade students were paired with tutors in the same grade as themselves or two grades ahead (DePaulo, Tang, Webb, Hoover, Marsh, & Litowitz, 1989). Presumably, the older tutors were the more talented helpers, yet, as predicted by social comparison theory, some students (fourth-graders who were especially competent themselves) performed much better when tutored by smart tutors from the same grade rather than two grades ahead. These effects seem to occur because social comparison concerns are maximized (cf. Tesser, in press; Wills, 1983).

On the other hand, various factors not clearly relevant to the instrumental quality of aid have been shown to affect the positivity of recipients' reactions to help, and are likely to predict willingness to seek help as well. These include the helper's physical attractiveness (Nadler, 1980; Nadler et al., 1982; Stokes & Bickman, 1974); the recipients' liking for the helper (DePaulo, 1978a; Stapleton, Nacci, & Tedeschi, 1973); the helper's (DiMatteo, Hays, & Prince, 1986; Whitcher-Alagna, 1983) and the help-seeker's (DePaulo & Fisher, 1981) nonverbal communication skills; whether the helper is a friend or a stranger (Nadler, Fisher, & Ben-Itzhak, 1983; Nadler, Fisher, & Streufert, 1974; Shapiro, 1980); the amount of imposition on the helper (DePaulo & Fisher, 1980; DePaulo, Leiphart, & Dull, 1984); the amount and appropriateness of the help that the helper provided (e.g., DePaulo, Brittingham, & Kaiser, 1983); and whether the helper provided the help voluntarily or involuntarily (Goranson & Berkowitz, 1966; Greenberg & Frisch, 1972).

Other Coping Attempts Employed for the Problem

Because the proportion of needy individuals who seek help is often low, it would not be surprising to find that people often engage in a variety of other ways of coping before deciding to seek help. In fact, people typically utilize a variety of coping mechanisms to deal with a stressful event; in over 90% of such events, they employ both problem-focused and emotion-focused coping strategies as well as social coping (Folkman & Lazarus, 1980, 1985; Perri, 1985). Among people experiencing symptoms that could be indicative of heart disease, some used a variety of strategies for appraising their symptoms, such as discussing them with others; those people were slower to seek help from physicians (Matthews et al., 1983; see also Safer, Tharps, Jackson, & Leventhal, 1979).

Even when people do seek help, they often do not begin by seeking help directly from the most appropriate helpers. They might begin, for example, by trying some implicit, disguised attempts to solicit help (e.g., Blau, 1955; Glidewell, Tucker, Todt, & Cox, 1983). They might then progress to the use of direct requests for help, but from helpers who are not necessarily the most competent to deal with their problems. For instance, as noted previously, psychological problems are often presented first to friends, clergy, or physicians, and only later (if at all) to helpers trained in psychology. This may indicate that people begin by seeking help for one type of problem (e.g., instrumental or physical) and then progress to discussions about other types of problems (e.g., interpersonal or emotional).

PERSONALITY FACTORS

Self-Esteem and Achievement Motivation

A psychologically troublesome aspect of seeking help is that it can feel like an admission of inadequacy and dependency. It might seem reasonable to expect that this threatening aspect of seeking help would be especially daunting to people with low self-esteem, who perhaps would be most vulnerable to such an acknowledgment of ineptitude. Yet, a number of studies have found low, rather than high, self-esteem people most willing to ask for help (Nadler, 1986). Alcoholics with low self-esteem, for example, are more likely to seek treatment (Charalampous, Ford, & Skinner, 1976; Miller, 1985) and to agree to more extensive treatment (Corotto, 1963) than are those with high self-esteem. Women who blame themselves for being mistreated, or who are low in self-acceptance, are more likely to join women's counseling groups (Frieze, 1979; Gross, Fisher, Nadler, Stiglitz, & Craig, 1979). In organizational settings, too, self-esteem predicts help-seeking, with low self-esteem employees more likely to seek needed advice (Burke & Weir, 1976). For undergraduates in the laboratory, too, low self-esteem predicts willingness to ask for help (e.g., Harris et al., 1977; Nadler & Fux, 1984).

In all of these instances, it is the people with high self-esteem who are more resistant to seeking help, perhaps because they believe that they should be able to succeed at the task by themselves. In fact, in one study in which half of the participants were made to feel inadequate by learning that most other participants in their situation had done much better (and that, by implication, they should have, too), those participants were more likely than the others (who were told that their performance, though deficient, was better than most others in their situation) to resist seeking help (Morris & Rosen, 1973).

In situations that are especially threatening to self-esteem, people may try to avoid seeking help (Folkman et al., 1986), but this sensitivity to threat seems to characterize people with high self-esteem even more than those with low self-esteem. For example, if performance at a task is described as indicative of intelligence or creativity, people with high self-esteem are even more reluctant than lows to seek help at the task (Tessler & Schwartz, 1972). Their reluctance is further exacerbated if the person from whom help is to be sought is similar to themselves, thus making them appear even more incompetent in comparison (Nadler, 1987). People with high self-esteem also are especially reluctant to seek help when they anticipate no opportunity to reciprocate the help (Nadler, Mayseless, Peri, & Tchemennski, 1985). In addition, traditional males with high self-esteem are especially resistant to seeking help on stereotypically masculine tasks (Wallston, 1976), probably because they feel that they should be able to succeed at those tasks by themselves.

In some instances, it may be appropriate for people with low self-esteem to be especially receptive to help, and there is evidence that people with low self-esteem profit from their willingness to seek advice. In work settings, for example, lows succeed more often than highs on tasks that require cooperation and consultation (Weiss & Knight, 1980). But there can also be hazards to seeking help for people who are low in self-esteem. To the extent that they feel incapable of improving, they might respond to the receipt of help with feelings of dependence and with impaired performance, rather than with persistence and enhanced performance as often shown by highs (e.g., DePaulo, Brown, Ishii, & Fisher, 1981; Miller, 1985; Nadler & Fisher, 1986). In the study of battered women, for example, those who blamed themselves were more likely to seek therapy than those who blamed their husbands, but they also were less likely to regard their therapy as successful (Frieze, 1979).

In situations that are threatening to self-esteem, is it possible for people to seek help and still avoid feeling demoralized by their need for help? Ames and Lau (1982) addressed this question in a study of students' willingness to attend an academic help session in preparation for a second exam after learning the results of their performance on the first exam. In this context it is, of course, the students who failed the first exam who are likely to feel most vulnerable. Ames and Lau (1982) predicted, and found, that of the students who had failed the first test, those who would be most likely to take the constructive step of attending the help sessions were those who made help-relevant attributions. Such students do not feel that their overall ability has been called into question by their performance on the first test, nor do they blame their performance on external forces; instead, they decide they did not try hard enough the first time, and that if they try harder the second time, they will succeed. They are, in essence, compartmentalizing their failure and construing it as a very specific (rather than global) deficit that can be remedied (Weiner, 1979). The results of the Ames and Lau (1982) research are consistent with Nadler and Fisher's (1986) threat to self-esteem model of reactions to help. Students who had failed the first test were motivated by the potential threat to their self-esteem to improve their performance; those who also made self-relevant attributions believed that the potential for improved performance was under their control—that is, that they could do better if they tried. Together, these two factors—motivation to improve and belief in one's control over the potential for improvement—predicted instrumental help-seeking.

A process analogous to the psychological compartmentalizing performed by the Ames and Lau (1982) help-seekers may be what allows certain paraplegics to be more open than others to seeking help (Nadler, in press). Paraplegics who are especially reluctant to seek help are those who regard their disability as central to their lives. For example, they see it as interfering with many important activities and they feel that they would be better people if they were not disabled. In contrast, those who see their disabilities as specific limitations in circumscribed domains that do not threaten their worth as a person are more open to seeking and receiving help from others (Nadler, Sheinberg, & Jaffe, 1981; cf. Nadler, Lewinstein, & Rahav, in press).

We have argued that asking for help can be threatening to self-esteem, and it is largely this threat that deters people with high self-esteem from seeking needed aid. But continuing to fail also can be threatening to self-esteem. Thus, in situations in which the embarrassment inherent in persistent failure supercedes the embarrassment of admitting the need for help, people with high self-esteem may be even more willing than people with low self-esteem to ask for help.

There is still another set of conditions under which people with high self-esteem may be willing to avail themselves of needed help. When seeking help is cast as an instrumental behavior that is likely to facilitate effective task performance, people with high self-esteem may be more willing than those with low self-esteem to utilize the available helpful resources. Esteem threats become essentially irrelevant, and the focus is instead on effective routes to the attainment of important goals (e.g., DePaulo, Brown, & Greenberg, 1983). Ames (1983b) has found, for example, that teachers who value being competent are especially willing to make use of a variety of sources of help.

The foregoing analysis does not necessarily imply that people who have a high motivation to achieve will be more willing to seek help than low-need achievers (Nadler, 1983). Achievement-oriented people may have the goal of mastering tasks completely independently (DePaulo, Brown, & Greenberg, 1983), or of using their level of performance at a task as an index of their own ability level (Trope, 1983). In either case, help-seeking would interfere with their goal.

Both self-esteem and achievement motivation were measured in the Tessler and Schwartz (1972) study. The two constructs were positively correlated ($r = .40$), and both independently predicted reluctance to seek help. That is, even after controlling for the fact that people with high self-esteem were somewhat more resistant to seeking help, it was still found that people highly in need for achievement were significantly less likely to seek help than were people low in need for achievement.

Shyness

One of the most reliable findings about people who are shy is that they are low in self-esteem (Cheek, Melchior, & Carpentieri, 1986). Typical correlations are quite robust, hovering around $-.50$. In that people with low self-esteem are often more willing to seek help than are people with high self-esteem, it might be expected that shy people also will be willing to ask for help. However, shyness is more than simply low self-esteem. Rather, it is a decidedly interpersonal syndrome. For people who are shy, social interactions are fraught with danger. Shy people would like very much to make a good impression on others, but doubt that they can do so (Leary, 1983). They feel anxious and act inhibited in the presence of other people (Cheek & Buss, 1981; DePaulo, Epstein, & LeMay, 1989), and they sometimes try to avoid social interactions altogether. Because help-seeking often involves initiating a social interaction, then, it can be quite problematic for people who are shy.

By their own self-reports, shy people concur with the conclusion that asking for help is hard for them. They acknowledge they have a smaller percentage of people in their social networks to whom they can turn for help and in whom they can confide. They also see others as offering less support, and they feel less satisfied with the support that they do receive (Jones & Carpenter, 1986). In educational contexts, they seek help less frequently from advisors (Friedman, 1980) and make fewer attempts to seek information from others about careers that interest them (Bruch, Giordano, & Pearl, 1986; Phillips & Bruch, 1988). Although about one in every four shy people indicates a willingness to seek help to overcome their shyness (Pilkonis, 1977), many also note that it would be difficult to do so, in part because they fear that others do not take shyness very seriously (Harris, 1984). On the basis of extensive questionnaires and interviews with people who are shy, Zimbardo (1977) concluded that the reluctance to ask for help is one of the most serious consequences of being shy.

In one of the few studies of shyness in which behavioral measures of help-seeking were collected (DePaulo, Dull, Greenberg, & Swaim, 1989), subjects attempted to do an impossible task in the presence of another person who was said to have just successfully completed the task. Shy subjects were not any less likely overall than were subjects who were not shy to seek help from the other person; however, they were less likely to seek help when the other person was a member of the opposite sex. In a second study, subjects were required to call strangers and ask them if they would be willing to complete a questionnaire. All respondents agreed to do so. However, when the subjects placing the calls were shy (compared with when they were not shy), and the respondents were of the opposite sex, the questionnaires actually were less likely to be returned (DePaulo et al., 1989).

Self-Disclosure

When people ask for help, even in the most perfunctory way, the mere fact of seeking the help can be a sort of self-disclosure; it can reveal, for instance, the help-seeker's dependence and need for help. Many help-requests, though, are not barren. Rather, the help-seeker, in requesting aid, often discloses something about the feelings or problems that are the basis of the need for assistance. It should follow, then, that people who are dispositionally more self-disclosing should also be more willing to ask for help. The evidence for this hypothesis is mostly indirect. For example, Fischer and Turner (1970) developed a scale of attitudes toward seeking professional help that successfully postdicts contacts with therapists. One of the four subscales was "interpersonal openness," a measure of willingness to disclose intimate facts and feelings. Also relevant to the hypothesized link between disclosure and help-seeking are studies showing that people who are interested in hearing feedback about themselves are particularly likely to seek psychological help (Snyder, Ingram, & Newburg, 1982); one way to solicit feedback is, of course, to self-disclose.

There is evidence that people who are high self-disclosers are more likely to form supportive relationships (Cohen, Sherrod, & Clark, 1986), to feel that social support is available to them (Burke, Weir, & Harrison, 1976), and to receive needed help (Burke, Weir, & Duncan, 1976). The effectiveness of self-disclosure in eliciting help may lie in the fact that in describing their distress, self-disclosers also are providing potential helpers with a cue to offer help and with information about the type of help that might be most appropriate and most appreciated (Coates & Winston, 1987). In many instances, perhaps particularly in interac-

tions with close friends and family members, self-disclosures may function as implicit requests for help. The mere fact of having mentioned one's distress may be sufficient to elicit an offer of help from people with whom one enjoys a communal relationship. And in fact, if it is necessary explicitly to request help in those relationships, the relationships may be troubled ones (cf. Pearlin & Schooler, 1978).

There are risks, though, to the persistent disclosure of distress. After a certain point, network members may become less helpful, rather than more helpful, as implicit demands for help continue unrelentingly (Coates & Winston, 1987). Conversely, both network members and professionals, in providing help, may make demands for continued self-disclosure from the help recipient, which can breed resentment and suppress future requests for help (cf. Merton, Merton, & Barber, 1983).

Belief System

People's beliefs about themselves, about helpers and the helping process, and about others' views of psychological problems are important predictors of their willingness to seek help. Three of the subscales of the Fischer and Turner (1970) measure of attitudes toward professional help are measures of such beliefs. Specifically, people with more positive attitudes toward professional help are those who believe that it is important and useful to seek help for psychological problems, who have confidence in mental health practitioners, and who are unconcerned with the potential stigma involved in seeking professional help.

Fischer and Turner (1970) also found that people with an internal locus of control (i.e., those who believe that they can control important outcomes in their lives) reported more positive attitudes toward professional help than did externals, who believe that their own outcomes are in the hands of fate, luck, or powerful other people. In medical contexts, too, internals are more likely to seek help, in that they search for more information relevant to their physical disorders. It is likely that internals preferentially seek the kinds of help that allow them some control over the helping process and outcomes. For example, they are more successful in self-directed and nondirective forms of treatment than in structured and directive forms (Miller, 1985).

People's beliefs about the nature of their problems are also important. For example, students who had been taught a disease model of mental illness, compared with those who were taught a social learning approach, were less likely to report that they would take active steps to deal with their own emotional problems, such as seeking help from a mental health center (Fisher & Farina, 1979), and more likely to say that they would resort to drugs and alcohol instead.

SOCIAL CONTEXT

One of the striking findings in the help-seeking literature is the preference for seeking help from friends rather than strangers. This has been demonstrated in laboratory studies (Corrigan, 1978; DePaulo, 1978a; DePaulo & Fisher, 1980; Shapiro, 1980; Tausig & Michello, 1988) showing that the probability of help-seeking increases markedly when the potential helper is a friend. Epidemiological studies also are notably consistent in showing that most help-seeking occurs within the informal network.

Several factors can be noted that would be relevant in naturalistic settings. One is that friends and family are easily accessible compared with professionals, who are physically distant. Another is that help from informal networks is less costly in terms of effort, time, and money. While these factors are probably relevant, however, we do not think that they are the sufficient factors for predicting help-seeking, because the major findings about help-seeking remain when these factors are controlled in laboratory and field studies. What other processes, then, may be relevant for help-seeking and social networks?

Emotional Support and Self-Disclosure

One consideration derives from a functional analysis of social support and help-seeking (Wills, 1985, 1987). This suggests that the major supportive function sought from social networks is emotional support, namely reassurance of self-worth, ability to talk about worries and negative feelings, and affirmation of acceptance by another person. There is little direct evidence about the desired functions from informal support, but a variety of studies suggest that emotional support is a major function of informal networks (see Cohen & Wills, 1985; Wills, in press).

This type of support involves self-disclosure, talking sometimes about negative aspects of the self, performances that have been negatively evaluated, or worries that might seem unfounded. The ability to self-disclose depends on the existence of a relationship where intimacy is possible. It is perhaps trivial to note that self-disclosure is facilitated by a close relationship, but a number of studies have demonstrated the importance of this process (e.g., Berg, 1984; Cohen, Sherrod, & Clark, 1986; Reis, Senchak, & Solomon, 1985). The crucial aspect of informal networks is that there is a history of self-disclosure where people learn that they are accepted despite negative aspects.

Reciprocal Comparison Process

Another aspect of informal networks is that they involve enduring relationships where reciprocal helping is possible. Helping interactions in which the recipient is unable to reciprocate the help received are perceived as aversive, whereas interactions in which some type of repayment is possible are perceived more positively (see Greenberg & Westcott, 1983). Such reciprocation is unlikely in relationships with strangers, but more likely in continuing relationships.

Social comparison is another relevant process. When a person receives help on a dimension central for self-definition, an unfavorable comparison is produced relative to the helper (Wills, 1983). The unfavorable comparison process could, in principle, present a source of strain to relationships where help-seeking occurs. The unfavorable comparison may be ameliorated, however, if the focal person has a subsequent opportunity to provide help to the other on a different task, perhaps a task that is central to the other's self-esteem. Tesser has shown that a kind of balancing of favorable and unfavorable comparisons seems to occur in close relationships, so that each participant has a source of comparisons that is favorable to central dimensions of his or her self-esteem (see Tesser, in press). Ideally, each participant in the network could be supportive to others in ways that would provide reciprocal enhancement of the individuals' self-esteem; for example, receiving support on emotional dimensions and giving support on instrumental dimensions. In everyday settings, behavior that has sometimes been construed as "disguised help-seeking" (Glidewell et al., 1983) may be based on this kind of process. Interactions focused on instrumental problems help to build a history of acceptance that promotes further help-seeking. A series of interactions of this type also may be constructive because it helps to build competence and hence reduces the prospect of dependence in future situations.

There are many unanswered questions. Do network members tend to minimize the seriousness of problems, as some have suggested (Sanders, 1982; cf. Timko, 1987; Turk, Litt, Salovey, & Walker, 1985)? Do they tend to make physical attributions for problems, which would tend to steer distressed persons toward medical practitioners (Tessler & Mechanic, 1978)? Or do they tend to accept simple solutions rather than encouraging more effortful problem-solving (Toro, Rappaport, & Seidman, 1987; Wahler, 1990). Currently there is little understanding of how network members actually respond to presentations of mild or severe problems and how this affects their help-seeking recommendations.

SELF-PROCESSES

There is reason to consider help-seeking behavior within the context of self-esteem maintenance. There is a general tendency for people to maintain self-esteem in the face of possible threats by processes such as social comparison (Wills, 1981), changes in self-perception (Tesser, in press), or information selection (Pyszczynski, Greenberg, & LaPrelle, 1985). Aspects of help-seeking that can present a potential threat to self-esteem include admission of inability to accomplish a goal (see Rosen, 1983), unfavorable comparison with others (Wills, 1983), and the prospect of continued dependence on others (Nadler & Fisher, 1986). Conditions that produce high levels of these factors should minimize help-seeking, whereas conditions that serve to reduce the salience of these factors should increase help-seeking. The question is, What conditions operate to reduce self-esteem concerns in help-seeking?

Labeling of Behavior

One cognitive mechanism for dealing with potential esteem issues is the labeling of the help-seeking behavior. Through cognitive mechanisms, people may construe help-seeking behavior as representing instrumental rather than emotional difficulties, and esteem concerns may be reduced. The source chosen for initial help efforts may be guided by a labeling process. For example, consulting a medical practitioner suggests that difficulties are physical, not emotional. This would occur both because the practitioner customarily treats physical illness and because the context of initial interaction is focused on discussion of physical symptoms. What is known about the typical course of help-seeking suggests that consultations with medical practitioners may reflect this type of labeling process. In the development of a medical consultation the patient may introduce some emotional concerns, with the expectation that some attention may be obtained and a relatively noncostly treatment (e.g., tranquilizers) will be provided. When the problem is extremely severe, the patient can go to a physician with reports of imminent mental breakdown, with the expectation that appropriate referral of supportive treatment can be obtained.

One way in which persons may deal with esteem concerns is to decrease the perceived centrality of a dimension on which esteem is threatened (Tesser & Campbell, 1983). This approach seems less available in the case of help-seeking because the person must decide to seek help specifically for the problematic dimension, which would emphasize rather than minimize its importance. Hence relabeling of the behavior may be easier than altering the perceived importance of the dimension.

Attributions for Help-Seeking

The implications of different types of attributions for a problem present a double-edged sword. If the problem is attributed to dispositional factors, then seeking help would presumably be more likely; but if this kind of personal attribution is made, then the corresponding degree of self-esteem threat would be increased. Laboratory studies are consistent with this, showing help-seeking to be decreased when performance problems are attributed to internal factors (Tessler & Schwartz, 1972; Morris & Rosen, 1973).

Evidence on the role of attributional processes in naturalistic help-seeking is lacking. We could predict that people will be more likely to seek professional help if an external attribution for their problem is available (e.g., stress). Retrospective studies with clinic samples show that the clients are virtually unanimous in attributing their problems to dispositional factors (Calhoun, Dawes, & Lewis, 1972; Robbins, 1981), but because the samples are highly selected and have been influenced by participation in treatment, these data are difficult to interpret.

Help-seeking may also be influenced if people make physical rather than psychological attributions for problems. Seeking treatment for stomach pain would, presumably, evoke fewer esteem issues than seeking treatment for neuroticism. The difficulty with this hypothesis is the lack of a determination of whether people really tend to confuse psychological distress and physical symptomatology. There are several studies showing that global ratings of perceived health status are significantly correlated with measures of psychological distress (Tessler & Mechanic, 1978; Garrity, Somes, & Marx, 1978). But because one would expect and find a correlation between poor health and depression (e.g., Frerichs, Aneshensel, Yokopenic, & Clark, 1982), it is hard to know what interpretation to make of this. There are few data on how attributions influence selection into treatment.

Consensus and Comparison Information

Perceptions of social consensus for behavior may be quite relevant for help-seeking. Studies of what has been termed the *false consensus effect* show a general tendency to perceive that one's own behavior and opinions are also characteristic of others (Marks & Miller, 1987). There is also a tendency to enhance social comparisons through perceptions that one's desirable attributes are relatively infrequent in the population (Marks, 1984; Campbell, 1986) and that one's undesirable attributes are relatively common (Suls & Wan, 1987).

Experimental studies have suggested that help-seeking is increased when perceived consensus is high (Gross et al., 1979; Nadler & Porat, 1978). These may be reflecting the operation of self-processes: If information provided to the subjects suggests that consensus for help-seeking is high, then esteem implications are reduced. Snyder and Ingram (1983) manipulated consensus information and showed that among symptomatic people, high-consensus information increased the tendency to seek help, apparently because it reduced the esteem threat of help-seeking; there was a reversed effect among nonsymptomatic people. Medical help-seeking, being a relatively frequent occurrence, may also be influenced by consensus perceptions; if people perceive this type of help-seeking as prevalent, they may regard it as more normative.

IMPLICATIONS FOR SOCIAL/CLINICAL PSYCHOLOGY

In this chapter we have presented descriptive data on help-seeking in community settings, and discussed evidence on processes in help-seeking behavior. From this discussion one should emerge with several conclusions. One is that the study of help-seeking is an important area for social and clinical psychology because there seem to be situations in which people could seek help, but do not. Understanding the factors that create reluctance to seek help would have bearing on a number of questions in the theory of coping and service utilization. Another conclusion is that a body of knowledge is available on factors in help-seeking behavior and suggests some predictable aspects of help-seeking. Our suggestion is that help-seeking is guided by concerns of dependence versus independence, and that this framework may serve to illuminate some basic issues in help-seeking research. At the same time, we suggest that many important questions in this area currently do not have definitive answers. In the following section, we suggest some general issues and directions for further research.

Sequence of Help-Seeking

From studies in community settings it is apparent that there may be a consistent progression in help-seeking. It is evident that of persons with significant psychological problems, many receive some kind of help within informal social networks but relatively few receive professional help. The suggestion is that there is a pyramidal process, such that (a) relatively minor problems and worries are dealt with through emotional and cognitive support from family and friends, (b) more persistent problems are taken to first-line helping agents such as clergy and general medical practitioners, and (c) serious problems are referred to appropriate specialists. While this model of help-seeking is logical and plausible, it is largely inferential and there is little direct evidence on stages of help-seeking. There is a need for studies that follow a general population or a high-risk subsample over time and try to delineate, through repeated measures, what types of help-seeking actions are pursued at different points in time.

Another reason for such studies is that there is little understanding of the consequences of assistance provided by various help resources. For example, one can find evidence suggesting that informal helpers may discourage medical help-seeking when it is in fact appropriate (see Matthews et al., 1983; McKinlay, 1973), or may sometimes have negative rather than positive effects on health behaviors (Baranowski & Nader, 1985; Wills, 1990, in press-a). Other studies suggests that some types of helping arouse negative affect in the short term but increase competence in the long term (e.g., DePaulo et al., 1989). The examples suggest caution about a straightforward generalization that if people receive informal help, then the help is necessarily appropriate or effective. Such issues indicate a need for detailed information on how help from informal networks affects efficacy and coping ability.

Finally, research on informal help-seeking suggests an issue for evaluation of professional help resources. Literature on professional psychotherapy shows evidence that it produces improved outcomes for most clients (e.g., Smith, Glass, & Miller, 1980), but community studies indicate that only a small minority of troubled people seek professional help; so the suggestion is that psychotherapy research is conducted on a highly selected sample of people. Additionally, there is reason to believe that participation in psychotherapy increases utilization of informal help resources (Cross et al., 1980; Veroff, Kulka, & Douvan, 1981), which introduces a possible confound in evaluation of formal psychotherapy. These considerations suggest a need for research on the interaction between formal and informal help resources.

Typology of Help-Seeking

Our analysis also suggests that help-seeking comprises a number of dimensions, hence, simply determining whether a person sought help provides limited information. The preceding discussion has suggested several dimensions that may be used to form a typology of help-seeking. These include (a) the type of helper (e.g., formal vs. informal), (b) the type of problem (e.g., instrumental vs. emotional), (c) the severity of the problem (e.g., minor vs. serious), (d) the relation to other coping efforts (e.g., none vs. many). We think that these dimensions may relate to an overall perception of the goal of help-seeking; that is, whether it will result in dependency versus increased competence in the long run. Another cross-cutting dimension is the type of relation-

ship, such that people may react very differently to dependence in the context of a close relationship, where dependence may be necessary and perhaps desirable, than they would in the context of a casual or exchange-oriented relationship (cf. Clark, 1983).

Our point is similar to that made by Stone and Neale (1984) about coping behavior in general; that is, a particular occurrence of a behavior may involve potentially different functions, and the person's goal in help-seeking could be a part of a typology. As we have noted previously, a given occurrence of a request for help may be based on functions such as an attempt at ingratiation with another person, an attempt to reduce dependence in the long term, or a response of helplessness with no perception that self-improvement will occur. Obviously these are very different functions that must have quite different consequences for coping and adjustment in the long run, yet without trying to elicit the person's perceived intent in the help-seeking, it could be difficult to tell these apart. At a minimum, one could get a subject's perception of how efficacy would be affected by a helping interaction, and how this would affect their feelings of intrinsic motivation and their perception of dependency on the helper (cf. Deci & Ryan, 1985).

This aspect remains somewhat ambiguous in laboratory studies. While present studies have provided tight control over situational variables that influence the probability of a help-seeking act, there is currently little information about the effects of help-seeking on the recipient, and in most cases there is little knowledge about how help-seekers perceive and construe their actions. What is surprising about data from laboratory studies is the low level of help-seeking in settings where one would think subjects would have little ego-investment, suggesting that even in a limited interaction with a stranger, people experience some conflict over esteem concerns and possible dependency. Obtaining more specific data on these types of variables may be an issue for further laboratory research.

Increasing Appropriate Utilization of Services

In applying the present model to help-seeking in community settings, considerations at both the institutional and individual levels are relevant. Considering institution-level factors, one suggestion is to find ways to routinize the process of help-seeking (Nelson, 1980) and to increase the ease of transitions between stages of help-seeking. For example, various types of resources (financial aid, academic advising, routine medical services, personal counseling) could be provided in the same physical location. In this setting, it would be easier for persons to enter the help-seeking area (e.g., for treatment of sexually transmitted diseases) because they would not be labeled by presenting for a particular type of treatment. It would be easier for people to make transitions from one type of help-seeking to another (e.g., from financial aid to personal counseling) because the referral process could be routinely suggested by staff members to all participants and would be physically convenient. Such a setting also might reduce administrative barriers to help-seeking, such as making appointments and determining the location of appropriate services.

With regard to individual-level factors, there is an issue about increasing choice about type of help. While practical considerations may be a limiting factor, in theory it seems desirable to offer potential clients a choice between several modalities (e.g., trained psychotherapist, group interaction, or self-help materials). Current research on reactions to help suggests that peer counselors may be a nonpreferred type of help (e.g., Nadler & Fisher, 1986); this issue deserves more research in professional help settings.

Also, there are approaches that could be used to advertise available helping services. One would be to provide consensus information, that is, data on the frequency of help-seeking among the relevant population. Another would be to provide information about the benefits of professional help so that people would be more aware of the potential benefits. Also, advertising material could emphasize the function of limited professional help for increasing independence (cf. Nelson & Barbaro, 1985). If attempting to increase utilization by underserved groups (e.g., older people, people of lower socioeconomic status), advertising material could provide examples of appropriate role models who have benefited from services.

Decreasing Inappropriate Utilization of Services

Psychological processes in help-seeking might create some situations that could be undesirable from a policy standpoint. For example, there are indications that a significant part of medical service utilization is attributable to mental health problems. From the standpoint of the individual, this may be a rational coping mechanism, although there is a question whether the typical outcome (drug treatment) is optimally matched to the person's needs (e.g., Caplan et al., 1984). From the standpoint of medical service provision, however, mental health treatment is time intensive, and presentation of psychological problems in medical clinics may result in less efficient treatment of medical patients. How could the concerns of the individual and the institution best be reconciled?

One suggestion is to screen patients for psychological distress and provide psychological services for people who appear to be most appropriate for psychological treatment. This is probably not a straightforward solution, first because utilization of psychological services is low even under optimal conditions (cf. Ware et al., 1984), and second because it directly counters the probable reason that the patients sought medical help in the first place (i.e., because they did not view psychological treatment as necessary). One suggestion is to develop educational approaches for teaching clients to discriminate better between physical and psychological conditions, perhaps, using terminology that is less esteem involving (e.g., reactions to stress) rather than stigmatizing (e.g., psychiatric condition). Another possibility is development of self-help material that is appropriate for particular populations (e.g., the elderly) and could be used in conjunction with established institutions (e.g., community centers). Finally, more research in medical settings is needed to understand the dynamics of this important issue.

REFERENCES

Ames, R. (1983a). Help-seeking and achievement orientation: Perspectives from attribution theory. In B. M. DePaulo, A. Nadler, & J. D. Fisher (Eds.), *New directions in helping: Vol. 2. Help-seeking* (pp. 165–186). New York: Academic Press.

Ames, R. (1983b). Teacher's attributions for their own teaching. In J. M. Levine & M. C. Wang (Eds.), *Teacher and student perceptions: Implications for learning.* Hillsdale, NJ: Lawrence Erlbaum Associates.

Ames, R., & Lau, S. (1982). An attributional

analysis of help-seeking in academic settings. *Journal of Educational Psychology, 74*, 414–423.

Bandura, A. (1982). Self-efficacy mechanism in human agency. *American Psychologist, 37*, 122–147.

Baranowski, T., & Nader, P. R. (1985). Family involvement in health behavior change programs. In D. C. Turk & R. D. Kerns (Eds.), *Health, illness, and families* (pp. 81–107). New York: John Wiley & Sons.

Berg, J. B. (1984). The development of friendship between roommates. *Journal of Personality and Social Psychology, 46*, 346–356.

Blau, P. M. (1955). *The dynamics of bureaucracy*. Chicago: University of Chicago Press.

Brickman, P., Rabinowitz, V. C., Karuza, J., Jr., Coates, D., Cohn, E., & Kidder, L. (1982). Models of helping and coping. *American Psychologist, 37*, 368–384.

Brown, B. B. (1978). Social and psychological correlates of help-seeking behavior among urban adults. *American Journal of Community Psychology, 6*, 425–439.

Bruch, M. A., Giordano, S., & Pearl, L. (1986). Differences between fearful and self-conscious shy subtypes in background and current adjustment. *Journal of Research in Personality, 20*, 172–186.

Burke, R. J., & Weir, T. (1976). Personality characteristics associated with giving and receiving help. *Psychological Reports, 38*, 343–353.

Burke, R. J., Weir, T., & Duncan, G. (1976). Informal helping relationships in work organizations. *Academy of Management Journal, 19*, 370–377.

Burke, R. J., Weir, T., & Harrison, D. (1976). Disclosure of problems and tensions experienced by marital partners. *Psychological Reports, 38*, 531–542.

Calhoun, L. G., Dawes, A. S., & Lewis, P. M. (1972). Correlates of attitudes toward help-seeking in outpatients. *Journal of Consulting and Clinical Psychology, 38*, 153.

Campbell, J. D. (1986). Similarity and uniqueness: Effects of attribute type, relevance, and self-esteem. *Journal of Personality and Social Psychology, 50*, 281–294.

Caplan, R. D., Abbey, A., Abramis, D. J., Andrews, F. M., Conway, T. L., & French, J. R. P., Jr. (1984). *Tranquilizer use and well-being: A longitudinal study of social and psychological effects*. Ann Arbor: Institute for Social Research.

Charalampous, K. D., Ford, B. K., & Skinner, T. J. (1976). Self-esteem in alcoholics and nonalcoholics. *Journal of Studies on Alcohol, 37*, 990–994.

Cheek, J. M., & Buss, A. H. (1981). Shyness and sociability. *Journal of Personality and Social Psychology, 41*, 330–339.

Cheek, J. M., Melchior, L. A., & Carpentieri, A. M. (1986). Shyness and self-concept. In L. M. Hartman & K. R. Blankstein (Eds.), *Advances in the study of communication and affect: Vol. 2. Perception of self in emotional disorder and psychotherapy* (pp. 113–131). New York: Plenum Press.

Christensen, K. C., & Magoon, T. M. (1974). Perceived hierarchy of help-giving sources for two categories of student problems. *Journal of Counseling Psychology, 21*, 311–324.

Clark, M. S. (1983). Some implications of close social bonds for help-seeking. In B. M. DePaulo, A. Nadler, & J. D. Fisher (Eds.), *New directions in helping: Vol. 2. Help-seeking* (pp. 205–229). New York: Academic Press.

Cleary, P. D., Goldberg, I. D., Kessler, L. G., & Nycz, G. R. (1982). Screening for mental disorder among primary care patients. *Archives of General Psychiatry, 39*, 837–840.

Coates, D., Renzaglia, G. J., & Embree, M. C. (1983). When helping backfires: Help and helplessness. In J. D. Fisher, A. Nadler, & B. M. DePaulo (Eds.), *New directions in helping: Vol. 1. Recipient reactions to aid* (pp. 251–279). New York: Academic Press.

Coates, D., & Winston, T. (1987). The dilemma of distress disclosure. In V. J. Derlega & J. H. Berg (Eds.), *Self-disclosure: Theory, research, and therapy* (pp. 229–255). New York: Plenum Press.

Cohen, S., Sherrod, D. R., & Clark, M. S. (1986). Social skills and the stress-protective role of social support. *Journal of Personality and Social Psychology, 50*, 963–973.

Cohen, S., & Wills, T. A. (1985). Stress, social support, and the buffering hypothesis. *Psychological Bulletin, 98*, 310–357.

Corotto, L. V. (1963). An exploratory study of the personality characteristics of alcoholic patients who volunteer for continued treatment. *Quarterly Journal of Studies on Alcohol, 24*, 432–442.

Corrigan, J. D. (1978). Salient attributes of two types of helpers. *Journal of Counseling Psychology, 25*, 588–590.

Cowen, E. L. (1982). Help is where you find it: Four informal helping groups. *American Psychologist, 37*, 385–395.

Cross, D. G., Sheehan, P. W., & Khan, J. A. (1980). Alternative advice and counsel in psychotherapy. *Journal of Consulting and Clinical Psychology, 48*, 615–625.

Deci, J., & Ryan, M. (1985). *The psychology of self-determination.* New York: Plenum Press.

DePaulo, B. M. (1978a). Help-seeking from the recipient's point of view. *JSAS Catalog of Selected Documents in Psychology, 8*, 62 (MS No. 1721).

DePaulo, B. M. (1978b). Accepting help from teachers when teachers are children. *Human Relations, 31*, 459–474.

DePaulo, B. M. (1982). Social-psychological processes in informal help-seeking. In T. A. Wills (Ed.), *Basic processes in helping relationships* (pp. 255–279). New York: Academic Press.

DePaulo, B. M., Brittingham, G. L., & Kaiser, M. K. (1983). Receiving competence-relevant help: Effects on reciprocity, affect, and sensitivity to the helper's nonverbally expressed needs. *Journal of Personality and Social Psychology, 45*, 1045–1060.

DePaulo, B. M., Brown, P. L., & Greenberg, J. M. (1983). The effects of help on task performance in achievement contexts. In J. D. Fisher, A. Nadler, & B. M. DePaulo (Eds.), *New directions in helping: Vol. 1. Recipient reactions to aid* (pp. 223–249). New York: Academic Press.

DePaulo, B. M., Brown, P. L., Ishii, S., & Fisher, J. D. (1981). Help that works: The effects of aid on subsequent task performance. *Journal of Personality and Social Psychology, 41*, 478–487.

DePaulo, B. M., Dull, W. R. Greenberg, J. M., & Swaim, G. W. (1989). Are shy people reluctant to ask for help? *Journal of Personality and Social Psychology, 56*, 834–844.

DePaulo, B. M., Epstein, J. A., & LeMay, C. S. (1989). Responses of the socially anxious to the prospect of interpersonal evaluation. Manuscript submitted for publication.

DePaulo, B. M., & Fisher, J. D. (1980). The costs of asking for help. *Basic and Applied Social Psychology, 1*, 23–35.

DePaulo, B. M., & Fisher, J. D. (1981). Too tuned-out to take: The role of nonverbal sensitivity in help-seeking. *Personality and Social Psychology Bulletin, 7*, 201–205.

DePaulo, B. M., Leiphart, V. M., & Dull, W. R.

(1984). Help-seeking and social interaction: Person, situation, and process considerations. In D. Bar-Tal, J. Karylowski, J. Reykowski, & E. Staub (Eds.), *Development and maintenance of prosocial behavior* (pp. 337–357). New York: Plenum Press.

DePaulo, B. M., Nadler, A., & Fisher, J. D. (Eds.). (1983). *New directions in helping: Vol. 2. Help-seeking.* New York: Academic Press.

DePaulo, B. M., Tang, J., Webb, W., Hoover, C., Marsh, K., & Litowitz, C. (1989). Age differences in reactions to help in a peer tutoring context. *Child Development, 60*, 423–439.

Diener, E. (1984). Subjective well-being. *Psychological Bulletin, 95*, 542–575.

DiMatteo, M. R., Hays, R. D., & Prince, L. M. (1986). Relationship of physicians' nonverbal communication skill to patient satisfaction, appointment compliance, and physician workload. *Health Psychology, 5*, 581–594.

Dooley, D., & Catalano, R. (1984). Why the economy predicts help-seeking: A test of competing explanations. *Journal of Health and Social Behavior, 25*, 160–176.

Druian, P. R., & DePaulo, B. M. (1977). Asking a child for help. *Social Behavior and Personality, 5*, 33–39.

Fischer, E. H., & Turner, J. L. (1970). Orientations to seeking professional help: Development and research utility of an attitude scale. *Journal of Consulting and Clinical Psychology, 35*, 79–90.

Fischer, E. H., Winer, D., & Abramowitz, S. I. (1983). Seeking professional help for psychological problems. In A. Nadler, J. D. Fisher, & B. M. DePaulo (Eds.), *New directions in helping* (Vol. 3, pp. 163–185). New York: Academic Press.

Fisher, J. D., & Farina, A. (1979). Consequences of beliefs about the nature of mental disorders. *Journal of Abnormal Psychology, 88*, 320–327.

Fisher, J. D., Goff, B. A., Nadler, A., & Chinsky, J. M. (1989). Social psychological influences on help-seeking and support from peers. In B. H. Gottlieb (Ed.), *Marshalling social support* (pp. 267–304). Newbury Park, CA: Sage Publications.

Fisher, J. D., Nadler, A., & Whitcher-Alagna, S. (1982). Recipient reactions to aid. *Psychological Bulletin, 91*, 27–54.

Folkman, S., & Lazarus, R. S. (1980). An analysis of coping in a middle-aged community sample. *Journal of Health and Social Behavior, 21*, 219–239.

Folkman, S., & Lazarus, R. S. (1985). If it changes it must be a process: Study of emotion and coping during three stages of a college examination. *Journal of Personality and Social Psychology, 48*, 150–170.

Folkman, S., Lazarus, R. S., Dunkel-Schetter, C., DeLongis, A., & Gruen, R. J. (1986). Dynamics of a stressful encounter: Cognitive appraisal, coping, and encounter outcomes. *Journal of Personality and Social Psychology, 50*, 992–1003.

Fox, J. W. (1984). Sex, marital status, and age as social selection factors in recent psychiatric treatment. *Journal of Health and Social Behavior, 25*, 394–405.

Frerichs, R. R., Aneshensel, C. S., Yokopenic, P. A., & Clark, V. A. (1982). Physical health and depression. *Preventive Medicine, 11*, 639–646.

Friedman, P. G. (1980). *Shyness and reticence in students.* Washington, DC: National Education Association.

Frieze, I. H. (1979). Perceptions of battered wives. In I. Frieze, D. Bar-Tal, & J. S. Carroll (Eds.), *New approaches to social problems.* Washington, DC: Jossey-Bass.

Garrity, T. F., Somes, G. W., & Marx, M. B. (1978). Factors influencing self-assessment of health. *Social Science and Medicine, 12*, 77–81.

Gartner, A., & Riessman, F. (1977). *Self-help in the human services.* San Francisco: Jossey-Bass.

Glidewell, J. C., Tucker, S., Todt, M., & Cox, S. (1983). Professional support systems: The teaching profession. In A. Nadler, J. D. Fisher, & B. M. DePaulo (Eds.), *New directions in helping. Vol. 3: Applied perspectives on help-seeking and -receiving* (pp. 189–211). New York: Academic Press.

Goodman, S. H., Sewell, D. R., & Jampol, R. C. (1984). Contributions of life stress and social supports to the decision to seek psychological counseling. *Journal of Counseling Psychology, 31*, 306–313.

Goranson, R. E., & Berkowitz, L. (1966). Reciprocity and responsibility reactions to prior help. *Journal of Personality and Social Psychology, 3*, 227–232.

Gortmaker, S. L., Eckenrode, J., & Gore, S. (1982). Stress and the utilization of health services: Time series and cross-sectional analyses. *Journal of Health and Social Behavior, 23*, 25–38.

Gourash, N. (1978). Help-seeking: A review of the literature. *American Journal of Community Psychology, 6*, 413–423.

Granovetter, M. (1973). The strength of weak ties. *American Journal of Sociology, 78*, 1360–1380.

Greenberg, M., & Westcott, D. R. (1983). Indebtedness as a mediator of reactions to aid. In J. D. Fisher, A. Nadler, & B. M. DePaulo (Eds.), *New directions in helping. Vol. 1: Recipient reactions to aid* (pp. 85–112). New York: Academic Press.

Greenberg, M. S., & Frisch, D. M. (1972). Effect of intentionality on willingness to reciprocate a favor. *Journal of Experimental Social Psychology, 8*, 99–111.

Greenley, J. R., & Mechanic, D. (1976). Social selection in seeking help for psychological problems. *Journal of Health and Social Behavior, 17*, 249–262.

Gross, A. E., Fisher, J. D., Nadler, A., Stiglitz, E., & Craig, C. (1979). Correlates of help-utilization at a women's counseling service. *Journal of Community Psychology, 7*, 42–49.

Gross, A. E., & McMullen, P. A. (1983). Models of the help-seeking process. In B. M. DePaulo, A. Nadler, & J. D. Fisher (Eds.), *New directions in helping: Vol. 2. Help-seeking* (pp. 45–70). New York: Academic Press.

Gurin, G., Veroff, J. B., & Feld, S. C. (1960). *Americans view their mental health.* New York: Basic Books.

Harris, A., Tessler, R., & Potter, J. (1977). The induction of self-reliance: An experimental study of independence in the face of failure. *Journal of Applied Social Psychology, 7*, 313–331.

Harris, P. R. (1984). The hidden face of shyness. *Human Relations, 37*, 1079–1093.

Henderson, S., Byrne, D. G., Duncan-Jones, P., Scott, R., & Adcock, S. (1980). Social relationships, adversity and neurosis. *British Journal of Psychiatry, 136*, 574–583.

Hill, F. E., & Harmon, M. (1976). The use of telephone tapes in a telephone counseling program. *Crisis Intervention, 7*, 88–96.

Hingson, R., Mangione, T., Meyers, A., & Scotch, N. (1982). Seeking help for drinking problems: A study in the Boston metropolitan area. *Journal of Studies on Alcohol, 43*, 273–288.

Horwitz, A. (1977). Pathways into psychiatric treatment: Some differences between men and women. *Journal of Health and Social Behavior, 18*, 169–178.

Ickes, W. J., & Kidd, R. F. (1976). An attributional analysis of helping behavior. In J. Harvey, W. Ickes, & R. Kidd (Eds.), *New directions in attributional research* (Vol. 1). Hillsdale, NJ: Lawrence Erlbaum Associates.

Janoff-Bulman, R., Madden, M. E., & Timko, C. (1983). Victims' reactions to aid: The role of perceived vulnerability. In A. Nadler, J. D. Fisher, & B. M. DePaulo (Eds.), *New directions in helping: Vol. 2. Applied perspectives on help-seeking and -receiving* (pp. 21–42). New York: Academic Press.

Jones, E. E. (1964). *Ingratiation*. New York: Irvington.

Jones, W. H., & Carpenter, B. N. (1986). Shyness, social behavior, and relationships. In W. H. Jones, J. M. Cheek, & S. R. Briggs (Eds.), *Shyness: Perspectives and research on treatment* (pp. 227–238). New York: Plenum Press.

Kadushin, C. (1969). *Why people go to psychiatrists*. New York: Atherton.

Kessler, L. G., Burns, B. J., Shapiro, S., Tischler, G. L., George, L. K., Hough, R. L., Bodison, D., & Miller, R. H. (1987). Psychiatric diagnoses of medical service users: Evidence from the epidemiologic catchment area program. *Archives of General Psychiatry, 77*, 18–24.

Kessler, R. C., Brown, R. L., & Bowman, C. L. (1981). Sex differences in psychiatric help-seeking: Evidence from four large-scale surveys. *Journal of Health and Social Behavior, 22*, 49–64.

Langer, E. J., & Benevento, A. (1978). Self-induced dependence. *Journal of Personality and Social Psychology, 36*, 886–893.

Lazarus, R. S., & Folkman, S. (1984). *Stress, appraisal, and coping*. New York: Springer.

Leaf, P. J., & Bruce, M. L. (1988). Gender differences in the use of mental health–related services. *Journal of Health and Social Behavior, 28*, 171–183.

Leary, M. R. (1983). *Understanding social anxiety*. Beverly Hills, CA: Sage Publications.

Lewinsohn, P. M., Hoberman, H., Teri, L., & Hautzinger, M. (1985). An integrative theory of depression. In S. Reiss & R. Bootzin (Eds.), *Theoretical issues in behavior therapy* (pp. 331–359). New York: Academic Press.

Link, B., & Dohrenwend, B. P. (1980). Ratio of treated to untreated cases in true prevalence studies of functional psychiatric disorder. In B. P. Dohrenwend, B. S. Dohrenwend, M. J. Gould, B. Link, R. Neugebauer, & R. Wunsch-Hitzig, (Eds.). *Mental illness in the United States: Epidemiological estimates* (pp. 133–149). New York: Praeger.

Marks, G. (1984). Thinking one's abilities are unique and one's opinions are common. *Personality and Social Psychology Bulletin, 10*, 203–208.

Marks, G., & Miller, N. (1987). The false-consensus effect: An empirical and theoretical review. *Psychological Bulletin, 102*, 72–90.

Matthews, K. A., Siegel, J. M., Kuller, L. H., Thompson, M., & Varat, M. (1983). Determinants of decisions to seek medical treatment by patients with acute myocardial infarction symptoms. *Journal of Personality and Social Psychology, 44*, 1144–1156.

McCrae, R. R. (1984). Situational determinants of coping responses. *Journal of Personality and Social Psychology, 46*, 919–928.

McKinlay, J. B. (1972). Some approaches and problems in the use of services. *Journal of Health and Social Behavior, 13*, 115–152.

McKinlay, J. B. (1973). Social networks, lay consultation and help-seeking behavior. *Social Forces, 51*, 275–292.

Merton, V., Merton, R. K., & Barber, E. (1983). Client ambivalence in professional relationships: The problem of seeking help from strangers. In B. M. DePaulo, A. Nadler, & J. D. Fisher (Eds.), *New directions in helping. Vol. 2. Help-seeking* (pp. 13–44). New York: Academic Press.

Meyer, J. P., & Mulherin, A. (1980). From attribution to helping: An analysis of the mediating effects of affect and expectancy. *Journal of Personality and Social Psychology, 39*, 201–210.

Miller, P. M., & Ingham, J. G. (1979). The life events to illness link. In I. G. Sarason & C. D. Spielberger (Eds.), *Stress and anxiety* (pp. 313–336). New York: Hemisphere.

Miller, W. R. (1985). Motivation for treatment: A review with special emphasis on alcoholism. *Psychological Bulletin, 98*, 84–107.

Moos, R. H., & Billings, A. G. (1982). Conceptualizing and measuring coping resources and processes. In L. Goldberger & S. Breznitz (Eds.), *Handbook of stress* (pp. 212–230). New York: Macmillan.

Morris, S. C., & Rosen, S. (1973). Effects of felt adequacy and opportunity to reciprocate on help-seeking. *Journal of Experimental Social Psychology, 9*, 265–276.

Nadler, A. (1980). Good looks do not help: Effects of physical attractiveness and expectations for future interaction on help seeking. *Personality and Social Psychology Bulletin, 6*, 378–383.

Nadler, A. (1983). Personal characteristics and help-seeking. In B. M. DePaulo, A. Nadler, & J. D. Fisher (Eds.), *New directions in helping: Vol. 2. Help-seeking* (pp. 303–340). New York: Academic Press.

Nadler, A. (1986). Self-esteem and the seeking and receiving of help: Theoretical and empirical perspectives. In B. Maher & W. Maher (Eds.), *Progress in experimental personality research* (Vol. 14, pp. 115–163). New York: Academic Press.

Nadler, A. (1987). Determinants of help seeking behaviour: The effects of helper's similarity, task centrality and recipient's self esteem. *European Journal of Social Psychology, 17*, 57–67.

Nadler, A. (in press). Help-seeking behavior as a coping resource. In M. Rosenbaum (Ed.), *Learned resourcefulness: On coping skills, self-regulation, and adaptive behavior*. New York: Springer.

Nadler, A., & Fisher, J. D. (1986). The role of threat to self-esteem and perceived control in recipient reactions to aid: Theory development and empirical validation. In L. Berkowitz (Ed.), *Advances in experimental social psychology* (Vol. 19, pp. 81–83). New York: Academic Press.

Nadler, A., Fisher, J. D., & Ben-Itzhak, S. (1983). With a little help from my friend: Effects of single or multiple act aid as a function of donor and task characteristics. *Journal of Personality and Social Psychology, 44*, 310–321.

Nadler, A., Fisher, J. D., & DePaulo, B. M. (1983). *New directions in helping: Vol. 3. Applied perspectives on help-seeking and -receiving*. New York: Academic Press.

Nadler, A., Fisher, J. D., & Streufert, S. (1974). The donor's dilemma: Recipient's reactions to aid from a friend or a foe. *Journal of Applied Social Psychology, 4*, 275–285.

Nadler, A., & Fux, B. (1984). *Help seeking as a function of self-esteem and ego defensiveness*. Unpublished manuscript, Tel Aviv University.

Nadler, A., Lewinstein, E., & Rahav, G. (in press). Acceptance of child's mental retardation and parent's willingness to seek help. *Mental Retardation*.

Nadler, A., Mayseless, O., Peri, N., & Tchemerinski, A. (1985). Effects of self-esteem and ability to reciprocate on help-seeking behavior. *Journal of Personality, 53*, 23–35.

Nadler, A., & Porat, A. (1978). Effects of anonymity and locus of need attribution on help-seeking behavior. *Personality and Social Psychology Bulletin, 4*, 624–628.

Nadler, A., Shapiro, R., & Ben-Itzhak, S. (1982). Good looks may help: Effects of helper's physical attractiveness and sex of helper on males' and females' help seeking behavior. *Journal of Personality and Social Psychology, 42*, 90–99.

Nadler, A., Sheinberg, L., & Jaffe, Y. (1981). Coping with stress by helping: Help seeking and receiving behavior in male paraplegics. In C. Spielberger, I. Sarason, & N. Milgram (Eds.), *Stress and anxiety* (Vol. 8, pp. 375–386): Washington, DC: Hemisphere.

Nelson, B. J. (1980). Help-seeking from public authorities: Who arrives at the agency door. *Policy Sciences, 12*, 175–192.

Nelson, G. D., & Barbaro, M. B. (1985). Fighting the stigma: A unique approach to marketing mental health. *American Marketing Quarterly, 2*, 89–101.

Nelson-Le Gall, S., Gumerman, R. A., & Scott-Jones, D. (1983). Instrumental help-seeking and everyday problem-solving. In B. M. DePaulo, A. Nadler, & J. D. Fisher (Eds.), *New directions in helping: Vol. 2. Help-seeking* (pp. 265–283). New York: Academic Press.

Neugebauer, R., Dohrenwend, B. P., & Dohrenwend, B. S. (1980). Formulation of hypotheses about the true prevalence of functional psychiatric disorders among adults. In B. P. Dohrenwend, B. S. Dohrenwend, M. S. Gould, B. Link, R. Neugebauer, & R. Wunsch-Hitzig, (Eds.). *Mental illness in the United States* (pp. 45–94). New York: Praeger.

Norcross, J. C., & Prochaska, J. O. (1986). The psychological distress and self-change of psychologists, counselors, and laypersons. *Psychotherapy, 23*, 102–114.

Ostrove, N., & Baum, A. (1983). Factors influencing medical help-seeking. In A. Nadler, J. D. Fisher, & B. M. DePaulo (Eds.), *New directions in helping: Vol. 3. Applied perspectives* on help-seeking and -receiving (pp. 107–129). New York: Academic Press.

Pearlin, L. I., & Schooler, C. (1978). The structure of coping. *Journal of Health and Social Behavior, 19*, 2–21.

Perri, M. G. (1985). Self-change strategies for the control of smoking, obesity, and problem drinking. In S. Shiffman & T. A. Wills (Eds.), *Coping and substance use* (pp. 295–317). Orlando, FL: Academic Press.

Phillips, S. D., & Bruch, M. A. (1988). Shyness and dysfunction in career development. *Journal of Counseling Psychology, 35*, 159–165.

Pilisuk, M., Boylan, R., & Acredolo, C. (1987). Social support, life stress, and subsequent medical care utilization. *Health Psychology, 6*, 273–288.

Pilkonis, P. A. (1977). Shyness, public and private, and its relationship to other measures of social behavior. *Journal of Personality, 45*, 585–595.

Pyszczynski, T., Greenberg, J., & LaPrelle, J. (1985). Social comparison after success and failure: Biased search for information consistent with a self-serving conclusion. *Journal of Experimental Social Psychology, 21*, 195–211.

Reis, H., Senchak, S. M., & Solomon, B. (1985). Sex differences in the intimacy of social interaction. *Journal of Personality and Social Psychology, 48*, 1204–1217.

Robbins, J. M. (1981). Lay attributions of personal problems and psychological help-seeking. *Social Psychiatry, 16*, 1–9.

Rosen, S. (1983). Perceived inadequacy and help-seeking. In B. M. DePaulo, A. Nadler, & J. D. Fisher (Eds.), *New directions in helping: Vol. 2. Help-seeking* (pp. 73–107). New York: Academic Press.

Safer, M. A., Tharps, Q. J., Jackson, M. D., & Leventhal, H. (1979). Determinants of three stages of delay in seeking care at a medical clinic. *Medical Care, 17*, 11–29.

Sanders, G. S. (1982). Social comparison and perceptions of health and illness. In G. S. Sanders & J. Suls (Eds.), *Social psychology of health and illness* (pp. 129–157). Hillsdale, NJ: Lawrence Erlbaum Associates.

Schurman, R. A., Kramer, P. D., & Mitchell, J. B. (1985). Treatment of mental illness by nonpsychiatric physicians. *Archives of General Psychiatry, 42*, 89–94.

Shapiro, E. G. (1978). Effects of visibility of task performance on seeking help. *Journal of Applied Social Psychology, 8*, 163–173.

Shapiro, E. G. (1980). Is seeking help from a friend like seeking help from a stranger? *Social Psychology Quarterly, 43*, 259–263.

Shapiro, E. G. (1983). Embarrassment and help-seeking. In B. M. DePaulo, A. Nadler, & J. D. Fisher (Eds.), *New directions in helping: Vol. 2. Help-seeking* (pp. 143–163). New York: Academic Press.

Shapiro, S., Skinner, E. A., Kessler, L. G., Von Korff, M., German, P. S., Tischler, G. L., Leaf, P. J., Benham, L., Cottler, L., & Regier, D. A. (1984). Utilization of health and mental health services: Epidemiologic Catchment Area sites. *Archives of General Psychiatry, 41*, 971–978.

Skinner, B. F. (1976, January/February). The ethics of helping people. *The Humanist*, pp. 7–11.

Smith, M. L., Glass, G. V., & Miller, T. I. (1980). *The benefits of psychotherapy*. Baltimore, MD: Johns Hopkins University Press.

Snyder, C. R., & Ingram, R. E. (1983). The impact of consensus information on help-seeking for psychological problems. *Journal of Personality and Social Psychology, 45*, 1118–1126.

Snyder, C. R., Ingram, R. E., & Newburg, C. L. (1982). The role of feedback in help seeking and the therapeutic relationship. In T. A. Wills (Ed.), *Basic processes in helping relationships* (pp. 287–305). New York: Academic Press.

Srole, L., Langner, T. S., Michael, S. T., Opler, M. K., & Rennie, T. A. (1962). *Mental health in the metropolis: The Midtown Manhattan study*. New York: McGraw-Hill.

Stapleton, R. E., Nacci, P., & Tedeschi, J. T. (1973). Interpersonal attraction and the reciprocation of benefits. *Journal of Personality and Social Psychology, 28*, 199–205.

Stokes, S. J., & Bickman, L. (1974). The effect of physical attractiveness and role of the helper on help seeking. *Journal of Applied Social Psychology, 4*, 286–294.

Stone, A. A., & Neale, J. M. (1984). New measure of daily coping. *Journal of Personality and Social Psychology, 46*, 892–906.

Suls, J., & Wan, C. K. (1987). Fear and estimates of social consensus. *Journal of Personality and Social Psychology, 52*, 211–217.

Tausig, M., & Michello, J. (1988). Seeking social support. *Basic and Applied Social Psychology, 9*, 1–12.

Taylor, S. E., Falke, R. L., Shoptaw, S. J., & Lichtman, R. R. (1986). Social support, support groups, and the cancer patient. *Journal of Consulting and Clinical Psychology, 54,* 608–615.

Tesser, A. (in press). Emotion in social comparison and reflection processes. In J. Suls & T. A. Wills (Eds.), *Social comparison: Contemporary theory and research.* Hillsdale, NJ: Lawrence Erlbaum Associates.

Tesser, A., & Campbell, J. (1983). Self-definition and self-evaluation maintenance. In J. Suls & A. Greenwald (Eds.), *Psychological perspectives on the self* (Vol. 2, pp. 1–31). Hillsdale, NJ: Lawrence Erlbaum Associates.

Tessler, R., & Mechanic, D. (1978). Psychological distress and perceived health status. *Journal of Health and Social Behavior, 19,* 254–262.

Tessler, R., Mechanic, D., & Dimond, M. (1976). The effects of psychological distress on physician utilization. *Journal of Health and Social Behavior, 17,* 353–364.

Tessler, R. C., & Schwartz, S. H. (1972). Help-seeking, self-esteem, and achievement motivation: An attributional analysis. *Journal of Personality and Social Psychology, 21,* 318–326.

Testa, M., & Major, B. (in press). The impact of social comparisons after failure: The moderating effects of perceived control. *Basic and Applied Social Psychology.*

Timko, C. (1987). Seeking medical care for a breast cancer symptom. *Health Psychology, 6,* 305–328.

Tinsley, H. E. A., de St. Aubin, T. M., & Brown, M. T. (1982). College students' help-seeking preferences. *Journal of Counseling Psychology, 29,* 523–533.

Tischler, G. L., Henesz, J. C., Myers, J. K., & Boswell, P. C. (1975). Utilization of mental health services. *Archives of General Psychiatry, 32,* 411–415.

Toro, P. A., Rappaport, J., & Seidman, E. (1987). Social climate comparison of mutual help and psychotherapy groups. *Journal of Consulting and Clinical Psychology, 55,* 430–431.

Trope, Y. (1983). Self-assessment in achievement behavior. In J. M. Suls & A. G. Greenwald (Eds.), *Psychological perspectives on the self* (Vol. 2, pp. 93–121). Hillsdale, NJ: Lawrence Erlbaum Associates.

Turk, D. C., Litt, M. D., Salovey, P., & Walker, J. (1985). Seeking urgent pediatric treatment:

Factors contributing to frequency, delay, and appropriateness. *Health Psychology, 4,* 43–59.

Verbrugge, L. M. (1976). Females and illness: Recent trends in sex differences in the United States. *Journal of Health and Social Behavior, 17,* 387–403.

Veroff, J. B., Douvan, E., & Kulka, R. A. (1981). *The inner American: A self-portrait from 1957 to 1976.* New York: Basic Books.

Veroff, J. B., Kulka, R. A., & Douvan, E. (1981). *Mental health in America: Patterns of help-seeking 1957–1976.* New York: Basic Books.

Von Korff, M., Shapiro, S., Burke, J. D., Teitlebaum, M., Skinner, E. A., German, P., Turner, R. W., Klein, L., & Burns, B. (1987). Anxiety and depression in a primary care clinic. *Archives of General Psychiatry, 44,* 152–158.

Wahler, R. G. (1990). Functions of social networks in coercive mother-child interactions. *Journal of Social and Clinical Psychology, 9,* 43–53.

Wallston, B. S. (1976). The effects of sex role ideology, self-esteem, and expected future interaction with an audience on male help seeking. *Sex Roles, 2,* 353–365.

Ware, J. E., Jr., Manning, W. G., Jr., Duan, N., Wells, K. B., & Newhouse, J. P. (1984). Health status and the use of outpatient mental health services. *American Psychologist, 39,* 1090–1100.

Weiner, B. (1979). A theory of motivation for some classroom experiences. *Journal of Educational Psychology, 71,* 3–25.

Weiss, H. M., & Knight, P. A. (1980). The utility of humility: Self-esteem, information search, and problem-solving efficiency. *Organizational Behavior and Human Performance, 25,* 216–223.

Whitcher-Alagna, S. (1983). Receiving medical help: A psychosocial perspective on patient reactions. In A. Nadler, J. D. Fisher, & B. M. DePaulo (Eds.), *New directions in helping: Vol. 3. Applied perspectives on help-seeking and -receiving* (pp. 131–161). New York: Academic Press.

Wilcox, B. L., & Birkel, R. C. (1983). Social networks and the help-seeking process: A structural perspective. In A. Nadler, J. D. Fisher, & B. M. DePaulo (Eds.), *New directions in helping: Vol. 3. Applied perspectives on help-seeking and -receiving* (pp. 235–253). New York: Academic Press.

Williams, K. B., & Williams, K. D. (1983). A social-impact perspective on the social inhibition of help-seeking. In B. M. DePaulo, A. Nadler, & J. D. Fisher (Eds.), *New directions in helping: Vol. 2. Help-seeking* (pp. 187–204). New York: Academic Press.

Wills, T. A. (1978). Perceptions of clients by professional helpers. *Psychological Bulletin, 85*, 968–1000.

Wills, T. A. (1981). Downward comparison principles in social psychology. *Psychological Bulletin, 90*, 245–271.

Wills, T. A. (1982). Nonspecific factors in helping relationships. In T. A. Wills (Ed.), *Basic processes in helping relationships* (pp. 381–404). New York: Academic Press.

Wills, T. A. (1983). Social comparison in coping and help-seeking. In B. M. DePaulo, A. Nadler, & J. D. Fisher (Eds.), *New directions in helping: Vol. 2. Help-seeking* (pp. 109–141). New York: Academic Press.

Wills, T. A. (1985). Supportive functions of interpersonal relationships. In S. Cohen & L. Syme (Eds.), *Social support and health* (pp. 61 82). Orlando, FL: Academic Press.

Wills, T. A. (1987). Help-seeking as a coping mechanism. In C. R. Snyder & C. Ford (Eds.), *Coping with negative life events: Clinical and social-psychological perspectives* (pp. 19–50). New York: Plenum Press.

Wills, T. A. (1990). Multiple networks. *Journal of Social and Clinical Psychology, 9*, 78–90.

Wills, T. A. (in press-a). Social support and the family. In E. Blechman & M. McEnroe (Eds.), *Family influences on emotion and health*. Hillsdale, NJ: Lawrence Erlbaum Associates.

Wills, T. A. (in press-b). Social support and interpersonal relationships. *Review of Personality and Social Psychology, 12*.

Wortman, C. B., & Brehm, J. W. (1975). Responses to uncontrollable outcomes: An integration of reactance theory and the learned helplessness model. In L. Berkowitz (Ed.), *Advances in experimental social psychology* (Vol. 8, pp. 277–336). New York: Academic Press.

Zimbardo, P. G. (1977). *Shyness: What is it, what to do about it*. Reading, MA: Addison-Wesley.

CHAPTER 19

SOCIAL COMPARISON PROCESSES IN COPING AND HEALTH

Thomas A. Wills

This chapter considers the role of social comparison in coping with adversity. The field of social and clinical psychology encompasses a number of stressors that present challenges to well-being, such as depression, physical disability, and physical illness. Social comparison processes are a type of cognitive coping mechanism that may be used, possibly with other coping mechanisms, in the attempt to restore and maintain psychological well-being. The purpose of this chapter is to discuss the theory of social comparison and the role of comparison processes in coping with problems that are of concern for social and clinical psychology.

Research on social comparison has undergone considerable development in recent years (Suls & Wills, in press). The work originally was based in laboratory studies investigating the role of social comparison in self-evaluation of abilities and opinions (see Latané, 1966; Suls & Miller, 1977). In recent years attention has shifted to the role of social comparison in self-esteem maintenance, because theory has suggested that social comparison is influenced by self-esteem concerns (Goethals,

Arrowood, Wills, Suls, & Wheeler, 1986). This work provides a theoretical base for research in field studies, and this chapter discusses how social comparison is relevant for coping and adjustment in clinical and health settings.

This chapter begins with a presentation of the theory of social comparison, including upward comparison and downward comparison. I consider the current evidential base for social comparison theory and then discuss applications to four types of clinical problems. A final section summarizes the current state of research and suggests some additional questions about comparison and adjustment.

THEORY OF SOCIAL COMPARISON

Social comparison theory considers how a person's perceptions of his or her attributes are influenced through comparison with those of other persons. It is assumed that people compare with others in the social environment, that selection of comparison targets is predictable from specific principles, and that comparison may have effects on subjective well-being. The derivations from these postulates have been developed in several bodies of theory that proceed from somewhat different starting points.

Upward Comparison

Social comparison theory was originated by Leon Festinger in an attempt to understand aspiration-level and conformity processes in small group settings (cf. Festinger, 1950; Festinger, Schachter, & Back, 1950). The original theory was based on the proposition that some personal attributes (e.g., abilities, opinions) cannot be evaluated easily through objective measures; therefore, comparison with other people is useful to determine one's standing on a particular dimension. Through comparison with others, Festinger posited, people can obtain greater certainty concerning their standing on a particular dimension. Accurate evaluation was assumed to be the principal goal of social comparison and, by implication, for effective coping and adjustment.

Several hypotheses formed the basis of the theory. The principles are worth stating in detail, as they have stimulated much research.

1. There is a drive to evaluate one's opinions and abilities. This is the primary postulate of the theory and is known as the "drive for comparison." It was assumed that people desire accurate information about the level of their abilities and the sharing of their opinions; hence, comparison will be a common process.

2. There is a tendency to compare with similar others. It was posited that comparison with a target who is very different in ability or opinion does not provide useful information in evaluating the level of one's own attributes. Therefore, the prediction is that people will select comparison targets who are close to their own ability or opinion; a classic example is a tennis player who compares with other players who are in his or her own league, not with either tennis pros or rank amateurs.

3. There is a unidirectional drive upward in the case of abilities, which is absent in the case of opinions. Festinger assumed that cultural pressures for performance would lead people to compare with others of higher ability, because this could lead to self-improvement. This is principle known as "upward comparison." However, it was suggested that this would not be true for opinions because there is no standard for what is a better

or worse opinion, the only real criterion being that the opinion is similar to one's own.

4. When relevant comparisons are available, subjective evaluations of abilities and opinions will become more certain and more stable. This corollary follows from the postulate that comparison is pursued in order to obtain greater confidence in self-evaluations.

Support for the theory initially was based on studies of aspiration level, which showed that subjects' level of aspiration was changed by performance feedback only when subjects received information about performances similar to their own (Festinger, 1954). More specific support was provided by a group of studies that gave a subject some minimal feedback about his or her performance, presented the subject with brief information about the performances of several other people, and then examined specific social comparison choices or consequences of comparison. These studies indicated that subjects tend to select similar others for comparison (e.g., Wheeler, 1966; Thornton & Arrowood, 1966), and suggested that comparison produces increased certainty about one's attributes (Radloff, 1966; cf. Wrightsman, 1960). This work provided impressive support for Festinger's formulation and the view of social comparison it represented.

Studies with sophisticated designs subsequently tested other aspects of the theory. Broadening the range of comparison choices showed that when the dimension of comparison was unfamiliar, people tend to choose first the top score in the distribution, then the bottom score, in order to establish the range of the attribute (Wheeler et al., 1969). These findings on range-seeking were extended by a number of studies showing that under relatively neutral conditions, subjects show a preference for comparison with similar and better-off others (e.g., Brickman & Berman, 1971; Gruder, 1971; Nosanchuk & Erickson, 1985; Wilson & Benner, 1971).

Downward Comparison

Social comparison theory as originally formulated was based on situations in which people were in relatively good standing on an attribute. Another question is, How is comparison pursued in conditions where the person is not relatively well off? The theory of downward comparison was developed from the belief that comparison may operate differently when one departs from relatively neutral conditions. It addresses how comparison operates in conditions where people are not relatively well off (i.e., they are distressed or threatened).

Downward comparison theory derives from the postulate that subjective well-being may be improved through comparison with another person who is not well off (Wills, 1981). In conditions where people are temporarily or chronically distressed and where problems are not easily remediable through instrumental action, subjective appraisal of one's own situation may be altered if comparison targets are available who also are stressed. The comparison between the self and the other may enable the person to feel better about his or her own situation. The strong version of the theory posits comparison with a target who is worse off than the self (downward comparison); the weak version posits that subjective well-being may be improved through comparison with another who is distressed, but at the same level as the self (lateral comparison).

The basic principle of downward comparison produces several corollaries, which are summarized as follows:

1. Comparison choices will differ in situations where people are stressed or threatened, compared with relatively neutral conditions.
2. When people are stressed they will show a tendency to compare with relatively worse-off others.
3. Downward or lateral comparison will produce an increase in subjective well-being.
4. People are ambivalent about downward comparison.

The initial support for downward comparison theory was based on a range of evidence. From laboratory research, a direct test was a study by Hakmiller (1966), in which subjects were given negative versus positive personality feedback and then were given the opportunity to obtain information about personality attributes (ranging from very maladjusted to very adjusted) of five other people. Results indicated that subjects given negative personality feedback showed a shift toward comparison with a worse-off other, and in the high-threat condition the majority of comparison choices (54%) were with the worst-off comparison target. Similar shifts in comparison behavior as a function of situational stress or low self-esteem were observed in studies by Friend and Gilbert

(1973) and Wilson and Benner (1971). These findings supported the hypothesis that when people are distressed, there is a tendency to shift from upward to downward comparison.

Other evidence from a range of sources was consistent with the postulates of downward comparison theory. In studies of fear-affiliation, for example, it was noted that distressed subjects showed a preference for affiliation with other people who were worse off than themselves (Darley & Aronson, 1966; Schachter, 1959; Zimbardo & Formica, 1963), and Bell (1978) showed that subjects in a negative mood, given a range of affiliation choices, preferred affiliation with people in a more negative mood. Indirect evidence in several studies that pitted similarity against downward comparison suggested that similarity was not the crucial variable in the effect (Bell, 1978; Hakmiller, 1966). Additionally, a number of studies with various paradigms indicated that downward comparison effects occur only when the comparison target is exposed to the same stressor as the subject; when the target person is not stressed, different and typically opposite results occur (e.g., Berkowitz & Knurek, 1969; Buck & Parke, 1972; Feshbach & Singer, 1957; Kenrick & Johnson, 1979; Rotton, Barry, Frey, & Soler, 1978).

Also, mood change was observed in some studies. These included studies using paradigms from fear-affiliation (Amoroso & Walters, 1969; Kiesler, 1966), comparison choice (Hakmiller, 1966), and projection (Bennett & Holmes, 1975; Burish & Houston, 1979). When measures of affect are obtained from stressed subjects before and after exposure to a downward comparison target, results show a decrease in negative affect from pre- to postmeasures (i.e., an increase in subjective well-being).

It is postulated that people are ambivalent about downward comparison. Such comparison goes against normative prescriptions and empathic tendencies of concern with other people (e.g., Berkowitz, 1972); so the opportunity for comparison presents a person with some conflict between these tendencies and the potential benefits of downward comparison. Also, the motive for self-esteem maintenance may conflict somewhat with the desire for accurate evaluation of abilities and more certain self-understanding. These considerations suggest that people's attitudes toward downward comparison will show some contradictions.

This ambivalence was exemplified in a classic

study by Brickman (1975) in which subjects participated in groups that contained either a negatively skewed distribution of outcomes (i.e., one member was worse off than the subject), an equal distribution of outcomes, or a positively skewed distribution (i.e., one member was better off than the subject). Results showed that subjects expressed greater satisfaction with their own scores in the first condition, which represents a downward comparison situation. At the same time, they rated this condition as most unfair with respect to distribution of outcomes (even though outcomes supposedly were attributable to subjects' own performances). Thus, subjects' ratings displayed ambivalence about comparison situations. Subjects did not necessarily endorse negative outcomes to others as a philosophically desirable basis for producing happiness, but they were more satisfied in a situation where one member was worse off and less satisfied in a situation where one member was better off.

Forced Comparison

Models of upward and downward comparison have coexisted with several related models of social relations that focus on negative discrepancies between self and other. These include models of equity (Adams, 1965; Berkowitz & Walster, 1976) and relative deprivation (Crosby, 1976; Davis, 1959). Influential papers by Brickman and Campbell (1971) and Brickman and Bulman (1977) discussed the potential costs of social comparison for interpersonal and intergroup relations. While these models address somewhat different issues, they all concern situations in which a person faces comparison with others who are better off, either because of their own efforts or through social factors that produce vested advantage. Additionally, Tesser's model of self-evaluation maintenance addresses issues of comparison in close relationships (Tesser, 1980; Tesser, Campbell, & Smith, 1984) and delineates processes that may influence reactions to comparison in ongoing relationships (Tesser, 1986). A related model by Salovey and Rodin (1984) considers the role of social comparison in interpersonal jealousy and envy (Salovey, in press).

Because of the variety of models, there is no simple summarization of their postulates and derivations. One common principle is the proposition that people will be dissatisfied when they make a comparison with other people who are better off.

There is considerable evidence for this proposition (Cook, Crosby, & Hennigan, 1977; Pettigrew, 1976; Tesser, 1988). Other principles relevant for forced comparisons are that dissatisfaction is influenced by the magnitude of the discrepancy between self and other (large), the similarity between the self and the other (similar), and the centrality of the comparison dimension for self-concept (central rather than peripheral).

The fact that social comparison may produce dissatisfaction is of considerable importance and raises difficulties for other social comparison theories, which have yet to be resolved. At the same time there are some unresolved paradoxes for forced comparison theories. A primary question derives from the observation that inequity is typical in societies, but dissatisfaction is not. This has led to suggestions that people may deal with unequal distributions by defining others as dissimilar, finding other dimensions on which the self is relatively advantaged, or altering the perceived centrality of the comparison dimension. Other mechanisms are possible, such as simply avoiding comparison. However, direct evidence regarding these possible avenues for dissonance reduction currently is lacking.

The postulates of upward and downward comparison have both received support. In relatively neutral conditions, people compare with similar others and with others who are better off than themselves. These replicated findings, together with confirmation of other predictions, have supported the basic validity of Festinger's theory. Correspondingly, it is found that when people are stressed or threatened, their comparison choices tend to shift from upward to downward, and there is evidence that this type of comparison produces an increase in subjective well-being. Hence, downward comparison also has support. There is also a good deal of evidence for the proposition that comparison with better-off others may produce dissatisfaction, but the relation of forced comparison to other types of comparison theory is not well understood at present.

CURRENT RESEARCH

Continuing research in social comparison has supported and elaborated the basic theory while extending the evidential base for social comparison processes. In the following sections, I consider recent basic research that has extended the scope of social comparison theory.

Related Attributes

The theory of social comparison was extended by considering the attributional basis of judgments about performance. When a particular performance is observed, the performance may be attributed to the ability of the actor but also may be attributed to other attributes that are related to the performance, such as effort. Following this line of thinking, the statement of related-attributes comparison by Goethals and Darley (1977) predicted that in addition to comparisons on a dimension of interest, people also would seek comparison on other dimensions that were related to the performance.

Research on related attributes has shown that such comparisons are relevant (e.g., Gastorf & Suls, 1978; Suls, Gastorf, & Lawhon, 1978; Zanna, Goethals, & Hill, 1975). For example, Gastorf and Suls (1978) gave subjects feedback about their scores on a test together with equal or upward comparison information about the scores of other subjects, and then assessed the subject's certainty about his or her own ability. In the first study, subjects who were given performance comparison information did not show any significant change in certainty. In a second study, however, when undergraduate subjects were given feedback about their performance together with information about a related attribute of the comparison person (undergraduate student vs. graduate student), they did show increased certainty. This supported the related-attributes hypothesis.

Similarly, Wheeler, Koestner, and Driver (1982) formulated groups of nine subjects, gave subjects feedback about their own scores on a task (below midrank in the group) together with the distribution of scores, and then gave them the opportunity to select information about other members who represented various combinations of performance level and another attribute (amount of practice). The belief that the additional attribute either was or was not related to performance was also manipulated. Results indicated that when true related-attributes information was available (i.e., the attribute was related to performance), subjects rated their own performance higher, apparently because they could attribute their relatively poor performance to lack of practice. In this condition they also showed more interest in comparison information, apparently because they believed the comparison would be more informative. An ambiguity in these data, however, was

that subjects showed a preference for similar comparison, choosing the person just above themselves, irrespective of the related-attribute manipulation. Hence the role of similarity as a primary principle in comparison was still supported.

Another ambiguity in related-attributes research concerns whether the additional attributes must be related to performance. In several studies, subjects have shown a preference for comparison targets who are similar on general attributes (e.g., sex, age) even when the attributes supposedly are not related to performance (Feldman & Ruble, 1981; Miller, 1982; Suls, Gaes, & Gastorf, 1979). For example, in the study by Miller (1982) subjects given scores about a test performance tended to choose a comparison other who was physically attractive, even when told that physical attractiveness was unrelated to test performance. Data such as these suggest that social comparison is influenced by concerns above and beyond the specific arena of performance, which may include the role of attributes in general competitive standing or the central importance of the attribute for self-concept.

Subjective Distress and Comparison

The possibility that comparison choices are influenced by esteem threat was tested by Levine and Green (1984) with a sample of children aged 8 to 10 years. Subjects worked alone at a computer terminal that presented a series of 10 visual perception tasks. After each trial, subjects could elect to receive feedback about their own scores, the typical score of other children on the problem, or both. Experimental variables, provided through manipulated feedback, were the subject's improving versus declining performance over trials (intrapersonal comparison) and their superior versus inferior standing relative to other children (interpersonal comparison). An "intrapersonal × interpersonal" interaction indicated that in the improving condition subjects looked equally often at scores of superior and inferior others, whereas in the declining performance condition subjects looked more frequently at the scores of inferior others (i.e., a downward comparison effect). Repeated-measures analyses showed that preference for downward comparison increased over trials when performance was declining. This study confirmed the proposition that downward comparison is evoked by an esteem threat (from poor performance), and that this comparison process can be observed in a sample of relatively young children (cf. Ruble, Boggiano, Feldman, & Loebl, 1980).

Information selection as a function of failure was examined by Pyszczynski, Greenberg, and LaPrelle (1985). Subjects were given a test purportedly measuring social sensitivity, were given manipulated feedback about their performance, and then had an opportunity to examine information about the performance of other subjects. Results indicated a general tendency for subjects to avoid information about others who had done better than themselves and to prefer information about others who had done less well than themselves (i.e., downward comparison). The preference for information about worse-performing others was particularly marked among subjects who were told their performance was poor. This study also found that subjects who failed tended to disparage the accuracy of the test. These results are similar to data from Frey and Stahlberg (1986), who found that persons experiencing ego-threat because of negative feedback from intelligence tests results tended to disparage the validity of the test. The latter is not, strictly speaking, a comparison effect, but suggests related self-enhancement processes that may operate together with social comparison processes.

Smith and Insko (1987) tested whether social comparison for ability evaluation was affected by own standing and by the public versus private status of the comparison. In a factorial design, undergraduate subjects were given information indicating that they had scored low versus high on a test of "social intelligence," were told that they ranked 5 in a group of 7 people, and then had the opportunity to examine other subjects' scores in a forced-choice comparison paradigm. Trait self-esteem also was included as a factor in the design. Results showed that for high-scoring subjects with private comparison, the majority of choices were of the top score in the group (i.e., rank 1). However, there was a progressive downward shift (a) when comparison was public, (b) when the subject's score was low, and (c) for persons low in self-esteem.

This study provides evidence that ability evaluation in neutral conditions is consistent with upward comparison theory (replicating previous findings), but that it is influenced by esteem concerns when there are potential threats to the self. The data also support the proposition that comparison shifts will be more prevalent among people low in self-esteem (cf. Wills, 1981). These results are consistent with studies of test diagnosticity, which show that subjects who expect to perform well choose tests that are highly diagnostic of ability (e.g., Trope, 1979, 1980), but subjects with ego-protective motives, including low self-esteem and expectation of failure, show a preference for tests that are less diagnostic (Strube & Roemmele, 1985).

Social Cognition Effects

In addition to comparison choices, effects may be observed on social cognition measures. When subjective distress occurs, perceptions of other people may be shifted in a manner that presents a more favorable situation for the self. This possibility was tested by Sherman, Presson, and Chassin (1984) in laboratory research where subjects were given manipulated information indicating success versus failure on a task and then were given an opportunity to make ratings of the performance of other people. Two studies showed that failure produced a downward shift in subjects' ratings of the performance of other people (i.e., subjects who failed overestimated the percentage of the population who would fail). Relevant control conditions in this and another study (Sherman, Presson, Chassin, & Agostinelli, 1984) indicated that the shift was attributable to a self-enhancement mechanism, not simply attributive projection from one's own behavior, because consensus shifts were found mainly for undesirable but not for desirable behaviors. An opposite effect (underestimation of population proportions, or "false uniqueness") is obtained when subjects rate positive aspects of themselves (Campbell, 1986; Marks, 1984; cf. Gerard & Orive, 1987; Goethals, Messick, & Allison, in press). This effect also seems guided by a self-enhancement process; that is, if people perceive that their competencies are rare in the population, they appear advantaged relative to others.

A study by Suls and Wan (1987) examined social cognition as a function of specific fears. A population of undergraduates was screened on a 51-item fear survey and subjects were identified as high on specific fears on the basis of extreme responses to specific items (e.g., snake phobia, public-speaking anxiety). As subjects completed the fear survey, they also indicated the percent of other undergraduates they thought would have high fear for each item. In this population, the scoring criteria indicated generally high levels of fear, with 20% to 54% of the overall sample classified as high fear. Analyses comparing social perceptions of high- and low-fear subjects indicated that both groups tended to overestimate the prevalence of fear in comparison with actual population figures, but high-fear subjects were significantly more inaccurate in their estimates; that is, they tended to overestimate fear prevalence more than other subjects. The authors suggested that such perceptions make people feel better about themselves because they indicate that many other people have the same problem (i.e., a lateral comparison process).

Comparison and Subjective Well-Being

The relation between comparison and subjective well-being has been examined in both correlational and experimental designs. Heath (1984) obtained ratings of the level of local crime (i.e., in one's own city) and nonlocal crime (i.e., crime in other cities) as presented in 36 newspapers from different regions. Telephone interviews were then conducted with residents of the 36 cities to elicit data on fear of crime. Results showed that fear was lower in areas where the newspaper reported a higher level of nonlocal crime; the results apparently exemplify a process in which people compare the level of crime in their own area with that in other areas and arrive at a relatively favorable perception of their own situation (i.e., a downward comparison process). In an exemplary design, Heath then tested this process in a laboratory study with controlled independent variables and ratings of mood as dependent variables. Results of the laboratory study paralleled the findings from the field study.

Laboratory studies of comparison effects on mood by Gibbons (1986) also showed enhancement of subjective well-being. Subjects were selected to represent high versus low depressive affect on the basis of a prior screening. In the context of an impression formation experiment, subjects first wrote a self-disclosing statement about a positive versus negative event and then had an opportunity to choose one from a set of other statements reflecting a range of positive to negative affects. Results of the first study indicated that depressed subjects preferred to read negative statements, particularly when negative mood was induced; this preference was reversed among nondepressed subjects. In a second study,

subjects wrote a self-disclosure statement and then were given a statement (purportedly from another subject) that was negative in tone (i.e., a downward comparison manipulation). Self-ratings of mood obtained pre- and poststatement showed an improvement in subjective state among depressed subjects; for nondepressed subjects, the comparison experience had no effect on mood. These data are consistent with the proposition that downward comparison enhances subjective well-being, and that downward comparison effects occur primarily when subjective distress is present.

A subsequent study (Gibbons & Gerrard, 1989) employed a design in which subjects, preselected on self-esteem, were told they would be participating in support groups in which the topic was coping strategies for adjustment to college life. Subjects spent some time writing a self-disclosure statement about a problem they had in adjustment, and then were given a statement supposedly written by another participant. The experimental manipulation was that the statement reflected either upward comparison (no difficulty in adjustment), downward comparison (the individual was having trouble in adjusting to college), or severe life problems (the individual had experienced a number of life problems but felt he or she was coping pretty well). Results for the downward comparison condition showed improvement in mood state among subjects low in self-esteem, but not for high self-esteem subjects. For the upward comparison target, improvement in mood state was observed for high self-esteem subjects. For the third target, improvement in mood state was noted for both subject groups, though the tendency was for greater improvement among people with low self-esteem.

Other studies have examined comparison variables in relation to judgments of life satisfaction (see Diener, 1984, for a discussion of comparison theories of life satisfaction). For example, Emmons and Diener (1985) used a sample of undergraduates, administering a questionnaire that included measures of current affect, satisfaction in 11 life domains, and a rating of comparative standing in relation to the average college student. Objective measures of each domain also were obtained (e.g., grade point average, number of friends). While the objective measures were significantly related to overall life satisfaction, the social comparison measure was the best single predictor of satisfaction and positive affect. This pattern held when other contributing factors (aspirations and life change) were partialled out.

To summarize, basic research has confirmed and broadened the base of social comparison theory. Research on related attributes has supported the role of social comparison for increasing confidence about evaluations of ability, although there is still some ambiguity about whether related attributes are primarily employed for accurate evaluation or for the broader purpose of determining one's competitive standing in the social environment. Research on downward comparison has provided support for several theoretical principles, showing that downward comparison is evoked by ego-threat, that it produces improvement in subjective well-being, and that it is more characteristic of people with low self-esteem. The relation of downward comparison to other cognitive coping strategies relevant for self-esteem maintenance has been suggested in several studies. The correspondence of results from laboratory and field research also has increased the evidential base for downward comparison.

SOCIAL COMPARISON AND COPING

Recent research on social comparison has extended to investigations of coping with particular life events (Wills, 1983, 1987). In the following sections, I will discuss some recent work from the areas of physical illness, disabilities, group process, and depression.

Physical Illness

Because physical illness presents people with multiple coping demands, may be long term, and sometimes is not readily treatable, cognitive coping mechanisms may be utilized to help people adapt to chronic physical conditions (Moos & Billings, 1982). Research on comparison-oriented coping has suggested that social comparison is relevant for people's attempts to cope with chronic illness.

A sample of 78 cancer patients, all female, participated in a study by Wood, Taylor, and Lichtman (1985), which investigated social comparison constructs. Measures included structured ratings of how the respondent rated her own adjustment to illness relative to other patients, and codings of spontaneous statements from the interview protocol. Results suggested that the respond-

ents had a considerable amount of information about other cancer patients, and data from structured questions indicated that the majority of patients perceived their own coping and adjustment as better than that of other patients, consistent with a downward comparison process. Interview statements suggested the prevalence of comparisons in which the respondent compared with another person who was worse off on a related dimension, which the authors termed *dimensional comparison*. The investigators included measures to test for upward comparison, but overall the data showed little evidence of upward comparisons in this sample. These data suggested that the process of downward comparison was used by patients to help deal with distress evoked by their illness.

Arthritis is a disease condition that, although not life threatening, may involve considerable pain and functional limitations on activity. The role of social comparison for coping with the disease was examined by Affleck and colleagues in a sample of 130 arthritis patients who had the illness for an average of 10 years (Affleck, Tennen, Pfeiffer, Fifield, & Rowe, 1987; Affleck, Tennen, Pfeiffer, & Fifield, 1988; Affleck & Tennen, in press). The study employed measures similar to those of Wood et al. (1985). Interview procedures elicited open-ended statements from respondents about what it is like to have the disease, and structured questions indexed respondents' perceptions of their own coping relative to other patients. In this study, standardized measures of psychological outcomes were obtained, including subjective measures of mood state and ratings by practitioners (rheumatologists and nurse practitioners) of the patient's adjustment to illness. Data for interview codings indicated that spontaneous comparison statements were relatively rare (coded for only 17% of the sample), but the comparison statements that were made predominantly reflected downward comparisons (82% of spontaneous statements). These statements reflected patients' perceptions that they were able to remain physically active, to control negative emotions and attitudes, and to maintain an attitude of optimism about the future. Correlations of comparative ratings with outcome measures indicated significant relationships with practitioners' ratings of adjustment; and these correlations remained significant when the effects of actual disease activity, functional status, and illness duration were partialled out. The latter finding is important because it shows that comparative ratings are not simply reflections of disease status.

Related findings from another research program with arthritis patients showed some evidence of both upward and downward comparison processes, which depended on the context of comparison. Blalock, DeVellis, and DeVellis (in press) used a choice paradigm to elicit the comparison preferences of patients under two conditions: (a) when they were experiencing difficulties in functioning and (b) when they wished to set goals for themselves. These data showed that in the first condition subjects preferred downward types of comparison, that is, with patients who also were experiencing performance difficulties. In the second condition, however, patients tended to prefer information about patients who were not experiencing difficulties, that is, upward comparison. Another study (DeVellis et al., in press) examined comparison preferences and found a general tendency for downward comparisons, with some range-seeking (i.e., asking about patients who were functioning well). Subjects' comparative ratings indicated that they saw themselves as functioning better than the average patient. In this study, comparative ratings did not show a net contribution to outcome measures when disease activity was partialled.

Disabilities

Disabilities present another area where social comparison processes may be relevant. Here, in addition to the functional limitations posed by the disability, there may be some element of social stigma that presents a challenge to the person's self-esteem. Research on comparison among people with physical or intellectual disabilities has suggested that social comparison plays a role in efforts at adaptation.

Gibbons (1985a, 1985b; cf. Strang, Smith, & Rogers, 1978) investigated the operation of self-esteem processes in samples of mentally retarded (MR) adolescents. Respondents were asked about perceptions of retarded and nonretarded targets, as well as self-perceptions. Results showed that while subjects held fairly negative perceptions of MR persons in general, they rated themselves more favorably than other MR targets and about equal to nonretarded targets for outcomes such as likelihood of cognitive success. The inference was that subjects were arriving at relatively favorable ability perceptions through comparison with MR

targets whom they perceived to be worse off. However, no effects were noted for social dimensions, where subjects rated themselves quite negatively. These data suggested a possible negative consequence of downward comparison: If subjects make negative comparisons with members of their own group, it may reduce positive social relationships with these members.

Similar results were obtained by Harter and colleagues (Harter, 1985; Silon & Harter, 1985). Measuring self-perceptions of MR and nonretarded individuals in mixed classrooms, they found that the MR students rated themselves equal to nonretarded students, while learning-disabled (but not retarded) students rated themselves lower than nonretarded students. Questions about comparisons indicated that MR students were comparing themselves to their retarded peers, thus arriving at a relatively favorable comparison, while learning-disabled students were comparing themselves with normal students, thus arriving at a relatively unfavorable perception.

The reactions of parents of handicapped children were studied by Affleck and colleagues in neonatal units (Affleck et al., 1987; Affleck & Tennen, in press; cf. Tennen, Affleck, & Gershman, 1986). Mothers were interviewed shortly after the birth of a child with perinatal complications, and were reinterviewed 6 months later. In this study the mother's perception of the condition of her own infant, relative to other infants in the unit, was recorded in addition to her perception of her own coping ability. Data indicated that spontaneous comparison statements were more common in this population (coded for 73% of respondents) and that the majority of these statements represented downward comparison (86% of all statements); these included comparisons of the infant's medical condition relative to others, and comparison of the present outcome with potentially worse outcomes. Comparative ratings also indicated that mothers perceived the severity of the child's medical condition as less than average and their own coping as better than average. In this population currently facing a life crisis, spontaneous comparisons were more frequent than in the arthritis sample. For data obtained shortly after birth, correlations of comparison measures with indices of illness severity and adjustment were not significant, but follow-up data indicated that comparative ratings were significantly related to indices of mood and parenting competence, with control for baseline comparison index and current caretaking difficulty. This suggested a delayed effect of comparison-oriented coping on psychological outcomes.

With regard to adults' perception of their own disability, Schulz and Decker (1985) interviewed a sample of 100 spinal cord–injured people who had incurred the disability an average of 20 years previously. Data from this study are somewhat indirect because respondents generally declined to answer a direct question about their comparison preferences. Further probing produced data indicating that 25% of respondents said they compared with other disabled persons, 16% said they compared with nondisabled persons, and 59% said they just compared to "people in general," not any specific target. However, comparative ratings indicated that the respondents perceived their own life situation to compare favorably with that of other people, both disabled and nondisabled. Qualitative responses suggested that this occurred because disabled people focus on particular dimensions, such as intellectual ability and social sensitivity, on which they perceive themselves as advantaged relative to the comparison targets.

Group Processes

The possibility that social comparison processes operate in group therapy settings was investigated in a series of studies (Gerrard, Gibbons, & Sharp, 1985; Gibbons & Gerard, in press; Gibbons, Gerrard, Lando, & McGovern, 1989). Participants in self-help groups for eating disorders were initially studied. In Gerrard et al. (1985), participants assessed at intake were told they could examine case studies of other people with eating disorders and could choose from among cases with a more versus less severe problem, and with greater versus less success in coping with the problem. Subjects were blocked into two groups based on responses to the Beck Depression Inventory (though all subjects scored relatively high on this measure). Results indicated that all participants wished to read about a case that was fairly severe. Analyses for the coping question showed that low-depression subjects preferred a case with complete coping success, but high-depression subjects preferred a case with lower coping success. This is suggestive of the shift toward downward comparison as a function of distress noted in other studies, although the predominant tendency in this group was for downward comparison.

Measures of comparison were obtained from 120 participants in smoking cessation groups over 16 sessions by Gibbons et al. (1989). At the first and last sessions, participants completed questionnaire measures concerning seriousness of their problem, absolute and relative to other smokers; perceptions of the typical smoker; and comparison preference for other (potential) group members, in terms of amount of smoking and difficulty in quitting. Specific effects for comparison preference indicated that over all subjects, the relationship between problem seriousness and preference for downward comparison targets was significant: The more serious a subject thought his or her smoking problem was, the more preference he or she showed for targets with serious problems and lower coping success. The strength of this relationship was modest in the baseline measurement, probably because threat levels were relatively high for all subjects, but longitudinal analyses showed that the strength of the relationship in the total sample increased over time, because some subjects quit and the variability in the severity measure increased. Moreover, within-subject analyses showed that as perceived problem seriousness declined over time, so did preference for downward comparison targets. It should be noted that in this study the comparison targets were outside the group; data on ratings of other group members showed no indications of derogation within the group, and in fact the participants rated other group members quite favorably.

Depression and Social Comparison

Some other research not encompassed under the above categories has been directed toward the relationship between social comparison and depression. For the most part this research has not been conducted with clinically depressed subjects, so there is some qualification to the external validity of the studies. For example, in conceptually related studies one can find evidence either that distressed people in clinical settings show evidence of self-protective attributions (Tennen et al., 1986) or that in student samples, self-protective attributions are more characteristic of high self-esteem subjects (Tennen & Herzberger, 1987). Whether the latter type of result is more typical of college samples, where subjects represent the upper end of the self-esteem distribution, is currently unknown because few studies have been conducted with actual clinical populations. Nonetheless, this research may have theoretical implications for processes of coping.

A first issue concerns the prevalence of self-enhancement tendencies in the general population. A number of studies have shown the existence of such an effect. For example, Alicke (1985) obtained ratings from college student subjects concerning various personality traits that varied in desirability and controllability. Subjects rated the extent to which a given trait characterized (a) themselves and (b) the average college student. Results showed that subjects viewed desirable traits as more characteristic of themselves than of others. Also, a crossover interaction with controllability was found: Subjects rated desirable/controllable traits as more characteristic of themselves (relative to others), whereas they rated undesirable/controllable traits as more characteristic of others (relative to the self). This effect was attenuated for traits low in controllability.

Similar data by Marks (1984) derived from studies in which subjects defined attributes that they regarded as their best ability and most important opinion, and then estimated the prevalence of these attributes in the population. For attributes named in the original subjects' responses, ratings of actual prevalence for the abilities and opinions were obtained from an independent sample. Results showed a crossover interaction, in which subjects underestimated the prevalence of their best ability (i.e., false uniqueness) and overestimated the prevalence of their important opinion (i.e., false consensus). Data from a similar paradigm using sample-based prevalences (Campbell, 1986) indicated that subjects overestimated the prevalence of their own opinions and low abilities, but underestimated the prevalence of their own high abilities. The results were interpreted as reflecting a self-enhancement process in which subjects perceive prevalence figures in a way that produces a positive evaluation of the self.

A further issue concerns the relative importance of cognitive consistency versus self-enhancement in reactions to feedback. The consistency model posits that people will respond positively to feedback that is consistent with their self-concept; that is, people with negative self-concepts will accept negative feedback, and people with positive self-concepts will accept positive feedback. A self-enhancement formulation, in contrast, predicts that people will respond only to feedback that produces a favorable image of the self. Each formulation is internally consistent and has some

supporting evidence (Jones, 1973; Shrauger, 1975). The contrasting predictions of these models were tested in a study by Swann, Griffin, Predmore, and Gaines (1987). Subjects, prescreened on social self-esteem were given negative feedback about a task performance. Reactions to feedback were assessed both through cognitive measures (e.g., competence of evaluator) and through affective measures (mood adjective checklists for depression, anxiety, and hostility). Results for cognitive measures showed a main effect for feedback, with all subjects responding more positively to favorable feedback. There was also an interaction: Cognitive reactions to favorable feedback were more positive for high- compared with low-esteem subjects, whereas cognitive reactions to unfavorable feedback were more positive for low- compared with high-esteem subjects. In contrast, results for affective reactions were consistent with a self-enhancement model; all subjects had more positive affective reactions to favorable than unfavorable feedback, and there were no interactions with self-esteem level. These data provide evidence for self-enhancement as a determinant of affective processes in the general population. However, there is currently no direct test of consistency versus enhancement models using social comparison choices or consequences as the dependent measure.

Relations between social comparison and dysphoric symptomatology in college student samples have been assessed by several investigators. For example, Weary, Elbin, and Hill (1987) presented subjects, prescreened on depressive symptoms, with several case histories about events occurring to other persons, and gave subjects manipulated feedback indicating that another subject had made either quite similar or quite dissimilar attributions about the events. The dependent variable was a single rating of the extent to which the feedback had influenced the subject's feeling about him or herself. Results showed a marginal main effect for depression, with dysphoric subjects reporting being more affected, and a significant main effect for similarity of feedback, with subjects who received similar feedback more affected by the feedback they received, compared with subjects who received dissimilar feedback. The data were interpreted as indicating that depressed people are more sensitive to social comparison. In this study, however, social comparison choices were not assessed, nor were effects on behavior or subjective well-being measured.

Tabachnik, Crocker, and Alloy (1983) presented

subjects, blocked on depressive symptomatology, with a list of 60 trait adjectives. The set of traits was grouped by the experimenters into subsets representing items that were positive, negative, or neutral in descriptive content. The experimenters obtained subjects' ratings of (a) the extent to which a given item was true of themselves and (b) of the average college student, (c) the estimated percentage of students whom each item characterized, and (d) the percentage of students who would say that the item characterized themselves. Self-ratings by an independent sample of students on the 60 items, (i.e., population prevalence figures) also were obtained. Comparisons of a with b showed that depressed subjects rated themselves higher on negative traits and lower on positive traits than they rated the average student, a result that was consistent with the original measure of depression (i.e., perceiving oneself negatively). Analyses of variance comparing subjects' estimates of the prevalence of an item (rating c) with population prevalence figures showed a "depression × trait type" interaction. Depressed subjects, relative to nondepressed subjects, were more inaccurate in social perceptions because they overestimated the prevalence of negative attributes, underestimated the prevalence of positive attributes, and did not differ on neutral attributes. The data indicate a processing of social consensus information in a self-enhancing manner by depressed subjects. These results are consistent with the study previously discussed by Suls and Wan (1987), which showed that people who had a specific fear tended to overestimate the prevalence of that fear in the population. Both sets of data seem to reflect a tendency for distressed people to perceive social information in a manner that indicates there are many other people who have the same problem (i.e., a lateral or downward comparison process).

A converse view of this issue has been presented by Swallow and Kuiper (1988). Their model proposes that individuals become depressed because of excessive concern with upward comparison. It is suggested that if a person continually makes what he or she perceives as unfavorable comparisons with other people, and is unable to make compensating comparisons that provide favorable information about the self, then depressive affect might ensue because of negative self-image and feelings of lack of self-worth. It is suggested that if people are at risk for depression because of low self-complexity and high self-awareness, then negative life events may lead the person to focus on unfavorable comparisons with other people, leading to development and perhaps maintenance of a negative self-concept (cf. Pyszczynski & Greenberg, 1987). If individuals are uncertain about their self-concept (Warren & McEachren, 1983), maintain a set of excessively high standards for performance evaluation (Kuiper & Olinger, 1986), are inclined to compare on central dimensions of self-concept (Tesser & Campbell, 1980; Harter, 1983), and overperceive similarity between self and others (Swallow & Kuiper, 1987), then a process could be set in motion that would lead to a series of unfavorable comparisons. Swallow and Kuiper (1988) further proposed that depressive individuals fail to perceive the contribution of related attributes to others' performances, which again would tend to produce unfavorable comparisons for the self. This model contains many promising suggestions about how comparison processes may relate to affect and adjustment. At present, however, there is little direct evidence for the basic postulates of the model.

GENERAL DISCUSSION

This chapter has outlined the theoretical basis for the study of social comparison and discussed recent research on comparison conducted in laboratory and field settings. This work has provided consistent support for social comparison theory. The predictions of upward comparison theory and related attributes theory have been extended in current research, and the propositions of downward comparison theory have been supported in a number of settings. Social comparison theory continues to provide predictions that may lead to better understanding of self-evaluation and self-concept maintenance (Goethals et al., 1986; Wood, 1989).

One conclusion of this chapter is that downward comparison processes are observed with high prevalence in clinical settings. While results vary somewhat according to the measure employed and the population studied, the evidence indicates that comparison with other distressed people is observed in populations with physical illness, disability, and other health problems (eating disorder, smoking). The suggestion of these findings is that comparison is being employed as a coping mechanism, and the further question is whether downward comparison provides functional benefit for distressed people; that is, does it lead to better adjustment?

A convergence of findings from clinical populations suggests that this is the case, as both concurrent and prospective studies have shown comparison measures significantly related to adjustment (e.g., Affleck & Tennen, in press). Experimental studies (e.g., Gibbons, 1986) also have shown downward comparison conditions to improve subjective well-being. The concordance of results from controlled experiments and naturalistic studies conforms to theoretical predictions, and together this evidence suggests that downward comparison does provide functional benefit. At the same time there are still a number of methodological issues unresolved in this research (Wills, 1987), so conclusions about the status of downward comparison as a coping process remain somewhat qualified. It should be noted as well that upward comparison is observed in clinical populations, so this aspect of comparison theory should not be ignored. In the following sections I discuss some issues raised by current studies, and make some suggestions for further research.

Temporal Effects in Comparison

One question deriving from the health-related research is whether comparison processes are temporally linked. In theory, comparison-oriented coping should be employed during times of intense emotional distress, so the derivation is that downward comparison should be observed with greatest prevalence among people who are recently confronted with a health problem, either their own or another person's. The evidence is limited but seems consistent with this suggestion, because the clearest evidence has been obtained from samples assessed immediately after a health crisis (Affleck & Tennen, in press) or in the process of self-change of a health behavior (Gibbons et al., 1989). Studies of samples surveyed at longer intervals after illness onset (Affleck & Tennen, in press; Schulz & Decker, 1985) have shown less evidence of coping effects. Wood et al. (1985), studying a sample with an intermediate time frame (mean 2 years postsurgery), found comparison measures inversely related to time since diagnosis, so these data also are consistent with a temporal trend.

If a predictable time course exists, it may represent an intense period of comparison-oriented coping occurring around the time of disease onset, followed by a period where cognitive mechanisms decline and are replaced by information- or behaviorally oriented coping. From this perspective, the possibility is that a shift from downward to upward comparison will occur as people deal successfully with anxiety and emotional distress, and turn attention to instrumental types of coping. Another formulation suggests that patients are initially dealing with the effect of the disease on self-concept, but when these issues are dealt with, then people shift attention from the self to other people, and to issues of maintaining interpersonal relationships (Moos, 1986).

Correlation with Other Cognitive Mechanisms

Another issue concerns whether downward comparison is part of a larger class of cognitive coping mechanisms. In the previous discussion there were suggestions that downward comparison is accompanied by several other cognitive mechanisms that also operate to produce enhancement of self-esteem; for example, overestimating the prevalence of negative attributes in the population (e.g., Suls & Wan, 1987). There is no reason to believe that comparison-oriented coping will be employed to the exclusion of other coping mechanisms (Wills & Shiffman, 1985), so the question is whether there is significant association with other cognitive mechanisms, either those that might be classified as avoidant (e.g., denial, distraction) or those that might be classified as attentional (e.g., situation redefinition, focus on positive aspects).

This leads to the suggestion that coping research attempts to obtain measures of different coping mechanisms and test for unique effects as well as for shared variance (Wills, 1987). The contribution of comparison-oriented coping might be unique, but it is quite possible that the contributions to adjustment occur through the application of a variety of coping mechanisms, in which case the shared variance would be most important (cf. Perri, 1985; Shiffman, 1985). Alternatively, it is conceivable that relations of comparison-oriented coping to adjustment are spurious, deriving from their association with other mechanisms that are causally important, or with third factors. Further descriptive research is needed to determine the correlation among coping mechanisms and to test for differential relationships to outcomes. This is combined with the need for multiple measures of comparison as a coping mechanism (cf. Affleck & Tennen, in press).

Effects of Downward Comparison

At present there is little understanding of the precise effects of downward comparison. There are suggestions that downward comparison may decrease anxiety or fear, and increase optimism or life satisfaction. These seem, on the face of it, to be different processes, and so there is a need for more exact specification of the cognitive or behavioral consequences of downward comparison. If comparison served simply to produce short-term decreases in anxiety, then its predicted consequences would be rather different than would be the case if comparison produced enduring shifts in optimism. More attention to this issue is needed.

In addition, there is the question of whether downward comparison produces changes in self-concept. Going with a straight derivation from upward comparison theory, one would say it should not; lateral comparison produces no information about one's relative standing in the population, and downward comparison in its simplest form only produces a suggestion that one is better off than someone else. If downward comparison were employed after a period of range-seeking (Wheeler et al., 1969), then this difficulty might be alleviated; but there has been no test of such a sequential process. Neither is there any requirement in downward comparison theory that the comparison target be a similar other. Since the field evidence is ambiguous on this point, there is at present no compelling basis for believing that downward comparison requires a similar other as a target (Wills, in press).

There is, then, no clear requirement that downward comparison must change self-concept. But if not, why would it be a prevalent coping mechanism? One possibility is that downward comparisons produce only short-term fluctuations in subjective well-being, which are useful for affect regulation but have no long-term impact on self-perception. The question is, What processes are responsible for the high stability of self-concept over time and the observation that self-concept may be unaffected by severe negative life events? This question needs further investigation.

There is also a question about possible negative effects of downward comparison. It could be suggested that if people rely exclusively on coping through comparison, then other types of coping mechanisms may be reduced. People could fall into passivity, lose the benefits of self-improvement through upward comparison, and, through indiscriminate comparisons, arrive at self-images that are out of touch with actual personality attributes. I think this perspective is oversimplified, because it assumes that people will use only one coping mechanism (I don't believe this is the case), but it is worth considering. Also, there is a question as to whether a reliance on downward comparison would lead to negative perceptions of other people (Gibbons, 1985a). I think this is a real concern (see Wills, 1981) and should be investigated in detail. Social cognition is not a zero-sum process, but a coping mechanism that leads one to focus on negative attributes of other people, and as such, may have potential cost for the overall process of coping and supportive relationships.

Upward Comparison and Clinical Psychology

There has been relatively little attention paid to the process of upward comparison in clinical populations. This is not unreasonable as downward comparison has been the prevalent process observed in clinical samples. But it is possible that upward comparison has been short-changed. In theory, upward comparison could be useful to people who are undergoing a process of change. At the same time, there are a number of indications that distressed people wish to avoid social comparisons, because the comparisons are generally unfavorable to themselves. This tendency is supported by studies that have shown negative effects of forced comparison information (e.g., Marsh & Parker, 1984; Salovey & Rodin, 1984; Tesser, 1986). What then are the barriers to social comparison in distressed populations, and what processes of comparison theory could be employed to increase the ability of distressed people to obtain useful information from their social environments? Is there a rationale for introducing some downward comparison into clinical procedure to produce short-term change in self-concept so that people can be motivated for further coping efforts? It seems worthwhile to think about this issue.

Finally there is the question of whether psychological distress is produced through excessive upward comparison, or a focus on noncentral performance dimensions (Harter, 1983; Swallow & Kuiper, 1988). It is possible that psychological distress arises through underutilization of mechanisms normally used to produce positive self-concept (Snyder & Higgins, 1988), or that depression is maintained because of excessive focus on negative attributes of the self, with a consequent inability to consider one's favorable standing relative to others on some dimensions (Pyszczynski & Greenberg, 1987). It is apparent that upward comparison also may have mixed effects, and understanding the balance of these effects may have significant implications for social and clinical psychology.

REFERENCES

Adams, J. S. (1965). Inequity in social exchange. In L. Berkowitz (Ed.), *Advances in Experimental Social Psychology* (Vol. 2, pp. 267–299). New York: Academic Press.

Affleck, G., & Tennen, H. (in press). Social comparison and coping with medical disorders. In J. Suls & T. A. Wills (Eds.), *Social comparison: Contemporary theory and research*. Hillsdale, NJ: Lawrence Erlbaum Associates.

Affleck, G., Tennen, H., Pfeiffer, C., & Fifield, J. (1988). Social comparisons in rheumatoid arthritis: Accuracy and adaptational significance. *Journal of Social and Clinical Psychology, 6*, 219–234.

Affleck, G., Tennen, H., Pfeiffer, C., Fifield, J., & Rowe, J. (1987). Downward comparison and coping with serious medical problems. *American Journal of Orthopsychiatry, 57*, 570–578.

Alicke, M. D. (1985). Global self-evaluation as determined by the desirability and controllability of trait adjectives. *Journal of Personality and Social Psychology, 49*, 1621–1630.

Amoroso, D. M., & Walters, R. H. (1969). Effects of anxiety and socially mediated anxiety reduction on paired-associate learning. *Journal of Personality and Social Psychology, 11*, 338–396.

Bell, P. A. (1978). Affective state, attraction, and affiliation. *Personality and Social Psychology Bulletin, 4*, 616–619.

Bennett, D. H., & Holmes, D. S. (1975). Influence of denial and projection on anxiety associated with threat to self-esteem. *Journal of Personality and Social Psychology, 32*, 915–921.

Berkowitz, L. (1972). Social norms, feelings, and other factors affecting helping and altruism. In L. Berkowitz (Ed.), *Advances in experimental social psychology* (Vol. 6, pp. 63–108). New York: Academic Press.

Berkowitz, L., & Knurek, D. A. (1969). Label-mediated hostility generalization. *Journal of Personality and Social Psychology, 13*, 200–206.

Berkowitz, L., & Walster, E. (Eds.). (1976). *Equity theory: Toward a general theory of social interaction*. New York: Academic Press.

Blalock, S., DeVellis, B., & DeVellis, R. (in press). Social comparison among individuals with rheumatoid arthritis. *Journal of Applied Social Psychology*.

Brickman, P. (1975). Adaptation level determinants of satisfaction with equal and unequal outcome distributions in skill and chance situations. *Journal of Personality and Social Psychology, 32*, 191–198.

Brickman, P., & Berman, J. J. (1971). Effects of performance expectancy and outcome certainty on interest in social comparison. *Journal of Experimental Social Psychology, 7*, 600–609.

Brickman, P., & Bulman, R. J. (1977). Pleasure and pain in social comparison. In J. M. Suls & R. M. Miller (Eds.), *Social comparison processes: Theoretical and empirical perspectives* (pp. 149–186). Washington, DC: Hemisphere.

Brickman, P., & Campbell, D. T. (1971). Hedonic relativism and planning the good society. In M. H. Appley (Ed.), *Adaptation-level theory: A symposium* (pp. 287–304). New York: Academic Press.

Buck, R. W., & Parke, R. D. (1972). Behavioral and physiological response to the presence of a friendly or neutral person in two types of stressful situations. *Journal of Personality and Social Psychology, 24*, 143–153.

Burish, T. G., & Houston, B. K. (1979). Causal projection, similarity projection, and coping with threat to self-esteem. *Journal of Personality and Social Psychology, 47*, 57–70.

Campbell, J. D. (1986). Similarity and uniqueness: Effects of attribute type, relevance, and self-esteem. *Journal of Personality and Social Psychology, 50*, 281–294.

Cook, T. D., Crosby, F., & Hennigan, K. M. (1977). The construct validity of relative deprivation. In J. M. Suls & R. M. Miller (Eds.),

Social comparison processes: Theoretical and empirical perspectives (pp. 307–333). Washington, DC: Hemisphere.

Crosby, F. (1976). A model of egoistical relative deprivation. *Psychological Review, 83*, 85–113.

Darley, J. M., & Aronson, E. (1966). Self-evaluation vs. direct anxiety reduction as determinants of the fear-affiliation relationship. *Journal of Experimental Social Psychology, 2*(Suppl. 1), 66–79.

Davis, J. A. (1959). A formal interpretation of the theory of relative deprivation. *Sociometry, 22*, 280–296.

DeVellis, R., Holt, K., Renner, B., Blalock, S., Blanchard, L., Cook, H., Klotz, M., Mikow, V., & Harring, K. (in press). The relationship of social comparison to rheumatoid arthritis symptoms and affect. *Basic and Applied Social Psychology*.

Diener, E. (1984). Subjective well-being. *Psychological Bulletin, 95*, 542–575.

Emmons, R. A., & Diener, E. (1985). Factors predicting satisfaction judgments. *Social Indicators Research, 16*, 157–167.

Feldman, N. S., & Ruble, D. N. (1981). Social comparison strategies: Dimensions offered and options taken. *Personality and Social Psychology Bulletin, 7*, 11–16.

Feshbach, S., & Singer, R. (1957). The effects of personal and shared threats upon social prejudice. *Journal of Abnormal and Social Psychology, 54*, 411–416.

Festinger, L. (1950). Informal social communication. *Psychological Review, 57*, 271–282.

Festinger, L. (1954). A theory of social comparison processes. *Human Relations, 7*, 117–140.

Festinger, L., Schachter, S., & Back, K. (1950). *Social pressures in informal groups*. New York: Harper & Row.

Frey, D., & Stahlberg, D. (1986). Selection of information after receiving more or less reliable self-threatening information. *Personality and Social Psychology Bulletin, 12*, 434–441.

Friend, R. M., & Gilbert, J. (1973). Threat and fear of negative evaluation as determinants of locus of social comparison. *Journal of Personality, 41*, 328–340.

Gastorf, J. W., & Suls, J. (1978). Performance evaluation via social comparison: Performance similarity vs. related-attributes similarity. *Social Psychology, 41*, 297–305.

Gerard, H. B., & Orive, R. (1987). The dynamics of opinion formation: An informational social comparison model. In L. Berkowitz (Ed.), *Advances in experimental social psychology* (Vol. 20, pp. 171–202). San Diego: Academic Press.

Gerrard, M., Gibbons, F. X., & Sharp, J. (1985, August). Social comparison in a self-help group for bulimics. Paper presented at the meeting of the American Psychological Association, Los Angeles.

Gibbons, F. X. (1985a). A social-psychological perspective on developmental disabilities. *Journal of Social and Clinical Psychology, 3*, 391–404.

Gibbons, F. X. (1985b). Social comparison among mentally retarded persons. *American Journal of Mental Deficiency, 90*, 98–106.

Gibbons, F. X. (1986). Social comparison and depression: Company's effect on misery. *Journal of Personality and Social Psychology, 51*, 140–148.

Gibbons, F. X., & Gerrard, M. (1989). Effects of upward and downward social comparison on mood states. *Journal of Social and Clinical Psychology, 8*, 14–31.

Gibbons, F. X., & Gerrard, M. (in press). Downward comparison in special populations. In J. Suls & T. A. Wills (Eds.), *Social comparison: Contemporary theory and research*. Hillsdale, NJ: Lawrence Erlbaum Associates.

Gibbons, F. X., Gerrard, M., Lando, H. A., & McGovern, P. G. (1989). Social comparison and smoking cessation. Unpublished manuscript, Iowa State University.

Goethals, G. R., Arrowood, A. J., Wills, T. A., Suls, J., & Wheeler, L. (1986). Social comparison theory: Lost and found. *Personality and Social Psychology Bulletin, 12*, 261–299.

Goethals, G. R., & Darley, J. (1977). Social comparison theory: An attributional approach. In J. M. Suls & R. M. Miller (Eds.), *Social comparison processes: Theoretical and empirical perspectives* (pp. 259–278). Washington, DC: Hemisphere.

Goethals, G. R., Messick, D. M., & Allison, S. T. (in press). The uniqueness bias: Studies of constructive social comparison. In J. Suls & T. A. Wills (Eds.), *Social comparison: Contemporary theory and research*. Hillsdale, NJ: Lawrence Erlbaum Associates.

Gruder, C. L. (1971). Determinants of social comparison choices. *Journal of Experimental Social Psychology, 7*, 473–489.

Hakmiller, K. L. (1966). Threat as a determinant of downward comparison. *Journal of Experimental Social Psychology, 2(Suppl. 1), 32–39.

Harter, S. (1983). Processes underlying the construction, maintenance, and enhancement of the self-concept in children. In J. Suls & A. G. Greenwald (Eds.), Psychological perspectives on the self (Vol. 3, pp. 137–181). Hillsdale, NJ: Lawrence Erlbaum Associates.

Harter, S. (1985). The need for a developmental perspective in understanding child disorders. Journal of Social and Clinical Psychology, 3, 484–499.

Heath, L. (1984). Impact of newspaper crime reports on fear of crime: Multimethodological investigation. Journal of Personality and Social Psychology, 47, 263–276.

Jones, S. C. (1973). Self and interpersonal evaluations: Esteem theory versus consistency theory. Psychological Bulletin, 79, 185–199.

Kenrick, D. T., & Johnson, G. A. (1979). Interpersonal attraction in aversive environments. Journal of Personality and Social Psychology, 37, 572–579.

Kiesler, S. B. (1966). Stress, affiliation and performance. Journal of Experimental Research in Personality, 1, 227–235.

Kuiper, N. A., & Olinger, L. J. (1986). Dysfunctional attitudes and a self-worth contingency model of depression. In P. C. Kendall (Ed.), Advances in cognitive-behavioral research and therapy (Vol. 5, pp. 115–142). New York: Academic Press.

Latané, B. (1966). Studies in social comparison: Introduction and overview. Journal of Experimental Social Psychology, 2(Suppl. 1), 1–5.

Levine, J. M., & Green, S. M. (1984). Acquisition of relative performance information: The roles of intrapersonal and interpersonal comparison. Personality and Social Psychology Bulletin, 10, 385–393.

Marks, G. (1984). Thinking one's abilities are unique and one's opinions are common. Personality and Social Psychology Bulletin, 10, 203–208.

Marsh, H. W., & Parker, J. W. (1984). Determinants of student self-concept. Journal of Personality and Social Psychology, 47, 213–231.

Miller, C. T. (1982). The role of performance-related similarity in social comparison of abilities: A test of the related-attributes hypothesis. Journal of Experimental Social Psychology, 18, 513–523.

Moos, R. H. (Ed.). (1986). Coping with physical illness (Vol. 2). New York: Plenum Press.

Moos, R. H., & Billings, A. G. (1982). Conceptualizing and measuring coping resources and processes. In L. Goldberger & S. Bresnitz (Eds.), Handbook of stress (pp. 212–230). New York: Macmillan.

Nosanchuk, T. A., & Erickson, B. H. (1985). How high is up: Calibrating social comparison. Journal of Personality and Social Psychology, 48, 624–634.

Perri, M. G. (1985). Self-change strategies for the control of smoking, obesity, and problem drinking. In S. Shiffman & T. A. Wills (Eds.), Coping and substance use (pp. 295–317). Orlando, FL: Academic Press.

Pettigrew, T. F. (1967). Social evaluation theory: Convergences and applications. In D. Levine (Ed.), Nebraska Symposium on Motivation (Vol. 15, pp. 241–315). Lincoln, NE: University of Nebraska Press.

Pyszczynski, T., & Greenberg, J. (1987). Self-regulatory perseveration and the depressive self-focusing style: A self-awareness theory of reactive depression. Psychological Bulletin, 102, 122–138.

Pyszczynski, T., Greenberg, J., & LaPrelle, J. (1985). Social comparison after success and failure: Biased search for information consistent with a self-serving conclusion. Journal of Experimental Social Psychology, 21, 195–211.

Radloff, R. (1966). Social comparison and ability evaluation. Journal of Experimental Social Psychology, 2(Suppl. 1), 6–26.

Rotton, J., Barry, T., Frey, J., & Soler, E. (1978). Air pollution and interpersonal attraction. Journal of Applied Social Psychology, 8, 57–71.

Ruble, D. N., Boggiano, A. K., Feldman, N. S., & Loebl, J. H. (1980). Developmental analysis of the role of social comparison in self-evaluation. Developmental Psychology, 16, 105–115.

Salovey, P. (in press). Social comparison processes in envy and jealousy. In J. Suls & T. A. Wills (Eds.), Social comparison: Contemporary theory and research. Hillsdale, NJ: Lawrence Erlbaum Associates.

Salovey, P., & Rodin, J. (1984). Some antecedents and consequences of social-comparison jealousy. Journal of Personality and Social Psychology, 47, 780–792.

Schachter, S. (1959). The psychology of affiliation. Palo Alto, CA: Stanford University Press.

Schulz, R., & Decker, S. (1985). Long-term adjustment to physical disability. Journal of Personality and Social Psychology, 48, 1162–1172.

Sherman, S. J., Presson, C. C., & Chassin, L. (1984). Mechanisms underlying the false consensus effect: The special role of threats to the self. *Personality and Social Psychology Bulletin, 10*, 127–138.

Sherman, S. J., Presson, C. C., Chassin, L., & Agostinelli, G. (1984). The role of evaluation and similarity principles in the false consensus effect. *Journal of Personality and Social Psychology, 47*, 1244–1262.

Shiffman, S. (1985). Coping with temptations to smoke. In S. Shiffman & T. A. Wills (Eds.), *Coping and substance use* (pp. 223–242). Orlando, FL: Academic Press.

Shrauger, J. S. (1975). Responses to evaluation as a function of initial self-perceptions. *Psychological Bulletin, 82*, 581–596.

Silon, E. L., & Harter, S. (1985). Assessment of perceived competence and motivational orientation in segregated and mainstreamed mentally retarded children. *Journal of Educational Psychology, 77*, 217–230.

Smith, R. H., & Insko, C. A. (1987). Social comparison choice during ability evaluation: The effects of comparison publicity, performance feedback, and self-esteem. *Personality and Social Psychology Bulletin, 13*, 111–122.

Snyder, C. R., & Higgins, R. L. (1988). Excuses: Their effective role in the negotiation of reality. *Psychological Bulletin, 104*, 23–35.

Strang, L. Smith, M. D., & Rogers, C. M. (1978). Social comparison, multiple reference points, and self-concepts of academically handicapped children before and after mainstreaming. *Journal of Educational Psychology, 70*, 487–497.

Strube, M. J., & Roemmele, L. A. (1985). Self-enhancement, self-assessment, and self-evaluative task choice. *Journal of Personality and Social Psychology, 49*, 981–993.

Suls, J., Gaes, G., & Gastorf, J. (1979). Evaluating a sex-related ability: Comparison with same-, opposite-, and combined-sex norms. *Journal of Research in Personality, 13*, 294–304.

Suls, J., Gastorf, J., & Lawhon, J. (1978). Social comparison choices for evaluating a sex- and age-related ability. *Personality and Social Psychology Bulletin, 4*, 102–105.

Suls, J. M., & Miller, R. L. (1977). *Social comparison processes: Theoretical and empirical perspectives*. Washington, DC: Hemisphere.

Suls, J., & Wan, C. K. (1987). In search of the false-uniqueness phenomenon: Fear and estimates of social consensus. *Journal of Personality and Social Psychology, 52*, 211–217.

Suls, J. M., & Wills, T. A. (in press). *Social comparison theory: Contemporary theory and research*. Hillsdale, NJ: Lawrence Erlbaum Associates.

Swallow, S. R., & Kuiper, N. A. (1987). The effects of depression and cognitive vulnerability to depression on similarity judgments between self and other. *Motivation and Emotion, 11*, 157–167.

Swallow, S. R., & Kuiper, N. A. (1988). Social comparison and negative self-evaluations: An application to depression. *Clinical Psychology Review, 8*, 55–76.

Swann, W. B., Jr., Griffin, J. J., Jr., Predmore, S. C., & Gaines, B. (1987). The cognitive-affective crossfire: When self-consistency confronts self-enhancement. *Journal of Personality and Social Psychology, 52*, 881–889.

Tabachnik, N., Crocker, J., & Alloy, L. B. (1983). Depression, social comparison, and the false consensus effect. *Journal of Personality and Social Psychology, 45*, 688–699.

Tennen, H., Affleck, G., & Gershman, K. (1986). Self-blame among parents of infants with perinatal complications: The role of self-protective motives. *Journal of Personality and Social Psychology, 50*, 690–696.

Tennen, H., & Herzberger, S. (1987). Depression, self-esteem, and the absence of self-protective attributional biases. *Journal of Personality and Social Psychology, 52*, 72–80.

Tesser, A. (1980). Self-esteem maintenance in family dynamics. *Journal of Personality and Social Psychology, 39*, 77–91.

Tesser, A. (1986). Some effects of self-evaluation maintenance on cognition and action. In R. M. Sorrentino & E. T. Higgins (Eds.), *Handbook of motivation and cognition: Foundations of social behavior* (pp. 435–464). Chichester, England: John Wiley & Sons.

Tesser, A. (1988). Toward a self-evaluation maintenance model of social behavior. In L. Berkowitz (Ed.), *Advances in experimental social psychology* (Vol. 21, pp. 181–227). New York: Academic Press.

Tesser, A., & Campbell, J. (1980). Self-definition: The impact of the relative performance and similarity of others. *Social Psychology Quarterly, 43*, 341–347.

Tesser, A., Campbell, J., & Smith, M. (1984).

Friendship choice and performance: Self-evaluation maintenance in children. *Journal of Personality and Social Psychology, 46*, 561–574.

Thornton, D., & Arrowood, A. J. (1966). Self-evaluation, self-enhancement and the locus of social comparison. *Journal of Experimental Social Psychology, 2*(Suppl. 1), 40–48.

Trope, Y. (1979). Uncertainty-reducing properties of achievement tasks. *Journal of Personality and Social Psychology, 37*, 1505–1518.

Trope, Y. (1980). Self-assessment, self-enhancement, and task preference. *Journal of Experimental Social Psychology, 16*, 116–129.

Warren, L. W., & McEachren, L. (1983). Psychological correlates of depressive symptomatology in adult women. *Journal of Abnormal Psychology, 92*, 151–160.

Weary, G., Elbin, S., & Hill, M. G. (1987). Attributional and social comparison processes in depression. *Journal of Personality and Social Psychology, 52*, 605–610.

Wheeler, L. (1966). Motivation as a determinant of upward comparison. *Journal of Experimental Social Psychology, 2*(Suppl. 1), 27–31.

Wheeler, L., Koestner, R., & Driver, R. E. (1982). Related attributes in the choice of comparison others: It may be there, but it isn't all there is. *Journal of Experimental Social Psychology, 18*, 489–500.

Wheeler, L., Shaver, K. G., Jones, R. A., Goethals, G. R., Cooper, J., Robinson, J. E., Gruder, C. L., & Butzine, K. W. (1969). Factors determining the choice of comparison others. *Journal of Experimental Social Psychology, 5*, 219–232.

Wills, T. A. (1981). Downward comparison principles in social psychology. *Psychological Bulletin, 90*, 245–271.

Wills, T. A. (1983). Social comparison in coping and help-seeking. In B. M. DePaulo, A. Nadler, & J. D. Fisher (Eds.), *New directions in helping: Vol. 2. Help-seeking* (pp. 109–141). New York: Academic Press.

Wills, T. A. (1987). Downward comparison as a coping mechanism. In C. R. Snyder & C. Ford (Eds.), *Coping with negative life events: Clinical and social-psychological perspectives* (pp. 243–268). New York: Plenum Press.

Wills, T. A. (in press). Similarity and self-esteem in downward comparison. In J. Suls & T. A. Wills (Eds.), *Social comparison: Contemporary theory and research*. Hillsdale, NJ: Lawrence Erlbaum Associates.

Wills, T. A., & Shiffman, S. (1985). Coping and substance use: A conceptual framework. In S. Shiffman & T. A. Wills (Eds.), *Coping and substance use* (pp. 3–24). Orlando, FL: Academic Press.

Wilson, S. R., & Benner, L. A. (1971). The effects of self-esteem and situation on comparison choices during ability evaluation. *Sociometry, 34*, 381–397.

Wood, J. V. (1989). Theory and research concerning social comparisons of personal attributes. *Psychological Bulletin, 106*, 231–248.

Wood, J. V., Taylor, S. E., & Lichtman, R. R. (1985). Social comparison in adjustment to breast cancer. *Journal of Personality and Social Psychology, 49*, 1169–1183.

Wrightsman, L. S., Jr. (1960). Effects of waiting with others on changes in level of felt anxiety. *Journal of Abnormal and Social Psychology, 61*, 216–222.

Zanna, M. P., Goethals, G., & Hill, J. (1975). Evaluating a sex-related ability: Social comparison with similar others and standard setters. *Journal of Experimental Social Psychology, 11*, 86–93.

Zimbardo, P. G., & Formica, R. (1963). Emotional comparison and self-esteem as determinants of affiliation. *Journal of Personality, 31*, 141–162.

CHAPTER 20

ADJUSTMENT AND COPING IMPLICATIONS OF LONELINESS

Warren H. Jones
Margaret D. Carver

A considerable amount of recent research converges on the conclusion that close personal relationships as well as less intimate social involvements are essential to psychological adjustment and well-being. In a sense, psychologists have simply documented something many people take for granted; specifically, that interpersonal commitments are more than commonplace in human experience, they are essential to life, growth, and happiness. In this context, an understanding of people who are socially isolated or whose relationships are in disarray assumes particular significance. Although there have been many conceptual approaches to interpersonal disruption and isolation, one concept that affords a unique perspective from which to study the role of relationships in health and well-being is the concept of loneliness.

We begin with a detailed review of the literature on loneliness, including issues of conceptualization and measurement. Next, in order to explore its determinants and consequences, we examine the individual differences and the demographic,

developmental, interpersonal, and social correlates of loneliness. In addition, we examine the evidence concerning the association between loneliness and indices of psychological as well as medical complaints, and the patterns of coping that appear to emanate from feelings of loneliness. Also, we discuss the research on helping people who are lonely. Finally, we summarize all the literature with particular emphases on its self-defeating nature and other issues at the nexus of social and clinical psychology.

BASIC ISSUES

Definition and Conceptualization

Several definitions of loneliness have been suggested. For example, Sermat (1978) described loneliness as the experience associated with a discrepancy between the kinds of relationships one perceives that one has versus one's ideal. Peplau and Perlman (1982) defined loneliness as the unpleasant experience that derives from important

deficiencies (both qualitative or quantitative) in
one's network of social relations. Sullivan (1953)
conceived of loneliness as both unpleasant and
motivating and as arising from an unmet need for
interpersonal intimacy. By contrast, Moustakas
(1961) conceptualized loneliness as an experience
that inevitably arises from the "separateness" of
human existence.

Despite such divergence, various definitions of
loneliness typically share three points of emphasis
(Peplau & Perlman, 1982). First, virtually all definitions imply that loneliness results from deficiencies in the lonely person's social relationships.
Second, loneliness is seen as a subjective psychological phenomenon and is therefore not synonymous with solitude or aloneness. It is assumed
that virtually everyone has at least minimal social
contact. Therefore, loneliness is typically seen as
representing dissatisfaction with the number or
quality of contacts one does have rather than the
total absence of social contact. Third, loneliness is
most often conceptualized as distressing and
motivating. Even those theorists who posit a "creative potential" for loneliness (e.g., Moustakas,
1961) draw distinctions between such states and
other forms of loneliness that are seen as debilitating.

Peplau and Perlman (1982) further argued that
what distinguishes various models and definitions
of loneliness is the nature of the interpersonal deficiencies that are assumed to give rise to it. For
example, several of the earlier writers on the subject suggested that people have inherent and lifelong needs for intimacy and that loneliness results
from the failure to satisfy those needs (e.g., Sullivan, 1953; Weiss, 1973). By contrast, cognitive
approaches to loneliness assume individual differences in the need for intimacy and social contact,
suggesting that loneliness occurs when intimacy
and social contact are suboptimal (e.g., Lopata,
1969; Peplau & Perlman, 1982; Sermat, 1978).
Furthermore, Peplau and Perlman (1982) characterized loneliness as an end-point on a continuum
that includes suboptimal intimacy (i.e., loneliness) at one pole and feelings of privacy invasion
at the other. Unfortunately, empirical research on
loneliness has proceeded more or less independently of theorizing about it. Thus, with few exceptions, research agendas have not been guided
by theoretical expectations and theories generally
have not been informed by subsequent results
(Jones, 1987; Weiss, 1987).

Measurement

Similarly, a wide variety of instruments and
strategies have been used to measure loneliness.
These have included Q-sort statements (Eddy,
1961), rating scales (e.g., Rubenstein & Shaver,
1982; Russell, Peplau, & Cutrona, 1980; Russell,
Peplau, & Ferguson, 1978), single-item self-label-
ing measures (Berg, Mellstrom, Persson, & Svanborg, 1981; Dean, 1962), protective techniques
(Krulik, 1978) and interviews (e.g., Lowenthal,
Thurner, & Chiribuga, 1975). A loneliness scale
for children is available (Asher & Wheeler, 1985).
Although most scales yield a single, global index
of loneliness, multidimensional scales also have
been devised (cf. Belcher, 1973; deJong-Gierveld,
1987; Scalise, Ginter, & Gerstein, 1984; Schmidt
& Sermat, 1983; Young, 1982).

On the other hand, the UCLA Loneliness Scale
(Russell, 1982; Russell et al., 1980; Russell et al.,
1978) has been used much more frequently than
any other measure, particularly in recent research.
The UCLA scale contains 20 items assessing theoretically relevant experiences (e.g., dissatisfaction
with one's relationships, feelings of being left out,
etc.), but does not refer directly to loneliness. Research has strongly supported the utility of the
UCLA scale as a measure of loneliness. For example, estimates of coefficient alpha have typically
exceeded .90 and test-retest reliability has been
found to be approximately .75 for two months
and .60 for six months (Cutrona, 1982; Russell,
1982; Russell et al., 1978; Sarason, Sarason,
Hacker, & Basham, 1985).

The validity of the UCLA scale has been established in a variety of ways. For example, UCLA
scale scores have been found to predict self-selection into a loneliness treatment clinic, number of
close friends, social support, amount of social
contact, frequency of social activity, and social
satisfaction. Scores from the UCLA scale also
correlate in predicted directions with a variety of
affective, personality, and self-reported behavioral variables (e.g., shyness, depression, anxiety,
risk-taking, etc.), suggesting the construct validity
of the scale (Jones, Freemon, & Goswick, 1981;
Russell et al., 1980; Russell et al., 1978). Furthermore, the discriminant validity of the scale has
been demonstrated. In one study, for example,
UCLA scores were more strongly related to a self-
labeling measure of loneliness than to measures of
related constructs such as extraversion, social risk-

taking, and affiliative tendency (Russell et al., 1980). The divergence of loneliness and other similar constructs such as social support has been demonstrated also (Russell, Kao, & Cutrona, 1987). Finally, evidence generally supports the psychometric adequacy of alternative measures of loneliness as well, although far less information is available on these scales as compared with the UCLA scale (e.g., Schmidt & Sermat, 1983).

THE PSYCHOLOGY OF LONELINESS

Much of what is known about loneliness concerns the psychological factors and processes with which it is reliably associated, including, for example, its developmental, self-concept, personality, cognitive, and emotional correlates. To some extent, such analyses suggest hypotheses regarding potential causes of loneliness, its development over the life-course, and the personal characteristics that may make some people more vulnerable to its occurrence. To a greater extent, these data shed light on the phenomenology of loneliness; that is, the emotions, thoughts, and beliefs experienced by people who are lonely.

Biographic Factors in Loneliness

Demographic Correlates

As is the case with most unpleasant psychological conditions, loneliness is associated with single marital status, and inversely related to income, socioeconomic status, and education (Bahr & Harvey, 1979; Baum, 1982; Hanley-Dunn, Maxwell, & Santos, 1985; Wenz, 1977). Also, several studies have reported inverse correlations between loneliness and age (Schmidt & Sermat, 1983). Other studies have found significantly greater loneliness among blacks and other minority ethnic groups (e.g., Cutrona, 1982) and among the unemployed (Hansson, 1986; Siassi, Crocetti, & Spiro, 1974).

However, some assessment of the demographic correlates of loneliness have resulted in nonsignificant findings. With respect to many demographic variables, the lack of significant findings is undoubtedly often due to inadequate sampling (i.e., groups that are too small and/or homogenous on the demographic variable in question). In addition, the relationship between loneliness and some variables may be nonlinear. For example, available evidence suggests that loneliness decreases with age from adolescence or early adulthood up to approximately the age of 80, after which there may be a sharp increase (e.g., Dean, 1962).

Two additional explanations for the inconsistencies in demographic correlates of loneliness may be relevant. First, several studies have indicated that it is satisfaction with one's life that predicts loneliness rather than demographic standing per se. For example, satisfaction with income (Hornung, 1981) and housing (Woodward, Gingles, & Woodward, 1974) were found to be significantly related to loneliness whereas objective indexes of these variables were not. Second, there is evidence that demographic variables are better predictors of objective social isolation than the subjective state of loneliness. For example, Munnichs (1964) compared loneliness and social isolation with several types of variables, including personal opinions and demographic, social, and personal characteristics, finding that whereas social isolation was related to some demographic and social variables, loneliness was exclusively related to personal characteristics, in particular being dissatisfied with life. Thus, it seems reasonable to conclude that broad demographic characteristics are related to loneliness, but that their contribution to its development is either modest or mediated by other psychological processes.

Gender Differences

Comparisons between gender and loneliness also have produced inconsistent findings with some studies finding women and girls more lonely (Kivett, 1979; Wenz, 1977), others finding men and boys more lonely (Avery, 1982; Berg et al., 1981; Franzoi & Davis, 1985; Schmitt & Kurdek, 1985), and yet other studies yielding nonsignificant gender differences (Russell et al., 1980). Borys and Perlman (1985) have presented evidence suggesting that these inconsistencies can be explained as a function of the type of measure used to assess loneliness. First, they conducted a meta-analysis of the literature on gender differences in which either the UCLA scale (which does not contain the words lonely or loneliness) or a single-item measure was used. For the UCLA scale, only 4 of 28 studies (14.3%) showed a statistically significant gender effect and, in all four cases, male respondents yielded significantly higher loneliness scores. By contrast, in 9 of 11 (81.9%) single-item surveys (for which the measure of loneliness was a sentence containing the words lonely or loneliness), women were found to have significantly higher scores. Subsequently, in ratings of lonely male and female hypothetical stimulus people, Borys and Perlman (1985) found that lonely men were evaluated significantly more negatively than lonely women by both male and female raters. Thus, these investigators concluded that women are more likely to directly acknowledge their loneliness because the negative social consequences for doing so are less severe.

Developmental Factors in Loneliness

Age of Onset

Sullivan (1953) argued that loneliness cannot occur until preadolescence, at which time individuals seek validation of self-worth through relationships external to the family, in particular peer relationships. More contemporary writers have suggested that loneliness may occur much earlier (e.g., Rubin, 1982), perhaps as early as infancy (Ellison, 1978). Available empirical evidence does indicate that loneliness may be reliably measured among peer-rejected children as young as seven and eight years of age (Asher, Hymel, & Renshaw, 1984; Asher & Wheeler, 1985).

Age Differences

As indicated earlier, loneliness appears to be most common among adolescents and young adults, declining thereafter except perhaps for people over the age of 80 (e.g., Dean, 1962; Lobdell & Perlman, 1986; Perlman, Gerson, & Spinner, 1978; Perlman, Locke, & Bond, 1985; Revenson & Johnson, 1984; Rubenstein & Shaver, 1982; Schmitt & Kurdek, 1985; Schultz & Moore, 1984). In addition, the psychological correlates of loneliness have been compared among various age cohorts in an effort to determine if loneliness is related to different factors at differing ages. Perlman (1988) has summarized this literature by noting three typical findings. First, certain personality and affective variables such as self-esteem, depression, social anxiety, and so forth tend to be associated with loneliness at all age levels. Second, loneliness is related to judgments of deficient social relationships regardless of age. Third, indexes of the quality of respondents' relationships are better predictors of loneliness than are

quantitative indicators at all ages. By contrast, what varies with age is the interpersonal domain that is most strongly related to loneliness. For example, the status of one's peer relations as compared with family ties is more strongly related to loneliness among college-age adults, whereas the opposite is true of preadolescents (Perlman et al., 1985). Family relationships and, in particular, marital quality predicts loneliness among middle-aged adults better than relationships with friends and neighbors, whereas contact and satisfaction with friends and neighbors appear to be more important for loneliness among the elderly than is contact with family such as one's adult children (Arling, 1976; Perlman et al., 1978; Perlman et al., 1985).

Parent-Child Relationships

Another area of investigation that has received attention concerns the potential influence of early experience (especially the type and quality of parent-child contact) on subsequent loneliness. For example, loneliness has been related to parental divorce at an early age for respondents (Shaver & Rubenstein, 1980). Also, several studies have shown that current loneliness is related to retrospective accounts of one's parents as being cold, distant, nonnurturing, remote, punishing, absent, and lacking in warmth, guidance, emotional support, and encouragement (Bergenstal, 1981; Hojat, 1982; Paloutzian & Ellison, 1982). Furthermore, there is evidence for the cross-generational transmission of loneliness, that is, parents' loneliness scores are significantly correlated with the loneliness scores of their adult children (Lobdell & Perlman, 1986), lending further credence to the notion that problems in parent-child relationships contribute to the subsequent development of loneliness among offspring.

Personality and Individual Differences

Self-Concept and Self-Esteem

Numerous studies have compared measures of loneliness with self-reported indices of individual differences, that is, self-concept, personality (especially social skill), emotions, and beliefs. For example, loneliness has been inversely related to measures of self-esteem in several studies (e.g., Jones et al., 1981; Russell et al., 1980), particularly social aspects of self-esteem (Goswick & Jones, 1981). In one study, loneliness was inversely related to certainty with regard to one's self-view (Loucks, 1980). Further evidence suggests that the convergence between measures of loneliness and self-regard is extensive and fundamental. For example, loneliness and self-esteem clustered together in a factor analysis of adjustment-related variables (Remondet, Hansson, Rule, & Winfrey, 1987) and the relationship between loneliness and self-esteem remains significant even when the statistical contributions of personality and social network variables are partialled out (e.g., Carpenter, Hansson, Rountree, & Jones, 1984). Also, loneliness is directly related to composite scores derived from factor analyses of self-descriptions, including, for example, factors labeled as self-deprecation (Rubenstein & Shaver, 1982) and inferiority feelings (Goswick & Jones, 1982).

Personality and Social Skill

Similarly, there is considerable evidence that loneliness is related to various dimensions of personality, particularly those involving social skill and confidence. For example, loneliness is strongly related to measures of shyness and social anxiety (Jones & Carpenter, 1986; Moore & Schultz, 1983) and inversely with extraversion and sociability (Hojat, 1982; Stokes, 1985). Lonely college students report having difficulty making friends naturally and with ease (Horowitz & French, 1979). Also, loneliness is inversely related to the various skills involved in dating, conflict resolution, and social initiation (Wittenberg & Reis, 1986), as well as attachment quality (Hecht & Baum, 1984), likeability (Moore & Schultz, 1983; Schultz & Moore, 1984), communication competence (Bell, 1985; Spitzberg & Canary, 1985), empathy (Franzoi & Davis, 1985), interpersonal competence (Sarason et al., 1985), social risk-taking (Moore & Schultz, 1983; Schultz & Moore, 1984), and assertiveness (Carpenter et al., 1984; Russell et al., 1980; Wittenberg & Reis, 1986), and directly related to attachment threat, (Hecht & Baum, 1984), avoidance of others (Jones, Cavert, Snider, & Bruce, 1985b), communication apprehension (Bell, 1985; Zakahi & Duran, 1982), and sensitivity to rejection (Jones et al., 1985b; Russell et al., 1980). Loneliness has been consistently related to measures of both masculinity and femininity among both male and female respondents (Avery, 1982; Berg & Peplau, 1982; Jones, Carpenter, & Quintana, 1985a; Wittenberg & Reis, 1986). Thus, in sex role terminology, loneliness is inversely related to androgyny.

Additional personality constructs have been related to loneliness as well, typically with less consistent results, however. For example, contrary to expectation, public and private self-consciousness, defined as attention to the internal aspects of experience and awareness of oneself as a social object, respectively, were unrelated to loneliness in one study (Schultz & Moore, 1984). On the other hand, a longitudinal investigation of adolescents suggested that private self-consciousness may mediate the relationship between loneliness and self-disclosure. Franzoi and Davis (1985; Davis & Franzoi, 1986) used structural equation techniques to examine the causal relationships among loneliness, self-disclosure to peers and parents, and antecedent variables. They found that adolescents high in private self-consciousness were more willing to self-disclose to peers, resulting in reduced feelings of loneliness.

An even more complex pattern of results has emerged with respect to the relationship between loneliness and self-disclosure. Some researchers have reported significant inverse correlations (Wittenberg & Reis, 1986) and some have reported nonsignificant findings (Jones et al., 1981), whereas other researchers have found significant inverse correlations for women but not men (Berg & Peplau, 1982) for one cultural group, but not for another (Jones et al., 1985a), or for some targets of disclosure (e.g., peers, mother, father, strangers, etc.) but not others (Berg & Peplau, 1982; Franzoi & Davis, 1985; Solano, Batten, & Parish, 1982). One study even indicated a positive relationship between loneliness and self-disclosures among elderly respondents for high-intimacy topics only (Perlman et al., 1978).

Emotions and Feelings

Loneliness has also been extensively related to various emotional states and traits. In particular, loneliness appears to be strongly associated with the experience of depression, anxiety, and interpersonal hostility (e.g., Hansson, Jones, Carpenter, & Remondet, 1986; Jones et al., 1985a; Moore & Schultz, 1983; Perlman et al., 1978; Russell et al., 1978; Russell et al., 1980; Schultz & Moore, 1984). Furthermore, research has yielded direct correlations with such variables as tension, fatigue, confusion (Loucks, 1980), boredom, restlessness (Perlman et al., 1978; Rubenstein & Shaver, 1982; Russell et al., 1978), and emptiness (Perlman et al., 1978), and inverse correlations with vigor or energy, and morale (Hansson et al., 1986; Loucks, 1980; Perlman et al., 1978). Check, Perlman, and Malamuth (1985) reported positive correlations between loneliness and hostility among male college students. Also, studies have supported the expectation of an association between loneliness and emotional arousal in general as reflected in emotionality scales and the composite score on the Profile of Mood States (Loucks, 1980).

Beliefs and Attributions

Loneliness also appears to be related to one's opinions about people, life, and society in a manner suggesting that lonely people subscribe to negativistic, cynical, and pessimistic views of relationships, specific other people, and people in general. Measures of loneliness have been inversely correlated with acceptance of others, beliefs in the trustworthiness, altruism, and favorability of human nature, and positive family and friendship attitudes (Jones et al., 1981; Jones et al., 1985a; Wittenberg & Reis, 1986). Similarly, loneliness has been found to be directly related to several dimensions of alienation including powerlessness, normlessness, and perceived social isolation (Jones et al., 1981; Jones et al., 1985a). Also, Check et al. (1985) found positive correlations between loneliness among male college students and anger toward women, acceptance of violence toward women, and subscription to adversarial sex beliefs.

Furthermore, there is an inverse relationship between loneliness and the tendency to find satisfaction and meaning in life. For example, loneliness consistently correlates inversely with measures of happiness, life satisfaction (Moore & Schultz, 1983; Perlman et al., 1978; Russell et al., 1978; Sadava & Matejcic, 1987; Schultz & Moore, 1984), purpose in life (Baum, 1982; Jones et al., 1985a), spiritual well-being, and religiosity (Ellison & Paloutzian, 1979; Paloutzian & Ellison, 1982).

Hansson et al. (1986) reported that among a group of elderly respondents, loneliness was inversely related to beliefs about the safety of one's environment and predictability regarding what is likely to happen. Not surprisingly, then, loneliness has been found by several investigators to be positively correlated with externality, external locus of control, and the components of externality such as lack of choice and powerful others (Baum, 1982; Hansson et al., 1986; Jones et al., 1981;

Jones et al., 1985a; Hojat, 1982; Schultz & Moore, 1984; Moore & Schultz, 1983).

Another consistently replicated pattern of findings concerns the role of causal attributions in the development and maintenance of loneliness. Peplau and her colleagues (Michela, Peplau, & Weeks, 1982; Peplau, Russell, & Heim, 1978; Peplau, Miceli, & Morasch, 1982; Peplau & Caldwell, 1978) have reported a series of studies in which participants who make internal and stable attributions (e.g., personality, attractiveness) as opposed to external and unstable attributions (e.g., lack of effort, impersonal social environments) for interpersonal difficulties are found to score higher on measures of loneliness. Moreover, these results have been replicated and extended by several other researchers (Anderson & Arnoult, 1985; Anderson, 1983; Dufton, & Perlman, 1986). Also, the tendency to make internal and stable rather than strategy and effort attributions has been found in longitudinal studies to predict subsequent loneliness (Cutrona, 1982; Shaver, Furman, & Buhmeister, 1985), and interventions that are directed toward changing attributional processes have been found to result in significant reductions in loneliness (Conoley & Garber, 1985).

Given the variety and magnitude of the correlations between loneliness and certain aspects of personality, self-regard, emotions, and beliefs, two central questions arise. First, it is likely that many of the personality correlates of loneliness are themselves correlated. Thus, which personality variables or combinations of variables best predict loneliness? Second, to what extent is loneliness determined by preexistent personality factors or to what extent does the development of loneliness result in the decline of social skill and confidence? Fortunately, there are preliminary data with which to address both issues.

Jones et al. (1985a) factor analyzed a large number of self-reported personality and attitudinal variables previously found to be associated with loneliness and then compared the resultant factor scores with scores on the UCLA Loneliness Scale using a hierarchical regression procedure. Two factors appeared to be most strongly and more or less equally related to loneliness in terms of the proportion of variance in loneliness scores explained. One composite variable, which was termed relational competence, included positively loaded scales such as masculinity and assertiveness and negatively loaded variables such as shyness. The second factor, termed communality, contained variables such as empathy, self-esteem, self-disclosure, femininity, and trust, all of which were positively loaded. This basic pattern of results has been replicated by Wittenberg and Reis (1986). Thus, in general, loneliness appears to be related to individual differences associated with problems in initial interactions with strangers as well as problems in achieving intimacy with significant relational partners.

Regarding the issue of directionality, there is now sufficient evidence from longitudinal studies to tentatively favor the hypothesis that the personality correlates of loneliness precede and contribute to the development of loneliness rather than vice versa (e.g., Cheek & Busch, 1981; Jones & Moore, 1987; Shaver et al., 1985). Also, several studies have demonstrated that social skills training procedures and other intervention strategies designed to improve skills and reduce social anxiety not only do so but also result in at least short-term reductions in loneliness (Jones, Hansson, & Cutrona, 1984; Rook, 1984b).

Stability and Change

Stability

Despite initial expectations, research suggests that loneliness is a relatively stable characteristic. For example, test-retest correlations for the UCLA and other scaled measures of loneliness typically exceed .75 over a 1 to 2 month period (Belcher, 1973; Bradley, 1969; Hojat, 1983; Jones et al., 1985b; Jones & Moore, 1987; Russell, 1982; Russell et al., 1978; Russell et al., 1980; Sarason, Sarason, & Shearin, 1986; Weeks, Michela, Peplau, & Bragg, 1980), with lower but substantial coefficients for longer periods of time, including 6 months (Cutrona, Russell, & Rose, 1986), 7 months (Cutrona, 1982), and 36 months (Sarason et al., 1986). Other studies indicate that whereas loneliness tends to be transitory in response to situational events (e.g., geographical mobility, beginning college, etc.) for people more vulnerable to loneliness (e.g., by virtue of shyness), loneliness initiated by situational factors tends to persist (Cutrona, 1982; Jones et al., 1985b; Shaver et al., 1985). Even when loneliness in response to situational stressors, such as beginning college, dissipates among such people, they still tend to remain lonelier than the general population (Cheek & Busch, 1981). Not surprisingly, loneliness follow-

ing widowhood tends to persist until a romantic relationship is reestablished or the person remarries (Bahr & Harvey, 1979; Glick, Weiss, & Parkes, 1974). Also, it has been demonstrated that ratings of lonely people by others remain relatively stable over time despite continued interactions among participants (Jones et al., 1981).

State versus Trait Loneliness

Several studies have demonstrated the utility of distinguishing between loneliness that has persisted (i.e., chronic or trait loneliness) and loneliness of recent origin or brief duration (transitory or state loneliness). For example, trait as opposed to state lonely people yield more negative scores on various psychological dimensions such as self-esteem and hostility (Hanley-Dunn et al., 1985; Hojat, 1983) and the length of loneliness or loneliness chronicity appears to be more strongly related to dysfunctional styles of coping with loneliness, whereas transitory loneliness may be more closely associated with heightened affective arousal (Gerstein & Tesser, 1987; Jones et al., 1985b).

As would be expected, Shaver et al. (1985) found that chronic loneliness was more stable than state loneliness among first-year college students and that the relative stability of state loneliness was accounted for by the stability of trait loneliness. Also, although trait loneliness significantly predicted state loneliness, it did so best during periods of relative stability in respondents' lives as compared with periods of change. Finally, Shaver et al. (1985) reported that trait loneliness was more strongly related to respondents' levels of social skill, whereas state loneliness had more to do with current satisfaction with one's social network. Similarly, persistence of loneliness over time appears to be related to certain personality variables, particularly shyness, social anxiety, empathy, and sociability (Jones et al., 1985b).

THE SOCIAL PSYCHOLOGY OF LONELINESS

Loneliness refers to the status and quality of an individual's relationships and therefore much of the research on loneliness has involved assessments of the frequency and satisfaction with which respondents engage in various kinds of interpersonal activities. A smaller body of literature focuses on specific interpersonal and conversational behaviors associated with loneliness.

Relational Status and
Interpersonal Contact

Quantitative Variables

Numerous studies have demonstrated that loneliness is related to deficiencies in intimate and social relationships. The connection between loneliness and one's relationships is more complex than was initially anticipated, however. Not surprisingly, greater loneliness is associated with being single, divorced, separated, and widowed (Bahr & Harvey, 1979; Gubrium, 1974; Rubenstein & Shaver, 1982; Woodward, Zabel, & Decosta, 1980) and there is evidence that the more recent the loss and the longer the prior marriage, the greater the loneliness following divorce, separation, or the death of a spouse (Bahr & Harvey, 1979; Hornung, 1981; Kivett, 1979).

Similarly, loneliness has been found to be inversely related to self-reported number of both casual and intimate friends (Jones et al., 1985a; Moore, 1974), having a steady dating or romantic partner among not married respondents (Jones et al., 1985a), the size and density of one's social support network (Dufton & Perlman, 1986; Jones & Moore, 1987; Levin & Stokes, 1986; Sarason et al., 1985; Sarason et al., 1986; Stokes, 1985), as well as receiving support from one's friends and family (Carpenter et al., 1984; Corty & Young, 1981; Schmitt & Kurdek, 1985). Also, Levin and Stokes (1986) found an inverse relationship between loneliness and the proportion of the social network identified as confidants.

A similar pattern of relationships has emerged with respect to the connections between loneliness and contact with other individuals, groups, and organizations. On the one hand, loneliness has been found to be inversely related to frequency of contact with other people generally among college students (Cutrona, 1982), adolescents (Brennan, 1982) and the elderly (Berg et al., 1981; Kivett, 1979) as well as contact with friends, neighbors, family, and one's children (Arling, 1976; Berg et al., 1981; Brennan, 1982). Not surprisingly, loneliness has been found to be negatively correlated with dating frequency among adolescents and college students (Brennan, 1982; Cutrona, 1982; Hoover, Skuja, & Cosper, 1979; Jones et al., 1985a), as well as elderly widows (Glick et al., 1974). Also, people who participate in religious organizations and extracurricular school activities report themselves to be less lonely (Bahr & Har-

vey, 1979; Brennan, 1982; Evans, 1983; Hornung, 1981; Kivett, 1978). Finally, loneliness is often directly correlated with the self-report of spending time alone and more frequently engaging in certain "social" activities (e.g., eating) by oneself (Hoover et al., 1979; Munnichs, 1964; Russell et al., 1980), and living alone (Berg et al., 1981), and the frequency of problematic contact with significant others (Brennan, 1982; Rook, 1984a), and inversely correlated with frequency of receiving support from others (Brennan, 1982; Jones & Moore, 1987; Levin & Stokes, 1986; Stokes, 1985) and frequency of talking with friends and family on the telephone (Kivett, 1978).

Qualitative Variables

On the other hand, in several instances loneliness was found to be unrelated to such quantitative indicators of social support, friendship, and romantic status (e.g., Austin, 1983; Baum, 1982; Corty & Young, 1981; Hoover et al., 1979; Kivett, 1979). The reason for this is likely that loneliness has less to do with the number of relevant relationships — given some minimal number — than one's satisfaction with such relationships. For example, several studies have used both quantitative and qualitative or satisfaction measures of relational status to predict loneliness, finding that the qualitative and satisfaction measures account for a larger proportion of the variance in loneliness scores (e.g., Hecht & Baum, 1984; Jones et al., 1985a; Rubenstein & Shaver, 1982).

Additional qualitative variables inversely associated with loneliness include satisfaction with the support received from the social network (Sarason et al., 1985; Sarason et al., 1986), helpfulness of the network (Schultz & Saklofske, 1983), closeness to parents, siblings, and friends (Sarason et al., 1985; Jones et al., 1985a; Hojat, 1982; Mishara, 1975; Lobdell & Perlman, 1986), and marital satisfaction (Lobdell & Perlman, 1986).

Other researchers have demonstrated that loneliness is related to the discrepancy between desired and perceived relational status (Perlman et al., 1985), lower attachment (Hecht & Baum, 1984), the presence of problematic social ties (Rook, 1984a), and that initial loneliness is a significant predictor of subsequent social support (Jones & Moore, 1987; Sarason et al., 1986). Williams and Solano (1983) reported that loneliness was related to the proportion of reciprocated friendship choices. Rook (1987) found that the relationship between loneliness and self-reported reciprocity of interpersonal exchanges was U-shaped, that is, loneliness was related to giving more than one receives and receiving more than one reported giving. Also, Cutrona et al. (1986) found that social support and stress interacted to predict loneliness. Finally, children who listed friends rather than parents as "first comfort figures" scored highest on a measure of parental loneliness (Marcoen & Brumagne, 1985).

Interaction Diary Studies

Several studies have examined the relationship between loneliness and social contact more directly by requesting participants to record in diaries various aspects of their interactions with others immediately or soon after the occurrence of the interaction. Such research has produced several interesting findings. First, when alone both adolescents and single adults are more likely to report feeling lonely, and this is particularly so for adolescent and single adults who find themselves alone on Friday and Saturday evenings (Larsen, Csikszetmihalyi, & Graef, 1982). On the other hand, several studies failed to produce significant correlations between loneliness and the average number of interactions per day or the amount of time spent with others (Corty & Young, 1981; Hecht & Baum, 1984; Jones, 1981; Reis, Wheeler, Nazlek, Kernis, & Spiegal, 1985; Orchard, 1986), even though loneliness has been found to be directly related to the diversity (i.e., number of different people) of the respondent's actual interactional network (Jones, 1981). Instead, most of the significant findings have involved the quality of the interaction or various characteristics of one's interactional partners. For example, loneliness has been found to be inversely related to the emotional quality of the interaction as well as to the degree of acquaintance with members of the interactional network (Jones, 1981), and for both male and female respondents, the proportion of interactions with females or mixed-sex groups (Reis et al., 1985).

Interpersonal Perceptions of Self and Others

Perceptions Among Strangers

Another way of assessing loneliness in a social context is to examine its connections to others' impressions of the lonely person and the manner in which lonely people view other people. Several studies assessing interpersonal perceptions and loneliness among strangers have been reported (Bell, 1985; Jones et al., 1981; Jones, Sansone, & Helm, 1983; Solano et al., 1982). Typically, college students who do not know one another are placed in dyads or groups and told to engage in brief conversations after which they rate themselves and their partners (or fellow group members) on several relevant dimensions (e.g., quality of the interaction, interpersonal attraction, friendliness, etc.).

Such data may be examined from each of two perspectives: (a) the association between loneliness and ratings given and (b) the association between loneliness and ratings received. For ratings given, several studies have demonstrated that highly lonely as compared with less lonely participants tend to rate themselves as having been less honest, less open, and less friendly in both dyadic and group settings (Jones et al., 1981; Jones et al., 1983). In these studies, loneliness has been associated with more negative expected ratings (i.e., student's rating of how his or her partner or fellow group members will rate him or her) along the dimensions of honest, open, and friendly. Similarly, Bell (1985) found that highly lonely participants expected their partners to be less interested in continued interactions with them. Also, participants with higher loneliness scores tend to rate their partners more negatively and indicate less interest in continued interactions with their partners themselves, less interpersonal attraction for partners, and less interest in developing a friendship with their partner (Bell, 1985; Jones et al., 1981; Jones et al., 1983). Finally, it has been found that lonelier participants obtain less objective information about their partners during such interactions and that the above pattern of results remains stable despite continued interactions (Jones et al., 1981).

In other words, following brief interactions with strangers, lonely people rate themselves and their fellow participants negatively and expect negative ratings if not outright rejection from their fellow participants. Also, loneliness appears to involve getting to know others less well in initial interactions. This latter finding might be due to partners' revealing less information to lonely people or to lonely people paying less attention to their partners. Research on loneliness and actual interpersonal behavior favors the latter hypothesis.

Results regarding ratings received have been somewhat less consistent, although significant results have always been in the expected direction. Jones and his colleagues found only modest support for the expectation that the partners of lonely participants in these studies would rate them more negatively (Jones et al., 1981; Jones et al., 1983). Similarly, Sloan & Solano (1984) found no differences in communication satisfaction among partners of lonely as compared with partners of not lonely participants, and Chelune, Sultan, and Williams (1980) found no significant relationships between confederates' ratings of participants' social skills and participants' self-rated loneliness.

On the other hand, Bell (1985) reported several inverse rating correlates of loneliness, including partners' rating of participants' desire for future interactions. Similarly, Spitzberg and Canary (1985) found that partners rated lonely participants as less socially competent. Gerson and Perlman (1979) found that transient loneliness was related to clarity in emotional expressiveness. Also, partners of lonely participants rate them as "liking themselves less" (Jones et al., 1983), as "less interested in future interactions" (Bell, 1985), and as "more difficult to get to know" (Solano et al., 1982).

Perceptions Among Ongoing Relational Partners

Only a few studies have examined interpersonal perceptions among ongoing relationships and almost all of these have focused on ratings received. These studies have generally indicated stronger correlations between self-ratings of loneliness and the perceptions of others. Two notable exceptions involved nonsignificant correlations between loneliness and ratings of popularity among Merchant Marine cadets (Eddy, 1961; Sisenwein, 1964). All other studies have resulted in at least some significant findings. For example, among college students, loneliness has been found to be inversely correlated with roommates' ratings of social skills, disclosure, positive attributes, social self-esteem, and friendship (Williams & Solano, 1983; Wittenberg & Reis, 1986). Among children, loneliness is inversely related to ratings of one's desirability as a playmate and popularity choices (Asher & Wheeler, 1985) and social sensitivity (Marcoen & Brumagne, 1985).

Loneliness and Social Behavior

There is some evidence that loneliness is related to problematic conversational behaviors during interactions with strangers. For example, highly lonely as compared with less lonely college students have been found to talk less, ask fewer questions, change the topic more frequently, and to attend less to their interaction partners (Bell, 1985; Jones, Hobbs, & Hockenbury, 1982; Lemmon, 1984; Sloan & Solano, 1984). Some studies have failed to confirm behavioral differences between low and highly lonely participants, however (Chelune et al., 1980; Orchard, 1986). In addition, Sloan and Solano (1984) reported that loneliness was associated with greater attention to one's partner and Sarason et al., (1985) found a small but significant direct correlation between loneliness and ratings of the proportion of time spent looking at and listening to one's interaction partner. Moreover, Vitkus and Horowitz (1987) demonstrated that lonely people do not lack social skills in the sense of not knowing what to do in such interactions. Instead, the problems lonely people have in this regard appear to involve the adoption of a passive role.

Examinations of loneliness in response to laboratory and hypothetical manipulations also suggest that lonely people often deviate from the social norm. For example, in two separate studies of responses to the influence of others, a gender by loneliness interaction was observed (Hansson & Jones, 1981). Specifically, highly lonely male participants conformed to and modeled others significantly less than both low lonely men and women, whereas highly lonely women modeled and conformed to a greater degree. This apparent tendency of lonely people to engage in social behaviors at variance with normative expectations has been found with respect to self-disclosure as well (Chelune et al., 1980; Solano et al., 1982). For example, Solano et al. (1982) found that highly lonely as contrasted with less lonely participants tended to select less intimate topics to disclose personal information to opposite as compared with same-sex strangers in an acquaintanceship exercise, a pattern of disclosure at variance with normative data among college students.

Furthermore, highly lonely as contrasted with less lonely participants have been found to be less willing to engage in social comparison with similar others regarding their opinions on controversial topics (Hansson & Jones, 1981), and to use coercive power strategies more frequently (which are typically less effective) in response to hypothetical scenarios calling for attempts to influence others (Gerson & Perlman, 1979).

External Factors in Loneliness

Environmental Factors

It has been widely assumed that stress and other situational factors that prevent or interfere with one's relationships are major contributors to the experience of loneliness. This expectation is, of course, confirmed by research indicating that loneliness is related to such environmental and interpersonal factors as relative social isolation, lower social support, lower participation in organizations and social events, unattached marital and romantic status, less time spent with friends, family, and significant others, living alone, and so on. In addition, research more clearly focused on these issues suggests that stress is an important determinant of loneliness, particularly with respect to state loneliness or the initial onset of loneliness. For example, there is evidence that loneliness is directly related to the number of negative and problematic social ties that an individual has (Rook, 1984a) and to the number of recent negative events (Cutrona et al., 1986), and not to the number of positive events (Sarason, Shearin, Pierce, & Sarason, 1987) in a person's life. Also, loneliness is related to the number of psychological problems experienced (Corty & Young, 1981) and to feelings of uncertainty associated with life changes (Jones et al., 1985a). Being in new situations that require the reestablishment of social ties also appears to result in loneliness (Brodkin, Shrier, Alger, Layman, & Buxton, 1983; Cutrona, 1982), but such increases appear to occur primarily for measures of state as opposed to trait loneliness (Shaver et al., 1985).

Several studies have confirmed that the onset of loneliness closely follows the loss of one's spouse due to death or divorce. Divorced adults who feel rejected by their exspouses are more lonely than those who do not feel rejected (Woodward et al., 1980), and divorce apparently increases feelings of loneliness when the divorced person feels "out of place," continues to have unpleasant interactions with the exspouse, as the date for the final divorce degree approaches, and, among women only,

if she faces a financial problem, responsibilities, or decisions in the absence of a helpmate (Woodward et al., 1980). Widows are more lonely than their married cohorts (Bahr & Harvey, 1979; Lopata, 1969), but time since the death of the spouse is strongly and inversely correlated with loneliness among widows (e.g., Hornung, 1981; Hansson et al., 1986), suggesting that loneliness deriving from widowhood tends to dissipate with time.

Despite generally significant findings among the divorced and widowed, however, some researchers have argued that such groups are not particularly lonely, or at least not as lonely as one might expect, suggesting that the loss of an important relationship may not be the most critical external determinant of loneliness (e.g., Hornung, 1981; Woodward et al., 1980). Instead, how the relationship is terminated and whether the termination was anticipated may extensively modify the degree of loneliness following relational loss.

Similarly, loneliness has been related to perceptions of parental disinterest and rejection as well as peer rejection, disapproval, and being ignored or left out of social activities among children, adolescents, and college students (Asher & Wheeler, 1985; Brennan, 1982; Goswick & Jones, 1982; Greene, 1980; Hojat, 1982). Children and adolescents may also experience relational loss through the death of a parent or parental divorce, and such events are associated with greater loneliness among adults even when the loss occurred several years before, during the respondent's childhood (Shaver & Rubenstein, 1980).

Several studies have indicated that loneliness is more likely to occur at certain times and seasons (e.g., at night, on weekends, in spring; Wenz, 1977; Woodward et al., 1980), and when lack of money, inadequate transportation, or time constraints interfere with one's involvement with significant others (Kivett, 1979; Bahr & Harvey, 1979; Perlman et al., 1978). Surprisingly, loneliness also has been related to extraneous sources of threat and failure that are not inherently interpersonal, such as battle intensity among soldiers (Solomon, Mikulincer, & Hobfoll, 1986), failing an exam (Cutrona, 1982), and academic failure in high school and college (Brennan, 1982; Goswick & Jones, 1982).

Because of the diversity of situations and external factors associated with loneliness and because of the general lack of agreement among psychologists as to what a situation is, some researchers have used open-ended questions in an effort to determine the frequency and underlying structure of the situations that appear to lead to loneliness. For example, Cutrona (1982) asked college students what made them feel lonely. The percentage of respondents' most frequent answers were as follows: (a) leaving home to go to college, 40%; (b) romantic break-ups, 15%; (c) problems with friends, 11%; (d) difficulties with school work, 11%; (e) family problems (e.g., parental divorce), 9%; and (f) isolated living situations, 6%. By contrast, Rubenstein and Shaver (1982) reported that two factors—being unattached and alienation—accounted for 67% of the variance of loneliness scores among adult respondents. Less common categories included forced isolation, being alone, and residential dislocation.

Relational Stress

The situational determinants of loneliness also have been investigated under the rubric of relational stress (Jones et al., 1985b). In one series of investigations, college students were asked what made them feel lonely in an open-ended response format. Respondents' answers were used to generate items that were scaled for their "loneliness-eliciting potential." Subsequent analyses suggested that relational stress consists of the following kinds of events and situations: (a) emotional threats to relationships (e.g., arguments, failure); (b) social isolation (e.g., few friends, being left out); (c) social marginality (e.g., being with strangers or others with whom one has little in common); (d) and romantic conflict (e.g., romantic break-ups). Additional research indicated that these events and situations are considered threatening because, as is the case with stress generally, they are unpleasant but difficult to predict or control. Also, results indicated that relational stress situations (a) tend to last a relatively long time but are experienced relatively infrequently; (b) increase the desire to affiliate with others, but at the same time are associated with increased use of coping strategies that do not include other people; and (c) increase feelings of dissimilarity from others. Moreover, exposure to relational stress was found to predict loneliness concurrently as well as 2 months later. Finally, some of the psychological characteristics previously associated with loneliness were more strongly associated with relational stress (e.g., anxiety, sensitivity to rejection), whereas other characteristics were more strongly

related to current or typical loneliness (e.g., self-esteem).

LONELINESS AND CLINICAL PSYCHOLOGY

Adjustment and Health

To the extent that loneliness is a transitory reaction to normal fluctuations in relationships and interpersonal encounters, it is primarily of interest to social psychologists. However, within clinical psychology there is a strong tradition of examining interpersonal conflicts and failures as major causes as well as consequences of classical syndromes of psychopathology (e.g., Sullivan, 1953). In addition, research directly focused on the construct of loneliness suggests, at least in general terms, important linkages between interpersonal dissatisfaction and problems in living.

Psychological Problems

Given the extensive pattern of correlations between loneliness and various negative psychological conditions, it is legitimate to ask to what degree loneliness implies adjustment problems of clinical significance. Several types of data are available with which to assess this issue. First, individuals undergoing psychological treatment, counseling, or imprisonment tend to have significantly higher loneliness scores; for example, psychiatric in-patients, prison inmates, hospitalized alcoholics, abusive parents, general hospital patients, suicide attempters, medical outpatients, and so forth (Carpenter et al., 1984; Kudoh & Nishikawa, 1983; Kugler & Hansson, 1988; Nerviano & Gross, 1976; Russell et al., 1978). On the other hand, it is difficult to determine whether there is some unique connection between loneliness and poor adjustment or whether individuals in these groups are simply experiencing extensive problems that might contribute both to their loneliness and their need for intervention. Also, in some instances such people are confined to hospitals and prisons and thus their loneliness may derive as much from restricted interpersonal opportunities as from poor adjustment.

Second, a number of studies have reported significant correlations between loneliness and self-reported measures of putative clinical syndromes, including neurosis, personality disorder, rape potential, chronic depression, lack of personality integration, general maladjustment, suicide risk, drug and alcohol abuse, sleep disturbances, and so forth (Baum, 1982; Berg et al., 1981; Check et al., 1985; Corty & Young, 1981; Cutrona et al., 1986; Goswick & Jones, 1981; Hojat, 1982; Kudoh & Nishikawa, 1983; Levin & Stokes, 1986; Loucks, 1980; Reis et al., 1985; Shaver & Rubenstein, 1980; Stokes, 1985; Wenz, 1977). Also, loneliness has been related to practitioners' ratings of mental status and adjustment (Berg et al., 1981).

Although suggestive, these studies generally fail to disentangle the loneliness and adjustment issue and, in particular, none has established the point at which loneliness signals adjustment problems of clinical significance. Moreover, none of these studies attempted to differentiate between chronic and situational loneliness.

Medical Problems

It also has been found that loneliness is associated with the self-report of medical problems and complaints, including greater frequency of everyday medical symptoms and behaviors (e.g., more headaches, backaches, fatigue, use of sedatives, frequency of physician visits, health worries, lower medical compliance, poorer health habits; Carpenter et al., 1984; Reis et al., 1985), and global self-ratings of health (Baum, 1982; Berg et al., 1981; Kivett, 1978, 1979; Rook, 1984a). Also, both children and adults hospitalized with life-threatening illnesses indicate that they experience problems with loneliness (Carpenter et al., 1984; Dubrey & Terrill, 1975; Francis, 1972; Krulik, 1978). More important, loneliness has been found to be related to physician ratings of medical compliance, general health, and specific medical diagnoses (Berg et al., 1981; Carpenter et al., 1984; Reis et al., 1985) and the time since the onset of legal blindness (Evans, 1983). Also, prospective studies among the elderly indicate that initial loneliness predicts subsequent nursing home admissions and, once in a nursing home, mortality (Cutrona et al., 1986; Russell & Cutrona, 1985). Although health correlates are often the focus of gerontological research on loneliness, these relationships have been observed in a variety of populations, including college students (Reis et al., 1985).

One study suggested that the relationship between loneliness and health is mediated by locus of control (Schill, Toves, & Ramanaiah, 1980);

specifically, the relationship between loneliness and self-rated health on a medical index was higher among internally as opposed to externally oriented respondents. Another study suggested that loneliness, but not actual amount of social contact, significantly predicted self-rated health among college students (Corty & Young, 1981). Several of these studies involved college students, a relatively healthy population, raising the question as to whether the strength of association between loneliness and health would be greater among older populations, in particular the elderly. Although this issue has not been extensively investigated, available evidence confirms higher correlations between loneliness and health among the elderly as compared with young adults (Schmitt & Kurdek, 1985).

Because single-item general health measures have been used in several studies and yet other studies have focused on a single medical population—all suffering from the same disorder—a major question in this area is with which medical problem is loneliness most closely associated? For college students, Reis et al. (1985) found that loneliness was related to actual diagnoses for nervous system and mental disorders and inversely with accidents, but among male participants only. By contrast, Berg et al., (1981) reported nonsignificant comparisons between loneliness and several types of physician-diagnosed illnesses (e.g., chronic bronchitis, hypertension, anginal pain, diabetes, congestive heart failure) among elderly Swedish participants. Berg et al. (1981) also found that lonely as contrasted with not lonely respondents reported greater fatigue, more negative health, and, for women only, greater consumption of hypnotic and sedative drugs and more frequent requests for medical advice. Thus, whereas it seems clear that loneliness is related to health, it is not yet clear which specific medical ailments may be involved.

Assuming a connection between loneliness and poor health, another issue concerns the physiological mechanisms that may account for such statistical relationships. Using psychiatric patients and medical students as participants, Kiecolt-Glaser and her associates have demonstrated that loneliness is associated with lowered immunocompetency (Kiecolt-Glaser, Speicher, Holliday, & Glaser, 1984; Kiecolt-Glaser, Ricker, Messick, Speicher, Holliday, Garner, & Glaser, 1984). For example, in one study, subjects high as compared with low in loneliness had significantly higher and abnormal levels of Epstein-Barr virus, which is the etiological agent responsible for mononucleosis. In another study, higher loneliness was associated with lower transformation levels of B lymphocytes, which means a greater vulnerability to manifesting the symptoms of Epstein-Barr virus.

Coping with Loneliness

Weiss (1974) suggested that loneliness results in two different and seemingly incompatible patterns of coping. First, what Weiss termed *searching* was defined as a frantic attempt to find those people or groups of people who would presumably alleviate one's feelings of loneliness by restoring satisfying relationships. At the same time, however, the lonely person tends to be keenly vigilant to possible rejection or disinterest on the part of others, resulting in the pattern that Weiss termed *sensitivity*. Additional research suggests, however, that the coping styles associated with feeling lonely may be more complex than is suggested by Weiss' dichotomy. In particular, several studies suggest that a common coping response to loneliness is avoidance or withdrawal from other people.

For example, Rubenstein and Shaver (1982) reported that the most common reactions to loneliness elicited in large surveys of adults included watching television (60%), listening to music (57%), calling a friend (55%), and reading (50%). Factor analyses of these responses resulted in four coping style clusters as follows: (a) sad passivity (e.g., crying, sleeping, sitting and thinking, doing nothing); (b) active solitude (e.g., studying, working, writing, listening to music, exercising); (c) spending money (e.g., shopping); and (d) social contact (e.g., calling a friend, visiting someone). Rubenstein and Shaver also reported that current loneliness was directly correlated with sad passivity factor scores and inversely correlated with social contact.

In a similar study among college students, Paloutzian and Ellison (1979) found several coping strategies associated with loneliness including (a) sensually oriented responses (e.g., drinking, taking drugs, sexual encounters); (b) religious responses (e.g., prayer, reading the Bible); (c) searching responses (e.g., going to a dance, driving around); (d) nonsocial diversions (e.g., keeping busy, reading, studying, working); (e) intimacy contact (e.g., talking to a close friend about one's feelings; spending time with a close friend just to be together); and (f) passivity (e.g., sleep). Furthermore, these researchers reported that students who evaluated their social skills more positively reported themselves as less likely to engage in sensual or diversionary activities when lonely and somewhat more likely to engage in intimacy-oriented and religious activities. Also, participants who viewed their social skills more positively saw the sensual and diversionary reactions as less effective and the intimacy contact reactions as more effective in reducing one's feelings of loneliness.

Berke and Peplau (1976) asked college students which of four alternatives they would choose to alleviate their feelings of loneliness. Results indicated that most students said that they would try to change the situation (60%). Twenty-three percent of the respondents chose exerting greater effort (e.g., trying to be friendlier), 11% said they would passively wait for things to improve, and 6% suggested they would try to improve their ability to make new friends. Consistent with the attributional analysis of loneliness, Berke and Peplau also found that those students who attributed loneliness to internal qualities of the lonely person chose trying harder more frequently as the recommended strategy for coping with loneliness, whereas students attributing loneliness to situational factors more frequently chose changing the situation.

Other studies have found that lonelier respondents are more likely to indicate coping with loneliness by avoiding others, sensual and diversionary activities (Jones et al., 1985b), sensitivity to rejection (Russell et al., 1980), passivity (Dubrey & Terrill, 1975), and less likely to engage in active social functions (Evans, 1983; Moore & Schultz, 1983; Schultz & Moore, 1984). Not surprisingly, religious people are more likely to use religious coping responses such as prayer and reading the Bible (Carroll, 1984; Dufton & Perlman, 1986). Also, personality and social skill has been linked to coping styles in response to loneliness (Gerstein & Tesser, 1987; Jones et al., 1985b; Shaver et al., 1985), with higher levels of social skill associated with more active coping styles that involve approaches to other people. However, in a longitudinal study Cutrona (1982) found that overcoming loneliness among first-year college students was unrelated to social contact and coping strategies (e.g., joining social groups). Instead, students who overcome their loneliness tended to maintain high expectations for their relationships despite their initial loneliness and to attribute the causes of their initial loneliness to external and unstable factors (e.g., large impersonal social environments, a lack of effort). By contrast, students who failed to overcome their loneliness tended to revise their expectations for relationships downward, invoked internal and stable attributions for their loneliness (e.g., personality, physical attractiveness), and consoled themselves with thoughts of accomplishments in noninterpersonal areas of endeavor.

Therapeutic Intervention for Loneliness

Some research has been directed toward the efficacy of therapeutic interventions for loneliness (cf. Jones et al., 1984; Natale, 1986; Rook, 1984b). Although relatively few controlled studies have been reported thus far, several techniques have been investigated including group and individual psychotherapy (Evans, Werkhoven, & Fox, 1982; Gallup, 1981), social skills training (Jones et al., 1982; Orchard, 1986), pastoral counseling (Parsons & Wicks, 1986), cognitive therapy (Conoley & Garber, 1985; Orchard, 1986; Young, 1982), didactic groups (Weiss, 1974), network building (Anderson, 1984; Evans, 1983), and, among children, play therapy (Bolea, 1986). With one exception, these studies suggest the conclusion that various approaches result in significant reductions in loneliness both simultaneously and at follow-up (Jones et al., 1984). The one exception involved discussion groups for lonely widows, which appeared to fail because participants felt that loneliness was an appropriate form of grieving for the deceased spouse (Weiss, 1974). Otherwise, on the basis of current evidence it would appear that almost any form of intervention carries with it some chance of relieving feelings of loneliness.

Several considerations, however, argue against unrestrained optimism regarding therapeutic interventions of loneliness. For example, in the available studies, samples have been relatively small and homogenous, leaving open the question of generalization to diverse populations. Similarly, follow-up intervals have been relatively short; thus, it is not yet clear whether reductions of loneliness resulting from therapy are permanent. Also, when significant reductions in loneliness have been achieved, participants have tended to remain significantly more lonely than average (e.g., Jones et al., 1982).

Moreover, most people who feel lonely do not seek counseling or therapy for their problems and, as was the case with coping patterns characterisc of loneliness, there is evidence that greater loneliness is associated with greater reluctance to seek outside professional help (Paloutzian & Ellison, 1979). Thus, additional research is needed to determine the permanence of reductions in loneliness induced with therapy as well as on the strategies that are available to lonely people to reduce their loneliness on their own.

SUMMARY

To summarize, available evidence makes it clear that loneliness — conceptualized as either a temporary experience or an enduring characteristic — is unpleasant and indicative of serious interpersonal problems. Furthermore, in our view, although loneliness frequently occurs as a function of stressful situations and events, it also appears that certain individuals are particularly vulnerable by virtue of a constellation of dysfunctional personality traits, beliefs, and cognitive habits, in particular poor social skills and hostile, passive, and reticent interpersonal styles. Obviously, such persons may be more likely to develop serious and possibly pathological loneliness given extraordinary or persistent relational stress. Less obviously, we suspect that such people are also more vulnerable to loneliness in response to the interpersonal stressors of everyday life (e.g., geographical mobility, meeting strangers, developing new relationships, etc.). Furthermore, the evidence suggests that for some, loneliness becomes a chronic and persistent problem requiring clinical attention.

Ironically, the more serious loneliness becomes as a personal problem, the less likely it appears that the lonely person will take appropriate measures to alleviate his or her loneliness. For example, in interactions with strangers who potentially might become friends and companions, lonely people assume rejection that has not occurred and tend to behave in a passive and unresponsive manner. Their judgments of themselves and other people with whom they interact tend to be hostile and pessimistic. Similarly, when asked how to cope with loneliness, lonelier respondents indicate that they typically engage in activities that often do not involve other people (taking drugs, watching television), whereas less lonely respondents indicate that they seek out good friends for companionship and understanding. Furthermore, although a variety of therapeutic modalities and approaches appear to afford effective treatment, lonelier respondents have been found to be less likely to seek professional forms of help and intervention. As a consequence, as loneliness intensifies, it appears that the capacity of lonely people to overcome their problems is lessened, which in turn increases the probability of loneliness that is chronic and of clinical significance.

REFERENCES

Anderson, C. A. (1983). Motivational and performance deficits in interpersonal settings: The effect of attributional style. *Journal of Personality and Social Psychology, 45*, 1136–1147.

Anderson, C. A., & Arnoult, L. H. (1985). Attributional style and everyday problems in living: Depression, loneliness, and shyness. *Social Cognition, 3*, 16–35.

Anderson, L. (1984). Intervention against loneliness in a group of elderly women: A process evaluation. *Human Relations, 37*, 295–310.

Arling, G. (1976). The elderly widow and her family, neighbors and friends. *Journal of Marriage and the Family, 38*, 757–768.

Asher, S. R., Hymel, S., & Renshaw, P. D. (1984). Loneliness in children. *Child Development, 55*, 1456–1464.

Asher, S. R., & Wheeler, V. A. (1985). Children's loneliness: A comparison of rejected and neglected peer status. *Journal of Consulting and Clinical Psychology, 53*, 500–505.

Austin, B. A. (1983). Factorial structure of the UCLA Loneliness Scale. *Psychological Reports, 53*, 883–889.

Avery, A. W. (1982). Escaping loneliness in adolescence: The case for androgyny. *Journal of Youth and Adolescence, 11*, 451–459.

Bahr, H. M., & Harvey, C. D. (1979). Correlates of loneliness among widows bereaved in a mining disaster. *Psychological Reports, 44*, 367–385.

Baum, S. K. (1982). Loneliness in elderly persons: A preliminary study. *Psychological Reports, 50*, 1317–1318.

Belcher, M. (1973). *The measurement of loneliness: A validation study of the Belcher extended loneliness scale (BELS)*. Unpublished doctoral dissertation, Illinois Institute of Technology, Chicago.

Bell, R. A. (1985). Conversational involvement and loneliness. *Communication Monographs, 52*, 218–235.

Berg, J., & Peplau, L. A. (1982). Loneliness: The relationship of self-disclosure and androgyny. *Personality and Social Psychology Bulletin, 8*, 624–630.

Berg, S., Mellstrom, D., Persson, G., & Svanborg, A. (1981). Loneliness in the Swedish aged. *Journal of Gerontology, 36*, 342–349.

Bergenstal, W. K. (1981). *The relationship of father support and father availability to adolescent sons' experience of loneliness and separation anxiety*. Unpublished doctoral dissertation, California School of Professional Psychology, San Diego.

Berke, B., & Peplau, L. A. (1976, April). *Loneliness in the university*. Paper presented at the meeting of the Western Psychological Association, Los Angeles.

Bolea, A. S. (1986). Treating loneliness in children. In S. M. Natale (Ed.), *Psychotherapy and the lonely patient* (pp. 16–27). New York: Haworth Press.

Borys, S., & Perlman, D. (1985). Gender differences in loneliness. *Personality and Social Psychology Bulletin, 11*, 63–74.

Bradley, R. (1969). *Measuring loneliness*. Unpublished doctoral dissertation, Washington State University, Pullman, WA.

Brennan, T. (1982). Loneliness at adolescence. In L. A. Peplau & D. Perlman (Eds.), *Loneliness: A sourcebook of current theory, research and therapy* (pp. 269–290). New York: Wiley-Interscience.

Brodkin, A. M., Shrier, D., Alger, E., Layman, W. A., & Buxton, M. (1983). Allaying loneliness in freshman medical students: An outcome of an elective course. *Journal of Medical Education, 58*, 722–727.

Carpenter, B. N., Hansson, R. O., Rountree, R., & Jones, W. H. (1984). Relational competence and adjustment in diabetic patients. *Journal of Social and Clinical Psychology, 1*, 359–369.

Carroll, L. J. (1984). *Changes in loneliness: The effects of attributions, coping strategies, changes in personality variables and changes in social networks*. Unpublished doctoral dissertation, University of Manitoba, Winnipeg.

Check, J. V. P., Perlman, D., & Malamuth, N. M. (1985). Loneliness and aggressive behavior. *Journal of Social and Personal Relationships, 2*, 243–252.

Cheek, J. M., & Busch, C. M. (1981). The influence of shyness on loneliness in a new situation. *Personality and Social Psychology Bulletin, 7*, 572–577.

Chelune, G. J., Sultan, F. E., & Williams, C. L. (1980). Loneliness, self-disclosure and interpersonal effectiveness. *Journal of Counseling Psychology, 27*, 462–468.

Conoley, C. W., & Garber, R. A. (1985). Effects of reframing and self-control directives on loneliness, depression, and controllability. *Journal of Counseling Psychology, 32*, 139–142.

Corty, E., & Young, R. D. (1981). Social contact and perceived loneliness in college students. *Perceptual and Motor Skills, 53*, 773–774.

Cutrona, C. E. (1982). Transition to college: Loneliness and the process of social adjustment. In L. A. Peplau & D. Perlman (Eds.), *Loneliness: A sourcebook of current theory, research and therapy* (pp. 291–309). New York: Wiley-Interscience.

Cutrona, C. E., Russell, D., & Rose, J. (1986). Social support and adaptation to stress by the elderly. *Journal of Psychology and Aging, 1*, 47–54.

Davis, M. H., & Franzoi, S. L. (1986). Adolescent loneliness, self-disclosure, and private self-consciousness: A longitudinal investigation. *Journal of Personality and Social Psychology, 51*, 595–608.

Dean, L. R. (1962). Aging and the decline of affect. *Journal of Gerontology, 17*, 440–446.

de Jong-Gierveld, J. (1987). Developing and testing a model of loneliness. *Journal of Personality and Social Psychology, 53*, 119–128.

Dubrey, R. J., & Terrill, L. A. (1975). The loneliness of the dying person: An exploratory study. *Omega, 6*, 357–371.

Dufton, B. D., & Perlman, D. (1986). Loneliness and religiosity: In the world, but not of it. *Journal of Psychology and Theology, 14*, 135–145.

Eddy, P. D. (1961). *Loneliness: A discrepancy with the phenomenological self.* Unpublished doctoral dissertation, Adelphi College, Garden City, NY.

Ellison, C. W. (1978). Loneliness: A social-developmental analysis. *Journal of Psychology and Theology, 6*, 3–17.

Ellison, C. W., & Paloutzian, R. F. (1979, August). *Assessing quality of life, spiritual well-being and loneliness.* Paper presented at the annual meeting of the American Psychological Association, Toronto.

Evans, R. L. (1983). Loneliness, depression and social activity after determination of legal blindness. *Psychological Reports, 52*, 603–608.

Evans, R. L., Werkhoven, W., & Fox, H. R. (1982). Treatment of social isolation and loneliness in a sample of visually impaired elderly persons. *Psychological Reports, 51*, 103–108.

Francis, G. M. (1972). *Loneliness: A study of hospitalized adults.* Unpublished doctoral dissertation, University of Pennsylvania, Philadelphia.

Franzoi, S. L., & Davis, M. H. (1985). Adolescent self-disclosure and loneliness: Private self-consciousness and parental influence. *Journal of Personality and Social Psychology, 48*, 768–780.

Gallup, C. S. C. (1981). *A study to determine the effectiveness of a social skills training program in reducing the perceived loneliness of social isolation.* Unpublished doctoral dissertation, Ohio University, Athens, OH.

Gerson, A. C., & Perlman, D. (1979). Loneliness and expressive communication. *Journal of Abnormal Psychology, 88*, 258–261.

Gerstein, L. H., & Tesser, A. (1987). Antecedents and responses associated with loneliness. *Journal of Social and Personal Relationships, 4*, 329–363.

Glick, I., Weiss, R. S., & Parkes, C. M. (1974). *The first year of bereavement.* New York: John Wiley & Sons.

Goswick, R. A., & Jones, W. H. (1981). Loneliness, self-concept and adjustment. *Journal of Psychology, 107*, 237–240.

Goswick, R. A., & Jones, W. H. (1982). Components of loneliness during adolescence. *Journal of Youth and Adolescence, 11*, 373–384.

Greene, M. B. (1980). *Children's self-rated loneliness: Who gets lonely when?* Unpublished doctoral dissertation, Columbia University, New York.

Gubrium, J. F. (1974). Marital desolation and the evaluation of everyday life in old age. *Journal of Marriage and the Family, 36*, 107–113.

Hanley-Dunn, P., Maxwell, S. E., & Santos, J. F. (1985). Interpretation of interpersonal interactions: The influences of loneliness. *Personality and Social Psychology Bulletin, 11*, 445–456.

Hansson, R. O. (1986). Relational competence, relationships and adjustment in old age. *Journal of Personality and Social Psychology, 50*, 1050–1058.

Hansson, R. O., & Jones, W. H. (1981). Loneliness, cooperation and conformity. *Journal of Social Psychology, 115*, 103–108.

Hansson, R. O., Jones, W. H., Carpenter, B. N., & Remondet, J. (1986). Loneliness and adjustment to old age. *International Journal of Aging and Human Development, 24,* 41–53.

Hecht, D. T., & Baum, S. K. (1984, January). Loneliness and attachment patterns in young adults. *Journal of Clinical Psychology, 40,* 193–197.

Hojat, M. (1982). Loneliness as a function of selected personality variables. *Journal of Clinical Psychology, 38,* 137–141.

Hojat, M. (1983). Comparison of transitory and chronic loners on selected personality variables. *British Journal of Psychology, 74,* 199–202.

Hoover, S., Skuja, A., & Cosper, J. (1979). Correlates of college students' loneliness. *Psychological Reports, 44,* 1116.

Hornung, K. L. (1981). *Loneliness among older urban widows.* Unpublished doctoral dissertation, University of Nebraska, Lincoln, NE.

Horowitz, L. M., & French, R. D. (1979). Interpersonal problems of people who describe themselves as lonely. *Journal of Consulting and Clinical Psychology, 47,* 762–764.

Jones, W. H. (1981). Loneliness and social contact. *Journal of Social Psychology, 113,* 295–296.

Jones, W. H. (1987). Research and theory on loneliness: A response to Weiss' reflections. *Journal of Social Behavior and Personality, 2,* 27–30.

Jones, W. H., & Carpenter, B. N. (1986). Shyness, social behavior and relationships. In W. H. Jones, J. M. Cheek, & S. R. Briggs (Eds.), *A sourcebook on shyness: Research and treatment* (pp. 227–238). New York: Plenum Press.

Jones, W. H., Carpenter, B. N., & Quintana, D. (1985a). Personality and interpersonal predictors of loneliness in two cultures. *Journal of Personality and Social Psychology, 48,* 1503–1511.

Jones, W. H., Cavert, C. W., Snider, R. L., & Bruce, T. (1985b). Relational stress: An analysis of situations and events associated with loneliness. In S. Duck & D. Perlman (Eds.), *Understanding personal relationships* (pp. 221–242). London: Sage Publications.

Jones, W. H., Freemon, J. A., & Goswick, R. A. (1981). The persistence of loneliness: Self and other determinants. *Journal of Personality, 49,* 27–48.

Jones, W. H., Hansson, R. O., & Cutrona, C. (1984). Helping the lonely: Issues of intervention with young and older adults. In S. Duck (Ed.), *Personal relationships 5: Repairing personal relationships* (pp. 143–161). London: Academic Press.

Jones, W. H., Hobbs, S. A., & Hockenbury, D. (1982). Loneliness and social skill deficits. *Journal of Personality and Social Psychology, 42,* 682–689.

Jones, W. H., & Moore, T. L. (1987). Loneliness and social support. *Journal of Social Behavior and Personality, 2,* 145–156.

Jones, W. H., Sansone, C., & Helm, B. (1983). Loneliness and interpersonal judgments. *Personality and Social Psychology Bulletin, 9,* 437–441.

Kiecolt-Glaser, J. K., Ricker, D., Messick, G., Speicher, C., Holliday, J., Garner, W., & Glaser, R. (1984). Urinary cortisol levels, cellular immunocompetency, and loneliness in psychiatric inpatients. *Psychosomatic Medicine, 46,* 15–24.

Kiecolt-Glaser, J. K., Speicher, C. E., Holliday, J. E., & Glaser, R. (1984). Stress and the transformation of lymphocytes by Epstein-Barr virus. *Journal of Behavioral Medicine, 7,* 1–11.

Kivett, V. R. (1978). Loneliness and the rural widow. *The Family Coordinator, 27,* 389–394.

Kivett, V. R. (1979). Discriminators of loneliness among the rural elderly: Implications for intervention. *The Gerontologist, 19,* 108–115.

Krulik, T. (1978). *Loneliness in school age children with chronic life-threatening illness.* Unpublished doctoral dissertation. University of California, San Francisco.

Kudoh, T., & Nishikawa, M. (1983). A study of the feelings of loneliness: 1. The reliability and validity of the revised UCLA loneliness scale. *Japanese Journal of Experimental and Social Psychology, 22,* 99–108.

Kugler, K. E., & Hansson, R. O. (1988). Relational competence and social support among parents at risk of child abuse. *Family Relations, 37,* 328–332.

Larsen, R., Csikszentmihalyi, M., & Graef, R. (1982). Time alone in daily experience: Loneliness or renewal? In L. A. Peplau & D. Perlman (Eds.), *Loneliness: A sourcebook of current theory, research and therapy* (pp. 40–53). New York: Wiley-Interscience.

Lemmon, G. R. (1984). *Behavioral rehearsal of partner attention: Social skill remediation of loneliness among the separated and divorced.* Unpublished doctoral dissertation, Virginia Commonwealth University, Richmond, VA.

Levin, I., & Stokes, J. P. (1986). An examination of the relation of individual differences variables to loneliness. *Journal of Personality, 54*, 717–733.

Lobdell, J., & Perlman, D. (1986). The intergenerational transmission of loneliness: A study of college females and their parents. *Journal of Marriage and the Family, 48*, 589–595.

Lopata, H. Z. (1969). Loneliness: Forms and components. *Social Problems, 17*, 248–261.

Loucks, S. (1980). Loneliness, affect and self-concept: Construct validity of the Bradley loneliness scale. *Journal of Personality Assessment, 44*, 142–147.

Lowenthal, M. F., Thurner, M., & Chiriboga, D. (1975). *The four stages of life*. San Francisco: Jossey-Bass.

Marcoen, A., & Brumagne, M. (1985). Loneliness among children and young adolescents. *Developmental Psychology, 21*, 1025–1031.

Michela, J. L., Peplau, L. A., & Weeks, D. G. (1982). Perceived dimensions of attributions for loneliness. *Journal of Personality and Social Psychology, 43*, 929–936.

Mishara, T. T. (1975). *A social self approach to loneliness among college students*. Unpublished doctoral dissertation, University of Maine, Orono.

Moore, D., & Schultz, N. R. (1983). Loneliness at adolescence. Correlates, attributions and coping. *Journal of Youth and Adolescence, 12*, 95–100.

Moore, J. A. (1974). Loneliness: Self-discrepancy and sociological variables. *Canadian Counsellor, 10*, 133–135.

Moustakas, C. E. (1961). *Loneliness*. Englewood Cliffs, NJ: Prentice-Hall.

Munnichs, J. M. (1964). Loneliness, isolation and social relations in old age. *Vita Humana, 7*, 228–238.

Natale, S. M. (Ed.). (1986). *Psychotherapy and the lonely patient*. New York: Haworth Press.

Nerviano, V. J., & Gross, W. F. (1976). Loneliness and locus of control for alcoholic males: Validity against Murray need and Cattell trait dimensions. *Journal of Clinical Psychology, 32*, 479–484.

Orchard, J. M. (1986). *The comparative effectiveness of social skill training and cognitive restructuring in the treatment of loneliness*. Unpublished doctoral dissertation, University of Manitoba, Winnipeg.

Paloutzian, R. F., & Ellison, C. W. (1979, April). *Loneliness and spiritual well-being as functions of living environment and professional status in adult women*. Paper presented at the annual meeting of the Western Psychological Association, San Diego.

Paloutzian, R. F., & Ellison, C. W. (1982). Loneliness, spiritual well-being and the quality of life. In L. A. Peplau & D. Perlman (Eds.), *Loneliness: A sourcebook of current theory, research, and therapy* (pp. 224–237). New York: John Wiley & Sons.

Parsons, R. D., & Wicks, R. J. (1986). Cognitive pastoral psychotherapy with religious persons experiencing loneliness. In S. M. Natale (Ed.), *Psychotherapy and the lonely patient* (pp. 47–60). New York: Haworth Press.

Peplau, L. A., & Caldwell, M. A. (1978). Loneliness: A cognitive analysis. *Essence, 2*, 207–220.

Peplau, L. A., Miceli, M., & Morasch, B. (1982). Loneliness and self-evaluation. In L. A. Peplau & D. Perlman (Eds.), *Loneliness: A sourcebook of theory, research and therapy* (pp. 135–151). New York: John Wiley & Sons.

Peplau, L. A., & Perlman, D. (Eds.). (1982). *Loneliness: A sourcebook of current theory, research and therapy*. New York: Wiley-Interscience.

Peplau, L. A., Russell, D., & Heim, M. (1978). An attributional analysis of loneliness. In I. Frieze, D. Bar-Tal, & J. Carroll (Eds.), *Attribution theory: Applications to social problems*. San Francisco: Jossey-Bass.

Perlman, D. (1988). Loneliness: A life-span developmental perspective. In R. M. Milardo (Ed.), *Families and social networks* (pp. 190–220). Newbury Park, CA: Sage Publications.

Perlman, D., Gerson, A. C., & Spinner, B. (1978). Loneliness among senior citizens: An empirical report. *Essence, 2*, 239–248.

Perlman, D., Locke, J., & Bond, J. (1985, August). *Loneliness among university students and their grandparents*. Paper presented at the meeting of the American Psychological Association, Los Angeles.

Reis, H. T., Wheeler, L., Nazlek, J., Kernis, M. H., & Spiegal, N. (1985). On specificity in the impact of social participation on physical and psychological health. *Journal of Personality and Social Psychology, 48*, 456–471.

Remondet, J. H., Hansson, R. O., Rule, B., & Winfrey, G. (1987). Rehearsal for widowhood. *Journal of Social and Clinical Psychology, 5*, 285–297.

Revenson, T. A., & Johnson, J. L. (1984). Social and demographic correlates of loneliness in late life. *American Journal of Community Psychology, 12*, 71–85.

Rook, K. S. (1984a). The negative side of social interaction: Impact on psychological well-being. *Journal of Personality and Social Psychology, 46*, 1097–1108.

Rook, K. S. (1984b). Interventions for loneliness: A review and analysis. In L. A. Peplau & S. E. Goldston (Eds.), *Preventing the harmful consequences of severe and persistent loneliness* (pp. 47–79) (DHHS Publication No. ADM 84-1312). Washington, DC: U.S. Government Printing Office.

Rook, K. S. (1987). Social support versus companionship: Effects on life stress, loneliness, and evaluations by others. *Journal of Personality and Social Psychology, 52*, 1132–1147.

Rubenstein, C. M., & Shaver, P. (1982). *In search of intimacy*. New York: Delacorte Press.

Rubin, Z. (1982). Children without friends. In L. A. Peplau & D. Perlman (Eds.), *Loneliness: A sourcebook of current theory, research, and therapy* (pp. 255–268). New York: John Wiley & Sons.

Russell, D. (1982). The measurement of loneliness. In L. A. Peplau & D. Perlman (Eds.), *Loneliness: A sourcebook of current theory, research and therapy* (pp. 81–104). New York: Wiley-Interscience.

Russell, D., & Cutrona, C. (1985, August). *Loneliness and physical health among the rural elderly*. Paper presented at the meeting of the American Psychological Association, Los Angeles.

Russell, D., Kao, C., & Cutrona, C. E. (1987, June). *Loneliness and social support: Same or different constructs?* Paper presented at the Iowa Conference on Personal Relationships, Iowa City.

Russell, D., Peplau, L. A., & Cutrona, C. E. (1980). The revised UCLA loneliness scale: Concurrent and discriminate validity evidence. *Journal of Personality and Social Psychology, 39*, 472–480.

Russell, D., Peplau, L. A., & Ferguson, M. (1978). Developing a measure of loneliness. *Journal of Personality Assessment, 42*, 290–294.

Sadava, S. W., & Matejcic, C. (1987). Generalized and specific loneliness in early marriage. *Ca-nadian Journal of Behavioral Science, 19*, 56–66.

Sarason, B. R., Sarason, I. G., Hacker, T. A., & Basham, R. B. (1985). Concomitants of social support: Social skills, physical attractiveness, and gender. *Journal of Personality and Social Psychology, 49*, 469–480.

Sarason, I. G., Sarason, B. R., & Shearin, E. N. (1986). Social support as an individual difference variable: Its stability, origins, and relational aspects. *Journal of Personality and Social Psychology, 50*, 845–855.

Sarason, B. R., Shearin, E. N., Pierce, G. R., & Sarason, I. G. (1987). Interrelations of social support measures: Theoretical and practical implications. *Journal of Personality and Social Psychology, 52*, 813–832.

Scalise, J. J., Ginter, E. J., & Gerstein, L. H. (1984). A multidimensional loneliness measure: The loneliness rating scale (LRS). *Journal of Personality Assessment, 48*, 525–530.

Schill, T., Toves, C., & Ramanaiah, N. (1980). Coping with loneliness and locus of control. *Psychological Reports, 47*, 1054.

Schmidt, N., & Sermat, V. (1983). Measuring loneliness in different relationships. *Journal of Personality and Social Psychology, 44*, 1038–1047.

Schmitt, J. P., & Kurdek, L. A. (1985). Age and gender differences in and personality correlates of loneliness in different relationships. *Journal of Personality Assessment, 49*, 485–496.

Schultz, B. J., & Saklofske, D. H. (1983). Relationship between social support and selected measures of psychological well-being. *Psychological Reports, 53*, 847–850.

Schultz, N. R., & Moore, D. (1984). Loneliness: Correlates, attributions, and coping among older adults. *Personality and Social Psychology Bulletin, 10*, 67–77.

Sermat, V. (1978). Sources of loneliness. *Essence, 2*, 271–276.

Shaver, P., Furman, W., & Buhmeister, D. (1985). Transition to college: Network changes, social skills, and loneliness. In S. Duck & D. Perlman (Eds.), *Understanding personal relationships* (pp. 193–220). London: Sage Publications.

Shaver, P., & Rubenstein, C. (1980). Childhood attachment experience and adult loneliness. In L. Wheeler (Ed.), *Review of Personality and Social Psychology* (Vol. 1, pp. 42–73). Beverly Hills, CA: Sage Publications.

Siassi, I., Crocetti, G., & Spiro, H. R. (1974). Loneliness and dissatisfaction in a blue collar population. *Archives of General Psychiatry, 30*, 261–265.

Sisenwein, R. J. (1964). *Loneliness and the individual as viewed by himself and others*. Unpublished doctoral dissertation, Columbia University, New York.

Sloan, W. W., Jr., & Solano, C. H. (1984). The conversational style of lonely males with strangers and roommates. *Personality and Social Psychology Bulletin, 10*, 293–301.

Solano, C. H., Batten, P. G., & Parish, E. A. (1982). Loneliness and patterns of self-disclosure. *Journal of Personality and Social Psychology, 43*, 524–531.

Solomon, Z., Mikulincer, M., & Hobfoll, S. E. (1986). Effects of social support and battle intensity on loneliness and breakdown during combat. *Journal of Personality and Social Psychology, 51*, 1269–1276.

Spitzberg, B. H., & Canary, D. J. (1985). Loneliness and relationally competent communication. *Journal of Social and Personal Relationships, 2*, 387–402.

Stokes, J. (1985). The relationships of social network and individual difference variables to loneliness. *Journal of Personality and Social Psychology, 48*, 981–990.

Sullivan, H. S. (1953). *The interpersonal theory of psychiatry*. New York: W. W. Norton.

Vitkus, J., & Horowitz, L. M. (1987). Poor social performance of lonely people: Lacking a skill or adopting a role? *Journal of Personality and Social Psychology, 52*, 1266–1273.

Weeks, D. G., Michela, J. L., Peplau, L. A., & Bragg, M. E. (1980). The relation between loneliness and depression: A structural equation analysis. *Journal of Personality and Social Psychology, 39*, 1238–1244.

Weiss, R. S. (Ed.). (1973). *Loneliness: The experience of emotional and social isolation*. Cambridge, MA: MIT Press.

Weiss, R. S. (1974). The provisions of social relationships. In Z. Rubin (Ed.), *Doing unto others* (pp. 17–26). Englewood Cliffs, NJ: Prentice-Hall.

Weiss, R. S. (1987). Reflections on the present state of loneliness research. *Journal of Social Behavior and Personality, 2*, 1–16.

Wenz, F. V. (1977). Seasonal suicide attempts and forms of loneliness. *Psychological Reports, 40*, 807–810.

Williams, J. G., & Solano, C. H. (1983). The social reality of feeling lonely: Friendship and reciprocation. *Personality and Social Psychology Bulletin, 9*, 237–242.

Wittenberg, M. T., & Reis, H. T. (1986). Loneliness, social skills, and social perception. *Personality and Social Psychology Bulletin, 12*, 121–130.

Woodward, H., Gingles, R., & Woodward, J. C. (1974). Loneliness and the elderly as related to housing. *The Gerontologist, 14*, 349–351.

Woodward, J. C., Zabel, J., & Decosta, C. (1980). Loneliness and divorce. *Journal of Divorce, 4*, 73–82.

Young, J. E. (1982). Loneliness, depression and cognitive therapy: Theory and application. In L. A. Peplau & D. Perlman (Eds.), *Loneliness: A sourcebook of current theory, research and therapy* (pp. 379–405). New York: John Wiley & Sons.

Zahaki, W. R., & Duran, R. L. (1982). All the lonely people: The relationship among loneliness, communicative competence and communication anxiety. *Communication Quarterly, 30*, 202–209.

CHAPTER 21

CLINICAL JUDGMENT AND DECISION-MAKING

Peter Salovey
Dennis C. Turk

Clinicians make judgments frequently about the possible causes and consequences of their clients' behaviors. They must decide on the best possible treatment for clients and try to predict how clients are likely to behave in the future. When prediction is based on intuitive, subjective, and idiosyncratic variables, it is often referred to as *clinical judgment*. Clinical judgment is often contrasted in reliability and validity with *statistical* or *actuarial prediction*, which is based on the quantitative combination of objectively gathered data.

The relative accuracy of statistical versus clinical predictions was a source of considerable debate after the publication of several highly influential articles by Sarbin (1941, 1943, 1944) and, especially, upon publication of Meehl's (1954) *Clinical Versus Statistical Prediction*, which summarized a number of studies pointing to the advantages of statistically based approaches to diagnosis and assessment. Nearly 35 years after publication of his book, Meehl (1986) claimed that no more than 5% of it needs to be retracted or in any way qualified. Even Holt, Meehl's most persistent critic (e.g., Holt, 1958, 1970, 1978), recently acknowledged that "maybe there are still lots of clinicians who believe that they can predict anything better than a suitably programmed computer; if so, I agree that it is not only foolish but at times unethical of them to do so" (Holt, 1986, p. 378). Given this seeming rapprochement between the clinical and statistical camps, it is probably most useful in a handbook such as this one to describe the cognitive processes that impinge on the validity of clinical judgment rather than to continue to polarize the issue as a debate about the advantages of objective, statistical prediction over intuitive, clinical judgment.

In this chapter, we will discuss research that is

Preparation of this manuscript was supported in part by National Institutes of Health Biomedical Research Support Grant S07 RR07015, National Cancer Institute Grant CA 42101, and National Center for Health Statistics Contract 200-88-7001 to Peter Salovey, and National Institute of Dental Research Grant DE07514 and National Institute of Arthritis and Musculoskeletal and Skin Diseases Grant ARNS38698 to Dennis C. Turk. We thank C. R. Snyder and Sasha van der Sleesen for their comments on an earlier draft of this chapter.

relevant to the cognitive processes underlying the judgments of mental health professionals, including clinical psychologists. Our goal is not to demonstrate that clinicians are somehow deluded into believing that they possess especially acute judgmental skills and that they should perhaps be punished, or, better yet, hospitalized for these delusions. Rather, we hope to emphasize the basic notion that clinicians are decision makers just like any other decision makers, and their judgmental powers are probably no better and no worse than anyone else's. Moreover, the manner by which a clinician makes a judgment or decision is identical to such processes in the lay person. This statement is not intended to be pejorative, but one of existing facts as we know them. Meehl (1954) underscored this point right from the outset of the clinical judgment debate when he noted that "psychologists should be sophisticated about errors of observing, recording, retaining, and recalling to which the human brain is subject. We, of all people, ought to be highly suspicious of ourselves. We have no right to assume that entering the clinic has resulted in some miraculous mutation and made us singularly free from ordinary errors" (pp. 27–28).

Meehl's (1954) monograph summarized the literature on clinical judgment available at that time: 22 studies that could be reviewed in a brief chapter. Since the publication of Meehl's volume, the literature has grown from 22 to perhaps more than 1000 articles directly relevant to clinical judgment and decision-making. There has been considerable speculation about the origins of the present interest in this area (Sarbin, 1986; Scriven, 1979). Kleinmuntz (1984) outlined five developments that have contributed to the recent scientific interest in clinical judgment. These include (a) lingering aspects of the original clinical versus statistical prediction controversy, (b) the growing interest in artificial intelligence and decision-making technologies among cognitive scientists, (c) the vast growth of behavioral decision theories and the decision sciences in the past 20 years, (d) a greater attention to formal approaches to medical reasoning among physicians, and (e) the emergence of the desktop computer as an information-processing machine.

In the remainder of this chapter, we will discuss some of the cognitive processes that affect the judgmental tasks of clinicians (see also Turk & Salovey, 1985; 1986). This description will be organized roughly in terms of how these tasks are sequenced in a typical clinical setting: (a) forming a first impression, (b) using a classification system, (c) making a diagnosis, (d) assessing covariation, and (e) making decisions and predicting the future. We will conclude with a discussion of how both clinical judgment and research on clinical judgment might be improved.

COGNITIVE PROCESSES IN CLINICAL JUDGMENT

Forming a First Impression

Prior Expectancies and Implicit Theories

Prior experiences, training, theoretical orientation, and influential authority figures often direct the expectations with which clinicians initiate an encounter with a potential client. When well organized, these sets of expectations can be referred to as schemas. Schemas play an important role in helping us filter and organize incoming information and attend primarily to important and relevant features of it. Without schemas, clinicians (or anyone else) would have difficulty making sense of the barrage of incoming information available in the clinical setting. Moreover, without schemas they would be unable to make decisions quickly.

These sets of expectations, however, can bias the processing of new information by focusing clinicians' attention on information consistent with the schema and causing them to ignore or discount information irrelevant to these expectations. As a result, there is a tendency to process information confirming an initial expectation or impression (Bieri, Atkins, Briar, Leaman, Miller, & Tripodi, 1966; Hastie, 1981; Taylor & Crocker, 1981).

The potential biases fostered by the existence of prior expectations have been demonstrated in dramatic ways. Temerlin (1968) developed a tape that portrayed a man as happy and effective in his work, involved in warm and satisfying relationships, self-confident, and secure with little arrogance, competitiveness, or grandiosity. The man identified with his father, was happily married, and reported having pleasurable sexual experiences. He reported a happy childhood, had a good sense of humor, few role anxieties, and reasonable worries. In short, he displayed no ostensible symptoms of pathology and seemed to be a "normal, healthy man."

Psychologists, psychiatrists, and graduate students were asked to observe the tape and determine whether this man was psychotic, neurotic, or healthy. In one condition of the experiment, a prestigious clinician introduced the tape by noting that the man portrayed was a "rare case of a mentally healthy individual." In another condition, he suggested that the man "looks neurotic but is actually quite psychotic." A control group received no suggestion at all. In the first condition, all of the clinicians rating the tape agreed that the man was in fact a healthy individual. However, in the condition during which they were told to expect "latent" psychosis, 44% of the clinicians evaluated the man as psychotic, 50% as neurotic, and only 6% as healthy. When no suggestion at all was given, 57% of the clinicians thought the man was healthy, none of the clinicians rated the man as psychotic, although 43% thought he was neurotic. The prior expectation of psychosis (or, at least, "looking neurotic") in the psychosis suggestion condition may have caused the clinicians to pay particular attention to and remember evidence consistent with pathology. The bias was most strongly held by psychiatrists and least strongly held by graduate students of clinical psychology. Professional clinical psychologists were moderately influenced by the prestigious psychotherapist.

In another study, when a taped actor was labeled a "job applicant," he was seen as much less psychologically disturbed than when the identical behavior was portrayed but the actor labeled a "patient" (Langer & Abelson, 1974). The impact of this prior expectation was stronger for psychodynamically oriented clinicians than for behaviorists. Perhaps the behaviorists attended only to the patient's objectively observable behaviors (but see Snyder, 1977, for an alternative explanation.) Other experiments like these have been conducted and the effects observed by Temerlin, and Langer and Abelson have largely been replicated (e.g., Sushinsky & Wener, 1975). However, this line of research has been criticized on theoretical grounds (e.g., Davis, 1979, who argues that the clinicians in these experiments are appropriately utilizing base-rate information).

Even when prior expectancies are not explicitly provided, a set of expectations may develop rapidly after initial patient contact, often based on very little information. For example, after determining that someone is intelligent, we may expect him or her to have a good sense of humor even though we have never seen any evidence of witti-

ness. These *implicit personality theories* (Asch, 1946; Bruner & Tagiuri, 1954) are then used as the basis for subsequent judgments about the individual even if the clinician no longer can recall the origins of the implicit theory itself (Carlston, 1977; Srull & Wyer, 1979). Unfortunately, individuals adhere tenaciously to initial diagnostic conceptualizations, largely ignoring new information (Rubin & Shontz, 1960).

The clinicians in Rosenhan's (1973) classic study, in which normal individuals falsified a single psychotic symptom (hearing voices), readily diagnosed these pseudopatients as pathological (usually schizophrenic) and admitted them as inpatients for 7 to 52 days in the absence of any subsequent evidence of psychosis (see Spitzer, 1975, 1976; Weiner, 1975, for critiques, however). The initial impression of pathology made it difficult for these clinicians to recognize "normal" behavior in the pseudopatients. Meehl (1960) observed that the basic impression of a patient formed during the first few sessions is retained intact after 24 sessions, and the initial diagnostic impression of a patient may be formed in the first minute of therapy (Gauron & Dickinson, 1969; see also Sandifer, Hordern, & Green, 1970). This diagnostic tenacity may be in part a result of tendencies to seek or elicit information confirming initial hypotheses, a judgmental phenomenon that will be dealt with in the next section of this chapter.

Confirmatory Strategies

Prior expectations, schemas, and implicit theories all affect initial impressions, as we have described. Additionally, they profoundly influence subsequent data gathering. When these expectations are organized into hypotheses, there is a pervasive tendency to seek information that confirms them and to ignore disconfirming information. This data-gathering style has been labeled "behavioral confirmation" or "seek and ye shall find" (Snyder, 1981). Snyder defines behavioral confirmation as the process by which an individual's preconceived beliefs and prior expectations guide interaction in such a way that these initial beliefs, even when false, come to be confirmed by the other person's behavior (Snyder & Thomsen, 1988).

Individuals tend to use their interactions with others as opportunities to test the accuracy of hypotheses they hold about them. But we are not objective observers of them. Rather, we often act as if the hypotheses are true, eliciting hypothesis-confirming behavior from others. Some years ago, Merton (1948) referred to such an interaction sequence as a self-fulfilling prophecy. For example, when college students were asked to find out whether another person was an extrovert or an introvert, they selected questions based on whether the initially provided hypothesis was one of introversion or extroversion (Snyder & Swann, 1978b). If they were trying to confirm whether the person was an extrovert, they would ask questions that solicited evidence of extroverted behavior (e.g., "What would you do if you wanted to liven things up at a party?"). If they were trying to confirm the introvert hypothesis, they might select a question such as, "What factors make it hard for you to really open up to people?" Not only do these questions elicit a biased set of information, but they may cause the other person to behave in a way that confirms the hypothesis (e.g., one is more likely to behave in an outgoing way while discussing how to liven up a party as compared with discussing what makes it hard to open up to others).

The pervasiveness of the hypothesis-confirmation strategy is quite breathtaking. Individuals engage in this information-seeking style no matter what the origins of the initial hypothesis (e.g., self-generated, provided by others), whether the hypothesis is likely to be accurate or inaccurate, whether clear incentives for accurate hypothesis testing are offered, or whether the hypothesis contains disconfirming attributes (Snyder, 1981). Surprisingly, subjects in Snyder's experiments treated all hypotheses with equal weight when selecting questions to ask, and these hypothesis-confirming strategies even generalized to drawing inferences about oneself.

The seeking of hypothesis-confirming information may create a tendency among clinicians to overpathologize the behavior of others. Because in the clinical context clinicians expect to observe pathology, there may be a pervasive tendency to interpret ambiguous client behaviors as evidence for pathology (Sarbin, Taft, & Baily, 1960). Another danger of hypothesis-confirming strategies in the clinical setting is that clinicians at times are motivated to elicit experiences from their clients that confirm their theoretically based hypotheses. After a time in therapy, clients' behaviors may come to match the theoretical frameworks of their therapists (Frank, 1974; Scheff, 1966). In fact, a therapeutic cure might be defined as the conversion of the client's value and belief systems to that

of the therapist (Bandura, Lipsher, & Miller, 1960; Rosenthal, 1955; Welkowitz, Cohen, & Ortmeyer, 1967). After a time in psychotherapy, clients will even report dream material that is consistent with the therapist's orientation (Whitman, Kramer, & Baldridge, 1963).

Salience, Vividness, and Availability

Another variable influencing the forming of an initial impression is the notion that some people and some features of other people are more noticeable than others. *Salience* refers to the properties of a stimulus that make it likely to attract attention relative to its context. *Vividness* is often used to denote the inherent properties of a stimulus that attract attention independent of its context (Fiske & Taylor, 1984). People become salient when they are novel in a social context (e.g., the only blond in a room full of brunets or the only schizophrenic in a room of "normals"), by behaving in unexpected ways, or by being relevant to the perceiver's goals. On the other hand, a description of a specific traffic accident is more vivid than statistics about traffic accidents, no matter the context in which they are presented.

It might be expected that particularly salient or vivid aspects of an individual would exert greater impact on judgment. That is, the mundane is forgotten while the unusual remembered. Salient individuals are seen as more in personal control of their behavior rather than as buffeted by external forces (Fiske, Kenny, & Taylor, 1982). When a person acts especially crazy among a crowd of people acting normally, we assume that the crazy person is responsible for his or her odd behavior, discounting the role of environmental factors. Moreover, unpleasant salient others are likely to be judged as especially unpleasant (Fiske & Taylor, 1984). Surprisingly, though, these attributional and evaluative consequences of salience may not be mediated by memorability (McArthur, 1981; Taylor & Fiske, 1978; Taylor & Thompson, 1982). That is, salience may influence attributions and evaluations even when there is no evidence of increased recall of salient others.

On those occasions, however, when especially salient or vivid material is encoded better into memory, it can exert a pronounced and systematic effect on judgment. Information that is especially easy to bring to mind is said to be more *available*. When individuals estimate the probability of an event or outcome by the ease with which it is brought to mind, they are using the *availability heuristic* (Tversky & Kahneman, 1973). When forming an impression of a new client, it is easy to overestimate the frequency of the client's unusual behaviors because such behaviors are more available. For example, a clinician might decide that a client is suicidal because the client once mentioned thinking about suicide. The memorability of the client's revelation leads to an overestimation of its likelihood.

Another example concerns judgments about the dangerousness of released mental patients. Often, the dangerousness of discharged mental patients is overestimated because the occasional violent patient is easily recalled, with help from media coverage, but the more typical expatient who lives out a quiet and uneventful life is not remembered. Hence, a clinician easily recalling a dramatically violent former patient may form an impression of a new client as being more dangerous than he or she actually is. Similarly, we may overestimate the proportion of the homeless who are mentally ill because "normal" acting homeless individuals are not especially memorable.

Emotional Influences on Person Perception

A final variable that influences initial impressions is affect. The moods and emotions of the perceiver influence judgments made about the characteristics of other people. For example, whether one's mood is created by a recent failure (Lerner, 1965), receipt of a desirable prize (Lott & Lott, 1968), viewing of an evocative film (Gouaux, 1971), or ambient temperature (Griffitt, 1970), we find others to be more attractive and desirable when we are in pleasant rather than dysphoric moods ourselves.

When incoming information is ambiguous, moods may be especially likely to bias initial impressions. For example, happy individuals are more likely to rate the illustration on a Thematic Apperception Test (TAT) card as containing pleasant content than are angry individuals (Bower, 1981), and they are more likely to interpret ambiguous written material in a similar mood-congruent manner (Clore, Schwarz, & Kirsch, 1983). In general, judgments about others follow a mood-congruent pattern (Forgas & Bower, 1988). When people are in good moods, their judgments are positive, and when in bad moods, negative (Mayer & Bremer, 1985; Mayer & Volanth, 1985). One reason why moods might affect judgment is that they make mood-congruent events stored in memory more easily retrievable, and the greater

availability of such memories leads to predictions of greater likelihood for similar future events (Bower, 1981; Isen, 1970, 1984). An alternative explanation (Mayer, 1986) is that such judgment effects are rooted in recategorizations in memory rather than memory enhancements or failures. According to this view, individuals in a good mood may classify a mildly negative event as a neutral or positive event (Mayer & Salovey, 1988).

Using a Classification System

Clinical judgment in psychology is often based on a taxonomy. In order to communicate, conduct research, and prescribe treatment, it is essential that some consensually validated criteria are used to describe groups of individuals who are similar on some relevant attributes. For clinical psychologists, the most recent edition of the *Diagnostic and Statistical Manual of Mental Disorders* (DSM-III-R; American Psychiatric Association, 1987) serves as the guiding taxonomic framework for the ultimate classification of individuals into diagnostic categories. The construction of a classification system and its eventual use are psychological processes, no matter how objective they may seem, and it is to these issues that we will turn briefly.

Development and Use of a Taxonomy

A taxonomy of taxonomies would divide them into either natural or artificial and hierarchic or nonhierarchic (Rasch, 1987). When the criteria used to classify individuals (as in the case of psychologists) are based on characteristics fundamental to those individuals, the taxonomy is termed *natural*. *Artificial* taxonomies classify individuals on the basis of an accidental or arbitrary attribute. A taxonomy based on height or eye color clearly would be a natural one, whereas one based on shirt color would be artificial. The DSM-III-R was intended to be a natural taxonomy, purportedly describing differences inherent within individuals. Critics, however, who argue that DSM-III-R diagnostic categories lie primarily in the minds of the diagnostician rather than in the observable attributes of clients and patients might claim that the DSM-III-R is actually an artificial taxonomy (cf. Rosenhan, 1975). That is, they would claim that the defining criteria "reside" in the observer and his or her context, not in the observed.

Hierarchic taxonomies attempt to group individuals into successively more inclusive classes based on fewer attributes to define a particular category. Nonhierarchic taxonomies use a single attribute or set of attributes to define a category (Lowry, 1981). The DSM-III-R is largely non-hierarchic, but it does contain some hierarchical elements. For example, in the DSM-III-R, the category of schizophrenic disorders is subdivided further into disorganized, catatonic, paranoid, and residual types.

Taxonomies may be developed inductively or deductively (Mezzich, 1980; Walker & Avant, 1983). Some classification schemes in psychology are developed inductively or empirically. That is, individuals are observed until some attribute on which they can be differentiated is discovered. Individual differences in the members of these categories are then ascertained such that the categories can be divided into sets of subcategories. After individuals are categorized, a taxonomy can be developed that specifies the rules and procedures for further classification of individuals. These rules were thus derived inductively by observing differences among individuals.

A deductively derived taxonomy begins with a theoretically based statement about how individuals should differ and subsequently be categorized. Its utility is then tested by actually employing it to classify individuals. Does assignment of an individual to a class facilitate treatment decisions or predictions of future behavior? It is probably accurate to say that the major categories of the DSM-III-R (e.g., schizophrenic disorders, organic mental disorders, affective disorders, anxiety disorders) were derived deductively, and that the specific subtypes within these general categories were constructed inductively.

Several structural issues, reviewed by Mezzich, Goodpastor, and Mezzich (1987), constrain the ways in which clinicians make clinical judgments in response to a diagnostic taxonomy. The first of these issues is that of polydiagnosis, the fact that several sets of diagnostic criteria are used to describe the same disorder (Berner, Katschnig, & Lenz, 1982). Most classification systems used in psychology or medicine (e.g., DSM-III-R, or International Classification of Diseases, ninth edition [ICD-9]) are based on the consensus of a group of professionals and in that sense reflect the elimination of certain diagnostic features on which agreement could not be obtained. Berner and Katschnig (1983) argued for the utility of considering multiple classification systems and cate-

gorization criteria when making a diagnosis. This polydiagnostic approach would allow individuals to carry diagnoses based on different taxonomies. Although potentially confusing, the advantage would be a clear statement of a patient's diagnosis according to each of a set of taxonomies (e.g., DSM-III-R, research diagnostic criteria, and Bleuler's [1908] standard). The argument for polydiagnosis also includes the notion that systematic discrepancies among diagnostic systems would be more easily identified and ameliorated. In clinical research, polydiagnosis would increase the comparability of results across research teams using different diagnostic criteria.

The second of these structural issues is the hierarchical arrangement of clinical disorders such that the diagnosis of one precludes the diagnosis of another. In the most parsimonious hierarchy, no one individual could be diagnosed with more than one disorder (Jaspers, 1963). In fact, when most taxonomies are used, such as the DSM-III-R, the presence of one disorder increases the probability that a second disorder might be diagnosed. For DSM-III-R, the receipt of any diagnosis increases the probability of receiving almost any other diagnosis. Mezzich et al. (1987) suggest that explicit exclusion criteria might be developed in order to minimize inaccuracies resulting from such category overlap. At present, only some disorders listed in the DSM-III-R contain exclusion criteria.

A third structural issue is determining how multiple diagnoses should be integrated when the criteria for several different disorders are met. For example, a patient might be diagnosed as having a simple phobia, being an abuser of alcohol, and behaving like a depressive. Such multiple diagnoses can be handled in a variety of ways. They can be combined into syndromes when their co-occurrence is systematic. Alternatively, the person can be treated as if the diagnoses were conceptually (and etiologically) distinct.

Finally, Mezzich et al. (1987) urged us to consider multiaxial diagnosis in which several different aspects of a psychological disorder are considered systematically. A multiaxial system asks the clinician to make a diagnostic judgment across a set of aspects (termed *axes*). The DSM-III-R introduced multiaxial diagnosis to most clinicians. Judgments about patient diagnoses are now made on five (not necessarily orthogonal) dimensions: primary psychiatric syndromes, personality and developmental disorders, physical disorders, psychosocial stressors and their severity, and highest level of adaptive functioning during the past year. Use of the third (physical illness), fourth (stress), and fifth (level of functioning) axes have been promoted, especially, by the health psychology movement in clinical psychology. In practice, however, often only the first and sometimes the second axis are used. Limits on the use of the full multiaxial system are often imposed by (a) insurance companies who demand that patients be labeled on the first axis primarily, (b) clinicians who are trained to accentuate this pathology dimension, (c) diagnosticians who may have difficulty simultaneously conceptualizing clients on a large number of dimensions, and (d) the time and financial pressures on the practicing clinician that reward quick and parsimonious decisions.

Diagnostic Categories and the Processing of Prototypes

Cantor and her colleagues (e.g., Cantor, Smith, French, & Mezzich, 1980; Genero & Cantor, 1987) have noted that diagnostic categories based on taxonomies such as the DSM-III-R have some special properties. First, it is difficult to specify the defining features that all category members possess. Further, these categories (i.e., diagnoses) are vague or "fuzzy" (cf. McCloskey & Glucksberg, 1978); that is, they sometimes lack consensually defined and specific necessary and sufficient criterial properties. As a result, diagnostic categories may be better defined by specific prototypes rather than criterial features (Horowitz, Post, French, Wallis, & Siegelman, 1981; Horowitz, Wright, Lowenstein, & Parad, 1981). In other words, diagnosticians may think about a category such as "paranoid schizophrenic" by retaining in memory a prototypic paranoid schizophrenic rather than a list of features common to all paranoid schizophrenics.

The implications of the idea that diagnostic categories are fuzzy sets best characterized by prototypes who possess a set of correlated features are that there is considerable heterogeneity among similarly diagnosed patients, that similarly diagnosed patients can vary in terms of how typical they are for (i.e., how well they fit) a particular diagnosis, and that diagnosis is the process by which a clinician matches the features presented by a patient with those of category prototypes (Genero & Cantor, 1987). The diagnostic process, then, is characterized by a similarity-matching procedure whereby a particular client is compared with a prototype for each potentially relevant diagnostic category. This is a very different process than simply affirming the existence of a small group of requisite features. As a result, some clients will be more easily classified and subsequently remembered than others—those clients who most closely match the category prototype. Imagine that each category is a circle. The exact center of the circle depicts the prototype for people who fit in the circle (i.e., the category). However, an individual can be closer to the periphery than the center of the circle yet still have enough of the defining characteristics to be classified within the category depicted by the circle. The difficulties of diagnosis by prototype-matching will be discussed momentarily.

Making a Diagnosis

After forming an initial impression of a client, clinicians often must get down to the business of using a taxonomy to make a formal diagnosis. Although many of the same cognitive processes operate for this task as were described in initial impression formation, the process of diagnosis also lends itself to other judgmental difficulties.

Prototype-Matching

As described earlier, clinical diagnosis proceeds through prototype-matching, whereby a patient's characteristics are compared with those of a category prototype (Genero & Cantor, 1987). This diagnostic process may pose some judgmental difficulties. Because diagnostic categories are fuzzy, the individuals receiving a particular diagnosis are a heterogeneous group. Hence, it can be difficult to recognize even typical category members. For example, among a group of individuals diagnosed as depressed, there may be individuals with different subsets of depressive characteristics. One person might be agitated, another lethargic, and so forth. Moreover, even clients who match a category prototype quite closely may also bare some resemblance to another category prototype. For example, a paranoid schizophrenic may also seem somewhat like a person with bipolar affective disorder (i.e., manic-depressive psychosis) in a manic phase.

Representative Thinking

The diagnostic process is essentially a judgment that an individual is a member of a particular category or that a given outcome can be explained by a particular set of antecedents. The decision-making strategy frequently employed for judgments of this kind is the *representativeness heuristic* (Kahneman & Tversky, 1972, 1973; Tversky & Kahneman, 1974). Representativeness refers to judgments based on the degree to which a given stimulus or evidentiary base matches the essential features of some category, schema, or prior expectation. To make an accurate decision, clinicians must consider the probability of encountering a category member as well as a nonmember by chance, given that both exhibit some diagnostic sign. However, much of this important base-rate information is ignored, and decision-makers tend to attend selectively instead to information that fits preexisting sets of expectations, as we discussed previously.

It is the representativeness heuristic that makes us think that a bright college student who is a poor speller might be dyslexic, even though there are innumerable individuals who are not dyslexic but are still poor spellers (Dawes, 1986). We are ignoring the high base-rate of poor-spelling non-dyslexics in the population and instead focusing our attention on a presumed link between spelling and dyslexia. As a general rule, we tend to ignore the base-rate of a particular disorder independent of some characteristic of the disorder, and vice versa (Dawes, 1963; Meehl & Rosen, 1955). We may believe that someone giving a color response on the Rorschach is emotionally labile, ignoring the number of people who are emotional who do not give color responses as well as the number of people who do not give color responses but are emotionally labile.

Use of the representativeness heuristic gives rise to a classic judgmental error called *illusory correlation*, the perception that events are associated even when the relationship between them is incidental (Chapman, 1967; Tversky & Kahneman, 1980). In a classic set of studies, for example, clinicians readily assumed that certain signs on projective drawing tests (e.g., the Draw a Person Test) are associated with clinically relevant patient characteristics, even in the absence of any demonstrated association. For example, the vast majority of clinicians assumed that drawings containing unusual eyes indicate suspiciousness and that muscular physiques indicate a concern with masculinity (Chapman & Chapman, 1967). Interestingly, untrained subjects espoused these same illusory associations. Again, the actual base-rates of the symptom (suspiciousness) in the presence or

absence of the sign (unusually drawn eyes) are ignored, as is the base-rate of perfectly normal people drawing unusual eyes when presented with this task.

Similar results have been obtained using the Rorschach inkblots. Diagnosticians consistently overestimate the association between popular responses (e.g., seeing an anus) and stereotypically associated conditions (e.g., homosexuality) (Chapman & Chapman, 1969). Illusory correlations have been demonstrated using behavioral rating systems as well (Berman & Kenny, 1976). The bias is especially tenacious. Even after being told that correlations are illusory or being taught alternative diagnostic strategies, diagnosticians still adhere to the illusory associations. In fact, they tend to become even more confident of their veracity (Einhorn & Hogarth, 1978; Kurtz & Garfield, 1978; Mowrey, Doherty, & Keeley, 1979; Waller & Keeley, 1978). We consider such illusory correlations as the result of representative thinking. However, the problem of illusory correlation extends beyond this domain and will be dealt with in its own right in the next section of this paper.

Assessing Covariation

Many clinical judgment tasks, at all phases of diagnosis and treatment, involve covariation assessment, the determination of a relationship between two events; in particular, that one event occurs more in the presence than in the absence of the other event (Kayne & Alloy, 1988). As Kayne and Alloy described, much of the therapeutic process is taken up with assessing covariation. For instance, some of the biases that we have discussed under other rubrics can also be considered as instances of covariation assessment gone awry. The illusory correlations reported by Chapman and Chapman (1967, 1969) and discussed by us as an example of representative thinking can be considered a failure in accurately assessing the covariation between psychodiagnostic test results and patients' symptoms. Similarly, the confirmatory biases we have discussed, such as the labeling bias demonstrated by Temerlin's (1968), Rosenhan's (1973), and Langer and Abelson's (1974) subjects, can all be considered distortions in the assessment of actual covariation between behaviors implied by such labels and the patient's behavior. Difficulties in assessing covariation also tend to bias clinicians to be overconfident about the likely success of treatments consistent with their schooling.

Errors in Detecting Covariation

The literature on the ability to detect covariation accurately has been well described by Kayne and Alloy (1988), so we will only summarize it briefly here. In short, if individuals are asked to judge the covariation of sets of continuous stimuli about which they have no prior expectations (e.g., lists of number pairs), they can do it quite accurately (Beach & Scopp, 1966; Erlick & Mills, 1967). However, when asked to make dichotomous judgments about stimuli for which individuals have strong prior expectancies, the evidence for accuracy is weaker (Alloy & Abramson, 1979; Dickinson, Shanks, & Evenden, 1983; Peterson, 1980; Ward & Jenkins, 1965). In these studies, typically, when subjects expected to observe covariation they in fact did, unless encouraged to consider noncontingency as an alternative hypothesis. Finally, when judging one's own behaviors, there is a marked tendency, so long as we are not depressed (see Abramson & Alloy, 1981; Alloy & Abramson, 1979, 1982; Alloy, Abramson, & Viscusi, 1981; Alloy, Crocker, & Tabachnik, 1980), to overestimate the degree of covariation between our actions and environmental outcomes (Langer, 1975; Langer & Roth, 1975; Wortman, 1975).

The Sources of These Errors

Why do individuals have difficulty accurately assessing covariation, especially when they have strong expectations about contingencies among events? Kayne and Alloy (1988) suggested that there are five points in the judgmental process from which biases in the assessment of covariation can emanate: (a) gathering confirming and disconfirming data, (b) sampling cases, (c) classifying instances, (d) recalling evidence and estimating frequencies, and (e) combining evidence and formulating a judgment. Suppose a clinician is trying to decide whether clients who are late for their first appointments tend to show little improvement in therapy. This clinician, then, is trying to assess the covariance between being late and improvement and expects to see a negative association. In order to assess whether there is a relationship between these two variables, the clinician would have to think about four different kinds of clients: those who were late and those who were not late crossed with those who improved and those who did not improve. As discussed earlier, however, individuals are more prone to attend to and remember cases that confirm the late/no-im-

provement, not-late/improvement hypotheses and to ignore the disconfirming cases that could be found in the other two cells (Snyder & Cantor, 1979; Snyder & Swann, 1978a, 1978b; Wason & Johnson-Laird, 1972). For the most part, people are more likely to attend to cases that confirm the primary hypothesis; in this case, the late/no-improvement combination (Crocker, 1982; Schustack & Sternberg, 1981).

The second point at which error is introduced into the assessment of covariance is when deciding on which cases to include as evidence. First, when the clinician is seeking to test the late/no-improvement hypothesis, he or she can easily forget that the available data base (i.e., that clinician's case load) is neither a random nor especially large sample of cases (Tversky & Kahneman, 1971). Moreover, if the clinician tries to enlarge the sample by asking colleagues, the question is likely to be formulated as, "Do you have any patients who came late to their first session and then never improved?" forgetting about the three other possible combinations of these variables, especially the two that disconfirm the expected association (Alloy, Crocker, & Tabachnik, 1980; John, Scott, & Bettman, 1986).

Individuals also have great difficulty correctly classifying cases as confirming or as disconfirming the initial covariance hypothesis. In the example that we have been using, what is considered a "late" client? One who arrived 5 minutes late? Ten minutes late? It is quite possible that a client who arrived 5 minutes late and subsequently did not improve might inadvertently be classified as "late" at the same time that a 10-minute-late client who was "cured" was not (Crocker, 1981). The subjective classification of clients as improved or not improved is probably even more difficult. The initial hypothesis about covariation is likely to influence the manner in which ambiguous cases are classified (Nisbett & Ross, 1980).

After classifying cases as confirming or disconfirming the covariation hypothesis, individuals must total them up. If the cases are aggregated over a long period of time, recall biases may make covariation estimation inaccurate. As mentioned earlier, cases consistent with initial hypotheses are more likely to be recalled than irrelevant or inconsistent cases (Arkes & Harkness, 1983; Trolier & Hamilton, 1986).

Once the cases in the four cells are recalled and combined, individuals must somehow arrive at an estimate of the actual level of covariation between the two variables; in our example, being late and therapeutic improvement. It is unlikely that individuals compute some statistic—an odd ratio, chisquare, or correlation coefficient. Rather, they rely on a more intuitive approach, although this question has not been studied directly through think-aloud or other thought-sampling procedures (Kayne & Alloy, 1988). Such intuitive estimates of covariation are notoriously inaccurate.

Making Decisions and Predicting the Future

Decision-Making Processes

The kind of decision-making faced by clinicians is generally referred to as decision-making under conditions of uncertainty. The study of such decision-making processes is called *decision analysis* (Elstein, 1988). Decision analysis is the examination of normative processes in decision-making (Keeney, 1982; Raiffa, 1968; Weinstein & Fineberg, 1980), especially logical, rational decisions that follow from the application of axiomatic principles such as the theory of expected utility (Schoemaker, 1980; Von Neumann & Morgenstein, 1947). However, psychological research on decision-making suggests that people often deviate from the decision-making outcomes predicted by decision theorists and expected utility theory (Fischhoff, 1980; Kahneman & Tversky, 1979; Tversky & Kahneman, 1981). Recently, Tversky and Kahneman (1986) argued that actual human decision-making processes will never consistently fit normative models. Rather, normative models, like expected utility, are ideals rather than actual representations of human decision-making processes (for an excellent review of decision analysis and decision theory, see Abelson & Levi, 1985).

Elstein (1988) nicely summarized the ways in which decision-makers deviate typically from normative or ideal models of decision-making. The first difficulty is in estimating probabilities for clinically relevant outcomes. Normatively, the determination of the probability of a particular clinical outcome (e.g., depression, schizophrenia) given a diagnostic sign is based on Bayes's Theorem, which instructs the decision-maker to attend to (a) the frequency that the diagnostic sign occurs in the population, (b) the frequency or base-rate of the clinical outcome in the population, (c) the probability that a person with the clinical outcome will display the diagnostic sign, and (d) the probability that normal individuals will display

the diagnostic sign, as we have discussed earlier. However, individuals deviate from Bayes's Theorem considerably. Clinical decision-makers often attend only to a test's sensitivity (its accuracy in identifying individuals with a disorder) and ignore its specificity (its accuracy in identifying people who do not have the disorder) (Balla, Elstein, & Gates, 1983). They ignore the base-rates and attend to a few vivid cases (Nisbett, Borgida, Crandall, & Reed, 1976; Nisbett & Ross, 1980). Even if a diagnostic sign displays few false positives, when the base-rate of a disorder in a population is small, many people will be falsely labeled as pathological (Wiggins, 1973).

A second deviation of human decision-makers from normative decision theories reviewed by Elstein (1988) concerns the minimization of maximum possible losses (i.e., the minimization of regret, Feinstein, 1985). Clinicians will often make decisions that minimize possible aversive outcomes rather than ones that might maximize health. For example, clinicians might be inclined to overdiagnose pathology because that would minimize the risk of a grossly impaired person being labeled healthy and not receiving any treatment. Often such decisions are accompanied by an overconfidence in clinicians' beliefs about the salubriousness of their therapeutic actions (Cohen & Oyster-Nelson, 1981; Kayne & Alloy, 1988).

Finally, the estimates of the utility of various therapeutic options varies widely depending on how these options are framed (Tversky & Kahneman, 1981). For example, clinicians often come to different decisions if they focus on the probability of a positive outcome if an action is taken versus the probability of a negative outcome if an action is not taken. The framing postulate suggests that decision-makers organize information relevant to decisions in terms of potential gains or potential losses as compared with a present referent point (e.g., present level of health). Factually equivalent material can be presented to individuals such that they encode it as either a gain or a loss. For example, in a classic Tversky and Kahneman (1981) study, subjects were presented with a situation in which the outbreak of a disease is expected to kill 600 people. Subjects must decide whether to endorse a program guaranteeing that 200 people will be saved and 400 will die or one that says there is a .33 probability that all 600 will be saved and a .67 probability that all 600 will die. When the question emphasizes the fact that the first program will save 200 people, subjects tend to endorse this "sure thing" option. But when the question emphasizes that this option will result in 400 deaths, subjects tend to endorse the risky, probabilistic alternative.

Affective Influences on Risk-Taking and Decisions

Earlier we reviewed some of the evidence for the idea that moods and emotions influence judgment in a direction congruent with their affective valence. In addition, affect seems to influence decision-making under conditions of risk or uncertainty (reviewed by Isen, 1987). For example, when the outcome of a decision is not especially important, happy moods tend to produce riskier decision-making. However, when there is a potential for a great loss, individuals tend to become more conservative when in a positive mood (Arkes, Herren, & Isen, 1988; Isen & Geva, 1987; Isen, Means, Patrick, & Nowicki, 1982; Isen & Patrick, 1983). When the risk of loss is great, happy subjects seem to behave so as to maintain their happiness. Happy individuals view the consequences of such losses as more dire or extreme than individuals in a more neutral mood state (Isen, Nygren, & Ashby, 1985). Moreover, moods have a rather systematic influence on perceptions of the probability of positive and negative outcomes. The probability of future negative events such as diseases, natural disasters, and other catastrophes looms much larger when we are sad than happy (Johnson & Tversky, 1983; Salovey & Birnbaum, 1989).

The decision-making strategies used by individuals vary depending on mood. Happy individuals are likely to try to reduce the complexity of a decision-making task in order to engage in quick and simple kinds of cognitive processing (Isen & Daubman, 1984). Moreover, when happy, individuals are more likely to use intuitive (and potentially error-prone) strategies as compared with more taxing, logical ones (Isen et al., 1982). As we have described elsewhere (Salovey & Turk, 1988), it seems that happy decision-makers may be more inclined to rely on their "gut" instincts.

The Hindsight Bias

After a decision is made, clinicians can be influenced by the tendency of their colleagues to claim that they could have predicted the outcome in advance. Labeled the *hindsight bias* by Fischhoff (1975), individuals believe that certain outcomes are easier to predict when thinking about them after the fact. Such "Monday morning quarter-

backing" can often be found at medical and psychological case conferences (Dawson, Arkes, Siciliano, Blinkhorn, Lakshmanan, & Petrelli, 1988). After listening to a case history and learning of the outcome, individuals often succumb to the belief that they "knew it all along." The unfortunate implication of the hindsight bias is that on hearing a case history, individuals tend to believe that case is not very informative. After all, they could have predicted the results in advance. Similarly, the hindsight bias is associated with underestimating the power of judgmental biases and overconfidence in one's inferential skills.

HUMAN INFORMATION-PROCESSING LIMITATIONS

The bulk of this chapter thus far has been devoted to the specific ways in which clinical judgment can be suboptimal. We have tried to emphasize that it is judgment per se that is fallible, not necessarily clinicians. In this section, we will discuss those aspects of the human cognitive system that limit judgmental capacities in all of us.

Faust (1986) has suggested that two cognitive limitations may be the major contributors to judgmental difficulties: the capacity to use additional information and the ability to perform multiple cue tasks. Individuals have great difficulty integrating new, additional information within an existing set of information. As additional information is provided, it is often ignored or discounted (Sines, 1959). For example, clinicians have great difficulty integrating new test results with an existing battery of scores (Golden, 1964) or with data gleaned from a clinical interview (Winch & More, 1956).

Second, clinicians often believe they are integrating various sources of data in a complex, interactional, configural analysis. However, in reality, studies using multiple cue tasks that provide information pertaining to two or more dimensions indicate that clinicians actually combine information in simple linear ways (Wiggins & Hoffman, 1968). This is probably why linear models provide such an accurate representation of human judgment processes (Goldberg, 1968). In short, individuals have great difficulty combining multiple cues even when the judgmental task requires the integration of only two or three bits of information. We seem to lack the cognitive capacity for such operations (for a more thorough review see

Slovic & Lichtenstein, 1971). These limitations on cognitive processing reflect what has been termed *bounded rationality* (Newell & Simon, 1972; Simon, 1979), the idea that humans possess a limited capacity for rational thought. Bounded rationality is primarily attributable to the limits of human memory so that complex problems must be somehow simplified in order to reduce their load on the cognitive system.

IMPROVING CLINICAL JUDGMENT

One of the reasons why the literature on bias in clinical judgment and inference processes has had little impact on clinical practice is that often such limitations are described in a derogatory tone and few hints about their reduction are provided. With great amusement, investigators in this field have documented our judgmental shortcomings and other "irrational" inferential processes. But it is much easier to be critical than constructive. Behavior is difficult to change, and sometimes the suggestions of nonpractitioners are overly cumbersome. For discussions of clinical judgment to have impact in clinical settings, however, they must be provided in the context of practical as well as helpful advice. In the remainder of this chapter, we will discuss some of the procedures that have been suggested for improving clinical judgment and some ideas for improving research in this area as well.

Direct Training in Reasoning Skills

It is often thought that if psychological and medical decision-makers could be instructed directly in judgmental skills and warned against inferential limitations and biases, they could learn to be more accurate and less overconfident judges. For example, Howe, Holmes, and Elstein (1984) offered a three-term course in decision analysis to medical students organized around the discussion of cases. Although the students often found presentations about the limitations of clinical judgment unsettling, they were able to learn to recognize and quantify sources of uncertainty and error.

The impact of such direct training programs on judgment has been assessed, but the results are mixed. Individuals do not seem to have difficulty learning abstract (not domain-specific) reasoning skills (Nisbett, Fong, Lehman, & Cheng, 1987). Moreover, statistics courses do increase the

chances that individuals will recognize the operation of statistical principles in common events (Fong, Krantz, & Nisbett, 1986). However, the direct provision of corrective feedback to clinical decision-makers has not proved to be especially effective (Goldberg, 1968; Graham, 1971), nor have warnings provided in advance of decision-making (Fischhoff, 1977; Kurtz & Garfield, 1978; Wood, 1978).

General Correctives

Although merely pointing out the existence of judgmental shortcomings may not be an especially effective way in which to reduce their impact, a certain amount of self-reflection might be helpful. Faust (1986) described three general strategies that yield easily implemented corrective procedures. These include (a) testing the validity of diagnostic signs, (b) using disconfirmatory strategies, and (c) recognizing predictive uncertainty. To these we add, as others have advised (e.g., Dawes, 1986), suggestions regarding how to avoid being influenced by client acceptance of faculty judgments and how to reduce the burden on memory inherent in judgmental tasks.

Tests for Diagnostic Signs

Faust (1986) recommended that clinicians examine supposedly diagnostic tests and signs very carefully for evidence of their validity. In particular, three tests should be applied to a diagnostic sign before it is accepted as useful. The first test is to determine if there is a true association between the sign and the disorder. The disorder must appear more frequently in the presence of the sign than in its absence. As discussed earlier, the probability of finding a clinical case in each of four cells must be evaluated: (+)sign/(+)disorder, (+)sign/(−)disorder, (−)sign/(+)disorder, (−)sign/(−)disorder. Validity cannot be confirmed unless data for all four of these cells are gathered. Such Bayesian thinking seems essential to improving clinical judgment (see also Arkes, 1981).

The second test is to make sure that the sign increases diagnostic accuracy. A sign may be strongly associated with a disorder, but it also must not falsely identify pathology at a rate greater than the frequency of the pathology itself. Finally, one must assure oneself that use of a diagnostic sign results in incremental validity. That is, the sign must not be redundant with other diagnostic signs; it must contribute new information or predictive power. If it does not, the clinician can become overconfident being falsely reassured by each new (but redundant) sign. It is rare when more than a handful of diagnostic signs are needed to maximize predictive accuracy.

Using Disconfirming Strategies

Faust (1986) also noted that clinicians would be more accurate if they emphasized the disconfirmation of hypotheses rather than confirming evidence for an a priori hypothesis. Unless one accurately searches for disconfirming information, one often will not obtain evidence that a hypothesis is absolutely wrong. "Signs associated with more than one condition or with many conditions (e.g., anxiety) are much less useful for differential diagnosis than exclusionary signs or criteria" (p. 427). As a general rule, the clinician should try to generate several alternative explanations for their clinical hypotheses. In particular, it is helpful to generate a set of confirmatory ("why might I be correct?") and a set of disconfirmatory ("why might I be incorrect?") explanations. Multiple competing hypotheses should be considered so that the data obtained can rule out some while supporting an alternative.

When individuals are forced to generate alternative explanations for outcomes, errors in reasoning such as the hindsight bias are reduced because generated alternatives are then judged as more likely to occur (Ross, Lepper, Strack, & Steinmetz, 1977; Slovic & Fischhoff, 1977), thus reducing overconfidence and consequently premature closure (Elstein, Shulman, & Sprafka, 1978). Generating multiple alternative explanations also increases the probability that one of them might be correct (Arnoult & Anderson, 1988).

Beware of Client Acceptance
of Faulty Judgment

The term *Barnum effect* has been used by Meehl (1956) to describe the situation in which people willingly accept personality interpretations from experts even though they are based on vague horoscopelike statements that are likely to apply to most people in the general population (e.g., "Although you generally think well of yourself, at times you doubt your abilities"). This remarkably consistent phenomenon was reviewed by Snyder, Shenkel, and Lowery (1977), who noted that acceptance of Barnum interpretations is enhanced by situational features common to the clinical diagnostic situation. The client assumes that the in-

terpretation was specifically developed for him or her, derived from the results of valid psychological assessment techniques, and delivered by an expert, high-status clinician. After accepting such interpretations, clients increase their faith in psychological testing and their confidence in the skills of their clinician (Snyder, Larsen, & Bloom, 1976; Snyder & Shenkel, 1976).

It is important that clinicians not be reinforced by their clients' enthusiastic acceptance of personality interpretations (even when they are not Barnum statements). The Barnum effect literature establishes clearly that clients will accept any reasonable-sounding interpretation delivered by an authority figure so long as it seems somewhat tailored to them personally. We have even been able to replicate the Barnum effect in our Abnormal Psychology classes in which all students take a brief personality scale and later in the semester all receive the same description of their personalities on a form with their personalized code number. Nearly all of these students rate the description as a good or excellent formulation of their personality characteristics. Snyder et al. (1977) aptly pointed out that the "sucker" in the Barnum situation may not be the naive client who believes generic feedback, but the clinician who interprets such client acceptance as valid feedback about his or her clinical skills.

Recognizing Predictive Uncertainty

Given that prediction is filled with uncertainty, clinicians should accept this uncertainty and recognize that a certain amount of error is unavoidable. By accepting such fallibility, clinicians will not too hastily abandon good but imperfect predictors and will not be overconfident in stating predictions and diagnoses. Recognition that as clinicians we are fallible should allow us to accept research on judgment and decision-making processes less defensively.

Minimizing Reliance on Memory

As discussed earlier, most judgmental biases are the result of limitations of our cognitive systems to deal simultaneously with multiple bits of information. To minimize bias, then, we should be motivated to minimize reliance on memory. Along these lines, Dawes (1986) suggested that it is helpful to rely on external aids—the computer, pencil and paper—when we need to estimate frequencies, and that it makes sense to actually write down base-rates and probability ratios. Unfortunately, decision-makers often reject such external aids. They often believe that they can improve on them by using inferences based on theoretical viewpoint and clinical experience, even though these are likely to worsen prediction (Arkes, Dawes, & Christensen, 1986).

Minimizing reliance on memory has other useful functions. For example, it can reduce the likelihood that information not presented at a case conference that is consistent with a case summary is misremembered as having been presented. Unpresented symptoms that are consistent with a diagnosis tend to be remembered as having been presented (Arkes & Harkness, 1980). Moreover, previously presented symptoms that are not consistent with the diagnosis are often forgotten.

There are a multitude of creative solutions to reducing the load on memory during judgmental tasks. For example, Arnoult and Anderson (1988) suggested using multiple judges, role-playing, videotape, rating scales, balance sheets, graphics, and hypothetical questions. And Nisbett and Ross (1980) have provided some helpful maxims. By not burdening working memory, clinicians may be less likely to rush to choose a seemingly satisfactory but perhaps wrong solution to a judgmental problem.

IMPROVING RESEARCH ON CLINICAL JUDGMENT

After nearly 40 years of research on judgment, inference, and decision-making, the influence of this corpus of data on actual clinical practice is not very evident. Few volumes have been written attempting to translate research of laboratory-oriented social and cognitive psychologists into a language understandable by the practicing clinician (but see Turk & Salovey, 1988). The investigators complain that clinicians react defensively to their suggestions concerning improving judgmental accuracy. But often these suggestions have been made in the context of books and articles ignoring or discounting the difficulties faced by the clinician and, at times, questioning the intelligence of the clinician him or herself. For research on judgmental processes to have any impact on clinical practice, such "clinician bashing" must cease. Clinicians may operate from a different "assumptive world" than decision theorists, but if presented empathically, the messages of such investigators need not be lost on them. To the extent that psychology as a discipline can reaffirm its

commitment to training clinicians who are also scientists (the fading scientist-practitioner model), we increase the likelihood that important research on judgment and decision-making will find its way to the clinic.

Recently, the clinical judgment literature has also been criticized as suffering from an inadequate framework for understanding different types of judgment and, especially, for failing to attend to the context in which judgments are made (Rock, Bransford, Maisto, & Morey, 1987). These authors suggest that a more "ecological" approach be taken in studying judgment that explicitly attends to "(a) characteristics of the therapist, (b) information processing strategies made available to the clinician, (c) critical tasks that define the major focus of specific judgments, and (d) the nature of the clinical materials that provide the basis for judgments" (p. 645).

For many years, Holt (1958, 1961, 1970, 1988) and others have argued that the literature on judgment, which is based primarily on laboratory experiments, may not be directly generalizable to the kinds of clinical judgment tasks faced by the practicing clinician. He has described six discrepancies between clinical judgment as studied versus practiced. As summarized by Rock et al. (1987), Holt questioned the ecological validity of the extant research on clinical judgment. The debate about ecological validity of the laboratory paradigm in cognitive psychology now rages in a variety of contexts (compare Neisser, 1982, with Banaji & Crowder, 1989). It is sufficient here to note, however, that Rock et al. (1987) suggested that the experimental literature on clinical judgment would have greater impact if relevant variables affecting the context in which judgments are made are considered. For example, they suggested (based on Jenkins, 1979) (a) that investigators measure the explicit characteristics of their subjects relevant to the judgment task such as abilities, knowledge, preferences, experience, and orientation, and (b) that the criterial tasks— diagnosis, prognosis, formulation, and description—be made explicit. Furthermore, they recommended that characteristics of the clinical materials on which judgments are based be attended to, such as in-person interviews, taped interviews, case notes, case conference, case history, test battery, or the reports of others; and that the specific information-processing activities required of the clinician be measured explicitly: single versus multiple judgment trials, opportunity for feedback, and ability to debug problems in making judgments.

In analyzing the data collected from experiments considering all of these variables, interactions should be emphasized. What combinations of variables accumulated in what ways produce especially good or especially poor judgmental outcomes? In recent years, the ecological approach to clinical judgment has motivated reviews of the situational factors impinging on person perception during the clinical interview (Cline, 1985) and studies of the judgments of physicians (LaDuca, Engel, & Chovan, 1988).

SUMMARY

This chapter describes some of the difficulties faced by clinicians in the course of making judgments at five stages in the diagnostic process: (a) forming a first impression, (b) using a classification system, (c) making a diagnosis, (d) assessing covariation, and (e) making decisions and predicting the future. At each of these steps, various factors conspire to produce suboptimal judgment mostly emanating from the limited capacity of our cognitive systems. Several suggestions are made concerning the reduction of these biases, and we conclude with some thoughts regarding how to make research in this area more accessible to the practicing clinician in his or her daily activities. In particular, clinical judgment is improved when diagnosticians examine the validity of tests very carefully, use a disconfirming rather than confirmatory hypothesis-testing process, reduce reliance on client acceptance of interpretations as evidence of their validity, accept the presence of predictive uncertainty, and use any expedient possible to reduce demand on working memory. Conversely, research on clinical judgment will be more likely to influence the practicing clinician when it attends to the real conditions in which clinical decisions are made and is communicated in a context that acknowledges the difficulties inherent in clinicians' work. Perhaps the scientist-practitioner perspective that is being revived through the health psychology movement will serve to increase communication between investigators of clinical judgment and clinicians themselves.

REFERENCES

Abelson, R. P., & Levi, A. (1985). Decision making and decision theory. In G. Lindzey & E. Aronson (Eds.), *Handbook of social psychology* (3rd ed., Vol. 1, pp. 231–310). New York: Random House.

Abramson, L. Y., & Alloy, L. B. (1981). Depression, nondepression, and cognitive illusions: A reply to Schwartz. *Journal of Experimental Psychology: General, 110*, 436–447.

Alloy, L. B., & Abramson, L. Y. (1979). Judgment of contingency in depressed and nondepressed students: Sadder but wiser? *Journal of Experimental Psychology: General, 108*, 441–485.

Alloy, L. B., & Abramson, L. Y. (1982). Learned helplessness, depression, and the illusion of control. *Journal of Personality and Social Psychology, 42*, 1114–1126.

Alloy, L. B., Abramson, L. Y., & Viscusi, D. (1981). Induced mood and the illusion of control. *Journal of Personality and Social Psychology, 41*, 1129–1140.

Alloy, L. B., Crocker, J., & Tabachnik, N. (1980). *Depression and covariation judgments: Expectation-based distortions in information search and recall.* Paper presented at the annual meeting of the American Psychological Association, Montreal.

American Psychiatric Association. (1987). *Diagnostic and statistical manual of mental disorders* (3rd ed., rev.). Washington, DC: Author.

Arkes, H. R. (1981). Impediments to accurate clinical judgment and possible ways to minimize their impact. *Journal of Consulting and Clinical Psychology, 49*, 323–330.

Arkes, H. R., Dawes, R. M., & Christensen, C. (1986). Factors influencing the use of a decision rule in a probabilistic task. *Behavior and Human Decision Processes, 37*, 93–110.

Arkes, H. R., & Harkness, A. R. (1980). The effect of making a diagnosis on subsequent recognition of symptoms. *Journal of Experimental Psychology: Human Learning and Memory, 6*, 568–575.

Arkes, H. R., & Harkness, A. R. (1983). Estimates of contingency between two dichotomous variables. *Journal of Experimental Psychology: General, 112*, 117–135.

Arkes, H. R., Herren, L. T., & Isen, A. M. (1988). The role of potential loss in the influence of affect on risk-taking behavior. *Organizational Behavior and Human Decision Processes, 42*, 181–193.

Arnoult, L. H., & Anderson, C. A. (1988). Identifying and reducing causal reasoning biases in clinical practice. In D. C. Turk & P. Salovey (Eds.), *Reasoning, inference, and judgment in clinical psychology* (pp. 209–232). New York: Free Press.

Asch, S. E. (1946). Forming impressions of personality. *Journal of Abnormal and Social Psychology, 41*, 258–290.

Balla, J. I., Elstein, A. S., & Gates, P. (1983). Effects of prevalence and test diagnosticity upon clinical judgments of probability. *Methods of Information in Medicine, 22*, 25–28.

Banaji, M. R., & Crowder, R. (1989). The bankruptcy of everyday memory. *American Psychologist, 44*, 1185–1193.

Bandura, A., Lipsher, D. H., & Miller, P. E. (1960). Psychotherapists' approach-avoidance reactions to patients' expressions of hostility. *Journal of Consulting Psychology, 24*, 1–8.

Beach, L. R., & Scopp, T. S. (1966). Inferences about correlations. *Psychonomic Science, 6*, 253–254.

Berman, D. S., & Kenny, D. A. (1976). Correlational bias in observer ratings. *Journal of Personality and Social Psychology, 34*, 263–273.

Berner, P., & Katschnig, H. (1983). Principles of "multiaxial" classification in psychiatry as a basis of modern methodology. In T. Helgason (Ed.), *Methodology in evaluation of psychiatric treatment*. Cambridge, England: Cambridge University Press.

Berner, P., Katschnig, H., & Lenz, G. (1982). Poly-diagnostic approach: A method to clarify incongruencies among the classification of the functional psychoses. *The Psychiatric Journal of the University of Ottawa, 7*, 244–248.

Bieri, J., Atkins, A. L., Briar, S., Leaman, R. L., Miller, H., & Tripodi, T. (1966). *Clinical and social judgement*. New York: John Wiley & Sons.

Bleuler, E. (1908). Die prognoe der dementia praecox schizophrenic gruppe. *Allemeine Zeitschrift von Psychiatrie, 65*, 436–464.

Bower, G. H. (1981). Mood and memory. *American Psychologist, 36*, 129–148.

Bruner, J. S., & Tagiuri, R. (1954). The perception of people. In G. Lindzey (Ed.), *Handbook of social psychology*. Reading, MA: Addison-Wesley.

Cantor, N., Smith, E., French, R., & Mezzich, J. (1980). Psychiatric diagnosis as prototype categorization. *Journal of Abnormal Psychology, 89*, 181–193.

Carlston, E. D. (1977). *The recall and use of observed behaviors and inferred traits in social inferences processes*. Unpublished doctoral dissertation, University of Illinois, Urbana, IL.

Chapman, L. J. (1967). Illusory correlation in observational reports. *Journal of Verbal Learning and Verbal Behavior, 6*, 151–155.

Chapman, L. J., & Chapman, J. P. (1967). Genesis of popular but erroneous psycho-diagnostic observations. *Journal of Abnormal Psychology, 72*, 193–204.

Chapman, L. J., & Chapman, J. P. (1969). Illusory correlation as an obstacle to the use of valid psychodiagnostic signs. *Journal of Abnormal Psychology, 74*, 271–280.

Cline, T. (1985). Clinical judgment in context: A review of situational factors in person perception during clinical interviews. *Journal of Child Psychology and Psychiatry, 26*, 369–380.

Clore, G. L., Schwartz, N., & Kirsch, J. (1983). *Generalized mood effects on evaluative judgments*. Paper presented at the meeting of the Midwestern Psychological Association, Chicago.

Cohen, L. H., & Oyster-Nelson, C. K. (1981). Clinicians' evaluations of psychodynamic psychotherapy: Experimental data on psychological peer review. *Journal of Consulting and Clinical Psychology, 49*, 583–589.

Crocker, J. (1981). Judgment of covariation by social perceivers. *Psychological Bulletin, 90*, 272–292.

Crocker, J. (1982). Biased questions in judgment of covariation studies. *Personality and Social Psychology Bulletin, 8*, 214–220.

Davis, D. A. (1979). What's in a name? A Bayesian rethinking of attributional biases in clinical judgment. *Journal of Consulting and Clinical Psychology, 47*, 1109–1114.

Dawes, R. M. (1963). A note on base rates and psychometric efficiency. *Journal of Consulting Psychology, 26*, 422–424.

Dawes, R. M. (1986). Representative thinking in clinical judgment. *Clinical Psychology Review, 6*, 425–441.

Dawson, N. V., Arkes, H. R., Siciliano, C., Blinkhorn, R., Lakshmanan, M., & Petrelli, M. (1988). Hindsight bias: An impediment to accurate probability estimation in clinicopathologic conferences. *Medical Decision Making, 8*, 259–264.

Dickinson, A., Shanks, D., & Evenden, J. (1983). Judgment of act-outcome contingency: The role of selective attribution. *Quarterly Journal of Experimental Psychology, 36*, 29–50.

Einhorn, H. J., & Hogarth, R. M. (1978). Confidence in judgment: Persistence of the illusion of validity. *Psychological Review, 85*, 395–416.

Elstein, A. S. (1988). Cognitive processes in clinical inference and decision making. In D. C. Turk & P. Salovey (Eds.), *Reasoning, inference, and judgment in clinical psychology* (pp. 17–50). New York: Free Press.

Elstein, A. S., Shulman, A. S., & Sprafka, S. A. (1978). *Medical problem solving: An analysis of clinical reasoning.* Cambridge, MA: Harvard University Press.

Erlick, D. E., & Mills, R. G. (1967). Perceptual qualification of conditional dependency. *Journal of Experimental Psychology, 73*, 9–14.

Faust, D. (1986). Research on human judgment and its application to clinical practice. *Professional Psychology: Research and Practice, 5*, 420–430.

Feinstein, A. R. (1985). The "chagrin factor" and qualitative decision analysis. *Archives of Internal Medicine, 145*, 1257–1259.

Fischhoff, B. (1975). Hindsight = / foresight: The effect of outcome knowledge on judgment under uncertainty. *Journal of Experimental Psychology: Human Perception, 1*, 288–299.

Fischhoff, B. (1977). Perceived informativeness of facts. *Journal of Experimental Psychology: Human Perception and Performance, 3*, 349–358.

Fischhoff, B. (1980). Clinical decision analysis. *Operations Research, 28*, 28–43.

Fiske, S. T., Kenny, D. A., & Taylor, S. E. (1982). Structural models of the mediation of salience effects on attribution. *Journal of Experimental Social Psychology, 18*, 105–127.

Fiske, S. T., & Taylor, S. E. (1984). *Social cognition.* Reading, MA: Addison-Wesley.

Fong, G. T., Krantz, D. H., & Nisbett, R. E. (1986). The effects of statistical training on thinking about everyday problems. *Cognitive Psychology, 18*, 253–292.

Forgas, J., & Bower, G. H. (1988). Affect in social and personal judgments. In K. Fiedler & J. Forgas (Eds.), *Affect, cognition, and social behavior* (pp. 183–208). Toronto: C. J. Hogrefe.

Frank, J. D. (1974). *Persuasion and healing* (rev. ed.). New York: Schocken Books.

Gauron, E. F., & Dickinson, J. K. (1969). The influence of seeing the patient first on diagnostic decision-making in psychiatry. *American Journal of Psychiatry, 126*, 199–205.

Genero, N., & Cantor, N. (1987). Exemplar prototypes and clinical diagnosis: Toward a cognitive economy. *Journal of Social and Clinical Psychology, 5*, 59–78.

Goldberg, L. R. (1968). Simple models or simple processes? Some research on clinical judgments. *American Psychologist, 23*, 483–496.

Golden, M. (1964). Some effects of combining psychological tests on clinical inferences. *Journal of Consulting Psychology, 28*, 440–446.

Gouaux, C. (1971). Induced affective states and interpersonal attraction. *Journal of Personality and Social Psychology, 20*, 37–43.

Graham, J. R. (1971). Feedback and accuracy of clinical judgments from the MMPI. *Journal of Consulting and Clinical Psychology, 36*, 286–291.

Griffitt, W. B. (1970). Environmental effects of interpersonal affective behavior: Ambient effective temperature and attraction. *Journal of Personality and Social Psychology, 15*, 240–244.

Hastie, R. (1981). Schematic principles in human memory. In E. T. Higgins, C. P. Herman, & M. P. Zanna (Eds.), *Social cognition: The Ontario symposium* (Vol. 1, pp. 39–88). Hillsdale, NJ: Lawrence Erlbaum Associates.

Holt, R. R. (1958). Clinical *and* statistical prediction: A reformulation and some new data. *Journal of Abnormal and Social Psychology, 56*, 1–12.

Holt, R. R. (1961). Clinical judgment as a disciplined inquiry. *Journal of Nervous and Mental Disease, 133*, 369–382.

Holt, R. R. (1970). Yet another look at clinical and statistical prediction: Or, is clinical psychology worthwhile? *American Psychologist, 25*, 337–349.

Holt, R. R. (1978). A historical survey of the clinical-statistical prediction controversy. In R. R. Holt (Ed.), *Methods in clinical psychology: Vol. 2. Prediction and research* (pp. 3–18). New York: Plenum Press.

Holt, R. R. (1986). Clinical and statistical prediction: A retrospective and would-be integrative perspective. *Journal of Personality Assessment, 50*, 376–386.

Holt, R. R. (1988). Judgment, influence, and reasoning in clinical perspective. In D. C. Turk & P. Salovey (Eds.), *Reasoning, inference, and judgment in clinical psychology* (pp. 233–250). New York: Free Press.

Horowitz, L. M., Post, D., French, R., Wallis, K., & Siegelman, E. (1981). The prototype as a construct in abnormal psychology: 2. Clarifying disagreement in psychiatric judgments. *Journal of Abnormal Psychology, 90*, 575–585.

Horowitz, L. M., Wright, J. C., Lowenstein, E., & Parad, H. W. (1981). The prototype as a construct in abnormal psychology: 1. A method for deriving prototypes. *Journal of Abnormal Psychology, 90*, 568–574.

Howe, K. R., Holmes, M., & Elstein, A. S. (1984). Teaching clinical decision making. *The Journal of Medicine and Philosophy, 9*, 215–228.

Isen, A. M. (1970). Success, failure, attention, and reactions to others: The warm glow of success. *Journal of Personality and Social Psychology, 15*, 294–301.

Isen, A. M. (1984). Toward understanding the role of affect in cognition. In R. S. Wyer & T. K. Srull (Eds.), *Handbook of social cognition* (Vol. 3, pp. 179–236). Hillsdale, NJ: Lawrence Erlbaum Associates.

Isen, A. M. (1987). Positive affect, cognitive processes, and social behavior. In L. Berkowitz (Ed.), *Advances in experimental social psychology* (Vol. 20, pp. 203–253). Orlando, FL: Academic Press.

Isen, A. M., & Daubman, K. A. (1984). The influence of affect on categorization. *Journal of Personality and Social Psychology, 47*, 1206–1217.

Isen, A. M., & Geva, N. (1987). The influence of positive affect on acceptable level of risk: The person with a large canoe has a large worry. *Organizational Behavior and Human Decision Processes, 39*, 145–154.

Isen, A. M., Means, B., Patrick, R., & Nowicki, G. (1982). Some factors influencing decision-making strategy and risk-taking. In M. S. Clark & S. T. Fiske (Eds.), *Affect and cognition: The 17th annual Carnegie symposium on cognition* (pp. 243–261). Hillsdale, NJ: Lawrence Erlbaum Associates.

Isen, A. M., Nygren, T. E., & Ashby, F. G. (1985). *The influence of positive affect on the subjective utility of gains and losses: It's not worth the risk*. Paper presented at the meeting of the Psychonomic Society, Boston.

Isen, A. M., & Patrick, R. (1983). The effect of positive feelings on risk-taking: When the chips are down. *Organizational Behavior and Human Performance, 31*, 194–202.

Jaspers, K. (1963). *General psychopathology*. Manchester, England: The University of Manchester Press.

Jenkins, J. J. (1979). Four points to remember: A tetrahedron model of memory experiments. In L. S. Cermak & I. M. Craik (Eds.), *Levels of processing in human memory* (pp. 429–446). Hillsdale, NJ: Lawrence Erlbaum Associates.

John, D. R., Scott, C. A., & Bettman, J. R. (1986). Sampling data for covariation assessment: The effect of prior beliefs on search patterns. *Journal of Consumer Research, 13*, 38–47.

Johnson, E. J., & Tversky, A. (1983). Affect, generalization, and the perception of risk. *Journal of Personality and Social Psychology, 45*, 20–31.

Kahneman, D., & Tversky, A. (1972). Subjective probability: A judgment of representativeness. *Cognitive Psychology, 3*, 430–454.

Kahneman, D., & Tversky, A. (1973). Intuitive prediction: Biases and corrective procedures. *TIMS studies in the management sciences, 12*, 313–327.

Kahneman, D., & Tversky, A. (1979). Prospect theory: An analysis of decision under risk. *Econometrica, 47*, 263–291.

Kayne, N. T., & Alloy, L. B. (1988). Clinician and patient as aberrant actuaries: Expectation-based distortions in assessment of covariation. In L. Y. Abramson (Ed.), *Social cognition and clinical psychology* (pp. 295–365). New York: Guilford Press.

Keeney, R. L. (1982). Decision analysis: An overview. *Operations Research, 30*, 803–836.

Kleinmuntz, B. (1984). The scientific study of clinical judgment in psychology and medicine. *Clinical Psychology Review, 4*, 111–126.

Kurtz, R. M., & Garfield, S. L. (1978). Illuscry correlation: A further exploration of Chapman's paradigm. *Journal of Consulting and Clinical Psychology, 46*, 1009–1015.

LaDuca, A., Engle, J. D., & Chovan, J. D. (1988). An exploratory study of physician's clinical judgement: An application of social judgement theory. *Evaluation and the Health Professions, 11*, 178–200.

Langer, E. J. (1975). The illusion of control. *Jour-*

nal of Personality and Social Psychology, 32, 311-328.

Langer, E. J., & Abelsen, R. P. (1974). A patient by any other name . . . : Clinical group differences in labeling bias. Journal of Consulting and Clinical Psychology, 42, 4-9.

Langer, E. J., & Roth, K. (1975). Heads I win, tails it's chance: The illusion of control as a function of the sequence of outcomes in a purely chance task. Journal of Personality and Social Psychology, 32, 951-955.

Lerner, M. J. (1965). The effect of responsibility and choice on a partner's attractiveness following failure. Journal of Personality, 33, 178-187.

Lott, A. J., & Lott, B. E. (1968). A learning theory approach to interpersonal attitudes, In A. G. Greenwald, T. C. Brock, & T. M. Ostrom (Eds.), Psychological foundations of attitudes (pp. 67-88). New York: Academic Press.

Lowry, L. F. (1981). Learning about learning: Classification abilities. Berkeley: University of California.

Mayer, J. D. (1986). How mood influences cognition. In N. E. Sharkey (Ed.), Advances in cognitive science I (pp. 290-314). Chichester, England: Ellis Horwood.

Mayer, J. D., & Bremer, D. (1985). Assessing mood with affect-sensitive tasks. Journal of Personality Assessment, 49, 95-99.

Mayer, J. D., & Salovey, P. (1988). Personality moderates the interaction of mood and cognition. In K. Fiedler & J. Forgas (Eds.), Affect, cognition, and social behavior (pp. 87-99). Toronto: C. J. Hogrefe.

Mayer, J. D., & Volanth, A. J. (1985). Cognitive involvement in the emotional response system. Motivation and Emotion, 9, 261-275.

McArthur, L. Z. (1981). What grabs you? The role of attention in impression formation and causal attribution. In E. T. Higgins, C. P. Herman, & M. P. Zanna (Eds.), Social cognition: The Ontario symposium (Vol. 1, pp. 201-246). Hillsdale, NJ: Lawrence Erlbaum Associates.

McCloskey, M., & Glucksberg, S. (1978). Natural categories: Well-defined or fuzzy sets? Memory and Cognition, 6, 462-472.

Meehl, P. E. (1954). Clinical versus statistical prediction. Minneapolis: University of Minneapolis Press.

Meehl, P. E. (1956). Wanted—A good cookbook. American Psychologist, 11, 262-272.

Meehl, P. E. (1960). The cognitive activity of the clinician. American Psychologist, 15, 19-27.

Meehl, P. E. (1986). Causes and effects of my disturbing little book. Journal of Personality Assessment, 50, 370-375.

Meehl, P. E., & Rosen, A. (1955). Antecedent probability and the efficiency of psychometric signs, patterns, or cutting scores. Psychological Bulletin, 52, 194-216.

Merton, R. K. (1948). The self-fulfilling prophecy. Antioch Review, 8, 193-210.

Mezzich, J. E. (1980). Taxonomy and behavioral science: Comparative performance of grouping methods. New York: Academic Press.

Mezzich, J. E., Goodpastor, W., & Mezzich, A. C. (1987). Structural issues in diagnosis. In C. G. Last & M. Hersen (Eds.), Issues in diagnostic research (pp. 87-98). New York: Plenum Press.

Mowrey, J. D., Doherty, M. E., & Keeley, S. M. (1979). The influence of negation and complexity on illusory correlation. Journal of Abnormal Psychology, 88, 334-337.

Neisser, U. (Ed.). (1982). Memory observed. San Francisco, CA: W. H. Freeman.

Newell, A., & Simon, H. A. (1972). Human problem solving. Englewood Cliffs, NJ: Prentice-Hall.

Nisbett, R. E., Borgida, E., Crandall, R., & Reed, H. (1976). Popular induction: Information is not always informative. In J. S. Carroll & J. W. Payne (Eds.), Cognition and social behavior (pp. 227-236). Hillsdale, NJ: Lawrence Erlbaum Associates.

Nisbett, R. E., Fong, G. T., Lehman, D. R., & Cheng, P. W. (1987). Teaching reasoning. Science, 238, 625-631.

Nisbett, R. E., & Ross, L. (1980). Human inference: Strategies and shortcomings of social judgment. Englewood Cliffs, NJ: Prentice-Hall.

Peterson, C. R. (1980). Recognition of noncontingency. Journal of Personality and Social Psychology, 38, 727-734.

Raiffa, H. (1968). Decision analysis: Introductory lectures on choice under uncertainty. Reading, MA: Addison-Wesley.

Rasch, R. F. R. (1987). The nature of taxonomy. IMAGE: Journal of Nursing Scholarship, 19, 147-149.

Rock, D. L., Bransford, J. D., Maisto, S. A., & Morey, L. (1987). The study of clinical judgment: An ecological approach. Clinical Psychology Review, 7, 645-661.

Rosenhan, D. L. (1973). On being sane in insane places. *Science, 179*, 250–258.

Rosenhan, D. L. (1975). The contextual nature of psychiatric diagnosis. *Journal of Abnormal Psychology, 84*, 462–474.

Rosenthal, D. (1955). Changes in some moral values following psychotherapy. *Journal of Consulting Psychology, 19*, 431–436.

Ross, L., Lepper, M. R., Strack, F., & Steinmetz, J. (1977). Social explanation and social expectation: Effects of real and hypothetical explanations on subjective likelihood. *Journal of Personality and Social Psychology, 35*, 817–829.

Rubin, M., & Shontz, F. C. (1960). Diagnostic prototypes and diagnostic processes of clinical psychologists. *Journal of Consulting Psychology, 24*, 234–239.

Salovey, P., & Birnbaum, D. (1989). The influence of mood on health-relevant cognitions. *Journal of Personality and Social Psychology, 57*, 539–551.

Salovey, P., & Turk, D. C. (1988). Some effects of mood on clinician's memory. In D. C. Turk & P. Salovey (Eds.), *Reasoning, inference, and judgment in clinical psychology* (pp. 107–123). New York: Free Press.

Sandifer, M. G., Hordern, A., & Green, L. M. (1970). The psychiatric interview: The impact of the first three minutes. *American Journal of Psychiatry, 126*, 968–973.

Sarbin, T. R. (1941). Clinical psychology: Art or science? *Psychometrika, 6*, 391–401.

Sarbin, T. R. (1943). A contribution to the study of actuarial and individual methods of prediction. *American Journal of Sociology, 48*, 593–602.

Sarbin, T. R. (1944). The logic of prediction in psychology. *Psychological Review, 51*, 210–228.

Sarbin, T. R. (1986). Prediction and clinical inference: Forty years later. *Journal of Personality Assessment, 50*, 362–369.

Sarbin, T. R., Taft, R., & Bailey, D. E. (1960). *Clinical inference and cognitive theory*. New York: Holt, Rinehart & Winston.

Scheff, T. J. (1966). *Being mentally ill: A sociological theory*. Chicago: Aldine.

Schoemaker, P. J. H. (1980). *Experiments in decisions under risk: The expected utility hypothesis*. Boston: Martinus Nijhoff.

Schustak, M. W., & Sternberg, R. J. (1981). Evaluation of evidence in causal inference. *Journal of Experimental Psychology: General, 110*, 101–120.

Scriven, M. (1979). Clinical judgment. In H. T. Engelhardt, Jr., S. F. Spicker, & B. Towers (Eds.), *Clinical judgment: A critical appraisal* (pp. 3–16). Dordrecht, The Netherlands: D. Reidel.

Simon, H. A. (1979). Information processing models of cognition. *Annual Review of Psychology, 30*, 363–396.

Sines, L. K. (1959). The relative contribution of four kinds of data to accuracy in personality assessment. *Journal of Consulting Psychology, 23*, 483–492.

Slovic, P., & Fischhoff, B. (1977). On the psychology of experimental surprises. *Journal of Experimental Psychology: Human Perception and Performance, 3*, 544–551.

Slovic, P., & Lichtenstein, S. C. (1971). Comparison of Bayesian and regression approaches to the study of information processing in judgment. *Organizational Behavior and Human Performance, 6*, 659–744.

Snyder, C. R. (1977). "A patient by any other name" revisited: Maladjustment or attributional locus of problem. *Journal of Consulting and Clinical Psychology, 45*, 101–103.

Snyder, C. R., Larsen, D., & Bloom, L. J. (1976). Acceptance of personality interpretations prior to and after receiving diagnostic feedback supposedly based on psychological, graphological, and astrological assessment procedures. *Journal of Clinical Psychology, 32*, 258–265.

Snyder, C. R., & Shenkel, R. J. (1976). Effects of "favorability," modality, and relevance upon acceptance of general personality interpretations prior to and after receiving diagnostic feedback. *Journal of Consulting and Clinical Psychology, 44*, 34–41.

Snyder, C. R., Shenkel, R. J., & Lowery, C. R. (1977). Acceptance of personality interpretations: The "Barnum effect" and beyond. *Journal of Consulting and Clinical Psychology, 45*, 104–114.

Snyder, M. (1981). "Seek and ye shall find. . . . " In E. T. Higgins, C. P. Herman, & M. P. Zanna (Eds.), *Social cognition: The Ontario symposium on personality and social psychology* (pp. 277–303). Hillsdale, NJ: Lawrence Erlbaum Associates.

Snyder, M., & Cantor, N. (1979). Testing hypotheses about other people: The use of historical knowledge. *Journal of Experimental Social Psychology, 15,* 330–342.

Snyder, M., & Swann, W. B., Jr. (1978a). Behavioral confirmation in social interaction: From social perception to social reality. *Journal of Experimental Social Psychology, 14,* 148–162.

Snyder, M., & Swann, W. B., Jr. (1978b). Hypothesis-testing processes in social interaction. *Journal of Personality and Social Psychology, 36,* 1202–1212.

Snyder, M., & Thomsen, C. J. (1988). Interactions between therapists and clients: Hypothesis testing and behavioral confirmation. In D. C. Turk & P. Salovey (Eds.), *Reasoning, inference, and judgment in clinical psychology* (pp. 124–152). New York: Free Press.

Spitzer, R. L. (1975). On pseudoscience in science, logic in remission, and psychiatric diagnosis: A critique of Rosenhan's "On being sane in insane places." *Journal of Abnormal Psychology, 84,* 442–452.

Spitzer, R. L. (1976). More on pseudoscience in science and the case for psychiatric diagnosis. *Archives of General Psychiatry, 33,* 459–470.

Srull, T. K., & Wyer, R. S., Jr. (1979). The role of category accessibility in the interpretation of information about persons: Some determinants and implications. *Journal of Personality and Social Psychology, 37,* 1660–1672.

Sushinsky, L. W., & Wener, R. (1975). Distorting judgments of mental health: Generality of the labeling bias effect. *Journal of Nervous and Mental Disease, 161,* 82–89.

Taylor, S. E., & Crocker, J. (1981). Schematic bases of social information processing. In E. T. Higgins, C. P. Herman, & M. P. Zanna (Eds.), *Social cognition: The Ontario symposium* (Vol. 1, pp. 89–134). Hillsdale, NJ: Lawrence Erlbaum Associates.

Taylor, S. E., & Fiske, S. T. (1978). Salience, attention, and attribution: Top of the head phenomena. In L. Berkowitz (Ed.), *Advances in experimental social psychology* (Vol. 11, pp. 250–288). New York: Academic Press.

Taylor, S. E., & Thompson, S. C. (1982). Stalking the elusive "vividness" effect. *Psychological Review, 89,* 155–181.

Temerlin, M. K. (1968). Suggestion effects in psychiatric diagnosis. *Journal of Nervous and Mental Disease, 147,* 349–353.

Trolier, T. K., & Hamilton, D. L. (1986). Variables influencing judgments of correlational rela-

tions. *Journal of Personality and Social Psychology, 50,* 879–888.

Turk, D. C., & Salovey, P. (1985). Cognitive structures, cognitive processes, and cognitive-behavior modification: II. Judgments and inferences of the clinician. *Cognitive Therapy and Research, 9,* 19–33.

Turk, D. C., & Salovey, P. (1986). Clinical information processing: Bias inoculation. In R. E. Ingram (Ed.), *Information processing approaches to clinical psychology* (pp. 305–323). Orlando, FL: Academic Press.

Turk, D. C., & Salovey, P. (Eds.). (1988). *Reasoning, inference, and judgment in clinical psychology.* New York: Free Press.

Tversky, A., & Kahneman, D. (1971). Belief in the law of small numbers. *Psychological Bulletin, 76,* 105–110.

Tversky, A., & Kahneman, D. (1973). Availability: A heuristic for judging frequency probability. *Cognitive Psychology, 5,* 207–232.

Tversky, A., & Kahneman, D. (1974). Judgement under uncertainty: Heuristics and biasis. *Science, 185,* 1124–1131.

Tversky, A., & Kahneman, D. (1980). Causal schemas for judgments under uncertainty. In M. Fishbein (Ed.), *Progress in social psychology* (Vol. 1, pp. 49–72). Hillsdale, NJ: Lawrence Erlbaum Associates.

Tversky, A., & Kahneman, D. (1981). The framing of decisions and the psychology of choice. *Science, 211,* 453–458.

Tversky, A., & Kahneman, D. (1986). Rational choice and the framing of decisions. *Journal of Business, 59,* 5251–5278.

Von Neumann, J., & Morgenstein, O. (1947). *Theory of games and economic behavior.* Princeton: Princeton University Press.

Walker, L. O., & Avant, K. C. (1983). *Strategies for theory construction in nursing.* Norwalk, CT: Appleton-Century-Crofts.

Waller, R. W., & Keeley, S. M. (1978). Effects of explanation and information on the illusory correlation phenomenon. *Journal of Consulting and Clinical Psychology, 46,* 342–343.

Ward, W. D., & Jenkins, H. M. (1965). The display of information and the judgment of contingency. *Canadian Journal of Psychology, 19,* 231–241.

Wason, P. C., & Johnson-Laird, P. N. (1972). *Psychology of reasoning: Structure and content.* London: D. T. Batsford.

Weiner, B. (1975). "On being sane in insane

places:" A process (attributional) analysis and critique. *Journal of Abnormal Psychology, 84,* 433–441.

Weinstein, M. C., & Fineberg, H. V. (1980). *Clinical decision analysis.* Philadelphia: W. B. Saunders.

Welkowitz, J., Cohen, J., & Ortmeyer, D. (1967). Value system similarity: Investigation of patient-therapist dyads. *Journal of Consulting Psychology, 31,* 48–55.

Whitman, R. M., Kramer, M., & Baldridge, B. (1963). Which dream does the patient tell? *Archives of General Psychiatry, 8,* 277–282.

Wiggins, J. S. (1973). *Personality and prediction: Principles of personality assessment.* Reading, MA: Addison-Wesley.

Wiggins, N., & Hoffman, P. J. (1968). Three models of clinical judgment. *Journal of Abnormal Psychology, 73,* 70–77.

Winch, R. F., & More, D. M. (1956). Does TAT add information to interview? Statistical analysis of the increment. *Journal of Clinical Psychology, 12,* 316–321.

Wood, G. (1978). The knew-it-all-along effect. *Journal of Experimental Psychology: Human Perception and Performance, 4,* 345–353.

Wortman, C. B. (1975). Some determinants of perceived control. *Journal of Personality and Social Psychology, 31,* 282–294.

CHAPTER 22

INTERPERSONAL METHODS OF ASSESSMENT AND DIAGNOSIS

Donald J. Kiesler

This chapter attempts to encapsulate contemporary interpersonal theory, assessment, and research as relevant to diagnosis of adaptive and maladaptive human functioning. Although an in-depth coverage is impossible, it is hoped that a wide-band synopsis might prove heuristic to both social and clinical psychologists.

In what follows I address, in turn, four central topics: (a) interpersonal behavior and personality, (b) interpersonal behavior and maladjustment, (c) interpersonal assessment, and (d) interpersonal diagnosis. Major emphasis will be placed on the last two topics.

INTERPERSONAL BEHAVIOR AND PERSONALITY

At a minimum, interpersonal behavior refers to our actions in the presence of other humans—our social behavior. Interpersonal theorists, however, do not focus study on what an individual does with others in one or various situations and do not concentrate on the behavior of an individual

in situations, be they social (dyads, families, groups, etc.) or impersonal.

> Interpersonal study focuses on human transactions, not on the behavior of individuals. What needs to be studied is not conceptually isolated "human behavior," but rather the behavior of persons relating to and interacting in a system with other persons. That human activity to be understood and explained is interpersonal or social, which necessitates focus on at least a dyad or two-person group. (Kiesler, 1982a, p. 5)

Measurement of interpersonal behavior requires, at a minimum, measurement of at least two people's conjoint behaviors during their interactions with each other. Assessment focuses on what person A and person B do reciprocally to and with each other during their transactions. Interpersonal meaning cannot be extracted by aggregating measures of what A does with B, thereby summarizing A's behavior in that particular social context. Rather, by measuring both A's and B's interactional behaviors, interpersonal meaning is extracted from the lawful interrelationships of each person's unfolding behaviors to those of the other. As many others have suggested, what needs to be studied is interaction (action-reaction) rather than action.

The basic unit of interpersonal behavior is the interaction unit (Peterson, in press), variously referred to as the "interpersonal proceeding" (Murray, 1951), "interaction sequence" (Raush, 1965; Peterson, 1979a), "interaction episode" (Kelley et al., 1983), and "relational scenario" (Gergen, 1987). The interaction unit consists of an action by A and the accompanying reaction by B, and in communications terminology consists of a speech turn by A and the subsequent speech turn of B. In studying interaction units over various temporal lengths of a dyad's transactions, researchers can draw conclusions regarding the probabilities of recurrent sequences of their actions-reactions. Importantly, as Murray (1951) cogently observed (Peterson, in press; Thorne, 1986), in understanding interaction units, person B must be given the same conceptual status as person A; our explanation must include as much formulation of person B's thought and action as of person A's thought and action.

Murray's comments highlight another central emphasis. Interpersonal behavior encompasses not merely overt, observable transactions between two individuals, but also refers to the private, unobservable, symbolic (fantasized) interactions and dialogues with the self and other conducted by either. Study of these symbolic interactions attempts to understand not only the nature of the cognitive schemas (Sullivan's [1953] "personifications") for both the other member of the dyad and for persons more generally, but the reciprocal relationships of each person's cognitive events (both person and self schemas) to the action-reaction sequences occurring in the arena of their conjoint overt behavior.

In sum, interpersonal behavior refers to recurrent patterns of reciprocal relationship present among two people's covert and overt actions and reactions studied over some period (sequence) of their transactions with each other. The length of period studied can range from a single interaction unit (cycles) to phases, episodes, sequences, and so on (Peterson, in press), all the way to the entire history of transactions between two individuals. Accordingly, the concept of interpersonal behavior overlaps, to a great extent, that of interpersonal communication (Kiesler, 1979, 1988; Kiesler, Bernstein, & Anchin, 1976), which refers

to recurrent patterns of reciprocal relationship present among two people's verbal-nonverbal message exchanges over some period of their communications with each other.

Interpersonal Assumptions for Human Personality

The assumptions that interpersonal theorists adopt in their study of personality, psychopathology, and psychotherapy are interspersed in Sullivan (1953) and in more contemporary pivotal volumes (Anchin & Kiesler, 1982; Carson, 1969; Leary, 1957).

Kiesler (1982a) summarized these embedded themes in the form of six "interpersonal assumptions for human personality":

1. As just elaborated, interpersonal study focuses on human transactions, not on the behavior of individuals. That activity to be understood and explained is interpersonal, which necessitates focus on at least a dyad or two-person group.

2. A central theoretical position is accorded to the construct of self, a self that is interpersonal and transactional in its development and functioning throughout life. A central and pervasive feature of our transactions is self-presentation — the automatic, predominantly unaware, and recurrent manner in which we centrally view ourselves, which in turn leads to acted out claims or bids to others (evoking messages) regarding the kind of reactions and relationships we seek from them. In pursuit of our transactions, we seek to impose distinctive interpersonal climates — to produce constricted covert responses in others (impact messages) that lead to constricted overt (complementary) reactions confirmatory of our self-presentations. Sullivan (1953) labeled the essential constructs governing these processes self and other *personifications*; the contemporary equivalent would be self and other *schemas* (Carson, 1969; Safran, 1984b).

3. A person's recurrent pattern of interpersonal situations (person A's covert and overt behaviors, along with interactant B's covert and overt reactions) represents distinct combinations or blends of two basic dimensions of interpersonal behavior: control (dominance-submission) and affiliation (friendliness-hostility). The empirical domain of individual differences in interpersonal behavior can be validly summarized by an interpersonal circle (e.g., Kiesler, 1983), a circumplex organized around the vertical and horizontal axes of control

and affiliation, respectively. This circle can validly characterize both A's actions and B's reactions over various temporal sequences of their transactions.

4. Interpersonal transactions consist of two-person mutual influence. Causality is simultaneously bidirectional; that is, circular (Danziger, 1976) rather than linear. Interpersonal behavior is embedded in a feedback network in which the effect influences or alters the cause—in which person A both shapes and is shaped by the environment (especially by person B).

5. At a minimum, interpersonal theorists adopt an interactionist position in which person A's behaviors are an interactive product of both A's predispositions toward transactions and situational/environmental events. Further, the most important class of situations is that of other people, especially significant others; the environment as perceived by A (the psychological environment) is prepotent. A recent transactional alternative to interactionism, Duke's (1987) situational stream hypothesis, is even more congruent to the interpersonal perspective.

6. The vehicle for human transactions is communication; that is, the verbal and nonverbal messages exchanged between person A and interactant B over the course of the transactions. Because nonverbal messages predominate in emotional and relational communication, understanding of interpersonal behavior requires simultaneous study of both the report (linguistic) and, especially, the command (nonverbal) levels of human communication (Duke & Nowicki, 1982; Kiesler, 1979; Kiesler, Bernstein, & Anchin, 1976).

Interpersonal Complementarity

A key interpersonal construct, embedded in the self-confirmation process just described, is that of reciprocity or complementarity in human transactions. When anchored empirically in the interpersonal circle, the principle serves as a guide to specific transactional predictions in a wide range of applied areas, including diagnosis and treatment. Derived originally from Sullivan's (1953) theorem of reciprocal emotion, its broadest meaning is that "our interpersonal actions are designed to invite, pull, elicit, draw, entice, or evoke 'restricted classes' of reactions from persons with whom we interact, especially from significant others" (Kiesler, 1983, p. 198). Leary (1957) called this the "principle of reciprocal interpersonal relations;"

Carson (1984) more recently has referred to this interpersonal situation as "interbehavioral contingency."

Carson (1969) was the first to define explicitly how this principle relates to the interpersonal circumplex, as follows: "Complementarity occurs on the basis of reciprocity in respect to the dominance-submission axis (dominance tends to induce submission, and vice versa), and on the basis of correspondence in respect to the hate-love axis (hate induces hate, and love induces love)" (p. 112). Kiesler (1983) summarized and clarified the propositions of complementarity articulated by Carson (1969), offered expanded and new propositions for personality tied operationally to the 1982 interpersonal circle, and articulated other propositions that related to psychopathology and to the goals and procedures of psychotherapy. The result was 11 propositions of complementarity as they apply in personality, psychopathology, and psychotherapy.

Orford (1985, 1986) critically examined the evidence for interpersonal complementarity and concluded that the only prediction finding support was on the friendly side of the circle; that is, friendly-dominant and friendly-submissive behaviors are mutually evoking. Disconfirming findings reported by Orford were (a) that hostile-dominant acts are frequently responded to with further hostile-dominant behavior (rather than with predicted hostile-submissive behavior), and (b) that hostile-submissive behavior is frequently met with friendly-dominance (rather than with predicted hostile-dominance). Orford also discussed in detail the conceptual and methodological problems with research into complementarity and provided an expanded discussion and emphasis regarding setting, status, and temporal factors that were addressed earlier in Kiesler's (1983) propositions.

Kiesler (1987c) suggested caution regarding Orford's conclusions and offered clarifications to place Orford's review in a more balanced perspective. First, because multiple interpersonal circles exist, valid tests of complementarity for any particular circle require the use of measures that fit the structure of that circle. Orford draws strong conclusions about the Kiesler and Wiggins circles from studies that exclusively used the Interpersonal Check List (ICL), a measure tied specifically to Leary's circle and one that provides a poor fit to the Kiesler and Wiggins circles. Second, all available studies of complementarity have analyzed only the action/overt-reaction chain of the circular transaction cycle, whereas propositions of complementarity seem most veridically applicable to the action/covert-reaction link of the chain (i.e., person A's overt action, person B's covert-impact response). Third, as Orford notes, few available studies have analyzed interaction units (action-reaction sequences), in contrast to aggregated data; the most valid tests of complementarity can be discovered only by looking at the moment-by-moment sequential negotiations occurring between dyadic interactants. Fourth, interpersonal theory does not postulate that any relationship between two interactants will show complementary patterns of behavior as defined by the interpersonal circle. What the theory does postulate is that one interactant's interpersonal behavior tends to pull complementary behaviors from the other interactant; whether a complementary outcome occurs for one interactant in a particular dyad depends crucially on what the other person concurrently wants, seeks, and is most comfortable with. When the self-presentation behaviors of two interactants mesh and are mutually confirming, the outcome is complementarity; when they clash, the outcome is anticomplementarity; when they only partially mesh, the outcome is acomplementarity (Kiesler, 1983). Theoretically, then, one does not expect to find complementary pairings in all (or even most) interpersonal encounters, as Orford's thesis assumes. Depending on interactant mixes and the other important contextual and intervening factors amplified by Orford, one can expect to find any one of the three outcomes.

Nowicki and Manheim (in press) noted that investigators have yet to determine how much time is required for complementarity to make its impression on a relationship. "It is possible that the lack of consistent empirical support for the complementary hypothesis reported by Orford (1986) may be due, in part, to an inability to pinpoint precisely when interactants are engaged in transactions which are affected by interpersonal complementarity. Consistent with the results of the present study, investigators who have found support for the complementary hypothesis are usually those who went beyond a single brief interaction or studied interpersonal behavior over differing lengths of time (e.g., Dietzel & Abeles, 1975; Rausch, 1965; Shannon & Guerney, 1973)" (Nowicki & Manheim, in press, p. 18). A summary of research on reciprocity using the Social Relations Model (Kenny & LaVoie, 1984) similarly concludes that only in long-term relationships is there compelling evidence for reciprocity; in short-term relationships (e.g., interactions with strangers) no evidence emerges.

Interpersonal research has a long way to go before a heuristic body of data becomes available that can offer replicable answers to interpersonal complementarity theory. Some crucial issues, besides the ones just articulated, include (a) the necessity of using circle measures demonstrating close fit to circumplex structure (at present, only Wiggins' Interpersonal Adjective Scales [IAS] and Interpersonal Adjective Scales-Revised [IAS-R] [see "Interpersonal Assessment" section] satisfy this requirement); (b) whether axis, quadrant, octant, or segment scores are used in calculations (segment scores represent the most conservative and powerful test); (c) whether the scores used are raw (normative) or ipsatized (Block, 1957; Paddock, Potts, Kiesler, & Nowicki, 1986); (d) whether the complementarity index is constructed from a correlation coefficient between interactants' profiles, a summed difference score squared, a summed absolute value difference score, or from cross-product scores in regression analysis; (e) whether the complementarity index is summarized from the entire circle, various hemispheres (especially hostile vs. friendly), or quadrants; (f) whether data are from self-reports, participant ratings, or nonparticipant observations; (g) whether nonverbal as well as verbal interactant behaviors are being rated in observational studies; (h) where on the temporal dimension of a dyadic relationship one obtains one's measures (e.g., the choice, beginning, deepening, or termination phase of a particular dyad's relationship) (Duke & Nowicki, 1982; Nowicki & Manheim, in press); (i) whether the interactional context is structured (with clear roles or rules for each participant) or unstructured (novel, or unfamiliar); (j) whether the transactants are strangers, acquaintances, friends (in general, significant others or not); (k) whether noticeable age or status differences exist among the interactants; (l) whether the interactants are of the same or opposite gender; (m) whether the study assesses the effects of the interactants individual reciprocity or the unique dyadic reciprocity (Kenny & LaVoie's [1984] Social Relations Model); (n) whether the investigator measures all seven of the possibilities of covert and overt reactions to noncomplementary situations detailed by Secord and Backman (1961, 1965); and (o) how the interpersonal proposition of "transactional escalation" (Van Denburg, 1988; an individual's preferred pattern of interpersonal behavior escalates under stressful conditions) interacts with propositions of complementarity in stressful contexts (see also Swann & Read, 1981).

Cognition in Interpersonal Theory

Although a major focus of interpersonal research has been the study of overt interpersonal behavior through applications of interpersonal circle measures, considerable emphasis also has been placed on the covert, cognitive events that are central to human transactions. It seems evident that an individual's characteristic cognitive or construal style, whether disordered or not, contributes significantly to both encoding and decoding processes inherent in interpersonal transactions.

Sullivan's (1953) original interpersonal statement put a heavy emphasis on the schema-equivalent constructs of personification of self and of others. Leary (1956, 1957) provided a five-level model for measurement of interpersonal behavior that included assessment of overt and covert behaviors along a continuum of awareness to unconsciousness: (a) public communication, (b) conscious description, (c) private communication or perception, (d) unexpressed (significant omissions), (e) values (ego ideal). He also emphasized the importance of empirical indices that documented the degree of variability or inconsistency in characterizations from these multiple perspectives (see also Madison & Paddock, 1983).

Carson (1969, 1971, 1979, 1982, 1984, 1989) has provided an in-depth analysis of interpersonal behavior with particular emphasis on cognitive components. His 1969 volume provides an incisive review of Sullivanian constructs, which he translates into the cognitive language of "plans" and "strategies" in the tradition of Miller, Galanter, and Pribram (1960). Reviewing evidence for the circumplex arrangement of interpersonal behavior, Carson analyzed interpersonal complementarity using constructs from Secord and Backman's (1961, 1965) balance theory. In the final section of his book, Carson merged the four quadrants of the interpersonal circle with "rewards" and "costs" derived from Thibaut and Kelley's (1959) exchange theory, then constructed a 4 × 4 matrix for classifying interaction sequences for the study of interpersonal transactions in personality, psychopathology, and psychotherapy.

Carson (1982) offered the fundamental cognitive hypothesis that a person's behavior is designed to produce consequences in and reactions from others that confirm the principal hypotheses (perceptions, expectations, or construals of other people) organizing his or her world. In Carson's view, an "unbroken causal loop" (p. 66) exists among (a) a person's social perceptions or cognitions, (b) his or her behavioral enactments, and (c) reactions of interactants that confirm the person's cognitions or expectancies. Carson (1979) further speculated that people who are dispositionally passive count on others to assume the dominant position with them; consequently, their world is largely populated by assertive and dominant individuals. Affiliative people, on the other hand, do not usually bring an expectation into a relationship, but instead wait to see what the other person is going to be like; if anything, these people tend to have a generalized positive attributional set toward others, thereby judging differences along the affiliation-hostility dimension to be more salient than differences in dominance-submission.

Safran (1984a), like Carson, argued that "cognitive activities, interpersonal behaviors, and repetitive interactional or *me-you patterns* are linked together and maintain one another in an unbroken causal loop," which he named the "cognitive interpersonal cycle" (p. 342). Safran concluded that "a full assessment in the context of a *cognitive-interpersonal* therapy requires that the therapist conduct a comprehensive exploration of both the specific interpersonal behaviors and *me-you patterns* that impair the client's interpersonal relations, and the particular cognitive activities that are linked to them" (pp. 345–346). Kiesler (1986a) developed both Carson's and Safran's notions of causal loops into a more comprehensive model for general psychopathology, the Maladaptive Transaction Cycle.

Other explorations of the cognitive components of interpersonal behavior can be found in Andrews and Moore (in press), Conway (1980, 1983), Crowley (1985), Gascoyne (1984), Golding (1977, 1978), Golding, Valone, and Foster (1980), Horowitz (1979), Horowitz, Weckler, and Doren (1983), and Safran and Segal (1990). Golding (1977), for example, reported that individuals who describe themselves as aggressive, hostile, and suspicious (i.e., hostile-dominant) have generally negative attributional sets. They tend to attend to the dominance-submission dimension in a relationship far more than the love-hate dimension, thereby overattributing both hostility and submissiveness to others.

Applications to Behavior Theory and Social Learning

Several theorists have drawn important implications of interpersonal principles for behavioral and social learning analyses. DeVogue and Beck (1978) argued that "behavioral technology has become limited by the failure of behaviorists to incorporate into their viewpoint a broad theory of human relationship" (p. 204). Applying Leary's (1957) interpersonal model to their review of the social reinforcement literature, they concluded that "only in friendly dominant/friendly submissive dyads . . . would social 'reinforcement' in the form of praise and approval have its maximum effect. In any nonreciprocal [i.e., noncomplementary] dyad . . . we could predict less frequent use of the target response by the subject in this reciprocal dyad. . . . Especially when the subject attempts to use hostile dominance vis-a-vis the reinforcer, the subject may show a decrease in the target response in order to avoid the aversive stimulation of praise and approval" (p. 221). Hence, in psychotherapy and other helping relationships, "the utility of a warm, empathic approach quite possibly is limited to those clients who present themselves initially to the therapist as friendly and submissive, since they would constitute the only clients who would find the approach nonaversive" (p. 235).

In a similar vein, Brokaw and McLemore (1983) argued that a significant portion of current social-reinforcement research utilizes friendly reinforcers assumptively, without demonstrating their reinforcement efficacy for the particular behaviors targeted. Their study contrasted the assumptive notion with the interpersonal prediction that different reinforcers are required for different behaviors. Their findings supported the interpersonal principle that "reinforcers will vary according to the *complements* of targeted behaviors" (p. 1018); for subjects' targeted hostile-dominant behaviors, confederates' hostile-submissive reactions produced significantly more frequent continued hostile-dominant target behaviors than did confederates' friendly-submissive reactions. Brokaw and McLemore concluded that "the interpersonal conceptualization of complementarity represents an important component of the reinforcement construct" (p. 1019).

Kiesler, Bernstein, and Anchin (1976) argued that behavior therapies have ignored, deemphasized, or have not developed constructs and operational assessments for key therapeutic factors that loom central in interpersonal communication theory. Various chapters of their manuscript developed the assertion that the multiple phenomena of the client-therapist relationship need to be systematically incorporated into behavior therapy theory and practice. They analyzed traditional constructs of resistance and transference from their interpersonal communication perspective, highlighting that the self-defeating interpersonal relationship messages a patient sends the therapist may be representative of the patient's central self-defeating interactions with other significant people. Kiesler (1979) detailed a list of operational indices of relationship in psychotherapy and elsewhere.

Safran (1984a, 1984b) has argued convincingly for a rapprochement between cognitive-behavioral and interpersonal therapies. Safran (1984b) documented how Sullivan's concepts of personification, parataxic distortion, selective inattention, security operations, and dynamism predated and are both compatible with contemporary theory and research in cognitive psychology, and contributory to important amplifications of contemporary approaches to cognitive therapy. Safran (1984a; Safran, Vallis, Segal, & Shaw, 1986) detailed specific ways in which incorporation of interpersonal principles can broaden and enrich cognitive therapy's theoretical and practical scope; namely, (a) understanding and dealing with problems in both therapeutic compliance and maintenance, (b) broadening its conceptualization of the role of emotions in psychotherapy, and (c) incorporating the technique of pinpointing dysfunctional automatic thoughts of a client as part of the interpersonal intervention of metacommunication (Kiesler, 1988).

INTERPERSONAL BEHAVIOR AND MALADJUSTMENT

Maladjusted behavior resides in a person's recurrent transactions with others, especially significant others. Defined as disordered, inappropriate, inadequate, and self-defeating interpersonal actions, maladaptive behavior results originally and cumulatively from an individual's failure to attend to and correct the self-defeating, interpersonally unsuccessful aspects of his or her interpersonal acts. The disturbed person consistently broadcasts a rigid and extreme self-presentation and simultaneously pulls for a rigid and constricted relationship from others. The individual imposes a rigid program on transactions, a program he or she is unwilling or unable to modify, despite the initially varying interpersonal stances of others. For the disturbed person, then, the ability to modify his or her definition of self and others in line with varying situational factors seems strikingly absent. Maladjusted people attend to some aspects of their claims as to how to define self in important relationships; they do not attend to other aspects of their interpersonal acts nor do they attend to the aversive interpersonal consequences they unaccountably and automatically produce.

In contrast, as Carson (1969) describes, the more normal individual has a sufficiently broad style of interacting, reflecting a more flexible definition of self and others. The normal person enacts varied sets of interpersonal actions appropriately tuned to the interactant. In each instance, he or she negotiates a mutually agreed upon definition of self and other, responding to the unique aspects of the particular interpersonal situation.

Maladjusted behavior, then, has three important characteristics: (a) extremeness (the more extreme an interpersonal behavior, the more maladaptive it is, the more aversive its effects on interactants); (b) rigidity (with varying interactants, a maladjusted individual's interpersonal acts are constricted to expressions of only a few classes of the total range of possible interpersonal behaviors); (c) cross-channel incongruity (the complex of verbal and nonverbal messages that constitute the interpersonal acts of maladjusted individuals yield discrepant, mixed, and inconsistent information to interactants, in turn evoking from them discrepant, mixed, and inconsistent interpersonal reactions).

Duke and Nowicki (1982) further clarified this interpersonal analysis by documenting that "not only may incongruence sometimes be 'normal' and appropriate, but that incongruence may actually be the prevalent mode of adult human interaction" (pp. 82–83). The effect of cross-channel incongruity depends crucially on situational parameters. In their view, the result is at least four categories of dyadic congruence/incongruence situational patterns: adaptive congruence, adaptive incongruence, maladaptive congruence, and maladaptive incongruence. They concluded that incongruence "must be viewed as associated with maladjustment only in certain situationally defined instances . . . failure to learn when, where, and with whom to be congruent or incongruent may have more to do with the development of maladjustment than with simple incongruence per se" (p. 83).

Kiesler's (1986a, pp. 7–10) Maladaptive Transaction Cycle is a model that defines the essential components of the maladjusted person's action-reaction sequence with others—a conceptual guide that predicts the specific components of the recurrent pattern of actions and reactions that define the person's self-defeating maladaptive transactions with others. The model, together with complementarity predictions from the interpersonal circle, provides the framework for specifying the covert and overt aspects of the maladjusted person's behavior that are chained circularly to the covert and overt aspects of the interactant's reactions. It specifies, further, how the maladjusted individual's transactions with others typically move to "impasse"; that is, to recurrent enactment of the cycle of maladaptive self-fulfilling prophecy and behavior. The Maladaptive Transaction Cycle is depicted in Figure 22.1.

The principles of interpersonal therapy have been presented in detail by Anchin (1982b), Carson (1969), Kiesler (1979, 1982a, 1982b, 1983, in press), Kiesler, Bernstein, and Anchin (1976), Leary (1957), and Strong (1987a, 1987b, 1987c). Summaries of various approaches to interpersonal therapy can be found in Anchin and Kiesler (1982) and Kiesler (1986a). Several therapeutic volumes have appeared recently: Andrews (in press-b), Benjamin (in press-a, in press-b), Cashdan (1988), Kiesler (1988), Klerman, Weissman, Rounsaville, and Chevron (1984), Safran and Segal (1990), and Strong and Claiborn (1982).

In interpersonal therapy the therapist's essential task is to disrupt the patient's vicious cycle of self-defeating actions depicted in the Maladaptive Transaction Cycle. In attempting to accomplish this task, the therapist has available important components of intervention that are derivable from the interpersonal circle (Kiesler, 1983). Having identified prototypic segments on the circle that define a particular disorder, theoretically derivable interventions can be systematically designated, including (a) the goal of therapy, (b) the precise overt and covert reactions (objective countertransference) that will be "pulled" from the

STAGE 1

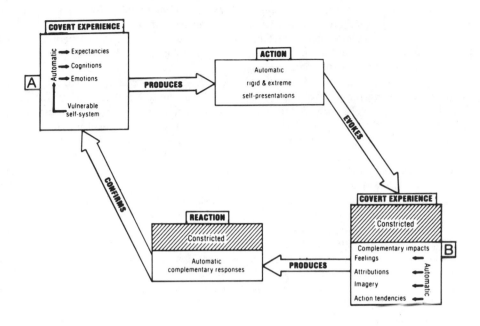

STAGE 2

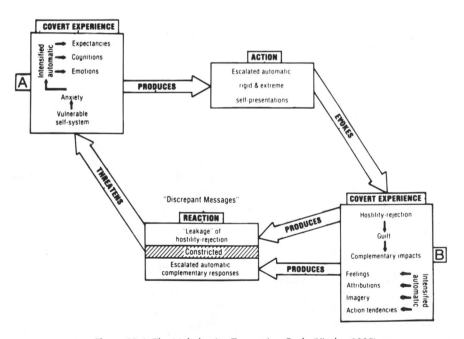

Figure 22.1. The Maladaptive Transaction Cycle (Kiesler, 1985).

therapist in early transactions, (c) the therapist's shift to therapeutic "asocial" responses (Beier, 1966) to effect cognitive ambiguity and uncertainty as the first step toward disrupting the patient's maladaptive style, and (d) the specific anticomplementary responses the therapist can initiate to exert the greatest pressure for positive change in the patient. Kiesler (in press) has provided a pictorial summary of this "Interpersonal Treatment Plan" as a clinical guide for psychotherapy applications.

Although interpersonal therapists have yet to articulate comprehensive treatment packages applying these principles to specific disorders, some important first steps have been taken (Andrews, 1966, 1984, in press-a, in press-b, in press-d; Beier & Young, 1984; Benjamin, 1982, in press-a, in press-b; Cashdan, 1971, 1982, 1988; Coyne, 1976a, 1976b; Coyne & Segal, 1982; Kiesler, 1977, 1979, 1982b, 1988, in press; Klerman, Weissman, Rounsaville, & Chevron, 1984; McLemore & Hart, 1982; Safran & Segal, 1990; Wachtel, 1982; Weissman, Klerman, Rounsaville, Chevron, & Neu, 1982; Young & Beier, 1982). Summaries of many of these various approaches to interpersonal therapy can be found in Anchin and Kiesler (1982) and Kiesler (1986a).

INTERPERSONAL ASSESSMENT

As the Maladaptive Transaction Cycle shows, the basic blocks of transactional behavior are four: person A's covert experience about B, A's overt behavior (action) toward B, person B's covert engagements (impacts) in response to A's action, and B's overt reaction to A. Any comprehensive study of interpersonal behavior, then, requires measurement of each of these four transactional blocks, measurement of both A's and B's covert and overt actions and reactions, and methodologies that draw conclusions about the patterns present between and among these four links of the circular interactional chain. Measurement of the basic blocks requires delineation of some duration of the A-B-A-B interaction sequence. As we have seen, the duration period focused on can range from the interaction unit (A's speech turn, B's speech turn) through phases, episodes, sequences, all the way to the entire history of transaction between A and B.

Also, if our analysis focuses on the interpersonal behavior of A, we can extend our measurement to A's behavior, not only with B, but with various other people with whom A interacts (or has interacted) in his or her life. Study of A's interactions with these other people also will ultimately involve characterizations of the environmental contexts in which these interactions occur, the defined roles of both A and the others in each of these contexts, the interface of the various A-B dyadic units with larger interpersonal systems (e.g., family, group, subculture) in which the dyad is embedded, and so on.

At the most microanalytic level of interpersonal behavior, the interaction unit, characterization of A's interpersonal behavior, is in terms of "acts" (A's actions, B's reactions; B's actions, A's reactions). At the most macroanalytic level, where A's (or B's) interpersonal behavior is measured from the viewpoint of a wide band of time and people-situations, characterization of A's interpersonal behavior is in terms of style or disposition. At levels between micro and macro, A's interpersonal behavior can be characterized only with newly invented terms, because the available language of psychology offers no appropriate words.

Most, if not all, interpersonal measures evolved first as inventories designed to measure interpersonal style. This evolution was tied intimately to the many normative attempts to characterize and assess the comprehensive domain of interpersonal behavior—attempts that resulted in the various interpersonal circles constituting the conceptual-empirical models that guide both interpersonal theory and research. However, many of these same measures also have been adapted for ratings of acts (within interaction units) as part of sequential analysis studies.

Another difference among measures that is conceptually related to the act-style continuum just articulated concerns the adjective versus verb-phrase format of the various inventories. Verb-phrase items seem designed, and necessary, for coding or rating of interpersonal acts; adjectival items seem designed for ratings of individuals' styles or dispositions. The pioneers in the empirical study of interpersonal behavior, the Kaiser Permanente research group, were acutely aware of this difference. "In rating the observed and recorded interactions [of group therapy participants], it was noticed that transitive verbs were the handiest words for describing what the subjects did to each other, e.g., *insult, challenge, answer, help*. In rating the content of the spoken or written descriptions of self-or-other, it was noted that adjectives were more often suitable . . . [e.g.] 'I am *friendly, helpful, strong*; they are *hostile, selfish, wise, helpful*.' A clear relationship seemed to exist between these two types of interpersonal description, such that the adjectives seemed to express an interpersonal attribute or potentiality for action, while the verbs described the action directly" (Leary, 1957, p. 63). More recently, Buss and Craik (1983a) defined an act as a specific behavior in context (e.g., "When I am on a committee, I take charge of things"). A trait or disposition, in contrast, refers to a label that summarizes frequently occurring acts of a particular class. Importantly, in their view there is no one-to-one correspondence between a single act and its signified disposition; rather, to validly reflect a disposition, multiple constituent acts need to be sampled across situations and time. The upshot is that interpersonal measures vary along an adjective (style, disposition) to verb-phrase (act) continuum of item format that affects, in some presently unknown manner, the results from studies of interpersonal behavior.

Interpersonal measures can be used differently depending on the design focus of a particular investigation (Kiesler, 1987a, p. 17). The focus essentially can be on the actor, the inventory respondent (rater, interactant), or the actor-respondent transaction. In "actor-focused" studies, the central aim of the investigator is to characterize the overt behavior of actor A, or the individual differences present in the overt interpersonal behaviors of selected groups of actors. The design strategy is to eliminate any variance present in the actor(s)'s interpersonal scores that derives from real differences in the interpersonal decoding styles of the respondent(s). The investigator accomplishes this by using a sample of respondents to rate the actor's interpersonal behavior. In "respondent-focused" studies, the aim of the investigator is to characterize the covert decoding or construal style of respondent B, or of a group of respondents. The design strategy is to randomize any variance present in the respondent(s)' item responses that derives from real differences in the overt interpersonal behavior of the actor(s). By standardization or randomization of actor subjects or conditions, the investigator attempts to ensure that the respondent(s)' item responses averaged across actors will be good estimates of the true variance attributable to the respondent(s)' characteristic interpersonal decoding style. Finally, "transaction-focused" studies incorporate the most complicated design strategy but the one most relevant to testing interpersonal hypotheses. In these studies, the investigator's central purpose is to characterize patterns in the conjoint, systemic, transactional behavior evident in some sample of actor-respondent dyads. A clearly distinguishing feature of these studies is that actor and respondent labels are interchangeable, in that each interactant's actions are coded in sequential analysis, or each interactant fills out an inventory on the other and dyadic scores are derived from the set. These studies, thus, always produce two sets of interpersonal measures: either one for A and one for B in act studies, or, in style studies, with each of two samples of subjects alternatively taking the respondent role. The focus of analysis is on description of the system properties of various combinations of actor-respondent matches. As a result, neither the interpersonal behavior of the actor nor that of the respondent is of interest in and of itself. Instead, it is the degree and/or kind of fit, match, or complementarity of interpersonal actions or styles that is the crucial concern.

It seems that a comprehensive and sophisticated understanding of interpersonal behavior requires studies with all three concentrations: actor, respondent, and transaction. This is especially the case for studies attempting to test the various propositions of interpersonal complementarity as articulated within the context of the interpersonal circle (Kiesler, 1983). Wright and Ingraham (1986), further underlining the importance of these distinctions, have argued and demonstrated that Kenny and LaVoie's (1984) Social Relations Model provides a method to separate individual difference (actor or respondent) effects from relationship-specific (transaction) effects in analysis of interpersonal behavior. The Social Relations Model addresses both relationship effects and outgoing and incoming individual differences in social behavior by providing a method to partial out three separate sources of variance in a dyadic system: A's average behavior toward a sample of other people (actor effect), B's average behavior toward a sample of other people (partner effect), and the dyad-specific adjustment A and B make to each other (relationship effect). Relationship effect, then, is the regular variability in an individual's behavior associated with interaction in a specific relationship, above and beyond individual differences of either member. Using round robin analyses of variance (Warner, Kenny, & Stoto, 1979) of graduate students' ratings of each other in experiential groups, Wright and Ingraham (1986) tested for interpersonal complementarity and found clear support for correspondence of affiliative behavior but inconclusive results for reciprocity of control behavior.

Interpersonal Circle Inventories

An authoritative historical and psychometric summary of interpersonal inventories can be found in LaForge, Freedman, and Wiggins (1985) and Wiggins (1982). More recent summaries of interpersonal assessment can be found in Anchin and Kiesler (1982), Benjamin (1984, 1987b), Carson (1984), Kiesler (1986a, 1986b), and Brokaw and McLemore (in press). This section will provide a tabular summary of circle inventory measures that are being used currently in programs of research as well as brief summaries of other more recent measures and approaches to the assessment of interpersonal behavior.

"It is a well-established empirical generalization that interpersonal variables have a circular structure. This fact can contribute to systematic assessment and prediction in the absence of any theoretical speculations about the nature of interpersonal behavior" (Wiggins, 1982, p. 214). However, when circumplex (Guttman, 1954) and other specific interpersonal geometric properties also are incorporated (e.g., Kiesler, 1983), the circular representation becomes a powerful structure for generation of theoretical propositions regarding interpersonal behavior. In this latter case, the interpersonal circle becomes "a formal geometrical model of the interrelations among indicants of constructs derived from an interpersonal theory of personality. Under this interpretation, the specific angular location of person variables (indicants) and their distance from the center of the circle should provide an empirical basis for testing hypotheses derived from interpersonal theory" (Wiggins, Phillips, & Trapnell, 1989, p. 296).

The research evidence upon which circle representations of interpersonal behavior have been based has been summarized in Berzins (1977), Bierman, (1969), Carson, (1969), Foa (1961), Plutchik and Conte (1986), and Wiggins (1982, in press). Evidence for the convergence of interpersonal behavior across methods of measurement (e.g., self-report inventories, self-ratings, peer ratings) has been reported by Golding and Knudson (1975) and Mungas, Trontel, and Winegardner (1981).

Historically, four two-dimensional interpersonal circles have been published as contemporary attempts to define and summarize the interrelationships among categories of adult interpersonal behavior. The earliest circle was that provided by Leary (1957), followed by Lorr and McNair (1965), Wiggins (1979a, 1979b, 1982), and the 1982 Interpersonal Circle (Kiesler, 1983, 1985). A party game version is also available (Oden, 1976).

Kiesler (1983) constructed the 1982 circle as a comprehensive taxonomy of the domain of two-dimensional interpersonal behavior by integrating and expanding the content of four major adult interpersonal measures: the Interpersonal Check List (ICL; LaForge & Suczek, 1955; Leary, 1957), the Interpersonal Behavior Inventory (IBI; Lorr & McNair, 1965, 1967), the Interpersonal Adjective Scales (IAS; Wiggins, 1979a, 1979b, 1981), and the Impact Message Inventory (IMI; Kiesler, Anchin, Perkins, Chirico, Kyle, & Federman, 1985). The result was a circle taxonomy consisting of 16 segments, 128 subclasses, 2 levels, and 350 bipolar items. Kiesler subsequently derived the Check List of Interpersonal (or Psychotherapy) Transactions (CLOIT-CLOPT; Kiesler, 1984, 1987b) as an inventory measure of the 1982 circle structure. Supporting empirical evidence for the validity of the 1982 circle structure has been found in studies by Conte and Plutchik (1981), Kiesler and Chapman (1988), Paddock and Nowicki (1986, 1987), and Wiggins, Trapnell, and Phillips (1988b). Benjafield and Carson (1985) present empirical evidence that the octant categories of the 1982 circle can be ordered historicodevelopmentally. That is, words belonging to octants closest to the circle axes of control or affiliation (LM, DE, PA, HI) have the earliest "dates of entry" into the language, as determined by Oxford English Dictionary counts, whereas words belonging to octants falling in the middle of the circle quadrants (NO, BC, FG, JK) had significantly later dates of entry. Figure 22.2 presents Kiesler's 1982 Interpersonal Circle.

The original and all subsequent two-dimensional circles are constructed on the assumption that human interpersonal behavior represents blends of two basic motivations: the need for control (power, dominance) and the need for affiliation (love, friendliness). That is, people interacting with each other continually are negotiating two major relationship issues: how friendly or hostile they will be with each other, and how much in charge or in control each will be in their en-

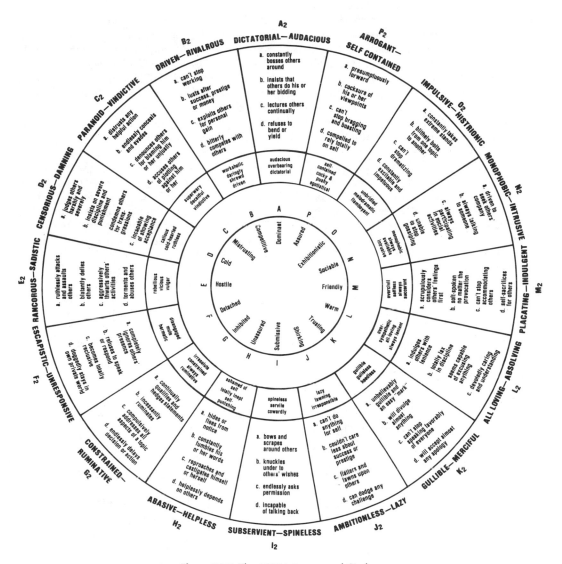

Figure 22.2. The 1982 Interpersonal Circle.

counters. Interpersonal circles directly incorporate this assumption by placing control (dominance-submission) and affiliation (friendliness-hostility) along their vertical and horizontal axes, respectively.

Any interpersonal action represents a composite or blend of relative components of these two factors—so many units of control, so many units of affiliation. The 16 segments found on the circle circumference define the range of possible blends of the two underlying dimensions. For example,

on the 1982 circle, exhibitionistic actions fall at segment O and represent approximately 2 units of dominance and 2 units of friendliness. In contrast, inhibited actions (segment G) represent the polar opposite to O and represent approximately 2 units of submission and 2 units of hostility.

The sixteen circle radii represent continua of normal (near the midpoint) to abnormal (near the circumference) versions of each segment's interpersonal acts. In other words, component actions subsumed by each segment vary in terms of their intensity or extremeness; the more extreme the act, the more maladjusted it is, and the more aversive its effects on interactants. For example, along the range of segment O, exhibitionistic acts, level 2 histrionic actions (loquacious/divulging, histrionic, impulsive, hypersuggestible) are more maladaptive than milder segment O versions at level 1 (talkative/disclosing, demonstrative, causal/spontaneous, suggestive). Note that Figure 22.2 provides level 1 (mild-moderate) and level 2 (extreme) labels for each of the 16 segments of interpersonal behavior.

Interpersonal circle inventories are designed to assess the comprehensive domain of interpersonal behavior as classified and conceptualized on the various interpersonal circles; they yield scores for categories (most usually 16) arranged in circumplex order around the circumference of one of these interpersonal circles. The circular and circumplicial structure of the circle arrangement provides for a distinct pattern of intercorrelations among the 16 categories such that circle axis categories are orthogonal, adjacent categories are positively correlated, and categories opposite on the circle are negatively correlated. For more detail regarding the logical, mathematical, and circumplicial characteristics of interpersonal circles and their measures, see Guttman (1954), Kiesler (1983), LaForge (1977), McCormick and Kavanagh (1981), Phillips (1983), Wiggins (1982), and Wiggins, Steiger, and Gaelick (1981). Inventories are differentiated into those with adjective format and those with verb-phrase item format. All inventories, to greater or lesser degrees, can be used to measure individuals' self-report characterizations of their own behavior, interactants' characterizations of each other's behaviors, or observers' ratings of interactant behavior.

Tables 22.1, 22.2 and 22.3 present a sumary of eight interpersonal circle inventories used by contemporary interpersonal researchers, including respective act-by-act coding version derivatives that have been applied in sequential analysis studies. Table 22.1 highlights key inventory properties of each and provides key references for obtaining copies and more detailed information. A masterful historical and psychometric analysis of almost all of these inventories can be found in Wiggins (1982).

Two of these inventories deserve a few comments because of their uniqueness as circle measures.

1. In contrast to the seven other two-dimensional circle inventories, Benjamin's (1974) structural analysis of social behavior constitutes what can be called a three-dimensional, or two-plane, model that adds new categories of interpersonal behavior and provides, on a third plane, assessment of a covert dimension of intrapersonal behavior. Benjamin's model uniquely defines autonomy as the opposite of control and submission as its complement. The first two diamond-shaped planes or surfaces of her model contain not only the four Leary-tradition quadrants (in Benjamin's terms, "friendly-influence," "hostile-power," "friendly-accept," "hostile-comply"), but also four additional quadrants ("encourage friendly autonomy," "invoke hostile autonomy," "enjoy friendly autonomy," "take hostile autonomy"). Her third surface, intrapersonal or introject, assesses people's behaviors toward themselves ("manage, cultivate self," "oppress self," "accept, enjoy self," "reject self").

2. The six other inventories besides Kiesler and colleagues' IMI and Wiggins' Affective Reactions Questionnaire (ARQ) are designed to designate the overt interpersonal behavior of target people by measuring perceptions of the targets themselves (self-report), of interactants, or of external observers. In contrast, the IMI and ARQ are designed to designate the overt behavior of target people by measuring the covert reactions targets induce or evoke in interactants or observers. Uniquely, both are self-report transactional inventories used to identify the interpersonal behavior of individuals by measuring the covert consequences occurring within interactants that result from the individuals' interpersonal behavior patterns.

Inventory of Interpersonal Problems (IIP)

Horowitz and his colleagues (Horowitz, 1979, 1988; Horowitz & French, 1979; Horowitz, French, & Anderson, 1982; Horowitz, French, Lapid, & Weckler, 1982; Horowitz, Post, French, Wallis, & Siegelman, 1981; Horowitz, Rosenberg, Baer, Ureno, & Villasenor, 1988; Horowitz, Rosenberg, Ureno, Mertz, & O'Halloran, 1988; Horowitz, Sampson, Siegelman, Weiss, & Goodfriend, 1988; Horowitz & Vitkus, 1986; Horowitz, Weckler, & Doren, 1983; Horowitz, Wright, Lowenstein, & Parad, 1981; see also Youngren & Lewinsohn, 1980) set out to investigate the relationships among three classes of complaints that bring patients into psychotherapy: symptoms, specific behavioral difficulties, and self-defeating thoughts. In the process they examined complaints in the form of interpersonal problems (e.g., "I can't seem to make friends"; "I find it

Table 22.1. Summary Characteristics of Contemporary Interpersonal Circle Inventories

INVENTORY	REFERENCE	S	TI	NIS	IF	IS
ICL	LaForge & Suczek (1955)	16	128	8	ADJ-VRB	Checklist
IBI	Lorr & McNair (1967)	15	140	7-11	VRB	Checklist
ISI	Lorr & Youniss (1983)	15	300	20	sentence	T-F
	Lorr & DeJong (1986) (SF)	15	150	10	sentence	T-F
IAS	Wiggins (1979b, 1981)	16	128	8	ADJ	8-pt Likert
	Wiggins (1988) (IASR)	8[a]	64	8	ADJ	8-pt Likert
CLOIT	Kiesler (1984, 1987b)	16	96	6	VRB	Checklist
IMI	Kiesler et al. (1985)	15	90	6	ADJ-VRB	4-pt Likert
ARQ	Wiggins (1984)	8[a]	32	4	ADJ	8-pt Likert
SASB	Benjamin (1983)	8[a]	144	4-5	ADJ-VRB	11-pt Likert
	Benjamin (1987a) (SF)	8[a]	32	1	ADJ-VRB	11-pt Likert

Note. S=number of scales; TI=total number of items; NIS=number of items per scale; IF=item format (ADJ=adjectives; VRB=verb phrases); IS=item scale; ICL=Interpersonal Check List; IBI=Interpersonal Behavior Inventory; ISI=Interpersonal Style Inventory; IAS=Interpersonal Adjective Scales; IASR=IAS Revised; CLOIT=Check List of Interpersonal (Psychotherapy) Transactions; IMI=Impact Message Inventory; ARQ=Affective Reactions Questionnaire; SASB=Structural Analysis of Social Behavior; SF=short form.
[a]Octant scales (rather than sixteenths). Benjamin provides eight octant scores on each of her three surfaces.

hard to say no to my friends") gathered from samples of patients about to begin therapy. Observers viewed videotaped intake interviews and recorded each problem that began with the phrase "I find it hard to . . ." or with a synonym such as "I can't . . .", as well as statements that began "I find it hard not to . . ." or with a synonym such as "I can't stop. . . ." Nearly 200 problems were identified and over three-quarters were judged to be interpersonal in nature.

By various sorting and scaling procedures, three major problem dimensions were identified among the 200 problem statements: control, degree of psychological involvement, and nature of the involvement (friendly to hostile). A clustering procedure grouped the problems further into five thematic clusters concerning intimacy, aggression, compliance, independence, and socializing. A final analysis yielded a list of 127 problem state-

ments scored under one of these five clusters. These 127 items represent the present version of the IIP (Horowitz, 1979; Horowitz, Rosenberg, Baer, et al., 1988; Horowitz et al., 1983).

The IIP is a 127-item inventory with each item rated by a subject or patient on a 5-point scale ranging from "not at all" to "extremely." It demonstrates acceptable test-retest reliability and convergent validity both with other interpersonal measures and with clinicians' ratings of patients' behaviors (Horowitz, Rosenberg, Baer, et al., 1988). It has been shown to be responsive to changes that occur during psychotherapy (Horowitz, Rosenberg, Ureno, et al., 1988).

Alden, Wiggins, and Phillips (1987) reported clear circulant relationships between the IAS-R (Wiggins, Trapnell, & Phillips, 1988b) and the IIP. Circumplex analyses revealed that the first two dimensions to emerge from the IIP were prob-

Table 22.2. Summary Characteristics of Contemporary Interpersonal Circle Inventories (Part 2)

INVENTORY	INVENTORY MANUAL REFERENCE	CODING MANUAL REFERENCE
ICL	LaForge (1977)	O'Dell (1966, 1968)
	Leary (1956, 1957)	Alexander (1970)
	Lees-Haley (1981)	Duke (1978)
		Strong, Hills, & Nelson (1988)
IBI	None	None
ISI	Lorr (1986)	None
IAS	None	None
CLOIT	Kiesler, Goldston, & Schmidt (in preparation)	Kiesler (1985)
IMI	Kiesler (1987a)	None
ARQ	None	None
SASB	Benjamin (1987c, in press-a, in press-b)	Benjamin, Giat, & Estroff (1981)

Table 22.3. Summary Characteristics of Contemporary Interpersonal Circle Inventories (Part 3)

		EMPIRICAL STUDIES
ICL	Bibliographies	Clark & Taulbee (1981); Taulbee & Clark (1982)
	Critiques	Chartier & Conway (1984); Kiesler (1983); Lorr & McNair (1965); Paddock & Nowicki (1986, 1987); Stern (1970); Wiggins (1979a, 1982)
	Acts Codings	Strong, Hills, Kilmartin, et al. (1988).
IBI	Review	Lorr & McNair (1966)
	Studies	Lorr, Bishop, & McNair (1965); Lorr & McNair (1963, 1965); Lorr, Suzidelis, & Kinnane (1973); McNair & Lorr (1965)
	Critiques	Kiesler (1983); Wiggins (1982)
ISI	Manual	Lorr (1986)
IAS	Studies	Alden, Wiggins, & Phillips (1987); Buss & Barnes (1986); Buss, Gomes, Higgins, & Lauterbach (1987); Gifford & O'Connor (1987); Wiggins & Broughton (1985); Wiggins & Holzmuller (1978, 1981); Wiggins, Phillips, & Trapnell (1989); Wiggins, Steiger, & Gaelick (1981); Wiggins, Trapnell, & Phillips (1989a); Yarnold, Grimm, & Lyons (1987); Yarnold & Lyons (1987)
	Critique	Kiesler (1983)
CLOIT	Manual	Kiesler, Goldston, & Schmidt (in preparation)
	Studies	Carson & Shapiro (1985); Kiesler & Chapman (1988); Kiesler & Goldston (1988); Kiesler, Goldston, Paddock, & Van Denburg (1986); Kiesler, Schmidt, & Larus (1988, 1989); Kiesler, Van Denburg, Sikes, Larus, & Goldston (1988); Kiesler & Watkins (in press); Mahalik, Hill, Thompson, & O'Grady (1989); Thompson, Hill, & Mahalik (1989); Van Denburg (1988); Weinstock-Savoy (1986); Wilkie (1987)
IMI	Manual	Kiesler (1987a)
	Critiques	Borgen (1985); Kiesler (1983); McCarthy (1985); Strong (1985); Wiggins (1982)
ARQ		Wiggins, Trapnell, & Phillips (1988a)
SASB	Questionnaires	
	Manual	Benjamin (1987c, in press-a, in press-b; see also Benjamin, 1979b, 1984);
	Critique	Alpher (1988); Wiggins (1982)
	Coding System	
	Manual	Benjamin, Giat, & Estroff (1981); see also Benjamin (1979a; 1986b); Benjamin, Foster, Giat-Roberto, & Estroff (1986)
	Critique	Grotevant & Carlson (1987); Weick (1984)
	Bibliography for both	L. S. Benjamin (personal communication, 1988); Humphrey & Benjamin (1986)

lem versions of the same two dimensions of the interpersonal circle, and also identified eight-item subset scales from the 127 IIP items that both were equally spaced within the two-dimensional space and met statistical criteria for a circumplex ordering. The 64-item, eight-scale version of the IIP that correlates strongly with Wiggins's IAS-R measure is described and listed in Horowitz (1988).

Comprehensive interpersonal assessment requires some form of inventory of interpersonal problems. As Alden et al. (1987) noted, self-report interpersonal inventories "ask an individual to describe his or her characteristic traits and do not specifically include statements of interpersonal problems. Trait endorsements do not necessarily imply interpersonal problems" (p. 5). Study of interpersonal problems can provide not only

an interpersonal translation of presenting complaints, but also can illuminate the correspondence of patient presenting problems to clusters of overt interpersonal behaviors defined by the 16 segments of the interpersonal circle (e.g., Alden et al., 1987) and to various physical and mental disorders. The IIP shows considerable promise for serving these important functions as a standard component of an emerging battery of interpersonal measures.

Assessment of Significant Others

Within interpersonal theory, the preeminent situational determinants of a patient's maladaptive actions are other people, especially those whom a person considers "significant." "Significant persons are those whose opinions about the [person] 'as a person' matter, with whom the [person] spends considerable time in either imaginary or real transactions, and who serve as potential sources of intimacy and regard in the [person's] life" (Kiesler, 1986a, p. 11). Until recently, however, no systematic procedures have been available to the clinician or researcher to help chart the scope and nature of these past and present relationships. Until very recently, empirical research on significant others has been virtually nonexistent (Shrauger & Schoeneman, 1979).

Interpersonal Inventory

Klerman et al. (1984, pp. 86–87), as part of their interpersonal treatment of depression, emphasize an assessment procedure called the "interpersonal inventory," which is completed through the process of the therapist's questions in early therapy sessions. The questioning has as its goal a review of key people and issues in the patient's life, past and present. The therapist has the option of pursuing this exploration further by asking the patient to write an autobiographical statement containing interpersonal information.

Either exploration seeks to gather the following information about each person who is important in the patient's life: (a) interactions with the patient, including frequency of contact, activities shared, and so forth; (b) the expectations of each party in the relationship, including some assessment of whether the expectations were or are fulfilled; (c) a review of satisfactory and unsatisfactory aspects of the relationship with specific, detailed examples of both kinds of interactions; and (d) the ways the patient would like to change the relationships, whether through changing his or her own behavior or bringing about changes in the other person.

Significant Other Survey

Chewning (1983a, 1983b) constructed the Significant Other Survey for standardized use in interpersonal research and therapy. Her survey asks the respondent to "list the names of all the persons who you consider to be highly significant in your life" (p. 1). For each person listed, the respondent then supplies the following information: (a) a rating of the importance of the person's opinion of the respondent as a person; (b) a rating of how much imaginary and real time is devoted by the respondent to each person; (c) a list of three positive and three negative "traits, characteristics, or behavior patterns" characteristic of the respondent; (d) a list of three positive and three negative traits that characterize each significant person listed; (e) a rating of the extent to which the respondent has actually discussed each of his or her traits in actual conversation with each significant other; and (f) a rating of the extent to which each significant other has actually discussed his or her traits in actual conversation with the respondent.

More recently, Larus, Chewning, and Kiesler (1988) have developed a revised inventory, the Significant Other Inventory (SOI), that is more simple in both size and structure. Respondents are asked (a) to list three to six of the most significant people in their lives, (b) to characterize the most prominent role each significant other (SO) occupies vis a vis their particular relationship, and (c) to rate each SO on a series of 21 characteristics chosen to represent different definitions of SOs and other theoretical features present in the literature. In a preliminary validation study, Larus (1989) examined psychometric, structural, and logical features of the SOI preparatory to applications within the psychotherapy context.

In order to understand the complex workings of interpersonal behavior, it is clear that important situational factors need to be identified and their interactive effects demonstrated (Kiesler, 1982a). It is also clear that a central source of situational influence resides in the dispositional patterns of interpersonal behavior characteristic of interactants (Kiesler, 1982a). The interpersonal propositions of complementarity are postulated to operate most straightforwardly in situations without structure and clearly defined expectations (Kiesler, 1983). Further, as Orford (1986) documents, there is considerable evidence that interpersonal contingencies are affected by factors of role and status. It is within this multivariate complex of interactive situational influence, also including various types of personal relationships (e.g., with strangers, acquaintances, close friends), that the measurement and study of significant others becomes so critical. Moreover, in interpersonal therapy it is crucial that the therapist be able to identify the significant relationships in a patient's life in order to explore, define, and alter the patient's Maladaptive Transaction Cycle. Perhaps the assessment procedures of both Larus et al. (1988) and Klerman et al. (1984) may become part of an eventual standardized interpersonal assessment battery.

Sequential Analysis of Interpersonal Transactions

The potentially most powerful procedures for identifying specific components of the Maladaptive Transaction Cycle are various possibilities of sequential or stochastic analysis of the evolving patterns of action-reaction between individuals and various significant others.

We have seen above that various interpersonal measures have been adapted to act-by-act coding systems that yield nominal scores ready for various sequential analysis statistics. Benjamin has applied structural analysis of social behavior codings (Benjamin, Giat, & Estroff, 1981) in a series of clinical applications (Benjamin, 1977, 1979b, 1982, in press-c; Benjamin, Foster, Giat-Roberto, & Estroff, 1986; see also Brokaw & McLemore, 1988; Henry, Schacht, & Strupp, 1986). Strong has applied ICL codings (Strong, Hills, & Nelson, 1988) in a series of studies summarized in Strong, Hills, Kilmartin, DeVries, Lanier, Nelson, Strickland, and Meyer (1988). Wilkie (1987) applied a 1982 Circle Acts Version (Kiesler, 1985) in a sequential analysis of complementarity in dyadic interaction.

The Interaction Record and Functional Analysis of Interpersonal Behavior

Peterson has developed and applied several sequential analysis methods that are relevant to clinicians and researchers alike (Boals, Peterson, Farmer, Mann, & Robinson, 1982; Peterson, 1977, 1979a, 1979b, 1979c, 1982, in press; Peterson & Rapinchuk, in press). A central method that Peterson and colleagues employ is the Interaction Record (IR; Peterson, 1979a, 1979b) and its accompanying manual (Peterson, 1979c), which they have applied primarily to studies of marital therapy. Peterson argued that the flow of actions and reactions that occurs as spouses meet, deal with one another, and then part must first be described at a very specific and concrete level; this is accomplished through administration of the IR. Only subsequently should the therapist attempt to understand this flow in terms of deeper relationship meanings.

On separate IR forms each spouse describes the most important interaction they had on a given day. In their own words, and from their respective viewpoints, each independently describes in specific detail the conditions under which the exchange took place, how the interaction started, and what happened then. The third point is especially crucial in that the spouse is asked to write a fairly detailed account of the exchange from start to finish, including, Who did and said what to whom? What were you thinking and feeling as the action went on? What ideas and emotions did your partner seem to have? How did it all come out?

In interpreting interaction records, Peterson first identifies the major acts or moves that each person has made in the course of the exchange; then an interpersonal meaning or message is inferred for each act. Each message contains three kinds of meaning: a report of the emotion the person is feeling at the time, a report of the way the person construes the situation, and an expectation about the response of the other. Peterson reports that, despite the rather high level of inference required for these interpretations, clinicians agree fairly closely about them. He finds interesting differences between normal and disturbed couples regarding the kinds of affect, construal, and expectation they report with this procedure.

Peterson also advocates use of videotaped samples of "analog interactions" between spouses for which they are directed to discuss conflicts, plan vacations, and so on. Descriptions of recurrent interaction patterns can be derived from these videotapes by clinicians or other observers. Once obtained, the causal governing regularities in interpersonal behavior between marriage partners or other dyads can be inferred provisionally. Peterson uses the phrase "functional analysis of interpersonal behavior" to designate this "cyclical process of describing interaction patterns, formulating ideas about the conditions that maintain the patterns, testing the propositions by planned interventions, and describing the interaction patterns that follow" to determine whether changes have or have not occurred. Changes "in predicted directions confirm hypotheses about the causes of the disorder. Persistence of the problem tends to disconfirm the hypothesis and requires conceptual reformulation" (Peterson, 1982, p. 164).

Peterson's modifications of behavior procedures for study of interpersonal disorders have much to offer interpersonal assessment, especially with regard to discovery of specific components of Maladaptive Transaction Cycles prototypical of distinct individual, marital, and family psychiatric disorders.

INTERPERSONAL DIAGNOSIS

Various authors have argued that contemporary interpersonal theories of personality and psychopathology can provide taxonomies to guide assessment of the mental disorders as defined in the *Diagnostic and Statistical Manual of Mental Disorders* (DSM-III-R; American Psychiatric Association, 1987; Adams, 1964; Frances, 1982; Kiesler, 1986a, 1986b; Leary, 1957; Leary & Coffey, 1955; McLemore & Benjamin, 1979; McLemore & Brokaw, 1987; Plutchik & Conte, 1986; Widiger & Frances, 1985, 1988; Widiger, Frances, Spitzer, & Williams, 1988; Widiger & Kelso, 1983; Wiggins, 1982). These authors have proposed adoption of one or another version of the interpersonal circle to serve as a taxonomy of individual differences for the domain of normal to maladjusted adult interpersonal behavior. Other authors have provided more in-depth analyses of principles and procedures of interpersonal diagnosis (Andrews, in press-c; Benjamin, 1984, 1986a, in press-a, in press-b; Boghosian, 1982; Buss & Craik, 1986b, 1987; Horowitz & Vitkus, 1986; Horowitz et al., 1983; Kiesler, 1986a, 1986b; Leary, 1957; Safran, 1984a; Widiger & Trull, 1987; Wiggins, 1982).

Several authors also have made a priori attempts to translate DSM characterizations of personality disorders into prototypic patterns of maladaptive interpersonal behavior at distinctive segments or octants of the interpersonal circle (Kiesler, 1986b; Leary, 1957; McLemore & Brokaw, 1987; Widiger & Kelso, 1983; Wiggins, 1982). At present, however, few empirical studies have addressed these interpersonal predictions. Several investigators (Lorr, Bishop, & McNair, 1965; Plutchik & Platman, 1977) have examined patterns of interpersonal behavior associated with DSM-III-R symptomatic (axis I) disorders. Three studies (Blashfield, Sprock, Pinkston, & Hodgin, 1985; Plutchik & Platman, 1977; Widiger, Trull, Hurt, Clarkin, & Frances, 1987) have examined the circumplex properties of interpersonal behavior on samples of personality disorder patients. Only Morey (1985) and Kiesler, Van Denburg, Sikes, Larus, and Goldston (1988), however, have directly examined distinctive profiles of interpersonal behavior for the axis II disorders, with mixed results. Obviously, much empirical work remains to be done by interpersonal researchers.

Since Leary (1957) first observed the pattern, it still seems the case that DSM-III-R disorders are classified predominantly in the hostile (left) half

of the interpersonal circle; further, they are underrepresented in the bottom-right (friendly-submissive) and extreme top left (dominant-competitive) circle categories. These patterns of interpersonal behavior undoubtedly reflect interactive effects of societal preferences and values. These societal contributions, however, need to be both explicitly conceptualized and empirically demonstrated before interpersonal diagnosis can provide a comprehensive paradigm for mental disorder.

At present, interpersonal diagnosis is most clearly relevant to the DSM-III-R personality disorders. Future theory and research will determine the extent to which interpersonal conceptualizations and measurement might be useful for diagnosis of DSM-III-R axis I disorders (Widiger & Hyler, 1987). Also, as Kiesler, Van Denburg, et al. (1988) noted, self-report data are suspect as the sole basis for determining either diagnosis of personality disorder or profiles of interpersonal behavior, because it is the pattern of a patient's overt behavior as assessed from interactants' or observers' ratings that produces the maladaptive aversive effects in others emphasized both by DSM-III-R and by interpersonal theory.

Principles of Interpersonal Diagnosis

Kiesler (1986b) has detailed six principles that guide interpersonal diagnosis using the circle as a conceptual framework: (a) Circle diagnosis focuses exclusively on assessment of overt social-interpersonal behaviors of abnormal people; these observable actions include both verbal and nonverbal behaviors. It thereby avoids inferences about patients' motives, feeling states, cognitions, or other covert events. (b) Circle diagnosis of mental disorders needs to designate both the exact circle segments as well as the exact level on each segment (mild, moderate, extreme) that characterize the maladaptive behavior for each disorder. (c) The task of interpersonal diagnosis is to establish the empirical profile of circle segments that represents the distinctive prototype (Horowitz, 1979; Horowitz, French, & Anderson, 1982; Horowitz, French, et al., 1982; Horowitz, Post et al., 1981; Horowitz et al., 1983; Horowitz, Wright et al., 1981; Rosch, 1975, 1978; Wiggins, 1982) of exemplary behaviors for each of the mental disorders. Because diagnostic categories represent fuzzy sets, there is no reason to expect an exact one-to-one correspondence between specific mental disorders and circle segments. (d) There is no compelling reason to assume that the circle structure of the prototypes defining each of the various disorders will be identical or isomorphic. Prototypic descriptions of various disorders may incorporate different levels and segment-bands, may subsume more than one circle octant, and in some cases may include octants from different quadrants. (e) For comprehensive interpersonal diagnosis of mental disorders, classes of situations associated with and most relevant to each defining prototype need to be clearly specified so that assessment can target these environmental contexts. The distinctive situational band width (classes of situations and interpersonal contexts) in which the prototypical behavior pattern is most likely to be expressed must be specified as an essential component of the assessment procedure. (f) The therapeutic situation must be distinctively included in this situational specification. Both the expected counterpull of the therapy situation and the distinctive complementary covert engagements the therapist can expect to experience as operative for each prototypical disorder need to be designated as, by employing circle principles, they define for the therapist the first stage of sequential interventions (Kiesler, 1983, 1988) designed to progressively alter the patient's style toward less extreme and rigid self-presentations.

Issues in Interpersonal Diagnosis

It is important to realize, however, that basic understanding both of interpersonal diagnosis and intervention requires use of two conceptual models: the interpersonal circle and the Maladaptive Transaction Cycle (Kiesler, 1986a). The interpersonal circle specifies the range of individual differences in normal and abnormal interpersonal behavior. Through use of one or more of the inventories described in the previous section, one can assess a patient's interpersonal behavior and precisely locate that behavior on the surface of the interpersonal circle. This placement, in turn, permits both exact specification of the patient's maladaptive pattern of living as well as precise prediction of various components of the optimal treatment program for the patient (Kiesler, 1983, 1988). The Maladaptive Transaction Cycle provides a framework for depicting the specific transactional pattern present in any patient's self-defeating interpersonal relationships. It also pinpoints covert (cognitive, emotional, etc.) and overt behavioral components that need to be

targeted for intervention in order to disrupt the patient's pattern of maladaptive transactions.

Covert Interpersonal Assessment

What the Maladaptive Transaction Cycle makes abundantly evident is that comprehensive assessment of mental disorders will require, in addition to present interpersonal circle inventories that target overt behavior, additional inventories or measures that target patients' *covert* behaviors and experiences (Kiesler, 1983, 1986a, 1986b; Widiger, Frances, & Trull, 1987). Ideally, models of covert events will be developed that permit predictions of one-to-one correspondence with the categories of overt behavior depicted on the interpersonal circle.

To date, this bridging work has occurred primarily in the area of emotion. Plutchik (1980) showed that circumplex models of personality traits can be mapped onto structural models of the emotion domain. Schaefer and Plutchik's (1966) factor analytic findings supported their hypothesis that circular configurations would be found for trait and emotion signs and for diagnostic constructs. They concluded that most of the variance of traits and emotions associated with psychiatric diagnostic categories falls within a two-dimensional space so that trait and emotion terms can be plotted within the same semantic configuration. Russell (1980) provided evidence of a clear circumplex structure in the domain of personal affect. Kiesler, Horner, Larus, and Chapman (1988) showed that (a) interpersonal acts located at the poles of the two 1982 circle axes evoke distinctive patterns of emotion as measured by Russell's (1980) personal affect scales, and (b) Russell's list of affect adjectives exhibits a circumplex structure equivalent to that found for personal affect when used to measure the "evoked emotion" characteristic of interpersonal encounters.

Empirical studies of the traditional cognitive realm are necessary to determine whether similar structural models can be found for construal, perceptual, expectational, and other cognitive events that provide covariate matches to the categories of overt behavior anchored on the circumference of the interpersonal circle. Seminal work has begun by Carson (1969, 1979, 1982), Andrews and Moore (in press), Conway (1980, 1983), Crowley (1985), Golding (1977, 1978), Golding, Valone, and Foster (1980), Horowitz (1979), Horowitz et al. (1983), Safran (1984a, 1988), and Safran and Segal (1990).

Situational and Temporal Assessment

If interpersonal diagnosis is to contribute to full understanding of mental disorders, its assessment must systematically incorporate the important situational and temporal factors relevant to expression of each disorder's prototypical maladaptive interpersonal pattern, including both central and peripheral components (Anchin, 1982a; Duke & Nowicki, 1982; Kiesler, 1982a, 1983, 1986a, 1986b; Orford, 1986; Strong, in press). An important move in this direction is the "act-frequency approach" of Buss (1985a, 1985b) and Buss and Craik (1980, 1981, 1983a, 1983b, 1983c, 1984, 1986a, 1986b, 1987; Buss, Gomes, Higgins, & Lauterbach, 1987), which conceptualizes interpersonal dispositions as cognitive categories of acts that summarize general trends in behavior. Their prototypical (act in-context) interpersonal descriptors anchor interpersonal assessment simultaneously in both overt behaviors and situations.

Interpersonal behavior and diagnosis need to be viewed from the perspective of relationship development as well. Duke and Nowicki (1982) proposed that relationships progress through four phases: choice, beginning, deepening, and termination. From their perspective, negotiation of relationship definition is not as essential during the earliest stages of a relationship, but becomes more important as the interaction continues over time.

Assessment of Nonverbal Behavior

Kiesler (1983) emphasized that "basic aspects of nonverbal communication need to be integrated both with the interpersonal circle and with interpersonal theory more generally" (p. 211). Kiesler (1977, 1979, 1982a, 1988; Kiesler et al., 1976) provided a theoretical integration of nonverbal behavior with interpersonal theory. Nowicki and colleagues have pursued a program of research examining the nonverbal and verbal correlates of interpersonal behavior (Cooley & Nowicki, in press; McGovern, 1985; McLeod & Nowicki, 1985; Nowicki & Manheim, in press; Oxenford & Nowicki, in press), as have Perlmutter, Paddock, and Duke (1985) and Schmidt (1988).

It is clear that nonverbal messages predominate in emotional and relationship communication, and in the arena of interpersonal behavior. The factor structure underlying both domains is identical. Increasingly, complexes of specific nonverbal behaviors have been identified for control and affiliation relationship messages; these complexes need to be interfaced with the traditional acts used to define the interpersonal circle categories, and need to become an essential part of assessment of interpersonal behavior.

Assessment of Significant Others

Duke and Nowicki's (1982) analysis, that relationship definition becomes more important as an interaction continues over time, also leads to the conclusion, emphasized by Kiesler (Kiesler et al., 1976), that significant others are crucial to the task of interpersonal diagnosis — that assessment of patients' maladaptive behavior must include transactant ratings by people currently significant in each patient's life. Use of the Significant Other Inventory (Larus et al., 1988) may provide the initial methodology for identification of these people.

CONCLUSION

Contemporary interpersonal theory, together with its two central conceptual/empirical models (the interpersonal circle and the Maladaptive Transaction Cycle), has much to offer to assessment, diagnosis, and differential treatment of mental disorders.

Psychometrically sophisticated inventories and coding systems are increasingly available to assess the transactional domain of interpersonal behavior. Continuing attempts to chart the covert behavioral domains of interactants may gradually provide conceptual bridges to the categories of overt behavior organized on the interpersonal circle, bridges that also lawfully link together the covert and overt blocks of interactants' behaviors conceptualized in the Maladaptive Transaction Cycle. Kiesler and colleagues' (1985) Impact Message Inventory provides a preliminary and unique probe into this covert transactional arena.

Availability of other interpersonal assessment procedures can address more directly the complexity of the diagnostic task. Horowitz and colleagues' (Horowitz, Rosenberg, Baer et al., 1988) Interpersonal Problem Inventory is directly relevant to diagnosis and treatment, and already has shown important relationships to interpersonal circle categories. Preliminary methods for assessment of significant others (Larus et al.'s, [1988] Significant Other Inventory, Klerman and colleagues' [1984] Interpersonal Inventory method) offer opportunities both for assessing significant others' perceptions of the interpersonal behavior of patients and charting patient improvement over the course of treatment. Peterson's (1982) applications of Interaction Records and sequential analysis of interpersonal behavior have already demonstrated clinical utility in diagnosis and treatment of marital couples. Benjamin's (in press-a, in press-b) structural analysis of social behavior models, including questionnaires and codings, has shown considerable utility in both diagnostic and treatment settings.

Much remains to be done, but much has been accomplished. Contemporary interpersonal theory of maladjustment, diagnosis, and treatment is complex and needs to become even more complex to capture the multiple facets of human transactions. The "carrot" that interpersonal theory extends is the specificity of explanation and prediction that the interpersonal circle (and, eventually, the Maladaptive Transaction Cycle) provides—together with the capacity for falsification that this level of concreteness offers.

Finally, interpersonal diagnosis and interpersonal treatment are inherently inseparable. The ultimate predictive power of the interpersonal circle (and the Maladaptive Transaction Cycle) resides in its propositions for psychotherapeutic intervention (Kiesler, 1983, 1986b). The real promise of the interpersonal circle is that, having identified prototypic segments that define a particular disorder, theoretically derivable interventions can be systematically designated. Kiesler's (in press) Interpersonal Treatment Plan offers a practical guide for individual clinical cases. What is available, however, is only a skeleton of an ultimately comprehensive treatment package for mental patients. Many additional components are necessary, including guidelines for analysis of situational manifestations of maladaptive interpersonal behavior; specification of interventions that target cognitive, affective, and other covert events lawfully associated with a patient's overt behavior patterns; specific rules that guide the therapist's metacommunicative use of covert complementary responses or impact messages with different patients; and rules that govern optimal sequencing over sessions of asocial, acomplementary, and anticomplementary therapist responses.

Hopefully, an ever increasing number of psychological researchers will pursue the fascinating challenges that remain.

REFERENCES

Adams, H. B. (1964). "Mental illness" or interpersonal behavior? *American Psychologist, 19*, 191–197.

Alden, L., Wiggins, J. S., & Phillips, N. (1987). *Interpersonal problems and interpersonal dispositions: A circumplex analysis.* Unpublished manuscript, University of British Columbia, Vancouver, Canada.

Alexander, J. F. (1970, April). *Videotaperecorded family interaction: A systems approach.* Paper presented at the annual meeting of the Western Psychological Association, Los Angeles, CA.

Alpher, J. S. (1988). Structural analysis of social behavior. In D. J. Keyser & R. C. Sweetland (Eds.), *Test critiques* (Vol. 7). Kansas City, MO: Test Corporation of America.

American Psychiatric Association. (1987). *Diagnostic and statistical manual of mental disorders* (3rd ed., rev.). Washington, DC: Author.

Anchin, J. C. (1982a). Sequence, pattern, and style: Integration and treatment implications of some interpersonal concepts. In J. C. Anchin & D. J. Kiesler (Eds.), *Handbook of interpersonal psychotherapy* (pp. 95–131). Elmsford, NY: Pergamon Press.

Anchin, J. C. (1982b). Interpersonal approaches to psychotherapy: Summary and conclusions. In J. C. Anchin & D. J. Kiesler (Eds.), *Handbook of interpersonal psychotherapy* (pp. 313–330). Elmsford, NY: Pergamon Press.

Anchin, J. C., & Kiesler, D. J. (1982). *Handbook of interpersonal psychotherapy.* Elmsford, NY: Pergamon Press.

Andrews, J. D. W. (1966). Psychotherapy of phobias. *Psychological Bulletin, 66*, 455–480.

Andrews, J. D. W. (1984). Psychotherapy with the hysterical personality: An interpersonal approach. *Psychiatry, 47*, 211–232.

Andrews, J. D. W. (in press-a). Self-confirmation theory: A paradigm for psychotherapy integration. *Journal of Integrative and Eclectic Psychotherapy.*

Andrews, J. D. W. (in press-b). *The active self in psychotherapy.* New York: Gardner.

Andrews, J. D. W. (in press-c). Integrating visions of reality: Interpersonal diagnosis and the existential vision. *American Psychologist.*

Andrews, J. D. W. (in press-d). Psychotherapy of depression: A self-confirmation model. *Psychological Review*.

Andrews, J. D. W., & Moore, S. (in press). Social cognition in the histrionic/overconventional personality. In P. Magaro (Ed.), *Annual review of psychopathology*.

Beier, E. G. (1966). *The silent language of psychotherapy: Social reinforcement of unconscious processes*. Chicago: Aldine.

Beier, E. G., & Young, D. M. (1984). *The silent language of psychotherapy: Social reinforcement of unconscious processes* (2nd ed.). New York: Aldine.

Benjafield, J., & Carson, E. (1985). An historico-developmental analysis of the circumplex model of trait descriptive terms. *Canadian Journal of Behavioral Science, 17*, 339–345.

Benjamin, L. S. (1977). Structural analysis of a family in therapy. *Journal of Abnormal Psychology, 45*, 391–406.

Benjamin, L. S. (1979a). Use of structural analysis of social behavior (SASB) and Markov chains to study dyadic interactions. *Journal of Abnormal Psychology, 88*, 303–319.

Benjamin, L. S. (1979b). Structural analysis of differentiation failure. *Psychiatry, 42*, 1–23.

Benjamin, L. S. (1982). Use of structural analysis of social behavior (SASB) to guide intervention in psychotherapy. In J. C. Anchin & D. J. Kiesler (Eds.), *Handbook of interpersonal psychotherapy* (pp. 190–212). Elmsford, NY: Pergamon Press.

Benjamin, L. S. (1983). *Intrex questionnaires*. Madison, WI: Intrex Interpersonal Institute.

Benjamin, L. S. (1984). Principles of prediction using structural analysis of social behavior (SASB). In R. A. Zucker, J. Aronoff, & A. J. Rabin (Eds.), *Personality and the prediction of behavior* (pp. 121–173). New York: Guilford Press.

Benjamin, L. S. (1986a). Using SASB to add social parameters to axis I of DSM-III. In T. Millon & G. L. Klerman (Eds.), *Contemporary issues in psychopathology: Toward the DSM-IV* (pp. 599–638). New York: Guilford Press.

Benjamin, L. S. (1986b). Operational definition and measurement of dynamics shown in the stream of free associations. *Psychiatry, 49*, 104–129.

Benjamin, L. S. (1987a). *Intrex short form questionnaires*. Madison, WI: Intrex Interpersonal Institute.

Benjamin, L. S. (1987b). An interpersonal approach. *Journal of Personality Disorders, 1*, 334–339.

Benjamin, L. S. (1987c). *Intrex shortform user's manual*. Madison, WI: Intrex Interpersonal Institute.

Benjamin, L. S. (in press-a). *Interpersonal diagnosis and treatment: The SASB approach*. New York: Guilford Press.

Benjamin, L. S. (in press-b). *Diagnosis and treatment of personality disorders: A structural approach*. New York: Guilford Press.

Benjamin, L. S. (in press-c). Commentary on the inner experience of the borderline self-mutilator. *Journal of Personality Disorders*.

Benjamin, L. S., Foster, S. W., Giat-Roberto, L., & Estroff, S. E. (1986). Breaking the family code: Analyzing videotapes of family interactions by structural analysis of social behavior. In L. S. Greenberg & W. M. Pinsof (Eds.), *The psychotherapeutic process: A research handbook*. New York: Guilford Press.

Benjamin, L. S., Giat, L., & Estroff, S. E. (1981). *Manual for coding social interactions in terms of structural analysis of social behavior*. Madison: University of Wisconsin Press.

Berzins, J. I. (1977). Therapist-patient matching. In A. S. Gurman & A. M. Razin (Eds.), *Effective psychotherapy: A handbook of research* (pp. 222–251). Elmsford, NY: Pergamon Press.

Bierman, R. (1969). Dimensions of interpersonal facilitation in psychotherapy and child development. *Psychological Bulletin, 72*, 338–352.

Blashfield, R., Sprock, J., Pinkston, K., & Hodgin, J. (1985). Exemplar prototypes of personality disorder diagnoses. *Comprehensive Psychiatry, 26*, 11–21.

Block, J. (1957). A comparison between ipsative and normative ratings of personality. *Journal of Abnormal and Social Psychology, 54*, 50–54.

Boals, G. F., Peterson, D. R., Farmer, L., Mann, D. F., & Robinson, D. L. (1982). The reliability, validity, and utility of three data modes in assessing marital relationships. *Journal of Personality Assessment, 46*, 85–96.

Boghosian, J. (1982). Interpersonal dimensions of mental health. *Dissertation Abstracts International, 43*, 397A.

Borgen, F. H. (1985). Review of the impact message inventory, form II. In J. V. Mitchell (Ed.), *Ninth mental measurements yearbook*. Lincoln, NE: Buros Institute of Mental Measurements.

Brokaw, D. W., & McLemore, C. W. (1983). Toward a more rigorous definition of social reinforcement: Some interpersonal clarifications. *Journal of Personality and Social Psychology, 44*, 1014–1020.

Brokaw, D. W., & McLemore, C. W. (1988). *Markov chains and master therapists: An interpersonal analysis of psychotherapy process.* Unpublished manuscript, Relational Dynamics Institute, Pasadena, CA.

Brokaw, D. W., & McLemore, C. W. (in press). Interpersonal models of personality and psychopathology. In D. Gilbert (Ed.), *Personality, social skills, and psychopathology*. New York: Plenum Press.

Buss, D. M. (1985a). The temporal stability of acts, trends, and patterns. In C. Spielberger & J. N. Butcher (Eds.), *Advances in personality assessment* (Vol. 5, pp. 165–196). Hillsdale, NJ: Lawrence Erlbaum Associates.

Buss, D. M. (1985b). The act frequency approach to the interpersonal environment. *Perspectives in Personality, 1*, 173–200.

Buss, D. M., & Barnes, M. L. (1986). Preferences in human mate selection. *Journal of Personality and Social Psychology, 50*, 559–570.

Buss, D. M., & Craik, K. H. (1980). The frequency concept of disposition: Dominance and prototypically dominant acts. *Journal of Personality, 48*, 379–392.

Buss, D. M., & Craik, K. H. (1981). The act frequency analysis of interpersonal dispositions: Aloofness, gregariousness, dominance, and submissiveness. *Journal of Personality, 49*, 175–192.

Buss, D. M., & Craik, K. H. (1983a). The act frequency approach to personality. *Psychological Review, 90*, 105–126.

Buss, D. M., & Craik, K. H. (1983b). The dispositional analysis of everyday conduct. *Journal of Personality, 51*, 393–412.

Buss, D. M., & Craik, K. H. (1983c). Act prediction and the conceptual analysis of personality scales: Indices of act density, bipolarity, and extensivity. *Journal of Personality and Social Psychology, 45*, 1081–1095.

Buss, D. M., & Craik, K. H. (1984). Acts, dispositions, and personality. In B. A. Maher & W. B. Maher (Eds.), *Progress in experimental personality research: Normal personality processes* (Vol. 13, pp. 241–301). New York: Academic Press.

Buss, D. M., & Craik, K. H. (1986a). The act

frequency approach and the construction of personality. In A. Angleitner, A. Furnham, & G. Van Heck (Eds.), *Personality psychology in Europe* (pp. 141–156). Lisse, The Netherlands: Swets & Zeitlinger.

Buss, D. M., & Craik, K. H. (1986b). Acts, dispositions, and clinical assessment: The psychopathology of everyday conduct. *Clinical Psychology Review, 6*, 387–406.

Buss, D. M., & Craik, K. H. (1987). Act criteria for the diagnosis of personality disorders. *Journal of Personality Disorders, 1*, 73–81.

Buss, D. M., Gomes, M., Higgins, D. S., & Lauterbach, K. (1987). Tactics of manipulation. *Journal of Personality and Social Psychology, 52*, 1219–1229.

Carson, R. C. (1969). *Interaction concepts of personality*. Chicago: Aldine.

Carson, R. C. (1971). Disordered interpersonal behavior. In W. A. Hunt (Ed.), *Human behavior and its control*. Cambridge, MA: Schenkman.

Carson, R. C. (1979). Personality and exchange in developing relationships. In R. L. Burgess & T. L. Huston (Eds.), *Social exchange in developing relationships*. New York: Academic Press.

Carson, R. C. (1982). Self-fulfilling prophecy, maladaptive behavior, and psychotherapy. In J. C. Anchin & D. J. Kiesler (Eds.), *Handbook of interpersonal psychotherapy* (pp. 64–77). Elmsford, NY: Pergamon Press.

Carson, R. C. (1984). The social-interactional viewpoint. In M. Hersen, A. E. Kazdin, & A. S. Bellack (Eds.), *The clinical psychology handbook*. New York: Pergamon Press.

Carson, R. C. (1989). Personality. *Annual Review of Psychology, 40*, 227–248.

Carson, R. C., & Shapiro, J. H. (1985). *Mood, gender-typing, and interpersonal orientation: On "masculine" imperturbability*. Unpublished manuscript, Duke University.

Cashdan, S. (1971). *Interactional psychotherapy: Stages and strategies in behavioral change.* New York: Grune & Stratton.

Cashdan, S. (1982). Interactional psychotherapy: Using the relationship. In J. C. Anchin & D. J. Kiesler (Eds.), *Handbook of interpersonal psychotherapy* (pp. 215–226). Elmsford, NY: Pergamon Press.

Cashdan, S. (1988). *Object relations therapy: Using the relationship*. New York: W. W. Norton.

Chartier, B. M., & Conway, J. B. (1984, August). *A psychometric comparison of the Leary and*

Wiggins interpersonal scales. Paper presented at the meeting of the American Psychological Association, Toronto, Canada.

Chewning, M. C. (1983a). *Significant other survey*. Richmond, VA: Virginia Commonwealth University.

Chewning, M. F. (1983b). *Interpersonal distance, interaction frequency, and the nature of relationships as a function of locus of control orientation and three classes of others*. Unpublished master's thesis, Virginia Commonwealth University, Richmond, VA.

Clark, T. L., & Taulbee, E. S. (1981). A comprehensive and indexed bibliography of the interpersonal check list. *Journal of Personality Assessment, 45*, 505–525.

Conte, H. R., & Plutchik, R. (1981). A circumplex model for interpersonal personality traits. *Journal of Personality and Social Psychology, 40*, 701–711.

Conway, J. B. (1980). *Biases in cognitive-affective processing across interpersonal styles and stress*. Unpublished manuscript, University of Saskatchewan, Saskatoon, Canada.

Conway, J. B. (1983). *Individual differences in biased interpersonal construal of self and others*. Unpublished manuscript, University of Saskatchewan, Saskatoon, Canada.

Cooley, E. L., & Nowicki, S., Jr. (in press). Discrimination of facial expressions of emotion by depressed subjects. *Genetic Psychology Monographs*.

Coyne, J. C. (1976a). Depression and the response of others. *Journal of Abnormal Psychology, 85*, 186–193.

Coyne, J. C. (1976b). Toward an interactional description of depression. *Psychiatry, 39*, 28–40.

Coyne, J. C., & Segal, L. (1982). A brief, strategic interactional approach to psychotherapy. In J. C. Anchin & D. J. Kiesler (Eds.), *Handbook of interpersonal psychotherapy* (pp. 248–261). Elmsford, NY: Pergamon Press.

Crowley, R. M. (1985). Cognition in interpersonal theory and practice. In M. J. Mahoney & A. Freeman (Eds.), *Cognition and psychotherapy* (pp. 291–312). New York: Plenum Press.

Danziger, K. (1976). *Interpersonal communication*. Elmsford, NY: Pergamon Press.

DeVogue, J. T., & Beck, S. (1978). The therapist-client relationship in behavior therapy. In M. Hersen, R. M. Eisler, & P. M. Miller (Eds.), *Progress in behavior modification* (Vol. 6). New York: Academic Press.

Dietzel, C. S., & Abeles, N. (1975). Client-therapist complementarity and therapeutic outcome. *Journal of Counseling Psychology, 22*, 264–272.

Duke, M. P. (1978). *A new method for measuring the circumplex*. Paper presented at the Southeastern Psychological Association meeting, Atlanta, GA.

Duke, M. P. (1987). The situational stream hypothesis: A unifying view of behavior with special emphasis on adaptive and maladaptive behavior patterns. *Journal of Research in Personality, 21*, 239–263.

Duke, M. P., & Nowicki, S., Jr. (1982). A social learning theory analysis of interactional theory concepts and a multidimensional model of human interaction constellations. In J. C. Anchin & D. J. Kiesler (Eds.), *Handbook of interpersonal psychotherapy* (pp. 78–94). Elmsford, NY: Pergamon Press.

Foa, U. G. (1961). Convergences in the analysis of the structure of interpersonal behavior. *Psychological Review, 68*, 341–353.

Frances, A. (1982). Categorical and dimensional systems of personality diagnosis: A comparison. *Comprehensive Psychiatry, 23*, 516–527.

Gascoyne, S. (1984). *Interpersonal perceptions as a function of personality styles*. Unpublished doctoral dissertation, Virginia Commonwealth University, Richmond, VA.

Gergen, K. J. (1987). *Exploration of emotional scenarios*. Unpublished project description, Swarthmore College, Swarthmore, PA.

Gifford, R., & O'Connor, B. (1987). The interpersonal circumplex as a behavioral map. *Journal of Personality and Social Psychology, 52*, 1019–1026.

Golding, S. L. (1977). Individual differences in the construal of interpersonal interactions. In D. Magnuson & N. Endler (Eds.), *Personality at the crossroads: Current issues in interactional psychology*. New York: John Wiley & Sons.

Golding, S. L. (1978). Toward a more adequate theory of personality: Psychological organizing principles. In H. London & N. Hirschberg (Eds.), *Personality: A new look at metatheories*. Washington, DC: Hemisphere.

Golding, S. L., & Knudson, R. M. (1975). Multivariable-multimethod convergence in the domain of interpersonal behavior. *Multivariate Behavioral Research, 10*, 425–448.

Golding, S. L., Valone, K., & Foster, S. W. (1980).

Interpersonal construal: An individual differences framework. In N. Hirschberg (Ed.), *Multivariate methods in the social sciences: Applications*. Hillsdale, NJ: Lawrence Erlbaum Associates.

Grotevant, H. D., & Carlson, C. I. (1987). Family interaction coding systems: A descriptive review. *Family Process, 26*, 49–74.

Guttman, L. (1954). A new approach to factor analysis: The radex. In P. R. Lazarsfeld (Ed.), *Mathematical thinking in the social sciences*. Glencoe, IL: Free Press.

Henry, W. P., Schacht, T. E., & Strupp, H. H. (1986). Structural analysis of social behavior: Application to a study of interpersonal process in differential psychotherapeutic outcome. *Journal of Consulting and Clinical Psychology, 54*, 27–31.

Horowitz, L. (1979). On the cognitive structure of interpersonal problems treated in psychotherapy. *Journal of Consulting and Clinical Psychology, 47*, 5–15.

Horowitz, L. (1988). *Inventory of interpersonal problems: Scoring procedures*. Unpublished manuscript, Stanford University, Stanford, CA.

Horowitz, L. M., & French, R. deS. (1979). Interpersonal problems of people who describe themselves as lonely. *Journal of Consulting and Clinical Psychology, 57*, 762–764.

Horowitz, L. M., French, R. deS, & Anderson, C. A. (1982). The prototype of a lonely person. In L. Peplau & D. Perlman (Eds.), *Loneliness: A sourcebook of current theory, research, and therapy* (pp. 183–205). New York: Wiley-Interscience.

Horowitz, L. M., French, R. deS, Lapid, J. S., & Weckler, D. A. (1982). Symptoms and interpersonal problems: The prototype as an integrating concept. In J. C. Anchin & D. J. Kiesler (Eds.), *Handbook of interpersonal psychotherapy* (pp. 168–189). Elmsford, NY: Pergamon Press.

Horowitz, L. M., Post, D. L., French, R. deS, Wallis, K. D., & Siegelman, E. Y. (1981). The prototype as a construct in abnormal psychology: 2. Clarifying disagreement in psychiatric judgments. *Journal of Abnormal Psychology, 90*, 575–585.

Horowitz, L. M., Rosenberg, S. E., Baer, B. A., Ureno, G., & Villasenor, V. S. (1988). The inventory of interpersonal problems: Psychometric properties and clinical applications. *Journal of Consulting and Clinical Psychology, 56*, 885.

Horowitz, L. M., Rosenberg, S. E., Ureno, G., Mertz, M., & O'Halloran, P. (1988). *The psychodynamic formulation, the modal response method, and interpersonal problems*. Unpublished manuscript, Stanford University, Stanford, CA.

Horowitz, L. M., Sampson, H., Siegelman, E. Y., Weiss, J., & Goodfriend, S. (1988). Cohesive and dispersal behaviors: Two classes of concomitant change in psychotherapy. *Journal of Consulting and Clinical Psychology, 46*, 556–564.

Horowitz, L. M., & Vitkus, J. (1986). The interpersonal basis of psychiatric symptoms. *Clinical Psychology Review, 6*, 443–469.

Horowitz, L. M., Weckler, D. A., & Doren, R. (1983). Interpersonal problems and symptoms: A cognitive approach. In P. Kendall (Ed.), *Advances in cognitive-behavioral research and therapy* (pp. 81–125). London: Academic Press.

Horowitz, L. M., Wright, J. C., Lowenstein, E., & Parad, H. W. (1981). The prototype as a construct in abnormal psychology: 1. A method for deriving prototypes. *Journal of Abnormal Psychology, 90*, 568–574.

Humphrey, L. L., & Benjamin, L. S. (1986). Using structural analysis of social behavior to assess critical but elusive family processes: A new solution to an old problem. *American Psychologist, 41*, 979–989.

Kelley, H. H., Berscheid, E., Christensen, A., Harvey, J. H., Huston, T. L., Levinger, G., McClintock, E., Peplau, L. A., & Peterson, D. R. (1983). *Close relationships*. New York: W. H. Freeman.

Kenny, D. A., & La Voie, L. (1984). The social relations model. In L. Berkowitz (Ed.), *Advances in experimental social psychology*. New York: Academic Press.

Kiesler, D. J. (1977). *Communications assessment of interview behavior of the "obsessive" personality*. Unpublished manuscript, Virginia Commonwealth University, Richmond, VA.

Kiesler, D. J. (1979). An interpersonal communication analysis of relationship in psychotherapy. *Psychiatry, 42*, 299–311.

Kiesler, D. J. (1982a). Interpersonal theory for personality and psychotherapy. In J. C. Anchin & D. J. Kiesler (Eds.), *Handbook of interpersonal psychotherapy*. Elmsford, NY: Pergamon Press.

Kiesler, D. J. (1982b). Confronting the client-therapist relationship in psychotherapy. In J. C. Anchin & D. J. Kiesler (Eds.), *Handbook of interpersonal psychotherapy*. Elmsford, NY: Pergamon Press.

Kiesler, D. J. (1983). The 1982 interpersonal circle: A taxonomy for complementarity in human transactions. *Psychological Review, 90*, 185–214.

Kiesler, D. J. (1984). *Check list of psychotherapy transactions* and *Check list of interpersonal transactions*. Richmond, VA: Virginia Commonwealth University.

Kiesler, D. J. (1985). *The 1982 interpersonal circle: Acts version*. Unpublished manuscript, Virginia Commonwealth University, Richmond, VA.

Kiesler, D. J. (1986a). Interpersonal methods of diagnosis and treatment. In J. O. Cavenar, Jr. (Ed.), *Psychiatry* (Vol. 1, pp. 1–23). Philadelphia: J. B. Lippincott.

Kiesler, D. J. (1986b). The 1982 interpersonal circle: An analysis of DSM-III personality disorders. In T. Millon & G. L. Klerman (Eds.), *Contemporary directions in psychopathology: Towards the DSM-IV* (pp. 57–597). New York: Guilford Press.

Kiesler, D. J. (1987a). *Research manual for the impact message inventory*. Palo Alto, CA: Consulting Psychologists Press.

Kiesler, D. J. (1987b). *Check list of psychotherapy transactions-revised* and *Check list of interpersonal transactions-revised*. Richmond, VA: Virginia Commonwealth University.

Kiesler, D. J. (1987c, October). Complementarity: Between whom and under what conditions? *Clinician's Research Digest: Supplemental bulletin, 5*, No. 20.

Kiesler, D. J. (1988). *Therapeutic metacommunication: Therapist impact disclosure as feedback in psychotherapy*. Palo Alto, CA: Consulting Psychologists Press.

Kiesler, D. J. (in press). Supervision in interpersonal communication psychotherapy. In A. K. Hess (Ed.), *Psychotherapy supervision: Theory, research and practice* (Vol. 2). New York: John Wiley & Sons.

Kiesler, D. J., Anchin, J. C., Perkins, M. J., Chirico, B. M., Kyle, E. M., & Federman, E. J. (1985). *The impact message inventory: Form II*. Palo Alto, CA: Consulting Psychologists Press.

Kiesler, D. J., Bernstein, A. B., & Anchin, J. C.

(1976). *Interpersonal communication, relationship, and the behavior therapies*. Richmond, VA: Virginia Commonwealth University.

Kiesler, D. J., & Chapman, R. C. (1988). *A multidimensional scaling analysis of the 1982 interpersonal circle*. Unpublished manuscript, Virginia Commonwealth University, Richmond, VA.

Kiesler, D. J., & Goldston, C. S. (1988). Client-therapist complementarity: An analysis of the Gloria films. *Journal of Counseling Psychology, 35*, 127–133.

Kiesler, D. J., Goldston, C. S., Paddock, J. M., & Van Denburg, T. F. (1986). *An initial validation of the check list of interpersonal transactions*. Unpublished study, Virginia Commonwealth University, Richmond, VA.

Kiesler, D. J., Goldston, C. S., & Schmidt, J. A. (in preparation). *Manual for the Check List of Interpersonal Transactions-Revised*. Virginia Commonwealth University, Richmond, VA.

Kiesler, D. J., Horner, M. S., Larus, J. P., & Chapman, R. C. (1988). *Measurement of evoked emotion in interpersonal transactions*. Unpublished manuscript, Virginia Commonwealth University, Richmond, VA.

Kiesler, D. J., Schmidt, J. A., & Larus, J. P. (1988). *Internal consistency and test-retest reliability of the self-report version of the check list of interpersonal transactions (CLOIT)*. Unpublished study, Virginia Commonwealth University, Richmond, VA.

Kiesler, D. J., Schmidt, J. A., & Larus, J. P. (1989). *The interpersonal adjective scales (IAS) and the check list of interpersonal transactions (CLOIT): Convergent validity evidence*. Unpublished study, Virginia Commonwealth University, Richmond, VA.

Kiesler, D. J., Van Denburg, T. F., Sikes, V. M., Larus, J. P., & Goldston, C. S. (in press). *Interpersonal behavior profiles of eight cases of DSM-III personality disorder*. Unpublished manuscript. Commonwealth University, Richmond, VA.

Kiesler, D. J., & Watkins, L. M. (1989). Interpersonal complementarity and the therapeutic alliance: A study of relationship in psychotherapy. *Psychotherapy, 26*, 183–194.

Klerman, G. L., Weissman, M. M., Rounsaville, B. J., & Chevron, E. S. (1984). *Interpersonal psychotherapy of depression*. New York: Basic Books.

LaForge, R. (1977). *Using the ICL: 1976.* Unpublished manuscript, Mill Valley, CA.

LaForge, R., & Suczek, R. F. (1955). The interpersonal dimensions of personality: III. An interpersonal check list. *Journal of Personality, 24*, 94–112.

LaForge, R., Freedman, M. B., & Wiggins, J. S. (1985). Interpersonal circumplex models: 1948–1983 (Symposium). *Journal of Personality Assessment, 49*, 613–631.

Larus, J. P. (1989). Significant other inventory: Towards charting the nature of significant others. Unpublished master's thesis, Virginia Commonwealth University, Richmond, VA.

Larus, J. P., Chewning, M. F., & Kiesler, D. J. (1988). *Significant other inventory.* Richmond, VA: Virginia Commonwealth University.

Leary, T. (1956). *Multilevel measurement of interpersonal behavior: A manual for the use of the interpersonal system of personality.* Berkeley, CA: Psychological Consultation Service.

Leary, T. (1957). *Interpersonal diagnosis of personality.* New York: Ronald Press.

Leary, T., & Coffey, H. S. (1955). Interpersonal diagnosis: Some problems of methodology and validation. *Journal of Abnormal and Social Psychology, 50*, 110–124.

Lees-Haley, P. R. (1981). College norms for the Leary interpersonal checklist. *Journal of Consulting and Clinical Psychology, 49*, 302–303.

Lorr, M. (1986). *Interpersonal style inventory (ISI) manual.* Los Angeles: Western Psychological Services.

Lorr, M., Bishop, P. F., & McNair, D. M. (1965). Interpersonal types among psychiatric patients. *Journal of Abnormal Psychology, 70*, 468–472.

Lorr, M., & DeJong, J. (1986). A short form of the interpersonal style inventory (ISI). *Journal of Clinical Psychology, 42*, 466–469.

Lorr, M., & McNair, D. M. (1963). An interpersonal behavior circle. *Journal of Abnormal and Social Psychology, 67*, 68–75.

Lorr, M., & McNair, D. M. (1965). Expansion of the interpersonal behavior circle. *Journal of Personality and Social Psychology, 2*, 823–830.

Lorr, M., & McNair, D. M. (1966). Methods relating to evaluation of therapeutic outcome. In L. A. Gottschalk & A. H. Auerbach (Eds.), *Methods of research in psychotherapy.* New York: Appleton-Century-Crofts.

Lorr, M., & McNair, D. M. (1967). *The interpersonal behavior inventory, form 4.* Washington, DC: Catholic University of America.

Lorr, M., Suziedelis, A., & Kinnane, J. F. (1973). Modes of interpersonal response to peers. *Multivariate Behavioral Research, 8*, 427–438.

Lorr, M., & Youniss, R. P. (1983). *The interpersonal style inventory, form E.* Los Angeles, CA: Western Psychological Services.

Madison, J. K., & Paddock, J. R. (1983). Assessing variability in circumplex models of personality. *Journal of Personality Assessment, 47*, 390–395.

Mahalik, J. R., Hill, C. E., Thompson, B. J., & O'Grady, K. E. (1989). *Predicting rater bias: Variables affecting ratings on Kiesler's interpersonal circle.* Unpublished manuscript, University of Maryland, College Park, MD.

McCarthy, P. R. (1985). Impact message inventory. In D. J Keyser & R. C. Sweetland (Eds.), *Test critiques* (Vol. 3). Kansas City, MO: Test Corporation of America.

McCormick, C. C., & Kavanagh, J. A. (1981). Scaling interpersonal checklist items to a circular model. *Applied Psychological Measurement, 5*, 421–447.

McGovern, S. R. (1985). *Degree of congruence between verbal and nonverbal behavior, expressed personality correlates, and interpersonal functioning.* Unpublished master's thesis, Emory University, Atlanta, GA.

McLemore, C. W., & Benjamin, L. S. (1979). Whatever happened to interpersonal diagnosis? A psychosocial alternative to DSM-III. *American Psychologist, 34*, 17–34.

McLemore, C. W., & Brokaw, D. W. (1987). Personality disorders as dysfunctional interpersonal behavior. *Journal of Personality Disorders, 1*, 270–285.

McLemore, C. W., & Hart, P. P. (1982). Relational psychotherapy: The clinical facilitation of intimacy. In J. C. Anchin & D. J. Kiesler (Eds.), *Handbook of interpersonal psychotherapy* (pp. 227–247). Elmsford, NY: Pergamon Press.

McLeod, M., & Nowicki, S., Jr. (1985). Interpersonal style and cooperative behavior in preschool age children. *Journal of Personality, 117*, 85–96.

McNair, D. M., & Lorr, M. (1965). Differential typing of psychiatric outpatients. *The Psychological Record, 15*, 33–41.

Miller, G. A., Galanter, E., & Pribram, K. H.

(1960). *Plans and the structure of behavior*. New York: Holt, Rinehart & Winston.

Morey, L. C. (1985). An empirical comparison of interpersonal and DSM-III approaches to classification of personality disorders. *Psychiatry, 48*, 358–364.

Mungas, D. M., Trontel, E. H., & Winegardner, J. (1981). Multivariable-multimethod analysis of the dimensions of interpersonal behavior. *Journal of Research in Personality, 15*, 107–121.

Murray, H. A. (1951). Toward a classification of interaction. In T. Parsons & E. A. Shils (Eds.), *Toward a general theory of action*. New York: Harper Torchbooks.

Nowicki, S., Jr., & Manheim, S. (in press). Interpersonal complementarity and time of interaction in female relationships. *Journal of Research in Personality*.

O'Dell, J. W. (1966). *Group size and emotional interaction*. Unpublished doctoral dissertation, University of Michigan, Ann Arbor, MI.

O'Dell, J. W. (1968). Group size and emotional interaction. *Journal of Personality and Social Psychology, 8*, 75–78.

Oden, T. C. (1976). *TAG: Transactional awareness game*. New York: Harper & Row.

Orford, J. (1985). *The rules of interpersonal complementarity: Does hostility beget hostility and dominance submission?* Unpublished manuscript, University of Exeter, Exeter, England.

Orford, J. (1986). The rules of interpersonal complementarity: Does hostility beget hostility and dominance, submission? *Psychological Review, 93*, 365–377.

Oxenford, C., & Nowicki, S., Jr. (in press). The relation of hostile nonverbal communication styles and popularity in pre-adolescent children. *Journal of Genetic Psychology*.

Paddock, J. R., & Nowicki, S. (1986). The circumplexity of Leary's interpersonal circle: A multidimensional scaling perspective. *Journal of Personality Assessment, 50*, 279–289.

Paddock, J. R., & Nowicki, S. (1987). An examination of the Leary circumplex through the interpersonal check list. *Journal of Research in Personality, 20*, 107–144.

Paddock, J. R., Potts, M. A., Kiesler, D. J., & Nowicki, S. P., Jr. (1986). *Ipsative scoring of interpersonal circle measures*. Paper read at the annual Southeastern Psychological Association meeting, Kissimmee, FL.

Perlmutter, K. B., Paddock, J. R., & Duke, M. P.

(1985). The role of verbal, vocal, and nonverbal cues in the communication of evoking message styles. *Journal of Research in Personality, 19*, 31–43.

Peterson, D. R. (1977). A functional approach to the study of person-person interactions. In D. Magnusson & N. S. Endler (Eds.), *Personality at the crossroads: Current issues in interactional psychology* (pp. 305–313). Hillsdale, NJ: Lawrence Erlbaum Associates.

Peterson, D. R. (1979a). Assessing interpersonal relationships by means of interaction records. *Behavioral Assessment, 1*, 221–236.

Peterson, D. R. (1979b). Assessing interpersonal relationships in natural settings. *New Directions for Methodology of Behavioral Science, 2*, 33–54.

Peterson, D. R. (1979c). *Instructions for collecting and interpreting interaction records*. New Brunswick, NJ: Rutgers State University.

Peterson, D. R. (1982). Functional analysis of interpersonal behavior. In J. C. Anchin & D. J. Kiesler (Eds.), *Handbook of interpersonal psychotherapy* (pp. 149–167). Elmsford, NY: Pergamon Press.

Peterson, D. R. (in press). Interpersonal goal conflict. In L. A. Pervin (Ed.), *Goal concepts in personality and social psychology*. Hillsdale, NJ: Lawrence Erlbaum Associates.

Peterson, D. R., & Rapinchuk, J. G. (in press). Patterns of affect in destructive and constructive marital conflicts. *Journal of Personality and Social Psychology*.

Phillips, N. (1983). *Selection of items with circumplex properties*. Unpublished manuscript, University of British Columbia, Vancouver.

Plutchik, R. (1980). *Emotion: A psychoevolutionary synthesis*. New York: Harper & Row.

Plutchik, R., & Conte, H. R. (1986). Quantitative assessment of personality disorders. In J. O. Cavenar, Jr. (Ed.), *Psychiatry* (Vol. 1, pp. 1–13). Philadelphia: J. B. Lippincott.

Plutchik, R., & Platman, S. R. (1977). Personality connotations of psychiatric diagnosis: Implications for a similarity model. *Journal of Nervous and Mental Disease, 165*, 418–422.

Rausch, H. L. (1965). Interaction sequences. *Journal of Personality and Social Psychology, 2*, 487–499.

Rosch, E. (1975). Cognitive reference points. *Cognitive Psychology, 7*, 532–547.

Rosch, E. (1978). Principles of categorization. In E. Rosch & B. B. Lloyd (Eds.), *Cognition and* categorization. Hillsdale, NJ: Lawrence Erlbaum Associates.

Russell, J. A. (1980). A circumplex model of affect. *Journal of Personality and Social Psychology, 39,* 1161–1168.

Safran, J. D. (1984a). Assessing the cognitive interpersonal cycle. *Cognitive Therapy and Research, 8,* 333–348.

Safran, J. D. (1984b). Some implications of Sullivan's interpersonal theory for cognitive therapy. In M. A. Reda & M. J. Mahoney (Eds.), *Cognitive psychotherapies: Recent developments in theory, research and practice.* Cambridge, MA: Ballinger.

Safran, J. D., & Segal, Z. V. (1990). *Cognitive therapy: An interpersonal process perspective.* New York: Basic Books.

Safran, J. D., Vallis, T. M., Segal, Z. V., & Shaw, B. F. (1986). Assessing core cognitive processes in cognitive therapy. *Cognitive Therapy and Research, 10,* 509–526.

Schaefer, E. S., & Plutchik, R. (1966). Interrelationships of emotions, traits, and diagnostic constructs. *Psychological Reports, 18,* 399–410.

Schmidt, J. A. (1988). *Interpersonal ratings of channel incongruence of normal versus personality disordered individuals.* Master's thesis in progress, Virginia Commonwealth University, Richmond, VA.

Secord, P. F., & Backman, C. W. (1961). Personality theory and the problem of stability and change in individual behavior: An interpersonal approach. *Psychological Review, 68,* 21–32.

Secord, P. F., & Backman, C. W. (1965). An interpersonal approach to personality. In B. A. Maher (Ed.), *Progress in experimental personality research* (Vol. 2, pp. 91–125). New York: Academic Press.

Shannon, J., & Guerney, B., Jr. (1973). Interpersonal effects of interpersonal behavior. *Journal of Personality and Social Psychology, 26,* 142–150.

Shrauger, J. S., & Schoeneman, T. J. (1979). Symbolic interactionist view of self-concept: Through the looking glass darkly. *Psychological Bulletin, 86,* 549–573.

Stern, G. G. (1970). *People in context: Measuring person-environment congruence in education and industry.* New York: John Wiley & Sons.

Strong, S. R. (1985). Review of the impact message inventory. In J. V. Mitchell (Ed.), *The ninth mental measurements yearbook.* Lincoln, NE: University of Nebraska Press.

Strong, S. R. (1987a). Interpersonal change processes in therapeutic interactions. In J. Maddux, C. Stoltenberg, & R. Rosenwein (Eds.), *Social processes in clinical and counseling psychology* (pp. 68–82). New York: Springer-Verlag.

Strong, S. R. (1987b). Interpersonal influence theory and therapeutic interactions. In F. J. Dorn (Ed.), *Social influence processes in counseling and psychotherapy* (pp. 17–30). Springfield, IL: Charles C Thomas.

Strong, S. R. (1987c). Interpersonal influence theory as a common language for psychotherapy. *Journal of Integrative and Eclectic Psychotherapy, 6,* 173–184.

Strong, S. R. (in press). Interpersonal influence theory: The situational and individual determinants of interpersonal behavior. In R. V. Dawis & D. Lubinski (Eds.), *Assessing individual differences in human behavior: New concepts, methods, and findings.* Minneapolis, MN: University of Minnesota Press.

Strong, S. R., & Claiborn, C. D. (1982). *Change through interaction: Social psychological processes of counseling and psychotherapy.* New York: John Wiley & Sons.

Strong, S. R., Hills, H. I., Kilmartin, C. T., DeVries, H., Lanier, K., Nelson, B. N., Strickland, D., & Meyer, C. W. III. (1988). The dynamic relations among interpersonal behaviors: A test of complementarity and anticomplementarity. *Journal of Personality and Social Psychology, 54,* 798–810.

Strong, S. R., Hills, H. I., & Nelson, B. N. (1988). *Interpersonal communication rating scale (revised).* Richmond, VA: Virginia Commonwealth University.

Sullivan, H. S. (1953). *The interpersonal theory of psychiatry.* New York: W. W. Norton.

Swann, W. B., Jr., & Read, S. J. (1981). Self-verification process: How we sustain our self-conceptions. *Journal of Experimental Social Psychology, 17,* 351–372.

Taulbee, E. S., & Clark, T. L. (1982). *A comprehensive annotated bibliography of selected psychological tests: Interpersonal check list, MMPI short forms, the Blacky pictures.* Troy, NY: Whitson.

Thibaut, J. W., & Kelley, H. H. (1959). *The social*

psychology of groups. New York: John Wiley & Sons.

Thompson, B. J., Hill, C. E., & Mahalik, J. R. (1989). *A test of interpersonal theory of psychotherapy: Multiple case comparisons.* Unpublished manuscript, University of Maryland, College Park, MD.

Thorne, A. (1986). *Toward an interpersonology.* Paper presented at the annual convention of the American Psychological Association, Washington, DC.

Van Denburg, T. F. (1988). *Transactional escalation in rigidity and intensity of interpersonal behavior under stress.* Unpublished doctoral dissertation, Virginia Commonwealth University, Richmond, VA.

Wachtel, P. L. (1982). Interpersonal therapy and active intervention. In J. C. Anchin & D. J. Kiesler (Eds.), *Handbook of interpersonal psychotherapy* (pp. 46–63). Elmsford, NY: Pergamon Press.

Warner, R. M., Kenny, K. A., & Stoto, M. (1979). A new round robin analysis of variance for social interaction. *Journal of Personality and Social Psychology, 37*, 1742–1757.

Weick, K. E. (1984). Systematic observation methods. In *Handbook of social psychology* (3rd ed.). Reading, MA: Addison-Wesley.

Weinstock-Savoy, D. E. (1986). *The relationship of therapist and patient interpersonal styles to outcome in brief dynamic psychotherapy.* Unpublished doctoral dissertation, Boston University, Boston, MA.

Weissman, M. M., Klerman, G. L., Rounsaville, B. J., Chevron, E. S., & Neu, C. (1982). Short-term interpersonal psychotherapy (IPT) for depression: Description and efficacy. In J. C. Anchin & D. J. Kiesler (Eds.), *Handbook of interpersonal psychotherapy* (pp. 296–310). Elmsford, NY: Pergamon Press.

Widiger, T. A., & Frances, A. (1985). The DSM-III personality disorders: Perspectives from psychology. *Archives of General Psychiatry, 42*, 615–623.

Widiger, T. A., & Frances, A. J. (1988). Personality disorders. In J. Talbott, R. Hales, & S. Yudofsky (Eds.), *The American Psychiatric Press Textbook of Psychiatry* (pp. 621–648). Washington, DC: American Psychiatric Press.

Widiger, T. A., Frances, A., Spitzer, R. L., & Williams, J. B. W. (1988). The DSM-III-R personality disorders: An overview. *American Journal of Psychiatry, 145*, 786–795.

Widiger, T. A., Frances, A., & Trull, T. J. (1987). A psychometric analysis of the social-interpersonal and cognitive-perceptual items for the schizotypal personality disorder. *Archives of General Psychiatry, 44*, 741–745.

Widiger, T. A., & Hyler, S. (1987). Axis I/axis II interactions. In J. O. Cavenar, Jr. (Ed.), *Psychiatry*. Philadelphia: J. B. Lippincott.

Widiger, T. A., & Kelso, K. (1983). Psychodiagnosis of axis II. *Clinical Psychology Review, 3*, 491–510.

Widiger, T. A., & Trull, T. J. (1987). Behavioral indicators, hypothetical constructs, and personality disorders. *Journal of Personality Disorders, 1*, 82–87.

Widiger, T. A., Trull, T., Hurt, S., Clarkin, J., & Frances, A. (1987). A multidimensional scaling of the DSM-III personality disorders. *Archives of General Psychiatry, 44*, 557–563.

Wiggins, J. S. (1979a). A psychological taxonomy of trait-descriptive terms: The interpersonal domain. *Journal of Personality and Social Psychology, 37*, 395–412.

Wiggins, J. S. (1979b). *Taxonomy of interpersonal trait-descriptive terms.* Unpublished manuscript, University of British Columbia, Vancouver.

Wiggins, J. S. (1981). *Revised interpersonal adjective scales.* Vancouver: University of British Columbia.

Wiggins, J. S. (1982). Circumplex models of interpersonal behavior in clinical psychology. In P. C. Kendall & J. N. Butcher (Eds.), *Handbook of research methods in clinical psychology* (pp. 183–221). New York: John Wiley & Sons.

Wiggins, J. S. (1984). *Affective reactions questionnaire.* Vancouver: University of British Columbia.

Wiggins, J. S. (1988). *Interpersonal adjective scales, form IASR-B5.* Vancouver: University of British Columbia.

Wiggins, J. S., & Broughton, R. (1985). The interpersonal circle: A structural model for the integration of personality research. In R. Hogan & W. H. Jones (Eds.), *Perspectives in personality* (Vol. 1, pp. 1–47). Greenwich, CT: JAI Press.

Wiggins, J. S., & Holzmuller, A. (1978). Psychological androgyny and interpersonal behavior.

Journal of Consulting and Clinical Psychology, 46, 40–52.

Wiggins, J. S., & Holzmuller, A. (1981). Further evidence on androgyny and interpersonal flexibility. *Journal of Research in Personality, 15*, 67–80.

Wiggins, J. S., Phillips, N., & Trapnell, P. (1989). Circular reasoning about interpersonal behavior: Evidence concerning some untested assumptions underlying diagnostic classification. *Journal of Personality and Social Psychology, 56*, 296–305.

Wiggins, J. S., Steiger, J. H., & Gaelick, L. (1981). Evaluating circumplexity in personality data. *Multivariate Behavioral Research, 16*, 263–289.

Wiggins, J. S., Trapnell, P., & Phillips, N. (1988a). *The measurement of affective reactions to interpersonal stimuli*. Unpublished manuscript, University of British Columbia, Vancouver.

Wiggins, J. S., Trapnell, P., & Phillips, N. (1988b). Psychometric and geometric characteristics of the revised Interpersonal Adjective Scales (IAS-R). *Multivariate Behavioral Research, 23*, 517–530.

Wilkie, C. F. (1987). *Interpersonal complementarity in dyadic interaction*. Unpublished master's thesis, University of Saskatchewan, Saskatoon, Canada.

Wright, T. L., & Ingraham, L. J. (1986). A social relations model test of the interpersonal circle. *Journal of Personality and Social Psychology, 50*, 1285–1290.

Yarnold, P. R., Grimm, L. G., & Lyons, J. S. (1987). The Wiggins interpersonal behavior circle and the type A behavior pattern. *Journal of Research in Personality, 21*, 185–196.

Yarnold, P. R., & Lyons, J. S. (1987). Norms for college undergraduates for the Bem sex-role inventory and the Wiggins interpersonal behavior circle. *Journal of Personality Assessment, 51*, 595–599.

Young, D. M., & Beier, E. G. (1982). Being asocial in social places: Giving the client a new experience. In J. C. Anchin & D. J. Kiesler (Eds.), *Handbook of interpersonal psychotherapy* (pp. 262–273). Elmsford, NY: Pergamon Press.

Youngren, M. A., & Lewinsohn, P. M. (1980). The functional relation between depression and problematic interpersonal behavior. *Journal of Abnormal Psychology, 89*, 333–341.

CHAPTER 23

LABELING: THE NEED FOR GREATER PERSON-ENVIRONMENT INDIVIDUATION

Beatrice A. Wright

The problem of labeling will always be a problem. This assertion embraces two quite different meanings of the word *problem*. In the first instance, the problem refers to perplexing questions proposed for investigation and academic discussion. In the second instance, the reference is to problems that add to disadvantagement caused by negative labeling. This chapter concerns both types of "problems" and concludes with specific recommendations for at least mitigating the serious affronts to human dignity and potential that can be created by a label.

The relevant literature is vast. It ranges over work on impression formation (interpersonal perception), prejudice (attitudes), discrimination (behavior), deviancy (societal edicts), ethnocentrism (ingroup vs. outgroup), semantics and semiotics (meaning of speech and symbols), labels (identity, diagnosis), and stereotypes (beliefs). Even research on categorizing objects (object perception) is relevant. The present chapter does not review this literature as a whole, but does draw on theory and research in making a case for its primary theme — namely, that the current focus in clinical diagnosis on labeling *problem behavior* must be broadened by a lens that also sharply focuses on *positive personal characteristics* as well as on *environmental factors* for diagnostic and treatment purposes. Such a mission might seem disheartening in that it requires greater cognitive complexity, not less. Yet, broadening the diagnostic lens is crucial if two system concepts — whole person and behavior as a function of person in interaction with environment — are to be taken seriously (Lewin, 1935). Anything short of this does a disservice to remediation potential and personal integrity.

LABELING, DISTINCTIVENESS, AND DEINDIVIDUATION

To label is to give a name to things grouped together according to a shared characteristic(s). Because labels stand for something, they are abstractions. They occur naturally and are necessary. They serve to organize and simplify the world, to make it seemingly more understandable. For labeling purposes, differences among members of the labeled group are secondary, if not unimportant, so long as they do not violate the rules of inclusion. Thus, the label "American" or the label "fruit" encompasses an enormous diversity within each of these categories.

Grouping and labeling also require differentiating an outgroup. "American" and "fruit" are communicable labels because there are other people and edibles that are excluded from these classifications. It can be expected, therefore, that labeling groups leads to a muting of perceived within-group differences and a highlighting of perceived between-group differences. Such muting and highlighting of differences have received considerable support in a variety of laboratory studies. Two experiments are described here: one involves objects and the other, people. They were selected to underscore the fact that the process of grouping (labeling, categorizing) involves basic dynamic properties regardless of whether the grouping is of people or objects.

In the first experiment (Tajfel & Wilkes, 1963), research participants were shown a series of eight lines whose lengths differed from each other by a constant ratio. In one condition, the letter A appeared above each of the four shorter lines and the letter B above each of the four longer lines. In other conditions, the four A's and the four B's were either attached to the lines indiscriminately or did not appear. The participants estimated the length of the lines in random order. The results indicated that lines belonging to the two systematically labeled classes A and B were judged as farther apart in length than in the unclassified or haphazardly classified conditions. Moreover, the repeated experience of estimating the lines in successive trials led to an increase in the judged similarity of stimuli belonging to the same systematically labeled class, as compared with the other two conditions. In short, the participants tended to overestimate differences in adjacent lines across categories A and B, but to underestimate differences in length within the categories.

The second experiment concerns social perception (Doise, Deschamps, & Meyer, 1978). The research participants were asked to describe photographs of children using a list of trait adjectives. There were two conditions. In one condition, the participants were presented with six photographs at one time, grouped according to sex (three boys, three girls), and described each photograph. In the second condition, the research participants were initially presented with only three same-sex

photographs (boys or girls) to describe. Following that, they were shown the three photographs of the other sex to describe. Thus, these participants did not know in advance that they would rate photographs of both sexes, whereas the participants in the first condition realized this from the beginning. The results indicated that those participants who had the two sexes in mind at the outset tended to perceive smaller intrasex differences and larger intersex differences than participants who did not anticipate rating photographs of the other sex.

The two experiments demonstrate that the perception of within-group differences tend to be diminished, whereas between-group differences tend to be exaggerated. Another way to put this is that group members tend to be perceived as more similar to each other and more dissimilar to out-group members than when they remain as unclassified objects or individuals.

A different type of evidence for within-group deindividuation (attenuation of differences) emerges when "the stream of behavior" of group members is divided into meaningful units. Wilder (1984) took advantage of the idea that behavior, rather than being perceived as a continuous stream, is "chunked" in order to impart meaning (Barker & Wright, 1955; Barker, 1963). He reasoned that behavior would be divided into larger chunks when the person is viewed as a member of a group rather than as an individual. In the experiment, research participants were asked to divide the videotaped behaviors of one of four people into meaningful action units. In the group condition, the four people were identified as a group, whereas in the nongroup condition they were described as having come together by chance. The results showed that subjects chunked the behavior of group members into fewer meaningful units than when the people were seen as aggregates of individuals. The inference is that the behavior of an individual who is perceived as a member of a group is less informative.

Deindividuation has other consequences. Experiments have shown that the beliefs as well as the behavior of people perceived as members of a group tend to be seen as more similar than in the case of people viewed as individuals (Wilder, 1978). Also, more information that is consistent than inconsistent with the group label will tend to be remembered. In one study, for example, more "librarianlike" behavior was recalled about the person when she was presented as a librarian than as a waitress (Cohen, 1981). For further research on the implications of the categorization process, the reviews by Tajfel (1978) and by Wilder (1986) are recommended.

What needs to be emphasized is that human perception is coerced by the mere act of grouping things together. Within-group attentuation and between-group accentuation of differences is a product of categorization and may well be a general law that operates in the case of classification of both objects and people. Moreover, inasmuch as labeling serves to identify group membership, the mere act of labeling leads to both deindividuation of group members and accentuation of differences with outgroups. Such coercion poses an enormous challenge to psychology, whether with respect to clinical practice or research. Fundamental questions surface: Does deindividuation have negative consequences? When, what are they, and for whom? What are the costs of emphasizing distinctiveness between groups? If differences are accentuated, what happens to the similarities between groups? And where is the environment in all this? The challenge to psychology will be explored further and partial solutions formulated in the remainder of this chapter.

LABELING AND THE FUNDAMENTAL NEGATIVE BIAS

The discussion thus far has dealt with the effects of perceiving something as a member of a group (category, class of things) regardless of whether the affixed label is neutral or evokes a value-laden train of thought. But labels that identify group memberships of people (or of objects for that matter) are usually not neutral, but instead signal positive or negative evaluations. These value differentials, as compared with "neutral" categories, have been shown to enhance still further perceived similarities within categories and perceived differences between categories (Tajfel, 1978, p. 62), thereby compounding the problem of within-group deindividuation.

Basic Proposition

The basic proposition of the fundamental negative bias involves the concepts of saliency, value, and context (Wright, 1988). (a) If something stands out sufficiently (saliency), and (b) if, *for whatever reason*, it is regarded as negative (value), and (c) if its context is vague or sparse (context),

then the negative value of the object of observation will be a major factor in guiding perception, thinking, and feeling to fit its negative character.

This proposition has a parallel in the positive side of bias; namely, where something is perceived as salient, positive, and in a sparse context, then positivity will be a major factor in guiding subsequent cognitive-affective events. Because the fundamental negative bias contributes so insidiously to prejudice and disadvantagement, the focus is on this bias in the following discussion.

That the affective value of something, in the absence of counteracting contextual factors, can become a potent force in influencing what a person thinks about and feels can be understood in terms of the concept of similarity as a unit-forming factor (Heider, 1958; Wertheimer, 1923). Similarity between entities, be they external objects or intrapsychic events, is a powerful factor in perceiving them as a unit; that is, as belonging together. An especially salient type of similarity among entities is their affective quality. Things that are positive are alike in engendering a force toward them; negative things, a force away from them. Combining positive and negative qualities subjects the person to forces opposite in direction.

Experiments on Context

External Context

Context refers to the set of conditions within which something is perceived and that influences that thing's meaning. The context can refer to conditions external to the perceiver or to intrapsychic predispositions of various sorts. A few experiments bearing on the significance of external context with regard to the fundamental bias are presented below.

In an important yet simple experiment, reactions to the label "blindness" as compared with "blind people," and "physical handicap" as compared with "physically handicapped people" were examined (Whiteman & Lukoff, 1965). That the condition itself was evaluated far more negatively than were people with the condition is not surprising. Still, the question remains as to how to account for the difference. The explanation can be found in the fundamental negative bias. Blindness, the salient condition, generally is valued negatively. When no context existed to alter its meaning, its negativity guided the reaction accordingly. When, however, the positive concept "person" was added, a context was provided that moderated the dominant position of the negative condition. It was the context that in effect changed the concept to be rated. And that is just the point. Contexts bring about diverse structures of meaning. The classical work of Asch (1952), which clearly demonstrated the importance of context in perception of people, should be especially noted.

The context can be positive or negative. In the above example, the concept of "person" provided a positive context and therefore constrained the negative spread. Research also has shown that, as the positive character of the context becomes even more salient, attitudes become more favorable. This was demonstrated, for example, in an experiment in which attitudes toward a person who was labeled with a particular problem (e.g., former mental patient, amputee) became more positive when that person was described as functioning adequately than when the negative label stood alone (Jaffe, 1966).

If a positive context can constrain negative evaluation, we might surmise that a negative context could increase the negativity of the object of observation, thereby adding to the grip of the fundamental negative bias in controlling attitudes. Thus, in one experiment attitudes toward a person described as physically disabled and as having undesirable personality traits tended to be more negative than toward a comparably described, able-bodied person (Leek, 1966). Such intensified reactions also have been demonstrated with respect to race (Dienstbier, 1970) and people with mental disorders (Gergen & Jones, 1963).

Besides affecting the *processing* of information presented about a person, the fundamental negative bias also influences information *sought* about a person. This was demonstrated in a study specifically designed to explore implications of the fundamental negative bias (Pierce, 1987). The research participants, simulating the role of a counselor, were asked what they would like to know about a client. The client was either identified as just having been released from a psychiatric ward (salient negative) or as just having graduated from college (salient positive). In both cases, she was further described as seeking help because she was "feeling somewhat anxious and uncertain about her future, including a job and other issues in her life." The subjects selected 24 items of information they would like to know about Joan, the client, from a list of 68 items, half of which referred to something positive (e.g., "Is Joan intelligent?") and half to something negative (e.g., "Is Joan cruel?"). Significantly more negative items were selected in the case of the former psychiatric patient than the college graduate, apparently reflecting the belief that the negative information would be more relevant. Although there may be some bias in fact for this belief, the differential preference for negatives in the two cases poses a particular challenge for those who believe in the importance of calling special attention to positive personal traits. Bear in mind that the only revealed difference between the clients was identification as former psychiatric patient versus college graduate. Parenthetically, the subjects also rated Joan, as they believed the helping agency would, less positively in the former case.

The meaning of *external context* should be clarified. External context is not limited to a network of externally presented personal attributes but includes the external situation as well. The fact that the meaning of observations can be altered by the situation in which person perception takes place is well known. In the above study (Pierce, 1987), two simulated situations were compared. One was that of a counseling center that "seeks out the strengths and assets of people"; the other was a psychological clinic that "deals with the emotional and behavioral problems of people." When the client was identified as attending a psychological clinic, whether as a former mental patient or as a college student, the research participants checked significantly more negative-information items that would be sought by the agency and the client was evaluated less positively than when she was identified as attending a counseling center. In this experiment, the orienting function of the helping agency (the external situational context) played an important role in determining the affective course that cognition would take.

Research on the effect of being helped on the recipient's liking for the help-giver provides a different type of example of the context effect of situations on affect. It has been shown that whereas a decrease in liking for the helper occurs under specified conditions when the recipient and donor of the help are working independently, there is an increase under the same set of conditions when the two are interdependent (e.g., members of the same team; Cook & Pelfrey, 1985). Of interest is the fact that the increase in liking holds even though the helper is the object of the recipient's racial prejudice.

Intrapsychic Context

In addition to conditions externally imposed, factors internal to the person also can provide the main context for influencing perception. A variety of personal dispositions, such as personality traits and values, are potentially important in this regard. With respect to the fundamental negative bias, it is known that people who are more ethnocentric are more likely to view minority group members negatively than people who are less ethnocentric (English, 1971a, 1971b). This personality trait could provide the kind of internal context that maximizes the saliency of any negative attribute presented by the external stimulus conditions of an outgroup; it could even have the power to lead the perceiver to ignore positive attributes. The same line of reasoning holds for values. It seems plausible that a strong value placed on human dignity, for example, would have the potential to exert a significant influence in organizing perception in a way that forestalls the fundamental negative bias.

Motivation should be mentioned as still another potentially important internal factor that can affect the potency of the fundamental negative bias. For example, the evaluator might benefit in some way by devaluating another, as when there is a need to feel superior. Such a motive could easily reinforce the fundamental negative bias, even to the extent ot discrediting what would ordinarily be regarded as positive aspects of the other person. The converse is also true. Thus, humanistic and religious concerns could be a motivating force that creates a positive context of beliefs and principles in which to view people. There are a few examples of personal dispositions that conceivably support or compete with the power of the fundamental negative bias. The reader will be able to think of others.

Insider Versus Outsider Perspectives

The contrasting viewpoints of the *insider* and *outsider* corral a different set of context conditions in terms of which judgments are made (Dembo, 1964, 1970). The insider (also referred to as "actor") is the person experiencing his or her own behavior, feelings, or problems. The outsider is the person observing or evaluating someone else. Both clinicians and researchers are outsiders with respect to the views of the clients and subjects they are studying. Several types of investigations involving insider-outsider perspectives are described later.

Research on the *mine-thine problem* is especially revealing because the research participant is placed in the position of both insider and outside-observer as he or she engages the assigned task (Wright, 1983). A simple way to conduct the experiment is to ask participants to list the initials of five people they know well in one column and beside each initial to indicate that person's worst handicap (limitation, shortcoming, disability, or problem). Then, next to each of the five handicaps they are asked to write what they regard as their own worst handicap. They are then asked to circle the one from each pair they would choose for themselves if they had a choice. Next, they write two numbers on a slip of paper to indicate the number of times their own and the others' worst handicaps were chosen, the sum of the two normally being five. These slips are then collected so that the number frequencies can be displayed and discussed.

The results are dramatic and consistent. The number of times one's own handicap or problem is reclaimed clearly exceeds the frequency of choosing the others'. Among the five choices, it is common for subjects to select their own handicap five, four, or three times — rarely less frequently.

The difference between what is taken into account by the insider and outsider becomes appreciated in a personally direct way in the group's attempt to explain the results. Explanations include the following: they are used to their own handicap (familiarity); they have learned how to deal with it (coping); it is a part of the self and one's history (self-identity). Keep in mind that the subject is an insider when considering his or her own handicap, and an outsider when regarding the other person's. Consequently, the other person's handicap more or less stands alone as a labeled negative condition and is therefore perceptually more insulated from context factors that could check the spread of its negative affect.

Other investigations have shown that patients (the insiders) tend to have a more positive outlook than do others viewing their situation (Hamera & Shontz, 1978; Mason & Muhlencamp, 1976). Still other research has shown that mental hospital patients, mothers on welfare, and clients at a rehabilitation center (i.e., the insiders) tend to rate themselves as above average in how fortunate they are, whereas people viewing their situation from the outside judge them to be below average

(Wright & Howe, 1969). This phenomenon, known as the "fortune phenomenon," was first noted by Dembo, Leviton, and Wright (1956/1975).

To my knowledge, all research bearing on the perspectives of insiders and outsiders shows not only that the meaning of the experience or label differs, but also that insiders are generally more inclined than outsiders to take into account positives in their troubling situations. It seems clear that the context in which the judgments are made differs greatly in the two cases. Insiders place the significance of the problem in a life context so that the span of realities connected with it is wide. Only some aspects are negative; others are clearly positive (e.g., coping, identity), and it is this broad context that restrains the spread of negative effects. On the other hand, to outsiders the other person's problem more or less tends to stand alone, especially when it is represented by a label. In this case, the context is sparse or simplified and the negativity of the problem dominates the train of thought.

Relative Potency of Positives Versus Negatives

The problem of context raises the question of the relative potency of positive and negative attributes. There is strong and accumulating evidence that under many conditions people tend to weigh negative aspects more heavily than positive aspects (Kanouse & Hanson, 1971). The following experiment is illustrative (Feldman, 1966). Research participants rated each of 25 statements containing a different adjective to describe the person, given the context "He is a [e.g., wise] man." A nine-point rating scale was used ranging from good to bad. The participants also rated the statement when it included both a positive and a negative adjective (e.g., wise and corrupt). The potency of each adjective was determined by comparing the ratings of the statement when the adjective was used alone and when it appeared as a pair. The results were clear. The most powerful trait-adjectives were negative. That is, overall ratings of people described by both a positive and negative label were more negative than would be predicted by simply averaging the scale values assigned to each used singly.

The study previously described on the fundamental negative bias (Pierce, 1987) also offers evidence concerning the potency-value of negatives.

You will recall that in that study, subjects sought information about a client from the perspective of a counseling center that focused on strengths and assets, or a psychological clinic that focused on emotional and behavior problems. At the end of the experiment, the subjects were asked to write an essay expressing their views as to whether the kind of information sought about the client would have been different had the client gone to the alternate agency for help (the psychological clinic in the case of the client at the counseling center, and vice versa). Whereas none of the subjects spontaneously indicated that the problem-oriented psychological clinic would have been less adequate than the counseling center to meet the client's needs, some subjects questioned whether a strength-focused agency could help the client resolve her problems even though she might feel better about herself for a short while.

Several explanations of the greater potency (weight) given to negatives than positives have been proposed. First, negative information may become more salient because it arouses vigilance. Also, negative experiences do not "let go" of the person; the person ruminates about them, thereby increasing their presence and potency. Moreover, the norms of society are positive. Any negative deviation stands out and is given added weight because of its normative violation. Another explanation for the disproportionate weight given to negative attributes is that they are more likely to reduce or cancel the value of positive attributes than vice versa. Finally, it has been suggested (Kogan & Wallach, 1967) that the special saliency of negatives may have a physiological basis insofar as evidence exists for the relative independence of reward and punishment systems in the brain. These separate systems may have evolved in the Darwinian sense, producing approach and avoidance tendencies of unequal strength.

The greater potency of negatives, however, should not be taken to mean that negatives facilitate a broader, more flexible, or more integrated organization of cognitive material. On the contrary, the evidence suggests that positive affect is superior in this regard. For example, a variety of studies have shown that both positive affect and positive material cue a wider range of associations than negative material (Isen, 1987). This point is especially relevant when considering action to change matters for the better, as in the case of treatment settings. A further point needs to be emphasized; namely, that the added potency of negatives places a heavy demand on context factors in holding the fundamental negative bias in check.

LABELING AND NEGLECT OF ENVIRONMENTAL CONSIDERATIONS

Thus far, the discussion has dealt with the general effects of grouping people and objects by some labeling device and the effects when the label connotes something negative. The results indicate that within-group deindividuation and between-group accentuation of differences tend to occur. The results also indicate that when a label is both negative and salient within a sparse context, it tends to invite more negative associations than when the context is expanded to include positive aspects. Furthermore, the negative preoccupation is exacerbated by the added weight ordinarily given to negatives. The point was stressed that the negative preoccupation can be checked by imbedding the label in a cognitive-affective context (external/intrapsychic) that alters the significance of the label. Now let us turn our attention to the obscurity of the environment in the labeling process.

Person and Environment as Figure and Ground

We begin with the observation that frequently people are labeled (grouped) solely by personal attributes: race, gender, age, intellectual level, physical condition, emotional status, and so forth. These attributes describe the person, not the environment. Even in cases where the label alludes to a particular environment, the label is generally interpreted as providing information about the person. Thus, such labels as mental hospital patients, rehabilitation clients, librarians, prisoners, and third-graders essentially define the kind of person one is referring to, not the kind of environment. The label directs attention to patients, not hospitals; prisoners, not prisons; librarians, not libraries. At best, the environment remains as a vague background against which the person is featured.

The prominence of the person as figure and the vagueness of the environment is further supported by the nature of environments and people. People are active, moving in space, commanding attention by their behavior. Environments are less visible when perceiving persons and therefore less apprehendable. The environment provides the medium that allows the person to act, just as sound waves are the medium that allows the person to hear (Heider, 1926). In both cases, the sound heard and the person behaving are more easily apprehended than the mediating conditions. Unless the environment stands out because it is the object of study (in ecology, for example), or because of some commanding event, as when an earthquake strikes (physical environment), or a child is sexually abused (social environment), the environment remains hidden in thinking about and evaluating a person.

An additional factor contributing to the saliency of the person and the eclipse of the environment is that the person and his or her behavior are tied together by proximity; that is, the person is present whenever the behavior occurs. Proximity, like similarity, has long been recognized as a unit-forming factor. Thus, closeness in time and space between person and behavior creates a strong force toward accounting for the person's behavior in terms of properties of the person to the neglect of the environment. Even the expression "the person's behavior" uses the possessive case to tie the behavior to the person and not to the environment. Moreover, as the person moves from place to place, the constancy is the person, not the environment. Small wonder, then, that in thinking about a person, personal attributes override environmental considerations.

Causal Attribution

Major consequences for seeking and understanding the causes of behavior follow from the figure-ground relationship between person and environment. Despite the fact that most people would agree that both physical and social environments affect behavior, the role of the environment is easily neglected just because of its obscurity. The aforementioned study of information sought about a client bears on this point (Pierce, 1987). When the research participants were asked to indicate which of the initial pool of about 100 information items were irrelevant to the problems presented, a much larger percentage of environmental than person-attribute items were so judged (77% vs. 17%), this in spite of the fact that these items were not trivial ones. They touched on crime, pollution, standard of living, and education—environmental areas that clearly could be considered significant.

Additional factors affecting the relative saliency of person and environment in causal attribution are discussed below; namely, insider versus outsider perspectives, covariation, just world phenomenon, focal task, and values and motivation.

Insider Versus Outsider Perspectives

The difference in the two perspectives was introduced in connection with the fundamental negative bias where it was shown that the insider is relatively more inclined than the outsider to take positives in a troubling situation into account. Now let us examine how the two perspectives influence the saliency of person versus environment and therefore causal attribution.

The overall conclusion, based on several lines of investigation, is that the insider is more apt than the outsider to attribute his or her own behavior to properties of the environment, whereas the outside observer relatively more frequently sees the other person's traits as the source of the behavior (Goldberg, 1978). This general result is nicely shown in an experiment in which the research participants were asked to describe five people, including themselves, by selecting from each of 20 pairs of trait opposites (e.g., energetic vs. relaxed) the trait that most nearly applied to the person, or by checking the alternative option, "depends on the situation" (Nisbett, Caputo, Legant, & Maracek, 1973). The participants more frequently checked "depends on the situation" when describing themselves (the insider) than when they were in the position of observers describing someone else (e.g., best friend, peer acquaintance).

A second study demonstrated that the weight given to person and environment depends on the focus of attention of the insider and outsider (Storms, 1973). In this experiment, the focus of the insider's attention was shifted to approximate the visual focus of an observer. There were two parts to this experiment. Part 1 was a live situation in which two participants conversed with each other. This session was videotaped with separate cameras focused on each of the conversants. In part 2, each member of the dyad watched the videotape that had been focused on himself or herself, thereby assuming the visual vantage point of an outsider observer.

In both the live and video situations, the participants indicated the degree to which they felt their own behavior (how friendly, talkative, nervous, and domineering they were) was affected (a) by their own personality, and (b) by the nature of the situation (e.g., other person's behavior). In the live situation, the subjects as insiders attributed their behavior significantly more frequently to the environment than in the videotape situation where their visual attention approximated that of an observer. It also should be pointed out that in this experiment, as well as the preceding one in which five persons were rated, the research participants attributed their own behavior to personal traits more frequently than to the situation whether or not they were in the position of insiders or outside observers. This is because behavior still remains "attached to the person" even when the person is the insider, although in this position the person is more sensitive to the environment than when in the position of an outsider.

In a third study, the insider and outsider roles were simulated (Snyder, Shenkel, & Schmidt, 1976). Research participants assumed the role of counselor (outsider) or client (insider) as they listened to a taped therapy interview ostensibly of a client who was either seen for the first time or who was chronic (in counseling five different times). In the interview, the client asserted that her situation caused her problems. Once again, the problems of the client were seen as significantly more personality based when the ratings were made from the point of view of the counselor than of the client, a difference that held in the case of both the first-time and chronic client.

Covariation

The perception of "what varies with what" is a powerful factor in the determination of causes (Kelley, 1973). That is, where behavior is perceived to vary with the person, explanation is sought in terms of personal attributes. Where behavior is seen to vary with the situation, characteristics of the situation are held accountable. It is now proposed that because of the saliency of the person in understanding a person's behavior, the attributes of the person initially become the arena for the explanatory search (Wright, 1983). Only when this probe proves unrewarding is the search expanded to include the environment.

As an illustration, consider the difference in attribution outcome when the behavior under scrutiny is atypical or typical. In his classical work, Heider (1958) pointed out, "If we know that only one person succeeded or only one person failed out of a large number in a certain endeavor, then we shall ascribe success or failure to this person — to his great ability or to his lack of ability. On the other hand, if we know that practically everyone who tries, succeeds, we shall attribute the success to the task" (p. 89). We then say that the task was easy, or in the case of general failure, that the task was hard.

The inferential process in the two cases can be described as follows. The judgment that a particular behavior is typical or deviant requires comparing the behavior of people at the start, simply because behavior is "tied to" people. At this stage, the environment does not enter. If an adequate explanation of the behavior can be found in person characteristics, person attribution takes place. In the interest of parsimony, the explanatory process then stops because there is no felt need to seek further explanation by examining the environment. It is only when cogent personal characteristics do not readily surface that the need to explain shifts attention to the environment, thus ushering in an additional stage in the inferential process.

It is further proposed that in the case of atypical behavior, personal characteristics more readily emerge than in the case of typical behavior. It is relatively easy to account for a child's inattentiveness, for example, in terms of presumed hyperactivity, mental retardation, or some other characteristic of the child when most children are able to attend to the task. With such closure in the attribution search, there is no need to pursue the matter further by inquiring about possible contributing situational factors, such as class size or home difficulties. There is even no felt need to ask whether the child is inattentive in other situations, such as on the playground. In short, the atypical behavior is seen to covary with the person, not with the situation. Research has shown that a person-based attribution of behavior correlates significantly and positively with the perceived degree of the person's maladjustment (Snyder, 1977).

In the case of typical behavior, however, the course of events often takes a different turn. Consider the case where almost all members of a classroom are inattentive. It is not ordinarily concluded that the class is hyperactive or mentally retarded or delinquent. An observer would tend to reserve such judgment for special classes of labeled children. Instead, the teacher's skill in keeping order might be questioned or the overcrowded classroom noted. These probes enlarge the causal network to include the situation. Thus, when the search for personal traits is not adequate to the task of accounting for common behavior, the perceiver moves to the next possible explanatory source — the situation.

Apparently, once attention is directed to the situation, other situations are drawn into the comparative process. If an observer holds overcrowding accountable for the inattentiveness, it is because the inattentiveness is felt to contrast with behavior in less crowded classes. Similarly, behavior typical at a tennis match is ascribed to the nature of the situation, only because the behavior is understood to change with the situation. The side-to-side head-turning occurs when the ball is volleyed from court to court, not during interludes; or it occurs at tennis matches, not at concerts. However, if a few individuals were observed engaged in "nontennis"-oriented activity, the behavior would likely be attributed to boredom or some other personal attribute.

The covariation process described above is particularly threatening to minority groups, however they are labeled (e.g., mentally ill, disabled, etc.). This is because once they and their behavior are identified as atypical — nonnormative, deviant — the covariation process captures many seemingly plausible personal traits in its causal net, thereby aborting the causal search. The result is that environmental considerations are effectively screened out.

The Just World Phenomenon

A third factor in causal attribution involves consideration of both reality and what ought to be. Theory and research support the idea that human beings are inclined to feel that suffering and punishment, like joys and rewards, should be deserved (Asch, 1952; Heider, 1958). This sentiment is aptly referred to as the "just world phenomenon" (Lerner, 1970). Belief in a just world can be maintained by *blaming the victim*. This has been shown in a series of laboratory experiments summarized by Lerner (1970). Blaming is manifested when the suffering is viewed as a consequence or punishment of some form of sin, wrongdoing or irresponsibility. Because of the need to bring "ought" and "reality" into balance, the poor tend to be blamed for their poverty and the person who is raped is blamed for the rape.

A scale has been developed to measure individual differences concerning belief in a just world (Rubin & Peplau, 1975). Results indicate that believers are more likely to admire fortunate people and derogate victims than nonbelievers, thus maintaining the notion that people in fact get what they deserve.

To be sure, "ought and reality" can be aligned by altering reality to fit what ought to be. Such is the goal of reformers and activists whose efforts are directed at environmental change (legal, political, social, economic). Yet, as we have seen, because it is the suffering of a person (or people) that is being explained, the focus quite naturally becomes the person, not the environment. It takes a broader view to be able to scan other situations and to recognize the possible covariation between suffering and situations.

Although the just world phenomenon applies equally to advantaged and disadvantaged groups, it adds to the problems of those who are already burdened. Whenever the suffering is justified by perceiving the person as its main cause, possible environmental circumstances are overlooked.

Task Focus

The explanatory search in understanding behavior also is guided by the task undertaken by the investigator. Where the task is to form an impression of the person, to understand the person's behavior, to characterize the person in terms of descriptions, labels, or diagnoses, the task itself directs the perceiver's attention to the person.

However, where the task is to describe the environment in which people function, the focus of attention shifts to families, homes and schools, neighborhoods and parks, places of work and worship, and so forth. A vocabulary then emerges to describe and label the characteristics of situations that influence behavior (Stokols & Altman, 1987). Ecological Psychology is one representative of this focus (Barker, 1963; Schoggen, 1989). Its vocabulary includes such phrases as *behavior settings; penetration,* which refers to the power of different functional positions in *the* setting; and *action patterns,* which refers to the human needs to which settings cater. Another representative of systematic environmental attention is behavior modification approaches that focus on the connection between environmental contingencies and the reinforcement and extinction of behavior. Terms used are schedules of reinforcement, discriminative stimuli, chaining, and conditioned reinforcers. More global reference to environments

includes such descriptive terms as urban, rural, ghetto, integrated, autocratic, democratic, permissive, sympathetic, violent, and so forth.

The focus of helping agencies varies. Some concentrate on changing the person's situation, as is the case of social service and employment agencies. Others focus on changing the person: schools and treatment centers are examples. People are referred to one or another agency according to whether the problem is seen to be intrinsic to the person or to the environment.

Thus, the perceived source of difficulties critically affects referral decisions. This was clearly shown in an experiment in which participants, serving as counselors in a simulated referral agency, assigned clients to one or another agency after learning of the problem (Batson, 1975). When the client's situation was held primarily accountable for the problem, referrals were more likely to be directed to social service agencies than to institutions oriented toward changing the person, whereas the reverse was true when the problem was judged to reside in the client.

Where the primary mission of a treatment center is to change the person, assessment procedures will be directed toward describing and labeling person attributes. The danger is that the environment scarcely enters the equation in understanding behavior.

Other Factors in Neglect of Environmental Considerations

Just as intrapsychic factors were mentioned as supporting or diminishing the power of the fundamental negative bias, so do these factors need to be recognized in the mix of factors that influence the figure-ground relationship between person and environment. The ideology of rugged-individualism, for example, focuses on the person as the responsible agent. On the other hand, values and ideology can direct attention to the environment, as in the case of reformers and activists who argue for integration or segregation. Also, ego-defensive forces may create a need to blame the person or the environment. By blaming the poor, for example, one may feel personally competent or unobliged to contribute to remediation. Or, by blaming the environment one may see a way to assuage personal guilt by shifting responsibility from the self to others. Snyder (1990) has drawn attention to the need to preserve a sense of control, this being a principal motivation on the part of both society and the individual in holding people responsible for their actions.

Additionally, the environment may be perceived as fixed, as too difficult to change. Effort may therefore be expended on changing the person. A case in point is the misperception that job tasks and the work environment are immutable. Instead of trying to modify them, the potential worker may be denied employment, directed elsewhere, or trained for a different occupation. The net effect is that the person needs to change, not the environment. The concept of "reasonable accommodations," however, shifts the focus to the environment. Increasingly, modifying the environment, physically or through rule change, is becoming evident. Examples include removing architectural barriers, establishing flex-time and parental leave, rearranging task assignments, and providing supportive employment (e.g., when a coach is at hand).

Sorely needed to resolve the problem of environmental neglect is clarification of basic conceptual and methodological issues. Without that, corrective measures will remain limited, a basic reason being that the forces toward perceiving people and their attributes are overpowering. Fortunately, the Conference on Conceptualization and Measurement of Organism-Environment Interaction (1989) holds promise. The stated goals are (a) to develop a set of conceptual guidelines that would enable us to predict which organismic and environmental factors are most likely to interact to influence development, and (b) to develop a set of methodological criteria that would maximize our chances of identifying existing interactions.

IMPLICATIONS FOR PROFESSIONAL PRACTICE AND RESEARCH

The wide array of factors discussed thus far alert us to psychological decoys that easily lead the professional astray in practice and research. Recommendations based on this understanding are offered as safeguards. First we turn to clinical settings in which to examine the impact of the issues raised, and then to the research enterprise.

Clinical Settings

Clinical settings are established to help solve problems — physical, mental, or emotional. And that is part of the problem. Being problem-

oriented, the clinician easily concentrates on pathology, dysfunction, and troubles, to the neglect of discovering those important assets in the person and resources in the environment that must be drawn upon in the best problem-solving efforts (Wright & Fletcher, 1982).

Consider the following example. A counselor, seeking consultation concerning the rehabilitation of a delinquent youth, presented the case of 14-year-old John. The following 10 symptoms were listed: assault, temper tantrums, stealing (car theft), fire-setting, self-destructive behavior (jumped out of a moving car), threats of harm to others, insatiable demand for attention, vandalism, wide mood swings, and underachievement in school. On the basis of these symptoms, the diagnosis on Axis I of the *Diagnostic and Statistical Manual of Mental Disorders* (DSM-III-R; American Psychiatric Association, 1987) was conduct disorder, undersocialized, aggressive, and with the possibility of a dysthymic disorder; on Axis II, passive aggressive personality. No physical disorders were listed on Axis III. The psychosocial stressors, rated extreme on Axis IV, noted the death of his mother when John was a baby and successive placement with various relatives and homes. On Axis V, John's highest level of adaptive functioning was rated as poor.

Following perusal of this dismal picture, I asked the counselor whether John had anything going for him. The counselor then mentioned that John kept his own room in order, took care of his personal hygiene, liked to do things for others (although on his own terms), liked school, and had an IQ of 140. Notice how quickly the impression of John changes, once positives in the situation are brought out to share the stage with the problems. Before that, the fundamental negative bias reigned supreme. Whereas the fact of John's delinquency had led to the detection of all sorts of negatives about John's conduct and situation, the positives remained unconsidered. Is this case atypical? Only in its extreme neglect of strengths, I venture to say. Even a casual review of psychological reports of cases at mental health facilities will reveal how common it is for troublesome aspects to overshadow those that hold promise.

Notice, also, that the positives in John's case had been neglected with respect to both personal characteristics and significant environments. Environmental stresses are briefly noted on Axis IV, the Axis that requires such specification. But the counselor did not indicate any environmental supports that could be provided by John's relatives, his school, or community. Were such environmental resources nonexistent or did they remain hidden and unexplored?

There are at least two reasons that contribute to the elusiveness of environmental resources in the assessment procedures of person-centered treatment settings. Because it is the person who is to be treated, attention is focused on the person. The consequence is that assessment procedures are inclined toward the person, not the environment. Adequate attention to resources in the environment also is made more difficult by the fundamental negative bias. Just as the negative train of thought gives short shrift to assets of the person, so it also does the resources in the environment. The affective shift required makes it more "natural" to disregard positives in the environment when trying to understand problems.

Hardly anyone would argue that the environment should be ignored, and yet we know how easily the environment fades into oblivion. Some may take the position that no one profession can do the entire job of assessment, pointing out that it is the psychologist's responsibility to examine people, whereas social workers are specifically trained to examine circumstances in the home, school, and other community settings. However, the conclusion that psychologists are therefore absolved from seriously considering environmental factors is not warranted.

The covariation principle discussed earlier provides a readily available self-monitoring check to assist in bringing environmental issues to the foreground. The general question, "Does this behavior or problem occur in all situations?" forces one to review the many types of situations in the person's life.

To ensure that positives are not submerged by negatives, a second recommendation is offered. It is proposed that assets and deficits approximate an equal amount of space in psychological reports and equal time at case conferences. This "equal space and time" guideline serves as a concrete reminder of the importance of seriously attending to both aspects. It follows that psychologists need to work as hard at discovering positives as negatives. In support of this effort, it is essential that psychological tests are selected that are designed to uncover strengths and assets just as tests are selected that are sensitive to deficits and pathology.

The Four-Front Approach

Once the power of the fundamental negative bias and the forces that keep the environment at bay are recognized, it becomes clear that the assessment and diagnostic processes need to be engaged on four fronts. Professionals must give serious attention to (a) deficiencies and undermining characteristics of the person, (b) strengths and assets of the person, (c) lacks and destructive factors in the environment, and (d) resources and opportunities in the environment.

Highlighting positives as well as negatives in both the person and the environment serves vital purposes. It provides a framework to counteract deindividuation. It affects the significance of the negatives and enlarges remediation possibilities. It also encourages the *discovery* of assets and resources that can be developed in serving human potential.

A brief example of the efficacy of using assets to remediate deficits involves the case of a middle-aged man whose visual-spatial skills were impaired by a stroke (Chelune, 1983). The neuropsychologist was able to demonstrate the potential utility of using the client's intact verbal skills as a means of compensating for the considerable difficulty he had performing such construction tasks as copying a cross. When instructed to "talk himself through" such tasks, he was able to do them without difficulty. If only the impaired side of his functioning had been attended to, remediation possibilities would have been limited.

In accord with the approach on four fronts, an attempt was made to correct common oversights that appeared in the behavior checklists on children's intake forms at mental health centers (Fletcher, 1979). These checklists essentially pointed up child problems but rarely, if at all, included items pertaining to child assets or the environment. A checklist was therefore constructed consisting of four separate parts: (a) Child Problems (39 items; e.g., temper outbursts, mean to others); (b) Child Assets (39 items; e.g., affectionate, finishes tasks); (c) Environmental Problems (21 items; e.g., family fights, lack of recreational opportunities); (d) Environmental Resources (21 items; e.g., grandparent(s), school). Notice that the problems and assets on the child side were made equal in number, as were the problems and resources on the environmental side, but that the child items far exceeded the environmental items.

This disparity occurred in spite of a serious attempt to correct it and reflects the greater availability of person categories in our lexicon than environmental categories.

The *Diagnostic and Statistical Manual of Mental Disorders*

Following its third revision (American Psychiatric Association, 1980), the *Diagnostic and Statistical Manual of Mental Disorders* (DSM-III) has been widely accepted in the United States as *the* diagnostic tool of mental health clinicians and researchers. It also has had a major influence internationally. The last revision, DSM-III-R (American Psychiatric Association, 1987), describes over 200 categories of mental disorder in terms of major features, symptoms, and distinguishing criteria. Five Axes are provided for recording basic information. The first three constitute the official diagnostic assessment:

I. Clinical Syndromes
II. Developmental and Personality Disorders
III. Physical Disorders (related to understanding and management)

The last two Axes (also included in DSM-III) represent a major innovation:

IV. Severity of Psychosocial Stressors
V. Global Assessment of Functioning

An enormous amount of research and care has gone into the DSMs. Because DSM is such an important *evolving* document, it is fitting that we examine some of the ideas that have determined its current nature. The discussion and recommendations center around the problems of deindividuation, the fundamental negative bias, and neglect of environmental considerations.

Deindividuation

The evidence is clear. Affixing a label (diagnosis in the present instance) leads to a muting of differences within the labeled group. The working groups involved in DSM-III and its revision (DSM-III-R) were not naive. They remind the user that a "misconception is that all people described as having the same mental disorder are alike in all important ways. Although [they] . . . have at least the defining features of the disorder, they may well differ in other important respects that may affect

clinical management and outcome" (DSM-III-R, 1987, p. xxiii).

But within-group deindividuation is so insidious that all too readily it reaches the ultimate point of dehumanization—the person is then made equivalent to the mental disorder. Once again the DSM working group, alert to this danger, cautions, "A common misconception is that a classification of mental disorders classifies people, when actually what are being classified are disorders that people have. For this reason, the text of DSM-III-R (as did the text of DSM-III) avoids the use of such expressions as 'a schizophrenic' or 'an alcoholic,' and instead uses the more accurate, but admittedly more cumbersome, 'a person with Schizophrenia' or 'a person with Alcohol Dependence'" (DSM-III-R, 1987, p. xxiii). My belief, however, is that the two caveats, wise as they are, cannot stem the tide of deindividuation so long as a few diagnostic labels dominate perception. What is needed is greater individuation in terms of the four-front approach.

The Fundamental Negative Bias

It is my conviction that so long as the main diagnostic categories are disorders, relatively little effort will be expended on personal assets and environmental resources. The DSM working groups made a beginning attempt to offset this danger by including Axis V, which requires a rating of the person's current psychological, social, and occupational functioning as well as the highest functioning level achieved during the past year. The Global Assessment of Functioning Scale is provided to assist this assessment. However, a scant *two pages* is concerned with Axis V in contrast to the *hundreds of pages* devoted to diagnosing mental disorders. Small wonder that the aforementioned report of the delinquent youth was so negatively one-sided, and small wonder that attention to deficits and pathology so commonly overwhelms the reporting of strengths and assets in mental health agencies.

The rejoinder may be that it is the job of mental health agencies to diagnose and deal with problems, and that problems refer to dysfunction, not to well-functioning areas. But the rejoinder to this point of view is that inasmuch as the person functions as a whole system in which healthy and dysfunctional characteristics affect each other, both aspects must be given serious attention in diagnosis and treatment plans. Surely it makes a difference to both diagnosis and treatment if a client is aware of his or her difficulties, is willing to accept help, is responsible, is kind, and gets along with others. Systematic research can help to clarify which personal assets need to be singled out, how they cluster, and how to present them; on profiles, checklists, rating scales, for example.

Neglect of Environmental Considerations

Axis IV was devised in recognition of the fact that the environment is not inconsequential in understanding and diagnosing mental disorder. Still, Axis IV must be considered barely a first step in meeting the challenge. First to be observed is that this Axis refers to psychosocial *stressors, not resources.* The Axis is helpful insofar as its guidelines draw attention to the environment—problems regarding family, occupation, living circumstances, and so forth. Even so, *very little space* is committed to Axis IV. Only three pages are devoted to presenting the Severity of Psychosocial Stressors Scale and its instructions. The fact that attention to the environment has barely begun is also evident in the authors' statement "that it should . . . be noted that DSM-III-R does not attempt to classify disturbed dyadic, family, or other interpersonal relationships" (1987, p. xxv.)

The second point to be noted is that the rating of the severity of the stressor is based on the clinician's judgment of the stress of an average person in similar circumstances, not on the reaction of the client, "even though . . . the client may be especially vulnerable" (1987, p. 19). It is not clear why such deindividuation should prevail, especially in light of the difference in perspectives between the insider who experiences the environment and the outsider who merely observes it.

An additional point to be noted is that there is no Axis that directs attention to environmental supports. In my view, this is a serious omission for the same reason that applies to relegating positive personal attributes to the background.

DSM-III-R states that "each of the mental disorders is conceptualized as a clinically significant behavioral or psychological syndrome or pattern that occurs *in a person* [italics added]. . . . Whatever its original cause, it must currently be considered a manifestation of a . . . dysfunction *in the person* [italics added] (1987, p. xxii). Although the intent of this conceptualization is well taken—namely, to exclude "deviant behavior" and con-

flicts that are primarily between the individual and society from being considered mental disorders—one can see how the concept of "in the person" contributes to a fine-grained picture of the person within a more or less environmental vacuum.

Future Revisions

"DSM-III is only one still frame in the ongoing process of attempting to better understand mental disorders. DSM-III-R represents still another frame" (1987, p. xxvii). So spoke the authors, a beautifully stated affirmation that reflects the integrity of both scientist and clinician in recognizing the limitations of current knowledge.

The themes of this chapter, with its focus on the problems of deindividuation, the fundamental negative bias, and neglect of environmental considerations, strongly suggest that the recommended four-front approach become the model for future DSM revisions. How else can positives as well as negatives in both the person and the environment be made sufficiently salient to allow an integrated assessment of the whole person-in-environment? Is it too impractical to envision four DSM volumes, one volume devoted to each of the fronts? Can anything short of that do justice to the goal of diagnosing and remediating problems with which a person is struggling? Does this mean that there would be separate "diagnoses" pertaining to each of the fronts? That remains for future DSM working groups to decide, but probably a clear characterization of each front would have to be indicated.

The DSM working group was encouraged by the "increased commitment . . . to reliance on data as the basis for understanding mental disorders" (DSM-III-R, 1987, p. xxvii). But the question is, "What kind of data do we need to rely on?" The authors explicitly state that "it should be understood that for most of the categories the diagnostic criteria . . . have not yet been fully validated by data about such important correlates as clinical course, outcome, family history, and treatment response. Undoubtedly, with further study, the criteria will be further refined" (p. xxiv). It is my view that further study will require collecting data on all four fronts recommended here in order for diagnoses to be validated by clinical course and treatment response.

The DSM authors recognize that "additional information about the person being evaluated beyond that required to make a DSM-III-R diagnosis will invariably be necessary" (1987, p. xxvi). What is not recognized is that the additional information must detail personal strengths and environmental difficulties and resources with the same investigatory acumen as is currently devoted to symptoms of pathology. The earlier mentioned (p. 479) Conference on Organism-Environment Interaction (1989) can be expected to contribute guidelines toward conceptual and methodological clarification to assist in gathering relevant information.

Whatever the nature of future DSMs, however, the recommendations proposed here can be instituted in clinical practice. These recommendations refer to the four-front approach, approximating equal time and space to assets as to deficits in psychological reports and at case conferences, and to uncovering the environment by covarying problematic behavior with situations in the person's life.

The main themes argued in the present paper also raise issues bearing on the conduct and interpretation of research. A few examples are discussed below.

Comparing Conditions and Groups in Research

The difference in perspectives of the outsider and insider, and the power of the fundamental negative bias alert us to certain pitfalls that need to be avoided in interpreting research. Consider an experiment that compared reactions of able-bodied persons to confederate interviewers with and without a simulated disability. (Because there is no need to indict a particular researcher, this study is not identified here.) All things were kept equal in the two conditions except for the independent variable. Although the major finding was that the interviewer with the disability was *consistently* rated more favorably on a variety of personality characteristics (e.g., more likable, better attitude), the results were interpreted as supporting research indicating the operation of a sympathy effect to avoid the appearance of rejection or prejudice.

A number of points need to be emphasized. First, the investigator was seduced into attending to the disability variable as the salient factor in the experiment because "all other things were kept equal." Second, these controls kept the investigator, as observer, from attending to the context of the interview as experienced by the research participants. The negative value attributed to the disability, therefore, stood alone in determining the negative flow of thoughts and feelings, leaving the investigator to become trapped by the fundamental negative bias, even to the extent of treating findings favoring the interviewer with the disability as if they were negative.

For the research participants, however, the situation appeared very different. They knew nothing about the behavior of the interviewer being held constant in two experimental conditions in which only the interviewer's physical appearance varied. All they were aware of was an interviewer whose status and behavior were positive. Thus, instead of the context being obliterated, the context was decidedly positive. Under these circumstances, response intensification occurred, a response that fits with other research. The research participants may have appreciated the interviewer's apparent success in meeting the challenges of his or her disability and therefore perceived the interviewer as having special qualities as a cause or consequence of such success. The conclusion is compelling that two vastly different situations were evaluated, one as perceived by the research participants and a very different one by the experimenter.

Researchers must become sensitized to possible differences in perspective between themselves and subjects, especially in terms of the saliency and context of variables under study. They must also become aware of the power of the fundamental negative bias to influence their own thinking when the independent variable carries a negative connotation or label (disability in the above experiment).

The preceding discussion relates to research in which research participants are assigned to different conditions, not to research in which the behavior of distinct groups of people are compared. In the latter case, special precautions need to be taken lest the label identifying the groups control the investigator's thinking. Countless numbers of studies compare males and females, blacks and whites, people with and without disabilities, heterosexuals and homosexuals, and so forth. All too often, between-group differences are attributed solely to the group characteristic made visible by the label (e.g., gender, race). What is frequently ignored or discounted are the generally large overlap in behavior between groups, within-group differences, and differences in the groups' life circumstances. The consequent between-group distinctiveness, within-group deindividuation, and environmental neglect have serious societal implications that need to be thought through by researchers. At the very least, the "something else perhaps" notion, proposed by the philosopher Herbert Feigl (1953), bears reemphasizing to avoid "nothing but" interpretations based on a salient, labeled variable. Feigl also reminded us that the investigator must be pressed to discover "what's what" by systematic research.

The Problem of Statistical Significance

The fact that the null hypothesis cannot be proven statistically (Fisher, 1955) adds to the complexity of the issues raised above. Similarities between groups, typically regarded as null findings, are therefore discounted. The consequence for understanding different groups is serious, and in the case of groups that are already disadvantaged, ignoring similarities adds to the disadvantagement.

A variety of statistical procedures to help eliminate the bias against accepting the null hypothesis (i.e., similarities between groups) have been proposed. Traditionally, researchers use the .01 or .05 alpha level of significance to refer to the small probability that the obtained difference between groups could be due to chance. One proposal is that the high end of the probability range could be used to suggest the likelihood of similarity (rather than exact equivalence) between groups (Wright, 1988, p. 16). While it is true that the null hypothesis cannot logically be proven and can "at most be confirmed or strengthened" (Fisher, 1955), it should be noted that large p values do in fact "confirm or strengthen" the hypothesis that group differences are small or nonexistent. In that case, one could conclude that the obtained difference is unreliable as a difference but reliable as a similarity. The similarity, then, would have to be judged as to whether it is of psychological importance, just as a statistically significant difference has to be so judged.

The point is that investigators, by giving weight to similarities as well as to differences between groups, achieve better understanding of the data and help to stem the automatic slide toward between-group accentuation of differences. A further fact not to be overlooked is that perceived similarities promote positive intergroup relations. Additional arguments, evidence, and procedures

to counteract prejudice against accepting the null hypothesis can be found in Greenwald (1975).

The Problem of Attitude Tests of Stereotypes

When measuring attitudes toward a particular group, the intent is to get at stereotypes, at attitudes that are tied to the label designating the group. If the label connotes something negative to the respondent, as is often the case with regard to mental disorder, disability, poverty, and homosexuality, for example, then the label is likely to give rise to a negative mindset in answering the items, especially because the label, as an abstraction, is separated from particular people and circumstances.

Contributing to this mindset is a preponderance of negatively focused items that frequently, although not always, characterize attitude tests about groups stigmatized in some way. This negative loading may be a manifestation of the fundamental negative bias inasmuch as the test constructor may be led by the group's stigmatized status to formulate items that imply devaluation. It also may be felt to be a way to minimize the influence of "social desirability"; that is, a subject's inclination to respond favorably to items expressing what is proper.

In any case, the negative loading can have several unacceptable consequences. First, we should be concerned lest a preponderance of negatively worded items orients thinking toward the negative side of possibilities, thereby strengthening a negative-response bias. Also, rejecting a negative statement is not the same, affectively and cognitively, as affirming a positive statement. Rejecting the idea, for example, that a particular group is often conniving or lazy does not imply the opposite belief, that the group is often honest or eager to work. Both types of statements are needed to guard against a negative bias as well as to offer respondents the opportunity to express attitudes that reflect genuinely positive, as well as negative, feelings and beliefs.

In addition, an overload of negatively worded items could provide a misleading educational experience, leading the respondent to begin to believe disparaging statements that had not been entertained before. The possibility of this happening is increased by evidence showing that people tend to give more weight to negative aspects of something than to positive aspects. To counteract the excessive weight that might be given to negative items, the most obvious suggestion is to include at least the same number, and preferably a greater number, of positively worded items.

Another concern relates to the nature of stereotyping itself. Although it is understandable that attitude tests avoid differentiations among group members captured by the label, the possible deleterious effects of an ostensible scientific instrument that homogenizes people in this way are of concern. Deindividuation flies in the face of decades of research showing that a label or diagnosis tells us very little about what a person is like inasmuch as individuals are unique in their combination of interests, values, abilities, circumstances, and so forth. Because of the nature of stereotypes, however, the tests themselves have to ignore this uniqueness. To minimize stereotyping effects of such tests, it is recommended that research participants be cautioned against this possibility during debriefing.

Another urgently needed recommendation is that researchers spend at least as much effort searching for and uncovering positive attitudes as they do negative ones. To agree with this recommendation depends on believing that positive attitudes toward disadvantaged groups not only exist, but are as important as negative attitudes. They are important for two reasons. (a) Attitudes are typically ambivalent, and when evaluated within this more complex matrix, the perception of the group is likely to change. A telling example discussed earlier is the attitude change that took place toward the delinquent youth as soon as positive traits were brought to the fore. (b) Positive attitudes are also important because it is these attitudes that have to be drawn on, built on, and spread in the effort to overcome disparaging beliefs and feelings of one group toward another.

Many issues were raised in this chapter. It is hoped that readers will be encouraged to consider the conceptual reasoning, evidence, and recommendations in both their ongoing scholarly work and clinical practice.

REFERENCES

American Psychiatric Association. (1980). *Diagnostic and statistical manual of mental disorders* (3rd ed.). Washington, DC: Author.

American Psychiatric Association. (1987). *Diagnostic and statistical manual of mental disorders* (3rd ed., rev.). Washington, DC: Author.

Asch, S. E. (1952). Forming impressions of personality. *Journal of Abnormal and Social Psychology, 41*, 258–290.

Barker, R. G. (Ed.). (1963). *The stream of behavior*. New York: Appleton-Century-Crofts.

Barker, R. G., & Wright, H. F. (1955). *Midwest and its children*. New York: Harper & Row.

Batson, C. D. (1975). Attribution as a mediator of bias in helping. *Journal of Personality and Social Psychology, 32*, 455–466.

Chelune, G. J. (1983). *Neuropsychological assessment: Beyond deficit testing*. Paper presented at the 91st annual convention of the American Psychological Association, Anaheim, CA.

Cohen, C. E. (1981). Person categories and social perception: Testing some boundaries of the processing effects of prior knowledge. *Journal of Personality and Social Psychology, 40*, 441–452.

Conference on Conceptualization and Measurement of Organism-Environment Interaction, American Psychological Association. (1989). *Science Agenda, 2*(1), 4.

Cook, S. W., & Pelfrey, M. (1985). Reactions to being helped in cooperating interracial groups: A context effect. *Journal of Personality and Social Psychology, 49*, 1231–1245.

Dembo, T. (1964). Sensitivity of one person to another. *Rehabilitation Literature, 25*, 231–235.

Dembo, T. (1970). The utilization of psychological knowledge in rehabilitation. *Welfare Review, 8*, 1–7.

Dembo, T., Leviton, G. L., & Wright, B. A. (1956/1975). Adjustment to misfortune: A problem of social-psychological rehabilitation. *Artificial Limbs, 3*(2), 4–62. (Reprinted in *Rehabilitation Psychology*, 1975, *2*, 1–100.)

Dienstbier, R. A. (1970). Positive and negative prejudice with race and social desirability. *Journal of Personality, 38*, 198–215.

Doise, W., Deschamps, J. C., & Meyer, G. (1978). The accentuation of intracategory similarities. In H. Tajfel (Ed.), *Differentiation between social groups: Studies in the social psychology of intergroup relations* (pp. 159–168). (European Monograph in Social Psychology 14.) London: Academic Press.

English, R. W. (1971a). Correlates of stigma toward physically disabled persons. *Rehabilita-*

tion Research and Practice Review, 2, 1–17.

English, R. W. (1971b). Assessment, modification and stability of attitudes toward blindness. *Psychological Aspects of Disability, 18*(2), 79–85.

Feigl, H. (1953). The scientific outlook: Naturalism and humanism. In H. Feigl & M. Brodbeck (Eds.), *Readings in the philosophy of science* (pp. 8–18). New York:.Appleton-Century-Crofts.

Feldman, S. (1966). Motivational aspects of attitudinal elements and their place in cognitive interaction. In S. Feldman (Ed.), *Cognitive consistency: Motivational antecedents and behavioral consequences* (pp. 75–108). New York: Academic Press.

Fisher, R. (1955). Statistical method and scientific induction. *Journal of the Royal Statistical Society, 17*, 69–78.

Fletcher, B. L. (1979). *Creating a child intake form for use in a mental health center*. Unpublished manuscript. University of Kansas, Lawrence.

Gergen, K. L., & Jones, E. E. (1963). Mental illness, predictability and affective consequences as stimulus factors in person perception. *Journal of Abnormal and Social Psychology, 67*, 95–104.

Goldberg, L. R. (1978). Differential attribution to trait-descriptive terms to oneself as compared to well-liked, neutral, and disliked others: A psychometric analysis. *Journal of Personality and Social Psychology, 36*, 1012–1028.

Greenwald, A. G. (1975). Consequences of prejudice against the null hypothesis. *Psychological Bulletin, 82*, 1–20.

Hamera, E. K., & Shontz, F. C. (1978). Perceived positive and negative effects of life-threatening illness. *Journal of Psychosomatic Research, 22*, 419–424.

Heider, F. (1926). Ding und Medium. *Symposion, 1*, 109–157.

Heider, F. (1958). *The psychology of interpersonal relations*. New York: John Wiley & Sons. (Republished by Lawrence Erlbaum Associates, Hillsdale, NJ.)

Isen, A. M. (1987). Positive affect, cognitive processes, and social behavior. In L. Berkowitz (Ed.), *Advances in experimental social psychology* (Vol. 20, pp. 203–254). Orlando, FL: Academic Press.

Jaffe, J. (1966). Attitudes of adolescents toward the mentally retarded. *American Journal of Mental Deficiency, 70*, 907–912.

Kanouse, D. E., & Hanson, L. R., Jr. (1971). Negativity in evaluations. In E. E. Jones et al. (Eds.), *Attribution: Perceiving the causes of behavior* (pp. 47–62). Morristown, NJ: General Learning Press.

Kelley, H. H. (1973). Process of causal attribution. *American Psychologist, 28*, 107–128.

Kogan, N., & Wallach, M. A. (1967). Risk taking as a function of the situation, the person, and the group. In G. Mandler, P. Mussen, N. Kogan, & M. A. Wallach (Eds.), *New directions in psychology III*, pp. 111–278. New York: Holt, Rinehart, & Winston.

Leek, D. F. (1966). *Formation of impressions of persons with a disability*. Unpublished master's thesis, University of Kansas, Lawrence.

Lerner, M. J. (1970). The desire of justice and reactions to victims. In J. Macaulay & L. Berkowitz (Eds.), *Altruism and helping behavior* (pp. 205–229). New York: Academic Press.

Lewin, K. (1935). *A dynamic theory of personality*. New York: McGraw-Hill.

Mason, Ł., & Muhlenkamp, A. (1976). Patients' self-reported affective states following loss and caregivers' expectations of patients' affective states. *Rehabilitation Psychology, 23*, 72–76.

Nisbett, R. E., Caputo, C., Legant, P., & Maracek, J. (1973). Behavior as seen by the actor and as seen by the observer. *Journal of Personality and Social Psychology, 27*, 154–164.

Pierce, D. L. (1987). *Negative bias and situation: Perception of helping agency on information seeking and evaluation of clients*. Unpublished master's thesis, University of Kansas, Lawrence.

Rubin, Z., & Peplau, L. A. (1975). Who believes in a just world? *Journal of Social Issues, 31*, 65–89.

Schoggen, P. (1989). *Behavior settings: A revision of Barker's ecological psychology*. Stanford, CA: Stanford Press.

Snyder, C. R. (1977). "A patient by any other name" revisited: Maladjustment or attributional locus of problem? *Journal of Consulting and Clinical Psychology, 45*, 101–103.

Snyder, C. R. (1990). Self-handicapping processes and sequelae: On the taking of a psychological dive. In R. L. Higgins, C. R. Snyder, & S. Berglas, *Self-handicapping: The paradox that isn't*. New York: Plenum Press.

Snyder, C. R., Shenkel, R. J., & Schmidt, A. (1976). Effects of role perspective and client psychiatric history on locus of problem. *Journal of Consulting and Clinical Psychology, 44*, 467–472.

Stokols, D., & Altman, I. (Eds.). (1987). *Handbook of environmental psychology* (Vols. 1 & 2). New York: John Wiley & Sons.

Storms, M. D. (1973). Videotape and the attribution process: Reversing actors' and observers' points of view. *Journal of Personality and Social Psychology, 27*, 165–175.

Tajfel, H. (Ed.). (1978). *Differentiation between social groups: Studies in the social psychology of intergroup relations.* (European Monographs in Social Psychology 14.) London: Academic Press.

Tajfel, H., & Wilkes, A. (1963). Classification and quantitative judgment. *British Journal of Psychology, 54*, 101–114.

Wertheimer, M. (1923). Untersuchungen zur Lehre von der gestalt [Examination of the lessons of gestalt]. II. *Psychologishe Forschung, 4*, 301–350.

Whiteman, M., & Lukoff, I. F. (1965). Attitudes toward blindness and other physical handicaps. *Journal of Social Psychology, 66*, 135–145.

Wilder, D. A. (1978). Perceiving persons as a group: Effects on attributions of causality and beliefs. *Social Psychology, 1*, 13–23.

Wilder, D. A. (1984). *Effects of perceiving persons as a group on the information conveyed by their behavior.* Unpublished manuscript, Rutgers University, New Brunswick, NJ. Reported in Wilder (1986).

Wilder, D. A. (1986). Social categorization: Implications for creation and reduction of intergroup bias. In L. Berkowitz (Ed.), *Advances in experimental social psychology* (Vol. 19, pp. 291–355). Orlando, FL: Academic Press.

Wright, B. A. (1983). *Physical disability: A psychosocial approach* (2nd ed.). New York: Harper & Row.

Wright, B. A. (1988). Attitudes and the fundamental negative bias. In H. E. Yuker (Ed.), *Attitudes toward persons with disabilities* (pp. 3–21). New York: Springer.

Wright, B. A., & Fletcher, B. L. (1982). Uncovering hidden resources: A challenge in assessment. *Professional Psychology, 13*, 229–235.

Wright, B. A., & Howe, M. (1969). *The fortune phenomenon as manifested in stigmatized and non-stigmatized groups.* Unpublished manuscript, University of Kansas, Lawrence.

CHAPTER 24

TOWARD A GENERAL MODEL OF PERSONAL CHANGE

Ronnie Janoff-Bulman
Steven S. Schwartzberg

Although we might agree that change is a condition of existence, we nevertheless appear to take for granted constancy and stability in our own natures. It is as if we recognize that the world changes around us, yet we cling to a view of ourselves as relatively unchanging. People generally hold low expectations for personal change in themselves and others and regard such change as difficult to achieve (Silka, 1989). Nevertheless, there are times in some people's lives when they confront dramatic personal change, whether imposed or freely sought. How do people change? What psychological processes underlie personal change? What, if any, are the common elements of deep-seated personal changes that may follow events as disparate as victimization and psychotherapy?

In this chapter we will attempt to address these questions, with the intent of developing a general understanding of personal change. First, we will discuss several parameters that are important for defining and limiting the phenomenon we refer to as personal change. We will then propose a heuristic model of the common process underlying personal change. We believe that common processes are likely to underlie personal change, whether it results from psychotherapy, consciousness-raising, victimization, brainwashing, or seemingly spontaneous religious conversion; the proposed model represents an attempt to delineate the common elements of diverse change phenomena. Finally, this model will be applied specifically to two domains that are often associated with personal change: the aftermath of extreme negative events and psychotherapy.

PARAMETERS OF PERSONAL CHANGE

People can and do change in many ways. We move from infancy to adolescence and adulthood. Along the way we presumably learn about ourselves and our world. A person may go from playing no instrument to becoming a violin virtuoso. An individual may become a great soccer player or mathematician, or may learn to be a wonderful teacher; these clearly involve personal changes. When people say that someone has changed, they are essentially claiming that the person is different from the way he or she was (Silka, 1989). These examples illustrate instances involving perceptions of difference, yet they do not seem to capture the type of personal change we have chosen to address in this chapter.

We are committed to an understanding of personal change in terms of the basic assumptions people hold about themselves and their world; that is, people have changed to the extent that changes occur at the level of people's conceptual systems. All of us hold basic assumptions that enable us to make sense of our world and serve as guides for our behavior. Parkes (1971, 1975) is referring to this set of basic assumptions when he discusses his concept of "assumptive world." Epstein's (1973, 1979, 1980) "theory of reality," Bowlby's (1969) "world models," and Marris' (1975) "structures of meaning" all describe a basic conceptual system, developed over time, that provide us with expectations about ourselves and the world. Similarly, Snyder (1989; Snyder & Higgins, 1988) has developed the construct of a personal theory of self and discusses the process of "reality negotiation," which involves incorporating new information into one's self-theory. These assumptions—about the world and ourselves—provide us with a sense of order and predictability, and generally are unquestioned and unchallenged. Our fundamental assumptions generally serve us well, and we therefore take them for granted. Yet, it is change in our assumptive worlds that constitutes "real" personal change.

Certainly, change occurs in people's behaviors; individuals may alter their behaviors because of situational demands or volitional decision. We would argue, however, that personal change has occurred to the extent that this behavior change is represented in one's conceptual system. Changes in behavior may reflect changes in one's assumptions, and one would expect behavioral changes to follow changes in people's assumptive worlds. However, behavioral changes also may precede changes in people's conceptual systems, a phenomenon often reported by social psychologists (consider, for example, the large literature on cognitive dissonance; e.g., Festinger, 1957; Brehm & Cohen, 1962; Wicklund & Brehm, 1976). In such cases, one's behaviors are used as data to be conceptually understood and incorporated at the level of one's assumptions. It is change in the conceptual system, whether derived from perceptions of one's own behavior, one's experiences, or other incoming information, that best defines personal change.

This assumptive world perspective is a broad explanatory framework that can be used to understand both major and minor instances of change. Thus, changes such as learning a new instrument or becoming an expert at some sport are no doubt represented at the level of one's conceptual system, as are instances of deep-seated personal change. To arrive at a better understanding of the latter, of what might be referred to as personality change, one needs to consider the parameters for defining such change. What are the important dimensions for understanding different types of personal change? Two dimensions seem particularly worth considering. The first involves the depth and breadth of the change in question; the second involves the extent to which a change is gradual and incremental versus more "catastrophic." Differences among types of personal change can largely be understood in terms of placement along these dimensions. The type of change addressed in this chapter falls toward the extreme end of the two continua: change that is deep and broad, as well as accelerated and dramatic.

The depth and breadth of personal change can be understood in terms of where change occurs in one's assumptive world. As Epstein (1980) has argued, our conceptual systems are hierarchically organized, with higher and lower order postulates. The basic assumptions considered above represent our highest order postulates. They are the most abstract, global, generalized assumptions that we hold and are at the foundation of the system. Lower order postulates are narrow, more specific generalizations; "I am a good piano player" or "I am a good basketball player" represent lower order postulates, whereas "I am a good person" represents a higher order postulate. Lower level postulates, or assumptions, are more directly reflections of our experience, involving specific abilities or interactions with the world. They are subjected to the "direct test of experience" (Epstein, 1980).

As one moves up the hierarchy of postulates, change becomes more difficult. Thus, with broader assumptions, such as those reflecting beliefs about interactions of groups of people, political beliefs, or strongly held cultural notions (e.g., the appropriate roles of men and women), change will be far more difficult to effect than at the lower level of postulates. The highest order postulates, our most general beliefs about the world and ourselves, are still more difficult to alter. Change at this level represents the most deep-seated personal change, for the assumptions here are not only our deepest, but our broadest. Change here, at the foundation of the conceptual system, is most apt to affect assumptions at all of the other levels.

Change can occur at any level of our assumptive world. The more global and generalized the belief, the greater the personal change. Although most recent work on schemas has stressed the extent to which people's schemas do not change (for a review, see Fiske & Taylor, 1984), change is no doubt far more common than attested to in this literature. Every time we learn something new, some schema is changing. The acquisition of skills and knowledge is no doubt represented by changes in our conceptual system, although these changes typically occur among our lower order postulates, reflecting beliefs about particular stimuli and evaluations of specific abilities. Further, these changes generally involve adding to prior assumptions rather than invalidating and changing them; in this sense there is no clash with the old, but rather a process of building on the old. This additive process is typical of gradual change, an endpoint of the second dimension that may define personal change.

Just as change at the level of our lower order postulates is quite common and gradual, it typically occurs incrementally. Such changes are rarely noticed as they occur, just as the gradual changes in a child's physical growth are not noticed on a day-to-day basis, but rather must be compared with some relatively distant past marker to be recognized as substantial. Small, gradual changes in our more narrow generalizations are common; they represent ordinary learning and daily interactions. We generally think of learning as "adding to" our knowledge base. These are the types of changes that Kuhn (1962) refers to when he discusses the "additive adjustment of theory." These do not create a condition of crisis or scientific revolution, but rather involve cumulative, incremental changes to the theory. Watzlawick and his colleagues (Watzlawick, Weakland, & Fish, 1974) are referring to this type of change when they write of "first-order change," which involves change in a system without any fundamental changes occurring in the system. This type of change also is described by Rothbart (1981) in his discussion of the "bookkeeping model" of changing stereotypes. In this case, schemas change slowly, bit by bit, in the face of incongruent in-

formation; the change involves minor adjustments, made over time.

Compare this with a second model of change — the conversion model — also proposed by Rothbart (1981). This type of change involves a few extremely critical instances that are very salient; the information provided is highly incongruent, and the change is more or less "catastrophic." These instances involve a type of "gestalt switch" and characterize a more dramatic personal change. Watzlawick (Watzlawick et al., 1974) writes of "second-order change" as a change "whose occurrence changes the system itself" (p. 10). Kuhn's conception of change in the aftermath of scientific revolutions also reflects this more catastrophic change. The scientific theory has been stretched too far; it cannot account for the anomalies that confront the theory, and the theory must therefore be altered, not gradually or in a minor way. Rather, a new theory is required, one that can account for both the old and new data. Similarly, dramatic personal change is neither additive nor gradual, but involves noncumulative changes in people's fundamental assumptions about the world.

Personal change may occur as a consequence of many distinct life experiences, including victimization, psychotherapy, groups devoted to support or consciousness-raising, or even particularly persuasive written material. In most cases, this type of dramatic personal change occurs as a result of nonnormative events that are pursued by or imposed on an individual. More normative life events, such as normative role changes, can at times trigger deep-seated, dramatic changes, although we would argue that for most people these changes are gradual and, more important, additive; they are added to one's preexisting views of oneself and do not challenge these views. Thus, the woman in our society who has been raised to view herself as a caregiver and nurturer is not apt to make fundamental changes in the way she sees herself when she becomes a mother for the first time. The "data" she incorporates will be added to her assumptions about herself.

Those people whose beliefs are fundamentally changed rather than added to as a result of new roles are those whose personal changes are more deep-seated and dramatic. Thus, for some, becoming a parent for the first time may fundamentally change views of oneself; what one learns generalizes to fundamental beliefs about oneself that challenge preexisting beliefs. In these instances, basic assumptions are altered; the process does not involve small, incremental additions to one's prior assumptions, but more dramatic changes in one's assumptions.

Again, personal change is far more common than we generally realize. Most changes, however, are of the sort represented by knowledge learning and physical growth—gradual and incremental. These are certainly instances of change; the person changes as a result. In these instances, however, assumptions are not challenged or threatened; the change is additive, the new beliefs essentially fit. The more dramatic instances of personal change addressed in this chapter are reflections of challenge, threat, and change at the level of one's basic assumptions. There is a qualitative shift at this level of belief, not simply a quantitative one. Just as new scientific theories arise out of crisis, when prior theories are stretched too far, we believe dramatic personal change, at the level of our higher order postulates, involves crisis and confrontation.

A HEURISTIC MODEL OF PERSONAL CHANGE

Using the framework of assumptive worlds, we propose that there are four central elements involved in the process of dramatic personal change: confrontation, resistance, validation, and integration. This process involves recognizing anomalous "data" (confrontation), opposing any change implied by the new information, typically through ignoring or reinterpreting the new data (resistance), realizing the validity and "truth value" of the new information (validation), and finally, integrating the new data and one's prior assumptions (integration). Although we regard these as core ingredients of the process, we do not claim that this list is exhaustive. Rather, these elements are intended as the rudiments of a heuristic model of change, which is presented in Figure 24.1.

The four elements are essentially microprocesses, and they are temporarily ordered such that confrontation represents the first stage of the overall process and integration the last. The arrows between resistance and validation indicate that these interim processes often alternate in occurrence; that is, resistance is apt to appear soon after confrontation, to be followed by the process of validation, which in turn often results in some new resistance, which may again be followed by validation. When the process of validation is complete, the person moves on to the stage of integra-

tion. The process of personal change may be foreclosed at any point along this continuum; the greater the movement to the right, however, the greater the likelihood of change. This movement, from confrontation through resistance and validation to integration, constitutes a general model of change that we believe can be used to describe the process of personal change, regardless of triggering event. An understanding of the four components of the model, described in general as follows, will be enriched in the last sections of the chapter, in which the model is applied to instances of personal change following victimization and psychotherapy.

Confrontation

Confrontation entails the recognition of anomalous data. In other words, an individual comes face to face with information that simply does not fit preexisting assumptions. This information can be presented in the form of powerful personal experiences, such as serious illness or loss, or through the intervention of others, such as parents, teachers, and therapists. In either case, the viability of our fundamental assumptions is threatened; there is a discrepancy between one's beliefs and the new data.

Generally, our fundamental assumptions are outside of our awareness; we take them for granted and function on the basis of these basic postulates, but they are ordinarily likely to be preconscious (Epstein, 1984) rather than in our day-to-day awareness. Confrontations with anomalies generally force us to objectify and examine these assumptions. The preexisting beliefs, which had never been questioned or challenged, are suddenly brought into awareness to be evaluated, worked on, and worked over.

It is probably the case that the psychological confrontation between old and new beliefs can take place outside of conscious awareness; the emotional concomitants of this confrontation—characterized primarily by anxiety, which signals cognitive disintegration (Averill, 1976)—would still be evident. Nevertheless, it is probably more often the case that the anomalous information "brings to consciousness" the preexisting assumptions. It is interesting to note that consciousness-raising, which aims at altering fairly high order postulates in one's assumptive world, has a label that is descriptive of this process. Such groups involve bringing to consciousness those very basic

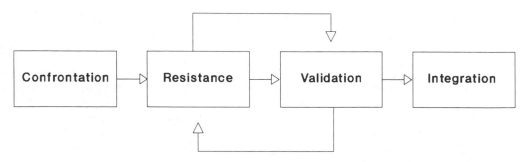

Figure 24.1. Heuristic model of personal change.

assumptions that are assumed to reflect one's own oppression (e.g., Nassi & Abramonwitz, 1981). The early stages of consciousness-raising involve the revelation and sharing of personal experiences, the communal creation of data that are used, in the end, to transform the members' basic assumptions.

Confrontation with anomalous data essentially calls forth and challenges our basic assumptions. It is the initial impetus for change. Such anomalous data are essential for the process of change. Generally, new information is not threatening and does not lead to major changes in our assumptive worlds. Rather, it leads to relatively small changes in our narrow generalizations, or lower order postulates, that respond to daily interactions and direct feedback; or, at the level of more fundamental assumptions, it is assimilated through incremental, additive changes rather than qualitative shifts in these high order postulates. With minimal massage or reinterpretation, even discrepant or anomalous new information can be altered to fit our preexisting assumptions. Occasionally, however, we are confronted by new information that is clearly anomalous; it cannot be readily assimilated nor easily altered to fit. In such cases there is a confrontation between the new data and the old assumptions. The latter are challenged, yet do not bend gracefully. Rather, we respond to this "threat" with resistance.

Resistance

The process of personal change is rarely a smooth one. People have a need for stability and coherence in their conceptual systems (Epstein, 1980, 1984; Nisbett & Ross, 1980). This stability provides us with a sense of psychological equilibrium. We eschew changes in our assumptive worlds, and we are particularly threatened by challenges posed to our most basic assumptions about the world and ourselves.

Psychological research on schemas, our stored knowledge about particular stimuli, has demonstrated that cognitively we are very conservative; we reinterpret and misremember data to fit our preexisting schemas (for a review see Fiske & Taylor, 1984). Our basic assumptions about the world are essentially our most abstract, generalized cognitive-emotional schemas, and we strive to incorporate new information within the framework of our basic assumptions rather than alter our assumptions. When the viability of such assumptions is called into question by anomalous information, we resist the changes implied by these anomalies. We may ignore or deny the new data, or continue to work at reinterpreting the new information so that it no longer poses a great threat.

Once confronted with anomalous data, the process of change remains a difficult one, for it is extremely unsettling to give up prior views of oneself and the world. These are the basic assumptions that have been developed over years of experience and have provided the person with a sense of coherence and comfort. In a sense, then, this resistance to change is a positive component of the change process, for it suggests that the required change in assumptions is likely to be an important, fundamental one. The absence of resistance raises the question of the depth or significance of the personal change to be effected.

In understanding resistance, it is not the valence of the basic assumptions that is important, but rather the stability and coherence they have afforded the individual in the past. Thus, data that threatens deeply held positive or negative views of oneself are apt to be forcefully resisted, for it is the stability of the system rather than its valence that is crucial to an understanding of this process. Change is never easy, for it involves a cognitive crisis. A person is confronted with new, anomalous data; an assumptive world must be established that can account for this new information. Resistance to such change is to be expected if the assumptions that are affected are fundamental to the person's conceptual system.

Validation

Challenges to one's assumptive world will be resisted, sometimes so successfully that the process of change is foreclosed. Sometimes, however, the anomalous data simply do not go away. The new data are too real, too compelling to leave alone, and must be accounted for by the individual. The process of validation is central to an understanding of change, for it is only in the face of "real" or "valid" anomalies that the process of change continues to unfold, such that personal change may be effected.

Given our need for stability and our general resistance to change, it is in many ways remarkable that people ever experience major personal changes. Our cognitive conservatism generally serves us well, and one can argue, very rationally, that we should not change old theories unless there is a very good reason for doing so; in fact, philosophers of science have made precisely this argument (e.g., Popper, 1963). We should not readily give up theories, but should give them more than a fair chance to survive. Yet, humans have the ability to learn, and this learning is generally in the service of developing theories that are useful maps of ourselves and our world, theories that are accurate enough to serve as viable guides to everyday living. Just as scientists test the validity of data, so too do individuals in their daily lives; the process of validation is no doubt more informal, yet nevertheless important, because valid information is not readily ignored. Anomalous data are only problematic when regarded as valid and well grounded; in other words, people must try to account for the anomalous when it is too real and too compelling to ignore, deny or discount. How, then, do we establish that something is worthy of belief?

The basis for establishing "truth value" is related to our ways of knowing. Traditionally, a primary distinction in sources of knowledge has been made between perception and apperception. Perception involves our knowledge of the external world, which is gained through our senses (e.g., hearing, seeing), and apperception involves our knowledge of our internal world, which is gained through an awareness of ourselves, particularly our emotions. Brickman's (1978) proposal of two types of validity roughly parallels this distinction. He has argued that there are really two types of validity, inferential and phenomenological validity. The former corresponds to ways of knowing used in science; evidence is provided by calculation, typified by experiments, and unambiguous outcomes are sought. In the case of phenomenological validity, evidence is provided by involvement and is typified by personal experience. Further, meaningful rather than unambiguous outcomes are sought. Brickman (1978) asserted that the question of calculation versus involvement as a way of knowing is an old one. He wrote

> It is captured in the contrast between the pull of a case study and the power of a statistical sample. . . . We are surprised, and sometimes despairing, at the extent to which people allow a single case or several dramatic cases to override the evidence of a statistical sample. . . . Yet, the present analysis suggests that it may not always be wrong to do so. Phenomenological validity can only be found in direct experience or in its next best form, vicarious experience gained through the vivid portrayal of someone else's direct experience. (Brickman, 1978, p. 24)

These two types of validity correspond to Epstein's (1980, 1985) cognitive-experiential self-theory of personality. Epstein argued that we have two minds, a rational mind and an "experiential" mind. The former is logical and analytic and expresses itself in words and numbers. The experiential mind is intimately connected with emotions; it is more directly tied to experience and represents reality primarily through images. The experiential mind operates automatically, providing us with an automatic way of responding to the world. These minds can be integrated, but also at times may be a source of conflict. Thus, Epstein (1985) wrote of the person who rationally decides to become a physician because of the high pay, high status, and high respect given to this profession; further, the person's parents have always wanted him or her to be a doctor, so the decision would please them. On the other hand, the individual's experiential conceptual system, which is influenced by emotions derived from past experiences, views becoming a physician as extremely unappealing. Both sources of information provide valid information. Epstein (1985) argued that although most people tend to consciously identify themselves with their rational conceptual system, in fact their behaviors are often far more determined by their experiential systems, by what "feels" good and bad. It is also possible that people differ in the extent to which they rely on different types of knowing and validity in establishing the truth value of data and experiences.

Considering the perspective of Brickman (1978) and Epstein (1985), there are two different ways of knowing; one is a logical-rational means, represented by inferential validity and established by our intellect. The other is represented by phenomenological validity and is established by our emotions. Interestingly, recent work on the two sides of the brain presents an anatomical analog to these two ways of knowing. The left side of the brain is associated with reason and intellectual knowledge, thereby paralleling the rational mind, whereas the right side of the brain is associated with feelings and emotions, thereby paralleling the experiential mind. Whether the two types of knowing are actually processed in distinctly different parts of the brain and in different ways remains an open question. Nevertheless, the two sides of the brain present an intriguing metaphor for thinking about our two ways of knowing.

There are no doubt particular rules of evidence that are used to calculate validity by the rational mind (i.e., inferential validity). We would argue that a primary rule is that of consensus (see Brickman, 1978); that is, a very significant piece of evidence used by the rational mind in calculating validity is the belief of others. In the case of an experiment, qualified scientists agree on the criteria for inferential validity. The rational mind engages in a logical analysis of data, and a primary component of this analysis involves attention to the beliefs of qualified or important others. Do well-respected authorities in the field, or those qualified to make a judgment, believe this? Do other people important to me believe this? Consciousness-raising groups and support groups make good use of this consensual criteria of validity. Propositions appear more valid and convincing when attested to by important others. As we will argue below, the impact of therapy may in part be attributable to the power of the therapist to convince the client of the validity of the anomalous data (see Frank, 1961). The validity of information provided by clinicians, then, is no doubt

derived in part from their roles as qualified observers of human behavior.

We believe, however, that these analyses of change are incomplete; rather, personal change that involves shifts in people's fundamental assumptions requires experiential, or phenomenological, validity as well. In other words, deep-seated change requires emotional "knowledge" of the new information's truth value, knowledge that is generally attained through direct personal experience rather than through the persuasive efforts of others or any rational calculation of what is worthy of belief.

The special significance or emotional experience in changing people's assumptions can be illustrated in the domain of people's stereotypes of minority groups. There is considerable literature that attests to the great difficulties involved in changing people's stereotypes of other groups (see, e.g., Hamilton, 1981; Rothbart & Oliver, 1985). Simply providing people with incongruous information about outgroups (i.e., information that does not fit their stereotypes) is not effective in changing people's attitudes toward specific outgroups. Yet, in an intriguing classroom demonstration aimed at teaching students about prejudice and discrimination, a teacher in a small Iowa town gave children the experience of being members of ingroups and outgroups. As described in a television documentary in the 1980s, the teacher divided her class on the basis of eye color and arbitrarily gave one group greater privileges than another; the privileged eye color was changed the second day of the demonstration so that all children had a chance to be a member of the favored group and the discriminated group. Even 10 to 15 years after the demonstration, the now-grown children testified to the powerful impact of this demonstration, claiming that it had a profound impact on their understanding of others and their treatment of outgroup members. Evidently, the understanding achieved by these children resulted because they experienced rejection themselves.

Anomalous data, when regarded as valid, are not ignored, but set the wheels of personal change in motion. In the process of accepting the validity of new information, resistance is likely to alternate with validation, as the threat to the old assumptions is increasingly apparent. Validation can come in the form of rational evidence, largely involving consensual validation by others. It also can come in the language of emotions. In the case of dramatic personal change, rational calculation is not apt to be sufficient. The validity derived from direct experience involves emotional knowing, and it is this that is most likely to lead to an acceptance of anomalies and the ultimate integration of new data and old assumptions.

Integration

In the end, a person rebuilds or establishes a new, viable set of basic assumptions. The new, anomalous data are regarded as valid, not simply to be denied, discounted, or ignored. In most instances, the individual will not simply discard preexisting views, but, rather, will integrate the old and new. Old assumptions will not remain intact, assimilating the new beliefs or existing, in whole, beside new assumptions. Rather, these assumptions will be altered. The process is largely dialectical, resulting in a synthesis of the old and new assumptions. For most people this does not represent a complete break with old ways of seeing oneself and the world; even when there is dramatic personal change and people see themselves very differently, a sense of continuity of self is largely maintained. Not simply the new, but the old must make sense.

For some individuals, the new assumptive world is, on balance, primarily a reflection of the new, powerful data. For others, it is largely representative of prior postulates. Here, the valence of the beliefs may play an important role, in contrast to the irrelevance of valence for the process of resistance. To the extent that the prior beliefs were more positive, an individual may be more motivated to retain them in the new assumptive world; to the extent that the new views are more positive, the motivation may be to minimize the prior assumptions. In either case, the process of resolving the cognitive crisis is an arduous one, involving powerful emotions and creative coping strategies. The rebuilt assumptive world is qualitatively different from what existed before, and the person feels like a changed individual. The difficult task of presenting oneself to others—for feedback and support—now begins.

PERSONAL CHANGE FOLLOWING TRAUMATIC NEGATIVE EVENTS

To a considerable extent, our interest in personal change originally stemmed from our interest in the psychological aftermath of victimization. Victims of crime, disease, early loss of a loved one, and natural disasters often report having changed considerably as a result of their misfortune (e.g., Janoff-Bulman, 1979; Taylor, 1983; Veronen & Kilpatrick, 1983). In the words of one rape victim we interviewed, "It's like I've walked through a door." Things are not the same on the other side. Interestingly, despite people's generally low expectations of change in individuals, we have very clear expectations of change for people who have been victimized through such events as sexual assault or life-threatening illness (Silka, 1989).

As a result of her work with a variety of victimized populations, including victims of rape, serious accidents, divorce, and early loss of a loved one, Janoff-Bulman (1985; 1989; Janoff-Bulman & Frieze, 1983; Janoff-Bulman & Timko, 1987) has argued that a common psychological process underlies the reactions of victims, regardless of their victimization. The trauma of victimization, she claims, is best understood in terms of the intense challenge posed to victims' basic assumptions about themselves and their world.

Among the most fundamental assumptions we hold are beliefs about our self-worth and about the meaningfulness and benevolence of the world (Janoff-Bulman, 1985, 1989). People's assumptions in our culture tend to be positively biased. Such biased assumptions begin during an early period of responsive caregiving, at which time the child begins to develop preverbal conceptions of a good, predictable world in which one is worthy of care (Janoff-Bulman, in press); they also are supported by (and are reflections of) a society that views optimism and happiness as the normal condition of humankind. In general, people believe in a world that is benevolent and meaningful, and they believe in their own self-worth. In other words, we believe that we are good, decent people, that the world and other people are good, and that events in our world "make sense" and do not happen randomly; that is, we believe things happen to people because they deserve it (i.e., we invoke principles of justice; Lerner, 1980) or because they have acted so as to bring about the outcome (i.e., we invoke principles of control; Seligman, 1975). Together, these beliefs about benevolence, meaningfulness, and self-worth provide us with a sense of safety and security. We maintain an "illusion of invulnerability" or "unrealistic optimism" (Janoff-Bulman & Lang-Gunn, 1989; Perloff, 1983; Weinstein, 1980; Weinstein & Lachendro, 1982). We overestimate the likelihood of positive events happening to us and underestimate the likelihood of negative events. Assumptions about the benevolence and meaningfulness of the world and the worthiness of the self are among the highest order postulates in our conceptual systems. These fundamental assumptions provide us with a sense of relative invulnerability. And it is these very basic assumptions that are changed by the experience of victimization which, we maintain, can be understood in terms of the processes of confrontation, resistance, validation, and integration.

Confrontation in Victimization-Induced Change

There are events in people's lives that simply cannot be accounted for by our basic assumptions, the assumptions we have developed and maintained over years of experience. Victimizations—crimes, life-threatening illnesses, serious accidents, natural disasters—force people to question their most fundamental assumptions about themselves and the world (Janoff-Bulman, 1985, 1989; Janoff-Bulman & Frieze, 1983). The data from their negative experience do not fit; the data cannot be readily integrated. Suddenly the victim is confronted with the possibility of a conceptual system that does not work—a system that cannot account for what has happened. The individual who has maintained a belief in his or her own relative invulnerability, by believing in the benevolence and meaningfulness of the world and his or her own self-worth, has been victimized and can no longer believe, "It can't happen to me."

Extreme negative events pose a dramatic assault on the victim's basic assumptions (Janoff-Bulman, 1985, 1989; Janoff-Bulman & Frieze, 1983). The powerful feelings of anxiety, confusion, and depression that are frequently experienced in the immediate aftermath of victimization reflect the victim's cognitive-emotional crisis, the potential threat of complete disintegration of the victim's assumptive world. The data of this experience — that the world is not benevolent or meaningful, or that the victim is not worthy—does not fit with preexisting assumptions. The crisis is profound, because it is the fundamental assumptions that are attacked. We have a need for stability and coherence in our conceptual systems, and yet the experience of victimization leads people to question the very assumptions that had afforded them such stability and coherence. It is not sur-

prising, then, that resistance to change, primarily in the form of denial, is extremely common following victimization.

Resistance in Victimization-Induced Change

Denial is an extremely common response to victimization. It usually involves disbelief that some traumatic event has occurred, or more commonly, a lack of recognition of the seriousness of the negative event. In a review of studies reporting victims' reactions, Janoff-Bulman and Timko (1987) concluded, "From an examination of the literature, it becomes very apparent that researchers investigating reactions to negative life events frequently find a great deal of denial, and the denial is generally regarded as a normal part of the coping process" (p. 148). Extensive denial has been reported as an early response by burn and polio victims (Hamburg & Adams, 1967), terminally ill patients (Hackett & Weisman, 1969; Weisman, 1972; Weisman & Hackett, 1967), patients with chronic lung failure (Dudley, Verney, Masuda, Martin, & Holmes, 1969), cardiac patients (Cassem & Hackett, 1971; Druss & Kornfeld, 1967), crime victims (Bard & Sangrey, 1979), and concentration camp victims (Eitinger, 1982). The reality of their victimization is too threatening to confront immediately and all at once. The data do not fit, and they are confronted with the possibility of a complete breakdown of their conceptual systems.

Through the early use of denial, victims resist the onslaught of threatening information. Although it has often been regarded as maladaptive in the psychiatric literature, denial may in fact play a very adaptive role in the early stages of the victim's coping process (Janoff-Bulman & Timko, 1987; Epstein, 1967, 1983; Horowitz, 1980, 1982, 1983; Lazarus, 1983). Denial precludes total psychological breakdown by enabling victims to pace their recovery following trauma; excessive amounts of anxiety and confusion are reduced. "A dramatic, unmodulated attack on the primary postulates of one's assumptive world is controlled by the process of denial, which allows the individual to face slowly and gradually the realities of the external world and incorporate them into his or her internal world" (Janoff-Bulman & Timko, 1987, p. 147).

In the case of victimization, personal change is

not freely sought, but rather imposed. An extreme, negative event occurs and the data from the experience powerfully challenges old assumptions. Change in these basic assumptions is resisted, not because the new assumptions would be more negative, but rather because the stability of the old system, which had been developed and solidified over many years, is now seriously threatened.

The common process of denial following victimization reflects the depth of the assumptions that are challenged by victimization. Yet, denial also serves the adaptive function of pacing information, so that victims are not overwhelmed by the assault on their assumptions. Typically, denial decreases over time, and victims recognize the "truth value" of their experience and work to integrate the new data.

Validation in Victimization-Induced Change

Victimization provides the victim with anomalous new data, data that may include such "facts" as the world is not always good, there are events that don't make sense, good people cannot always avoid misfortune. In the case of extreme negative events, the validity of this new data is rarely questioned. Phenomenological validity is extremely high. The victim's experience is too vivid and emotionally compelling to be ignored or dismissed. The traumatic event has not been read about in a book or newspaper, or related by another person; it has been powerfully, directly experienced by the victim.

Rationally, we know that negative events such as crime and serious disease happen, but emotionally, at some gut level, we do not believe such events will happen to us. Reading about these events (i.e., being provided with facts about real cases of victimization) has little effect on people and their basic assumptions about the world. We change our basic assumptions by directly experiencing such events, or, in some cases, by indirectly experiencing them through other people very close to us who have been victimized. In these cases, empathic responses also make the event very emotionally real and personal change may be forthcoming. Validity is not a problematic process in the case of victimization; victims know—emotionally and experientially—the "truth value" of the data derived from their experience.

Integration in Victimization-Induced Change

The legacy of victimization is often a change in people's assumptive worlds. Victims' basic assumptions are challenged by anomalous data. Resistance in the form of denial is commonly used and, with time, dissipates. The data are too valid to be denied over the long run. They must be dealt with, worked on, and integrated at the level of the victim's assumptive world. Coping with victimization involves rebuilding a viable set of basic assumptions of the world and oneself, a set of assumptions that can account for the data of the victimizing experience. This is not an easy task; the assumptions in question are the fundamental ones, the assumptions that form the foundation of the victim's assumptive world. Further, in arriving at a viable set of assumptions, the victim is motivated not only by the need to account for the new negative experience, but also by the need to account for his or her past experiences, which had been well served by the victim's prior assumptions. People resist change in their conceptual systems, and yet victims cannot ignore their seemingly anomalous, powerful negative experience.

How do victims integrate their experience? This difficult process is facilitated by a number of coping strategies. These strategies minimize the challenge posed to the victim's assumptive world by minimizing the negative implications of the victimization. Thus, several strategies enable victims to bolster positive assumptions of self-worth and the benevolence of the world. Thus, victims try to compare themselves with others worse off than themselves and invent hypothetical others for this social comparison if real others do not seem to exist (Taylor, Wood, & Lichtman, 1983; Wills, 1981). Victims often reinterpret their experience, at least partially, in a positive light; they look for benefits to be derived from their experience (Bulman & Wortman, 1977; Silver & Wortman, 1980; Taylor, 1983; Taylor, Wood, & Lichtman, 1983). Victims often report a newfound appreciation of life and a recognition of what is really important, as well as a newfound sense of their own strengths and possibilities.

Another coping strategy that is far more adaptive than meets the eye is self-blame, which is extremely common following victimization (for a review, see Janoff-Bulman & Lang-Gunn, 1989). Given its association with depression (e.g., Beck,

1967), self-blame is generally regarded as a maladaptive strategy for victims. Nevertheless, it appears that self-blame is not a monolithic concept, but refers to at least two distinct self-attributional phenomena: behavioral and characterological self-blame (Janoff-Bulman, 1979). Although the latter, which involves blaming the kind of person you are (i.e., one's character or stable traits) is maladaptive, there is considerable empirical evidence indicating that behavioral self-blame—blaming some action you engaged in or failed to engage in—is adaptive (e.g., Affleck, Allen, Tennen, McGrade, & Ratzan, 1985; Baum, Flemming, & Singer, 1983; Janoff-Bulman, 1979; Peterson, Schwartz, & Seligman, 1981; Tennen, Affleck, & Gerschman, 1986; Timko & Janoff-Bulman, 1985). Behavioral self-blame enables victims to minimize the need for change in their assumptive world. Victims who blame their behaviors are largely able to maintain their preexisting assumptions, particularly regarding the meaningfulness of the world and their own self-worth. If the victimization can be understood in terms of their own behaviors, then the world remains meaningful (i.e., people control outcomes); further, victims can believe that they did a foolish thing without generalizing this to a belief that they are foolish people. Positive self-worth is thereby minimally affected.

Victims use a number of cognitive strategies to help them resolve their cognitive-emotional crisis. These strategies, involving particular interpretations of their victimization, minimize the need for conceptual change by bolstering some prior assumptions. A complete overthrow of the old system is thereby generally avoided. In the end, victims integrate the old assumptions and new data, such that old and new experiences can be accounted for by their assumptive world.

Victims do change. Their basic assumptions generally do not look the same following their experience. Some victims, such as those exhibiting posttraumatic stress disorder, seem unable to rebuild a viable conceptual system; their lives are pervaded by anxiety and a state of cognitive disintegration. Others rebuild a system based almost entirely on the negative implications of their victimization. These victims have often experienced an event that is particularly difficult to assimilate; and these events are often those that seem to preclude the use of some common strategies (e.g., deriving benefit, behaviorally self-blaming). There is evidence, for example, that rape victims

who were raped in seemingly safe situations, such as when they were sleeping in their beds in a locked home, have the most difficult time years after the event (Scheppele & Bart, 1983). Recent research on the long-term negative effects of the unexpected loss of a child or spouse in auto accidents suggests the difficulty of assimilating these types of extreme events.

Most victims, however, rebuild a set of assumptions that reflects their experience yet provides some continuity with past assumptions (Janoff-Bulman, 1989). The world does not look the same, but it is not entirely negative. They recognize the limitations of our existence; people cannot control everything, bad things do happen, all events do not make sense. As one rape victim told us:

> An event like rape separates you from the mainstream. It forces you to develop a personal philosophy; you have to do thinking and searching. The world is more dangerous to me now. I know there is evil, that really anything could happen. I could die tomorrow.

And these are the words of a cancer patient we interviewed:

> The world isn't what it was to me. I don't see things the same way. I know about chance now, that bad things happen when you don't expect them.

People's expectations about the impact of traumatic life events seem well-founded (Silka, 1989). Victims do experience personal change following their negative experience, and this change takes place at the level of their basic assumptions about the world. Generally, there is a qualitative change in their basic assumptions that reflects some new combination of their traumatic experience and their preexisting assumptions.

APPLICATIONS TO PSYCHOTHERAPY

Personal change is generally regarded as one of the primary goals, if not the preeminent goal, of people who seek psychotherapy. Given the tremendous diversity of theories and styles that inform psychotherapy, it is not surprising that clinicians' beliefs differ widely regarding how this change should be effected. Fundamental theoretical differences about the role of insight, the necessity of addressing specific symptoms, the nature and importance of the therapeutic relationship, and the relative benefit of behavioral change versus increased self-knowledge all lead to widely divergent approaches to therapeutic change.

The disarmingly basic question, "How does therapy work?" has yet to be answered satisfactorily. The literature on psychotherapy process and outcome is enormous, complex, and daunting in its scope (see Garfield & Bergin, 1986, for a comprehensive review). A vast number of factors have been implicated in therapeutic change. Orlinsky and Howard (1986) list 34 variables relevant to therapeutic outcome, categorizing them in terms of provision and implementation of a therapeutic contract, interventions made by the therapist, patient participation, and dimensions of the therapeutic bond. In a review chapter of psychotherapy effectiveness, Lambert, Shapiro, and Bergin (1986) suggest that "a major factor in maintaining treatment gains seems to be the degree to which patients . . . recognize that changes are partially the result of effective patient effort" (p. 165). Factors as diverse as the amount of patient speech during therapy sessions (e.g., McDaniel, Stiles, & McGaughey, 1981; Staples & Sloane, 1976) and the timeliness with which therapy is begun after a patient makes initial contact (e.g., Roth, Rhudick, Shaskan, Slobin, Wilkinson, & Young, 1964; Uhlenhuth & Duncan, 1968; Zeiss, Lewinsohn, & Munoz, 1979) have been implicated in the process of therapeutic change.

Given the amalgam of treatment approaches and change-related variables that represent the current state of the art, is it possible to discuss a metaprocess for understanding therapeutic change? We would like to posit that the heuristic model of personal change presented above, involving the processes of confrontation, resistance, validation, and integration, provides a suitable template across modalities. Although different types of therapy will use different clinical strategies, we believe that they can all be described within the explanatory framework provided by the proposed model. Thus, for example, confrontation or validation may appear distinctly different across therapist orientations, yet they nevertheless will be reflected in the therapeutic process. Further, the present model may provide one means of organizing, and thereby better understanding, the complex literature on psychotherapy outcome. Specific change-related variables (e.g., client motivation, client-therapist relationship) may be associated with distinct components of the proposed model.

In applying this model, we are first committing ourselves to an understanding of therapeutic change in terms of people's basic assumptions. The goal of therapy is to alter people's basic assumptions about themselves and/or their world so that they may feel good and function better. Frank (1961) similarly argued for understanding the aim of psychotherapy in terms of changes in people's assumptive worlds. He, too, recognized the significance of people's fundamental assumptions—those that are our most abstract, highest order postulates—for understanding people's views of themselves and interactions in the world. However, he then equated these assumptions with attitudes, and maintained that therapy could best be understood as an influence process. According to Frank (1961), the therapist's sources of influence—power and similarity—provide the primary basis for understanding successful psychotherapeutic change. As will be discussed below, we believe that the therapist-as-persuader plays a role, though not the primary role, in understanding personal change through therapy.

Given the tremendous diversity of psychotherapy modalities, any attempt to apply the proposed model of personal change in a comprehensive way would be a task of immense scope. Our aim is more modest. Rather than fully describe all or most psychotherapy orientations from the perspective of the model, we instead hope to illustrate its applicability by presenting specific examples of strategies and processes drawn from a number of different therapy modes, including behavioral, cognitive, psychoanalytic, paradoxical, and gestalt treatments. The complexity and richness of specific theories are afforded less priority than is optimal. Rather, our interest is in examining what we regard as broad therapy-related phenomena, the underlying or metaprocess of personal change. Certainly, therapy does not always result in deep personal change. People may experience very little change, or change some specific behavior and some concomitant narrow generalization about themselves or their world. Sometimes, however, people experience deep-seated change, change in basic assumptions about themselves and their world. We believe that when this happens, it is because the process of psychotherapy proceeds along a course delineated by our heuristic model of personal change. How, then, can psychotherapeutic change be understood in terms of confrontation, resistance, validation, and integration?

Confrontation in
Psychotherapy-Induced Change

Confrontation entails the recognition of new data, or information, that do not fit; these anomalous data lead to the questioning of basic assumptions. The early stages of therapy involve clarifying the discrepancy between new information or experiences and prior assumptions. Often this discrepancy is explicit to clients prior to their first therapy session; it is what got them to therapy in the first place. Sometimes anomalous data have been presented in the form of particular life events (e.g., divorce or some relationship termination, being fired from a job, a specific illness, failing in school) that cannot be assimilated. Sometimes it involves bumping into one's limits, not achieving what one set out to do. In these instances, the confrontation between old assumptions and anomalous information is largely prepackaged for the therapist and is "delivered" to the therapist for help in effecting change.

For others entering psychotherapy, the nature of personal distress is not well articulated or understood. These clients may be experiencing a great deal of anxiety or may report being stuck or demoralized. Something is not working. With these individuals, the therapist attempts to find, objectify, and label the difficulty; the therapist leads the client to question old assumptions by presenting new "data" in the course of therapy. Whether made explicit first by the client or the therapist, the endpoint of this first process involves challenging old assumptions. Just as victimization leads individuals to objectify and come face to face with old assumptions, similarly psychotherapy leads clients to objectify and question old assumptions. The therapist may do this through verbal discourse or direct behavioral intervention; in either case, a threat to the client's conceptual system is established through the confrontation of new, anomalous data.

It should be noted that "confrontation" is meant here to specify a challenge within, or to, the assumptive belief system of an individual. We do not mean to imply that a confrontational or oppositional interpersonal stance is a prerequisite, or even a preferred method, of achieving this confrontation. Rather, we are asserting that confronting an individual's maladaptive assumptions can be seen as an integral and fundamental aspect of psychotherapy across a range of modalities.

Confrontation counteracts complacency and sets the stage for change. In some therapies, direct challenge of old assumptions is an explicit, obvious aspect of treatment. For example, cognitive therapists elicit and test "automatic thoughts," which are those "thoughts that intervene between outside events and the individual's emotional reactions to them. They often go unnoticed because they are part of a repetitive pattern of thinking . . . " (Beck & Young, 1985, p. 215). The automatic, unquestioned nature of these thoughts suggests the conceptual link between these cognitions and people's basic assumptions, although the latter can best be understood as our deepest cognitive-emotional schemas, and not solely cognitions that may exist at any level of the conceptual system. In cognitive therapy, therapists explicitly identify and challenge people's automatic thoughts and attempt to provide other more adaptive cognitions to take their place.

The psychoanalytic process of interpretation also can be regarded as representing confrontation. According to Malan (1979), interpretation partly involves presenting to a patient a succinct and relevant statement of how his or her current actions or emotions are influenced by past events. By relating the present to the past, new experiences are used to uncover old, unquestioned assumptions. Translated into the language of the current model, the act of psychoanalytic interpretation involves uncovering and objectifying some of the fundamental assumptions by which clients make sense of themselves and the world, and discerning where those assumptions are maladaptive, outdated, or discrepant with new experience.

While the process of confrontation exists across modalities, the mechanics vary greatly, as does the theoretical framework for understanding pathology and conceptualizing the appropriate path for change. Thus, in psychoanalytic therapies, challenging old assumptions often occurs through an exchange that emphasizes the continued effects of early infancy and childhood. Behavior therapists emphasize the actual behaviors in which a person is engaged, and how these might be self-defeating or inappropriate; client attention to and practice of new behaviors are the routes to questioning old assumptions. Cognitive therapists emphasize and challenge the adaptiveness of specific cognitions. Therapists practiced in paradoxical interventions may not verbalize a confrontation, but instead set a task for the client that exemplifies it.

These differences in theory and technique yield significantly different means of clinical assessment, formulation, and intervention. Yet while the guidelines by which a clinical problem is formulated differ from theory to theory, the need to formulate the problem remains constant. Regardless of orientation, this formulation can be conceptualized in terms of assumptive worlds. For the individual in psychotherapy, the first element of change involves questioning basic assumptions. Anomalous data, provided by significant events prior to therapy or by the therapist during treatment (through, for example, testing, interpretation, behavioral exercises, or paradoxical treatments), serve to identify and challenge fundamental aspects of the client's assumptive world.

Resistance in Therapy-Induced Change

Resistance reflects the difficulty of relinquishing the fundamental rules by which an individual has come to make sense of him or herself and the world. Because of its strong connection with certain schools of thought, the concept of resistance has been disclaimed by other schools. As used here, resistance is regarded as the deep hesitancy to abandon or alter old assumptions. As such, it can be used as a transtheoretical construct, bridging concepts as divergent as psychoanalytic defense mechanisms and failure to complete cognitive-behavioral homework assignments.

Changing old assumptions, even if maladaptive, threatens the person's sense of stability and coherence. The resistance to change no doubt also reflects the fear of an unknown, new conceptual system; there may be a fear of losing the old and having nothing, no new framework of understanding, to replace it. The old system, even if dysfunctional, is familiar and comfortable; a dysfunctional set of assumptions may be preferable to none at all. Behavior therapists argue that it is not enough to eradicate maladaptive behaviors; equal emphasis must be placed on creating and positively reinforcing new behaviors. In object relations theory, Fairbairn (1952) theorized that having a bad internal object relation was better than having no object at all. According to Ogden (1983),

Fairbairn's thinking stems from the idea that a human being's sanity and survival depend on object-relatedness, and a person experiences the terror of impending annihilation when he feels that all external and internal object ties are being severed. Therefore, he clings desperately to any object tie (external or internal), even ones that are experienced as bad, when that is all that is available. (p. 236)

Given that a "dysfunctional reality" is better than no reality at all, resistance in psychotherapy can be seen as the inability, or fear, to accept the demands of a new reality and set of assumptions. These demands will be variously defined, according to the dictates of the theory and the prescribed nature of the interventions. Thus, while object relations theory may emphasize the difficulty of abandoning an internal object, behavior therapies may focus on the difficulty of breaking entrenched patterns of interaction, and family systems theories will highlight the interpersonal pressure to maintain old ways of being.

Regardless of the type of therapy, however, resistance by clients is an all-too-familiar phenomenon. Clients commonly reject either the provider of care (i.e., the therapist) or the advice given by the provider (Pomerleau & Rodin, 1986). In rejecting the provider, clients may devalue the therapist, arguing, for example, that he or she is too inexperienced with specific problems, not smart enough, only interested in money, too distant, too uncaring, or not a good match; the role of the therapist in the client's life may be minimized, thereby lessening the therapist's presumed influence, and, in turn, the client's impetus to change.

Clients' resistance can take varied behavioral forms as well. A client may stop coming to treatment after an initial session or two, or in midcourse. In behavioral or cognitive therapies, clients may not do their homework assignments; they may not engage in new behaviors or practice self-efficacy statements, for example. Clients may come late to therapy sessions. They may identify their problem, but then fill the therapy session with boring, superficial information, to save only the last minute or two for a discussion of anxiety-laden material. Patients also may engage in denial, rationalization, and intellectualization (the classic psychoanalytic defense mechanisms), and may externalize blame onto others, thereby attempting to minimize the need for personal change.

Although it creates problems in therapy, resistance can be understood as an indication that basic assumptions have been challenged and questioned. People defend against threats, and clients that make some progress in therapy will naturally experience a threat to their conceptual system. Resistance should be expected if the viability of fundamental assumptions are at stake. For personal change to occur, however, resistance must be overcome. This involves realizing and accepting the "truth value" of new data and changed assumptions. Individuals must feel confident that their acceptance will not entail the need to abandon prior assumptions, with nothing to replace them. Overcoming or working through resistance goes hand in hand with the process of validation, and the two may in fact be defined in terms of one another: resistance is the inability to accept the validity of the new beliefs, and validation is the process by which resistance can be overcome. These two processes often alternate over the course of therapy; as new data and assumptions are increasingly validated, the conceptual system is threatened and resistance emerges as a protective response. Over time, resistance subsides, as the process of validation gains momentum. The cycle of resistance-validation-resistance will continue until the process of validation is completed. What does this process entail in psychotherapy?

Validation in Therapy-Induced Change

Validation in psychotherapy is the process by which clients are able to accept the discrepant data, overcome resistance to change, and begin to incorporate new beliefs about themselves and the world into their fundamental assumptive framework. In some therapies, the necessity for validation is made quite explicit and becomes a focal point of intervention. It may take the form of active permission to change granted by the therapist, or the encouraged repetition of self-efficacy statements (e.g., Bandura, 1977, 1978). It may involve strategies to enlist social support or change the client's patterns of interpersonal activity, or to provide the opportunity for clients to practice new roles or behaviors, such as in role-playing or psychodrama.

These strategies attempt to address the patient's need for validation, but provide an incomplete picture of the processes involved. We believe validation in therapy is a two-stage process. The first stage is a "readiness" to accept new truth value; the client must be willing to listen and be open to the new data and assumptions implicit or explicit in the therapeutic exchange. The second stage entails making the leap and actually accepting this new therapy-induced perspective. The two

types of validity discussed above — inferential and phenomenological (Brickman, 1978) — are related to these two stages. We believe that inferential validity and rational, logical analysis play the primary role in the first stage of validation; in contrast, phenomenological validity and emotional experience (Epstein, 1985) play the crucial role in the second part of this process.

In the first stage, clients must convince themselves that the challenge posed to their assumptive world is worthy of attention. Why not continue to resist the threat? The answer for the client rests with the social influence features of the therapy. At this stage, the client's rational analysis suggests that there are two reasons to listen to the therapist. To the extent that the therapist is regarded as qualified — as an "expert" of sorts on human behavior — and, in addition, appears to truly want to help the client, the client should, over time, move through this first phase of validation. These social influence aspects of psychotherapy are those discussed by Frank (1961). He wrote, "The success of all methods and schools of psychotherapy depends in the first instance on the patient's conviction that the therapist cares about him and is competent to help him" (Frank, 1961, p. 165). The therapist functions, at first, as a person who persuades, by virtue of his or her personal strengths (e.g., self-confidence, expertise, apparent concern for others) and the status accorded psychotherapies as helping agents in our society.

This part of the validation process is by far the easier of the two to complete. The second phase involves more than a willingness to listen, for it entails acceptance, and with acceptance, change in fundamental assumptions. It may be that much of therapeutic activity can be seen as satisfying the first phase of the validation process, that of creating an environment in which change is given ample opportunity to occur. By laying the groundwork for the validation of new beliefs, many of the details of therapeutic business can facilitate change — but will not be sufficient in and of themselves to produce change. A warm, supportive "holding" environment, for example, may allow an individual to listen to possibilities for change, to test hypotheses, and to voice fears and anxieties, but it will not bring on the change. Or, the frequent repetition of an idea or interpretation may gradually make it more accessible and tenable, but is alone unlikely to lead to personal change.

The tenacity of individuals' inability to change

is one of the central, most vexing problems of psychotherapy. Clients can arrive at dazzling insights regarding their difficulties. They can earnestly apply themselves to the most detailed behavioral regimens, or dedicate themselves to attempting new roles in their lives. Yet still, amid real desire and heartfelt cries of "Why can't I change?" the struggle to alter old dysfunctional patterns or reach new levels of functioning remains enormously difficult. Clients in psychotherapy may rationally believe the "data" that are exchanged in therapy; the new assumptions may seem valid and therefore acceptable from a reasoned, intelligent analysis. Yet, we believe, this is not sufficient for completion of the validation process. Such rational belief is not sufficient for change.

Reflecting a somewhat similar perspective, Hollon and Beck (1986) wrote, "There is not, as yet, compelling evidence that cognitive therapy works, when it works, *by virtue of changing beliefs and/ or information processing* [italics added], although that remains a very viable possibility" (p. 451). By implication, addressing cognitions alone may be insufficient to create the necessary "truth value" for new fundamental assumptions. In the psychoanalytic literature, the concept of "abreaction" (Freud & Breuer, 1924) conveys an analogous message. Abreaction, the process by which verbally reliving previous events can have a therapeutic or cathartic benefit, necessarily involves an emotional investment in the disclosure for change to occur (see La Planche & Pontalis, 1973, for a fuller definition). For true belief and acceptance to transpire, and change to occur, the client must validate the new data and assumptions through the language of experience and emotions (Epstein, 1985). Phenomenological validity (Brickman, 1978), and not inferential validity, provides the crucial test. Somehow the client must come to "feel" that the new assumptions are valid. Emotions must be powerfully involved. Through actual emotional experience we must come to understand the maladaptive nature of our prior assumptions and the validity of the perspectives provided in therapy.

The therapeutic relationship itself may facilitate this emotional, experiential component of the validation process. The client-therapist relationship consistently emerges as a crucial variable in successful psychotherapy (Garfield & Bergin, 1986). A warm, supportive therapeutic environment may facilitate important emotional experiences, for a person may feel free to experiment with new roles, with new ways of interacting. A client may feel safe enough to deeply, emotionally experience or reexperience powerful events and interactions. Consistent with this perspective is the orientation of client-centered therapists, who assert that a therapist's unconditional positive regard is an extremely important component in effecting therapeutic change (Rogers, 1961). In psychoanalysis, therapeutic treatment includes analysis of the transference. In this case, the "here and now" interpersonal interactions between client and therapist are used to highlight the client's unconscious assumptions. The interpersonal interactions of client and therapist may provide an important experiential, emotional component for validation. Also from a psychoanalytic perspective, Kohut (1971) wrote of mirroring, which involves providing a reflective emotional experience for clients, thereby allowing and tacitly encouraging them to voice the emotions that may have been unacceptable in the person's early history.

A concept that appears to be reemerging in current discussions of therapeutic change is that of the "corrective emotional experience." It is likely that modern usage of the term differs from that originally intended by Alexander and French (1946). In its original usage, the authors were proposing a specific model of brief psychoanalytic therapy that involved a very active role for the therapist. They argued that the therapist needs to provide, for the purposes of counterbalance, the emotions that were presumed to be lacking from caregivers in the patient's early development. In modern usage, the term is theoretically broader, and also implies a consistently empathic and warm stance on the part of the therapist. The assumption is that in therapy the client is able to relive certain emotional experiences to correct for past errors. In this manner, clients may experience and thereby validate, phenomenologically, new ways of seeing themselves and their world.

Behavioral techniques that provide experiences with personal mastery, role-playing, and "cognitive rehearsal," in which a client imagines, step by step, successfully performing new activities, may also provide validating experiences, particularly to the extent that these new behaviors involve strong emotions. Therapies that focus on paradoxical interventions may also facilitate the process of phenomenological validity. As discussed above, the presentation of a paradox can represent a confrontation to the assumptive system. The validation comes with the experiential understanding of a different way of functioning, which is achieved perhaps by rejecting the paradox, perhaps by embracing it. This new understanding need not rely on insight, nor on dictated cognitive changes, but the result is the same: a change in an individual's beliefs about him or herself.

Integration in Therapy-Induced Change

The process of change eventually involves integrating one's new experiences and assumptions into a new, synthesized conceptual system. There is an integration of new and old assumptions, and an assumptive world that is different from both emerges. This new set of assumptions provides the individual with a more adaptive way of functioning in the world, while simultaneously providing the individual with a sense of continuity with the past.

Often a person becomes completely immersed in new views of the self or world validated by the therapeutic experience. Over time, however, these new views become somewhat tempered and integrated with older, preexisting beliefs. This process of integration has been exemplified in models that address identity formation within minority cultures. For example, Hall, Cross, and Freedle's (1972) model of black identity formation, or Cass' (1979) model of gay/lesbian identity formation both postulate that once an individual has successfully passed through the struggle of self-acceptance (i.e., after the new assumptions have been validated), he or she then becomes immersed in the minority subculture. Old beliefs and assumptions are rejected and only new ones are considered viable. This period of immersion in the new yields, however, to a process of synthesis, in which old and new beliefs are incorporated into a new assumptive world.

Similarly, in those cases where therapy has served as catalyst for dramatic growth and change, it is likely that the changes will be tempered in time, as an altered, synthesized assumptive framework emerges. This often involves, in part, a reconceptualization of one's past. The process of discovering new meaning for old events or feelings is an example of how the assumptive framework can be modified and reinvested with a bias toward new, more positive basic assumptions. Frankl (1973) discussed how the significance of a specific moment or a specific realization can ret-

roactively reshape the meaning of one's entire life. The work of therapy and its aftermath need not involve only introducing new assumptions, but also redefining the old ones, so that they may continue to reflect the data of a person's changing life.

SUMMARY AND CONCLUSIONS

The model we have proposed is an attempt to delineate processes that we believe are common to the experience of personal change, regardless of the catalyst for change. Confrontation, resistance, validation, and integration are themselves complex processes that we believe describe the course of personal change. Although a person's experience of these four model components may differ dramatically across types of change (e.g., victimization-induced vs. psychotherapy-induced), we maintain that the metalevel descriptions of these four components, which include functional analyses of the four processes, are actually quite similar. Confrontation involves recognizing the anomalous and the challenge posed to one's old assumptions. Resistance entails attempts to ward off change through cognitive (e.g., denial, denigration of a therapist) or behavioral (e.g., missing therapy sessions) means. Validation involves establishing the "truth value" of new data and new assumptions. It is probably the crux of change, particularly psychotherapeutic change, but should be understood as one component of the entire model. Finally, integration is the synthesis of old and new assumptions, so that personal change is recognized and yet continuity with the past is preserved.

This chapter no doubt raises many questions, perhaps many more than it answers. The applications of the model to victimization and therapy are intended to promote interest rather than make converts. To date, personal change is a poorly understood, little-studied, yet extremely compelling psychological phenomenon. We hope that the proposed model can serve as a heuristic for exploring and understanding the fundamental elements of this extraordinary human process.

REFERENCES

Affleck, G., Allen, D. D. A., Tennen, H., McGrade, B. J., & Ratzan, S. (1985). Causal and control cognitions in parent coping with a chronically ill child. *Journal of Social and Clinical Psychology, 3*, 369–379.

Alexander, F., & French, T. M. (1946). *Psychoanalytic therapy: Principles and application*. New York: Ronald Press.

Averill, J. (1976). Emotion and anxiety: Sociocultural, biological, and psychological determinants. In M. Zuckerman & C. D. Spielberger (Eds.), *Emotion and anxiety: New concepts, methods and applications*. New York: Erlbaum-Wiley.

Bandura, A. (1977). Self-efficacy: Toward a unifying theory of behavioral change. *Psychological Review, 84*, 191–215.

Bandura, A. (1978). Reflections on self-efficacy. *Advances in Behavior Research and Therapy, 1*, 237–269.

Bard, M., & Sangrey, D. (1979). *The crime victim's book*. New York: Basic Books.

Baum, A., Flemming, R., & Singer, J. E. (1983). Coping with victimization by technological disaster. *Journal of Social Issues, 39*, 119–140.

Beck, A. T. (1967). *Depression: Clinical, experimental, and theoretical aspects*. New York: Harper & Row.

Beck, A. T., & Young, J. E. (1985). Depression. In D. H. Barlow (Ed.), *Clinical handbook of psychological disorders*. New York: Guilford Press.

Bowlby, J. (1969). *Attachment and loss: Vol. 1. Attachment*. London: Hogarth.

Brehm, J. W., & Cohen, A. R. (1962). Exploration in cognitive dissonance. New York: John Wiley & Sons.

Brickman, P. (1978). Is it real? In J. H. Harvey, W. Ickes, & R. F. Kidd (Eds.), *New directions in attribution research* (Vol. II). Hillsdale, NJ: Lawrence Erlbaum Associates.

Bulman, R. J., & Wortman, C. B. (1977). Attributions of blame and coping in the "real world": Severe accident victims react to their lot. *Journal of Personality and Social Psychology, 35*, 351–363.

Cass, V. C. (1979). Homosexual identity formation. *Journal of Homosexuality, 4*, 219–235.

Cassem, N. H., & Hackett, T. P. (1971). Psychiatric consultation in a coronary care unit. *Annals of Internal Medicine, 75*, 9–14.

Druss, R. G., & Kornfeld, D. S. (1967). The survivors of cardiac arrest. *Journal of the American Medical Association, 201*, 291–296.

Dudley, D. L., Verney, J. W., Masuda, M., Martin, C. J., & Holmes, T. H. (1969). Long-term adjustment, prognosis, and death in irreversible diffuse obstructive pulmonary syndromes. *Psychosomatic Medicine, 31*, 310–325.

Eitinger, L. (1982). The effects of captivity. In F. M. Ochberg & D. A. Soskis (Eds.), *Victims of terrorism*. Boulder, CO: Westview Press.

Epstein, S. (1967). Toward a unified theory of anxiety. In B. A. Maher (Ed.), *Progress in experimental personality research* (Vol. 4). New York: Academic Press.

Epstein, S. (1973). The self-concept revisited, or a theory of a theory. *American Psychologist, 28*, 404–416.

Epstein, S. (1979). The ecological study of emotions in humans. In P. Pliner, K. R. Blanstein, & I. M. Spigel (Eds.), *Advances in the study of communication and affect: Vol. 5. Perception of emotions in self and others*. New York: Plenum Press.

Epstein, S. (1980). The self-concept: A review and the proposal of an integrated theory of personality. In E. Staub (Ed.), *Personality: Basic issues and current research*. Englewood Cliffs, NJ: Prentice-Hall.

Epstein, S. (1983). Natural healing processes of the mind: Graded stress inoculation as an inherent coping mechanism. In D. Meichenbaum & M. E. Jarcmko (Eds.), *Stress reduction and prevention*. New York: Plenum Press.

Epstein, S. (1984). Controversial issues in emotion theory. In P. Shaver (Ed.), *Review of personality and social psychology: Emotions, relationships, and health*. Beverly Hills, CA: Sage Publications.

Epstein, S. (1985). The implications of cognitive-experiential self-theory for research in social psychology and personality. *Journal for the Theory of Social Behavior, 15(3)*, 283–310.

Fairbairn, W. R. D. (1952). Schizoid factors in the personality. In *Psychoanalytic studies of the personality*. London: Routledge Kegan Paul.

Festinger, L. (1957). A theory of cognitive dissonance. Evanston, IL: Row, Peterson.

Fiske, S. T., & Taylor, S. E. (1984). *Social cognition*. Reading, MA: Addison-Wesley.

Frank, J. (1961). *Persuasion and healing*. Baltimore, MD: Johns Hopkins University Press.

Frankl, V. E. (1973). *The doctor and the soul*. New York: Alfred A. Knopf. (Original work published 1946)

Freud, S., & Breuer, J. (1924). On the psychical mechanisms of hysterical phenomena. In S. Freud, *Collected papers*, Vol. 1. London: Hogarth Press and The Institute of Psychoanalysis. (Original work published 1893)

Garfield, S. L., & Bergin, A. E. (Eds.). (1986). *Handbook of psychotherapy and behavior change*. New York: John Wiley & Sons.

Hackett, T. P., & Weisman, A. D. (1969). Denial as a factor in patients with heart disease and cancer. *Annals New York Academy of Sciences, 164*, 802–811.

Hall, B., Cross, W., & Freedle, A. (1972). Stages in the development of black awareness. In Jones (Ed.), *Black psychology*. New York: Harper & Row.

Hamburg, D. A., & Adams, J. E. (1967). A perspective on coping behavior. *Archives of General Psychiatry, 17*, 277–284.

Hamilton, D. (Ed.). (1981). Cognitive processes in stereotyping and group behavior. Hillsdale, NJ: Lawrence Erlbaum Associates.

Hollon, S., & Beck, A. T. (1986). Research on cognitive therapies. In S. L. Garfield & A. E. Bergin (Eds.), *Handbook of psychotherapy and behavior change*. New York: John Wiley & Sons.

Horowitz, M. (1980). Psychological response to serious life events. In V. Hamilton & D. Warburton (Eds.), *Human stress and cognition*. New York: John Wiley & Sons.

Horowitz, M. J. (1982). Stress response syndromes and their treatment. In L. Goldberger & S. Breznitz (Eds.), *Handbook of stress*. New York: Free Press.

Horowitz, M. J. (1983). Psychological response to serious life events. In S. Breznitz (Ed.), *The denial of stress*. New York: International Universities Press.

Janoff-Bulman, R. (1979). Characterological versus behavioral self-blame: Inquiries into depression and rape. *Journal of Personality and Social Psychology, 37*, 1798–1809.

Janoff-Bulman, R. (1985). The aftermath of victimization: Rebuilding shattered assumptions. In C. R. Figley (Ed.), *Trauma and its wake*. New York: Brunner/Mazel.

Janoff-Bulman, R. (1989). Assumptive worlds and the stress of traumatic events: Applications of the schema concept. *Social Cognition, 7*, 113–136.

Janoff-Bulman, R. (in press). Understanding people in terms of their assumptive worlds. In D. J. Ozer, J. M. Healy, & A. J. Stewart (Eds.), *Perspectives on personality: Self and emotion*. Greenwich, CT: JAI Press.

Janoff-Bulman, R., & Frieze, I. H. (1983). A theoretical perspective for understanding reactions to victimization. *Journal of Social Issues, 39*, 1–17.

Janoff-Bulman, R., & Lang-Gunn, L. (1989). Coping with disease and accidents: The role of self-blame attributions. In L. Y. Abramson (Ed.), *Social-personal inference in clinical psychology*. New York: Guilford Press.

Janoff-Bulman, R., & Timko, C. (1987). Coping with traumatic life events: The role of denial in light of people's assumptive worlds. In C. R. Snyder & C. Ford (Eds.), *Coping with negative life events: Clinical and social psychological perspectives*. New York: Plenum Press.

Kohut, H. (1971). *The analysis of the self*. New York: International University Press.

Kuhn, T. S. (1962). *The structure of scientific revolutions*. Chicago: The University of Chicago Press.

Lambert, M. J., Shapiro, D. A., & Bergin, A. E. (1986). The effectiveness of psychotherapy. In S. L. Garfield & A. E. Bergin (Eds.), *Handbook of psychotherapy and behavior change*. New York: John Wiley & Sons.

La Planche, J., & Pontalis, J. B. (1973). *The language of psychoanalysis*. New York: W. W. Norton.

Lazarus, R. S. (1983). The costs and benefits of denial. In S. Breznitz (Ed.), *The denial of stress*. New York: International Universities Press.

Lerner, M. J. (1980). *The belief in a just world*. New York: Plenum Press.

Malan, D. H. (1979). *Individual psychotherapy and the science of psychodynamics*. London: Butterworths.

Marris, P. (1975). *Loss and change*. Garden City, NY: Anchor/Doubleday.

McDaniel, S. H., Stiles, W. B., & McGaughey, K. J. (1981). Correlations of male college students' verbal response mode use in psychotherapy with measures of psychological disturbance and psychotherapy outcome. *Journal of Clinical and Consulting Psychology, 49*, 571–582.

Nassi, A. J., & Abramowitz, S. I. (1981). Raising consciousness about women's groups: Process and outcome research. In S. Cox (Ed.), *Female psychology: The emerging self*. New York: St. Martin's Press.

Nisbett, R. E., & Ross, L. (1980). *Human inference: Strategies and shortcomings of so-*

cial judgment. Englewood Cliffs, NJ: Prentice-Hall.

Ogden, T. H. (1983). The concept of internal object relations. *International Journal of Psychoanalysis, 64*, 227–241.

Orlinsky, D. E., & Howard, K. I. (1986). Process and outcome in psychotherapy. In S. L. Garfield & A. E. Bergin (Eds.), *Handbook of psychotherapy and behavior change*. New York: John Wiley & Sons.

Parkes, C. M. (1971). Psycho-social transitions: A field of study. *Social Science and Medicine, 5*, 101–115.

Parkes, C. M. (1975). What becomes of redundant world models? A contribution to the study of adaptation to change. *British Journal of Medical Psychology, 48*, 131–137.

Perloff, L. S. (1983). Perceptions of vulnerability to victimization. *Journal of Social Issues, 39*, 41–62.

Peterson, C., Schwartz, S. M., & Seligman, M. E. P. (1981). Self-blame and depressive symptoms. *Journal of Personality and Social Psychology, 41*, 253–259.

Pomerleau, O. F., & Rodin, J. (1986). Behavioral medicine and health psychology. In Garfield & Bergin (Eds.), *Handbook of psychotherapy and behavior change*. New York: John Wiley & Sons.

Popper, K. R. (1963). *Conjectures and refutations: The growth of scientific knowledge*. New York: Harper & Row.

Rogers, C. (1961). *On becoming a person*. New York: Houghton Mifflin.

Roth, I., Rhudick, P. J., Shaskan, D. A., Slobin, M. S., Wilkinson, A. E., & Young, H. (1964). Long-term effects on psychotherapy of initial treatment conditions. *Journal of Psychiatric Research, 2*, 283–297.

Rothbart, M. (1981). Memory processes and social beliefs. In D. Hamilton (Ed.), *Cognitive processes in stereotyping and group behavior*. Hillsdale, NJ: Lawrence Erlbaum Associates.

Rothbart, M., & Oliver, J. (1985). Social categorization and behavioral episodes: A cognitive analysis of the effects of intergroup contact. *Journal of Social Issues, 41*, 81–104.

Scheppele, K. L., & Bart, P. B. (1983). Through women's eyes: Defining danger in the wake of sexual assault. *Journal of Social Issues, 39*, 63–81.

Seligman, M. E. P. (1975). *Helplessness: On depression, development, and death*. San Francisco: W. H. Freeman.

Silka, L. (1989). *Intuitive judgments of change*. New York: Springer-Verlag.

Silver, R. L., & Wortman, C. B. (1980). Coping with undesirable life events. In J. Garber & M. E. P. Seligman (Eds.), *Human helplessness: Theory and application*. New York: Academic Press.

Snyder, C. R. (1989). Reality negotiation: From excuses to hope and beyond. *Journal of Social and Clinical Psychology, 8*, 130–157.

Snyder, C. R., & Higgins, R. L. (1988). Excuses: Their effective role in the negotiation of reality. *Psychological Bulletin, 104*, 23–35.

Staples, F. R., & Sloane, R. B. (1976). Truax factors, speech characteristics, and therapeutic outcome. *Journal of Nervous and Mental Disease, 163*, 135–140.

Taylor, S. E. (1983). Adjustment to threatening events: A theory of cognitive adaptation. *American Psychologist, 38*, 1161–1173.

Taylor, S. E., Wood, J. V., & Lichtman, R. R. (1983). It could be worse: Selective evaluation as a response to victimization. *Journal of Social Issues, 39*, 19–40.

Tennen, H., Affleck, G., & Gerschman, K. (1986). Self-blame among parents of infants with perinatal complications: The role of self-protective motives. *Journal of Personality and Social Psychology, 50*, 690–696.

Timko, C., & Janoff-Bulman, R. (1985). Attributions, vulnerability, and psychological adjustment: The case of breast cancer. *Health Psychology, 4*, 521–544.

Uhlenhuth, E. H., & Duncan, D. B. (1968). Subjective change with medical student therapists: II. Some determinants of change in psychoneurotic outpatients. *Archives of General Psychiatry, 18*, 532–540.

Veronen, L. J., & Kilpatrick, D. G. (1983). Rape: A precursor of change. In *Life-span developmental psychology: Non-normative life events*. New York: Academic Press.

Watzlawick, P., Weakland, J., & Fish, R. (1974). *Change: Principles of problem formation and problem resolution*. New York: W. W. Norton.

Weinstein, N. D. (1980). Unrealistic optimism about future life events. *Journal of Personality and Social Psychology, 39*, 806–820.

Weinstein, N. D., & Lachendro, E. (1982). Egocentrism as a source of unrealistic optimism. *Personality and Social Psychology Bulletin, 8,* 195–200.

Weisman, A. D. (1972). *On dying and denying.* New York: Behavioral Publications.

Weisman, A. D., & Hackett, T. P. (1967). Denial as a social act. In S. Levin & R. J. Kahana (Eds.), *Psychodynamic studies on aging: Creativity, reminiscing, and dying.* New York: International Universities Press.

Wicklund, R. A., & Brehm, J. W. (1976). Perspectives on cognitive dissonance. Hillsdale, NJ: Lawrence Erlbaum Associates.

Wills, T. A. (1981). Downward comparison principles in social psychology. *Psychological Bulletin, 90,* 245–271.

Zeiss, A. M., Lewinsohn, P. M., & Munoz, R. F. (1979). Nonspecific improvement effects in depression using interpersonal, cognitive and pleasant events focused treatments. *Journal of Consulting and Clinical Psychology, 47,* 427–439.

CHAPTER 25

COGNITIVE-BEHAVIORAL INTERVENTIONS

Rick E. Ingram
Philip C. Kendall
Audrey H. Chen

Psychological health represents the core concern of clinical psychological theory, research, and treatment. While efforts aimed at maintaining mental health have received increasing attention, the fundamental emphasis of clinical psychological science remains the restoration of healthy functioning through the treatment of psychological disorders. To treat these disorders, several major schools of psychological theory have spawned literally hundreds of specific therapies. Among the recent and most widely used intervention methods are those based on cognitive and cognitive-behavioral strategies.

The extensive development of cognitive approaches over the last decade is evidenced by the numerous volumes discussing the theoretical foundations, empirical research, and practical applications of these methods (e.g., Beck & Emery, 1985; Dobson, 1988; Ingram, 1986; Kendall, in press; Kendall & Hollon, 1979, 1981; Meichenbaum, 1977). The advent of a number of journals specializing in cognitive clinical theory, research, and interventions further attests to the prominence of this perspective. In a survey reported by

D. Smith (1982), for example, clinical and counseling psychologists identified their "school" of thought. Though most were eclectic (approximately 40%), cognitive-behavioral and psychodynamic approaches were second (approximately 10% each). Considering the relative recency of cognitive-behavioral approaches, there appear to be a great number of professionals who have integrated these approaches into their practice. Indeed, as at least some practitioners accept cognitive-behavioral therapy as a form of eclecticism, many of the 40% who self-defined as eclectic also may make use of cognitive-behavioral procedures.

Given the prominence of cognitively oriented therapy approaches, the purpose of this chapter is to provide an overview of the cognitive/cognitive-behavioral treatment paradigm. In particular, we first discuss the definitions, assumptions, and features that both characterize the cognitive-behavioral approach and that differentiate it from other approaches. To place these features and assumptions into a proper context, we also briefly discuss the historical foundations of these current interventions. Finally, to illustrate the fundamental elements of cognitive-behavioral treatment, we provide some examples of specific cognitive-behavioral therapies.

It is important to note that the emphasis of this chapter is on cognitive-behavioral treatments as they apply to issues of psychological health. However, the essential assumptions and features of the approach are also relevant to physical health questions. In this vein, Bradley and Kay (1985) have provided an excellent discussion of the expanding role of cognition in health psychology.

HISTORICAL PRECIS OF COGNITIVE-BEHAVIORAL APPROACHES TO TREATMENT

To fully appreciate the present assumptions and characteristics of cognitive-behavioral treatment, it is useful to consider the origins of this approach. While many clinical scientist-practitioners may prefer to view themselves as experimental psychologists who specialize in clinical issues, the evolution of clinical psychology does not always parallel the evolution of experimental psychology. For instance, while behaviorism was taking root in experimental psychology, clinical psychology was shifting from a reliance on Freudian concepts to an emphasis on Humanistic/Rogerian concepts. Clinical behaviorism was not far behind, however, and was soon established as the dominant paradigm in scientific clinical psychology. Buoyed by empirical literature interpreted as demonstrating the effectiveness of behaviorist interventions, clinical behaviorism enjoyed much success. Numerous researchers, for example, sought to delineate the stimulus-response links that would explain behavior and thus allow for the prediction and modification of abnormal behavior. Other researchers tested the effectiveness of learning principles developed in experimental laboratories in analog treatment studies of behavior disorders, most notably conditioned anxious behavior. Journals specializing in behavioral therapy and applied behavior analysis also were initiated and professional associations were developed to advance behavior therapy and applied behavior analysis.

While the behavioral paradigm was similarly influential in experimental psychology, researchers started to question the adequacy of strict behavioral concepts to explain complex behavior. Accordingly, experimental psychologists began to return to an earlier interest in cognitive variables, this time from a more scientific perspective. Cog-

nitive constructs, models, and methodologies soon boomed in experimental and developmental psychology, while social psychology and clinical psychology eventually followed suit. However, the acknowledgment and incorporation of cognition in behaviorally dominated clinical psychology was a gradual shift rather than an abrupt change.

There seem to be three reasonably distinct stages in this conceptual shift to cognitive concepts. First, given the belief of some learning theorists that the study of cognition was not scientific, initial shifts to a cognitive perspective were of necessity quite subtle. For instance, in developing the tenets of social learning theory, which emphasized vicarious learning processes, Bandura (1969) and Mischel (1973) suggested the importance of cognitive variables, but placed these variables within the context of "covert behavior." It was this context that allowed them access to "legitimate" scientific status. These social learning approaches thus represented the early antecedents of contemporary cognitive therapy.

Second, the gradual inclusion of cognitive variables into the realm of scientific respectability was followed primarily by a group of clinical researchers who were interested in the development of effective treatment procedures. As such, they focused considerable attention on explicitly cognitive targets and developed both cognitive and behavioral procedures designed to affect these targets. The emphasis at this stage was on effective treatment development rather than on refinement and development of cognitive conceptual frameworks. Nevertheless, these researchers moved away from the notion of cognitions as simply internal behaviors and maintained that the cognitive system operated according to sets of principles that could be substantially different from traditional learning principles. Moreover, such cognitions were viewed as having legitimate causal implications in dysfunctional behavior. Thus, emphasis was generally on how individuals cognitively structure their experience and, in particular, on modifying specific dysfunctional cognitions. Employing the term *cognitive-behavioral* for probably the first time, this group included works by Kendall and Hollon (1979, 1981), Mahoney (1974), Lazarus (1981), and Meichenbaum (1977). Additionally, Beck (1976; Beck, Rush, Shaw, & Emery, 1979), and Ellis (1963) were central among this group, although they came from traditions that were not originally behaviorist.

The third stage is represented by contemporary

work in cognitive-behavioral psychology. Activities here are too diverse to identify a particular focus. However, one can distinguish several general themes. One such theme in contemporary cognitive-behavioral theory and research is an increased emphasis on the conceptual development of models of cognition and the role of cognition in psychological dysfunction. Given that some previous cognitive constructs in cognitive-behavioral psychology developed independently of ongoing efforts in basic cognitive psychology (Winfrey & Goldfried, 1986), much current conceptual work has focused on adaptation of the methods, data, and constructs from experimental cognitive psychology to cognitive-behavioral clinical psychology (e.g., Ingram, 1986; Merluzzi, Glass, & Genest, 1981).

An additional theme concerns the conceptual understanding and modification of emotion in cognitive-behavioral therapy paradigms (e.g., Greenberg & Safran, 1987; Guidano & Liotti, 1983; Kendall, 1985). An emphasis on elucidating the disordered processes that are modified by cognitive-behavioral interventions, and thus responsible for therapeutic improvement, is also a current focus of contemporary theory and research efforts (Hollon, Evans, & DeRubeis, 1987; Simons, Garfield, & Murphey, 1984). Relatedly, investigators continue to empirically examine the effectiveness of cognitive-behavioral approaches, but with an increased precision that reflects the methodological advances in the field (see Hollon & Beck, 1986). Finally, at both the conceptual and empirical levels, efforts also are underway to broadly integrate cognitive-behavioral interventions with other diverse psychotherapeutic approaches to human change (Goldfried, 1980, 1982; Wolfe & Goldfried, 1988; see also Haaga, 1986). Interventions that integrate cognitive and behavioral approaches may be a part of, or the stimulus for, this larger trend.

DESCRIPTIVE FEATURES OF COGNITIVE-BEHAVIORAL TREATMENT

Delineation of the descriptive features of cognitive interventions is important for two reasons. First, examination of these features allows for distinguishing between what constitutes cognitive-behavioral treatment from what does not. Second, once the domain of cognitive-behavioral treatment is understood, the key commonalities

and distinctions between various cognitive-behavioral approaches can be identified. In considering what constitutes cognitive-behavioral therapy, however, it is important to guard against extending uniformity myths (Kiesler, 1966), which would imply that all cognitive-behavioral treatments are essentially the same in both procedures and underlying theoretical conceptualizations of psychological disturbance; however, this is not the case (Hollon & Beck, 1986; Kendall & Bemis, 1983). While there are a set of features and assumptions that, by definition, characterize cognitive-behavioral interventions, it is important to keep in mind that these various interventions can be distinguished by different clinical procedures, by demonstrated treatment effectiveness, and occasionally by specific theoretical assumptions. For present purposes, we refer to "the cognitive-behavioral approach" as a group of cognitive-behavioral therapies that share a core set of assumptions and characteristics. We do not intend to suggest, however, that this approach represents a consolidated, uniform, or single approach to treatment; there are meaningful differences among specific cognitive-behavioral interventions.

Definitions

As a core definition, cognitive-behavioral therapy emphasizes both theoretical and procedural elements. Specifically, cognitive-behavioral therapy is defined as those sets of therapeutic procedures that (a) embody theoretical conceptualizations of change that place primary importance on cognitive processes and (b) procedurally target at least some therapeutic maneuvers, especially at altering aspects of cognition.

Such a definition has several functions. For example, it suggests certain implications for conceptualizations of human change processes, and consequently, for translating these theoretical ideas into further therapeutic development, modifications, and refinements. Additionally, such a definition provides a basis for discriminating between cognitive-behavioral and non–cognitive-behavioral approaches. Approaches solely concerned with the modification of behavior, for instance, would not qualify as cognitive-behavioral even though they may unwittingly modify cognitive processes. Hollon and Beck (1986) argued in this regard that systematic desensitization would not be considered a cognitive-behavioral approach as behavioral rather than cognitive change is the therapeutic goal as well as the presumed causal mechanism. Similarly, as Dobson and Block (1988) noted, approaches employing operant techniques with the sole purpose of modifying behavior, even though they may alter some aspect of cognitive functioning, would not be cognitive-behavioral any more than would approaches emphasizing childhood traumas and cathartic expression.

A cognitive-behavioral model of psychopathology and psychotherapy places major emphasis on (a) both the learning process and the influence of the contingencies and models in the environment while (b) underscoring the centrality of mediating/information-processing factors in both the development and remediation of disorders (Kendall, 1985). The model does not concern itself with efforts to uncover unconscious early trauma, nor does it belabor biological, neurological, and genetic aspects of pathology. Rather, these latter factors are accepted as influential in certain disorders but of less concern in many others. Similarly, affective processes, family systems, and social context are not given primary emphasis, but these factors are recognized and integrated. Cognitive-behavioral analyses of psychological disorders involve considerations of numerous features of the client's internal and external environment and represent an integrationist perspective.

A further differentiation can be made regarding the type of pathology generally seen as appropriate for cognitive intervention: *cognitive deficits* versus *cognitive distortion*. Deficits refer to an absence of thinking (lacking cognitive activity where it would be beneficial), whereas distortions refer to dysfunctional thinking processes (Kendall, 1985). This distinction highlights the differences between the forerunners of adult cognitive-behavioral therapy that focused on modifying dysfunctional thinking in adults (e.g., Beck, Ellis) and early cognitive-behavioral training with children that dealt mostly with teaching to remediate deficiencies in thinking (e.g., self-instructions; Kendall, 1977; Meichenbaum & Goodman, 1971). The distinction can be furthered when types of psychopathology are considered. Depression and anxiety are more related to cognitive distortions, whereas other disorders such as hypomania may reflect cognitive deficiencies. Some data support this distinction in children where depressed and/or socially isolated children have problems that resemble distorted thinking (misperceiving demands of the environment; excessive self-criticism) while hyperactive/impulsive children have problems related to an absence of thinking (Kendall & Morison, 1984; Kendall, Stark, & Adams, in press). Thus, the deficiency/distortion distinction appears to offer promise as a way of conceptualizing different types of cognitive disorders.

Assumptions

Cognitive-behavioral procedures also can be distinguished by their underlying assumptions. While there are no universally agreed upon assumptions, the following list based on Dobson (1988), Kendall and Bemis (1983), Kendall and Hollon (1979), and Mahoney and Arnkoff (1978) seems reasonable according to current theory and data.

1. Individuals respond to cognitive representations of environmental events rather than to the events per se.
2. Learning is cognitively mediated.
3. Cognition mediates emotional and behavioral dysfunction. It should be noted that this assumption does not imply a linear focus where cognition is primary, but rather that cognitive variables are interrelated with affective and behavioral variables and thus affects these variables (and vice versa).
4. At least some forms of cognition can be monitored.
5. At least some forms of cognition can be altered.
6. As a corollary to numbers 3, 4, and 5, altering cognition can change dysfunctional patterns of emotion and behavior.
7. Both cognitive and behavioral therapeutic change methods are desirable and can be integrated.

It would be premature to say that we know what it takes "cognitively" to attain and maintain satisfactory adjustment. Differences in definitions of adjustment obviously exist, yet there is sufficient information to propose that (a) realistic, rational, and flexible cognitive styles are desirable over unrealistic, irrational, and rigid styles (cf. Arnkoff & Glass, 1982); and (b) having access to and engaging in the cognitive processes necessary for problem resolution is superior to deficient processing (cf. Spivack & Shure, 1974). Thus, the cognitive-behavioral model does not offer a unitary explanation as much as a series of guideposts for adjustment. For example, the model does not prescribe that all people think positive thoughts or that they avoid all negative thinking. The model does hold, however, that positive and negative thinking and the relationships between them (e.g., sequence and other topological characteristics) are important (Kendall, Howard, & Hays, 1989).

Features

Although we have offered potential defining features of cognitive-behavioral therapy (i.e., the theoretical importance of cognitive causal factors and methods intended specifically to alter these cognitive variables), interventions falling within this class of therapeutic procedures may vary on a number of different dimensions. It is therefore often difficult to distinguish what does or does not constitute a cognitive-behavioral therapy. In clarifying the nature of cognitive-behavioral therapy, a construct borrowed from experimental cognitive psychology, cognitive prototypes, can be quite helpful. According to Rosch (1973, 1975), prototypes represent abstractions of superordinate natural categories. The degree of "relatedness" of category members depends on the number of features these members share with the category. Hence, if the natural category is "bird," a robin is seen as more typical than a penguin because it shares more features with the prototypical bird, although both qualify as birds. Such prototype constructs have previously been employed in psychopathology research to facilitate diagnosis (see Horowitz, French, Lapid, & Weckler, 1982; Horowitz, Weckler, & Doren, 1983; Nasby & Kihlstrom, 1986).

In determining therapy class membership, as in all cases of natural categories, it is helpful to examine the number of features that the particular case has in common with the prototype. The prototype construct suggests that it is not only possible to identify those interventions that are cognitive therapy, but also to distinguish among varying degrees of cognitive-behavioral. While some therapies may represent prototypical instances of the cognitive-behavioral approach, others may approximate this to a much lesser degree and be considered only somewhat cognitive-behavioral. Although we suggest that any therapeutic set of procedures possessing the two core assumptions that we earlier defined can be considered cognitive-behavioral (i.e., conceptualizations of change emphasizing cognition, as well

as treatments aimed at altering cognitions), the greater the number of other features present, the more cognitive-behavioral a given therapy can be considered.

In line with the assumptions underlying cognitive-behavioral therapy, there is no universally agreed upon set of defining features. We think the following list, however, is both reasonably accurate and comprehensive. As we have noted before, the first two features represent the core characteristics of any therapy considered to be cognitive-behavioral.

1. Cognitive variables are assumed to be important causal mechanisms. This does not imply that there are not other meaningful causal mechanisms as well, but that cognitive variables are important in the constellation of processes that elicit the onset and course of a disorder.
2. Following from the assumption that cognitive variables are presumed to be causal agents, at least some of the methods and techniques of the intervention are aimed specifically at cognitive targets.
3. A functional analysis of the variables maintaining the disorder (including cognitive, behavioral, and affective variables) is undertaken.
4. Cognitive-behavioral approaches employ both cognitive and behavioral therapeutic strategies. Typically, even behavioral tactics are aimed at cognitive objectives, such as in the case of Beck's (Beck et al., 1979) approach to depression, which employs behavioral homework assignments intended to help modify dysfunctional thoughts and beliefs.
5. There is a strong emphasis on empirical verification. This emphasis is manifested in two different domains. The first is in empirical research designed to establish the efficacy of the therapeutic procedures and help determine the processes by which these procedures function. The second is an emphasis within actual therapy on employing objective assessment to examine therapeutic progress. Again turning to treatment for depression, Beck (Beck et al., 1979) recommended a session-by-session client Beck Depression Inventory (BDI), to help objectively assess the range and degree of the client's depressive symptoms.
6. Cognitive-behavioral approaches are typically time limited (not considered long-term therapy in the classic sense) with plans for booster,

maintenance, and related sessions to buttress and improve treatment efforts. For example, cognitive-behavioral programs for childhood/adolescent anxiety disorders last for typically 16 to 20 sessions (e.g., Kendall, Kane, Howard, & Siqueland, 1989) and approximately 20 sessions for adult depression (Beck et al., 1979) is common.

7. Cognitive-behavioral approaches are collaborative enterprises (e.g., collaborative empiricism) where the client and therapist form a working alliance to alleviate dysfunctional thinking and behavior.

8. Cognitive-behavioral therapists are active and make recommendations and suggestions (directive) rather than being passive and nondirective.

9. Cognitive-behavioral approaches are educational in nature. Clients learn about the cognitive-behavioral model of dysfunction, the role of their thinking in the maintenance of dysfunction, and the need to modify dysfunctional cognition and behavior.

REPRESENTATIVE COGNITIVE-BEHAVIORAL PROCEDURES

Many specific cognitive-behavioral therapies exist. While it is outside the scope of this chapter to describe all of these specific interventions, we will first discuss several major categories of cognitive-behavioral therapy (summaries and reviews of specific interventions can be found in Dobson, 1988; Hollon & Beck, 1986; and Kendall, 1987), and then describe typical examples of therapies that fall within these categories.

Categories of Cognitive-Behavioral Interventions

Dobson and Block (1988) and Mahoney and Arnkoff (1978) described three general classes of cognitive-behavioral interventions that vary according to the general goal of the therapy: coping skills, cognitive restructuring, and problem-solving. Such approaches are not seen as exclusive but rather differ in terms of emphasis.

Coping skills approaches are those that focus on helping individuals develop skills for adapting to stressful circumstances that are beyond their current level of mastery. Meichenbaum's (1985) *Stress Inoculation Training* (SIT) is a relevant ex-

ample of coping skills approaches. After an extensive review of the literature on stress, Meichenbaum (1985) outlined a set of guidelines that were incorporated into his treatment program and that emphasized the systematic acquisition of coping skills. Specifically, these concepts parallel Orne's (1965) immunization model, which suggests that learning to deal with smaller amounts of stress helps to inoculate against the deleterious effects of stress in larger amounts. Following this model, Meichenbaum argued that if individuals learn to cope with small, manageable amounts of stress, they will be "inoculated" against future levels of stress that may be much more significant and less controllable.

Stress inoculation training involves three specific stages. The first stage is referred to as the educational phase and seeks to provide clients with a conceptualization of their stress responses and how self-statements exacerbate or even create this stress. This conceptualization emphasizes the link between maladaptive emotions and critical self-statements in potentially stressful situations. Adequate client conceptualization of SIT is essential for therapeutic improvement because clients must accept at some level that their thoughts (self-statements) are causally related to maladaptive emotions before they will be willing to alter these cognitions. During the educational stage, clients also are asked to monitor and record the types of self-statements they generate.

In the second phase of training, the acquisition stage, clients are taught a number of cognitive and behavioral coping skills, such as relaxation, replacement of negative self-statements with coping self-statements, and self-reinforcement. The therapist strives to ensure that coping skills are mastered with regard to four specific aspects of the stress experience: (a) the preparatory stage, in which the client makes self-statements to aid in preparing for the stressful experience; (b) self-statements that assist the client in managing negative emotions when beginning to experience the stressful event; (c) self-statements that aid in coping with certain elements of the event that may increase arousal; and (d) reinforcing attempts to cope effectively.

Once these four aspects can be adequately mastered, the third and final stage of SIT, the application phase, is introduced. In this stage, the client is exposed to the stressful situation in graduated steps and encouraged to practice the skills and utilize the information he or she has acquired in the first two stages of treatment. While the stressful situation is sometimes in vivo, it also may be imaginal.

A study by Kendall et al. (1979) illustrates a stress inoculation approach for health-related problems. Kendall et al. compared the effectiveness of a cognitive-behavioral (stress inoculation–like) treatment and a patient education treatment in reducing the stress of patients undergoing cardiac catheterization. To control the effects of the increased attention given to treated patients, an attention-placebo control group was employed. A final control group completed the assessment measures but received only the typical, current hospital experience (i.e., current conditions control). The results of the study indicated that the patient's self-reported anxiety was significantly lower after the intervention for the cognitive-behavioral, patient education, and attention-placebo groups than for the current-hospital conditions control. However, self-reported anxiety levels during the catheterization were significantly lower only for the cognitive-behavioral and patient-education groups. Physicians and technicians independently rated the patients' behavior during catheterization, and these ratings indicated that the patients receiving cognitive-behavioral treatments were best adjusted (e.g., least tense, least anxious, most comfortable). The patient education group was rated as better adjusted than the two control groups, but significantly less well adjusted than the cognitive-behavioral group.

Cognitive restructuring methods focus on increasing the individual's accurate appraisal of information by altering some aspect of his or her cognitive structures, or belief system. Here the emphasis is clearly on the modification of distorted cognitive processing. Examples of cognitive restructuring methods include Ellis' Rational Emotive Therapy (RET) and Beck's (Beck et al., 1979) cognitive therapy approach. RET will be discussed first.

RET is one of the earliest approaches to psychotherapy classified as cognitive-behavioral, having been formulated by Ellis (see Ellis, 1963). Like Beck, Ellis had been extensively trained in the psychoanalytic tradition. However, following this training and some experience in psychoanalytic treatment, Ellis questioned many of the therapeutic tenets of psychoanalysis such as the extensive length of treatment thought to be required for positive effects. He began experimenting with more active and directive therapy methods, which

gradually evolved into his theory of psychological dysfunction and treatment. Although developed in the 1950s, RET remained a frequently employed approach throughout the 1970s and 1980s.

RET is based on an A-B-C (and sometimes D and E) paradigm. The A, activating experience, is the event to which the individual is exposed. B stands for belief, or the series of thoughts and self-statements the individual has in response to the activating event. These cognitions are part of a core set of irrational beliefs that dysfunctional individuals possess. While many cognitive clinical theorists suggest that specific dysfunctional or irrational beliefs influence maladaptive emotional responses to certain events, Ellis is unique in proposing a standard set of negative beliefs that specifies that the individual must do, think, feel, or have something in order to be happy (e.g., "I must be successful at everything I do to be happy"). C represents the consequences, or behaviors and emotions that result from the belief just experienced.

The ABC paradigm serves as a convenient pneumonic device for clients and thus can help to facilitate an understanding of the link between cognition and affect. In therapy, Ellis seeks to add D and E to the system. D (disputation) stands for the debating, defining, and discriminating that occur between the therapist and client surrounding the irrational belief. Finally, E represents the desired effect that occurs after confronting the irrational beliefs. The therapist directly confronts and encourages the client to discriminate between self-statements that may be objectively true and those that may be irrational. In order to maximize learning and minimize the client's chances to revert to his or her irrational thoughts, RET often includes homework assignments, which may include cognitive exercises, in vivo sensitization, and rational-emotive imagery. Imagery may be used to aid client in holding the worst possible scenario he or she fears. This allows the client an opportunity to practice modifying the negative self-thoughts and verbalizations and replace them with more objective and rational thoughts.

Unfortunately, beyond stressing the need to confront clients and debate their irrational beliefs, Ellis offers few specific therapeutic procedures for helping clients to decrease irrational thinking. From the practicing therapist's standpoint, this lack of specificity makes it difficult to employ procedures that accurately reflect the theoretical rationale underlying RET. Additionally, such a lack of specificity makes it difficult for researchers to adequately test the efficacy of the approach, a difficulty that may account in part for the inconsistent empirical data on RET's effectiveness (T. Smith, 1982; see also Haaga & Davison, 1989).

A cognitive restructuring approach that does offer a specific set of procedures is Beck's cognitive therapy. Based somewhat loosely on schema constructs developed in experimental cognitive psychology, the methods Beck describes are intended to alter the cognitive structures that precipitate maladaptive information processing and either initiate or exacerbate psychological dysfunction. The approach has been found to have beneficial effects, yet there is some debate concerning whether it works in the manner proposed by Beck (see Hollon et al., 1987; Ingram & Hollon, 1986; Simons, Garfield, & Murphey, 1984).

Beck's approach is considered a metacognitive approach, and as such it aims to help individuals test the validity of their belief systems rather than assuming that they are necessarily accurate. This approach presents somewhat of a paradox for clients in that it facilitates a return to normal thinking and functioning by virtue of learning an "unusual" mode of thinking (Evans & Hollon, 1988). Beck suggests several specific cognitive and behavioral procedures to aid this metacognitive shift. As with virtually all cognitive therapy, an early step in the process is to provide a cognitive rationale for the treatment so that clients understand the importance of thinking processes in their emotional and behavioral dysfunction. Behavioral and cognitive self-monitoring methods teach the client to carefully keep track of events, thoughts, and feelings in situations that cause them distress. Cognitive strategies are aimed at helping the client to identify and then alter problematic and presumably inaccurate beliefs. Thus, upon identifying dysfunctional thoughts and beliefs, for example, the client might be taught a series of questions: (a) What is the evidence for the belief? (b) Are there more accurate alternatives to this belief (are there other ways to explain things)? (c) What is the actual meaning of the belief? These questions are thus intended to test the hypothesis that the belief is valid and, if not, to generate more accurate beliefs.

Behavioral homework assignments also are employed and represent a powerful therapeutic tool. These assignments, developed in collaboration by both the therapist and client, are designed to challenge beliefs through direct experience. Thus, a mother who believes that she is a bad mother because she occasionally wishes that she did not have kids may have the assignment to ask several women who she thinks are good mothers if they ever have similar thoughts. Even though Beck's approach is typically referred to as a cognitive therapy, these behavioral assignments attest to the fact that the approach is indeed a cognitive-behavioral system.

Although Beck's cognitive therapy was originally developed for the treatment of depression, it has been recently extended into several different clinical domains. Beck and Emery (1985), for example, have described cognitive therapy applications to anxiety disorders, while Clark (1986) has suggested the utility of cognitive therapy for panic-based disorders. Most recently, the utility of cognitive therapy approaches for marital therapy have been suggested and there also has been discussion of cognitive approaches for personality disorders. While the excursion of cognitive therapy into these different areas is both logically and intuitively appealing, empirical data are needed before conclusions can be drawn with regard to the effectiveness. Caution is particularly apt in the case of personality disorders, because these problems are widely acknowledged as resistant to treatment.

The final category of cognitive-behavioral approaches consists of problem-solving approaches. As the name implies, the purpose of this group of cognitive-behavioral therapies is to help teach clients effective methods for solving the problems of daily living. Contemporary problem-solving therapies have their roots in the era during the late 1960s and early 1970s when social competence and the social context of human problems were recognized as important issues in developing clinical interventions and prevention strategies (D'Zurilla & Goldfried, 1971; D'Zurilla, 1986; Spivak & Shure, 1974; also see Heppner in this volume).

D'Zurilla and Goldfried's (1971) problem-solving therapy represents a prime example of this type of approach (see also D'Zurilla, 1986). They proposed that to facilitate generalized behavior change, problem-solving therapy should serve as a form of therapy in which clients are trained to solve problems and become their own therapists. By training individuals to cope more effectively with problematic situations, they would be able to deal independently and more effectively with situations as they arose in daily living. Further, by increasing the number of effective coping responses that the individual would be capable of making in a problem situation, D'Zurilla and Goldfried (1971) hypothesized that the likelihood of being able to select the most effective response from these number of responses also would be increased.

As outlined by D'Zurilla (1986), problem-solving therapy is conceptualized as occurring in five stages: (a) general orientation, (b) problem definition and formulation, (c) generation of alternatives, (d) decision-making, and (e) verification. There is no specification that the precise order of these steps must be followed for problem-solving to be effective; an individual usually moves back and forth from one stage to another. Therapeutically, however, these steps may be viewed as a way of organizing therapeutic procedures. In the first phase of problem-solving therapy, general orientation, the client's beliefs, values, and appraisals of problematic situations are examined. Therapy at this stage focuses on helping clients to change their individual cognitive sets so that they can learn to assume that problems are a part of everyday life. The client also is taught to identify problem situations as soon as they occur and to inhibit their first impulses in favor of using problem-solving behaviors instead. Problem definition and formulation, the second stage, consists of teaching the client to operationally define and accurately classify the various aspects of the problem situation. The third stage in problem-solving involves the generation of alternative solutions, the core of which lies in brainstorming. Decision-making, the next step, involves choosing which of the different alternatives is best, and verification consists of evaluating the effectiveness of the solution. Thus, problem-solving therapy emphasizes not only teaching clients basic problem-solving skills, but also guides the client in applying these skills to problematic situations.

Problem-solving approaches also have been applied to childhood disorders (e.g., Kendall & Braswell, 1985; Weissberg, Cowen, Lotyczewski, & Gesten, 1983). Cognitive-behavioral therapy for children consists of a class of interventions including self-instructional and social problem-solving training, coping, modeling, affective education, role-playing, and the management of behavioral contingencies. One version of cognitive-behavioral therapy is for the treatment of children with deficits in self-control (e.g., hyperactive, impulsive children). Following several preliminary studies where positive outcomes were found (see Braswell & Kendall, 1987), Kendall and Braswell (1982) conducted a components analysis of a problem-solving treatment for children. As in the previous studies, 8- to 12-year-old subjects were selected via teacher referral for the exhibition of behavior that interfered with academic and social performance in the classroom. The cognitive-behavioral condition received self-instructional training via coping modeling and behavioral contingencies, whereas the behavioral treatment condition involved only task-modeling and contingencies. Dependent measures included teacher rating, task performance, and behavioral observations of off-task behavior in the classroom. The cognitive-behavioral group showed significant improvement and maintenance of improvement on a teacher rating form, while the behavioral and control groups did not. On the teacher ratings of hyperactivity, both the cognitive-behavioral and behavioral groups showed significant change at posttest and maintenance of change at follow-up. Only the subjects in the cognitive-behavioral group, however, showed improvement on a measure of self-concept.

The classroom observations yielded a high degree of variability, but the cognitive-behavioral group displayed relative improvement in the categories of off-task verbal and physical behaviors. Parent ratings of behavior in the home environment did not reveal significant treatment effects. Thus, treatment generalization to the classroom did occur, as indicated by teacher ratings and classroom observations, but generalization to the home did not.

More recently, the cognitive-behavioral problem-solving approach has been applied successfully with conduct-disordered youth. Kazdin and colleagues (Kazdin, Esveldt-Dawson, French, & Chis, 1987) reported improvements on ratings of externalizing problems, while Kendall and associates (Kendall, Rober, McLear, Epps, & Ronan, in press) found significant gains on prosocial behavior. These studies are illustrative of the types of cognitive-behavioral programs used with some children—a focus on overcoming cognitive deficiencies. Alternatively, treatment for childhood disorders such as depression and anxiety (see Kendall, in press) are geared toward correction of distorted information-processing.

Efficacy of Cognitive-Behavioral Treatments

Perhaps most noteworthy in examining issues regarding cognitive-behavioral therapy is the increasing appearance of empirical data evaluating the efficacy of various cognitive-behavioral approaches. Such data have been reported in a myriad of investigations, and a variety of summaries, both meta-analytic and qualitative, are currently available (e.g., Dobson, 1988; Hollon & Beck, 1986; Kendall, 1987, in press; Kendall & Bemis, 1983; Mahoney & Arnkoff, 1978; Steinbrueck, Maxwell, & Howard, 1983). In examining the results of these summaries, several factors preclude simple statements regarding the effectiveness of cognitive interventions. For example, the diversity of distinct cognitive-behavioral approaches prevents a simple answer to the question of effectiveness. Also, significant variations in definitions and duration of outcome criteria, disparate skill levels of the therapists used in studies, the different disorders treated, and variations in methodological adequacy all preclude clear and universal conclusions. Nevertheless, a review of the empirical data suggest that cognitive and cognitive-behavioral procedures appear to have "generally established their efficacy in a variety of disorders" (Hollon & Beck, 1986, p. 476). While not uniform, the empirical data are certainly quite promising.

Although several specific therapies have received support from empirical studies, Beck's cognitive therapy (Beck et al., 1979) for depression has been widely studied and found to be effective in a clear majority of studies. An early study providing support for Beck's treatment model was reported by Rush, Beck, Kovacs, & Hollon (1977). The authors found that depressed outpatients treated with cognitive therapy improved significantly more than outpatients treated with a standard anti-depressant medication regimen. While this study was not without some criticism, it not only precipitated a series of controlled outcome trials that compared the effectiveness of cognitive therapy and pharmacological treatments on both immediate outcome and relapse prevention, but it also facilitated the development of a large multi-center NIMH collaborative project on the psychological treatment of depression. In each case, cognitive therapy has been, at minimum, as effective as pharmacological treatment (Beck, 1986). The empirical picture for cognitively based therapies in general, and for Beck's cognitive therapy in particular, is therefore quite positive.

Is Clinical Psychology a Prescriptive or Conceptual Clinical Science?

Having discussed examples of specific cognitive-behavioral treatment approaches, it is important to attend to several empirical considerations regarding the effectiveness of therapy procedures and the information that such empirical data provide us. As we have previously noted, while not uniform, the research data on the efficacy of cognitive-behavioral approaches are encouraging. What are the practical implications of these encouraging data?

To answer this question it is necessary to look at some possible objectives of therapy outcome research. For example, one goal of therapy outcome research might be to determine which methods are effective for treating which clients with which problems (Kiesler, 1966): "Which specific procedures obtain which results with which patients, in what amount of time, and are these differential results equally enduring" (p. 162, Bergin & Lambert, 1978). This proposal suggests that, in principle, eventually it should be possible to empirically catalog effective treatment techniques for specific problems. According to this philosophy, the purpose of research data is to provide potential "recipes" of well-specified strategies/techniques that have been empirically proven to be successful for well-specified problems, thus allowing for the prescription of certain techniques for certain problems. Behavioral and cognitive-behavioral approaches have been seen as offering the greatest promise for achieving this laudable goal. For instance, the emphasis on employing specific techniques or methods in these approaches conforms nicely to the premises underlying this philosophy. In addition, the reliance on rigorous empirical verification of therapeutic efficacy implies a mechanism for eventually being able to reach the goal of empirical cataloging.

It is worthwhile to briefly examine the assumptions behind this prescriptive philosophy. Earlier we suggested that cognitive-behavioral approaches generally have proven their worth in the outcome literature, and it might thus be suggested that clinical science is steadily progressing toward a body of knowledge that allows for clear recommendations regarding particular therapeutic methods for specific problems. There are two interrelated problems with this assumption, however. The first has to do with the prescriptiveness of empirical findings, and the second concerns what actually is demonstrated when an approach has been found to be effective for a psychological problem. A prescriptive philosophy assumes something analogous to a medical treatment model. For example, different psychopharmacological doses of a medication prescribed by different practitioners for a disorder represent an identical treatment; the medication will always be the same and the dose always measured in the same way no matter who measures it and in which setting. This analogy obviously does not hold for psychological treatment. Even using the same methods for the same disorder, different therapists will "administer" the treatment quite differently due to a variety of factors such as their particular personal attributes and backgrounds, training backgrounds, and the vicissitudes of client circumstances and behaviors. Moreover, study therapists are supervised and closely follow detailed therapy manuals; this is seldom if ever the case in clinical practice. With few exceptions, it is simply not realistic to assume that a method or technique found effective in experimentally rigorous outcome studies is employed in the same way in actual practice.

It is therefore unlikely that clinical researchers will ever be able to prescribe certain treatments for certain disorders, at least in the manner that the treatments are actually tested. Does this then suggest that empirical research that tests the effectiveness of various treatment strategies is unimportant or not useful? Absolutely not; a strong emphasis on empirical testing is the hallmark of both behavioral and cognitive-behavioral approaches and is unequivocally essential. The problem, however, revolves around whether applied clinical psychology is a conceptual or a prescriptive science. As a conceptual science, empirical research informs therapists about human change principles and how these principles tend to be affected by various classes of therapist behaviors. These data then allow therapists to put this knowledge into practice, not in a prescriptive sense, but in a scientific-conceptual sense. Indeed, therapists can be seen as applied scientists who bring to bear their empirically derived knowledge of basic science (the functioning of various change variables)

on particular scientific (client) problems to be solved. Thus, these scientist-practitioners are characterized by a flexibility to apply their basic scientific knowledge in a way that fits best with their personalities and backgrounds, with the clients' personalities and backgrounds, and with the multitude of problems clients bring to therapy. It follows then that outcome research, which tells us most about scientific change principles, will be the most effective in helping clients. On the other hand, "horse race" studies comparing different methods to see what is the most effective are less valuable unless they can provide meaningful information about the therapist and client processes underlying the changes effected by the different treatments. Ultimately, outcome research that explicitly examines questions of process (once a beneficial outcome has been demonstrated) will be of the greatest use in a conceptual science such as clinical psychology.

SUMMARY AND CONCLUSIONS

Cognitive-behavioral treatments are among the most widely employed groups of interventions for improving psychological health. In this chapter we have reviewed the basic definitions, assumptions, and features of this family of approaches and have discussed several prototypic examples of cognitive-behavioral treatment. While acknowledging the encouraging outcome data for several specific cognitive-behavioral strategies, we also have suggested several caveats regarding the interpretation and practical utility of these approaches. Caveats aside, however, it is clear that cognitive-behavioral methods have found their way into the practice of numerous scientists/professionals and, as such, will continue to influence the field of clinical and health psychology for some time to come. While use of these methods is promising, it is clear that much work remains to be done, particularly work examining the process by which cognitive-behavioral methods may impact psychological health, as well as the development of theoretical models describing the role of cognitive-behavioral variables in both healthy and unhealthy functioning. These areas of emphases, along with the activity of numerous cognitive-behavioral researchers, offer considerable promise in providing a more thorough picture of cognitive-behavioral theories and procedures as they pertain to people's psychological health.

REFERENCES

Arnkoff, D. B., & Glass, C. R. (1982). Clinical cognitive constructs: Examination, evaluation, and elaboration. In P. C. Kendall (Ed.), *Advances in cognitive-behavioral research and therapy* (pp. 1–34). New York: Academic Press.

Bandura, A. (1969). *Principles of behavior modification*. New York: Holt, Rinehart, & Winston.

Beck, A. T. (1976). *Cognitive therapy and the emotional disorders*. New York: International University Press.

Beck, A. T. (1986). Cognitive therapy: A sign of retrogression or progress? *The Behavior Therapist, 9*, 2–3.

Beck, A. T., & Emery, G. (1985). *Anxiety and phobias: A cognitive perspective*. New York: Basic Books.

Beck, A. T., Rush, A. J., Shaw, B. F., & Emery, G. (1979). *Cognitive therapy of depression*. New York: Guilford Press.

Bergin, A. E., & Lambert, M. J. (1978). The evaluation of therapeutic outcomes. In S. L. Garfield & A. E. Bergin (Eds.), *Handbook of psychotherapy and behavior change* (2nd ed., pp. 139–190). New York: John Wiley & Sons.

Bradley, L. A., & Kay, R. (1985). The role of cognition in behavioral medicine. In P. C. Kendall (Ed.), *Advances in cognitive-behavioral research and therapy* (Vol. 4, pp. 137–217). Orlando, FL: Academic Press.

Braswell, L., & Kendall, P. C. (1987). Treating impulsive children via cognitive-behavior therapy. In N. S. Jacobson (Ed.), *Psychotherapists in clinical practice* (pp. 153–189). New York: Guilford Press.

Clark, D. M. (1986). A cognitive approach to panic. *Behavior Research and Therapy, 24*, 461–470.

Dobson, K. S. (1988). *Handbook of cognitive-behavioral therapies*. New York: Guilford Press.

Dobson, K. S., & Block, L. (1988). Historical and philosophical bases of the cognitive-behavioral therapies. In K. S. Dobson (Ed.), *Handbook of cognitive-behavioral therapies*. New York: Guilford Press.

D'Zurilla, T. (1986). *Problem-solving therapy: A social competence approach to clinical intervention*. New York: Springer.

D'Zurilla, T., & Goldfried, M. (1971). Problem solving and behavior modification. *Journal of Abnormal Psychology, 78*, 107–126.

Ellis, A. (1963). *Reason and emotion in psychotherapy*. New York: Lyle Stuart.

Evans, M. D., & Hollon, S. D. (1988). Patterns of personal and causal inference: Implications for the cognitive therapy of depression. In L. B. Alloy (Ed.), *Cognitive processes in depression* (pp. 344–377). New York: Guilford Press.

Goldfried, M. R. (1980). Toward the delineation of therapeutic change principles. *American Psychologist, 35*, 991–999.

Goldfried, M. R. (1982). On the history of therapeutic integration. *Behavior Therapy, 13*, 610–623.

Greenberg, L. S., & Safran, J. D. (1987). *Emotion in psychotherapy*. New York: Guilford Press.

Guidano, V. F., & Liotti, G. (1983). *Cognition processes and emotional disorders*. New York: Guilford Press.

Haaga, D. A. (1986). A review of the common principles approach to integration of psychotherapies. *Cognitive Therapy and Research, 10*, 527–538.

Haaga, D. A., & Davison, G. C. (1989). Outcome studies of rational-emotive therapy. In M. E. Bernard & R. DiGuiseppe (Eds.), *Inside rational-emotional therapy: A critical appraisal of the theory and therapy of Albert Ellis*. New York: Academic Press.

Hollon, S. D., & Beck, A. T. (1986). Research on cognitive therapies. In S. L. Garfield & A. E. Bergin (Eds.), *Handbook of psychotherapy and behavior change* (3rd ed., pp. 443–482). New York: John Wiley & Sons.

Hollon, S. D., Evans, M., & DeRubeis, R. (1987). Causal mediation of change in treatment for depression: Discriminating between nonspecificity and noncausality. *Psychological Bulletin, 102*, 139–149.

Horowitz, L. M., French, R., Lapid, J. S., & Weckler, D. (1982). Symptoms and interpersonal problems: The prototype as an integrating concept. In J. C. Andin & D. J. Kiesler (Eds.), *Handbook of interpersonal psychotherapy*. Oxford: Pergamon Press.

Horowitz, L. M., Weckler, D., & Doren, R. (1983). Interpersonal problems and symptoms: A cognitive approach. In P. C. Kendall (Ed.), *Advances in cognitive-behavioral research and therapy* (Vol. 2). New York: Academic Press.

Ingram, R. E. (1986). *Information processing approaches to clinical psychology. Orlando, FL: Academic Press.

Ingram, R. E., & Hollon, S. D. (1986). Cognitive therapy of depression from an information processing perspective. In R. E. Ingram (Ed.), *Information processing approaches to clinical psychology* (pp. 261–284). Orlando, FL: Academic Press.

Kazdin, A. E., Esveldt-Dawson, K., French, N. H., & Chis, A. S. (1987). Problem-solving skills training and relationship therapy in the treatment of antisocial child behavior. *Journal of Consulting and Clinical Psychology, 55,* 76–85.

Kendall, P. C. (1977). On the efficacious use of verbal self-instructional procedures with children. *Cognitive Therapy and Research, 1,* 331–341.

Kendall, P. C. (1985). Toward a cognitive-behavioral model of childhood psychopathology and a critique of related interventions. *Journal of Abnormal Child Psychology, 13,* 357–372.

Kendall, P. C. (1987). Cognitive processes and procedures in behavior therapy. In G. T. Wilson, C. M. Franks, P. C. Kendall, & J. P. Foreyt (Eds.), *Review of behavior therapy: Theory and practice* (11th ed., pp. 114–152). New York: Guilford Press.

Kendall, P. C. (Ed.). (in press). *Child and adolescent therapy: Cognitive-behavioral procedure.* New York: Guilford Press.

Kendall, P. C., & Bemis, K. M. (1983). Thought and action in psychotherapy: The cognitive-behavioral approaches. In M. Hersen, A. E. Kazdin, & A. S. Bellack (Eds.), *The clinical psychology handbook.* Elmsford, NY: Pergamon Press.

Kendall, P. C., & Braswell, L. (1982). Cognitive-behavioral self-control therapy for children: A components analysis. *Journal of Consulting and Clinical Psychology, 50,* 672–689.

Kendall, P. C., & Braswell, L. (1985). *Cognitive behavioral therapy for impulsive children.* New York: Guilford Press.

Kendall, P. C., & Hollon, S. D. (1979). *Cognitive-behavioral interventions: Theory, research, and procedures.* New York: Academic Press.

Kendall, P. C., & Hollon, S. D. (1981). *Assessment strategies for cognitive-behavioral interventions.* New York: Academic Press.

Kendall, P. C., Howard, B. L., & Hays, R. (1989). Self-talk and psychopathology: The balance of positive and negative thinking. *Cognitive Therapy and Research, 13,* 583–598.

Kendall, P. C., Kane, M. T., Howard, B. L., & Siqueland, L. (1989). *Cognitive-behavioral therapy for anxious children: Treatment manual.* (Available from P. C. Kendall, 288 Meeting House Lane, Marion, PA 19066.)

Kendall, P. C., & Morison, P. (1984). Integrating cognitive and behavioral procedures for the treatment of socially isolated children. In A. W. Meyers & W. E. Craighead (Eds.), *Cognitive behavior therapy with children.* New York: Plenum Press.

Kendall, P. C., Rober, M., McLear, S., Epps, J., & Ronan, K. (in press). Cognitive-behavioral treatment of conduct-disordered children. *Cognitive Therapy and Research.*

Kendall, P. C., Stark, K., & Adams, T. (in press). Cognitive deficit or cognitive distortion in childhood depression. *Journal of Abnormal Child Psychology.*

Kendall, P. C., Williams, L., Pechacek, T. F., Graham, L., Shisslak, C., & Herzoff, N. (1979). Cognitive-behavioral and patient education interventions in cardiac catheterization procedures: The Palo Alto medical psychology project. *Journal of Consulting and Clinical Psychology, 47,* 49–58.

Kiesler, D. J. (1966). Some myths of psychotherapy research and the search for a paradigm. *Psychological Bulletin, 65,* 110–136.

Lazarus, A. A. (1981). *The practice of multimodal therapy.* New York: McGraw-Hill.

Mahoney, M. J. (1974). *Cognition and Behavior Modification.* Cambridge, MA: Ballinger.

Mahoney, M. J., & Arnkoff, D. (1978). Cognitive and self-control therapies. In S. Garfield & A. E. Bergin, (Eds.), *Handbook of psychotherapy and behavior change: An empirical analysis* (2nd ed., pp. 689–772). New York: John Wiley & Sons.

Meichenbaum, D. (1977). *Cognitive behavior modification.* New York: Plenum Press.

Meichenbaum, D. (1985). *Stress Inoculation Training.* Elmsford, NY: Pergamon Press.

Meichenbaum, D. H., & Goodman, J. (1971). Training impulsive children to talk to themselves: A means of developing self-control. *Journal of Abnormal Psychology, 77,* 115–126.

Merluzzi, T. V., Glass, C. R., & Genest, M. 1981). *Cognitive Assessment.* New York: Guilford Press.

Mischel, W. (1973). Toward a cognitive social learning reconceptualization of personality. *Psychological Review, 80,* 252–283.

Nasby, W., & Kihlstrom, J. F. (1986). Cognitive assessment of personality and psychopathology. In R. E. Ingram (Ed.), *Information processing approaches to clinical psychology* (pp. 217–239). New York: Academic Press.

Orne, M. (1965). Psychological factors maximizing resistance to stress with special reference to hypnosis. In S. Klausner (Ed.), *The quest for self-control.* New York: Free Press.

Rosch, E. (1973). On the internal structure of perceptual and semantic categories. In T. M. More (Ed.), *Cognitive development and the acquisition of language.* New York: Academic Press.

Rosch, E. (1975). Cognitive representations of semantic categories. *Journal of Experimental Psychology: General, 104,* 192–233.

Rush, A. J., Beck, A. T., Kovacs, M., & Hollon, S. D. (1977). Comparative efficacy of cognitive therapy and pharmacotherapy in the treatment of depressed outpatients. *Cognitive Therapy and Research, 1,* 17–38.

Simons, A. D., Garfield, S. L., & Murphey, G. E. (1984). The process of change in cognitive therapy and pharmacotherapy of depression: Changes in mood and cognition. *Archives of General Psychiatry, 41,* 45–51.

Smith, D. (1982). Trends in counseling and psychotherapy. *American Psychologist, 37,* 802–809.

Smith, T. W. (1982). Irrational beliefs in the cause and treatment of emotional distress: A critical revision of the RET model. *Clinical Psychology Review, 2,* 505–522.

Spivack, G., & Shure, M. B. (1974). *Social adjustment of young children: A cognitive approach to solving real-life problems.* San Francisco: Jossey-Bass.

Steinbrueck, S. M., Maxwell, S. E., & Howard, G. S. (1983). A meta-analysis of psychotherapy and drug therapy in the treatment of unipolar depression with adults. *Journal of Consulting and Clinical Psychology, 51,* 856–863.

Weissberg, R. P., Cowen, E. L., Lotyczewski, B. S., & Gesten, E. L. (1983). The primary mental health project: Seven consecutive years of program outcome research. *Journal of Consulting and Clinical Psychology, 51,* 100–107.

Winfrey, L. L., & Goldfried, M. R. (1986). Information processing and the human change process. In R. E. Ingram (Ed.), *Information processing approaches to clinical psychology.* Orlando, FL: Academic Press.

Wolfe, B. E., & Goldfried, M. R. (1988). Research on psychotherapy integration: Recommendations and conclusions from an NIMH workshop. *Journal of Consulting and Clinical Psychology, 56,* 448–451.

CHAPTER 26

GENERAL FRAMEWORK FOR THE STUDY OF ATTITUDE CHANGE IN PSYCHOTHERAPY

John T. Cacioppo
Charles D. Claiborn
Richard E. Petty
Martin Heesacker

> In opinion change research, a communicator attempts to influence his audience in a predetermined direction; in counseling, the counselor attempts to influence his client to attain the goals of counseling. In both fields . . . characteristics of the communicator . . . the audience, and . . . the communication affect the success of influence attempts. (Strong, 1968, p. 215)

Attitudes represent global and enduring favorable or unfavorable response disposition toward a person, object, or issue. Studies from the structure of motivation (e.g., Dickinson & Dearing, 1979) to the structure of language (e.g., Osgood, Suci, & Tannenbaum, 1957), and from the conceptual organization of transient emotions (e.g., Russell, 1983) and daily moods (e.g., Diener, Larsen, Levine, & Emmons, 1985) to the organization of facial expressions of emotion (e.g., Abelson & Sermat, 1962; Osgood, 1966) have consistently revealed that people organize their perceptions of the world in terms of their evaluative responses (i.e., attitudes) toward stimulus categories. This evaluative categorization of stimuli is so dominant that it can emerge prior to people's recognition of what specifically are the discriminating features of these stimulus categories (Kunst-Wilson & Zajonc, 1980; Zajonc, 1980).

Attitudes, of course, are not the only determinants of behavior in any given situation (cf. Fishbein & Ajzen, 1975), and the importance of factors such as impression management, social norms, response control, and personality are discussed elsewhere in this volume. Attitudes and attitude changes are nevertheless important in psychotherapy because attitudes can influence how people perceive and feel about their world and can have direct and indirect effects on behavior across a wide range of situations.

The direct effect of attitudes on behavior represents the tendency for people to approach, acquire, support, protect, and promote liked, in contrast to disliked objects, persons, and issues. Although there may be intervening psychological operations between attitudes and behavior such as attitude accessibility and behavioral intentions, the emphasis here is on the response side of the information-processing sequence (e.g., response execution). Evidence that existing attitudes predict behaviors has been summarized by Ajzen and Fishbein (1977, 1980). In an illustrative study, Hoyt and Janis (1975) found compliance with an exercise regimen and weight-loss program was enhanced by preceding the exercise program with an attitude change treatment. Briefly, subjects were induced to think carefully (through use of a "balance sheet" procedure) about the costs and benefits of the exercise program or an unrelated health behavior. Subjects who completed the balance sheet for the relevant behavior attended more classes and lost more weight than subjects who completed the balance sheet for an unrelated behavior.

Similarly, clients enter psychotherapy with a set of attitudes that contribute to related behavioral responses. Psychotherapy reveals both information that is discrepant from a subset of these attitudes and inconsistencies among attitudes. These discrepancies might become apparent, for example, in discussions with or among clients, reconceptualizations of events and behaviors, or new behaviors observed or emitted by clients. Because people are motivated to hold internally consistent (Abelson, Aronson, McGuire, Newcomb, Rosenberg, & Tannenbaum, 1968) and veridical (Petty & Cacioppo, 1986a) beliefs and attitudes, these discrepancies can lead to change in one or more attitudes. As the client's attitudes change, so too can the accessibility of related thoughts, feelings, behavioral options, and associated behavioral responses. Hence, although observable responses rather than attitudes are likely to be the ultimate target of change, the general influence of a person's attitudes in effecting and maintaining this change across situations—and the behavioral resistance, noncompliance, and recidivism that can result in the absence of such changes—have rendered attitudes an important construct in counseling and clinical psychology.

The indirect effect of attitudes on behavior stems from the influence of attitudes on people's selective attention to, interpretation of, and recollection of people and events in their world and, subsequently, on their behavior and on the behavior of others toward them. In contrast to focusing on the direct behavioral effects of attitudes, the emphasis here is on the effect of attitudes on an individual's experience and representation of the world (e.g., selective attention, encoding). Lord,

Ross, and Lepper (1979), for instance, exposed students to information about the crime-deterring effectiveness of capital punishment. Half of the students favored capital punishment prior to the message and half of the students opposed capital punishment. In addition, the message was constructed such that half the evidence suggested that capital punishment was an effective deterrent to crime, whereas half the evidence suggested that it was not an effective deterrent. Because the information presented in the message presented both sides of the issue, the gap between the attitudes of students who initially favored or opposed capital punishment might be expected to diminish somewhat. Lord et al. (1979) found the opposite to be the case: each group accepted the evidence supporting their initial attitude and was critical of the evidence contradicting their attitude toward capital punishment. Consequently, each group perceived the evidence presented in the message to support their initial position, and the gap between the beliefs and attitudes of these subjects widened as a result of their exposure to the same "edifying" information. Behavioral measures were not taken in this study, but one would expect the disagreements between these two groups of subjects to have been enhanced rather than lessened by the arguments to which they were all exposed.

Although prior studies of attitudes in psychotherapy have focused primarily on the direct behavioral effects of attitude changes, the effects of attitudes on people's representation of their world and the indirect behavioral effects of attitudes may prove to be equally or more important. Attitudes and attitude changes could be pivotal in psychotherapy, even if attitudes influenced only how people perceived and felt about their world.

The present chapter concerns the attitude change literature and its implications for psychotherapy and psychotherapeutic change. A basic assumption of the present chapter was first articulated by Jerome Frank (1963), who, in his comparative study of the various schools of psychotherapy, noted that research on attitude change is "pertinent to our interests . . . since in psychotherapy the therapist tries to influence his patients" (p. 97). We begin by briefly reviewing historical developments in the field. We then outline a social psychological theory of communication and persuasion—the elaboration likelihood model (ELM; Petty & Cacioppo, 1981, 1986a, 1986b)—which provides a general integrative framework for thinking about attitudes and attitude change. We conclude with a discussion of research using the ELM to study change in psychotherapy.

HISTORICAL CONTEXT

The idea that psychotherapy can be conceptualized as an influence process has perhaps its clearest roots in the work of Frank (1963), Levy (1963), and Strong (1968) and his colleagues. Frank's *Persuasion and Healing*, first published in 1961, set forth a "common factors" view of psychotherapeutic change in which the therapist's verbal and nonverbal communications with the client represented persuasive appeals and constituted the principal mechanism of behavior change. Frank held that the locus of therapeutic change was the client's assumptive world, the "highly structured, complex, interacting set of values, expectations, and images of oneself and others, which guide and in turn are guided by . . . [one's] perceptions and behavior" (p. 27). Regardless of the specific target of the therapist's interventions — for example, the depth of the client's experiencing or the client's skill acquisition — the interventions also could be said to have an influential impact on the client's assumptive world. Changes in the assumptive world were expected in turn to enhance the persistence of client gains in therapy.

Levy (1963) also argued that attitude change research was relevant to the process of interpretation in psychotherapy. He linked variables such as the status of the communicator and the discrepancy between the client's initial attitude and the position advocated by the therapist to the comprehension, interpretation, and acceptance by the client of the therapeutic process and of therapist recommendations (cf. Claiborn & Dowd, 1985). Analog research on the effects of discrepancy indicate that message manipulations can contribute to attitude change, but what constitutes an optimal level of discrepancy and why are not clear from this model.

Strong (1968) developed a two-stage model of interpersonal influence in psychotherapy that was derived from the work by Festinger (1957) and Hovland and his colleagues (e.g., Hovland, Janis, & Kelley, 1953). In the first stage, therapists achieve credibility (expertise, trustworthiness, attractiveness) and power in the eyes of the client. In the second stage, the therapist attempts to influence the client by recommending positions that are dissonant to the client. By virtue of having achieved high credibility before the influence attempt, the therapist theoretically avoids the client reducing his or her cognitive dissonance simply by derogating the source or by discounting the importance of the issue (cf. Bochner & Insko, 1966).

Strong's (1968) model stimulated research on two fronts: (a) how particular features of a therapist contribute to his or her perceived expertise, trustworthiness, and attractiveness; and (b) how these characteristics affect the therapist's ability to influence the client. The focus of this research, like the model itself, is on the therapist rather than on the interaction between the therapist and client as the active agent in the influence process. Consequently, source factors, in contrast to characteristics of the message, recipient, modality, and context, have received the most attention in research on psychotherapy and attitude change. This is problematic because by focusing on the attitudinal effects of source factors, interactions involving message, recipient, modality, and contextual factors are masked, and the impression is created that there are no general principles of attitude change. For instance, prior research has found that highly credible (e.g., expert) therapists sometimes lead to more attitude change (e.g., Heppner & Dixon, 1978; Strong & Schmidt, 1970), sometimes lead to about the same attitude change (e.g., Greenberg, 1969; Sprafkin, 1970), and sometimes lead to less attitude change (e.g., Heesacker, 1986) than therapists low in credibility. These conflicting results are similar to the pattern in the social psychological literature that led Himmelfarb and Eagly (1974) to conclude that "after several decades of research, there are few simple and direct empirical generalizations that can be made concerning how to change attitudes" (p. 594).

The belief that there are no general principles of attitude change has been further fueled by the use of different theories to account for the various findings obtained in studies of psychotherapy and attitude change. When attitude change is enhanced by source credibility, investigators generally favor the message learning approach championed by Hovland and his colleagues (e.g., Craighead & Craighead, 1980; DiMatteo & DiNicola, 1982); but when attitude change is unrelated (or inversely related) to source credibility or message learning, investigators seem to favor Festinger's (1957) theory of cognitive dissonance as the basis for understanding attitude change and for designing therapeutic interventions (e.g., Brehm, 1976). Recent reviews of these theoretical perspectives and conflicting findings are provided by Corrigan, Dell, Lewis, and Schmidt (1980), Heppner and Claiborn (1989), and Heppner and Dixon (1981).

Importantly, the emphasis on the simple main effects of source, message, recipient, modality, and contextual factors on attitudes has been replaced over the past decade in the social psychological literature by an emphasis on the recipient (client) as a cognitively active participant in persuasion and on the interactive nature of the influence process. In the next section, we review an integrative framework of attitude change processes that has emerged from this research, and we discuss conceptual and methodological issues in the translation of this framework to psychotherapy. The approach taken here is based on Petty and Cacioppo's (1981, 1986a, 1986b) ELM of persuasion, which explicates how people relate incoming information to their previous experiences, knowledge, and attitudes. According to the ELM, for instance, the client is an active agent in the change process. Attitudes are a function of the thoughts and feelings evoked by an influence attempt, which in turn are a (sometimes complex) function of factors such as the person's knowledge, involvement, and motives, as well as the context and message content.

Effective and persisting persuasion within this framework does not rest on some invariant of the therapist or message, but rather requires an understanding of the functions served by the target attitudes and behaviors and the idiosyncratic manner in which clients think about the message arguments. This is because persisting attitude change is posited to be the consequence of idiosyncratic, issue-relevant thinking that favors the recommendation. For instance, what from the perspective of classical rhetoric theory might seem brilliant, persuasive arguments are anticipated by the ELM to provoke heated counterarguments and resistance in certain circumstances, whereas what might appear to one person to be logically flawed arguments could produce favorable thoughts and acceptance in others. The ELM may be of some general interest in the study of psychotherapy, then, because it provides a coherent means of thinking about the effects of many kinds of variables that come into play in persuasion and provides a means of understanding what some-

times appears to be conflicting results on attitude change attributed to these variables.

ELABORATION LIKELIHOOD MODEL

Prior to the development of the ELM, there were two major approaches to the study of persuasion. In the first, attitude change was viewed as resulting from a change in the salient beliefs about a particular position, whereas in the second, attitude change was viewed as resulting from an association between positive or negative stimuli (e.g., credible sources, unconditioned stimuli) and a particular position. For instance, people were conceived as being students of the message arguments who agreed to the extent that they attended to and learned the arguments and incentives for a new position (e.g., Eagly, 1974; Eagly & Warren, 1976; Hovland et al., 1953). This view began to be questioned by research demonstrating that (a) people's attitudes were frequently unrelated to message-learning (e.g., Greenwald, 1968; Insko, Lind, & LaTour, 1976); (b) subject-generated information and attributes were considered in addition to the explicit information provided in persuasive communications (cf. Petty, Wells, & Brock, 1976); (c) attitudes were influenced by biased as well as objective message-processing (e.g., Cacioppo, Petty, & Sidera, 1982; McGuire, 1981; Petty & Cacioppo, 1979a); and (d) attitudes and preferences could also be influenced by what appear to be only superficially related cues, such as the communicator's speed of speech (e.g., Miller, Maruyama, Beaber, & Valone, 1976). Research using retrospective verbal protocol analyses (e.g., "thought-listing" techniques; see Cacioppo & Petty, 1981) further suggested that the informational basis for attitudes was sometimes quite elaborate, but other times inconsistent, incoherent, or impoverished (Cacioppo & Petty, 1981; Petty, Cacioppo, & Goldman, 1981).

Central and Peripheral Routes to Attitude Change

The primary goal of the ELM is to provide a comprehensive framework for organizing, categorizing, and understanding the basic processes underlying the effectiveness of persuasive communications. That is, the ELM attempts to integrate the many seemingly conflicting research findings and theoretical orientations under one conceptual umbrella. After reviewing the literature on attitude persistence, Petty and Cacioppo (1978; Petty, 1977) concluded that the many different empirical findings and theories in the field might profitably be viewed as emphasizing one of two relatively distinct "routes to persuasion." The first was attitude change that likely occurred as a result of a person's careful and thoughtful consideration of the true merits of the information presented in support of an advocacy (central route). The other type of persuasion was what more likely occurred as a result of some simple cue in the persuasion context (e.g., an attractive source) that induced change without necessitating scrutiny of the merits of issue-relevant information (peripheral route). This conceptualization, which is depicted in Figure 26.1, illustrates the interesting possibility that attitudes are multiply determined, and that attitudes that appear on the surface to be the same may have different antecedents and consequences. For instance, the issue-relevant elaboration typifying the central route to persuasion can result in new arguments, or one's personal translations of them, being integrated into one's underlying belief structure for the attitude object, and extensive issue-relevant thinking can increase factors such as the informational coherence, accessibility, and generalizability of the consequent attitude. Attitudes formed through the central route, therefore, were expected to be relatively persistent, resistant to counterpersuasion, and predictive of behavior. The accumulated literature supports these predictions (cf. Petty & Cacioppo, 1986a).

Of course, it would be paralyzing if people were to try to adopt only those attitude positions about which they had thought carefully. This is true even though people are motivated generally to hold correct attitudes. According to the ELM, the numerous attitude stimuli to which people must respond daily, coupled with their limited time and cognitive resources, make it imperative that simple cues, habits, or rules of thumb can be used to guide acceptance or rejection of at least some attitude positions. The resultant attitudes are based on information that is really only superficially or peripherally related to the actual merits of the chosen attitude position, so these attitudes are said to be formed through the peripheral route. Note that whereas taking cognitive shortcuts to arrive at reasonably veridical attitude positions may prove adaptive in the long run, an immediate cognitive consequence is that people are less likely to elaborate on or integrate the message arguments into a core position within their attitude schema. In a psychotherapy setting, the client may comprehend but not engage in the cognitive elaboration required to personalize or internalize the therapist's rationale or position.

(By *personalize* we mean the assimilation of a message argument or recommendation to one's initial point of view, whereas by *internalize* we mean to adopt a message argument or recommendation as one's own.) Hence, attitudes reached through the peripheral route have been shown to be relatively susceptible to change and not highly predictive of behavior (see Figure 26.1; see also the review by Petty & Cacioppo, 1986a).

The Elaboration Likelihood Continuum

The ELM also provides a general theoretical framework for understanding how a variety of factors, such as speed of speech and source credibility, can increase, decrease, or have no effect on attitude change. If the central route is followed, the subjective cogency of the message arguments is predicted to be an important determinant of the individual's acceptance or rejection of the recommendation, and factors in the persuasion setting that might serve as peripheral cues are relatively unimportant determinants of attitudes. If, on the other hand, the peripheral route is followed, then the strength of the message arguments becomes less important and peripheral cues become more important determinants of attitudes.

The ELM also specifies in general terms the conditions that lead to influence through the central versus the peripheral route (see Figure 26.1). For instance, many attitudes and decisions are either perceived to be personally inconsequential or involve matters about which people are uninformed. In these situations, people may still want to be correct in their attitudes and actions, but they are not willing or able to think a great deal about the arguments for or against a particular position. Peripheral cues provide a means of maximizing the likelihood that one's position is correct while minimizing the cognitive requirements for achieving this position. Implicit in the central route, on the other hand, is that people must relate the incoming message arguments to their prior knowledge in such a way as to evaluate the agency and scope of the arguments, that is, they must elaborate cognitively on the information

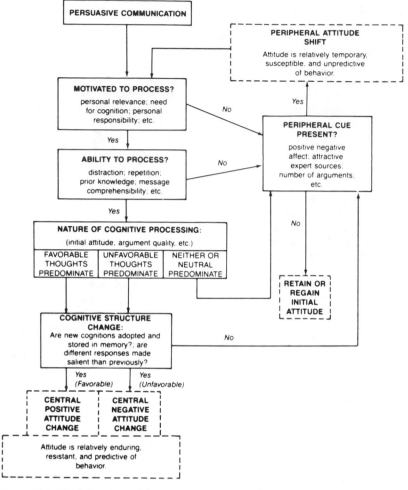

Figure 26.1. Central and peripheral routes to persuasion. The two anchoring endpoints on the elaboration likelihood continuum. From *Communication and Persuasion: Central and Peripheral Routes to Attitude Change* by R. E. Petty and J. T. Cacioppo, 1986, New York: Springer-Verlag. Copyright 1986 by Springer-Verlag. Reprinted by permission of authors.

they perceive to be relevant to the central merits of the advocacy. When conditions foster people's motivation and ability to engage in issue-relevant thinking, the "elaboration likelihood" is said to be high. This means that people are likely to attend to the appeal, attempt to access relevant information from both external and internal sources, scrutinize and make inferences about the message arguments in light of any other pertinent information available, draw conclusions about the merits of the arguments for the recommendation based on their analyses, and consequently derive an overall evaluation of, or attitude toward, the

recommendation. It should be apparent that given the nature of the processing constituting the central and peripheral routes to persuasion, these routes can be viewed as anchors on a continuum ranging from minimal to extensive message elaboration or issue-relevant thinking:

> We view the extent of elaboration received by a message as a continuum going from no thought about the issue-relevant information presented, to complete elaboration of every argument, and complete integration of these elaborations into the person's attitude schema. The likelihood of elaboration will be determined by a person's mo-

tivation and ability to evaluate the communication presented. (Petty & Cacioppo, 1986a, p. 8)

Motivational variables are those that propel and guide people's information-processing and give it purposive character. There are a number of variables that have been found to affect a person's motivation to elaborate on the content of a message. These include (a) task variables, such as the personal relevance of the recommendation (e.g., Petty & Cacioppo, 1979b); (b) individual difference variables, such as the individual's level of need for cognition (e.g., Cacioppo & Petty, 1982; Cacioppo, Petty, & Morris, 1983); and (c) contextual variables such as the number of sources advocating a position (e.g., Harkins & Petty, 1981). Petty and Cacioppo (1986a, chap. 9) noted that these kinds of variables seem to have in common that they act upon a directive, goal-oriented component that might be termed intention, and a nondirective, energizing information-processing component that might be termed effort or exertion. Intention is not sufficient for motivation, for instance, because one can want to think about a message or issue but not exert the necessary effort to move from "intending" to "acting" or "thinking."

If both intention and effort are present, then motivation to think about the advocacy may exist, but message elaboration may still be low because the individual does not have the ability to scrutinize the message arguments. There are a number of variables that can affect an individual's ability to engage in message elaboration, including task variables, such as message comprehensibility (e.g., Eagly, 1974); individual difference variables, such as intelligence (e.g., Eagly & Warren, 1976); and contextual variables, such as distraction (e.g., Petty, Wells, & Brock, 1976) and message repetition (Cacioppo & Petty, 1979, 1989). Note that contextual variables that affect a person's ability to elaborate cognitively on issue-relevant argumentation also can be characterized as factors affecting a person's opportunity to process the message arguments.

If task, individual, and contextual variables in the influence setting combine to render motivation and ability to process high, then the arguments presented in support of a change in attitudes or behavior will be thought about carefully. If the person generates predominantly favorable thoughts toward the message, then the likelihood of acceptance is enhanced, whereas if the person generates predominantly unfavorable thoughts

(e.g., counterarguments), then the likelihood of resistance or boomerang (attitude change opposite to the direction advocated) is enhanced. The nature of this elaboration (i.e., whether favorable or unfavorable issue-relevant thinking) is predicted by the ELM to be determined by whether the motivational and ability factors combine to yield relatively objective or relatively biased information-processing and by the nature of the message arguments. If elaboration likelihood is low, however, then the nature of the issue-relevant thinking is less important, and peripheral cues become more important determinants of attitude change (see Figure 26.1).

Inhibiting or Enhancing Message Elaboration

Many of the experiments examining the ELM have explored ways to stimulate or impair thinking about the message arguments in a persuasive appeal. For example, distraction can interfere with a person's careful scrutiny of the arguments in a message and thereby alter its persuasive impact. Petty et al. (1976), for instance, reported two experiments in which subjects listened to a persuasive message over headphones while monitoring in which of the four quadrants of a screen a visual image was projected (a distractor task). In the low-distraction condition, images were presented once every 15 seconds, whereas in the high-distraction condition, images were presented once every 5 seconds. Neither rate of presentation was so fast as to interfere with the subjects' comprehension of the simultaneously presented persuasive message, but the subjects' argument elaboration was much more disrupted in the high- than low-distraction condition. Consequently, subjects were less persuaded with distraction when the arguments were strong, but more persuaded with distraction when the arguments were weak.

A variety of task, contextual, and individual difference variables have been identified that enhance or impair argument elaboration by affecting a person's motivation or ability (see Petty & Cacioppo, 1986a). For instance, moderate levels of repetition of a complicated message can provide individuals with additional opportunities to think about the arguments and thereby enhance argument-processing (Cacioppo & Petty, 1989). Messages worded to underscore the self-relevance of the arguments facilitate the evaluation of the personal merits of the message arguments (Burnkrant & Unnava, 1989). And being the only one rather than one of many assigned to evaluate a recommendation can induce thinking on the part of people who would normally be uninterested in the issue (Petty, Harkins, & Williams, 1980).

Message Elaboration Vs. Peripheral Cues as Determinants of Attitude Change

According to the ELM, there is a trade-off between argument scrutiny and peripheral cues as determinants of a person's susceptibility or resistance to persuasion (see Figure 26.1). In an illustrative study, Petty, Cacioppo, and Goldman (1981) established two kinds of persuasion contexts: one in which the likelihood of relatively objective argument elaboration was high, and one in which the elaboration was low. This was accomplished by varying the personal relevance of the recommendation: subjects were exposed to an editorial favoring the institution of senior comprehensive exams at their university, but some subjects were led to believe these comprehensive exams would be instituted the following year (high personal relevance) whereas others were led to believe the exams would be instituted in 10 years (low personal relevance). To investigate the extent to which subjects' argument scrutiny determined attitudes, half of the subjects heard eight cogent message arguments favoring comprehensive exams, and the remaining subjects heard eight specious message arguments favoring the exams. Finally, to examine the extent to which peripheral cues were important determinants of attitudes, half of the subjects were told the recommendation they would hear was based on a report prepared by a local high school class (low expertise), whereas half were told the tape was based on a report prepared by the Carnegie Commission on Higher Education (high expertise). Following the presentation of the message, subjects rated their attitudes concerning comprehensive exams, listed the arguments they could recall, and completed ancillary measures.

According ot the ELM, argument quality should be the most important determinant of the students' attitudes toward comprehensive exams when they listened to the message with the belief that the recommendation was consequential for them personally, whereas the purported status or expertise of the source would be the most important determinant of the students' attitudes when

they listened to the message with the belief that the recommendation would not affect them personally. The results supported these predictions even though the subjects across the various conditions of the experimental design exhibited equal comprehension/recall of the message arguments to which they were exposed, and subjects in both the low and high personal relevance conditions made comparable assessments of the expertise of the source. These results suggest that the attitudinal effects observed in this study cannot be attributed simply to differences in the information the students extracted from the persuasion appeal, but rather it is the associations generated by subjects (see also Petty & Cacioppo, 1984).

Objective Versus Biased Argument-Processing

When a person is motivated to scrutinize arguments for a position, there are no assurances that the person will come to the "truth" or that the person's issue-relevant thinking will be objective or rational. By relatively objective message-processing, we simply mean that a person is trying to seek the truth wherever that may lead. When a variable enhances argument scrutiny in a relatively objective manner, the strengths of cogent arguments and the flaws in specious arguments should become more apparent. Conversely, when a variable reduces argument scrutiny in a relatively objective fashion, the strengths of cogent arguments and the flaws of specious arguments become less apparent. Objective processing, therefore, has much in common with the concept of "bottom-up" processing in cognitive psychology (Norman, 1976) because elaboration is postulated to be relatively impartial and guided by data (in this case, message arguments).

When a person is motivated to process a message in a biased fashion, the activation thresholds for eliciting favorable or unfavorable thoughts about the advocacy are asymmetrical. As a consequence, the person's knowledge base or situational factors make it more likely that one side will be supported over another. Biased processing, therefore, has more in common with "top-down" than "bottom-up" processing because the elaboration of the arguments is governed by existing cognitive structures, such as a relevant attitude schema, which guide processing in a manner favoring the maintenance or strengthening of the original schema. For instance, Cacioppo et al.

(1982) found that messages written to activate an important dimension of the subjects' self-concept increased biased argument-processing even though the attitude topic did not bear directly on their self-concept. This study illustrates that people are capable of augmenting even specious arguments to arrive at a more cogent line of reasoning for their desired position.

Variables Can Have Multiple Effects on Elaboration

One of the striking predictions from the ELM is that the effects on attitudes of fairly simple variables can change dramatically as a function of other task, individual, or contextual variables due to the interactive effects of these variables on the nature and extent of issue-relevant thinking. The first clear evidence that some variables increase argument-processing at one level of another factor, but may actually decrease argument-processing at a different level of that factor, was provided in a study on the use of rhetorical questions in a message (Petty, Cacioppo, & Heesacker, 1981). Prior to this study, rhetorical questions in a message were thought to enhance persuasion due to their usual association with strong arguments (Zillman, 1972). Petty, Cacioppo, and Heesacker (1981) reasoned that rhetoricals would enhance persuasion only if the message arguments were strong. If the message arguments were weak, then rhetoricals would enhance counterargumentation and lessen attitude change. This reasoning is based on the assumption that presenting the message arguments in rhetorical rather than declarative form increases a person's propensity to think about the message arguments. When the recommendation is already personally involving, Petty, Cacioppo, and Heesacker (1981) reasoned that the insertion of rhetorical questions might actually interfere with the recipients' ongoing idiosyncratic message elaboration. Consistent with this reasoning, pilot testing in which subjects were exposed to a personally relevant audiotaped message in either declarative or rhetorical form revealed that subjects actually reported being distracted from thinking about the recommendation when the topic was personally involving and the message was delivered in rhetorical form (see also Swasy & Munch, 1985). In sum, the ELM can account for a rather complicated pattern of data even though the intervening processes are fairly straightforward: (a) rhetorical questions enhance processing when the motivation to elaborate is low, but disrupt ongoing processing when motivation is already high; and (b) increasing argument-processing can increase or decrease persuasion depending on the quality of the message arguments.

To test this possible account, a study was conducted varying the use of rhetorical questions and argument quality along with a variable known to affect subjects' motivation to process issue-relevant arguments—the personal relevance of the message (Petty, Cacioppo, & Heesacker, 1981). Results revealed that under conditions of low personal relevance, message arguments in rhetorical rather than declarative form increased attitude change when the arguments were cogent but decreased attitude change when arguments were specious. Under conditions of high personal relevance, however, the opposite pattern was observed, and subjects who heard the rhetorical message arguments rated themselves as experiencing more distraction during the message than did subjects who heard the message arguments in declarative form.

The distracting effect of rhetorical questions is likely to be confined to situations in which the presentation rate of the message is controlled externally rather than by the subject (see Petty & Cacioppo, 1986a). If the presentation rate is controlled by the subject, as in a typical written message, then the disruption effect of rhetoricals should be eliminated. Evidence for this was provided by Burnkrant and Howard (1984).

In sum, the introduction of new factors or procedures (e.g., arguments presented in rhetorical rather than declarative form) can have striking but explicable effects on people's cognitive processes and attitudes. The research we have discussed thus far has not been conducted in a context resembling psychotherapy. Therefore, we turn next to the ELM within the context of psychotherapy.

ELM AND THE STUDY OF ATTITUDE CHANGE

The ELM places the recipient of influence—the client, in the case of psychotherapy—in the realistic role of being an active, willful, and sometimes biased participant in the influence process. The ELM also emphasizes the interactive effects of factors in the influence setting in producing attitude change or resistance to attitude change. Significant challenges can therefore be expected in extrapolating from the ELM to psychotherapeutic practice. We discuss five illustrative challenges in this section. The point of these illustrations is that the ELM can provide a general framework within which to study attitudes and attitude changes in psychotherapy, but the operationalization of postulates from the ELM in psychotherapy settings requires additional theory about and research on the effects of contextual factors in this setting.

As with social influence research generally, the ELM has the advantage of dealing with the process of attitude change. That is, predictions from the ELM are not dependent on the specific topic, position, or psychotherapeutic approach employed (e.g., rational emotive therapy, object-relations therapy), but rather on the general attributes of the persuasive communication and setting. However, many topics discussed in psychotherapy are moderately to highly involving, are counterattitudinal, and pertain to issues about which clients have prior knowledge. These attributes suggest that clients may be especially likely to exhibit biased rather than objective message-processing; or more precisely, under what general conditions clients may be likely to exhibit biased message processing. Simply assuming that a client will be relatively objective in his or her processing of a therapist's message because the message is personally relevant ignores the powerful biasing influence of the prior knowledge and beliefs accessed by the client (cf. Petty & Cacioppo, in press). General features of the issues addressed in psychotherapy, such as their personal relevance, pro- or counterattitudinal nature, and knowledge base, may also need to be considered.

Second, goals in psychotherapy often target both direct and indirect behavioral effects of attitudes as well as the direct effect of attitudes on clients' representation of their worlds. For instance, one goal in psychotherapy may be to convert a client's biased argument-processing to objective argument-processing and thereby achieve a more adaptive attitude. Prior research on the ELM has examined various means of enhancing or impeding argument elaboration, and conditions that evoke biased versus objective argument elaboration. However, little attention has been paid to the problem of transforming an individual's biased argument scrutiny to relatively objective argument-processing. On the positive side, this heretofore unexplored focus promises to enrich both psychotherapy theory and the ELM.

Third, the ELM does not specify what are the specific qualities that render some arguments cogent and others specious, but rather points to the idiosyncratic nature of this assessment and to the importance of personally tailored arguments to achieve enduring attitude change. Snyder and De-Bono (1985), for instance, reasoned that people who score high versus low on the self-monitoring scale (Snyder, 1974) differ in the kind of information that is most important when an individual is evaluating the central merits of an argument or issue. Specifically, Snyder and DeBono reasoned that individuals high in self-monitoring (i.e., who tend to monitor the social impact of their behavior) should especially be susceptible to advertisements employing an image campaign, whereas individuals low in self-monitoring should be relatively susceptible to advertisements espousing the specific attributes of a product. After exposure to a series of image and attribute advertisements in one study, subjects were asked to indicate how much they would be willing to pay for each of the advertised products. Results supported the predictions that high self-monitoring individuals were willing to pay more for the products advertised with image campaign, whereas low self-monitoring individuals were willing to pay more for the products in the attribute campaign. Snyder and DeBono characterized both groups of individuals as following the central route to persuasion, because both groups of subjects were attempting to evaluate the central merits of the product; what features were believed to be central simply differed for low and high self-monitors. We discuss procedures for operationalizing argument quality in the following section. An alternative perhaps more appropriate in psychotherapeutic practice is to develop strong and weak arguments tailored to match particular clients' cognitive structures and traits and to verify the subjectively cogent (or specious) nature of these arguments in discussions with the client.

Fourth, while persuasive messages in previous research on the ELM have often been presented in a one-way written communication, clients in psychotherapy receive most of their communications verbally in a dialogue with the therapist. Oral rather than written one-way communications may reduce a client's opportunity to process issue-relevant arguments because exposure is forced rather than self paced. Two-way communications may enhance a client's opportunity to process issue-relevant arguments because the therapist is able to monitor the client's nonverbal and verbal cues for comprehension and elaboration, and the client is, for example, able to ask for clarification. Thus, whether the modality of persuasive communications in psychotherapy should enhance or impair message elaboration should depend on other factors in the setting. For instance, presenting messages in written form should be especially important when the arguments are complex and difficult to process rapidly. This is particularly true when the therapist does not attend to the nature and extent of the client's message-processing. Under these conditions, simple cues in the persuasion context also should be relatively powerful determinants of persuasion. Studies in which the modality of presentation and source cues have been manipulated have supported this proposition; both source credibility (Andreoli & Worchel, 1978) and likability (Chaiken & Eagly, 1983) have had a greater impact on attitudes when a message was presented on video- or audio tape rather than in written form.

In sum, the translation of postulates of the ELM to psychotherapy itself raises interesting theoretical questions about the simple and interactive effects of task, individual difference, and contextual variables in the psychotherapy setting. Procedures such as the thought-listing technique (Cacioppo & Petty, 1981) and the manipulation of argument quality (Petty & Cacioppo, 1986a, see pp. 30–36; Petty et al., 1976) to assess the nature and extent of issue-relevant thinking have proven revealing in work on the development of the ELM and may be useful in the study of attitude change in psychotherapy as well.

Empirical Research Applying the ELM to Psychotherapy

Several studies have attempted to apply the ELM to analogs of psychotherapy context, with mixed results. This literature was reviewed recently by McNeil and Stoltenberg (1989). Rather than duplicating their review, which was optimistic in tone, we focus here on some of the conceptual and methodological problems encountered in attempts to generalize the ELM to psychotherapy. Before proceeding, however, it is worth noting that a number of basic effects predicted by the ELM have been confirmed in the analog studies of counseling and psychotherapy. For example, message content has consistently been shown in these applied studies to affect subjects' attitudes following an analog counseling session. McNeil and Stoltenberg (1988), for instance, manipulated ar-

gument quality and counselor expertise in an analog study concerning career goals. In addition, subjects were classified as being in low- or high-involvement conditions based on their responses to scores on a career decisiveness scale. Results revealed that argument quality exerted a strong effect on attitude and behavioral intention measures. This and related studies, therefore, have highlighted the importance of message factors in psychotherapy and have provided a necessary corrective to earlier studies that focused almost exclusively on source factors.

More problematic in several of the existing studies are (a) predictions attributed to the ELM but which, in fact, are not accurately derived from the ELM; and (b) operationalizations of crucial independent or dependent variables that differ in ways that seriously threaten the construct validity of these variables. For example, Stoltenberg and McNeil (1984) hypothesized that under conditions of high elaboration likelihood, source credibility enhances message scrutiny and the tendency for subjects to travel the central route to persuasion. As discussed above, however, the ELM holds that under conditions of high elaboration likelihood, subjects should think carefully about the merits of the recommendation(s) regardless of peripheral cues such as source credibility. It is under conditions of moderate elaboration likelihood that factors such as source credibility may affect the extent of message-processing.

Potential problems in the operationalization of crucial independent and dependent variables range from the use of correlational rather than experimental designs, a mismatch between the message recommendation and the target of the attitude measure, and the manipulation of argument quality without regard to the profile (e.g., positivity) of issue-relevant thinking evoked by the "strong" and "weak" versions of the persuasive communication. Because the manipulation of argument quality is an important methodological tool by which both the nature and extent of argument-processing can be inferred (Petty & Cacioppo, 1986b; Figure 26.2), we focus on this particular problem in some detail.

Briefly, the ELM prescribes an operational definition for strong and weak arguments. One begins developing arguments for a topic by generating a large number of arguments, both intuitively compelling and specious ones, in favor of some target position (e.g., adopting a healthy life-style). Next, members of the appropriate subject popula-

I. No Effect:

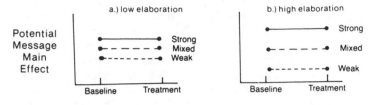

II. Cue Effect:

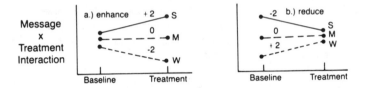

III. Objective Processing:

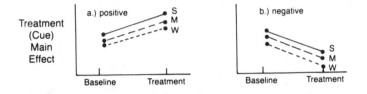

IV. Biased Processing:

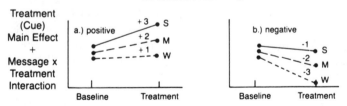

Figure 26.2. Impact of variables on attitude change according to the ELM. Under conditions of high-elaboration likelihood, attitudes are affected mostly by argument quality (I). Under conditions of low elaboration likelihood, attitudes are affected mostly by peripheral cues (II). Under conditions of moderate elaboration likelihood, variables may enhance or reduce message processing in either a relatively objective (III) or relatively biased (IV) manner. From *Communication and Persuasion: Central and Peripheral Routes to Attitude Change* by R. E. Petty and J. T. Cacioppo, 1986, New York: Springer-Verlag. Copyright 1986 by Springer-Verlag. Reprinted by permission of authors.

tion are given these arguments to rate for persuasiveness. Based on these scores, arguments with high and low ratings are selected to comprise at least one "strong" and one "weak" message. These arguments also are matched prior to their use on overall believability, comprehensibility, complexity, and familiarity. Other subjects are given one of these messages and are told to think about and evaluate it carefully. Following examination of the message, subjects list everything they thought about while examining the message, and these listed thoughts are coded as being favorable, unfavorable, or neutral toward the position advocated (see Cacioppo & Petty, 1981). A "strong" message is defined as one containing arguments such that when subjects are instructed to think about the message, the thoughts they generate are predominately favorable. A "weak" message is one that is also ostensibly in favor of the advocacy, but the arguments are constructed such that when subjects are instructed to think about the arguments they generate predominantly unfavorable thoughts. Because the message arguments are developed to elicit primarily favorable (strong), primarily unfavorable (weak), or neither predominantly favorable or unfavorable (mixed) issue-relevant thinking when subjects are instructed to think about the arguments, the various patterns of results depicted in Figure 26.2 can be predicted based on the nature and extent of message-processing actually evoked in a specific setting.

Implementation of this procedure is straightforward when working with relatively homogeneous subject populations, since the cognitive associations and elaborations of subjects in the pilot testing and those in the subsequent research are quite similar. This is less often the case in psychotherapeutic practice or research. One option is to block on the same individual difference variable(s) during pilot testing as in the planned research in order to identify message arguments that are strong and weak for each subgroup of subjects (see Cacioppo et al., 1983). A second option is to develop strong and weak arguments drawing upon a theory of the particular individual difference of interest. This second tack has the disadvantage of rendering disconfirmations of ambiguous theoretical import but has nevertheless proven informative in the social psychological literature (see Snyder & DeBono, 1985).

A third concern with the existing research on the ELM and attitude change in psychotherapy is that the theoretical implications of moderate elaboration likelihood have been ignored. Consequently, authors have concluded that the ELM was not applicable when the data fit neither those predicted by the central or the peripheral route to persuasion even though the ELM has provisions for more complex outcomes — such as source factors interacting with argument quality to produce attitude change. The ELM predicts that when the elaboration likelihood is low, subjects are more likely to base their attitudes on peripheral cues rather than on issue-relevant thinking. When the elaboration likelihood is high, subjects are more likely to base their attitudes on issue-relevant thinking than on peripheral cues. When the elaboration likelihood is moderate, however, subjects may use source and other factors to determine whether the message and issue are worth careful scrutiny (Petty & Cacioppo, 1986a). Under these circumstances, an interaction is predicted of the form that issue-relevant thinking (e.g., argument scrutiny) is greater under one level of a factor (e.g., high source credibility) than under the other (e.g., low source credibility). Thus, attitudes may be more sensitive to variations in argument quality when source credibility is high than low. The predicted interaction has been obtained in several experiments (cf. Heesacker, Petty, & Cacioppo, 1983; Puckett, Petty, Cacioppo, & Fisher, 1983), although this portion of the model has not been explored extensively in basic laboratory research on the ELM. Because several of the applied studies of the ELM also have found interactions between source and message factors (e.g., Heesacker, 1986; Neimeyer, Guy, & Metzler, 1989), it will be important for future studies to clarify when and why such interactions occur and whether these interactive effects are occurring under conditions of moderate elaboration likelihood. In sum, applied studies of attitude change in psychotherapy promise to lead to important refinements of this portion of the model, although it is important to note that simply detecting an interaction between source and message factors does not constitute a disconfirmation of the ELM.

Future Directions

The main question in psychotherapy process research is, "How do clients change?" The ELM suggests that they change in response to persuasive messages from the therapist after scrutinizing the message — and elaborating their thoughts in a relatively objective or biased fashion—in the context of their own prior beliefs. This change is affected by three general conceptual variables: message arguments, or information addressing the merits of a particular recommendation; peripheral cues, or stimuli that are not related specifically to the veridicality of a particular recommendation but rather signal in a general way (e.g., heuristics) that the associated recommendation is correct; and the elaboration-likelihood continuum, or people's motivation and ability to engage in issue-relevant thinking. Several nuances of the ELM may be of special importance as research moves from highly controlled laboratory settings using relatively homogeneous subject populations to the psychotherapy setting:

1. Specific factors can operate predictably in more than one of these capacities. For instance, the mere number of arguments in a heavily documented advocacy may serve as a cue regarding the likely support for a particular position under conditions of low elaboration likelihood, whereas these message arguments can be scrutinized for merit under conditions of high elaboration likelihood (Petty & Cacioppo, 1984).

2. The effect on cognitive responding of other factors (e.g., message repetition) has been found to vary as their level increases; for instance, moderate message repetition tends to increase objective argument-processing, whereas high levels of argument repetition tends instead to trigger biased argument-processing (e.g., Cacioppo & Petty, 1979, 1989).

3. Attitude changes achieved through the peripheral route, although relatively short-lasting and susceptible to counterpersuasion, may provide an opening through which irrational resistance and more enduring attitude change can be reached (e.g., see Cacioppo, Petty, & Stoltenberg, 1984).

4. Finally, whereas we have focused on the influence processes that characterize low- versus high-elaboration likelihood conditions, people often encounter recommendations under conditions of moderate-elaboration likelihood conditions. According to the ELM, people use cues in these circumstances to help decide whether or not to expend the time and effort to scrutinize the message arguments (Moore, Hausknecht, & Thamodaran, 1986; Petty & Cacioppo, 1984). These nuances make it clear that attempts to identify specific factors (e.g., argument number) with single conceptual variables within the ELM—and

predictions based on simply adding the previous empirical effects of variables tested separately rather than considering their possible interactive effects on the conceptual variables outlined by the ELM—are likely to be disappointing.

A second important focus of research on attitudes in psychotherapy concerns the differential consequences of attitude change achieved through various psychotherapy interventions. According to the ELM, attitudes changed through cognitive restructuring, whether achieved through cognitively or behaviorally oriented therapies, will be relatively enduring, resistant to counterpersuasion, and predictive of behavior more so than agreements reached through the peripheral route (Cacioppo et al., 1984).

Finally, Heppner and Claiborn (1989) concluded recently that substantive research on attitude change in psychotherapy will require the study of variables, many of which have not yet been incorporated into the ELM but that are relevant to the psychotherapy process as practitioners think of it. The target of influence in psychotherapy can range from global self-perceptions, such as self-esteem; to more particular self-perceptions, such as self-efficacy with respect to a particular behavior; to attitudes toward others in their social context, such as their colleagues or spouses. As these attitudes are defined, appropriate procedures for assessing the efficacy of generally or specifically focused psychotherapy interventions can be developed (cf. Fishbein & Ajzen, 1975). Both the conceptualization of these attitudes and the operationalization of the conceptualizations in psychotherapy research is a content matter, and perhaps can best be determined by personality and psychotherapy theory. Research on the processes underlying attitude change, on the other hand, may be indifferent to content, and, hence, an overarching conceptual formulation such as the ELM may organize what have previously appeared to be complicated or inconsistent results.

REFERENCES

Abelson, R. P., Aronson, E., McGuire, W. J., Newcomb, T. M., Rosenberg, M. J., & Tannenbaum, P. H. (Eds.). (1968). *Theories of cognitive consistency: A sourcebook*. Chicago: Rand McNally.

Abelson, R. P., & Sermat, V. (1962). Multidimensional scaling of facial expressions. *Journal of Experimental Psychology, 63*, 546–554.

Ajzen, I., & Fishbein, M. (1977). Attitude-behavior relations: A theoretical analysis and review of empirical research. *Psychological Bulletin, 84*, 888–918.

Ajzen, I., & Fishbein, M. (1980). *Understanding attitudes and predicting social behavior.* Englewood Cliffs, NJ: Prentice-Hall.

Andreoli, V., & Worchel, S. (1978). Effects of media, communicator, and message position on attitude change. *Public Opinion Quarterly, 42*, 59–70.

Bochner, S., & Insko, C. A. (1966). Communicator discrepancy, source credibility, and opinion change. *Journal of Personality and Social Psychology, 4*, 614–621.

Brehm, S. S. (1976). *The application of social psychology to clinical practice.* New York: Halsted Press.

Burnkrant, R., & Unnava, R. (1989). Self-referencing: A strategy for increasing processing of message content. *Personality and Social Psychology Bulletin, 15*, 628–638.

Burnkrant, R. E., & Howard, D. J. (1984). Effects of the use of introductory rhetorical questions versus statements on information processing. *Journal of Personality and Social Psychology, 47*, 1218–1230.

Cacioppo, J. T., & Petty, R. E. (1979). Effects of message repetition and position on cognitive responses, recall, and persuasion. *Journal of Personality and Social Psychology, 37*, 97–109.

Cacioppo, J. T., & Petty, R. E. (1981). Social psychological procedures for cognitive response assessment. The thought-listing technique. In T. V. Merluzzi, C. R. Glass, & M. Genest (Eds.), *Cognitive assessment* (pp. 309–342). New York: Guilford Press.

Cacioppo, J. T., & Petty, R. E. (1982). The need for cognition. *Journal of Personality and Social Psychology, 42*, 116–131.

Cacioppo, J. T., & Petty, R. E. (1989). Effects of message repetition on argument processing, recall, and persuasion. *Basic and Applied Social Psychology, 10*, 3–12.

Cacioppo, J. T., Petty, R. E., & Morris, K. (1983). Effects of need for cognition on message evaluation, recall, and persuasion. *Journal of Personality and Social Psychology, 45*, 805–818.

Cacioppo, J. T., Petty, R. E., & Sidera, J. (1982). The effects of a salient self-schema on the evaluation of proattitudinal editorials: Top-down versus bottom-up processing. *Journal of Experimental Social Psychology, 18*, 324–338.

Cacioppo, J. T., Petty, R. E., & Stoltenberg, C. D. (1984). Processes of social influence: The elaboration likelihood model of persuasion. In P. Kendall (Ed.), *Advances in cognitive-behavioral research and practice* (Vol. 4, pp. 218–275). New York: Academic Press.

Chaiken, S. E., & Eagly, A. H. (1983). Communication modality as a determinant of persuasion: The role of communicator salience. *Journal of Personality and Social Psychology, 45*, 241–256.

Claiborn, C. D., & Dowd, E. T. (1985). Attributional interpretations in counseling: Content versus discrepancy. *Journal of Counseling Psychology, 32*, 188–196.

Corrigan, J. D., Dell, D. M., Lewis, K. N., & Schmidt, I. D. (1980). Counseling as a social influence process: A review. *Journal of Counseling Psychology, 27*, 395–441.

Craighead, I. W., & Craighead, W. E. (1980). Implications of persuasive communication research for the modification of self-statements. *Cognitive Therapy and Research, 4*, 117–134.

Dickinson, A., & Dearing, M. F. (1979). Appetitive-aversive interactions and inhibitory processes. In A. Dickinson & R. A. Boakes (Eds.), *Mechanisms of learning and motivation.* Hillsdale, NJ: Lawrence Erlbaum Associates.

Diener, E., Larsen, R. J., Levine, S., & Emmons, R. A. (1985). Frequency and intensity: The underlying dimensions of affect. *Journal of Personality and Social Psychology, 48*, 1253–1265.

DiMateo, M. R., & DiNicola, D. D. (1982). *Achieving patient compliance.* Elmsford, NY: Pergamon Press.

Eagly, A. H. (1974). Comprehensibility of persuasive arguments as a determinant of opinion change. *Journal of Personality and Social Psychology, 29*, 758–773.

Eagly, A. H., & Warren, R. (1976). Intelligence, comprehension, and opinion change. *Journal of Personality, 44*, 226–242.

Festinger, L. (1957). *A theory of cognitive dissonance.* Stanford, CA: Stanford University Press.

Fishbein, M., & Ajzen, I. (1975). *Belief, attitude, intention, and behavior.* Reading, MA: Addison-Wesley.

Frank, J. D. (1963). *Persuasion and healing.* New York: Schocken Books.

Greenberg, R. P. (1969). Effects of presession counseling on perception of the therapist and receptivity to influence in a psychotherapy analogue. *Journal of Consulting and Clinical Psychology, 33*, 425–429.

Greenwald, A. G. (1968). Cognitive learning, cognitive response to persuasion, and attitude change. In A. G. Greenwald, T. C. Brock, & T. M. Ostrom (Eds.), *Psychological foundations of attitudes.* New York: Academic Press.

Harkins, S. G., & Petty, R. E. (1981). The multiple source effect in persuasion: The effects of distraction. *Personality and Social Psychology Bulletin, 7*, 627–635.

Heesacker, M. (1986). Counselor pretreatment and the elaboration likelihood model of attitude change. *Journal of Counseling Psychology, 33*, 107–114.

Heesacker, M., Petty, R. E., & Cacioppo, J. T. (1983). Field dependence and attitude change: Source credibility can alter persuasion by affecting message-relevant thinking. *Journal of Personality, 51*, 653–666.

Heppner, P. P., & Claiborn, C. D. (1989). Social influence research in counseling: A review and critique. *Journal of Counseling Psychology, 36*, 365–384.

Heppner, P. P., & Dixon, D. M. (1981). A review of the interpersonal influence process in counseling. *Personnel and Guidance Journal, 59*, 542–550.

Heppner, P. P., & Dixon, D. N. (1978). Effects of client perceived need and counselor role on clients' behaviors. *Journal of Counseling Psychology, 25*, 514–519.

Himmelfarb, S., & Eagly, A. H. (1974). Orientations to the study of attitudes and their change. In S. Himmelfarb & A. H. Eagly (Eds.), *Readings in attitude change.* New York: John Wiley & Sons.

Hovland, C. I., Janis, I. L., & Kelley, H. H. (1953). *Communication and persuasion.* New Haven, CT: Yale University Press.

Hoyt, M. F., & Janis, I. L. (1975). Increasing adherence to a stressful decision via a motivational balance-sheet procedure: A field experiment. *Journal of Personality and Social Psychology, 31*, 833–839.

Insko, C. A., Lind, E. A., & LaTour, S. (1976). Persuasion, recall, and thoughts. *Representative Research and Social Psychology, 7*, 66–78.

Kunst-Wilson, W. R., & Zajonc, R. B. (1980). Affective discrimination of stimuli that cannot be recognized. *Science, 207*, 557–558.

Levy, L. H. (1963). *Psychological interpretation.* New York: Holt, Rinehart & Winston.

Lord, C. G., Ross, L., & Lepper, M. R. (1979). Biased assimilation and attitude polarization: The effects of prior theories on subsequently considered evidence. *Journal of Personality and Social Psychology, 37*, 2098–2109.

McGuire, W. J. (1981). The probabilogical model of cognitive structure and attitude change. In R. E. Petty, T. M. Ostrom, & T. C. Brock (Eds.), *Cognitive responses in persuasion.* Hillsdale, NJ: Lawrence Erlbaum Associates.

McNeil, B. W., & Stoltenberg, C. D. (1988). A test of the elaboration likelihood model for therapy. *Cognitive Therapy and Research, 12*, 69–80.

McNeil, B. W., & Stoltenberg, C. D. (1989). Reconceptualizing social influence in counseling: The elaboration likelihood model. *Journal of Counseling Psychology, 36*, 24–33.

Miller, N., Maruyama, G., Beaber, R., & Valone, K. (1976). Speed of speech and persuasion. *Journal of Personality and Social Psychology, 34*, 615–625.

Moore, D. L., Hausknecht, D., & Thamodaran, K. (1986). Time compression, response opportunity, and persuasion. *Journal of Consumer Psychology, 13*, 85–99.

Neimeyer, G. J., Guy, J., & Metzler, A. (1989). Changing attitudes regarding the treatment of disordered eating: An application of the elaboration likelihood model. *Journal of Social and Clinical Psychology, 8*, 70–86.

Norman, D. A. (1976). *Memory and attention* (2nd ed.). New York: John Wiley & Sons.

Osgood, C. E. (1966). Dimensionality of the semantic space for communication via facial expression. *Scandanavian Journal of Psychology, 7*, 1–30.

Osgood, C. E., Suci, G. J., & Tannenbaum, P. H. (1957). *The measurement of meaning.* Urbana, IL: University of Illinois Press.

Petty, R. E. (1977). *A cognitive response analysis of the temporal persistence of attitude changes induced by persuasive communications.* Unpublished doctoral dissertation, The Ohio State University, Columbus.

Petty, R. E., & Cacioppo, J. T. (1978). *A cognitive response approach to attitudinal persistence.* Paper presented at the annual meeting of the American Psychological Association, Toronto, Canada.

Petty, R. E., & Cacioppo, J. T. (1979a). Effects of forewarning a persuasive intent and involvement on cognitive responses and persuasion.

Personality and Social Psychology Bulletin, 5, 173–176.

Petty, R. E., & Cacioppo, J. T. (1979b). Issue-involvement can increase or decrease persuasion by enhancing message-relevant cognitive responses. *Journal of Personality and Social Psychology, 37*, 1915–1926.

Petty, R. E., & Cacioppo, J. T. (1981). *Attitudes and persuasion: Classic and contemporary approaches*. Dubuque, IA: Wm. C. Brown.

Petty, R. E., & Cacioppo, J. T. (1984). The effects of involvement on responses to argument quantity and quality: Central and peripheral routes to persuasion. *Journal of Personality and Social Psychology, 46*, 69–81.

Petty, R. E., & Cacioppo, J. T. (1986a). *Communication and persuasion: Central and peripheral routes to attitude change*. New York: Springer-Verlag.

Petty, R. E., & Cacioppo, J. T. (1986b). The elaboration likelihood model of persuasion. *Advances in Experimental Social Psychology, 19*, 123–205.

Petty, R. E., & Cacioppo, J. T. (in press). Involvement and persuasion: Tradition versus integration. *Psychological Bulletin*.

Petty, R. E., Cacioppo, J. T., & Goldman, R. (1981). Personal involvement as a determinant of argument-based persuasion. *Journal of Personality and Social Psychology, 41*, 847–855.

Petty, R. E., Cacioppo, J. T., & Heesacker, M. (1981). The use of rhetorical questions in persuasion: A cognitive response analysis. *Journal of Personality and Social Psychology, 40*, 432–440.

Petty, R. E., Harkins, S. G., & Williams, K. D. (1980). The effects of group diffusion of cognitive effort on attitudes: An information processing view. *Journal of Personality and Social Psychology, 38*, 81–92.

Petty, R. E., Wells, G. L., & Brock, T. C. (1976). Distraction can enhance or reduce yielding to propaganda: Thought disruption versus effort

justification. *Journal of Personality and Social Psychology, 34*, 874–884.

Puckett, J., Petty, R. E., Cacioppo, J. T., & Fisher, D. (1983). The relative impact of age and attractiveness stereotypes on persuasion. *Journal of Gerontology, 38*, 340–343.

Russell, J. A. (1983). Pancultural aspects of the human conceptual organization of emotions. *Journal of Personality and Social Psychology, 45*, 1281–1288.

Snyder, M. (1974). The self-monitoring of expressive behavior. *Journal of Personality and Social Psychology, 30*, 526–537.

Snyder, M., & DeBono, K. G. (1985). Appeals to image and claims about quality: Understanding the psychology of advertising. *Journal of Personality and Social Psychology, 49*, 586–597.

Sprafkin, R. P. (1970). Communicator expertise and change in word meaning in psychological treatment. *Journal of Counseling Psychology, 17*, 191–196.

Stoltenberg, C. D., & McNeil, B. W. (1984). Effects of expertise and issue involvement on perceptions of counseling. *Journal of Social and Clinical Psychology, 2*, 314–325.

Strong, S. R. (1968). Counseling: An interpersonal influence process. *Journal of Counseling Psychology, 15*, 215–224.

Strong, S. R., & Schmidt, L. D. (1970). Expertness and influence in counseling. *Journal of Counseling Psychology, 17*, 81–87.

Swasy, J. L., & Munch, J. M. (1985). Examining the target of receiver elaborations: Rhetorical question effects on source processing and persuasion. *Journal of Consumer Research, 11*, 877–886.

Zajonc, R. B. (1980). Feeling and thinking: Preferences need no inferences. *American Psychologist, 35*, 151–175.

Zillmann, D. (1972). Rhetorical elicitation of agreement in persuasion. *Journal of Personality and Social Psychology, 21*, 159–165.

CHAPTER 27

SOCIAL INFLUENCE AND CHANGE IN THERAPEUTIC RELATIONSHIPS

Stanley R. Strong

A woman in her thirties reveals that she is depressed. Her therapist responds with empathy and gently queries about her feelings and the events related to her feelings. She elaborates about how helpless and inadequate she is, how her failures lead to numerous problems, how poorly others treat her, and how her husband is exacting and demanding. After exploring the difficulties she has experienced, the therapist states his admiration for her responsible and self-sacrificing devotion to her husband. He admires how she, by taking responsibility for their problems, enables her husband to feel confident and competent. She responds with dismay and more extreme demonstrations of helplessness. The therapist persists with his construction of her situation. He notes many instances in which she protected her husband by taking responsibility for problems through self-sacrificing acts of helplessness and inadequacy. He admires her responsible and altruistic concern for her husband's fragility.

In their next meeting, the client hesitatingly suggests that she does take responsibility for the difficulties she and her husband experience. She expresses doubt that her husband is as fragile as she apparently has believed. In the remaining sessions, time is devoted to working out how she can take responsibility in ways that are more respectful of her husband as a mature adult and of herself as a person of worth. Each session begins with a review of her experiences in trying new ways of exercising responsibility and ends in planning ways to meet challenges that she expects to arise in the next week. The client emerges from therapy no longer depressed and with different ways of behaving in many aspects of her life.

While many theoretical perspectives offer cogent accounts of the processes involved in the client's change in thinking and acting in the above case summary, the interpersonal perspective stresses the role played by social influence. The therapist presented and steadfastly elaborated a view of the client's situation that was highly discrepant from the view she presented to him. She accepted the view, albeit after strenuous efforts to dissuade the therapist of his unexpected view. The client's change is an example of social influence. When one person affects another's behavior, social influence has occurred.

Social influence is one of the most pervasive facts of human experience. People spend much of their time in behavioral exchanges with others. The exchanges are marked with striking evidence of social influence as seen in the coordination of the responses interactants exchange with one another (Strong et al., 1988). Social influence in the exchanges frequently results in changes in interactants' constructions of social reality and of themselves, changes that affect participants' behavior in future interactions (Strong, 1984).

In the above brief description of the behavioral exchange between client and therapist, the client's presentation of herself as depressed influenced the therapist to listen sympathetically. The therapist's empathic responses and queries influenced the client to elaborate on her experiences and feelings. The therapist's interpretation was followed by strenuous efforts by both client and therapist to influence each other's views. The therapy sessions were continuous streams of reciprocal influences that resulted in profound changes in the client's views of herself and others, and in her behavior.

The purposes of this chapter are to present a theory of the dynamics of social influence and to apply the theory to how change is achieved in therapeutic relationships.

INTERPERSONAL INFLUENCE IN RELATIONSHIPS

The scientific study of social influence can be traced to Kurt Lewin, to his topological and vector psychology and his concept of group dynamics (Cartwright, 1959a; Kelley & Thibaut, 1978). To Lewin, and to Ernst Cassirer, the philosopher of science under whom Lewin studied, observed events are symptoms of underlying dynamic processes. The job of the scientist is to posit theories of the underlying dynamic processes that account for and find expression in observed events (Cassirer, 1923; Lewin, 1935, pp. 1–42). To them, the purpose of science is to explain the known with the unknown and thus push back the frontiers of the unknown.

Lewin and Cassirer proposed that the first step in constructing a theory is to determine the phenomenon for which the theory is to account. The scientist then develops theoretical constructs, identifies relations among the constructs, and identifies connections between the constructs and potentially observable events. The theory should suggest how the theoretical constructs and potentially observable events are to be measured. A theory is a representation model of an unseen reality posited to underlie and account for observed events. What follows is a representational model of the unseen reality of social influence.

Key Social Influence Concepts

The phenomenon for which the theory of interpersonal influence is intended to account is the coordination of the responses people exchange as they interact in interpersonal relationships. Not only are we interested in accounting for moment to moment response exchanges, but also for changes in the relations among the responses exchanged over time. Change over time indicate developmental effects that reflect changes in the participants' interpersonal characteristics, changes of the sort therapeutic relationships are intended to foster.

The coordination of responses between people in interpersonal interactions is readily observed in the everyday exchanges we have with others. Goffman (1959) proposed that people coordinate their social behavior with one another to construct the social realities that define them as social beings. Laboratory studies have demonstrated that how one person responds to another profoundly affects how the other responds to the person on a moment-to-moment basis (Strong et al., 1988). As social beings, we are heavily invested in how others behave with respect to us. This investment reflects our dependence on other people for many of the substances and conditions we need for daily sustenance and growth, substances and conditions that are embedded in or controlled by others' responses. Dependence, a state induced by our needs for substances and conditions another controls, is the basic theoretical construct of social influence.

Dependence renders us responsive to the other in social exchanges. We are inclined to respond to the other in ways that encourage him or her to behave in ways that serve our needs. We also are inclined to be responsive to the other's needs for substances and conditions we control. The other's willingness to serve our needs is based fundamentally on our ability and willingness to serve the other's needs, to exchange benefit for benefit. Traditionally, social influence has been viewed in terms of the responsiveness to another's needs that dependence on the other generates. Dependence on another gives the other the ability to influence us, an ability labeled social power. Lewin conceived of social influence in terms of social power (Lewin, 1951, pp. 228–304 & 335–337), as did the pioneers who initially construed the dynamics of social influence (Cartwright, 1959a, 1959b; French & Raven, 1959; Emerson, 1962).

Early formulations of the dynamics of social influence regarded social influence as a one-way process. While theorists acknowledged that members of a relationship are dependent on each other and thus that both possess social power, they conceived of the outworkings of these dynamics in terms of imbalances in power, with the more powerful demanding concessions and the less powerful haplessly complying. Moscovici and his colleagues (Moscovici, 1985; Moscovici & Mugny, 1983) have shown that this conception of social influence is inadequate. A theory of social influence must account for the simultaneous effects of both participants' dependence on both participants' ongoing behavior: Interdependence must be the central construct.

Lewin defined a group in terms of the interdependence of its members (Lewin, 1948, p. 84). In a discussion of how the behavior of a marital dyad might be studied, he noted that, because of their interdependence, the behavior of each spouse was heavily influenced by his or her conceptions of the other's situation, character, needs, intentions, perceptions, and likely responses (Lewin, 1951, pp. 195–199). Kelley and Thibaut, who have developed a complex and fruitful theory of interdependence (Kelley, 1979; Kelley & Thibaut, 1978; Thibaut & Kelley, 1959), pointed out that interdependence profoundly affects the motives and behaviors of people in relationships. In order to maintain the other in the relationship and thus ultimately realize the potential benefits available through the other, both parties must delay personal gratification and serve the other's needs. Interdependence generates the motives and behaviors denoted by the concepts of altruism, loyalty, fairness, trust, equality, and equity, as well as competition and egocentrism.

Categorizing and Measuring Interpersonal Responses

In an interpersonal interaction, a person's behavior at a given time is a function of the person's psychological situation at that time. Interpersonal responses are conceived of as tools for affecting the other's psychological situation and thus the other's behavior. Interpersonal interactions are construed as processes of exchanging resources (substances and conditions related to needs) and information about resources and needs that could be exchanged and met in the interactions. Interpersonal responses are assumed to convey resources and information about resources and needs. In pursuit of their interests in interpersonal interactions, people are assumed to select and employ interpersonal responses in terms of the anticipated effects of the resources and information the responses convey on the other's psychological situation.

Categorizing Interpersonal Responses

The Strong et al. (1988) interpersonal circle categorizes interpersonal responses in terms of the resources and information they convey. Timothy Leary and his colleagues at the Kaiser Foundation introduced the interpersonal circle in the 1950s (Leary, 1957). It organizes interpersonal responses in terms of their loadings on two dimensions: status (dominant to submissive) and affiliation (friendly to hostile). The Strong et al. circle, patterned after Leary's circle, is presented in Figure 27.1. The Strong et al. circle divides interpersonal response space, defined by orthogonal status and affiliation dimensions, into eight categories: leading, self-enhancing, critical, distrustful, self-effacing, docile, cooperative, and nurturant. The responses in each category are organized in four levels of intensity, with the least intense responses occurring near the center of the circle and the most intense near the perimeter of the circle. Figure 27.1 presents representative interpersonal responses in each category and level of the Strong et al. circle.

Several other versions of the interpersonal circle have been published (Benjamin, 1974; Chance, 1966; Foa, 1961; Kiesler, 1983; Lorr & McNair, 1966; Perkins, Kiesler, Anchin, Chirico, Kyle, & Federman, 1979; Wiggins, 1979). The versions are intended to correct perceived inadequacies in Leary's circle and/or modify it for some specific use (Kiesler, 1983). Most of the models, including Leary's, are intended for interpersonal diagnosis of personality, and are linked to personality inventories. Psychometric studies of the structural properties of circle-based inventories support the two-dimensional structure of personality attributes and the general order of personality types

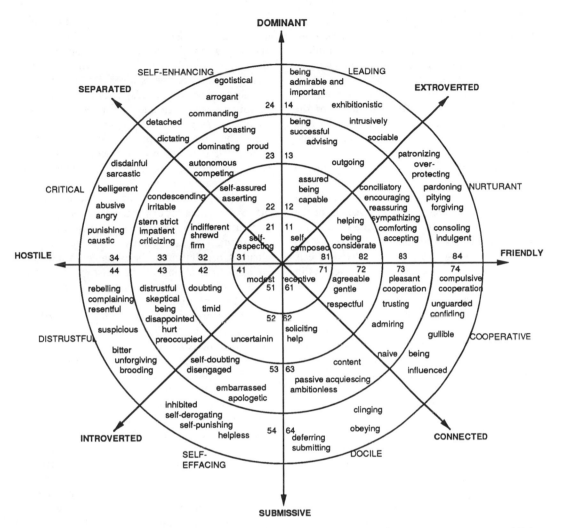

Figure 27.1. The Strong et al. (1988) interpersonal circle. From ''The Dynamic Relations Among Interpersonal Behaviors: A Test of Complementarity and Anticomplementarity'' by S. R. Strong et al., 1988, *Journal of Personality and Social Psychology, 54,* p. 799. Copyright 1988 by the American Psychological Association. Reprinted by permission.

within the circle (Wiggins, 1979; Perkins et al., 1979; Lorr & McNair, 1966).

Numerous efforts to empirically identify the psychometric structure of personality traits, emotions, and social behaviors have found circular structures and/or primary dimensions similar to Leary's circle (Becker & Krug, 1964; Conte & Plutchik, 1981; Falbo & Peplau, 1980; Russell, 1980; Schaefer, 1961; Stiles, 1980). Studies of self-reports of "how I get my way" in relationships have derived categories of influence strategies that are similar to the response categories of the Strong et al. circle (Buss, Gomes, Higgins,

& Lauterbach, 1987; Cowan, Drinkard, & Mac-Gavin, 1984; Falbo & Peplau, 1980; Howard, Blumstein, & Schwartz, 1986). The categories and dimensions of Bales' SYMLOG (Bales, Cohen, & Williamson, 1979) are also similar to those of the Strong et al. circle.

Strong et al. (1988) assessed the validity of the structure of their interpersonal circle in a study of the perceptual and behavioral effects of the eight types of responses in interactions between pairs of women working on a laboratory task. One of the women in each pair was a confederate trained to enact a high percentage of one type of response while she and a subject constructed and reached consensus about the best stories for two pictures. The eight response types defined eight conditions in the study. After the 16-minute interactions, subjects indicated their impressions of their partner's characteristics using the Impact Message Inventory (Perkins et al., 1979). The items of the inventory are scored on 15 personality scales that are organized in a circle along status and affiliation dimensions.

Differences on the personality scales due to conditions reflected the expected effects of response types on the subjects' impressions of the confederates. Strong et al. derived vectors in the interpersonal impression space defined by the inventory's status and affiliation dimensions to identify the response types' overall relative effects or impressions. The placement of the vectors in the interpersonal impression space closely corresponded to the placement of the response categories in the Strong et al. circle.

Responses in each category of the Strong et al. circle communicate specific information about resources, needs, and perceptions. The information the responses communicate is presented in Figure 27.2. Along the vertical axis of the model, information varies from the assertion of possession of dominant resources to the assertion of possession of submissive resources. Along the horizontal axis, information varies from the assertion of an altruistic focus on the other's needs to the assertion of an egotistic focus on own needs. The information communicated by responses in each category reflects the interpersonal significance of a particular combination of values on the two dimensions. The two diagonal axes in Figure 27.2 describe the overall thrust of the information communicated by responses that lie along them. One diagonal axis extends from "asserts resources" to "denies resources." The other extends from "asserts needs" to "denies needs." The specific resources the responses in each category assert are presented toward the center of the circle in Figure 27.2. The overall meanings of the information that the responses in each category communicate are presented inside the circle near the perimeter, whereas the attributions that the responses in each category encourage are presented outside the circle near the perimeter.

Leading and self-enhancing responses assert the possession of dominant resources, while docile and self-effacing responses assert the possession of submissive resources. Leading responses in-

form the other that the person has good resources and is considering the other's needs: They encourage attributions of competence and equitableness. Docile responses inform the other that the person has few resources and is looking to the other to consider the person's needs: They encourage attributions of deference and low involvement. Self-enhancing responses inform the other that the person has superior resources and that the other is in need of the person's consideration: They encourage attributions of superiority and autonomy. Self-effacing responses inform the other that the person has poor resources and is dependent on the other to consider his or her needs: They encourage attributions of helplessness and dependence.

Nurturant and cooperative responses assert an altruistic orientation in the exchange with the other, while critical and distrustful responses assert an egotistic orientation. Nurturant responses inform the other that the person believes the other to have resources of value and to be worthy of having his or her needs considered: They encourage attributions of trustworthiness and fairness. Cooperative responses inform the other that the person believes that the other values the person's resources and is considerate of the person's needs: They encourage attributions of trust and loyalty. Critical responses inform the other that his or her responses have no value and that he or she is not worthy of consideration: They encourage attributions of strength and dangerousness. Distrustful responses inform the other that the person feels that he or she is not being appreciated and that the other is not considering his or her needs: They encourage attributions of victimization and martyrdom.

Measuring Interpersonal Responses

The Interpersonal Communication Rating Scale (Strong, Hills, & Nelson, 1988) is a system for coding all of the responses enacted in an interpersonal interaction into the categories and levels of the Strong et al. circle. Coding the responses participants employ in an interaction into the categories of the scale provides a direct measure of the responses that participants exchange. While the percentages of total responses that fall into each category are useful in describing an interaction, hypotheses about relationship processes are better tested using continuous measures derived from the systematic arrangement of the categories in the circle.

A response is conceived of as a vector in inter-

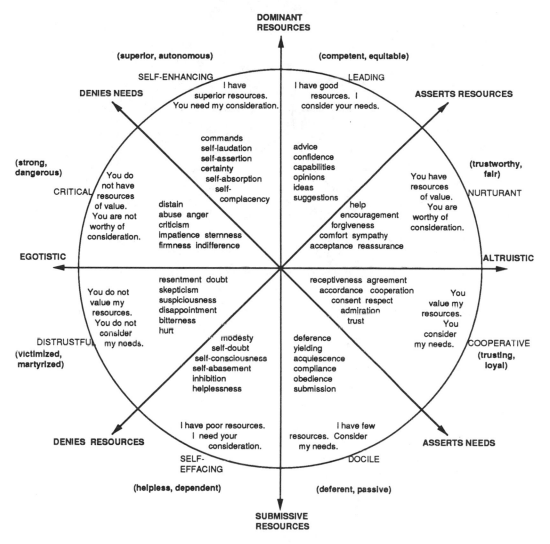

Figure 27.2. Information communicated by interpersonal responses.

personal response space that is described by its coordinates on the status and affiliation dimensions, and by its magnitude, the radius of the circle. The vector for responses coded in each category is the radius of the circle that bisects the category. The degrees of the arcs on the circle between the response vectors and radii perpendicular to the midpoint of the dimensions identify the degrees of the categories' central angles on the dimensions, as shown in Figure 27.3. The angles on the submissive and hostile sides of the dimensions are given minus ($-$) signs to distinguish them from angles on the dominant and friendly sides. Thus, the range of angles on each dimension is from $-67.5°$ to $67.5°$. The status and affiliation dimension coordinates of the response vectors are derived from the trigonometric functions of the categories' central angles on the dimensions, as illustrated in Figure 27.4.

This scoring method collapses the eight categories into two continuous measures: the status and affiliation coordinates. Using these measures, response differences can be directly assessed between participants in the same or different interactions or between time periods. In addition, the pattern of an individual's responses over time can be assessed using time series analysis.

The systematic relations of response categories

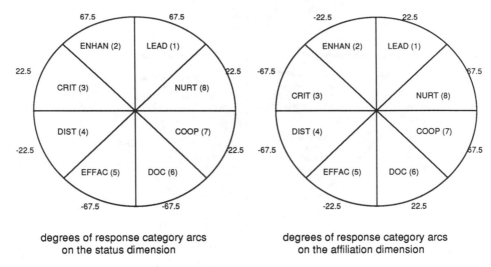

degrees of response category arcs
on the status dimension

degrees of response category arcs
on the affiliation dimension

Figure 27.3. Degrees of the response category arcs on the status and affiliation dimensions.

to each other in the interpersonal circle led Carson (1969) to propose the "principle of complementarity." The principle asserts that response categories that are reciprocal to one another on the status dimension and correspondent on the affiliation dimension are complements of each other (complementary category pairs are nurturant and cooperative, leading and docile, self-enhancing and self-effacing, and critical and distrustful). As seen in Figure 27.2, the messages of responses in the category pairs complement each other. For example, the message of responses in

the critical category is, "You do not have resources of value. You are not worthy of consideration." The message of responses in the distrustful category, the complement of critical, is, "You do not value my· resources. You do not consider my needs." The principle of complementarity posits that employing a particular response potentially encourages an interactant to reciprocate with its complement, an assertion in keeping with relations among the messages interpersonal responses convey.

Interpersonal responses have the potential to

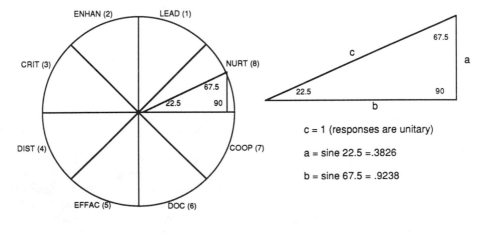

c = 1 (responses are unitary)

a = sine 22.5 =.3826

b = sine 67.5 = .9238

a = status dimension coordinate.
b = affiliation dimension coordinate.
c = magnitude of the response vector.

Figure 27.4. Derivation of response vector coordinates.

generate pressure on an interactant to respond with their complements. The principle of complementarity thus identifies the instrumental value of responses in potentially influencing the other's subsequent response. When a participant responds to another with the complement of the other's previous response, he or she communicates acceptance of the other's assertions about each other's characteristics and of the momentary state of their relationship, and potentially asserts pressure on the other to maintain the current pattern of exchange. When a participant responds to another with a noncomplementary response, he or she reveals a different understanding and potentially asserts pressure on the other to change his or her subsequent response in the direction of the complement of the received response.

How another responds to a specific influence attempt depends on the psychological significance of the received message to the other; that is, on its impact on the other's psychological situation. For example, the other may find the person's assertion that he or she is victimizing the person consistent with how he or she wants to be viewed or abhorrent to his or her self-image. The influence pressures that responses potentially arouse in an interactant, both in terms of direction and magnitude of pressure, are presented in Figures 27.5 and 27.6.

Using the continuous scoring method and the pythagorean theorem, vectors can be calculated that describe the influence pressure (both magnitude and direction) that one participant's response potentially arouses in the other to maintain the current exchange pattern (convergence) or to change the pattern (divergence) in the next exchange. A vector depicting the extent to which the first party changes in response to the influence attempt also can be calculated. From these two measures, magnitudes of conformity, anticonformity, innovation, unresponsiveness, and other indices of relationship behavior can be calculated. Using these measures, the dependencies acting on participants can be inferred from how they attempt to influence each other and from how they respond to each other's attempts to influence. The measures are functions of the relations between the responses of the two participants, and thus they provide indices of the ongoing process of relationship negotiation in the dyad. The indices provide ways of assessing and comparing the relationship processes of different dyads and the relationship behaviors of members within a dyad. In addition, the pattern of relationship negotiation in a dyad over time can be assessed using time series analysis.

Interpersonal Life Space

Behavior at a given time is a function of a person's psychological situation at that time. A person's psychological situation is composed of the psychological realities experienced by the person that arise from the interaction of the characteristics of the person with the characteristics of the person's environment. Thus, a person's psychological situation is the joint product of the characteristics of the person and of his or her environment, the meaning of Lewin's famous formula $B = f(P,E)$. The life space was Lewin's method of representing a person's psychological situation at a given time. In discussions of the life space, Lewin often used analogies to physical space, but he included in the life space anything that was real for the person, such as behaviors and perceptions of possible future events.

To conceptually represent the facts of social interaction, let us conceive of the life space as consisting of the ongoing response exchange between the person and the other and the response exchanges the person perceives to be possible in the future. A response exchange is a person's ongoing response and the context in which it is being enacted, including the other's immediately preceding response. A response exchange is labeled an event. The interpersonal life space is composed of the ongoing event and all events the person perceives to be possibilities in the future of the interaction with the other. Events are the regions of the interpersonal life space. To provide a concrete link between the theoretical representation of the person's psychological situation at a given time and the person's behavior at that time, the regions (events) of the interpersonal life space are represented as interpersonal circles.

The interpersonal life space is composed of two kinds of events: the ongoing event and potential events. The ongoing event is the region of the interpersonal life space in which the person is currently located. It contains the other's immediately preceding response, the response possibilities available to the person, and the factors acting on the person to which he or she is in the process of responding. Potential events are the person's concepts of possible future response exchanges in the relationship. Potential events are regions in the

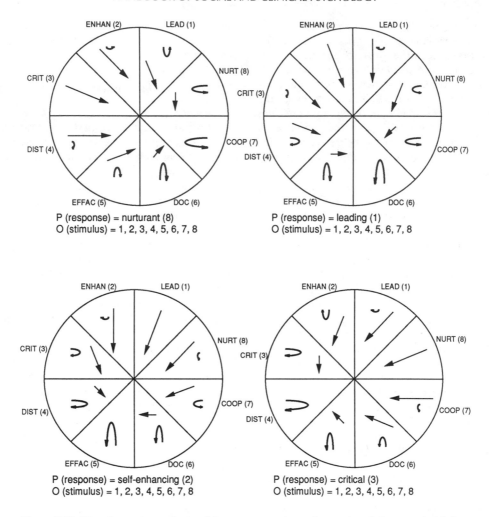

Figure 27.5. Direction and magnitude of the convergent (curved arrows) and divergent (→) influence pressures P's dominant responses potentially arouse in O.

interpersonal life space that surround the ongoing event. Each potential event contains the facts of the situation as the person currently conceives they would be if he or she were located in the potential event. Thus, potential events contain the other's immediately preceding response, the responses available to the person, and the factors acting on the person, all as the person anticipates they would be if he or she were currently located in the event.

Potential events are arranged in the interpersonal life space in terms of what the person conceives to be their connection to the ongoing event. Potential events adjacent to the ongoing event are those that the person believes are immediately accessible as a function of which response he or she chooses to enact in the ongoing event. Adjacent events are potential events that the person anticipates could be realities in the immediate future, depending on how he or she responds to the ongoing event. Potential events not adjacent to the ongoing event are those that the person conceives not to be immediately accessible from the ongoing event. These distant events are connected to the ongoing event through adjacent events. One or more potential event may lie between a distant event and the ongoing event. The potential events that lie between the ongoing event and some distant event are elements of a path through which the person believes he or she can access the distant event from the ongoing event. Paths are one or more potential events that the person believes must be sequentially accessed to achieve some distant event.

Through his or her responses, the person transforms an adjacent event into the ongoing event. In Lewin's terms, the person's response is a form of locomotion by which the person moves from the ongoing event into an adjacent event. Because the regions in the interpersonal life space are behavioral events rather than physical locations, conceiving of the results of a person's response as transforming the event seems more suitable than moving the person. To access a distant event, the person must sequentially transform into ongoing events the potential events that lie on the path

between the ongoing event and the distant event. This process is analogous to pulling on a chain. To lay my hands on some distant link, I must pull the chain toward me by grasping each successive link that lies between the link currently in hand and the desired distant link. When a person transforms a potential event into an ongoing event, that event becomes the center of the life space, and the life space is restructured around its new center. A person's response and the other's subsequent response are time units that mark the transition of the person's life space from one state to another.

Figure 27.7 presents an interpersonal life space. The center circle in Figure 27.7 is the ongoing event. The person is represented in the ongoing event with the "P" in the distrustful category, the

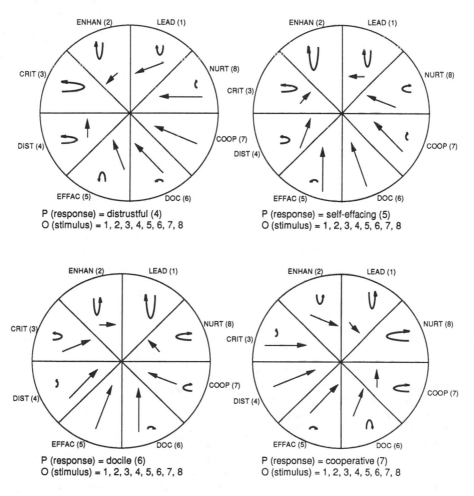

Figure 27.6. Direction and magnitude of the convergent (curved arrows) and divergent (→) influence pressures P's submissive responses potentially arouse in O.

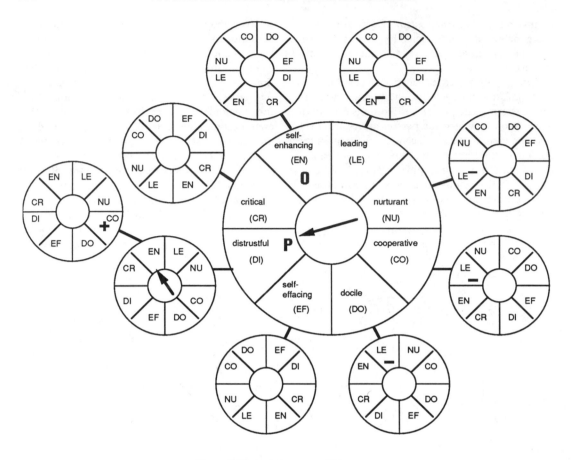

Figure 27.7. An interpersonal life space.

response the person is in the process of enacting. The eight categories of the circle are the response possibilities available to the person. The other's immediately preceding response to which the person is in the process of responding is indicated by the "O" placed in the self-enhancing category. The lines drawn from the eight response possibilities available to the person connect the ongoing event to adjacent events. These are the potential events that the person believes to be immediately available for transformation into the ongoing event by his or her response. The lines connect the person's possible responses in the ongoing event to the response they are expected to generate from the other in the adjacent events. One distant event, in which the other is expected to have enacted a cooperative response, is presented in Figure 27.7. This distant event is connected to the on-

going event through an adjacent event in which the other is expected to have enacted a nurturant response. By enacting a distrustful response in the ongoing event, the person expects to embark on a path leading from the ongoing event, in which the other enacted a self-enhancing response, to a distant event, in which the other is expected to have enacted a cooperative response.

Dependence

Dependence is a psychological force. It is generated by a valence located in a response that another is expected to have enacted in a potential event. The valence is a result of the co-occurrence of two facts in the person's interpersonal life space, a need of the person and the response potentially available from the other that conveys or controls resources related to the need. The other's valenced response is a goal, a resource potentially available from the other. The response may be rewarding or punishing in itself, or it may control access to some other rewarding or punishing environmental feature. The strength of the valence is a function of the need and the extent to which the potential response offers satisfaction or arousal of the need. The valence generates a dependency force that acts on the person. The direction of a dependency force is a function of the location of the potential event that contains the valence relative to the ongoing event. The magnitude of the force is a function of the magnitude of the valence and the number and nature of potential events that lie on the path from the ongoing event to the potential event that contains the valence. A positive dependency force inclines the person to respond to the other in the ongoing event in a way intended to transform it into an event that contains, or is on the path to, the other's valenced response. A negative dependency force has the opposite effect.

In Figure 27.7, the plus (+) sign in the cooperative category of the distant event indicates that the person's goal is to receive a cooperative response from the other. The dependency force acting on the person as a function of the positive valence in the distant event inclines the person to embark on the path toward this goal. By enacting a distrustful response, the person expects to transform the ongoing event into one in which the goal is immediately accessible. The minus (−) signs in the leading and self-enhancing categories of several adjacent events indicate negative valences for receiving leading and self-enhancing responses from the other. The dependency forces acting on the person as a function of these valences incline the person to avoid transforming adjacent events that contain the negative valences into the ongoing event.

Several dependency forces are acting on the person simultaneously. The forces combine according to the principles of vector algebra into a resultant force. The direction of the resultant force determines the direction of the person's response (toward potential events containing positive valences and away from those containing negative valences). A vector (an arrow) in the center of the ongoing event in Figure 27.7 indicates the resultant force acting on the person. The resultant force is the combined effect of the several dependency forces acting on the person. Due to the resultant force, the person is in the process of enacting a distrustful response. The person expects the distrustful response to bring the positively valenced potential event closer and avoid the negatively valenced events.

Dependency forces may have conflicting directions and thus incline the person to embark on different paths. Conflict among forces generates stress. Stress is manifest as negative affect, which is experienced as frustration, anxiety, anger, or fear. Its magnitude is the sum of the magnitudes of dependency forces that cancel one another and thus are not represented in the resultant force. Stress functions as a need. It motivates efforts to restructure the interpersonal life space. When a restructuring plan is believed to offer significant stress reduction, it becomes a goal. The psychological force the goal generates inclines the person to cognitively restructure his or her life space, a form of locomotion (Lewin, 1938). A high level of conflict among dependency forces generates high stress. High stress generates strong negative affect and persistent efforts to restructure the life space in a way that reduces conflict among forces and thus reduces stress.

Interdependence

The dependency forces acting on the other are functions of valences imparted to the person's potential responses by their relations to the other's needs. The other's dependencies determine how the other will respond to the person's behaviors and thus define the transformation values of the person's responses. To achieve desired potential events efficiently, the person must have accurate concepts of the nature of the dependency forces acting on the other. The person's concepts of the dependency forces acting on the other determine the person's perceptions of the transformation values of his or her responses. These concepts define the paths the person perceives to be available to transform desired potential events into the ongoing event. Concepts of the other's dependencies define the structure of the person's interpersonal life space. Likewise, the other's concepts of the nature of the person's dependencies define the other's perceptions of the paths to his or her goals. The person's response in the ongoing event affects the other's concepts of goals and the paths that lead to them, and thus influences the other's subsequent response.

In Figure 27.7, lines connect the person's available responses to the responses the person expects them to generate from the other. These lines reflect the person's concepts of the nature of the other's dependencies on the person. Overall, the person believes that the other wishes to receive cooperative responses (which convey admiration and accordance) or docile responses (which convey deference and compliance) from the person. This concept of the other's dependencies is reflected in the anticipation that six of the person's available responses will generate dominant responses from the other: leading (which conveys advice and suggestions), self-enhancing (which conveys certainty and self-laudation), or critical (which conveys disdain and criticism). On the other hand, the person perceives that the other is greatly concerned about being seen as fair and considerate. The person anticipates that enacting a distrustful response (which conveys disappointment and resentment) will motivate the other to enact a nurturant response (which conveys sympathy and reassurance), an effort to appear fair and considerate. The person anticipates that he or she will then be able to generate a cooperative response from the other by enacting a self-enhancing response.

The person's dependencies on the other determine the goals and thus direction of the person's behavior. The person's concepts of the other's dependencies determine the paths that lead to goals, and thus the responses the person employs in the interaction. The same is true for the other. Thus, interdependence renders the parties in a relationship responsive to each other's needs. Each is inclined to emit valenced responses (both positive and negative) to the other to influence the other to conform his or her responses to needs. Interactants' perceptions of the nature of their interdependence determine the behavioral content of their relationship.

Alternative Relationships

The magnitude of dependency forces acting on a person in a relationship is a function of (a) the strength of underlying needs, (b) the quality of the other's resources and their distance from the ongoing event and, (c) the extent to which the resources potentially available from the other are superior to those potentially available in alternative relationships. The availability of alternative relationships powerfully affects the strength of de-

pendency forces. A lack of alternatives creates profound dependencies and, as a result, profound social influence. Young children have no alternative relationships to those with their parents. As a result, their parents have profound influence on them. The emergence of alternative relationship possibilities is an important factor in psychological development. With the emergence of alternatives, the possibility of choice of relationships emerges. With choice, how the exchange of resources is coordinated becomes more important than the quality of the resources that could be exchanged.

Perceptual and Cognitive Processes

The dependency forces acting on a person, and the paths the person sees as leading to goals, are functions of the person's cognitive construction of the relationship with the other. The person generates a construction of the relationship by observing facts about the circumstances of the relationship and the events that transpire within it and deducing the meanings of the facts. The person attends to what he or she considers to be the most important features of ongoing events. The observed facts are then processed according to rules of evidence to determine their underlying causes. Underlying causes are construed as demand properties of the situation, the dispositions of the other, or the dispositions of the self. The person's conclusions generate new or confirm or contradict previous concepts of the features of the relationship. The person's construction of the relationship is embellished with new conclusions and revised when conclusions about the meaning of events are at variance with previous concepts. What the person attends to and the attributional principles and conventions he or she applies to determine underlying causes are crucial determinants of the cognitive construction of the relationship.

The person's cognitive construction of a relationship is composed of the following concepts:

1. The demand properties of the situation, including the restraints and demands the person expects to affect conduct in the relationship.

2. The dispositions that underlie the other's behavior. They are revealed in how the other's behavior departs from what the person expects as a function of the demand properties of the situation. They include the other's personal goals for the relationship, the other's needs and capabili-

ties, and the other's interpersonal values that underlie his or her strategy for taking the person's needs into consideration. This constellation of characteristics defines the *opportunity structure* the person believes that the other presents for meeting the person's needs (McCall & Simmons, 1966; Swann, 1987).

3. The dispositions that underlie the person's behavior. The person reveals his or her dispositions in, as well as deduces them from, how his or her behavior departs from the demand properties of the situation. They include personal goals for the relationship, needs and capabilities, and interpersonal values which underlie strategies for taking the other's needs into consideration. This constellation of characteristics defines the opportunity structure the person believes that he or she presents to the other.

4. Opportunity structures potentially available to self and other in alternative relationships. These concepts limit the strengths of the dependency forces that are perceived to be acting on self and other in the relationship.

5. Concepts of congruencies and discrepancies between obtained and desired resources and between achieved and desired impressions in the relationship. The person immediately experiences the consequences of the other's responses in terms of needs met or aroused. These experiences may or may not conform to the person's concepts of resources available in the relationship. Discrepancies between obtained and desired resources identify variances between reality and the person's construction of the opportunity structure the other presents.

Concepts of the other's impressions of the person are derived from observations of how the other seeks to influence the person. Discrepancies between achieved and desired impressions indicate variances between the other's impressions and the opportunity structure the person intended to present to the other.

Discrepancies between obtained and desired resources and between achieved and desired impressions generate changes in the person's concepts of goals and paths in the relationship.

Sources of Change

Behavior is the relationship between stimulus and response (Klir & Valach, 1967). Behavior change is a change in that relationship. Behavior change is a function of changes in the person's conceptions of the goals and paths available in the relationship. Change in conceptions of goals and paths is a function of changes in the person's construction of the relationship. Changes in construction of the relationship result from the following:

1. New or discrepant information about one or more concepts of the features of the relationship.
2. Cognitive restructuring of the interpersonal life space motivated by conflicts among dependency forces.
3. Alterations in (a) what the person attends to in relationships, (b) how the person processes the "facts," or (c) the information the person believes responses convey.

Changes of all three types, and especially in conceptions of the self, are most likely to occur in relationships in which the person has strong dependencies. Change is fostered when the person finds that his or her construction of the relationship does not predictably generate desired behavioral events.

Research Support for the Theory

From the perspective of interpersonal influence theory, a relationship is a dynamic and evolving social entity. Partners actively seek to conform their relationship to their needs. Through their behaviors, they construct its realities. In turn, their psychological constructions of its realities shape their behaviors. The evolving characteristics of a relationship are functions of the partners' characteristics. In turn, the evolving characteristics of the partners are functions of the relationship's characteristics. Social psychological research has accumulated a good deal of evidence that is consistent with this picture of relationships. Some of the evidence is reviewed below in terms of the reciprocal effects of social cognition and social behavior on each other.

Demand Properties of the Situation

According to the theory, people's understanding of the demand properties of the situation in which a relationship occurs affects behavior and determines baseline expectations for behavior. Characteristics of the other and of the self are deduced from how behavior deviates from these expectations. McClintock and Liebrand (1988) and Gruszkos (1986) have shown that demand properties of the situation affect behavior. McClintock and Liebrand had subjects play four dyadic decision games that had different outcome matrices. They found that the differences in outcome structures, which were explained to subjects before the games began, systematically affected the subjects' choice behaviors in interactive effects with the subjects' interpersonal values and their partners' game strategies. Gruszkos (1986) varied the demand properties of the situation by assigning leader or assistant roles to subjects in an experiment similar to the Strong et al. (1988) study. These differences in demand properties generated systematic differences in how subjects responded to confederate stimulus behaviors overall and in interactive effects with the types of responses the confederates enacted.

In the classic demonstration of how the perceived demand properties of a situation affect attribution, Jones, Davis, and Gergen (1961) found that observers made correspondent inferences to account for job applicants' behaviors in selection interviews only when the applicants' self-presentations violated the expectation that applicants would present themselves as personally suited to the demands of the job. Jones et al. (1981) have shown that when people observe themselves behaving in ways that they perceive to deviate from situational demands, they change their self-concepts. Festinger and Carlsmith's (1959) original demonstration of dissonance can be construed as the same effect. The subjects' protestation of enjoyment of an experimental task that was clearly boring, without some clear situational demand that could justify their behavior, led to self-concept change (Bem, 1974; Tedeschi, Schlenker, & Bonoma, 1971).

Dispositions of the Other

According to the theory, people's construction of the other's dispositions affects their behavior. McClintock and Liebrand (1988) systematically varied how the other responded to subjects in the decision games. They found that, as the games progressed, subjects increasingly and systematically varied their choices in accord with the dispositional implications of the others' choices. Strong et al. (1988) analyzed the relations among confederate and subject responses in two time periods corresponding to the women's work on two pic-

tures. They found that changes over time in the relations among responses varied systematically by condition. As shown by the personality measures, each response style generated distinct conceptions of the confederates' characteristics. These conceptions emerged as subjects gained experience with the confederates. The systematic behavior changes in time reflected the emerging conceptions. Similarly, Swann and Ely (1984) found that the questions subjects asked of another were initially a function of prior information they had about the other, but changed over time as the information the other provided contradicted the dispositional implications of the prior information.

The impression a person believes another has formed about the person's characteristics is an aspect of the person's conception of the other. Baumeister and Jones (1978) found that subjects' initial presentations of self to another systematically varied as a function of the impressions subjects believed their partners had about them. Swann's research, described below, also demonstrates the effects of behavior of conceptions of the other's impressions of one's characteristics.

Dispositions of the Self

According to the theory, people's constructions of their dispositions affect their behavior. McClintock and Liebrand (1988) selected groups of subjects on the basis of personal values for cooperation, competition, or individualism in relationships. They found that the self-concepts systematically affected subjects' choices in the games. In a post hoc analysis of subjects' self-ratings of dominance and affiliation in the Strong et al. (1988) study, Strong (in press) found that these self-concepts systematically affected how subjects responded in the various conditions. Swann and his colleagues (Swann, 1987; Swann & Ely, 1984; Swann & Hill, 1982) have shown that responses to feedback from another about the other's impressions of the person are largely a function of the correspondence of the feedback to the person's self-concept. When feedback was inconsistent with self-concept, Swann's subjects behaved in ways that contradicted the feedback and affirmed the self.

Discrepancy, Dependency, and Change in Self-Concept

The theory proposes that change in construction of a relationship is a function of discrepant information, and that change in the self-concept component of that construction is most likely when the person has strong dependencies in the relationship. Swann's (1987) research on identity negotiation in relationships has shown that feedback that is discrepant from a person's self-concept results in changes in self-concept only when the person is uncertain of his or her views and the other is certain of his or her feedback (Swann & Ely, 1984), or when the subject's intimate other agrees with the feedback (Swann & Predmore, 1985). Otherwise, discrepancy leads to conceptions of the other as a source of inaccurate information.

The effect of the strength of dependencies on how discrepancies are resolved is suggested in laboratory studies in which subjects are led to believe that they have no alternative but to continue a relationship with a specific other. According to the theory, perceptions of the availability of alternative relationships affect the strength of dependency forces acting on the person. In such studies (Kiesler, Zanna, & DeSalvo, 1966; Pallak & Heller, 1971; Wolf, 1979), subjects who believed that they must continue relationships with disagreeable others ingratiated the others with opinion conformity more than did subjects who did not anticipate subsequent contact. Similar effects of anticipated future contact have been found on interpersonal behavior (Gergen & Wishnov, 1965) and accounts for group failures and successes (Forsyth, Berger, & Mitchell, 1981; Norvell & Forsyth, 1984). Field studies of committed couples have found that the level of commitment and the presence of children, both of which suggest the degree to which alternative relationships are psychologically available, are systematically related to self-reports of behavior in the relationships (Howard et al., 1986).

SOCIAL INFLUENCE AND CHANGE IN THERAPEUTIC RELATIONSHIPS

The therapeutic relationship is formed with the objective of changing one member's behavior in other relationships such as with spouse, children, parents, friends, or employer. The change is generated through the information therapists and clients exchange in their responses to each other. To affect behavior in other relationships, therapy generates changes in clients' concepts of the demand properties of situations, of others' dispositions, or of their own dispositions. Such changes alter perceptions of the goals and paths in relationships and thus change behavior.

Voluntary clients enter therapy because of stress. Their current understandings of the features of important relationships are generating high levels of conflict among the dependency forces acting on them. Their current behaviors serve their strongest needs but frustrate other important needs. They turn to therapists in the hope of receiving help in cognitively restructuring problematic interpersonal life spaces in ways that reduce the stress they are experiencing. Relationships with therapists are sought because they are socially sanctioned as legitimate sources of expert help on interpersonal problems. Clients will maintain the relationships as long as they continue to experience high stress and perceive the relationships to offer some hope of receiving help. They give therapists the ability to influence them as long as they perceive that doing so is to their ultimate benefit.

Clients expect therapists to offer opportunity structures that contain (a) an overall goal of aiding them with their problems; (b) a need to be seen as competent, trustworthy, and likeable; (c) resources of acceptance, reassurance, help, encouragement, suggestions, confidence, ideas, and advice; and (d) a dedication to their ultimate welfare. The resources clients anticipate to be available from therapists define the avenues initially open to therapists to influence them. As clients' trust and confidence in their therapists as sources of help grow, a greater range of resources becomes available to therapists to influence them. Therapists expect clients to offer opportunity structures that contain (a) a goal of restructuring one or more interpersonal life spaces; (b) stress from conflicts among forces, a need to be seen as people of worth and integrity, and needs to protect themselves from dangerous interpersonal events; (c) resources of acceptance, accordance, and capabilities; and (d) an inclination to be somewhat considerate of the therapists' needs in the situation.

Therapists' notions about the resources available from clients are drawn from models of mental health. Anticipated client resources are goals in the distant events that therapists seek to generate in therapy. Models of psychological health champion flexible interpersonal functioning and emphasize resources conveyed in leading, nurturant, and cooperative responses. Therapists believe that clients are capable of such functioning even if there is little evidence to support this belief in initial ongoing events. At first, therapists do not know the paths to desired potential events. As a result, they seek to gain information about the opportunity structures clients present, a strategy they carry out by enacting nurturant and leading responses to whatever responses clients enact (Friedlander, Siegel, & Brenock, 1989). As therapists deduce paths that may lead to their goals, their behavior becomes more variable.

Therapists' single-minded dedication to achieving distant therapeutic goals is crucial to the success of therapy. If therapists allow clients' responses to generate reactions not directed at these goals, the objectives of therapy are not likely to be achieved. Therapists must not allow themselves to be influenced to respond nontherapeutically by responses that convey opinions, advice, self-absorption, commands, anger, criticism, resentment, skepticism, helplessness, acquiescence, admiration, accordance, or sympathy. Personal (nontherapeutic) responsiveness to such resources will confirm rather than contradict clients' concepts of the features of relationships, and thus will diminish rather than enhance the possibility of achieving the objective of therapy (Kell & Mueller, 1966).

Typically, clients manifest rigid, inflexible, and strident behavior patterns. Dynamically, these repetitive patterns are the behavioral effects of powerful negative valences located in potential responses from others. The stress clients are experiencing usually is a function of conflict among forces generated by the strong negative valences and weaker positive valences. The powerful negative valences are the result of clients' constructions of the meaning of some painful past and/or current experiences. In these experiences, clients have found that being seen by another as asserting the possession of certain resources has disastrous consequences, such as depreciation, rejection, abandonment, abuse, exploitation, bitterness, or martyrdom. Clients studiously avoid enacting responses that are anticipated to lead to these consequences. The inflexible behavior patterns in ongoing events represent attempts to avoid transforming dangerous potential events into the ongoing event.

Therapists' strategy for aiding clients to cognitively restructure problematic interpersonal life spaces includes the following:

1. Encourage clients to enact in therapy the inflexible and rigid behavior patterns associated with the conflict among forces in problematic relationships. This task must be carried out in a way that fosters trust and belief in the therapists' usefulness.

2. Deduce from the symptom pattern (a) the impressions clients are striving to create, (b) the impressions clients are striving to avoid creating, (c) the responses from others that are negatively valenced, (d) the responses from others that are positively valenced but are not being sought due to the effects of the negative valences, and (e) the cognitive concepts that are generating the valences.

3. Enact responses that convey information that is inconsistent with the concepts generating the valences. This task must be carried out in a way that (a) maintains clients' participation in therapy, (b) decreases the strength of negative valences, and (c) increases the strength of positive valences.

4. Aid clients in the task of extending and integrating new or altered concepts and resulting behavior patterns into problematic relationships.

Encouraging Symptomatic Behavior

Clients enter therapy expecting to describe their problems and receive insight into how they can be solved. Clients expect therapists to show interest in their difficulties and to help them focus on the most important features of the problems. They also are concerned that therapists view them in a positive and sympathetic light. They are reluctant to reveal actions and thoughts that they believe are morally unacceptable and are inclined to present their problems as due to others' inequitable and egotistical dispositions and actions or to personal dispositions over which they have little voluntary control.

Clients' self-presentations intended to secure positive and sympathetic hearings from therapists are driven by the same motivational factors that underlie their behaviors in problematic relationships. Therapist responses that convey receptiveness, acceptance, sympathy, and comfort encourage clients to enact the symptom pattern in therapy. These responses also encourage trust and kindle hope that the therapist may prove useful.

Therapists direct clients' disclosures to the most important features of problems by focusing on and responding to indications of negative affect. Stress generates negative affect, such as fear, anger, anxiety, and frustration. Responses with affectively negative components identify circumstances in which the underlying motivational structure contains conflicting forces. Empathic responses to the affectively negative components of responses direct clients' disclosures to the circumstances that are generating stress. Clients' reactions to their therapists' interest in the affective components of responses, both in terms of responses enacted and responses studiously avoided, are the basic facts from which therapists deduce the nature of the forces acting on clients, the concepts that are generating them, and the paths to therapeutic goals.

Diagnosis

The first step in deducing the causes of symptoms is to identify the impressions clients are striving to achieve in therapy. The responses clients enact are attempts to convey these impressions. Therapists note the impressions they are forming of clients and note how they are inclined to respond to clients. The most frequent impressions clients attempt to generate are those of being victims of unscrupulous others, martyrdom, helplessness, and dependence (Strong, 1986). These impressions are conveyed by distrustful and self-effacing responses. They generate inclinations in therapists to sympathize, reassure, and advise (nurturant and leading responses) and to show irritation, impatience, self-assertion, and self-laudation (critical and self-enhancing responses).

Psychological forces combine according to the principles of vector algebra. Therefore, strident efforts to generate a particular impression suggest that the impression being avoided is conveyed by responses located in the category opposite the enacted responses in the interpersonal circle. When clients enact self-effacing and distrustful responses, they maximally avoid impressions conveyed by leading and nurturant responses (see Figure 27.2).

Conflicting negative and positive valences are located in potential responses likely to be encouraged by the avoided impression. Leading and nurturant responses are most likely to generate self-enhancing and critical responses from others who are competitive or dissatisfied in the relationship and cooperative and docile responses from others who are affiliative or satisfied (Nutall, Strong, & McTaggart, 1988; Strong, in press). This suggests that the stress probably is a function of negative valences located in others' potential

self-enhancing and critical responses and positive valences located in other's potentially cooperative and docile responses. The enactment of distrustful and self-effacing responses probably reflects convictions (based on painful experiences) that enacting leading and nurturant responses will lead to exploitation, disregard, or, worse yet, rejection and abandonment.

The valences generating the conflicting forces stem from concepts of the features of relationships, such as the attributes of others and the self. The strength of the negative valences in others' potential self-enhancing and critical responses suggest that clients believe that self-absorption, criticism, and rejection from others are likely to occur and would be disastrous. On the other hand, the weaker positive valences located in potential cooperative and docile responses suggest that clients believe that the resources they have to convey in leading and nurturant responses are of little value to others. Such beliefs could stem from a number of concepts including (a) others are pernicious, dangerous, and egocentric, (b) I do not have dominant resources of much value to others, (c) others have resources superior to mine and, (d) I do not have good alternative relationships while others do.

Generating Change

The identification of concepts that may be generating the valences that underlie stress allows therapists to formulate and implement plans of how to foster changes in concepts. Change is stimulated by conveying information that (a) contradicts the impressions and behavioral effects clients expect their responses to generate and (b) implies how interpersonal concepts should be changed. One of many methods to foster changes is to enact cooperative responses that positively reframe symptomatic behaviors (i.e., paradoxical reframing; Strong, 1984, 1987a, 1987b; Swann, Pelham, & Chidester, 1988). These cooperative responses convey admiration and trust. They assert that symptomatic behaviors are motivated by desires to be responsible and to serve others through self-sacrificing acts. The responses convey highly discrepant information to clients. When clients enact self-effacing and distrustful responses, they intend to appear helpless and victimized and to solicit help. They are dismayed to learn that they conveyed impressions of responsibility and altruism and solicited admiration.

The cooperative responses imply that clients have valuable dominant resources to impart to others and altruistic motives to use them to benefit others. The responses assert that clients have achieved the impression they most feared to convey. But their therapist's response to the impression is admiration and trust, not the expected criticism and rejection. The responses imply that clients are attractive potential partners to others and thus that they have good alternatives to current relationships. In terms of the forces that underlie clients' symptomatic behaviors, the responses convey information that simultaneously attacks the concepts that are generating the predominant negative valences and reinforces the concepts that are generating the weaker positive valences. Because of clients' needs to be seen as people of worth and integrity, they are inclined to accept the implications of the responses, but only after strenuous efforts to test therapists' sincerity and confidence in their assertions.

Extending Change

Initial acceptance of the positive reframe of symptoms initiates a process of aiding clients' efforts to integrate its meaning into cognitive constructions of relationships and to enact responses that reflect its meaning in problematic relationships. This process may take considerable effort. Partners in problematic relationships seldom appreciate changes in clients' behaviors and often strive to influence them to return to the more predictable and familiar patterns. Therapists become their clients' coaches on how to encourage partners to change. Therapists become sources of encouragement and admiration for the clients' hard work. When clients master the interpersonal skills necessary to conform important relationships to their new concepts and when they achieve stability in them, they no longer need their therapists. The therapeutic relationship dissolves.

From the perspective of interpersonal influence theory, clients carry primary responsibility for the therapeutic relationship. Clients seek out the professional services of therapists in the responsible pursuit of solutions to interpersonal problems and accompanying personal distress. Clients decide at all points in the process whether the relationship is to be continued. Clients decide how much influence to allow therapists to exert on their thinking and acting. Clients are continually engaged in conforming personal relationships to their needs

before, during, and after therapy. The therapist's job is to assist clients to become more effective in these life-defining efforts.

Research on Change Processes in Therapeutic Relationships

Therapists pursue the job of enhancing clients' interpersonal effectiveness by guiding the therapeutic relationship through three developmental stages: (a) developing trust, (b) stimulating change, and (c) extending change. Distinctive patterns of interaction between therapist and client mark these developmental stages in successful therapeutic relationships (Strong & Claiborn, 1982; Tracey, 1985; Tracey & Ray, 1984). Research in counseling and clinical psychology has focused on some aspects of the processes of each stage. Some of this research, and needs for further research, are noted below.

Developing Trust

The therapist's objectives in the first stage of therapy are to increase the client's trust and confidence in the therapist, identify the relationship aspects generating stress, and diagnose the dynamics underlying interpersonal problems. Carl Rogers and his colleagues (Rogers & Dymond, 1954; Rogers, Gendlin, Kiesler, & Truax, 1967; Truax & Carkhuff, 1967) have shown that therapist enactment of nurturant responses that express empathy, unconditional regard, and nonpossessive warmth accomplishes the first two objectives of the first stage. These responses facilitate the client's depth of experiencing (expression of emotionally laden material through self-effacing, distrustful, and critical responses). The therapist's nurturant responses reassure the client of the therapist's positive regard for and understanding of him or her, and thus encourage the client to accept influence from the therapist. By focusing on stress-induced negative affect, empathic responses direct the client's attention to the issues creating problems in his or her relationships. Rogers and his colleagues have documented that, with continued assistance of this kind, clients can sort out many of their problems. This approach is a sufficient, though not an efficient, method of helping clients change (Rogers, 1957).

The least developed aspect of the first stage is diagnosis. Virtually no research has addressed how symptoms (rigid response patterns and emotional manifestations of stress) relate to the underlying dynamics identified in interpersonal influence theory.

Stimulating Change

The objective of the second stage of therapy is to stimulate change in the client's symptomatic behavior and in the dynamics that underlie it. The therapist accomplishes this objective by presenting information to the client that is discrepant with the client's concept of the therapeutic relationship. A large body of research has accumulated that addresses this process (Garfield & Bergin, 1986). However, surprisingly little systematic knowledge has emerged from the vast effort that has been expended. The paucity of attention to the development of adequate theories of change in relationships has greatly hampered research on, and the accumulation of systematic knowledge about, this process (Forsyth & Strong, 1986).

Interpersonal influence theory is an attempt to identify key aspects of the change process in therapeutic relationships. Systematic and theory-driven research on its concepts is needed, research that uses experimental methodologies such as those Ascher, Strong, and their colleagues have introduced (Ascher, 1981; Ascher & Turner, 1980; Beck & Strong, 1982; Feldman, Strong, & Danser, 1982; Strong, Wambach, Lopez, & Cooper, 1979), and controlled methods of field investigation such as Heppner and Claiborn (1989) have proposed. Crucial to the success of such efforts is a theoretically meaningful method of categorizing therapist and client responses. The Interpersonal Communication Rating Scale (Strong, Hills, & Nelson, 1988) was developed for this purpose.

Extending Change

The objective of the third stage of therapy is to extend the changes stimulated in therapy into the client's ongoing relationships. As Swann (1987) has noted, if changes generated in therapy are to survive, clients must implement them in ongoing relationships. The task is not easy. Partners usually act to counter and eliminate the changes. This fact probably accounts for Lieberman, Yalom, and Miles' (1973) finding that changes stimulated in group therapy survived best when the groups actively focused attention on extending changes into ongoing relationships. The growing popularity of family therapy is due largely to the growing recognition that therapeutic change must be supported by changes in clients' personal relationships. Little if any research has addressed how therapists equip and support clients to accomplish this crucial task.

REFERENCES

Ascher, L. M. (1981). Employing paradoxical intention in the treatment of agoraphobia. *Behaviour Research and Therapy, 19*, 533–547.

Ascher, L. M., & Turner, R. M. (1980). A comparison of two methods for administration of paradoxical intention. *Behaviour Research and Therapy, 18*, 121–126.

Bales, R. F., Cohen, S. P., & Williamson, S. A. (1979). *SYMLOG: A system for the multiple level observation of groups*. New York: Free Press.

Baumeister, F. R., & Jones, E. E. (1978). When self-presentation is constrained by the target's knowledge: Consistency and compensation. *Journal of Personality and Social Psychology, 36*, 608–618.

Beck, J., & Strong, S. R. (1982). Stimulating therapeutic change with interpretations: A comparison of positive and negative connotation. *Journal of Counseling Psychology, 29*, 551–559.

Becker, W. C., & Krug, R. S. (1964). A circumplex model for social behavior in children. *Child Development, 35*, 371–396.

Bem, D. J. (1974). Self-perception theory. In L. Berkowitz (Ed.), *Advances in experimental social psychology* (Vol. 6). New York: Academic Press.

Benjamin, L. S. (1974). Structural analysis of social behavior. *Psychological Review, 81*, 392–425.

Buss, D. M., Gomes, M., Higgins, D. S., & Lauterbach, K. (1987). Tactics of manipulation. *Journal of Personality and Social Psychology, 52*, 1219–1229.

Carson, R. C. (1969). *Interaction concepts of personality*. Chicago: Aldine.

Cartwright, D. (1959a). A field theoretical conception of power. In D. Cartwright (Ed.), *Studies in social power* (pp. 183–220). Ann Arbor, MI: Institute for Social Research.

Cartwright, D. (Ed.). (1959b). *Studies in social power*. Ann Arbor, MI: Institute for Social Research.

Cassirer, E. (1923). *Substance and function and Einstein's theory of relativity*. New York: Dover.

Chance, E. (1966). Content analysis of verbalizations about interpersonal experience. In L. A. Gottschalk & A. H. Auerbach (Eds.), *Methods of research in psychotherapy* (pp. 127–145). New York: Appleton-Century-Crofts.

Conte, H. R., & Plutchik, R. (1981). A circumplex model for interpersonal personality traits. *Journal of Personality and Social Psychology, 40,* 701–711.

Cowan, G., Drinkard, J., & MacGavin, L. (1984). The effects of target, age, and gender on use of power strategies. *Journal of Personality and Social Psychology, 47,* 1391–1398.

Emerson, R. M. (1962). Power-dependence relations. *American Sociological Review, 27,* 31–41.

Falbo, T., & Peplau, L. A. (1980). Power strategies in intimate relationships. *Journal of Personality and Social Psychology, 38,* 618–628.

Feldman, D. A., Strong, S. R., & Danser, D. B. (1982). A comparison of paradoxical and nonparadoxical interpretations and directives. *Journal of Counseling Psychology, 29,* 572–579.

Festinger, L., & Carlsmith, J. M. (1959). Cognitive consequences of forced compliance. *Journal of Abnormal and Social Psychology, 58,* 203–210.

Foa, U. G. (1961). Convergences in the analysis of the structure of interpersonal behavior. *Psychological Review, 68,* 341–353.

Forsyth, D. R., Berger, R., & Mitchell, T. (1981). The effects of self-serving vs. other-serving claims of responsibility on attraction and attribution in groups. *Social Psychology Quarterly, 44,* 59–64.

Forsyth, D. R., & Strong, S. R. (1986). The scientific study of counseling and psychotherapy: A unificationist's view. *American Psychologist, 41,* 113–119.

French, J. R. P., Jr., & Raven, B. (1959). The bases of social power. In D. Cartwright (Ed.), *Studies in social power* (pp. 150–167). Ann Arbor, MI: Institute for Social Research.

Friedlander, M. L., Siegel, S. M., & Brenock, K. (1989). Parallel processes in counseling and supervision: A case study. *Journal of Counseling Psychology, 36,* 149–157.

Garfield, S., & Bergin, A. (Eds.) (1986). *Handbook of psychotherapy and behavior change* (3rd ed.). New York: John Wiley & Sons.

Gergen, K. J., & Wishnov, B. (1965). Other's self-evaluations and interaction anticipation as determinants of self-presentation. *Journal of Personality and Social Psychology, 2,* 348–358.

Goffman, E. (1959). *The presentation of self in everyday life.* New York: Doubleday.

Gruszkos, J. (1986). *The effects of situational motivations on interpersonal behavior.* Unpublished doctoral dissertation, Virginia Commonwealth University, Richmond, VA.

Heppner, P. P., & Claiborn, C. D. (1989). Social influence research in counseling: A review and critique. *Journal of Counseling Psychology, 36,* 365–387.

Howard, J. A., Blumstein, P., & Schwartz, P. (1986). Sex, power, and influence tactics in intimate relationships. *Journal of Personality and Social Psychology, 51,* 102–109.

Jones, E. E., Davis, K. E., & Gergen, K. J. (1961). Role playing variations and their informational value for person perception. *Journal of Abnormal and Social Psychology, 63,* 302–310.

Jones, E. E., Rhodewalt, F., Berglas, S., & Skelton, J. A. (1981). Effects of strategic self-presentation on subsequent self-esteem. *Journal of Personality and Social Psychology, 41,* 407–421.

Kell, B. L., & Mueller, W. J. (1966). *Impact and change.* New York: Appleton-Century-Crofts.

Kelley, H. H. (1979). *Personal relationships.* Hillsdale, NJ: Lawrence Erlbaum Associates.

Kelley, H. H., & Thibaut, J. W. (1978). *Interpersonal relations.* New York: John Wiley & Sons.

Kiesler, C. A., Zanna, M., & DeSalvo, J. (1966). Deviation and conformity: Opinion change as a function of commitment, attraction, and the presence of a deviate. *Journal of Personality and Social Psychology, 3,* 458–467.

Kiesler, D. J. (1983). The 1982 interpersonal circle: A taxonomy for complementarity in human transactions. *Psychological Review, 90,* 185–214.

Klir, G. J., & Valach, M. (1967). *Cybernetic modeling.* Princeton, NJ: Van Nostrand.

Leary, T. (1957). *Interpersonal diagnosis of personality.* New York: Ronald Press.

Lewin, K. (1935). *A dynamic theory of personality.* New York: McGraw-Hill.

Lewin, K. (1938). *The conceptual representation and the measurement of psychological forces.* Durham, NC: Duke University Press.

Lewin, K. (1948). *Resolving social conflicts.* New York: Harper & Row.

Lewin, K. (1951). *Field theory in social science.* New York: Harper & Row.

Lieberman, M. A., Yalom, I. D., & Miles, M. B. (1973). *Encounter groups: First facts*. New York: Basic Books.

Lorr, M., & McNair, D. M. (1966). Methods relating to evaluation of therapeutic outcome. In L. A. Gottschalk & A. H. Auerbach (Eds.), *Methods of research in psychotherapy* (pp. 573–594). New York: Appleton-Century-Crofts.

McCall, G. J., & Simmons, J. L. (1966). *Identities and interactions: An examination of human associations in everyday life*. New York: Free Press.

McClintock, C. G., & Liebrand, W. B. G. (1988). *Journal of Personality and Social Psychology, 55*, 396–409.

Moscovici, S. (1985). Social influence and conformity. In G. Lindzey & E. Aronson (Eds.), *Handbook of social psychology* (3rd ed., Vol. 2). New York: Random House.

Moscovici, S., & Mugny, G. (1983). Minority influence. In P. B. Paulus (Ed.), *Basic group processes*. New York: Springer-Verlag.

Norvell, N., & Forsyth, D. R. (1984). The impact of inhibiting or facilitating causal factors on group members' reactions after success and failure. *Social Psychology Quarterly, 47*, 293–297.

Nutall, S. B., Strong, S. R., & McTaggart, M. J. (1988). *Effects of satisfaction, role, and race on behavior in marital dyads: A test of interpersonal influence theory*. Unpublished manuscript, Department of Psychology, Virginia Commonwealth University, Richmond, VA.

Pallak, M. S., & Heller, J. F. (1971). Interactive effects of commitment to future interaction and threat to attitudinal freedom. *Journal of Personality and Social Psychology, 17*, 325–331.

Perkins, M. J., Kiesler, D. J., Anchin, J. C., Chirico, B. M., Kyle, E. M., & Federman, E. J. (1979). The impact message inventory: A new measure of relationship in counseling/psychotherapy and other dyads. *Journal of Counseling Psychology, 26*, 363–367.

Rogers, C. R. (1957). The necessary and sufficient conditions of therapeutic personality change. *Journal of Consulting Psychology, 27*, 95–103.

Rogers, C. R., & Dymond, R. (1954). *Psychotherapy and personality change*. New York: Roland.

Rogers, C. R., Gendlin, E., Kiesler, D., & Truax, C. (1967). *The therapeutic relationships and its impact: A study of psychotherapy with schizo-phrenics*. Madison: University of Wisconsin Press.

Russell, J. A. (1980). A circumplex model of affect. *Journal of Personality and Social Psychology, 39*, 1161–1178.

Schaefer, E. S. (1961). Converging conceptual models for maternal behavior and for child behavior. In J. C. Glidewell (Ed.), *Parental attitudes and child behavior*. Springfield, IL: Charles Thomas.

Stiles, W. B. (1980). Comparison of dimensions derived from rating versus coding of dialogue. *Journal of Personality and Social Psychology, 38*, 359–374.

Strong, S. R. (1984). Experimental studies in explicitly paradoxical interventions: Results and implications. *Journal of Behavior Therapy and Experimental Psychiatry, 15*, 189–194.

Strong, S. R. (1986). Interpersonal influence theory and therapeutic interactions. In F. J. Dorn (Ed.), *Social influence processes in counseling and psychotherapy*. Springfield, IL: Charles Thomas.

Strong, S. R. (1987a). Interpersonal change processes in therapeutic interactions. In J. Maddux, C. Stoltenberg, & R. Rosenwein (Eds.), *Social processes in clinical and counseling psychology*. New York: Springer-Verlag.

Strong, S. R. (1987b). Interpersonal influence theory as a common language for psychotherapy. *International Journal of Integrative and Eclectic Psychotherapy, 6*, 173–184.

Strong, S. R. (in press). Interpersonal influence theory: The situational and individual determinants of interpersonal behavior. In R. V. Dawis & D. Lubinski (Eds.), *Assessing individual differences in human behavior*. Minneapolis: University of Minnesota Press.

Strong, S. R., & Claiborn, C. D. (1982). *Change through interaction: Social psychological processes of counseling and psychotherapy*. New York: Wiley-Interscience.

Strong, S. R., Hills, H. I., Kilmartin, C. T., DeVries, H., Lanier, K., Nelson, B. N., Strickland, D., & Meyer, C. W. III. (1988). The dynamic relations among interpersonal behaviors: A test of complementarity and anticomplementarity. *Journal of Personality and Social Psychology, 54*, 798–810.

Strong, S. R., Hills, H. I., & Nelson, B. N. (1988). *Interpersonal Communication Rating Scale*. Unpublished manuscript, Virginia Commonwealth University, Richmond, VA.

Strong, S. R., Wambach, C. A., Lopez, F. B., & Cooper, R. K. (1979). Motivational and equipping functions of interpretation in counseling and psychotherapy. *Journal of Counseling Psychology, 26*, 98–107.

Swann, W. B. (1987). Identity negotiation: Where two roads meet. *Journal of Personality and Social Psychology, 53*, 1038–1052.

Swann, W. B., & Ely, R. J. (1984). A battle of wills: Self-verification versus behavioral confirmation. *Journal of Personality and Social Personality, 46*, 1287–1302.

Swann, W. B., & Hill, C. A. (1982). When our identities are mistaken: Reaffirming self-conceptions through social interaction. *Journal of Personality and Social Psychology, 43*, 59–66.

Swann, W. B., Pelham, B. W., & Chidester, T. R. (1988). Change through paradox: Using self-verification to alter beliefs. *Journal of Personality and Social Psychology, 54*, 268–273.

Swann, W. B., & Predmore, S. C. (1985). Intimates as agents of social support: Sources of consolation or despair? *Journal of Personality and Social Psychology, 49*, 1609–1617.

Tedeschi, J. T., Schlenker, B. R., & Bonoma, T. V. (1971). Cognitive dissonance: Private ratiocination or public spectacle? *American Psychologist, 26*, 685–695.

Thibaut, J. W., & Kelley, H. H. (1959). *The social psychology of groups*. New York: John Wiley & Sons.

Tracey, T. J. (1985). Dominance and outcome: A sequential examination. *Journal of Counseling Psychology, 32*, 119–122.

Tracey, T. J., & Ray, P. B. (1984). The stages of successful time-limited counseling: An interactional examination. *Journal of Counseling Psychology, 31*, 13–27.

Truax, C. B., & Carkhuff, R. R. (1967). *Toward effective counseling and psychotherapy: Training and practice*. Chicago: Aldine.

Wiggins, J. S. (1979). A psychological taxonomy of trait descriptive terms: The interpersonal domain. *Journal of Personality and Social Psychology, 37*, 395–412.

Wolf, S. (1979). Behavioral style and group cohesiveness as sources of minority influence. *European Journal of Social Psychology, 9*, 381–395.

CHAPTER 28

ATTRIBUTION-BASED TREATMENTS

Nancy L. Murdock
Elizabeth M. Altmaier

Attributions are causal statements formulated by individuals to explain life events. These causal judgments have been investigated in a wide range of contexts, varying from person perception to self-perception to emotional reactions to success and failure. Attributional approaches to understanding human behavior rest on the assumption that people are inclined to consider their own behavior and that of others and to make judgments of the likely causes of such behavior. These judgments can then operate in a scientific manner, serving as hypotheses for future information-gathering and deliberation. In this chapter, we examine the treatment process from an attributional perspective. First, the ways in which people's attributions can cause or exacerbate dysfunctional behaviors are noted. Then we examine how therapist attributions of client behavior and life problems influence the therapy process. Finally, we consider the various ways in which changing a client's attributions might prove to be a therapeutic intervention.

ROLE OF ATTRIBUTIONS IN CLIENT PROBLEMS

Evidence indicates that attributions play a significant role in the genesis and maintenance of psychological difficulties. Much of the research in this area has focused on the link between attribution and depression, drawing on the learned helplessness model of depression (e.g., Abramson, Seligman, & Teasdale, 1978; Peterson & Seligman, 1984). Learned helplessness initially was thought to occur when an individual experienced a negative event that she or he perceived as uncontrollable. This helplessness produced three types of deficits: cognitive deficits (an inability to perceive control over the situation), motivational deficits (failure to adequately respond to the situation), and affective deficits (depression and other forms of negative mood) (Seligman, 1975).

Abramson et al. (1978), in a revision of learned helplessness theory, postulated that three dimensions of attribution were critical in determining whether a negative, uncontrollable experience would lead to pervasive helplessness and its associated deficits. When the individual explains the uncontrollable event as the result of internal factors, the result is personal helplessness. Universal helplessness occurs when the individual finds the cause of uncontrollability in external factors. While both types of helplessness produce the cognitive and motivational deficits generally associated with helplessness, personal helplessness is also likely to result in self-esteem deficits. Further, the generality and chronicity of helplessness is predicted by the attributional dimensions of stability and globality. For instance, an individual explaining a negative event as the result of causes that are stable across time (stability) and pervasive across situations (globality) will formulate a generalized expectancy of noncontingency and will consequently experience a generalized helplessness and greater depression.

Observations that certain individuals show consistent attributional patterns across situations led Abramson et al. (1978) to postulate that some individuals are more susceptible to depression as a result of an attributional style; that is, a tendency to attribute negative events to internal, stable, and global causes. These individuals are thought to be more prone to helplessness and, therefore, to depression.

Research on the reformulated learned helplessness model has produced mixed results (Brehm & Smith, 1986; Brewin, 1985; Coyne & Gotlib, 1983; Hammen, 1987; Peterson & Seligman, 1984). In general, it appears that individuals' causal statements for life events can influence depression and self-esteem, but the relationship may not be as direct as that postulated by the learned helplessness model (Brewin & Furnham, 1986; Cutrona, 1983; Gong-Guy & Hammen, 1980; Hammen & deMayo, 1982). Some studies have found support for the hypothesized depressive attributional style (Raps, Peterson, Reinhard, Abramson, & Seligman, 1982), whereas others have noted results that are inconsistent with the model. For example, Manly, McMahon, Bradley, and Davidson (1982) found no relationship between attributional style and depression following childbirth. Cutrona (1983), who also studied cognitive patterns in perinatal depression, demonstrated that attributional style weakly predicted depression following childbirth. Her results also revealed that attributional style did not predict

causal attributions for negative events occurring after delivery. Both of these studies are open to the speculation that postpartum depression is a special case of depression, and the relationship of this depression to attributional patterns may not follow predictions generated by the learned helplessness model. In a more general sample, Hamilton and Abramson (1983) found that depressed individuals demonstrated expected attributional patterns, but also noted that nearly half of their depressed sample showed cognitive patterns more like nondepressed individuals.

These and other studies relied primarily on the Attributional Style Questionnaire (ASQ; Seligman, Abramson, Semmel, & von Baeyer, 1979), a measure developed to assess a relatively enduring tendency to attribute outcomes along various attributional dimensions. The ASQ asks participants to rate hypothetical events on the attributional dimensions of internality, stability, globality, and importance. In contrast, attributions for specific events may have more utility in predicting depression. For example, Gong-Guy and Hammen (1980) found no differences between depressed and nondepressed individuals on a combined index of disturbing events, but found strong differences when attributions for the "most upsetting" recent event were examined. Norman and Antaki (1988) recently created the Real Events Attributional Style Questionnaire (REASQ), a revision of the ASQ that asks subjects to rate actual negative events in their lives. Their results indicated that REASQ scores for negative events moderately correlated with depression, while the original ASQ showed a nonsignificant relationship with BDI scores. These results are preliminary, however, and await further verification.

Numerous other arguments have been advanced to account for the inconsistent results within the research on attribution and depression. Hammen (1987) suggested that certain events may be "depressogenic"; that is, the characteristics of events may have more influence in determining affective responses than previously thought. Brewin and Furnham (1986) further argued that important factors in depression may be "preattributional" variables, such as consensus and consistency information. Consensus information refers to the degree to which the individual sees other people as experiencing some outcome, and whether the individual has experienced similar outcomes in the past determines consistency judgments. In two studies of cognition and depression, Brewin and

Furnham (1986) found evidence that depression and self-esteem were directly affected by consistency and (most notably) consensus information. Attributional information had little effect on affective variables when analyzed in combination with the preattributional variables. Brewin and Furnham argued that studies not including consistency and consensus measures were probably tapping these dimensions indirectly through standard attributional measures.

It is noteworthy that most of the research on the reformulated learned helplessness model has not addressed attributions along the dimension of controllability of cause, although this dimension has been identified by some as an important determinant of reactions to life events (Glass, 1977; Janoff-Bulman, 1979; Langer, 1983; Rothbaum, Weisz, & Snyder, 1982; Weiner, 1979). It is possible that perceived controllability of the cause (distinct from locus, stability, or globality) is an important determinant of emotional response. That is, if an individual experiences a negative life event, and attributes the event to causes that are not under his or her control, depression may result. In a related vein, research on the effectiveness of excuses (see Snyder & Higgins, 1988) suggests that the process of changing attributions for negative outcomes to less "central" sources enhances perceived control and self-esteem.

Preliminary research concerning the influence of attributions in other psychological domains, such as shyness (Brodt & Zimbardo, 1981; Girodo, Dotzenroth, & Stein, 1981), social anxiety (Haemmerlie & Montgomery, 1982, 1984), health-related issues (Affleck, Tennen, Croog, & Levine, 1987), marital and familial issues (Epstein, 1982; Harvey & Galvin, 1984), and child abuse (Larrance & Twentyman, 1983) has supported the contention that attributions play a role in a wide range of psychological functioning. For instance, Girodo et al. (1981) investigated the role of attributions in self-esteem and self-confidence for shy males, demonstrating that individuals with higher self-esteem formulated internal attributions for past social successes and external attributions for past failures and had greater expectancies for future success in social relationships as compared with individuals with low self-esteem. In a different domain, Larrance and Twentymen (1983) compared women who abused and neglected their children with a group of nonabusing control mothers. Abusing women had negative expectations about their children when compared with

controls, and tended to report stable and internal attributions for their children's transgressions. When their children succeeded, abusing mothers gave external and unstable attributions for these successes. The opposite pattern was found when other children failed; abusing mothers' attributed other children's transgressions to unstable and external factors.

Although the data appear to be somewhat mixed, the majority of studies suggest that causal attributions play an important role in psychological difficulties. Most theorists agree that counselors should determine what attributions are formulated by their clients in order to more fully understand each client's view of the problematic situation, paying particular attention to those causal statements that appear to undermine the client's sense of personal control over life events.

COUNSELOR ATTRIBUTIONS

Like clients, counselors also compose causal explanations for client difficulties. Counselor attributions for client problems would appear to be a critical influence upon the counseling process as causal hypotheses have been linked to choice of treatment (e.g., Batson, 1975; Murdock & Fremont, 1989). Also, counselor attributions that are directly or indirectly communicated to the client would influence the client's perceptions of his or her difficulties. Unfortunately, research on counselor attribution has been limited compared with the larger body of literature on client attributions.

It might be argued that, in a clinical setting, counselors and clients would view the clients' situations similarly, because information is more readily available than in an experimental setting. However, Sherrard and Batson (1979), comparing clients' and counselors' perceptions of the locus of client problems, demonstrated a lack of agreement between the groups. A further complicating feature in a clinical setting is the possibility of targeting treatment to perceived internal versus external causes. Batson (1975) found that subjects referred simulated clients to social service agencies when situational attributions were made for clients' problems, whereas more traditional therapy referrals were matched to dispositional attributions. Clearly, the act of presenting oneself for therapy carries with it a "set" for dispositional causes (cf. Snyder, 1977) for both client and therapist in the current psychotherapy milieu.

Strohmer and his associates (Haase, Strohmer,

Biggs, & Keller, 1983; Strohmer, Biggs, Keller, & Thibodeau, 1984; Strohmer, Haase, Biggs, & Keller, 1982) have conducted a series of studies on counselor decision-making relevant to attributional influence. In this research, Strohmer et al. (1982) initially proposed a model of counselor judgment in which counselor observations (i.e., of personality) and inferences of current status and cause (attributions) influence the counselor's ultimate judgment of client-anticipated progress in counseling. In the initial study (Strohmer et al., 1982), counselors (graduate students) were asked to make sequential judgments about case materials. This methodology yielded results supporting a model where observations influence inferences, which, in turn, influence clinical predictions. Attributional information did not have a critical effect on counselor judgment. The later studies used a larger sample size and counselor judgments within a specific diagnostic context (affective disorder). Again, attributions failed to account for significant variance in counselor judgment with the minor exception of distinguishing bipolar from unipolar affective disorder.

Other researchers (Murdock & Fremont, 1989) have investigated treatment assignments as a function of counselor attribution. These results suggest that attribution of client problems to stable causal factors was associated with referral to long-term individual counseling. In contrast, when the client's problems were seen as resulting from unstable factors, shorter-term interventions were offered.

While the results of these studies seem inconsistent, the discrepancies most likely result from the models from which they originated and the tasks that were assigned to therapist-participants. In particular, the experimental tasks have varied from assigning global attribution (personal vs. environmental causation) to therapist ratings on a number of more discrete dimensions (internality, stability, globality, controllability) to modeling therapist decision-making via sequential judgments on several variables. Clearly, more research is needed in this area to identify the influences of attributional variables on the various cognitive tasks undertaken by therapists.

ATTRIBUTIONS AND PSYCHOLOGICAL CHANGE

Attribution approaches to counseling postulate that altering causal statements can play a significant role in promoting and/or maintaining psychological change on the part of the client (An-

taki & Brewin, 1982; Claiborn, 1982; Forsterling, 1986; Strong, 1978). Several types of attribution-based interventions have been identified, including misattribution interventions, attribution retraining, and the use of attribution to promote maintenance of therapeutic change.

Misattribution Therapy

The earliest applications of attribution theory to treatment relied on the notion of misattribution: leading clients to attribute their negative arousal states to external, as opposed to internal, sources. The misattribution approach was based on Schachter's (1964) two-factor theory of emotions, which postulated that physiological arousal was generic and specific emotions were elicited by the cognitive labels individuals adopt. The term "misattribution" was used because the individual may incorrectly attribute arousal to a source other than that which produced it. For example, in Schachter and Singer's (1962) classic study, subjects were given an arousing drug (epinephrine) but were told that the injection was a vitamin supplement. Some participants were informed about the arousing effects of the drug, but a second group was not. A third group was misinformed about the effects of the drug (they were told that the supplement should produce numbness, itching, and a slight headache). Finally, a control group was given an injection of saline. The participant was then joined by a confederate who acted either angry or euphoric. Participants who had no prior explanation for their arousal or who were misinformed attributed their arousal to the confederate (i.e., either reported being angry or euphoric), while the subjects who were actually informed earlier did not make this misattribution. These findings suggested that emotional arousal could be reattributed to a source different from what actually caused the arousal.

Early laboratory research generally supported the misattribution approach. In one of the first investigations of misattribution therapy, Ross, Rodin, and Zimbardo (1969) induced fear in participants by leading them to believe they were to receive shock in a later stage of the experiment. Half of the participants were given the opportunity to misattribute fear-related symptoms to noxious noise, while the remaining participants were not presented with this misattribution procedure. Results of the study demonstrated that participants not given the noise explanation were more fearful than those who were, and they also expended more energy trying to avoid subsequent shock than those who were given misattribution therapy.

Using a similar method, Brodt and Zimbardo (1981) employed a misattribution intervention with chronically shy women. Their participants were bombarded with noxious noise in the presence of an attractive male confederate. Some shy subjects were told that their (presumably shyness-related) arousal was a side effect of the noise. Other shy subjects were misinformed about the effects of the noise; they were told that noise-related effects would be a dry mouth and tremors. A comparison group of not shy women also was misinformed about the effects of the noise. The male confederate was instructed "to provide an atmosphere in which the participant may talk if she so chooses" (p. 441). Interaction between the subject and confederate was monitored during a 5-minute period, ostensibly a readjustment period following the noise bombardment. Results revealed that shy women who had been given misattribution information interacted to the same degree as did the more outgoing comparison group. Interestingly, when asked to identify the shy and not shy women, the confederate, who was unaware of an experimental condition, had the most difficulty classifying the shy participants who received the misattribution intervention. He was quite accurate in identifying the not shy women (81%), and somewhat accurate in identifying the shy-misinformed participants (64%). However, he was much more ambivalent about the shy women who received the misattribution intervention.

Perhaps the most controversial misattribution therapy study was Storms and Nisbett's (1970) insomnia study. In this study, insomniac subjects were given a placebo pill. Some of the participants were told that the pill would relax them, others that it would precipitate arousal. Paradoxically, participants given the arousal explanation reported falling asleep more quickly than usual. Participants who received the relaxation explanation reported taking more time than usual to fall asleep. Storms and Nisbett contended that participants in the arousal condition misattributed their arousal to the placebo, rather than to insomnia, and thus were able to fall asleep more easily. However, no direct evidence was collected to support this interpretation of the findings.

Several subsequent investigations failed to replicate Storms and Nisbett's findings. Among these was a study conducted by Kellogg and Baron (1975). They offered an attribution for behavior

(as opposed to arousal) explanation, arguing that participants who agreed to take arousal pills might have decided that their insomnia was mild that week, and therefore, fell asleep more easily. In contrast, those taking relaxation pills could have decided that they did so because their insomnia was much worse than usual. Extending this justification hypothesis, Kellogg and Baron hypothesized that participants given strong external justification for taking the pills (which was not present in the original study) would attribute the pill-taking behavior to the external source, and no reverse placebo effect would appear. The results of Kellogg and Baron's study did not strongly support either of the hypotheses. The participants most similar to those in Storms and Nisbett's original study (those who were given no strong external justification for taking the pills), in fact, reported the longest latencies to sleep of any of the groups. This finding was even contrary to Kellogg and Baron's reformulation hypotheses. The authors noted that, while the justifications given participants did seem to have some effects, the source of these effects was unclear. These results are consistent with those of Bootzin, Herman, and Nicassio (1976) who also found a direct placebo effect in a study similar to the previous work.

Although later studies have provided some support for the misattribution position (Barefoot & Girodo, 1972; Lowery, Denney, & Storms, 1979), overall the research remains inconsistent. The contradictory results found with this approach have not been theoretically or empirically explained. In the context of these inconsistencies, Brehm and Smith (1986) pointed out that misattribution approaches appear to function effectively when the arousal is mild and the source of the arousal is ambiguous. Therefore, this approach may not be useful when arousal is intense because the source of the arousal is presumably more salient. Further, clients are likely to present themselves for treatment having already formulated some explanation for their troubles, and therefore the misattribution approach may not be as widely applicable in general counseling contexts as early research indicated.

Attribution Retraining

Changing maladaptive client attributions to ones that promote more positive psychological functioning is a second intervention derived from attribution theory (Abramson, Seligman, & Teasdale, 1978; Forsterling, 1985). Advocates of this approach generally argue that attributions for negative life events are more useful if they emphasize factors that have fewer implications for self-esteem or that produce positive affect. The reformulated learned helplessness model suggests that the most useful attributional therapy should emphasize attributing failure experiences to external, unstable, and specific factors. However, other attributional therapists (Dweck, 1975; Weiner, 1979) argue that the most effective attributional pattern in alleviating psychological difficulties is to focus upon internal, unstable, and specific causes. This attributional pattern would presumably increase the individual's sense of control over life outcomes and thus enhance psychological functioning (Bulman & Wortman, 1977; Glass & Singer, 1972; Janoff-Bulman, 1979; Langer & Rodin, 1976; Schultz, 1976).

Reattribution to External, Unstable, or Specific Factors

Skilbeck (1974) initially presented a case study in which the client, a female undergraduate student, came to counseling feeling anxious and depressed. She attributed these symptoms to her "disturbed family background" (Skilbeck, 1974, p. 372). Brief crisis counseling was used to locate the source of the client's difficulties in stress from an important upcoming class examination. Thus, causal analysis of her current circumstances reportedly altered the original internal and uncontrollable attribution (family background) to one that was external and controllable (reaction to a particularly difficult examination).

More recently, Wilson and Linville (1982) assessed the effects of an attribution therapy—leading individuals to attribute a negative outcome to unstable factors—on academic performance among first-year college students. Students who were experiencing academic difficulties were given information that low grades usually improve as students progress through their education (presumably an unstable attribution for performance). This intervention had positive effects: students receiving therapy showed improved grade point averages a year later, and fewer students of this group dropped out of college as compared with students in a control group who received no "therapy." In response to methodological criticism (Block & Lanning, 1984), Wilson and Linville later conducted two replication studies (1985). The combined results of the three studies supported their initial arguments, and further clarified

that the attributional treatments appeared to be more influential for male participants. The authors reasoned that the effects were stronger for males because female participants, more likely to seek social support when under stress, had already learned from others that causes of poor grades may be unstable in nature. Therefore, the heightened treatment effectiveness for male participants was presumably due to their learning new information from the intervention.

Research investigating attribution and mood states indicates that retraining individuals to attribute failure to external, unstable, and specific factors can allay the depressive mood that often accompanies uncontrollable negative events. Green-Emrich and Altmaier (1990) identified participants who were "adaptive" attributors (i.e., they most often attributed failure to external, unstable, and specific factors) and "nonadaptive" attributors (more often attributing negative outcomes to internal, stable, and global factors). Some participants from the nonadaptive group then received attributional retraining, in which participants were taught to attribute uncontrollable negative events to external, unstable, and specific factors. During an experimental session, all participants were confronted with an uncontrollable negative outcome and then attempted to solve a set of soluble anagrams. No differences were found for performance on the anagram task, but the treatment group showed lower depression scores than the untreated nonadaptive attributors. Depression levels were also similar for the treatment and adaptive, untreated groups. Thus, while attributional and performance measures appeared to be unaffected by the attributional intervention, the intervention did have effects on participants' mood states.

Reattribution to Internal and Controllable Factors

Altering attributions for failure experiences from internal and stable (ability) factors to internal and unstable (effort) factors appears to influence persistence on difficult tasks. Dweck (1975) initially demonstrated that teaching children to attribute failure outcomes to insufficient effort (an internal but controllable cause) was an effective attributional therapy. Chronically helpless children (i.e., who consistently perceived outcomes as uncontrollable) who were taught to attribute failure to lack of effort were more persistent on subsequent tasks compared with children who experienced only success in the training phase. Chapin and Dyck (1976) employed a similar paradigm to aid children with reading difficulties. They found that training these children to make effort attributions for negative outcomes increased persistence on a posttest, but also noted that this effect varied depending on reinforcement schedules used in training procedures. Longer reinforcement intervals produced increased persistence regardless of whether the children received attribution therapy, while attribution retraining showed positive effects when short reinforcement intervals were operating.

Zoeller, Mahoney, and Weiner (1983) targeted the performance-oriented attributions of mentally handicapped participants identified as having problems with motivation prior to the study. The attributional training was given after participants experienced repeated failure on an experimental task. Participants who learned to attribute failure to effort, and success to ability and effort, showed improved performance on subsequent psychomotor tasks relative to other participants who received no training.

In a partial replication of Chapin and Dyck's research, Fowler and Peterson (1981) varied schedules of reinforcement and type of attributional training given to children who had difficulties with reading. The type of attributional information given in previous research (i.e., telling the child that "you have tried hard") was conceptualized as relatively indirect, compared with their second treatment, which combined this information with cognitive modeling procedures. Children receiving direct training first heard an audiotape of another child who modeled effort attributions and then practiced verbalizing effort attributions overtly and covertly. Results generally supported Chapin and Dyck's findings with regard to reinforcement schedules, but did not suggest differential effectiveness of the type of attributional interventions. Children who were exposed to both direct and indirect effort attribution therapy showed increased persistence on difficult problems relative to children who received no attribution therapy paired with short reinforcement intervals. When reinforcement intervals were longer, children who received no attributional training performed no differently than those who did.

Fowler and Peterson (1981) also provided some evidence that attributional retraining was effective in changing children's attributions for outcomes in the direction of increased effort. Previous research had not undertaken the task of verifying the effects of attribution retraining; the assumption was made that these interventions changed attributions in the desired directions. Fowler and Peterson assessed the effects of their retraining on the Intellectual Achievement Responsibility Scale (IAR; Crandall, Katkovsky, & Crandall, 1965), a forced-choice instrument that measures participants' perceptions of responsibility for positive and negative achievement outcomes. On this scale, scores can be derived for responsibility taken (i.e., internal attributions) for positive and negative events, and the internal scores can be subdivided into scores reflecting attributions to effort and ability. Using the overall internal scores, all of Fowler and Peterson's treatments produced significant increases in attributions to internal factors from pre- to postmeasurements; specific attributions to effort changed in a similar manner.

Andrews and Debus (1978) examined the influence of attributional training on persistence with concept formation tasks. Participants in the training phase of their study were children (all male) who had least frequently attributed failure to lack of effort in the first phase of the research. Two groups of these participants were reinforced for making effort attributions (verbal/social and verbal/social plus token reinforcements) for both success and failure at a block design task. The control group was given no training. Treatment groups showed greater persistence on a perceptual reasoning task at both immediate and delayed posttests. Using both the IAR and a task-specific measure of attribution, Andrews and Debus found strong evidence for changes in attributional patterns over treatment, primarily with their task-specific attribution measure. Their results indicated that both treatment groups resulted in increased effort attribution for success and failure trials compared with the control group.

Effort retraining and persistence and performance on visual discrimination tasks were examined by Medway and Venino (1982). They reasoned that children who experienced an increasing pattern of successes (as opposed to a random pattern) on these problems would show greater attributions to effort and improved task persistence. The data were similar to those of previous research: effort retraining produced increased task persistence on a posttest. However, no differences in attributions to effort emerged when the trained and untrained groups were compared. The hypothesized increase in effort attributions under ascending success patterns also was not apparent.

Anderson (1983) also studied the influence of reattribution procedures on persistence, expectancies, and motivation using an interpersonal persuasion task (calling people on the telephone and trying to persuade them to donate blood). Some participants were told that either effort or "wrong strategies" were responsible for task outcomes, while others were informed that success was related to stable factors (character dispositions and ability). Results indicated that individuals receiving the attributional training toward unstable factors had higher initial expectancies with less decline following failure than did participants receiving training emphasizing stable factors. In addition, the unstable attribution group was more effective than the comparison group in its recruitment of blood donors.

A series of studies by Schunk (1981, 1982, 1983, 1984) employed attributional retraining with children in order to facilitate performance on arithmetic tasks. These studies focused on the effects of effort and ability attribution. Initially, Schunk (1981) found that attributional training had no effect on persistence, performance, or self-efficacy ratings. In contrast, Schunk (1982) demonstrated that a critical variable was whether the attributional intervention highlighted past or future achievement. "Effort therapy" was effective if it stressed that results of previous achievement (as opposed to future achievement) were dependent on the effort expended by the child. In another study (Schunk, 1983), effort or ability feedback was given to children, or the two were combined in one intervention. All three types of therapy improved performance, but ability feedback was superior in this respect and also had strong effects on self-efficacy. An interesting feature of this last study was that the arithmetic tasks used in the study were of average difficulty, and children were given significant training in completing them. Thus, the ability attribution was consistent with the children's experience with the problems—they were actually performing well. However, ability attributional information may be more risky when, as in most studies, failure experiences are added to the experimental tasks.

Other Variables

Other studies of attributional therapy have suggested that the operation of attributional interven-

tions may be more complex than previously thought. Factors such as the timing of the intervention (Altmaier, Leary, Forsyth, & Ansel, 1979), personality characteristics of the client (Forsyth & Forsyth, 1982), and the degree to which the intervention disagrees with the client's attributional scheme (Claiborn, 1982) may influence the effectiveness of attributional counseling.

Altmaier et al. (1979) investigated the effects of intervention timing and participant locus of control on the effectiveness of attributional interventions. Individuals who held an internal locus of control responded more positively when they received an attributional intervention prior to the negative event (interpersonal failure) or when the intervention was delayed. In contrast, external locus of control participants responded most positively when they received the intervention immediately after the negative event.

Forsyth and Forsyth (1982) found that, for clients who endorsed an internal locus of control, emphasizing internal and controllable causes (as opposed to external and controllable) was more effective in relieving social anxiety. They conducted a pair of studies to manipulate directly individuals' attributions for negative interpersonal events in an attempt to reduce overall social anxiety. Interventions focusing on reattribution to internal and controllable factors were more helpful for internal individuals than were interventions emphasizing external and controllable causes for "externals."

Some authors have suggested (e.g., Claiborn, 1982; Strong & Claiborn, 1982) that the content of attributional interventions is not as important as the discrepancy between client and counselor beliefs. According to this view, an intervention should moderately disagree with what the client thinks in order to produce the most change. Attempting to drastically alter a client's attributions, then, would undermine the change effort as would matching the client's explanations too closely.

Claiborn and Dowd (1985) compared the content model (i.e., certain attributions are more helpful than others) and the discrepancy model (described above) in a study that focused on interventions aimed at depression. Two treatments were offered: a characterological interpretation treatment (Janoff-Bulman, 1979) that located the source of negative emotions in personal characteristics, and a behavioral interpretation treatment that stressed behavioral and cognitive causes of negative emotions. All participants receiving interpretation treatment showed a decrease in depression over time, and interestingly, differing attributional patterns on the two attributional measures. The more global attributional measure (ASQ) revealed that participants' attributions became more specific and external as a result of treatment. However, for the actual problems they brought to therapy, clients became more internal. With regard to the two models being tested, the results of the study did not strongly support either model of attributional retraining. The discrepancy model received weak support from a finding that clients who initially held characerological styles decreased their judgments of stability of problem cause. The authors argued that this pattern fit the discrepancy model because the positive change occurred in a moderate, as opposed to highly discrepant, interpretation condition.

Other research has supported the contention that the content of the interpretation is not important. Hoffman and Teglasi (1982) studied the effects of two types of causal explanations with shy individuals. They exposed participants to either cognitive-behavioral or psychoanalytic interpretive explanations. These two groups were compared with a control condition in which no causal explanations were presented. The cognitive-behavioral explanation was assumed to represent internal and controllable causes for shyness, whereas the analytic formulations was presented as an external, uncontrollable explanation. Both attributional interventions increased motivation to change, expectancies of change, and involvement in and utilization of counseling sessions, as compared with the control condition. No differences emerged between the two attributional treatments.

In reviewing the literature on attribution retraining, it appears that both content and discrepancy models have received some support. However, the processes involved in attribution therapy are still unclear. Strong support is found for "effort therapy" when the behavior of interest is persistence. Some evidence seems to indicate that performance is affected by reattribution to effort, as well. Interventions aimed at changing attributions in the directions advocated by learned helplessness theory (external, specific, and unstable attributions for negative events) appear somewhat less successful when performance indices are examined. Wilson and Linville's (1982, 1985) studies focused on attribution to unstable factors, although it is unclear whether these factors were

perceived as internal or external by the participants. Green-Emrich and Altmaier's (1990) research suggested that affect was improved by altering attributions in an external direction, but not performance on an experimental task. Claiborn and Dowd's (1985) research indicated that, whereas content of the attributional intervention was unimportant, clients who attended therapy learned to be external attributors overall and internal attributors for presenting problems. One possible explanation for these divergent findings is implied in the above summary: attributional retraining is differentially effective depending on the target of the intervention.

Individuals who come to therapy are usually in great pain, and are often using internal attributions for negative life events. This process has been identified by Beck and others (i.e., the cognitive triad; Beck 1976; see Coyne & Gotlib, 1983, for a review), particularly with regard to depression. At the same time, the client may be using external attributions for actual symptomatic behavior (i.e., failing to take responsibility for changing problematic situations). The process of therapy may help the client formulate external, unstable, and specific attributions for many situations, thereby improving overall affect and raising self-esteem. In addition, modifying external attributions for specific dysfunctional behaviors (analogous to the achievement behaviors studied in the persistence studies) to ones that are more internal may prove beneficial to the client in increasing his or her sense of control over salient life events. Therefore, both types of attributional change probably operate, and the effects observed depend on the level at which change is measured. Future research should address these possibilities by including both specific and global attributional measures as well as taking into account various outcome criteria (e.g., persistence, affect, problem-solving).

ATTRIBUTION AND MAINTENANCE OF CHANGE

Attributional approaches to enhancing maintenance suggest that if clients attribute positive behavior change to internal (self-relevant) causes, change is more likely to persist. For example, Jeffrey (1974) compared self-control and environmental-control interventions in maintenance of weight loss. Self-control interventions emphasized the client's personal responsibility for change, whereas the environmental-control intervention stressed the therapist's role in weight loss. Both interventions were effective in producing weight loss over a 7-week period. Six weeks after treatment, however, the self-control directives were superior to the environmental-control interventions in maintenance of weight loss. The self-control group also demonstrated a more internal locus of control when compared with the environmental-control group.

Sonne and Janoff (1979) also investigated the influence of attribution in maintenance of weight loss. Clients who were told that weight loss was a matter of self-control attributed their success more to personal causes, and demonstrated superior maintenance of weight change at follow-up assessments, than did clients given other attributional explanations. In fact, the participants' perceptions of their control over weight loss and the degree to which they personally contributed to their behavior change accounted for 22% of the variance in weight loss 11 weeks after treatment.

Other research has supported the hypothesis that attributing positive change to internal factors may enhance the longevity of the change. Davison, Tsujimoto, and Glaros (1973) investigated the role of attribution in helping insomniacs maintain changes in sleep patterns. Their participants were given a sleep-producing drug (chloral hydrate) and were also instructed in relaxation and scheduling procedures. The drug given was known to shorten sleep attainment latencies in the dose administered. After using the drug and other procedures for a week, some participants were told that they had taken an optimal dose of the drug while others were informed that the amount they had taken was subclinical. All participants were told to stop using the drug, but to continue relaxation and scheduling procedures. The authors reasoned that participants who received the minimal dose explanation would be led to attribute their changes in sleep latencies to controllable factors (i.e., the procedural interventions) and therefore should show greater maintenance of change compared with the group told their drug dose was optimal. Results supported this prediction, and evidence was collected that substantiated the attributional pattern expected by these researchers. In a related vein, Colletti and Kopel (1979) and Colletti and Stern (1980) found that self-attribution was related to long-term reduction of cigarette smoking.

Brehm and Smith (1986) sensibly cautioned,

however, that the role of attribution in the explanation for relapse, or negative change, should be reversed. When a client experiences no change, or change in an undesirable direction, attribution to internal factors may be debilitating. In this instance, the counselor might be wiser to assist clients in formulating more external causal statements for their behavior. In consideration of failure or relapse "inoculation," counselors could consider developing an attributional set for the client that anticipates failure and attributes it to normal change-promoting processes.

ATTRIBUTION THERAPY IN A HEALTH CONTEXT

Much of the attribution therapy research has been conducted in achievement contexts using measures of persistence, performance, and affect. Thus, the link between this body of research and problems occurring within a health context is unclear. For people experiencing negative health outcomes, such as a recurrence of cancer, unremitting low back pain, or an unfavorable prognosis, the likelihood of attributions being made for the physical condition is high (Turnquist, Harvey, & Andersen, 1988), but the relation of these attributions to outcome is less clear. Further, the need to engage patients in attributions retraining within a health context is undefined.

Research evidence suggests that patients dealing with illness do indeed make attributions about their illness. Taylor, Lichtman, and Wood (1984) studied 78 breast cancer patients, using both interview and questionnaire methods. Their results indicated that almost all of the patients had made attributions for their cancer, in many cases using more than one causal element. These results are supported by data revealing that patients with a variety of diseases report one or more causes of their illness (e.g., Affleck, Allen, Tennen, McGrade, & Ratzan, 1985; Tennen, Affleck, & Gershman, 1986). The content of such attributions ranges widely over domains such as "others' actions," "self," "environmental events," and "chance."

In addition to variations in content, investigators have reported differences in the strength with which causal attributions are held. Turnquist et al. (1988), in reviewing research on attributions of illness, noted that severity of disease appeared to influence both frequency of attribution and the strength of belief. Individuals with severe illnesses, such as cancer, hold more beliefs but hold them less strongly than individuals with less severe illnesses. It may be, as Taylor (1983) proposed, that the cognitive adaptation problem posed by a threatening illness necessitates holding several specific cognitions so that any disconfirmation can result in a change to another attribution. A similar argument was put forth by Snyder (1989) in proposing a hope motive that is partially formed through attributional dissociation from bad outcomes. Such cognitive adaptation might precede emotional or behavioral adaptation; unfortunately, research on attitude-behavior sequencing is sparse in the attribution literature as a whole (Harvey & Weary, 1984) as well as in the health context.

How are health attributions related to adjustment? Although it would seem intuitively appealing that particular attributions would enhance adjustment to difficult treatment regimens or negative diagnoses, strong evidence of such a relationship is lacking. Generally, attributing cause of illness to others predicts a poor adjustment (i.e., Affleck et al., 1987), but there is no clear relationship for self-attributions and outcome. Some evidence for the positive role of self-blame (e.g., Bulman & Wortman, 1977) is contradicted by research suggesting that self-blame can serve as a predictor for negative outcomes (e.g., Kiecolt-Glaser & Williams, 1987).

A second aspect of attribution and outcome concerns patients' general beliefs about the likely course of their disease and their ability to exert control over this outcome. For example, for the breast cancer patients studied by Taylor et al. (1984), belief that one could control one's cancer and belief that others could control the cancer were both associated with good adjustment. Related research has shown that people who have a stronger belief in their own control have achieved better postoperative outcomes (Johnson, Leventhal, & Dabbs, 1971) and are more likely to engage in preventive health behaviors (Williams, 1972).

Asserting some type of personal control may be associated with better adjustment than considering a situation as uncontrollable. The distinction posed by Rothbaum et al. (1982) between primary and secondary control is relevant here. Primary control involves the individual changing the environment to improve outcome, while secondary control suggests changing oneself to improve the fit with the environment. Within a health context, both sources of control probably operate in an interactive manner. Individuals may experience negative health outcomes as a disconfirmation of control, and thus shift from primary control (e.g., making changes in diet, reducing stress) to secondary control methods (attributing likelihood of outcome to powerful others).

Attributions in health contexts can be considered to serve as representations about sources of control. The models of helping defined by Brickman, Rabinowitz, Karuza, Coates, Cohn, and Kidder (1982) provide a useful conceptualization of attributions and health processes. In these models, people vary in their attribution of problem responsibilty (to self or to others) and in their attribution of solution responsibilities (to self or to others). Interestingly, the usual mode of medical treatment is to place control in the hands of a powerful other, and such a model is characterized by Brickman et al. as one in which attribution for both problem and solution is external. When the medical model is utilized, the person perceives himself or herself as "ill" and experts as the ones who have control over treatment. Altmaier (1986) argued that the compensatory model was better suited to rehabilitation health outcomes, where responsibility for solution rested with the individual in consultation with powerful others. The compensatory model would suggest, as a practical implication, that patients be given as much control as possible over treatment, including increased participation in treatment decision-making. In addition, attributions to internal controllable sources for gradual successes would be critical.

An alternative understanding of the role of attributions in health outcomes has been proposed by Leventhal and colleagues (Leventhal, Meyer, & Nerenz, 1980). In this model, patients form representations of their disease and treatment along several dimensions: identity, cause, timeline, and consequences. The representation of cause most closely parallels a traditional definition of attribution, although all of the representations could be argued to serve attributional functions. These representations then influence subsequent plans and actions and the emotional responses patients have to the initial situational stimuli. Research has suggested for the most part that varying illness representations influence health-care utilization and compliance with treatment. For example, Bauman and Leventhal (1985) demonstrated that monitoring blood pressure primarily occurred in the presence of particular symptoms, indicating an acute as opposed to chronic illness representation.

Given the many sources of influence in health contexts, it is difficult to specify how attributional training might improve outcomes. Spontaneous cognitions are difficult to measure and are often correlated with mood, disease status, and treatment regimen. Thus, making confident predictions about the advisability of altering attributions is difficult. However, based on the preceding research, attributions that simultaneously work toward achieving a desired outcome and preparing for failure may be most adaptive within health contexts. The danger of promoting attribution of perceived control is that fostering a sense of control also can increase self-blame and negative affect when control failures occur. For example, recent treatment adjuncts for cancer that instruct a patient to assist in disease control through imagery can easily lead to self-blame if the cancer recurs. Disconfirmation of control (see Thompson, Cheek, & Graham, 1988, for review) is a likely event and suggests the importance of preparing for it. Indeed, preparing for failure is an integral component of most coping skills treatments (see Turk, Meichenbaum, & Genest, 1983) and may represent a promising avenue for attributional treatments in health contexts.

INTEGRATION

As with almost any area of research, the literature on attributional interventions is complex and, at times, confusing. Although our sample is by no means an exhaustive compilation of the applied attribution literature, the wealth of research in this area presents the difficult task of assimilating and using the knowledge gathered thus far (without formulating an internal attribution for our struggles). With all of the usual qualifications, the following are tentatively offered:

1. The misattribution approach seems less likely to apply to normal treatment situations because clients are likely to come to therapy as a last resort. Because they have probably lived with their negative affect for quite some time, they are likely to have formulated strong causal explanations (whether they wish to "consciously" acknowledge them or not) for their problems prior to seeing the therapist.

2. Within the attribution area, attributional retraining (or attribution therapy) is the most energetically researched intervention. The primary issue seems to reside in whether specific attributions are more helpful than others and in whether cli-

ents get better simply through forming new cognitive schemata.

3. This question (number 2) leads to the usual question found in psychotherapy outcome research: Better in what way? Almost all of the studies of attribution retraining showed positive effects, but the types of interventions offered and the selection of outcome variables varied widely.

4. Studies of attribution retraining to effort ("effort therapy") have generally supported Weiner's (1979) contention that such attributions should lead to increased motivation and persistence for difficult tasks. Some evidence also was gained for improvement in performance, but these results were not as consistent as the findings regarding persistence. Because not all studies gather performance data, this conclusion may largely be an artifact of the studies reviewed.

5. Studies involving more "traditional" therapy problems, such as depression or interpersonal problems, present inconsistent results. Some studies support the content model, some can be interpreted to support both content and discrepancy models, and others provide confirmation mainly for the discrepancy model of attribution therapy. This area deserves further research with a particular emphasis on relation of intervention to type of problem.

6. Unlike the studies in the persistence area, the quasitherapy studies do not use similar outcome measures and are inconsistent in assessing and reporting attributional processes of their client-subjects. For example, Claiborn and Dowd (1985) found evidence for two levels of attributional patterns that seemed to operate in opposite directions. Forsyth and Forsyth (1982, study 1) found differential attributional change dependent on the locus of control of subjects. Thus, it is difficult to generalize about this group of studies, but, as suggested earlier, these data do provide further research ideas.

7. Maintenance of therapeutic change appears to be facilitated by self attribution for successful behavioral change. As with the persistence studies, the maintenance research most often deals with easily measurable outcomes. Also, it should be clear that attribution to personal factors may only be facilitative for positive change; interventions after relapse may be quite different.

More research is needed, but generally, an attributional approach to treatment seems useful with some clients and some types of psychological difficulties. Therapists should be flexible in their use of attributional interventions, keeping in mind that the route to more positive psychological functioning can take different directions for different clients. As with any approach to treatment, a wholesale adoption of the tenets of attributional interventions is probably inappropriate; on the other hand, a significant body of research has indicated that this approach can be helpful. Obviously, it remains to the therapist to determine how attributional interventions can best be used to help clients in distress.

REFERENCES

Abramson, L. Y., Seligman, M. E. P., & Teasdale, J. D. (1978). Learned helplessness in humans: Critique and reformulation. *Journal of Abnormal Psychology, 87*, 49–74.

Affleck, G., Allen, D., Tennen, H., McGrade, B., & Ratzan, S. (1985). Causal and control cognitions in parents coping with a chronically ill child. *Journal of Social and Clinical Psychology, 3*, 369–379.

Affleck, G., Tennen, H., Croog, S., & Levine, S. (1987). Causal attribution, perceived control and recovery from a heart attack. *Journal of Social and Clinical Psychology, 5*, 356–364.

Altmaier, E. M. (1986). Processes in rehabilitation: A social psychological analysis. In J. E. Maddux, C. D. Stoltenberg, & R. Rosenwein (Eds.), *Social processes in clinical and counseling psychology* (pp. 171–184). New York: Springer-Verlag.

Altmaier, E. M., Leary, M. R., Forsyth, D. R., & Ansel, J. C. (1979). Attribution therapy: Effects of locus of control and timing of treatment. *Journal of Counseling Psychology, 26*, 481–486.

Anderson, C. A. (1983). Motivational and performance deficits in interpersonal settings: The effects of attributional style. *Journal of Personality and Social Psychology, 45*, 1136–1147.

Andrews, G. R., & Debus, R. L. (1978). Persistence and the causal perception of failure: Modifying cognitive attributions. *Journal of Educational Psychology, 70*, 154–166.

Antaki, C., & Brewin, C. (Eds.). (1982). *Attributions and psychological change*. New York: Academic Press.

Barefoot, J. C., & Girodo, M. (1972). The misattribution of smoking cessation symptoms. *Canadian Journal of Behavior Science, 4*, 358–363.

Batson, C. D. (1975). Attribution as a mediator of bias in helping. *Journal of Personality and Social Psychology, 32*, 455–466.

Baumann, L. J., & Leventhal, H. (1985). "I can tell when my blood pressure is up: Can't I?" *Health Psychology, 4*, 203–218.

Beck, A. T. (1976). *Cognitive therapy and the emotional disorders*. New York: International Universities Press.

Block, J., & Lanning, K. (1984). Attribution therapy requestioned: A secondary analysis of the Wilson-Linville study. *Journal of Personality and Social Psychology, 46*, 705–708.

Bootzin, R. R., Herman, C. P., & Nicassio, P. (1976). The power of suggestion: Another examination of misattribution and insomnia. *Journal of Personality and Social Psychology, 34*, 673–679.

Brehm, S., & Smith, T. W. (1986). Social psychological approaches to psychotherapy and behavior change. In S. L. Garfield & A. E. Bergin (Eds.), *Handbook of psychotherapy and behavior change* (3rd ed., pp. 69–115). New York: John Wiley & Sons.

Brewin, C. R. (1985). Depression and causal attributions: What is their relation? *Psychological Bulletin, 90*, 297–309.

Brewin, C. R., & Furnham, A. (1986). Attributional versus preattributional variables in self-esteem and depression: A comparison and test of learned helplessness theory. *Journal of Personality and Social Psychology, 50*, 1013–1020.

Brickman, P., Rabinowitz, V. C., Karuza, J., Coates, D., Cohn, E., & Kidder, L. (1982). Models of helping and coping. *American Psychologist, 37*, 368–384.

Brodt, S. E., & Zimbardo, P. G. (1981). Modifying shyness-related behavior through symptom misattribution. *Journal of Personality and Social Psychology, 41*, 437–449.

Bulman, R. J., & Wortman, C. B. (1977). Attributions of blame and coping in the "real world": Severe accident victims react to their lot. *Journal of Personality and Social Psychology, 35*, 351–365.

Chapin, M., & Dyck, D. G. (1976). Persistence in children's reading behavior as a function of N length and attribution retraining. *Journal of Abnormal Psychology, 85*, 511–515.

Claiborn, C. D. (1982). Interpretation and change in counseling. *Journal of Counseling Psychology, 29*, 439–453.

Claiborn, C. D., & Dowd, E. T. (1985). Attributional interpretations in counseling: Content versus discrepancy. *Journal of Counseling Psychology, 32*, 188–196.

Colletti, G., & Kopel, S. A. (1979). Maintaining behavior change: An investigation of three maintenance strategies and the relationship of self-attribution to the long-term reduction of cigarette smoking. *Journal of Consulting and Clinical Psychology, 47*, 614–617.

Colletti, G., & Stern, L. (1980). Two-year follow-up of a nonaversive treatment for cigarette smoking. *Journal of Consulting and Clinical Psychology, 48*, 292–293.

Coyne, J. C., & Gotlib, I. H. (1983). The role of cognition in depression: A critical appraisal. *Psychological Bulletin, 94*, 472–505.

Crandall, V. C., Katkovsky, W., & Crandall, V. J. (1965). Children's beliefs in their own control of reinforcement in intellectual achievement situations. *Child Development, 36*, 91–109.

Cutrona, C. E. (1983). Causal attributions and perinatal depression. *Journal of Abnormal Psychology, 92*, 161–172.

Davison, G. C., Tsujimoto, R. N., & Glaros, A. G. (1973). Attribution and the maintenance of behavior change in falling asleep. *Journal of Abnormal Psychology, 82*, 124–133.

Dweck, C. S. (1975). The role of expectations and attributions in the alleviation of learned helplessness. *Journal of Personality and Social Psychology, 23*, 109–116.

Epstein, N. (1982). Cognitive therapy with couples. *The American Journal of Family Therapy, 10*, 5–16.

Forsyth, N. L., & Forsyth, D. R. (1982). Internality, controllability and the effectiveness of attributional interventions in counseling. *Journal of Counseling Psychology, 29*, 140–150.

Forsterling, F. (1985). Attributional retraining: A review. *Psychological Bulletin, 98*, 495–512.

Forsterling, F. (1986). Attributional conceptions in clinical psychology. *American Psychologist, 41*, 275–285.

Fowler, J. W., & Peterson, P. L. (1981). Increasing reading persistence and altering attributional style of learned helpless children. *Journal of Educational Psychology, 73*, 251–260.

Girodo, M., Dotzenroth, S. E., & Stein, S. J. (1981). Causal attribution bias in shy males: Implications for self-esteem and self-confidence. *Cognitive Therapy and Research, 5*, 325–338.

Glass, D., & Singer, J. (1972). *Urban Press*. New York: Academic Press.

Glass, D. C. (1977). *Behavior patterns, stress, and coronary disease*. Hillsdale, NJ: Lawrence Erlbaum Associates.

Gong-Guy, E., & Hammen, C. (1980). Causal perceptions of stressful events in depressed and nondepressed outpatients. *Journal of Abnormal Psychology, 89*, 662–669.

Green-Emrich, A., & Altmaier, E. M. (1990). *Attribution retraining as a structured group counseling intervention*. Manuscript submitted for publication.

Haase, R. F., Strohmer, D. C., Biggs, D. A., & Keller, K. E. (1983). Mediational inferences in the process of counselor judgment. *Journal of Counseling Psychology, 30*, 275–278.

Haemmerlie, F. M., & Montgomery, R. L. (1982). Self-perception theory and unobtrusively biased interactions: A treatment for heterosocial anxiety. *Journal of Counseling Psychology, 29*, 362–370.

Haemmerlie, F. M., & Montgomery, R. L. (1984). Purposefully biased interventions: Reducing heterosocial anxiety through self-perception theory. *Journal of Personality and Social Psychology, 47*, 900–908.

Hamilton, E. W., & Abramson, L. Y. (1983). Cognitive patterns and major depressive disorder: A longitudinal study in a hospital setting. *Journal of Abnormal Psychology, 92*, 173–184.

Hammen, C. (1987). The causes and consequences of attribution research on depression. *Journal of Social and Clinical Psychology, 4*, 485–500.

Hammen, C., & deMayo, R. (1982). Cognitive correlates of teacher stress and depressive symptoms: Implications for attributional models of depression. *Journal of Abnormal Psychology, 91*, 96–101.

Harvey, J. H., & Galvin, K. S. (1984). Clinical implications of attribution theory and research. *Clinical Psychology Review, 4*, 15–34.

Harvey, J. H., & Weary, G. (1984). Current issues in attribution theory and research. *Annual Review of Psychology, 35*, 427–459.

Hoffman, M. A., & Teglasi, H. (1982). The role of causal attributions in counseling shy subjects. *Journal of Counseling Psychology, 29*, 132–139.

Janoff-Bulman, R. (1979). Characterological versus behavioral self-blame: Inquiries into depression and rape. *Journal of Personality and Social Psychology, 37*, 1798–1809.

Jeffrey, D. B. (1974). A comparison of the effects of external-control and self-control on the modification and maintenance of weight. *Journal of Abnormal Psychology, 83*, 404–410.

Johnson, J., Leventhal, H., & Dabbs, J. (1971). Contribution of emotion to instrumental response process in adaptation to surgery. *Journal of Personality and Social Psychology, 20*, 55–64.

Kellogg, R., & Baron, R. S. (1975). Attribution theory, insomnia, and the reverse placebo effect: A reversal of Storms and Nisbett's findings. *Journal of Personality and Social Psychology, 32*, 231–236.

Kiecolt-Glaser, J. K., & Williams, D. A. (1987). Self-blame, compliance, and distress among burn patients. *Journal of Personality and Social Psychology, 53*, 187–193.

Langer, E. J. (1983). *The psychology of control.* Beverly Hills, CA: Sage Publications.

Langer, E. J., & Rodin, J. (1976). The effects of choice and enhanced responsibility for the aged: A field experiment in an institutional setting. *Journal of Personality and Social Psychology, 33*, 951–955.

Larrance, D. T., & Twentyman, C. T. (1983). Maternal attributions and child abuse. *Journal of Abnormal Psychology, 92*, 449–557.

Leventhal, H., Meyer, D., & Nerenz, D. (1980). The common sense representation of illness danger. In S. Rachman (Ed.), *Medical psychology* (Vol. II). Elmsford, NY: Pergamon Press.

Lowery, C. R., Denney, D. R., & Storms, M. D. (1979). Insomnia: A comparison of the effects of pill attributions and nonpejorative self-attributions. *Cognitive Therapy and Research, 3*, 161–164.

Manly, P. C., McMahon, R. J., Bradley, C. F., & Davidson, P. O. (1982). Depressive attributional style and depression following childbirth. *Journal of Abnormal Psychology, 91*, 245–254.

Medway, F. J., & Venino, G. R. (1982). The effects of effort feedback and performance patterns on children's attributions and task persistence. *Contemporary Educational Psychology, 7*, 26–34.

Murdock, N. L., & Fremont, S. K. (1989). Attributional influences in counselor decision making. *Journal of Counseling Psychology, 36*, 417–422.

Norman, P. D., & Antaki, C. (1988). Real events attributional style questionnaire. *Journal of Social and Clinical Psychology, 2/3*, 97–100.

Peterson, C., & Seligman, M. E. P. (1984). Causal explanations as a risk factor for depression: Theory and evidence. *Psychological Review, 91*, 347–374.

Raps, C. S., Peterson, C., Reinhard, K. E., Abramson, L. Y., & Seligman, M. E. P. (1982). Attributional style among depressed patients. *Journal of Abnormal Psychology, 91*, 102–108.

Ross, L., Rodin, J., & Zimbardo, P. G. (1969). Toward an attribution therapy: The reduction of fear through induced cognitive-emotional misattribution. *Journal of Personality and Social Psychology, 4*, 279–288.

Rothbaum, F., Weisz, J., & Snyder, S. (1982). Changing the world and changing the self: A two-process model of perceived control. *Journal of Personality and Social Psychology, 42*, 5–37.

Schachter, S. (1964). The interaction of cognitive and physiological determinants of emotional state. In L. Berkowitz (Ed.), *Advances in experimental social psychology* (Vol. 1). New York: Academic Press.

Schachter, S., & Singer, J. (1962). Cognitive, social and physiological determinants of emotional state. *Psychological Review, 69*, 379–399.

Schulz, R. (1976). Effects of control and predictability of the psychological well-being of the institutionalized aged. *Journal of Personality and Social Psychology, 33*, 563–573.

Schunk, D. H. (1981). Modeling and attributional effects on children's achievement: A self-efficacy analysis. *Journal of Educational Psychology, 73*, 93–105.

Schunk, D. H. (1982). Effects of effort attributional feedback on children's perceived self-efficacy and achievement. *Journal of Educational Psychology, 74*, 548–556.

Schunk, D. H. (1983). Ability versus effort attributional feedback: Differential effects on self-efficacy and achievement. *Journal of Educational Psychology, 75*, 848–856.

Schunk, D. H. (1984). Sequential attributional feedback and children's achievement behaviors. *Journal of Educational Psychology, 76*, 1159–1169.

Seligman, M. E. P. (1975). *Helplessness: On depression, development, and death.* San Francisco: W. H. Freeman.

Seligman, M. E. P., Abramson, L. Y., Semmel, A., & von Baeyer, C. (1979). Depressive attributional style. *Journal of Abnormal Psychology, 88*, 242–247.

Sherrard, P. A., & Batson, C. D. (1979). Client and counselor perception of the client's problem: An analysis of initial assessment based on attribution theory. *Journal of College Student Personnel, 20*, 14–23.

Skilbeck, W. M. (1974). Attributional change and crisis intervention. *Psychotherapy: Theory, Research and Practice, 11*, 371–375.

Snyder, C. R. (1977). "A patient by any other name" revisited: Maladjustment or attributional locus of problem? *Journal of Consulting and Clinical Psychology, 45*, 101–103.

Snyder, C. R., (1989). Reality negotiation: From excuses to hope and beyond. *Journal of Social and Clinical Psychology, 8*, 130–157.

Snyder, C. R., & Higgins, R. L. (1988). Excuses: Their effective role in the negotiation of reality. *Psychological Bulletin, 104*, 23–35.

Sonne, J., & Janoff, D. (1979). The effect of treatment attributions on the maintenance of weight reduction: A replication and extension. *Cognitive Therapy and Research, 3*, 389–397.

Storms, M. D., & Nisbett, R. E. (1970). Insomnia and the attribution process. *Journal of Personality and Social Psychology, 16*, 319–328.

Strohmer, D. C., Biggs, D. A., Keller, K. E., & Thibodeau, J. R. (1984). Clinical judgment and affective disorders. *Journal of Counseling Psychology, 31*, 99–103.

Strohmer, D. C., Haase, R. F., Biggs, D. A., & Keller, K. E. (1982). Process models of counselor judgment. *Journal of Counseling Psychology, 29*, 597–606.

Strong, S. R. (1978). Social psychological approach to psychotherapy research. In S. L. Garfield & A. E. Bergin (Eds.), *Handbook of psychotherapy and behavior change: An empirical analysis* (2nd ed., pp. 101–135). New York: John Wiley & Sons.

Strong, S. R., & Claiborn, C. D. (1982). *Change through interaction*. New York: John Wiley & Sons.

Taylor, S. E. (1983). Adjustment to threatening events. *American Psychologist, 38*, 1161–1173.

Taylor, S., Lichtman, R., & Wood, J. (1984). Attributions, beliefs about control, and adjustment to breast cancer. *Journal of Personality and Social Psychology, 46*, 489–502.

Tennen, H., Affleck, G., & Gershman, K. (1986). Self-blame among parents of infants with perinatal complications: The role of self-protective motives. *Journal of Personality and Social Psychology, 50*, 690–696.

Thompson, S. C., Cheek, P. R., & Graham, M. A. (1988). The other side of perceived control: Disadvantages and negative effects. In S. Spacapan & S. Oskamp (Eds.), *The social psychology of health* (pp. 69–94). Newbury Park, CA: Sage Publications.

Turk, D., Meichenbaum, D., & Genest, M. (1983). *Pain and behavioral medicine*. New York: Guilford Press.

Turnquist, D., Harvey, J. R., & Andersen, B. (1988). Attributions and adjustment to life-threatening illness. *British Journal of Clinical Psychology, 27*, 55–65.

Weiner, B. (1979). A theory of motivation for some classroom experiences. *Journal of Educational Psychology, 71*, 3–25.

Williams, A. F. (1972). Personality characteristics associated with preventive dental practices. *Journal of American College of Dentists, 39*, 225–234.

Wilson, T. D., & Linville, P. W. (1982). Improving the academic performance of college freshmen: Attribution therapy revisited. *Journal of Personality and Social Psychology, 42*, 367–376.

Wilson, T. D., & Linville, P. W. (1985). Improving the performance of college freshmen with attributional techniques. *Journal of Personality and Social Psychology, 49*, 287–293.

Zoeller, C., Mahoney, G., & Weiner, B. (1983). Effects of attribution training on the assembly task performance of mentally retarded adults. *American Journal of Mental Deficiency, 88*, 109–112.

CHAPTER 29

SELF-MANAGEMENT IN HEALTH-CARE AND ILLNESS PREVENTION

Paul Karoly

Every day, all over the world, patients are being advised, instructed, even cajoled or threatened to carry out health-care behaviors (for those sick or injured) or health-promoting (for those "at risk" for illness) in the natural environment, over prolonged periods of time, and with minimal or no input from health professionals. Requiring patients to look after themselves, at least in Western societies, is a cultural convention that follows from biomedicine's "acute episodes" or "problem-awaiting" perspective. That is, sick people are generally expected to present themselves for medical help and, after receiving diagnostic and interventive care, to return to their homes either to mend, to self-administer further treatment (where feasible), to practice prevention, or to wait for new illness flare-ups. No one, not even the most hypochondriacal in the population, expects physicians to offer continuous, uninterrupted service. Hence, the capacity for self-management of health and illness is presumed, for all but the most severely physically or mentally handicapped or experientially limited.

One might therefore expect a topic as pivotal as

self-management to be included in every medical school curriculum or at least be a subject taught to all of us as part of our elementary education. After all, if this capacity is lacking or undeveloped, the health-care system as we know it cannot operate smoothly. Of course, self-management training is compulsory neither for doctors nor for patients. One reason (perhaps the main one) for this apparent oversight is the flawed logic that suggests (a) when doctor's orders are followed, self-management is self-evidently operating and (b) when patients fail to look after themselves, it is because they are "insufficiently motivated" (i.e., they are not scared enough, not sure enough that they are sick or at risk, or they have learned to feel helpless in the face of stress). The price being paid to verify this line of reasoning is the continued disregard of self-management as a scientific (theory-directed, testable, correctable) enterprise within those domains most likely to benefit from its empirical exploration; namely, medicine, education, and public health.

Although defining self-management will not be easy, let us, for the present, assume that it is a process by which an individual deliberately employs certain cognitive and/or behavioral skills to facilitate achieving a goal that would otherwise be difficult to attain because social forces or his or her own habits impede or discourage its pursuit. Thus, if a patient was always too busy to engage in certain taxing and time-consuming physical exercises as prescribed by her doctor, the resolve to try to "get control over her life" (i.e., to self-manage) is only expected to succeed if certain cognitive and/or behavioral skills are now brought into play. It should be obvious, however, that a person can attain many unconflicted goals, large and small, without having to exert special volitional control; and, therefore, it would be incorrect to say that in pursuing these goals anything other than simple stimulus-response connections are involved.

Goal attainment per se is not a synonym for self-management! However, in common parlance, this is precisely how the term is often used. Particularly because self-management is a dynamic process that may (or may not) aid in the attainment of a personally valued objective (e.g., a therapeutic health-care activity like jogging, dieting, giving up cigarettes, or engaging in "safe sex"), it is incorrect to assume the prior operation of this motivational strategy by reference only to observed outcomes. This, in fact, is a classic example of the fallacy of circular reasoning or affirming the consequent. When self-management was defined in a recent textbook as referring "to the *performance* of preventive or therapeutic health care activities . . . " (Tobin, Reynolds, Holroyd, & Creer, 1986, p. 29), even a sophisticated audience might well have been confused.

A problem closely related to the presumption of a self-directive process from its putative effects is the widespread assumption that performing an activity by oneself is necessarily an example of self-management. This misinterpretation is particularly common among marketers of so-called self-help materials (a growing industry, especially in the physical health field). For example, over the years clinical psychologists have found that teaching their fearful, tense, or phobic clients to muscularly relax has had very beneficial consequences (cf. Morris, 1986; Wolpe, 1982). Relaxation exercises can be tape-recorded and given to clients to use as a means of practicing their skills between sessions. However, anyone can now purchase a relaxation tape for their private use under the presumption that faithful listening constitutes self-directed relaxation. This is no more true than would reading the collected works of Freud constitute an example of self-directed psychoanalysis. Proper use of tapes may require a level of self-regulatory skill that the patient may not yet possess. For our present purposes, it is essential to emphasize that when books, recordings, or other devices for handling tension, obesity, cigarette smoking, alcoholism, and the like are sold to consumers as self-management materials, we cannot adequately judge the extent to which self-management, as I have defined it, is involved. The potential exists for both overestimating and underestimating the utility of the approach to be outlined in this chapter, because everyday successes and failures in what is presumed to be self-directed health care can so easily be misattributed, mislabeled, and misunderstood.

Despite what Reaganites might call "disinformation" in the domain of self-directed health behavior, there has been a growing recognition within the medical and allied health-care community of the importance of an empirical analysis of self-influence processes in the day-to-day regulation of health and illness behavior. Several coalescing lines of force provide justification for the current rebirth of patient responsibility as a societal ethic.

In recent years, the cost of health-care and the need to optimize the allocation of scarce economic resources between today's needs and the prevention of tomorrow's ills have become a concern of government, the medical profession, the insurance industry, and the average person. In a country where 750 billion dollars will be spent on health-care (in 1990), where tens of thousands remain underserved while hundreds of thousands with primarily psychosocial needs overutilize medical resources, and where the major causes of illness, pain, disability, and death (namely, cancer, stroke, heart disease, and accidents) are linked to personal life-style choices (e.g., smoking, tobacco use, alcohol consumption, illicit drugs, and the like), it is not surprising that the spotlight has fallen on the individual (cf. Broskowski, 1981; Fuchs, 1986; *Healthy People*, 1979; Kiesler & Morton, 1988).

Progress and positive forces also have had the effect of reawakening interest in self-directive processes. Changes in patterns of mortality and morbidity away from acute infectious diseases toward long-term, chronic conditions that are treated, for the most part, in the context of home and family (rather than hospital or consulting room) have contributed to the national raising of consciousness about individual or "life-style" contributors to the quality of life. The consumerist movement has made Americans defensive in their purchasing of products and services, including things medical, and is aided by television and the print media who continue to blitz us with "investigative reports" of fraud and incompetence in the professional community. Finally, the concern with physical fitness and diet has become more than a mere "craze" among many segments of the American population, bolstering the interest in, if not the display of, self-managed health-care.

Of course, it is difficult (perhaps imprudent at this time) to seek to estimate the success of unstructured and unmonitored self-regulatory efforts on the part of the general public. Sociological and epidemiological indicators do not tell the whole story. The publication and sales of self-help books, for example, may be increasing, but we don't know if the books are being read, or if read, understood, or if understood, actualized, or if actualized, indicative of genuine improvements in self-directed health maintenance or illness prevention.

It is fitting, therefore, that we address the self-management of health and illness primarily at the level of cognition, action, and interpersonal process. Particularly important is the question of how effective applied psychologists can be in the design and implementation of training programs to systematically enhance patients' control over their awareness and expression of symptoms, their reaction to illness triggers (e.g., stress, fear), their display of high-risk (usually addictive) behavior patterns, and/or their day-to-day performance of complex and effortful, therapeutic regimes or preventive health-care activities.

Because systematic interventions are (or should be) based on testable concepts regarding the onset and maintenance of adaptive successes and failures, I shall begin with consideration of (a) theory and metatheory in human self-determination and (b) the nature of the hypothesized relationships between self-regulatory processes and health.

CONCEPTUAL FOUNDATIONS

"Self-direction," according to a popular textbook on adjustment (Watson & Tharp, 1989), "means that your own behavior is under your control—that when it is necessary to change, you can" (p. 4). Writing about chronic illness management, Nerenz and Leventhal (1983) proposed the following account of what taking control of one-self actually entails; namely, the idea that the patient is always "actively constructing a definition or representation of his or her illness (or stress) episode . . . and basing or regulating his or her behavior in terms of this representation . . . " (p. 14). Rosenbaum (1988) proposed that representation is best viewed as phase one of a three-phase process of self-regulation that also includes the process of evaluation (appraisal) and a final action phase in which coping or risk-reduction behaviors are initiated. This analytic approach, emphasizing the unfolding of often covert processes, is consistent with the earlier work of Kanfer and Karoly (1972, 1982), Meichenbaum (1977), and others. On the other hand, self-direction, particularly by cognitive means, may be an attribution error, largely the product of our linguistic heritage. As Skinner (1989) sees it:

> . . . we cannot report any internal event, physical or metaphysical, accurately. The words we use we learned from people who did not know precisely what we were talking about, and we have no sensory nerves going to the parts of the brain in which the most important events presumably occur. (p. 17)

Thus, in a Skinnerian manner, Fisher (1986) defined self-control in health as "a social label for those interbehavior relationships by which problem behaviors or temptations are altered in ways that social norms hold to be beneficial" (p. 547).

Each of the above attempts at defining self-management captures the thread of an argument/debate over the essential nature of human function and over humankind's relation to the natural world that, while traceable to the ancient Greeks, impacts significantly not only on modern psychology and medicine, but on contemporary philosophy, theology, law, and education. As the arguments run, we are either free to steer our own course in life or we are not; we are controlled by mechanisms either within us or in the external world; we are either passive in the face of physical forces or we are active in shaping them. Self-management can, therefore, be construed alternatively as a practical set of skills, an internalized array of mental processes, or the end-result of the operation of environmental cues and contingencies whose controlling influence is often inappropriately ascribed to indwelling agents or determinants (such as ego-strength, will power, symbolic processes, self-conceptions, values, intentions, and the like). However, in each case, self-management implies that the actor functions effectively despite limited contact with or dependence on socializing/authority figures like physicians, psychotherapists, teachers, or parents (Karoly, 1982).

After more than 2,000 years of point and counterpoint, the clear lesson we can draw from debates over the nature of human adaptation is that the framing of the questions, in large part, limits the quality of the answers obtained. For example, assuming that freedom and determinism are diametrically opposing worldviews has, over the years, forced scholars to choose between qualitative versus quantitative models, between descriptive versus experimental methods of analysis, between acknowledging the role of experiential phenomena (such as conscious thought and imagery) or denying their utility. The freedom-determinism dichotomy is simply a misguided metatheoretic stance. As stated by Bandura (1986),

> Self-generated influences operate deterministically on behavior the same way as external sources of influence do. Given the same environmental conditions, persons who have the capabilities for exercising many options and are adept at regulating their own behavior will have greater freedom than will those who have limited means of personal agency. It is because self-influence operates deterministically on action that some measure of freedom is possible. (p. 39)

Thus, instead of conceiving of self-direction as "spontaneous outpourings or outflows, unaffected by tangible factors . . . " (Nuttin, 1984, p. 189), we allow for causal influence from various loci in addition to the external environment — including biochemical parameters and the cognitive or "personalized" elaboration of experience. This latter set of codeterminants of action involves the processing of information along with the potential for representation or rerepresentation of events in accordance with learned, personal preferences, standards, or goals (cf. Nuttin, 1984, chap. 5).

Similarly, while debate over the "freeness" (unknowableness) of self-directive processes has proven fruitless, so too has the even more common mistake of seeking to localize "ultimate" control over behavior in accordance with a simple, either-or, spatial (inside vs. outside) analogy. Many theorists, particularly those with a radical behavior bent, have aptly criticized the attempt to locate control under the skin or inside the head because the internal causative agent or process is so often linked to its behavioral effect — as when alcoholic "craving" is indexed by drinking or when

"commitment to therapy" is measured by appointment keeping. Purists in the cognitive camp, however, point out that no two people in the same setting are likely to perform exactly alike, with much of the difference attributable to their unique perception and understanding of events. Yet, in neither case does it provide much of purchase to apportion control or to rankle over first (ultimate) causes.

Fortunately, a theory of self-management does not depend on resolution of the philosophic locus of control debate. The operant perspective and the cognitive social learning viewpoint need not be pitted against one another because the concern of the investigator should not be to situate control, but rather to determine how best to operationalize multiple controlling variables (cravings or discriminative stimuli) and to select a level of analysis appropriate to the phenomenon at hand.

The levels of analysis approach is especially salient because it recognizes the general utility of multiple viewpoints while acknowledging the special merit of a particular analytic mode as determined by context and investigative intent. When the context involves such demands as the monitoring of bodily events (symptoms), the elaboration of current information in terms of future (delayed) consequences, or the appraisal of input in terms of internalized values or enduring standards, and when the investigative intent is not only to describe, but to set the stage for lasting behavior change, then, I believe, the so-called mediational approach to self-management becomes both relevant and defensible.

Self-management as a set of behaviors that are "obedient" to objectively delimitable environmental or organismic constraints is a valid point of departure (as, for example, when an obese child chooses to refrain from eating dessert in the presence of her diet-controlling mother), but one that loses much of its analytic strength when (a) the conflict is intraorganismic and the environment neutral (the obese child is alone in her bedroom and is deciding between going out for ice cream vs. a piece of fruit), (b) the conflict is intraorganismic and the environment is pulling for "inappropriate" behavior (the drug addict on the street corner), (c) the conflict is based not on competition of cues but on the organism's perception of temporal incongruity (overindulge now, pay for it later), or (d) the contingencies in the environment are in conflict (a restaurant that offers the would-be cigarette abstainer the choice of smoking or nonsmoking sections). Under circumstances such as these (and others) and when the environment cannot be (ethically or practically) manipulated, a mediational perspective on behavior dynamics seems warranted.

Some readers may be disappointed at this juncture, assuming that I have violated my previous interdiction concerning the either-or assignment of control to the person or the environment. However, I am not claiming that control rests solely or ultimately within the individual; but merely, that, under certain circumstances, the individual is the most sensible focus of analysis. As shall be made clear later, control does not rest at all; instead it is an emergent function of an interdependent network of coacting elements (mind, body, and context). Also, to be perfectly fair to those espousing the positivist (operant) perspective, it should be noted that they have not been oblivious to the question of boundary conditions or to the logic of a levels-of-analysis argument. Baer, Wolf, and Risley (1987), pioneers in the experimental analysis of behavior, have acknowledged that

> . . . the problems of today are not as delimited as those of our beginnings. They are called lifestyles in recognition of their systematic nature. The behaviors called delinquency, substance abuse, safety, exercise, and diet, for example, represent complex classes of topographies serving complex functions involving many agents of reinforcement/punishment and stimulus control all of whom interact to constitute and maintain the system as such. Thus, entry at just one point of such systems is likely to yield only limited, short-term behavior changes. . . . (p. 323)

Because, as I have noted, most of the health psychology applications of so-called self-management methods provide a conceptual warrant and a practical, clinical justification for employing the mediational approach, elaborating this perspective shall be the major objective of the present chapter.

Mediational Models

When the reflex arc and the stimulus-response associative bond took their place as the elementary units of motivational analysis in psychology, a number of thorny issues, served by a host of elusive concepts such as volition, self, intention, hope, desire, foresight, preference (value), and the like, seemed to dissolve. The topics and questions articulated fully 100 years ago by William James (1976) were seemingly retired, or left to the musings of philosophers. Yet, while accepting the

mechanistic "laws" of learning as highly descriptive of the passive animal in the constrained and predictable world of the laboratory runway, a number of empirically oriented thinkers in the 1960s and 1970s began to resurrect or redefine the Jamesian agenda (if not his conceptual formulations) in order to accommodate the proactive, idiosyncratic, self-conscious, anticipatory, and field-independent manner in which we humans traverse the unmarked and often unpredictable world of personal relationships, long-range (delayed) outcomes, and conflicting social ideals. Stimulus-Response (S-R) connections were supplemented by considering the role of images and plans (Miller, Galanter, & Pribram, 1960), language (Dollard & Miller, 1950; Staats, 1968, 1975), preferences and act-outcome expectancies (Irwin, 1970; Rotter, 1954), attentional focusing and the cognitive transformation of goal objects (Mischel, 1974; Mischel & Ebbesen, 1970), observational learning (Bandura, 1969), and the self-imposition of re warding and punishing consequences (Bandura & Perloff, 1967; Kanfer & Marston, 1963; Kanfer, 1971).

Information is the basic element within a mediational approach, and its intake, storage, retrieval, and transformation are its basic operations. As far as fundamental units of analysis are concerned, it is proposed that self-regulation of action is built on the individual's apprehension of environmental settings' offering alternative outcomes for alternative courses of action. Beliefs about situation-act-outcome (SAO) probabilities are dependent not only on direct experience, but on information transmitted verbally, imaginally, or via the observation of others. As the person matures, much of his or her activity is dependent on rules (many of which are inaccessible to conscious recall) concerning preferred SAO patterns. Means-end structures in the form of SAO representations are dynamic units in the sense that they respond to information about temporal relationships (an outcome that is rewarding at time 1, but eventuates in an aversive state at time 2), to alterations in environmental contingencies (certain acts, once rewarded, are no longer), to setting fluctuations, historical forces, and the like, and to higher order (hierarchically organized) programs (e.g., a set of actions with predictably positive outcomes may be deferred because they are inconsistent with a self-presentational motive currently activated).

Two different but equally important SAO functions are at the center of human self-directiveness.

The first reflects the capacity to think about the future, to anticipate as well as to simply imagine upcoming SAO sequences. Whether it is called forethought, planning, goal-setting, or is assigned other similar labels, the function involves the inferential processing of information about possible end states (the world, the self, and the self-world relation) in ways that can lead to adaptive change in stagnant or malfunctioning systems. The process by which a self-reflective organism sets its objectives and sometimes even introduces an internal conflict (i.e., a mismatch between desires and current accomplishments) can be termed a command or directive function (Ford, 1987). Its more technical name, in the context of control theory, is the feed forward function.

A complementary function reflects the actor's ability to process information about actual performance outcomes in a tangible manner relative to specific reference values or standards. The creation of stability in self-regulating systems requires this second kind of SAO function in which the consequences of an action are known to (fed back to) the actor for the express purpose of reducing any discrepancy or mismatch between what is desired (the reference value) and what is obtained. This more commonly discussed function is called negative feedback (negative = discrepancy reducing).

For any complex, self-steering organism to operate effectively and to grow in its ever-changing environment, both the feedback and feed forward functions are necessary. As noted by Ford (1987),

> When feedback and feedforward are combined, a dynamic control system potential emerges that *can combine information about past, present, and projected future events to guide the flow of its current activity in a variable environment either to maintain or alter its current steady states.* (p. 69)

Because feed forward and feedback functions operate in fallible information processors—that is, in human beings—the potential for adaptive control is always in question, subject to the vicissitudes of mechanisms yet to be explored. A number of theorists have offered roadmaps depicting the direct and indirect routes, obstacles, shortcuts, and misdirections that can result when self-management is pursued. I shall review several (though by no means all of the interesting) models of self-direction, highlighting those whose comprehensiveness, testability, and relevance to health psychology make them especially useful for our present purposes.

Kanfer's Multistage Model

It has been almost four decades since B. F. Skinner (1953) conceptualized self-control solely in terms of environmental contingencies, and more than 20 years since F. H. Kanfer and colleagues, noting the practical problem of the "initial predominance of available reinforcement for the undesirable response" (Kanfer & Phillips, 1970, p. 413), sought to personalize the process of self-control in order to understand how clinically dysfunctional behaviors with conflicting contingencies (i.e., rewarded in the short run, but punished in the long run) could be handled by the individual serving both as agent and object of change.

To accomplish a modification of a habitual (high-probability) response, the individual was said to make use of the same kinds of devices available to an external agent seeking to modify or shape the behavior of another organism: the ability to sense or detect outcomes, the setting of a criterion of performance, and the capacity to provide response-contingent reward or punishment as a result of either success or failure in matching the criterion. The external monitoring, evaluation, and consequation processes are taken over by the actor, yielding a three-stage, mediated model consisting of self-monitoring, self-evaluation, and self-reinforcement/punishment (cf. Kanfer, 1971; Kanfer & Karoly, 1972). The three stages, which were originally fashioned in an open or linear configuration, when viewed as a closed-loop (feedback-sensitive) pattern convey the essential elements of a control system, including the requisite feedback functions (knowledge of both the problem-engendering and corrective behavior) and the feed forward function (criterion or standard setting, presumably based on prior learning). Factors hypothesized to facilitate or impede the operation of these self-steering components include environmental inputs, cognitive and metacognitive activities, and physiological/genetic influences and their interactions (Kanfer & Karoly, 1972; Kanfer & Schefft, 1988). The three-stage model was proposed to account for the maintenance of goal-directed action in the relative absence of external contingencies (a process called self-regulation) as well as for the self-directed alteration of behavior under the influence of an immediate conflict or of conflicting temporal contingencies (a process called self-control).

The practical and heuristic value of the three-stage model continues to register in the applied (clinical) literature and in the emerging domain of health psychology (Holroyd & Creer, 1986; Karoly & Kanfer, 1982; Kirschenbaum & Tomarken, 1982; Watson & Tharp, 1989) despite reformulations and elaborations by Kanfer and his associates and criticisms from other self-management theorists.

Kanfer and Hagerman (1981, 1987) have differentiated the three-stage process into five sequences, the final four of which incorporate hitherto neglected processes: the actor's attributions of causality or relevance. Let us use as an illustration the case of a person trying to abstain from smoking cigarettes. Once the initial self-monitoring process is activated (as, for example, when a conflictive choice between lighting up or not signals that a "problem" exists), the individual must next decide (sequence 2) whether the cause of the general dilemma is primarily a function of situational, intrapsychic, or biologic parameters (alpha, beta, or gamma variables, respectively). If the attribution is to external causes (e.g., pressure from others) or to uncontrollable physiological factors (an inherited disposition or an illness), then the sequence may stop. If the problem is attributed to such beta variables as personal choice, a lack of willpower or effort, a history of prior bad decisions, or a desire to avoid an early and painful death, then the problem is potentially correctable and the process moves on to sequence three. The criterion selection and performance evaluation stages are entered only if the actor sees the problem at hand as being relevant to his or her "current concerns" (dominant goals). Further, a problem behavior (such as the desire to light up a cigarette) may access either a short-term or long-term concern or goal, and the ensuing evaluation may be impacted differentially as a result of the particular temporal standard invoked. After the evaluation is made of the discrepancy between outcome and reference value, the person enters sequence 4. Again, a causal attribution process is activated, this time having to do with whether the sensed discrepancy is personally or environmentally mediated. As Kanfer and Hagerman (1987) noted,

... our earlier self-regulation model lacked specification of the point at which attributions can affect both the self-evaluative and self-rein-

forcement processes. Empirical research from various laboratories suggests that subsequent behavior may differ when the individual attributes the discrepancy in reaching the self-set standard either to him or herself or to external events. (p. 301)

Note that the sequence 2 attribution dealt with characterizing the source of the smoking problem in general ("I smoke because I feel I want to"), whereas the sequence 4 attribution focuses on the reason(s) why the actor either succeeds or fails to resist the temptation to smoke. If the sequence 4 attribution is external, then the process terminates. An internal attribution means the sequence moves on to the self-reinforcement/self-punishment stage. The full model is illustrated in Figure 29.1.

It should be mentioned before moving on that Kanfer and his colleagues do not expect that the various attributional decisions will operate in a fully rational manner. Defensive attributions can short-circuit the regulatory process in various ways (implying that interventions based on the model will not likely succeed in the absence of clinical sensitivity).

Carver and Scheier's Focal Attention Approach

Like Kanfer and associates, Carver and Scheier (1981, 1982) were influenced by cybernetic concepts originating in biology and engineering. Particularly important to Carver and Scheier's theorizing were the ideas of W. T. Powers, an engineer, whose book *Behavior: The Control of Perception* (1973) presented a sophisticated hierarchical structural analysis of neuropsychological control systems. Also, as in the previous model, Carver and Scheier emphasize the structural importance of the negative feedback apparatus. Important differences emerge, however, with regard to what specific components of the control system are stressed and their hypothesized determinants.

For a system to operate in accordance with the principle of feedback control, there must be a function to detect (sense or monitor) information and one to take the information collected and compare it with the desired state of affairs (the standard, set point, or reference signal). This second function is often called the comparator function and it presumably serves a pivotal motivational role because it triggers actions (behaviors) designed to reduce perceived discrepancies between the input and the reference signal (cf. Miller et al., 1960; Powers, 1973). The activation of this

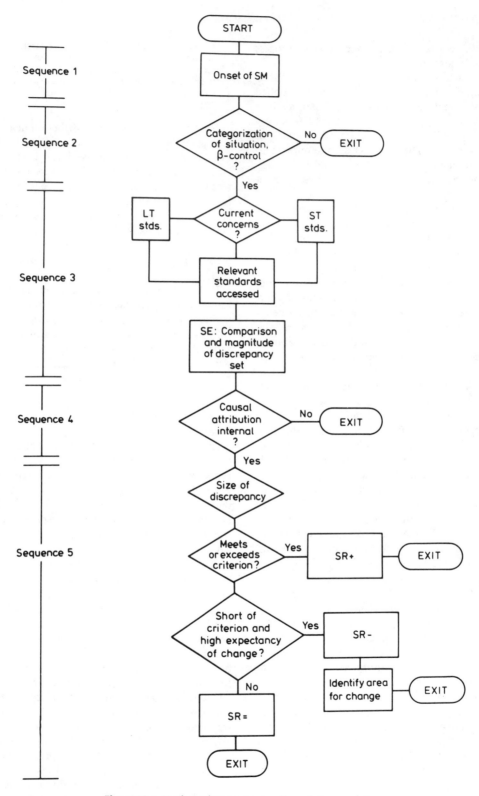

Figure 29.1. Kanfer and Hagerman's self-regulation model.

comparator has been a central concern in Carver and Scheier's work.

Because self-management comes into play if automatized or habitual behaviors are interrupted or challenged (e.g., a message on the cigarette smoker's package of cigarettes indicates that today's quota has been consumed), it is reasonable to assume that a state of "mindlessness" (Langer, Blank, & Chanowitz, 1978) is replaced by a certain degree of self-reflection or self-awareness. In the absence of self-awareness, the comparator may not engage; hence, the process of action control via negative feedback will fail to be initiated. In their research program, Carver and Scheier have sought to induce self-awareness via environmental manipulations (having subjects appear before an audience or work in front of a mirror) or they have assumed differential propensities toward self-attention as a function of subjects' scores on a paper-and-pencil scale (the Self-Consciousness Scale). It has been shown, in several experiments, that people are more likely to seek out information relevant to their ostensible values (standards, reference levels) when they are made to be focally self-aware (e.g., when seated before a mirror) than when such manipulations are omitted.

Self-focused attention comes into play not only by evoking a behavioral standard but also by motivating the individual to act to reduce any perceived discrepancies between the standard and current input. Carver and Scheier have likewise produced a body of empirical work to support the view that self-focus heightens conformity to salient standards or norms (cf. Carver & Scheier, 1981, 1982).

Finally, Carver and Scheier have highlighted a fundamental aspect of self-regulatory systems— their hierarchical nature—which, although articulated in detail by Powers (1973), appears to have gone unnoticed by many investigators. Basically, the human control system is believed to consist not of a single reference standard, but of multiple standards hierarchically interconnected. The system is so constituted that "each successive superordinate level of feedback systems 'behaves' by specifying reference values for the next lower level of control (Carver & Scheier, 1982, p. 101). Powers (1973) originally proposed nine levels of control, with one's idealized identity and values at the most abstract (highest) level and first-order control systems made up of muscular reflexes (the most concrete level). In answer to the key question, "Which level is functionally dominant at any

point in time?" Carver and Scheier argue that the level being attended to is superordinate. When the system is operating properly all levels are being served. This implies that we humans are complex in our goal-directedness: a single action can serve multiple objectives and different reference levels can become superordinate at different times. Among the important clinical implications of a hierarchial model is that it admits to intergoal conflict both within and between levels.

In sum, by emphasizing the role of self-awareness in comparator activation, performance motivation, and hierarchial control, Carver and Scheier have greatly expanded our ability to identify potential sources of self-regulatory success and failure.

Models Emphasizing Feed Forward Mechanisms

Both of the preceding approaches tend to stress postgoal, cognitive-comparison processes. That is, where the person wishes to go is somewhat less important than the feedback-driven process of getting there. However, while discrepancy-reduction mechanisms are clearly necessary, they are only half the story; as I noted previously, the feedback function requires a feed forward function to "drive" it (Ford, 1987). Bandura (1988) has similarly stated that

> in the negative feedback control system, if performance matches the standard, the person does nothing. A regulatory process in which matching a standard begets inertness does not characterize human self-motivation . . . Negative feedback may help to keep (people) going, but it is not present antecedently to start them. (p. 47)

While a distinction between initiation and continued control of motivation is important, it is also necessary to recall that after the first performance feedback, the feed forward and feedback operations are mutually influential, creating what Bandura (1988) calls a "dual cyclic process of disequilibrating discrepancy production followed by equilibrating discrepancy reduction" (p. 47).

Detailing the precise nature of feed forward mechanisms in self-direction is a critical requirement, one that is addressed but not empirically exploited in the previously noted conceptual accounts. Bandura (1988) has recently suggested the following "evaluative agentive properties" as likely feed forward operations: (a) predictive anticipatory control of effort expenditure, (b) self-efficacy attributions, (c) value systems that give rise to affective postperformance reactions, and (d) meta-cognitive activities (thinking about one's thinking relative to goals, actions, and self-appraisals). Each of these, and others, are disequilibrating in the sense that they function, not to set the organism's motivation energy to zero, but rather to infuse the system with a surplus of information to yield what control theorists call a dynamic equilibrium (cf. Ford, 1987; Powers, 1973). Human self-regulatory systems, unlike machines, are designed to grow and change, not to maintain unchanging order. Self-managing systems add flexibility to the process of adaptation, but not necessarily predictability.

A number of control systems theories, and a number of intervention programs based on these theories, have yet to fully appreciate the elaborative (self-constructing) nature of systems. They seem to focus an inordinate amount of attention on the content of a person's goal(s) rather than recognizing that it is how one wants, not just what one wants, that determines the success of a long-term self-change enterprise. A number of writers are beginning to formalize the study of feed forward processes in motivation (cf. Frese & Sabini, 1985; Pervin, 1989; Sorrentino & Higgins, 1986); and their research programs may provide the material for improvements in clinical self-change programs in the domain of health (and elsewhere). I shall return to these points in the final section.

Self-Management and Health

The basic tactical rationale behind the current renaissance of interest in individually guided action in health-care was stated forcefully by the Surgeon General (*Healthy People*, 1979): "It is the controllability of many risks — and, often, the significance of controlling even only a few — that lies at the heart of disease prevention and health promotion" (p. 13).

The unique perspective that each of us has on our own life circumstances renders the self-management approach essential to the success of modern medical technology, which, whatever other wonders it may perform, cannot (and should not) penetrate into our subjective worlds and private lives. Pointing to medicine's relative neglect of patient autonomy, Levy and Howard (1982) have outlined five "domains of patient power" or expertise, whose recognition is considered essential to the humanization of health-care. Patients are said to possess (a) experiential expertise, because only they can feel pain and the early warning signs

of incipient disease; (b) integrative expertise, because they must "integrate the multitude of physical as well as interpersonal systems that influence their health and illness behavior" (Levy & Howard, 1982, p. 564); (c) initiator expertise, because consulting a physician represents an advocacy role that only patients can undertake; (d) informative expertise, reflecting the power to give informed consent to medical procedures or experimentation; and (e) implementive expertise, or the power to comply with or to undermine the therapeutic, rehabilitative, or preventive regimens outlined by medical and/or allied health professionals. Thus, Levy and Howard (1982) construe health-care delivery as a bidirectional process, and self-management can therefore be viewed as the patient's contribution to the achievement of society's health agenda.

The patient-centered approach to health is, however, a bounded conception. Self-determination is relative, not absolute; and it is the "system" of which the patient is a vital part that truly "manages" the ultimate outcomes. Arguing too strongly for a self-directional model can sometimes foster a "blaming the victim" mentality. Self-management, likewise, should not be invoked as an excuse for inadequate physician participation (cf. Southam & Dunbar, 1986). Because the self-management credo is ultimately only as worthy as the methodologies/tactics it engenders, we will turn next to a survey of clinical interventions developed (in part) out of the theoretical models reviewed above.

CLINICAL FUNDAMENTALS OF SELF-MANAGEMENT

The mediational models just presented, along with the operant perspective, have been an extremely rich source of ideas for the clinician. At the interventive level of analysis, it has proven useful to view a complex, multilayered process more simply — as a set of interrelated skills capable of being taught (within limits) to children as well as adults (Karoly, 1977, 1981; Mahoney & Arnkoff, 1979). A number of procedures have emerged over the years that have been applied with the general objective of empowering clients to alter problematic response patterns that are either infrequent, beyond the scope of external surveillance, under the influence of cognitive or affective mediation, or highly likely to yield counterregulatory maneuvers if under the express direction of outside agents. A nonexhaustive listing of common self-management procedures is presented in Table 29.1.

Most of the procedures shown in Table 29.1 can be used for a variety of purposes other than the attainment of effective self-management. However, when a methodology is consistent with theoretical accounts and is employed for the purpose of enhancing self-change or self-maintenance, it can potentially be included. Thus, how an intervention is used is far more critical than the mere fact that it is used. The systematic employment of component procedures such as are listed in Table 29.1 turns out, however, to be a rare event in clinical practice. By *systematic*, I mean that the techniques are (a) chosen by the clinician after a thorough assessment of the client's specific needs (excesses or deficits), (b) realistic in light of the client's life circumstances, including factors "beyond" his or her control, (c) integrated with the client's existing skills repertoire, and (d) actually utilized by the client in accordance with the treatment plan (e.g., used at the proper time or in the proper sequence).

Given the diversity of available and potential self-management procedures, a conceptually driven categorization scheme is used as an organizational aid. A brief description of each of the seven related types of training (listed in Table 29.2) will be presented next, followed by illustrative examples drawn from the health psychology literature.

Early-Stage Motivation Enhancement

The techniques described in this category serve to activate and maintain the patient's desire to change, the expectation that change is possible, and the belief that the potential outcome is worth the effort, cost, or sacrifice involved. Both active and passive forms of "resistance" to change are assumed to be operative in most psychotherapy settings, and, at least early in therapy, some special procedures or tactics are needed to help overcome them (cf. Kanfer & Schefft, 1988, chap. 5). Later in the therapeutic process, particularly after the enactment of new behaviors produces tangible results (e.g., the dieter loses some weight; the smoker cuts back on the number of cigarettes smoked per day, etc.), then any procedure that contributes to treatment success can rightfully be termed a motivation enhancer.

The use of contracts, task (homework) assignments, and goal-setting/goal clarification methods are among the most effective means of motivation enhancement. They also help to accent several important dimensions of clinical self-management as a philosophy and a technology of change. First, such methods build a conceptual bridge between the consulting room and the patient's extratherapy world where the "real work" takes place. The procedures also highlight the role of the clinician as an essential but temporary facilitator of client change. The explicit statement of goals and the pursuit of specific behavioral objectives by means of newly acquired strategies likewise makes clear to the patient how self-directed change differs from naturally occurring (unplanned) change. Further, these methods should theoretically help to activate the patient's self-evaluative standards and do so at the appropriate level of control. And, finally, the use of such methods emphasizes an all too often neglected aspect of self-management—that it is a temporally extended process rather than merely a technology aimed at achieving a time-bound outcome or product (Kanfer & Gaelick, 1986; Mahoney & Arnkoff, 1979; Shelton & Levy, 1981).

Clarifying the patient's goals and breaking them down into small, achievable subgoals with clear behavioral referents is only a part of the goals analysis, albeit a vital one. Because goals are fundamental units of analysis (both as feed forward signals and as pivotal references in a feedback loop), they merit careful scrutiny throughout all phases of treatment. Goals also are considered basic to the individual's appraisal of self, world, and the self-world reaction; and an appreciation of the contents and organization of the patient's end-state cognitions is likely to provide valuable information about functional and dysfunctional higher order self-governance structures (cf. Emmons, 1989; Karoly, in press; Little, 1983; Pervin, 1989).

Behavioral Enactment Training

In many instances, the instrumental behaviors necessary to alter a self-defeating, high-probability response (such as smoking, drinking, overeating) do not need to be expressly taught; they are already in the individual's repertoire. However, the patient may well require assistance in the sequencing of his or her actions and in the selective inhibition/exhibition of well-learned behaviors in the pursuit of long-range (delayed) objectives. Thus, skills practice, mental as well as physical rehearsal, performance feedback (such as provided by a videotape replay), guided participation, relaxation training, and the like may be uti-

Table 29.1. Self-Management Training Strategies Frequently Employed

Goal(s) clarification and specification
Contracting/task assignments
Self-monitoring (self-observation and recording)
Stimulus control (environment manipulation)
Self-instructional training (for self-cueing or coping)
Self-generated positive consequences (tangible and/or imagined)
Self-generated negative consequences (tangible and/or imagined)
Training in problem-solving/decision-making
Training in planning/forethought
Covert conditioning (including covert sensitization, covert modeling, etc.)
Thought stopping/thought starting (cognitive distraction and/or cognitive
    activation)
Reattribution training (including self-efficacy enhancement)
Attitude modification
Imaginal rehearsal
Reinforcer sampling
Training in the solicitation of social support
Self-directed relaxation (self-hypnosis)/cue-controlled relaxation; meditation;
    anger control
Performance practice (rehearsal)
Information acquisition
Relapse (lapse) prevention training
Training in metacognitive activities (e.g., memory; self-management theory)
Biofeedback

lized. Effective self-management depends on what I have called integrated behavioral routines or programs (Karoly, 1985), implying that unless simple component skills (like saying no to drugs) are part of a broader set of action programs articulating what to do, where to do it, when to start, when to stop, and when to resume, they are unlikely to pilot the individual through life's changing landscape.

Cognitive Regulator Development and/or Modification

Humans transform their experiences, and ultimately themselves, through the symbolic manipulation of information. The information can exist in the form of factual knowledge, judgments or preferences, memories, wishes, or fantasized depictions of "possible selves" (Markus & Nurius, 1986) or "possible worlds" (Stalnaker, 1984). The dynamic control capabilities of people are clearly dependent on the extent and flexibility of cognitive regulatory options, such as those provided by language, visualization, memory, problem-solving, planning, goal-setting, self-reflection, evaluative judgment, information acquisition and retrieval habits, belief systems, self-instructional skills, attention deployment, propositional logic, and a host of capacities often summarized under the umbrella of "intelligence" (cf. Bandura, 1986; Cantor & Kihlstrom, 1987). These cognitive determinants of self-regulatory efficiency are among the most difficult to assess but among the most vital to the long-term success and generalization of clinical interventive efforts. The neglect of such mediators probably accounts for the limited success heretofore obtained in many empirical evaluations of self-management training with adults and particularly with children (for whom the develop-

Table 29.2. Suggested Categories of Self-Management Intervention

(a) Early-stage motivation enhancement
(b) Behavioral enactment training
(c) Cognitive regulator development and/or modification
(d) Pre- and postperformance monitoring and evaluation training
(e) Environmental manipulation
(f) Affect management
(g) Persistence training

mental emergence of information-processing skills is so obviously in need of attention).

As I shall argue in more detail in the final section of this chapter, it is rarely a question of whether an individual is cognitively regulating, but of how and to what purpose. Packaged training programs that seek to enhance specific mediational pathways can, therefore, run afoul of existing, maladaptive regulatory habits left undiagnosed and untreated.

Pre- and Postperformance Monitoring and Evaluation Training

Because of the centrality of the negative feedback loop in the emergence of self-management models in psychology, it is not surprising that control functions tied to the feedback reference signal — namely, the information collection and comparator functions — have figured so prominently in clinical work. To function adequately, the self-directive system must access information relevant to the variable being controlled (e.g., the number of cigarettes smoked) and then feed the information to the comparator, where the standard is matched against this input. If corrective action is taken, the information collection function monitors the consequences of said action and again transmits the information to the comparator (Carver & Scheier, 1981; Ford, 1987; Kanfer & Karoly, 1972; Powers, 1973). Thus, the self-monitoring of negatively valenced action (cigarette smoking) and/or of positively valenced, incompatible responding (such as cigarette refusal) is an essential clinical tactic.

Self-monitoring is the initial mechanism in multistage theories and has been viewed as prerequisite to other self-change techniques. More accurately, however, self-awareness in the form of a perceptual-cognitive focus on the consequences of one's continued display of health-compromising actions (drug-taking, overeating, use of unsterilized needles, etc.) is the necessary starting point (Karoly, 1980, 1981). Believing that one has a problem precedes the process of counting and recording problematic and corrective responses. However, in most cases, problem recognition occurs prior to the first clinical contact.

Self-monitoring proper refers to the process of attentional tracking of self-relevant attributes — attributes that may reflect emitted actions or behaviors (e.g., keeping count of cigarettes smoked), physiologic responses (e.g., attending to "urges" or "cravings"), biochemical processes (e.g., assessing one's own blood alcohol level), physical status

(e.g., weight) or thoughts (e.g., focusing on one's depressogenic cognitions). One can monitor such states or events prior to the performance of some designated controlling behaviors (as when the dieter monitors his or her intentions, urges, or efficacy attributions prior to eating meals), during the performance (counting calories consumed), or subsequent to it (monitoring post-meal levels of satiety or hunger). Self-monitoring depends not only on attention, but also on memory. To concretize the self-monitoring process and introduce a certain permanence into evanescent acts of attention, clinicians have developed methods to assist clients in the collection and storage of self-monitored data. To be maximally useful, self-recording devices must be unobtrusive and conveniently portable.

Currently, self-monitoring and self-recording remain among the most frequently assessed and trained skills in the self-management armamentarium (cf. Holroyd & Creer, 1986; Kanfer & Gaelick, 1986), employed not only for treatment purposes but for diagnosis and planning. As an intervention, self-monitoring has been employed by itself — as a means of interrupting automatized habits such as cigarette smoking — or in combination with other techniques (cf. Karoly & Doyle, 1975; Kazdin, 1974; O'Banion, Armstrong, & Ellis, 1980).

In the preceding discussion of cognitive regulator development and modification, I noted that self-reflective and evaluative tendencies are among the key information-processing operations available to the autonomous and flexible problem-solver. Interestingly, it is quite difficult in practice to clearly separate the act of self-monitoring from the process of evaluative judgment, particularly after the performance of a deliberate (nonautomatic) goal-directed act. Both Kanfer, in his early three-stage model (Kanfer & Karoly, 1972), and Bandura (1986), in his discussion of self-regulatory subfunctions, highlighted the fact that between self-observation and corrective action there exists a set of judgmental processes that determine the form and intensity of self-reactions and subsequent performance.

The complexity of the mediating judgmental processes has not been fully appreciated in clinical applications of self-management theory. Due largely to the influence of control theory, the process of matching-to-standard has been most often invoked as the evaluative subfunction responsible for directing and energizing performance

(Carver & Scheier, 1981). In addition, performance attributions have been recognized as potentially important to self-directed action (Bandura, 1986; Kanfer & Hagerman, 1981). Consequently, goals (standard) clarification and reattributional training have been accorded the lion's share of clinical attention (Ickes, 1988; Kanfer & Schefft, 1988; Miller & Porter, 1988). Notwithstanding the importance of these domains, the fact remains that the diversity of evaluative, self-regulated appraisals that can follow self-monitoring is only beginning to be explored conceptually and clinically. There is, for example, more than one type of performance standard (Bandura, 1986; Higgins, 1987; Karoly, 1985), more than one class of referential anchor (Higgins, 1987; Karoly & Decker, 1979; Miller, Turnbull, & McFarland, 1988), and distinct personal preferences and situational pressures capable of influencing the person's time-limited choice of judgment frame (Dweck & Leggett, 1988; Schwarzer, 1986). Further, the realism, objectivity, or accuracy of postperformance self-appraisals cannot be assumed.

Environmental Manipulation

Early learning-theory–inspired models of self-management placed a great deal of emphasis on the need to prearrange one's environment so as to (a) restrict or eliminate exposure to cures that would normally elicit maladaptive behavior or (b) increase exposure to cues that tend to elicit desirable (but low-probability) responses. Thus, the smoker is asked to remove ashtrays from various rooms in his or her home, or to confine smoking to one place and time, or to avoid both smoking and eating. This prearrangement of cues strategy is called stimulus control or stimulus narrowing (see, e.g. Goldiamond, 1965; Mahoney & Thoresen, 1974; Stuart, 1967). Generally, this type of strategy was seen to work best when used in combination with other interventions, particularly those designed to provide incentives for behaviors incompatible with the problem or target (Bandura, 1969). In addition, some investigators included covert cues (e.g., thoughts, urges) as stimuli capable of being controlled in an analogous fashion (cf. Homme, 1965).

Engineering of environmental forces also includes the prearrangement of response consequences. Arranging for significant others to reward adaptive behavior or to punish or ignore (extinguish) maladaptive responses is an example of such contingency management.

To those who view environmental determinants as distinct from mediational processes, the strategies in this category are erroneously considered to fall outside the self-direction domain, by definition. Or it is believed that the strategy of environmental management requires less self-directiveness than the other types because problems or conflictful decisions are eliminated before they occur, thereby obviating the need to "stare temptation in the face" (Mahoney & Thoresen 1974). However, within a control systems framework, one recognizing the dialectic nature of controlling events, such an analysis clearly falters.

Affect Management

Relaxation, self-hypnosis, biofeedback, meditation, autogenic training, desensitization, anger control, and various fantasy-based procedures can be employed to eliminate the affective reaction tendencies (such as fear, depression, or hostility) involved in the etiology or maintenance of such self-defeating, illness-engendering patterns as the Type A pattern, alcoholism, obesity, or cigarette smoking (Rudestam, 1980). Positive emotions may be viewed either as discriminative interoceptive stimuli linked to prohealth behaviors or they may be seen as naturally incompatible with stress, thus constituting clinical endpoints in their own right (Fisher, 1986). For our present purposes, it is also important to note that aversive or unpleasant emotions are associated with acute illness (e.g., pain) as well as with the day-to-day management of chronic disease (e.g., the fatigue, boredom, frustration, or embarrassment often tied to complex self-care regimens). Notably, the widespread use of emotion-based techniques may stem from a stronger connection to traditional models of psychotherapy (Greenberg & Safran, 1989) than to such theories of self-direction as were earlier reviewed.

Persistence Training

If the mobilization of feedback and feed forward processes is to provide effective solutions to life-style problems, then it is assumed that the underlying skills will remain potent, even if abeyant, and readily applied to novel or unforeseen challenges. Given the trend toward relapse associated with the treatment of additive disorders and training in health-care compliance (Marlatt & Gordon, 1985; Meichenbaum & Turk, 1987), the credibility of self-management methods is intrinsically linked to their long-term, rather than to their immediate, effects. As stated by Kanfer and Schefft (1988), "When clients learn to regulate their own actions, their dependency on external settings is decreased. Maintenance of gains can be supported by self-generated cues and reinforcements" (p. 62).

At this juncture, it is necessary to invoke an old, but very relevant, distinction—that between learning and performance. Often associated with the debate over whether reinforcers operate by strengthening S-R bonds or by providing incentives to act, the learning-performance distinction nonetheless justifies the assumption that the principles of response acquisition can be meaningfully separated from the principles determining the subsequent display of learned behaviors (cf. Bandura, 1969). In this regard, note that Kanfer and Schefft (1988) claimed only that "maintenance of gains can be supported by self-generated cues and reinforcement" (p. 62), not that such gains will inevitably be so supported. Therefore, although by their nature self-management techniques may possess a greater potential for maintenance, transfer, and generalization, they enjoy no special immunity to the disabling effects of memory decay, environmental disruption, competition of situational incentives, or conflict among activated reference standards in one's hierarchy of values.

One could add to the myths or misunderstandings about self-management the notion that, once acquired, self-management skills and tactics will inevitably be utilized, and that the problem of relapse or recidivism, having been solved, does not need to be further assessed.

Indeed, a general strategy for maintenance enhancement has been to anticipate the form and intensity of potential (high-risk) disruptive influences (personal, situational, or biochemical) and to train patients to cope with them prior to the termination of therapeutic contact. Included in this general relapse prevention approach is training that ostensibly equips the patient to foresee and forestall high-risk (usually stress-related) events—a kind of lifestyle management or primary prevention effort (cf. Marlatt & Gordon, 1985; Meichenbaum & Turk, 1987).

Having briefly considered the diverse objectives and formats of self-management training, it remains to be noted that the mode of delivery can likewise vary. The procedures I have outlined may be instigated either through direct training, through observational means (e.g., modeling), via mass media (television and newspaper), transmis-

sion of information and/or incentives through reading (bibliotherapy), or via some combination of these. The mode of delivery chosen should be appropriate to the nature and accessibility of the target problem. If reducing highway fatalities due to failure to use seatbelts is the self-management objective, then mass media campaigns may well be preferred over the use of individually based interventions. On the other hand, teaching young diabetic patients to monitor their glucose levels and self-inject insulin usually requires direct contact (at least initially) with a health professional.

APPLICATIONS OF SELF-MANAGEMENT IN HEALTH

Contemporary applications of self-management methods in health occur mainly in four domains: (a) chronic illness adjustment, particularly involving medical regimen adherence; (b) high-risk life-style control, typically involving such "addictive," health-compromising behaviors as overeating, excessive drug or alcohol use, and cigarette smoking; (c) pain management; and (d) regulation of nonaddictive, health-compromising patterns of affectivity, such as depression, hostility, fear, and the so-called stress reactions or physiologically based "illness triggers." A thorough review of any one of these fields of application would require more than a chapter-length treatment. I will, therefore, provide an overview of the first two (for reading on pain management see Blanchard, Andrasik, Guarnieri, Neff, & Rodichok, 1987; Turk, Meichenbaum & Genest, 1983; on stress and affect management see Olton & Noonberg, 1980; Wickramasekera, 1988).

Self-Managed Adaptation to Chronic Illness

Sustained self-management is mandated for chronic medical conditions treated mainly on an outpatient basis, under the day-to-day guidance of the patient (or the patient's family), that depend on continued vigilance and corrective action to prevent serious illness flare-ups or physical deterioration. Traditionally, both knowledge (of the disease and how to care for oneself) and motivation (desires, beliefs, and expectancies) have been emphasized by medical sociologists as necessary conditions for effective self-ministration, acting in concert with illness characteristics (e.g., Becker & Maiman, 1983). However, viewing self-management as a dynamic, self-constructive, socially embedded process requires that a complex task-analytic approach be undertaken to gauge the multiple goals and life demands acting on the patient, both generally and with respect to the illness. The patient's skills and skill deficiencies, along with the supportive and obstructive characteristics of the social and physical setting, need to be assessed and remediated as well. Finally, an appreciation of and training in specific cognitive and metacognitive operations associated with the feedback and feed forward system functions are entailed (particularly with children for whom age-related or experientially based attainment limitations place unique boundaries on the potential for self-direction).

Although no clinical intervention program has yet articulated and operationalized all of the elements I have ascribed to systematic self-management, a growing body of literature exists in which one or more training modalities have been employed to assist chronic patients to cope with one or more of the adaptive tasks of illness. Based on self-management models and extant conceptions of illness coping (e.g., Moos & Schaefer, 1984), Table 29.3 illustrates the compass of actual and potential applications. Many of the cells of the 7 (methods) by 10 (tasks) matrix are presently unexplored; yet sufficient light has been cast to justify our critical attention.

Diabetes

Insulin-dependent diabetes mellitus (IDDM) is a disease characterized by chronic high blood glucose concentration due mainly to destruction of the beta cells of the pancreas. Because the blood glucose concentration cannot be biologically self-regulated (as is the case in the nondiabetic), behavioral self-regulation is called for, usually in the form of a complex self-care regimen consisting of the self-measurement of glucose levels, single or multiple daily injections of insulin, diet and exercise regulation, and other patient-managed activities (Cox, Gonder-Frederick, Pohl, & Pennebaker, 1986; Pohl, Gonder-Frederick, & Cox, 1984; Surwit, Feinglos & Scovern, 1983). Described by Pohl et al. (1984) as "a nearly pure example of behavioral medicine" (p. 6), the self-care of IDDM can hardly be considered successful in the absence of educational and psychological intervention, as the rate of regimen noncompliance is quite high (Surwit et al., 1983; Wing, Epstein, Nowalk, & Lamparski, 1986).

Reasoning from a control theory perspective, Wing et al. (1986) suggested that the methods ar-

ticulated in Kanfer's three-stage conception (Kanfer & Karoly, 1972) could be brought to bear on tasks 1, 2, 4, and 8 (as listed in Table 29.3). These methods include self-monitoring and self-evaluation (category d, Table 29.2) and self-reinforcement (category c cognitive regulator).

As the process of error detection is seen as the "most important element of self-regulation system" (Wing et al., 1986, p. 79), blood sugar and urine monitoring have received a great deal of attention in terms of their accuracy and compliance rates. The most common method of self-assessment, urine testing, does not provide a sensitive index of blood glucose (BG), as it only measures excess amounts of the substance that have spilled into the urine, and a "negative test yields no information concerning BG levels below the renal threshold" (Gonder-Frederick, Cox, Pohl, & Carter, 1984, p. 12). Thus, the use of a self-administered blood test, wherein the patient pricks his or her finger and places a droplet of blood on a chemically-treated strip, is widely encouraged. By comparing the reagent with a color chart (or by using a reflectance photometer) the patient can obtain accurate and relatively immediate feedback about blood glucose levels — including dangerously low levels (hypoglycemia). Accurate feedback permits what are called flexible insulin regimens to be instituted. That is, corrective responding in the form of diet or exercise modification or the administration of insulin can be precisely attuned to the body's momentary needs, rather than being employed in accordance with a prearranged, daily schedule.

Better self-monitoring is, unfortunately, complex and error prone, and methods of improving the use and accuracy of blood glucose monitoring are now beginning to be developed. Further, because error detection alone does not constitute a self-regulating system, researchers also have stressed the need to train corrective or "controlling" responses in addition to blood glucose or urine monitoring. Diet, exercise, stress, and insulin adjustments (tasks 2, 4, and 8) are the adaptive responses most often studied (cf. Wing et al., 1986; Zinman, 1984) as instigated by direct training, information-giving, goal-setting, modeling, contingency-contracting, relaxation or meditation methods, and intensified medication and enhanced supervisory control (Cox et al., 1986; Geffner, Kaplan, Lippe, & Scott, 1983; Gross, 1982; Rose, Firestone, Heick, & Faught, 1983; Schafer, Glasgow, & McCaul, 1982). Neither the

Table 29.3. Matrix of Self-Management Interventions Applicable to the Varied Adaptive Tasks of Chronic Illness Adjustment

	ADAPTIVE TASKS (MAINTENANCE OF . . .)									
	1. Symptom (or symptom trigger) monitoring	2. Medication adjustment	3. Momentary help-seeking	4. Diet or exercise management	5. Social relationships (family, friends)	6. Vocational, school performance	7. Relations w/health-care staff	8. Emotional balance	9. Self-image (efficacy beliefs)	10. Growth potential/goal directedness
early-stage motivation enhancement										
behavioral enactment training										
cognitive regulator development/modification										
pre- postperformance monitoring and evaluation training										
environment manipulation										
affect management										
persistence training										

individual nor the combined potency of these motivation-enhancement, performance-monitoring, affect-management, and/or environmental-manipulation techniques is yet firmly established owing to the frequent use of small (possibly unrepresentative) clinical samples, the potential for self-report bias, the differences in measures of glycemic control employed, the lack of standardization in the training procedures used, and the failure to assess whether the techniques taught were actually learned or utilized by the study participants (both during the training and at follow-up).

The most frequently discussed cognitive regulators are goal-setting and self-reinforcement. In most cases, however, the use of symbolic, internal mechanisms is an inference to be drawn from the initial external manipulation of objectives and reinforcers (by physicians, nurses, or parents). By negotiating contracts and instituting point systems for the distribution of tangible rewards, the therapist uses early-stage motivation-enhancement procedures to "set the stage" for subsequent covert self-guidance (e.g., Schafer, Glasgow, & McCaul, 1982). Unfortunately, the systematic and verified use of symbolic regulators has not yet been empirically established in the domain of diabetes-regimen adherence. On the one hand, such a step may be superfluous if, as has been suggested, contingency-contracting and goal-setting per se are sufficient to ensure adherence (Cox et al., 1986). Yet, theory would propose that for a lifelong pattern to be established in a diverse and changing environment, some internalization of values and meanings and the use of self-generated cues and reinforcers would be required (Kanfer & Karoly, 1982; Karoly, 1982). Establishing the role of cognitive regulators in chronic illness adjustment is a logical prerequisite to the clinical training of such strategies; and some preliminary data are available. Tennen, Affleck, Allen, McGrade, and Ratzan (1984), for example, reported that children (mean age = 11.2 years) who manifested a feeling of personal responsibility for their diabetes (so-called behavioral self-blame) were rated by physicians as coping better and were under better metabolic control (assessed biochemically) than were children who manifested an external cause orientation. Studies employing locus of control indices, on the other hand, have tended to reveal that internality is a counterproductive orientation insofar as metabolic control is concerned (Burns, Green, & Chase, 1986; Rainwater, Jackson, &

Burns, 1982). Clearly, a number of factors, such as the patient's age, time since diagnosis, the status of the disease, family systems parameters, and the like, may converge to determine which attributional style will have what effect for which disease entity. Nonetheless, attributional processes do relate in important ways to illness adaptation. Judgments of self-efficacy, for example, correlate with or affect a patient's choice of action, energy mobilization, stress reactivity, and the direction of cognitive regulatory efforts (cf. Bandura, 1986; chapter 4 in this volume).

In a study of goal-oriented cognition among diabetic youngsters, Karoly and Bay (1990) found that children (mean age = 14) could distinguish between self-selected and imposed self-care goals, and that goal dimensions (determined factor analytically) are capable of accounting for significant variance (31%) in metabolic control (indexed by means of hemoglobin assays). Interestingly, only the socially-referenced goal factors were predictive of metabolic control, suggesting that youngsters (mostly preadolescents) do not rebel against the fact of health goal socialization, but may react adversely to the form in which it is offered (i.e., a factor labeled "coercion" was significantly negatively related to metabolic control).

Other Chronic Conditions

Attempts to utilize a self-management perspective have not been confined to diabetes. Applications to such illnesses as asthma, hypertension, and gastrointestinal disorders (and others) are described in Holroyd and Creer's (1986) edited volume. While most programs tend to make use of categories a, d, e, and f interventions (see Table 29.2), inroads into higher order mediational dimensions are being made.

In their study of self-directed hemodialysis, for example, Kirschenbaum, Sherman, and Penrod (1987) sought to increase self-directedness in four elderly patients with chronic renal disease through a multidimensional training program that included the provision of a conceptual rationale and the use of a "decisional balance sheet" procedure. The latter incorporated an assessment of advantages versus disadvantages of taking over the setup and use of a dialysis unit, and an "awareness of rationalizations" procedure designed to counter the convincing, but manageable disadvantages that the patients might have envisioned. Thus, although this process might be labeled an early-stage motivation enhancement, the emphasis on building a "top-down" conceptionalization of self-management also serves to mark it as an imaginative approach to cognitive regulation. The long-term effects of the training were not assessed (cf. also Witenberg, Blanchard, McCoy, Suls, & McGoldrick, 1983).

Tasks other than symptom-monitoring and medication or procedural compliance can and should be targeted via self-directed means. For example, the regulation of diet and exercise regimens has been pursued, both in the context of chronic illness (Wing, Epstein, & Nowalk, 1984; Zinman, 1984) and within a health promotion framework (Belisle, Roskies, & Levesque, 1987; Epstein, Wing, Valoski, & DeVos, 1988) using interventions that reflect some (though not all) of the components of a self-management perspective. Because the need to control weight and maintain aerobic fitness levels may remain as lifetime goals, persistence training procedures should see increased utilization in the years ahead. Of course, the same is true for symptom-monitoring and medication adjustment; and, thus, in these areas, relapse prevention methods should likewise find a fertile soil for application and elaboration.

In sum, the employment of the seven related self-management approaches to assist patients in dealing with the multiple tasks of adjustment to chronic illness is a developing enterprise, supported mainly by single case experiments and small N research, usually with convenience samples. To collect on the promissory note that self-directive methods represent, future research must attend more closely to methodological issues and seek wider penetration into the methods-by-tasks matrix.

High-Risk Life-Style Management

Heavy alcohol consumption, cigarette smoking, overeating, and leading a sedentary life are widely recognized as placing the person at risk for a variety of medical disorders and for shortening life expectancy (*Healthy People*, 1979; Matarazzo, Weiss, Herd, Miller, & Weiss, 1984). Further, from the initial stages of the behavioral health movement, self-management methods were identified as essential in the control or prevention of various health-compromising life-style patterns (Farquhar, 1987; Knowles, 1977; Mahoney & Arnkoff, 1979; Schwartz, 1979). Having thus enjoyed a long tenure in the field of high-risk behavior, self-

management methods have been allotted considerable empirical scrutiny and ample time, some would say, to prove themselves. They have not. Or, to be more explicit, self-management methods work as well as most so-called cognitive-behavioral interventions and better than many traditional forms of behavior change. What they do not do is provide for a permanent resolution of addictive disorders. The reasons for their failure, however, can be quite instructive.

The standards of proof in the case of therapeutic self-management would appear to be set at a higher level than those imposed for most other forms of clinical intervention. Because the addictive behaviors against which self-management procedures are directed have had a notoriously high rate of relapse or recidivism (Hunt, Barnett, & Branch, 1971; Leventhal & Cleary, 1980; Marlatt & Gordon, 1985; Shiffman, 1982), the treatment is usually judged in relation to problem levels at 1, 3, or 5 years posttermination.

Hall (1980) pointed to the problem of treatment implementation, suggesting that complex procedures require time, patience, and clinical experience to be rendered fully operational.

> . . . [the] failure of self-management behaviors to be maintained is due to the relatively short time periods in which new behaviors are taught and practice is encouraged . . . Since these behaviors are to supplant those the individual has employed throughout life, it has been argued that a relatively long treatment period . . . must be employed. (p. 276)

She also remarks that we generally know very little about the factors responsible for long-term success, when it is achieved, and wonders whether failures reflect a lack of learning of self-management principles or a client's disinclination to use them over time (the learning-performance distinction once again).

Further, although behaviorally oriented investigators were initially drawn to disorders such as obesity and alcoholism in the late 1960s and early 1970s, partly as a result of their ability to assess clinical outcomes in reproducible and reliable ways (e.g., pounds lost or blood alcohol level), contemporary self-management investigators are increasingly cognizant of the biopsychology of addictions and eating disorders. Alcoholism researchers can point to familial (genetic) transmission, possibly having to do with an inherited ability/inability to metabolize ethanol; drug researchers posit conditioning of positive affective states, mediated cortically (the dopaminergic ventral tegmental system), linked to drug-acquisition behavior; whereas researchers of eating disorders are investigating serotonin dysregulation in bulimics, and a loss of interoceptive control over eating in the obese (cf. Baker, Morse, & Sherman, 1987; Hill, Steinhauer, & Zubin, 1987; Mitchell & Eckert, 1987; Polivy & Herman, 1987; Schuckit, 1987).

Finally, we can (with hindsight) criticize first-generation self-management enthusiasts for their neglect of the emotional interpersonal and cultural contexts in which life-style problems are played out in their zeal to target readily delimitable, instrumental responses. Only recently has the complexity inherent in the concept of life-style been recognized and addressed. Bruhn (1988), for example, views behavior as one component of life-style that is contained within an individual's philosophy of life. The latter is ecologically embedded and a developmentally emergent product of socialization. Thus, health beliefs and habits are shaped by the physical environment (why give up smoking if the air is polluted?), by cultural values (good health is a commodity that can be bought), by subcultural realities (good health is a commodity that the poor cannot afford to buy or make time for), by social (peer) pressure, and by personal factors, such as a sense of mastery or control. As we know comparatively little of the natural history of health-relevant life-style socialization across diverse segments of our society, clinical programs designed simply to encourage one type of behavior (e.g., abstinence from premarital sex; the wearing of seatbelts) or to discourage others (e.g., drug experimentation, purging in order to keep weight off) are likely to face an uphill battle.

The overall lesson to be drawn from the limited successes of first-generation self-management forays into life-style modification is that the pursuit of high-risk pattern regulation (prevention or control) should be an interdisciplinary enterprise. If not yet truly inter- or multidisciplinary, the contemporary self-management literature at least reflects a genuine respect for the field of interacting forces that impinge on the at-risk child and adult. The smoking cessation research currently being conducted illustrates the new look in self-change psychology (contemporary efforts at enhancing the persistence of therapeutic learning are discussed in a separate chapter in this handbook).

Smoking Cessation

The important developments in this domain have included efforts to understand the natural history of smoking—particularly the determinants of initiation, self-quitting, and relapse.

Among the important insights of recent years is the view that addictions and other health-compromising habits may best be described in cyclical process terms rather than in static, categorical terms (Prochaska & DiClemente, 1986; Prochaska, Velicer, DiClemente, & Fava, 1988). For example, I have found it helpful to view self-defeating life-style patterns as multiphasic processes consisting of (a) initial exposure and use, (b) habit development and maintenance (automaticity phase), (c) preparation for change (includes several subphases), (d) habit cessation, (e) maintenance of cessation, (f) a lapse-relapse pattern, (g) recovery of cessation, (h) cycling between f and g, including experimentation with different controlling devices, (i) development of incompatible habit patterns, and (j) maintenance of healthy life-style. Some individuals do not stray past point a. Some end the process at point e. But many traverse the longer sequence, some never moving beyond point h, and some eventually becoming successful life-style managers (at least with respect to their former problem). The clinician's choice of intervention (self-managemental or otherwise) cannot be arbitrary or narrowly conceived and needs to be sensitive to environmental and patient readiness variables.

Prevention efforts, aimed at phases 1 and 2, are highly desirable (Evans, 1984) and depend on both cross-sectional and longitudinal studies of child and adolescent motives regarding smoking and the determinants of smoking initiation (e.g., Chassin, Presson, Sherman, Montello, & McGrew, 1986). The research of Chassin et al. (1986) on the role of parent and peer influences, for example, illustrates that a sweeping "Just Say No!" campaign would benefit from knowledge of whom to say no to and when.

Similarly, after a habit has developed, it would be helpful to know where the person is in the evolving process of change and what change strategies would be maximally helpful to employ. Prochaska, DiClemente, and colleagues have made strides in addressing these questions. Their model highlights four stages in the change process—precontemplation, contemplation, action, and maintenance—and 10 processes of change (assessed by means of a 40-item Processes of Change Questionnaire). They include a relapse phase and the possibility that individuals will cycle between relapse and cessation (a so-called revolving door model). Their processes-by-stages approach (analogous to the methods-by-task analysis I suggested in the previous section) has revealed an abundance of clinically useful data. For example, across several problem areas (psychic distress, smoking, and weight control), it was shown that helping relationships, consciousness-raising (e.g., being mindful of the problem), and self-liberation (e.g., self-instruction) were the highest ranked self-change methods and reinforcer management and stimulus control the lowest ranked (Prochaska & DiClemente, 1986).

Other recent studies, focusing on naturally occurring events in the process of self- and/or therapeutically assisted change have likewise proven theoretically and clinically provocative. Both cognitive factors and interpersonal exchange processes have emerged as promising avenues of exploration. Curry, Marlatt, and Gordon (1987), pursuing Marlatt and Gordon's (1985) relapse prevention model, investigated the assumption that a smoker's cognitive-affective reaction to an early slip or lapse of control can escalate into a complete relapse if the individual focuses on internal, stable, and global causal elements (e.g., "It's my fault; my problem is going to arise in many future situations; and my problem isn't just confined to smoking"). This mindset is what Mahoney and Arnkoff (1979) called the "saint or sinner syndrome," but is now better known as the abstinence violation effect (AVE). Participants completed questionnaires prior to enrollment in a smoking cessation project and retrospectively after their first lapse or smoking episode. Interestingly, no evidence for an AVE emerged in the responses of the group prior to actual quit attempts; instead the would-be quitters employed "face-saving" attributions (external, unstable, and specific). However, after their initial failures, the AVE was in evidence and proved to be a significant predictor of return to regular smoking subsequent to an initial lapse. The question of whether the attributional pattern differs for relapsers (those who return to smoking after their first slip) versus lapsers (those who return to abstinence) was addressed by O'Connell and Martin (1987). Their data tended to support the view that AVE is an effect rather than a cause of relapse (as relapsers were more likely to make internal attributions as

compared with lapsers). The data of Curry et al. (1987) lend further support to the view that preexisting attributional styles do not predispose smokers to failure in their quit attempts (however, see Harackiewicz, Sansone, Blair, Epstein, & Manderlink, 1987, for some intriguing suggestions about how attributional styles may interact with treatment modality to determine initial success and/or maintenance patterns).

If internal attributions for treatment failure are deleterious, so too are external attributions for treatment success—at least according to classical attribution theory (e.g., Davison & Valins, 1969). Yet, there are times (see Harackiewicz et al., 1987) when viewing one's successful self-generated efforts as being abetted by significant others leads to propitious long-range results. As self-management occurs in a social context (and is not seen as antithetical to external management), findings such as those reported by Morgan, Ashenberg, and Fisher (1988) help to contextualize a perspective that too often looks only "inside the heads" of would-be self-managers. These investigators found that at 2, 3, and 8-weeks posttherapy, abstainers could be distinguished from relapsers by their reports of having received help from friends. And, in a study comparing unaided quitters, relapsers, and current smokers, Karoly and McKeeman (1989) noted that quitters retrospectively reported not only more social support but less social hindrance than did relapsers or current smokers. In addition, quitters experienced less internal (goal-related) conflict than the other two groups. The smoking literature is poised to catch up with the obesity literature in the sense that instigators of weight loss via operant and self-managed methods have, for some time, recruited the aid of significant others in their change programs (cf. Brownell, Heckerman, Westlake, Hayes, & Monti, 1978; Saccone & Israel, 1978; Zitter & Fremouw, 1978) with varying degrees of success.

In sum, then, the application of self-management to health-compromising habits like smoking, drinking, or overeating has been maturing since the early behavior modification days, with investigators learning from their failures (or short-term successes) and embracing their science at levels of complexity appropriate to the nature of the problem(s) at hand. This is, after all, the essence of parsimony, which means (contrary to popular misconception) being as complex as you need to be (not thinking as simply as you can).

THEORY AND PRACTICE: CLOSING THE GAPS

The "signs of theoretical and conceptual refinement" in self-management applications to health which Mahoney and Arnkoff (1979) envisioned a decade ago are today landmarks that are plainly visible and readily appraised. Cautious optimism is still warranted. However, with a sharpening of analytic focus, our appreciation of the fissures and fine points of clinical self-direction has likewise matured. Where we go in the next 10 years shall depend in large measure on how vigorously researchers, clinicians, and theoreticians from diverse backgrounds pursue the as yet unasked or unanswered questions, the available methodological options, and full spectrum of implementation.

Among the important gap-closing tasks that remain are the following.

1. The need to evaluate the individual and the combined treatment effectiveness of self-management strategies. A trend toward congregating modalities (self-management, social skills training, community support, etc.) into megaprograms may well benefit clients, if a powerful change-inducing and change-maintaining recipe is formed. Yet, eventually, cost-effectiveness concerns will dictate that the truly potent ingredients be sifted from the mix.

2. The need to approach the processes and contents of consciousness (and in a less self-conscious manner). Feed forward and feedback mechanisms, although vitally linked to environmental conditions and to recordable instrumental behaviors, are internal events, and not equivalent to the conditions that surround them. For example, being trained in the use of self-instructional techniques is not a sufficient condition for assuming that self-instructional techniques were learned or used (cf. Locke, 1972). Similarly, assessing the content of a reference value, memory, inference, or causal attribution is not equivalent to mapping the unfolding processes that activate, maintain, or transform these self-regulatory constituents (Robertson, 1986).

3. The need to examine the higher order control systems elements, especially the relatively stable as well as the continuously negotiated aspects of self-relevant cognition called identity. We must recall that, just as Wittgenstein saw the meaning of words in their use (not their object or referent), so too does control theory conceive of the meaning of self-regulatory strategies and tactics as their utility vis-à-vis the higher level reference values of the actor. In this regard, the clinician's view of the importance or usefulness of any self-management method is secondary to the patient's. The clinical assessor must therefore determine when it is necessary to teach new strategies or seek to influence the goals, values, or self-presentational motives that strategies exist to serve.

4. The need to formalize and systematize the clinical study of affective/arousal functions in self-management. Not only are different kinds of negative affective states generated by awareness of discrepancies between reference standards and input (e.g., Higgins, 1987) but so too does positive arousal result from meeting, exceeding, imagining, or anticipating a goal (Markus & Ruvolo, 1989). Just as depression or dejection can interrupt or distort problem-solving, positive mood can enhance it (Hoffman, 1986). Self-management training should therefore address not only the clinical target (compliance, pain, the urge to smoke cigarettes, etc.), but also the affect generated both by pursuing and avoiding the target. Affect management, for its part, should not be restricted to "getting rid of" unwanted emotions, because development of a positive affect is often required, and because even some discomforting emotions convey information relevant to adaptation (Ford, 1987).

5. The need to continue the study of self-managemental failure. An appreciation of the diversity of self-evaluational and postperformance judgmental processes, including rationalization, affectively induced cognitive errors, goal-resetting, and the like would, I believe, contribute to improving clinical effectiveness. So too would a focus on skills training to a meaningful set of criteria. This involves more than the patient's being able to repeat the rules or make the correct choice on a paper-and-pencil inventory. For a control system to work effectively, it needs to engage in error correction in a timely fashion and mobilize its energies efficiently. These qualities, which can be engineered into a machine system, are in humans the joint result of feedback-based practice, external support, and a firm belief in the worthiness of one's objectives (Wright & Brehm, 1989) and one's abilities (Bandura, 1986). Such qualities may not be readily purchased through 10 one-hour sessions of prepackaged therapy.

6. The need to approach the issue of human self-directedness from the macro level of social/political/economic reform. Considering the weight of

the social forces at work in the case of an inner-city youth on drugs, the upwardly mobile 25-year-old constantly on a diet, or the senior citizen trying to live with osteoarthritis, it would not be unreasonable to plan now to alter the cues and contingencies for future cohorts through societal restructuring, thus making the pursuit of an independent and healthful life-style more imaginable and thereby more feasible than it is today.

REFERENCES

Baer, D. M., Wolf, M. M., & Risley, T. R. (1987). Some still-current dimensions of applied behavior analysis. *Journal of Applied Behavior Analysis, 20*, 313–327.

Baker, T. B., Morse, E., & Sherman, J. E. (1987). The motivation to use drugs: A psychobiological analysis of urges. In P. C. Rivers (Ed.), *Nebraska symposium on motivation, 1986: Alcohol and addictive behavior* (pp. 257–323). Lincoln, NE: University of Nebraska Press.

Bandura, A. (1969). *Principles of behavior modification*. New York: Holt, Rinehart & Winston.

Bandura, A. (1986). *Social foundations of thought and action: A social cognitive theory*. Englewood Cliffs, NJ: Prentice-Hall.

Bandura, A. (1988). Self-regulation of motivation and action through goal systems. In V. Hamilton, G. H. Bower, & N. H. Frijda (Eds.), *Cognitive perspectives on emotion and motivation* (pp. 37–61). Dordrecht: Kluwer Academic Publishers.

Bandura, A., & Perloff, B. (1967). Relative efficacy of self-monitored and externally-imposed reinforcement systems. *Journal of Personality and Social Psychology, 7*, 111–116.

Becker, M. H., & Maiman, L. A. (1983). Models of health-related behavior. In D. Mechanic (Ed.), *Handbook of health, health care, and the health professions* (pp. 539–568). New York: Free Press.

Belisle, M., Roskies, E., & Levesque, J. M. (1987). Improving adherence to physical activity. *Health Psychology, 6*, 159–172.

Blanchard, E. B., Andrasik, F., Guarnieri, P., Neff, D. F., & Rodichok, L. D. (1987). Two-, three-, and four-year follow-up on the self-regulatory treatment of chronic headache. *Journal of Consulting Clinical Psychology, 55*, 257–259.

Broskowski, A. (1981). The health-mental health connection. In A. Broskowski, E. Marks, & S. H. Budman (Eds.), *Linking health and mental health services* (pp. 13–25). Beverly Hills, CA: Sage Publications.

Brownell, K. D., Heckerman, C. L., Westlake, R. J., Hayes, S. C., & Monti, P. N. (1978). The effect of couples training and partner cooperativeness in behavioral treatment of obesity. *Behaviour Research and Therapy, 16*, 323–333.

Bruhn, J. G. (1988). Lifestyle and health behavior. In D. S. Gochman (Ed.), *Health behavior: Emerging research perspectives* (pp. 71–86). New York: Plenum Press.

Burns, K. L., Green, P., & Chase, H. P. (1986). Psychosocial correlates of glycemic control as a function of age in youth with insulin-dependent diabetes. *Journal of Adolescent Health Care, 7*, 311–319.

Cantor, N., & Kihlstrom, J. F. (1987). *Personality and social intelligence*. Englewood Cliffs, NJ: Prentice-Hall.

Carver, C. S., & Scheier, M. F. (1981). *Attention and self-regulation: A control theory approach to human behavior*. New York: Springer-Verlag.

Carver, C. S., & Scheier, M. F. (1982). An information-processing perspective on self-management. In P. Karoly & F. H. Kanfer (Eds.), *Self-Management and behavior change: From theory to practice* (pp. 93–128). Elmsford, NY: Pergamon Press.

Chassin, L., Presson, C. C., Sherman, S. J., Montello, D., & McGrew, J. (1986). Changes in peer and parent influence during adolescence: Longitudinal versus cross-sectional perspectives on smoking initiation. *Developmental Psychology, 22*, 327–334.

Cox, D. J., Gonder-Frederick, L., Pohl, S., & Pennebaker, J. W. (1986). Diabetes. In K. A. Holroyd & T. L. Creer (Eds.), *Self-management of chronic disease* (pp. 305–346). Orlando, FL: Academic Press.

Curry, S., Marlatt, G. A., & Gordon, J. R. (1987). Abstinence violation effect: Validation of an attributional construct with smoking cessation. *Journal of Consulting and Clinical Psychology, 55*, 145–149.

Davison, G. C., & Valins, S. (1969). Maintenance of self-attributed and drug-attributed behavior change. *Journal of Personality and Social Psychology, 11*, 25–33.

Dollard, J., & Miller, N. E. (1950). *Personality and psychotherapy*. New York: McGraw-Hill.

Dweck, C. S., & Leggett, E. L. (1988). A social-cognitive approach to motivation and personality. *Psychological Review, 95,* 256–273.

Emmons, R. A. (1989). The personal striving approach to personality. In L. A. Pervin (Ed.), *Goal concepts in personality and social psychology* (pp. 87–126). Hillsdale, NJ: Lawrence Erlbaum Associates.

Epstein, L. H., Wing, R. R., Valoski, A., & DeVos, D. (1988). Long-term relationship between weight and aerobic-fitness change in children. *Health Psychology, 7,* 47–53.

Evans, R. I. (1984). A social inoculation strategy to deter smoking in adolescents. In J. D. Matarazzo, S. M. Weiss, J. A. Herd, N. E. Miller, & S. Weiss (Eds.), *Behavioral health: A handbook of health enhancement and disease prevention* (pp. 765–774). New York: John Wiley & Sons.

Farquhar, J. W. (1987). *The American way of life need not be hazardous to your health* (rev. ed.). Reading, MA: Addison-Wesley.

Fisher, E. B. (1986). A skeptical perspective: The importance of behavior and environment. In K. A. Holroyd & T. L. Creer (Eds.), *Self-Management of chronic disease.* Orlando, FL: Academic Press.

Ford, D. H. (1987). *Humans as self-constructing living systems: A developmental perspective on behavior and personality.* Hillsdale, NJ: Lawrence Erlbaum Associates.

Frese, M., & Sabini, J. (Eds.). (1985). *Goal-directed behavior: The concept of action in psychology.* Hillsdale, NJ: Lawrence Erlbaum Associates.

Fuchs, V. R. (1986). *The health economy.* Cambridge, MA: Harvard University Press.

Geffner, M. E., Kaplan, S. A., Lippe, B., & Scott, M. L. (1983). Self-monitoring of blood glucose levels and intensified insulin therapy. *Journal of the American Medical Association, 249,* 2913–2916.

Goldiamond, I. (1965). Self-control procedures in personal behavior problems. *Psychological Reports, 17,* 851–868.

Gonder-Frederick, L., Cox, D. J., Pohl, S., & Carter, W. (1984). Patient blood glucose monitoring: Use, accuracy, adherence, and impact. *Behavioral Medicine Update, 6,* 12–16.

Greenberg, L. S., & Safran, J. D. (1989). Emotion in psychotherapy. *American Psychologist, 44,* 19–29.

Gross, A. M. (1982). Self-management training and medication compliance in children with diabetes. *Child and Family Behavior Therapy, 4,* 47–55.

Hall, S. M. (1980). Self-management and therapeutic maintenance: Theory and research. In P. Karoly & J. J. Steffen (Eds.), *Improving the long-term effects of psychotherapy: Models of durable outcome* (pp. 263–300). New York: Gardner Press.

Harackiewicz, J. M., Sansone, C., Blair, L. W., Epstein, J. A., & Manderlink, G. (1987). Attributional processes in behavior change and maintenance: Smoking cessation and continued maintenance. *Journal of Consulting and Clinical Psychology, 55,* 372–378.

Healthy people: The Surgeon General's report on health promotion and disease prevention. U.S. Department of Health, Education, and Welfare, 1979. PHS Publication No. 79-55071.

Higgins, E. T. (1987). Self-discrepancy: A theory relating self to affect. *Psychological Review, 94,* 319–340.

Hill, S. Y., Steinhauer, S. R., & Zubin, J. (1987). Biological markers for alcoholism: A vulnerability model conceptualization. In P. C. Rivers (Ed.), *Nebraska symposium on motivation, 1986: Alcohol and addictive behaviors* (pp. 207–256). Lincoln, NE: University of Nebraska Press.

Hoffman, M. L. (1986). Affect, cognition, and motivation. In R. M. Sorrentino & E. T. Higgins (Eds.), *Handbook of motivation and cognition* (pp. 244–280). New York: Guilford Press.

Holroyd, K. A., & Creer, T. L. (Eds.). (1986). *Self-management of chronic disease.* Orlando, FL: Academic Press.

Homme, L. E. (1965). Perspectives in psychology: XXIV. Control of coverants, the operants of the mind. *Psychological Record, 15,* 501–511.

Hunt, W. A., Barnett, L. W., & Branch, L. G. (1971). Relapse in addiction programs. *Journal of Clinical Psychology, 27,* 455–456.

Ickes, W. (1988). Attributional styles and the self-concept. In L. Y. Abramson (Ed.), *Social cognition and clinical psychology: A synthesis* (pp. 66–97). New York: Guilford Press.

Irwin, F. W. (1970). *Intentional behavior and motivation: A cognitive theory.* Philadelphia: J. B. Lippincott.

James, W. (1976). *The principles of psychology* (3 vols.). Cambridge, MA: Harvard University Press. (Original work published 1890)

Kanfer, F. H. (1971). The maintenance of behavior by self-generated stimuli and reinforcement. In A. Jacobs & L. B. Sachs (Eds.), *The psychology of private events* (pp. 39–59). New York: Academic Press.

Kanfer, F. H., & Gaelick, L. (1986). Self-management methods. In F. H. Kanfer & A. P. Goldstein (Eds.), *Helping people change; A textbook of methods* (3rd ed., pp. 283–345). Elmsford, NY: Pergamon Press.

Kanfer, F. H., & Hagerman, S. (1981). The role of self-regulation. In L. P. Rehm (Ed.), *Behavior therapy for depression* (pp. 143–179). New York: Academic Press.

Kanfer, F. H., & Hagerman, S. (1987). A model of self-regulation. In F. Halisch & J. Kuhl (Eds.), *Motivation, intention, and volition* (pp. 293–307). Berlin: Springer-Verlag.

Kanfer, F. H., & Karoly, P. (1972). Self-control: A behavioristic excursion into the lion's den. *Behavior Therapy, 3*, 398–416.

Kanfer, F. H., & Karoly, P. (1982). The psychology of self-management: Abiding issues and tentative directions. In P. Karoly & F. H. Kanfer (Eds.), *Self-management and behavior change: From theory to practice* (pp. 571–599). Elmsford, NY: Pergamon Press.

Kanfer, F. H., & Marston, A. R. (1963). Determinants of self-reinforcement in human learning. *Journal of Experimental Psychology, 66*, 245–254.

Kanfer, F. H., & Phillips, J. S. (1970). *Learning foundations of behavior therapy*. New York: John Wiley & Sons.

Kanfer, F. H., & Schefft, B. K. (1988). *Guiding the process of therapeutic change*. Champaign, IL: Research Press.

Karoly, P. (1977). Behavioral self-management in children: Concepts, methods, issues, and directions. In M. Hersen, R. M. Eisler, & P. M. Miller (Eds.), *Progress in behavior modification* (Vol. 5, pp. 197–262). New York: Academic Press.

Karoly, P. (1980). Person variables in therapeutic change and development. In P. Karoly & J. J. Steffen (Eds.), *Improving the long-term effects of psychotherapy: Models of durable outcome* (pp. 195–261). New York: Gardner Press.

Karoly, P. (1981). Self-management problems in children. In E. J. Mash & L. G. Terdal (Eds.), *Behavioral assessment of childhood disorders* (pp. 79–126). New York: Guilford Press.

Karoly, P. (1982). Perspectives on self-management and behavior change. In P. Karoly & F. H. Kanfer (Eds.), *Self-management and behavior change: From theory to practice* (pp. 3–31). Elmsford, NY: Pergamon Press.

Karoly, P. (1985). The logic and character of assessment in health psychology. In P. Karoly (Ed.), *Measurement strategies in health psychology* (pp. 3–45). New York: John Wiley & Sons.

Karoly, P. (in press). Goal systems and health outcomes across the life span: A proposal. In H. E. Schroeder (Ed.), *New directions in health psychology: Assessment*. New York: Hemisphere.

Karoly, P., & Bay, R. C. (1990). Diabetes self-care goals and their relation to children's metabolic control. *Journal of Pediatric Psychology, 15*, 83–95.

Karoly, P., & Decker, J. (1979). Effects of personally and socially referenced success and failure upon self-reward and self-criticism. *Cognitive Therapy and Research, 3*, 399–405.

Karoly, P., & Doyle, W. (1975). Effects of outcome expectancy and timing of self-monitoring on cigarette smoking. *Journal of Clinical Psychology, 31*, 351–355.

Karoly, P., & Kanfer, F. H. (Eds.). (1982). *Self-management and behavior change: From theory to practice*. Elmsford, NY: Pergamon Press.

Karoly, P., & McKeeman, D. (1989). *Social and goal-related conflict among cigarette smokers, unaided quitters, and relapsers*. Unpublished manuscript, Arizona State University, Department of Psychology, Tempe, AZ.

Kazdin, A. E. (1974). Self-monitoring and behavior change. In M. J. Mahoney & C. E. Thoresen (Eds.), *Self-control: Power to the person* (pp. 218–246). Monterey, CA: Brooks/Cole.

Kiesler, C. A., & Morton, T. L. (1988). Psychology and public policy in the "health care revolution." *American Psychologist, 43*, 993–1003.

Kirschenbaum, D. S., Sherman, J., & Penrod, J. D. (1987). Promoting self-directed hemodialysis: Measurement and cognitive-behavioral intervention. *Health Psychology, 6*, 373–385.

Kirschenbaum, D. S., & Tomarken, A. J. (1982). On facing the generalization problem: The study of self-regulatory failure. In P. C. Kendall (Ed.), *Advances in cognitive-behavioral research and therapy* (Vol. 1, pp. 119–200). New York: Academic Press.

Knowles, J. (Ed.). (1977). *Doing better and feeling*

worse: Health in the United States. New York: W. W. Norton.

Langer, E. J., Blank, A., & Chanowitz, B. (1978). The mindlessness of ostensibly thoughtful action: The role of "placebic" information in interpersonal interaction. *Journal of Personality and Social Psychology, 36*, 635–642.

Leventhal, H., & Clearly, P. D. (1980). The smoking problem: A review of the research and theory in behavioral risk modification. *Psychological Bulletin, 88*, 370–405.

Levy, S. M., & Howard, J. (1982). Patient-centric technologies: A clinical-cultural perspective. In T. Millon, C. Green, & R. Meagher (Eds.), *Handbook of clinical health psychology* (pp. 561–585). New York: Plenum Press.

Little, B. (1983). Personal projects: A rationale and method for investigation. *Environment and Behavior, 15*, 273–309.

Locke, E. A. (1972). Critical analysis of the concept of causality in behavioristic psychology. *Psychological Reports, 31*, 175–197.

Mahoney, M. J., & Arnkoff, D. G. (1979). Self-management. In O. F. Pomerleau & J. P. Brady (Eds.), *Behavioral medicine: Theory and practice* (pp. 75–96). Baltimore, MD: Williams & Wilkins.

Mahoney, M. J., & Thoresen, C. E. (1974). *Self-control: Power to the person*. Monterey, CA: Brooks/Cole.

Markus, H., & Nurius, P. (1986). Possible selves. *American Psychologist, 41*, 954–969.

Markus, H., & Ruvolo, A. (1989). Possible selves: Personalized representations of goals. In L. A. Pervin (Ed.), *Goal concepts in personality and social psychology* (pp. 211–241). Hillsdale, NJ: Lawrence Erlbaum Associates.

Marlatt, G. A., & Gordon, J. R. (1985). *Relapse prevention: Maintenance strategies in the treatment of addictive behaviors*. New York: Guilford Press.

Matarazzo, J. D., Weiss, S. M., Herd, J. A., Miller, N. E., & Weiss, S. (Eds.). (1984). *Behavioral health: A handbook of health enhancement and disease prevention*. New York: John Wiley & Sons.

Meichenbaum, D. (1977). *Cognitive behavior modification: An integrative approach*. New York: Plenum Press.

Meichenbaum, D., & Turk, D. C. (1987). *Facilitating treatment adherence: A practitioner's guidebook*. New York: Plenum Press.

Miller, D. T., & Porter, C. A. (1988). Errors and biases in the attribution process. In L. Y. Abramson (Ed.), *Social cognition and clinical psychology: A synthesis* (pp. 3–30). New York: Guilford Press.

Miller, D. T., Turnbull, W., & McFarland, C. (1988). Particularistic and universalistic evaluation in the social comparison process. *Journal of Personality and Social Psychology, 55*, 908–917.

Miller, G. A., Galanter, E., & Pribram, K. H. (1960). *Plans and the structure of behavior*. New York: Henry Holt.

Mischel, W. (1974). Process in delay of gratification. In L. Berkowitz (Ed.), *Advances in experimental social psychology* (Vol. 7, pp. 249–292). New York: Academic Press.

Mischel, W., & Ebbesen, E. B. (1970). Attention in delay of gratification. *Journal of Personality and Social Psychology, 16*, 329–337.

Mitchell, J. E., & Eckert, E. D. (1987). Scope and significance of eating disorders. *Journal of Consulting and Clinical Psychology, 55*, 628–634.

Moos, R., & Schaefer, J. A. (1984). The crisis of physical illness: An overview and conceptual approach. In R. H. Moos (Ed.), *Coping with physical illness 2: New perspectives* (pp. 3–25). New York: Plenum Press.

Morgan, G. D., Ashenberg, Z. S., & Fisher, E. B. (1988). Abstinence from smoking and the social environment. *Journal of Personality and Social Psychology, 56*, 298–301.

Morris, R. J. (1986). Fear reduction methods. In F. H. Kanfer & A. P. Goldstein (Eds.), *Helping people change* (pp. 145–190). Elmsford, NY: Pergamon Press.

Nerenz, D. R., & Leventhal, H. (1983). Self-regulation theory in chronic illness. In T. G. Burish & L. A. Bradley (Eds.), *Coping with chronic disease*. New York: Academic Press.

Nuttin, J. (1984). *Motivation, planning, and action: A relational theory of behavior dynamics*. Hillsdale, NJ: Lawrence Erlbaum Associates.

O'Banion, D., Armstrong, B., & Ellis, J. (1980). Conquered urge as a means of self-control. *Addictive Behaviors, 5*, 101–106.

O'Connell, K. A., & Martin, E. J. (1987). Highly tempting situations associated with abstinence, temporary lapse, and relapse among participants in smoking cessation program. *Journal of Consulting and Clinical Psychology, 55*, 367–371.

Olton, D. S., & Noonberg, A. R. (1980). *Biofeedback: Clinical applications in behavioral medicine.* Englewood Cliffs, NJ: Prentice-Hall.

Pervin, L. A. (Ed.). (1989). *Goal concepts in personality and social psychology.* Hillsdale, NJ: Lawrence Erlbaum Associates.

Pohl, S., Gonder-Frederick, L., & Cox, D. J. (1984). Diabetes mellitus: An overview. *Behavioral Medicine Update, 6,* 3–7.

Polivy, J., & Herman, C. P. (1987). Diagnosis and treatment of normal eating. *Journal of Consulting and Clinical Psychology, 55,* 635–644.

Powers, W. T. (1973). *Behavior: The control of perception.* Chicago: Aldine.

Prochaska, J. O., & DiClemente, C. C. (1986). Toward a comprehensive model of change. In W. R. Miller & N. Heather (Eds.), *Treating addictive behaviors* (pp. 3–27). New York: Plenum Press.

Prochaska, J. O., Velicer, W. F., DiClemente, C. C., & Fava, J. (1988). Measuring processes of change: Applications to the cessation of smoking. *Journal of Consulting and Clinical Psychology, 56,* 520–528.

Rainwater, N., Jackson, G. G., & Burns, K. L. (1982, August). *Relationships among psychological, metabolic, and behavioral measures in juvenile diabetics.* Paper presented at the 90th Annual Meeting of the American Psychological Association, Washington, DC.

Robertson, I. (1986). Cognitive processes in addictive behavior change. In W. R. Miller & N. Heather (Eds.), *Treating addictive behaviors: Processes of change* (pp. 319–329). New York: Plenum Press.

Rose, M. I., Firestone, P., Heick, H. M. C., & Faught, A. K. (1983). The effects of anxiety management training on the control of juvenile diabetes mellitus. *Journal of Behavioral Medicine, 6,* 381–395.

Rosenbaum, M. (1988). Learned resourcefulness, stress, and self-regulation. In S. Fisher & J. Reason (Eds.), *Handbook of life stress, cognition, and health* (pp. 483–496). Chichester, England: John Wiley & Sons.

Rotter, J. B. (1954). *Social learning and clinical psychology.* Englewood Cliffs, NJ: Prentice-Hall.

Rudestam, K. E. (1980). *Methods of self-change: An abc primer.* Monterey, CA: Brooks/Cole.

Saccone, A. J., & Israel, A. C. (1978). Effects of experimenter versus significant other-controlled reinforcement and choice of target behavior on weight loss. *Behavior Therapy, 9,* 271–278.

Schafer, L. C., Glasgow, R. E., & McCaul, K. D. (1982). Increasing the adherence of diabetic adolescents. *Journal of Behavioral Medicine, 5,* 353–362.

Schuckit, M. A. (1987). Biological vulnerability to alcoholism. *Journal of Consulting and Clinical Psychology, 55,* 301–309.

Schwartz, G. (1979). The brain as a health care system. In G. C. Stone, F. Cohen, & N. E. Adler (Eds.), *Health psychology: A handbook* (pp. 549–571). San Francisco: Jossey-Bass.

Schwarzer, R. (1986). Self-related cognitions in anxiety and motivation: An introduction. In R. Schwarzer (Ed.), *Self-related cognitions in anxiety and motivation* (pp. 1–17). Hillsdale, NJ: Lawrence Erlbaum Associates.

Shelton, J. L., & Levy, R. L. (1981). *Behavioral assignments and treatment compliance: A handbook of clinical strategies.* Champaign, IL: Research Press.

Shiffman, S. (1982). Relapse following smoking cessation: A situational analysis. *Journal of Consulting and Clinical Psychology, 50,* 71–86.

Skinner, B. F. (1953). *Science and human behavior.* New York: Macmillan.

Skinner, B. F. (1989). The origins of cognitive thought. *American Psychologist, 44,* 13–18.

Sorrentino, R. M., & Higgins, E. T. (Eds.). (1986). *Handbook of motivation and cognition: Foundations of social behavior.* New York: Guilford Press.

Southam, M. A., & Dunbar, J. (1986). Facilitating patient compliance with medical interventions. In K. A. Holroyd & T. L. Creer (Eds.), *Self-management of chronic disease* (pp. 163–187). Orlando, FL: Academic Press.

Staats, A. W. (1968). *Learning, language, and cognition.* New York: Holt, Rinehart & Winston.

Staats, A. W. (1975). *Social behaviorism.* Homewood, IL: Dorsey Press.

Stalnaker, R. C. (1984). *Inquiry.* Cambridge, MA: MIT Press.

Stuart, R. B. (1967). Behavioral control of overeating. *Behaviour Research and Therapy, 5,* 357–365.

Surwit, R. S., Feinglos, M. N. & Scovern, A. W. (1983). Diabetes and behavior. *American Psychologist, 83,* 255–262.

Tennen, H., Affleck, G., Allen, D. A., McGrade,

B. J., & Ratzan, S. (1984). Causal attributions and coping with insulin-dependent diabetes. *Basic and Applied Social Psychology, 5*, 131–142.

Tobin, D. L., Reynolds, R. V. C., Holroyd, K. A., & Creer, T. L. (1986). Self-management and social learning theory. In K. A. Holroyd & T. L. Creer (Eds.), *Self-management of chronic disease* (pp. 29–55). Orlando, FL: Academic Press.

Turk, D. C., Meichenbaum, D., & Genest, M. (1983). *Pain and behavioral medicine: A cognitive-behavioral perspective.* New York: Guilford Press.

Watson, D. L., & Tharp, R. G. (1989). *Self-directed behavior: Self-modification for personal adjustment.* Pacific Grove, CA: Brooks/Cole.

Wickramasekera, I. E. (1988). *Clinical behavioral medicine.* New York: Plenum Press.

Wing, R. R., Epstein, L. H., & Nowalk, M. P. (1984). Dietary adherence in patients with diabetes. *Behavioral Medicine Update, 6*, 17–21.

Wing, R. R., Epstein, L. H., Nowalk, M. P., & Lamparski, D. M. (1986). Behavioral self-regulation in the treatment of patients with diabetes mellitus. *Psychology Bulletin, 99*, 78–89.

Witenberg, S. H., Blanchard, E. B., McCoy, G., Suls, J., & McGoldrick, M. D. (1983). Evaluation of compliance in home and center hemodialysis patients. *Health Psychology, 2*, 227–237.

Wolpe, J. (1982). *The practice of behavior therapy* (3rd ed.). Elmsford, NY: Pergamon Press.

Wright, R. A., & Brehm, J. W. (1989). Energization and goal attractiveness. In L. A. Pervin (Ed.), *Goal concepts in personality and social psychology* (pp. 169–210). Hillsdale, NJ: Lawrence Erlbaum Associates.

Zinman, B. (1984). Diabetes mellitus and exercise. *Behavioral Medicine Update, 6*, 22–25.

Zitter, R. E., & Fremouw, W. J. (1978). Individual versus partner consequation for weight loss. *Behavior Therapy, 9*, 808–813.

CHAPTER 30

INTERVENING TO ENHANCE PERCEPTIONS OF CONTROL

Suzanne C. Thompson

Luck, chance, or fate may fortuitously bring about the ends we seek, but a far surer route is to have the ability to gain those ends through our own actions. Not surprisingly, the sense that one has this ability, termed personal control or mastery, has been proposed as an important component to one's self-concept and a necessary part of mental health. For example, one view of depression is that it is the result of learning that one's outcomes are not contingent on one's actions; in other words, believing that one does not have the control required to achieve desired ends (Seligman, 1974).

Research on the effects of situationally specific enhancements of control and on more enduring dispositions, such as a sense of mastery, has confirmed, for the most part, the importance of feeling that one has the ability to obtain desired ends through one's own actions. A sense of agency serves many important functions, including providing a sense of hope for positive future outcomes (Snyder, 1989). Interventions that give individuals control over some part of a stressful or noxious event have been found to reduce anxiety

and stress while awaiting the event and to improve poststress performance (Thompson, 1981); moreover, individuals with a generalized sense of control or mastery are better able to cope physically and psychologically with stressful life events (Kobasa, 1979; Taylor, 1983).

There is a general tendency for individuals to overestimate the amount of control they can exercise in their lives and to assume that they have control in areas where the objective evidence indicates otherwise (Langer, 1983). Presumably, a modest degree of overoptimism about the amount of control one can exercise is one of a number of illusions that serve adaptive functions, such as maintaining feelings of hope (Snyder, 1989) and a positive self-image (Taylor & Brown, 1988).

In contrast to this general illusion of control, some individuals experience debilitating feelings of helplessness and hopelessness due to very low estimates of the amount of control they have over the outcomes that are important to them. According to the theory of learned helplessness (Seligman, 1974), these feelings are due to previous experience with a lack of contingency between one's actions and one's outcomes. In the reformulated helplessness theory, the role of attributions that the actor makes for outcomes is emphasized (Abramson, Garber, & Seligman, 1980). Helplessness is seen as resulting from the attribution of negative experiences to internal, stable, and global causes. Thus, the new view is that just being exposed to noncontingency does not produce helplessness; rather, the individual's judgment that she or he has little possibility of affecting future outcomes is critical.

Learned helplessness theory proposes that feelings of helplessness are the source of chronic depression, but the depressed are not the only group for whom perceptions of low control over outcomes may be an issue. Feelings of helplessness and a loss of control are common among those who have experienced a major traumatic event, such as disability, diagnosis of a serious disease, or loss of a family member (Janoff-Bulman & Frieze, 1983). Some groups, such as the lonely or those with marital problems, may feel helpless in one major area of their lives, but may not have such feelings in other areas. For other groups, such as the aged, feelings of helplessness may gradually increase as health and mobility decline (Schulz, 1980). Thus, there are a number of groups for whom feelings of helplessness may be a major problem.

The purpose of this paper is to use the body of theory and research in social and clinical psychology to analyze what is involved in the process of exerting control and to use that analysis to suggest an intervention to help alleviate low perceptions of control. In keeping with the health focus of this volume, the emphasis will be on how individuals generate and maintain feelings of mastery and control and how to enhance these perceptions, rather than on the genesis of feelings of helplessness.

CONTROL-RELATED CONCEPTS

A variety of terms that are synonymous with or close in meaning to control, including self-efficacy, locus of control, self-control, and perceived control, are used in the literature.

Self-efficacy is one of three basic concepts in Bandura's theory of human behavior (Bandura, 1977; also see Maddux, this volume). It refers to a belief that one has the ability to execute a particular behavior. Self-efficacy in combination with

outcome expectancies (beliefs that a particular behavior will lead to certain outcomes) and outcome values (the value placed on the outcomes) determine the behavior undertaken by an individual. Because control over an outcome is a function of both the ability to perform an action and the degree to which the outcome depends on the action (Weisz, 1986), self-efficacy, as originally defined, is one component of a sense of personal control.

Locus of control is a concept derived from Rotter's (1966) social learning theory. Internal locus of control refers to an enduring disposition to believe that events are contingent on personal action. Locus of control is equivalent to outcome expectancies in self-efficacy theory, beliefs that actions will produce certain outcomes. It is not the same as self-efficacy or a sense of personal control. Internals in locus of control, for example, believe that personal action determines the reinforcements one receives, but also may feel incapable of executing those actions and, therefore, have a low sense of personal control.

Self-control is defined by Blankstein and Polivy (1982) as "a person's influence over and regulation of his or her own psychological, behavioral, and physical processes" (p. 1). Thus, self-control refers to a subset of personal control, one that is concerned with influencing one's own actions and reactions and not with the control of external environmental events per se.

Situationally specific perceived control refers to a belief that one can influence the outcome of an event in a particular situation. It has been investigated by making available a response that the individual can use to affect the event, such as being able to self-administer a stressor, making a decision relevant to the event, or getting instructions in cognitive techniques that can help modulate one's reactions (Averill, 1973; Thompson, 1981). It is assumed that the availability of these options increases perceptions of control, although that is usually not measured as part of the research.

The perception of control, as it will be used here, refers to a broader concept than situationally specific perceived control. Perceived control is defined here as the belief that one can obtain desired outcomes through one's own actions. Feelings of control may be influenced by features of the situations, but the perception of control resides within the person, not within the situation.

FACTORS THAT INFLUENCE PERCEPTIONS OF CONTROL

People have a sense of personal control when they are able to recognize what can and cannot be influenced through personal action in a situation, when they focus on the elements that can be controlled through personal action, and when they believe that they possess the skills necessary to successfully complete those actions. For example, an aspiring author would have a strong sense of personal control if she felt that she was aware of what affects whether or not a manuscript gets accepted by a publisher, believed that some of the causes of acceptance could be affected by authors' actions and focused on these controllable causes of acceptance (e.g., strong story line) rather than the uncontrollable causes (e.g., an editor's personal taste, distrust of first authors), and believed that she could successfully undertake those actions that could affect the controllable elements (e.g., could write a strong story line).

On the other hand, the potential author would not feel that she had much control in this area if she had no idea why manuscripts get accepted or rejected, believed that there was little that authors could do to affect the probability of acceptance, focused entirely on the causes of acceptance that were out of her control, or did not believe that she possessed the skills that would make a manuscript more acceptable.

Awareness of and Focus on Controllable Causes

Being Aware of Causes

Some knowledge about the causes of events is necessary if we are to feel that we are able to exert some control over them. That knowledge need not entail a deep understanding or an elaborate theoretical perspective on the topic, but, at a minimum, may consist of a simple observation of contingencies that can suggest possible causal influences.

The importance of awareness or knowledge of contingencies is emphasized in most analyses of the process of self-control. Knowledge about the thoughts, people, and situations that lead to certain reactions and behaviors is essential if one is eventually to develop control over one's actions and reactions (Mikulas, 1986). Rosenbaum sees this ability to monitor events as one type of process-regulating cognition by which individuals

regulate their own behavior (Rosenbaum & Smira, 1986). For this reason, the first step in a number of self-control enhancement programs is to develop clients' recognition of potentially risky situations and understanding of the influences that shape their choices and actions (Gilchrist & Schinke, 1985; Kanfer & Karoly, 1972; Omizo, Cubberly & Longano, 1984).

Knowledge of the contingencies that guide external events is equally important if some control is to be exerted on them. A feeling of control in the area of academic achievement, for example, would not be possible if one was not aware of what kinds of answers on exams or what kinds of papers are likely to be evaluated highly by teachers. Not surprisingly, a common reaction when faced with a new situation is for individuals to avidly seek information about the influences that affect various outcomes in order to exert control in the situations. For example, many people respond to a diagnosis of cancer with an intense search for information about its causes and treatment (cf. Fay, 1983, p. 52).

What is important for a sense of control and mastery is that individuals be able to identify causes of desired outcomes that may be influenced by personal action. This is related to Bandura's (1977) concept of outcome expectancies, beliefs about the outcomes associated with various actions. Individuals need to believe that there are one or more actions with high outcome expectancies for the desired outcome.

How do people identify influences on an outcome and judge what is and is not controllable through personal action? This, of course, is the crux of the often-repeated advice that was first given in a sermon by Reinhold Niebuhr (cited in Lefcourt, 1976). It calls for individuals to have the ability to control what can be controlled, to accept what cannot be controlled, and to have the wisdom to know the difference.

One way people may learn the influences and the "difference" is by observation. We can discover for ourselves what thoughts, persons, and situations influence our behavior by attending to the covariation between our reactions and various internal and external events. That is the logic behind the cognitive-behavioral technique of self-monitoring (Meichenbaum, 1985) in which clients are engaged in a conscious strategy of self-observation in order to identify influences on their behavior and actions.

Some studies have examined the effects of making it obvious that one's outcomes are contingent on one's performance. Heightening the contingency between action and outcome improved health status and increased activity in the elderly (Schulz & Hanusa, 1979) and reduced depressive cognitions in a student group (Stern, Berrenberg, Winn, & Dubois, 1978). Presumably, these positive effects came from participants' heightened perceptions that some of their actions were effective in controlling outcomes.

Another way that people learn what actions have high outcome expectancies (i.e., are likely to lead to desired outcomes) is through instruction or information from others. Several studies have examined the effect of telling subjects that the "broken record" technique, a strategy of continually repeating one's desires, is an effective assertiveness technique. Those who get this information have higher outcome expectancies for the technique and higher intentions of using the method than do those who hear it is not effective or who get no information (Maddux, Norton, & Stoltenberg, 1986; Maddux, Sherrer, & Rogers, 1982).

Psychotherapy is an experience that often provides both information about controllable outcomes and direct experience with the contingency between one's actions and outcomes. Many therapies emphasize the individual's contribution to and ability to control emotional reactions. In addition, changes induced by the therapeutic experience enable clients to have control over emotional responses that they previously experienced as being out of their control. A number of studies find that various types of psychotherapeutic interventions increase internality in locus of control, the disposition to perceive a contingency between personal behavior and outcomes (Craig & Andrews, 1985; Gillis & Jessor, 1970; Omizo, Cubberly, & Longano, 1984; Swink & Buchanan, 1984). Training in relaxation techniques also has been found to encourage a more internal locus of control in those with a diagnosis of alcoholism (Marlatt & Marques, 1977) and in hyperactive children (Porter & Omizo, 1984), perhaps because the training allows some control over reactions to stressful situations.

Focusing on Controllable Causes

Believing that some desired outcomes can be influenced by individual action will not contribute to a sense of control if the person does not focus on the causes that are controllable. Those who emphasize uncontrollable influences will feel helpless and unable to act to get what they want, despite the fact that they recognize that some causes are open to influence by personal action. For example, an overweight individual may believe that weight control is influenced both by uncontrollable factors, such as heredity, and by factors that can be influenced by personal action, such as exercise and diet. If the person focuses on the uncontrollable factors, he or she will feel helpless about weight loss or control.

Incomplete or Biased Processing

People are presumably motivated to perceive themselves as having control and to act to get the outcomes they desire (e.g., deCharms, 1968). Why does this process of searching for and focusing on controllable causes sometimes go awry, resulting in people who are seemingly unaware of ways they could influence the outcomes they desire? We will consider several reasons why someone's search for causes, especially for controllable causes, may be incomplete or biased.

For one, an incomplete search for causes may be linked to a coping style of denial or repression. Those who manage the anxiety associated with a potential loss or failure by denying the seriousness of the situation or by refusing to think about it are unlikely to invest much energy in a search for causes. Repressors do not seem to be interesting in obtaining information about an upcoming stressor. Field, Alpert, Vega-Lahr, Goldstein, and Perry (1988), for example, found that among children hospitalized for minor surgery, repressors were less likely than sensitizers to observe the medical procedures or to seek information about them. Not only are repressors not likely to want more information about a stressor, but they seem to cope better without it (Andrew, 1970).

A second influence on the completeness of a search for causes is individual differences in the disposition to be introspective and concerned with causality. Fletcher, Danilovics, Fernandez, Peterson, and Reeder (1986) have developed a measure of attributional complexity, the disposition to consider the causes of behavior, to prefer more complex causal explanations, and to reflect on the process by which one generates causal explanations. Attributional complexity is not related to intelligence within the normal range. Psychology students, for example, are probably not more intelligent than natural science students as measured by standardized test scores, yet psychology majors score twice as high as their natural science counterparts on a measure of attributional complexity (Fletcher et al., 1986). Those who are low in attributional complexity are probably less likely than more complex individuals to be aware of a variety of causal influences.

In addition to an incomplete search in which both uncontrollable and controllable causes are overlooked, some individuals may be especially prone to overlook controllable causes. This may occur if these individuals have some psychological investment in attributing their past failures and misfortunes to external, uncontrollable causes. Snyder and Higgins (1988; Higgins & Snyder, this volume) proposed that there is a general motivation to decrease linkages between the self and negative outcomes, so people tend to offer excuses, deny responsibility, and point to external causes when their actions have undesirable consequences. The identification of internal, controllable causes may be threatening if one has maintained self-esteem in the past by denying responsibility. The idea that personal action could control a current outcome raises the question of whether or not one was responsible for failures related to similar outcomes in the past.

Those who have low self-efficacy for actions that could influence an outcome may be another group that is unaware of ways that personal action could influence the attainment of goals. An important source of information about contingencies comes from our own experience with the consequences of our actions. People who do not possess a skill or who do not believe that they possess the skill may be missing information about the effectiveness of personal action.

Low feelings of efficacy also may motivate individuals to discount and not focus on those ways in which personal action could influence the outcome. One reason this could happen is because the perception that others can control an outcome, but you cannot, called personal helplessness, is seen as more devastating than universal helplessness, the feeling that no one can control the outcome (Abramson et al., 1980). Focusing on causes that no one can control may be less stressful than feeling unique in one's helplessness.

A second reason why low self-efficacy individuals may focus on uncontrollable outcomes is because identifying and focusing on controllable outcomes may make them feel obliged to try to exercise control, an effort that in their assessment is bound to fail. In the example of overweight people who see both heredity and a lack of exercise as contributing to obesity, those who focus on heredity as the cause need not try to do anything to change the situation, but if the lack of exercise is a focus, then the message is that they should begin an exercise program, something they may be loathe to do if they have low self-efficacy. There is some evidence that, at least in animals, it is more stressful to attempt to have control and fail than never to make the attempt (Weiss, 1971). By focusing on uncontrollable outcomes, low self-efficacy individuals may be protecting themselves from the stresses of trying to exercise control and failing. Snyder, Smoller, Strenta, and Frankel (1981) make a similar point in their analysis of giving up following a failure. If the chances of success are seen as slim, some people may protect their self-esteem by not trying to succeed.

This suggests that many people may be unaware of or not focus on controllable causes of an outcome they are seeking because their coping style is one of denying or ignoring an impending stress, because they tend not to be predisposed to identifying causal influences, or because they have had little success themselves in influencing this outcome. In addition, some individuals may be motivated to focus on uncontrollable influences because they have externalized responsibility in the past to maintain self-esteem or because they feel that they personally lack the skills to affect an outcome and do not want to feel obliged to attempt the actions and fail.

Focusing on Controllable Outcomes

What happens when people face situations in which there does not appear to be any way for them to get their most desired outcome through personal action? Irretrievable losses, such as permanent disability or the death of a loved one, represent situations in which the most desired outcome, full restoration of faculties or the return of the loved one, is not possible. Relationships sometimes deteriorate beyond the point where one person's actions could save them. In many other instances, people lose or fail to obtain desired outcomes and have no realistic reason to hope for eventually getting what they want.

These are situations in which control over obtaining the most desired outcome does not seem to be possible, but they are not situations in which people necessarily feel helpless and hopeless. Rothbaum, Weisz, and Snyder (1982) suggested that one way of asserting control when one cannot directly get what one wants is to use what they term "secondary control." This is achieved by identifying with powerful others, aligning oneself with fate, predicting events to avoid disappointment, or by reinterpreting the meaning of events. Although people who use these techniques may appear to have given up, Rothbaum et al. (1982) argued that people need not feel helpless if they use these secondary control procedures.

Another way in which some individuals maintain a sense of personal control in uncontrollable circumstances is by finding and focusing on alternative outcomes that can be influenced through personal action. It is not uncommon for individuals who have undergone some major loss to reevaluate their goals and focus on outcomes that can still be reached despite their loss. For example, when stroke patients and their caregivers were asked if they had found meaning in their experience, some of them responded that they had done so by changing to goals, such as living life one day at a time and appreciating family and friends, that can be reached even in their diminished circumstances (Thompson, Sobolew-Shubin, Graham, & Janigian, 1989). Thompson and Janigian (1988) suggested that one way in which people find meaningfulness in a traumatic event and restore a sense of control is by redirecting their energy to outcomes that are still reachable.

These ideas are consistent with Victor Frankl's (1963) perspective on the search for meaningfulness in everyday life. Frankl maintained that a sense of meaningfulness and control is possible whatever the restrictions of the circumstances. Even in the most extreme circumstances, it is possible (although it may not be at all easy) for people to choose the attitude with which they face their future. Thus, people can maintain a sense of control by focusing on their ability to control their approach to the situation.

Even in less extreme circumstances, people may have valued goals that turn out to be unreachable or unlikely to be attained. To the extent that they focus on less valued but still attainable goals, a sense of control can be maintained. The alternative goals may be substitutes for the original goal, such as switching from a premedicine concentration to other career goals, or they may involve focusing on alternative outcomes that do not substitute for the original goal, such as focusing on going through an unavoidable painful medical procedure with a minimum of pain and emotional distress.

Why do people not always find and focus on an alternative controllable outcome when it appears that a desired goal is not reachable? One major reason is that one cannot focus on alternative, competing goals if one is still heavily invested in and committed to the original goal. Klinger's (1977) Incentive Disengagement Theory predicts that there are five stages to the process of giving up a goal: invigoration, aggression, downswing into depression, depression, and recovery. When goal attainment appears to be permanently blocked, disengagement from the goal is not immediate. It is only after going through this sequence of increased effort to get the goal, anger about the blockage, and depression over the realization that it is unattainable that one is able to disengage from the goal and invest one's energies in other alternatives. Thus, immediately after a serious loss and perhaps for some time after that, people will find it difficult or impossible to find and focus on substitutes for the original goal. They may, however, be able to focus on outcomes that are not substitutes for the original goal and use that to maintain a sense of control. For example, those who have lost a spouse may be unwilling or unable to redirect their interest to other potential partners for a considerable amount of time, but they may be able to focus on actions they can take to deal with feelings of loneliness and depression.

A second reason why people may not focus on alternative controllable outcomes is because consciously or unconsciously they derive some secondary benefits from having others see them as victims. The behavioral concomitants of helplessness — apathy and expressions of depression — are an indication of the extent of someone's loss and serve as signals to others that the person needs and deserves sympathy and help. Others may withdraw their material and emotional support if the person suffering the loss exerts control by focusing on other, reachable outcomes. The benefits of regaining a sense of control may not seem worth the loss of a favored status as someone deserving attention and care.

Thus, one way to exert control is to find and focus on reachable outcomes. Individuals may fail to do this, however, because they are unable to disengage from the original goal or because they derive secondary benefits from being helpless.

Self-Efficacy for Relevant Actions

In addition to being able to identify and focus on causes and outcomes that can be influenced through personal action, it is also important to believe that one has the ability to perform those actions. This third component to perceptions of control is self-efficacy, the belief that one possesses the ability to carry out relevant personal actions.

Why would people have low self-efficacy beliefs for a particular action? One possible reason is that the perception is accurate and they do not possess the needed skill. However, there are also many instances in which people have the skill and have had successful experiences using their ability, but have not internalized this experience. Bandura (1977, 1982) suggests that experience is the best source of efficacy information, but it may not always have the impact it should on beliefs about self-efficacy. The processing of information about experience needs to be considered. This involves interpretation, inference, and attention.

Processing Information
About Experience

Interpretation. For some events in life, one receives clear feedback on the level of one's performance and whether or not that performance constitutes a success or failure. Placing first in a race or contest, for example, can clearly be labeled a success. For many other experiences, however, this type of explicit feedback is rare; it is far more common not to get any information on how one performed. Even for situations in which there is a clear rating of performance (e.g., grades in school or number of pounds lost in a week), there is considerable variability in what gets labeled a success or failure. For one person a grade of B+ is a success; to another person it is a failure. The interpretation of an outcome as a success or failure is important because performance that's not seen as successfully enacted will not increase feelings of self-efficacy regarding one's ability to reach a goal.

Inference. Causal attributions for direct experience are presumed to play an important role in judgments of self-efficacy, but there is no clear statement linking specific attributions to self-efficacy.

The important question is, What attributions are associated with high self-efficacy? According to Bandura (1982, p. 29), self-efficacy is enhanced by attributions of success to ability, especially in combination with attributions that discount other explanations for success, such as effort, low task difficulty, or luck. The reformulated learned helplessness model states that feelings of control are the result of internal, stable, and global attributions for success (Abramson et al., 1980). Thus, both self-efficacy theory and helplessness theory agree that ability attributions for success are associated with high control, but they make different predictions about the effects of effort, which is an internal attribution and can be stable and global.

There is evidence that both ability and effort attributions play an important role in judgments of self-efficacy. Schunk (1982) found that children who were encouraged to attribute their performance to the effort they expended showed increases in self-efficacy relative to those for whom the need to work hard was stressed and those who received no feedback. In a second study with a factorial design, he compared the effects of both ability and effort attributional feedback on perceptions of self-efficacy for math problems (Schunk, 1983). Ability feedback by itself resulted in the greatest increase in self-efficacy. The effort alone and effort plus ability feedback groups did not differ from one another and were both superior to the no feedback group in enhancing self-efficacy.

A related issue concerns the attributions that actors make for failure. Again, there is some confusion as to which attributions have the greatest effects on perceptions of self-efficacy. Presumably, external attributions would indicate that the failure can be dismissed as not reflecting on one's ability to perform the behavior and so would be least destructive to perceptions of self-efficacy or control. Learned helplessness theory proposes, for example, that external, variable, and specific attributions for failure are most adaptive (Abramson et al., 1980). However, an attribution of failure to an internal factor, lack of effort, has several advantages over some external attributions. One, effort is usually seen as a controllable factor, so if a lack of effort is the problem, success can be attained on future tries if the actor chooses to exert the needed effort, whereas if the failure is due to external factors, such as the difficulty of the task, bad luck, or unfair circumstances, then the actor has no control over the outcome of future performances. Two, although effort is an internal factor, it is less central to a person's sense of self than is ability. In their analysis of the effects of excuses, Snyder and Higgins (1988) proposed that lack of effort can be an adaptive attribution for failure because it is an acceptable excuse that does not threaten a central part of one's sense of self. In their review of the literature, they found that manipulations that promote the attribution of failure to low effort have positive effects on future performance. Thus, low effort attributions for failure may be more consistent with high self-efficacy beliefs than are external attributions.

Attention. A performance can be interpreted as a success and attributed to internal factors, but may not affect self-efficacy judgments if the performance is not remembered, is not the focus of attention, or is dismissed as unimportant in the light of past failures (Bandura, 1982). Individuals need to focus on their successes and see them as more relevant than past failures in order to enhance perceptions of efficacy. However, this may be particularly difficult to do for those with a pattern of past failure. Those who expect failure may ignore or discount successes because they are inconsistent with a negative self-image.

Thus, people may have low self-efficacy because they quite accurately perceive that they do not possess a skill. Alternatively, low self-efficacy may reflect the person's tendency to interpret achievement events as failures, to attribute success to external, uncontrollable factors, and to focus on failures rather than on successes.

INTERVENING TO ENHANCE PERCEPTIONS OF CONTROL

A model of the process of perceiving and exerting control with the three components of finding controllable causes, focusing on controllable outcomes, and perceiving oneself to have the skills necessary to enact the control has been presented here. This analysis suggests how to intervene to increase perceptions of control for those who are temporarily or chronically experiencing feelings of helplessness. This intervention is presented as a series of questions that individuals should ask themselves when faced with situations in which they might wish to have control. These are laid out in a flow chart in Figure 30.1.

There are eight questions that can be addressed in this process, but whether or not a particular question is relevant depends on the answer to pre-

vious questions. The eight questions refer to goal identification, the identification of controllable influences, the identification of alternative goals, an assessment of skills, identification of ways to acquire skills, an assessment of the accuracy of one's self-efficacy judgments, identification of ways to increase self-efficacy, and an assessment of the costs and benefits of exerting control. The idea is that learning to address control-relevant issues in this fashion will increase perceptions of control.

In the discussion that follows, it will be assumed that the intervention is administered by a therapist or other psychologically trained professional, either in individual or group sessions. However, many individuals, in particular those who are functioning well in most areas of their lives, may be able to acquire these techniques on their own through instructional materials or brief instructional interventions.

Goal Identification

Before people can consider exerting control in some area of their lives, they need to have a clear idea of what outcomes they wish to bring about or to avoid. It is difficult to take concrete action toward obtaining what you want unless you have a good sense of what that goal is. In many cases, of course, people are quite clear about what they want. The stroke patient's most preferred outcome is likely to be full recovery of functioning, and an untenured assistant professor has no trouble identifying a positive tenure decision as the outcome of choice. Frequently people know that they are dissatisfied with the current situation, but have only a very vague idea of what they want. For example, some depressed individuals may know that they are unhappy, but do not have a clear idea of how they want things to change, and an unhappy spouse may have difficulty saying what specific changes he or she wants in the partner's behavior. The first step toward achieving control is to define the outcome concretely enough so that it is possible to identify specific actions that can be taken to achieve it.

The consideration of desired outcomes should not be limited to goals that in the past people have thought themselves capable of influencing. It is premature to reject goals before there has been a new look at the possibility of attaining them within the current framework. The idea here is to give serious consideration to what one wants regardless

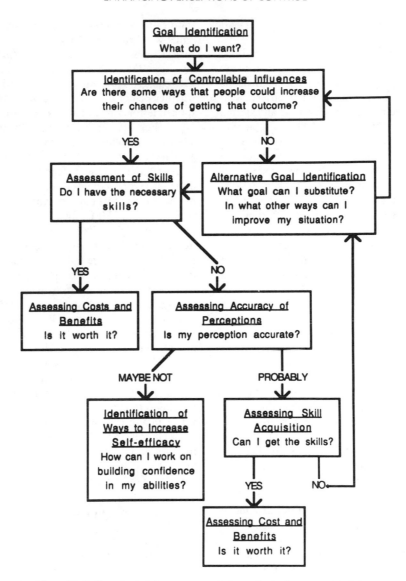

Figure 30.1. Flowchart of the components to control enhancement training.

of whether or not it seems that it would be easy to get one's desire. However, there probably does have to be some weight given to how realistic the goal is. Individuals who consistently identify very unlikely events and very difficult goals as desired outcomes may need to consider if they are setting themselves up for disappointment. They can be encouraged to focus on less spectacular but more realistic ambitions. For example, a person who thought that winning the lottery was a main goal may need to focus on other more easily obtained goals, at least for the purposes of this training.

Identification of Controllable Influences

The second step is to begin to identify ways that the outcome could be influenced through personal action. The key question is, Are there some ways that a person who wanted that outcome could influence her or his chances of getting it? The consideration of controllable causes should not be limited to actions that participants personally believe themselves capable of performing. They should be encouraged to save the question of their ability to carry out the action for a later part of the process.

There are a number of techniques that could be used to widen the pool of possible causes that are brought into consideration. Participants might be given an exercise to systematically observe and keep a log of their own behavior or of an external event they wish to control. It might be a topic that one could get written information on or it may be possible to ask knowledgeable others about the sorts of factors that influence one's chances of getting the desired outcome. For example, someone who was interested in getting his manuscripts published could ask editors about influences on whether or not papers get accepted or could talk to published authors about their experiences.

The analysis presented earlier of how the search of controllable causes can be incomplete or biased suggests that there are a number of difficulties some people will have with this step. If some individuals appear to be unable or unwilling to think about the causes of a stressful experience because they typically repress thoughts about this type of situation, then they might profit from a discussion of this tendency and a consideration of the costs and benefits of approaching stressful situations in this manner. They might decide that the use of repression or denial to manage anxiety is not worth losing the chance to control some part of the process. Or they might conclude that benefits of avoiding some anxiety are worth passing up the opportunity to have control in this area and consciously decide to continue using repression. Even if they make the latter choice, feelings of control are likely to be enhanced because the use of repression is now a conscious choice. The alternatives were considered and a decision was made, one that can be reviewed at a later date if there is a desire to do so.

Participants can be encouraged to make similar analyses of other blockages to considering controllable causes. If some people find it threatening to identify controllable causes because it implies responsibility for other failures, they can be helped to reconsider the beliefs and assumptions underlying that threat. It is likely that some of the irrational beliefs identified by Ellis make taking responsibility particularly threatening (Ellis & Harper, 1975). The rational-emotive perspective on these types of beliefs and their effects can be presented. Another approach is for those who find controllable causes threatening to think about using the distinction between responsibility for a cause and responsibility for taking action to remedy a situation (Brickman, Rabinowitz, Karuza, Coates, Cohn, & Kidder, 1982), which may be a less threatening way to conceive of controllable causes. They also may be asked to consider whether or not there are advantages of feeling responsible for a misfortune and if the benefits of not feeling responsible are worth giving up the chance to exert control and have an opportunity to get what they want.

In a similar fashion, if fear of failure appears to be an issue, participants can analyze with the help of the therapist whether or not that is a realistic concern. Even if it is, alternative perspectives on failure can be discussed, such as the idea that courageous people take more chances, so perhaps they experience more failure: Being willing to fail is a sign of courage. Another approach to countering fear of failure is to have participants use a technique like paradoxical intent (Frankl, 1963), in which people intentionally try to bring about some outcome that they have been trying to avoid out of fear. In this case, they might allow themselves two free failures, in which they are allowed to fail without any self-recriminations.

The point in all three of these examples of blockages to considering controllable causes is to get people to examine their assumptions and implicit choices and to have them work on changing the assumptions so that they can exert control or to at least make the choices explicit so they have a sense of control over the choice process.

Alternative Goal Identification

For some desired outcomes, there is obviously not any way that an individual can increase the chances of getting the desired outcome. The death of a family member, some disabilities, or losses of valued objects are permanent. In other cases, people may decide that although the chances of getting their primary outcome is not zero, the probability is low enough that for them it is not worth the effort that would be necessary. In those circumstances, it is important that people find and focus on alternative controllable goals in order to maintain a sense of personal control. The question that they need to ask themselves is, Given that I can't get what I most want, what can I do to get other goals that are also important to me or to improve my situation? (See also Heppner, this volume.)

Those who have suffered a major loss may not

be ready to look for a substitute goal for a considerable length of time, but their feelings of control can be increased in two other ways. A number of studies find that predictability is a factor that increases feelings of control (Miller, 1979). Information about the feelings that one is likely to experience following a loss and the process of adjusting to that loss help people anticipate what the experience will be like. The predictability increases perceptions of control because one is better able to deal with situations when they are expected. So, one way to increase control is to get information from others who have been in similar situations about what to expect. Another way to gain control when one's primary outcome is not possible is to focus on getting through the experience of dealing with that loss with a minimum of suffering and distress. For example, some cancer patients may not be able to get the most desired outcome—complete remission of the disease—but can focus on ways to reduce negative feelings or the amount of stress caused by the treatment.

Knowing when to give up a goal because the probability of ever obtaining it is low is a difficult decision and one that individuals need to make for themselves. Clients can benefit from an open consideration of the advantages and disadvantages of persistence in their situations. Perceptions of control will be enhanced if the goal is given up on the basis of an explicit choice to do what is in one's best interests, given the situation.

The goal of the therapist is to help people disengage from a goal that they have decided is unreachable, to help them consider a number of alternative outcomes, and to focus on these alternatives rather than on the lost outcome. Through group discussion or conversations with others in similar situations, additional possible goals can be identified so that people are basing their decisions on a view of the range of possibilities.

Assessment of Skills

Given that people have identified what they want and have some idea about how the outcome could be obtained through individual action, the next question is whether or not they possess the necessary skills to enact those actions. If people judge that they possess or could easily acquire the skills, then they need to decide whether or not the costs of exerting control are worth the potential benefits. This process of weighing costs and bene-

fits will be discussed later in the paper. If self-efficacy perceptions are low, then the next step to consider is whether or not those judgments are accurate.

Assessing the Accuracy of Self-Efficacy Expectations

Because it is possible for people to be able to successfully execute an action and still feel doubtful about their ability to do so (Bandura, 1982), some consideration needs to be given to whether or not one's feelings of low self-efficacy are justified. Questioning and feedback from the therapist would be useful here to help people decide whether or not they possess a skill. For example, some students might have a very low rating of their ability to write well. Through questioning about past experiences, however, it may be determined that in the past some papers have received good grades. Gently pushing someone to explain a discrepancy between performance and feeling may help reveal to them ways in which they discount success.

If the assessment made at this stage indicates that the person probably does not possess the needed skills, then the next question is whether or not the skills can be acquired. This will be considered following the next section. If the person decides that it is likely that he or she has the needed abilities, but lacks confidence in those abilities, he or she needs to work on increasing his or her self-efficacy.

Ways to Increase Self-Efficacy

For those who have unrealistic ways of evaluating their performance, more adaptive interpretations can be encouraged by calling attention to and challenging perfectionistic standards for the self. Many individuals may not realize that their standards are inappropriately high. Goldfried and Robins (1982) suggest that clients benefit from comparing their distorted subjective views of their own behavior with their more objective perspective of others' achievements. Appropriate comparison models to use to evaluate one's performance can be discussed. For example, those who use difficult to match comparison models may recognize the arbitrariness of the standards they use if they role play what their reactions to a performance would be if they used less difficult comparisons. Practice in finding and giving proper appreciation to the elements in a performance that were successful also may be useful. Strecher, Devellis, Becker, and Rosenstock (1986) suggested that therapists break target behaviors into easily managed components, arrange components so that initial tasks are easily mastered, and highlight clients' relative progress toward the target behavior.

Some individuals may need to learn to attribute their successes to their own behavior and their failures to external factors or to an internal, controllable factor (lack of effort) where appropriate. Forsterling (1986) has proposed that maladaptive attributions arise when individuals either do not have needed sources of information (consensus, consistency, and distinctiveness) or have inaccurate estimates of their values. He discussed how therapists can encourage clients to make correct, adaptive attributions by providing expert opinion about other people's behavior and by pointing out overlooked sources of consistency and distinctiveness information. For example, through examples and persuasion, a therapist may help a dieter to see that almost everyone occasionally violates his or her diet (high consensus for failure; therefore, not to be attributed to a lack of ability), that on many occasions the dieter has been able to resist temptation (high consistency for success; therefore, it can be attributed internally), and that the dieter is very successful at not eating between meals and at other times although he or she occasionally fails to follow the diet at mealtime (high distinctiveness for failure; therefore, not to be attributed internally).

Goldfried and Robins (1982) suggested that clients can profit from a discussion of their tendencies to discount success so they are aware that they do not give themselves full credit for accomplishments. In addition to awareness of one's propensity to discount success, keeping a written log of successful experiences and periodic reminders from the therapist of past effective responses can serve to keep accomplishments in attention so they are incorporated into the self-schema.

Assessing Skill Acquisition

In many cases, people may simply not possess the skills that they need to exert control and increase their chances of getting a desired outcome. For example, some students may need to learn adaptive study techniques, some dieters may be lacking in skills that help them to avoid forbidden foods, and some parents may not have acquired successful parenting abilities. For those who do not possess the requisite skills for a successful experience, the first step may involve instruction and practice in a technique, such as social skills training, relaxation or stress-reduction techniques, self-control management, cognitive restructuring, systematic desensitization, assertiveness training, decision-making, parenting skills, or role-playing of a target behavior. The acquisition of skills need not involve formal training, however. One might improve one's writing abilities, for example, by having colleagues read one's paper and getting feedback that can be incorporated into the next draft.

An important part of a feeling of control and mastery is to be able to recognize when one does not possess needed skills and to be willing and able to find out how one goes about acquiring them. The therapist's role is to encourage this kind of questioning and to serve as an expert source of information about the types of training that may be helpful.

If people decide that it is not possible for them to acquire the needed abilities, then the process should be focused on the identification of alternate goals. If skill acquisition seems to be a possibility, then the next step is to assess from the participant's perspective whether or not the benefits of learning a new skill are worth the costs.

Assessing Costs and Benefits

Although a number of theorists assume that possessing control is always desired and beneficial, there are indications that people do not always prefer to have control over some event that may affect them. Thompson, Cheek, and Graham (1988) reviewed the evidence that perceptions of control sometimes have negative effects. They found four types of situations in which a fair number of individuals would prefer not to have control: when the effort involved in exercising the control was not worth the outcome, when having or exercising control would adversely affect other goals, when failure seemed possible or probable, and when a more effective agent was available to get the desired outcome. Thus, there will be circumstances in which people will choose not to seek control or not to exercise it if they have it.

It is important to note that having no option available to influence a desired outcome is a very different situation in terms of overall feelings of control and mastery from a situation where one perceives that an opportunity to influence the outcome is available, but one chooses to forgo it. In the latter case, the individual has had some say in whether or not he or she has control, so would be aware of having some control over the process, especially if the decision not to attempt to influence the outcome has been consciously made. The point of this stage of the training for control is for individuals to consider the costs and benefits of gaining or using control and to be aware of their choices.

The role of the therapist is to encourage individuals to consider the advantages and disadvantages of gaining or exercising control in that particular situation, to make sure that they are aware of the full range of costs and benefits, and to highlight the idea that they are choosing for themselves whether or not to have control.

Additional Considerations

Iterative Progress

For the sake of simplicity, the process of enhancing feelings of mastery has been presented as a matter of progressing through discrete stages. A more realistic view, however, is that this is an iterative, rather than a linear, progression. Decisions made at one point in the process may lead one back to an earlier stage. For example, deciding not to exercise one's control brings one back to the point of considering other ways to influence the outcome or other goals one might try to influence.

The process is iterative in another way as well. The outcomes of efforts to exercise control provide valuable feedback about how effective an action is in obtaining an outcome, the costs and benefits of exercising control, and the accuracy of one's judgments of self-efficacy. Probably most important is the feedback regarding the effectiveness of one's efforts to exert control. As Carver and Scheier's (1981) cybernetic theory of control makes clear, an important part of the process of controlling an outcome is the use of feedback from earlier attempts at control. The feedback helps one to learn how to adjust actions to better exert control. The goal is for participants to see gaining control as an ongoing process of trial actions that are evaluated for their success and used to adjust future efforts.

Style of Therapy

A final consideration in enhancing client's perceptions of control is whether or not the interactions between the therapist and the participants in this training encourage or discourage the internalization of control. Types of therapies and styles of therapists differ in the attributions of control they convey to clients (Brehm & Smith, 1982). To the extent that a therapy leads clients to attribute the source of change to the therapist rather than themselves and teaches them to rely on the therapist's skills to help them change rather than learning to initiate change on their own, the therapy is not likely to produce lasting increases in perceptions of control (Blittner, Goldberg, & Merbaum, 1978).

There are three ways to encourage the internalization of control. First, participants should be actively involved in the process of training. Whenever possible, decisions about the problems to focus on and the course of treatment should be choices that are made by participants. Not only is client involvement with the decisions made in therapy more likely to increase feelings of control, but it is also the case that client-generated cognitive strategies are more effective than those provided by a therapist (Shumate & Worthington, 1987). This does not mean that direction or guidance is not provided by the therapist. Making decisions without a framework for change or without needed information or guidance from experts is not likely to increase feelings of control (Thompson et al., 1988). The therapist presents the framework and is available for expert advice, but whenever possible choices are up to the individual. For example, the therapist can provide information about the advantages and disadvantages of starting with a difficult to achieve outcome rather than one that is easy to obtain and leave the choice up to the participant.

Second, dependency on the therapist should be minimized. The intervention can be presented as a way to learn a skill that one can use in everyday life. There can be an explicit discussion of how one would go about using this procedure by oneself. Problems that might be encountered, such as the need for an objective perspective, can be discussed and alternatives can be identified.

Third, the therapist should continually throughout the intervention encourage clients to make internal attributions for change. Successes in exerting control should be explicitly tied to clients' skills at using this framework. Therapists can provide positive feedback for clients' abilities to master all parts of the process, including gathering information about controllable causes and finding alternative goals. When clients choose not to exert control because the benefits do not outweigh the costs, it can be emphasized that they are not exerting control because of a conscious choice that can be reevaluated at a future date. The decision to have or not have control is one that they are making, based on their assessment of the situation.

Illustration of Control Enhancement Training

To illustrate how these ideas can be applied, we will consider a young man whose feelings of helplessness stem from loneliness. The first step is to identify the specific outcome he would like to have: Is it more social contacts for leisure activities, a close friend, or a romantic relationship? If he has a number of goals, which one would he most prefer to start working on? The second step is to consider what factors might influence whether or not people in general get that outcome—a friendship, for example. During the discussion, the following influences might come up: having an outgoing personality, working around a lot of people so it is easy to meet others, being willing to approach others and suggest activities, having good social skills. The next question is, Which of those influences could someone change or develop so he or she could increase the chances of having a good friend? The client and therapist might agree that being willing to initiate contact with others seems like a controllable influence, but the client states that he has tried this and it does not work. This leads to an exploration of what exactly the client has tried and whether or not those attempts were unsuccessful. It turns out that the client has initiated contact with others twice in the last year and was turned down one of those times. The other time the new acquaintance did not reciprocate with an invitation, so they have had no more contact. At this point, the discussion can go a number of different directions, including whether or not that should be labeled a failure, how often one would want to be the initiator before one abandoned the attempts, or whether or not one's style of approaching others needed work. If the client decided that the attempts had not been a total failure, but proposed that feeling rejected when an acquaintance did not reciprocate an overture was not worth taking the chance, the discussion might move into an examination of the costs and benefits of initiating contact. The client's feelings about rejection and ways of handling those

feelings can be discussed. The focus of the discussion would switch to why one felt rejected and whether or not there were things one could do to deal with those feelings. Eventually the discussion would return to whether or not it was worth initiating social contact with others. If, after considering the costs and benefits, the client decided that it was worth trying this strategy again, the session could focus on how he was going to do this and what problems might come up. He would report back on how it went at the next session. If, however, he decided that the benefits of trying this did not outweigh the disadvantages, then the next step would be to consider other ways of increasing one's chances of having friends. If the discussion of these other ways also results in a decision that the attempts would not be worth the effort, then the session could move to a consideration of what one does when there is no way to act to get a desired outcome. A discussion of the issues and his feelings about them can help the client to decide whether or not he wants to give up the goal of having close friends. If giving up the goal is unacceptable, it might be useful to return to a consideration of the costs and benefits of different ways of influencing the outcome. One can have a different perspective on the disadvantages of some ways of exerting control if the alternative is to give up a highly desired goal. If the client decides that it is very unlikely that he will get what he wants and the best course is to adjust to that idea, then the discussion can cover several issues: how one goes about accepting the loss of a highly desired goal, what one can do to minimize the pain associated with the loss, and what the alternative goals are.

One of the therapist's goals throughout this process is to turn over the decision-making to the client while at the same time providing the guidance and information necessary to make informed decisions. Another goal is to make the framework (assessing what one wants, figuring out how to get it, assessing the costs and benefits, and making a decision about what to do) explicit so the client can begin to adopt this approach as a way of dealing with problems on his or her own.

SUMMARY

An approach to enhancing perceptions of control among individuals who feel a lack of control in one or many areas of their lives has been presented. This framework was generated from research and theory in both clinical and social psychology in areas such as self-control, self-efficacy, self-handicapping, and the search for meaning following a loss. The approach is based on an explicit consideration of ways to influence desired outcomes, of the skills that one has to do that, and of alternative goals when one cannot control the most desired outcome. The idea is that using this framework people will be more likely to find ways to exert control when that is possible and to have feelings of control even in situations where they cannot or choose not to act to get their most desired outcomes. The next step is to test the intervention with various groups, such as the aged, those with chronic illness, or those who have experienced a major loss, to see if it has the predicted effects on long-term perceptions of control.

REFERENCES

Abramson, L. Y., Garber, J., & Seligman, M. E. P. (1980). In J. Garber & M. E. P. Seligman (Eds.), *Human helplessness*. New York: Academic Press.

Andrew, J. (1970). Recovery from surgery with and without preparatory instructions for three coping styles. *Journal of Personality and Social Psychology, 15*, 223–226.

Averill, J. R. (1973). Personal control over aversive stimuli and its relationship to stress. *Psychological Bulletin, 80*, 286–303.

Bandura, A. (1977). Self-efficacy: Toward a unifying theory of behavioral change. *Psychological Review, 84*, 191–215.

Bandura, A. (1982). Self-efficacy mechanisms in human agency. *American Psychologist, 37*, 122–147.

Blankstein, K. R., & Polivy, J. (1982). Emotions, self-control, and self-modifications. An introduction. In K. R. Blankstein & J. Polivy (Eds.), *Advances in the study of communication and affect: Vol. 7. Self-control and self-modification of emotional behavior*. New York: Plenum Press.

Blittner, M., Goldberg, J., & Merbaum, M. (1978). Cognitive self-control factors in the reduction of smoking behavior. *Behavior Therapy, 9*, 553–561.

Brehm, S. S., & Smith, T. W. (1982). The application of social psychology to clinical practice: A range of possibilities. In G. Weary & H. L. Mirels (Eds.), *Integration of clinical and social psychology*. New York: Oxford University Press.

Brickman, P., Rabinowitz, V. C., Karuza, J., Jr., Coates, D., Cohn, E., & Kidder, L. (1982). Models of helping and coping. *American Psychologist, 37*, 368–384.

Carver, C. S., & Scheier, M. F. (1981). *Attention and self-regulation: A control-theory approach to human behavior*. New York: Springer-Verlag.

Craig, A., & Andrews, G. (1985). The prediction and prevention of relapse in stuttering. *Behavior Modification, 9*, 427–442.

deCharms, R. (1968). *Personal causation*. New York: Academic Press.

Ellis, A., & Harper, R. A. (1975). *A new guide to rational living*. North Hollywood, CA: Wilshire Books.

Fay, M. (1983). *A mortal condition*. New York: Coward-McCann.

Field, T., Alpert, B., Vega-Lahr, N., Goldstein, S., & Perry, S. (1988). Hospitalization stress in children: Sensitizer and repressor coping styles. *Health Psychology, 7*, 433–445.

Fletcher, G., Danilovics, P., Fernandez, G., Peterson, D., & Reeder, G. D. (1986). Attributional complexity: An individual differences measure. *Journal of Personality and Social Psychology, 51*, 875–884.

Forsterling, F. (1986). Attributional conceptions in clinical psychology. *American Psychologist, 41*, 275–285.

Frankl, V. E. (1963). *Man's search for meaning*. New York: Pocket Books.

Gilchrist, L. E., & Schinke, S. P. (1985). Improving smoking prevention programs. *Journal of Psychosocial Oncology, 3*, 67–78.

Gillis, J. S., & Jessor, R. (1970). Effects of brief psychotherapy on belief in internal control: An exploratory study. *Psychotherapy: Theory, Research, and Practice, 7*, 135–137.

Goldfried, M. R., & Robins, C. (1982). On the facilitation of self-efficacy. *Cognitive Therapy and Research, 6*, 361–380.

Janoff-Bulman, R., & Frieze, I. H. (1983). A theoretical perspective for understanding reactions to victimization. *Journal of Social Issues, 39*, 1–17.

Kanfer, F. H., & Karoly, P. (1972). Self-control: A behavioristic excursion into the lion's den. *Behavior Therapy, 3*, 398–416.

Klinger, E. (1975). Consequences of commitment to and disengagement from incentives. *Psychological Review, 82*, 1–25.

Kobasa, S. C. (1979). Stressful life events and

health: An inquiry into hardiness. *Journal of Personality and Social Psychology, 37,* 1–11.

Langer, E. J. (1983). *The psychology of control.* Beverly Hills, CA: Sage Publications.

Lefcourt, H. M. (1976). *Locus of control: Current trends in theory and research.* Hillsdale, NJ: Lawrence Erlbaum Associates.

Maddux, J. E., Norton, L. W., & Stoltenberg, C. D. (1986). Self-efficacy expectancy, outcome expectancy, and outcome value: Relative effects on behavioral intentions. *Journal of Personality and Social Psychology, 51,* 783–789.

Maddux, J. E., Sherer, M., & Rogers, R. W. (1982). Self-efficacy and outcome expectancy: Their relationship and their effects on behavioral intentions. *Cognitive Therapy and Research, 6,* 207–211.

Marlatt, G. A., & Marques, J. K. (1977). Meditation, self-control and alcohol use. In R. B. Stuart (Ed.), *Behavioral self-management: Strategies, techniques, and outcomes.* New York: Brunner/Mazel.

Meichenbaum, D. (1985). *Stress inoculation training.* Elmsford, NY: Pergamon Press.

Mikulas, W. L. (1986). Self-control: Essence and development. *The Psychological Record, 36,* 297–308.

Miller, S. M. (1979). Controllability and human stress: Method, evidence and theory. *Behavioral Research and Therapy, 17,* 287–304.

Omizo, M. M., Cubberly, W. E., & Longano, D. M. (1984). The effects of group counseling on self-concept and locus of control among learning disabled children. *Humanistic Education and Development, 23,* 69–79.

Porter, S. S., & Omizo, M. M. (1984). The effects of group relaxation training/large muscle exercise, and parental involvement on attention to task, impulsivity, and locus of control among hyperactive boys. *The Exceptional Child, 31,* 54–64.

Rosenbaum, M., & Smira, K. B. (1986). Cognitive and personality factors in the delay of gratification of hemodialysis patients. *Journal of Personality and Social Psychology, 51,* 357–364.

Rothbaum, F., Weisz, J. R., & Snyder, S. S. (1982). Changing the world and changing the self: A two-process model of perceived control. *Journal of Personality and Social Psychology, 42,* 5–27.

Rotter, J. B. (1966). Generalized expectancies for internal versus external control of reinforcement. *Psychological Monographs, 80* (whole No. 609), 1.

Schulz, R. (1980). Aging and control. In J. Garber & M. E. P. Seligman (Eds.), *Human helplessness.* New York: Academic Press.

Schulz, R., & Hanusa, B. H. (1979). Environmental influences on the effectiveness of control- and competence-enhancing interventions. In L. C. Perlmuter & R. A. Monty (Eds.), *Choice and perceived control.* New York: John Wiley & Sons.

Schunk, D. H. (1982). Effects of effort attributional feedback on children's perceived self-efficacy and achievement. *Journal of Educational Psychology, 74,* 548–556.

Schunk, D. H. (1983). Ability versus effort attributional feedback: Differential effects on self-efficacy and achievement. *Journal of Educational Psychology, 75,* 848–856.

Seligman, M. E. P. (1974). Depression and learned helplessness. In R. J. Friedman & M. M. Katz (Eds.), *The psychology of depression: Contemporary theory and research.* Washington, DC: Winston.

Shumate, M., & Worthington, Jr., E. L. (1987). Effectiveness of components of self-verbalization for control of cold pressor pain. *Journal of Psychosomatic Research, 31,* 301–310.

Snyder, C. R. (1989). Reality negotiation: From excuses to hope and beyond. *Journal of Social and Clinical Psychology, 8,* 130–157.

Snyder, C. R., & Higgins, R. L. (1988). Excuses: Their effective role in the negotiation of reality. *Psychological Bulletin, 104,* 23–35.

Snyder, M. L., Smoller, B., Strenta, A., & Frankel, V. E. (1981). A comparison of egotism, negativity, and learned helplessness as explanations for poor performance after unsolvable problems. *Journal of Personality and Social Psychology, 40,* 24–30.

Stern, G. S., Berrenberg, J. L., Winn, D., & Dubois, P. L. (1978). Perceived control. Contingent and noncontingent feedback in pulse-rate change and reduction in depressive cognitions. *Biofeedback and Self-Regulation, 3,* 277–285.

Strecher, V. J., Devellis, B. M., Becker, M. H., & Rosenstock, I. M. (1986). The role of self-efficacy in achieving health behavior change. *Health Education Quarterly, 13,* 73–91.

Swink, D. F., & Buchanan, D. R. (1984). The effects of sociodramatic goal-oriented role play and non–goal-oriented role play on locus of control. *Journal of Clinical Psychology, 40,* 1178–1183.

Taylor, S. E. (1983). Adjustment to threatening events: A theory of cognitive adaptation. *American Psychologist, 38,* 1161–1173.

Taylor, S. E., & Brown, J. D. (1988). Illusion and well-being: A social psychological perspective on mental health. *Psychological Bulletin, 103,* 193–210.

Thompson, S. C. (1981). Will it hurt less if I can control it? A complex answer to a simple question. *Psychological Bulletin, 90,* 89–101.

Thompson, S. C., Cheek, P. R., & Graham, M. A. (1988). The other side of perceived control: Disadvantages and negative effects. In S. Spacapan & S. Oskamp (Eds.), *The social psychology of health.* Beverly Hills, CA: Sage Publications.

Thompson, S. C., & Janigian, A. S. (1988). Life schemes: A framework for understanding the search for meaning. *Journal of Social and Clinical Psychology, 7,* 260–280.

Thompson, S. C., Sobolew-Shubin, A., Graham, M. A., & Janigian, A. S. (1989). Psychosocial adjustment following a stroke. *Social Science and Medicine, 28,* 239–247.

Weiss, J. M. (1971). Effects of punishing the coping response (conflict) on stress pathology in rats. *Journal of Comparative and Physiological Psychology, 77,* 14–21.

Weisz, J. R. (1986). Contingency and control beliefs as predictors of psychotherapy outcomes among children and adolescents. *Journal of Consulting and Clinical Psychology, 54,* 789–795.

CHAPTER 31

PARADOX-BASED TREATMENTS

Howard Tennen
Glenn Affleck

Paradoxical interventions are therapeutic strategies that are in seeming opposition to the treatment goals they try to achieve. Case illustrations are provocative and have raised many questions regarding the efficacy and mechanisms of this treatment approach. The following examples from the literature, to which we will return later, convey the uncommonsensical nature of these interventions as well as their range of application:

1. A patient complaining of panic attacks is asked to have such an attack deliberately so as to help bring the symptom under her control (Weakland, Fisch, Watzlawick, & Bodin, 1974).
2. A depressed stroke victim improves when his wife and children are told to stop trying to help him and to be ineffectual and helpless in his presence (Watzlawick & Coyne, 1980).
3. The father of a boy who regularly wets his bed at night is told that he must promise to follow the therapist's instructions *before* hearing what they were. After he agrees, he is told to give his son a large glass of water every evening and

demand that the son urinate on the bed and go to sleep on the wet bed (Madanes, 1980).
4. A patient with a long history of headaches is told by her therapist that her condition is probably irreversible and that therapy should concentrate on helping her live with the problem (Watzlawick, Beavin, & Jackson, 1967).
5. A young man diagnosed as schizophrenic is praised for acting crazy, since he is thus able to protect his father. By occupying mother's time with fights and tantrums, he allows father more time for work and relaxation (Selvini-Palazzoli, Cecchin, Prata, & Boscolo, 1978).

Our purpose in this chapter is to review the experimental, conceptual, and clinical literature related to paradox-based therapeutic intervention. We begin with a review of the clinical outcome literature. We then describe and evaluate clinical and social psychological explanations for paradoxical interventions. We next differentiate the key components of paradoxical interventions and place them in the context of a brief strategic therapy. Finally, we suggest implications for clinical and social psychological theory and research.

CLINICAL EFFICACY OF PARADOXICAL INTERVENTIONS

The most important question we can ask about any therapeutic technique is, Does it work? Any discussion of theory or technique must await an affirmative answer to this question. We therefore begin our review by examining three areas of the outcome literature: case studies, single case experimental designs, and randomized between-group designs. Together these investigations make a strong case for the efficacy of paradox-based treatments.

Case Studies

Case studies depict vividly the successful development of paradox-based interventions. The range of clinical problems to which they have been applied is impressive and includes tics (Yates, 1958), phobias (Malleson, 1959); depression (Johnston, Levis, & L'Abate, 1986), obsessive disorders (Frankl, 1960; Gertz, 1966; Gibson, 1985; Solyom, Garza-Perez, Ledwidge, & Solyom, 1972), urinary retention (Mozdzierz, 1985), sexual disorders (Frankl, 1966; Vandereycken, 1982), anorexia (Hsu & Liberman, 1982; Selvini-Palazzoli, 1974; Yapko, 1986), insomnia (Espie & Lindsay, 1987), anxiety-related somatic complaints (Greene & Sattin, 1985), problem prisoners (Chase, Shea, & Dougherty, 1984), transvestism (Cliffe, 1987), panic attacks (Dattilio, 1987), alcoholism (Weinstein, 1985), temper tantrums (Hare-Mustin, 1975), stuttering (Frankl, 1966), schizophrenia (Bergman, 1982; Selvini-Palazzoli et al., 1978; Walker & McLeod, 1982), school problems (Williams & Weeks, 1984), migraine headaches (Gentry, 1973), hypertension refractory to treatment (Sluzki, 1985), and family problems (Madanes, 1980).

Despite the plethora of successful case examples, it has become commonplace to describe the clinical outcome of paradoxical interventions as "untested" (Schwartz & Perrotta, 1985). The inherent unreliability of the case study method makes it impossible to draw valid conclusions about the generality of paradox-based interventions despite the apparent success suggested by these reports (Kazdin, 1980). Threats to internal validity, such as patient selection, present another

problem (Campbell & Stanley, 1963). Finally, therapist bias and the exclusion of experimental controls severely limit the usefulness of case studies (Wilson & Bornstein, 1984).

Empirically minded clinicians also have complained that published outcome data are sparse (Coyne & Biglan, 1984; Tennen, Eron, & Rohrbaugh, 1985), that most evidence about paradoxical techniques is impressionistic (Kolko & Milan, 1983; Soper & L'Abate, 1977), and that "there has been very little empirical work of any kind" (Weeks & L'Abate, 1982, p. 219). They have urged the publication of empirical research findings (Cade, 1984). We will demonstrate that there is now a sizable and consistent empirical literature supporting the therapeutic efficacy of paradoxical interventions. This literature consists of single-case experimental designs and comparative studies of paradoxical and nonparadoxical interventions.

Single-Case Experimental Studies

Single-case experimental designs or intrasubject-replication designs (Kazdin, 1980) are best applied to interventions that are targeted to a specific symptom or behavior, that produce rapid improvement, and that are flexible enough to allow the clinician to implement or withdraw treatment as necessary. Paradox-based interventions are thus well suited for this approach.

The most widely employed intrasubject-replication design is the ABAB design in which a baseline is established (A), followed by an intervention (B), subsequent withdrawal of the intervention (A), and finally its reimplementation (B). Symptom changes should parallel changes in implementation and withdrawal. ABAB designs have been employed successfully in the paradox-based treatment of constipation and encopresis (Bornstein, Sturm, Retzlaff, Kirby, & Chong, 1981) and sleep-onset insomnia (Ascher & Efran, 1978). Simpler AB designs have been used to treat agoraphobia (Kolko, 1984) and school truancy (Szykula & Morris, 1986). An ABC design was employed for obsessional flatulence ruminations (Milan & Kolko, 1982). After baseline (A) and an unsuccessful cognitive intervention (B), the authors successfully employed a paradoxical directive that resulted in the rapid and continued elimination of the rumination.

Several studies have employed multiple baseline designs, in which the length of the baseline is altered after each intervention (Kazdin, 1980;

Wilson & Bornstein, 1984). This design has been applied to the paradox-based treatment of agoraphobia (Ascher, 1981), insomnia (Relinger & Bornstein, 1979), and delinquent behavior (Kolko & Milan, 1983). Taken together, these studies provide consistent empirical support for the efficacy of paradoxical interventions.

Between-Group Studies

Studies comparing paradoxical and nonparadoxical treatments through randomized between-group designs are even more impressive (Katz, 1984; Strong, 1984). Two meta-analytic reviews (Hill, 1987; Shoham-Salomon & Rosenthal, 1987) document the effectiveness of paradoxical interventions in alleviating specific symptoms. The studies included in these reviews are summarized in Table 31.1.

Hill (1987) reviewed 15 published studies comparing paradoxical interventions and nonparadoxical treatments and computed the magnitude of the therapeutic effects. The effect size is computed by subtracting the mean of the control group from the mean of the treatment group and dividing by the standard deviation of the control group (cf. Smith, Glass, & Miller, 1980). The results make a strong case for the effectiveness of paradoxical interventions. The effect size for paradoxical interventions compared with no-treat-

Table 31.1. Outcome Studies Included in the Meta-Analytic Reviews of Hill (1987) and Shoham-Salomon & Rosenthal (1987)

STUDY	SYMPTOM
Ascher & Turner (1979)	Insomnia
Ascher & Turner (1980)	Insomnia
Turner & Ascher (1982)	Insomnia
Lacks, Bertelson, Gans, & Kunkel (1983)	Insomnia
Fogel & Dyal (1983)	Insomnia
Ott, Levine, & Ascher (1983)	Insomnia
Ascher (1981)	Agoraphobia
Mavissakalian, Michelson, Greenwald, Kornblith, & Greenwald (1983)	Agoraphobia
Feldman et al. (1982)	Depression
Beck & Strong (1982)	Depression
Conoley & Garber (1985)	Depression
Kraft et al. (1985)	Depression
Lopez & Wambach (1982)	Procrastination
Wright & Strong (1982)	Procrastination
Shoham-Salomon & Jancourt (1985)	Stress

ment controls indicated that an individual at the mean of the intervention group would be at the 84th percentile of the control group. Even when compared with placebo treatments, individuals who received paradoxical interventions experienced significantly more symptom relief.

The effect size for nonparadoxical treatments (usually behavioral or cognitive-behavioral interventions) was not significantly different from the effect of paradoxical approaches. But several of the studies included in the meta-analysis contained numerous effect sizes, which could bias the results. To correct for this bias, Hill computed the mean effect size for paradox-based and alternative treatments. Paradox-based treatment proved superior.

Shoham-Salomon and Rosenthal (1987) reviewed 10 outcome studies, including many reviewed by Hill. Their findings support and extend Hill's conclusions. They found that subjects receiving paradoxical interventions showed substantial symptom reduction compared with subjects receiving no treatment. Paradox-based treatments also showed a modest and nonsignificant advantage when compared with behavioral and cognitive-behavioral interventions. Moreover, their analysis of the durability of the treatment effect, its relation to the severity of the presenting symptom, and the differential impact of types of paradoxical interventions, provide an even more impressive picture of the efficacy of paradoxical treatments.

The effect of paradoxical treatments is durable and actually appears to increase with time. At 1 month follow-up, paradoxical interventions were superior to other treatments. This superiority is not due to the waning effects of the alternative modes, but rather to ongoing symptom reduction after the completion of paradoxical interventions. Shoham-Salomon and Rosenthal (1987) suggested that paradoxical interventions may require an incubation period before their full effect is obtained. But the enhanced effect over time is also consistent with a fundamental premise of those who employ these techniques: that change begets change (Watzlawick, Weakland, & Fisch, 1974).

It has been asserted (Watzlawick et al., 1967; Weeks & L'Abate, 1982) that paradoxical interventions are most helpful when the presenting symptom is severe. To test this assertion, Shoham-Salomon and Rosenthal (1987) computed the correlation between symptom severity and treatment effectiveness. Although the necessary data were available for only two studies, the findings are intriguing: greater symptom severity is associated with poorer outcome for nonparadoxical treatments, but greater severity is associated with better outcome for paradoxical interventions. The difference between these correlations is highly significant and, although tentative, suggests that paradoxical treatment approaches may be most effective where behavioral and cognitive-behavioral treatments fail.

In their landmark work on the benefits of psychotherapy, Smith et al. (1980) compared 17 types of therapy. Shoham-Salomon and Rosenthal (1987) rank ordered the effect size of these treatments and found that the paradox-based treatments evaluated in their meta-analysis ranked third following only cognitive therapies and hypnosis. They concluded that studies employing paradoxical interventions yield an effect size that is larger than the effect of 95% of the interventions reported by Smith et al. (1980).

One concern not yet addressed in our review is whether paradoxical interventions have an unacceptable proportion of iatrogenic outcomes. Might there be significant risk in asking a patient to exaggerate his or her symptom? Hill (1987) found that only 1 of 39 effect sizes was in a negative direction compared with no-treatment controls. The one negative effect was reversed by the time of follow-up, supporting Shoham-Salomon and Rosenthal's (1987) contention that paradoxical interventions may produce "sleeper effects." This rate of untoward effects (3%) compares favorably with the 12% rate for other modes of psychotherapy (Smith & Glass, 1977).

Since the publication of these meta-analyses, four controlled studies have appeared employing paradoxical interventions. One study (Westerman, Frankel, Tanaka, & Kahn, 1987) included individuals with a broad range of problems applying for treatment at a mental health clinic. The other three studies investigated the treatment of agoraphobia. Westerman et al. (1987) reported that behavior therapy and paradoxical interventions were equally effective. Ascher, Schotte, and Greyson (1986) and Schwartz and Michelson (1987) found that paradoxical intervention was as effective as behavioral techniques in the treatment of carefully diagnosed agoraphobic patients. Michelson, Mavissakalian, Marchione, Dancu, and Greenwald (1986) found that although effective, paradoxical intervention was not as effective as behavioral treatments of agoraphobics.

Overall, our review of the outcome literature indicates that the effectiveness of paradoxical interventions is substantial. Case studies and single-subject experimental designs support its efficacy. Controlled studies comparing paradoxical with other treatments reveal that paradoxical interventions are not only adequate, but may be superior. The studies reviewed include both carefully diagnosed patients and university students. The symptoms addressed are fairly wide ranging. The findings are compelling and demand an adequate explanation. We now examine the plethora of clinical and social psychological models proposed to explain the efficacy of paradoxical interventions.

CLINICAL EXPLANATIONS OF PARADOXICAL INTERVENTIONS

The relation between clinical theory and paradoxical interventions is akin to the fable of the blind men and the elephant: Every theory has attempted to take paradox out of context so that it is no longer contrary (*para*) to common opinion (*doxa*). The explanations, however, are inchoate and have stimulated neither research nor innovative clinical application.

Examples of paradoxical clinical interventions appear as early as the 19th century (cf. Foucault, 1965). The first modern application is described by Dunlap (1932), who explained paradox in terms of learning theory and called the technique "negative practice." Dunlap hypothesized that when a symptom is prescribed by a therapist and practiced by a patient, two things happen. First, the symptom, which was uncontrollable, is now under voluntary control. Second, it is subject to extinction. Thus, by practicing the symptom, the patient will remove it.

Conditioned inhibition and satiation are related learning theory constructs that have been used to explain paradox-based treatment (Rabkin, 1977). Conditioned inhibition refers to the observation that the repetition of a habit leads to its extinction even if the habit is followed by a reward. Satiation, on the other hand, explains the success of paradoxical interventions by noting that with continued presentation, a reinforcer loses its rewarding properties. These learning theory explanations may have some heuristic value when the patient actually repeats the symptom on many occasions. Most reports indicate, however, that symptom prescription is successful after only one or a few trials—an outcome that cannot be explained by conditioned inhibition or satiation. Nonetheless, behavior therapists continue to view paradoxical interventions as another tool in their armamentarium (cf. Michelson & Ascher, 1984).

Frankl (1960) explained the effects of paradoxical treatment with existential (logotherapy) concepts. He suggested that paradoxical interventions, specifically symptom prescription, produces change through "hyperintention" and humor. In theory, hyperintention means trying in an exaggerated way to produce a symptom. This very effort counteracts anticipatory anxiety or "fear of fear." By trying to bring on his or her fear or obsession, the phobic or obsessional patient finds that he or she is less ruminative or fearful. Humor provides a context of detachment from the symptom. Hyperintention may explain why many patients lose their symptoms with little practice (see example 1 at the beginning of this chapter), but it cannot explain situations in which the therapist tells the patient to not get better (example 4) or those situations in which another family member is asked to change his or her behavior (examples 2 and 3). Moreover, we will demonstrate later that the interventions that are best explained by existential concepts are least likely to have an adequate clinical effect. Despite these limitations, the logotherapeutic literature is replete with suggestions for refining the application of hyperintention and humor (Fabry, 1982; Riveros, 1984; Shaughnessy, 1984).

Adlerian therapy (Corsini, 1982; Main & West, 1987; West, Main, & Zarski, 1986), gestalt therapy (Seltzer, 1984; Peterson & Melcher, 1981), reality therapy (Wubbolding, 1984, 1985), transactional analysis (Massey, 1986; Price, 1986; Wathney, 1982), and psychoanalysis (Gurman, 1982) also have been used as conceptual bases for paradoxical interventions. The differences among these explanations is dramatic. Reality therapy explains paradox in terms of "conflict in need fulfillment" (Wubbolding, 1984); transactional analysis employs "duplex communication" and "stroking the client" (Massey, 1986); whereas psychoanalytic theory claims that paradoxical interventions are effective because they "express the most central and powerful psychodynamic themes . . . and . . . reveal both the positive and negative elements of intimate collusion" (Gurman, 1982, pp. 72–73).

We believe that the proliferation of these unsupported theories is more interesting than their heuristic value. This proliferation has two implications. The first is that behavior, whether patient's or therapist's, is easily absorbed into one's existing worldview. Second, attempts to persuade people that their view is incorrect by presenting evidence or alternative explanations seems to have no impact on their position. This attempted solution may even exacerbate the problem by making people more entrenched in their position. These implications will form the basis for our eventual conceptualization of paradoxical interventions.

SOCIAL PSYCHOLOGICAL EXPLANATIONS

The mystique of paradoxical interventions and an increasing interest by social psychologists in clinical phenomena (Strong, 1987) have led to social psychological explanations for the effects of paradox, and to models of clinical technique. Like most schools of psychotherapy, each social psychological theory explains paradoxical interventions within its own framework, and each leaves many unanswered questions.

Cognitive Dissonance

Kercher and Smith (1985) and Bogdan (1982) have offered explanations based on cognitive dissonance theory (Festinger, 1957). They hypothesize that prior to treatment, patients possess a cognitive consonance: they view problematic behaviors as maladaptive and also are concerned about those behaviors. To have a problem and not be concerned would create dissonance. When clinicians invoke paradoxical interventions, they arouse dissonance, which patients then try to reduce. Dissonance may be aroused by prescribing the symptom (see example 1 at the beginning of this chapter) or by relabeling it as good instead of bad (example 5). A symptom prescription is dissonant with the view that the symptom is bad. To reduce the dissonance, the patient may change behavior associated with the symptom. For example, the phobic may stop avoiding fear-inducing situations. When dissonance is aroused by relabeling a symptom, it can be reduced by not trying to change the symptom. For example, a depressed individual may be told that her depression is not to be avoided because it helps her understand herself. She can reduce dissonance by not trying to change her depression.

Although intriguing, the dissonance explanation is based on an assumption that is beyond the domain of the theory. Specifically, it assumes that people's attempts to solve problems can actually create larger problems. This can be seen in both of the examples presented to support the theory. The phobic's problem is not his or her fear, but the attempt to solve that problem by avoiding certain situations. Similarly, the depressed patient's problem is not her sadness per se, but her unsuccessful attempts to ward it off. As we hope to demonstrate, the concept of "problem-maintaining solutions" is central to an adequate conceptualization of paradoxical interventions. Nonetheless, it falls beyond the domain of dissonance theory.

Attribution Theory

L'Abate (1986) and Strong and associates (Beck & Strong, 1982; Hills, Gruszkos, & Strong, 1985; Strong & Claiborn, 1982) employ attribution theory to explain the effects of paradoxical interventions. Beck and Strong (1982) hypothesize that paradox-based treatments are successful because behavior change is attributed to internal stable sources. For example, when a therapist associates a patient's depression with sensitivity and caring, he or she is suggesting an internal stable attribution for any change in the symptom. An attributional explanation of paradoxical interventions faces two problems. First, it cannot account for those interventions in which someone other than the identified patient is the agent of change (see examples 2 and 3 at the beginning of this chapter). Moreover, the formulation does not stand up to empirical scrutiny. Strong is one of the few clinicians to test clinical hypotheses empirically, and he has not been able to provide support for his attributional formulation (Feldman, Strong, & Danser, 1982).

Reactance Theory

Another application of social psychological theory to paradoxical interventions appears in the work of Tennen, Rohrbaugh, and associates (Tennen, Rohrbaugh, Press, & White, 1981; Rohrbaugh, Tennen, Press, & White, 1981; Rohrbaugh, Tennen, & Eron, 1982; Tennen et al., 1985), who presented a model of therapeutic intervention based on reactance theory (J. W. Brehm, 1966; Brehm, 1976). Their model has generated both clinical (Ascher, 1986; Cade, 1984; Dowd & Swoboda, 1984; Kolko & Milan, 1986) and research (Westerman et al., 1987) interest.

Reactance theory is based on the assertion that

people experience certain behaviors, thoughts, and attitudes as "free," meaning that they could engage in that behavior, thought, or attitude at any given time. The central premise of the theory is that a person will experience an aversive motivational state, psychological reactance, when any free behavior is threatened. In response to this threat, he or she will try to restore the free behavior, thought, or attitude. If someone's free behavior is threatened by a request or directive, the simplest way to restore freedom is to disobey or do other than what is requested. Drawing on this premise, we differentiated two types of paradoxical intervention: those in which therapeutic change derives from complying with the therapist's directive, and those in which change results from defying the directive.

Compliance-based interventions are effective because complying with the directive interrupts the process that maintains the symptoms. Symptom prescription is thought to be most effective with obsessions, anxiety, and insomnia because these problems are maintained by attempts to stave them off. When a patient complies with a symptom prescription and attempts to create the symptom, he or she is interrupting a usual tactic of trying to prevent it.

Defiance-based interventions are effective because people change by defying the therapeutic directive. Consider the example of disengaging an overprotective mother from a symptomatic child (Haley, 1976). The therapist encourages the mother to spend even more time with her child to warn him about all of life's dangers. As Haley (1976) noted, "If this approach is done well, the mother will react by rebelling against the therapist and hovering over the child less" (p. 71). The reader might notice that as was true of dissonance theory, reactance theory requires the additional assumption of a problem-maintaining solution. Both compliance- and defiance-based interventions imply that the therapist is trying to get the patient to do less of something. That something is often the patient's well-intended but misguided solution to a problem.

We reasoned that two factors, both derived from reactance theory, determine whether to use compliance- or defiance-based paradoxical strategies. One factor is the probability that the person to be influenced will experience psychological reactance in response to the planned intervention. The second factor concerns the behavior or attitude to be influenced: Does the individual believe that it is "free?" Defiance-based strategies are most effective when the target behavior is free and reactance potential is high. Compliance-based paradox is most effective with "unfree" behaviors such as symptoms and when reactance potential is low. When reactance potential is low and the target behavior is free, paradoxical interventions are not necessary.

The most difficult clinical situations are encountered when reactance potential is high and the target behavior is unfree. In these cases, Tennen et al. (1981) recommend that the intervention be shifted to a collateral or supporting behavior. They offer the example of the depressed individual who believes that his or her depressive symptoms are unfree, but who could enumerate behaviors related to the depression that are free, such as calling an employment agency or walking to the neighborhood tavern. After having the defiant patient describe what he or she could do, the therapist might then suggest explicitly that he or she avoid doing these things.

The compliance-defiance model need not be applied to the problem-bearer. In fact, the behavior of others—usually family members—is usually a better prospect for defiance-based paradoxical interventions, because significant others usually define their behavior as free. Haley's (1976) case of the overprotective mother is a good example of this type of defiance-based intervention. But recall that while Haley endorsed this approach if it is done well, he did not specify the components of a well-presented intervention. Similarly, Tennen et al.'s model remains incomplete without an exposition on how to carry out effectively a compliance- or defiance-based paradoxical intervention. The model, like other social psychological models, also requires the concept of problem-maintaining solutions; that is, attempted solutions that exacerbate the problem. This concept is beyond the scope of the model. We now present a comprehensive model of behavior change, the strategic therapy approach, that we believe provides the best context from which to understand paradox-based treatment.

THE STRATEGIC THERAPY APPROACH

Most schools of psychotherapy require that the patient come to accept the therapist's definition of reality or at least comply with therapeutic directives or suggestions. But patients often resist our attempts to redefine their reality and only some-

times follow our suggestions. The "strategic" approach to therapy, most clearly described in the work of Jackson, Watzlawick, Weakland, Fisch, Coyne, and others at the Mental Research Institute in Palo Alto, California, advances the position that changing people's behavior does not require that we challenge their cherished assumptions about themselves and the world. Profound changes can occur with minimal interventions that merely extend existing assumptions. Consistent with Erickson's (Erickson & Rossi, 1975; Erickson, Rossi, & Rossi, 1976) principle of accepting and using what the patient offers in a manner analogous to psychological judo (Bandler & Grinder, 1975), strategic therapists propose to patients variations of their existing personal paradigms (Mahoney, 1980) or world images (Watzlawick, 1978).

We believe that the strategic therapist's application of paradox-based interventions turns on five central concepts: worldviews, reframing, problem-maintaining solutions, positive connotations, and behavioral prescription or restraint. We will attempt to elucidate these concepts and their relation to paradox-based treatment.

WORLDVIEWS, REFRAMING, AND THERAPEUTIC CHANGE

Our worldviews or world images are those cherished assumptions that we hold about the nature of things. Watzlawick (1978) referred to them as "second-order realities," as opposed to first-order reality, which is the world that exists independently of our appraisals. Drawing on the constructivist position (Dell, 1987; Efran, Lukens, & Lukens, 1988; Keeney, 1987; Maturana, 1975; von Glaserfeld, 1984), Watzlawick argued that the world "out there" is not accessible to us, and that our problems in life derive from our second-order realities.

In practice, a patient's worldview (which includes a view of oneself) is usually inferred. Consider the following example of a mother who brought her daughter for treatment of thumb-sucking. She had not complied with the therapist's request that she initiate a home-based program in which the girl was to be rewarded for not sucking her thumb and placed in her room for five minutes (time out) each time she sucked her thumb (Szykula & Morris, 1986):

Therapist: What has interfered with your using the suggestions for using incentives and time out?

Patient: Well, . . . I don't know if it's going to help . . . to reward and punish Nancy's behavior. I think Nancy has the problem because of her father's and my divorce. Do you think she's suffered emotional damages?

Therapist: . . . Her *emotionality* . . . and sulking are more a result of her feeling that the two secure people in her life have changed. And she is unaware whether they will really offer future security. . . . The structure of a point program . . . gives children a sense of security that they can both *see* and *feel*. It alleviates any thoughts that "mommy" can't take care of things because "daddy's not living at home any more."

Patient: Gee, I never thought of it that way. I just thought it . . . so superficial . . .

Therapist: It seems superficial to us adults, but to a child's view of the world, it's security and stability. (pp. 176–177)

In keeping with this mother's definition of the problem, the therapist redefines reward and punishment as sources of security and stability. The redefinition presents a reality that is so plausible, we need to remind ourselves that it is, in fact, an invented reality that is congruent with the mother's views. Equally plausible realities can be constructed for this or any situation.

In some circumstances, rather than working directly with the patient's worldview, the therapist cultivates a frame by gently crafting a new way to view the presenting complaint (Jones, 1986; Snyder, Higgins, & Stucky, 1983). Consider the case of a wife who is critical of her husband, whom she views as not caring and indifferent to her needs (Fisch, Weakland, & Segal, 1982). The therapist meets alone with the husband to understand his "flaw," and then with the wife. To cultivate a new frame, he asks her some leading questions:

Would I be correct that his parents might be described as cold and overly controlled . . . ? When you have pointed out to him his failure to be thoughtful to you, does he get angry, angrier than one would normally get . . . ?

The stage has now been set to redefine the husband's behavior not as evidence of his lack of caring, but rather of his inability to do otherwise:

What you have confirmed and helped me to see clearly is that, in a sense, Bob is a person who has been crippled, most likely in his early rearing. But it's a particular kind of crippling. You see, he can be a bright person, but he lacks the ability to be normally perceptive of others' needs and sensibilities, and this is all the more so with people

he is most close to. I myself do not understand it, but he can have less difficulty with people who are not important to him; yet the closer and more meaningful the relationship, the more this deficit will show up. What makes it a more sticky problem is that it's hard for him to be aware of it, and so he will get very angry when accused, even rightly, of being uncaring or thoughtless, since, as far as he knows, there is nothing he can perceive that needs taking care of. In a manner of speaking, it is almost as if he were retarded, not intellectually but perceptively. (Fisch et al., 1982, p. 106)

Jones (1986) pointed out that this kind of intervention makes intuitive use of what social psychologists have learned about schemas (Fiske & Linville, 1980), schema activation (Cohen & Ebbeson, 1979), and category accessibility (Weyer, 1980).

For both the mother of the emotional child and the wife of the uncaring husband, the reason that the reframe or redefinition is therapeutic is because it interdicts a problematic sequence of behavior. In the process of viewing the problem in a new light (yet one consistent with their own world image), these individuals behave differently. They no longer try to solve the problem by doing things to perpetuate it. As we mentioned in our discussion of social psychological perspectives on paradox, the idea that people engage in problem-maintaining solutions is central to nearly all explanations of paradoxical interventions.

PROBLEM-MAINTAINING SOLUTIONS

Problem-maintaining solutions are well-intended behaviors that are meant to alleviate a difficulty but instead change that difficulty into a problem. Tennen et al. (1985) describe three labels, premises, or expectations that appear to be tied repeatedly to problem maintenance: the expectation of mastery and control, utopian expectations, and labeling behavior as mad or bad. These views, when applied rigidly, lead to three kinds of problem-maintaining behavior: action where none is needed, no action where some is needed, and the wrong kind of action.

The expectation of control may be the most pervasive problem-maintaining premise. The problematic expectation is that people are masters of their fates and they should take responsibility for their own behavior. Problems maintained by the expectation of mastery include those where a person tries to produce an outcome that by its very nature requires not trying. Action is thus taken where none is needed. Tennen et al. (1985) offered the example of a man who is having difficulty maintaining an erection. This difficulty becomes a problem when he tries to create an erection by willing one: "The problem-maintaining premise of course is that there is a correlation between effort expenditure and intensity of erection. The harder he tries, the softer he becomes, which is interpreted as evidence that he is not trying hard enough . . . " (p. 193).

Utopian assertions (Watzlawick et al., 1974; Watzlawick, 1978) can also create a problem-maintaining solution. The assertion is that all is well in situations where some action is needed. Tennen et al. (1985) offered as an example the father of a delinquent adolescent referred by the courts, who talks about his son as if he were selected class valedictorian rather than someone who persists in making trouble. The therapist's task is to redefine the meaning of the boy's behavior in a way that produces appropriate action by the father. The details of this redefinition depend in part on the father's worldview. In any event, the therapist would not challenge the father to "face the facts."

A third group of problem-maintaining beliefs involves whether behavior is labeled as mad or bad. As labels have significant effects on those labeled (Berger & Luckmann, 1966), the therapist's task is to shift the meaning of the labeled behavior, which in turn influences how people behave. In the case of the frustrated wife whose husband was "not caring" (bad), the therapist redefined his behavior as inept and determined by deep-seated psychological forces (mad). This redefinition interdicted the wife's problem-maintaining pattern of accusations, which had led regularly to the husband's withdrawal, which, of course, the wife defined as more evidence that he is uncaring. There are other situations in which the problem-maintaining label is "mad" and the therapist reframes the behavior as "bad" so as to initiate new interaction patterns (e.g., Hoffman, 1976).

We can now identify problem-maintaining behaviors in each of the examples presented at the beginning of this chapter. In the first example of panic attacks, the problem-maintaining behavior is avoiding situations that may bring on an attack. The therapist therefore prescribes the symptom to interrupt the problem-maintaining cycle. In the second example, the children of the depressed stroke victim are taking the wrong kind of action. Their efforts are well intentioned, but it is not until they act in a helpless manner that their formerly "take charge" father begins to take charge again. In the third example, action is needed, but none is being taken. By extracting a promise in advance, the therapist gets the father to create an "ordeal" for his son in which bedwetting is no longer a viable alternative.

In the case of the patient with chronic headaches (example 4), the therapist attempts to interrupt the problem-maintaining solution of trying to eradicate the headaches. Finally, the young man in example 5 was diagnosed as schizophrenic. The therapist believes that this "mad" label plays a role in maintaining crazy behavior, and redefines the craziness to the family as the patient's noble attempt to protect his father. In this last example, the therapist indicates that the patient's symptoms are not only tolerable, but actually praiseworthy. This tactic of connoting a problem in a positive light plays a key role in the armamentarium of clinicians who employ paradoxical interventions. We now review the clinical and empirical evidence supporting this technique.

POSITIVE CONNOTATION AS A PARADOXICAL THERAPEUTIC STRATEGY

Despite the protestations of the constructivists, in our everyday activities we view reality as something "out there" that we perceive in a valid way. There are circumstances, however, that remind us of the fragility of that external reality. For example, in 1988 when massive forest fires swept through large sections of Yellowstone National Park, many people were horrified by what was to them without doubt massive destruction. But environmentalists were not at all concerned, nor did they view the fire as destructive. Rather, they viewed it as a natural phenomenon with many benefits, such as richer plant life, more nutrition for wildlife, and new information about the process of rejuvenation. These divergent views suggest very different actions. Those who witnessed destruction demanded that the fire be contained. Those who witnessed a positive and beneficial event suggested that nothing be done to protect the forest. This example demonstrates that a positive interpretation can be placed on almost any situation, and sets the stage for our discussion of one particular subset of reframes — those in which a problem is given a positive meaning, which is critical to our discussion of paradoxical interventions.

Clinical examples highlight both the power and potential perils of positive connotation: A depressed 12-year-old withdraws from others frequently, particularly when he is encouraged to interact with his peers. After the therapy team reviewed a series of problem-maintaining solutions, "He was told that, after thinking about this issue, we supported his withdrawal, inasmuch as it most likely represented an attempt to get in touch with his sad feelings. We further observed that only after he had truly come to know himself well, could he begin to interact with others" (Jessee, Jurkovic, Wilkie, & Chiglinsky, 1982, p. 316).

Coyne (1987) described the use of similar tactics with couples:

> With a couple, the therapist may ask the partners individually how they have been able to make it as long as they have, despite their problems. . . . [I]f the client merely states that they have stayed together because of fear or the welfare of the children, the therapist may reply that for many that would not be enough, and that somehow the client had found the personal resources to endure. If the client expresses longstanding hostility toward the partner, the therapist may comment that this may represent a real loyalty . . . and that remaining hostile, at least for now, may be a way of keeping enough distance to reduce the hurt. (p. 541)

As Coyne (1987) noted, such positive connotations are central to paradoxical interventions. Before implementing them, however, he advised the therapist to grasp the patient's existing perspectives (worldviews) and actively accept them. He noted that it is preferable for the client to volunteer evidence of strength or resources. Even then, he urged the therapist to not confront people with their strengths in a way that may burden them or demonstrate the therapist's lack of understanding.

Coyne's concern is well founded in view of the perfunctory application of positive connotation in the clinical literature. For example, a couple with chronic relationship problems is told that they really love each other and that changing for the better would be a sign of rejection (Soper & L'Abate, 1977). Or consider the patient who is commended for his symptoms. The therapist expresses admiration for the patient's "extraordinary sensitivity," "generosity," and "willingness to suf-

fer and make unparalleled sacrifices" for the family (Selvini-Palazzoli et al., 1978). We believe that the patient's acceptance of this positive connotation depends on the parameters mentioned by Coyne: that the connotation fit well within an existing worldview and that it neither burden the patient nor demonstrate the therapist's lack of understanding. Much has been made by family therapists of redefining symptomatic behavior as "heroic" (Sluzki, 1983). We fear, however, that the burden of superior qualities associated with hero status may turn some connotated heroes into tragic heroes.

The application of positive connotation in research studies is particularly troublesome, though understandable in view of the demands of randomized group designs. For example, Kraft, Claiborn, and Dowd (1985) offered six identical positive connotations to their mildly depressed subjects. Each connotation labeled the subject's characteristics or behavior as a sign of strength or good fortune. The exigencies of well-designed research may require that each subject receive identical instructions. But by not tailoring positive connotations to subjects' existing worldviews, outcome research underestimates the efficacy of paradox-based treatment.

Despite the constraints imposed by research design, there is now empirical evidence that positive connotations are a key ingredient in paradoxical interventions. In their meta-analytic review, Shoham-Salomon and Rosenthal (1987) investigated separately the effects of positive connotation and symptom prescription. The findings were provocative: Positive connotations were more effective than nonpositive connotations, increasing the mean therapeutic success rate from 14% to 85%. Moreover, positively connoted paradoxical interventions were significantly more effective than behavioral and cognitive-behavioral treatments. This is particularly impressive because systematic desensitization is considered the treatment of choice for the anxiety-based disorders investigated in these studies (Brehm & Brehm, 1981; Kazdin & Wilcoxon, 1976). Finally, Shoham-Salomon and Rosenthal found that in the absence of positive connotation, symptom prescriptions, the cornerstone of the logotherapeutic approach to paradoxical interventions, were less effective than other treatments.

We conclude this section with a reminder that positive connotations simply provide plausible and workable realities. Skynner (1981) suggested that these connotations express "the most essential truth" (p. 76). We must disagree. There are many truths, some more helpful than others.

PRESCRIBING AND RESTRAINING: THE FINAL INGREDIENTS

We have described four key components of paradoxical intervention: assessing and endorsing the patient's worldview, identifying problem-maintaining solutions, reframing the problem in a manner consistent with the patient's worldview, and employing positive connotation as part of the reframing process. The final component of the process is either prescribing the symptom or some related behavior, or restraining the patient from change.

Throughout this chapter, we have stressed that the meaning one attributes to events influences behavior, and that by rearranging meaning we can make significant therapeutic changes. It would be incorrect, however, to assume that one must change meaning to change behavior. Changes in behavior can themselves lead to new worldviews, views that would never occur without the new behavior. Therefore, behavioral directives play an important role in paradox-based interventions.

Ironically, the best known case of a single small behavior leading to significant changes comes not from the literature on paradox, but from psychoanalysis. Balint (1968) described a young woman who complained of not being able to achieve anything because of an overwhelming fear whenever she had to take a risk or make a decision. In the course of psychoanalytic treatment, she mentioned that despite many efforts, she had never been able to do a somersault. When Balint inquired further, she got off the analytic couch and to her amazement performed a somersault. Balint documented many positive changes in her emotional, social, and professional life that followed this seemingly minor event. Her view of herself and her relation to the world had apparently changed because of one small behavior.

Watzlawick (1985) reminded us that sometimes people's worldviews do not allow them to engage in behavior that could have a lasting impact, no matter how effortless that behavior may be. This is why reframes and positive connotations are employed; not only to infuse new meaning into a symptom or interaction pattern, but also to provide a rationale for one of two behavioral directives — behavioral prescription or restraint. Prescribing means telling people what to do either by giving them tasks or making suggestions. Prescribing the symptom is a common paradoxical tactic, but the literature is unclear as to whether the therapist should provide a rationale or simply instruct the patient to have his or her symptoms. Thus, some investigators employ no rationale (Westerman et al., 1987). Others provide a straightforward rationale such as "this activity could vitiate therapy" (Turner & Asher, 1982, p. 36) or tell patients that engaging in the symptom can "be used as a coping procedure to reverse the vicious cycle of fearful responding" (Michelson et al., 1986, p. 96). Our concern with these rationales is that they neither take full advantage of the patient's worldview nor provide a positive connotation to the problem behavior. As we have seen, the empirical literature supports our concern. Paradoxical interventions in the absence of positive connotations are less effective clinically.

Some investigators, nonetheless, have found that negative connotation can have a positive therapeutic impact. Kolko and Milan (1983), following the reactance theory model, successfully maximized opposition to a paradoxical directive that a young school truant not attend school by suggesting to him that he may not be mature enough to handle the attendant responsibilities. We believe that negative connotations may be more difficult than positive connotations to implement, and their potential effectiveness awaits stronger empirical support.

Behavioral prescriptions are targeted to interrupt problem-maintaining solutions, as demonstrated by the first three examples at the beginning of the chapter. Example 1 is a symptom prescription designed to interrupt the attempted solution of avoiding panic attacks. Example 2 is a behavioral prescription directed to the problem-maintaining behavior of well-meaning family members. The third example captures well Watzlawick's (1985) contention that existing worldviews often restrict potentially helpful actions. The father is directed to create an ordeal for his son, but only after the therapist extracted a promise from him that he would follow whatever the therapist requested. The father would never have let his son sleep in a wet bed had a promise not been given in advance. Yet this very behavior eliminated his son's symptom and enhanced their relationship, the son's esteem, and the father's sense of competence. This intervention demonstrates both the power of behavioral directives and the fact that changes in behavior can precede or lead to changes in one's view of the self, others, and the world.

Restraint is another way of influencing behavior to interrupt problem-maintaining sequences. Tennen et al. (1985) distinguish among implicit restraint, soft restraint, and hard restraint. Implicit restraint allows the patient to do less of the same. In fact, the entire process of paradoxic-based treatment is directed toward restraining usual attempts to change the problem. Thus, the therapist sets minimum goals and suggests starting slowly (Coyne, 1987).

Soft restraint involves the suggestion or implication that the patient should not change the very behavior that brings him or her to treatment. The therapist might voice concern about the dangers of improvement or the unfavorable consequences of change. Examples of soft restraint are found in our earlier vignettes of the withdrawn 12-year-old and the hostile couple. The 12-year-old is told, in essence, to continue to withdraw. The couple is told to remain hostile toward each other. Although potentially powerful, restraining maneuvers are easily misused because the therapist is saying things that could be interpreted as insulting. Yet, benevolent concern (Haley, 1976), the use of the patient's worldview, and positive connotation help assure that the intervention will succeed.

Hard restraint is the most extreme of the restraining strategies and we now believe that it may be unnecessary. It requires the therapist to suggest that the patient probably cannot change. Greenberg and Pies (1983) reported the following interaction between a patient diagnosed as having a borderline personality disorder and her therapist:

Ms. A.: I want you to know I'm very sick.

Th.: I realize that. I think it's going to be very, very difficult for you to get well.

Ms. A.: I think it's going to be very, very, very, *very* difficult.

Th.: I agree. In fact, I'd say the chances of your getting well are about 1 in 100. (p. 68)

The patient grew increasingly suicidal. Greenberg and Pies (1983) concluded that paradoxical techniques may produce adverse outcomes with borderline patients. They support this conclusion with the psychodynamic idea that in response to paradoxical interventions "the split object-relations unit may be projected onto the therapist" (p. 68). Another explanation is that the intervention failed because the therapist did not attempt to positively connote the patient's symptoms, did not attempt soft restraint, and did not assess or attempt to interdict a problem-maintaining se-

quence. In short, the therapist did not apply the fundamental principles of paradox-based interventions. Nonetheless, in view of the potential abuse of hard restraint, we now recommend against its use.

In summary, we have delineated the central features of paradoxical interventions: (a) an appreciation of the patient's or family's "worldview"; (b) an assessment of problem-maintaining behaviors or interactions; (c) a positive connotation or re-definition of the problem behavior that is either consistent with the patient's worldview or derives directly from the "cultivation" of a useful frame; and (d) behavioral prescription or restraint. The most important guidelines for the implementation of paradoxical interventions is that theory and technique should be inseparable. Before telling patients to change or not to change, the clinician must understand that attempted solutions turn difficulties into problems, that people are more willing to accept suggestions that simply extend their own point of view, and that certain constructions of reality are more useful than others.

CHALLENGES TO CLINICAL AND SOCIAL PSYCHOLOGY

We began this chapter with a review of clinical and social psychological explanations of paradoxical interventions. We will end with implications of these interventions and their constructivist underpinnings for clinical and social psychology. Attempts to "explain" paradox from other perspectives have not been productive. These interventions have their most heuristic explanation in the strategic-constructivist model of behavior change. Clinical and social psychology might profit from a change in perspective. Rather than attempt to explain paradoxical interventions within existing frameworks, existing frameworks might benefit from considering the challenge posed by the efficacy of paradoxical interventions. To this end, we offer some implications for theory, research, and practice.

Clinical Theory and Practice

Discovering Truth

There are several challenges for clinicians. The first has to do with truth and its relation to well-being. Schools of practice as diverse as cognitive behavior therapy and psychoanalysis agree that there is a truth, which if discovered, will enhance emotional well-being. Psychoanalytic truth lies in repressed memories and transference manifestations. Cognitive behavioral truth lies in irrational beliefs. But which truth do we select? Consider the issue of guilt. Cognitive-behavioral truth regarding guilt was depicted by Beck, Rush, Shaw, and Emery (1979):

> Some patients may feel guilty about their thoughts or wishes, rather than actions. A female patient experienced no feelings of guilt about having an affair with a married man, but she felt extremely guilty about wishing that the man's sick wife would die. The therapist pointed out that thoughts are not actions and that since the patient wasn't omnipotent, her wishes could not influence reality. The therapist also explained that her wish, although contrary to her value system, was understandable in view of the patient's desire to marry her lover. (p. 177)

This sounds true enough. But now consider the psychoanalytic truth about guilt put forth by Freud (1955):

> When there is a misalliance between . . . the intensity of the self-reproach and the occasion for it, the layman will say that the affect is too great for the occasion — that it is exaggerated — and . . . that consequently the inference that the person is guilty, is false. On the contrary, the affect is justified. The sense of guilt cannot itself be further criticized. But it belongs to another content, which is unknown and which requires to be looked for. (pp. 175–176)

These contradictory positions both claim to be true. But clinicians need not discover truth. They can construct workable points of view or plausible realities. In fact, one therapist's discovered truth is another's constructed reality. Consider the therapist who tells a patient that his or her guilt is justified. Is he or she a psychoanalyst following Freud's (1955) dictum, or is this a positive connotation and implied restraint? We believe that clinical theory and practice have suffered by insisting that there is truth in a realm of interpersonal relationships. The constructivist underpinnings of paradoxical interventions offers a challenge to this point of view.

Insight Precedes Change

A second challenge to clinical theory derived from paradoxical interventions is that insight or understanding is not a necessary precursor of meaningful behavior change or emotional well-being. With few exceptions, schools of psycho-therapy dictate that for lasting change to occur, an individual must understand the nature of his or her problems. This position, of course, rests on the assumption that there is a reality to understand. Yet as we hope we have demonstrated, significant changes can occur without insight. In fact, insight into former problem-maintaining sequences may only emerge after new behavior. We are not saying simply that insight is unnecessary for behavior change. Behaviorists have known this for decades. We are suggesting that we understand our world in part through our behaviors, and that new and more helpful understandings can derive only from a change in behavior.

The practical implications of this position are significant. It suggests that we need not challenge people's beliefs through interpretation (Strachey, 1934), cognitive restructuring (Meichenbaum, 1977), attribution retraining (Forsterling, 1985), and the like. Such challenges are difficult to enact, because people rightfully protect themselves from what they believe is an assault on their most cherished assumptions (Janoff-Bulman & Timko, 1987), and we interpret our failures to change these assumptions as proof that we must try harder. This may be a quintessential problem-maintaining solution.

Big Problems Require Big Interventions

Implicit in most approaches of psychotherapy is the idea that big problems require massive interventions. Thus, even clinicians who have witnessed the big effects of small interventions (Balint, 1968; Gurman, 1982) insist that the small intervention cannot replace interpretation, working through transference responses, and lifting repressions. At its core, the strategic-constructivist position is a minimalist position (Coyne, 1987) in which the therapist acts as a repairperson not an omnipotent healer (Watzlawick, 1985). Big problems become big because the wrong solution has been applied to one of life's difficulties, and when this solution has been unsuccessful, it is applied even more. Thus, the original difficulty is amplified by a recursive process so that the current problem has little resemblance to the difficulty (Maruyama, 1963; Szykula & Morris, 1986). To intervene effectively, one helps interrupt the attempted solution. Big problems can thus be resolved with small interventions.

The Past Influences the Present

The final implication of paradoxical interventions for clinical theory is that we may be able to change the past by redefining it in the present. Many schools of psychotherapy are based on the logical premise that since a cause must occur prior to an effect, events of the past create current problems. We maintain that current behaviors create current problems. If, however, those current behaviors are guided by premises about the past, we can more benignly redefine the past so as to interpret current problem-maintaining solutions. The vast literature on state-dependent memory (e.g., Singer & Salovey, 1988) documents just how our views of the past can be influenced by our current situation.

Social Psychological Theory and Research

The strategic-constructivist perspective that guides paradoxical interventions also has significant implications for social psychology. We will discuss briefly its implications for the definition of social support, for our understanding of responses to threatening events, and for our perspectives on well-being.

What Is Social Support?

The value of social support as a coping resource has been well documented. Social support appears to buffer individuals from stress (Cohen & Wills, 1985) by meeting a wide range of needs, including intimate interactions, advice, information, tangible aid, and social participation (Barrera, 1981; Cohen & McKay, 1984). Most functional theories define social support as perceived support (Cohen, 1988). Yet the strategic-constructivist perspective suggests that our current definitions of social support may be inadequate to explain certain adaptation-enhancing social interventions.

Consider, for example, an attempt to interrupt a cycle of problem maintenance by someone in a victim's support network. Do we characterize this attempt as supportive only if the victim experiences it as meeting a need? If so, how do we conceptualize defiance-based suggestions by perceptive friends or family members in which a problem-maintaining sequence is successfully interrupted, but the victim believes that he or she is doing well despite, rather than because of, the suggestions?

The concept of worldview also has implications for support-providers. If problem cycles are to be effectively interrupted, comments, suggestions, and other supportive attempts must be framed in a way that is consistent with the victim's worldview. Many well-intended support-providers offer to a victim interpretations of the victimizing event that are offensive because they are not in keeping with an existing worldview. We have found that encouraging a philosophical perspective is appraised as helpful by some victims, but as hurtful by others (Affleck, Tennen, Rowe, Walker, & Higgins, in press). Thus, people who, for example, do not already believe in "God's will" are unlikely to benefit from well-intentioned interpretations that invoke the will of God.

An important reason why intimate support providers may not be helpful in their interactions with victims is that the potential support-provider may have an overriding interest in seeing the victim recover quickly from the crisis (Lehman, Ellard, & Wortman, 1986). In contrast, the strategic perspective suggests that the best start is a slow start and that trying to recover may itself maintain emotional distress. Rather than supplying victims with cognitive coping strategies, which try to place a positive frame on an aversive event, the strategic perspective suggests that a positive connotation be placed on the victim's response to that event. We believe that the concepts of a problem-maintaining solution, worldview, and positive connotation might add a productive perspective to the social support literature.

Responses to Threatening Events and the Nature of Behavior Change

Recent advances in our understanding of how people respond to threatening events pose sobering implications for the process of recovery following victimization. Taylor (Taylor, 1983; Taylor & Brown, 1988) and Snyder (Snyder & Higgins, 1988) provide evidence to support their contention that in the face of threatening information about their physical health or self-esteem, individuals maintain a resilient set of illusions that ward off these threats. Janoff-Bulman (Janoff-Bulman & Timko, 1987) agreed that our assumptions about the nature of things are so robust that they can be shattered only by catastrophic events. Although the resilience of our "assumptive worlds" (Janoff-Bulman & Timko, 1987) or "adaptive illusions" (Taylor & Brown, 1988) have been framed as a protective mechanism, many victims (and nonvictims) maintain assumptive worlds or beliefs that are problem maintaining rather than problem alleviating. If it is true that people effectively ward off threats to these assumptions, then attempts to change maladaptive assumptions by direct challenge may be doomed to failure.

The strategic-constructivist approach to behavior change offers an intriguing alternative. Its minimalist perspective suggests that despite apparent evidence to the contrary, assumptive worlds can change without massive challenge by getting people to behave as if they held a more adaptive view. A change in the assumptive world will follow. Another suggestion is that attempts to directly challenge worldviews (Meichenbaum, 1977; Ellis & Harper, 1975) face a formidable task. Social psychological inquiry in this area has been based on the reasonable assumption that beliefs influence behavior. We might expand our perspective on adapting to threatening events by considering how behavior influences beliefs.

Defining Well-Being

Recent interest by social psychologists in adaptation to negative events raises the question of how to define emotional well-being. In a recent review of social psychological investigations of emotional well-being following threatening events, Tennen and Affleck (in press) found that every study assumed depression to signal maladaptation. A more positive connotation of depression in the face of threat is that the capacity to tolerate these feelings is not only nonpathological, but an emotionally mature response. The inability to experience or bear depression in the face of loss may signal a failure to mobilize available resources after accepting what cannot be controlled (Shur, 1953; Zetzel, 1965). Rather than something to be eliminated, depression becomes something to be experienced.

The Interactional Nature
of Emotional Disorders

As its core, the strategic approach focuses on interactional, problem-maintaining sequences. This poses a challenge to current social psychological theory, which, as Strong (1987) noted, has focused on intrapsychic events. There is a paucity of social psychological studies that view clinical disorders from an interactional perspective (Coyne, 1976; Forrest & Hokanson, 1975; Shaw, 1982), and even fewer consider symptom-maintaining sequences. The strategic-constructivist perspective guiding paradoxical interventions holds considerable promise as a framework from which to view the maintenance and alleviation of emotional disorders.

REFERENCES

Affleck, G., Tennen, H., Rowe, J., Walker, L., & Higgins, P. (in press). Mother's interpersonal relationships and adaptation to hospital and homecare of high risk infants. In R. Antonak & J. Mulick (Eds.), *Transitions in mental retardation: Vol. V. Life Cycles*. Norwood, NJ: Ablex.

Ascher, L. M. (1981). Employing paradoxical intention in the treatment of agoraphobia. *Behavior Research and Therapy, 19*, 533–542.

Ascher, L. M. (1986). Several suggestions for the future of paradox in therapy. *The Counseling Psychologist, 14*, 291–296.

Ascher, L. M., & Efran, J. (1978). The use of paradoxical intention in cases of delayed sleep onset insomnia. *Journal of Consulting and Clinical Psychology, 8*, 547–550.

Ascher, L. M., Schotte, D. E., & Greyson, J. B. (1986). Enhancing effectiveness of paradoxical intention in treating travel restriction in agoraphobia. *Behavior Therapy, 17*, 124–130.

Ascher, L. M., & Turner, R. M. (1979). Paradoxical intention and insomnia: An experimental investigation. *Behavior Research and Therapy, 17*, 408–411.

Ascher, L. M., & Turner, R. M. (1980). A comparison of two methods of the administration of paradoxical intention. *Behavior Research and Therapy, 18*, 121–126.

Balint, M. (1968). *The basic fault: Therapeutic aspects of regression*. London: Tavistock Publications.

Bandler, R., & Grinder, J. (1975). *Patterns of hypnotic techniques of Milton H. Erickson, M.D.* (Vol. 1). Cupertino, CA: Meta.

Barrera, M. (1981). Social support in the adjustment of pregnant adolescents: Assessment issues. In B. H. Gottlieb (Ed.), *Social networks and social support*. Beverly Hills, CA: Sage Publications.

Beck, A. T., Rush, A. J., Shaw, B. F., & Emery, G. (1979). Cognitive therapy of depression. New York: Guilford Press.

Beck, J. T., & Strong, S. R. (1982). Stimulating therapeutic change with interpretations: A comparison of positive and negative connotation. *Journal of Counseling Psychology, 29*, 551–559.

Berger, P., & Luckmann, T. (1966). *The Social Construction of Reality*. Garden City, NY: Doubleday.

Bergman, J. S. (1982). Paradoxical interventions with people who insist on acting crazy. *American Journal of Psychotherapy, 36*, 214–222.

Bogdan, J. L. (1982). Paradoxical communication as interpersonal influence. *Family Process, 21*, 443–452.

Bornstein, P. H., Sturm, C. A., Retzlaff, P. D., Kirby, K. L., & Chong, H. (1981). Paradoxical instruction in the treatment of encopresis and chronic constipation: An experimental analysis. *Journal of Behavior Therapy and Experimental Psychiatry, 12a*, 167–170.

Brehm, J. W. (1966). *A theory of psychological reactance*. New York: Academic Press.

Brehm, S. S. (1976). *The application of social psychology to clinical practice*. Washington, DC: Hemisphere.

Brehm, S. S., & Brehm, J. W. (1981). *Psychological reactance: A theory of freedom and control*. New York: Academic Press.

Cade, B. (1984). Paradoxical techniques in therapy. *Journal of Child Psychology and Psychiatry, 25*, 509–516.

Campbell, D. T., & Stanley, J. C. (1963). *Experimental and quasiexperimental designs for research*. Chicago: Rand McNally.

Chase, J. L., Shea, S. J., & Dougherty, F. I. (1984). The use of paradoxical interventions within a prison facility. *Psychotherapy, 21*, 278–281.

Cliffe, M. G. (1987). Paradoxical psychotherapy in a case of transvestism. *British Journal of Medical Psychology, 60*, 283–285.

Cohen, L., & Ebbeson, E. (1979). Observational goals and schema activation: A theoretical framework for behavior perception. *Journal of Experimental Social Psychology, 15*, 305–329.

Cohen, S. (1988). Psychosocial models of the role of social support in the etiology of physical disease. *Health Psychology, 7*, 269–297.

Cohen, S., & McKay, G. (1984). Social support, stress, and the buffering hypothesis: A theoretical analysis. In A. Baum, S. Taylor, & J. Singer (Eds.), *Handbook of psychology and health* (Vol. IV). Hillsdale, NJ: Lawrence Erlbaum Associates.

Cohen, S., & Wills, T. A. (1985). Stress, social support, and the buffering hypothesis. *Psychological Bulletin, 98*, 1562–1571.

Conoley, C. W., & Garber, R. A. (1985). Effects of reframing and self-control directives on loneliness, depression, and controllability. *Journal of Counseling Psychology, 32*, 139–142.

Corsini, R. J. (1982). The relapse technique in counseling and psychotherapy. *Individual Psychology, 38*, 380–385.

Coyne, J. C. (1976). Toward an interactional description of depression. *Psychiatry, 39*, 28–40.

Coyne, J. C. (1987). The concept of empowerment in strategic therapy. *Psychotherapy, 24*, 539–545.

Coyne, J. C., & Biglan, A. (1984). Paradoxical techniques in strategic family therapy: A behavioral analysis. *Journal of Behavior Therapy and Experimental Psychiatry, 15*, 221–227.

Dattilio, F. M. (1987). The use of paradoxical intention in the treatment of panic attacks. *Journal of Counseling and Development, 66*, 102–103.

Dell, P. F. (1987). Maturana's constitutive ontology of the observer. *Psychotherapy, 24*, 462–466.

Dowd, E. T., & Swoboda, J. S. (1984). Paradoxical interventions in behavior therapy. *Journal of Behavior Therapy and Experimental Psychiatry, 15*, 229–234.

Dunlap, K. (1932). *Habits: Their making and unmaking*. New York: Liveright.

Efran, J. S., Lukens, R. J., & Lukens, M. D. (1988, September–October). Constructivism: What's in it for you. *Family Therapy Networker*, pp. 17–18.

Ellis, A., & Harper, R. (1975). *A new guide to rational living*. Englewood Cliffs, NJ: Prentice-Hall.

Erickson, M. H., & Rossi, E. L. (1975). Varieties of double bind. *American Journal of Clinical Hypnosis, 17*, 143–157.

Erickson, M. H., Rossi, E. L., & Rossi, S. I. (1976). *Hypnotic realities. The induction of clinical hypnosis and forms of indirect suggestion*. New York: Irwington Publishers.

Espie, C. A., & Lindsay, W. R. (1987). Cognitive strategies for the management of severe sleep-maintenance insomnia. *Behavioral Psychotherapy, 15*, 388–395.

Fabry, J. (1982). Some practical hints about paradoxical intention. *International Forum for Logotherapy, 5*, 25–29.

Feldman, D. A., Strong, S. R., & Danser, D. B. (1982). A comparison of paradoxical and nonparadoxical interpretations and directives. *Journal of Counseling Psychology, 29*, 572–579.

Festinger, L. (1957). *A theory of cognitive dissonance*. Stanford, CA: Stanford University Press.

Fisch, R., Weakland, J., & Segal, L. (1982). *The tactics of change: Doing therapy briefly*. San Francisco: Jossey-Bass.

Fiske, S., & Linville, P. (1980). What does the schema concept buy us? *Personality and Social Psychology Bulletin, 6*, 543–557.

Fogel, D. O., & Dyal, J. A. (1983). Paradoxical giving up and the reduction of sleep performance anxiety in chronic insomniacs. *Psychotherapy: Theory, Research, and Practice, 20*, 21–30.

Forrest, M. S., & Hokanson, J. E. (1975). Depression and autonomic arousal reduction accompanying self-punitive behavior. *Journal of Abnormal Psychology, 84*, 346–357.

Forsterling, F. (1985). Attributional retraining: A review. *Psychological Bulletin, 98*, 495–512.

Foucault, M. (1965). *Madness and civilization: A history of insanity in the age of reason*. New York: Random House.

Frankl, V. E. (1960). Paradoxical intention: A logotherapeutic technique. *American Journal of Psychotherapy, 14*, 520–535.

Frankl, V. E. (1966). Logotherapy and existential analysis: A review. *American Journal of Psychotherapy, 20*, 252–260.

Freud, S. (1955). Notes upon a case of obsessional neurosis. In J. Strachey (Ed.), *The standard edition of the complete psychological works of Sigmund Freud* (Vol. 10, pp. 155–318). London: Hogarth. (Original work published 1909)

Gentry, D. (1973). Directive therapy techniques in the treatment of migraine headaches: A case study. *Psychotherapy: Theory, Research, and Practice, 10*, 308–311.

Gertz, H. O. (1966). Experience with the logotherapeutic technique of paradoxical intention in the treatment of phobic and obsessive compulsive patients. *American Journal of Psychiatry, 123*, 548–553.

Gibson, D. L. (1985). Doubting Thomas, the obsessive. *Journal of Psychology and Christianity, 4*, 34–36.

Greenberg, R. P., & Pies, R. (1983). Is paradoxical intention risk free? A review and case report. *Journal of Clinical Psychiatry, 44*, 66–69.

Greene, G. J., & Sattin, D. B. (1985). A paradoxical treatment format for anxiety-related somatic complaints: Four case studies. *Family Systems Medicine, 3*, 197–204.

Gurman, A. S. (1982). Using paradox in psychodynamic marital therapy. *The American Journal of Family Therapy, 10*, 72–74.

Haley, J. (1976). *Problem-solving therapy*. San Francisco: Jossey-Bass.

Hare-Mustin, R. (1975). Treatment of temper tantrums by paradoxical intervention. *Family Process, 14*, 481–486.

Hill, K. A. (1987). Meta-analysis of paradoxical interventions. *Psychotherapy, 24*, 266–270.

Hills, H. I., Gruszkos, J. R., & Strong, S. R. (1985). Attribution and the double bind in paradoxical interventions. *Psychotherapy, 22*, 779–785.

Hoffman, L. (1976). Breaking the homeostatic cycle. In P. J. Guerin (Ed.), *Family therapy: Theory and practice*. New York: Gardner.

Hsu, L. K., & Liberman, S. (1982). Paradoxical intention in the treatment of chronic anorexia nervosa. *American Journal of Psychiatry, 139*, 650–653.

Janoff-Bulman, R., & Timko, C. (1987). Coping with traumatic events: The role of denial in light of people's assumptive world. In C. R. Snyder & C. E. Ford (Eds.), *Coping with negative life events: Clinical and social psychological perspectives* (pp. 135–159). New York: Plenum Press.

Jessee, E. H., Jurkovic, G. J., Wilkie, J., & Chiglinsky, M. (1982). Positive reframing with children: Conceptual and clinical considerations. *American Journal of Orthopsychiatry, 52*, 314–322.

Johnston, T. B., Levis, M., & L'Abate, L. (1986). Treatment of depression in a couple with systematic homework assignments. *Journal of Psychotherapy and the Family, 2*, 117–128.

Jones, C. W. (1986). Frame cultivation: Helping new meanings take root in families. *American Journal of Family Therapy, 14*, 57–68.

Katz, J. (1984). Symptom prescription: A review of the clinical outcome literature. *Clinical Psychology Review, 4*, 703–717.

Kazdin, A. E. (1980). Research design in clinical psychology. New York: Harper & Row.

Kazdin, A. E., & Wilcoxon, L. A. (1976). Systematic desensitization and nonspecific treatment effects: A methodological evaluation. *Psychological Bulletin, 83*, 729–758.

Keeney, B. P. (1987). The construction of therapeutic realities (1987). *Psychotherapy, 24*, 469–476.

Kercher, G., & Smith, D. (1985). Reframing paradoxical psychotherapy. *Psychotherapy, 22,* 786–792.

Kolko, D. J. (1984). Paradoxical instruction in the elimination of avoidance behavior in an agoraphobic girl. *Journal of Behavior Therapy and Experimental Psychiatry, 15,* 51–57.

Kolko, D. J., & Milan, M. A. (1983). Reframing and paradoxical instruction to overcome "resistance" in the treatment of delinquent youths: A multiple baseline analysis. *Journal of Consulting and Clinical Psychology, 51,* 655–660.

Kolko, D. J., & Milan, M. A. (1986). Acceptability of paradoxical interventions: Some paradoxes of psychotherapy research. *Professional Psychology: Research and Practice, 17,* 824–827.

Kraft, R. G., Claiborn, C. D., & Dowd, E. T. (1985). Effects of positive reframing and paradoxical directives in counseling for negative emotions. *Journal of Counseling Psychology, 32,* 617–621.

L'Abate, L. (1986). *Systematic family therapy.* New York: Brunner/Mazel.

Lacks, P., Bertelson, A. D., Gans, L., & Kunkel, J. (1983). The effectiveness of three behavioral treatments for different degrees of sleep onset insomnia. *Behavior Therapy, 14,* 593–605.

Lehman, D. R., Ellard, J. H., & Wortman, C. B. (1986). Social support for the bereaved: Recipients' and providers' perspectives on what is helpful. *Journal of Consulting and Clinical Psychology, 54,* 438–446.

Lopez, F. G., & Wambach, C. A. (1982). Effects of paradoxical and self-control directives in counseling. *Journal of Counseling Psychology, 29,* 115–124.

Madanes, C. (1980). Protection, paradox, and pretending. *Family Process, 9,* 73–85.

Mahoney, M. J. (1980). Psychotherapy and the structure of personal revolutions. In M. J. Mahoney (Ed.), *Psychotherapy Process.* New York: Plenum Press.

Main, F. O., & West, J. D. (1987). Sabotaging adolescent depression through paradox. *Individual Psychology, 43,* 185–191.

Malleson, N. (1959). Panic and phobia. *Lancet, 1,* 225–227.

Maruyama, M. (1963). The second cybernetics: Deviation-amplifying mutual causative processes. *American Scientist, 51,* 164–179.

Massey, R. F. (1986). Paradox, double binding, and counterparadox: A transactional analysis

perspective: A response to Price. *Transactional Analysis Journal, 16,* 24–46.

Maturana, H. R. (1975). The organization of the living: A theory of the living organization. *International Journal of Man-Machine Studies, 7,* 313–332.

Mavissakalian, M., Michelson, L., Greenwald, D., Kornblith, S., & Greenwald, M. (1983). Cognitive-behavioral treatment of agoraphobia: Paradoxical intention vs. self-statement training. *Behavior Research and Therapy, 21,* 75–86.

Meichenbaum, D. (1977). *Cognitive-behavior modification: An integrative approach.* New York: Plenum Press.

Michelson, L., & Ascher, L. M. (1984). Paradoxical intervention in the treatment of agoraphobia and other anxiety disorders. *Journal of Behavior Therapy and Experimental Psychiatry, 15,* 215–220.

Michelson, L., Mavissakalian, M., Marchione, K., Dancu, C., & Greenwald, M. (1986). The role of self-directed in vivo exposure in cognitive, behavioral, and psychophysiological treatments of agoraphobia. *Behavior Therapy, 17,* 91–108.

Milan, M. A., & Kolko, D. J. (1982). Paradoxical intention in the treatment of obsessional flatulence ruminations. *Journal of Behavior Therapy and Experimental Psychiatry, 13,* 167–172.

Mozdzierz, G. J. (1985). The use of hypnosis and paradox in the treatment of a case of chronic urinary retention/"bashful bladder." *American Journal of Clinical Hypnosis, 28,* 43–47.

Ott, B. D., Levine, B. A., & Ascher, L. M. (1983). Manipulating the explicit demand of paradoxical intention instructions. *Behavioral Psychotherapy, 11,* 25–35.

Peterson, L., & Melcher, R. (1981). To change, be yourself: An illustration of paradox in gestalt therapy. *Personnel and Guidance Journal, 60,* 101–103.

Price, R. (1986). On mistaking windmills for giants: A reply to Massey. *Transactional Analysis Journal, 16,* 110–113.

Rabkin, R. (1977). *Strategic psychotherapy: Brief and symptomatic treatment.* New York: Basic Books.

Relinger, H., & Bornstein, P. H. (1979). Treatment of sleep onset insomnia by paradoxical instruction: A multiple baseline design. *Behavior Modification, 3,* 203–222.

Riveros, D. (1984). Maurice and Mr. Sleep. *Inter-*

national Forum for Logotherapy, 7, 55–56.

Rohrbaugh, M., Tennen, H., & Eron, J. (1982). Paradoxical interventions. In J. H. Masserman (Ed.), *Current Psychiatric Therapies* (Vol. 21), 67–74.

Rohrbaugh, M., Tennen, H., Press, S., & White, L. (1981). Compliance, defiance, and therapeutic paradox: Guidelines for strategic use of paradoxical interventions. *American Journal of Orthopsychiatry, 51,* 454–467.

Schwartz, R. C., & Perrotta, P. (1985). Let us sell no intervention before its time. *Family Therapy Networker, 9,* 18–25.

Schwartz, R. M., & Michelson, L. (1987). State-of-mind model: Cognitive balance in the treatment of agoraphobia. *Journal of Orthopsychiatry, 51,* 454–467.

Seltzer, L. F. (1984). The role of paradox in gestalt therapy and technique. *Gestalt Journal, 7,* 31–42.

Selvini-Palazzoli, M. (1974). *Self-starvation: From individual to family therapy in the treatment of anorexia nervosa.* New York: Jason Aronson.

Selvini-Palazolli, M., Cecchin, G., Prata, G., & Boscolo, L. (1978). *Paradox and counterparadox: A new model in the therapy of the family in schizophrenic transaction.* New York: Jason Aronson.

Shaughnessy, M. F. (1984). Humor in logotherapy. *International Forum for Logotherapy, 7,* 106–111.

Shaw, B. (1982). Stress and depression: A cognitive perspective. In R. W. J. Neufeld (Ed.), *Psychological stress and psychopathology* (pp. 125–148). New York: McGraw-Hill.

Shoham-Salomon, V., & Jancourt, A. (1985). Differential effectiveness of paradoxical interventions for more versus less stress-prone individuals. *Journal of Counseling Psychology, 32,* 449–453.

Shoham-Salomon, V., & Rosenthal, R. (1987). Paradoxical interventions: A meta-analysis. *Journal of Consulting and Clinical Psychology, 55,* 22–28.

Shur, M. (1953). The ego and anxiety. In R. M. Lowenstein (Ed.), *Drives, affects, and behavior* (pp. 279–375). New York: International Universities Press.

Singer, J. A., & Salovey, P. (1988). Mood and memory: Evaluating the network theory of affect. *Clinical Psychology Review, 8,* 211–251.

Skynner, A. C. R. (1981). An open systems, group-analytic approach to family therapy. In A. Gurman & D. Kniskern (Eds.), *Handbook of Family Therapy.* New York: Brunner/Mazel.

Sluzki, C. E. (1983). Process, structure and worldviews: Toward an integrated view of systemic models in family therapy. *Family Process, 22,* 469–476.

Sluzki, C. E. (1985). Family consultation in family medicine: A case example. *Family Systems Medicine, 3,* 160–170.

Smith, M. L., & Glass, G. V. (1977). Meta-analysis of psychotherapy outcome studies. *American Psychologist, 32,* 752–760.

Smith, M. L., Glass, G. V., & Miller, T. I. (1980). *The benefits of psychotherapy.* Baltimore, MD: Johns Hopkins University Press.

Snyder, C. R., & Higgins, R. C. (1988). Excuses: Their effective role in the negotiation of reality. *Psychological Bulletin, 104,* 23–35.

Snyder, C. R., Higgins, R. L., & Stucky, R. J. (1983). *Excuses: Masquerades in search of grace.* New York: Wiley-Interscience.

Solyom, L., Garza-Perez, J., Ledwidge, B. L., & Solyom, C. (1972). Paradoxical intention in the treatment of obsessive thoughts: A pilot study. *Comprehensive Psychiatry, 13,* 291–297.

Soper, P. H., & L'Abate, L. (1977). Paradox as a therapeutic technique: A review. *International Journal of Family Counseling, 5,* 10–21.

Strachey, J. (1934). The nature of the therapeutic action of psychoanalysis. *The International Journal of Psychoanalysis, 15,* 127–159.

Strong, S. R. (1984). Experimental studies in explicitly paradoxical interventions: Results and implications. *Journal of Behavior Therapy and Experimental Psychiatry, 15,* 189–194.

Strong, S. R. (1987). Social-psychological approach to counseling and psychotherapy: "A false hope"? *Journal of Social and Clinical Psychology, 5,* 185–194.

Strong, S. R., & Claiborn, C. D. (1982). Change through intersection. *Social psychological processes of counseling and psychotherapy.* New York: John Wiley & Sons.

Szykula, S. A., & Morris, S. B. (1986). Strategic therapy with children: Single subject case-study demonstrations. *Psychotherapy, 23,* 174–180.

Taylor, S. E. (1983). Adjustment to threatening events: A theory of cognitive adaptation. *American Psychologist, 38,* 1161–1173.

Taylor, S. E., & Brown, J. D. (1988). Illusion and well-being: A social psychological perspective on mental health. *Psychological Bulletin, 103*, 193–210.

Tennen, H., & Affleck, G. (in press). Blaming others for threatening events: An empirical and conceptual review. *Psychological Bulletin.*

Tennen, H., Eron, J. B., & Rohrbaugh, M. (1985). Paradox in context. In G. Weeks (Ed.), *Promoting change through paradoxical interventions* (pp. 187–214). Homewood, IL: Dorsey Press.

Tennen, H., Rohrbaugh, M., Press, S., & White, L. (1981). Reactance theory and therapeutic paradox: A compliance-defiance model. *Psychotherapy: Theory, Research, and Practice, 18*, 14–22.

Turner, R. M., & Ascher, L. M. (1982). Therapist factor in the treatment of insomnia. *Behavior Research and Therapy, 20*, 33–40.

Vandereycken, W. (1982). Paradoxical strategies in a blocked sex therapy. *American Journal of Psychotherapy, 36*, 103–108.

von Glaserfeld, E. (1984). An introduction to radical constructivism. In P. Watzlawick (Ed.), *The invented reality* (pp. 17–40). New York: W. W. Norton.

Walker, J. I., & McLeod, G. (1982, July). Group therapy with schizophrenics. *Social Work*, 364–367.

Wathney, S. (1982). Paradoxical interventions in transactional analysis and gestalt therapy. *Transactional Analysis Journal, 12*, 185–189.

Watzlawick, P. (1978). *The language of change: Elements of therapeutic communication*. New York: Basic Books.

Watzlawick, P. (1985). *If you desire to see, learn how to act*. Paper presented at the Evolution of Psychotherapy Conference, Phoenix, AZ.

Watzlawick, P., Beavin, J. H., & Jackson, D. D. (1967). *Pragmatics of human communication*. New York: W. W. Norton.

Watzlawick, P., & Coyne, J. C. (1980). Depression following stroke: Brief problem-focused treatment. *Family Process, 19*, 13–18.

Watzlawick, P., Weakland, J., & Fisch, R. (1974). *Change: Principles of problem formation and problem resolution*. New York: W. W. Norton.

Weakland, J. H., Fisch, R., Watzlawick, P., & Bodin, A. (1974). Brief therapy: Focused problem resolution. *Family Process, 13*, 141–168.

Weeks, G. R., & L'Abate, L. (1982). *Paradoxical psychotherapy: Theory and practice with individuals, couples and families*. New York: Brunner/Mazel.

Weinstein, D. L. (1985). Strategic treatment techniques in alcoholism treatment. Valuable tools for dealing with resistance. *Alcoholism Treatment Quarterly, 1*, 25–35.

West, J. D., Main, F. O., & Zarski, J. J. (1986). The paradoxical prescription in individual psychology. *Individual Psychology, 42*, 214–224.

Westerman, M. A., Frankel, A. S., Tanaka, J. S., & Kahn, J. (1987). Client cooperative interview behavior and outcome in paradoxical and behavioral brief treatment approaches. *Journal of Counseling Psychology, 34*, 99–102.

Weyer, R. (1980). Acquisition and use of social knowledge: Basic postulates and representative research. *Personality and Social Psychology Bulletin, 6*, 558–573.

Williams, J. M., & Weeks, G. R. (1984). Use of paradoxical techniques in a school setting. *The American Journal of Family Therapy, 12*, 47–57.

Wilson, G. L., & Bornstein, P. H. (1984). Paradoxical procedures and single-case methodology: Review and recommendations. *Journal of Behavior Therapy and Experimental Psychiatry, 15*, 195–203.

Wright, R. M., & Strong, S. R. (1982). Stimulating therapeutic change with directives: An exploratory study. *Journal of Counseling Psychology, 29*, 199–202.

Wubbolding, R. E. (1984). Using paradox in reality therapy: I. *Journal of Reality Therapy, 4*, 3–9.

Wubbolding, R. E. (1985). Paradoxical techniques in reality therapy: II. *Journal of Reality Therapy, 4*, 3–7.

Yapko, M. D. (1986). Hypnotic and strategic interventions in the treatment of anorexia nervosa. *American Journal of Clinical Hypnosis, 28*, 224–232.

Yates, J. (1958). The application of learning theory to the treatment of tics. *Journal of Abnormal and Social Psychology, 56*, 175–182.

Zetzel, E. (1965). Depression and the capacity to bear it. In M. Shur (Ed.), *Drives, affects, and behavior* (Vol. 2, pp. 243–274). New York: International Universities Press.

CHAPTER 32

HYPNOSIS, HYPNOTIZABILITY, AND HYPNOTHERAPY

Nicholas P. Spanos

Contemporary research in the area of hypnosis is organized around two competing paradigms, which have been labeled the special process and the sociocognitive perspectives (Spanos, 1986a, 1986b; Spanos & Chaves, 1989). In special process accounts hypnotic behavior is conceptualized as differing fundamentally from ordinary social behavior, and a variety of unusual psychological processes or mechanisms are posited to account for hypnotic responding (e.g., trance state, dissociation). Alternatively, sociocognitive approaches emphasize the continuity between hypnotic enactments and other forms of social behavior, eschew the positing of unusual mental processes, and attempt to account for hypnotic performance by using constructs regularly employed by social psychologists to explain other forms of social behavior (e.g., attitudes, expectations, attributions, role enactment, interpretational set).

The theoretical controversies between special process and sociocognitive formulations have usually been played out in the experimental laboratory where control over relevant antecedent variables can be attained with relative ease. However,

the procedures and ideas associated with the topic of hypnosis began in clinical practice and have been employed for clinical purposes from the late 18th century to the present.

Theoretical controversies have been much less prominent in the clinical than in the experimental literature. Frequently, the literature reviews (e.g., Frankel, 1987; Holroyd, 1980) and clinical reports (e.g., Oystraugh, 1989) in the clinical area begin with the tacit assumptions that the term hypnosis refers to a denotable psychological state, condition, or process, that the presence of this "state" can be readily recognized, that it can be induced with the use of varied sets of rituals labeled as hypnotic induction procedures, and that once induced, the hypnotic state in some manner (often unspecified) facilitates a therapeutic outcome.

All of the above assumptions, however, are open to very serious question. For example, after more than 200 years of research, the term *hypnosis* remains exceedingly vague and continues to be used in contradictory ways by different investigators (Barber, 1969; Barber, Spanos, & Chaves, 1974). Furthermore, physiological, behavioral, and verbal report indicators that unambiguously reflect a hypnotic state (as opposed to relaxation, expectancy-induced attributions, etc.) have yet to be identified (Edmonston, 1980; Radtke & Spanos, 1981; Spanos, 1986b). Most important, it has become increasingly clear that the available data in this research area can be better understood by rejecting rather than accepting outmoded notions such as "hypnotic trance state" (Spanos, 1986b). Explanatory concepts drawn from the contemporary literature in cognitive and social psychology have proven successful in generating and parsimoniously conceptualizing a wide array of laboratory findings concerning hypnotic behavior (Sarbin & Coe, 1972; Spanos & Chaves, 1989). This chapter reviews clinical findings in this area without adopting the tacit assumptions of special process theories.

Before addressing these issues, however, several limitations should be acknowledged. The term *hypnotherapy* does not refer to a delimited and agreed upon set of procedures. In fact, any therapeutic intervention that is defined by the therapist as involving hypnosis can be considered hypnotherapy. In some cases (e.g., Rock, Shipley, & Campbell, 1969) therapists have claimed to be "doing hypnotherapy" even though the treatment was never defined as hypnosis to the clients. Procedures as diverse as psychoanalytically oriented age regression and "uncovering" therapy (Raginsky, 1967), direct suggestion for symptom removal (Gelder, Bancroft, Gath, Johnston, Mathews, & Shaw, 1973), variants of systematic desensitization (Gibbons, Kilbourne, Saunders, & Castles, 1970), and other behavior therapies (Kroger & Fezler, 1976) have all been considered hypnotherapy. However, the only thing tying these diverse procedures together is the name "hypnosis" with its attendant mythologies of altered states and unusual psychological mechanisms.

Most clinical reports of hypnotic treatment are little more than anecdotal case reports or a series of such reports. Oftentimes criteria for inferring improvements are unclear, and frequently there are no control or comparison groups against which to evaluate the effects of the hypnotic treatment. When studies contain serious deficiencies of this kind then it is obviously impossible to draw meaningful conclusions about the effectiveness of hypnotic interventions. Consequently, this review is, for the most part, limited to studies in which the procedures labeled hypnotic are at least minimally described, the hypnotic treatments are compared with some non-

hypnotic psychological treatment and/or to a no-treatment control condition, and quantitative indexes of therapeutic effect are provided.

The effects of hypnotherapy are examined on six disorders. For three of these disorders the problem behaviors are under the client's self-control (i.e., phobic avoidance, smoking, obesity). The remaining three disorders are typically conceptualized as involuntary (asthma, warts, pain; Wadden & Anderton, 1982). These six disorders were chosen because in the case of each there are at least a few studies that compared hypnotic and nonhypnotic treatments and provided information about the relationship between treatment outcome and hypnotizability.

Evidence from laboratory studies strongly indicates that hypnotic procedures are no more effective than various nonhypnotic procedures (e.g., task-motivating instructions) at enhancing responsiveness to a wide range of suggestions (for reviews cf. Barber, 1969; Diamond, 1974; Spanos & Chaves, 1989). Despite this evidence, numerous clinicians argue that hypnotic procedures are more effective than nonhypnotic procedures for treating clinical problems (e.g., Gault, 1988; Graham, 1986), or, relatedly, that therapeutic suggestions and procedures given to hypnotic subjects are more effective than the same procedures given to nonhypnotic subjects (Astor, 1973; Dengrove, 1973). When confronted with the results of laboratory studies it is common for such investigators to argue that clinical hypnosis is somehow different from laboratory hypnosis and, therefore, that experimental findings should not be generalized to the clinic (Gault, 1988; Graham, 1986). One purpose of this review is to examine clinical studies that compared hypnotic and nonhypnotic therapeutic procedures in order to determine whether the available data in fact provide any support for the common contention that hypnotic procedures are more therapeutically beneficial than nonhypnotic ones.

Some investigators (Bowers & Kelly, 1979; Spinhoven, 1988; Wadden & Anderton, 1982) acknowledge that hypnotic procedures are unlikely to be any more effective than nonhypnotic procedures at inducing therapeutic gain. Nevertheless, these investigators contend that hypnotizability (i.e., responsiveness to hypnotic suggestions) is likely to moderate the success of many psychological treatments regardless of whether the treatments are formally labeled as hypnotic. This argument is based on the assumption that hypnotizability constitutes a stable trait or capacity and that subjects who possess high levels of this capacity utilize it in response to the suggestive components of whatever psychological treatment they are administered. For example, Wadden and Anderton (1982) argued that hypnosis should be regarded not in terms of the administration of an induction procedure, but instead "as a stable characteristic (trait) of the individual. . . . If the subject has high [hypnotizability] any communication can be turned into a therapeutic suggestion. Hypnotic ability can be used without labeling the situation as hypnosis . . . " (p. 217).

Despite such assertions, opinions about the relationship between hypnotizability and treatment outcome are divided, and a number of clinicians have argued that hypnotizability is irrelevant to treatment outcome (Barber, 1980; Gill & Brenman, 1959; Swirsky-Sacchetti & Margolis, 1986; Weitzenhoffer, 1953). Moreover, the experimental evidence for a stable trait conceptualization of hypnotizability is rather tenuous. Recent studies (reviewed by Spanos, 1986a) indicate that brief training procedures aimed at enhancing subjects' attitudes toward hypnosis, and teaching them appropriate interpretations of task demands, produce substantial enhancements in hypnotizability. Also, relationships between hypnotizability and responsiveness to at least some types of test suggestions are context dependent (Spanos, 1986b). These relationships appear to depend less on any special abilities or capacities held by high hypnotizables, and more on the degree to which subjects hold similar understandings, motivations, and expectations when enacting the responses to be correlated. A second purpose of this review is to examine the evidence for a relationship between hypnotizability and treatment outcome in each of the disorders under examination, and to determine whether the available data are more consistent with a stable trait or sociocognitive conceptualization of hypnotizability.

PHOBIAS

Hypnotic versus Nonhypnotic Treatments

Eight studies have compared hypnotic procedures with some form of behavior therapy (usually systematic desensitization) in the treatment of phobias. In four of these studies (Gibbons et al., 1970; Lang, 1969; McAmmond et al., 1971; Schubot, 1966) the hypnotic and behavior therapy procedures yielded equivalent reductions in phobic behavior; in three studies (Lang, Lazovik, & Reynolds, 1965; Marks, Gelder, & Edwards, 1968; Melnick & Russell, 1976) the behavior therapy procedure produced significantly greater fear reduction than the hypnotic procedure; and in only one study (O'Brien, Cooley, Ciotti, & Henninger, 1981) did the hypnotic procedure produce greater fear reduction than the behavior therapy procedure. It is important to keep in mind that many of these studies contain methodological difficulties that make any interpretation difficult. For example, O'Brien and colleagues (1981) compared desensitization alone against desensitization plus hypnotic sessions in which subjects were given posthypnotic suggestions to have dreams that would reduce their phobias. The desensitization alone group received four treatment sessions whereas the desensitization plus hypnosis group received nine sessions. In addition, the subjects assigned to the desensitization plus hypnosis group were preselected for high hypnotizability whereas those assigned to the desensitization alone group were unselected with respect to hypnotizability. Given that no subjects were given nonhypnotic dream suggestions and that type of treatment was confounded with both the number of treatment sessions and pretested hypnotizability, it is impossible to draw any conclusions from this study concerning the role played by hypnotic procedures in phobia reduction.

Unfortunately, the confounding of antecedent variables characterizes most of the studies in this area. Only two of the eight studies dealing with phobia reduction (Lang, 1969; Schubot, 1966) avoided such confounding by comparing systematic desensitization in which the initial relaxation procedure was replaced with a hypnotic induction, with standard systematic desensitization. In neither study did the two treatments differ significantly on any fear reduction index. Taken together, the results of these eight studies provide no support for the hypothesis that hypnotic treatments are intrinsically more effective than nonhypnotic treatments in the reduction of phobic behavior, and no support for the related hypothesis that hypnotic procedures facilitate the effectiveness of treatments such as systematic desensitization.

Hypnotizability and Outcome

Three studies assessed the relationship between treatment outcome and hypnotizability in phobic disorders. Horowitz (1970) found that three hypnotic treatments (i.e., recalling fear-related events while relaxed, recalling fear-related events while aroused, posthypnotic suggestion for fear reduction) were equally effective at reducing phobic avoidance behavior. When the subjects in her three treatment groups were combined, Horowitz (1970) found that the correlation between hypnotizability and improvement scores (i.e., posttest approach score − baseline approach score) were consistently low and nonsignificant. Lang (1969) also reported low and nonsignificant correlations between hypnotizability and fear reduction following either systematic desensitization or a hypnotic treatment. On the other hand, Schubot (1966) reported significant correlations between hypnotizability and fear reduction following hypnotic desensitization but no significant correlations between these variables following standard (nonhypnotic) desensitization.

SMOKING

A large number of studies have assessed changes in smoking behavior following hypnotic interventions designed to reduce smoking (see Holroyd, 1980, for a review). The particular kinds of interventions labeled as hypnotic in these studies varied greatly (e.g., imagining aversive consequences to smoking, "ego-enhancing" instructions, explanations of reasons for quitting), as did the number and length of treatment sessions, length of follow-up, drop-out rates, and abstinence rates associated with the various treatments. Furthermore, the large majority of these studies failed to include no treatment control or nonhypnotic comparison groups. Consequently, in these studies it is impossible to evaluate the role of spontaneous remission in smoking reduction or to determine whether the hypnotic components of these various treatments actually contributed anything to the results obtained.

Hypnotic Versus Nonhypnotic Treatments

Eleven studies (Barkley, Hastings, & Jackson, 1977; Hyman, Stanley, Burrows, & Horne, 1986; Francisco, 1972; MacHovec & Man, 1978; Pederson, Scrimgeour, & Lefcoe, 1975, 1979; Perry, Gelfand, & Marcovitch, 1979; Rabkin, Boyko, Shane, & Kaufest, 1984; Shewchuk et al., 1977; Spanos, De Faye, Gabora, & Jarrett, 1989; Williams & Hall, 1988) compared hypnotic with nonhypnotic treatments for smoking cessation. In seven of these studies some variant of a hypnotic cognitive restructuring procedure developed by Spiegel (1970) as a treatment for smoking was compared with various nonhypnotic treatments. In the Spiegel procedure, subjects were relaxed and repeatedly administered a standard set of "therapeutic messages" (e.g., "Smoking is poisonous to your body. You need your body to live."), in a context defined as hypnosis. As originally developed, the procedure involved only a single session, but clients were encouraged to practice self-hypnosis regularly, during which they self-administered the therapeutic messages. Common modifications of this procedure include the use of multiple treatment sessions (Francisco, 1972; Hyman et al., 1986) and group treatment (e.g., Spanos et al., 1989).

In four studies (Francisco, 1972; Hyman et al., 1986; Shewchuk et al., 1977; Spanos et al., 1989) the Spiegel procedure failed to produce significantly greater abstinence or smoking reduction at follow-up than did various nonhypnotic treatments (e.g., the Spiegel instructions defined nonhypnotically, nonhypnotic relaxation, individual counseling, placebo, group behavior modification), and in one of these studies (Spanos et al., 1989) the Spiegel procedure also failed to differ in these regards from no treatment. The Spiegel procedure was more effective than a nonhypnotic comparison treatment in only one study (Williams & Hall, 1988), and in that case the comparison treatment simply involved a one-session group discussion of reasons for smoking and attempts to quit. Finally, Perry et al. (1979) conducted two studies that found that the Spiegel treatment produced significantly lower abstinence rates at follow-up than did rapid smoking treatments. Barkley et al. (1977) also compared a hypnotic cognitive restructuring treatment with nonhypnotic rapid smoking and, in addition, included an attention placebo treatment. Rapid smoking led to significantly greater abstinence than did the placebo, whereas the hypnotic and placebo treatments failed to differ significantly.

Pederson et al. (1975) gave clients either (a) six sessions of group counseling that involved discussion of self-regulation techniques, the relative advantages of quitting versus cutting down, and so forth; (b) group counseling plus a single 1½-hour hypnotic session that emphasized relaxation procedures plus descriptions of the benefits of not smoking; or (c) hypnosis alone. Counseling plus hypnosis led to greater abstinence at follow-up than did either counseling alone or hypnosis alone. Subjects in the latter two treatments failed to differ in abstinence from waiting list controls.

In a second and related study, Pederson et al. (1979) again compared counseling and counseling plus hypnosis. Two other treatments also were compared: counseling plus videotaped hypnosis, in which subjects watched a videotape of others being administered the hypnotic treatment, and counseling plus relaxation hypnosis. In the latter treatment, subjects were administered hypnotic suggestions for relaxation but did not receive any suggestions or instructions concerning smoking cessation. The counseling plus hypnosis treatment produced significantly higher abstinence than did the remaining three treatments. Unfortunately, neither of the Pederson et al. (1975, 1979) studies included subjects who received nonhypnotic suggestions and instructions concerning smoking cessation in combination with counseling. Consequently, the role of hypnotic procedures in producing the superior effects found in the counseling plus hypnosis treatments remains unclear.

MacHovec and Man (1978) compared subjects who received individual hypnotherapy, group hypnotherapy, correct site acupuncture, pseudoacupuncture, and no treatment. The authors did not compute statistical analyses on their findings, but provided enough information about rates of smoking cessation in the various conditions to allow such analyses to be performed. Contrary to the implication given in some review articles (e.g., Holroyd, 1980), subjects in the two hypnosis conditions did not show significantly greater improvement than those given correct site acupuncture (χ^2 [1] = .01, p = not significant).

In summary, the available data provide no support for the notion that hypnotic treatments are more effective than nonhypnotic treatments for reducing smoking. On the other hand, two studies indicate that rapid smoking treatments are more effective than hypnotic cognitive restructuring in this regard. Cognitive restructuring procedures defined as hypnosis were no more effective than nonhypnotic cognitive restructuring in reducing smoking.

Hypnotizability and Outcome

Four studies have assessed relationships between hypnotizability and treatment-induced reductions in smoking. Perry and Mullen (1975) found a significant correlation (r = .32) between hypnotizability assessed before treatment and percentage reduction in smoking following the administration of Spiegel's (1970) one-session hypnotic cognitive restructuring treatment. Subjects also were divided into those who reduced smoking by more than 50% and those who reduced smoking by less than 50%. Significantly more high than low hypnotizables reported on follow-up that they had reduced smoking by more than 50%.

Perry et al. (1979) conducted two studies. As described earlier, the first compared hypnotic cognitive restructuring and rapid smoking. In neither treatment did hypnotizability, tested at follow-up, correlate significantly with smoking reduction. In Perry et al.'s (1979) second study, subjects received hypnotic cognitive restructuring plus rapid smoking. Hypnotizability tested both before treatment and again at follow-up failed to correlate significantly with smoking reduction. Finally, Spanos et al. (1989) found no significant correlation between hypnotizability assessed at follow-up and smoking reduction in either hypnotic or nonhypnotic cognitive restructuring treatments.

Despite their failure to find a relationship between hypnotizability and treatment outcome, Perry et al. (1979) found that the degree to which subjects rated themselves as motivated to stop smoking did predict treatment outcome. In other words, irrespective of hypnotizability, subjects who were strongly motivated to give up smoking benefited from their hypnotic treatment to a greater extent than those with relatively little motivation.

OBESITY

As pointed out by Mott and Roberts (1979), most of the literature dealing with hypnosis and weight loss consists of anecdotal case reports or uncontrolled clinical studies.

Hypnotic Versus Nonhypnotic Treatment

Only five experiments (Devine & Bornstein, 1980; Deyoub & Wilkie, 1980; Goldstein, 1981; Miller, 1975; Wadden & Flaxman, 1981) have compared hypnotic and nonhypnotic treatments for weight loss, and three of these studies compared covert modeling with or without a prior hypnotic induction procedure. Deyoub and Wilkie (1980) found that task-motivating instructions followed by covert modeling produced significantly more weight loss than hypnotic induction followed by covert modeling. On the other hand, neither Devine and Bornstein (1980) nor Wadden and Flaxman (1981) found significant differences between their hypnotic and nonhypnotic covert modeling treatments.

Goldstein (1981) compared a behavior modification treatment with two hypnosis plus behavior modification treatments. One of these hypnosis treatments included an arm levitation suggestion designed to prove to subjects who passed it that they were "really hypnotized." The other hypnotic treatment did not include the arm levitation suggestion. Subjects in the two hypnotic treatments were also administered various cognitive restructuring exercises that were not given to those in the behavior modification alone treatment. Subjects given behavior modification alone or hypnosis without arm levitation plus behavior modification did not differ significantly in weight loss. However, subjects in both of these treatments lost less weight than those in the hypnosis with arm levitation plus behavior modification treatment. Unfortunately, the confounding of the arm levitation suggestion with the hypnotic conditions, coupled with the extra cognitive restructuring exercises given only to the hypnotic groups, makes it impossible to determine the role played by hypnotic procedures in producing the obtained results.

Miller (1975) provided subjects with a treatment aimed at building a positive self-image and teaching good eating habits. For those in one condition the treatment was preceded by a hypnotic induction whereas those in another received the same treatment without an induction. Subjects in a third treatment practiced good eating habits in vivo. At follow-up, subjects in the three treatments failed to differ in weight loss. In summary, the available evidence does not support the hypothesis that hypnotic procedures are more effective than nonhypnotic procedures at inducing weight loss; and there is some evidence to suggest that task-motivating instructions coupled with covert modeling are more effective in this regard than hypnotic induction coupled with covert modeling.

Hypnotizability and Outcome

Table 32.1 outlines the results of studies that have assessed relationships between treatment-induced weight loss and hypnotizability. Andersen (1985) found a significant correlation between these variables for hypnotically treated subjects (nonhypnotic subjects were not tested). Relatedly, Goldstein (1981) reported that subjects who passed the arm levitation suggestion in his hypnosis plus arm levitation treatment lost significantly more weight than those who failed this suggestion.

Deyoub and Wilkie (1980) provided some evidence that the relationship between hypnotizability and treatment-induced weight loss might be dependent on the type of treatment administered. Those investigators found a substantial correlation between hypnotizability and weight loss in their hypnosis plus covert modeling treatment but no significant correlation between these variables in their task motivation plus covert modeling treatment. On the other hand, in six other studies (Cohen & Alpert, 1978; Devine & Bornstein, 1980; Deyoub, 1979a, 1979b; Miller, 1975; Wadden & Flaxman, 1981) no significant relationship was found between hypnotizability and weight loss in either hypnotic or nonhypnotic treatments. Despite a failure to find relationships between hypnotizability and treatment-induced weight loss, it is interesting to note that Wadden and Flaxman (1981) did find a significant correlation between expectancy for treatment success and weight loss in both hypnotic and nonhypnotic treatments.

WARTS

Warts are virally induced benign tumors of the skin (White & Fenner, 1986). Although a large number of anecdotal case reports and clinical studies have employed hypnotic interventions in an attempt to induce wart loss, most of these studies lacked no treatment control groups and, therefore, treatment effects could not be distinguished from spontaneous remission (for reviews see Johnson, 1989; Ullman & Dudek, 1960).

Hypnotic Versus Nonhypnotic Treatments

Only five experiments have compared hypnotic treatments with untreated control conditions and/ or to nonhypnotic treatments for wart regression (Johnson & Barber, 1978; Spanos, Stenstrom, & Johnston, 1988; Spanos, Williams, & Gwynn, 1990; Surman, Gottlieb, Hackett, & Silverberg, 1973). Surman et al. (1973) found that subjects given hypnotic suggestions to imagine that their warts were disappearing lost significantly more warts during a 3-month follow-up period than untreated controls. These findings certainly indicate that some aspect of Surman et al.'s (1973) hypnotic suggestion treatment was effective at inducing wart remission. However, the lack of a group administered suggestions without hypnosis makes it impossible to assess the contribution of the hypnotic procedure to the success of the treatment.

Johnson and Barber (1978) compared hypnotic

Table 32.1. Relationships Between Hypnotizability and Treatment Outcome in Studies Dealing with the Treatment of Phobias, Smoking, Obesity, Asthma, Warts, and Pain

STUDY	SIGNIFICANCE OF RELATIONSHIP	HYPNOTIZABILITY ASSESSMENT
Phobias		
Horowitz (1970)	−	S
Lang (1969)	−	S
Schubot (1966)	+ (hypnosis) − (nonhypnosis)	S
Smoking		
Perry & Mullen (1975)	+	NS
Perry et al. exp. 1 (1979)	−	S
Perry et al. exp. 2 (1979)	−	S
Spanos et al. (1989)	−	S
Obesity		
Andersen (1985)	+	S
Devine & Bornstein (1980)	−	S
Deyoub (1979a)	−	S
Deyoub (1979b)	−	S
Deyoub & Wilkie (1980)	+ (hypnosis) − (task-motivation)	S
Goldstein (1981)	+	NS
Miller (1975)	−	S
Wadden & Flaxman (1981)	−	S
Asthma		
Collison (1975)	+	NS
White (1961)	−	NS
Warts		
Asher (1956)	+	NS
Sinclair-Gieben & Chalmers (1959)	+	NS
Spanos et al. exp. 1 (1988)	−	S
Spanos et al. exp. 2 (1988)	−	S
Surman et al. (1973)	−	NS
Ullman & Dudek (1960)	+	NS
Pain		
Andreychuk & Skriver (1975)	+	NS
Barber (1976)	−	S
Cedercreutz et al. (1976)	+	NS
Cedercreutz (1978)	+	NS
Crowley (1980)	−	S
Friedman & Taub (1984)	+	S
Gillett & Coe (1984)	−	S
Gottfredson (1973)	+	S
Hilgard & Le Baron (1984)	+	S
Nolan et al. (1989)	−	S
Perchard (1960)	+	NS
Reeves et al. (1983)	+	S
Rock et al. (1969)	−	NS
Samko & Schoenfeld (1975)	−	S
Schafer (1975)	+	NS
Snow (1979)	−	S
Spinhoven et al. (1985)	+	S
Spinhoven et al. (1988)	−	S
Stam et al. (1984)	+	S
Venn (1987)	−	S
Wall & Womack (1989)	−	S
Smith, Womack & Chen (1989)	−	S

Note. + =significant relationship between hypnotizability and treatment outcome; − =no significant relationship between these variables; S=hypnotizability was assessed with a standardized, multi-item hypnotizability scale; NS=the procedure for assessing hypnotizability is unknown, involved only a single item, or involved an unknown or nonstandardized number of items.

and nonhypnotic suggestions for wart regression. However, so few subjects in either treatment lost warts that statistical comparisons could not be meaningfully conducted. Because this study failed to include a no-treatment control group, spontaneous remission could not be excluded as the cause of the small amount of wart loss that was obtained.

Two studies (Spanos et al., 1988, experiment 1; Spanos et al., 1989) found that subjects given hypnotic suggestions lost significantly more warts than those given either placebos or no treatment. In addition, Spanos et al. (1990) found that their hypnotic suggestion subjects lost significantly more warts than those who self-administered a commercially available nonprescription topical salicylic acid compound.

Spanos et al. (1988, experiment 2) compared hypnotic and nonhypnotic suggestions that asked subjects to imagine their warts tingling and disappearing. Hypnotic induction plus suggestion, nonhypnotic relaxation instructions plus suggestion, and suggestion alone were equally effective at inducing wart remission within a 6-week follow-up period, and more effective in this regard than no treatment. In short, hypnotic suggestions to imagine warts disappearing appear to be more effective than placebo treatments or no treatment at inducing wart loss. However, suggestions to imagine without any accompanying hypnotic procedures appear to be as effective in this regard as hypnosis plus suggestion.

Hypnotizability and Outcome

Three studies reported that highly hypnotizable subjects treated with hypnotic suggestions lost more warts than corresponding low hypnotizables (Asher, 1956; Sinclair-Gieben & Chalmers, 1959; Ullman & Dudek, 1960). On the other hand, Tenzel and Taylor (1969) reported that none of 20 highly hypnotizable subjects treated with hypnotic suggestions exhibited wart regression and three other studies (Spanos et al., 1988, experiments 1 & 2; Surman et al., 1973) found no significant correlation between wart loss and hypnotizability in subjects treated with hypnotic suggestions or suggestions alone.

ASTHMA

Although the etiology of asthma remains a controversial topic, there is general agreement that psychological factors are linked to this disorder (Creer, 1982). A large number of psychological interventions have been employed to treat this disorder, and claims of success have been registered in numerous studies, including some that employed hypnotic interventions (for reviews see Creer, 1982; DePiano & Salzberg, 1979; Purcell & Weiss, 1970). Nevertheless, most such studies suffer serious methodological problems that suggest caution against overoptimistic interpretation. With respect to hypnotic treatments, for example, DePiano and Salzberg (1979) pointed out that, "When self-report is used, most investigators report an improvement in the patient's symptoms. However, physiological measures show more equivocal results" (p. 1233). The importance of using physiological as opposed to self-report criteria when evaluating therapeutic reduction in asthmatic symptomatology was illustrated by Rubinfeld and Pain (1976). Those investigators found that patients who indicated by self-report that they were asthma free were actually exhaling less than 50% of what should have been their normal expiration rates.

Hypnotic Versus Nonhypnotic Treatments

Only two studies (Maher-Loughman, 1970; Moore, 1965) have compared hypnotic with nonhypnotic psychological interventions for asthma. Maher-Loughman (1970) gave subjects in one group extensive training in hypnotic and self-hypnotic procedures that included relaxation and ego-enhancing suggestions and information aimed at enhancing expectations of treatment success. Nonhypnotic subjects received progressive relaxation and breathing exercises. Males reported equivalent improvements under both treatments, but females reported significantly more improvement with the hypnotic intervention. Objective indicators of respiratory functioning were not assessed. The reasons for the marked sex difference in response to the two treatments are unclear. Furthermore, the confounding of the hypnotic treatment with ego-enhancing and expectancy suggestions precludes any conclusion about the role of hypnotic procedures per se in determining treatment outcomes. The failure to assess physiological indicators of respiratory functioning also suggests caution when evaluating these findings.

Moore (1965) treated asthmatic patients with either relaxation, relaxation (hypnosis) plus suggestions for improvement, or systematic desensitization. Patients in all three treatments reported equivalent levels of improvement, but only those treated by systematic desensitization exhibited improvement on objective indices of respiratory functioning.

Hypnotizability and Outcome

No studies have assessed relationships between degree of improvement following hypnotic interventions for asthma and hypnotizability as assessed by standardized scales. However, two studies assessed relationships between such improvement and ratings of patients' "hypnotic depth." Collison (1975) retrospectively analyzed the medical records of 121 asthmatic patients who had been treated with hypnotic treatments designed to enhance coping and relaxation. Patients rated as relatively good hypnotic subjects were classified as exhibiting substantially more improvement than those who were rated as poor hypnotic subjects. Unfortunately, the same investigator who performed the hypnotic treatments also rated hypnotic depth and retrospectively rated degree of improvement. Therefore, the possibility that the pattern of obtained results was influenced by subtle experimenter biases cannot be ruled out.

White (1961) reported that ratings of "hypnotic depth" were unrelated to improvement on either self-report or physiological indices in asthma patients treated with hypnotic suggestions. Unfortunately, White's (1961) study suffered from a small sample size and in both the Collison (1975) and White (1961) studies the reliability and validity of the procedures used to rate "hypnotic depth" are unknown.

PAIN

A large number of studies (reviewed by Tan, 1982; Turk, Meichenbaum, & Genest, 1983) now indicate that various cognitive-behavioral interventions (e.g., coping imagery suggestions, electromyogram biofeedback, relaxation training) can engender reports of reduced pain and distress for at least some kinds of acute and chronic clinical pain syndromes. A number of these studies compared hypnotic and nonhypnotic treatments and these will be discussed in terms of the pain syndromes toward which the treatments were directed.

Headache

Seven controlled outcome studies have compared hypnotic interventions with various nonhypnotic behavioral and/or cognitive treatments for the control of migraine, chronic tension, or mixed migraine/tension headaches (Andreychuk & Skriver, 1975; Friedman & Taub, 1984, 1985; Nolan, Hayward, Scott, & Spanos, 1989, experiments 1 & 2; Schlutter, Golden, & Blume, 1980; Spinhoven, Van Dyck, Zitman, & Linssen, 1985; Spinhoven, Linssen, Van Dyck, & Zitman, 1988). Four of these studies failed to include no treatment control conditions (Andreychuk & Skriver, 1975; Schlutter et al., 1980; Spinhoven et al., 1985; Spinhoven et al., 1988). All four found no differences between the hypnotic and nonhypnotic treatments that were compared, but the lack of no treatment control groups makes it unclear whether the treatments were equally effective or whether they all simply failed to influence headache activity.

Friedman and Taub (1984, 1985) reported that thermal biofeedback, relaxation alone, hypnotic relaxation plus thermal imagery, and hypnotic relaxation alone were all equally effective, and more effective than no treatment, at reducing the self-reported frequency and intensity of migraine headaches. Nolan et al. (1989, experiment 1) found that two sessions of hypnotic induction plus training in the use of coping imagery and two sessions of nonhypnotic imagery training were equally effective, and more effective than no treatment, at reducing self-reports of mixed migraine/tension headache both at posttreatment and at 3-months' follow-up. In a second experiment Nolan et al. (1989, experiment 2) employed the same treatments for chronic tension headache but, in addition, included a psychological placebo treatment and gave all subjects four rather than two treatment sessions. Both the hypnotic and nonhypnotic imagery group subjects reported equivalent reductions in headache activity from the baseline to the posttreatment intervals. However, at the 4-month follow-up interval, neither treatment any longer differed from baseline in reported headache activity. Placebo subjects reported no changes in headache activity across assessment intervals, while no treatment control subjects reported significant increments in headache across assessment intervals.

Anderson, Basker, and Dalton (1975) compared at least six sessions of hypnotic suggestions for enhanced coping, ego-strengthening, relaxation, and instructions for self-hypnosis with the administration of vasoconstrictive ergotamine medication for the treatment of migraine headache. Subjects were randomly assigned to the two treatments and followed at monthly intervals for a year. The assessment of headache activity was based on therapists' reports of patients' retrospective monthly reports of their headache activity. The hypnotic treatment was associated with significantly greater reported headache reduction than the medication treatment. Unfortunately, the retrospective nature of patients' monthly pain reports leaves open the possibility that memory distortions may have influenced the accuracy of subjects' pain estimates. Furthermore, the failure of Anderson et al. (1975) to include a group of non-hypnotic patients administered the same treatment suggestions as given to the hypnotic group means that the role of hypnotic procedures in producing the obtained results cannot be evaluated.

Taken together, the available data in this area indicate that cognitive restructuring procedures administered in a hypnotic context may sometimes be more effective than vasoconstrictive medication at controlling migraine headache. However, these data provide no support whatsoever for the hypothesis that hypnotic cognitive restructuring procedures are more effective than corresponding nonhypnotic procedures in reducing migraine or tension headache.

Obstetrical Pain

Hypnotic (and earlier mesmeric) procedures have been employed to aid in the alleviation of childbirth pain for well over a century (D'Eon, 1989). Nevertheless, there appear to be only five published studies that compared hypnotic and nonhypnotic interventions in this regard, and that provided at least rudimentary quantitative information concerning pain.

In the oldest of these studies, Perchard (1960) compared three parturient-mother groups. One group was administered information about childbirth plus three hypnotic sessions that emphasized relaxation and that included suggestions for pain reduction and comfort during delivery; a second group received educational talks about childbirth and in some cases nonhypnotic relaxation exercises; and a third group received no treatment. Unfortunately, the mothers' reports of pain during labor were not assessed until a week following delivery, and therefore, the validity of these reports is compromised. Perchard (1960) did not report statistical analyses on his data. The data provided suggest that the patients who received hypnosis or education/information reported less pain than controls, but in the absence of statistical analyses the findings remain unclear.

Davidson (1962) reported that six sessions of group self-hypnosis were more effective at reducing reported pain than either six sessions of Reid's prepared childbirth training or no special training other than "mothercraft." Unfortunately, instead of random assignment, subjects were allowed to choose their own treatment group. Moreover, only the hypnotic treatment included suggestions for pain reduction. The confounding of hypnotic and suggestion procedures coupled with subjects' self-selecting their own treatment makes it impossible to assess whether hypnotic procedures played a role in the results obtained.

Two studies (Davidson, Garbett, & Tozer, 1985; Rock, Shipley, & Campbell, 1969) assigned subjects to either hypnotic or standard antenatal preparation treatments. In both studies the hypnotic treatment included suggestions for relaxation and comfort during delivery. Rock et al. (1969) found that hypnotic subjects rated their delivery as less painful than did those given antenatal preparation. Davidson et al. (1985) found that hypnotic subjects rated the first stage of labor as less painful than did subjects given antenatal preparation. However, the subjects in these groups failed to differ significantly in their pain ratings of the second stage of labor. Once again, the confounding of hypnotic procedures with suggestions for analgesia makes it impossible to determine the role of hypnotic procedures in producing the findings of either study.

Finally, Venn (1987) compared parturient-mothers who self-selected Lamaze childbirth training, hypnotic treatment plus Lamaze training, or hypnotic treatment alone. The hypnotic treatment included an induction procedure and guided imagery suggestions for analgesia. Subjects in the three conditions failed to differ significantly in either self-reports or nurses' reports of labor pain, or in medication usage.

Cancer Pain

Six studies compared hypnotic and nonhypnotic interventions for the alleviation of pain associated with cancer or its treatment. Three of these studies (viz., Katz, Kellerman, & Ellenberg, 1987; Wall & Womack, 1989; Zelter & LeBaron, 1982) assessed pain in children undergoing bone marrow aspiration procedures, and three (Reeves, Redd, Storm, & Minagaua, 1983; Spiegel & Bloom, 1983; Syrjala, Cummings, Donaldson & Chapman, 1987) assessed pain relief in adults.

In a well-known study, Zelter and LeBaron (1982) compared pain reduction during bone marrow aspiration in a control group of children that received supportive counseling, distraction, and deep breathing procedures with a hypnotic group that received the same kinds of supports along with suggestions to carry out pleasant and interesting guided imagery. Children in both conditions exhibited reductions in pain, but hypnotic subjects showed greater reductions than controls. Although Zelter and LeBaron (1982) concluded that "hypnosis is more effective than nonhypnotic techniques" (p. 1035), the failure of these investigators to administer guided imagery procedures to their nonhypnotic as well as their hypnotic subjects precludes acceptance of this interpretation.

Katz et al. (1987) compared a group of children trained in hypnotic and self-hypnotic procedures with a group that received nondirected play sessions that controlled for the amount of attention and time the children were given by a professional. Girls did somewhat better in the hypnotic condition, whereas boys did somewhat better in the play condition. Overall, however, this study clearly indicates no superiority for hypnotic analgesia as compared with a control play condition in children undergoing a noxious medical treatment.

Wall and Womack (1989) taught children in a nonhypnotic treatment the use of active distraction strategies, while children in a hypnotic group received training in relaxation and guided imagery. The two treatments were associated with equivalent reductions in pain during the bone marrow aspirations.

The three studies that compared hypnotic and nonhypnotic interventions for the relief of cancer-related pain in adults have been reviewed in detail by Stam (1989). Spiegel and Bloom (1983) compared three groups of women with breast cancer. Those in one group constituted a no-treatment control sample, those in another condition received group therapy, and those in a third received group therapy plus a self-hypnosis exercise. Two of four self-reported pain measures were significantly reduced in the combined group therapy conditions as opposed to control condition. However, only one of the four pain report measures was reduced in the group therapy plus hypnosis condition as compared with the group therapy alone condition. Stam (1989) has detailed problems with Spiegel and Bloom's (1983) analyses of data that make interpretation of these findings difficult. In addition, Spiegel and Bloom (1983) confounded number of treatments (group therapy plus hypnotic treatment) with the use of a hypnotic procedure. Thus, it is impossible to determine whether the hypnotic procedures played any role in the results obtained.

Syrjala et al. (1987) compared hypnotic, cognitive-behavioral, therapist contact, and no-treatment control conditions in cancer patients who experienced oral pain as a side effect of chemotherapy and radiation treatments. The authors concluded that the hypnotic treatment was more effective in alleviating pain than the cognitive behavioral treatment. However, statistical analyses were carried out only after dropping the data from control subjects. As pointed out by Stam (1989), "It seems likely that, if the no treatment control group were included, it would have washed out *any* treatment effects" (p. 322).

Reeves et al. (1983) compared a group given two sessions of hypnotic training and a no-treatment control group in the reduction of pain induced by hyperthermia treatments. For all subjects pain was assessed on both pretreatment (baseline) and posttreatment trials. Hypnotic subjects exhibited significantly greater pain reduction than controls. Unfortunately, subjects administered nonhypnotic procedures for pain reduction were not included in the study.

Other Pain Syndromes

In a methodologically sound study, Stam, McGrath, and Brooke (1984) compared hypnotic and nonhypnotic cognitive-behavioral pain management treatments for the reduction of tempromandibular joint pain. Subjects were randomly assigned to treatments, and no treatment control subjects also were included. Subjects in the hypnotic and nonhypnotic treatments reported significant pain decrements of equivalent magnitude, and greater pain decrements than control subjects.

Snow (1979) compared one session of hypnotic suggestions for analgesia with an oral placebo for the reduction of chronic pain in male paraplegics. Subjects in the two treatments failed to differ significantly in degree of pain reduction. Crowley (1980) compared a single session of hypnotic suggestions for analgesia with local chemical analgesia on reductions in acute pain associated with podiatric surgery. Hypnotic analgesia was significantly less effective than the local analgesic at reducing reported pain. Werbel (1963) gave hypnotic suggestions for comfort, relaxation, and painless defecation to one group of patients who underwent surgery for the removal of hemorrhoids and no treatment to control patients who underwent the same type of surgery. Patients who received the hypnotic treatment required less postoperative medication and reported less pain during defecation than controls. Unfortunately, patients were not randomly assigned to groups. More important, the failure of Werbel (1963) to include patients who received nonhypnotic suggestions for analgesia makes it impossible to evaluate the role of hypnotic procedures in the results obtained.

Several investigators (Gault, 1988; Perry, Laurence, & Nadon, 1988) have employed anecdotal reports to argue that hypnotic procedures can greatly reduce or eliminate the pain of major surgery. However, these anecdotes contain so many methodological limitations that no firm conclusions concerning this topic are possible (Spanos & Chaves, 1989). Moreover, there are also anecdotal reports that indicate that nonhypnotic suggestions can be employed to reduce surgical pain (cf. Chaves, 1989, for a review). Controlled studies that compare hypnotic and nonhypnotic procedures for reducing the pain of major surgery are nonexistent.

Two studies (Patterson, Questad, & de Lateur, 1989; Wakeman & Kaplan, 1978) compared patients who received hypnotic analgesia plus analgesic medication during the treatment of burns with patients who received medication alone. Wakeman and Kaplan (1978) reported that hypnotic subjects required less analgesic medication than controls. Patterson et al. (1989) found that hypnotic subjects reported significant pain reductions (relative to pretreatment baseline levels), whereas medication alone controls reported no significant changes in pain. Unfortunately, neither study included patients who received nonhypnotic suggestions for pain relief. Furthermore, patients in the Patterson et al. (1989) study were not randomly assigned to treatments and those in the hypnotic group differed from those in the control group on a number of potentially important variables (e.g., controls suffered burns on significantly larger portions of their bodies than did hypnotic subjects).

The available data indicate that interventions labeled as hypnotic are often helpful in reducing the pain associated with a wide range of medical conditions and medical procedures. On the other hand, none of this evidence suggests that the hypnotic aspects of these interventions (i.e., administration of a hypnotic induction procedure) are important in facilitating pain reduction. On the contrary, the evidence from the best controlled studies (e.g., Stam et al., 1984) indicates that nonhypnotic suggestive treatments are as effective as hypnotic ones at producing reductions in clinical pain.

Hypnotizability and Outcome

Table 32.1 summarizes the results of 22 studies that assessed the relationship between hypnotizability and treatment-induced reductions in pain. Although 11 of these studies reported significant relationships between these variables, in 11 other studies the relationship between pain reduction and hypnotizability failed to attain significance. Furthermore, in several of the studies that reported significant relationships between these variables, methodological considerations complicate the interpretation of the findings.

Friedman and Taub (1985) reported that high hypnotizables given various hypnotic treatments reported significant decrements in headache pain at some posttreatment intervals, whereas low hypnotizables reported no significant decrements at any interval. However, while the high hypnotizables in this study were given hypnotic procedures without any unusual preliminary instructions, the low hypnotizables were instructed to simulate hypnosis. The experimental literature on hypnosis has made it abundantly clear that the effects of hypnotic procedures are often altered dramatically when subjects are instructed to simulate hypnosis (cf. Spanos, 1986b). Consequently, the confounding of hypnotizability level with instructions to simulate makes the high/low hypnotizability differences obtained by Friedman and Taub (1985) uninterpretable.

Schafer (1975) reported a strong relationship between hypnotically induced relief of pain in 20 burn patients and hypnotizability as assessed by response to a nonstandardized series of suggestions. Six of Schafer's (1975) patients (33.3%) reported no pain relief following the hypnotic intervention, and five of these six nonresponders also attained low hypnotizability scores. (Neither Schafer [1975] nor Rock et al. [1969] presented the correlation between hypnotizability and pain scores. I computed these correlations from the raw data presented in each article. This correlation was substantial and highly significant in the case of Schafer's data [$r = .77$], but failed to attain significance in the case of Rock et al.'s data.)

However, most of these nonresponders also were described as being too heavily drugged or in too high a state of panic to attend to the hypnotic analgesia procedures. If drugs and panic prevented these patients from attending to hypnotic suggestions for relaxation and pain relief, then it is likely that these same factors also prevented them from attending to the test suggestions used to assess hypnotizability. In short, the strong correlation between hypnotizability and pain relief obtained by Schafer (1975) may have been produced artifactually by high levels of drugs and panic that eliminated responsiveness to both hypnotic analgesia procedures and hypnotizability test suggestions in a subsample of his patients.

Andreychuk and Skriver (1975) combined into a single group headache patients who had been treated with a hypnotic procedure, alpha biofeedback, or temperature biofeedback. For the group as a whole they found a significant relationship between degree of headache reduction and hypnotizability. However, interpretation of this finding is complicated by several factors. To begin with, in all treatments baseline levels of pain were substantially higher in high than in low hypnotizables. Furthermore, the data presented in the article make it apparent that, despite an overall significant effect, the strength of the relationship between headache reduction and hypnotizability differed markedly among these three treatments. Curiously, this relationship was weakest and clearly nonsignificant in the hypnotic treatment. Hypnotic high hypnotizables reduced headache activity by 38.8% while the reduction for low hypnotizables was almost as large at 33.4%.

Cedercreutz, Lahteenmaki, and Tulikoura (1976) reported that "depth of hypnosis" as rated by the hypnotist on a 4-point scale correlated moderately ($r = .44$) with headache relief following hypnotic treatment. However, this correlation reflected the fact that patients classified as showing zero depth (12% of the sample) reported no relief whatsoever from the hypnotic treatment. There were no differences in treatment efficacy among subjects classified as exhibiting "light," "medium," or "deep" levels of hypnotic responsiveness.

The findings of both the Andreychuk and Skriver (1975) and Cedercreutz et al. (1976) studies, along with those from the 11 studies that found no significant relationship between hypnotizability and treatment-induced pain reduction, appear to contradict Hilgard's (1977) contention that large suggestion-induced reductions in

pain are attainable only by highly hypnotizable subjects.

OVERVIEW AND CONCLUSIONS

Hypnotic Versus Nonhypnotic Treatments

The clinical studies reviewed in this chapter vary substantially in quality. Many are difficult to interpret because they lack no treatment control groups and/or because they confound the administration of hypnotic procedures with particular suggestions, instructions, or procedures that were not administered to those who received nonhypnotic treatments. Despite such difficulties, and despite the fact that these studies dealt with the treatment of six different disorders, the results of studies that compared hypnotic and nonhypnotic psychological treatments show a surprising degree of consistency. Regardless of the disorder treated, the most common outcome of the studies was a failure to find significant differences between the particular hypnotic treatment under investigation and the nonhypnotic psychological treatment or treatments against which it was compared. A number of studies found that hypnotic treatments were less efficacious than nonhypnotic comparison treatments, and a few found that hypnotic treatments were more efficacious. However, studies that found a difference between hypnotic and nonhypnotic treatments invariably involved a confounding of antecedent variables. Those relatively few studies that administered the same therapeutic instructions and suggestions to both hypnotic and nonhypnotic subjects reported equivalent levels of therapeutic gain for both treatments.

Obviously, the findings reviewed in this chapter do not preclude the possibility that some clients may benefit more from hypnotic than nonhypnotic treatments. These findings do suggest, however, that any such benefit is likely to be due to variables such as the attitudes and expectations that subjects hold about hypnotic treatments rather than to any intrinsic effect (i.e., a hypnotic trance state) produced by hypnotic procedures. For example, Lazarus (1973) randomly assigned patients who requested hypnosis either to a behavior therapy procedure defined as hypnosis or a behavior therapy procedure defined as relaxation. Patients who reported no preference for either treatment also were assigned to the hypnotic and relaxation conditions.

The clients who requested and received the hypnotic treatment showed more improvement than those who requested hypnosis but received relaxation. However, the hypnotic and relaxation treatments did not produce differential improvement for clients who showed no initial preference for either treatment. Also relevant to this issue are the results of studies that found that therapeutic outcome in both hypnotic and nonhypnotic treatments was predicted by subjects' expectations of success and by their motivations to change problem behaviors rather than by hypnotizability (Perry et al., 1979; Wadden & Flaxman, 1981).

The effects of motivations, attitudes, and expectations on treatment success can, of course, cut both ways. For some clients the definition of the situation as hypnosis may engender fear and negative attitudes that can interfere with treatment. For example, Hendler and Redd (1986) found that cancer patients undergoing chemotherapy were significantly more likely to refuse participation in a relaxation treatment for nausea control when the treatment was defined as hypnosis as opposed to relaxation.

Taken together, the available data provide no support for the hypothesis that hypnotic procedures are intrinsically more effective than nonhypnotic procedures at inducing therapeutic gain, or for the related hypothesis that the addition of hypnotic procedures augments the potency of therapeutic instructions or suggestions. In short, the results obtained in these clinical studies are consistent with the large body of findings in the experimental literature that indicates that equivalent levels of responsiveness are attained when hypnotic subjects and motivated nonhypnotic subjects are administered the same suggestions.

Hypnotizability and Therapeutic Gain

The available data concerning relationships between hypnotizability and therapeutic gain are much less consistent than those that deal with the therapeutic efficacy of hypnotic versus nonhypnotic procedures. For each disorder examined, at least one study reported a significant relationship between some index of hypnotizability and therapeutic gain. Overall, however, the number of studies that found no relationship between these variables outnumbered those that found a relationship.

Both Wadden and Anderton (1982) and Spinhoven (1988) hypothesized that hypnotizability would be related to therapeutic outcome when the disorders treated were involuntary, but would be unrelated to hypnotizability when the problem behaviors were self-initiated or under voluntary control. Table 32.2 divides the studies reviewed in this chapter into those that treated the three "involuntary" disorders (i.e., asthma, warts, pain) and those that treated the more "voluntary" problem behaviors (i.e., phobic avoidance, smoking, overeating). Although significant relationships between treatment outcome and hypnotizability were more often found for the involuntary than the voluntary disorders, this difference did not attain statistical significance (χ^2 [1] = 1.88, p = not significant). Even in the case of the involuntary disorders, hypnotizability and treatment outcome failed to correlate significantly in half of the studies.

These findings are difficult to reconcile with a stable trait conceptualization of hypnotizability. If, for example, high hypnotizability scores reflect high levels of a stable capacity that augments the effects of therapeutic suggestions for, say, wart regression, then it is difficult to explain why in half of the available studies wart regression failed to correlate significantly with hypnotizability.

A sociocognitive alternative to the stable trait hypothesis suggests that the degree of relationship between hypnotizability and therapeutic outcome may be related to the expectations, understandings, and motivations that patients develop about these phenomena. For example, patients who are led to believe that their hypnotizability test performance is relevant to how well they will respond to treatment may well develop different motivations and expectations about both hypnotizability testing and treatment outcome than do patients who see their response to treatment as unrelated to their hypnotizability test performance. For instance, in patients who are led to construe hypnotizability and response to treatment as related, the attainment of a low hypnotizability score may engender expectations of low treatment success and a loss of motivation to follow treatment instructions and suggestions. Alternatively, the attainment of a high hypnotizability score by such patients may bolster their confidence in the success of the treatment and enhance the likelihood that they will abide by the treatment regimen provided. In short, contextual factors that lead subjects to construe their performance on hypnotizability tests as predictive of their response to treatment may play an important role in creating a correlation between these variables.

Standardized hypnotizability test situations differ from hypnotherapeutic treatment situations in a number of important respects. Frequently, hyp-

Table 32.2. Frequencies With Which Relationships Between Hypnotizability and Treatment Outcome Were Significant or Nonsignificant in Voluntary and Involuntary Diosorders

	TYPES OF DISORDERS	
	VOLUNTARY	INVOLUNTARY
Significant	5	15
Nonsignificant	12	15

Note. χ^2 (1)=1.88, p=not significant.

notizability is tested by someone other than the therapist in a context that is clearly defined to patients as not part of their therapy. Consequently, the patterns of rapport that develop between hypnotherapists and patients and that play a major role in motivating how patients respond to treatment are likely to be very different from the patterns of rapport that develop between patients and whoever tests them for hypnotizability using standardized scales. Moreover, the specific test suggestions employed on standardized scales may sometimes bear little resemblance to the suggestion/instruction procedures that constitute the hypnotherapeutic relationship. For reasons such as these, patients who are administered formal tests of hypnotizability may see little relationship between their performance on these tests and their response to treatment.

Investigators who assessed hypnotizability or "hypnotic depth" by using only a single item or by employing idiosyncratic, nonstandardized procedures appear to have integrated their assessment of hypnotizability into their ongoing hypnotherapeutic treatment to a much greater extent than have investigators who tested hypnotizability on standard scales. For example, when informal hypnotizability assessments were conducted, they ap-

pear almost always to have been conducted by the therapist who treated the patients. Moreover, these assessments were often performed in the hypnotherapeutic situation and, thereby, were likely to be construed by patients as part of, or at least as strongly related to, their therapy.

Table 32.3 collapses across type of disorder and divides studies into those in which hypnotizability was assessed with one or more of the standardized, multi-item scales, and those in which it was assessed with a single item or with some nonstandardized or unknown procedure. Informally assessed hypnotizability correlated significantly with therapeutic outcome much more frequently than did formally assessed hypnotizability (χ^2 [1] = 10.58, $p < .01$).

Obviously, this finding should be viewed as tentative and interpreted with caution. None of the studies reviewed here was designed to manipulate the extent to which patients construed their performance on hypnotizability tests as related to therapeutic outcome. On the other hand, this finding is consistent with the results of experimental findings that indicate that correlations between hypnotizability and suggestion-induced pain reductions are context dependent and related to subjects' perceptions of the similarities between the

Table 32.3. Frequencies With Which Relationships Between Hypnotizability and Treatment Outcome Were Significant or Nonsignificant When Hypnotizability Was Assessed With Standardized Multi-Item Scales or With Nonstandardized Procedures

	TYPES OF HYPNOTIZABILITY ASSESSMENT	
	STANDARDIZED	NONSTANDARDIZED
Significant	9	11
Nonsignificant	24	3

Note. χ^2 (1)=10.58, $p<.01$.

hypnotizability and pain-testing situations (cf. Spanos, 1989, for a review). At the very least, the present finding suggests that experiments aimed at varying the degree of connectedness between hypnotizability testing and therapy situations may provide fruitful information about the manner in which contextual variables influence the relationship between hypnotizability and treatment outcome.

REFERENCES

Andersen, M. S. (1985). Hypnotizability as a factor in the hypnotic treatment of obesity. *International Journal of Clinical and Experimental Hypnosis, 33*, 150–159.

Anderson, J. A. D., Basker, M. A., & Dalton, R. (1975). Migraine and hypnotherapy. *International Journal of Clinical and Experimental Hypnosis, 13*, 48–58.

Andreychuk, T., & Skriver, C. (1975). Hypnosis and biofeedback in the treatment of migraine headaches. *International Journal of Clinical and Experimental Hypnosis, 23*, 172–183.

Asher, R. (1956). Respectable hypnosis. *British Medical Journal, 2*, 309–313.

Astor, M. H. (1973). Hypnosis and behavior modification combined with psychoanalytic psychotherapy. *International Journal of Clinical and Experimental Hypnosis, 21*, 18–24.

Barber, J. (1976). *The efficacy of hypnotic analgesia for dental pain in individuals of both high and low hypnotic susceptibility*. Unpublished doctoral dissertation, University of Southern California.

Barber, J. (1980). Hypnosis and the unhypnotizable. *American Journal of Clinical Hypnosis, 23*, 4–9.

Barber, T. X. (1969). *Hypnosis: A scientific approach*. New York: Van Nostrand Reinhold.

Barber, T. X., Spanos, N. P., & Chaves, J. F. (1974). *Hypnosis, imagination and human potentialities*. Elmsford, NY: Pergamon Press.

Barkley, R. A., Hastings, J. E., & Jackson, T. L. (1977). The effects of rapid smoking and hypnosis in the treatment of smoking behavior. *International Journal of Clinical and Experimental Hypnosis, 25*, 7–17.

Bowers, K. S., & Kelly, P. (1979). Stress, disease, psychotherapy and hypnosis. *Journal of Abnormal Psychology, 88*, 490–505.

Cedercreutz, C. (1978). Hypnotic treatment of 100 cases of migraine. In F. H. Frankel & H. S.

Zamansky (Eds.), *Hypnosis at its bicentennial*. New York: Plenum Press.

Cedercreutz, C., Lahteenmaki, R., & Tulikoura, J. (1976). Hypnotic treatment of headache and vertigo in skull injured patients. *International Journal of Clinical and Experimental Hypnosis, 24*, 195–201.

Chaves, J. F. (1989). The hypnotic control of clinical pain. In N. P. Spanos & J. F. Chaves (Eds.), *Hypnosis: The cognitive-behavioral perspective*. Buffalo, NY: Prometheus.

Cohen, N. L., & Alpert, M. (1978). Locus of control as a predictor of outcome in treatment of obesity. *Psychological Reports, 42*, 805–806.

Collison, D. A. (1975). Which asthmatic patients should be treated with hypnotherapy? *Medical Journal of Australia, 1*, 776–781.

Creer, T. L. (1982). Asthma. *Journal of Consulting and Clinical Psychology, 50*, 912–921.

Crowley, R. (1980). Effects of indirect hypnosis (rapid induction analgesia) for relief of acute pain associated with minor podiatric surgery. *Dissertation Abstracts International. 40*, 4549.

Davidson, G. P., Garbett, N. D., & Tozer, S. G. (1985). An investigation into audiotaped self-hypnosis training in pregnancy and labor. In D. Waxman, P. C. Misra, M. Gibson, & M. A. Basker (Eds.), *Modern trends in hypnosis* (pp. 223–233). New York: Plenum Press.

Davidson, J. A. (1962). An assessment of the value of hypnosis in pregnancy and labour. *British Medical Journal, 2*, 951–953.

Dengrove, E. (1973). The uses of hypnosis in behavior therapy. *International Journal of Clinical and Experimental Hypnosis, 21*, 13–17.

D'Eon, J. L. (1989). Hypnosis and obstetrics. In N. P. Spanos & J. F. Chaves (Eds.), *Hypnosis: The cognitive-behavioral perspective*. Buffalo, NY: Prometheus.

DePiano, F. A., & Salzberg, H. C. (1979). Clinical applications of hypnosis to three psychosomatic disorders. *Psychological Bulletin, 86*, 1223–1235.

Devine, D. A., & Bornstein, P. H. (1980). Covert modeling-hypnosis in the treatment of obesity. *Psychotherapy: Theory, Research and Practice, 17*, 272–276.

Deyoub, P. L. (1979a). Hypnosis in the treatment of obesity and the relation of suggestibility to outcome. *Journal of the American Society of Psychosomatic Dentistry and Medicine, 26*, 127–149.

Deyoub, P. L. (1979b). Hypnotizability and obesity. *Psychological Reports, 45*, 974.

Deyoub, P. L., & Wilkie, R. (1980). Suggestion with and without hypnotic induction in a weight reduction program. *International Journal of Clinical and Experimental Hypnosis, 27*, 333–340.

Diamond, M. J. (1974). Modification of hypnotizability: A review. *Psychological Bulletin, 81*, 180–198.

Edmonston, W. E., Jr. (1980). *Hypnosis and Relaxation: Modern verification of an old equation*. New York: John Wiley & Sons.

Francisco, J. W. (1972). *Modification of smoking behavior: A comparison of three approaches*. Unpublished doctoral dissertation, Wayne State University, Wayne, NE.

Frankel, F. H. (1987). Significant developments in medical hypnosis during the past 25 years. *The International Journal of Clinical and Experimental Hypnosis, 35*, 231–247.

Friedman, H., & Taub, H. A. (1984). Brief psychological training procedures in migraine treatment. *American Journal of Clinical Hypnosis, 26*, 187–200.

Friedman, H., & Taub, H. A. (1985). Extended follow-up study of the effects of brief psychological procedures in migraine therapy. *American Journal of Clinical Hypnosis, 28*, 27–33.

Gault, A. (1988). Reflections of mesmeric analgesia. *British Journal of Experimental and Clinical Hypnosis, 5*, 17–24.

Gelder, M. G., Bancroft, J. H. J., Gath, D. H., Johnston, D. W., Mathews, A. M., & Shaw, P. M. (1973). Specific and non-specific factors in behavior therapy. *British Journal of Psychiatry, 123*, 445–462.

Gibbons, D., Kilbourne, L., Saunders, A., & Castles, C. (1970). The cognitive control of behavior: A comparison of systematic desensitization and hypnotically-induced "directed experience" techniques. *American Journal of Clinical Hypnosis, 12*, 141–145.

Gill, M. M., & Brenman, M. (1959). *Hypnosis and related states*. New York: International University Press.

Gillett, P. L., & Coe, W. C. (1984). The effects of rapid induction analgesia (RIA), hypnotic susceptibility and the severity of discomfort on reducing dental pain. *American Journal of Clinical Hypnosis, 27*, 81–90.

Goldstein, Y. (1981). The effects of demonstrating to a subject that she is in a hypnotic trance as a variable in hypnotic interventions with obese women. *International Journal of Clinical and Experimental Hypnosis, 29*, 15–23.

Gottfredson, D. K. (1973). *Hypnosis as an anesthetic in dentistry*. Unpublished doctoral dissertation, Brigham Young University, Provo, UT.

Graham, K. R. (1986). Explaining "virtuoso" hypnotic performance: Social psychology or experiential skill? *Behavioral and Brain Sciences, 9*, 473–474.

Hendler, C. S., & Redd, W. H. (1986). Fear of hypnosis: The role of labeling in patients' acceptance of behavioral interventions. *Behavior Therapy, 17*, 2–13.

Hilgard, E. R. (1977). The problem of divided consciousness: A neodissociation interpretation. *Annals of the New York Academy of Sciences, 296*, 48–59.

Hilgard, J. R., & LeBaron, S. (1984). *Hypnotherapy of pain in children with cancer*. Los Altos, CA: Kaufmann.

Holroyd, J. (1980). Hypnosis treatment for smoking: An evaluative review. *International Journal of Clinical and Experimental Hypnosis, 28*, 341–357.

Horowitz, S. L. (1970). Strategies within hypnosis for reducing phobic behavior. *Journal of Abnormal Psychology, 75*, 104–112.

Hyman, G. J., Stanley, R. O., Burrows, G. D., & Horne, D. J. (1986). Treatment effectiveness of hypnosis and behavior therapy in smoking cessation: A methodological refinement. *Addictive Behaviors, 11*, 355–365.

Johnson, R. F. (1989). Hypnosis, suggestion, and dermatological changes: A consideration of the production and diminution of dermatological entities. In N. P. Spanos & J. F. Chaves (Eds.), *Hypnosis: The cognitive-behavioral perspective*. Buffalo, NY: Prometheus.

Johnson, R. F. Q., & Barber, T. X. (1978). Hypnosis, suggestion and warts: An experimental investigation implicating the importance of "believed in efficacy." *American Journal of Clinical Hypnosis, 20*, 165–174.

Katz, E. R., Kellerman, J., & Ellenberg, L. (1987). Hypnosis in the reduction of acute pain and distress in children with cancer. *Journal of Pediatric Psychology, 12*, 379–394.

Kroger, W. S., & Fezler, W. D. (1976). Hypnosis and behavior modification: *Imagery conditioning*. Philadelphia: J. B. Lippincott.

Lang, P. J. (1969). The mechanisms of desensitization and the laboratory study of human fear (pp. 160–191). In C. M. Franks (Ed.), *Behavior therapy: Appraisal and status*. New York: McGraw-Hill.

Lang, P. J., Lazovik, A. D., & Reynolds, D. J. (1965). Desensitization, suggestibility and pseudotherapy. *Journal of Abnormal Psychology, 70*, 395–402.

Lazarus, A. A. (1973). "Hypnosis" as a facilitator in behavior therapy. *International Journal of Clinical and Experimental Hypnosis, 21*, 25–31.

MacHovec, S. J., & Man, S. C. (1978). Acupuncture and hypnosis compared: Fifty-eight cases. *American Journal of Clinical Hypnosis, 21*, 45–47.

Maher-Loughman, G. P. (1970). Hypnosis and autohypnosis for the treatment of asthma. *International Journal of Clinical and Experimental Hypnosis, 1*, 1–14.

Marks, I. M., Gelder, M. G., & Edwards, G. (1968). Hypnosis and desensitization for phobias: A controlled prospective trial. *British Journal of Psychology, 114*, 1263–1274.

McAmmond, D. M., Davidson, P. O., & Kovitz, D. M. (1971). A comparison of the effects of hypnosis and relaxation training on stress reactions in a dental situation. *American Journal of Clinical Hypnosis, 13*, 233–242.

Melnick, J., & Russell, R. W. (1976). Hypnosis versus systematic desensitization in the treatment of test anxiety. *Journal of Counseling Psychology, 23*, 291–295.

Miller, J. E. (1975). *Hypnotic susceptibility, achievement motivation, and the treatment of obesity*. Unpublished doctoral dissertation, University of Southern California, Los Angeles.

Moore, N. (1965). Behavior therapy in bronchial asthma: A controlled study. *Journal of Psychosomatic Research, 9*, 257–267.

Mott, T., & Roberts, J. (1979). Obesity and hypnosis: A review of the literature. *American Journal of Clinical Hypnosis, 22*, 3–7.

Nolan, R., Hayward, A., Scott, H., & Spanos, N. P. (1989). *Hypnotic and nonhypnotic imagery-based strategies in the treatment of tension and mixed tension/migraine headache*. Unpublished manuscript, Carleton University, Ottawa, Ontario.

O'Brien, R. M., Cooley, L. E., Ciotti, J., & Henninger, K. M. (1981). Augmentation of systematic desensitization of snake phobia through posthypnotic dream suggestion. *American Journal of Clinical Hypnosis, 23*, 231–238.

Oystragh, P. (1989). Vaginismus: A case study. *Australian Journal of Clinical and Experimental Hypnosis, 16*, 147–152.

Patterson, D. R., Questad, K. A., & de Lateur, B. J. (1989). Hypnotherapy as an adjunct to narcotic analgesia for the treatment of pain for burn debridement. *American Journal of Clinical Hypnosis, 31*, 156–163.

Pederson, L. L., Scrimgeour, W. G., & Lefcoe, N. M. (1975). Comparison of hypnosis plus counseling, counseling alone, and hypnosis alone in a community service smoking withdrawal program. *Journal of Consulting and Clinical Psychology, 43*, 920.

Pederson, L. L., Scrimgeour, W. G., & Lefcoe, N. M. (1979). Variables of hypnosis which are related to success in a smoking withdrawal program. *International Journal of Clinical and Experimental Hypnosis, 27*, 14–20.

Perchard, S. D. (1960). Hypnosis in obstetrics. *Proceedings of the Royal Society of Medicine, 53*, 458–460.

Perry, C., Gelfand, R., & Marcovitch, R. (1979). The relevance of hypnotic susceptibility in the clinical context. *Journal of Abnormal Psychology, 88*, 592–603.

Perry, C., Laurence, J. R., & Nadon, R. (1988). Hypnosis, surgery and the social-psychological position. *British Journal of Experimental and Clinical Hypnosis, 5*, 143–149.

Perry, C., & Mullen, G. (1975). The effect of hypnotic susceptibility on reduced smoking behavior treated by an hypnotic technique. *Journal of Clinical Psychology, 31*, 498–505.

Purcell, K. & Weiss, J. H. (1970). Asthma. In C. C. Costello (Ed.), *Symptoms of psychopathology*. New York: John Wiley & Sons.

Rabkin, S. W., Boyko, E., Shane, F., & Kaufest, J. (1984). A randomized trial comparing smoking cessation programs utilizing behavior modification, health education or hypnosis. *Addictive Behaviors, 9*, 157–173.

Radtke, H. L., & Spanos, N. P. (1981). Was I hypnotized? A social psychological analysis of hypnotic depth reports. *Psychiatry, 44*, 359–376.

Reeves, J. L., Redd, W. H., Storm, F. K., & Minagawa, R. Y. (1983). Hypnosis in the control of pain during hyperthermia treatment of cancer. In J. J. Bonica, U. Lindblom, & A. Iggo (Eds.), *Advances in pain research and therapy* (Vol. 5, pp. 857–861). New York: Raven.

Rock, N. L., Shipley, T. E., & Campbell, C. (1969). Hypnosis with untrained volunteer patients in labor. *International Journal of Clinical and Experimental Hypnosis, 17*, 25–36.

Rubinfeld, A. R., & Pain, M. C. F. (1976). Perception of asthma. *Lancet*, April 24, 882–884.

Samko, M. A., & Schoenfeld, L. S. (1975). Hypnotic susceptibility and Lamaze childbirth experience. *American Journal of Obstetrics and Gynecology, 121*, 631–636.

Sarbin, T. R., & Coe, W. C. (1972). *Hypnotic behavior: The social psychology of influence communication*. New York: Holt.

Schafer, D. W. (1975). Hypnosis use on a burn unit. *International Journal of Clinical and Experimental Hypnosis, 23*, 1–14.

Schlutter, I. C., Golden, C., & Blume, H. G. (1980). A comparison of treatments for prefontal muscle contraction headache. *British Journal of Medical Psychology, 53*, 47–52.

Schubot, E. D. (1966). *The influence of hypnotic and muscular relaxation in systematic desensitization of phobias*. Unpublished doctoral dissertation, Stanford University, Stanford, CA.

Shewchuk, L. A., Dubren, R., Burton, D., Forman, M., Clark, R. R., & Jassen, A. R. (1977). Preliminary observations on an intervention program of heavy smokers. *International Journal of the Addictions, 12*, 323–336.

Sinclair-Gieben, A. H. C., & Chalmers, D. (1959). Evaluation of treatment of warts by hypnosis. *Lancet, 2*, October 3, 480–482.

Smith, M. S., Womack, W. M., & Chen, A. C. N. (1989). Hypnotizability does not predict outcome of behavioral treatment of pediatric headache. *American Journal of Clinical Hypnosis, 31*, 237–241.

Snow, L. (1979). The relationship between "Rapid Induction" and placebo analgesia, hypnotic susceptibility and chronic pain intensity. *Dissertation Abstracts International, 40*, 937.

Spanos, N. P. (1986a). Hypnosis and the modification of hypnotic susceptibility: A social psychological perspective. In P. L. N. Naish (Ed.), *What is hypnosis?* (pp. 85–120). Philadelphia: Open University Press.

Spanos, N. P. (1986b). Hypnotic behavior: A social psychological interpretation of amnesia, analgesia and trance logic. *Behavioral and Brain Sciences, 9*, 449–502.

Spanos, N. P. (1989). Experimental research on hypnotic analgesia. In N. P. Spanos & J. F.

Chaves (Eds.), *Hypnosis: The cognitive-behavioral perspective* (pp. 206–240). Buffalo, NY: Prometheus.

Spanos, N. P., & Chaves, J. F. (Eds.). (1989). *Hypnosis: The cognitive-behavioral perspective*. Buffalo, NY: Prometheus.

Spanos, N. P., & Chaves, J. F. (1989). Hypnotic analgesia and surgery: In defense of the social-psychological position. *British Journal of Experimental and Clinical Hypnosis, 6*, 131–140.

Spanos, N. P., De Faye, B., Gabora, N., & Jarrett, L. (1989). *Comparison of hypnotic and nonhypnotic single session treatments for smoking cessation*. Unpublished manuscript, Carleton University, Ottawa, Ontario.

Spanos, N. P., Stenstrom, R. J., & Johnston, J. C. (1988). Hypnosis, placebo and suggestion in the treatment of warts. *Psychosomatic Medicine, 50*, 245–260.

Spanos, N. P., Williams, V., & Gwynn, M. I. (1990). Effects of hypnotic, placebo and salicylic acid treatments on wart regression. *Psychosomatic Medicine, 52*, 109–114.

Spiegel, D., & Bloom, J. R. (1983). Group therapy and hypnosis reduce metastatic breast carcinoma pain. *Psychosomatic Medicine, 45*, 333–339.

Spiegel, H. (1970). A single-treatment method to stop smoking using ancillary hypnosis. *International Journal of Clinical and Experimental Hypnosis, 18*, 235–250.

Spinhoven, P. (1988). Similarities and dissimilarities in hypnotic and nonhypnotic procedures for headache control: A review. *American Journal of Clinical Hypnosis, 30*, 183–194.

Spinhoven, P., Van Dyck, R., Zitman, F. G., & Linssen, A. C. G. (1985). *Treating tension headache: Autogenic training and hypnotic imagery*. Paper presented at the 10th International Congress of Hypnosis and Psychosomatic Medicine, Toronto, Canada, August 10–16.

Spinhoven, P., Linssen, A. C. G., Van Dyck, R., & Zitman, F. G. (1988). *Locus of control, cognitive strategies and hypnotizability in pain management: A preliminary report*. Paper presented at the 11th International Congress of Hypnosis and Psychosomatic Medicine, The Hague, The Netherlands, August 13–19.

Stam, H. J. (1989). From symptom relief to cure: Hypnotic interventions in cancer. In N. P. Spanos & J. F. Chaves (Eds.), *Hypnosis: The cognitive-behavioral perspective.* Buffalo, NY: Prometheus.

Stam, H. J., McGrath, P. A., & Brooke, R. I. (1984). The effects of a cognitive-behavioral treatment program on tempro-mandibular pain and dysfunction syndrome. *Psychosomatic Medicine, 46*, 534–545.

Surman, O. S., Gottlieb, S. K., Hackett, T. P., & Silverberg, E. L. (1973). Hypnosis in the treatment of warts. *Archives of General Psychiatry, 28*, 439–441.

Swirsky-Sacchetti, T., & Margolis, C. G. (1986). The effects of a comprehensive self-hypnosis training program on the use of factor VIII in severe hemophilia. *International Journal of Clinical and Experimental Hypnosis, 34*, 71–83.

Syrjala, K. L., Cummings, C., Donaldson, G., & Chapman, C. R. (1987). *Hypnosis for oral pain following chemotherapy and irradiation.* Paper presented at the 5th World Conference on Pain, Hamburg, West Germany, August.

Tan, S. Y. (1982). Cognitive and cognitive-behavioral methods for pain control: A review. *Pain, 12*, 201–228.

Tenzel, J. H., & Taylor, R. L. (1969). An evaluation of hypnosis and suggestion as treatment for warts. *Psychosomatics, 10*, 252–257.

Turk, D. C., Meichenbaum, D., & Genest, M. (1983). *Pain and behavioral medicine: A cognitive behavioral perspective.* New York: Guilford Press.

Ullman, M., & Dudek, S. (1960). On the psyche and warts: II. Hypnotic suggestion and warts. *Psychosomatic Medicine, 22*, 68–76.

Venn, J. (1987). Hypnosis and the Lamaze method: An exploratory study. *International Journal of Clinical and Experimental Hypnosis, 35*, 79–82.

Wadden, T., & Anderton, C. H. (1982). The clinical use of hypnosis. *Psychological Bulletin, 91*, 215–243.

Wadden, T., & Flaxman, J. (1981). Hypnosis and weight loss: A preliminary study. *International Journal of Clinical and Experimental Hypnosis, 29*, 162–173.

Wakeman, R. J., & Kaplan, J. Z. (1978). An experimental study of hypnosis in painful burns. *American Journal of Clinical Hypnosis, 21*, 3–12.

Wall, V. J., & Womack, W. (1989). Hypnotic versus active cognitive strategies for alleviation of procedural distress in pediatric oncology patients. *American Journal of Clinical Hypnosis, 31*, 181–191.

Weitzenhoffer, A. M. (1953). *Hypnotism: An objective study in suggestibility.* New York: John Wiley & Sons.

Werbel, E. W. (1963). Use of posthypnotic suggestions to reduce pain following hemorrhoidectomies. *American Journal of Clinical Hypnosis, 6*, 132–136.

White, D. O., & Fenner, F. (1986). *Medical virology.* New York: Academic Press.

White, H. (1961). Hypnosis in bronchial asthma. *Journal of Psychosomatic Research, 5*, 272–279.

Williams, J. M., & Hall, D. W. (1988). Use of single session hypnosis for smoking cessation. *Addictive Behaviors, 13*, 205–208.

Zelter, L., & LeBaron, S. (1982). Hypnosis and nonhypnotic techniques for reduction of pain and anxiety during painful procedures in children and adolescents with cancer. *Journal of Pediatrics, 101*, 1032–1035.

CHAPTER 33

CHANGE IN THERAPEUTIC GROUPS

Donelson R. Forsyth

People have been using groups to accomplish goals since ancient times. Noted group dynamicist Alvin Zander, in tracing the history of groups in society, pointed out that our ancestors protected themselves from dangerous animals, human enemies, and natural disasters by joining together in groups. In ancient Egypt workers combined their efforts to build dams, irrigation systems, and colossal monuments. By 300 B.C. Chinese workers and merchants had formed organized guilds to monitor business practices. The Romans made extensive use of groups, for their armies and their government were organized into various tribunes, legislative bodies, and associations. And, of course, people have traditionally conducted religious services in groups rather than in isolation (Zander, 1985).

This tradition continues today, for most social behavior takes place in a group context. Businesses, governments, educators, administrators, and the armed forces rely on groups to solve problems, create products, formulate standards, and communicate knowledge. Groups, too, have become useful tools in the field of mental health.

Springing from such divergent sources as Joseph Hershey Pratt's 1905 use of groups to ward off depression among patients suffering from tuberculosis, Moreno's psychodrama and sociometry (1932), Freud's *Group Psychology and the Analysis of Ego* (1922), and Lewin's (1936) training groups (t-groups), groups offer practitioners the means of achieving therapeutic change en masse. Indeed, the fervor and resolve of advocates of group-level interventions prompted Back (1973) to label this perspective a social movement rather than an emerging field.

This chapter explores the utility and dynamics of the therapeutic group. It begins by reviewing extant types of therapeutic groups and their typical characteristics. Next, we raise the question of effectiveness, and rely heavily on previously published reviews as well as on more recent empirical outcome studies to develop an answer. We then catalog the interpersonal processes that are common to many group therapies, making heuristic use of the concept of curative factors (Yalom, 1985). This chapter seeks to draw a general model of group therapy that integrates the clinical literature on change via group interaction and the social psychological literature on group structure and process.

THE VARIETY OF THERAPEUTIC GROUPS

People join groups to achieve a variety of goals and the vast assortment of currently available therapeutic groups reflects this variability. Traditional therapy groups, such as psychoanalytic or gestalt treatments, remain, but they are only one approach among many. Although the more extreme group interventions requiring marathon sessions or intense emotional stimulation are becoming increasingly rare, these groups have been replaced by a myriad of change-promoting groups. The encounter groups and sensitivity training groups of yesterday have become the jogging clubs, workshops, seminars, and self-help groups of today.

These groups, despite their many forms, generally fit one of three basic categories: group therapy, interpersonal learning groups, and self-help groups (Klein, 1983; Lakin, 1972; Lieberman, 1976; Rudestam, 1982). Like any individual therapy, group therapy is usually conducted by a mental health professional, and it focuses on helping individuals overcome relatively severe psychological and social problems. But unlike individual therapies, group therapies involve treating individuals "in groups, with the group itself constituting an important element in the therapeutic process" (Slavson, 1950, p. 42). Most group therapists tend to be eclectic in their choice of methods. They make use of the transference process to bring issues originating from parental and sibling relationships into the group, they use role-playing, psychodrama, and gestalt experiences, and they analyze events transpiring in the group as well as those outside of it. Many group therapists also rely heavily on principles of behavior therapy, including modeling, behavior rehearsal, and feedback (Hollander & Kazaoka, 1988; Rose, 1977, 1983).

Interpersonal learning groups, in contrast, involve attempts to help relatively well-adjusted individuals extend their self-understanding and improve their relationships with others (Forsyth, 1990). These groups spring from an intellectual heritage that can be traced back to Lewin's "training laboratories" (T-groups), as well as the more humanistically motivated sensitivity training and encounter groups of the 1960s and 1970s (Back, 1973; Lakin, 1972). In contemporary form, however, interpersonal learning groups tend to be much more structured and more behaviorally oriented. Although they are used to achieve a variety of goals from increasing assertiveness and leadership skills to eliminating ineffective listening habits and self-destructive cognitions, most of these interventions involve brief didactic presentations, structured experiential exercises, group discussion of the topic or process under scrutiny, and behavioral rehearsal.

Last, self-help groups are voluntarily formed groups of people who help one another cope with or overcome a common problem. Although drug and food addiction groups like Alcoholics Anonymous (AA) and Weight Watchers are among the best known self-help groups, self-help groups focus on a range of problems. Examples include groups composed of individuals suffering from illness, relatives of the terminally ill or handicapped, people seeking support during a time of life or family crisis, and members of minority groups seeking protection of their social rights. Like AA, many such groups form because the members' needs are not being met by existing educational, social, or health agencies, and are organized by laypeople (Cole, 1983; Robinson, 1980).

The gulf separating these various forms of therapeutic groups should not be minimized. Yet, despite their uniqueness, all these interventions are similar in that they are all groups. First, they include two or more interdependent individuals who influence one another through social interaction. In some groups (psychoanalytic groups, for example), interactions may center on a leader, but in all these groups influence occurs among members. Second, as groups these therapeutic entities develop structural qualities, including roles, norms, status, and attraction relations. These structures provide an underlying organization for relationships among members and they influence a variety of group processes. Individuals who occupy particular roles, for example, generally perform certain types of behaviors in their groups. In most groups a stable pattern of variations in status and attraction relations can also be discerned, and these patterns have a major impact on member satisfaction. Third, as groups these aggregates of individuals possess some modicum of cohesiveness. In many cases the group develops an identity of its own, and members share a bond of loyalty to one another and to the group itself. Fourth, these groups are dynamic in that they change gradually over time. Although different theorists highlight different patterns of change, most agree that groups progress through periods of tentative interaction, conflict, cohesion, productivity, and dissolution (Tuckman, 1965; Tuckman & Jensen, 1977). Last, the groups within these three categories are similar in that they all form for the purpose of facilitating change or adjustment in group members.

ARE THERAPEUTIC GROUPS THERAPEUTIC?

The use of groups as agents of change dates back many years, but it was Lewin who stated the "law" of group therapy in its most basic form: "It is easier to change individuals formed into a group than to change any of them separately" (1951, p. 228). In the years since Lewin articulated this hypothesis, researchers have busied themselves with the chore of gathering the evidence needed to evaluate the accuracy of his conjecture. Their efforts offer answers to these questions: (a) Are therapeutic groups effective? and (b) Are some forms of group treatment superior to others?

Overall Effectiveness of Group Interventions

Outcome studies of group treatments, although far from unanimous in their support of Lewin's law, are for the most part positive. Two major reviews of the outcome literature published before 1975 ruled in favor of therapeutic groups, although both bemoaned the methodological flaws that undermine the scientific adequacy of the data base (Back, 1974; Meltzoff & Kornreich, 1970). Meltzoff and Kornreich, (1970) for example, were guardedly optimistic about the utility of group therapies as they found that 80% of the methodologically sound studies reported either major or minor benefits for clients, whereas nearly all of the studies that reported no benefit were methodologically flawed.

More recent reviews concur with these initial assessments. Lieberman (1976), Hartman (1979), and Bednar and Kaul (1978), in their general reviews of group outcomes, were positive about current group methods and even more optimistic about future applications. Spitz (1984) presented a generally favorable review of the use of groups

with a variety of client populations, including borderline and narcissistic personality disorders, physically ill patients, and chronic psychiatric patients. Kanas (1986), after examining 33 inpatient and 10 outpatient studies dating back to 1950, concluded that group therapy was effective in 67% of the inpatient studies and 80% of the outpatient studies. He also reported that long-term therapy (more than 3 months) was especially useful, as were approaches that focused on interpersonal processes. Lastly, Toseland and Siporin (1986) reviewed over 30 studies that compared individual and group therapies, and concluded that in 25% of these studies the group therapy was significantly more effective than individual therapies. Indeed, Toseland and Siporin argued that group therapy should be the treatment of choice for most clients.

Reviews of experiential groups also are generally positive (Bates & Goodman, 1986; Knapp & Shostrom, 1976). Knapp and Shostrom (1976) found that in those studies that used the Personality Orientation Inventory (POI) to assess outcome, most participants showed a consistent pattern of increased self-actualizing scores. Berman and Zimpfer (1980), in a systematic review of 26 controlled studies of personal growth groups, restricted their analysis to studies that (a) used both pretest and posttest measures, (b) met for at least 10 hours, and (c) had a long-term follow-up (at least 1 month after termination). Summarizing these methodologically superior studies, Berman and Zimpfer concluded that group treatments result in enduring positive changes, particularly at the self-report level.

Studies of the use of group therapies with particular populations also have yielded generally positive results. Kilmann and his colleagues (Sotile & Kilmann, 1977), although initially frustrated by the low quality of the research procedures in studies of group treatments for sexual dysfunctions, eventually concluded that group therapy is an effective means of treating female orgasmic dysfunction and secondary erectile dysfunctional behavior (Mills & Kilmann, 1982). Zimpfer (1987), in his review of 19 studies of group therapy for the elderly, found that group treatments were differentially effective depending on the problems experienced by the client. He concluded that treatments that provide social support and sustain health-promoting actions and attitudes were most effective. Brandsma and Pattison (1985), after reviewing the empirical literature pertaining to group therapy with alcoholics, concluded that group interventions are an effective means of treating alcoholics who require therapeutic treatment.

Not all reviewers are convinced that groups work. Solomon (1982), for example, found that outcome studies that compare individual and group therapy for alcoholism do not recommend one treatment over the other. Parloff and Dies (1977), after reviewing the results of studies of group therapies with a range of client types (schizophrenics, psychoneurotics, juveniles, and adult offenders), concluded that the results are disappointing. Abramowitz (1977) reached a similar conclusion in her review of outcome research on children's activity, behavior modification, play, and verbal therapy groups. Rose, Tolman, and Tallant (1985), although they do not report negative findings about group therapy effectiveness, argued that most investigators do not take group-level process variables into consideration when designing their interventions or their assessments. Also, evidence pertaining to marathon groups is relatively negative (Kilmann & Sotile, 1976).

Negative reviews, however, are the exception; most summaries conclude that therapeutic groups are a useful means of helping individuals deal with psychological difficulties. As Bednar and Kaul (1979) wrote, "Group treatments have been more effective than no treatment, than placebo treatment, or than other accepted forms of psychological treatment" (p. 314). Given the impact of groups in virtually all aspects of our everyday lives, it would be surprising to find that they do not influence individuals in therapeutic settings.

Comparing Types of Group Therapies

Groups are generally effective, but recently researchers have sought to determine if variations in group technique are differentially effective. The category *therapeutic group* is extremely broad, for it includes methods that differ greatly in terms of purposes and procedures. A therapeutic group may be designed to accomplish such varied goals as social support (support groups), the improvement of members' social skills (T-groups), an increased insight into one's own emotions and motivations (encounter groups), or it may simply function as arenas for the delivery of traditionally individualistic therapy, including behavioral and psychodynamic therapies (Lakin, 1972; Rude-

stam, 1982). Groups also conform to no single set of procedures, for some groups are leader centered (psychoanalytic or gestalt groups) whereas others are group-focused (encounter and T-groups), and the group's activities can range from the highly structured (social skill training groups, such as assertiveness-training groups) to the unstructured (encounter groups). Group practitioners also vary greatly in their orientations and techniques, for some focus on emotions with gestalt exercises, others concentrate on the here-and-now of the group's interpersonal process, and others train members to perform certain behaviors through videotaped feedback, behavioral rehearsal, and systematic reinforcement.

Given this diversity in purposes and procedures, one might expect that some types may emerge as more effective than others. Yet, most studies attest to the relative equality of the different types of group therapy. Lieberman, Yalom, and Miles' (1973) classic investigation remains an excellent example of the apparent equivalence of group interventions. This triad investigated the overall impact of a 12-week experiential group on members adjustment (Lieberman, Yalom, & Miles, 1973; Yalom, 1985; Yalom, Tinklenberg, & Gilula, 1975, cited in Yalom, 1985). Using a pool of 206 Stanford University students who were enrolled for course credit, Lieberman, Yalom, and Miles randomly assigned each person to one of 18 different therapy groups representing 10 theoretical orientations: gestalt, transactional analysis, T-groups, Synanon, Esalen, psychoanalytic, marathon, psychodrama, encounter tape, and encounter. Trained observers coded the group's interactions, with particular attention to the leader's style. Before, during, immediately after, and 6 months following the participation they administered a battery of items assessing group members' self-esteem, attitudes, self-satisfactions, values, satisfaction with friendships, and so on. Measures also were completed by the comembers, the leaders, and by group members' acquaintances.

Somewhat unexpectedly, the project discovered that no one theoretical approach had a monopoly on effectiveness. For example, two separate gestalt groups with different leaders were included in the design, but the members of these two groups evidenced widely discrepant gains. One of the gestalt groups ranked among the most successful in stimulating participant growth, but the other group yielded fewer benefits than all of the groups.

These findings may have resulted from the lack

of experience of the group leaders, as Russell (1978) suggested, but more recent studies provide general confirmation for the equivalency among treatments reported by Lieberman, Yalom, and Miles. Looking first at comparative studies of psychotherapy groups, Gonzalez-Menendez (1985) assigned 40 inpatients to one of three directive psychotherapeutic groups. An informative group emphasized transmitting useful information to subjects, an introspective group stressed self-understanding, and an inspirational group encouraged members to develop health-sustaining behaviors. The informative and inspirational groups were somewhat more effective, but the differences among the three groups were slight.

Falloon (1981) assigned 51 psychiatric outpatients with specific interpersonal skills deficits to either role-rehearsal and modeling behavioral therapy groups or guided discussion group therapy. The role-rehearsal group had fewer dropouts and reported more liking for their groups, but both treatments were effective in changing participants' social skills levels. Coche, Cooper, and Petermann (1984) reported similar results. They assigned 41 psychiatric patients to one of two group therapy procedures: a brief interactive group therapy or a cognitively oriented, problem-solving training group. Both programs were effective, although in somewhat different spheres. The interactive therapy groups resulted in improvements in the interpersonal realm, whereas the problem-solving intervention was more effective in reducing complaints about distress and adjustment.

Turning to experimental studies of assertiveness training, we again see few differences between various types of group approaches. Berah (1981), for example, contrasted massed versus distributed practice in assertiveness training groups. Self-report measures, a role-play test, and peer ratings before, immediately after, and 4 weeks following training all indicated that the subjects improved relative to the controls, but that the mass-practice, distributed-practice, and combined mass and distributed-practice groups were equally effective. Similarly, Sanchez, Lewinsohn, and Larson (1980) compared group assertion training to traditional group psychotherapy for depressed outpatients. Self-report measures indicated that the assertion training was more effective than traditional psychotherapy initially, but differences between the two groups dissipated over time. Markham (1985) studied assertiveness training methods by assigning 45 women to one of three

conditions: a behavioral rehearsal group, a group systematic desensitization program, or a control group. Self-report and behavioral measures indicated that individuals in the two treatment groups improved relative to the controls, but the two treatments did not differ significantly from each other on any measure. These effects were still in evidence on a 3-month delayed posttest.

Studies of alcoholism and weight-loss similarly suggest that one group method is as good as another. Knauss, Jeffrey, Knauss, and Harowski (1983) assigned 68 overweight men and women to one of four weight-loss programs: a bibliotherapy effort group, a faded self-management group, a standard self-management group, and a self-management with additional group sessions. Attrition was lower in the group therapy conditions, and all subjects in the various group treatment conditions lost significant amounts of weight. Oei and Jackson (1984) divided 18 problem drinkers into two different therapeutic groups. In both groups the therapist utilized role-playing, modeling, and behavioral rehearsal to stimulate self-understanding, but in one group the therapist also (a) elicited and rewarded all positive self-statements, (b) challenged negative self-statements, and (c) personally self-disclosed. Self-reports and behavioral ratings based on coded videotapes of interpersonal behavior indicated that clients in both groups improved, but that the group with a self-disclosing therapist improved more. Rosenberg and Brian (1986) compared three different group treatments for repeat driving-under-the-influence offenders: a cognitive-behavioral intervention, a rational-emotive approach, and an unstructured insight-oriented therapy. Measures taken after 6 months in the programs indicated all were equally effective. Lastly, Hajek, Belcher, and Stapleton (1985) found that leader-centered groups were less effective than noncentralized groups. They assigned 132 smokers to 14 leader-centered groups and 138 smokers to 14 nondirective groups that emphasized social support and interpersonal pressure against smoking. After 1 year, more individuals in the nondirective groups had quit smoking, particularly if they were members of somewhat larger groups.

Differences among treatments, although rare, have been noted. In an experimental analysis of recently divorced women Graff, Whitehead, and LeCompte (1986) assigned 12 clients to a cognitive-behavioral therapy group, 12 to a supportive-insight group, and 22 to two control groups. Self-report measures, which included indices of depression, self-esteem, and neuroticism, indicated both group interventions were effective. A 4-month follow-up, however, indicated that the cognitive-behavioral intervention maintained its effectiveness more than the supportive-insight approach. Beutler, Milton, Schieber, Calvert, and Gaines (1984), too, found some differences among treatments. They randomly assigned 176 patients to a control group or to one of the following three treatment programs: interactive, process-oriented experiential, encounterlike, or behaviorally oriented groups. Beutler found that both the process-oriented and behaviorally oriented groups were effective, but that the experiential group resulted in deterioration among some patients. Lastly, Kivlighan, McGovern, and Corazzini (1984) used similar content and procedures in six therapy groups, but they varied the timing of the delivery of information pertaining to intimacy and expressing anger. As the forming-storming-norming-performing model of group development described by Tuckman (1965) suggests, interventions that matched the group's stages of development were more effective than mismatched interventions. Kaplan (1982) compared four types of group-oriented approaches with assertiveness training: a behavioral approach, cognitive assertion training, a behavioral-cognitive approach, and a self-awareness approach. The extensive dependent measures, which included self-report measures, a situation test, and two nonobtrusive measures, indicated that all approaches except the self-awareness method were effective. Finkelstein, Wenegrat, and Yalom (1982) in their analysis of est (Erhard seminar training) noted that this large-group change method has a significant group therapy component, but the benefits reported among est graduates result more from expectancy and response sets than from actual psychological change. Lastly, Kilmann and Sotile (1976) argued against the usefulness of marathon groups, and little new research has emerged in support of this technique (cf. Page, 1982, 1983, 1984, 1985).

The Equivalence of Groups and the Dodo's Verdict

The research reviewed here indicates that certain methods, particularly more radical interventions such as marathon groups, are not particularly effective means of achieving therapeutic change. However, the majority of the more traditional therapeutic groups, including psychodynamic group psychotherapy, support groups, social skills groups, assertiveness training groups, t-groups, Tavistock groups, experiential groups, gestalt groups, and structured groups, facilitate health-sustaining changes in participants. These findings, although somewhat perplexing given the considerable differences among these various interventions, correspond to results obtained in studies of individual therapy. Meta-analytic reviews of one-to-one therapeutic interventions indicate that these treatments are more effective than no treatment at all, but no one approach emerges as more powerful than any other (Smith, Glass, & Miller, 1980). As Luborsky, Singer, and Luborsky (1975) suggested, the verdict of the Dodo bird in *Alice's Adventures in Wonderland* seems to apply (Carroll, 1865/1962). At one point in her adventure, Alice and a collection of colorful characters raced against one another. The race was very disorganized, and finally ended when "the Dodo suddenly called out 'The race is over!'" All the characters then "crowded round it, panting and asking, 'but who has won?'" The Dodo's verdict: "Everybody has won and all must have prizes" (p. 45).

Drawing on Stiles, Shapiro, and Elliott's (1986) analysis of the apparent equivalence of individual therapies, a number of factors can be identified to account for this "no difference" result. First, the various group therapies may be differentially effective, but researchers' measures may not be sensitive enough to detect these variations. Second, as Kiesler's (1966) dismissal of the "uniformity myth" suggests, it may be that effectiveness is a complex product of the interaction of groups, therapists, clients, and circumstances. As Paul (1967) stated, the question is not, "Is therapy A more effective than therapy B?" but, "What type of group run by which therapist is effective for this individual with this type of problem?" When researchers ignore the fit between treatment, therapist, client, and problem, the result is global, but undifferentiated, effectiveness. Third, although extant group interventions are based on widely divergent theoretical assumptions, these assumptions may not lead to differences in practice. A leader of a gestalt group and the leader of a psychodynamic group, for example, may each explain their goals and methods in very different theoretical terms, but they may nonetheless rely on identical methods when in their groups.

A fourth plausible explanation remains. This

explanation suggests that despite their heterogeneity in purposes and procedures, therapeutic groups have certain characteristics in common. In all groups the members have the opportunity to learn from others. They can rely on one another for support and guidance. They receive feedback from other group members that is self-sustaining and corrective, and they also gain an audience for their self-disclosures. Might these common aspects of groups and their dynamics account for the therapeutic effects of group interventions? This possibility is examined below.

SOCIAL PROCESSES IN THERAPEUTIC GROUPS

Why are therapeutic groups therapeutic? Why, despite their heterogeneity in terms of purposes and procedures, are they generally equivalent in terms of effectiveness? Perhaps the solution to this puzzle lies in the fact that therapeutic groups, as groups, possess certain characteristics in common, and it is these characteristics that may account for their therapeutic impact.

Several theorists have specified the characteristics of therapeutic groups that enhance their effectiveness. Lakin (1972), for example, argued that the successful group must facilitate emotional expression and generate feelings of belongingness, but it must also stimulate interpersonal comparisons and provide members with the opportunity to interact with one another. Similarly, Bednar and Kaul (1978) recommend participation in a "developing social microcosm," "interpersonal feedback and consensual validation," and "reciprocal opportunities to be both helpers and helpees in group settings" (p. 781).

Yalom's interpersonal model of group psychotherapy, however, is by far the most comprehensive and well-researched analysis of why groups work (Yalom, 1975, 1985). Yalom proposed that certain therapeutic, or curative, factors underlie effective psychotherapeutic groups. Some of the factors on Yalom's list are mechanisms that are responsible for facilitating change, whereas others describe the general group conditions that should be present within effective therapeutic groups. The list includes the installation of hope, universality, imparting of information, altruism, the corrective recapitulation of the primary family group, development of socializing techniques, imitative behavior, interpersonal learning, group cohesiveness, catharsis, and existential factors. Self-

understanding is also a potential candidate for the curative factors list, although Yalom suggests that this factor may be more epiphenomena than mediator of change.

Yalom gleaned these factors from his clinical experience and empirical research. His list, however, is consistent with theoretical analyses of groups in general. Following a tradition established by William Graham Sumner, Charles Horton Cooley, and Kurt Lewin, social psychologists have long argued that groups are the shapers of individuals. Small groups are society's primary socializing agents, for they provide their members with a particular worldview, and then sustain that view through direct instruction, selective social reinforcement, and corrective social influence as necessary. Individuals, too, sustain their groups by defending them against other groups, by contributing their effort in group activities, and by changing the group when existing norms and forms of activity are antiquated or become maladaptive.

In the following sections, the curative factors in groups from a group dynamics perspective are examined. Where possible, empirical findings are discussed to substantiate the theoretical arguments offered, but in most cases the available evidence is so sparse that many of the ideas discussed are admittedly speculative. Nonetheless, five key processes that undergird change in therapeutic groups are examined below: social comparison, social learning, self-insight, social influence, and social provisions.

Social Comparison

In the early 1950s, Leon Festinger suggested that individuals often join groups to obtain information about their social world (1950, 1954). Festinger believed that physical reality rarely provides us with objective standards for the validation of personal opinions, beliefs, or attitudes. Therefore, we often compare our personal viewpoint to the views expressed by others to determine if they are "correct," "valid," or "proper." Festinger called this information-seeking process social comparison.

Through social comparison, members of therapeutic groups gain reassuring information about the nonuniqueness of their problems. Veridical information-seeking–social comparison with similar others in the group convinces members that their problems are more commonplace than they imagined. Also, the individuals may find reassurance by comparing themselves to others in the group who are experiencing more severe problems or coping less effectively than themselves. This downward social comparison process is likely to occur when we are uncertain of abilities and lack confidence in our beliefs, and hence may serve a protective, adaptive function (Wills, 1981, this volume). Studies of breast cancer patients, for example, indicate that women who compare themselves with superior copers describe their own adjustment in more negative terms. Perhaps as a result of these negative implications, over 60% of the women engaged in downward social comparison by choosing a comparison person who was not coping effectively (Wood, Taylor, & Lichtman, 1985).

Yalom (1985) noted that the act of joining together with people who share a particular problem is, in and of itself, reassuring because it reduces anxiety that emanates from uncertainty: "Fear and anxiety that stem from uncertainty of the source, meaning, and seriousness of psychiatric symptoms may so compound the total dysphoria that effective exploration becomes vastly more difficult" (p. 12). In support of his speculations, studies of uncertainty and social comparison indicate that individuals seek out other people whenever they feel uncertain of the validity of their attitudes or beliefs. Schachter (1959), for example, found that college women, when confronted by an ambiguous and anxiety-provoking situation, clearly preferred to wait with others, only if these others could provide them with information. Other studies suggest that affiliating individuals, particularly when fearful, interact more, both verbally and nonverbally, and also display withdrawal reactions and controlled nonreactions (Morris, Worchel, Bois, Pearson, Rountree, Samaha, Wachtler, & Wright, 1976). Schachter's studies prompted him to conclude that individuals prefer to face problems in groups rather than alone, because the groups provide members with anxiety-reducing information. As he concluded, "Misery doesn't love just any kind of company, it loves only miserable company" (p. 24).

Social Learning

Theorists have repeatedly underscored the value of groups as arenas for interpersonal learning (Lieberman, 1980; Yalom, 1975). By participating in a group, individuals gain information about themselves, their problems, and their social relationships with others. As Yalom (1985) noted, some of this information is conveyed through direct instruction, as clients trade advice and information and the therapist provides structure and direction. The group also provides members with the opportunity to implicitly gather data concerning their own interpersonal behavior. Interaction in the group setting is social behavior, and so it has implications for self-definition that go beyond the confines of the temporary group situation. Within the social microcosm of the small group, individuals "become aware of the significant aspects of their interpersonal behavior: their strengths, their limitations, their parataxic distortions, and their maladaptive behavior that elicits unwanted responses from others" (Yalom, 1975, p. 40). Through feedback from the group leader and other group members, as well as self-observations formulated within the group setting, individuals gain an increased understanding of their social selves, and this self-understanding provides the basis for changes in cognitions and actions. The value of interpersonal learning is also recognized by group members themselves, for when rating the most valuable aspect of the group experience they tend to emphasize feedback and interpersonal processes: "The group's teaching me about the type of impression I make on others"; "Learning how I come across to others"; and "Other members honestly telling me what they think of me" (Yalom, 1975, p. 79). Of the 12 curative factors noted by Yalom (1985), four of them pertain to social learning: guidance (direct instruction), interpersonal learning via feedback, interpersonal learning by examining relationships with others, and identification with others within the group.

Social learning processes play a role in all types of psychotherapies, but their utility in group settings is particularly noteworthy (Bandura, 1986). Behavioral group therapies, for example, highlight social learning processes by focusing on discrete skills that are modeled and practiced within the group setting (Bellack & Hersen, 1979; Curran, 1977; Galassi & Galassi, 1979). Although such interventions sometimes include structured analyses of participants' self-perceptions, emotions, and perceptions of others, these self-processes are generally tied to specific, identifiable behaviors. Similarly, interpersonal group therapies, like those advocated by Yalom, also stimulate change through social learning. Yalom argues that by concentrating on events within the group and treating them as the objects of analysis, the "here-and-now" focus gives clients the opportunity to directly observe the social ramifications of their actions. Through feedback from the group leader and other members, clients develop a clearer understanding of their own personal attitudes, values, and characteristics. Thus, the here-and-now focus not only increases self-insight, but also creates new choice points within clients' behavioral scripts. However, to be certain that these new scripts generalize to nontherapy interactions, some therapy time should be used to bring outside events into the group. As Anderson (1985) and Strong and Claiborn (1982) noted, group therapy is most effective with a here-and-now focus complemented by an excursion into the "then-and-there."

Self-Insight

Learning about one's personal and interpersonal characteristics via interaction with others is a particularly important form of social learning that occurs in groups. The need for self-understanding is a prominent motive in human beings, and individuals often seek therapy when they feel that they lack self-insight. Like individual therapies, group interventions promote self-understanding by providing members with feedback from multiple sources, by forcing members to recognize their impact on others, and by giving members the opportunity to reveal hidden aspects of themselves (Luft, 1984).

Achieving self-insight through interaction with others is consistent with symbolic interactionism's premise that our sense of self is created by our interpretations of the symbolic gestures expressed by others during social interaction (Mead, 1934). Some of these gestures are explicit: a group member may tell another, "You should try to be more sensitive" or "You are always so judgmental, it makes me sick." Alternatively, this feedback may be implicit, as when individuals' responses to one another convey information about their perceptions. As Cooley (1902) explained, other people are a mirror that can be used to gain self-understanding: "as we see our face, figure, and dress in the glass, and are interested in them because they are ours . . . so we perceive in another's mind some thought of our appearance, manners, aims, deeds, character, friends, and so on, and are variously affected by it" (p. 231).

Although the self is social in nature, it is hardly a social chameleon. Interpersonal feedback is selectively filtered by the self, with the result that negative feedback or disconfirming feedback is ignored. This self-protective bias, which is often achieved through the use of excuses (Higgins & Snyder, this volume), results in differential sensitivity to positive and negative feedback (Greenwald, 1981; Kivlighan, 1985). For example, in a series of investigations, Jacobs and his colleagues arranged for subjects to participate in a short-term, highly structured "sensitivity" group (Jacobs, 1974). When subjects rated one another on a series of adjectives, Jacobs found that they consistently accepted positive feedback, but consistently rejected negative feedback. This "credibility gap" occurred despite attempts to vary the source of the information (Jacobs, 1974), the sequencing of the information (Davies & Jacobs, 1985; Jacobs, Jacobs, Gatz, & Schaible, 1973; Schaible & Jacobs, 1975), the behavioral and affective focus of the feedback (Jacobs, Jacobs, Cavior, & Feldman, 1973), and the anonymity of the appraisals (Jacobs, Jacobs, Cavior, & Burke, 1974).

Therapeutic groups, however, circumvent these defenses. When several individuals provide similar feedback, the individual is more likely to internalize this information. Also, because the feedback is given in the context of a long-term, reciprocal relation, it cannot be as easily dismissed as biased or subjective. Group leaders, too, often reward members for accepting rather than rejecting feedback, and the setting itself works to intensify self-awareness. The effectiveness and popularity of sensation "games" and simulations in encounter groups possibly stem from their self-focusing qualities.

In sum, a change in self-insight is a key by-product of therapeutic groups. Even when few changes occur at the behavioral level, changes in self-reported insight are often found in posttherapy reviews (Budman, Demby, Feldstein, & Gold, 1984; Butler, 1977; Ware & Barr, 1977; Ware, Barr, & Boone, 1982). Lieberman et al. (1973), for example, found that most of the gains produced by the group experience were found for self-reported changes in the attitude and value realm, rather than actual behavioral changes. And while Miles (1965) found that executives who participated in National Training Laboratories programs received better ratings by their associates than control group subjects, the participants' self-ratings again revealed much greater change. These and other findings led Gibb (1970, p. 214) to conclude that participation in sensitivity groups yields changes in "ability to manage feelings, directionality of motivation, attitudes towards the self, attitudes towards others, and interdependence," even when little change in behavior occurs.

Studies of group members' evaluations of the therapeutic experience also attest to the importance of self-insight. Butler and Fuhriman (1983a), in a review of outcome studies that asked group members to rank or rate the importance of these curative factors, found that most group members emphasize three of them as most important: self-understanding, interpersonal learning, and catharsis (Butler & Fuhriman, 1983a; Markovitz & Smith, 1983; Maxmen, 1973, 1978; Rohrbaugh & Bartels, 1975; Rugel & Meyer, 1984; Sherry & Hurley, 1976). When these same researchers (Butler & Fuhriman, 1983b) later asked 91 outpatients from 23 psychotherapy groups to rate these factors, self-understanding, along with catharsis and interpersonal learning, were once more highly valued; and more important, those individuals who profited the most from their therapeutic experience were the ones who most emphasized the impact of increased self-understanding.

Social Influence

Many people have a negative view of social influence. They assume that influence is coercive in some way, that it violates the rights of others to choose freely. This pejorative view of social influence, however, is one sided. Individuals in any group, including a therapeutic group, change their behavior for a variety of reasons (Deutsch & Gerard, 1955; Kelley, 1952). Extreme social pressure may be a factor, but social influence takes many other shapes.

In some cases, individuals change their own personal position when they gain information about others' responses on the issue. This informational influence occurs because other people are a valuable source of information about the social world. As described earlier, social comparison theory notes that one primary reason for joining a group is to gain information about the accuracy of one's own perceptions and beliefs (Festinger, 1954; Goethals & Darley, 1977). If others suggest our views are inaccurate, we sometimes change them. Change also can be caused by normative influence. When a group member feels ashamed for losing her temper and making derog-atory statements about the group, strains to disclose an embarrassing personal secret, or tries to give support to a group member who becomes upset, these actions and reactions may reflect the group's norms. At one level, people feel compelled to act in accordance with group norms because a variety of negative consequences could result from nonconformity. Violating group norms can create conflict within the group and can lead to losses in status, to rejection, or even to ostracism. At another level, however, people obey norms in order to fulfill personal expectations about proper behavior. Norms are not simply external constraints but internalized standards; members feel duty bound to adhere to their group's norms because, as loyal members, they accept the legitimacy of the established norms and recognize the importance of supporting these norms.

Change in a group also can result from direct and indirect interpersonal influence. As Strong (1968) argued, therapy is itself a form of persuasive social influence. Clients seek help when they are dissatisfied or frustrated with their current behaviors, but do not feel that they can resolve these problems without assistance. The therapist, therefore, takes the role of the psychological expert who suggests interpretations of the client's experiences and ways to deal with current problems. Interpretations, in the social influence framework, are statements, suggestions, summaries, or questions that offer new ways of viewing the client's problems (Strong & Claiborn, 1982). As a result, therapists who possess certain characteristics that enhance their expertness, attractiveness, and legitimacy (or trustworthiness) influence their clients more strongly (Corrigan, Dell, Lewis, & Schmidt, 1980). These empirical studies also suggest specific techniques that therapists can use to increase the strength of their social influence. For example, professional-looking facilities, displays of credentials, and even manner of dress influence clients' perceptions and may enhance expertness. Group therapists also can increase their expertness by using appropriate (and abstract) psychological terminology, by asking appropriate, thought-provoking questions, and by adopting "an attentive, confident, and reassuring manner" (Corrigan et al., 1980, p. 434). Similarly, Strong (1968, p. 217) offers a number of techniques that therapists can adopt to increase their trustworthiness, including maintaining "a reputation for honesty," adopting a role that is associated with trust (e.g., physician or clergy), and emphasizing one's "sincerity and openness" and "lack of motivation for personal gain."

The strength of social influence processes in groups is considerable. Consider, as an example, Crandall's (1988) recent study of normative, informational, and interpersonal determinants of bulimia. Bulimia tends to run in certain social groups, such as cheerleading squads, dance troupes, sports teams, and sororities (Crago, Yates, Beutler, & Arizmendi, 1985; Garner & Garfinkel, 1980; Squire, 1983). In explanation, Crandall noted that such groups adopt norms that encourage binging and purging. Rather than viewing these actions as abnormal and a threat to health, the sororities that Crandall studied accepted purging as a normal means of controlling one's weight. He also found indirect evidence of interpersonal influence; to be popular in the group, one had to binge at the rate established by the group's norms. Also, as time passed, those who did not binge began to binge.

By harnessing these forces to stimulate health-promoting behaviors rather than unhealthy behaviors, the skilled group leader creates internalization rather than merely compliance or imitation. When internalization occurs, the individual "adopts the induced behavior because it is congruent with his value system. He may consider it useful for the solution of a problem or find it congenial to his needs" (Kelman, 1958, p. 53).

Social Provisions

When individuals encounter stressful experiences they require emotional support, advice and guidance, and positive feedback about their value. Across the life span, individuals need to give and receive nurturance. In many situations individuals require information about the nature of the social world and their own personal identities. In some cases the tasks they attempt are so difficult that they would be overwhelmed if they attempted them alone.

The concept of social provisions suggests that group membership is an efficient means of meeting these basic psychological and relational needs (Weiss, 1973, 1974). Across a variety of contexts and cultures, humans tend toward sociality rather than isolation (Mann, 1980). Studies indicate that human infants seem to be predisposed to form strong attachments to others and babies who are deprived of close human contact have higher mortality rates (Ainsworth, 1979; Bowlby, 1980). Even

adults are discomfited by protracted periods of social isolation (Zubek, 1973) and most prefer the company of others when threatened or distressed (Rofe, 1984). Sociobiologists, too, suggest that cooperative group life is a more evolutionary stable strategy than competition and individualism (Axelrod & Hamilton, 1981). As a result, individuals may be biologically driven to seek membership in groups, and they experience anxiety when threatened with exclusion from membership (i.e., Baumeister & Tice, 1990; Leary, 1990). As Moreland (1987, p. 104) noted in his theory of social integration, throughout history groups have formed "whenever people become dependent on one another for the satisfaction of their needs." The concept of social provisions suggests that therapeutic groups are effective because, as groups, they satisfy certain basic human needs.

The provisions supplied by groups have been described in a variety of ways by researchers and theorists, but the model recently proposed by Shaver and Buhrmester (1983) is particularly parsimonious and comprehensive. Drawing on previous studies of loneliness (Weiss, 1973), sociological analyses of the bases of society (Toennies, 1887/1961), and leadership in groups (Fiedler, 1978), they suggest that social needs and their corresponding social provisions fall into one of two fundamental categories: psychological intimacy and integrated involvement. The need for psychological intimacy can be met through membership in a group that provides emotional support and nurturance. According to Shaver and Buhrmester, (1983, p. 265), such groups provide members with "affection and warmth; unconditional positive regard; opportunity for self-disclosure and emotional expression; lack of defensiveness, lack of concern for self-presentation; giving and receiving nurturance; security and emotional support." Groups that provide members with integrated involvement, in contrast, provide members with "enjoyable and involving activities and projects; social identity and self-definition; [a sense of] being needed for one's skills; social comparison information; opportunity for power and influence; conditional positive regard; support for one's beliefs and values" (Shaver & Buhrmester, 1983, p. 265).

Therapeutic groups are effective, in part, because they satisfy one or both of these basic needs. Although intimacy needs are often satisfied by long-term dyadic pairings such as close friendships and love relationships, a highly cohesive therapeutic group also meets these needs. As Yalom (1985) noted, the effective group allows members to give and receive help (altruism), provides them with emotional support and positive feedback (cohesiveness), serves as an audience for self-disclosures and venting of emotions (catharsis), and offers answers to questions of value and meaning (existential factors). An intimate therapeutic group takes the place of the original family group and provides the member with a sense of belonging, protection from harm, and acceptance (recapitulation of the family). Second, group members often give advice to one another and offer new suggestions to problems (guidance). They also demonstrate ways to act (identification) and provide accurate feedback about personal qualities and impact on others (interpersonal learning).

The social provisions offered by group membership suggest that they are effective vehicles for increasing members' hope regarding future events, for they address the two components of hope identified by Snyder, Anderson, and Irving (this volume). First, a group helps members identify the goals that they wish to achieve. Lewin's classic studies of level of aspiration in groups, for example, clearly illustrate how groups help individuals set goals that match the capabilities of their members while blocking the formation of goals that will be too easy or too difficult to achieve (Lewin, Dembo, Festinger, & Sears, 1944). Second, groups provide members with the multiple means of achieving these goals. They not only provide individuals with social support, but they also help members develop the interpersonal skills needed to acquire these provisions from groups outside of the therapeutic setting, such as their families and friends (Mallinckrodt, 1989).

THE THERAPEUTIC GROUP QUA GROUP

As therapies go, group therapies are effective. That no one approach to treatment has emerged as particularly potent, however, suggests that their curative effects have more to do with the characteristics of groups per se than with the unique techniques utilized by group therapists.

A group dynamics perspective argues that the therapeutic group, qua group, has a profound impact on its members. Through membership in groups individuals define and confirm their values and beliefs and take on or refine a social identity.

When they face uncertain situations, in groups they gain reassuring information about their problems and security in companionship. In groups they learn about relations with others, the type of impressions they make on others, and the way they can relate with others more effectively. In groups, the individual's most basic needs find satisfaction. These needs may be instinctive, or they may be learned. They may be the end product of early childhood experiences or a reaction to temporary, but stressful, situations. They may reflect our uncertainty about our social world or a desire to achieve important goals. But no matter what their origin or nature, groups offer a means of satisfying these needs.

To close on an editorial note, the preceding analyses of the curative foundations of therapeutic groups are more speculative than they should be. The topic of group processes is one of the oldest and most researched areas within social psychology. The structural properties of groups are now well understood, and recent significant advances have been made in our understanding of leadership, social identity, socialization, and other processes in groups. These advances, however, have not added significantly to our understanding of change-producing groups. Much of the literature on therapeutic groups is devoted to descriptions of new variations on old themes, with little attention paid to the structural and interpersonal factors that mediate the effectiveness of these interventions. The lack of theory and empirical rigor bemoaned by Meltzoff and Kornreich in 1970 and Bednar and Kaul in 1978 remains unexorcized.

Future researchers must move past such basic questions as, "Do groups work?" and "Will this type of group intervention succeed?" to ask "Why do groups work?" They must develop more elaborate conceptualizations of groups that take into account both their change-producing properties and their properties as groups per se. Although daunting, this task requires the integration of recent theoretical developments within group dynamics with analyses of their therapeutic properties. Refinements in theoretical formulations offer very specific hypotheses about the impact of group size, levels of authority, and degree of intimacy or change in groups (Latané, 1981; Mullen, 1985). Recent studies of leadership have succeeded in identifying members' cognitive and perceptual reactions to leaders, and the impact of these reactions on leadership effectiveness (Lord, 1985).

Studies of decision-making groups reveal the polarizing impact of group discussion on members (Janis, 1982). Moreland and Levine's (1982) model of group socialization describes the predictable sequence of role transitions that occurs as members move through the investigations, socialization, role maintenance, resocialization, and exit phases during their tenure in the group. Although these theoretical developments are not specific to therapeutic groups, they may hold the key for understanding why such groups are effective in promoting change. Because therapeutic groups are groups first and therapeutic groups second, future efforts must build a theoretical context for understanding how therapeutic groups, as groups, promote change.

REFERENCES

Abramowitz, C. V. (1977). The effectiveness of group psychotherapy with children. *Annual Progress in Child Psychiatry and Child Development*, 393–408.

Ainsworth, M. D. S. (1979). Infant-mother attachment. *American Psychologist, 34*, 932–937.

Anderson, J. D. (1985). Working with groups: Little known facts that challenge well-known myths. *Small Group Behavior, 16*, 267–283.

Axelrod, R., & Hamilton, W. D. (1981). The evolution of cooperation. *Science, 211*, 1390–1396.

Back, K. W. (1973). *Beyond words: The story of sensitivity training and the encounter movement*. Baltimore, MD: Penguin Books.

Back, K. W. (1974). Intervention techniques: Small groups. In M. Rosenzweig & L. Porter (Eds.), *Annual Review of Psychology*, 367–387.

Bandura, A. (1986). *Social foundations of thought and action: A social cognitive theory*. Englewood Cliffs, NJ: Prentice-Hall.

Bates, B., & Goodman, A. (1986). The effectiveness of encounter groups: Implications of research for counselling practice. *British Journal of Guidance and Counselling, 14*, 240–251.

Baumeister, R. F., & Tice, D. M. (1990). Anxiety and social exclusion. *Journal of Social and Clinical Psychology, 9*, 165–175.

Bednar, R. L., & Kaul, T. (1978). Experiential group research: Current perspectives. In S. Garfield & A. Bergin (Eds.), *Handbook of psychotherapy and behavior change*. New York: John Wiley & Sons.

Bednar, R. L., & Kaul, T. (1979). Experiential group research: What never happened. *Journal of Applied Behavioral Science, 15*, 311–319.

Bellack, A., & Hersen, M. (1979). *Research and practice in social skills training*. New York: Plenum Press.

Berah, E. F. (1981). Influence of scheduling variations on the effectiveness of a group assertion-training program for women. *Journal of Counseling Psychology, 28*, 265–268.

Berman, J. J., & Zimpfer, D. G. (1980). Growth groups: Do the outcomes really last? *Review of Educational Research, 50*, 505–524.

Beutler, L. E., Milton, F., Schieber, S. C., Calvert, S., & Gaines, J. (1984). Comparative effects of group psychotherapies in a short-term inpatient setting: An experience with deterioration effects. *Psychiatry, 47*, 66–76.

Bowlby, J. (1980). *Attachment and loss* (Vol. 1). London: Hogarth.

Brandsma, J. M., & Pattison, E. M. (1985). The outcome of group psychotherapy alcoholics: An empirical review. *American Journal of Drug and Alcohol Abuse, 11*, 151–162.

Budman, S. H., Demby, A., Feldstein, M., & Gold, M. (1984). The effects of time-limited group psychotherapy: A controlled study. *International Journal of Group Psychotherapy, 34*, 587–603.

Butler, R. R. (1977). Self-actualization: Myth or reality? *Group and Organizational Studies, 2*, 228–233.

Butler, T., & Fuhriman, A. (1983a). Curative factors in group therapy: A review of the recent literature. *Small Group Behavior, 14*, 131–142.

Butler, T., & Fuhriman, A. (1983b). Level of functioning and length of time in treatment variables influencing patients' therapeutic experience in group psychotherapy. *International Journal of Group Psychotherapy, 33*, 489–505.

Carroll, L. (1962). *Alice's adventures in wonderland*. Harmondsworth, England: Penguin Books. (Original work published 1865)

Coche, E., Cooper, J. B., & Petermann, K. J. (1984). Differential outcomes of cognitive and interactional group therapies. *Small Group Behavior, 15*, 497–509.

Cole, S. A. (1983). Self-help groups. In H. I. Kaplan & B. J. Sadock (Eds.), *Comprehensive group psychotherapy* (2nd ed., pp. 144–150). Baltimore, MD: Williams & Wilkins.

Cooley, C. H. (1902). *Human nature and the social order*. New York: Charles Scribner's Sons.

Corrigan, J. D., Dell, D. M., Lewis, K. N., & Schmidt, L. D. (1980). Counseling as a social influence process: A review. *Journal of Counseling Psychology, 27*, 395–441.

Crago, M., Yates, Beutler, L. E., & Arizmendi, T. G. (1985). Height-weight ratios among female athletes: Are collegiate athletics the precursors to an anorexic syndrome? *International Journal of Eating Disorders, 4*, 79–87.

Crandall, C. S. (1988). Social contagion of binge eating. *Journal of Personality and Social Psychology, 55*, 588–598.

Curran, J. P. (1977). Skills training as an approach to the treatment of heterosexual-social anxiety: A review. *Psychological Bulletin, 1977, 84*, 140–157.

Davies, D., & Jacobs, A. (1985). "Sandwiching" complex interpersonal feedback. *Small Group Behavior, 16*, 387–396.

Deutsch, M., & Gerard, H. B. (1955). A study of normative and informational social influences upon individual judgment. *Journal of Abnormal and Social Psychology, 41*, 629–636.

Falloon, I. R. (1981). Interpersonal variables in behavioural group therapy. *British Journal of Medical Psychology, 54*, 133–141.

Festinger, L. (1950). Informal social communication. *Psychological Review, 57*, 271–282.

Festinger, L. (1954). A theory of social comparison processes. *Human Relations, 7*, 117–140.

Fiedler, F. E. (1978). The contingency model and the dynamics of the leadership process. In L. Berkowitz (Ed.), *Advances in experimental social psychology* (Vol. 12). New York: Academic Press.

Finkelstein, P., Wenegrat, B., & Yalom, I. (1982). Large group awareness training. *Annual Review of Psychology, 33*, 515–539.

Forsyth, D. R. (1990). *Group dynamics* (2nd ed.). Pacific Grove, CA: Brooks/Cole.

Freud, S. (1922). *Group psychology and the analysis of the ego*. London: Hogarth.

Galassi, J. P., & Galassi, M. D. (1979). Modification of heterosocial skills deficits. In A. S. Bellack & M. Hersen (Eds.), *Research and practice in social skills training*. New York: Plenum Press.

Garner, D. M., & Garfinkel, P. E. (1980). Sociocultural factors in the development of anorexia nervosa. *Psychological Medicine, 10*, 647–656.

Gibb, J. R. (1970). Effects of human relations training. In A. E. Bergin & S. L. Garfield (Eds.), *Handbook of psychotherapy and behavior change*. New York: John Wiley & Sons.

Goethals, G. R., & Darley, J. M. (1977). Social comparison theory: An attributional approach. In J. M. Suls & R. L. Miller (Eds.), *Social comparison processes: Theoretical and empirical perspectives*. Washington, DC: Hemisphere.

Gonzalez-Menendez, R. (1985). La psicoterapia de grupo didactica en psicoticos hospitalizados: Estudio comparativo de tres variantes. [Didactic group psychotherapy in hospitalized psychotic patients: Comparative study of 3 variations]. *Revista del Hospital Psiquiatrico de La Habana, 26*(Suppl.), 212–228.

Graff, R. W., Whitehead, G. I., & LeCompte, M. (1986). Group treatment with divorced women using cognitive-behavioral and supportive-insight methods. *Journal of Counseling Psychology, 33*, 276–281.

Greenwald, A. G. (1980). The totalitarian ego: Fabrication and revision of personal history. *American Psychologists, 35*, 603–618.

Greenwald, A. G. (1981). Self and memory. In G. H. Bower (Ed.), *The psychology of learning and motivation* (Vol. 15). New York: Academic Press.

Hajek, P., Belcher, M., & Stapleton, J. (1985). Enhancing the impact of groups: An evaluation of two group formats for smokers. *British Journal of Clinical Psychology, 24*, 289–294.

Hartman, J. J. (1979). Small group methods of personal change. *Annual Review of Psychology, 30*, 453–476.

Hollander, M., & Kazaoka, K. (1988). Behavior therapy groups. In S. Long (Ed.), *Six group therapies* (pp. 257–326). New York: Plenum Press.

Jacobs, A. (1974). The use of feedback in groups. In A. Jacobs & W. W. Spradlin (Eds.), *Group as an agent of change*. New York: Behavioral Publications.

Jacobs, A., Jacobs, M., Cavior, N., & Burke, J. (1974). Anonymous feedback: Credibility and desirability of structured emotional and behavioral feedback delivered in groups. *Journal of Counseling Psychology, 21*, 106–111.

Jacobs, M., Jacobs, A., Cavior, N., & Feldman, A. (1973). Feedback II: The "credibility gap": Delivery of positive and negative emotional and behavior feedback in groups. *Journal of Consulting and Clinical Psychology, 41*, 215–223.

Jacobs, M., Jacobs, A., Gatz, M., & Schaible, T.

(1973). Credibility and desirability of positive and negative structured feedback in groups. *Journal of Consulting and Clinical Psychology, 40*, 244–252.

Janis, I. L. (1982). *Victims of groupthink* (2nd ed.). Boston: Houghton-Mifflin.

Kanas, N. (1986). Group therapy with schizophrenics: A review of controlled studies. *International Journal of Group Psychotherapy, 36*, 339–351.

Kaplan, D. A. (1982). Behavioral, cognitive, and behavioral-cognitive approaches to group assertion training therapy. *Cognitive Therapy and Research, 6*, 301–314.

Kelley, H. H. (1952). Two functions of reference groups. In G. E. Swanson, T. M. Newcomb, & E. L. Hartley (Eds.), *Readings in social psychology* (2nd ed.). New York: Holt.

Kelman, H. C. (1958). Compliance, identification, and internalization: Three processes of attitude change. *Journal of Conflict Resolution, 2*, 51–60.

Kiesler, D. J. (1966). Some myths of psychotherapy research and the search for a paradigm. *Psychological Bulletin, 65*, 110–136.

Kilmann, P. R., & Sotile, W. M. (1976). The marathon encounter group: A review of the outcome literature. *Psychological Bulletin, 83*, 827–850.

Kivlighan, D. M., Jr. (1985). Feedback in group psychotherapy: Review and implications. *Small Group Behavior, 16*, 373–386.

Kivlighan, D. M., Jr., McGovern, T. V., & Corazzini, J. G. (1984). Effects of content and timing of structuring interventions on group therapy process and outcome. *Journal of Counseling Psychology, 31*, 363–370.

Klein, R. H. (1983). Group treatment approaches. In M. Hersen, A. E. Kazdin, & A. S. Bellack (Eds.), *The clinical psychology handbook* (pp. 593–610). Elmsford, NY: Pergamon Press.

Knapp, R. P., & Shostrom, E. L. (1976). POI outcomes in studies of growth groups: A selected review. *Group and Organization Studies, 1*, 187–202.

Knauss, M. R., Jeffrey, D. B., Knauss, C. S., & Harowski, K. (1983). Therapeutic contact and individual differences in a comprehensive weight loss program. *Behavior Therapist, 6*, 124–128.

Lakin, M. (1972). *Experiential groups: The uses of interpersonal encounter, psychotherapy groups, and sensitivity training*. Morristown, NJ: General Learning Press.

Latané, B. (1981). The psychology of social impact. *American Psychologist, 36*, 343–356.

Leary, M. R. (1990). Responses to social exclusion: Social anxiety, jealously, loneliness, depression, and low self-esteem. *Journal of Social and Clinical Psychology, 9*, 221–229.

Lewin, K. (1936). *Principles of topological psychology*. New York: McGraw-Hill.

Lewin, K. (1951). *Field theory in social science*. New York: Harper & Row.

Lewin, K., Dembo, T., Festinger, L., & Sears, P. S. (1944). Level of aspiration. In J. McV. Hunt (Ed.), *Personality and the behavior disorders*. New York: Ronald.

Lieberman, M. A. (1976). Change induction in small groups. *Annual Review of Psychology, 27*, 217–250.

Lieberman, M. A. (1980). Group methods. In F. H. Kanfer & A. P. Goldstein (Eds.), *Helping people change*. New York: Pergamon Press.

Lieberman, M., Yalom, I., & Miles, M. (1973). *Encounter groups: First facts*. New York: Basic Books.

Lord, R. G. (1985). An information processing approach to social perceptions, leadership, and behavioral measurement in organizations. In L. L. Cummings & B. M. Staw (Eds.), *Research in organizational behavior* (Vol. 7, pp. 87–128). Greenwich, CT: JAI Press.

Luborsky, L., Singer, B., & Luborsky, L. (1975). Comparative studies of psychotherapies: Is it true that "Everyone has won and all must have prizes?" *Archives of General Psychiatry, 32*, 995–1008.

Luft, J. (1984). *Groups process: An introduction to group dynamics* (3rd ed.). Palo Alto, CA: Mayfield.

Mallinckrodt, B. (1989). Social support and the effectiveness of group therapy. *Journal of Counseling Psychology, 36*, 170–175.

Mann, L. (1980). Cross-cultural studies of small groups. In H. C. Triandis & R. W. Brislin (Eds.), *Handbook of Cross-Cultural Psychology: Social Psychology* (Vol. 5). Boston: Allyn & Bacon.

Markham, D. J. (1985). Behavioral rehearsals vs. group systematic desensitization in assertiveness training with women. Special issue: Gender roles. *Academic Psychology Bulletin, 7*, 157–174.

Markovitz, R. J., & Smith, J. E. (1983). Patients' perceptions of curative factors in short-term group psychotherapy. *International Journal of Group Psychotherapy, 33*, 21–39.

Maxmen, J. (1973). Group therapy as viewed by hospitalized patients. *Archives of General Psychiatry, 28*, 404–408.

Maxmen, J. (1978). An educative model for inpatient group therapy. *International Journal of Group Psychotherapy, 28*, 321–338.

Mead, G. H. (1934). *Mind, self, and society*. Chicago: University of Chicago Press.

Meltzoff, J., & Kornreich, M. (1970). *Research in psychotherapy*. New York: Atherton Press.

Miles, M. B. (1965). Changes during and following laboratory training: A clinical-experimental study. *Journal of Applied Behavioral Science, 1*, 215–242.

Mills, K. H., & Kilmann, P. R. (1982). Group treatment of sexual dysfunctions: A methodological review of the outcome literature. *Journal of Sex and Marital Therapy, 8*, 259–296.

Moreland, R. L. (1987). The formation of small groups. Review of *Personality and Social Psychology, 8*, 80–110.

Moreland, R. L., & Levine, J. M. (1982). Socialization in small groups: Temporal changes in individual-group relations. In L. Berkowitz (Ed.), *Advances in experimental social psychology* (Vol. 15, pp. 137–192). New York: Academic Press.

Moreno, J. L. (1932). *Who shall survive?* Washington, DC: Nervous and Mental Disease Publishing Co.

Morris, W. N., Worchel, S., Bois, J. L., Pearson, J. A., Rountree, C. A., Samaha, G. M., Wachtler, J., & Wright, S. L. (1976). Collective coping with stress: Group reactions to fear, anxiety, and ambiguity. *Journal of Personality and Social Psychology, 33*, 674–679.

Mullen, B. (1985). Strength and immediacy of sources: A meta-analytic evaluation of the forgotten elements of social impact theory. *Journal of Personality and Social Psychology, 48*, 1458–1466.

Oei, T. P., & Jackson, P. R. (1984). Some effective therapeutic factors in group cognitive-behavioral therapy with problem drinkers. *Journal of Studies on Alcohol, 45*, 119–123.

Page, R. C. (1982). Marathon group therapy with users of illicit drugs: Dimensions of social learning. *International Journal of the Addictions, 17*, 1107–1115.

Page, R. C. (1983). Marathon group counseling with illicit drug users: A study of the effects of two groups for 1 month. *Journal for Specialists in Group Work, 8*, 114–125.

Page, R. C. (1984). The effects of 16 hour long marathon groups on the ways that female drug users perceive women. *Journal of Offender Counseling, Services and Rehabilitation, 8*, 13–26.

Page, R. C. (1985). The effects of marathon groups on the ways illicit drug users perceive counseling. *International Journal of the Addictions, 20*, 1675–1684.

Parloff, M. B., & Dies, R. R. (1977). Group psychotherapy outcome research 1966–1975. *International Journal of Group Psychotherapy, 27*, 281–319.

Paul, G. L. (1967). Strategy of outcome research in psychotherapy. *Journal of Consulting Psychology, 31*, 109–118.

Robinson, D. (1980). Self-help health groups. In P. B. Smith (Ed.), *Small groups and personal change* (pp. 176–193). New York: Methuen.

Rofe, Y. (1984). Stress and affiliation: A utility theory. *Psychological Review, 91*, 235–250.

Rohrbaugh, M., & Bartels, B. D. (1975). Participants' perceptions of curative factors in therapy and growth groups. *Small Group Behavior, 6*, 430–456.

Rose, S. D. (1977). *Group therapy: A behavioral approach*. Englewood Cliffs, NJ: Prentice-Hall.

Rose, S. D. (1983). Behavior therapy in groups. In H. I. Kaplan & B. J. Sadock (Eds.), *Comprehensive group psychotherapy* (2nd ed., pp. 101–108). Baltimore, MD: Williams & Wilkins.

Rose, S. D., Tolman, R., & Tallant, S. (1985). Group process in cognitive-behavioral therapy. *Behavior Therapist, 8*, 71–75.

Rosenberg, H., & Brian, T. (1986). Group therapy with alcoholic clients: A review. *Alcoholism Treatment Quarterly, 3*, 47–65.

Rudestam, K. E. (1982). *Experiential groups in theory and practice*. Monterey, CA: Brooks/Cole.

Rugel, R. P., & Meyer, D. J. (1984). The Tavistock group: Empirical findings and implications for group therapy. *Small Group Behavior, 15*, 361–374.

Russell, E. W. (1978). The facts about Encounter groups: First facts. *Journal of Clinical Psychology, 34*, 130–137.

Sanchez, V. C., Lewinsohn, P. M., & Larson, D. W. (1980). Assertion training: Effectiveness in the treatment of depression. *Journal of Clinical Psychology, 36*, 526–529.

Schachter, S. (1959). *The psychology of affiliation*. Stanford, CA: Stanford University Press.

Schaible, T., & Jacobs, A. (1975). Feedback III: Sequence effects: Enhancement of feedback acceptance and group attractiveness by manipulation of the sequence and valence of feedback. *Small Group Behavior, 6*, 151–173.

Shaver, P., & Buhrmester, D. (1983). Loneliness, sex-role orientation, and group life: A social needs perspective. In P. B. Paulus (Ed.), *Basic group processes*. New York: Springer-Verlag.

Sherry, P., & Hurley, J. R. (1976). Curative factors in psychotherapeutic and growth groups. *Journal of Clinical Psychology, 32*, 835–837.

Slavson, S. R. (1950). Group psychotherapy. *Scientific American, 183*, 42–45.

Smith, M. L., Glass, G. V., & Miller, T. I. (1980). *The benefits of psychotherapy*. Baltimore, MD: Johns Hopkins University Press.

Solomon, S. D. (1982). Individual versus group therapy: Current status in the treatment of alcoholism. *Advances in Alcohol and Substance Abuse, 2*, 69–86.

Sotile, W. M., & Kilmann, P. R. (1977). Treatments of psychogenic female sexual dysfunctions. *Psychological Bulletin, 84*, 619–633.

Spitz, H. I. (1984). Contemporary trends in group psychotherapy: A literature survey. *Hospital and Community Psychiatry, 35*, 132–142.

Squire, S. (1983). *The slender balance*. New York: Pinnacle.

Stiles, W. B., Shapiro, D. A., & Elliott, R. (1986). "Are all psychotherapies equivalent?" *American Psychologist, 41*, 165–180.

Strong, S. R. (1968). Counseling: An interpersonal influence process. *Journal of Counseling Psychology, 15*, 215–224.

Strong, S. R., & Claiborn, C. D. (1982). *Change through interaction*. New York: John Wiley & Sons.

Toennies, F. (1887/1961). Gemeinschaft and Gesellschaft. In T. Parsons, E. Shils, K. D. Naegele, & J. R. Pitts (Eds.), *Theories of society*. New York: Free Press.

Toseland, R. W., & Siporin, M. (1986). When to recommend group treatment: A review of the clinical and the research literature. *International Journal of Group Psychotherapy, 36*, 171–201.

Tuckman, B. W. (1965). Developmental sequences in small groups. *Psychological Bulletin, 63*, 384–399.

Tuckman, B. W., & Jensen, M. A. C. (1977). Stages of small group development revisited. *Group and Organizational Studies, 2*, 419–427.

Ware, R., & Barr, J. E. (1977). Effects of a nine-week structured and unstructured group experience on measures of self-concept and self-actualization. *Small Group Behavior, 8*, 93–100.

Ware, R., Barr, J. E., & Boone, M. (1982). Subjective changes in small group processes: An experimental investigation. *Small Group Behavior, 13*, 395–401.

Weiss, R. S. (1973). *Loneliness: The experience of emotional and social isolation*. Cambridge, MA: MIT Press.

Weiss, R. S. (1974). The provisions of social relationships. In Z. Rubin (Ed.), *Doing unto others*. Englewood Cliffs, NJ: Prentice-Hall.

Wills, T. A. (1981). Downward comparison principles in social psychology. *Psychological Bulletin, 90*, 245–271.

Wood, J. V., Taylor, S. E., & Lichtman, R. R. (1985). Social comparison in adjustment to breast cancer. *Journal of Personality and Social Psychology, 49*, 1169–1183.

Yalom, I. (1975). *The theory and practice of group psychotherapy* (2nd ed.). New York: Basic Books.

Yalom, I. (1985). *The theory and practice of group psychotherapy* (3rd ed.). New York: Basic Books.

Yalom, I. D., Tinklenberg, J., & Gilula, M. (1975). Curative factors in group therapy. Cited in I. D. Yalom, *The theory and practice of group psychotherapy*. New York: Basic Books.

Zander, A. (1985). *The purposes of groups and organizations*. San Francisco: Jossey-Bass.

Zimpfer, D. G. (1987). Groups for the aging: Do they work? *Journal for Specialists in Group Work, 12*, 85–92.

Zubek, J. P. (1973). Behavioral and physiological effects of prolonged sensory and perceptual deprivation: A review. In J. E. Rasmussen (Ed.), *Man in isolation and confinement*. Chicago: Aldine.

CHAPTER 34

PROBLEM-SOLVING TRAINING: IMPLICATIONS FOR REMEDIAL AND PREVENTIVE TRAINING

P. Paul Heppner
Eric T. Hillerbrand

How people cope with their personal problems and process information — how they think, feel, and behave when grappling with a real-life problem — is a complex and dynamic process that has defied simple descriptions. In spite of the importance of these issues, prior to 1980 researchers had not yet developed a technology for assisting people with their decision-making and problem-solving. While our sophistication in problem-solving training has increased in the last decade, the technology is still developing. The lack of a technology is most likely tied to the fact that little is known about how people cope with their real-life personal difficulties (Sternberg, 1982).

The purpose of this chapter is to examine and discuss the problem-solving training literature. First we will provide a definition of problem-solving that will set the parameters for the chapter. Next we will examine the evidence for the relationship between stress, problem-solving, and psychological health; in essence, we will conclude that there is sufficient empirical support to link problem-solving and psychological health. It is not surprising, then, to find considerable interest in

problem-solving training for both remedial and preventive strategies for the mental health problems of modern society. In the third section of the chapter, we briefly describe and review the problem-solving training literature for adults. Finally, in the last section, we will discuss future directions for research on problem-solving training by suggesting additional variables and new perspectives on this topic.

PROBLEM-SOLVING

Problem-solving is a topic that has been the focus of inquiry for many years in psychology. During that time many conceptions of the problem-solving process have been proposed, ranging from various learning approaches (Gagne, 1964; Kendler & Kendler, 1962; Skinner, 1974) to traditional cognitive gestalt approaches (Asher, 1963; Kohler, 1925; Maier, 1970; Sheerer, 1963), and also including computer simulation and mathematical models (Feigenbaum & Feldman, 1963; Newell, Shaw, & Simon, 1958; Newell, Shaw, & Simon, 1963; Restle & Davis, 1962). Differences in conceptions of the problem-solving process have sharply divided psychologists. On the one hand, investigators such as Gagne (1964) and Skinner (1974) have focused mainly on the past experience of the individual as the most important variable in problem-solving. Other investigators (e.g., Kohler, 1925; Maier, 1970) have maintained that it is largely the individual's perception of the situation that is of utmost importance in solving a problem.

The primary focus of this chapter is on real-life personal problem-solving, which is to be distinguished from either laboratory problems (e.g., anagram tasks) or hypothetical, impersonal problems (e.g., physics problems). Although we acknowledge that there is considerable overlap between laboratory and real-life problem-solving activities, we believe that it is important at this time to distinguish between laboratory and real-life problem-solving (see Wicklegren, 1974). In this chapter, problem-solving is conceptualized as a complex and dynamic process as described by Heppner and Krauskopf (1987):

> Real-life personal problem solving is defined as a goal-directed sequence of cognitive and affective operations as well as behavioral responses for the purpose of adapting to internal or external demands or challenges. Problem solving and coping are considered synonymous in this article. In a way, problem solving is the regulation of one's cognitive, affective, and behavioral responses. Problem solving refers to successful and unsuccessful activities, as well as conscious and unconscious activities aimed at approaching or avoiding a problem. Problem solving is not simply the rational, logical, cognitive processing of information. Rather, real-life problem solving is further conceptualized as being a complex, dynamic, highly interactive and intermittent process (rather than a linear, stage-sequential process). It is dynamic and interactive in that initial problem-solving responses affect later responses, alter initial perceptions, and goals often change over time. Problem solving is intermittent in that different problem-solving processes occur at various intervals, often without a specified sequence. Personal problem solving is also a highly complex process in that a typical problem might be solved immediately or might involve innumerable decisions, have multiple possible solutions, and be so ambiguous as to hamper evaluation. (p. 375)

In essence, real-life personal problem-solving is a very broad activity and involves rational and irrational processes, conscious and unconscious processes, as well as cognitive, affective, and behavioral processes.

Stress, Psychological Health, and Problem-Solving

Although the concept of stress has been around for centuries (Lazarus & Folkman, 1984), there is still no universally accepted definition. Definitions of stress fit primarily into three categories: stimulus-based definitions, intervening-process definitions, and response-based definitions (Houston, 1987). Stimulus-based definitions focus on stimuli that disrupt the individual, such as the death of a loved one (e.g., Holmes & Rahe, 1967). Stress, in this view, consists of stressful events. Intervening process definitions focus on the processes that occur between some stimulus and responses of the individual; Lazarus and Folkman (1984) proposed such a model that focuses on the interactive relationship between the person and environment, and particularly the balance between the person's resources and the environmental demands. Response-based definitions focus on the condition of being disturbed, such as the General Adaptation Syndrome described by Selye (1956). Houston (1987) extended the response-based definitions by distinguishing between physical stress and psychological stress. From this perspective, stress consists of physical and psychological outcomes. Regardless of the specific definition of stress, it is becoming increasingly clear that stress is a major factor in adaptational outcomes, such as physical and psychological health (e.g., Fisher, 1986; Houston, 1987; Lazarus & Folkman, 1984; Selye, 1983).

In essence, problem-solving, or coping, is a broad set of activities for responding to life situations, and especially stressful events. It also has been suggested for some time that ineffective problem-solving results in stressful outcomes and psychological maladjustment (D'Zurilla & Goldfried, 1971; Goldfried & D'Zurilla, 1969; Goldfried & Goldfried, 1975; Howard & Scott, 1965; Luchton, 1974; Mahoney, 1974; Mechanic, 1968, 1974; Scott & Howard, 1970; Spivack, Platt, & Shure, 1976; Spivack & Shure, 1974). As Durlak (1983) has noted, it is easy to accept the utility of effective problem-solving skills; it makes intuitive sense that "good problem-solvers . . . are flexible and adaptable in different social circumstances, able to deal effectively with stress, and able to develop suitable methods to attain personal goals and satisfy their needs" (p. 31). Conversely, ineffective problem-solvers are less able to adequately respond to problems, and in essence, deal less effectively with their environment.

One must ask, however, how much empirical support there is for linking problem-solving and psychological health. In this vein, the last several years have witnessed an abundance of research that has examined the relationship between stress and problem-solving or coping efforts aimed at alleviating stress. For example, investigators have made efforts to describe and assess coping efforts (Coyne, Aldwin, & Lazarus, 1981; Heppner & Petersen, 1982; Platt & Spivack, 1975; Worden & Sobel, 1978), identify coping resources (Antonovsky, 1979; Barefoot, Dahlstrom, & Williams, 1983; Brown, Brady, Lent, Wolfert, & Hall, 1987; Kobasa, Maddi, & Kahn, 1982), and identify stress precursors and correlates (Eysenck, 1983; Forsythe & Compas, 1987; Lazarus & Folkman, 1984; Selye, 1983; Snyder & Ford, 1987). The upshot of the last decade of research is that it is becoming increasingly clear that problem-solving or coping does play a role in adaptational responses to stress. We will briefly review two lines of research; both suggest a link between problem-solving and one particular adaptional outcome — psychological health.

Cognitive Deficit

Perhaps one of the earliest lines of research within the parameters of real-life problem-solving to link problem-solving and psychological maladjustment was that which examined cognitive deficiencies within problem-solving thinking. Specifically, George Spivack, Mryna Shure, and their associates have examined the relationship between psychological maladjustment and the following cognitive component skills within problem-solving: (a) problem sensitivity, (b) alternative solution thinking, (c) means-end thinking, (d) consequential thinking, and (e) causal thinking. The major assessment instrument used in this line of research has been the Means-Ends Problem Solving Procedure (MEPS; Platt & Spivack, 1975). These researchers have identified deficits in problem-solving cognition across several populations, such as poorly adjusted preschool children from disadvantaged environments (Shure, Spivack, & Jaeger, 1971), emotionally disturbed 10- to 12-year-old children (Shure & Spivack, 1972), institu-

tionalized impulsive teenagers (Spivack & Levine, 1963), adolescent psychiatric patients (Platt, Altman, & Altman, 1973), youthful incarcerated heroin addicts (Platt, Scura, & Hannon, 1973), and adult psychiatric patients (Platt & Spivack, 1972a, 1972b). Although the validity of the MEPS has been questioned and criticized (e.g., Butler & Meichenbaum, 1981; D'Zurilla, 1986), this line of research has shown that adaptive thinking ability as measured by the MEPS has differentiated between various adjusted and maladjusted groups. For more information about this line of research, readers are referred to Butler and Meichenbaum (1981), D'Zurilla (1986), D'Zurilla and Nezu (1982), Kendall, Pellegrini, and Urbain (1981), and Spivack, Platt, and Shure (1976).

Problem-Solving Appraisal

Another line of research has provided evidence that a person's beliefs or appraisals of his or her problem-solving capabilities are related to psychological adjustment. This research has been spawned by the notion of higher order or metacognitive variables in various cognitive processes (e.g., Brown, 1977; Flavell & Wellman, 1977; Meichenbaum & Asarnow, 1979). Metacognition refers to an individual's awareness of the processes that affect the efficient use of cognitive skills, such as the awareness of one's own cognitive abilities and the monitoring and regulation of cognitive processes. The focus is not on "the specific knowledge or processes that individuals may apply directly to the solution of problems, but with higher order variables that affect how (and whether) they will solve problems" (Butler & Meichenbaum, 1981, p. 219).

Butler and Meichenbaum hypothesized that one such variable, an individual's appraisal of his or her problem-solving ability, will affect problem-solving performance. Several other writers have suggested that one's appraisal of ability seems to be related to coping with stress (e.g., Antonovsky, 1979; Coyne & Lazarus, 1980; Kobasa, 1979). For example, Kobasa proposed that "hardiness" as a constellation of personality characteristics involves self-appraisal activities that mediate reactions to stressful life events and subsequent physical and psychological health (see Kobasa, 1982; Kobasa, Maddi, & Kahn, 1982; Maddi, Hoover, & Kobasa, 1982).

Heppner and Petersen (1982) have developed a measure of such self-appraisal, the Problem Solving Inventory (PSI). Factor analysis of the PSI revealed three factors: (a) problem-solving confidence, (b) approach-avoidance style, and (c) personal control (Heppner & Petersen, 1982). People who perceive themselves as effective problem-solvers (having confidence, personal control, and approaching problems; low PSI scores) differ significantly from those who perceive themselves as ineffective (lacking confidence and personal control, and avoiding problems; high PSI scores) on a range of cognitive, affective, and behavioral variables.

Several studies have examined the relationship between the PSI and several indices of psychological health. Briefly, results show that, when compared to those who scored high on the PSI, those who scored low reported (a) a more positive self-concept, and fewer dysfunctional thoughts and irrational beliefs (Heppner, Reeder, & Larson, 1983); (b) less social anxiety (DeClue, 1983); (c) less trait anxiety, more intuitive and dependent decision-making styles, and more interpersonal assertiveness (Neal & Heppner, 1982; Larson, 1984; Phillips, Pazienza, & Ferrin, 1984); (d) fewer physical health symptoms (Tracey, Sherry, & Keitel, 1986), and (e) better psychological adjustment as measured by the Minnesota Multiphasic Personality Inventory (MMPI) and SCL-90 (Heppner & Anderson, 1985; Heppner, Kampa, & Brunning, 1987).

In addition, considerable research has examined the relationship between problem-solving and depression. Initially, research found that perceived ineffective problem-solvers reported higher levels of depressive symptoms than did perceived effective problem-solvers (e.g., Heppner & Anderson, 1985; Heppner, Baumgardner, & Jackson, 1985; Heppner et al., 1987; Nezu, 1985; Nezu & Ronan, 1985; Nezu, Kalmar, Ronan, & Clavijo, 1986). More recent research, however, suggests that problem-solving appraisal moderates depressive symptoms in relationship to stressful events (Nezu & Ronan, 1988; Nezu, Nezu, Saraydarian, Kalmar, & Ronan, 1986). Specifically, it appears that perceived effective problem-solvers (as measured by the PSI) under high levels of stress reported significantly lower levels of depressive symptoms when compared with perceived ineffective problem-solvers under similar levels of high stress (Nezu, Nezu et al., 1986). Similar results were found utilizing the MEPS with both prospective and cross-sectional analyses (Nezu & Ronan, 1988). These results provide strong support for

the links between problem-solving, stress, and psychological health.

TRAINING LITERATURE

Much of the applied problem-solving research has conceptualized the problem-solving process as a constellation of relatively discrete, cognitive abilities (e.g., Feldhusen, Houtz, & Ringenbach, 1972) or thought processes (e.g., Spivack, Platt, & Shure, 1976). Most often the various thought processes have been conceptualized into problem-solving models that consist of five or more problem-solving stages (e.g., Dewey, 1933; D'Zurilla & Goldfried, 1971).

D'Zurilla and Goldfried's (1971) five-stage model has received considerable attention: general orientation (the cognitive and motivational set with which one approaches and recognizes problems in general), problem definition and formulation (the delineation of a problem into concrete and specific terms and the identification of specific goals), generation of alternatives (the production of an exhaustive list of appropriate solution possibilities), decision-making (the systematic evaluation of the range of alternative solutions regarding consequences and the selection of the most optimal choices), and solution implementation and verification (the monitoring and evaluation of the actual solution outcome after its implementation). One training approach has been to teach cognitive skills within a specific stage in a brief training session (e.g., generating alternatives). A more common approach has been to teach all five stages over an extended period of time. A third approach has been to combine problem-solving skill training with some other intervention, such as anxiety management. These three approaches will be briefly summarized; for additional information, the reader is referred to earlier reviews by D'Zurilla (1986), D'Zurilla and Nezu (1982), and Heppner, Neal, and Larson (1984).

Teaching Specific Component Skills

Several training studies have taught specific cognitive skills within a particular problem-solving stage. The studies follow a similar format. The treatment groups receive brief training (e.g., 45 minutes) in some specific problem-solving skill. Both the treatment and control groups are then asked to respond to hypothetical problems using the problem-solving skill under examination. The results from several investigations show that the treatment groups outperformed the control groups on problem-solving activities applied to hypothetical situations when given training on (a) problem definition (Nezu & D'Zurilla, 1981a, 1981b), (b) generation of alternatives (D'Zurilla & Nezu, 1980; Nezu & D'Zurilla, 1981b), (c) decision-making (Nezu & D'Zurilla, 1979; Nezu & D'Zurilla, 1981a), and combinations of the above components (Cormier, Otani, & Cormier, 1986).

This line of research has provided solid evidence that specific problem-solving skills can be taught in a relatively brief training session. Additional research is needed to examine the generalization of the problem-solving training to the participants' real-life personal problems, maintenance of these skills over time, and effects of such training on other variables involved in the problem-solving process (e.g., confidence in one's problem-solving skills).

Teaching Problem-Solving Models

A common approach in problem-solving training has been to teach the entire D'Zurilla and Goldfried (1971) five-stage model of problem-solving. Training typically consists of didactics and practice in each of the five stages across several sessions, followed by applied integration of the model and continued practice of the different skill components (Nezu, 1986). Training is usually conducted in small groups that include 6 to 10 sessions that often span 6 to 10 weeks. Training that has been based on or is similar to the five component areas in D'Zurilla and Goldfried's (1971) model has been effective in a wide variety of target populations and training goals: psychiatric patients (Edelstein, Couture, Cray, Dickens, & Lusebrink, 1980; Hansen, St. Lawrence, & Christoff, 1985), alcoholism (Intagliatia, 1978), depression (Hussian & Lawrence, 1981; Nezu, 1986), academic underachievement (Richards & Perri, 1978), and anger control (Moon & Eisler, 1983). One study that examined vocational indecision (Mendonca & Siess, 1976) did not support the effectiveness of training based on the component skills within the five stages.

The above studies provide encouraging support for the utility of problem-solving training based on the component skills of D'Zurilla and Goldfried's five stages. One study in this group provides particularly strong support for training based on the five component skills. Nezu (1986)

randomly assigned 26 clinically depressed community adults to one of three conditions: (a) problem-solving therapy (PST) based on the five component skills; (b) problem-focused therapy (PFT), which was a more general problem-oriented group therapy; and (c) a waiting-list control. Both therapy conditions were conducted in a group setting over eight weekly sessions. Nezu selected four dependent measures that not only assessed the subjects' target problem, depression, but also broadened his assessment to include a more general problem-solving appraisal and locus of control as well. Specifically, his dependent measures included the Beck Depression Inventory (BDI; Beck, 1972), the depression scale of the MMPI (MMPI-D; Dahlstrom & Dahlstrom, 1980), the PSI (Heppner & Petersen, 1982), and the Internal-External Locus of Control Scale (I-E; Rotter, 1966). He used these instruments as pretest, posttest, and as 6-month follow-up measures. The results indicated that the PST condition resulted in greater reductions in depression (which were maintained at the 6-month follow-up). In addition, the PST condition increased subjects' appraisal of their problem-solving effectiveness and also changed their locus of control orientation from external to internal. Thus, the training seemed to not only affect the target problem, but also more global but generalized constructs that appear to be important in the coping process.

Teaching Component Skills in Conjunction with Other Interventions

Another strategy in problem-solving training has been to develop new training programs designed to emphasize one or more problem-solving component skill in conjunction with other interventions such as communication skills, stress management skills, or study skills. Problem-solving training in these instances often consists of didactic information, practice, homework assignments, identifying problems, self-monitoring, analyzing obstacles, planning, encouragement, and brainstorming.

Three studies that developed new problem-solving training programs targeted ineffective coping in general. For example, Sarason and Sarason (1981) developed a problem-solving training program for problems typically encountered by high school students. Training consisted primarily of modeling and role-playing effective problem-solving behavior and cognitive processes (e.g., examining probable consequences of one's actions). Training resulted in better performance on two problem-solving tests and a job interview, and fewer problem behavior referrals. Likewise, Dixon, Heppner, Petersen, and Ronning (1979) developed a general problem-solving training program for college students based on didactic presentations, group discussions, directed practice, and homework assignments covering a broad range of problem-solving skills. The results revealed that training resulted in higher quality (not quantity) of responses, less impulsivity in solving problems, but no differences in decision-making skills.

Heppner, Baumgardner, Larson, and Petty (1988) also developed a generic problem-solving training program for college students that emphasized self-management principles in coping, such as self-reinforcement and self-punishment processes, approach and avoidant behaviors, irrational beliefs, self-statements, and effective reactions. The results indicated that problem-solving training was effective at enhancing students' problem-solving appraisal, and that the self-report changes were maintained at a 1-year follow-up. In particular, training seemed most useful for students who initially appraised their problem-solving very negatively.

Three other studies developed training programs aimed at alleviating stress and anxiety. Tableman, Marciniak, Johnson, and Rodgers (1982) developed a stress management training program for low-income women supported by public assistance. Their training program focused on providing training in four coping skills: (a) increasing belief in one's personal power and potential, (b) life planning and goals, (c) problem-solving aimed at changing the negative aspects of one's life, and (d) techniques for stress reduction. The results indicated that treatment resulted in important gains on a variety of inventories measuring psychological distress, such as depression and anxiety.

Likewise, Petty, Moeller, and Campbell (1976) used problem-solving discussions that emphasized brainstorming to treat elderly people experiencing stress and anxiety related to the aging process. The results indicated that subjects increased their awareness of events affecting physical and psychological discomfort, and learned new coping behaviors to deal with these symptoms. Toseland (1977) designed a problem-solving training workshop to improve the general coping skills of senior citizens, particularly for problems requiring as-

sertive behavior. Training consisted of teaching several traditional problem-solving skills (e.g., generating alternatives) as well as analyzing one's cognitive and affective processes. The results suggested that training resulted in positive gains in both self-report of assertiveness and a problem-solving performance test.

Several other investigators examined the efficacy of problem-solving training on marital and family problems. Ewart, Taylor, Kraemer, and Agras (1984) developed a communication and problem-solving training program for hypertensive patients experiencing marital conflicts. The results revealed that patients who learned effective problem-solving techniques engaged in fewer hostile exchanges and had greater reductions in blood pressure. Jacobson (1977a, 1977b; 1978) assessed problem-solving training and contingency contracting as a treatment for married couples. The problem-solving and contingency contracting group reported higher marital adjustment scores and better problem-solving scores than a control group or a nonspecific marital therapy group. Likewise, Robin and colleagues developed a problem-solving communication training program for treating parent-adolescent conflicts. Training consisted of teaching specific problem-solving and communication skills to individual mother-adolescent dyads by a therapist. Three outcome studies revealed that training tended to result in improvements in observational measures of problem-solving behavior in actual communications, and improvements in conflict resolution at home (Foster, Prinz, & O'Leary, 1983; Robin, 1981; Robin, Kent, O'Leary, Foster, & Prinz, 1977).

At least two studies investigated the effects of problem-solving training on weight-control problems. Black and his colleagues have developed a seven-step problem-solving training program that complements behaviorally oriented weight-control methods; Black's problem-solving approach focuses on identifying problems, generating alternatives, decision-making, and evaluating progress. Black and Scherba (1983) initially found that subjects who contracted to practice problem-solving (vs. behavioral weight control) lost significantly more weight following the completion of a weight-loss program. In another study, Black and Threlfall (1986) found that those subjects who complied with the requirements of the problem-solving training program lost significantly more weight than those who complied poorly.

Three other problem-solving training studies examined treating agoraphobia, psychiatric patients, and cigarette smoking. Jannoun, Munby, Catalan, and Gelder (1980) compared problem-solving training with programmed practice for the treatment of agoraphobia. Problem-solving training consisted of identifying relevant life problems and discussing general ways of reducing stressors. The results showed that the treatments were equally effective in reducing anxiety and phobic severity. Bedell, Archer, and Marlowe (1980) developed a didactic training program to help psychiatric patients understand problem-solving concepts and practice-oriented activities, such as role-playing and homework assignments, to facilitate skill enhancement. The training group (vs. a control group) improved significantly more on two problem-solving self-report measures. A final study (Karol & Richards, 1978) found that couples in problem-solving training combined with a buddy system compared with a behavioral treatment group (e.g., self monitoring, stimulus control, and alternative behavior planning) were smoking less at the end of treatment and at the 2-month, 4-month, and 8-month follow-ups.

FUTURE DIRECTIONS

After extensively reviewing the problem-solving literature, D'Zurilla (1986) concluded that taken together, the results of these studies have produced "very promising results" (p. 210). These results constitute support for the use of problem-solving training as a clinical intervention approach for a variety of clinical problems. It appears that problem-solving training "contributes not only to immediate treatment effects but to the maintenance of treatment effects as well" (D'Zurilla, 1986, p. 211). However, D'Zurilla (1986) and D'Zurilla and Nezu (1982) noted several methodological problems that qualify some of the results.

1. Problem-solving training is conducted as part of a treatment package that includes other treatments, and thus it is hard to isolate the problem-solving training effects.
2. Some studies do not include the necessary experimental control to eliminate extraneous variables.
3. Some studies do not include the necessary control groups to isolate the effects of nonspecific factors associated with treatment.

4. Some studies failed to include any measures of problem-solving among the outcome measures.
5. Some studies only used a problem-solving outcome measure without including any measures of adjustment, psychopathology, or maladaptive behavior.
6. Some studies do not include any follow-up evaluations.

We agree that much more is known about problem-solving training since D'Zurilla and Goldfried's (1971) landmark article, although we still have not developed a technology for helping people solve their problems. The purpose of this section is to stimulate both practitioners and researchers to think about problem-solving training for adults. Although the training in problem-solving skills is becoming more sophisticated and successful, there is a great deal that we do not know about problem-solving (Heppner, 1989) and, subsequently, problem-solving training.

Our central thesis is that problem-solving training can be enhanced by greater attention to more microscopic problem-solving processes. First, we need a greater understanding of the specific processes used in real-life problem-solving. This includes a more minute microscopic understanding of the cognitive and noncognitive processes used in coping and problem-solving. The second area concerns the generalizability of the training outcomes. Specifically, greater consideration needs to be given to understanding how problem-solving training programs generalize to real-life problems, across various types of problems, over time, and across individual differences. We will discuss these points subsequently in six sections: (a) descriptions of real-life problem solving, (b) cognitive processes, (c) noncognitive processes, (d) training generalizability over time, (e) problem types, and (f) individual differences.

Descriptive Information About Real-Life Problem-Solving

As Sternberg (1982) has noted, little is known about how people cope with their real-life personal difficulties. We need to attend more closely to and describe in more detail how people process information as they attempt to cope with these troublesome problems. In particular, we believe that problem-solving training needs to examine in greater detail clients' existing knowledge bases, how they process information, and how they use their knowledge bases to regulate their cognitions, affect, and behavior with specific problems.

It is also important to note that the models for problem-solving training were typically derived from research conducted in the well-controlled environment of the laboratory using mathematics or physics problems (what Simon [1973] calls "well-structured" problems) compared with the less defined, "ill-structured" problems of everyday life. These problems contain clear information and established solution paths. Ill-structured problems have ambiguous problem information, solution paths, and solution goals.

Real-life problems are far more complex and are never as neatly packaged and presented as those in the laboratory. Nor are the problems typically as simple and clear as they are when used in problem-solving training sessions. The result is that clients may be able to solve an overly simplified problem in the structure of the training setting but be unable to solve the problem when it occurs in a more complex real-life environment in part because of inadequate models of how people solve real-life problems.

Our clients need to know how to solve the ambiguous problems of real life, which may entail using something other than these laboratory models. Research on the solution of ill-structured problems suggests that individuals need skills to structure these poorly defined problems, translating them into smaller, and more clear, well-structured subproblems (Greeno, 1978). At present, however, we know little about this structuring process with real-life problems.

In short, we recommend that researchers in applied problem-solving training (a) describe in greater detail how people process information as they cope with real-life, troublesome problems, and (b) develop accurate, descriptive models of the real-life problem-solving process.

Cognitive Processes

We firmly believe that research in applied problem-solving could benefit from a more microscopic analysis of relevant cognitive processes within problem-solving activities. We suggest that three cognitive processes need consideration: (a) memory use, (b) acquisition and organization of problem-relevant knowledge, and (c) acquisition of problem recognition skills. These three will be briefly explored.

It is commonly noted in laboratory research that memory is a key cognitive component in problem-solving (e.g., Glaser & Chi, 1988). Learning new skills is cognitively laborious. Information related to new skills is often clumsily recalled in a highly inefficient process. The length of time necessary to learn new cognitive skills is directly related to the availability and efficiency of memory resources (e.g., Fredericksen, 1984). Memory capacity and use also is affected by client mood or anxiety level (e.g., Gagne, 1985). In order to optimally use memory capacity, it has been suggested that memory skills be taught (Fredericksen, 1984) or external aids developed to reduce the burden on memory resources (Perkins, 1987). In short, we recommend that researchers in applied problem-solving examine the utility of memory skills or aids in problem-solving training.

Effective problem solvers need both skills in how to solve problems as well as problem-relevant knowledge stored in memory. The importance of one's knowledge base in problem solution has long been acknowledged (Simon & Hayes, 1976). We need to understand the kind of knowledge base necessary for demonstrating particular problem-solving competencies in a given area. For example, what kinds of knowledge do nonassertive clients need about themselves, others, and interpersonal interactions in order for the clients to combine this knowledge with problem-solving skills in order to competently solve assertiveness problems.

The type of knowledge may not be as important as the way this knowledge is organized (in what have been called "knowledge structures" or "schemas"). More competent problem-solvers have their knowledge organized in highly efficient, easily accessible, and complexly organized patterns (e.g., Glaser & Chi, 1988). We have little understanding of this organization in specific problem domains.

In short, we recommend that researchers in applied problem-solving training give more attention to clients' existing knowledge bases and how that information is structured or organized (also see Heppner & Krauskopf, 1987). For a client, existing knowledge structures may need to be altered or new structures acquired apart from acquiring new problem-solving skills. We believe it is important for us to understand how this knowledge organization can be facilitated, how new information can be added to existing structures, and how clients can "learn to learn" how to alter structures. Flexibility in the acquisition and use of these structures seems to be an important ingredient (see Neves & Anderson, 1981). However, many clients exhibit considerable cognitive rigidity and do not demonstrate this flexibility. Perhaps it would be useful in training to explicitly focus on the role of existing knowledge bases (and how knowledge is organized) to facilitate self-management processes.

Finally, clients need to be able to accurately identify problem areas in which they have difficulty. Real-life problems often appear in a confusing, unclear manner. Thus, clients may have difficulty in recognizing problems and initiating their newly acquired problem-solving skills.

Research has shown that recognizing specific types of problems and problem features, sometimes referred to as pattern recognition skills, are important in problem-solving and can be taught if there are recurrent and constant patterns (Fredericksen, 1984). However, in the confusing and poorly defined problems of everyday living, pattern recognition becomes more complex. The knowledge necessary for the solution of poorly defined problems may be so broad that it does not fit an efficient and easily organized pattern that then can be used to recognize relevant problem features. The use of general pattern recognition heuristics or metacognitive skills (i.e., training clients to ask themselves if this is a problem) may be useful in this context. In short, because problem recognition plays such a critical role for later problem-solving activities, we recommend that researchers examine the specific activities involved in identifying and defining problems. We suspect that interventions aimed at the pattern recognition processes will be helpful to many clients.

Noncognitive Processes

The primary emphasis in most problem-solving training programs has been on cognitive skills and processes. We especially believe that the role of affect has received less attention than it deserves in problem-solving training, particularly the so-called "intuitive" process (Brammer, in press) as well as the negative states people try to regulate. Often when clients enter therapy, their presenting problem centers on negative emotional states. If our goal is to help clients with affective problems and processes, we need to focus specifically on affective processes in training.

People are often very rational, logical, and systematic in their thinking. But it is important to note that often people think in very irrational,

illogical, and unsystematic ways. Subsequently, we believe that how people distort information is a critical process in problem-solving, and therefore is an essential topic for training (Heppner, 1989; Strohmer & Blustein, in press).

Emotions may have a substantial impact on how information is processed during coping or problem-solving (Heppner & Krauskopf, 1987). Many times emotional reactions are ambiguous and difficult for clients to understand; furthermore, at times one's emotions become so painful that strong avoidant patterns or defenses are developed, such as denial or overcompensation. The outcome of such strong emotional reactions is that it is difficult for a person to cognitively process relevant information pertaining to the emotional reactions or problem. In short, a substantial portion of clients' problem-solving involves widely ranging affective reactions to problems that can inhibit, enhance, or distort cognitive and behavioral processes (Heppner, 1989).

We strongly recommend that researchers increase their attention to the regulation of affective processes within problem-solving and aim problem-solving interventions at increasing clients' understanding and effective regulation of their affective processes.

Training Generalizability

One of the issues that has hindered problem-solving training has been the apparent limited transfer of skills to new situations ("transfer-of-training"; Belmont, Butterfield, & Ferritti, 1982). In essence, problem-solving training research has had difficulty demonstrating that problem-solving skills acquired in a particular treatment setting are generalized to real-life or nontreatment settings, both immediately after training as well as over time. In part, the limited transfer of training exhibited in problem-solving training reflects an inconclusive debate among researchers and clinicians as to whether individuals should be trained in general or situation-specific knowledge about problems (Glaser, 1984).

It is clear from past laboratory research that individuals have difficulty in generalizing the specific problem-solving skills that they have learned (e.g., Glick, 1986) to new or novel problems. Concomitantly, when individuals are trained in more general problem-solving skills, they have difficulty learning how and when to apply this general knowledge to specific problem situations.

It is also important to carefully consider our clientele. To help a person become a better problem-solver is often not a small task, especially if the person has severe problem-solving deficits and has not consistently adapted well to his or her environment for several years. It is erroneous to assume that three or four sessions with problem-solving training will make much of a difference with a chronically poor problem-solver. It is important to remember that often clients have spent years learning maladaptive problem-solving styles, that these maladaptive styles usually serve some psychological function for the client, and that it will be difficult for training to erase these maladaptive styles.

Transfer issues may have implications for how training programs are formulated. Perkins and Solomon (1986) suggest that transfer can occur either consciously or spontaneously. Conscious transfer occurs when an individual identifies some aspects of a new problem (problem cues) that are similar to the trained problem, and then uses (transfers) existing skills. Transfer may occur spontaneously when a particular skill is practiced to the point that performance is automatic. A specific problem cue, occurring in a new or novel problem, may then serve as a stimulus for the automated performance of the specific skill.

Further, the bulk of the research has focused on the positive effects of training transfer. Little is known about negative transfer of training (Lohman, 1986). As a result, we presently have little knowledge about the detrimental effects of problem-solving training on the individual's existing problem-solving abilities and solutions.

The transfer issue is particularly important considering that practice with feedback is essential for skill acquisition to the point of automated performance. The importance of practice in attaining high levels of competence in skill usage has only recently been understood (Fredericksen, 1984). For example, practice entails long periods of exposure to problem tasks; Chase and Simon (1973) suggest over 10,000 practice hours are necessary for acquisition of chess expertise.

No problem-solving training program provides clients with this type of practice. At best, it is typically assumed that clients will continue to utilize the problem-solving skills acquired in the programs, practicing the skills correctly, and eventually obtaining sufficient levels of competence. However, it is unclear what our clients are practicing and learning. In short, we know little about the type of feedback that best facilitates skill acquisition during problem-solving training, and how practice following training, without expert feedback, affects skill acquisition. As part of understanding transfer, we need to know more about how clients practice, how performance is affected by in-session versus out-of-session practice, and how client performance is affected by the sparse, and possibly inaccurate, feedback clients obtain about performance.

Further, there is the issue of the long-term effects of training. We believe training outcomes need to be broadened considerably to more adequately evaluate training. Outcomes of training might include (a) traditional outcomes such as problem-solving component skills or problem-solving appraisal, as well as how clients (b) process information and (c) regulate their cognitive, affective, and behavioral processes (see Baron, Baron, Barber, & Nolen-Hoeksema, in press).

In short, we recommend that researchers give more attention to the extent that clients use their newly acquired problem-solving skills. We believe that problem-solving training needs to focus more directly on the issue of skill transfer or generalizability. In order for training programs to demonstrate the positive outcome of problem-solving training, we need to better understand how to facilitate this transfer process (see Fredericksen, 1984).

Problem Types

It is becoming increasingly clear that different types of problems lead to different problem-solving activities (e.g., Heppner, Hibel, Neal, Weinstein, & Rabinowitz, 1982; Perri & Richards, 1977) and may affect skill transfer. Thus, a second generalization issue pertains to different types of problems. Thus, experimental researchers have proceeded to examine how problem-solvers respond to domain-specific problems, such as chess problems (Chase & Simon, 1973), math problems (Marshall, 1982), or anagram problems (Davis, 1966). At present, it is unclear how people might organize or group personal problems into particular domains or categories. Heppner and Krauskopf (1987) have suggested several dimensions on which personal problems may vary, which might help explain how people organize personal problems (e.g., cause of the problem, problem difficulty).

The way in which clients organize problems

may be affected by the verbal component and subjective interpretation of interpersonal problems. Groen and Patel (1988) have noted that verbal comprehension constitutes an important, and unresearched, part of problem solution. This verbal component may make problems open to multiple interpretations. Thus, one client may interpret a problem in one manner, grouping it in one problem category, whereas another client will have a very different interpretation. Training in specific problem-solving skills, algorithmic approaches, may not be appropriate (Glaser, 1988). Rather, complex verbal tasks may require the acquisition of metacognitive skills rather than specific pattern-recognition skills (see Brown & Campione, 1986). Rather than learning specific comprehensive strategies, it may be more important to learn metacognitive skills that can be used to check comprehension and understanding. For example, it might be helpful to teach clients metacognitive skills that allow them to double-check ambiguities or unclear problems and problem features rather than specific pattern-recognition skills.

In short, we recommend that researchers give more attention to problem type during problem-solving training. While it is obvious that different types of problems lead to different problem-solving activities, we need to know more specifically how different problem characteristics affect the problem-solving process. In addition, the role of the client's verbal comprehension of particular problems merits attention.

Individual Differences

For many years it was assumed that clients seeking psychotherapy were a rather homogeneous group and would respond in similar ways to therapeutic interventions. Kiesler (1971) coined this assumption the "uniformity myth" and suggested that researchers must examine important differences across clients. Within problem-solving training, researchers seem to assume that participants are a homogeneous group, all having similar strengths and deficits, and all needing the same interventions to enhance a common set of problem-solving skills. However, different people most likely will have different skill deficits. Normally, and moreso under stress, individuals tend to emphasize the cognitive skills that they feel comfortable with and deemphasize the areas in which they feel deficient (Cronbach & Snow, 1977; Krauskopf & Davis, 1973). Clients in therapy already have a

well-rehearsed repertoire of skills and some type of organized knowledge base that is used in problem-solving. However, these skills and knowledge bases, often the source of their problem behavior, prove to be inadequate.

A critical part of our training efforts needs to involve identifying the role of individual differences variables in problem-solving in general, and especially in relationship to problem-solving training (see Heppner & Krauskopf, 1987; Larson, in press). Cronbach and Snow (1977) noted the significance of individual aptitude in interacting with treatment outcomes. Understanding a client's pre-existing cognitive aptitude, knowledge bases, and skill deficits has implications for the course of problem-solving training. Another feature is level of problem-solving expertise. Clients with little competence in problem-solving require a different training format than clients with greater expertise.

In short, we recommend that researchers attend more to the role that individual differences play within problem-solving in general, but in particular within problem-solving training interventions. How clients process information in the coping process is very directly related to a number of personality variables (Heppner & Krauskopf, 1987). Given the diversity of skills across clients, we suspect that the effectiveness of problem-solving training also could be enhanced by attending more to particular skill deficits within clients.

CONCLUSION

Problem-solving training has focused on a wide range of skills, from specific component skills (e.g., generating alternatives) to general problem-solving models. Training has been successful with a wide range of target problems, from study skills to depression. The results of these studies have produced "very promising results" (D'Zurilla, 1986, p. 210), and clearly support continued examination of problem-solving training as a clinical intervention for promoting physical and psychological health.

Obviously, problem-solving training holds considerable appeal for remedial interventions, which has been the focus of much of the previous research on problem-solving training. It is abundantly clear that stress is related to physical and psychological health. It also is becoming increasingly clear that problem-solving, or coping, plays a role in how one responds to stressful events.

Moreover, problem-solving training also could

be used proactively to augment the effectiveness of well-functioning high school and college students. Problem-solving training could be viewed as providing a generic set of self-management skills that could enhance students' coping abilities with regard to personal, career, and academic problems. In a way, it is startling to realize that a complex society such as ours does not provide systematic problem-solving training for the myriad of applied problems that its members will undoubtedly face. In a similar way, Sternberg (1985) has argued that our educational institutions fall dramatically short in teaching students about the complex process called problem-solving.

There is evidence that college students who function well in their environment benefit from problem-solving training. For example, one study (Heppner & Reeder, 1984) found that even resident assistants who were selected for having leadership and interpersonal skills and who had appraised themselves as effective problem-solvers benefited from brief problem-solving training. Besides increasing their awareness of how they solve problems, training also had a positive impact on how they later reported solving problems on their residence hall floors, both immediately after training and in a 4-month follow-up. Another group of college students who initially appraised themselves as very effective problem-solvers reported fewer personal problems after participating in eight 1½-hour problem-solving training sessions (Heppner et al., 1989). In addition, the effective problem-solvers reported higher levels of satisfaction with the training than did students who initially appraised themselves as very ineffective problem solvers. We suspect that because of the complexity of applied problem-solving, even those people who report being effective problem-solvers can receive substantial benefits from training.

While considerable progress has been made within the last 15 years with regard to problem-solving training, it is clear that much remains unknown about how to facilitate or enhance clients' coping and problem-solving efforts. More information is needed about real-life problem-solving processes and the effects of problem-solving training on specific microprocesses, for both remedial and preventive interventions.

REFERENCES

Antonovsky, A. (1979). *Health, stress, and coping*. San Francisco: Jossey-Bass.

Asher, J. J. (1963). Towards a new field theory of problem solving. *Journal of General Psychology, 68*, 3–8.

Barefoot, J. C., Dahlstrom, W. G., & Williams, R. B. (1983). Hostility, CHD incidence, and total mortality: A 25-year follow-up study of 255 physicians. *Psychosomatic Medicine, 45*, 59–63.

Baron, J., Baron, J. H., Barber, J. P., & Nolen-Hoeksema, S. (in press). Rational thinking as a goal of therapy. *Journal of Cognitive Psychotherapy: An International Journal*.

Beck, A. T. (1972). *Depression: Causes and treatment*. Philadelphia: University of Pennsylvania Press.

Bedell, J. R., Archer, R. P., & Marlowe, H. A., Jr. (1980). A description and evaluation of a problem solving skills training program. In D. Upper & S. M. Ross (Eds.), *Behavioral group therapy: An annual review* (pp. 3–35). Champaign, IL: Research Press.

Belmont, J. M., Butterfield, E. C., & Ferriti, R. P. (1982). To secure transfer of training instruction of self-management skills. In D. K. Detterman & R. J. Sternberg (Eds.), *How and why intelligence can be increased?* (pp. 147–154). Norwood, NJ: Ablex.

Black, D. R., & Sherba, D. R. (1983). Contracting to problem solve versus contracting to practice behavioral weight loss skills. *Behavior Therapy, 14*, 100–109.

Black, D. R., & Threlfall, W. E. (1986). A stepped approach to weight control: A minimal intervention and a bibliotherapy problem solving program. *Behavior Therapy, 17*, 144–157.

Brammer, L. (in press). Teaching personal problem solving to adults. *Journal of Cognitive Psychotherapy: An International Quarterly*.

Brown, A. L. (1977). Knowing when, where, and how to remember: A problem of metacognition. In R. Glaser (Ed.), *Advances in instructional psychology* (pp. 77–165). Hillsdale, NJ: Lawrence Erlbaum Associates.

Brown, A. L., & Campione, J. C. (1986). Psychological theory and the study of learning disabilities. *American Psychologist, 14*, 1059–1068.

Brown, S. D., Brady, T., Lent, R. W., Wolfert, J., & Hall, S. (1987). Perceived social support among college students: Three studies of the psychometric characteristics and counseling uses of the social support inventory. *Journal of Counseling Psychology, 34*, 337–354.

Butler, L., & Meichenbaum, D. (1981). The assessment of interpersonal problem-solving skills. In P. C. Kendall & S. D. Hollen (Eds.), *Assessment strategies for cognitive-behavioral interventions* (pp. 197–225). New York: Academic Press.

Chase, W. G., & Simon, H. A. (1973). Perception in chess. *Cognitive Psychology, 4*, 55–81.

Cormier, W. H., Otani, A., & Cormier, S. (1986). The effects of problem-solving training on two problem-solving tasks. *Cognitive Therapy and Research, 10*, 95–108.

Coyne, J. C., Aldwin, C., & Lazarus, R. S. (1981). Depression and coping in stressful episodes. *Journal of Abnormal Psychology, 90*, 439–447.

Coyne, J. C., & Lazarus, R. S. (1980). Cognitive style stress perception, and coping. In I. L. Kutash & L. B. Schlesinger (Eds.), *Handbook of stress and anxiety: Contemporary knowledge, theory, and treatment* (pp. 144–158). San Francisco: Jossey-Bass.

Cronbach, L. J., & Snow, R. E. (1977). *Aptitudes and instructional methods: A handbook for research on interactions*. New York: Irvington.

Dahlstrom, W. G., & Dahlstrom, L. E. (1980). *Basic readings on the MMPI: A new selection on personality measurement*. Minneapolis: University of Minnesota Press.

Davis, G. A. (1966). Current status of research and theory in human problem solving. *Psychological Bulletin, 66*, 36–54.

DeClue, G. S. (1983). *Patterns of intellectual functioning: Ability, personality, and problem solving style*. Doctoral dissertation, University of Missouri-Columbia.

Dewey, J. (1933). *How we think*. New York: D. C. Heath.

Dixon, D. R., Heppner, P. P., Petersen, C. H., & Ronning, R. R. (1979). Problem-solving workshop training. *Journal of Counseling Psychology, 26*, 133–139.

Durlak, J. A. (1983). Social problem solving as a primary prevention strategy. In R. D. Felner, L. A. Jason, J. N. Moritsugu, & S. S. Faber (Eds.), *Preventive psychology: Theory, research, and practice* (pp. 31–48). Elmsford, NY: Pergamon Press.

D'Zurilla, T. J. (1986). *Problem-solving therapy: A social competence approach to clinical intervention*. New York: Springer.

D'Zurilla, T. J., & Goldfried, M. R. (1971). Problem solving and behavior modification. *Journal of Counseling Psychology, 20*, 1976–1980.

D'Zurilla, T. J., & Nezu, A. (1980). A study of the generation-of-alternatives process in social problem solving. *Cognitive Therapy and Research, 4*, 67–72.

D'Zurilla, T. J., & Nezu, A. (1982). Social problem solving in adults. In P. C. Kendall (Ed.), *Advances in cognitive-behavioral research and therapy* (Vol. 1, pp. 201–274). New York: Academic Press.

Edelstein, B. A., Couture, E. T., Cray, M., Dickens, P., & Lusebrink, N. (1980). Group training of problem-solving with chronic psychiatric patients. In D. Upper & S. Ross (Eds.), *Behavioral group therapy: An annual review* (Vol. 2, pp. 85–102). Champaign, IL: Research Press.

Ewart, C. K., Taylor, C. B., Kraemer, H. C., & Agras, W. S. (1984). Reducing blood pressure reactivity during interpersonal conflict: Effects of marital communication training. *Behavior Therapy, 15*, 473–484.

Eysenck, H. J. (1983). Stress, disease, and personality: The "inoculation effect." In C. L. Cooper (Ed.), *Stress research: Issues for the eighties* (pp. 121–146). New York: John Wiley & Sons.

Feigenbaum, E. A., & Feldman, J. (1963). *Computers and thought*. New York: McGraw-Hill.

Feldhusen, J. F., Houtz, J. C., & Ringenbach, S. (1972). The Purdue Elementary Problem-Solving Inventory. *Psychological Reports, 31*, 891–901.

Fisher, S. (1986). *Stress and strategy*. London: Lawrence Erlbaum Associates.

Flavell, J. H., & Wellman, H. M. (1977). Metamemory. In R. V. Kail & J. W. Hagen (Eds.), *Perspectives on the development of memory and cognition* (pp. 3–34). Hillsdale, NJ: Lawrence Erlbaum Associates.

Forsythe, C. J., & Compas, B. E. (1987). Interaction of cognitive appraisals of stressful events and coping: Testing the goodness of fit hypothesis. *Cognitive Therapy and Research, 11*, 473–485.

Foster, S. L., Prinz, R. J., & O'Leary, K. D. (1983). Impact of problem-solving communication training and generalization procedures on family conflict. *Child and Family Behavior Therapy, 5*, 1–23.

Fredericksen, N. (1984). Implications of cognitive theory for instruction in problem solving. *Review of Educational Research, 54*, 363–407.

Gagne, E. D. (1985). *The cognitive psychology of school learning*. Boston: Little, Brown.

Gagne, R. M. (1964). Problem solving. In A. W. Melton (Ed.), *Categories of human learning* (pp. 293–323). New York: Academic Press.

Glaser, R. (1984). Education and thinking. *American Psychologist, 39*, 93–104.

Glaser, R. (1988, August). *The reemergence of learning theory within instructional research*. Paper presented at the meeting of the American Psychological Association, Atlanta, GA.

Glaser, R., & Chi, M. T. H. (1988). Overview. In M. T. H. Chi, R. Glaser, & M. J. Farr (Eds.), *The nature of expertise* (pp. xv–xxix). Hillsdale, NJ: Lawrence Erlbaum Associates.

Glick, M. L. (1986). Problem-solving strategies. *Educational Psychologist, 21*, 99–120.

Goldfried, M. R., & D'Zurilla, T. J. (1969). A behavior-analytic model for assessing competence. In C. D. Spielberger (Ed.), *Current topics in clinical and community psychology* (Vol. 1, pp. 151–196). New York: Academic Press.

Goldfried, M. R., & Goldfried, A. P. (1975). Cognitive change methods. In F. H. Kanfer & A. P. Goldstein (Eds.), *Helping people change* (pp. 89–116). Elmsford, NY: Pergamon Press.

Greeno, J. G. (1978). Natures of problem-solving abilities. In W. K. Estes (Ed.), *Handbook of learning and cognitive processes: Vol. 5. Human information processing* (pp. 239–270). Hillsdale, NJ: Lawrence Erlbaum Associates.

Groen, G. J., & Patel, V. L. (1988). The relationship between comprehension and reasoning in medical expertise. In M. T. H. Chi, R. Glaser, & M. F. Farr (Eds.), *The nature of expertise* (pp. 287–310). Hillsdale, NJ: Lawrence Erlbaum Associates.

Hansen, D. J., St. Laurence, J. S., & Christoff, K. A. (1985). Effects of interpersonal problem-solving training with chronic aftercare patients on problem-solving component skills and effectiveness of solutions. *Journal of Consulting and Clinical Psychology, 53*, 167–174.

Heppner, P. P. (1989). Identifying the complexities within clients' thinking and decision making. *Journal of Counseling Psychology, 36*, 257–259.

Heppner, P. P., & Anderson, W. P. (1985). The relationship between problem solving self-appraisal and psychological adjustment. *Cognitive Therapy and Research, 9*, 415–427.

Heppner, P. P., Baumgardner, A., & Jackson, J. (1985). Problem solving self-appraisal, depression, and attribution styles: Are they related? *Cognitive Therapy and Research, 9*, 105–113.

Heppner, P. P., Baumgardner, A. H., Larson, L. M., & Petty, R. E. (1988). The utility of problem-solving training that emphasizes self-management principles. *Counselling Psychology Quarterly, 1*, 129–143.

Heppner, P. P., Baumgardner, A. H., Larson, L. M., & Petty, R. E. (1989). The utility of problem-solving training that emphasizes self-management principles. *Counselling Psychology Quarterly, 1*, 129–143.

Heppner, P. P., Hibel, J. H., Neal, G. W., Weinstein, C. L., & Rabinowitz, F. E. (1982). Personal problem solving: A descriptive study of individual differences. *Journal of Counseling Psychology, 29*, 580–590.

Heppner, P. P., Kampa, M., & Brunning, L. (1987). The relationship between problem-solving self-appraisal and indices of physical and psychological help. *Cognitive Therapy and Research, 11*, 155–168.

Heppner, P. P., & Krauskopf, C. J. (1987). An information processing approach to personal problem solving. *The Counseling Psychologist, 15*, 371–447.

Heppner, P. P., Neal, G. W., & Larson, L. M. (1984). Problem-solving training as prevention with college students. *Personnel and Guidance Journal, 62*, 514–519.

Heppner, P. P., & Petersen, C. H. (1982). The development and implications of a personal problem-solving inventory. *Journal of Counseling Psychology, 29*, 66–75.

Heppner, P. P., & Reeder, B. L. (1984). Problem-solving training with residence hall staff: Who's most satisfied. *Journal of College Student Personnel, 25*, 357–360.

Heppner, P. P., Reeder, B. L., & Larson, L. M. (1983). Cognitive variables associated with personal problem-solving appraisal: Implications for counseling. *Journal of Counseling Psychology, 30*, 537–545.

Holmes, T. H., & Rahe, R. H. (1967). The social readjustment rating scale. *Journal of Psychosomatic Research, 11*, 213–218.

Houston, B. K. (1987). Stress and coping. In C. R. Snyder & C. E. Ford (Eds.), *Coping with negative life events: Clinical and social psychological perspectives* (pp. 373–399). New York: Plenum Press.

Howard, A., & Scott, R. (1965). A proposed

framework for the analysis of stress in the human organism. *Behavioral Science, 10,* 141–160.

Hussian, R. A., & Lawrence, P. S. (1981). Social reinforcement of activity and problem solving training in the treatment of depressed institutionalized elderly patients. *Cognitive Therapy and Research, 5,* 57–69.

Intagliatia, J. C. (1978). Increasing the interpersonal problem solving skills of an alcoholic population. *Journal of Consulting and Clinical Psychology, 46,* 489–498.

Jacobson, N. S. (1977a). Training couples to solve their marital problems: A behavioral approach to relationship discord. Part I: Problem-solving skills. *International Journal of Family Counseling, 5,* 22–31.

Jacobson, N. S. (1977b). Problem solving and contingency contracting in the treatment of marital discord. *Journal of Consulting and Clinical Psychology, 45,* 92–100.

Jacobson, N. W. (1978). Specific and nonspecific factors in the effectiveness of a behavioral approach to the treatment of marital discord. *Journal of Consulting and Clinical Psychology, 46,* 442–452.

Jannoun, L., Munby, M., Catalan, J., & Gelder, M. (1980). A home-based treatment program for agoraphobia: Replication and controlled evaluation. *Behavior Therapy, 11,* 294–305.

Karol, R. L., & Richards, C. S. (1978). *Making treatment effects last: An investigation of maintenance strategies for smoking reduction.* Paper presented at the Annual Convention of the Association for the Advancement of Behavior Therapy, Chicago.

Kendall, P. C., Pellegrini, D. S., & Urbain, E. S. (1981). Approaches to assessment for cognitive-behavioral interventions with children. In P. C. Kendall & S. D. Hollon (Eds.), *Assessment strategies for cognitive-behavioral intervention* (pp. 227–285). New York: Academic Press.

Kendler, H. H., & Kendler, T. S. (1962). Vertical and horizontal processes in problem solving. *Psychological Review, 69,* 1–16.

Kiesler, D. J. (1971). Experimental designs in psychotherapy research. In A. E. Bergin & S. L. Garfield (Eds.), *Handbook of psychotherapy and behavior change: An empirical analysis* (pp. 36–74). New York: John Wiley & Sons.

Kobasa, S. C. (1979). Stressful life events, personality, and health: An inquiry into hardiness. *Journal of Personality and Social Psychology, 37,* 1–11.

Kobasa, S. C. (1982). Commitment and coping in stress resistance among lawyers. *Journal of Personality and Social Psychology, 42,* 707–717.

Kobasa, S. C., Maddi, S. R., & Kahn, S. (1982). Hardiness and health: A prospective study. *Journal of Personality and Social Psychology, 42,* 168–177.

Kohler, W. (1925). *The mentality of apes* (E. Winter, Trans.). New York: Harcourt, Brace.

Krauskopf, C. J., & Davis, K. G. (1973). Studies of the normal personality. *JSAS Catalogue of Selected Documents in Psychology, 3,* 85.

Larson, L. M. (1984). *Training self-appraised effective and ineffective problem solvers in assertion.* Master's thesis: University of Missouri, Columbia, MO.

Larson, L. M. (in press). A critique of problem-solving training: Where to from here? *Journal of Cognitive Psychotherapy: An International Journal.*

Lazarus, R. S., & Folkman, S. (1984). *Stress, appraisal, and coping.* New York: Springer Publishing Company, Inc.

Lohman, D. F. (1986). Predicting mathematic effects in the teaching of higher-order thinking skills. *Educational Psychologist, 21,* 191–208.

Luchton, R. (1974). Crisis theory: Review and critique. *Social Science Review, 48,* 384–402.

Maddi, S. R., Hoover, M., & Kobasa, S. C. (1982). Alienation and exploratory behavior. *Journal of Personality and Social Psychology, 42,* 884–890.

Mahoney, M. (1974). *Cognition and behavior modification.* Cambridge, MA: Ballinger Publishing Co.

Maier, N. R. F. (1970). *Problem solving and creativity.* Belmont, CA: Brooks/Cole.

Marshall, S. P. (1982). Sex differences in mathematical errors: An analysis of distracter choices. *Journal for Research in Mathematics Education, 14,* 325–336.

Mechanic, D. (1968). The study of social stress and its relationship to disease. In D. Mechanic (Ed.), *Medical sociology* (pp. 294–322). New York: Free Press.

Mechanic, D. (1974). Discussion of research programs on relations between stressful life events and episodes of physical illness. In B. S. Dohrenwend & B. P. Dohrenwend (Eds.),

Stressful life events (pp. 87–97). New York: John Wiley & Sons.

Meichenbaum, D., & Asarnow, J. (1979). Cognitive-behavioral modification and metacognitive development: Implications for the classroom. In P. C. Kendall & S. D. Hollon (Eds.), *Cognitive-behavioral interventions: Theory, research, and procedure* (pp. 11–35). New York: Academic Press.

Mendonca, J. D., & Siess, T. F. (1976). Counseling for indecisiveness: Problem-solving and anxiety management training. *Journal of Counseling Psychology, 23*, 339–347.

Moon, J. R., & Eisler, R. M. (1983). Anger control: An experimental comparison of three behavioral treatments. *Behavior Therapy, 14*, 493–505.

Neal, G. W., & Heppner, P. P. (1982). *Personality correlates of effective personal problem solving*. Paper presented at the annual meeting of the American Personnel and Guidance Association, Detroit.

Neves, D. M., & Anderson, J. R. (1981). Knowledge compilation: Mechanisms for the automatization of cognitive skills. In J. R. Anderson (Ed.), *Cognitive skills and their acquisition* (pp. 57–84). Hillsdale, NJ: Lawrence Erlbaum Associates.

Newell, A., Shaw, J. C., & Simon, H. A. (1958). Elements of a theory of human problem solving. *Psychological Review, 65*, 151–166.

Newell, A., Shaw, J. C., & Simon, H. A. (1963). GPS, a program that simulates human thought. In E. A. Feigenbaum & J. Feldman (Eds.), *Computers and thought* (pp. 39–70). New York: McGraw-Hill.

Nezu, A. M. (1985). Differences in psychological distress between effective and ineffective problem solvers. *Journal of Counseling Psychology, 32*, 135–138.

Nezu, A. M. (1986). Efficacy of a social problem solving therapy approach for unipolar depression. *Journal of Consulting and Clinical Psychology, 54*, 196–202.

Nezu, A., & D'Zurilla, T. J. (1979). An experimental evaluation of the decision-making process in social problem solving. *Cognitive Therapy and Research, 3*, 269–277.

Nezu, A., & D'Zurilla, T. J. (1981a). Effects of problem definition and formulation on decision making in the social problem-solving process. *Behavior Therapy, 12*, 100–106.

Nezu, A., & D'Zurilla, T. J. (1981b). Effects of problem definition and formulation on the generation of alternatives in the social problem-solving process. *Cognitive Therapy and Research, 5*, 265–271.

Nezu, A. M., Kalmar, K., Ronan, G. F., & Clavijo, A. (1986). Attributional correlates of depression: An interactional model including problem solving. *Behavior Therapy, 17*, 50–56.

Nezu, A. M., Nezu, C. M., Saraydarian, L., Kalmar, K., & Ronan, G. F. (1986). Social problem solving as a moderating variable between negative life stress and depressive systems. *Cognitive Therapy and Research, 10*, 489–498.

Nezu, A. M., & Ronan, G. F. (1985). Life stress, current problems, problem solving, and depressive symptoms: An integrative model. *Journal of Consulting and Clinical Psychology, 53*, 693–697.

Nezu, A. M., & Ronan, G. F. (1988). Social problem solving as a moderator of stress-related depressive symptoms: A prospective analysis. *Journal of Counseling Psychology, 35*, 134–138.

Perkins, D., & Solomon, G. (1986). Transfer and teaching thinking. In D. Perkins, J. Bishop, & J. Lochhead (Eds.), *Thinking: Progress in research and teaching*. Hillsdale, NJ: Lawerence Erlbaum Associates.

Perkins, D. N. (1987). Thinking frames: An integrative perspective on teaching cognitive skills. In J. B. Baron & R. J. Sternberg (Eds.), *Teaching thinking skills* (pp. 41–61). New York: W. H. Freeman.

Perri, M. G., & Richards, C. S. (1977). An investigation of naturally occurring episodes of self-controlled behaviors. *Journal of Counseling Psychology, 24*, 178–183.

Petty, B. J., Moeller, T. P., & Campbell, R. Z. (1976). Support groups for elderly persons in the community. *Gerontologist, 16*, 522–528.

Phillips, S. D., Pazienza, N. J., & Ferrin, H. H. (1984). Decision making styles and problem solving appraisal. *Journal of Counseling Psychology, 31*, 497–502.

Platt, J. J., Altman, N., & Altman, D. S. (1973). *Dimensions of interpersonal problem-solving thinking in adolescent psychiatric patients*. Paper presented at the meeting of the Eastern Psychological Association, Washington, DC.

Platt, J. J., Scura, W. C., & Hannon, J. P. (1973). Problem-solving thinking of youthful incarcerated heroin addicts. *Journal of Community Psychology, 1*, 278–281.

Platt, J. J., & Spivack, G. (1972a). Problem-solving thinking of psychiatric patients. *Journal of Consulting and Clinical Psychology, 39*, 148–151.

Platt, J. J., & Spivack, G. (1972b). Social competence and effective problem-solving thinking in psychiatric patients. *Journal of Clinical Psychology, 28*, 3–5.

Platt, J. J., & Spivack, G. (1975). *Manual for the means-ends problem-solving procedure (MEPS): A measure of interpersonal cognitive problem solving skill*. Philadelphia: Department of Mental Health Science, Hanemann Medical College and Hospital.

Restle, F., & Davis, J. H. (1962). Success and speed of problem solving by individuals and groups. *Psychological Review, 69*, 520–536.

Richards, C. S., & Perri, M. G. (1978). Do self-control treatments last? An evaluation of behavioral problem solving and faded counselor contact as treatment maintenance strategies. *Journal of Counseling Psychology, 25*, 376–383.

Robin, A. L. (1981). A controlled evaluation of problem-solving communication training with parent-adolescent conflict. *Behavior Therapy, 12*, 593–609.

Robin, A. L., Kent, R., O'Leary, K. D., Foster, S., & Prinz, R. (1977). An approach to teaching parents and adolescents problem-solving communication skills: A preliminary report. *Behavior Therapy, 8*, 639–643.

Rotter, J. B. (1966). Generalized expectancies for internal versus external control of reinforcement. *Psychological Monographs, 80* (1, Whole No. 609).

Sarason, T. G., & Sarason, B. R. (1981). Teaching cognitive and social skills to high school students. *Journal of Consulting and Clinical Psychology, 49*, 908–918.

Scott, R., & Howard, A. (1970). Models of stress. In S. Levine & N. Scotch (Eds.), *Social stress* (pp. 259–278). Chicago: Aldine.

Selye, H. (1956). *The stress of life*. New York: McGraw-Hill.

Selye, H. (1983). The stress concept: Past, present, and future. In C. L. Cooper (Ed.), *Stress research: Issues for the eighties* (pp. 1–20). New York: John Wiley & Sons.

Sheerer, M. (1963). Problem solving. *Scientific American, 208*, 118–128.

Shure, M. B., & Spivack, G. (1972). Means-ends thinking, adjustment and social class among elementary school-aged children. *Journal of Consulting and Clinical Psychology, 38*, 348–353.

Shure, M., Spivack, G., & Jaeger, M. (1971). Problem-solving thinking and adjustment among disadvantaged preschool children. *Child Development, 42*, 1791–1803.

Simon, H. A. (1973). The structure of ill structured problems. *Artificial Intelligence, 4*, 181–201.

Simon, H. A., & Hayes, J. R. (1976). Understanding complex task instructions. In D. Klahr (Ed.), *Cognition and instruction* (pp. 269–285). Hillsdale, NJ: Lawrence Erlbaum Associates.

Skinner, B. F. (1974). *About behaviorism*. New York: Alfred A. Knopf.

Snyder, C. R., & Ford, C. E. (1987). *Coping with negative life events: Clinical and social psychological perspectives*. New York: Plenum Press.

Spivack, G., & Levine, M. (1963). *Self-regulation in acting-out and normal adolescents* (Report M-4531). Washington, DC: National Institute of Mental Health.

Spivack, G., Platt, J. J., & Shure, M. B. (1976). *The problem-solving approach to adjustment*. San Francisco, CA: Jossey-Bass.

Spivack, G., & Shure, M. G. (1974). *Social adjustment of young children*. San Francisco: Jossey-Bass.

Sternberg, R. J. (1982). Reasoning, problem solving, and intelligence. In R. J. Sternberg (Ed.), *Handbook of human intelligence* (pp. 225–307). New York: Cambridge University Press.

Sternberg, R. J. (1985). Teaching critical thinking, Part I. Are we making critical mistakes? *Phi Delta Kappan, 67*, 194–198.

Strohmer, D. C., & Blustein, D. L. (in press). The adult problem solver as person scientist. *Journal of Cognitive Psychotherapy: An International Quarterly*.

Tableman, B., Marciniak, D., Johnson, D., & Rodgers, R. (1982). Stress management for women on public assistance. *American Journal of Community Psychology, 10*, 357–376.

Toseland, R. A. (1977). A problem solving group workshop for older persons. *Social Work, 22*, 325–326.

Tracey, T. J., Sherry, P., & Keitel, M. (1986). Distressed and help seeking as a function of person-environment fit and self-efficacy: A causal model. *American Journal of Community Psychology, 14*, 657–676.

Wicklegren, W. A. (1974). *How to solve problems*. San Francisco: W. H. Freeman.

Worden, J. W., & Sobel, H. J. (1978). Ego strength and psychosocial adaptation to cancer. *Psychosomatic Medicine, 40*, 485–592.

CHAPTER 35

CLIENT-THERAPIST MATCHING

Larry E. Beutler
John Clarkin
Marjorie Crago
John Bergan

While attempting to develop a secular philosophy, Freud failed to escape the symbols and rituals of religion (Vitz, 1988). Denuded of their reliance on deity, these rituals and symbols were given a degree of scientific respectability by associating them with concepts of neurology, physiology, and physics. Likewise, Client Centered Therapy (Rogers, 1951), representing the first major departure from psychoanalytic symbolism, also incorporated religiouslike values. Coming from a forgiving, American Protestant tradition, Rogers incorporated concepts of "free will" and Christian acceptance into a view of personal change. With the general acceptance of client-centered assertions about the value of nonjudgmental attitudes and nonjudging acceptance, psychotherapy paradoxically has adopted the religious concepts that destine it to remain a value-laden procedure.

Corresponding with its implicit alliance with religious methods, it has always been an implicit clinical belief that treatment effectiveness can be enhanced by matching client and therapist for compatible backgrounds, attitudes, and belief systems. This process casts psychotherapy more into the mold of a social influence (i.e., benign persuasion) process than of a healing process. While the forces of persuasion are important processes in all mental health treatment, they are most directly observed in psychotherapy. It should be emphasized, nonetheless, that psychotherapy is not a distinct class of treatment. The specific applications of designated procedures, ranging from chemical agents to selective reinforcement, are not qualitatively different from the psychotherapy process, and they can be investigated as ingredients within the broader framework which that process implies. That broader process is one of persuading clients to change the attributions, attitudes, and even values that dictate treatment compliance, govern the nature of the doctor-client relationship, and result in client benefit. Understanding this relationship necessitates identifying the values that underlie the efforts of therapists to influence clients and exploring how and under

Work on this chapter was supported in part by National Institute of Mental Health Grant No. RO1-MH39859 to L. E. Beutler. Portions of this chapter were extracted from Beutler and Clarkin (1990).

what conditions these values facilitate or impede the effects of specific interventions.

Suggesting that psychotherapy is a process of social persuasion implies a certain degree of intent to exert influence. Certainly this intent is most directly observed in the cognitive change therapies that accept the explicit task of altering attitudes and beliefs. To the degree that any therapist intends the therapy process to create noncoerced changes in a client's feelings, insights, attitudes, viewpoints, or behaviors, however, all psychotherapies are based on interpersonal influence. Therapists have ideas about what constitutes emotionally healthy changes and these ideas influence treatment aims; he or she must rely on his or her own preferred values and beliefs to define what constitutes "healthy" changes. This fact implies that clients will be asked to accept, if not adopt, certain of the therapist's viewpoints.

Whether or not we can justify ethically the role of attitude conversion in psychotherapy, it is probable that attitude persuasion is best accomplished within the context of a collaborative, supportive, caring and respectful (i.e., compatible) relationship. Moreover, a compatible relationship is not accidental—it evolves from a complex interaction of the inherent dispositions contributed by the parties involved and therapeutic strategies that establish an environment that is conducive to change. In the final analysis, it may well be impossible to separate the so-called nonspecific qualities of the relationship and the procedures that the therapist uses (e.g., Rounsaville, Chevron, Prusoff, Elkin, Imber, Sotsky, & Watkins, 1987; Waterhouse & Strupp, 1984).

At least three separate but overlapping lines of research have addressed methods of enhancing therapeutic compatibility. These lines of investigation reflect the interplay among therapist, patient, and treatment variables in facilitating productive treatment matching. Some research, for example, has concentrated on discovering preexisting, personal qualities of clients and therapists (personal matching) that facilitate the development of a productive relationship; other research has attempted to enhance compatibility by educating clients in the nature and goals of treatment (client preparation), and thereby bringing their expectations into alignment with the demands of the treatment to be provided; the third type of research has concentrated on matching treatment interventions themselves to the nature of preexisting client characteristics (technical eclecticism).

Personal matching implies that the nature of compatibility is to be found in qualities of the client and therapist that interact independently of treatment technologies and professional theories. The subject matter of such investigations includes client-therapist personalities, values, attitudes, cognitive styles, and demographic characteristics. In contrast, the other two research approaches emphasize the importance of treatment rather than treater characteristics. Client preparation studies, for example, are based on an implicit assumption that treatment embodies a set of relatively immutable values that if acknowledged and adopted by the client will facilitate treatment gain. This form of client-therapy matching concentrates on altering clients' expectations of the length and frequency of treatment, and assumes the task of educating them in the roles that may be adopted by client and therapist. Its methods are devoted to alterations of clients to fit the parameters that are set by the treatment. Concomitantly, it gives little attention to modifications of the treatment or to variations among therapists who apply treatments.

The third area is one of still embryonic research and stands in contrast to the other areas of investigation by emphasizing the possibility that different treatment procedures may be more or less well suited to clients whose problems and personalities differ. Research of this latter type has focused on the selection of global treatment models (e.g., behavior therapy, cognitive therapy, insight therapy), the application of specific treatment procedures (i.e., interpretation, reflection, homework, etc.), and the assignment of therapists who favor either directive or nondirective approaches. The concepts studied fall within the purview of what Lazarus (1981) has called "technical eclecticism."

In this chapter we will consider these three types of research and their interrelationships. Because of the breadth of the topic of matching, a comprehensive review of current literature would far surpass the page limitations of this volume. Instead, we will summarize some conclusions from the most methodologically sound research currently available and illustrate these conclusions with references to more narrowly focused but exhaustive research reviews than our own.

PERSONAL COMPATIBILITY

It is now reasonably well established that patterns of similarity and difference at least partially dictate what constitutes an initially good therapist-client match and go far to determine the degree to which an effective therapeutic alliance can be established. Whereas research on personal compatibility has addressed similarity of demographic variables, attitudes and values, prior experiences, and personality (Atkinson & Schein, 1986), the first two of these areas has been the most productive and promising (cf. Beutler, 1981; Beutler, Crago, & Arizmendi, 1986) and will be the areas emphasized here.

Demographic Similarity

One's gender, aspects of appearance relating to ethnicity, and features that index one's age are easily observed (Shapiro & Penrod, 1986) and are used by clients to make relatively accurate judgments of therapists' status (Berry & McArthur, 1986). Because they are so readily observed, the effect of client-therapist demographic similarities on treatment commitment and outcome have been extensively researched. Unfortunately, most of this research has dealt with analog populations of clients and/or therapists, quasitherapy environments, and criteria that are far removed from those used to judge result in clinical settings. As a result of such disparity among methods and populations, the results of research in this area are far from consistent. Nonetheless, if one considers only the most clinically relevant studies, some tentative conclusions do emerge. Namely, demographic similarity between client and therapist (a) facilitates positive perceptions of the relationship in the beginning stages of treatment; (b) enhances commitment to remaining in treatment, especially among disenfranchised groups; and (c) sometimes accelerates the amount of improvement experienced by those who complete a course of treatment.

More specifically, both age (Luborsky, Crits-Christoph, Alexander, Margolis, & Cohen, 1983), ethnic (Jones, 1978), gender (Blase, 1979; Jones, Krupnick, & Kerig, 1987), and socioeconomic background (Carkhuff & Pierce, 1967) similarity have been associated with positive client perceptions of the treatment relationship. Of the various demographic dimensions studied, gender similarity and ethnic similarity appear to be the most strongly preferred by clients, and similarity in these domains generally enhances clients' perceptions of their therapist's understanding and empathy, increases clients' liking for their therapists, and results in the relationship being judged to be more helpful than when such similarity is lacking.

Ethnic similarity between client and therapist is especially preferred by black clients, and in this group such similarity is associated with an enhanced commitment to remain in treatment. Conversely, ethnic dissimilarity may be associated with early dropout rates (Turner & Armstrong, 1981; Neimeyer & Gonzales, 1983) and refusal to enter treatment after an initial evaluation (Abramowitz & Murray, 1983; Terrell & Terrell, 1984). It is notable, nonetheless, that the strength of this effect appears to be somewhat less among nonblack minorities than among blacks (Atkinson, 1983).

Overall, research on personal matching suggests that clients use relatively obvious similarities to establish a basis for trust and for assessing how likely they are to be understood. On the other hand, the relationship between similarity and treatment outcome is generally very small and probably not direct. For example, in spite of evidence both that ethnic similarity is preferred among black clients and that female therapists are more likely than their male counterparts to facilitate therapeutic change generally, these effects are quite modest compared with other contributors to outcome (e.g. Jones et al., 1987; Merluzzi, Merluzzi, & Kaul, 1977; Proctor & Rosen, 1981). Even more important, it appears to be the androgyny and flexibility of attitudes that one holds toward ethnic and sexual roles rather than gender or ethnicity per se that most likely account for even these modest effects. In gender-matching studies, in particular, the flexibility and acceptance of diversity that is embodied in androgynous and traditional female roles appear to contribute to client satisfaction and growth whether they are present in male or female therapists (Atkinson & Schein, 1986; Beutler, Crago, et al., 1986; Blier, Atkinson, & Geer, 1987).

Personal Beliefs

Personal beliefs represent the cognitive elements that both underwrite one's personal strivings and that derive from one's background. While the weight of evidence persuasively underlines that treatment outcome is related linearly to the degree to which clients acquire the global beliefs and values of their particular therapist (Beutler, 1981; Beutler, Crago, et al., 1986; Hamblin, Beutler, Scogin, & Corbishley, 1988), improvement is only enhanced by a complex pattern of similarity and dissimilarity between client and therapist belief and value systems (e.g., Beutler,

Jobe, & Elkins, 1974; Cheloha, 1986). Indeed, the specific beliefs that contribute to this value-conversion process remain open to question (Tjelveit, 1986).

The most consistent evidence available suggests that treatment outcome is enhanced when clients and therapists place similar value on such attributes as wisdom, honesty, intellectual pursuits, and knowledge. At the same time, the degree of difference that exists between client's and therapist's valuing of such qualities as a sense of personal safety (Beutler, Pollack, & Jobe, 1978), interpersonal treatment goals (Charone, 1981), social status and friendships (Arizmendi, Beutler, Shanfield, Crago, & Hagaman, 1985; Beutler, Arizmendi, Crago, Shanfield, & Hagaman, 1983; Beutler et al., 1974) facilitates improvement.

The mere observation that converging beliefs and values are associated with improvement may be enough to justify efforts directly to persuade clients to adopt therapists' value stances. However, most therapists are trained in the tradition of free will and self-selection and have difficulty morally or ethically justifying such a position. Some comfort may be found in the observations that therapists' values are more similar to those of their clients than they are different (Beutler et al., 1978), and that religious attitudes, those on which clients and therapists are most likely to differ (Bergin, 1980), are seldom listed among those that either change during treatment or contribute to improvement (Chesner & Baumeister, 1985; Houts & Graham, 1986; Lewis, 1983; Hill, Howard, & Orlinsky, 1970). Even more important, evidence suggests that it is the acceptability to the therapist of the client's viewpoint (Beutler et al., 1974) and the therapist's ability to communicate within the client's value framework (Probst, 1980; Probst, Ostrom, & Watkins, 1984) more than the particular values held by the therapist that contribute to client improvement. If they are sufficiently accepting of the client's religious values, even nonreligious therapists and therapists representing a very different religious orientation from the client can communicate within the client's value system and effect improvement without threatening the client's valued beliefs (Beutler, Crago, et al., 1986; Chesner & Baumeister, 1985).

Aside from client-matching, there appear to be some values that generally distinguish more and less effective therapists. Lafferty, Beutler, and Crago (1989) suggested that therapists who value intellectual pursuits and hard work tend to be

more effective than those who place relatively more value on social and economic status. It is interesting to note, however, that these productive values may be more characteristic of academic teachers than they are of therapy practitioners (Conway, 1988).

TREATMENT PREPARATION

Client role induction allows some opportunity to compensate for the limitations on therapist-client compatibility imposed by the self-selection of client and therapist. Most investigations of role induction, though varying in method, objectives, and client sample, have suggested that pretreatment preparation enhances the persuasive potency of the therapist (cf. Beutler, Crago, et al., 1986; Mayerson, 1984; Orlinsky & Howard, 1986; Parloff, Waskow, & Wolfe, 1978). These studies suggest that role induction improves treatment retention rates (LaTorre, 1977; Wilson, 1985), facilitates positive perceptions of the treatment process (Jacobs, Trick, & Withersty, 1976; Yalom, Houts, Newell, & Rank, 1967; Zwick & Attkisson, 1985), promotes treatment compliance (Meichenbaum & Turk, 1987), and enhances psychotherapy outcomes (Childress & Gillis, 1977; Strupp & Bloxom, 1973; Zwick & Attkisson, 1985).

The procedures of role induction can be subclassified into three subtypes (Beutler & Clarkin, 1990): (a) instructional methods, (b) observational and participatory learning, and (c) treatment contracting.

Instructional Methods

Instructional methods of inducing role behaviors among clients consist of providing direct written or verbal information about the nature of therapy and of the roles expected of the client and therapist. In their simplest form, role-instruction methods explain what to expect and how to respond to the treatment. However, most role-induction interviews are somewhat more elaborate than this.

In one of the best known studies of instructional methods, Hoehn-Saric, Frank, Imber, Nash, Stone, and Battle (1964) constructed a pretherapy interview that specifically described the nature of individual psychotherapy, outlined what behaviors were expected of client and therapist, described the nature of such therapeutic phenomenon as resistance and transference, provided suggestions for recognizing and dealing with these issues when they arose, and specified the length of time before improvement should be anticipated. When systematically compared with the treatment of clients who did not receive this pretraining, they found that the role-induction interview significantly enhanced the process and outcome of psychotherapy.

While there are some exceptions (e.g., Yalom et al., 1967), most of the current evidence indicates that instructional methods facilitate symptomatic change, encourage the adoption of role-appropriate attitudes, and promote the development of positive feelings about treatment (cf. Mayerson, 1984; Zwick & Attkisson, 1985). Other research suggests that direct instruction reduces nonproductive advice-seeking and enhances involvement in treatment (Turkat, 1979). Moreover, the procedures apply across client groups, impacting many who present special problems or who usually are considered to be poor risks for conventional psychotherapies, such as the poor and the uneducated (e.g., Heitler, 1976; Holliday, 1979).

Observational and Participatory Learning Methods

A second role-induction method of enhancing client-therapist compatibility consists of pretherapy modeling and/or practice. Truax and colleagues were among the first to report positive results with this procedure (Truax & Carkhuff, 1967; Truax & Wargo, 1969). Their induction procedure consisted of a 30-minute audio tape of representative therapy segments. The procedure was specifically aimed at facilitating group therapy process and modeled "good" and productive interchanges among group members.

In an effort to extend the procedure of Truax and his colleagues, Strupp and Bloxom (1973) employed a role-induction film to prepare clients of low socioeconomic status for conventional treatments. At the end of 12 treatment sessions, those clients who had been presented with film demonstrations before treatment reported more facilitative treatment relationships, exhibited more productive in-treatment behaviors, and experienced better treatment outcomes when contrasted with similar clients receiving a control film. A third group receiving a role-induction interview demonstrated similar effects to those observing the film. In other studies, role-induction films also have demonstrated a positive impact on dropout rates, even among clients with relatively severe psychopathology (Mayerson, 1984; Wilson, 1985).

In a variation of these procedures, Warren and

Rice (1972) suggested the value of adding therapy practice sessions to observations in order to stabilize or reinforce effective treatment behaviors. In this procedure, clients met with someone other than their own therapist for approximately half an hour following every third or fourth session of time-limited psychotherapy. During these meetings, clients were encouraged to talk about problems that arose with therapy or with the therapist, and then instruction and information were provided to enhance the client's response to these problems. The authors demonstrated that this procedure reduced dropout rates among poor prognosis clients.

Contracting Methods

Whereas therapeutic contracting has been discussed widely in family systems theory (Madanes, 1981), gestalt/transactional analysis (Goulding & Goulding, 1979), and cognitive therapy (Beck, Rush, Shaw, & Emery, 1979), behavior therapists have been most active and explicit in defining its use. The specific techniques used include signed agreements (Alexander, Barton, Schiavo, & Parsons, 1976) and requiring the client to deposit money that will be returned if the predetermined goals are achieved (e.g. Pomerleau, 1979; Pomerleau & Pomerleau, 1984). These various contracting procedures can be viewed as components of several lockstepped but supraordinate phases (Kirschenbaum & Flaner, 1984): (a) initial decision-making, (b) the generation or modification of expectancies, (c) the identification of target objectives of change, (d) monitoring progress, (e) delivering consequences, and (f) programming generalizations.

The role of contingency contracting is currently receiving wide usage in marital therapy where it is employed to facilitate communication and the provision of mutual support (Azrin, Naster, & Jones, 1973; Emmelkamp, 1986). Contracting has been especially well received among those who attempt systematically to train couples in communication skills (Weiss, Hops, & Patterson, 1973).

The use of behavioral contracting extends beyond treatment preparation to the instigation of therapeutic change (Emmelkamp, 1986). Hence, much of the activity in treatment programs that uses behavioral contracting has centered around negotiation of the contract itself and, concomitantly, on the acts of assessing and reinforcing compliance.

The role of contracting as a procedure for

enhancing client compliance is best seen in studies of time-limited psychotherapy. One of the most surprising conclusions to come from this literature is the serendipitous finding that an explicit, preset time limit results in clients remaining in treatment longer than when no such explicit contract is present. While the usual treatment duration in outpatient settings varies from five to eight sessions (Butcher & Koss, 1978; Koss & Butcher, 1986), a sampling of literature (e.g., Sloane, Staples, Cristol, Yorkston, & Whipple, 1975; Elkin, 1986; Beutler, Scoggin, Kirkish, Schretlen, Corbishley, Hamblin, Meredith, Potter, Bamford, & Levenson, 1987) led Beutler and Clarkin (1990) to conclude that time-limited therapies may have a mean treatment duration closer to twice the length of open-ended treatment. Moreover, clients who are explicitly contracted to a given treatment duration become more quickly involved in the treatment process than their peers in open-ended treatment (Koss & Butcher, 1986). Clearly, what we have traditionally thought of as "short-term" treatments, by this standard, are not short term at all.

TECHNICAL ECLECTICISM

Clinical wisdom has always held that the persuasive power of psychotherapy is enhanced when there is some type of compatibility between the client and problem variables, on the one hand, and the specific treatment procedures selected on the other. The usual term referring to the matching of clients to treatment procedures is *technical eclecticism*. However, the term eclectic, at least as it has been applied to mental health treatment, has been overused and, at times, has been used as the equivalent of "muddle-headedness" (Norcross, 1986b). In contemporary literature, there are really several different types of eclecticism (see Norcross, 1986a; Norcross & Prochaska, 1988; Lazarus, 1981; Wolfe & Goldfried, 1988 for a discussion of these terms). Technical eclecticism maintains that integration among various treatment approaches should take place at he level of specific procedures rather than at the level of theory. That is, a technically eclectic clinician endeavors to select the best and most useful procedures for a given client from among those advocated by the hundreds of procedures available, irrespective of the theories from which these procedures derive. Some technical eclectic variations have developed specific guidelines to help the clinician determine the procedures to be selected. These approaches are collectively referenced by attaching the adjective "systematic" to the term eclectic (Norcross, 1986a; Beutler, 1983).

Systematic, technical eclecticism arose from the awareness of the inconsistency between therapists' theoretical viewpoints and their in-therapy behavior. The foundation for this movement was in the joint observations that (a) therapists of equivalent experience but different theoretical positions behave quite similarly to one another (Fiedler, 1950; Sloane et al., 1975); and paradoxically, (b) there is great diversity in therapeutic behaviors and outcomes among therapists who are representative of any given theoretical orientation (e.g. Lieberman, Yalom, & Miles, 1973; Luborsky, Singer, & Luborsky, 1975). Collectively, the methodological and clinical concerns arising from these observations resulted in an effort to operationally define and standardize treatments (Luborsky & DeRubeis, 1984). "How to do it" manuals soon appeared for cognitive therapy (Beck et al., 1979), interpersonal psychotherapy (Klerman, Weissman, Rounsaville, & Chevron, 1984), psychoanalytic psychotherapy (Luborsky, 1984; Strupp & Binder, 1984), gestalt therapy (Daldrup, Beutler, Greenberg, & Engle, 1988), and various forms of group and family therapies (Jacobson & Margolin, 1979; Freeman, 1983; Sank & Shaffer, 1984).

Numerous studies have followed the lead of the National Institute of Mental Health Collaborative Study of Depression (Elkin, Parloff, Hadley, & Autry 1985) which was the first effort to test manual-driven psychotherapies. These studies have attempted to find the best type of treatment for clients who present with symptoms of both depression and psychogenic pain (e.g., Beutler, Daldrup, Engle, Guest, & Corbishley, 1988), generalized anxiety (e.g., Borkovec, et al., 1987), and age-associated depression (e.g. Thompson, Gallagher, & Breckenridge, 1987). As these initiatives have caught on, manuals have become increasingly more clinically oriented and less often geared only to specific research applications. With the advent of manuals that define what psychotherapists of various schools actually do, the degree of overlap and eclectic "borrowing" across therapies and populations has become apparent even to those who would like to maintain a pure view of theory and practice. Many researchers have come to believe that distinctions among theories is more artificial than real; others identify with the clinical impression that there are meaningful differences among the effects that can be attributed to different procedures and client characteristics.

While various types or modes of psychotherapy are associated with distinctive therapeutic processes, only a few dimensions are necessary to describe most variations among psychotherapy orientational strategies (Sundland, 1977). Some of these differences reflect differing outcome goals, others reflect differences in mediating changes, and still others reflect differences in the specific techniques employed. Beutler and Clarkin (1990) have attempted to consolidate a number of eclectic models with current research to propose client variables that can efficaciously be matched with each of these dimensions. In the absence of prospective research, however, these proposals remain speculative at the present time, but are presented here as promising hypotheses.

Goals

To the degree that there are systematic differences among practitioners from different orientations, these differences generally are consistent with the theoretical frameworks to which therapists adhere (Brunink & Schroeder, 1979; Larson, 1980; Sloane et al., 1975; Sundland, 1977). Yet, there are nearly 400 different theoretical systems, and it is unlikely that all of these embody unique aspects of either theory or practice. The probability that there are a relatively few clusters of representative approaches and theories has sponsored several efforts to find dimensions of basic commonality and distinction.

The principal method used for reducing the number of theoretical systems into clinically meaningful groupings has been to seek the common philosophical positions and/or developmental roots. As one views these efforts to collapse the number of theoretical systems, two points become clear: (a) there is currently no consensually accepted set of dimensions that allows one to make rational distinctions among theoretical systems, and (b) the effort to find commonalities is hampered by the tendency to equate theories with therapeutic procedures and formats.

Different forms of treatment are designed to induce outcomes that range along a dimension of breadth. The variations in desired outcomes can be seen in two extreme types—altered symptoms and resolution of internal conflicts. This definition parallels various distinctions between "action" and "insight" (London, 1986) or "reality-oriented" and "insight-oriented" (Thorpe, 1987) therapies. The differences between these two categories are most obvious when the effects of broadly focused psychological therapies are compared with more narrowly focused somatic therapies (Christensen, Hadzi-Pavlovic, Andrews, & Mattick, 1987; DiMascio et al., 1979; Klerman, DiMascio, Weissman, Prusoff, & Paykel, 1974). Somatic therapies are designed to effect change in the symptoms that constitute the client's diagnosis. Behavioral and cognitive psychotherapies, in a similar fashion, are directed specifically at altering symptomatic presentations over the course of treatment.

In contrast, therapies such as interpersonal, experiential, and psychodynamic therapies place higher priority on changing patterns of coping than on changing symptoms per se. Though not ignoring the importance of symptomatic change, these theories add to the definition of improvement, alterations of internal and nonobservable characteristics. Indeed, to most clinicians of these latter persuasions, it is not unthinkable that some improved clients will continue to have symptoms at treatment's end.

The importance of defining a focal objective and following the plan that evolves from this focus is seen in the observation that the amount of focal concentration on the problem constituting this formulation (Strupp, 1980a, 1980b, 1981), as well as the degree of adherence to the structure and processes defined by the therapeutic plan, are related to client outcome (Luborsky, McLellan, Woody, O'Brien, & Auerbach, 1985; Rounsaville, O'Malley, Foley, & Weissman, 1988). In other words, consistent attention to the relationships and goals that constitute the focus of treatment may well be more important to treatment outcome than either the strength of the techniques employed or the accuracy of the theory from which these techniques were originally derived.

Corresponding with the two types of therapeutic outcome goals—symptomatic and conflictual—clients present problems that vary in complexity. Beutler and Clarkin (1990) proposed that an effective treatment assignment is one that matches the nature and complexity of the client's problems with the nature of the targeted objectives.

In addition to the breadth of goals targeted by different procedures, theoretical systems also differ in the types of mediating changes valued as a means to achieve these ends. These valued changes range along a dimension of "depth" to complement the dimension of "breadth."

Mediating Changes

Just as a treatment plan must accommodate variations in the ultimate goals of intervention, it also must recognize that these different goals will be met most efficaciously by following different paths. Conflictual goals entail a different set of intermediate steps and require a different level of intervention than symptomatic goals. That is, treatment selection must recognize that different paths must be followed to modify an overt behavior as opposed to raising a repressed memory or recognizing a dysfunctional thought. The therapist's formulation of the problem must be consistent not only with the type of problem to be addressed but with the client's preferred method of coping with problems. Concomitantly, the methods of intervention selected must be able variously to support, circumvent, or alter the client's coping style.

For example, as problem complexity increases, technical procedures seem to become more important (e.g., Barker, Funk, & Houston, 1988). These technical procedures vary in terms of the level of client experience addressed, the phase objectives of the treatment process, and the characteristic coping styles to which they are best applied (Jones, Cumming, & Horowitz, 1988; Rounsaville et al., 1987). An understanding of the different depths of experience addressed by different procedures requires translating theoretical formulations into their implicit value systems. All theories value change at numerous levels, but some theories consider the means by which change occurs to be through the recovery of unconscious experience (i.e., insight), others attribute change to increasing awareness of feelings or sensations, and still others attribute change to alterations in either cognitive habits or overt behaviors.

Daldrup et al. (1988), for example, suggest that various therapies concentrate in various ways on one or more of five avenues to emotional change. These change processes range from accessing core beliefs through acknowledging emotions, intensifying emotional experiences, and reconceptualizing emotional experiences, to modifying emotional responses or behaviors. Most analyses of therapeutic depths or levels define three or four groupings of theories based on which combination of these levels of experience they most consistently attend.

Beutler and Clarkin (1990) propose that matching the client's style of coping with threatening experience to the level of experience affected by different procedures will allow the construction of menus composed of relatively specific treatments. Use of the procedures in these menus are thought to increase the persuasive power of the therapist.

At least one reason that the treatments cannot be specified more clearly is because of the dimensional nature of client coping patterns. Coping styles reflect a number of interrelated dimensions rather than nominal groupings (e.g., Freebury, 1984; Millon, 1969; Millon & Everly, 1985; Widiger, Trull, Hurt, Clarkin, & Frances, 1987), and clients tend to move among the dimensions as stressors vary, as levels of disturbance become more and less debilitating, and as the demand characteristics of the situation change. Hence, within some limits, variability of coping style is the norm rather than the exception for most people. Nonetheless, it is conventional (Gleser & Ihlevich, 1969; Loevinger, 1966) to classify clients into discrete groups based on the most dominant coping pattern represented.

While still embryonic, clinicians and researchers are coming to recognize the potential value of matching the level of experience addressed by the therapy intervention with the nature of client coping styles. For example, Freebury (1984) has proposed that client ego development and coping pattern may be used to determine both the intensity and level of intervention (uncovering therapy vs. crisis intervention and behaviorally focused intervention). Likewise, Clark, Beck, and Stewart (1989) defined two personality styles—"sociotropic" and "autonomous" types—that they suggest respond to different therapeutic methods. The sociotropic client is described as socially active and responsive (extroverted/externalized), and is thought to need reassurance, direction, and assistance in taking risks. In contrast, the autonomous style is considered to be self-directed, self-controlled, and insensitive to feeling or sensory states (internalized/introverted). Clark et al. (1989) propose that such clients require less behavioral direction than their counterparts and may benefit from treatment that encourages them to attend to internal experiences.

Likewise, interactions between client coping styles and the levels of experience addressed by the treatment have been shown to affect the nature of the therapeutic alliance among depressed and anxious clients (Gaston, Marmar, Thompson, & Gallagher, 1988), as well as to enhance treatment outcome among alcoholic clients (McLachlan, 1972). Most specifically, behaviorally targeted therapies appear to induce better results than those that focus on unconscious processes among clients who are prone to externalize their distress (e.g., Sloane et al., 1975; Beutler, 1979a). Conversely, the first author and his colleagues have confirmed that therapies that address unconscious motives and feelings are more effective than those that address the level of behavior change among these internalizing clients (Calvert, Beutler, & Crago, 1988). Other research from the same research program suggests that therapies that implement change by arousing awareness of sensations and feelings are somewhat more effective than therapies that address the level of unconscious motives, when applied to clients with externalizing coping styles (Beutler & Mitchell, 1981).

Collectively, these and other research findings suggest that there may be reliable differences in outcomes among psychotherapy procedures as a joint function of the type of intermediate changes sought and the nature of client coping or defensive styles (cf. Beutler, 1979a, 1983; Beutler & Crago, 1987).

Specific Techniques

Beutler and Clarkin (1990) proposed that there are three client dimensions, the recognition of which allows the therapist to selectively use treatment menus in order to respond to moment-to-moment changes in the therapeutic process: problem severity, reactance level, and problem-solving phase. Sensitivity to the first two of these dimensions will help the therapist optimally maintain client arousal, a condition that is deemed necessary in order to maintain therapeutic focus and client motivation. Specifically, problem severity, as indexed by client distress, serves as an indicator of whether increased arousal or decreased arousal is indicated, and client reactance level is a marker for determining how directive or evocative the therapist should be. With arousal at an optimal level, sensitivity to the client's problem-solving cycle will help the therapist maintain a helpful balance between addressing intrasession and extratherapy issues.

Because arousal is be either beneficial or inhibiting of treatment progress, depending on its level, all varieties of psychotherapy are largely devoted to managing the level of client arousal or distress in order to keep these experiences within a range that is conducive to effective work. Arkowitz and Hannah (1989) suggest that all therapies emphasize that treatment-relevant behavior must take place in the contest of affective arousal. They go on to suggest that if arousal level is optimal, it will facilitate self-observation, disconfirmation of pathognomic beliefs, and cognitive change. While different theories may value these latter consequences to a greater or lesser degree, virtually all theories acknowledge the reciprocal nature of these processes as the therapist appropriately manages client arousal level and therapy activity.

In all models of psychotherapy, the therapist introduces arousal by *exposure* to dissonant elements of functioning (Beutler, 1979b, 1981, 1983). Cognitive dissonance, as an exposure method, can be created either by confronting a client with those aspects of experience, behavior, and sensation that are being avoided, or by preventing the exercise of usual coping strategies. In either case, the process increases the client's arousal level. On the other hand, if problem severity and associated arousal are already very high, they can be felt as distress and subsequent efforts to reduce or cope with it may hamper the efficiency of any educative experience. A high distress level may indicate that the client's defenses are not working well. If this is a continuing aspect of the client's condition, the process of psychotherapy may be impeded and susceptibility to other illnesses is even likely to increase (Beutler, Engle, Oro'-Beutler, Daldrup, & Meredith, 1986; Brownlee-Duffeck, Peterson, Simonds, Goldstein, Kilo, & Hoette, 1987; Coyne & Holroyd, 1982). As extreme distress can impede the process of maintaining attentional focus, increases defensive activities, and reduces behavioral flexibility, reduction of distress may advantageously precede selective arousal induction around specific issues in such cases.

Some procedures specifically are designed to have the effect of increasing arousal, while others are designed to decrease arousal. As symptoms of distress increase and begin to interfere with motivation, flexibility, and the ability to retain attentional focus, procedures such as breathing control, attention to somatic sensations, cognitive control strategies, and managed exposure (e.g. Rapee, 1987) can be expected to be advantageous for bringing client arousal levels back into manageable limits. Likewise, if clients experience too little arousal, their motivation may suffer. Increasing the level of client exposure and therapist-client activity may facilitate the arousal needed to maintain involvement in treatment and new learning.

The experienced clinician will recognize that client arousal level also varies as a function of how the responsibilities for therapy tasks are distributed. Therapist directiveness alters the responsibility for session activity in favor of the therapist, while evocative therapy procedures, including silence, place more responsibility for the session on the client. Concomitantly, for most clients, the therapist's directiveness and assumption of responsibility are associated with reductions in client arousal level; reducing the amount of therapist directiveness will be reflected in corresponding increases in client arousal level (cf. Tracey, 1987; Beutler, 1983; Beutler, Crago, et al., 1986).

Whereas procedures such as these can be used productively to manage client arousal sufficiently to retain focus and motivation, it also should be observed that some clients respond to the intent of the procedures with a paradoxical effect. For example, most behavioral clinicians will recall clients that have become aroused and anxious when being taught to relax and those who feel quite relaxed when imagining their most feared events (e.g., Barlow & Waddell, 1985; Borkovec et al., 1987; Heide & Borkovec, 1983). These paradoxical responses identify a client as having high reactance (Brehm & Brehm, 1981) when faced with loss of perceived control or freedom. As a consequence, the methods of inducing therapeutic levels of arousal must incorporate decisions about the degree of directiveness to utilize in the therapeutic process and the degree to which extratherapy activities should receive attention.

Reactance refers to client resistance at an interpersonal level, in the way that coping style refers to client resistance at an intrapsychic level. Reactance is not only a stable trait, but is also a situationally responsive state that ebbs and flows. Indeed, when it was originally presented as a concept of clinical significance, reactance was described as a universal state that was induced by the threat of losing personal choice (Brehm, 1976). Only later was it expanded to include a characteristic and enduring response trait of significance in selecting treatments (Beutler, 1979a, 1983; Dowd & Pace, 1989).

Beutler and Clarkin (1990) proposed three working assumptions to govern therapist directiveness in response to client reactance level. First, they proposed that therapeutic effects will be enhanced if the use of evocative procedures is emphasized over directive ones among those clients for whom initial evaluation suggests high levels of reactance. Implied in this assumption are the corollary beliefs that (a) treatment will be enhanced by the use of directive procedures among clients who present with low levels of reactance, and (b) treatment may be affected negatively by mismatching client reactance levels and therapist directiveness. Indeed, there is some evidence for each of these assumptions (cf. Beutler, Crago, et al., 1986; Forsyth & Forsyth, 1982; Weary & Mirels, 1982).

The second and related assumption proposed by Beutler and Clarkin is that momentary changes of client reactance levels, occurring during the course of a session, will respond well to a therapist who shifts in counterpoint between directive and evocative procedures. These momentary changes will vary both as a function of client characteristic sensitivity to threatened loss of autonomy (trait reactance) and as a function of momentary changes in the distribution of perceived power within the relationship itself (state reactance).

Both of the foregoing points have been illustrated by Blau (1988). Emphasizing the need to differentiate among what he refers to as "unintrusive," "moderately intrusive," and intense or "probative" interventions, Blau asserted that relatively unintrusive interventions such as acceptance, empathy, encouragement, restatement, and the use of metaphor and analogy are most powerful for the client who exhibits—by disposition or by situation—high levels of resistance to the therapist's influence. In contrast, moderately intrusive interventions, including such therapist acts as structuring, asking direct questions, clarifying client feelings, setting limits and providing guidance and advice are most powerful among moderately reactant clients who, by nature or experience, have come to trust the level of safety and support provided by the therapist.

Blau emphasized that "probative" (p. 126) interventions only should be used when clients are very secure with the therapist and when their own strong and positive self-attitudes protect them from the need to resist the therapist's efforts. Such directed and interpretive activities as analysis of resistance and transference, the use of guided fantasy, dream analysis, magnification of client or therapist gestures and expressions, and confrontation of behaviors and fears tend to evoke reactance and should be employed carefully and slowly by the therapist in order to avoid negative responses and to preserve the therapeutic attachment. Even therapist humor can evoke resistance and should be applied cautiously with reactant clients (e.g., Saper, 1987). Because of considerations, the degree of intrusiveness characterizing a given intervention is modified in accordance both with the client's general resistance and with his or her reactance level at the moment.

An additional assumption proposed by Beutler and Clarkin is directed at the special case of paradoxical interventions. Dowd and Pace (1989) have suggested that paradoxical interventions should be given lower priority than more straightforward strategies and not used unless these latter procedures are ineffective. The type of paradoxical intervention to which Dowd and Pace referred include symptom prescription, countermanded change (i.e., suggesting that change will not or should not occur during a designated period of time), and magnifying or exaggerating symptoms. These procedures rely on the client to resist the therapist's influence. While some paradoxical injunctions are designed to provide a new framework within which the client observes a pattern of ongoing behavior, the so-called "defiance-based injunction" (Seltzer, 1986) assumes that the motivational force behind the symptom is reactance—the client's need to maintain or establish autonomy. Prescribing the symptom, in this case, resets the balance of autonomy on the side of giving up the symptom rather than maintaining it.

Shoham-Salomon and colleagues (Shoham-Salomon, Avner, & Zevlodever, 1988; Shoham-Saloman, & Rosenthal, 1987) have demonstrated that defiance-based paradoxical interventions have their most desirable effects among clients who exhibit high levels of reactance, especially if their symptoms are relatively intense. Among such highly reactant clients, paradoxical strategies are likely to be considerably more effective than those that rely on client cooperation. This research further suggests that, in contrast, clients who have low reactance levels respond better either to structured, directive interventions or to procedures that value client compliance than they do to defiance-based paradoxical ones.

CONCLUSIONS

To suggest that client-therapist similarities are central to developing a beneficial therapeutic alliance is a far too simplistic assertion. A good therapeutic alliance must also be built on the presence of different but relevant perspectives and evolves out of what transpires within the treatment to enhance or inhibit the growth of the relationship. This latter point is captured well in the writing of Kohut (1977, 1984) who proposed a tripolar concept of self, each aspect of which is associated with a certain environmental response. These tripolar needs to receive selective responses from the environment and the history of early environmental supply of these responses result in attributes that make the client selectively seek one of several types of relationships. The first two attributes, ambition and ideals, grow both from an environment that acknowledges the differences that exist between oneself and others and from a relationship with someone who embodies healthy values. If one's needs for acknowledgment are not met, anger and rebellion may become the norm. On the other hand, if desires for a stable value model are frustrated, one may attempt to construct an idealized relationship with others and consequently relate through a medium of dependency and self-depreciation. One sees in this logic the central role that a therapist may play in providing the model of personal values and ideals that the client lacked in the course of earlier experiences and on which therapeutic persuasion may depend.

Kohut also proposed that twinship needs reflect one's effort to see oneself as similar to significant others. Frustration of these needs for similarity when interacting with figures who are very different from or critical of oneself is thought to result in a sense of alienation, and in psychotherapy may drive the client to seek similarity with the therapist. Hence, to Kohut, clients both seek to know therapist's personal values and to adopt them in their search for human identity and safety. The fact that therapeutic benefit, especially as judged by the therapist, is associated with a process of client conversion to the therapist's personal beliefs (Beutler, 1981), is consistent with this viewpoint.

We may conclude that therapists who share similar humanitarian and intellectual values with their clients, and who have discrepant views of personal safety and the value of interpersonal intimacy and attachment, comprise optimally compatible pairings. When differences occur in other belief and value dimensions, therapists who are sufficiently tolerant of and able to communicate from within the client's framework may be as effective as those whose views are similar to their clients. Such therapists do not appear to exert undue influence over socially sensitive but valid social values.

The methods of role induction may facilitate the development of desired client-therapy matches, especially adding to the power of the therapeutic alliance, which tends to become stabilized early in treatment (Eaton, Ables, & Gutfreund, 1988). Role-induction procedures have several characteristics in common, whether constructed as direct instruction, through contracts, or through modeling and observation. Wilson (1985) noted that a central tenet of most procedures is that pretherapy training will help establish treatment as a collaborative venture. The various other aspects of role induction simply reinforce and operationalize this concept of collaboration.

Once one decides that certain client roles should be induced rather than adopting procedures that accommodate client expectations, the method to be used for role induction becomes a critical variable. A careful distinction between the induction and the treatment cannot always be maintained. Hence, the role induction should be selected to fit the client's needs for personal contact, structure, and reassurance, as well as their preferential defensive styles.

While it is clinically obvious that the nature of preparing clients for treatment should vary from client to client and from treatment to treatment, empirical literature is relatively silent on this issue. Overall, it is defensible to argue that combining procedures is more advantageous than single role-induction procedures (Mayerson, 1984), but this is seldom feasible in view of time demands and convenience. For most cases, we are left to rely on clinical experience and common sense to tell us how to prepare a given client for treatment.

Similarly, clinicians usually rely on intuition or theoretical logic in selecting specific means of intervention. Unfortunately, they are limited in their choices by their theoretical leanings and experience. A number of authors have proposed a superordinate model of interventions that would provide a method of selecting a wider variety of techniques than that encompassed in a single theoretical approach to treatment. While several of these models have been based on prevailing clinical wisdom and available empirical research, prospective research on the models themselves is just beginning. We have presented some of the conclusions and hypotheses developed by Beutler and Clarkin (1990), who have consolidated several

empirically derived treatment matching models around the concept of personal persuasion.

Beutler and Clarkin have proposed matching criteria to help select the focal objectives of treatment, the mediating goals of treatment, and the use of directive and evocative measures. These selections rely on corresponding client qualities of problem complexity, coping style, and reactance potential. This model attempts to extract from notions of persuasion the principles that will allow therapists to be maximally efficient in the selection of technical strategies, but is likely to be most effective if applied in compatible therapeutic dyads, and when clients themselves are prepared in advance for accepting the assumptions and expectations that are embodied in the procedures used.

REFERENCES

Abramowitz, S. I., & Murray, J. (1983). Race effects in psychotherapy. In J. Murray & P. R. Abramson (Eds.), *Bias in psychotherapy* (pp. 215–255). New York: Praeger.

Alexander, J. F., Barton, C., Schiavo, R. S., & Parsons, B. V. (1976). Systems-behavioral interventions with families of delinquents: Therapist characteristics, family behavior, and outcome. *Journal of Consulting and Clinical Psychology, 17*, 656–664.

Arizmendi, T. G., Beutler, L. E., Shanfield, S., Crago, M., & Hagaman, R. (1985). Client-therapist value similarity and psychotherapy outcome: A microscopic approach. *Psychotherapy: Theory, Research and Practice, 22*, 16–21.

Arkowitz, H., & Hannah, M. T. (1989). Cognitive, behavioral, and psychodynamic therapies: Converging or diverging pathways to change? In A. Freeman, K. Simon, L. E. Beutler, & H. Arkowitz (Eds.), *Comprehensive handbook of cognitive therapy* (pp.143–168). New York: Plenum Press.

Atkinson, D. R. (1983). Ethnic similarity in counseling psychology: A review of research. *The Counseling Psychologist, 11*, 79–92.

Atkinson, D. R., & Schein, S. (1986). Similarity in counseling. *The Counseling Psychologist, 14*, 319–354.

Azrin, N. H., Naster, B. J., & Jones, R. (1973). Reciprocity counselling: A rapid learning-based procedure for marital counselling. *Behavior Research and Therapy, 11*, 365–382.

Barker, S. L., Funk, S. C., & Houston, B. K. (1988). Psychological treatment versus nonspecific factors: A meta-analysis of conditions that engender comparable expectations for improvement. *Clinical Psychology Review, 8,* 579–594.

Barlow, D. H., & Waddell, M. T. (1985). Agoraphobia. In D. H. Barlow (Ed.), *Clinical handbook of psychological disorders: A step-by-step treatment manual* (pp. 1–68). New York: Guilford Press.

Beck, A. T., Rush, A. J., Shaw, B. F., & Emery, G. (1979). *Cognitive therapy of depression.* New York: Guilford Press.

Bergin, A. E. (1980). Psychotherapy and religious values. *Journal of Consulting and Clinical Psychology, 48,* 95–105.

Berry, D. S., & McArthur, L. Z. (1986). Perceiving character in faces: The impact of age-related craniofacial changes on social perception. *Psychological Bulletin, 100,* 3–18.

Beutler, L. E. (1979a). Toward specific psychological therapies for specific conditions. *Journal of Consulting and Clinical Psychology, 47,* 882–897.

Beutler, L. E. (1979b). Values, beliefs, religion and the persuasive influence of psychotherapy. *Psychotherapy: Theory, Research and Practice, 16,* 432–440.

Beutler, L. E. (1981). Convergence in counseling and psychotherapy: A current look. *Clinical Psychology Review, 1,* 79–101.

Beutler, L. E. (1983). *Eclectic psychotherapy: A systematic approach.* Elmsford, NY: Pergamon Press.

Beutler, L. E., Arizmendi, T. G., Crago, M., Shanfield, S., & Hagaman, R. (1983). The effects of value similarity and clients' persuadability on value convergence and psychotherapy improvement. *Journal of Social and Clinical Psychology, 1,* 231–245.

Beutler, L. E., & Clarkin, J. (1990). *Systematic treatment selection: Toward targeted therapeutic interventions.* New York: Brunner/Mazel.

Beutler, L. E., & Crago, M. (1987). Strategies and techniques of prescriptive psychotherapeutic intervention. In R. E. Hales & A. J. Frances (Eds.), *American Psychiatric Association: Annual Review* (Vol. 6, pp. 378–397). Washington, DC: American Psychiatric Association.

Beutler, L. E., Crago, M., & Arizmendi, T. G. (1986). Therapist variables in psychotherapy process and outcome. In S. L. Garfield & A. E. Bergin (Eds.), *Handbook of psychotherapy and behavior change* (3rd ed., pp. 257–310). New York: John Wiley & Sons.

Beutler, L. E., Daldrup, R., Engle, D., Guest, P., & Corbishley, A. (1988). Family dynamics and emotional expression among patients with chronic pain and depression. *Pain, 32,* 65–72.

Beutler, L. E., Engle, D., Oro'-Beutler, M. E., Daldrup, R., & Meredith, K. (1986). Inability to express intense affect: A common link between depression and pain? *Journal of Consulting and Clinical Psychology, 54,* 752–759.

Beutler, L. E., Jobe, A. M., & Elkins, D. (1974). Outcomes in group psychotherapy: Using persuasion theory to increase treatment efficiency. *Journal of Consulting and Clinical Psychology, 42,* 547–553.

Beutler, L. E., & Mitchell, R. (1981). Psychotherapy outcome in depressed and impulsive patients as a function of analytic and experiential treatment procedures. *Psychiatry, 44,* 297–306.

Beutler, L. E., Pollack, S., & Jobe, A. M. (1978). "Acceptance," values and therapeutic change. *Journal of Consulting and Clinical Psychology, 46,* 198–199.

Beutler, L. E., Scoggin, F., Kirkish, P., Schretlen, D., Corbishley, M. A., Hamblin, D., Meredith, K., Potter, R., Bamford, C. R., & Levenson, A. I. (1987). Group cognitive therapy and alprazolam in the treatment of depression in older adults. *Journal of Consulting and Clinical Psychology, 55,* 550–556.

Blase, J. J. (1979). A study of the effects of sex of the client and sex of the therapist on clients' satisfaction with psychotherapy. *Dissertation Abstracts International, 39,* 6107B–6108B.

Blau, T. J. (1988). *Psychotherapy tradecraft: The technique and style of doing therapy.* New York: Brunner/Mazel.

Blier, M. J., Atkinson, D. R., & Geer, C. A. (1987). Effect of client gender and counselor gender and sex roles on willingness to see the counselor. *Journal of Counseling Psychology, 34,* 27–30.

Borkovec, T., Mathews, A. M., Chambers A., Ebrahimi, S., Lytle, R., & Nelson, R. (1987). The effects of relaxation training with cognitive therapy or nondirective therapy and the role of relaxation-induced anxiety in the treatment of generalized anxiety. *Journal of Consulting and Clinical Psychology, 55,* 883–888.

Brehm, S. S. (1976). *The application of social psychology to clinical practice.* New York: John Wiley & Sons.

Brehm, S. S., & Brehm, J. W. (1981). *Psychological reactance: A theory of freedom and control.* New York: Academic Press.

Brownlee-Duffeck, M., Peterson, L., Simonds, J. F., Goldstein, D., Kilo, C., & Hoette, S. (1987). The role of health beliefs in regimen adherence and metabolic control of adolescents and adults with diabetes mellitus. *Journal of Consulting and Clinical Psychology, 55,* 139–144.

Brunink, S., & Schroeder, H. (1979). Verbal therapeutic behavior of expert psychoanalytically oriented, gestalt and behavior therapists. *Journal of Consulting and Clinical Psychology, 47,* 567–574.

Butcher, J. N., & Koss, M. P. (1978). Research on brief and crisis-oriented psychotherapies. In S. L. Garfield & A. E. Bergin (Eds.), *Handbook of psychotherapy and behavior change* (2nd ed., pp. 725–768). New York: John Wiley & Sons.

Calvert, S. J., Beutler, L. E., & Crago, M. (1988). Psychotherapy outcome as a function of therapist-patient matching on selected variables. *Journal of Social and Clinical Psychology, 6,* 104–117.

Carkhuff, R. R., & Pierce, R. (1967). Differential effects of therapist race and social class upon patient depth of self-exploration in the initial clinical interview. *Journal of Consulting Psychology, 31,* 632–634.

Charone, J. K. (1981). Patient and therapist treatment goals related to psychotherapy outcome. *Dissertation Abstracts International, 42,* 365B.

Cheloha, R. S. (1986). The relationship between client-therapist mental health value similarity and psychotherapy outcome. *Dissertation Abstracts International, 47,* 1716B.

Chesner, S. P., & Baumeister, R. F. (1985). Effect of therapist's disclosure of religious beliefs on the intimacy of client self-disclosure. *Journal of Social and Clinical Psychology, 3,* 97–105.

Childress, R., & Gillis, J. S. (1977). A study of pretherapy role induction as an influence process. *Journal of Clinical Psychology, 33,* 540–544.

Christensen, H., Hadzi-Pavlovic, D., Andrews, G., & Mattick, R. (1987). Behavior therapy and tricyclic medication in the treatment of obsessive-compulsive disorder: A quantitative review. *Journal of Consulting and Clinical Psychology, 55,* 701–711.

Clark, D. M., Beck, A. T., & Stewart, B. (1989, July). *Sociotropy and Autonomy: Cognitive vulnerability.* A paper presented at the World Congress on cognitive therapy. Oxford, England.

Conway, J. B. (1988). Differences among clinical psychologists: Scientists, practitioners, and scientist-practitioners. *Professional Psychology: Research and Practice, 19,* 642–655.

Coyne, J. C., & Holroyd, K. (1982). Stress, coping, and illness. In T. Millon, C. Green, & R. Meagher (Eds.), *Handbook of clinical health psychology* (pp. 103–127). New York: Plenum Press.

Daldrup, R. J., Beutler, L. E., Greenberg, L. S., & Engle, D. (1988). *Focused expressive psychotherapy: Freeing the overcontrolled patient.* New York: Guilford Press.

DiMascio, A., Weissman, M. M., Prusoff, B. A., Neu, C., Zwilling, M., & Klerman, G. L. (1979). Differential symptom reduction by drugs and psychotherapy in acute depression. *Archives of General Psychiatry, 36,* 1450–1456.

Dowd, E. T., & Pace, T. F. (1989). The relativity of reality: Second order change in psychotherapy. In A. Freeman, K. M. Simon, L. E. Beutler, & H. Arkowitz (Eds.), *Comprehensive handbook of cognitive therapy* (pp. 213–226). New York: Plenum Press.

Eaton, T. T., Abeles, N., & Gutfreund, M. J. (1988). Therapeutic alliance and outcome: Impact of treatment length and pretreatment symptomatology. *Psychotherapy, 25,* 536–542.

Elkin, I. (moderator). (1986, June). *NIMH treatment of depression collaborative research program: Part I.* Panel presented at the meeting of Society for Psychotherapy Research, Wellesley, MA.

Elkin, I. E., Parloff, M. B., Hadley, S. W., & Autry, J. H. (1985). NIMH treatment of depression collaborative research program. *Archives of General Psychiatry, 42,* 305–316.

Emmelkamp, P. (1986). Behavior therapy with adults. In S. L. Garfield & A. E. Bergin (Eds.), *Handbook of psychotherapy and behavior change* (3rd ed., pp. 385–442). New York: John Wiley & Sons.

Fiedler, F. E. (1950). The concept of an ideal therapeutic relationship. *Journal of Consulting Psychology, 14,* 239–245.

Forsyth, N. L., & Forsyth, D. R. (1982). Internality, controllability, and the effectiveness of attributional interpretation in counseling. *Journal of Counseling Psychology, 29*, 140–150.

Freebury, M. B. (1984). The prescription of psychotherapy. *Canadian Journal of Psychiatry, 29*, 499–503.

Freeman, A. (Ed.). (1983). *Cognitive therapy with couples and groups.* New York: Plenum Press.

Gaston, L., Marmar, C. R., Thompson, L. W., & Gallagher, D. (1988). Relation of patient pretreatment characteristics to the therapeutic alliance in diverse psychotherapies. *Journal of Consulting and Clinical Psychology, 56*, 483–489.

Gleser, G. C., & Ihlevich, D. (1969). An objective instrument to measure defense mechanisms. *Journal of Consulting and Clinical Psychology, 33*, 51–60.

Goulding, M., & Goulding, R. (1979). *Changing lives through redecision therapy.* New York: Brunner/Mazel.

Hamblin, D. I., Beutler, L. E., Scogin, F., & Corbishley, A. (1988, June). *Sensitivity to therapist values and outcome in group cognitive therapy.* Paper presented at the annual meeting of the Society from Psychotherapy Research, Santa Fe, NM.

Heide, F. J., & Borkovec, T. D. (1983). Relaxation-induced anxiety: Paradoxical anxiety enhancement due to relaxation training. *Journal of Consulting and Clinical Psychology, 51*, 171–182.

Heitler, J. B. (1976). Preparatory techniques in initiating expressive psychotherapy with lower-class, unsophisticated patients. *Psychological Bulletin, 83*, 339–352.

Hill, J. A., Howard, K. I., & Orlinsky, D. E. (1970). The therapist's experience of psychotherapy: Some dimensions and determinants. *Multivariate Behavioral Research, 5*, 435–451.

Hoehn-Saric, R., Frank, J. D., Imber, S. D., Nash, E. H., Stone, A. R., & Battle, C. C. (1964). Systematic preparation of patients for psychotherapy: I. Effects of therapy on behavior and outcome. *Journal of Psychiatric Research, 2*, 267–281.

Holliday, P. B. (1979). Effects of preparation for therapy on client expectations and participation. *Dissertation Abstracts International, 39*, 3517B.

Houts, A. C., & Graham, K. (1986). Can religion make you crazy? Impact of client and therapist religious values on clinical judgments. *Journal of Consulting and Clinical Psychology, 54*, 267–271.

Jacobs, M. K., Trick, O. L., & Withersty, D. (1976). Pretraining psychiatric inpatients for participation in group psychotherapy. *Psychotherapy: Theory, Research and Practice, 13*, 361–367.

Jacobson, N. S., & Margolin, G. (1979). *Marital therapy: Strategies based on several learning and behavior exchange principles.* New York: Brunner/Mazel.

Jones, E. E. (1978). Effects of race on psychotherapy process and outcome: An exploratory investigation. *Psychotherapy: Theory, Research and Practice, 15*, 226–236.

Jones, E. E., Cumming, J. D., & Horowitz, M. J. (1988). Another look at the nonspecific hypothesis of therapeutic effectiveness. *Journal of Consulting and Clinical Psychology, 56*, 48–55.

Jones, E. F., Krupnick, J. L., & Kerig, P. K. (1987). Some gender effects in brief psychotherapy. *Psychotherapy, 24*, 336–352.

Kirschenbaum, D. S., & Flaner, R. C. (1984). Toward a psychology of behavioral contracting. *Clinical Psychology Review, 4*, 597–618.

Klerman, G. L., DiMascio, A., Weissman, M. M., Prusoff, B., & Paykel, E. S. (1974). Treatment of depression by drugs and psychotherapy. *American Journal of Psychiatry, 131*, 186–191.

Klerman, G. L., Weissman, M. M., Rounsaville, B. J., & Chevron, E. S. (1984). *Interpersonal psychotherapy of depression.* New York: Basic Books.

Kohut, H. (1977). *The restoration of the self.* New York: International Universities Press.

Kohut, H. (1984). *How does analysis cure?* Chicago: University of Chicago Press.

Koss, M. P., & Butcher, J. N. (1986). Research on brief psychotherapy. In S. L. Garfield & A. E. Bergin (Eds.), *Handbook of psychotherapy and behavior change* (3rd ed., pp. 627–670). New York: John Wiley & Sons.

Lafferty, P., Beutler, L. E., & Crago, M. (1989). Differences between more and less effective psychotherapists: A study of select therapist variables. *Journal of Consulting and Clinical Psychology, 57*, 76–80.

Larson, D. G. (1980). Therapeutic styles and schoolism: A national survey. *Journal of Humanistic Psychology, 20*, 3–20.

LaTorre, R. A. (1977). Pretherapy role induction procedures. *Canadian Psychological Review, 18*, 308–321.

Lazarus, A. A. (1981). *The practice of multimodal therapy*. New York: McGraw-Hill.

Lewis, K. N. (1983, August). *The impact of religious affiliation on therapists' judgments of clients*. Paper presented at the American Psychological Association Convention, Anaheim, CA.

Lieberman, M. A., Yalom, I. D., & Miles, M. B. (1973). *Encounter groups: First facts*. New York: Basic Books.

Loevinger, J. (1966). The meaning and measurement of ego development. *American Psychologist, 21*, 195–206.

London, P. (1986). *The modes and morals of psychotherapy* (2nd ed.). Washington, DC: Hemisphere.

Luborsky, L. (1984). *Principles of psychoanalytic psychotherapy: A manual for supportive-expressive treatment*. New York: Basic Books.

Luborksy, L., Crits-Christoph, P., Alexander, L., Margolis, M., & Cohen, M. (1983). Two helping alliance methods for predicting outcomes of psychotherapy: A counting signs vs. a global rating method. *Journal of Nervous and Mental Disease, 171*, 480–491.

Luborsky, L., & DeRubeis, R. J. (1984). The use of psychotherapy treatment manuals: A small revolution in psychotherapy research style. *Clinical Psychology Review, 4*, 5–14.

Luborsky, L., McLellan, A. T., Woody, G. E., O'Brien, C. P., & Auerbach, A. (1985). Therapist success and its determinants. *Archives of General Psychiatry, 42*, 602–611.

Luborsky, L., Singer, B., & Luborsky, L (1975). Comparative studies of psychotherapies. *Archives of General Psychiatry, 32*, 995–1008.

Madanes, C. (1981). *Strategic family therapy*. San Francisco: Jossey-Bass.

Mayerson, N. H. (1984). Preparing clients for group therapy: A critical review and theoretical formulation. *Clinical Psychology Review, 4*, 191–213.

McLachlan, J. C. (1972). Benefit from group therapy as a function of patient-therapist match on conceptual level. *Psychotherapy: Theory, Research and Practice, 9*, 317–323.

Meichenbaum, D. J., & Turk, D. C. (1987). *Facilitating treatment adherence: A practitioner's guidebook*. New York: Plenum Press.

Merluzzi, T. V., Merluzzi, B. H., & Kaul, T.

(1977). Counselor race and power base: Effects on attitudes and behaviors. *Journal of Counseling Psychology, 24*, 430–436.

Millon, T. (1969). *Modern psychopathology*. Philadelphia: W. B. Saunders.

Millon, T., & Everly, G. S. (1985). *Personality and its disorders*. New York: John Wiley & Sons.

Neimeyer, G. J., & Gonzales, M. (1983). Duration, satisfaction, and perceived effectiveness of cross-cultural counseling. *Journal of Counseling Psychology, 30*, 91–95.

Norcross, J. C. (Ed.). (1986a). *Handbook of eclectic psychotherapy*. New York: Brunner/Mazel.

Norcross, J. C. (1986b). Eclectic psychotherapy: An introduction and overview. In J. C. Norcross (Ed.), *Handbook of eclectic psychotherapy* (pp. 3–24). New York: Brunner/Mazel.

Norcross, J. C., & Prochaska, J. O. (1988). A study of eclectic (and integrative) views revisited. *Professional Psychology: Research and Practice, 19*, 170–174.

Orlinsky, D. E., & Howard, K. I. (1986). Process and outcome in psychotherapy. In S. L. Garfield & A. E. Bergin (Eds.), *Handbook of psychotherapy and behavior change* (3rd ed., pp. 311–384). New York: John Wiley & Sons.

Parloff, M. B., Waskow, I. E., & Wolfe, B. E. (1978). Research on therapist variables in relation to process and outcome. In S. L. Garfield & A. E. Bergin (Eds.), *Handbook of psychotherapy and behavior change* (2nd ed., pp. 233–282). New York: John Wiley & Sons.

Pomerleau, O. F. (1979). Behavioral medicine: The contribution of the experimental analysis of behavior to medical care. *American Psychologist, 34*, 654–663.

Pomerleau, O. F., & Pomerleau, C. S. (1984). *Break the smoking habit: A behavioral program for giving up cigarettes*. W. Hartford, CT: Behavioral Medicine Press.

Probst, L. R. (1980). The comparative efficacy of religious and nonreligious imagery for the treatment of mild depression in religious individuals. *Cognitive Therapy and Research, 4*, 167–178.

Probst, L. R., Ostrom, R., & Watkins, P. (1984, June). *The efficacy of religious cognitive-behavioral therapy for the treatment of clinical depression in religious individuals*. Paper presented at the Society for Psychotherapy Research, Lake Louise, Alberta, Canada.

Proctor, E. K., & Rosen, A. (1981). Expectations and preferences for counselor race and their relation to intermediate treatment outcomes. *Journal of Counseling Psychology, 28,* 40–46.

Rapee, R. (1987). The psychological treatment of panic attacks: Theoretical conceptualization and review of evidence. *Clinical Psychology Review, 7,* 427–438.

Rogers, C. R. (1951). *Client-centered therapy.* Boston: Houghton Mifflin.

Rounsaville, B. J., Chevron, E. S., Prusoff, B. A., Elkin, I., Imber, S., Sotsky, S., & Watkins, J. (1987). The relation between specific and general dimensions of the psychotherapy process in interpersonal psychotherapy of depression. *Journal of Consulting and Clinical Psychology, 55,* 379–384.

Rounsaville, B. J., O'Malley, S. S., Folley, S., & Weissman, M. M. (1988). Role of manual-guided training in the conduct and efficacy of interpersonal psychotherapy for depression. *Journal of Consulting and Clinical Psychology, 56,* 681–688.

Sank, L. I., & Shaffer, C. S. (1984). *A therapist's manual for cognitive behavior therapy in groups.* New York: Plenum Press.

Saper, B. (1987). Humor in psychotherapy: Is it good or bad for the client? *Professional Psychology: Research and Practice, 18,* 360–367.

Seltzer, L. F. (1986). *Paradoxical strategies in psychotherapy: A comprehensive overview and guidebook.* New York: John Wiley & Sons.

Shapiro, P. N., & Penrod, S. (1986). Meta-analysis of facial identification studies. *Psychological Bulletin, 100,* 139–156.

Shoham-Salomon, V., Avner, R., & Zevlodever, R. (1988, June). *"You are changed if you do and changed if you don't": Cognitive mechanisms underlying the operation of therapeutic paradoxes.* A paper presented at the Society for Psychotherapy Research, Santa Fe, NM.

Shoham-Salomon, V., & Rosenthal, R. (1987). Paradoxical interventions: A meta-analysis. *Journal of Consulting and Clinical Psychology, 55,* 22–27.

Sloane, R. B., Staples, F. R., Cristol, A. H., Yorkston, N. J., & Whipple, K. (1975). *Psychotherapy versus behavior therapy.* Cambridge MA: Harvard University Press.

Strupp, H. H. (1980a). Success and failure in time-limited psychotherapy: A systematic comparison of two cases (Comparison 1). *Archives of General Psychiatry, 37,* 595–603.

Strupp, H. H. (1980b). Success and failure in time-limited psychotherapy: A systematic comparison of two cases (comparison 2). *Archives of General Psychiatry, 37,* 708–716.

Strupp, H. H. (1981). Toward the refinement of time-limited dynamic psychotherapy. In S. H. Budman (Ed.), *Forms of brief therapy* (pp. 219–242). New York: Guilford Press.

Strupp, H. H., & Binder, J. L. (1984). *Psychotherapy in a new key.* New York: Basic Books.

Strupp, H. H., & Bloxom, A. L. (1973). Preparing lower class patients for group psychotherapy: Development and evaluation of a role-induction film. *Journal of Consulting and Clinical Psychology, 41,* 373–384.

Sundland, D. M. (1977, June). *Theoretical orientation: A multiprofessional American sample.* Paper presented at the eighth annual meeting of the Society for Psychotherapy Research, Madison, WI.

Terrell, R., & Terrell, S. (1984). Race of counselor, client sex, cultural mistrust level, and premature termination from counseling among black clients. *Journal of Counseling Psychology, 31,* 371–375.

Thompson, L., Gallagher, D., & Breckenridge, J. (1987). Comparative effectiveness of psychotherapies for depressed elders. *Journal of Consulting and Clinical Psychology, 55,* 385–390.

Thorpe, S. A. (1987). An approach to treatment planning. *Psychotherapy, 24,* 729–735.

Tjelveit, A. C. (1986). The ethics of value conversion in psychotherapy: Appropriate and inappropriate therapist influence on client values. *Clinical Psychology Review, 6,* 515–537.

Tracey, T. J. (1987). Stage differences in the dependencies of topic initiation and topic following behavior. *Journal of Counseling Psychology, 34,* 123–131.

Truax, C. B., & Carkhuff, R. R. (1967). *Toward effective counseling and psychotherapy: Training and practice.* Chicago: Aldine.

Truax, C. B., & Wargo, D. G. (1969). Effects of vicarious therapy pre-training and alternate sessions on outcome in group psychotherapy with outpatients. *Journal of Consulting and Clinical Psychology, 33,* 440–447.

Turkat, D. M. (1979). Psychotherapy preparatory communications: Influences upon patient role expectations. *Dissertation Abstracts International, 39,* 4059B.

Turner, S., & Armstrong, S. (1981). Cross-racial psychotherapy: What the therapists say. *Psy-*

chotherapy: Theory, Research and Practice, 18, 375–378.

Vitz, P. C. (1988). *Sigmund Freud's christian unconscious.* New York: Guilford Press.

Warren, R. C., & Rice, L. N. (1972). Structuring and stabilizing of psychotherapy for low-prognosis clients. *Journal of Consulting and Clinical Psychology, 39*, 173–181.

Waterhouse, G. J., & Strupp, H. H. (1984). The patient-therapist relationship: Research from the psychodynamic perspective. *Clinical Psychology Review, 4*, 77–92.

Weary, G., & Mirels, H. L. (Eds.). (1982). *Integrations of clinical and social psychology.* New York: Oxford University Press.

Weiss, R. L., Hops, H., & Patterson, G. R. (1973). A framework for conceptualizing marital conflict, a technology for altering it, some data for evaluating it. In F. W. Clark & L. A. Hamerlynck (Eds.), *Critical issues in research and practice: Proceedings of the Fourth Banff International Conference in Behavior Modification.* Champaign, IL: Research Press.

Widiger, T. A., Trull, T. J., Hurt, S. W., Clarkin, J. F., & Frances, A. (1987). A multidimensional scaling of the DSM-III personality disorders. *Archives of General Psychiatry, 44*, 557–563.

Wilson, D. O. (1985). The effects of systematic client preparation, severity, and treatment setting on dropout rate in short-term psychotherapy. *Journal of Social and Clinical Psychology, 3*, 62–70.

Wolfe, B. E., & Goldfried, M. R. (1988). Research on psychotherapy integration: Recommendations and conclusions from an NIMH workshop. *Journal of Consulting and Clinical Psychology, 56*, 448–451.

Yalom, I. D., Houts, P. S., Newell, G., & Rank, K. H. (1967). Preparation of patients for group therapy. *Archives of General Psychiatry, 17*, 416–427.

Zwick, R., & Attkisson, C. C. (1985). Effectiveness of a client pretherapy orientation videotape. *Journal of Counseling Psychology, 32*, 514–524.

CHAPTER 36

ON THE ROBUSTNESS AND FLEXIBILITY OF CLINICAL HEALTH INTERVENTIONS

Paul Karoly

THE PSYCHOTHERAPY HERITAGE

Against the background of a client's usual performance variability, a therapist typically seeks to induce, via episodic contacts, a series of temporary disruptions in that client's preferred mode(s) of thinking, feeling, and/or behaving. Further, it is expected that, over time, certain permanent (nonreversible) adaptive changes will result in the content or pattern of cognition, affect, or actions — changes capable not only of sustaining current healthy adjustments, but of undergirding new ones. In popular clinical parlance, interventions (of whatever sort) are critically evaluated in terms of their ability to produce initial therapeutic change, to effect maintenance (persistence) of change over extended periods, and to ensure that the newly learned responses will be applied to different settings, in the company of different people, and toward the resolution of related, but distinct problems (generalization and transfer effects).

Because psychologists, psychiatrists, and social workers have been employed for many decades in medical hospitals and clinics, dealing with the so-called neurotic problems of the physically ill, the triad of concerns — change, maintenance, and transfer — naturally went with them. Today's health psychologist, whose agenda includes both illness management and health promotion, is expected to consider the need for durable and extendable interventions and to be mindful of the fact that these objectives are not easily attained (cf. Goldstein & Kanfer, 1979; Karoly & Steffen, 1980; Kazdin, 1989; Meichenbaum & Turk, 1987).

What can the health psychologist expect to find when turning to the psychotherapy literature for counsel and direction? To date, three approaches have been employed to deal with the issue of the persistence of therapy-based change. The first (and most common) strategy is to ignore the long-term effects of one's intervention because of (a) the difficulty and expense in monitoring posttreatment events, (b) strong theory-derived expectations (faith) that patient status at the end of treatment will automatically endure, or (c) the conviction that posttherapy recidivism or deterioration in patient functioning does not necessarily reflect on the quality of initial care. Until consumers or insurance companies insist on a different course, begging the admittedly important question of durability of effects will probably suffice in the world of private practice.

A second, more responsive, approach is to consider maintenance and generalization to be technical or engineering problems. The *behavioral engineering model* is built on the deliberate manipulation of in-therapy or extratherapeutic events designed to render therapy-based learning as resistant as possible to extinction and as transferrable as clinical foresight permits (Goldstein, Lopez, & Greenleaf, 1979; Marholin & Touchette, 1979; Wildman & Wildman, 1980). The operant or applied behavior analysis framework has for many years been in the forefront of maintenance and generalization enhancement research (Karoly & Harris, 1986; Kazdin, 1989; Snyder, 1989).

A third perspective can be termed *person-centered*, as it involves a social learning theory–inspired emphasis on the individual's cognitive construction of life events, as well as on individual differences in those mediational processes that ostensibly move (or fail to move) the individual through the various phases of treatment, including maintenance and transfer (cf. Haaga & Davison, 1986; Kanfer & Schefft, 1988; Karoly, 1980; Kirschenbaum & Tomarken, 1982; Kuhl, 1987; Marlatt & Gordon, 1985).

Although the aforementioned models dominate current thinking, two additional and promising frameworks are distinct enough from the first three to be listed and considered separately. A fourth point of departure for examining consistency in therapeutic learning might be termed *ecological*, because it pivots on the application of social network analysis to posttreatment environments in an effort to address the key questions of extratherapy maintenance and generalization (cf. Higginbotham, West, & Forsyth, 1988, chap. 7; Price, 1979).

Finally, a viewpoint I call a *dynamic adaptive systems* (DAS) model is needed to balance questions of treatment robustness (e.g., maintenance, generalization, and transfer of training) against considerations of the inevitability of environmental change, the continuous reorganization of adaptive patterns, and transitional aspects of performance. As a shorthand, I refer to this latter set of dimensions as open system constraints and assert that they set natural bounds on the effects of interventive strategies founded on the traditional

"learn it, store it, use it" philosophy of training (models 2, 3, and 4 above).

ROBUSTNESS AND HEALTH PSYCHOLOGY

Who Cares About Persistence of Effect?

What do needle aversion, treatment-induced pain, obtaining a second surgical opinion, hospital-related stress, and tracheostomy dependence have in common? They are among the very few clinical targets in contemporary health psychology/behavioral medicine that are time limited or context bound. Almost every other domain of basic and applied work involves problematic patterns (relating to acute or chronic disease or health promotion) requiring continued vigilance, effort, and motivation on the part of the patient. Thus, as in traditional psychotherapy, a concern for the stability and carryover potential of all manner of interventions should be mandated.

To appreciate how widespread and compelling the mandate actually is, one has only to peruse the health psychology journals. In the area of high risk life-style change (e.g., treatment of cigarette smoking, alcoholism, obesity, and the like) almost no studies are published without a follow-up assessment, often in months, sometimes in years posttreatment. This attention to persistence of effects may be due to the known relapse proneness of individuals with addictive problems or to the nature of the interventions themselves (often involving self-management components designed to provide patients with the skills to actively and continuously treat themselves). In the analysis of compliance or adherence to chronic illness treatment regimens, it has likewise become de rigueur to determine whether patients are using newly gained knowledge or skills in their extratherapy environments, and whether they are doing so correctly and consistently enough to bring about a medical stabilization of their disorder (cf. Haynes, Taylor, & Sackett, 1979; Karoly, this volume; Meichenbaum & Turk, 1987).

The problem of adherence or compliance with physicians' prescriptive or preventive instructions is often considered to be a variant of the maintenance problem (cf. Stuart, 1982). However, it is important to distinguish between the determinants of order- or instruction-following and the factors that contribute to the temporal persistence of learned and practiced behavior. In the former case, there may have been no information transmitted, no intention to act, and no new learning taking place. If the patient fails to follow through on a physician's (often unrealistic) expectations, such a "failure" must be distinguished from failures of motivation/performance that have traditionally been investigated within learning and social-cognitive theory.

Nevertheless, studies investigating a novel intervention, or those mainly concerned with short-term effects, continue to be published without benefit of continuity analysis. Recent interventive research on such topics as weight loss by means of worksite competition (Cohen, Stunkard, & Felix, 1987), biofeedback-assisted relaxation for high blood pressure (McGrady, Woerner, Bernal, & Higgins, 1987), compliance with cancer therapy (Richardson et al., 1987), self-directed hemodialysis (Kirschenbaum, Sherman, & Penrod, 1987), and feedback training for the self-control of tinnitus (Ince, Greene, Alba, & Zaretsky, 1987) all failed to incorporate a follow-up assessment. In each case, the effects noted from pretreatment to the termination of the clinical program could hardly be expected to persist or generalize automatically or perfectly.

Thus, a focus on the robustness of effects is widespread in health psychology, although not yet uniform. Considering the relative youth of the field, it is not entirely surprising that the experimental demonstration of a treatment's initial impact over any notably intractable problem is worthy of publication, irrespective of the staying power of the changes engendered.

However, the critical question at hand is not how much attention should ideally be paid to treatment robustness, but whether health-related interventions have yet proven themselves capable of yielding long-lasting and generalizable results when follow-up assessments are conducted. Unfortunately, this question is not an easy one to answer (or to answer with a simple yes or no).

Methodological Issues

All psychosocial interventions designed to enhance patient control over illness or illness risk are predicated on the assumed correctness and potency of the prescribed medical regimen, that "doing as instructed" relates in a predictable fashion to health status. When prescriptive potency is weak or moderate (as is apparently the case in many chronic illnesses; cf. Haynes et al., 1979), the effects of treatment are confounded with the

vagaries of neurobiology. The failure to note this possibility has no doubt yielded frequent Type I and II errors in the analysis of treatment efficacy.

However, even if there were a definite linear relation between health (including medication-taking) behavior and biologic status, interpretive problems would still arise. Consider, for example, the diversity of assessment questions and measurement methods available in health psychology. Different investigators undertaking a determination of whether treatment X yields strong and durable effects as applied to disease Y might (a) select different samples and sampling methods, (b) deliver and schedule treatment X differently, (c) examine divergent forms of program adherence (e.g., attendance at aftercare meetings vs. continued implementation of self-management strategies) via divergent means (e.g., self-report, observer ratings, etc.), (d) assess clinical (disease) end points differently, or (e) utilize disparate data analytic strategies (cf. Grady & Wallston, 1988; Karoly, 1985). Further, if the investigator wishes to pinpoint the determinants of nonadherence he or she may elect to study passive elements (forgetting), active resistance (missed appointments), or nonconscious forces (self-deception). Variability in such strategic decision-making will impact differentially on the internal and external validity of the research, making it unlikely that a ready consensus will be obtained in regard to the original question ("Are the effects of treatment X maintained?").

Some unique methodological and conceptual issues are likewise associated with robustness studies. The analysis of maintenance or generalization of effects requires one or more follow-up assessments. The expense of such measurement operations often leads to compromise and inconsistency; for example, when face-to-face contact is sacrificed for telephone interviewing, when standardized measures are discontinued, or when single measures are utilized in place of multidimensional indices (capable of providing convergent evidence for the lastingness of treatment effects) (cf. Mash & Terdal, 1980). Further, when contacting program participants is difficult (e.g., locating patients released from alcohol treatment programs), the tendency is to analyze data from participants who may be unrepresentative of the original sample. Indeed, some evidence suggests that better follow-up data (indicative of continued adaptive success) come from the easy-to-locate subjects (Lee & Owen, 1986).

In addition, some forms of generalization of health-relevant changes do not easily yield to analysis. While the study of temporal and spatial persistence (generalization over time and across settings) has been frequently attempted, response generalization—changes in responses similar to but not identical with those originally targeted for treatment—has rarely been investigated in health psychology applications. Perhaps this is because theoretical guidelines for what to expect are lacking or inconsistent. For example, if a person learns to give up cigarettes, can we reasonably expect him or her to be better able to control overeating or the abuse of alcohol? Similarly, if a person is trained to manage one aspect of a complex medical regimen, can we expect that other regimen demands will be likewise improved? Patterns of covariation among diverse health or illness behaviors are complex and not readily linked to common external or internal mediators (Carmody, Brischetto, Matarazzo, O'Donnell, & Connor, 1985; Harris & Guten, 1979; Mechanic & Cleary, 1980; Orme & Binik, 1989).

In view of (a) the apparent failure of conventional and behavioral interventions to permanently curb health-risk patterns, (b) the alarming picture of widespread patient nonadherence to chronic illness management regimens initiated within the traditional physician-patient exchange, and (c) the known methodological limitations within the field, a strongly cautious tone has been set for the fledgling enterprise of health psychology. The operative mode is to assume that psychosocial interventions (from group therapy to primary prevention) do not normally produce durable or transferrable effects unless special attention (both substantive and methodological) is directed to these considerations.

And what if this special attention is paid? As yet, it appears that investigators are still divided as to how best to specifically enhance their treatments to attain robust outcomes, and the division tends to be along "party" lines. Further, researchers tend to be disease or problem specific as well as method specific. We, therefore, must be content to render our critical judgments one disease, one intervention, one theory, and often one research team at a time.

In view of the nascent state of knowledge about treatment potency in health, I shall rely on the previously noted conceptual frameworks from the field of psychotherapy to provide an analytic frame of reference. Beginning with a discussion of the application of the behavioral engineering approach to the problems of health promotion and illness adjustment, I shall concisely and selectively review contemporary perspectives on the robustness of clinical health interventions.

BEHAVIORAL ENGINEERING

As noted previously, some may feel justified in ignoring questions of robustness by asserting that life is complex, and that events that follow therapy-based change can and will act capriciously to undermine learning and motivation. Yet, it is but a small step to the position that learning and performance are complex, and that transfer and generalization should be planned rather than lamented.

One avenue for acknowledging the complexity inherent in skilled action is to assume domain, task, or setting specificity. This view (popular within educational and human factors psychology) is predicated on the assumption that articulate performance is highly context dependent (rather than being solely practice dependent). Consider, for example, the seemingly simple act of taking one's medication every 6 hours. All that is apparently required is access to a watch or clock, a supply of pills, and the availability of water to facilitate swallowing. On the surface, it would appear that the skill of pill-taking could be trained in the doctor's office and would be readily transferrable to most other settings—work, home, indoors and out, night and day. Yet we know that at least one third of prescribed medications are not taken or are taken incorrectly (Haynes et al., 1979). Therefore, taking a pill might profitably be seen as an act strongly tied to environmental contingencies, as well as under the functional control of distinct stimulus conditions. Cues that remind the patient of the appropriate time to take a pill may not be as easily discernible at night as they are during the day, at work relative to home, or in the company of others versus when the patient is alone. The social response to pill-taking might likewise vary: One's spouse regards it with approval, but one's boss views it with suspicion. In addition, the sequence of behavioral steps necessary to follow through on doctor's orders may differ considerably depending on one's locale, especially if certain settings present real or perceived obstacles to task completion. Thus, an individual may well remember to take his pills at work and be reinforced for so doing, but find it logistically difficult to stop what he is doing, retrieve his medicine, and take it without impairing his job performance or concentration.

An important pragmatic implication follows from this line of reasoning: A thorough task analysis is a prerequisite to skills-training, and involves the construction of a normative model of necessary actions and decisions as well as a set of modified models matched to the unique demands of important and expectable situations.

After carefully analyzing the task requirements, monitoring ongoing performance, and instigating health-engendering behavior changes via contingent reinforcement, modeling (observational learning), extinction, time-out, contingency contracting, and similar training methods (see Kanfer & Goldstein, 1986), the behavioral engineer may have actually accomplished only half of his or her therapeutic mission. When powerful change-inducing procedures are withdrawn, client responses can revert to preprogram levels because the natural contingencies may favor old (maladaptive) behaviors and because the client can usually discriminate between the payoffs associated with the treatment and posttreatment environments (Karoly & Harris, 1986). Several practical methods of redress follow from this state of affairs.

To promote persistence (maintenance), generalization, and/or spread (transfer) of training, the behavior analyst relies on the fact that stimuli that resemble training stimuli come to acquire a degree of functional control over new learning in proportion to their sharing of common characteristics. Therefore, the programming of generalization (over time or across settings) can be deliberately implemented through procedures that allow a wide array of setting events to become associated with correct (reinforced) responding. Such procedures are directed at transcending the differentiation and specificity of learning processes that, although a tribute to our innate capacity to make fine stimulus and response distinctions, are clearly antithetical to generalization. In a sense, generalization occurs when discrimination (specificity) breaks down.

Table 36.1 lists several commonly employed strategies for enhancing the persistence and transfer potential of behaviors acquired by means of operant and/or classical conditioning or observational learning methods. Each attempts to render newly learned responses "extinction proof." The utilization of such procedures within health psychology appears to be expanding. However, the findings to date concerning the effectiveness of behaviorally engineered health behavior training have been mixed.

In a well-known recent study, Lund and Kegeles (1984) examined the maintenance process in the context of a preventive dental program for seventh-graders. In prior experiments, the authors had shown that contingent rewards could increase daily fluoride rinsing in children. To forestall a return to baseline rates of rinsing, the authors instituted two maintenance strategies: partial reward scheduling and self-management instruction. Seven hundred thirty-two boys and girls, almost equally divided into urban and suburban schools in eight different locales, participated in either partial or saturated reward programs with half also receiving self-management training or no additional instruction. Rewarded youngsters received prizes for frequency of mouth-rinsing and those instructed in self-management were allowed to chart (self-monitor) their own progress, select their own prizes, and were encouraged to associate mouth-rinsing with a high-frequency behavior.

Compliance with monitoring procedures (persistence of training) declined over time and dropped off sharply after rewards were initially discontinued, as would be expected. However, neither the partial schedule, nor the instruction in self-management, yielded any differential rates of maintenance. The failure of the partial reinforcement extinction effect clearly disconfirms scores of laboratory studies. Further, interpreting the ineffectiveness of the self-management program is complicated by the fact that the instruction seemed to assist urban students while actually being detrimental to suburban participants. The authors concluded that "If the goal is to obtain long-term behavior change through relatively short-term education/intervention, it is clear that we do not currently know how to achieve it, notwithstanding expressions of confidence in the power of psychological knowledge" (p. 366).

While it would be premature to conclude that behavioral methods for enhancing maintenance have been oversold, it seems reasonable to conclude that their complexity and subtlety have been insufficiently appreciated.

In commenting on the Lund and Kegeles results, Suls (1984) suggested that the level of analysis employed may have been too narrow. The dental rinsing behavior of the young participants may have interfered with other aspects of their daily health routines, may have been incompatible with broader goals, or may have already been well es-

Table 36.1. Some Procedures for Promoting Maintenance and Transfer Within a Behavioral Engineering Perspective

PROCEDURE	PRACTICE
Method of Sufficient Exemplars	Introducing enough samples of diverse settings and responses to permit the learner to function skillfully under different (even unforeseeable) circumstances. Expanded stimulus control permits the pill-taker (see text) greater freedom of action.
Method of Common Stimuli	Determining what stimuli or events will occur in the client's natural environment (generalization setting) and systematically introducing them during training (where possible).
Programming Natural Reinforcers	Utilizing real-life, normally available rewards and reward agents to strengthen desirable behavior. For example, it is insufficient for the dentist to reward a child's flossing; parent-provided praise can sustain the health-promoting actions far longer. Peers are also useful natural response facilitators.
Maximizing Response Availability	Training to criterion and allowing sufficient practice will ensure that the desired response (e.g., cigarette refusal) is available across contexts and times.
Intermittent Schedules and Schedule Thinning	Arranging to use less frequent reward subsequent to skill acquisition in order to enhance resistance to extinction. Rewards can likewise be delayed in delivery or gradually faded out altogether in order to strengthen performance under real-world conditions.
Method of Mediated Generalization	The operant equivalent of self-control. Learners are taught a verbal or cognitive technique to use either as a cue or reinforcer for themselves. The mediator helps maintain the adaptive response (but what maintains the mediator?).
Use of "Booster" Sessions	Denying the arbitrary dividing line between treatment and follow-up, clinicians provide periodic retraining and new training opportunities.

Note. Adapted from Baer (1982); Goldstein, Lopez, and Greenleaf (1979); and Kazdin (1989).

tablished but with a different brand of fluoride rinse. Thus, the interventive methods may have been adequate, but applied without benefit of necessary collateral knowledge. O'Leary (1984) inquired into the reinforcing power of the rewards (gliders, pens, yo-yos) used and also questioned both the immediate and long-term value of the target, fluoride rinsing, with adolescents. Again, it is not the utility of the behavioral or social learning models that is at issue, but their mode of application in the specific context of adolescent dental rinsing behavior.

Closer examination of the self-management intervention employed by Lund and Kegeles (1984) may shed further light on the meaning of the findings. As noted in my chapter on self-management earlier in this volume, the researcher must distinguish between exposure to self-management–based procedures (many of which are covert and designed to be carried out outside the surveillance of clinicians) and their acceptance and use by program participants. In this particular case, it is even doubtful whether the terms "training" or "treatment" are appropriate to describe the didactic portion of the intervention (the children were guided or encouraged rather than taught to use

certain strategies). However, my aim is not to defend the behavioral engineering framework (indeed, self-management is more correctly considered a person-centered approach), but rather to suggest that careful pretraining assessment, treatment tailoring, and the intensive analysis of learning and motivation over the course of therapy and beyond are frequently lacking in large-scale, group comparison studies.

My reading of the literature suggests that single-case (or small N) experimental analyses of behavioral engineering technologies applied to health behavior maintenance often yield more encouraging outcomes than do large N experiments such as the one carefully conducted by Lund and Kegeles (1984). As I have noted, careful attention to the details of assessment and training may simply be more common in small N research. However, it is also possible that, in single case designs, the participants are more highly motivated, less dysfunctional, and more likely to benefit from the heightened professional attention than those randomly assigned to standardized treatments in group studies. Therefore, until we can rationally decide whether the technology, its manner of application, or the clinical target are to blame for occasional maintenance failures, we also must attend to the periodic successes of behavioral engineering.

The inclusion of parents as natural reinforcers subsequent to traditional behavioral training has, for example, been shown to be a useful strategy for maintaining regimen compliance in juvenile diabetics (Epstein, Beck et al., 1981; Lowe & Lutzker, 1979). Unlike the approach taken in the Lund and Kegeles (1984) study (and in other attempts to manipulate in-therapy events to promote subsequent persistence of learning), these investigators did not make sharp distinctions between treatment and follow-up, assuming that the programming of maintenance involves, as Mash and Terdal (1980) have noted,

> provision of ongoing, contemporaneous, and presumably measurable contextual events that serve to influence behavior. Both initial effects *and* later effects (sometimes referred to as maintenance) should be directly related to continued representation of this programming. (p. 116)

Another means of transcending the distinction between treatment per se and follow-up involves the provision of additional professional treatment at periodic intervals subsequent to the formal termination of therapy. Popular in the domain of addictive disorders, the use of "booster sessions" has yielded mixed results (cf. Brandon, Zelman, & Baker, 1987; Perri et al., 1988). Because these sessions rarely involve additional trials of operant or classical conditioning interventions, the mechanism(s) behind "behavioral" boosters remain difficult to determine or evaluate. Multicomponent boosters (including cognitive and social psychological interventions) are, in fact, more the norm.

Programming reinforcers for health behavior at the worksite represents another means of extending the power of contingencies for the sake of achieving durable change. Cigarette smoking, weight control, dental health, stress management, and occupational safety are among the common targets of programs utilizing operant principles to induce both change and maintenance (Cataldo & Coates, 1986; Fisher, Lowe, Levenkron, & Newman, 1982). Results are promising, although often inconsistent insofar as long-term behavior change is concerned. As in all new applications, program variability is great. Further, many programs involve combinations of behavioral engineering, educational, and attitude modification elements (precluding specific assessment of the power of any single modality).

Finally, many behaviorally based studies of chronic health problems such as pain, eating disorders, asthma, elimination disorders, arthritis, and the like that did not specifically attempt to train for maintenance, have nonetheless found evidence of significant persistence at follow-up (cf. Siegel, 1983; Snyder, 1989; Varni, 1983). However, despite the success of token economies and contingency contracts in bringing about apparently robust changes, the majority of behavioral investigators still eschew the "train and hope" strategy in favor of explicit maintenance programming (Baer, 1982; Wildman & Wildman, 1980).

In sum, while not unequivocally positive and not without their interpretive difficulties, studies of maintenance that have been based presumably on learning principles have opened new vistas for acute and chronic illness management as well as for health promotion. Particularly when combined with other training methods, the behavioral engineering approach to clinical robustness merits continued investigation.

PERSON-CENTERED PERSPECTIVES

In recent years, epidemiological and sociopolitical trends have underscored the role of the individual in health-care and illness prevention (Matarazzo, 1984). Whereas the behavioral engineering approach just discussed does not ignore individual differences (indeed, behavioral clinicians have often been acutely sensitive to the need to particularize their interventions), it does not penetrate conceptually or procedurally to the level of mediation or to the active internal processes wherein personal and environmental events are detected, stored, and transformed over the course of adaptation. Personality portrays the learner (rather than the techniques of learning) as pivotal to the long-term display of health-promoting behavior.

Relatively stable aspects of functioning, in the form of personality traits and demographic characteristics, have long been popular in the literature on maintenance and compliance, probably because they can be expeditiously assessed. Data on trait and demographic differences have been employed to determine treatment assignment (matching) and to predict (or postdict) long-range outcomes (which in turn permits better therapy-patient matching). Psychosomatic models (circa 1950) and some contemporary personality conceptions (e.g., the hardiness concept, the coronary-prone [Type A] pattern, etc.) invoke etiological hypotheses as well, with indirect implications for treatment persistence.

In their classic review of medical adherence, Haynes et al. (1979) tabulated general patient characteristics (e.g., attitudes, knowledge, etc.), sociodemographics, psychosocial factors (e.g., family size and stability), and psychological factors (e.g., self-concept, dependency, locus of control, etc.) in terms of their positive, negative, or null associations with indices of compliance. Despite problems with "box score" sorts of outcome summaries, implications of the Haynes et al. review are widely cited (cf. Phillips, 1988) as suggesting that static person-centered concepts yield equivocal findings, with more "encouraging" patterns deriving from indices touching on family and related interpersonal processes.

On the other hand, it has been suggested (Kasl, 1975; Meichenbaum & Turk, 1987) that patient variables may prove to be useful predictors of adherence when considered in combination, that is, when aggregated into high-risk profiles. Svanum and McAdoo (1989), employing the 13 validity and clinical scales of the Minnesota Multiphasic Personality Inventory (MMPI), matched "rapid relapsers" and short-term successes following a residential chemical dependency treatment program, and found, for example, that maintenance failure in patients with clinical elevations could be accounted for by a profile of factors involving "psychological turmoil" (i.e., depression, anxiety, and sleep problems). Multivariate procedures are likely to prove instructive, and should be pursued in the future. However, I would suggest that, in addition to employing multitrait profiles, investigators pursue the interactive effects of personality patterns and treatment modes, as well as the three-way interaction between trait profile, treatment type, and the explicit type of maintenance training in the prediction of long-term adherence.

Being pathology centered, the MMPI and other popular clinical measures may not be the best or only multidimensional assessment tools to aid in the prediction of long-term health outcomes (cf. Leon, Finn, Murray, & Bailey, 1988). The NEO Personality Inventory (NEO-PI; Costa & McCrae, 1985) and the Hogan Personality Inventory (HPI; Hogan, 1986) are both designed to tap the "big five" personality dimensions (neuroticism, extraversion, openness to experience, agreeableness/sociability, and conscientiousness, as they are variously called) and consequently may prove to be more generally useful. For example, using a

battery of basic physical fitness tests (indirect indices of the persistence of individuals' health-promoting behaviors), Hogan (1989) showed that the HPI provided better and clearer predictive patterns than did the MMPI. She found, among other things, that physical endurance is the most predictable fitness variable and is most closely related to the conscientiousness dimension (labeled "prudence" in the HPI). McCrae and Costa (1989) likewise argued that their NEO-PI can predict the extended outcomes of psychoactive interventions.

Traitlike variables, when statistically related to adherence patterns, sometimes tend to evoke pessimistic prognostic verdicts owing to the widespread belief that durable characteristics (especially demographics) are not amenable to change. When employed cross-sectionally, trait concepts are also subject to misleading causal interpretations and to the effects of measurement artifacts (cf. Friedman & DiMatteo, 1989; Krantz & Hedges, 1987). Therefore, caution is advised for those who rely on traditional personality constructs, especially because medical system backlash can be the ultimate consequence of too heavy an emphasis on descriptive behavioral science in a functionalist biologic discipline (Angell, 1985).

An alternate model of person-centered analysis in health psychology is associated with a cognitive social learning perspective (Bandura, 1986; Kanfer & Karoly, 1972; Mischel, 1973). Traits are replaced by person variables, which are not expected to predict cross-situational consistencies. Rather, as Mischel (1986) noted, these constructs

> . . . suggest useful ways of conceptualizing and studying specifically how the qualities of the person influence the impact of stimuli ("environments", "situations", "treatments") and how each person generates distinctive complex behavior patterns in interaction with the conditions of his or her life. (p. 307)

Five types of person variables have been proposed by Mischel, including (a) the competencies involved in generating intellectual and behavioral responses, (b) categorization (encoding) strategies for unitizing events and construing self and others, (c) expectancies associated with behavior-outcome and stimulus-outcome relations, (d) subjective values (incentives and aversions), and (e) self-regulatory systems and plans. All of these person variables could conceivably be related to the processes through which patients achieve long-term control over aspects of acute and chronic illness and over risk-reducing and health-promoting behavior. Most have been studied empirically, either by themselves or as part of multidimensional intervention programs. Because several notable person-variable domains have been reviewed in depth elsewhere in this volume (e.g., problem-solving competencies, self and social cognition, self-efficacy expectations, and self-regulation), I shall devote the bulk of my attention to the multicomponent relapse prevention (RP) model, which seeks to integrate most, if not all, of the five social-learning functions articulated by Mischel (1973, 1986).

However, before addressing RP concepts and health applications, I turn briefly to a person variable that has been somewhat overshadowed by the others—the area of subjective values. Preferences and aversions (positive and negative incentives) are said to energize an individual's actions, providing the motivational impetus not only for short-term change, but for long-term maintenance of change. A person may well possess health-engendering thoughts and self-appraisals and the requisite health-promoting behavioral skills and still lack the motivational arousal necessary to overcome the inevitable physical and psychic obstacles that life sets forth along the bumpy path to success.

Arousal or action potential has traditionally been thought to depend on such factors as needs (internal states of deprivation), values associated with sought-after outcomes, and the perceived probabilities (expectancies) of success. These dimensions have recently been conceptualized, according to a model of energization developed by Brehm and his colleagues (cf. Brehm, Wright, Solomon, Silka, & Greenberg, 1983; Ford & Brehm, 1987; Wright, 1987; Wright & Brehm, 1989), as constituting potential motivation that offers an insufficient account of the conditions necessary to explain action. In the energization formulation, potential motivation represents an upper limit to arousal, which is translated into actual motivation only through the additional mediational link provided by the individual's appraisal of how much effort is necessary, possible, and warranted in the situation in order to obtain the outcome. Brehm and his colleagues argue that effort underlying instrumental behavior is related to, but partially independent of, the situation's potential motivation (needs, values, and expectancies). The joint effect of task difficulty and potential motivation needs to be determined when seeking to predict action because the degree of energization and the

attractiveness of the goal (its valence) are interactive products rather than main effects.

The energization hypothesis predicts that individuals will not be aroused by easy tasks, no matter how much they need or value a potential outcome, nor will they be aroused if the effort required for goal pursuit outweighs the importance (value) of the incentive. Such a viewpoint can be readily applied to explain the maintenance failure reported by Lund and Kegeles (1984) in their fluoride rinsing study (e.g., the response was simply too easy) and, perhaps, to the uncountable clinical failures that result when nonvoluntary patients are subjected to treatments that they neither truly desire nor comprehend.

A similar effort-centered model has been pursued by Eisenberger and his colleagues (cf. Eisenberger & Masterson, 1983; Eisenberger, Mitchell, & Masterson, 1985; Eisenberger, Mitchell, McDermitt, & Masterson, 1984; Eisenberger & Shank, 1985) and expressly addresses questions of persistence following learning. These investigators consider the investment of effort in a task as a response capable of being directly trained (reinforced), the so-called learned effort hypothesis, and one that pays dividends in terms of increased moral responding as well as enhanced robustness (maintenance and transfer).

The energization and learned-effort perspectives clearly deserve the attention of health psychologists interested in assessing motivation before the fact and assisting their patients to work persistently toward illness management or health promotion goals.

A perspective that has already changed the face of clinical intervention is the relapse prevention approach of Marlatt and his associates (cf. Marlatt & Parks, 1982; Marlatt & Gordon, 1985). Originally developed as a self-control-oriented, persistence-training intervention to combat relapse among people with addictive disorders (typically alcoholism, obesity, or cigarette smoking), the RP approach is broadly applicable to chronic disease management and to health promotion efforts—indeed to any domain in which disengagement from complex, health-facilitative tasks is a possibility (cf. Kirkley & Fisher, 1988; Meichenbaum & Turk, 1987).

Rather than asking how to make treatment more lasting, Marlatt and his colleagues have sought to identify the point in the posttherapy stream when learning or motivation break down and the conditions that surround that event. Because, in the addictions, most relapses occur within 90 days of treatment termination, Marlatt expected that a set of common elements might be found across habitual smoking, alcoholism, or heroin addiction. Although in his early work with chronic alcoholics Marlatt found that social stress and frustration were highly associated with recidivism, his RP model focuses on both situational factors and the cognitive interpretations that attend a lapse or relapse episode. Because I am here dealing with person-centered constructs, I shall focus on the latter set of elements.

Expectancies figure prominently in the RP framework. Relapse is a process that is seen as highly sensitive to three "interlocking cognitive mediators": self-efficacy, outcome expectancies, and attributions of causality. It is assumed that while an individual is voluntarily abstinent (that is, acting in accordance with an imposed set of rules governing the target behavior), he or she experiences a sense of self-efficacy. The sense of personal control continues until a high-risk situation is encountered (typically involving negative emotional states, interpersonal conflict, or social pressure). If a coping response is emitted, self-efficacy is enhanced. But if the person lacks the skills to cope, efficacy is diminished. Further, if the individual holds positive expectancies concerning the consequences of the prohibited or forbidden substance, relapse or lapse probability is heightened. If a lapse (a single slip or transgression) actually occurs, the possibility of total program cessation is further strengthened if the person additionally subscribes to an all-or-nothing attributional pattern called the abstinence violation effect (AVE). The AVE reflects guilt, self-blame, and loss of personal control as well as a cognitive dissonance component ("I can't be an abstainer if I just let myself indulge; thus, I must not want to abstain").

Combating the forces that press for relapse, then, requires a multicomponent program, drawing on a variety of cognitive, self-managemental, and behavioral skills training modalities and touching on the full range of Mischelian person variables. Both specific and global intervention strategies are involved, including self-monitoring to determine predictable high-risk contexts (based on previous lapses), coping skills training to deal with interpersonal stressors, educational and decision-making interventions to offset positive expectancies about the rule-violating behavior, and programmed relapse and cognitive restructuring to

defuse the AVE. To help develop a more adaptive life-style that can displace the addictive or unhealthful activity, RP also includes exposure to "positive addictions" (e.g., running, meditation, etc.), practicing a detached attitude toward one's urges, and stimulus control methods that seek to eliminate situational cues to problem behavior.

The effectiveness of RP methods and their variants in facilitating the robustness of training is impressive, despite the relative newness of the approach and its apparent complexity (cf. Brownell, Marlatt, Lichtenstein, & Wilson's 1986 review).

Relative to the behavioral engineering methods previously discussed, RP and other person-centered modalities are more time consuming, require greater patient involvement and psychological mindedness, and rely to a greater extent on patient self-report in both diagnosis and case management. Further, RP interventions in particular have not always been conducted such that their allegiance to Marlatt's formulations could be readily discerned. In addition, as Brownell, Marlatt, Lichtenstein, and Wilson (1986) have noted,

> Some studies can be faulted for small sample sizes, short follow-up periods, modest treatment effects, and so forth. . . . However, the studies with results in favor of relapse prevention outnumber those with negative results; therefore, at the very least, more vigorous testing of the model is warranted. (p. 778)

ECOLOGICAL APPROACHES

Despite the measurable, if inconsistent, successes of the health maintenance programmers, relapse nonetheless continues to occur. After failing to improve smoking abstinence rates subsequent to establishing several maintenance-enhancement training programs, Brandon et al. (1987) reached the sobering conclusion that

> Maintenance sessions prolonged abstinence only as long as such sessions were ongoing. This result is consistent with the fact that continual social support and contact is at the heart of effective self-help programs such as Alcoholics Anonymous. (p. 782)

Indeed, the assumption that the social and physical environment exerts a powerful influence (for better or for worse) over health practices has led investigators toward a rediscovery of ecological models of behavior control.

The critical role of the behavior setting is, of course, inherent in operant and other learning-based perspectives and is widely accepted within transactional or "reciprocal determinist" views of personality (Bandura, 1986; Kanfer & Karoly, 1972; Mischel, 1986). However, working in and with the environment to affect lasting personal change and targeting populations and the interactional network patterns, represents a relatively nontraditional approach for most clinicians. If spouses, friends, families, or communities are going to be included in the process of achieving durable health-relevant changes, new models, or at least extensions of existing frameworks, are required.

After reviewing attempts to extend learning theories toward a conceptualization of differential environmental impact, Higginbotham et al. (1988) characterized the resultant clinical case formulations as "coarse and inadequate," with settings seen as collections of either stimuli or significant others operating unilaterally or as reciprocal sources of stimulus control. Citing O'Donnell (1977), Higginbotham et al. (1988) averred that the generalization, maintenance, and transfer questions were not being formulated properly. As these investigators posed them, the key questions are, "Why has the natural environment not developed or supported the desired behavior?" and/or "Why are our procedures not readily adopted in natural settings?" They believe the answers are to be found not just in the clients or in the training, but within the settings and their specific transactional norms (cf. Heller's 1979 discussion of social support and Price's 1979 analysis of social ecological models as applied to issues of robustness).

Higginbotham et al. (1988) offered network analysis as a comprehensive guiding conceptual model for deciphering the structural organization of environments and for uncovering their capacities to strengthen (or weaken) individual behavior change. Among the basic propositions of a network approach are (a) the notion that while individuals freely choose to enter most social contexts, their opportunities and resources are constrained by their assigned or assumed position in the social system and by demographic factors; (b) the idea that networks can be characterized according to the individual's objectives (to obtain social support, to achieve a time-limited concrete goal, or to attain a long-term collective goal); and (c) the assumption that networks can be described along the dimensions of capacity (for providing support), resource exchange style (frequency, duration, and channel of delivery of support), and network intensity (or the degree to which the person is bound by ties and obligations).

Higginbotham et al. (1988) presented a series of intriguing hypotheses about deviance maintaining and aversive networks and about change-enhancing systems that apply as well to the health psychologist's clinical interests as they do to the concerns of the psychotherapist. For example, their Hypothesis 7.2 states that "Client network capacity characterized by weak delivery system infrastructure, i.e. small size, only one or two dense clusters, low reachability, and structural instability, will fail to provide social exchange resources capable of sustaining behavior change" (p. 189). Not only can such a social network structure be a direct source of stress, but, for individuals who are particularly dependent (the seriously chronically ill, the wheelchair bound) or inadequately skillful, it can exacerbate their existing problems, placing them at increased risk for illness, injury, and for medical noncompliance.

Problem-solving and self-regulatory capacities, among the most important of Mischel's (1973) person variables and among the most sought-after clinical commodities in health psychology (Holroyd & Creer, 1986; Karoly, this volume; Mahoney & Arnkoff, 1979), are themselves subject to disruptive environmental influences, as reflected in Higginbotham et al.'s Hypothesis 7.3:

> Client networks manifesting a resource exchange style dominated by nonreciprocal interactions and lacking multiplex ties decrease social support capacity over time while increasing dependency and powerlessness. Such conditions are devoid of opportunities for clients to initiate self-control procedures or receive social reinforcement for clinical behavior change. (p. 192)

The authors also describe hypotheses concerning the nature of networks capable of empowering the individual and sustaining therapeutic change (and interested readers are urged to consult the original source).

While the health literature has not yet been explicitly influenced by Higginbotham et al.'s (1988) hypotheses, the general trend in research has certainly been consistent with the fundamental tenet of network theory: that social contexts can create or constrain opportunities for the long-term implementation of health- and illness-management skills and motives. Applications differ with regard to how deeply they delve into structural and functional network characteristics and how extensively they analyze maintenance.

For example, McCrady (1989) has noted that the RP model tends to focus on coping at the individual level, but can logically be extended to consider significant others as sources of stress and as relapse prevention agents. She proposes that support network quality, the density of reinforcement received from family members for abstinence, and the probability of reward withdrawal from family contingent on misbehavior all combine to influence likelihood of successful maintenance. Similarly, spouse cognition (expectancy, attribution, self-efficacy beliefs, etc.) can influence coping probability for both self and patient. McCrady (1989) conjectured that the model becomes increasingly complex as it looks beyond the spouse to include family, friends, coworkers, and members of self-help groups.

Indeed, perhaps the unwieldy nature of network diagnosis and manipulation has worked to limit the kinds of interventions thus far attempted. In their studies of childhood obesity treatment, Epstein and his colleagues (Epstein, Wing, Koeske, Andrasik, & Ossip, 1981; Epstein, Wing, Koeske, & Valoski, 1987) have opted to treat obese children and obese parents together. This approach not only makes for cost-effective use of professional effort, but capitalizes on the modeling and reinforcing power of parents. A 5-year follow-up of this program (Epstein et al., 1987) revealed that maintenance of weight loss was best for children treated with their parents as compared with children treated alone or in a control group. Interestingly, when Perri and his associates (Perri et al., 1987) sought to use peers as supporters for adult obese patients, the evidence at 18-months' follow-up failed to confirm the incremental utility of a social network maintenance enhancer. Thus, it remains unclear precisely for whom (children vs. adults) network input is best applied and how far from home clinicians can look for support.

Moving away from high-risk addictive disorders to problems of medical regimen adherence, the work of Kaplan and Hartwell (1987) provides additional perspectives on the utility of a network model. Adults with non–insulin-dependent diabetes were randomly assigned to one of four treatments (diet, exercise, diet plus exercise, or diabetes education). Independent of their group assignment, patients provided data relevant to their support system by completing the Social Support Questionnaire (Sarason, Levine, Basham, & Sarason, 1983) when they entered the study. Employing diabetes control (assessed via glycosylated hemoglobin assay) as an index of maintenance, Kaplan and Hartwell found dif-

ferential patterns of relations between support dimensions (network size and satisfaction) and blood glucose for men and women. For women, the size of the support network varied directly with failure to attend sessions and failure to complete a diary, whereas network satisfaction was positively correlated with good metabolic control. For men, high social network satisfaction was associated with poor metabolic control. The authors argued that social support may serve as a stress buffer to a greater degree for women than for men, although acknowledging that the complex pattern of findings renders their explanations tentative.

It is noteworthy that Kaplan and Hartwell (1987) discovered ecological factors to be differentially associated with gender, a person-centered variable. Other investigators (Cohen, 1988; Higginbotham et al., 1988) have likewise outlined mediational models wherein social systems are seen to affect health status indirectly through their influence on cognitive processes, emotional states, habit patterns, or aspects of psychophysiological individuality. Higginbotham et al. (1988), for example, conclude that maintenance and generalization of treatment gains depend on the operation of a cognitive "meta-skill" consisting of three competencies: (a) awareness of how network characteristics facilitate or impede empowerment, (b) the capacity to self-monitor network configurations, and (c) behavioral skills for achieving favorable network characteristics when disruptions occur. This formulation bears a close resemblance to Mischel's (1973) person variables and to an early cognitive-behavioral account (Karoly, 1981) of self-regulation and its subcomponents. Therefore, insofar as treatment is concerned, the most cost-effective locus of intervention is still the individual.

I am not suggesting (nor were Higginbotham et al.) that ecological models are literally reducible to person-centered ones. On the contrary, I believe that interventions at the macro level should be pursued, and that linear formulations of causation in the analysis of robustness must eventually give way to truly transactional renderings, wherein serious account is taken of the qualities of the individual as well as of the situation (cf. Ford, 1987; Powers, 1973).

DYNAMIC ADAPTIVE SYSTEMS

We come now to the final conceptual framework, one that differs from the others in that it is offered primarily in the spirit of hypothesis generation, with only piecemeal empirical support. It is, however, a perspective capable of consolidating previous concepts concerning performance stability (maintenance) with models of patterned (predictable) variability, growth, and adaptive change.

I begin with an admonition for most (but by no means all) purveyors of psychosocial treatment. When psychotherapists or health psychologists speak of supporting patient change, what they really seem to mean is supporting patient constancy (albeit a supposedly "healthy" constancy). The model, with slight variation, is that the patient is being helped to stop doing X, which is psychically or physically inappropriate, and to start doing Y, which is defined as healthful and adaptive. On the assumption that X has become easy and familiar (preferred), highly likely to be reinforced in the short run, and/or automatic (overlearned) and therefore resistant to change, the clinician must bring sophisticated and subtly powerful methods to the task of displacing X and establishing Y (which is usually more difficult and less preferred for the patient, at least initially). Behaviors such as X would presumably persist indefinitely without intervention, whereas Y-like activities need considerable and continued psychological and social sustenance. It is, therefore, only the change from X to Y that is supported. Once Y is in place, the clinician and the patient would have it remain in effect for as long as possible, generalize to other settings and people, and assist in the learning of new Y-like responses (transfer of training). In essence, the goal is to infuse Y with the same sort of "psychological inertia" that X was said to possess.

Unfortunately, the aim of establishing a behavior or behavior pattern (and its accompanying affect and cognition) as a durable, change-resistant, inertially guided, or otherwise permanent dimension of one's life runs into both practical and conceptual difficulties. At the most fundamental theoretical level, what I have called open system constraints, such as time, situational forces, and internal growth processes, must be held constant for the notion of a fixed, adaptive habit pattern to make any real sense for mobile, proactive creatures living in an everchanging environment. Human action in the real world (outside the laboratory or consulting room) derives its meaning from the goals that push it, the contingencies that pull it, the settings that compel its form, duration, or intensity, and the idiosyncratic cognitive operations that link it both to the past and to the intended future. Because life's background variables are in flux everywhere (except in test tubes or arti-

ficially controlled settings), a person's hierarchically ordered goals move into and out of a dominant position in focal awareness as a result of being either temporarily satisfied or situationally postponed. Thus, no single action or action pattern—whether it be positively valenced (taking one's medication, engaging in physical exercise, monitoring one's blood sugar) or negatively valenced (avoiding alcohol, refusing cigarettes, etc.)—can retain invariant adaptive significance. At best, therapeutic goals can achieve periodic adaptive relevance. Therefore, it may be a serious tactical mistake to define compliance or adherence strictly in terms of strict rule-following or absolute behavioral continuity.

The concept of periodic adaptive relevance should not be taken to imply that health outcomes or health status vary in their importance. The threat of lung cancer is always real for the cigarette smoker, just as the threat of death or systemic damage is always relevant for the diabetic or asthmatic who fails to take needed medication. However, the specific actions that patients engage in during the normal course of self-care or self-directed risk reduction should not be thought of as rigidly scheduled or fixed in terms of their healing potential. The dieter, smoker, or diabetic is unlikely to remain committed to his or her health objectives if, during those times when eating, smoking, or taking insulin are not at issue, he or she remains nonetheless concerned, worried, or mindful of "staying on the program" (but see Kirschenbaum & Tomarken, 1982, for an opposing point of view).

I believe that most clinicians and their clients have an intuitive, if not explicit, understanding of the situation I have just described. Many instances of relapse, resistance, dropout, defaulting, and the like can readily be interpreted as reflecting goal or contextual realignments that may or may not threaten the patient's medical status. Although this relativistic point of view is implicitly appreciated, I contend that when disengagements from the therapeutic path do occur, most of us continue to operate as though the client has somehow lost sight of an unassailable objective, and that the only feasible clinical task is to seek to reinstate it.

The alternative I propose is that, in addition to focusing on X and Y and the psychological states or outcomes that they represent, we must also (a) consider the variables that control the transitions or oscillations between states and (b) learn to determine when these transitions are adaptive or maladaptive. Hence, in addition to training our clients in how to manage or control their states (of mind, affect, or behavior) we should seek to train them in the complex skill (or metaskill) of state transition management. This approach is predicated on the belief that variability (or change) is as fundamental in defining a person and his or her life circumstances as are the stable, prototypical elements. That we have considerable difficulty in adopting this mindset was expressed over a half century ago by Ralph Barton Perry (1938), a student of William James. Perry observed that

> The practically habituated mind flies from perch to perch, and is aware of the perch rather than the passage. This is James's famous distinction between transitive and substantive states. . . . The discovery of James is that these transitive states, despite their obscurity, are none the less *there*, for the sensitive and practised eye. (p. 81)

Although contemporary psychologists are actively investigating transitional phenomena, their emphasis has been on rather molar events, such as the so-called midlife crisis or the stress-engendering transitions from junior high to high school, from childlessness to childrearing, or from productive work life to retirement. I am merely suggesting that day-to-day, moment-by-moment transitions, typically orchestrated around specific goal pursuits, is a unit of study likewise worth pursuing. Further, such an undertaking may enhance our ability to assist clients to adjust in adaptive ways to the changing circumstances of their lives, whether the purpose is the long-term assurance of physical or of psychological health.

Paralleling the discipline-wide emphasis on experiential states (which produces an inordinate interest in stability) is the didactic focus on the content of learning, a practice many believe creates in clients a declarative knowledge base, but not necessarily a procedural one (Anderson, 1983; Kanfer & Schefft, 1988). Our interventions, in other words, teach what to do, but not often do they convey why or offer a dynamic representation of how. Consequently, action is inflexible because it is bound to rigid rules rather than to self-correcting principles or programs. Furthermore, the accentuation of imperatives minimizes the affective component of learning and motivation that depends on a hierarchy of personalized values or preferences (Goldstein, 1981). Thus, the person who takes up jogging because it is "the thing to do" is less apt to persist (particularly in the face of obstacles) or to experiment with other forms of exercise than is the person who has adopted health as a value or as an essential component of identity, and who thinks in terms of dynamic means-ends relations rather than in terms of fixed sequences of means and ends (cf. Dweck, 1986; Resnick, 1987, for similar arguments applied to the field of education).

Toward Therapeutic Flexibility

In the space remaining, I shall illustrate how "open system constraints" can potentially be addressed in our interventive work, as opposed to being widely ignored under the *ceteris paribus* assumption of scientific inquiry.

Essentially, I shall assert (somewhat boldly some might say) that state transition management be considered a sixth person variable, on a par with the five important constructs proposed by Mischel (1973, 1986) and intensively investigated by social learning theorists over the past several decades. Although strongly related to what Mischel has called construction competencies and self-regulatory systems, the mechanisms of state transition management are meant to transcend the acquisition and use of fixed rules, knowledge systems, personal attainments (skill-driven outcomes), and/or motives, which, not incidentally, have been the primary targets of most structured interventions in both clinical and health psychology.

Simply stated, I believe that there is an upper limit to the achievable robustness of any treatment program based solely on the inculcation of knowledge, rules, behavioral competencies, or specific attitudes—an upper limit that can nonetheless be extended via a consideration of the elaborative, inductive, or self-programming capacities of the human information processor. Such a consideration requires an appreciation of the importance of nonequilibrium forces operating in concert with stabilizing forces. The essence of a state transition model, then, is the recognition that the world is constantly changing, and that what is important about people is not how they typically act, think, feel, or believe (a summary description constructed by editing out transitional events), but rather how they seek to create stability out of the continuous changes in their states and how they likewise seek to create change at times of relative stabilization. In this context, neither stability nor change is more basic or essential than the other. (Another noteworthy characteristic of a state-transition management perspective is that, as applied in the domain of personality psychology, it defines stylistic change or the alteration of behavioral output to be an occurrence that is just as normative as the display of behavioral constancy. Few personality theories address variability and stability by means of similar mechanisms.) Further, the individual must be "in charge of" the state transition process, deliberately countering either forced movements away from prior states (e.g., seeking stability) or counteracting forced movements toward prior states (e.g., seeking change). Forced movements reflect the action of stressful life events, stimulus overload or underload, bodily or biochemical trauma, failure feedback, interpersonal pressures, and the like. Finally, it should be noted that the individual's periodic need to counteract constancy will, according to this formulation, inevitably run afoul of the clinician's desire to establish a permanent personality or life-style program. Because self-directed behavioral revision/change is misunderstood and understudied relative to self-stabilization (the subject of most personality research) and because I believe that teaching people how to effectively enlarge their repertoires can enhance the power of health-relevant interventions, I shall focus on two major contributors to personal flexibility: goal cognition and inductive rule systems.

First, it may be useful for me to offer a tentative definition of flexibility, as I use the term. Although control theorists employ terms like reorganization, self-construction, autopoises, second-order change, and the like (e.g., Ford, 1987; Powers, 1973), the word "flexibility" has a certain down-to-earth, familiar quality that better captures the essence of the intended meaning. Flexibility refers to both a process and state of mind underlying the pursuit of life goals that can be characterized, generally, as an openness to and a capacity to learn from experience. It refers, specifically, to the use of inductive models that include mechanisms for both revising and refining old rules and for generating new ones, particularly under conditions of novelty and uncertainty (cf. Holland, Holyoak, Nisbett, & Thagard, 1986, especially chap. 3). As a set of cognitive operations, flexibility falls midway between the obsessive use of rules, on the one hand, and automaticity (mindlessness) on the other. It is assumed that individuals possess some direct, conscious access to what transpires under the banner of flexible thinking. Despite its heavy cognitive patina, flexible problem-solving is seen as being triggered by

external (environmental) as well as internal factors, especially uncontrollable setting changes and/or the immediate failure of current programs. Thus, flexibility is not a trait or static disposition, but rather a negotiated construction, requiring environmental activation and support. Finally, it should be noted that the forces working toward robustness (stability) of learning and those operating in the service of flexibility are complementary rather than antagonistic. Flexibility undergirds stability by allowing people to select alternate routes to the same (or similar) ends. Likewise, stability in the form of situationally activated scripts, schemas, or implicit theories facilitates adaptive choice by selectively restricting one's access to information, presumably filtering out irrelevancies.

Goal Cognition

Within the framework of contemporary social cognition, flexibility in the interpretation of experience is believed to be directed by goals or personal strivings (Emmons, 1989; Karoly, in press; Little, 1983; Showers & Cantor, 1985). Goals have a particularly powerful role to play in assisting individuals to grow and to retain their freedom of movement (hopefully, therefore, imparting some immunity from the obsolescence of fixed habit patterns). This growth-enhancing role is connected to what has been called the feed forward function of goals. That is, as representations of possible future states of self and/or world, goals can prevent us from resting on our prior accomplishments or relying too strongly on action-outcome expectancies or rule systems that have, with the passing of time, outlived their usefulness. Whereas feedback permits us to match standards, feed forward allows us to set and reset personal objectives as circumstances and new learning warrant. Goals can, therefore, act as a destabilizing force capable of balancing the natural pressures toward homeostasis (cf. Ford, 1987; my chapter on self-management in this volume for further discussions of the feed forward function of personal goals).

Although the specific content focus of goals can be critical in terms of their adaptive significance, the interpretive dimensions by means of which goals are cognitively construed and the dynamic processes by which goal attainment is evaluated are particularly important as precursers of flexibility. For example, in their self-regulatory approach to medical compliance, Leventhal, Zimmerman, and Gutmann (1984) noted that the goal of health promotion is often evaluated by people in terms of attributions of control over risk factors. Thus, whether individuals make concerted efforts to restructure their lives so as to avoid the possibility of cancer or heart disease is determined, in part, by how they envision such health goals.

Inductive Rule Systems

Teaching our patients how to think about their health, as opposed to what to think (or do or believe) is another mechanism for transcending outmoded therapeutic objectives and achieving some degree of enactive flexibility. As noted earlier in this chapter, the link between conscious control and health-relevant action is far from perfectly understood. Similarly, the relation between health-relevant action and medical status is often imperfect. Under such conditions, it would not only be impractical to press patients to rigidly follow predetermined illness management or health-promotion plans, it would raise serious ethical questions as well.

Cognitive scientists and educators concerned with producing learning styles that are self correcting and capable of guiding adaptation even under conditions of change, instability, imperfect skill development, and uncertainty have recently focused on the individual's construction and use of mental models. These models, though dependent on the prior acquisition of information, values, and behavioral capacities, are flexibly attuned to current situational constraints and to future possibilities. As Holland, Holyoak, Nisbett, and Thagard (1986) noted,

> Because mental models are built by integrating knowledge in novel ways in order to achieve the system's goals, model construction provides the opportunity for new ideas to arise by recombination and as a consequence of disconfirmation of model-based predictions. (p. 14)

Induction refers to the process whereby the constituents of mental models are revised (updated) or totally replaced. The ability of inductive systems to not only rework existing adaptive patterns but to build new ones is a particularly powerful weapon in the fight against obsolescence of traditional "learn it, store it, use it"–based therapies.

The practical matter of teaching inductive processing is, of course, complex and unlikely to yield to the force of memorization, contingent reward of "correct" responses, social pressure, or other robustness builders. Extrapolating from nonclinical (often computer simulation) contexts, the fundamentals of flexible reasoning would include, among many other features, an emphasis on (a) if-then (condition-action) units capable of representing one's environment in a tentative (open) rather than a fixed manner; (b) process-oriented thinking; (c) rules that include default options and exceptions under special circumstances; (d) the person's ability to allow alternate rules to compete for retention by attending to how well the rules work in current situations; (e) the person's ability to detect covariation among current goals, situational demands, and feedback concerning state changes and to apply this information to the selection or generation of new rules; (f) a willingness to think counterfactually (in "what if" terms); (g) the ability to organize knowledge efficiently; and (h) the avoidance of both the mindless (automatic) or highly abstract processing of events and relations among events (cf. Holland et al., 1986; Showers & Cantor, 1985).

One of the major challenges in health life-style research centers on how to assess patients' inferential processes and how to design interventions that enhance rather than limit their operating range. As noted previously, many different therapeutic modalities (behavioral, cognitive, or environmental) may be potentially potent (yielding robust outcomes) only to the extent that flexibility is built in at the program level. Patients must be free to change their direction in pursuit of health-relevant objectives, to achieve consistency by managing patterns of variability, and to restore their preferred psychological states subsequent to disruption only when these prior states are again adaptively relevant in situational context and not in accordance with fixed prescriptions or schedules.

When working toward the goal of durable treatment effects and low rates of disengagement from therapeutic programs, clinicians are advised to consider robustness (maintenance potential) to be only one relevant consideration for judging success. Flexibility represents a second and orthogonal dimension. That is, program adherence can sometimes be bought through power of coercion, heavy surveillance, the rote accumulation of declarative knowledge, and powerful contingencies of reward or punishment, or contrariwise, through the inculcation of goal-directedness, a sensitivity to transitional phenomena, and tactical/procedural learning. Flexible adherence is preferrable to inflexible adherence. In addition, flexible nonadherence may well prove to be a better way to fail than nonadherence attendant to heavy-handed interventions.

REFERENCES

Anderson, J. (1983). *The architecture of cognition.* Cambridge, MA: Harvard University Press.

Baer, D. M. (1982). The role of current pragmatics in the future analysis of generalization technology. In R. B. Stuart (Ed.), *Adherence, compliance, and generalization in behavioral medicine* (pp. 192–212). New York: Brunner/Mazel.

Bandura, A. (1986). *Social foundations of thought and action: A social cognitive theory.* Englewood Cliffs, NJ: Prentice-Hall.

Brandon, T. H., Zelman, D. C., & Baker, T. B. (1987). Effects of maintenance sessions on smoking relapse: Delaying the inevitable? *Journal of Consulting and Clinical Psychology, 55,* 780–782.

Brehm, J. W., Wright, R. A., Solomon, S., Silka, L., & Greenberg, J. (1983). Perceived difficulty, energization, and the magnitude of goal valence. *Journal of Experimental Social Psychology, 19,* 21–48.

Brownell, K. D., Marlatt, G. A., Lichtenstein, E., & Wilson, G. T. (1986). Understanding and preventing relapse. *American Psychologist, 41,* 765–782.

Carmody, T. P., Brischetto, C. S., Matarazzo, J. D., O'Donnell, R. P., & Connor, W. E. (1985). Co-occurrent use of cigarettes, alcohol, and coffee in healthy, community-living men and women. *Health Psychology, 4,* 323–335.

Cataldo, M. F., & Coates, T. J. (Eds.). (1986). *Health and industry: A behavioral medicine perspective.* New York: John Wiley & Sons.

Cohen, R. Y., Stunkard, A. J., & Felix, M. R. J. (1987). Comparison of three worksite weight-loss competitions. *Journal of Behavioral Medicine, 10,* 467–479.

Cohen, S. (1988). Psychosocial models of the role of social support in the etiology of physical disease. *Health Psychology, 7,* 269–297.

Costa, P. T., & McCrae, R. R. (1985). *The NEO Personality Inventory manual.* Odessa, FL: Psychological Assessment Resources.

Dweck, C. S. (1986). Motivational processes affecting learning. *American Psychologist, 41,* 1040–1048.

Eisenberger, R., & Masterson, F. A. (1983). Required high effort increases subsequent persistence and reduces cheating. *Journal of Personality and Social Psychology, 44,* 593–599.

Eisenberger, R., Mitchell, M., & Masterson, F. A. (1985). Effort training increases generalized self-control. *Journal of Personality and Social Psychology, 49,* 1294–1301.

Eisenberger, R., Mitchell, M., McDermitt, M., & Masterson, F. A. (1984). Accuracy versus speed in the generalized effort of learning-disabled children. *Journal of the Experimental Analysis of Behavior, 42,* 19–36.

Eisenberger, R., & Shank, D. M. (1985). Personal work ethic and effort training affect cheating. *Journal of Personality and Social Psychology, 49,* 520–528.

Emmons, R. A. (1989). The personal striving approach to personality. In L. A. Pervin (Ed.), *Goal concepts in personality and social psychology* (pp. 87–126). Hillsdale, NJ: Lawrence Erlbaum Associates.

Epstein, L. S., Beck, S., Figueroa, J., Farkas, G., Kazdin, A. E., Daneman, D., & Becker, D. (1981). The effects of targeting improvements in urine glucose on metabolic control in children with insulin-dependent diabetes. *Journal of Applied Behavior Analysis, 14,* 365–375.

Epstein, L. S., Wing, R. R., Koeske, R., Andrasik, F., & Ossip, D. J. (1981). Child and parent weight loss in family-based behavior modification programs. *Journal of Consulting and Clinical Psychology, 49,* 674–685.

Epstein, L. H., Wing, R. R., Koeske, R., & Valoski, A. (1987). Long-term effects of family-based treatment of childhood obesity. *Journal of Consulting and Clinical Psychology, 55,* 91–95.

Fisher, E. B., Lowe, M. R., Levenkron, J. C., & Newman, A. (1982). Reinforcement and structured support of maintained risk reduction. In R. B. Stuart (Ed.), *Adherence, compliance, and generalization in behavioral medicine* (pp. 145–168). New York: Brunner/Mazel.

Ford, C. E., & Brehm, J. W. (1987). Effort expenditure following failure. In C. R. Snyder & C. E. Ford (Eds.), *Coping with negative life events* (pp. 81–103). New York: Plenum Press.

Ford, D. H. (1987). *Humans as self-constructing living systems: A developmental perspective on behavior and personality.* Hillsdale, NJ: Lawrence Erlbaum Associates.

Friedman, H. S., & DiMatteo, M. R. (1989). *Health psychology.* Englewood Cliffs, NJ: Prentice-Hall.

Goldstein, A. P. & Kanfer, F. H. (Eds.). (1979). *Maximizing treatment gains: Transfer enhancement in psychotherapy.* New York: Academic Press.

Goldstein, A. P., Lopez, M., & Greenleaf, D. O. (1979). Introduction. In A. P. Goldstein & F. H. Kanfer (Eds.), *Maximizing treatment gains* (pp. 1–22). New York: Academic Press.

Goldstein, H. (1981). *Social learning and change: A cognitive approach to human services.* New York: Tavistock.

Grady, K. E., & Wallston, B. S. (1988). *Research in health care settings.* Newbury Park, CA: Sage Publications.

Haaga, D. A., & Davison, G. C. (1986). Cognitive change methods. In F. H. Kanfer & A. P. Goldstein (Eds.), *Helping people change* (pp. 236–282). Elmsford, NY: Pergamon Press.

Harris, D. M., & Guten, S. (1979). Health protective behavior: An exploratory study. *Journal of Health and Social Behavior, 20,* 17–29.

Haynes, R. B., Taylor, D. W., & Sackett, D. L. (Eds.). (1979). *Compliance in health care.* Baltimore, MD: Johns Hopkins University Press.

Heller, K. (1979). The effects of social support: Prevention and treatment implications. In A. P. Goldstein & F. H. Kanfer (Eds.), *Maximizing treatment gains* (pp. 353–382). New York: Academic Press.

Higginbotham, H. N., West, S. G., & Forsyth, D. R. (1988). *Psychotherapy and behavior change: Social, cultural, and methodological perspectives.* Elmsford, NY: Pergamon Press.

Hogan, J. (1989). Personality correlates of physical fitness. *Journal of Personality and Social Psychology, 56,* 284–288.

Hogan, R. (1986). *Hogan personality inventory manual.* Minneapolis, MN: National Computer Systems.

Holland, J. H., Holyoak, K. J., Nisbett, R. E., & Thagard, P. R. (1986). *Induction: Processes of inference, learning, and discovery.* Cambridge, MA: MIT Press.

Holroyd, K. A., & Creer, T. L. (Eds.). (1986). *Self-management of chronic disease.* Orlando, FL: Academic Press.

Ince, L. P., Greene, R. Y., Alba, A., & Zaretsky, H. H. (1987). A matching-to-sample technique for training self-control in tinnitus. *Health Psychology, 6,* 89–99.

Kanfer, F. H., & Goldstein, A. P. (Eds.). (1986). *Helping people change: A textbook of methods.* Elmsford, NY: Pergamon Press.

Kanfer, F. H., & Karoly, P. (1972). Self-control: A behavioristic excursion into the lion's den. *Behavior Therapy, 3,* 398–416.

Kanfer, F. H., & Schefft, B. K. (1988). *Guiding the process of therapeutic change.* Champaign, IL: Research Press.

Kaplan, R. M., & Hartwell, S. L. (1987). Differential effects of social support and social networks on physiological and social outcomes in men and women with Type II diabetes mellitus. *Health Psychology, 6,* 387–398.

Karoly, P. (1980). Person variables in therapeutic change and development. In P. Karoly & J. J. Steffen (Eds.), *Improving the long-term effects of psychotherapy* (pp. 195–261). New York: Gardner Press.

Karoly, P. (1981). Self-management problems in children. In E. J. Mash & L. G. Terdal (Eds.), *Behavioral assessment of childhood disorders* (pp. 79–126). New York: Guilford Press.

Karoly, P. (Ed.). (1985). *Measurement strategies in health psychology.* New York: John Wiley & Sons.

Karoly, P. (in press). Goal systems and health outcomes across the lifespan: A proposal. In H. E. Schroeder (Ed.), *New directions in health psychology: Assessment.* New York: Hemisphere.

Karoly, P., & Harris, A. (1986). Operant methods. In F. H. Kanfer & A. P. Goldstein (Eds.), *Helping people change: A textbook of methods* (pp. 111–144). Elmsford, NY: Pergamon Press.

Karoly, P., & Steffen, J. J. (Eds.). (1980). *Improving the long-term effects of psychotherapy: Models of durable outcome.* New York: Gardner Press.

Kasl, S. V. (1975). Issues in patient adherence to health care regimens. *Journal of Human Stress, 1,* 5–18.

Kazdin, A. E. (1989). *Behavior modification in applied settings* (4th ed.). Pacific Grove, CA: Brooks/Cole.

Kirkley, B. G., & Fisher, E. B. (1988). Relapse as a model of nonadherence to dietary treatment of diabetes. *Health Psychology, 7,* 221–230.

Kirschenbaum, D. S., Sherman, J., & Penrod, J. D. (1987). Promoting self-directed hemodialysis: Measurement and cognitive-behavioral intervention. *Health Psychology, 6,* 373–385.

Kirschenbaum, D. S., & Tomarken, A. J. (1982). On facing the generalization problem: The study of self-regulatory failure. In P. C. Kendall (Ed.), *Advances in cognitive-behavioral research and therapy* (Vol. 1, pp. 119–200). New York: Academic Press.

Krantz, D. S., & Hedges, S. M. (1987). Some cautions for research on personality and health. *Journal of Personality, 55*, 351–357.

Kuhl, J. (1987). Action control: The maintenance of motivational states. In F. Halisch & J. Kuhl (Eds.), *Motivation, intention, and volition* (pp. 279–291). New York: Springer-Verlag.

Lee, C., & Owen, N. (1986). Community exercise programs: Follow-up difficulty and outcome. *Journal of Behavioral Medicine, 9*, 111–117.

Leon, G. R., Finn, S. E., Murray, D., & Bailey, J. M. (1988). Inability to predict cardiovascular disease from hostility scores or MMPI items related to Type A behavior. *Journal of Consulting and Clinical Psychology, 56*, 597–600.

Leventhal, H., Zimmerman, R., & Gutman, M. (1984). Compliance: A self-regulation perspective. In W. D. Gentry (Ed.), *Handbook of behavioral medicine* (pp. 369–436). New York: Guilford Press.

Little, B. (1983). Personal projects: A rationale and method for investigation. *Environment and Behavior, 15*, 273–309.

Lowe, K., & Lutzker, J. R. (1979). Increasing compliance to a medical regimen with a juvenile diabetic. *Behavior Therapy, 10*, 57–64.

Lund, A. K., & Kegeles, S. S. (1984). Rewards and adolescent health behavior. *Health Psychology, 3*, 351–369.

Mahoney, M. J., & Arnkoff, D. G. (1979). Self-management. In O. F. Pomerleau & J. P. Brady (Eds.), *Behavioral medicine: Theory and practice* (pp. 75–96). Baltimore, MD: Williams & Wilkins.

Marholin, D., & Touchette, P. E. (1979). The role of stimulus control and response consequences. In A. P. Goldstein & F. H. Kanfer (Eds.), *Maximizing treatment gains* (pp. 303–351). New York: Academic Press.

Marlatt, G. A., & Gordon, J. R. (1985). *Relapse prevention: Maintenance strategies in the treatment of addictive disorders*. New York: Guilford Press.

Marlatt, G. A., & Parks, G. A. (1982). Self-management of addictive disorders. In P. Karoly & F. H. Kanfer (Eds.), *Self-management and behavior change: From theory to practice* (pp. 443–488). Elmsford, NY: Pergamon Press.

Mash, E. J., & Terdal, L. G. (1980). Follow-up assessments in behavior therapy. In P. Karoly

& J. J. Steffen (Eds.), *Improving the long-term effects of psychotherapy* (pp. 99–147). New York: Gardner Press.

Matarazzo, J. D. (1984). Behavioral health: A 1990 challenge for the health sciences professions. In J. D. Matarazzo, S. M. Weiss, J. A. Herd, N. E. Miller, & S. Weiss (Eds.), *Behavioral health* (pp. 3–40). New York: John Wiley & Sons.

McCrady, B. S. (1989). Extending relapse prevention models to couples. *Addictive Behaviors, 14*, 69–74.

McCrae, R. R., & Costa, P. T. (1989). More reasons to adopt the five-factor model. *American Psychologist, 44*, 451–452.

McGrady, W., Woerner, M., Bernal, G., & Higgins, J. T. (1987). Effect of biofeedback-assisted relaxation on blood pressure and cortisol levels in normotensives and hypertensives. *Journal of Behavioral Medicine, 10*, 301–310.

Mechanic, D., & Cleary, P. D. (1980). Factors associated with the maintenance of positive health behavior. *Preventive Medicine, 9*, 805–814.

Meichenbaum, D., & Turk, D. C. (1987). *Facilitating treatment adherence: A practitioner's guidebook*. New York: Plenum Press.

Mischel, W. (1973). Toward a cognitive social learning reconceptualization of personality. *Psychological Review, 80*, 252–283.

Mischel, W. (1986). *Introduction to personality*. New York: Holt, Rinehart & Winston.

O'Donnell, C. R. (1977). Behavior modification in community settings. In M. Hersen, R. M. Eisler, & P. M. Miller (Eds.), *Progress in behavior modification* (Vol. 4, pp. 69–117). New York: Academic Press.

O'Leary, K. D. (1984). Commentary on rewards and adolescent health behavior. *Health Psychology, 3*, 377–379.

Orme, C. M., & Binik, Y. M. (1989). Consistency of adherence across regimen demands. *Health Psychology, 8*, 27–43.

Perri, M. G., McAdoo, W. G., McAllister, D. A., Lauer, J. B., Jordan, R. C., Yancey, D. Z., & Nezu, A. M. (1987). Effects of peer support and therapist contact on long-term weight loss. *Journal of Consulting and Clinical Psychology, 55*, 615–617.

Perri, M. G., McAllister, D. A., Gange, J. J., Jordan, R. C., McAdoo, W. G., & Nezu, A. M. (1988). Effects of four maintenance programs on the long-term management of obesity. *Journal of Consulting and Clinical Psychology, 56*, 529–534.

Perry, R. B. (1938). *In the spirit of William James*. New Haven, CT: Yale University Press.

Phillips, E. L. (1988). *Patient compliance: New light on health delivery systems in medicine and psychotherapy*. Toronto, Canada: Hans Huber.

Powers, W. T. (1973). *Behavior: The control of perception*. Chicago: Aldine.

Price, R. H. (1979). The social ecology of treatment gain. In A. P. Goldstein & F. H. Kanfer (Eds.), *Maximizing treatment gains* (pp. 383–426). New York: Academic Press.

Resnick, L. (1987). *Education and learning to think*. Washington, DC: National Academy Press.

Richardson, J. L., Marks, G., Johnson, C. A., Graham, J. W., Chan, K. K., Selser, J. N., Kishbaugh, C., Barranday, Y., & Levine, A. M. (1987). Path model of multidimensional compliance with cancer therapy. *Health Psychology, 6*, 183–207.

Sarason, I. G., Levine, H. M., Basham, R. B., & Sarason, B. R. (1983). Assessing social support: The social support questionnaire. *Journal of Personality and Social Psychology, 44*, 127–139.

Showers, C., & Cantor, N. (1985). Social cognition: A look at motivated strategies. *Annual Review of Psychology, 36*, 275–305.

Siegel, L. J. (1983). Psychosomatic and psychophysiological disorders. In R. J. Morris & T. R. Kratochwill (Eds.), *The practice of child therapy* (pp. 253–286). Elmsford, NY: Pergamon Press.

Snyder, J. J. (1989). *Health psychology and behavioral medicine*. Englewood Cliffs, NJ: Prentice-Hall.

Stuart, R. B. (1982). A natural history of health behavior decision-making. In R. B. Stuart (Ed.), *Adherence, compliance, and generalization in behavioral medicine* (pp. 3–27). New York: Brunner/Mazel.

Suls, J. M. (1984). Level of analysis and efforts to modify adolescent health behavior: A commentary on Lund and Kegeles. *Health Psychology, 3*, 371–375.

Svanum, S., & McAdoo, W. G. (1989). Predicting rapid relapse following treatment for chemical dependence: A matched-subjects design. *Journal of Consulting and Clinical Psychology, 57*, 222–226.

Varni, J. W. (1983). *Clinical behavioral pediatrics: An interdisciplinary biobehavioral approach*. Elmsford, NY: Pergamon Press.

Wildman, R. W. II, & Wildman, R. W. (1980). Maintenance and generalization of institutional behavior modification programs. In P. Karoly & J. J. Steffen (Eds.), *Improving the long-term effects of psychotherapy* (pp. 27–69). New York: Gardner Press.

Wright, R. A. (1987). Coping difficulty, energy mobilization, and appraisals of a stressor: Introduction of a theory and a comparison of perspectives. In C. R. Snyder & C. E. Ford (Eds.), *Coping with negative life events* (pp. 51–79). New York: Plenum Press.

Wright, R. A., & Brehm, J. W. (1989). Energization and goal attractiveness. In L. A. Pervin (Ed.), *Goal concepts in personality and social psychology* (pp. 169–210). Hillsdale, NJ: Lawrence Erlbaum Associates.

PART IV

NOW AND THEN:
PRESENT PARADIGMS AND
FUTURE DIRECTIONS

CHAPTER 37

METHODOLOGICAL CHALLENGES AT THE SOCIAL/CLINICAL INTERFACE

Timothy W. Smith
Frederick T. Rhodewalt

The integration of social and clinical psychology has matured. Early landmarks in the development of this interface are best characterized as cogent discussions of the relevance of social psychological theory for the explication and even refinement of clinical enterprises such as psychotherapy (Frank, 1961/1973; Heller, 1963; Goldstein, Heller, & Sechrest, 1966; Carson, 1969; Brehm, 1976). These efforts clearly established the potential contribution of social psychological models to the study of human adjustment and therapeutic change. More recent reviews of the interface between these fields (e.g., Brehm & Smith, 1986; Weary & Mirels, 1982) reflect a different, later stage in the development of a discipline. The intervening years were associated with a wide array of empirical studies evaluating the previous theoretical contributions and several more recent ones. The promissory note of clinical relevance was paid, at least in part, by a large and growing body of research.

Despite this progress, considerable challenges remain. In the past 20 years, clinical psychology has become a more empirically oriented field.

Forces from within and outside the discipline have encouraged and even required stronger evidence of the accuracy of theories of etiology, the validity of assessment procedures, and the effectiveness of interventions. To sustain and advance the process of integration, social-clinical research efforts must continue, and interface research must continue to grow more ambitious. Much of social-clinical research still consists of laboratory-based analog studies. Undergraduate samples are used, and the experimental manipulations are intentionally short-lived. Yet, the results of such studies are often interpreted as relevant to more severely disordered groups and the long processes of the development and remediation of dysfunction. In the years ahead, additional innovations in which social psychological concepts are applied to clinical topics can be tested appropriately in this manner, at least initially. However, a more substantial and lasting impact of the interface on mainstream clinical psychology will require more compelling evidence of the value of social psychological models. This more compelling evidence, in turn, requires more direct tests with clinical populations.

Research at the interface of social and clinical psychology must address the methodological problems common to the two component disciplines. But there are also methodological challenges that, if not unique, are particularly salient in integrative social-clinical research. If this enterprise is to continue and develop, research methods must evolve so as to yield additional evidence of the value of the integrative approach.

In this chapter, we attempt to articulate the methodological challenges faced by social-clinical researchers. The list is certainly not exhaustive, nor is the list of suggested solutions complete. However, our discussion should highlight the ways in which researchers must work to increase the scientific yield of their studies. Cook and Campbell (1979) provide a useful framework for organizing the methodological challenges at the interface. Statistical conclusion validity refers to inferences about the sensitivity and accuracy of tests of covariation among research operations, as well as presence and magnitude of covariation. Internal validity refers to inferences about whether or not apparent statistical covariation between research operations reflects spurious relations due to confounding factors. Construct validity refers to inferences about the extent to which research operations (and the covariation between them) actually reflect the construct(s) they are intended to reflect. Finally, external validity in the Cook and Campbell (1979) system refers to inferences about the extent to which the relationships observed generalize to other subjects, settings, and times. Although statistical conclusion validity is occasionally a problem in the social-clinical research literature (Sedlmeier & Gigerenzer, 1989), the major difficulties occur elsewhere. An overreliance on simple correlational methods weakens the internal validity of large portions of the social-clinical research literature, and many difficult challenges concern construct and external validity.

Our first major section describes methodological challenges in testing models of emotional and physical health. Difficulties in operationalizing predictors and outcomes, and associated threats to construct and external validity, are discussed. Common problems in testing the association between predictors and outcomes also are discussed. The second major section discusses problems in testing models of diagnosis and treatment. We conclude with a discussion of the more general issue of the relation between theory and research at the interface. Hopefully, this review of method-ological challenges will serve as a guide for the maintenance and continued development of the empirical foundation of the social-clinical interface.

TESTING MODELS OF EMOTIONAL AND PHYSICAL HEALTH

Certainly one of the largest areas in the integration of social and clinical psychology is the study of psychopathology and adjustment. Social psychological models of a wide variety of adjustment problems have been developed and at least partially tested. In recent years these models have expanded beyond emotional adjustment and psychopathology to include physical health as well. As indicated in previous chapters in this volume, many traditional social psychological concepts and paradigms have been employed in theoretical explanations of emotional and physical disorders.

In some cases, social psychological approaches have been accepted in the mainstream of psychopathology research. The learned helplessness model of depression (Seligman, 1975; Abramson, Seligman, & Teasdale, 1978) is an obvious example of this achievement. In other cases, social psychological models are gaining empirical support, but have not yet been accepted outside of the interface of social and clinical psychology. For the accepted models to retain their status and the developing models to achieve such acceptance, a variety of methodological challenges must be met. The causal constructs in the models—predictors of adjustment—must be operationalized in valid ways. The specific constructs explained—the adjustive outcomes—also must be assessed through valid operations. And finally, the association between the causal and outcome constructs must be tested in an appropriate and compelling manner. At first glance, these appear to be most elementary of methodological requirements. As we will argue, however, many of the current shortcomings in social-clinical research on adjustment involve these basic issues. As a result, the future of the interface will be determined, at least in part, by our ability to correct these limitations.

Operationalizing Predictors

Social psychological models of adjustment posit a variety of situational factors and person variables as causes or at least predictors of emotional and physical outcomes. The results of the studies testing these models are useful only to the extent that the specific research operations reflect the hypothesized causal or predictive constructs. In several areas, the construct validity of operational predictor variables is open to serious question.

Studies of Life Stress

Many social psychological models of adjustment assign a central role to the concept of stress. Such models identify aspects of stressful stimuli, such as controllability, as important predictors of health outcomes. Other models identify aspects of individuals or their social environments that make them more or less vulnerable to the negative effects of stress. Obviously, empirical tests of these models require the manipulation or measurement of stressful life circumstances.

Laboratory studies of stress in humans have employed a wide variety of well controlled aversive or threatening stimuli over the years (Lazarus & Folkman, 1984). Threats of physical discomfort (e.g., electric shock) or self-esteem threats (e.g., intelligence tests, etc.) successfully arouse the physiological, affective, and even behavioral signs of stress responses. The precise experimental control available in the laboratory and the consequent gains in internal validity are presumed to permit unambiguous interpretation of the research findings obtained in such studies.

It is also true, however, that laboratory studies typically do not entail severe or prolonged stressful stimulation. Thus, laboratory studies typically do not include manipulations of stress equivalent to those discussed in many models of emotional and physical disorder. Experimental operations may not adequately capture the theoretical constructs, and generalization to more severe stressors is unknown. This is one important incentive to study naturally occurring stressful life circumstances. Most of the work of this type has involved the measurement of stressful life events (e.g., death of a loved one, divorce, loss of a job, etc.) and the examination of the association between levels of life stress and either emotional or physical disorder. Several self-report instruments are now in wide use for measuring the number and even perceived stressfulness of recent life events (Monroe, 1982; Perkins, 1982).

As straightforward as such procedures might seem, they are the source of considerable controversy. Several authors have suggested that many of the individual stressful events might be the result of emotional or physical disorder (e.g., breakup

of a relationship, loss of a job) rather than an independent cause (Dohrenwend, Krasnoff, Askenasy, & Dohrenwend, 1982; Schroeder & Costa, 1984). Thus, concurrent associations between self-reports of stressful life events and adjustment may reflect precisely the opposite causal association as is central to most of these models.

A very similar criticism suggests that reports of stressful life events may be symptoms of psychological disorder. In an interesting test of this notion, Dohrenwend, Dohrenwend, Dodson, and Shrout (1984) asked a large sample of clinical psychologists to rate the items in several measures of stressful life events as to the extent to which they reflected symptoms of psychological disorder. Many of the items were rated as reflecting emotional disorder, and this confounding of predictor and outcome was particularly true of measures of minor stressful events (i.e., daily hassles; Delongis, Coyne, Dakoif, Folkman, & Lazarus, 1982). Thus, the correlations between measures of stressful events and emotional outcomes may be due, at least in part, to the fact that the two sets of research operations assess a single construct.

In a very important discussion of this issue, Depue and Monroe (1986) have underscored the possible role of chronic disorders and enduring personality characteristics in the life events–symptoms association. Individuals with chronic psychological disorders or high levels of certain personality characteristics such as neuroticism or negative affectivity are likely to report high levels of life stress and current emotional distress. Neuroticism or negative affectivity refers to a stable individual difference in the tendency to experience negative moods. As a result, the association between stressful event scores and current distress may reflect the operation of a third variable — the presence versus absence of chronic disorder or individual differences in neuroticism.

The problems of reverse causal direction, confounding of measures of events and symptoms, and chronic disorder or personality are all obviously serious threats to the validity of concurrent correlational studies of stressful life events. Despite these interpretive ambiguities, such studies are common at the interface of social and clinical psychology. Given the limitations of such designs, the results do not provide compelling evidence about the accuracy of the models being tested. The assessment and statistical control of chronic conditions and relevant personality dispositions seems essential in concurrent studies. Prospective studies, also including measurement and statistical control of possible confounding factors, would produce a substantially less ambiguous and therefore more compelling form of evidence.

Current models of stress and adaptation often emphasize the importance of the individual's appraisal of the stimulus (Lazarus & Folkman, 1984). Similar events may not be equally stressful for different people because of differences in the level of subjectively perceived harm or threat. A large body of research is consistent with this view. As a result, many stressful life event surveys (e.g., Sarason, Johnson, & Siegel, 1978) ask respondents not only to indicate whether or not they have experienced the listed events but also to rate the valence or impact of the event. While this approach is consistent with cognitive mediation models of stress and adaptation, it also has been criticized as confounding the event measure with the outcome under study (Dohrenwend et al., 1982). Subjective impact ratings may reflect emotional distress, thereby artificially inflating the association between predictor and outcome.

The potential gains from life stress research are substantial. As a result, this general approach certainly should remain as a methodological tool in testing social-clinical models. However, its uncritical use will add little truly useful information. Refined methodologies that attempt to rule out the alternative interpretations we have discussed will hopefully become more commonplace. Studies of predictable, naturally occurring stressful events such as childbirth or elective surgery provide an alternative way to operationalize the construct of stress in prospective designs with less interpretive ambiguity.

Studies of the Social Environment

One of the most widely studied moderators of the effects of stress is social support. As in the case of life stress research, the most common approach to operationalizing this variable has been self-report inventories (Heitzman & Kaplan, 1988). Respondents rate the quantity and/or quality of supportive social relationships available to them. Similar interpretive difficulties as those found in studies of life stress are associated with most studies involving self-reported social support. For example, in the Dohrenwend et al. (1984) study, clinical psychologists rated many social support scale items as likely to be symptoms of emotional disorder. Further, Depue and Monroe (1986) argued that subjects who score low on reported social support and high on measures of stressful life events are likely to be suffering from chronic disorder or to display high levels of neuroticism or negative affectivity. Because both life stress and social support are likely to be correlated with these stable subject characteristics, people scoring high on both types of inventories as opposed to only one are more likely to display some chronically dysphoric condition. Thus, the cell of the high versus low life stress by high versus low social support factorial design that is predicted to display the highest level of distress is also the most likely to include chronically disordered or high negative affectivity subjects.

The self-report methodology and the measured as opposed to manipulated nature of the social support variable are the source of these interpretive ambiguities. Descriptions of the social environment as unsupportive may reflect personality or chronic disorder rather than the actual situation. Even if veridical, however, such reports may still reflect enduring characteristics of the person rather than the independent influence of the social environment. As a result, studies of social support or related environmental characteristics must articulate and rule out these alternative explanations as best as possible.

There is an obvious intuitive appeal and a growing body of empirical support for the notion that a supportive social network has salubrious effects on emotional and physical health (Cohen & Wills, 1985; House, Landis, & Umberson, 1988). Researchers testing social-clinical models involving this construct must be aware of the interpretive difficulties associated with the most commonly used approaches. Although cumbersome, random assignment to supportive relations is possible. Two recent studies of expectant mothers, for example, found that random assignment to a condition in which a previously unacquainted, supportive companion was available throughout the labor and delivery process produced a 50% reduction in delivery complications and a similarly large reduction in the duration of the process, even among uncomplicated births (Sosa, Kennell, Klaus, Robertson, & Urrutia, 1980; Klaus, Kennell, Robertson, & Sosa, 1986). Thus, experimental approaches to the study of social support during significant stress are available.

Studies of Personality and Individual Differences

A common theme running through much of the social-clinical literature is that certain aspects of personality increase vulnerability to the development of emotional or physical dysfunction. Type A behavior, attributional style, and pessimism are only a few of the relevant examples of this general paradigm. Empirical tests of these models are valid only to the extent that the measures of the personality characteristic under study are valid assessment techniques. If scores on the individual difference assessment instrument do not reflect the construct under study, then the model has not been tested and results are not relevant to the theory. If the construct validity of the relevant assessment device is unknown or incompletely established, then obviously the relationship of research findings using the device to the theory is unknown. Evaluation of the construct validity of personality and individual difference assessment procedures has long been an important aspect of clinical psychology. These fundamental tenets of personality research methodology are, surprisingly, a source of difficulty in current social-clinical research.

As we discussed in our chapter on Type A behavior in this volume, the lack of traditional construct validity studies posed a problem in the early years of Type A research. The major measures of this construct are quite modestly related and show quite distinct patterns of association to other personality dimensions. Yet, early reviews of this literature pooled findings using this array of assessment procedures to evaluate the overall relationship between the construct of Type A behavior and coronary heart disease. Subsequent research has explored and even benefited from the differences between purported measures of this single construct. It is also true, however, that some of the waxing and waning of acceptance of the association between Type A and heart disease and the resulting confusion and controversy in both scientific and popular literature can be directly attributed to a lack of thorough, a priori construct validation research.

More recent entries into the list of individual difference dimensions in social-clinical research also suffer from this problem of incomplete construct validation. One example is the construct of optimism and the device intended to assess this dimension, the Life Orientation Test (LOT; Scheier & Carver, 1985). Consistent with self-regulation models of the process of coping and adjustment (Carver & Scheier, 1982), individual differences in optimism are important when confronting taxing situations. Optimists, given their positive expectations, are likely to cope actively with the difficulty and as a result are less

likely to suffer the emotional and physical consequences of stress. In contrast, pessimists, given their negative expectations, are likely to cope regressively when confronted with difficulty. Given this maladaptive response, they are more likely to suffer the emotional and physical effects of stress.

Scheier and Carver (1985) developed the eight-item LOT to assess individual differences in optimism-pessimism. This self-report scale correlates as expected with self-reports of coping behavior and physical symptoms (Scheier & Carver, 1985; Scheier, Weintraub, & Carver, 1986). As for evaluations of the construct validity of the scale, Scheier and Carver (1985, 1987) reported that moderate correlations with measures of depression, hopelessness, and similar dimensions provide evidence of convergent and discriminant validity. The authors argued that the correlations are large enough to be meaningful, (i.e., convergent validity), but not so large as to indicate that the LOT is assessing the same dimensions as assessed by the other scales (i.e., discriminant validity).

Traditional procedures for evaluating the convergent and discriminant validity of assessment devices are more specific than those employed by Scheier and Carver. At least two measures of at least two distinct constructs are employed (cf. Campbell & Fiske, 1959). Convergent validity is demonstrated by a large correlation between two measures of a given trait, while discriminant validity is demonstrated by correlations between two measures of separate traits that are smaller than the correlations between the measures of a single trait.

In a recent study, we evaluated the construct validity of the LOT using this more traditional approach (Smith, Pope, Rhodewalt, & Poulton, 1989). We selected the Generalized Expectancy of Success Scale (GESS; Fibel & Hale, 1978) as a second measure of optimistic expectations about the future. The construct described by these authors is very similar to optimism as articulated by Scheier and Carver (1985). The second trait selected for the validation procedure was neuroticism (Eysenck & Eysenck, 1964) or negative affectivity (Watson & Clark, 1984). We selected this dimension because it has similar self-report coping and physical symptom correlates as those reported for the LOT (Costa & McCrae, 1987; McCrae & Costa, 1986; Vitalliano et al., 1987; Watson & Pennebaker, 1989). Thus, if the LOT displayed poor discriminant validity in relation to measures of neuroticism, then it is possible that the previously reported findings regarding coping and health reports reflect this older, more established personality trait as opposed to the construct of optimism.

In three separate samples, the LOT and GESS were significantly correlated (average $r = .56$). However, the LOT was at least as closely correlated with measures of neuroticism (average $r = -.62$). Thus, given this lack of discriminant validity, it could be argued that the LOT is simply an inversely scored measure of neuroticism. Although we were able to replicate the previously described correlations of the LOT with coping and symptom reports, these associations were largely eliminated when neuroticism was controlled through partial correlation. Control of optimism scores, however, did not eliminate the significant correlations of neuroticism with coping and symptom reports. Therefore, it is quite plausible that the earlier findings reflect the trait of neuroticism rather than optimism.

Obviously, our results do not challenge the conceptual model that generated this line of research on optimism. Rather, our findings challenge the interpretation of the previous studies as supporting that model. Because of the questionable construct validity of the measure of optimism, the previous results are not clearly relevant to the model.

It would be misleading to imply that the LOT is a unique example of this problem. For example, very similar critiques have been presented concerning the construct of hardiness (Kobasa, 1979). Scales purported to assess this personality scale have been criticized for related measurement problems, with consequent ambiguities regarding the interpretation of previous tests of hardiness theory (Allred & Smith, 1989; Funk & Houston, 1987; Rhodewalt & Zone, 1989). Even though they have not been criticized, measures of other individual difference dimensions have not been subjected to thorough construct validation research. For example, Peterson, Seligman, and their colleagues have reported several very impressive prospective studies of the emotional and physical health consequences of explanatory style (Chapter 14). Even though multiple methods are available for assessing this construct, the obvious convergent-discriminant validation studies have not been reported. Without such independent evidence of construct validity, interpretation of this impressive set of findings as reflecting the effects of explanatory style is tentative at best.

Many researchers have called for greater empiri-

cal scrutiny of measures of personality in studies of emotional and physical health, and most of these authors have explicitly suggested that new measures be validated in reference to measures of established dimensions of personality such as neuroticism (Costa & McCrae, 1987; Depue & Monroe, 1986; Holroyd & Coyne, 1987; Watson & Pennebaker, 1989). This type of research would not only facilitate the interpretation of many existing and future studies, it would also "reduce the risk that we would reinvent constructs under new labels" (Holroyd & Coyne, 1987, p. 367). In any case, researchers who develop or employ individual difference measures should thoroughly evaluate and establish the construct validity of their trait measures. Incomplete efforts clearly undermine the value of the accumulated findings.

Studies of Cognitive Processes

As is the case in much of psychology, much of the activity at the social-clinical interface has a strong cognitive orientation (Brehm & Smith, 1986). Emotional and physical health are seen as influenced by a variety of cognitive processes. The research and theory regarding optimism or explanatory style, for example, could easily be viewed as representing cognitive models. Attributing a causal role to cognitive constructs creates a special challenge for the investigator. Valid methods of manipulating or measuring cognitive processes must be developed.

Many tests of cognitive models of adjustment are by necessity correlational. Predicted differences on a relevant cognitive dimension are tested in comparisons of functional and dysfunctional groups, such as nondepressed and depressed college students. These groups are often initially distinguished by selection of extreme scores on self-report measures of the dysfunctional condition. Unfortunately, the cognitive process under study also is often operationalized as scores on a self-report measure. For example, depressed and nondepressed groups might be compared as to their scores on a measure of dysfunctional attitudes, or socially anxious and nonanxious groups might be compared as to their scores on a paper-and-pencil measure of anxious self-statements. Coyne and Gotlib (1983) have pointed out that such studies often contain a "thinly veiled tautology" (p. 46). Groups that are distinguished on the basis of their relative endorsement of questionnaire items purported to measure the dysfunctional condition (e.g., depression, social anxiety, etc.) are compared on their relative endorsement of very similarly worded items intended to assess a cognitive process. Rather than a correlation between a dysfunctional emotional condition or disorder and a cognitive process or structure, such correlations may simply reflect the convergence of scores on similarly worded questionnaires (cf. Nicholls, Licht, & Pearl, 1982).

Interpretive ambiguities associated with studies of this type are not unique to the social-clinical interface. They are common in the literature testing many cognitive models of emotional disorder (Coyne & Gotlib, 1983; Smith, 1989b). At the very least, the producers and consumers of this type of cognitive research should explicitly acknowledge the interpretive problems inherent in such studies, and when possible the alternative explanations should be tested directly (e.g., Zurawski & Smith, 1987).

Researchers also should consider alternatives to self-report assessments of cognitive constructs. A variety of information-processing paradigms have been employed to test cognitive models of dysfunctional conditions (Ingram, 1986). Such studies have often produced results consistent with cognitive models of depression (Ingram, Smith, & Brehm, 1983), social anxiety (Smith, Ingram, & Brehm, 1983), and Type A behavior (Stern, Harris, & Elvenum, 1981) without the alternative interpretations associated with self-reports of cognition. Such procedures also circumvent difficulties arising from the influence of cognitive processes that are not easily tapped by verbal reports. The rapidly growing literature on social cognition (Taylor & Fiske, 1984) contains many experimental paradigms with demonstrated or at least potential utility for testing cognitive models of adjustment.

Operationalizing Outcomes

We stated earlier that tests of social psychological models of adjustment are useful only to the extent that the specific operational definitions of the predictors or causes of dysfunction measure or manipulate the construct these operations are intended to reflect. The same is true of the other end of the equation. These empirical tests are useful only to the extent that the operations used in measuring or classifying dysfunctional states or conditions have sufficient construct validity. The social-clinical literature includes several threats to our ability to interpret research operations as reflecting the adaptational constructs under study.

Emotional Functioning

Perhaps the largest part of the social-clinical literature consists of studies of dysfunctional emotional conditions such as depression and anxiety. Studies testing social psychological models of emotional adjustment often contain measurement problems that limit their contribution.

A common problem concerns the issue of the continuity of emotional disorders along the dimension of severity. Many studies test models of maladjustment by comparing groups of college students or groups from other essentially normal populations. The groups differ on the basis of their scores on a measure of a dysfunctional state, such as the Beck (1967) Depression Inventory (BDI). One possible problem with this procedure is that the difference in depression levels between groups of college students with high versus low BDI scores may be much smaller than the difference between clinically depressed and normal groups. Insufficient variability on the independent variable would pose a threat to statistical conclusion validity in the Cook and Campbell (1979) scheme. However, the continuity problem is somewhat different. Simply put, the question of continuity concerns whether or not the difference between groups selected in this manner resembles the difference between a group of clinically dysfunctional individuals and a group of demographically similar normal controls not simply in magnitude but in form. In the continuous model, the assumption is that the causes of mild dysfunctional conditions are similar to the causes of severe, clinically significant conditions. The discontinuous model suggests that the outward similarity between the two conditions is misleading, and in fact the subclinical and clinical dysfunctions represent different phenomena with distinct etiologies.

It is now generally agreed among psychopathology researchers that the continuity of seemingly similar dysfunctional states varying in outward severity might be fruitfully tested but should rarely if ever be assumed (Depue & Monroe, 1983, 1986). Analog studies have an obvious heuristic purpose, but are insufficient if a model of a clinical disorder is to be tested. Unfortunately, many social psychological models of emotional adjustment are tested only with college student populations. Although studies of college students selected on the basis of high scores on measures of social anxiety or depression might be relevant to our understanding of clinically significant social phobia or affective disorder, we cannot assume this to be true.

One response to this situation is to note that variations in emotional distress within the normal range are a worthy topic of study in their own right. The emotional problems of essentially healthy, adjusted individuals are certainly not trivial. Therefore, one could solve the problem posed by the threat of discontinuity by avoiding even the temptation to speculate about, let alone generalize to, clinical populations.

However, this solution certainly undermines the potential utility of many social psychological models of emotional functioning, and probably does not honestly reflect the ambitions of most social-clinical researchers. If the social-clinical integration is to move from an innovation to more lasting, mainstream contribution, promising analog research should be followed by more difficult studies of clinical populations. Although both types of research are useful, a lasting impact for the interface will require a solid foundation of clinical research.

A second major challenge to the validity of outcome measurements concerns the problem of specificity. If a model of depression is being tested, depressed and nondepressed groups are typically compared. If a model of social anxiety is under scrutiny, anxious and nonanxious groups are compared. Predicted differences are interpreted as supporting the model of a particular emotional problem under consideration.

Potential problems arise due to the fact that individuals scoring high on measures of one dysfunctional condition (e.g., depression) often have similarly extreme scores on measures of other emotional disorders (e.g., anxiety). Several studies have demonstrated that measures of different maladaptive emotions such as anxiety, depression, and others are so closely correlated in normal samples as to be virtually indistinguishable (Gotlib, 1984; Tanaka-Matsumi & Kameoka, 1986; Watson & Clark, 1984). As a result, groups selected on the basis of depression scores are likely to differ by almost as much, if not just as much, on anxiety and other characteristics. The obtained correlates of depression are quite likely to be just as closely related to anxiety.

The fact that the correlates of a particular emotional condition are not specific to that type of dysfunction may or may not be a problem depending on the theory being evaluated. If the theory is nonspecific (i.e., it concerns emotional adjustment broadly defined), then no difficulty is present. If, however, the theory purports to explain a specific form of emotional disorder, then the findings must reflect that level of specificity if they are to be considered supportive. For example, the reformulated learned helplessness model (Abramson et al., 1978) concerns depression as opposed to more general forms of distress. Some studies have found the predicted attributional style to be present in clinically depressed but not other clinical groups (Heimberg, Vermilyea, Dodge, Becker, & Barlow, 1987; Johnson, Petzel, & Munic, 1986), suggesting that depressive attributional style is specific to depression. Other research, however, has suggested that this attributional style is a correlate of global psychopathology in clinical populations rather than being unique to depression (Hamilton & Abramson, 1983; Miller, Klee, & Norman, 1982; Heimberg, Klosko, Dodge, Shadick, Becker, & Barlow, 1989).

Thus, if the theory to be tested makes predictions about a specific disorder, then additional controls are needed. Two-group comparisons are inadequate if the results are to be interpreted as relevant to a single type of pathology. If correlational designs are used literally, correlations with other dysfunctional dimensions must be tested simultaneously for specific interpretations to be justified. We should note that the failure to demonstrate predicted specificity may reflect poor discriminant validity of the measures of emotional functioning rather than the absence of unique effects. Thus, researchers must be cautious to avoid falsely rejecting specificity hypotheses.

One final difficulty in measuring emotional adjustment concerns interface research in medical populations. Several social psychological models have been developed to explain the development of depression or other emotional adjustment problems in the medically ill. This common and important clinical problem is certainly worthy of study, and the social psychological models offered to date are quite promising.

The primary threat to the validity of studies addressing this problem concerns the use of depression measures developed in psychiatric samples. In psychiatric populations, somatic symptoms such as lethargy, difficulty concentrating, concerns over physical appearance, reduced libido, and changes in appetite typically reflect depression. Endorsement of related items on self-report inventories validly reflect depression in this instance. In the medically ill, however, these symptoms may reflect the illness itself or the side effects of medication. As a result, scores on inventories including such items are likely to overestimate the severity of depression and create ambiguity in the interpretation of effects involving depression scores (e.g., Pincus, Callahan, Bradley, Vaughn, & Wolfe, 1986; Peck, Smith, Ward, & Milano, 1989).

Physical Functioning

Increasing amounts of the conceptual and empirical activity at the social-clinical interface concern physical rather than emotional health. As a result, the measurement of physical health outcomes becomes an essential methodological challenge. A key, often neglected distinction in operationalizing physical health is the difference between illness and illness behavior (Cohen, 1979; Mechanic, 1972). Illness refers to the tissue or physiological changes indicative of disease. Fever, infection, and elevated blood pressure are all examples of possible measures of illness. Illness behavior, in contrast, refers to all of the things people might do when they are ill, such as visit a physician, report symptoms or stay in bed.

Illness and illness behavior are obviously correlated. This is true logically, but there is also empirical evidence to indicate that subjective health reports are concurrently and prospectively related to objectively measured health status (Kaplan & Comacho, 1983). However, illness and illness behavior are far from perfectly correlated. Stoic individuals deny symptoms and refuse to see a physician even when clearly ill. Hypochondriacal persons, in contrast, report many symptoms and frequently seek medical attention when they are well. Thus, while measures of illness and illness behavior share some variance, they have a considerable amount of unique variance as well.

The problem arises when we use measures of illness behavior to operationalize physical health. It is easy to see why researchers might substitute measures of illness behavior for actual measures of illness. The two types of measures are related, and illness behavior is likely to be easier and less expensive to assess. However, there is no guarantee that the portion of illness behavior variance accounted for by predictor variables in a study is the same portion of variance in illness behavior scores that overlaps with actual illness. The findings observed might reflect the variance in illness behavior attributable to actual illness, but might instead reflect the variance in illness behavior that is independent of actual illness. If the latter is true, it would obviously be inappropriate to interpret the operational outcome as reflecting the outcome construct of physical health. Interpretive ambiguities arise from the fact that if only illness behavior is assessed, then it is virtually impossible to determine whether or not the covariation between predictors and outcome involves actual illness.

This problem becomes a larger threat when one considers the content of many social-clinical models of physical health. These models often include the constructs of life stress, social support, and a variety of personality dimensions. As mentioned in our discussion of operationalizing each of these classes of predictor variables, measures of these constructs are often substantially correlated with the personality trait of neuroticism or negative affectivity. Recent research suggests that this trait, in turn, is consistently related to somatic complaints or physical symptom reports but not actual illness (Costa & McCrae, 1987; Watson & Pennebaker, 1989). Therefore, associations between many predictor measures and health measures may reflect a correlation between neuroticism and somatic complaints in the absence of actual illness. Obviously, this possibility requires reinterpretation or at least reconsideration of associations of life stress, social support, and many personality traits with symptom reporting. Further, if social psychological models of influences on physical health are to be tested in a more compelling fashion, the possible confounding effects of neuroticism must be considered.

The cautionary note should not be taken to indicate that illness behavior in the absence of actual illness is simply a nuisance variable. Such behavior is extremely interesting, important, and even costly. As a result, it is certainly worth researching. Rather, we simply wish to point out the problems inherent in using measures of illness behavior to operationalize physical illness.

Testing Associations Between Predictors and Outcomes

From our discussion so far, it is clear that the value of social-clinical research depends on how predictors and outcomes are operationalized. The value is also influenced by the nature of the tests of their association. Here again, this statement is perhaps both obvious and far from unique to the social-clinical interface. Yet, given many of the research strategies employed in this area, this issue and its incumbent challenges are worth reviewing. We are not referring to basic threats to statistical conclusion validity (Cook & Campbell, 1979), such as low power, experimentwise error rates, and the reliability of outcome measures and treatment implementation. Rather, we are referring to the general approach to hypothesis testing in many social-clinical studies.

Theoretical Risks

It is perhaps unnecessary to point out that theories — or the less assuming structures, models — are never proven correct. Rather, the strongest statement one can make about the extent to which a theory has been corroborated is that it has been subjected to serious risk of disconfirmation and has survived. Popper (1959) argued that the degree of corroboration depends on "the severity of the various tests to which the hypothesis in question can be, and has been, subjected" (p. 267). The severity of the test depends, in part, on how likely it is that a prediction derived from the theory will be disconfirmed. Severe tests subject the prediction to clear risk of disconfirmation. Simple directional predictions would seem too sufficiently clear as to obviously risk refutation.

However, many such simple, directional tests provide a rather illusory form of risk of refutation. In his critique of "soft psychology" (the social-clinical interface is an example of this form of psychology), Meehl (1978) argued that one factor inhibiting the systematic accumulation of compelling theory-based scientific knowledge is the fact that hypotheses are rarely confronted with a "grave risk of refutation" (p. 821). For example, in testing the attributional reformulation of the learned helplessness model, a researcher might simply predict that higher scores on the measure of dysfunctional attributional style will be associated with higher scores on a depression scale. When one considers the host of methodological artifacts, potential confounds, as well as alternative processes that would possibly produce the hypothesized effect, it is clear that the effect is quite likely to occur, even if the theory is false. A supportive result is a very weak corroboration of the theory, because of its high prior probability given its many possible explanations. Thus, support for simple predictions often does not provide much in the way of corroboration because of their high prior probability of occurrence from many factors other than those specified by the theory.

Meehl (1978) argued that more complex or precise predictions entail a greater risk of refutation and provide more potential corroboration as a result. If the theory generates the prediction that depressed subjects should differ in their explanations of negative events from anxious subjects who will, in turn, be similar to normal controls, a somewhat larger degree of corroboration results from a predicted finding. A somewhat smaller pool of possible explanations produces a smaller prior probability of the pattern of differences. An even greater degree of corroboration results from a predicted finding indicating that these differences in attributions across groups are precisely opposite from a different class of events. A more complex prediction, with a resulting lower prior probability, is more useful.

Meehl's (1978) suggestion that psychology is often satisfied with increasing numbers of "tabular asterisks" (i.e., significant statistical tests of simple directional predictions) is no less true of research at the social-clinical interface. His recommendation that the accumulated body of research will be more valuable if more complex predictions are tested and theories, as a result, placed at greater risk is also potentially quite helpful for interface research.

On a practical level, this means the articulation of more complex pattern predictions rather than simple directional tests. Interactional or nonlinear predictions are preferred over linear main effects. Although the level of complexity Meehl suggests may well be unattainable, the criticism clearly describes possible improvements. Social psychological theories can generate complex predictions, and the empirical tests should reflect this richness. An equally valuable aspect of Meehl's advice is the acceptance of falsification when predicted effects fail to materialize. Of course, this requires the researcher to accept the validity of the operationalizations of the constructs under consideration. Such acceptance is prudent only after thorough empirical evaluations of construct validity.

Potentially Misleading Patterns

Although more complex, pattern predictions may ultimately produce a richer harvest, such patterns must not be accepted uncritically. Even a more complex effect can reflect something other than the constructs and processes under consideration. We have already referred to one example. Depue and Monroe (1986) described how the apparent interaction between life stress and social support might reflect something other than the buffering effect on emotional health. This pattern could reflect the fact that more chronically disturbed people—identified through the convergence of measures of problems associated with chronic disturbance—are more likely to experience current distress than are groups without a chronic disorder.

In a study of this type, Blumenthal, Burg, Barefoot, Williams, Haney, and Zimet (1987) reported that social support moderated the concurrent association between Type A behavior and the severity of coronary artery disease. This pattern could reflect, as the authors suggest, that a supportive social environment reduces the health risk associated with Type A behavior. It is also possible, however, that the combination of low levels of social support and the presence of Type A behavior effectively identified hostile individuals. Hostile people, in turn, may have had more severe coronary disease (cf. Cohen & Matthews, 1987). Thus, more complex predictions certainly do not remove potential interpretive ambiguities.

Recognizing Tested and Untested Patterns

In many cases, the association between predictors and outcomes that is actually tested is far less complex than the model that spawned the study. The results may be interpreted, however, as supporting the more complex conceptual structure. Krantz and Hedges (1987) have noted this potential problem in discussing research on personality and health. The theoretical models in this area typically assert that a given personality characteristic is associated with a health outcome by means of an intervening psychophysiological mechanism. For example, Type A behavior may lead to coronary disease through repeated episodes of exaggerated cardiovascular reactivity. Subsequent research may establish that (a) Type A behavior predicts the development of coronary disease, (b) Type A behavior is associated with reactivity, and (c) that reactivity predicts the development of coronary disease. Even if these three features of the nomological net are clearly established, the basic theory has not been tested directly.

It is also true that some researchers claim falsification when a pattern prediction from the theory has not actually been tested. For example, many conceptual models concerning personality factors hypothesized to increase vulnerability to illness are interactional models. In the presence of certain environmental or situational factors (e.g., high levels of stress, etc.), the personality dimension is related to disease risk. The operational tests of these models often fail to assess the relevant situational factor (Matthews, 1983; Smith, 1989a). As a result, the theoretically more accurate and possibly statistically more powerful interaction effect goes untested. Thus, researchers must take care not to claim support or disconfirmation for incompletely tested models.

Mediational Analyses and Theoretical Risk

Interactional predictions in which one independent variable moderates the effects of a second are one way to increase theoretical risk and consequent scientific yield. Moderator effects are, by definition, statistical interactions. As a result, the more complex prediction produces greater risk and potential corroboration. A second way involves tests of models where one variable mediates the effects of a second (Baron & Kenny, 1986). Mediational statistical techniques can test predictions regarding how predictors influence outcomes. The predicted set of associations is inherently more complex, and as a result a greater degree of corroboration is possible. In many instances mediational variables are specified in social psychological theories of adjustment, and recent developments in data analytic techniques make such hypotheses easily testable.

TESTING MODELS OF DIAGNOSIS AND TREATMENT

Social psychological models are not only useful in suggesting possible etiological and maintaining factors in adjustment difficulties. Many conceptual approaches to the clinical processes of assessment and intervention have been offered in recent years. Research in these areas is, unfortunately, less common than are studies of emotional and physical dysfunction. This is unfortunate because the potential practical benefits of social psychological models in this area are substantial. As noted above, however, the current zeitgeist in clinical psychology emphasizes empirical tests of such models in clinical populations. For the potential benefits of social psychological approaches to assessment and treatment to be realized, additional research is necessary. Such research, in turn, must address several methodological challenges.

Studies of Clinical Assessment

From a historical perspective, assessment has been perhaps the most central activity of clinical psychologists. As described by many authors, clinical assessment is essentially a special case of social judgment. Evidence is assembled and reviewed, dispositional characteristics are attributed to the person assessed, and predictions about future behavior are offered. Meehl (1960) was one of the earliest proponents of subjecting the cognitive activity of the clinician to empirical study. The research that has accumulated to date documents the fact that despite their professional training, clinicians often make similar mistakes in social judgment as those observed in nonclinical social knowing (see Chapter 21). Their active collection and recall of clinical evidence is likely to be influenced by their hypotheses to produce a confirmatory bias. Their judgments are susceptible to anchoring effects and illusory correlations, and they are prone to attribute client characteristics to dispositional rather than situational factors. Additional research would certainly be useful in redressing some of these drawbacks in the clinical assessment process.

Many studies of clinicians' cognitive processes in assessment contexts have employed analogue samples and role-play procedures. Obviously, studies of actual clinicians provide more compelling and relevant information. Interestingly, some studies have found that actual clinicians are more prone to cognitive errors in the assessment process than are untrained, naive subjects (e.g., Friedlander & Phillips, 1984). Other studies indicate that some biases, such as confirmatory hypothesis-testing strategies, actually increase with additional clinical experience (Hirsch & Stone, 1983). Thus, analog studies may underestimate the problematic features of social cognition in clinical assessment. As a result, studies of actual clinicians are important.

It may be useful to duplicate clinicians' typical working environments in studies of this type. Many clinicians, for example, must cope with large caseloads. Increasing the information-processing demands in clinical assessment tasks has been found to produce greater evidence of cognitive errors, such as illusory correlations (Leuger & Petzel, 1979). Increased ecological validity of studies of clinicians' judgments, therefore, may underscore the importance of the problem and its remediation.

One final methodological challenge to social psychological studies of the assessment process concerns the interactive nature of actual clinical assessment. Initial impressions or even the wording of referral questions may lead to the selection of some assessment procedures over others or some interview questions over other lines of inquiry. The resulting additional information elicited from the client shapes additional assessment selections in an at least temporarily ongoing interactive cycle. In contrast, many studies of the social psychology of clinical judgment are more static. A set of materials is presented, with some feature varied across experimental conditions. Although such studies are certainly valuable, this approach also may fail to capture the extent of the problem. Confirmatory hypothesis testing in an ongoing interaction as opposed to a more static review of test protocols is likely to produce compounding errors with stronger ultimate effects. Also, as the amount of available clinical material increases, clinicians' confidence in the accuracy of their judgments outstrips their actual accuracy (Oskamp, 1965). Thus, open-ended, clinician-guided assessment procedures seem to present the greatest opportunity for problems. Once again, the study of actual clinicians in as ecologically valid a setting and process as possible would be very useful.

Studies of Clinical Intervention

Many of the conceptual contributions of social psychology to clinical practice have been directed toward a better understanding and increased effectiveness of psychotherapy and behavior-change procedures. The empirical evaluation of the effectiveness of therapeutic interventions is an increasingly important aspect of clinical psychology, as is the study of therapy process. The result of these trends is that the potential contribution of social psychological models is great, but the methodological price of admission is steep.

Analog Studies of Psychotherapy

Large controlled trials of psychotherapy and related behavior-change techniques using clinical samples seeking treatment and experienced therapists are time consuming, expensive, and cumbersome. Given these disincentives, it is not surprising that many therapy studies are conducted as analogs of actual intervention procedures. Kazdin's (1978) discussion of the potential differences between analog therapy studies and more realistic procedures is essential reading for all researchers considering such an approach for testing a social psychological model of behavior change. Many times less severe target problems are addressed, college student populations are studied, subjects are recruited through incentives other than a desire to reduce their distress, and less experienced therapists are typically used. Whether or not these differences from actual clinical settings and procedures preclude generalization from analog research to clinical practice is an empirical question. Unfortunately, there are many more analog studies than there are answers to the empirical question about external validity.

Certainly analog therapy research has many uses, such as initial hypothesis testing. However, the potential impact of social psychological models will be reduced if interface researchers do not address the generalizability question directly. Psychotherapy researchers and practicing clinicians are much more likely to be persuaded by more realistic therapy studies than by analog research. Certainly research along the entire continuum from basic social psychological laboratory research to comparative psychotherapy trials involving social psychological models is useful (Brehm & Smith, 1982). Nevertheless, the future and potential contribution of the social-clinical interface would be well served by pushing the activity farther along the continuum more frequently.

Testing Social Psychological Therapies

As mentioned above, psychotherapy research has become increasingly more sophisticated in recent years. The central issues in this area are relevant to any researcher wishing to test a psychotherapy or related interventions derived from social psychological principles.

One basic issue concerns the selection of appropriate comparison or control conditions. At a simple level, much psychotherapy research asks the question, "Is treatment X effective?" An important follow-up question is, "Compared to what?" Historically, psychotherapy research design has emphasized controls for the natural history of the disorder under treatment (i.e., spontaneous remission) and for the nonspecific factors common to virtually all therapies (e.g., attention, expectancy for improvement, etc.). As a result, two logical choices for control groups were "no treatment" or "waiting list" controls and "nonspecific factors" or "placebo" controls (Hersen, Michelson, & Bellack, 1984).

Current discussions of appropriate comparison groups have questioned this long-standing practice and the associated conceptual models (Horvath, 1988; Parloff, 1986; Basham, 1986). Withholding treatment and administration of inert therapies presented as effective raise unpleasant ethical questions. It is also relatively rare that the question, "Is this therapy better than nothing?" is important given the large treatment literatures amassed for most disorders. Further, one researcher's "nonspecific factor" is another's innovative social psychological active ingredient. As a result, needed tests of social psychologically oriented therapies must carefully articulate the question to be asked, ensure that it is useful given the existing treatment literature, and select the necessary comparison condition so that groups differ only in the key construct under consideration.

Another recent development in psychotherapy research is the focus on the clinical significance of change (Jacobsen & Reuensto, 1988). Statistical differences may answer important conceptual questions, but in this arena the practical importance of observed changes is equally important. Evaluating the magnitude and meaning of observed changes is an evolving topic of clinical research, and social-clinical studies of psychotherapy should at least be informed by this work.

Social Psychological Studies
of Therapy Process

Unique therapies may be derived from social psychological models, and they can be tested meaningfully by the methods mentioned above. A different role for interface models, however, involves explanation of the mechanisms that underlie the effectiveness of existing interventions. Mediational models and associated analytic techniques are an established aspect of current social psychology (Baron & Kenny, 1986). Similar conceptual and statistical approaches are extremely relevant to the explication of psychotherapy process (e.g., Hollon, DeRubeis, & Evans, 1987).

The controlled evaluation of therapies derived from social psychological concepts is unnecessary in this pursuit. Rather, social psychological constructs hypothesized to mediate therapeutic effectiveness are assessed in the context of traditional therapy research designs, and included in appropriate mediational statistical tests.

CONCLUSIONS AND CURRENT ISSUES

Sound and increasingly ambitious research is necessary to sustain the impressive integration of social and clinical psychology observed in recent decades. Theories must be pressed to yield more precise and complex, falsifiable predictions. The operational definitions must be increasingly compelling in order that both positive and negative results have greater utility. Promising and intriguing results from analog research should be followed by conceptual replications of more direct clinical relevance, and the cumbersome complexity of research problems in psychopathology, psychotherapy, and clinical assessment must be confronted and managed rather than avoided. This tall order must be met if the integration of social and clinical psychology is to continue its movement from a primarily academic activity to an influence on mainstream clinical psychology and actual clinical practical.

Of course, there are already many examples of the kinds of social-clinical studies we are recommending. Some are decades old and others are quite recent. Thus, rather than suggesting a new type of research activity at the interface, we are simply recommending an increase in the proportion of research of this more involved and informative type.

Although they are not strictly methodological, there are several related issues that we have not addressed. One issue concerns the direction of the currents flowing at the interface. Our discussion has largely focused on generating more compelling tests of social psychological models of clinical problems and procedures. This type of interdisciplinary activity has had an important impact and will continue to do so. It is also true, however, that social psychological paradigms can offer useful tools for testing rich conceptual traditions in clinical psychology. For example, the concepts and methods of attribution research and specifically self-handicapping (Jones & Berghas, 1978) provided an opportunity to test Adler's decades-old notions about the strategic use of symptoms (Snyder & Smith, 1982). Recent advances in cognitive psychology provide an opportunity to operationalize many psychodynamic constructs pertaining to unconscious processes (Kihlstrom, 1987). Current cognitive-social approaches to personality (e.g., Cantor & Kihlstrom, 1981) similarly provide methods for testing a long theoretical tradition of interactional approaches to dysfunctional behavior (e.g., Sullivan, 1953; Carson, 1969; Anchin & Kiesler, 1982). Thus, social and clinical psychology both bring rich reserves of theory that when explored with the other discipline's research methods can yield a wealth of new information.

Even if the enormous amount of empirical activity we have outlined actually occurs, the explanation and remediation of dysfunctional conditions will not become a precise science. As a result, we must acknowledge that the more com-

pelling and difficult research we have discussed must be combined with an additional type of interface activity. In discussing the relationship between the science of psychology and the explanation and alteration of individual behavior, Manicas and Secord (1983) pointed out that empirically substantiated theories must be translated to have relevance for specific situations. This translation, of course, is based on the empirical science, but requires a great deal of additional historical, social, biographical and even biological information.

The methodological challenges we have discussed might help to refine and extend the science, but they do little to produce sophistication in the technical process of application. A very different, and perhaps less easily defined, set of methodological challenges must be met to produce compelling applications. Of course, high-quality application is precisely the kind of activity displayed by many of the pioneers at the social-clinical interface (Brehm, 1976; Heller, 1963). Coming full circle then, hopefully a more compelling body of empirical research will stimulate additional, artful applications to clinical activities.

REFERENCES

Abramson, L., Seligman, M., & Teasdale, J. (1978). Learned helplessness in humans: Critique and reformulation. *Journal of Abnormal Psychology, 87*, 49–74.

Allred, K. D., & Smith, T. W. (1989). The hardy personality: Cognitive and physiological responses to evaluative threat. *Journal of Personality and Social Psychology, 56*, 257–266.

Anchin, J. C., & Kiesler, D. J. (Eds.). (1982). *Handbook of interpersonal psychotherapy.* Elmsford, NY: Pergamon Press.

Baron, R. M., & Kenny, D. A. (1986). The moderator-mediator variable distinction in social psychological research: Conceptual, strategic, and statistical considerations. *Journal of Personality and Social Psychology, 51*, 1173–1182.

Basham, R. B. (1986). Scientific and practical advantages of comparative design in psychotherapy outcome research. *Journal of Consulting and Clinical Psychology, 54*, 88–94.

Beck, A. T. (1967). *Depression: Causes and treatment.* Philadelphia: University of Pennsylvania Press.

Blumenthal, J. A., Burg, M. M., Barefoot, J., Williams, R. B., Haney, T., & Zimet, G.

(1987). Social support, Type A behavior, and coronary heart disease. *Psychosomatic Medicine, 49*, 331–340.

Brehm, S. S. (1976). *The application of social psychology to clinical practice*. Washington, DC: Hemisphere.

Brehm, S. S., & Smith, T. W. (1982). The application of social psychology to clinical practice: A range of possibilities. In G. Weary & H. L. Mirels (Eds.), *Integration of clinical and social psychology* (pp. 9–24). New York: Oxford University Press.

Brehm, S. S., & Smith, T. W. (1986). Social psychological approaches to psychotherapy and behavior change. In S. L. Garfield & A. E. Bergin (Eds.), *Handbook of psychotherapy and behavior change* (3rd ed., pp. 69–115). New York: John Wiley & Sons.

Campbell, D. T., & Fiske, D. W. (1959). Convergent and discriminant validation by the multitrait-multimethod matrix. *Psychological Bulletin, 56*, 81–105.

Cantor, N., & Kihlstrom, J. F. (Eds.). (1981). *Personality, cognition, and social interaction*. Hillsdale, NJ: Lawrence Erlbaum Associates.

Carson, R. C. (1969). *Interaction concepts of personality*. Chicago: Aldine.

Carver, C. S., & Scheier, M. F. (1982). Control theory: A useful conceptual framework for personality-social, clinical, and health psychology. *Psychological Bulletin, 92*, 111–135.

Cohen, F. (1979). Personality, stress, and the development of physical illness. In G. C. Stone, F. Cohen, & N. E. Adler (Eds.), *Health psychology* (pp. 77–111). San Francisco: Jossey-Bass.

Cohen, S., & Matthews, K. A. (1987). Social support, Type A behavior, and coronary heart disease. *Psychosomatic Medicine, 4*, 325–330.

Cohen, S., & Wills, T. A. (1985). Stress, social support, and the buffering hypothesis. *Psychological Bulletin, 98*, 310–357.

Cook, T. D., & Campbell, D. T. (1979). *Quasi-experimentation: Design and analysis issues for field settings*. Chicago: Rand-McNally.

Costa, P. T., Jr., & McCrae, R. R. (1987). Neuroticism, somatic complaints, and disease: Is the bark worse than the bite? *Journal of Personality, 55*, 299–316.

Coyne, J. C., & Gotlib, I. H. (1983). The role of cognition in depression: A critical appraisal. *Psychological Bulletin, 94*, 472–505.

Delongis, A., Coyne, J. C., Dakoif, G., Folkman, S., & Lazarus, R. S. (1982). Relation of daily hassles, uplifts, and major life events to health status. *Health Psychology, 1*, 119–136.

Depue, R. A., & Monroe, S. M. (1983). Psychopathology research. In M. Hersen, A. E. Kazdin, & A. S. Bellack (Eds.), *The clinical psychology handbook: Vol. 1. The foundations* (pp. 239–264). Elmsford, NY: Pergamon Press.

Depue, R. A., & Monroe, S. M. (1986). Conceptualization and measurement of human disorder in life stress research: The problem of chronic disturbance. *Psychological Bulletin, 99*, 36–51.

Dohrenwend, B. S., Dohrenwend, B. P., Dodson, M., & Shrout, P. E. (1984). Symptoms, hassles, social supports, and life events: Problem of confounded measures. *Journal of Abnormal Psychology, 93*, 222–230.

Dohrenwend, B. S., Krasnoff, L., Askenasy, A. R., & Dohrenwend, B. P. (1982). The psychiatric epidemiology research interview life events scale. In L. Goldberger & S. Breznitz (Eds.), *Handbook of stress: Theoretical and clinical aspects* (pp. 332–363). New York: Free Press.

Eysenck, H. J., & Eysenck, S. B. G. (1964). *Manual for the Eysenck personality inventory*. London: University Press.

Fibel, B., & Hale, W. D. (1978). The generalized expectancy for success scale – A new measure. *Journal of Consulting and Clinical Psychology, 46*, 924–931.

Frank, J. D. (1973). *Persuasion and healing: A comparative study of psychotherapy* (rev. ed.). Baltimore, MD: The Johns Hopkins University Press. (Original material published 1961)

Friedlander, M. L., & Phillips, S. D. (1984). Preventing anchoring errors in clinical judgment. *Journal of Consulting and Clinical Psychology, 52*, 366–371.

Funk, S. C., & Houston, B. K. (1987). A critical analysis of the hardiness scale's validity and utility. *Journal of Personality and Social Psychology, 53*, 572–578.

Goldstein, A. P., Heller, K., & Sechrest, L. B. (1966). *Psychotherapy and the psychology of behavior change*. New York: John Wiley & Sons.

Gotlib, I. H. (1984). Depression and general psychopathology in university students. *Journal of Abnormal Psychology, 93*, 19–30.

Hamilton, E. W., & Abramson, L. Y. (1983). Cognitive patterns and major depressive disorder: A longitudinal study in a hospital setting. *Journal of Abnormal Psychology, 92,* 173–184.

Heimberg, R. G., Klosko, J. S., Dodge, C. S., Shadick, R., Becker, R. E., & Barlow, D. H. (1989). Anxiety disorders, depression, and attributional style: A further test of the specificity of depressive attributions. *Cognitive Therapy and Research, 13,* 21–36.

Heimberg, R. G., Vermilyea, J. A., Dodge, C. S., Becker, R. E., & Barlow, D. H. (1987). Attributional style, depression, and anxiety: An evaluation of the specificity of depressive attributions. *Cognitive Therapy and Research, 11,* 537–550.

Heitzmann, C. A., & Kaplan, R. M. (1988). Assessment of methods for measuring social support. *Health Psychology, 7,* 75–109.

Heller, K. (1963). Experimental analogues of psychotherapy: The clinical relevance of laboratory findings of social influence. *Journal of Nervous and Mental Disorders, 137,* 420–426.

Hersen, M., Michelson, L., & Bellack, A. S. (1984). *Issues in psychotherapy research.* New York: John Wiley & Sons.

Hirsch, P. A., & Stone, G. L. (1983). Cognitive strategies and the client conceptualization process. *Journal of Counseling Psychology, 30,* 566–572.

Hollon, S. D., DeRubeis, R. J., & Evans, M. D. (1987). Causal mediation of change in treatment for depression: Discriminating between nonspecificity and noncausality. *Psychological Bulletin, 102,* 139–149.

Holroyd, K. A., & Coyne, J. C. (1987). Personality and health in the 1980s: Psychosomatic medicine revisited? *Journal of Personality, 55,* 359–375.

Horvath, P. (1988). Placebos and common factors in two decades of psychotherapy research. *Psychological Bulletin, 104,* 214–225.

House, J. S., Landis, K. R., & Umberson, D. (1988). Social relationships and health. *Science, 241,* 540–545.

Ingram, R. E. (Ed.). (1986). *Information processing approaches to clinical psychology.* New York: Academic Press.

Ingram, R. E., Smith, T. W., & Brehm, S. S. (1983). Depression and information processing: Self-schemata and the encoding of self-relevant information. *Journal of Personality and Social Psychology, 45,* 412–420.

Jacobsen, N. S., & Revensto, D. (1988). Statistics for assessing the clinical significance of psychotherapy techniques: Issues, problems, and new developments. *Behavioral Assessment, 10,* 133–145.

Johnson, J. E., Petzel, T. P., & Munic, D. (1986). An examination of the relative contribution of depression versus global psychopathology to depressive attribution style in a clinical population. *Journal of Social and Clinical Psychology, 4,* 107–113.

Jones, E. E., & Berglas, S. (1978). Control of attributions about the self through self-handicapping strategies: The appeal of alcohol and the role of underachievement. *Personality and Social Psychology Bulletin, 4,* 200–206.

Kaplan, G. A., & Camacho, T. (1983). Perceived health and mortality: A nine-year follow-up of the human population laboratory cohort. *American Journal of Epidemiology, 117,* 292–304.

Kazdin, A. E. (1978). Evaluating the generality of findings in analogue therapy research. *Journal of Consulting and Clinical Psychology, 46,* 673–686.

Kihlstrom, J. F. (1987). The cognitive unconscious. *Science, 237,* 1445–1452.

Klaus, M. H., Kennell, J. H., Robertson, S. S., & Sosa, R. (1986). Effects of social support during parturition of maternal and infant morbidity. *British Medical Journal, 293,* 585–587.

Kobasa, S. C. (1979). Stressful life events, personality, and health: An inquiry into hardiness. *Journal of Personality and Social Psychology, 37,* 1–11.

Krantz, D. S., & Hedges, S. M. (1987). Some cautions for research on personality and health. *Journal of Personality, 55,* 351–357.

Lazarus, R. S., & Folkman, S. (1984). *Stress, appraisal, and coping.* New York: Springer.

Leuger, R. J., & Petzel, T. P. (1979). Illusory correlation in clinical judgment: Effect of amount of information to be processed. *Journal of Consulting and Clinical Psychology, 47,* 1120–1121.

Manicas, P. T., & Secord, P. F. (1983). Implications for psychology of the new philosophy of science. *American Psychologist, 38,* 399–413.

Matthews, K. A. (1983). Assessment issues in coronary-prone behavior. In T. M. Dembroski, T. H. Schmidt, & G. Blumchen (Eds.), *Biobehavioral bases of coronary heart disease* (pp. 62–78). Basel, Switzerland: Karger.

McCrae, R. R., & Costa, P. T., Jr. (1986). Personality, coping, and coping effectiveness in an adult sample. *Journal of Personality, 54*, 385–405.

Mechanic, D. (1972). Social psychological factors affecting the presentation of bodily complaints. *New England Journal of Medicine, 286*, 1132–1139.

Meehl, P. E. (1960). The cognitive activity of the clinician. *American Psychologist, 15*, 19–27.

Meehl, P. E. (1978). Theoretical risks and tabular asterisks: Sir Karl, Sir Ronald, and the slow progress of soft psychology. *Journal of Consulting and Clinical Psychology, 46*, 806–834.

Miller, I. W., Klee, S. H., & Norman, W. H. (1982). Depressed and nondepressed inpatients' cognitions of hypothetical events, experimental tasks, and stressful life events. *Journal of Abnormal Psychology, 91*, 78–81.

Monroe, S. M. (1982). Life events assessment: Current practices, emerging trends. *Clinical Psychology Review, 2*, 435–453.

Nicholls, J. G., Licht, B. G., & Pearl, R. A. (1982). Some dangers of using personality questionnaires to study personality. *Psychological Bulletin, 92*, 572–580.

Oskamp, S. (1965). Overconfidence in case-study judgments. *Journal of Consulting Psychology, 29*, 261–265.

Parloff, M. B. (1986). Placebo controls in psychotherapy research: A sine qua non or a placebo for research problems? *Journal of Consulting and Clinical Psychology, 54*, 79–87.

Peck, J. R., Smith, T. W., Ward, J. R., & Milano, R. (1989). Disability and depression in rheumatoid arthritis: A multitrait-multimethod investigation. *Arthritis and Rheumatism, 32*, 1100–1106.

Perkins, D. V. (1982). The assessment of stress using life events scales. In L. Goldberger & S. Breznitz (Eds.), *Handbook of stress: Theoretical and clinical aspects* (pp. 320–331). New York: Free Press.

Pincus, T., Callahan, L. F., Bradley, L. A., Vaughn, W. K., & Wolfe, F. (1986). Elevated MMPI scores for hypochondriasis, depression, and hysteria in patients with rheumatoid arthritis reflect disease rather than psychological status. *Arthritis and Rheumatism, 29*, 1456–1466.

Popper, K. R. (1959). *The logic of scientific discovery*. New York: Basic Books.

Rhodewalt, F., & Zone, J. (1989). Appraisal of life change, depression, and illness in hardy and nonhardy women. *Journal of Personality and Social Psychology, 56*, 81–88.

Sarason, I. G., Johnson, J. H., & Siegel, J. M. (1978). Assessing the impact of life changes: Development of the life experiences survey. *Journal of Consulting and Clinical Psychology, 46*, 932–946.

Scheier, M. F., & Carver, C. S. (1985). Optimism, coping, and health: Assessment and implications of generalized outcome expectancies. *Health Psychology, 4*, 219–247.

Scheier, M. F., & Carver, C. S. (1987). Dispositional optimism and physical well-being: The influence of generalized outcome expectancies on health. *Journal of Personality, 55*, 169–210.

Scheier, M. F., Weintraub, J. K., & Carver, C. S. (1986). Coping with stress: Divergent strategies of optimists and pessimists. *Journal of Personality and Social Psychology, 51*, 1257–1264.

Schroeder, D. H., & Costa, P. T. (1984). Influence of life event stress on physical illness: Substantive effects or methodological flaws: *Journal of Personality and Social Psychology, 46*, 853–863.

Sedlmeier, P., & Gigerenzer, G. (1989). Do studies of statistical power have an effect on the power of studies? *Psychological Bulletin, 105*, 309–316.

Seligman, M. E. P. (1975). *Helplessness: On depression, development, and death*. San Francisco: W. H. Freeman.

Smith, T. W. (1989a). Interactions, transactions, and the Type A pattern: Additional avenues in the search for coronary-prone behavior. In A. W. Siegman & T. M. Dembroski (Eds.), *In search of coronary-prone behavior* (pp. 91–116). Hillsdale, NJ: Lawrence Erlbaum Associates.

Smith, T. W. (1989b). Assessment in rational-emotive therapy: Empirical access to the ABCD model. In M. E. Bernard & R. DiGuisseppe (Eds.), *Inside rational-emotive therapy* (pp. 135–153). New York: Academic Press.

Smith, T. W., Ingram, R. E., & Brehm, S. S. (1983). Social anxiety, anxious self-preoccupation, and recall of self-relevant information. *Journal of Personality and Social Psychology, 44*, 1276–1283.

Smith, T. W., Pope, M. K., Rhodewalt, F., & Poulton, J. F. (1989). Optimism, neuroticism, coping, and symptom reports: An alternative interpretation of the life orientation test. *Jour-

nal of Personality and Social Psychology, 56, 640–648.

Snyder, C. R., & Smith, T. W. (1982). Symptoms as self-handicapping strategies: The virtues of old wine in a new bottle. In G. Weary & H. L. Mirels (Eds.), *Integrations of clinical and social psychology* (pp. 104–127). New York: Oxford University Press.

Sosa, R., Kennell, J., Klaus, M., Robertson, S., & Urrutia, J. (1980). The effect of supportive compassion on perinatal problems, length of labor and mother-infant interacting. *New England Journal of Medicine, 303,* 597–600.

Stern, G. S., Harris, J. R., & Elverum, J. (1981). Attention to important versus trivial tasks and salience of fatigue-related symptoms for coronary-prone individuals. *Journal of Research in Personality, 15,* 467–474.

Sullivan, H. S. (1953). *The interpersonal theory or psychiatry.* New York: W. W. Norton.

Tanaka-Matsumi, J., & Kameoka, V. A. (1986). Reliabilities and concurrent validities of popular self-report measures of depression, anxiety, and social desirability. *Journal of Consulting and Clinical Psychology, 54,* 328–333.

Taylor, S. E., & Fiske, S. T. (1984). *Social cognition.* Reading, MA: Addison-Wesley.

Vitaliano, P. P., Maiuro, R. D., Russo, J., & Becker, J. (1987). Raw versus relative scores in the assessment of coping strategies. *Journal of Behavioral Medicine, 10,* 1–18.

Watson, D., & Clark, L. A. (1984). Negative affectivity: The disposition to experience aversive emotional states. *Psychological Bulletin, 96,* 465–490.

Watson, D., & Pennebaker, J. W. (1989). Health complaints, stress, and distress: Exploring the central role of negative affectivity. *Psychological Review, 96,* 233–253.

Weary, G., & Mirels, H. L. (Eds.). (1982). *Integrations of clinical and social psychology.* New York: Oxford University Press.

Zurawski, R. M., & Smith, T. W. (1987). Assessing irrational beliefs and emotional distress: Evidence and implications of limited discriminant validity. *Journal of Counseling Psychology, 34,* 224–227.

CHAPTER 38

METATHEORETICAL AND EPISTEMOLOGICAL ISSUES

Donelson R. Forsyth
Mark R. Leary

The seeds of an interface between social and clinical psychology were sown in 1921 when the *Journal of Abnormal Psychology*, founded by Morton Prince in 1906, was transformed into the *Journal of Abnormal Psychology and Social Psychology*. Prince, along with managing editor Floyd Allport, decided to expand the scope of the journal to incorporate research that bridged the study of interpersonal and abnormal processes. They reasoned that researchers in these fields were interested in many common topics and pointed to the fact that social psychology had already benefited "in a peculiar way" from discoveries in psychopathology. As social psychology came into its own as a behavioral science, subsequent editor Gordon Allport argued that not only did social psychology profit from the study of dysfunctional processes, but that social psychology had much to offer those interested in abnormal behavior. Nearly two decades after Prince's and Floyd Allport's call for an integration of social and abnormal/clinical psychology, however, Gordon Allport admitted that few of the articles published in the journal had reflected the connections between so-cial and abnormal psychology they had envisioned (Allport, 1938). Even so, he continued to champion the "marriage of abnormal and social psychology" and called for the "creation of a unified dynamic psychology which, in time, will overarch the divisions of mental science drawn merely in terms of subject matter or in terms of schools of thought" (Allport, 1949, p. 439).

For the next 20 years social and clinical psychology rarely interwined. Indeed, when Goldstein, Heller, and Sechrest surveyed the connections between the two fields in 1966 they found little in the way of social psychology of psychotherapy. Nonetheless, they concluded that extrapolations from social psychological studies of behavior change to therapeutic settings offered a host of new methods for "altering patient behavior" (p. 4). Strong (1968) agreed, calling for psychologists who were interested in client change to draw on social psychological work on attitude change and social influence. But, again, the call went largely unheeded. Nearly a decade later, Brehm (1976) resurrected the idea once again in *The Application of Social Psychology to Clinical Practice*, urging others to join in the active application of social psychological principles in clinical realms.

Now, as we move into the 1990s, we see signs that this septuagenarian idea is at last taking hold as increasing numbers of theorists, researchers, and practitioners have begun to advocate the development of links between social psychology and fields that by tradition focus on abnormality and adjustment (Brehm & Smith, 1986; Dorn, 1984; Higgenbotham, West, & Forsyth, 1988; Leary & Maddux, 1987; Leary & Miller, 1986; Maddux, Stoltenberg, & Rosenwein, 1987; Sheras & Worchel, 1979; Snyder & Ford, 1987; Weary & Mirels, 1982). Yet, despite recent progress toward a viable interface between social and clinical psychology (see Leary & Maddux, 1987, for a review), theorists and researchers do not yet agree on a number of central issues pertaining to the social-clinical interface. To some, social psychology is a gold mine of methods for promoting therapeutic change (Harari, 1983), whereas others argue that clinicians should not make use of a theoretical system that views individual action as largely environmentally constrained (Rychlak, 1983; Strong, 1987). Some recommend that social psychologists themselves should get involved in the delivery of therapy (C. Hendrick, 1983), but others caution against their entry into the role of therapist (S. Hendrick, 1983). Some recommend the merging of the fields at the level of service delivery to create a new approach to psychological and somatic treatment (C. Hendrick, 1983; Strickland & Halgin, 1987), but others favor maintaining the current system of clinical training (Winer, 1987). Others wonder if social psychology will provide much useful information given that it relies so heavily on laboratory studies conducted with college students (Garfield, 1979; Gazda & Pistole, 1987), and others rebel at the thought of having to tote the theoretical baggage most social psychologists insist on carrying with them from study to study (Strong, 1987). Some, too, have wondered why anyone would even consider an alliance of clinical psychology with social psychology given the weaknesses in both disciplines (Sarason, 1981, 1987).

In this chapter we explore these and related issues. We recognize that such debates and disagreements are complex and brook no easy solution, but we assume that progress can be achieved by examining the ideas and assumptions that lie at the core of this growing interface between social and clinical psychology. Our approach assumes

that links between social psychology and clinical psychology can be forged at a number of different levels, and that the nature of the interface depends directly on the quality and quantity of these linkages. After identifying six levels where possible linkages between social and clinical psychology exist or could be created, we examine two of these possible linkages in greater detail.

THE NATURE OF AN INTERFACE

What is an interface? In some usages, an interface is a common ground between independent entities, an area of shared interest that provides a meeting point between otherwise unrelated partners. Alternatively, the term interface has been used to refer to improved communication between two systems, increased coordination between areas that once operated independently, if not at cross-purposes.

Maddux and Stoltenberg (1983) described the interface as a conceptual bridge between social and clinical psychology that makes possible the "use of social-psychological theories (e.g., attribution, attitude change, group process) in increasing our understanding of the development of psychological and behavioral problems and their modification" (p. 289). Similarly, Weary (1987, p. 160) argued that the interface of "social and clinical psychology is based on the notion that systematic attention to social psychological principles is essential to any understanding of the definition, development, maintenance, and modification of maladaptive behaviors." Harvey, Bratt, and Lennox (1987, p. 9) defined the interface in terms of "the study of human problems in living and illness (mental and physical) via an emphasis upon the broad literature of social psychology and social-psychological processes as central explanatory mechanisms."

Such views of social-clinical psychology treat the interface as a unitary, monolithic entity. However, in actuality, these two fields interface on at least six different levels. Specifically, one may speak of the social-clinical interface at an educational, practical, methodological, theoretical, metatheoretical, and epistemological level.

The Educational Interface

The strongest and most long-lasting link between the fields can be found in the educational domain. In 1947, the American Psychological Association's Committee on Training in Clinical Psychology agreed that training

> programs should consist mainly of basic courses in principles, rather than the multiplication of courses in technique. The specific program of instruction should be organized around a careful integration of theory and practice, of academic and field work, by persons representing both aspects. (Shakow, 1978, p. 151)

The areas considered to comprise the core in the training of a clinical psychologist have varied over the years, but social psychology has been regarded as a fundamental part of the core. However, this linkage has not been reciprocal. Clinical trainees are expected to study social psychology, but social psychology students are not encouraged to study abnormal behavior, clinical assessment, therapeutic methods, and the like.

The Practical Interface

A second linkage between the fields has occurred at the level of practice. The practical interface involves the potential link between social psychology's research findings and clinicians' therapeutic interventions. In elucidating their concept of "extrapolation," Goldstein et al. (1966) argued that empirical results in nonclinical areas such as social psychology should be used to develop clinical treatments and procedures. Similarly, Harari (1983, p. 176) described social psychology in clinical practice, which "deals with social psychology as a contributing factor in the enhancement of clinical practice." Attributional therapies, one of the most popular applications of social psychology in clinical practice, represent this level of interface, as do other social-psychology–inspired methods such as role-playing, reverse placebo interventions, and some forms of interpersonal skills training. Like the educational interface, the practical interface has traditionally been a one-way street, with clinicians borrowing from social psychology rather than vice versa. Increasingly, however, social psychologists are employing constructs, methods, and findings that originated in clinical practice and research.

The Methodological Interface

Social and clinical psychology also interface at a methodological level. Although social psychology can make no special claim for expertise in research methodology, the field's penchant for sophisticated statistical and methodological practices makes it a valuable resource for applied researchers. Conversely, the unique methodological problems faced by researchers in clinical, counseling, and community settings have stimulated a number of methodological developments. As more social psychologists moved out of the laboratory in the 1980s they took advantage of these methods in their own work (Higgenbotham et al., 1988).

Clinical and social psychologists, too, are united by their interest in the measurement of individual differences, and they can be found side by side building new depression inventories, exploring ways to measure stress, criticizing and improving methods for assessing social skills, and developing coding systems that can be used to structure observations of therapeutic interactions.

The Theoretical Interface

A fourth, less well developed facet of the interface occurs at the level of theory. The theoretical interface involves the integration of facets of clinical and social psychology in constructing conceptual models that are more encompassing than those developed in either field in isolation. Clinical psychology, by tradition, has drawn on personality psychology and behaviorism for its models of abnormality and treatment and as a result the theoretical links between social and clinical have not been fully developed (Rosenzweig, 1949).

Moreover, the linkage is often viewed as a one-way relationship. As noted earlier, Maddux and Stoltenberg (1983) argued for the use of social-psychological theories when studying the origin of dysfunctional behavior and methods of treatment, and Weary (1987, p. 160) proposed that social-psychological principles are critical for understanding "the definition, development, maintenance, and modification of maladaptive behaviors." The chapters of this handbook, however, are evidence that interface theorists and researchers are developing theoretical models that fill the gap between the two disciplines (Leary & Miller, 1986).

The Metatheoretical Interface

Educational, practical, methodological, and theoretical linkages make up the bulk of the explicit cross-disciplinary ties between social and clinical psychology, but they do not exhaust all the possible linkages. Reaching beyond theory, we find that social and clinical psychologists, qua psychologists, are also linked by certain metatheoretical assumptions. As the philosopher of science Thomas Kuhn argued in his provocative book *The Structure of Scientific Revolutions*, scientists working in a particular field share a set of assumptions about the phenomena they study (Kuhn, 1970). Although these metatheoretical assumptions are rarely discussed explicitly, they provide an undergirding structure that guides the theories formulated and methods used by researchers (Fiske, 1986; Meehl, 1986). The concept of metatheory is relevant here because it suggests that the interface of social and clinical psychology is based not only on shared methodological and theoretical beliefs, but also on implicit beliefs about psychology and about human beings. What is the nature of men and women? Are humans free? Is behavior caused by exogenous or endogenous factors? Are humans governed more by rationality or irrationality? It also suggests that weaknesses in the social-clinical interface may be due in part to differences in the metatheoretical assumptions that characterize social versus clinical psychology. The degree to which social and clinical psychologists agree and disagree on these fundamental questions has direct implications for the viability of an interface between them. We will explore the metatheoretical interface and its implications for social-clinical psychology in greater detail momentarily.

The Epistemological Interface

One last linkage remains to be examined, because how psychologists deal with issues that arise at the level of education, practice, methodology, theory, and metatheory reflects, in many cases, their epistemological assumptions. Put simply, how should our knowledge of human behavior be refined and extended? Should we continue to emulate the methods used in the physical sciences, or should we turn instead to the interpretative disciplines for suggestions and methods of expanding our knowledge? Do theories play an indispensable role in the growth of knowledge or do they blind us to alternative ways of knowing? Should we strive to develop general, lawlike statements about the causes of behavior, or should we focus on single-case, ideographic descriptions? Should theories be judged on their internal consistency and

predictive power or on their ability to generate solutions to practical problems? The answers to these questions are tied closely to one's personal and professional philosophy of science, a philosophy that for most psychologists is implicit and unarticulated. We return to the epistemological interface below.

Table 38.1 summarizes the preceding discussion of the various levels of integration between social and clinical psychology. In the sections that follow we will examine these linkages in more detail, focusing on the metatheoretical and epistemological interfaces between the two fields. First, we describe some of the divergent assumptions that structure theorists' analysis of psychological processes and consider how these divergences both hinder and facilitate metatheoretical integration. We then address several epistemological controversies that create divisions between social psychologists and clinical psychologists. The controversies pertain primarily to the nature and conduct of scientific inquiry, the nature of theories and models, and the relationship between empirical evidence and theory in science. We also consider theoretical and practical linkages between the fields, but only briefly because the authors of other chapters in this volume examine these two interface levels in detail. In addition, Smith and Rhodewalt (Chapter 37) discuss methodological linkages and Hendrick and Hendrick (Chapter 39) address the educational/training linkages between social and clinical psychology.

THE METATHEORETICAL INTERFACE

Scientists, whether physicists, psychologists, or chemists, embrace assumptions about their subject matter that are not explicitly acknowledged within the defined domain of their theoretical systems. Scientists, if stripped of their metatheoretical assumptions and reduced to raw empiricists, would be overwhelmed by the countless alternative and correct interpretations of reality. These metatheoretical assumptions are essential because they provide us with an orientation to our subject matter, they identify which questions are worth asking and which ones are not, and they shape the way we see and speak about the world.

Coan (1968), Rosenberg and Gara (1983), and Watson (1967) present a sampling of the divergent metatheoretical assumptions that have characterized various approaches in psychology since the

Table 38.1. A Six-Level Model of a Comprehensive Interface Between Social Psychology and Clinical Psychology

LEVEL OF INTERFACE	EXAMPLE ISSUES
Educational	What educational experiences should be included in the training of therapists? Should the training of academic social psychologists include work in clinical settings? What areas define basic studies in psychology?
Practical	How can the utility of group psychotherapies be increased? Why do paradoxical therapies work? How can we prevent premature termination of treatment? How does the client-therapist match influence treatment outcome?
Methodological	How can the results of multiple independent studies be combined statistically? How can the placebic effects of a treatment be distinguished from the treatment-specific effects? How can the key the qualties of one's social support network be assessed?
Theoretical	What interpersonal and intrapersonal factors work to promote adjustment and what factors contribute to dysfunction? How do individuals cope with stressful environmental events? What factors are involved with recovery from psychological and physical illness?
Metatheoretical	What is the essential nature of the human being? Is behavior caused by exogenous or endogenous factors? Are humans governed more by rationality or irrationality? Is the human species unique?
Epistemological	How should human thought, feeling, and emotion be studied? What is the relationship between conceptual understanding and empirical findings? Is psychology a science, in the same sense that physics is a science? Do laws of human behavior exist?

field's inception. Psychologists have debated such metatheoretical issues as

- Should we be concerned with unconscious processes, or focus only on observable behavior?
- Is behavior caused by forces present in the immediate external environment, or historical factors whose force is still felt in the distant future?
- Can psychological processes be broken down into specific elements, or should we take a holistic approach that avoids analysis?

Our answers to these questions summarize our beliefs about the prime causes of behavior and the nature of human beings.

Watson (1967) has noted that these bipolar themes, which he called "prescriptions," serve to orient researchers and theorists when they conceptualize problems within psychology. His analysis, extended to the social-clinical interface, suggests that if social and clinical psychologists share metatheoretical assumptions then they would also be united in their theoretical and methodological orientations. If, however, the two fields embrace disparate metatheories, then disunity is to be expected. Here we compare and contrast three assumptions that, although rarely explicitly stated, constitute basic differences between much of contemporary social and clinical psychology.

Sociogenicism-Psychogenicism

In a tradition dating back to the field's founding, social psychologists focus first on exogenous causes of behavior before turning their attention to endogenous causes (Snyder & Forsyth, Chapter 1). Asked why an individual self-aggrandizes, acts altruistically, or engages in aberrant actions, the social psychologist's first inclination is to examine the social forces in the situation. Intrapersonal processes are not ignored, but they are typically viewed as dependent variables or as mediators of external causes. Social psychological models tend to stress environmental determinism over biological determinism, situationism over personologism, and sociogenicism over psychogenicism.

An equally long tradition, which has roots in Freud's psychodynamic theory, prompts many clinicians to focus on the internal, psychogenic determinants of behavior. With behaviorists providing a notable exception, the theorists who provided the foundations for much contemporary clinical conceptualization and intervention offered models that included reference to the structure of personality, dynamic intrapsychic mechanisms, and the relationships between the individual's particular qualities and his or her behavior. Adler, Freud, Jung, Horney, Maslow, Murray, and others were generalists, but at the core their theories assumed that personality, needs, motivations and other psychogenic mechanisms play a pivotal role in adjustment and dysfunction. The psychogenic orientation was summarized by Urban (1983, p. 163), who argued strongly that when psychologists look for causes outside of the individual they "deny and distort the essential quality of human existence. Everything of significance with regard to this entire process occurs within the inner or subjective experience of the individual." Psychogenicism is also compatible with general endogenism, in which behaviors are attributed to a host of internal processes such as genetic factors, past events, and biological processes.

These divergent meta-assumptions regarding sociogenicism and psychogenicism influence social psychologists' and clinical practitioners' analyses of human behavior at a variety of levels. Whereas psychodynamic concepts have trouble taking hold in social psychology (Hall & Lindzey, 1969), they are the cornerstone of much current thinking in clinical psychology (Blatt & Lerner, 1983; Robbins, 1989). Aside from the content of psychoanalytic theory per se, its psychogenic emphasis is inconsistent with most social psychologists' metatheoretical bent toward sociogenicism.

Much of clinical psychology also stresses the causal importance of the individual's past and future, suggesting that previous experiences determine current level of adjustment in tandem with striving for future outcomes. Because these factors must be represented within the individual, social psychology tends to ignore them, choosing instead to focus on contemporaneous causes present in the immediate setting. The result: Social psychologists view the person in mechanistic, static, nontelic ways, whereas clinical psychologists highlight motivational, goal-seeking, and dynamic processes in their analyses.

These metatheoretical differences lead social and clinical psychology to take quite different tacks when addressing the same processes. In the study of attraction, for example, social psychologists spent decades examining the impact of situationally specific factors—similarity in expressed attitudes, propinquity, approval, and so on—on liking. When clinical psychologists began to study the nature of the therapeutic relationship—a topic that also involves interpersonal attraction—they focused not on contextual factors, but on the match between the unique personal characteristics of the two individuals involved (Beutler, Clarkin, Crago, & Bergen, Chapter 35).

A similar difference unfolded as social and clinical psychologists explored attributional processes. Social psychologists, stimulated by Heider's (1958) provocative theoretical notions, erected sophisticated theoretical models about how people identify causes of their and others' actions. These models specified the dimensionality of attribution thought and the basic processes involved in causal thinking, but theories assumed everyone made attributions and that these attributions were affected by certain aspects of the situation. Clinical psychologists, in contrast, were drawn to the study of attributions by perplexing experimental findings pertaining to the effects of uncontrollable circumstances on motivation and by conflicting symptoms reported by depressed individuals. Clinical models also were based on Heider's work, but in this case the focus was on individual differences in attributional tendencies. The core idea was that certain styles of attribution are healthy, whereas others are maladaptive (Peterson, 1985).

Although experimental social psychologists have long been interested in personal factors such as attitudes and values, historically the field has been ambivalent about the importance of personality variables. This stance, however, is changing. Many social psychologists are now interested in how individual differences moderate people's reactions to various situations. Much of this work is occurring in the context of studying interactionistic models that strive to understand how dispositional and situational factors combine to influence behavior.

Indeed, much current work that is regarded as social-clinical in focus, even that conducted by scholars who identify themselves as social psychologists, involves not extrapolations of experimental social psychology, but rather the study of personality variables in the development and treatment of dysfunctional behavior. Recent clinically relevant research on topics such as attributional styles, self-esteem maintenance, social anxiety, loneliness, stress, sex roles, and the like involves an emphasis on individual differences and personality processes.

Put differently, the growth of the social-clinical interface has been stimulated by growth of the social-personality interface. Blass (1984), for example, noted that the theoretical assumptions and methodological tools of social and personality psychology are being used by the other with increasing frequency (see also Baron & Boudreau,

1987; Ryff, 1987). In many cases researchers have reached beyond the individual difference definition or situational definition of a variable to define the construct in terms that apply at both levels. Self-attention, for example, has been studied by examining the reactions of individuals who vary in dispositional self-consciousness and by manipulating subjects' level of self-awareness in the research setting. Blass also notes that social psychologists have extended their long-standing interest in the relationship between attitudes and behaviors to a more general interest in the relationship between personal factors (personality, traits, attitudes, attributions) and action.

This growing recognition of the interaction of social and personality factors by social psychologists complements the movement toward interactionism in clinical psychology that dates back to the 1970s. In response to Mischel's (1968) challenges, clinical theorists continue to shift from a pure trait view of personality toward an interactional perspective (Magnusson & Endler, 1977; Snyder & Ickes, 1985). Interpersonal theory, too, offers an alternative to traditional psychogenicism. This approach, as summarized by Anchin and Kiesler's (1982) *Handbook of Interpersonal Psychotherapy*, affirms Sullivan's (1950, p. 92) claim that "the general science of psychiatry seems to me to cover much the same field as that which is studied by social psychology, because scientific psychiatry has to be defined as the study of interpersonal relations" (Kiesler, Chapter 22; Strong, Chapter 27). Sullivan's ideas concerning the interpersonal bases of both abnormal and normal behavior are being extended actively by researchers, who are finding that maladaptive behaviors can be both defined and treated interpersonally. Still, given the intrapsychic bent of many clinicians, interpersonal theory is rarely put into practice. As Carson explained, "one of the more extraordinary characteristics of interpersonal theory is the extent to which it is ignored, particularly among writers who purport to survey the field of personality theory" (1983, pp. 148–149).

Despite movement toward an integration of sociogenicism and psychogenicism, some have questioned whether these perspectives are, in fact, reconcilable. For example, Berglas (1988) argued that these two paradigms are so different that the results that they yield are incommensurate with one another, and Rychlak (1983) expressed doubts about the reconciliation of these views. Furthermore, some have condemned social psychologists'

interest in intrapersonal variables altogether (e.g., Carlson, 1984).

In sum, despite the traditional inward and outward focus of clinical and social psychology, recent developments suggest a gradual weakening of this posture and growing openness to the alternative view. The acceptance of social causes as primary is fundamental in social psychology, but single-minded sociogenicism constrains the study of behavior, whether normal or abnormal. Similarly, clinical psychology's psychogenicism forces theorists, researchers, and clinicians to rely too heavily on traditional personality theories, traits, and dispositional variables. The limitations of such myopia were vividly lamented by Sarason (1981):

> Built into psychology, part of its world view, is the polarity man *and* society. Call it a polarity or a dichotomy or even a distinction, it makes it easy for psychology to focus on one and ignore the other, to avoid dealing with the possibility that the distinction is arbitrary and misleading, that it does violence to the fact that from the moment of birth the individual organism is a social organism, that social means embeddedness in patterned relationships that are but a part of an array of such relationships rooted, among other things, in a social history and a distinctive physical environment. (p. 175)

Humanism-Egoism

The story is well known in psychology circles. Dismayed by the narrow views of human beings proffered by Freudians and behaviorists, a clique of influential theorists including Maslow (1971), Rogers (1942), and Fromm (1955) called for a more humanistic orientation. Their arguments went unheeded within much of academic psychology, but in time many psychologists engaged in clinical practice came to embrace many of the assumptions of humanistic psychology: our ability to rise above limiting situational constraints; to make sense of ourselves and our social world; to imagine alternative futures and undertake steps to increase the likelihood that the ones we favor will occur; and to identify what gives our lives meaning. Urban (1983) summarized this humanistic view when he wrote

> Humans have the capacity to transcend the immediacy of the present and to envision alternate states and possibilities; this provides the opportunity for one to invest meaning into one's existence, specifically to formulate intention, sense, purpose, and significance into the pursuit of

one's life. To be authentically human is to become increasingly open to experience, to accept the inherent freedom associated with one's fate, to assume fully the responsibility for developing and constantly refashioning one's identity, one's personal commitments, and one's life. (p. 163)

Few would argue that social psychology is a humanistic discipline. Although not radically behavioristic, most social psychologists assume that the minimax principle dictates most of our actions. Our choices, our relationships, and even our apparently altruistic actions can be traced to our desire to maximize our positive outcomes while minimizing our costs. Although the cognitive movement in social psychology led researchers to pay attention to the ways in which people make sense of the world and themselves, the person is still viewed as a relatively passive information-processor who takes shortcuts. Also, even though social psychologists acknowledge the existential strivings of human beings, most assume that these strivings are muted by our unremitting egoism. The individual views the world from his or her own perspective, and the biases inherent in this limited viewpoint are never wholly escaped.

This assumption, although occasionally challenged, suggests that the self is a primary psychological mechanism. However, the social psychological notion of the self bears little resemblence to the self described by humantistic psychologists. Most social psychologists view the drive for self-promotion as stronger than the drive for other-promotion. Human beings are so fundamentally egocentric that social psychologists are skeptical about the inherent goodness of individuals, to the point that moral behaviors such as altruism are viewed as impossible (cf. Campbell & Specht, 1985; Kelley & Thibaut, 1985; Wispe, 1985). In brief, social psychologists tend to share the metatheoretical assumption that people are, on the whole, egoistic and self-serving.

Social psychology's reverence for studies that demonstrate the powerful impact of external factors on the individual illustrate the antihumanistic flavor of the field. Asch's (1955) studies of conformity, Milgram's (1974) classic studies of obedience, the countless studies of people competing in the Prisoners' Dilemma, and Latané and Darley's (1970) analysis of bystander apathy all affirm the image of the human being as easily swayed by situation concerns, willing to violate personal values, and hungry for self-enhancement. Studies of attitude change following counterattitudinal be-

havior, for example, indicate that most individuals, with very little situational pressure, willingly misrepresent their actual attitudes and beliefs to others. Although the causes and consequences of this counterattitudinal advocacy are still debated, a self-presentational explanation suggests that individuals lie in such settings so that they can project an image of rationality and consistency. They realize that what they are saying is not true, but they state certain attitudes to present a socially acceptable impression to the experimenter and others (Schlenker, Forsyth, Leary, & Miller, 1980). Thus, even instances of apparent consistency and rationality may be a facade.

Despite social psychology's long disdain for things humanistic, recently researchers have begun exploring the waters beyond this metatheoretical assumption. Self theorists, for example, are beginning to recognize that the self system does more than simply maintain and promote oneself (Epstein, 1985; Hales, 1985). Perhaps the most boundary-stretching of these new views is Solomon, Greenberg, and Pyszczynski's (Chapter 2) terror-management theory, which argues that the self-serving attributional bias that so thrilled social psychologists who were interested in egocentric biases is caused by the existential terror we experience when we come face to face with the realization that death is inescapable.

Studies of helping behavior provide yet another example of changes in social psychologists' view of the human being. For years this topic has been dominated by models that argue that people help others only to maximize their own personal outcomes. Recently, however, researchers in social psychology have begun to search for nonegoistic, other-serving helping. Batson, for example, offered evidence of two different classes of helping—egoistic helping that results in positive feelings for the helper and empathic helping that is motivated by an altruistic desire to reduce the distress of the person in need. Although questions remain, preliminary findings suggest that unlike the egoistic helper, the empathic, altruistic helper is truly other-serving (Batson & Coke, 1981; Batson, Duncan, Ackerman, Buckley, & Birch, 1981).

These advances argue in favor of an expanded model of human beings that reconciles their egoistic and humanistic capabilities. A social psychology based completely on egoism and selfishness as primary social motives is a restricted social psychology (Vitz, 1977, 1985; Wallach & Wallach, 1983). Social psychology strives to provide a cross-cultural view of human behavior, but clearly not all cultures prize selfishness as much as the Western world. As Hogan and Sloan (1985) asked, is it just coincidence that a social psychology rooted in a culture that praises independence and self-seeking strivings implicitly assumes that individuals are egoistically motivated? Similarly, a purely humanistic psychology has difficulties coping with nonconscious motivations, with irrational, aggressive behavior, and with the tremendous impact of society on the human individual. These flaws, however, are not fundamental ones. Therefore, rather than rejecting either view and replacing it with another, an integrative approach argues for a synthesis that retains the strengths of each while avoiding the weaknesses of each.

Rationality-Nonrationality

Social psychological theorizing, in many regards, highlights humans' rationality. People are viewed as processors of information who constantly seek data about themselves and others, then base their behavior on the available information. Of course, the available information is sometimes inaccurate and/or distorted (often by the egoistic biases discussed above). Even so, people are viewed as conscious thinkers who, despite their episodes of irrationality, do their best to process information. Social psychologists admit that reinforcements play a major role in shaping behavior and that nonconsciousness processes may influence thought and feeling, but the social psychologist adds that cognitive processes, including goal-seeking and information-processing systems, also must be considered. In brief, the social psychologist tends to emphasize conscious thought.

Clinical psychology, in contrast, considers the less rational side of human existence. The clinician deals with individuals whose cognitive, motivation, and emotional rigidities are overriding their ability to adapt to situational influences. Whereas the rational person processes information and responds accordingly, the abnormal individual reacts automatically, inappropriately, and consistently across settings. Their actions, too, are caused by nonconscious factors that are only glimpsed by the individual, if not outside of conscious awareness entirely. Viewed from this perspective, behavior and emotion are seen to be products of nonconscious motives that spring from unseen intrapsychic wells. In many models, the individual cannot be rational even under the

best of circumstances because most of the forces that guide behavior remain largely hidden. In brief, clinical models tend to regard conscious thought as relatively unimportant.

Even when thoughts are in awareness, most classic theories of dysfunction stress the role of irrational thought in behavioral and emotional problems, if not in the human condition. Psychoanalytic approaches, for example, focus on identifying and correcting outdated and unrealistic views of oneself and others. Cognitive-behavioral approaches often stress the effects of maladaptive cognitions on dysfunctional behavior and emotion. Approaches based on rational-emotive therapy are perhaps prototypical in this respect because they try to demonstrate the irrational and self-defeating nature of the client's belief system.

Of course, the human being portrayed by both the social psychological and clinical psychological perspectives is but a caricature. People are, at times, both rational and irrational, and their behavior is controlled by factors of which they both are and are not aware. Thus, again, we see that a metatheoretical integration of social and clinical psychology provides a broader, more realistic view of human behavior than does either alone.

Metatheory at the Interface

We have examined three issues that sit squarely in the center of the methatheoretical interface of social and clinical psychology. On all three, traditional social and clinical psychology divaricate, with social psychology stressing external causes, the egoism of human beings, and our rationality, and clinical psychology stressing internal causes, humanism, and nonrational processes, including emotions and unconscious motivations.

Fortunately, these orienting prescriptions are not necessarily the binding (or biasing) world-defining postulates of a Kuhnian paradigm. If accepted as paradigmatic givens, then the psychologist could not escape their constraints to view behavior from a different perspective. The humanist could not step back and look at human actions as motivated by biological urges that are common in many species. The behaviorist could not admit that, in some cases, individuals are motivated by existential strivings and personally salient goals. The ecological psychologists could not recognize that different individuals react uniquely to the same behavior setting. Rather, these assumptions provide the underlying defining structure of theory of psychology and ensure a constant dialectical interplay among opposing theoretical camps. These differences between social and clinical psychology reach down to the theoretical core of these disciplines, and to their interface as well. The social-clinical interface offers theorists the means of achieving greater understanding of human behavior through the synthesis of two disciplines that embrace opposing goals, methods, and philosophies.

THE EPISTEMOLOGICAL INTERFACE

For centuries psychology was an integral part of philosophy. When questions about the nature of the mind, the relationship between mental events and physiological processes, and the innate propensities of the human being arose, they were settled through philosophical discussion. This tradition changed radically, however, when psychology broke from philosophy to strike out as a science. Rather than generating knowledge only through insight and discourse, these new psychologists advocated supplementing conceptualization with observation and analysis of objective evidence. Rather than rely on debate to settle disagreements, psychologists turned to data as the final arbiter. And rather than rely on folk wisdom and common sense when explaining the nature of thought, feeling, and action, psychologists spun their own theories and tested these theories empirically.

As social and clinical psychology emerged as subfields within psychology, both of these subfields adopted—at least implicitly—these overarching epistemological assumptions of the psychologist qua scientist (Forsyth & Strong, 1986). Their unique interests and objectives, however, took them in somewhat different directions. Researchers (both social and clinical psychologists alike) sought to identify general tendencies in human behavior and to construct logically coherent models that would account for these tendencies. Practicing clinicians, in contrast, confronted a veritable sea of unique human beings seeking to overcome personal limitations and psychological dysfunction. Rather than searching for lawlike generalities, clinicians required heuristic guidelines that offered insights on a person-by-person basis.

The bifurcation of psychology into two opposing camps split on epistemological issues has been decried by many (Harcum, 1988; Kimble, 1984; Koch, 1981; O'Hara, 1986; Rogers, 1986; Staats, 1981), but Chein's (1966) distinction between scientistic and clinicalistic psychology captures the essence of the issues. Chein argued that small differences between research-oriented psychologists and applications-oriented psychologists became exaggerated over time, and eventually resulted in two different subcultures within psychology: scientism and clinicalism.

Scientism, which is the doctrine of many social psychologists (and academic clinical psychologists as well), advocates the strict application of the hypothetico-deductive method of science, including theory construction, experimentation, quantitative methods, prediction, and the use of appropriate terminology. Wrote Chein:

> The most extreme expressions of scientism involve doctrinaire views on the nature of science and on proper rules of scientific conduct and expression. . . . The scientismist is given to *respectable* language, respectability being far more important in practice than the rationalizing value of precision. Scientism [also] tends to seize upon a particular set of primitive terms and propositions (typically, but not necessarily, drawn from physics, chemistry, or physiology) and to assume it to be optimal and sufficient. The particular set may vary from one scientismist to another, but both operate in terms of such sets, tolerate one another's sets, and dismiss anything not included in or deducible from the union of sets selected by themselves and fellow scientismists as unreal or inconsequential. (pp. 337–338)

Chein (p. 341) suggested that the basic theme of scientism is summarized by the question, "How can knowledge grow if we do not get started on knowing at least something definitively?"

Clinicalism, in contrast, is the doctrine of many, but by no means all that of practicing clinicians. According to Chein (1966, p. 338) this "approach to knowledge" rejects scientism, and replaces it with personal comprehension. From Chein:

> The clinicalist tends to be suspicious of any fixed scheme of classification, preferring to pick the concepts that best fit the case, and hence to select from a nonsystematic array of concepts. . . . He may espouse a particular theory, but only as a helpful guide to observation. . . . Controlled observation is, for him, constituted of intensive and extensive probing and feedback from test interventions. . . . Although he may express some generalization, he does not intend it be taken literally and is apt to feel badgered when one persists in trying to hold him to it. . . . The clinicalist does not seek to discover, formulate, or

prove any general laws. . . . He assumes that determinants—inner and outer—are in continual flux, in ever changing configurations of varying subsets, and doubts the discoverability of laws. . . . Evidence of the predictability of behavior in controlled laboratory conditions evokes a suspicion that laboratory situations are so abnormal that no generalizations from them are warranted. (p. 338)

Chein (p. 341) suggested that the basic theme of clinicalism is summarized by the question, "How can knowledge grow if we keep blocking growth by prematurely freezing categories and the dimensions of inquiry into functional relationships, thereby losing contact with the primary data of all knowledge, the manifold particularities?" (p. 341).

The implications of Chein's analysis are powerful and far-reaching. If psychologists adopt such differing epistemologies, then how can the interface hope to bridge the gap between them? Keeping in mind that the diversity of opinion and outlook within each of these disciplines makes sweeping statements about these differences oversimplifications, several aspects of their epistemological outlooks are examined below.

Positivism

In the first half of this century, logical positivists were kept busy trying to describe how science worked. Mach (1897/1914), for example, argued that theories are summaries of empirically verifiable relationships among variables. Because it only summarizes the data, a good theory should not go beyond these data, he argued. If it does, it becomes metaphysical. The logical positivists also stressed the power of deduction as the most adequate means of achieving an understanding of the regularities underlying observed phenomena. For Popper (1959, p. 59), the "explanation of an event means to deduce a statement which describes it, using as premises of the deduction one or more universal laws, together with certain singular statements, the initial condition." In like fashion, Hempel and Oppenheim's (1948) deductive-nomological model argued for the axiomatization of theory by forming general lawlike statements, the specification of antecedent-limiting conditions, deriving hypotheses from theories, operationalizing definitions, and the potential disconfirmability of theoretical systems (Hempel, 1966).

The work of such philosophers as Kuhn (1970),

Feyerabend (1970), Achinstein (1968), and Hanson (1958) did much to temper the strict arguments offered by the logical positivists. Although their viewpoints varied, all agreed that no science—not physics, not chemistry, not psychology—works in the way described by logical positivists. Newton did not deduce his laws, Einstein did not rely solely on data to develop his theory of relativity, and the rejection of Bohr's theory of the atom depended more on logical argument than on empirical findings. Moreover, sciences come in many variations, and it is doubtful that any single philosophy describes the methods and foundations of the growth of scientific knowledge. As D'Andrade (1986) noted, sciences such as physics, chemistry, and astronomy deal with aspects of the universe that are relatively unchanging and strive to make generalizations that will hold across diverse times and places. Biologists, geologists, and some social scientists, in contrast, examine aspects of the world that are more transient and situationally specific. Biologists, for example, recognize that the organic processes they study occur here on the planet Earth, but might not occur in other environments. These disciplines do not conform to the dictates of Hempel's deductive-nomological model, yet they are still scientific.

Postpositivism

Many contemporary social and clinical psychologists recognize the limitations of logical positivism as a model of how science works, but they accept a modified version of positivism, often termed postpositivism. This view maintains that science, as an epistemological system, relies on methods that are different from alternative epistemologies. More than other approaches to gaining knowledge, science advocates the long-term goal of increasing and systematizing our knowledge about the subject matter. It requires relating observations back to theoretical constructs that provide the framework for interpreting data and generating predictions. In addition, science insists that the test of theory be based on objective, empirical methods rather than on logical claims, subjective feelings, or authorities' opinions. Science also involves a striving for consensus among members of the discipline concerning acceptable and unacceptable explanations of empirical observations. Psychological studies, if they are to be scientific, must remain within these boundaries. Hypotheses offered must be empirically testable, using methods that other scientists accept as adequate. Although values undoubtedly play a role in determining which topics are investigated and the researcher's bias for one interpretation over another, values should have no impact on the data collection procedures or statistical analyses.

Constructivism

Other theorists, however, believe that even post-positivism provides a limited view of how science works and argue in favor of an alternative philosophy of science. These various viewpoints include sociorationalism (Gergen, 1978, 1984), hermeneutics (Alexander, 1988), dialectics (Rychlak, 1968), ethnomethodology (Garfinkel, 1967), ethogenics (Harre & Secord, 1972), realism (Manicas & Secord, 1983), and semiotics (D'Andrade, 1986). Although these alternatives differ from one another in a variety of ways, most argue that social scientists should stop trying to emulate an approach that is suited for the natural sciences. Rather, they suggest that social scientists must develop methods that take into full account the reflexive, interpretive, constructivistic nature of all human activity. Rather than assuming facts exist, that observation is a neutral process, that causality is linear, and that individual action can be examined in mechanistic terms, these viewpoints champion the in-depth study of behavior as it occurs in ongoing settings using ethnography and detailed interviewing, the intimate involvement of the researcher in the data collection processes, and close scrutiny of the participants' construction of the situation.

Constructivistic philosophies of science do not dominate clinical theory or clinical practice, but these approaches are quite consistent with the idiographic and phenomenological-humanistic traditions that imbue much of clinical psychology. Gordon Allport's distinction between idiographic and nomothetic approaches to psychological issues is still relevant, still debated, and still unresolved (Brooks & Johnson, 1978; Dukes, 1965; Holt, 1962; Marceil, 1977). Allport (1937), in a prophetic statement, argued

> Psychology in the main has been striving to make of itself a completely nomothetic discipline. The idiographic sciences, such as history, biography, and literature, on the other hand, endeavor to understand some particular event in nature or in society. A psychology of individuality would be essentially idiographic. (p. 22)

Humanistic psychologists also reject the mechanistic, biological models of human behavior in favor of a view that highlights our sense-making capabilities (Frankl, 1962). Phenomenologists, including Rogers (1942) and Snygg and Coombs (1949), argued that behavior cannot be understood until we discover the meaning that the individual attaches to it. Existentialists, when they emphasize awareness, human choice and freedom, and the fragility and plasticity of the human experience, are espousing a view that is well suited to a constructivistic epistemology.

Constructivism also minimizes the gulf between the clinical researcher and the clinical practitioner. As Higgenbotham, West, and Forsyth (1988) noted, clinical practice requires tremendous amounts of interpretive activity. Clinicians must employ an interpretive corpus drawn from some socially sanctioned system of reality (e.g., psychodynamic theory, cognitive-behavioral theory, or whatever), then construct their client's condition and their subjective interpretation of the problem. Through interpretive work the clinician identifies (or, in the language of constructivism, "makes") behavioral and psychological particulars, abstracts the complex totality of the distressed client, interprets the abstracted data, and constructs a clinical reality that then becomes the object of a therapeutic endeavor. Often, too, the clinician must translate across two systems of meaning — the view of clinical psychology and the view of the client (e.g., Good & Good, 1982; Kleinman, 1986; Labov & Fanshel, 1977). Although a positivist would argue that the practitioner is being non-scientific when engaged in such a highly interpretative process, the constructivist would argue that the reality-building, data-making work of the clinician is no different from the theory-building, data-collection work of the researcher.

The Dialectical Epistemology of the Interface

Most psychologists embrace the dictates of a positivistic philosophy of science that argues scientists must generate lawlike statements that can be tested via research. Some, however, advocate constructivism, for they feel that if one is to understand an individual, then theory and research must be ideographic rather than nomothetic. The positivist argues that data are not particularly meaningful unless embedded in a theoretical context, whereas the constructivistic prefers to use theories as heuristic guides rather than as constraining frameworks. Given that positivists and constructivists seek the growth of knowledge via different, and immediately incompatible, routes, which route will be chosen by researchers seeking to link social and clinical psychology?

If history and tradition provide an indication, then positivism will probably hold sway over constructivism, at least in academic circles (O'Hara, 1986; Kimble, 1984). If, however, researchers remain both rational and flexible, then a choice may not be necessary. Although the logical positivists argued for a view of science founded an unidirectional causality, explanation of the whole through analysis of the component parts, and an accretive research process that more and more accurately describes the world, progress in science often results from a dialectical process involving thesis, antithesis, and synthesis (Rychlak, 1968, 1977). Rather than staunchly defending a viewpoint against attack, the dialectician searches for the means to reconcile multiple, yet inconsistent, interpretations of reality. Such an approach requires taking the best from positivism and the best from constructivism and synthesizing them in a dialectical philosophy of science.

Chein (1966) herself favors this synthesis as the solution to the schism between scientism and clinicalism. She wrote:

> Let there be free competition of ideas, of methodologies, and even of doctrinaire views. But let us also beware of permitting, if only by default, extremists to curtail the competition or to build walls that block channels of free communication. . . . Let us also recognize the need to expose our students to both subcultures and to meaningful approach to integrating them. Our students are the ones who will be carrying psychology forward, and we can do them no greater service than to expand their epistemological horizons.

CONCLUSIONS AND IMPLICATIONS

Is an interface between social and clinical psychology possible? The history of psychology gives cause for optimism, for the idea of achieving greater understanding of human behavior by linking two subfields of psychology is not a new one. In the late 1940s several regional and national conferences were held to discuss the then radical idea of integrating clinical psychology and personality psychology. At the end of World War II the role of the clinical psychologist expanded to include

treatment, but these treatments often lacked a theoretical foundation. As Snyder (1949) complained,

> I believe that it is time for us to face reality, and to admit that in the field of psychotherapy there is very little basic theoretical underlying structure that is at all convincing. Many clinical psychologists, as a matter of fact, seem not to recognize the need of an integrated theory of behavior. . . . (p. 22)

To deal with this problem, both therapists and researchers recommended the integration of personality theory with clinical work. Rosenzweig, who presided at two of the conferences (1949, p. 5), called for an integration of academic psychology and clinical psychology:

> To solve the implied problem it would seem that the clinical worker has need to recognize the theoretical implications of his tools and his concepts; the academic psychologist may reasonably be expected to reorient some of his efforts toward the study of the total individual. . . . By fostering all possible relationships between personality, including social and abnormal psychology, and the·clinical study of the individual, the objective could be realistically implemented. (p. 6)

Discussants varied, however, in their optimism concerning such integration, and in their remarks they identified a number of problems that would have to be surmounted before such a united effort would be successful. First, many wondered about the tremendous gap between the academic personality psychologist's view of the person and the view adopted by most clinicians. Championing an idiographic approach, Rosenzweig (1949, p. 5) doubted that "one can deduce from general laws of segmental behavior the structure and function of individuals. If one is to learn about individuals it seems probable that one will need to begin with them, in all their intricacies, as the units of observation and conceptualizations." Because academicians preferred a nomothetic approach to personality, the clinicians doubted that much could be achieved through an integration.

Second, Rosenzweig questioned the content of personality theory itself when he argued that clinical psychology cannot be applied psychology, because no "basic" science foundation exists: "Since historically there is no clear relationship of dependence between academic psychology and the practical work of the clinician, considerable doubt exists as to just what is being applied" (p. 5). Angyal (1941) made the same point when he said that psychiatry is the application of a basic science that does not exist.

Third, the discussants wondered how the theories themselves would translate in clinical practice. As Rosenzweig noted,

> . . . theories of the academic psychologist and the practices of the clinical psychologist have for the most part developed independent of one another. On occasion, to be sure, the one field has fertilized the other and there has been a fruitful consummation. . . . Many such instances, however, would be difficult to find. (p. 4)

Fifty years later these doubts sound familiar, but they are the doubts we express about the unity of clinical and social psychology. The problems that Rosenzweig and the other discussants identified were gradually overcome, and the interface of personality theory and clinical practice has largely been achieved. Likewise, the problems that confront social-clinical integrationists are sizable, but not insurmountable.

REFERENCES

Achinstein, P. (1968). *Concepts of science*. Baltimore, MD: Johns Hopkins Press.

Alexander, J. C. (1988). The new theoretical movement. In N. J. Smelzer (Ed.), *Handbook of sociology* (pp. 77–101). Newbury Park, CA: Sage Publications.

Allport, G. W. (1937). *Personality: A psychological interpretation*. New York: Holt.

Allport, G. W. (1938). An editorial. *Journal of Abnormal and Social Psychology, 33*, 3–13.

Allport, G. W. (1949). Editorial notes. *Journal of Abnormal and Social Psychology, 44*, 439–442.

Anchin, J. C., & Kiesler, D. J. (Eds.). (1982). *Handbook of interpersonal psychotherapy*. Elmsford, NY: Pergamon Press.

Angyal, A. (1941). *Foundations for a science of personality*. New York: Commonwealth Fund.

Asch, S. E. (1955). Opinions and social pressures. *Scientific American, 193*, 31–35.

Baron, R. M., & Boudreau, L. A. (1987). An ecological perspective on integrating personality and social psychology. *Journal of Personality and Social Psychology, 53*, 1222–1228.

Batson, C. D., & Coke, J. S. (1981). Empathy: A source of altruistic motivation for helping? In J. P. Rushton & R. M. Sorrentino (Eds.), *Altruism and behavior*. Hillsdale, NJ: Lawrence Erlbaum Associates.

Batson, C. D., Duncan, B. D., Ackerman, P., Buckley, T., & Birch, K. (1981). Is empathic emotion a source of altruistic motivation? *Journal of Personality and Social Psychology, 40*, 290–302.

Berglas, S. (1988). The three faces of self-handicapping: Protective self-presentation, a strategy for self-esteem enhancement, and a character disorder. In S. L. Zelen (Ed.), *Self-representation* (pp. 133–169). New York: Springer-Verlag.

Blass, T. (1984). Social psychology and personality: Toward a convergence. *Journal of Personality and Social Psychology, 47*, 1013–1027.

Blatt, S. J., & Lerner, H. (1983). Psychodynamic perspectives on personality theory. In M. Hersen, A. E. Kazdin, & A. S. Bellack (Eds.), *The clinical psychology handbook* (pp. 87–106). Elmsford, NY: Pergamon Press.

Brehm, S. S. (1976). *The application of social psychology to clinical practice*. Washington, DC: Hemisphere.

Brehm, S. S., & Smith, T. W. (1986). Social psychological approaches to psychotherapy and behavior change. In S. L. Garfield & A. E. Bergin (Eds.), *Handbook of psychotherapy and behavior change* (3rd ed.). New York: John Wiley & Sons.

Brooks, G. P., & Johnson, R. W. (1978). Floyd Allport and the master problem of social psychology. *Psychological Reports, 42*, 295–308.

Campbell, D. T., & Specht, J. C. (1985). Altruism: Biology, culture, and religion. *Journal of Social and Clinical Psychology, 3*, 33–42.

Carlson, R. (1984). What's social about social psychology? Where's the person in personality research? *Journal of Personality and Social Psychology, 47*, 1304–1309.

Carson, R. C. (1983). The social-interactional viewpoint. In M. Hersen, A. E. Kazdin, & A. S. Bellack (Eds.), *The clinical psychology handbook* (pp. 143–153). Elmsford, NY: Pergamon Press.

Chein, I. (1966). Some sources of divisiveness among psychologists. *American Psychologist, 21*, 333–342.

Coan, R. W. (1968). Dimensions of psychological theory. *American Psychologist, 23*, 715–722.

D'Andrade, R. (1986). Three scientific world views and the covering law model. In D. W.

Fiske & R. A. Shweder (Eds.), *Metatheory in social science: Pluralisms and subjectivities* (pp. 19–41). Chicago: University of Chicago Press.

Dorn, F. J. C. (1984). *Counseling as applied social psychology*. Springfield, IL: Thomas.

Dukes, W. F. (1965). N = 1. *Psychological Bulletin, 64*, 74–79.

Epstein, S. (1985). The implications of cognitive-experiential self-theory for research in social psychology and personality. *Journal for the Theory of Social Behaviour, 15*, 283–310.

Feyerabend, P. (1970). Problems of empiricism. In R. Colodny (Ed.), *Beyond the edge of certainty* (Vol. 2). Englewood Cliffs, NJ: Prentice-Hall.

Fiske, D. W. (1986). Specificity of method and knowledge in social science. In D. W. Fiske & R. A. Shweder (Eds.), *Metatheory in social science: Pluralisms and subjectivities* (pp. 61–82). Chicago: University of Chicago Press.

Forsyth, D. R., & Strong, S. R. (1986). The scientific study of counseling and psychotherapy: A unificationist view. *American Psychologist, 41*, 113–119.

Frankl, V. E. (1962). *Man's search for meaning*. New York: World Publishing.

Fromm, E. (1955). *The sane society*. New York: Rinehart.

Garfield, S. L. (1979). Editorial. *Journal of Consulting and Clinical Psychology, 47*, 104.

Garfinkel, H. (1967). *Studies in ethnomethodology*. Englewood Cliffs, NJ: Prentice-Hall.

Gazda, G. M., & Pistole, M. C. (1987). Interface: Thoughts from counseling psychology. *Journal of Social and Clinical Psychology, 5*, 176–184.

Gergen, K. J. (1978). Toward generative theory. *Journal of Personality and Social Psychology, 36*, 1344–1360.

Gergen, K. J. (1984). An introduction to historical social psychology. In K. J. Gergen (Ed.), *Historical social psychology* (pp. 3–36). Hillsdale, NJ: Lawrence Erlbaum Associates.

Goldstein, A. P., Heller, K., & Sechrest, L. B. (1966). *Psychotherapy and the psychology of behavior change*. New York: John Wiley & Sons.

Good, B., & Good, M. J. (1982). Toward a meaning-centered analysis of popular illness categories: "Fright illness" and "heart distress" in Iran. In A. J. Marsella & G. White (Eds.), *Cultural conceptions of mental health and therapy*. Boston: D. Reidel.

Hales, S. (1985). The inadvertent rediscovery of self in social psychology. *Journal for the Theory of Social Behaviour, 15*, 237–282.

Hall, C. S., & Lindzey, G. (1969). The relevance of Freudian psychology and related viewpoints for the social sciences. In G. Lindzey & E. Aronson (Eds.), *The handbook of social psychology* (Vol. 1, 2nd ed., pp. 245–319). Reading, MA: Addison-Wesley.

Hanson, N. R. (1958). *Patterns of discovery*. Cambridge, MA: Cambridge University Press.

Harari, H. (1983). Social psychology of clinical practice and in clinical practice. *Journal of Social and Clinical Psychology, 1*, 173–184.

Harcum, E. R. (1988). Defensive reactance of psychologists to a metaphysical foundation for integrating different psychologies. *Journal of Psychology, 122*, 217–235.

Harre, R., & Secord, P. F. (1972). *The explanation of social behavior*. Oxford: Blackwell.

Harvey, J. H., Bratt, A., & Lennox, R. D. (1987). The maturing interface of social-clinical-counseling psychology. *Journal of Social and Clinical Psychology, 5*, 8–20.

Heider, F. (1958). *The psychology of interpersonal relation*. New York: John Wiley & Sons.

Hempel, C. G. (1966). *Philosophy of natural science*. Englewood Cliffs, NJ: Prentice-Hall.

Hempel, C. G., & Oppenheim, P. (1948). Studies in the logic of explanation. *Philosophy of Science, 15*, 134–175.

Hendrick, C. (1983). Clinical social psychology: A birthright reclaimed. *Journal of Social and Clinical Psychology, 1*, 66–78.

Hendrick, S. (1983). Ecumenical (social and clinical and x, y, z . . .) psychology. *Journal of Social and Clinical Psychology, 1*, 79–87.

Higgenbotham, H. N., West, S. G., & Forsyth, D. R. (1988). *Psychotherapy and behavior change: Social, cultural, and methodological perspectives*. Elmsford, NY: Pergamon Press.

Hogan, R., & Sloan, T. (1985). Egoism, altruism, and psychological ideology. *Journal of Social and Clinical Psychology, 3*, 15–19.

Holt, R. (1962). Individuality and generalization in the psychology of personality. *Journal of Personality, 30*, 377–404.

Kelley, H. H., & Thibaut, J. W. (1985). Self-interest, science, and cynicism. *Journal of Social and Clinical Psychology, 3*, 26–32.

Kimble, G. A. (1984). Psychology's two cultures. *American Psychologist, 39*, 833–839.

Kleinman, A. (1986). Some uses and misuses of

the social sciences in medicine. In D. W. Fiske & R. A. Shweder (Eds.), *Metatheory in social science: Pluralisms and subjectivities* (pp. 222–245). Chicago: University of Chicago Press.

Koch, S. (1981). The nature and limits of psychological knowledge: Lessons of a century qua "Science." *American Psychologist, 36,* 257–275.

Kuhn, T. S. (1970). *The structure of scientific revolutions* (2nd ed.). Chicago: University of Chicago Press.

Labov, W., & Fanshel, D. (1977). *Therapeutic discourse: Psychotherapy as conversation.* New York: Academic Press.

Latané, B., & Darley, J. M. (1970). *The unresponsive bystander: Why doesn't he help?* New York: Appleton-Century- Crofts.

Leary, M. R., & Maddux, J. E. (1987). Progress toward a viable interface between social and clinical-counseling psychology. *American Psychologist, 42,* 904–911.

Leary, M. R., & Miller, R. S. (1986). *Social psychology and dysfunctional behavior: Origins, diagnosis, and treatment.* New York: Springer-Verlag.

Mach, E. (1914). The analysis of sensation. La Salle: Open Court. (Original work published 1897).

Maddux, J. E., & Stoltenberg, C. D. (1983). Clinical social psychology and social clinical psychology: A proposal for peaceful coexistence. *Journal of Social and Clinical Psychology, 1,* 289–299.

Maddux, J. E., Stoltenberg, C. D., & Rosenwein, R. (1987). *Social processes in clinical and counseling psychology.* New York: Springer-Verlag.

Magnusson, D., & Endler, N. S. (Eds.). (1977). *Personality at the crossroads: Current issues in interactional psychology.* Hillsdale, NJ: Lawrence Erlbaum Associates.

Manicas, P. T., & Secord, P. F. (1983). Implications for psychology of the new philosophy of science. *American Psychologist, 38,* 399–413.

Marceil, J. C. (1977). Implicit dimensions of idiography and nomothesis. *American Psychologist, 32,* 1046–1055.

Maslow, A. H. (1971). *The farther reaches of human nature.* New York: Viking.

Meehl, P. E. (1986). What social scientists don't understand. In D. W. Fiske & R. A. Shweder (Eds.), *Metatheory in social science: Plural-*

isms and subjectivities (pp. 315–338). Chicago: University of Chicago Press.

Milgram, S. (1974). *Obedience to authority.* New York: Harper & Row.

Mischel, W. (1968). *Personality and assessment.* New York: John Wiley & Sons.

O'Hara, M. (1986). Comment of Carl Roger's "Toward a more human science of the person." *Journal of Humanistic Psychology, 25,* 25–30.

Peterson, C. (1985). Learned helplessness: Fundamental issues in theory and research. *Journal of Social and Clinical Psychology, 3,* 248–254.

Popper, K. R. (1959). *The logic of scientific discovery.* New York: Basic Books.

Robbins, S. B. (1989). Role of contemporary psychoanalysis in counseling psychology. *Journal of Counseling Psychology, 36,* 267–278.

Rogers, C. (1986). Toward a more human science of the person. *Journal of Humanistic Psychology, 25,* 7–24.

Rogers, C. R. (1942). *Counseling and psychotherapy.* Boston: Houghton Mifflin.

Rosenberg, S., & Gara, M. A. (1983). Contemporary perspectives and future directions of personality and social psychology. *Journal of Personality and Social Psychology, 45,* 57–73.

Rosenzweig, S. (1949). The systemetic intent of clinical psychology. *Journal of Abnormal and Social Psychology, 44,* 3–6.

Rychlak, J. F. (1968). *A philosophy of science for personality theory.* Boston: Houghton-Mifflin.

Rychlak, J. F. (1977). *The psychology of rigourous humanism.* New York: Wiley-Interscience.

Rychlak, J. F. (1983). Exclusivity in psychological specialization: A conceptual or practical problem? *Journal of Social and Clinical Psychology, 1,* 185–192.

Ryff, C. D. (1987). The place of personality and social structure research in social psychology. *Journal of Personality and Social Psychology, 53,* 1192–1202.

Sarason, S. B. (1981). An asocial psychology and a misdirected clinical psychology. *American Psychologist, 36,* 827–836.

Sarason, S. B. (1987). A house, a home, an interface. *Journal of Social and Clinical Psychology, 5,* 222–226.

Schlenker, B. R., Forsyth, D. R., Leary, M. R., & Miller, R. S. (1980). Self-presentational analysis of the effects of incentives on attitude change following counterattitudinal behavior.

Journal of Personality and Social Psychology, 39, 553–577.

Shakow, D. (1978). Clinical psychology seen some 50 years later. *American Psychologist, 33*, 148–158.

Sheras, P. L., & Worchel, S. (1979). *Clinical psychology: A social psychological approach.* New York: Van Nostrand.

Snyder, C. R., & Ford, C. E. (Eds.). (1987). *Coping with negative life events: Clinical and social psychological perspectives.* New York: Plenum Press.

Snyder, M., & Ickes, W. (1985). Personality and social behavior. In G. Lindzey & E. Aronson (Eds.), *Handbook of social psychology* (Vol. 2, 3rd ed., pp. 883–947). New York: Random House.

Snyder, W. U. (1949). Some contributions of psychotherapy to personality theory. *Journal of Abnormal and Personality Psychology, 44*, 22–28.

Snygg, D., & Coombs, A. W. (1949). *Individual behavior.* New York: Harper & Row.

Staats, A. W. (1981). Paradigmatic behaviorism: Unified theory construction methods, and Zeitgeist of separatism. *American Psychologist, 16*, 125–179.

Strickland, B. R., & Halgin, R. P. (1987). Perspectives on clinical, counseling, and social psychology. *Journal of Social and Clinical Psychology, 5*, 150–159.

Strong, S. R. (1968). Counseling: An interpersonal influence process. *Journal of Counseling Psychology, 15*, 215–224.

Strong, S. R. (1987). Social-psychological approach to counseling and psychotherapy: "A false hope?" *Journal of Social and Clinical Psychology, 5*, 185–194.

Sullivan, H. S. (1950). Tensions interpersonal and international: A psychiatrist's view. In H. Cantril (Ed.), *Tensions that cause war.* Urbana, IL: University of Illinois Press.

Urban, H. B. (1983). Phenomenological-humanistic approaches. In M. Hersen, A. E. Kazdin, & A. S. Bellack (Eds.), *The clinical psychology handbook* (pp. 155–175). Elmsford, NY: Pergamon Press.

Vitz, P. C. (1977). *Psychology as religion: The cult of self-worship.* Grand Rapids, MI: Eerdmans.

Vitz, P. C. (1985). The dilemma of narcissism. *Journal of Social and Clinical Psychology, 3*, 9–14.

Wallach, M. A., & Wallach, L. (1983). *Psychology's sanction for selfishness: The error of egoism in theory and therapy.* San Francisco: W. H. Freeman.

Watson, R. I. (1967). Psychology: A prescriptive science. *American Psychologist, 22*, 435–443.

Weary, G. (1987). Natural bridges: The interface of social and clinical psychology. *Journal of Social and Clinical Psychology, 5*, 160–167.

Weary, G., & Mirels, H. L. (Eds.). (1982). *Integrations of clinical and social psychology.* New York: Oxford University Press.

Winer, J. L. (1987). Counseling-clinical-social psychology: A counseling psychologist's comment. *Journal of Social and Clinical Psychology, 5*, 216–221.

Wispe, L. (1985). Selfishness, society, and sympathy: A kind of a review. *Journal of Social and Clinical Psychology, 3*, 20–25.

CHAPTER 39

EDUCATION AT THE INTERFACE

Susan S. Hendrick
Clyde Hendrick

Most of the chapters in this volume attend to the ever-growing content of health research and health service delivery in the interface between social and clinical psychology. The breadth and depth of this content are testimony to Harvey and Weary's (1979) vision, because they called for not just a rapprochement but an active, integrated collaboration of the social and clinical areas in psychology. The sweep of the topics—from self processes and individual differences, to interpersonal processes, to diagnosis and treatment—indicates just how much of psychology can be included within the health area of the interface.

It appears to us that if these multiple topics compose the "what" of health research and training at the interface, then several of the chapters in the current section comprise the "where"; for instance, where the current emphases will go in terms of methodological and theoretical issues, and where our future focus might be (e.g., prevention). The present chapter offers a modest "how" that must necessarily be added to any consideration of what or where—the "how" of training and education at the interface.

Most of the past attention to interface work has assumed the existence of social and clinical psychologists who could profit from more frequent and wide-ranging collaboration in research and practice. Although this volume attests to the validity of this basic assumption, the achievement of maximal productivity in interface efforts (with health representing only one such effort) will necessitate careful and purposive efforts in education of the coming generations of psychologists.

In dealing with the "what," "where," and "how" of the interface, it is important not to forget the "who." In our view, any individual who is involved in either research or practice with explicit attention paid to both clinical and social psychology may be considered as operating within the interface. Thus, traditional social psychologists who want to study social influence processes in therapy settings are operating within the interface. And traditionally trained clinicians who conceptualize therapy as "attitude change" are also operating within the interface. We will not argue in this chapter that working within the interface requires training in a specific type of education/training model. Rather, we observe that if we wish to foster increased growth of the interface area, we may make more rapid gains to the extent that our training is intentional.

Such education can follow different models, and several of these models are presented in this chapter. The first two sections emphasize the past decade's development of the interface area and the somewhat parallel development of health psychology and behavioral medicine. The third section focuses on the intersection of these two forces as we discuss health within the social and clinical interface. The fourth section reviews some education/training models already in place and also describes some of the factors promoting, and mitigating against, true interface education. We conclude with a proposal for how education at the interface may offer one prototype for future educative efforts in the multifaceted and currently fragmented discipline of psychology.

It is important to state at the outset that we do not propose that the interface between social and clinical psychology and health psychology are one and the same. Rather, we view health psychology as one forum in which the interface issues can be usefully examined. All interface issues are not health psychology issues, but many of the content and process issues (e.g., what would be included in training, who should provide the training) that have occurred in the health psychology arena are directly applicable to interface issues in other arenas (e.g., psychopathology, relationship research and therapy). Thus, whereas complete overlap between health and the interface is not implied, our thesis is that a very close relationship exists.

THE SOCIAL-CLINICAL INTERFACE

The social-clinical interface is a complex area. Any serious consideration of education and training of graduate students for interface activities requires some background understanding of what we mean by the interface, of the span of concerns encompassed by the interface, and of the issues involved in interface training activities. These topics will be considered in turn.

Basis of the Interface

Social and clinical psychology have always had a loose association with each other, although as the professional roles of the two disciplines have developed the activities shared have become in-

creasingly infrequent. During previous years, interface activity was discussed primarily in terms of whether the two disciplines could contribute jointly to the practice of psychotherapy. Weary (1987) argued that the focus on psychotherapy is shifting toward an increased concern with the role of social-psychological factors in the development and maintenance of dysfunctional behaviors. Thus, the area of mutual concern may be in a point of transition. Be that as it may, it is relatively clear that the initial focus was on psychotherapy, a central area of endeavor for clinical psychology.

One of us (C. Hendrick, 1983) made a strong polemical argument that social psychology should have the same right to practice psychotherapy as clinical psychology. This argument was based on the assumption that psychotherapy is first and foremost a species of human interaction. It is true that psychotherapy evolved to treat mental illness, which was conceived as a disease entity within the organism that must be exorcised. Medicine developed primarily as a discipline for the cure of disease. As psychiatry emerged it was natural to consider mental illness as a disease that should be treated and cured by medicine. But increasingly over the years, psychiatry and clinical psychology have come to view mental illness as a disturbance in interpersonal relations. We do not argue, of course, that it is only that, but simply that one primary construal of mental illness has come to be a notion of disturbed interpersonal interactions. C. Hendrick (1983) argued that any human interaction involves three generic classes of behavior: social cognition about the interaction, emotionality as a tenor and tone of the interaction, and a variety of interpersonal processes, including communication, persuasion, exchange, conformity, and so forth. These are the concepts that are the woof and warp of social psychology as a discipline. Further, they are the sorts of conceptions with which Strong (1978) has made such a compelling case over the years for the incorporation of social-psychological knowledge into a basic paradigm for effective psychotherapy. It was on this basis that C. Hendrick (1983) argued that a clinical social-psychology has a right to exist. He implied that social psychology should be the central discipline in psychotherapy because its concepts provide the underlying ideological structure on which current psychotherapy is practiced, notwithstanding the many problems of translating social psychological concepts into specific theories of psychotherapy.

This polemic in favor of social psychology inspired a response (S. S. Hendrick, 1983) that argued for an ecumenical social, counseling, and "x, y, z" psychology. The point was made that all the basic disciplines in psychology have a great deal to contribute to psychotherapy, as well as to other emerging areas, such as health psychology. The particular point that "social psychology should have the same right to practice psychotherapy as clinical psychology" is clearly a controversial one. Social psychology is the discipline that focuses on interpersonal processes, but it concentrates primarily on basic research rather than application. If someone trained in social psychology relied on this view to treat people with psychological problems, would not that person be engaged in clinical psychology? Not unless one assumes that only clinical psychologists can deal with psychological problems. However, this issue raises controversial questions about whether extensive therapy training, as well as professional licensing, are necessary for the therapeutic enterprise. Although these authors are less troubled than many about the concept of social psychologists engaging in psychotherapeutic practice, our purpose in this chapter is not to define "who can do what," and thus perhaps narrow the interface, but rather to paint the interface with as broad a brush stroke as possible.

Broadening the Interface

During the past few years, the concept of an interface has been generalized to include counseling as well as clinical and social psychology. A special issue of the *Journal of Social and Clinical Psychology* (C. Hendrick, 1987) dealt with a wide variety of issues involved in this triadic interface, including training issues. Because of its focus on healthy functioning in everyday environments, counseling psychology was recognized as having a substantial contribution to make to the interface. The set of articles dealt with a wide variety of possibilities and problems concerned with the interface of the three disciplines. A large number of positive suggestions were made, but there was also considerable pessimism. For example, Strong (1987), a substantial contributor in previous years, did a serious appraisal as to whether a successful integration is possible. He noted that not a single innovation to therapy had resulted from the application of social psychology to therapy in the previous 20 years. Despite his pessimistic appraisal of the fruits of collaboration between clinical and social psychology, he concluded that because of changes in social psychology in recent years there was still some hope for the future.

In a brief commentary article on the previous articles in the special issue, Sarason (1987) showed some pessimism, using the metaphor that although psychology is a vast house of many mansions, few would call it a happy home. Further, he feared that the request for interface activities is more of a plea than a real trend. In part, the conservative nature of training programs serves as a barrier to the integrative tendency. He did, however, see some hope in the fact of the existence of a special issue as a sign that at least some number of psychologists still want the house of psychology to become a home.

The range of attitudes expressed in this series of articles, from pessimistic to optimistic, indicates once again the importance of human interest and commitment in the achievement of innovation. A full integration of clinical, counseling, and social psychology to create a true interface is as simple as a great many people willing and wanting it to be so. However, to the extent that there are reservations, turf issues, suspicions of people in other disciplines, and so forth, such an interface probably cannot occur.

Leary (1987) contributed a valuable conceptual perspective on the interface, taking an approach somewhat different than any previously taken by writers in the area. Leary distinguished among social-dysgenic, social-diagnostic, and social-therapeutic psychology in describing in detail the conceptual delineation of each area. Social-dysgenic psychology is concerned with the understanding of interpersonal processes involved in problem behaviors. In previous years, this approach was relatively narrow and was the province of psychopathologists, particularly in terms of the search for classificatory entities within the individual psyche. During the recent past a wide variety of problem processes have been recognized as suitable for consideration by the mental health professions, including such things as loneliness, shyness, depression, insomnia, spouse abuse, and the like. It is apparent that this list of topics overlaps considerably with interests that have been pursued by social psychologists as well as clinicians. This broader approach to dysfunctional behavior provides, of course, a ready meeting ground for the three disciplines currently under discussion.

Social-diagnostic psychology is Leary's term for the identification and classification of interpersonal problems. He makes the valuable point that the diagnosis of such problems always involves social inference. Further, such inferential processes appear to be on a continuum between the lay inference processes of everyday life and the formal inference process of the clinician in the act of diagnosis. It is an easy step to note the extensive research and literature within social psychology that deal with person perception, attribution, judgmental biases, and the like. It would be highly desirable to begin to integrate those literatures and develop them in such a way that they can apply formally to the diagnostic situations dealt with by the clinician.

Finally, social-therapeutic psychology involves the treatment of dysfunctional behavior, which may be subdivided into (a) the particular set of problems that brought a client to therapy in the first place and (b) the role of interpersonal factors in the ongoing process of counseling and psychotherapy. These three facets of dysfunctionality, diagnosis, and treatment form an interdependent triad that has substantial relevance to all three disciplines of social, clinical, and counseling psychology. Further, as Leary developed these conceptions, it is clear that all three disciplines are intimately involved conceptually, and by inference ought to be involved in varying proportions practically, with clinicians receiving better training in social psychology and social psychologists increasingly turning their attention to studying clinical problems.

Training Considerations

At this point in our history, training considerations for the interface are as varied as the conceptions of what the interface substantively involves. No more than a few examples may be given at this point. Strickland and Halgin (1987) advocated a human services psychology that would include a merger of counseling and clinical psychology, but expand their doctoral training to include social and developmental psychology, thereby creating a kind of "super" discipline that follows the Boulder model of training. Winer (1987) took a strong exception to this model of graduate training, in part because of the probability that in the merger of clinical and counseling, counseling would cease to exist as a viable discipline.

As clinical psychologists have become more aware of the cultural and social factors that impinge on and disturb behavior (Weary, 1987), there has been a reduced emphasis on psychotherapy per se and an attempt to broaden the spectrum of problem behaviors dealt with by professional psychologists. This broadening of perspective of course includes much of the domain of research interests of social psychologists. Such liberation of conceptual boundaries makes possible the joint training, even if with different emphases, of social, clinical, and counseling psychologists. A common curriculum focusing on dysfunctional behavior and the role of social factors in pathology is highly viable, although, as Weary noted, there are substantial professional barriers against the integration of social and clinical psychology.

The approach described by Leary (1987) also has many joint training possibilities. Leary made the sane observation that knowledge of dysfunctional behavior and its diagnosis does not prepare one for the practical considerations of therapy. Further, it works both ways. Many psychotherapists are very poorly trained in the social bases of dysfunctional behavior, in the same way that social psychologists are ordinarily totally untrained in therapeutic activities to ameliorate such dysfunctional behavior. In an ideal curriculum, social psychology would have much to offer in the training of counseling and clinical psychologists, and those two disciplines in turn would have much to offer to the enrichment of the training of social psychologists. Exact professional specialization might differ, but all three disciplines could emerge from a common but variegated core of training activities, to the mutual benefit of all three disciplines.

Statements concerning what might be feasible (and even desirable) for interface training appear inherently reasonable, and we believe that the area of health psychology/behavioral medicine offers a useful prototype for future activity in the interface.

DEVELOPMENT OF HEALTH PSYCHOLOGY/BEHAVIORAL MEDICINE

The field of health psychology has blossomed, particularly over the past decade. Behavioral medicine also has thrived. There is some apparent confusion about the relation between health psychology and behavioral medicine, although we believe that the definitions accorded each in the literature fairly clearly delineate the similarities and differences between the two. Health psychology has been defined as " . . . a generic field of psychology, with its own body of theory and knowledge, which is differentiated from other fields in psychology" (Stone, 1983). Behavioral medicine appears to cast its net somewhat more widely as " . . . the interdisciplinary field concerned with the development and integration of behavioral and biomedical science knowledge and techniques relevant to health and illness" (Schwartz & Weiss, 1978). For our purposes, the areas of health psychology and behavioral medicine will be considered as two separate but overlapping entities, with health psychology functioning as one of the several components of behavioral medicine (by definition, an interdisciplinary field).

Beyond Definitions

Definitions are just a beginning, though in the case of the definition of health psychology offered above, it marked a process well past its beginning. The National Working Conference on Education and Training in Health Psychology, which met in the spring of 1983 and offered the definition of health psychology noted above, was a formal recognition that health psychology was alive and well and growing at a rapid rate, albeit without benefit of definitions, educational curricula, specified training experiences, and mandated licensing and credentialing. The conference did not initiate health psychology, but rather legitimized it. The (carefully selected) conference participants intended to address both the reality of the existing field of health psychology and to set in place the mechanisms with which to shape its future (similar to the contributors to this volume).

Participants in the conference came from different areas of psychology (e.g., experimental, social, physiological, and clinical) and from various work settings (e.g., universities, professional schools, medical schools, hospitals, rehabilitation settings, and governmental agencies). The diversity of the participants was matched only by the diversity of topics focused on by the task groups. These reports included

- Basic research
- Applied research
- Health-care services
- Public health/community health psychology

- Health policy
- Industrial/organizational settings
- Accreditation
- Credentialing
- Ethical concerns
- Legal issues
- Women and ethnic minorities
- Life-cycle health psychology
- Training venues
- Relationship of health psychology to other areas of psychology and other disciplines and professions

Out of this diversity, however, evolved considerable consensus concerning an appropriate future for health psychology, such as endorsement of the scientist-practitioner model, the value of generic psychological training for health psychologists, need for interdisciplinary education and training, special attention to legal and ethical problems, and so on. Although the interrelationships between mental and physical health were duly noted, and knowledge of aspects of clinical psychology was deemed important for health psychologists in both service delivery and research positions, it was agreed that health psychology was greater than the sum of any of its psychological parts (including clinical) and " . . . should become an independent specialty" (Stone, 1983).

This movement toward recognition of health psychology as a separate entity appeared congruent with the fact that those psychologists who " . . . are making the most visible contributions to health psychology . . . have come to health psychology via training and backgrounds of experience in *every* major specialty area of psychology" (Matarazzo, 1983, p. 87). The conference participants also acknowledged the reality that health psychology is important enough and cohesive enough to qualify as a specialty area.

Issues about the specific academic and professional preparation of health psychologists center largely, though not wholly, on scientist-practitioner differences and predoctoral versus postdoctoral specialization. In regard to the former issue, the National Working Conference elected to endorse overlapping scientist and practitioner training paths. In regard to the latter issues, health psychology appears to have a twofold emphasis, with predoctoral health psychology training encompassing generic psychology work as well as a health "track" and health-related practical training, and postdoctoral training encompassing a 2-year specialized training experience (Matarazzo,

1983; Stone, 1983). More recently, Sheridan, Matarazzo, Ball, Perry, Weiss, & Belar (1988) outlined a model for postdoctoral health psychology training and education that attempts to delineate necessary previous preparation of postdoctoral candidates, general structure of postdoctoral experiences, and techniques and skills to be learned during the postdoctoral years.

It is certainly the case that disciplines other than health psychology — notably clinical psychology and counseling psychology — also have defined their spheres of activity and training models through conferences similar to the National Working Conference on Education and Training in Health Psychology. However, it seems to us that the breadth of topics considered and, even more important, the breadth of disciplines and work settings represented make this conference directly relevant to issues of the interface.

Choice Points

Although health psychology is still expanding and does not appear to have yet reified either its entrance requirements or its training approaches, to the extent that it becomes the "property" of any one area of psychology or endorses any narrow view of appropriate education and training, it is likely that the yeasty new specialty will lose some of its vitality. Some mixing of genes ensures a species' survival; too much inbreeding ensures its eventual demise.

In a recent article, Taylor (1987) wrote on the present progress and future prospects of health psychology. While noting the major achievements of the area (e.g., "documenting the importance of quality of life, identifying the psychological impact of treatment intervention for chronic disorders, and inducing medical care-givers to consider these factors . . . " [p. 74]), Taylor also outlined the need to document treatment effectiveness, demonstrate cost-effectiveness, and deal with logistical issues such as publication outlets for health psychology materials.

Particularly compelling is Taylor's stance that " . . . the entry-level credential (in health psychology) can be pre-doctoral training . . . " (p. 81). Noting that any requirement of 2 years of postdoctoral training for an entry-level credential may drive the best and brightest young scholars to other areas within and without psychology, she also pointed out a reality that those professionals who are obsessed with licensing and credentialing appear to have overlooked:

There is also a certain irony to the extended and complex curriculum that many in health psychology are outlining for future students, and it is the fact that none of the present ranks in the field went through anything like it. Most of us who are now in health psychology came to it from other disciplines in psychology. When we converted to health psychology, we educated ourselves through whatever haphazard and piecemeal methods were available to us, and if our track record to date is any indication, we have done a fine job of it. Of course, the field is now in a position to offer much better courses and training in research and methods directly relevant to health psychology. But in addition, students deserve some credit for being entrepreneurial about their skills, and we must assume that they will acquire some of the skills they need on their own. (Taylor, 1987, p. 82)

In line with Taylor's emphasis on openness and flexibility in health psychology is a training component recently discussed by Bresler (1988) that offers both theory and practice in community health promotion within a more traditional clinical psychology curriculum. The training emphasis includes a seminar, student involvement as a member of a risk-factor modification group, and various campus and community intervention projects, including health-promotion activities in a church, and a health-promotion package offered in connection with a local insurance group to 1,100 of its clients. Although Bresler acknowledged the difficulties of integrating additional work in health promotion/health psychology into an already demanding clinical training curriculum, the rewards appear to more than balance out the costs. Being on the cutting edge of a rapidly growing area engenders enthusiasm in students and faculty alike.

Our brief look at health psychology has allowed us to examine the professional questions that confront a new and rapidly growing discipline. The diverse perspectives on education and training in health psychology (e.g., predoctoral vs. postdoctoral training), and the probable evolution of that discipline have implications for the interface of social and clinical psychology and its future development.

HEALTH IN THE INTERFACE

Although we noted earlier that health psychology and the interface are not one and the same, we view health psychology as a "model" for the interface, in terms of the former's growth, boundary definitions, and training issues. In addition, the topic of "health" can itself be considered within the domain of the social-clinical interface, as it is in the current volume. This placement is exceedingly appropriate, judging by the breadth of the chapters included. Both the range of contributions and the range of contributors testify that health is a great showcase for the talents of the interface. Why is this the case?

A preliminary attempt to answer this question is shown by the model in Figure 39.1. Figure 39.1, adapted from an earlier article (Hendrick & Hendrick, 1984), shows in some detail the vast array of concepts pertaining to health and disease. In the following discussion, we will borrow liberally from that article.

Although psychological concepts can be readily and usefully applied to health behavior and disease states (attribution of cause is one example), such concepts only get at part of the health-disease gestalt. Other, more behavioral and environmental variables related to health and disease (e.g., housing quality, exercise, air and water pollution) might be described as life-style/environmental concepts. Still other concepts, such as ethnicity, socioeconomic status, and the like, might be labeled sociological concepts. Sociological concepts are related to both psychological and environmental factors; however, they are qualitatively different. For example, exercise, in some form, occurs within every social stratum. For the poor migrant laborer, it may occur in the natural course of trying to eke out a living. For the upper middle-class person, however, specific kinds of exercise to attain specific kinds of physiological ends may be carefully planned. Intentional exercise may produce somewhat different results than does naturally occurring exercise.

Thus, the three distinct but related classes of concepts termed psychological, life-style, and sociological bear on the social bases of illness and health. These three systems of concepts may be thought of as three large sets of independent variables, in turn impinging on two sets of dependent variables — illness behavior and health behavior.

If research and intervention efforts are to be effectively directed toward prediction and eventual control among these five interconnected sets of variables, then those professionals involved in such efforts either need tremendous breadth of knowledge or they need to participate in collaborative research.

The latter alternative appears to be the more pragmatic one, and thus there is a seemingly perfect fit of health into the interface area. In their attempt to fit psychobiology within the interface, Spring and her colleagues (Spring, Chiodo, & Bowen, 1987) reprised some of the research on stress, linking early work by social psychologists on crowding, to psychobiological studies on control and cancer, to social-clinical work on stress, competition, and aggression, and to personality psychology theorizing on the "hardy personality" as a healthy response to stress. As these authors wisely noted, one of the reasons for the fecundity of health psychology has been the fact that little of its time (at least up to this point) has been spent in disciplinary turf issues. Although it is possible that current trends to license and credential those who are to be involved in patient-related aspects of health psychology service delivery will needlessly define boundaries of those who "can" and those who "cannot," such a direction appears to us less promising than a yeasty eclecticism.

This eclecticism welcomes the separate but highly congenial contributions of the social psychologist, the clinical psychologist, and the counseling psychologist. The social psychologist brings with him or her a tradition of empiricism as a major approach to finding out answers to individual and group questions. Theoretical curiosity, followed by systematic exploration, are essential to solving some of the highly complex issues related to health and disease. This research tradition has included studies of specific disease states, such as cancer, coronary-prone behavior, and smoking, as well as research concerning the health-care delivery system (e.g., interpersonal interaction among health-care professionals, physician-patient communication).

Clinical psychology brings to health research a respected tradition of concern with the organism gone awry; a push to understand the etiology of physical and mental disease states, the course of such disease states, and various approaches to treatment; and, perhaps, ultimate cure of these disease states. The involvement in health within the interface is quite natural for clinical psychology, as indicated by the significant interface contributions made by clinical psychologists (e.g., Brehm, 1976; Weary & Mirels, 1982).

The historical roots and contemporary foci of counseling psychology as well as the natural bridges between counseling and social psychology have been detailed elsewhere (S. S. Hendrick, 1987). Most relevant to the discussion of health, however, is counseling's long-term involvement

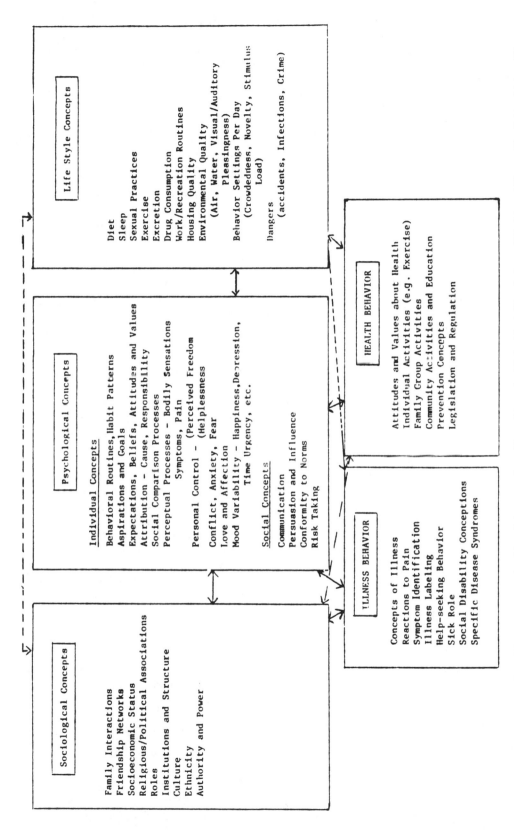

Figure 39.1. Five sets of variables pertaining to health and disease. Adapted from "Toward a Clinical Social Psychology of Health and Disease" by C. Hendrick and S. S. Hendrick, 1984, *Journal of Social and Clinical Psychology, 2,* p. 185. Copyright 1984 by The Guilford Press. Adapted by permission.

with rehabilitation psychology and career/vocational psychology, and its reliance on short- and intermediate-term therapeutic approaches (Tipton, 1983). Although a disease-focused, remediative approach to illness is entirely defensible, so also is a wellness-focused, preventive approach. It is no accident that the developing area of psychology on which we have concentrated so much attention is called health psychology. There is a historical tendency in psychology to focus on pathology (physiological, cognitive, emotional); however, there also has been an emphasis on articulating processes of normal human development, and counseling psychology has nearly always worked within the latter framework. Thus, counseling is in a rather special position in respect to health within the interface. It is oriented to deal fully with both the personal and professional disruptions evoked by acute and chronic illnesses, as well as to play a prominent role in prevention. This, indeed, is the perspective that really ought to be driving the entire health psychology "machine."

Although we have directed our comments to social, clinical, and counseling psychology, it is apparent to us that "the challenges of health psychology are such that nearly all branches of psychology must contribute to problem definition and solution if more effective prevention and remediation strategies are to be employed" (Hendrick & Hendrick, 1984, p. 191). And if psychology is to contribute in a wide-ranging fashion to problem definition and solution, then it must contribute even more widely to the education and training of those psychologists who will deal with health issues.

MODELS FOR EDUCATION/TRAINING

Although the topic of research and practice in "health" appears to fit quite neatly into the interface of social and clinical psychology and may represent the "where" many psychologists have ended up, the "how" of getting here is less clear. As we noted earlier, training in health psychology has become increasingly formalized, with nearly 100 doctoral and postdoctoral health psychology training programs documented (e.g., Belar & Siegel, 1983; Belar, Wilson, & Hughes, 1982). We describe three different approaches to training. The fertile diversity of these programs suggests that premature formalization of curricula may be

detrimental to the evolution of the interface of social and clinical psychology.

A Multifaceted Model

This model evolved in a southeastern university familiar to us. The psychology department offers training in traditional areas of clinical and experimental psychology, as well as specialized training in applied developmental, clinical-child, and pediatric health psychology. The health area evolved such that it is represented in three distinct programs in biopsychology, behavioral medicine, and health psychology.

The biopsychology program was designed to offer consistent research training in the areas of neuroscience and behavior. Students take a set of psychology core courses as well as neuroscience/behavioral medicine/health psychology courses. In addition, coursework in anatomy, physiology, pharmacology, and immunology is encouraged. Research emphasizes health-related neuroanatomical and electrophysiological studies relevant to health and disease.

The behavioral medicine program provides systematic research training and relevant coursework geared toward the psychosocial and biobehavioral factors involved in the etiology, pathogenesis, and treatment of disease as well as disease prevention in people at high risk. The program is built on a traditional scientific paradigm emphasizing experimental methods, statistics, and psychophysiology. Interdisciplinary research is encouraged, and in fact research is the continuous thread tying the program together.

The health psychology program is geared toward students who wish to be both academically and clinically prepared for careers as clinicians and researchers in health settings. The program includes traditional clinical coursework, some of the behavioral medicine coursework, and both research and practicum experience in health psychology. Although this program is relatively more oriented to clinical than experimental psychology (requiring a predoctoral internship in clinical psychology), there is nevertheless an ongoing emphasis both on research and practice.

A Mixed Model

The training methods described so far are geared toward psychology students, albeit students who may have varied backgrounds and interests. A heartening example of an innovative, and truly interdisciplinary, training approach was offered by Winder, Michelson, and Diamond (1985). They discussed a pediatric practicum training model that includes a multi-focus training approach geared toward pediatric medical residents and graduate students from both developmental and clinical psychology. The intensive, 2-year practicum training experience involves multiple components. For the psychology students, background coursework (required for clinical, encouraged for developmental), group supervision (a minimum of 8 work hours per week in a medical setting), and specialized workshops are a central part of the training process. Additional components involving both pediatric residents and psychology students include advanced coursework in normal child development, a course of pediatric and perinatal medicine, a series of workshops, and interdisciplinary case conferences.

Several aspects of the program are noteworthy. What is apparent from the program description offered above is the substantial time commitment required of both students and supervising faculty. A 2-year training program is much more than what is involved in a typical practicum; it is a substantial training experience that produces pediatric psychologists. Another important aspect is the truly interdisciplinary nature of the program. Psychologists and physicians learn together, consult together, and although the process is imperfect (e.g., difficulties emerged with the physician-to-psychologist referral process), it represents a truly collaborative learning experience.

Finally, the collaborative learning experience occurs within psychology as well as between psychology and medicine, combining " . . . both clinical and developmental models in an integrative approach to the learning of psychology in both theory and practice" (Winder et al., 1985, p. 734). Although the authors noted that some psychologists may object to shared training for both developmental and clinical psychology students, they also acknowledge that "the philosophy of training subscribed to by this program includes the recognition that psychologists may become health care providers by a variety of routes" (p. 736).

The wisdom of this catholic approach to training is underscored by research that obtained responses from 686 pediatric and health psychologists. Assessing graduate training, Stabler and Mesibov (1984) noted

Although about 65% of both pediatric and health psychologists were trained in clinical psychology training programs, another 33% had very different training experiences. Pediatric psychologists who were not trained in clinical programs were primarily trained in developmental, educational, and school psychology programs . . . Health psychologists who were not trained in clinical programs were primarily trained in social and experimental psychology programs. (p. 149)

Social-Counseling Training

As noted earlier, there has been some suggestion (S. S. Hendrick, 1987) that social psychology would find a much happier, more natural alliance with counseling psychology than it has ever found with clinical psychology. Reasons cited were counseling's basic stance of cooperativeness, a likely egalitarian relationship between social and counseling, and the traditional concern of both areas with normal (rather than deviant) human behavior.

Rather than continue to talk about the potential for cooperativeness, several faculty in the Department of Psychology at Texas Tech University (Lubbock) decided to try to develop a social-counseling track to train a few select students. The program admitted three students in the fall-winter of 1986 in a training pilot study. Admission of the students was followed, rather than preceded, by some formalization of course requirements, qualifying examination emphases, and norms for ongoing research. Development of the track was done with two particular goals in mind. First, several social and counseling faculty were doing research in and/or were particularly interested in the interface area and wished to further legitimize the area within the Psychology Department. Second, there was a real desire among the faculty to train students who would have the professional training so useful in today's competitive job market as well as the thorough grounding in the research process that is the real basis of traditional psychology. It is worth noting that at least one other program at another university, attempting some of the same goals, has added a 5th year of training to the traditional 4-year curriculum in order to accommodate specialized training in health psychology. It was Texas Tech's intention to try to integrate coursework in such a way as to add as little as possible to a student's courseload (perhaps just one semester). An essential requirement was, of course, ongoing involvement in research, preferably research within the interface. An example social-counseling course plan is shown in Table 39.1.

Because all graduate students in the Psychology Department are required to take a number of courses known as the departmental core (e.g., two statistics, personality, social, developmental, history, physiology, learning), these courses would serve "double duty" for the social-counseling student. In addition, students typically have a 15-hour minor in an area outside the major (though often within the department itself). Thus, hours in each of the two areas could count as a formal minor for the other area. Counseling students are required to take four practica, though students frequently take more. Social-counseling students are urged to take only the required practica and to use any extra time fulfilling other requirements and conducting research. Not infrequently, students in social or industrial/organizational take courses in intelligence testing, vocational psychology, and ethics as part of their graduate training, so these courses can be considered as contributing to a student's training in both social and counseling. Still other courses may be counted as electives for either social or counseling. Although research involvement is required of counseling students for at least two semesters prior to beginning work on the dissertation (and is encouraged for all semesters), students in social and social-counseling have ongoing research involvement, which adds to the workload. In addition, certain courses in assessment and selected other areas may be less relevant to social psychology but are essential for a fully trained professional counseling psychologist.

Although planning coursework was not too difficult, other important graduate training experiences that had to be addressed were qualifying examinations, dissertation, and internship. It was determined that, at least on a preliminary basis, the social-counseling student would take qualifying examinations in the counseling area, with part of that examination, or a separate, somewhat more circumscribed examination, administered to fulfill the social requirement. The dissertation and internship were easier to design. The dissertation would involve a topic within the interface area and would be directed by either a social or counseling psychologist, with a member of the "other" faculty serving on the committee. The question on internship was relevant to the counseling training as well as to the student's potential licenseability as a psychologist. It was decided that any internship in a traditional counseling psychology setting would be acceptable, unless or until true interface internship sites might be developed (which could be done relatively easily in college counseling centers or community mental health facilities).

We are still in the early stages of this training program at Texas Tech and are not yet in a position to evaluate its success. Our first students are progressing well, though none have actually graduated as of this writing. We hope to attract other students to the track, but we will have somewhat more wisdom about the program they might follow. We have found that laying out a sequence of courses on paper is quite different from living through those courses with a particular student. Courses do not always get offered when they should; sometimes it seems that every needed course is offered in the same semester, if not at the same time. In addition, taking three courses, practicum, research, and typically working half-time is exhausting. Thus, proceeding through the curriculum outlined in Table 39.1 in lock-step fashion is probably not possible, and not necessarily desirable, for many doctoral students. In this respect, the social-counseling track is no different than any other graduate training program. Down the road, it may be that to be both realistic and honest with students, we will have to describe the track as "5 years plus internship" rather than the current "4 years plus internship."

On the up side, we have attracted quality students who have good ideas and are willing to work on them, and who effectively bring together both concepts and faculty from social and counseling psychology. More faculty time and energy will have to be devoted to program formalization in the near future if this special training experience is to succeed. However, reifying the program is not one of our goals. Currently, many things are not even written down, much less written in stone.

Although these various training models are interesting, it is reasonable to wonder whether they offer us anything drastically different from the Boulder model, or even from the training/education that preceded that model. Psychologists have always been encouraged to read widely, beyond narrow and parochial limits. In fact many psychology programs employ a core curriculum that draws broadly from the varying areas of psychology. Applied psychologists read the works of interpersonal theorists and explore the implementation of various social psychological theories in the

Table 39.1. Sample Course Schedule for Students in the Social/Counseling Program at Texas Tech University, Lubbock

	FALL	SPRING	SUMMER I	SUMMER II
Year 1	Experimental design Social seminar Vocational 1 Prepracticum Research	Multivariate Physiological Vocational 2 Social applications to counseling Research	Personality	Research
Year 2	Learning Social-Attitudes Intelligence testing Practicum Research	Social (core) Social-small groups MMPI Practicum Research	Counseling women Ethics	Research
Year 3	Advanced Child Social-applied Advanced theories Practicum Research	History & systems assessment Social systems Practicum Research	Assessment	Research
Year 4	Dissertation	Dissertation	Internship	
Year 5	Internship	Internship		

therapy context, although similar training of experimental psychologists in "applied" knowledge occurs less frequently. And certainly the Boulder model stresses that clinical and counseling psychologists should be trained as scientists first and practitioners second.

We believe that these specific training models offer new commentary, above and beyond what has gone before, however. They make explicit what has been implicit and formalize what has been done sometimes on an ad hoc basis. To the extent that formalization turns interface training into just one more rigid professional training paradigm, we have regressed. But to the extent that it legitimizes interface training, we have progressed. In addition, to the extent that such models pay more than lip service to scientist-practitioner training, with "scientist" assuming its rightful place, we need to employ them more widely.

THE FUTURE

We have reprised the history of the social-clinical counseling interface and have presented health psychology as a rapidly growing specialty area that has some lessons to teach the interface, another rapidly growing specialty area. We also have offered several training models that might serve as the basis for training in the area of social-clinical-counseling. However, we have thus far been more interested in raising issues and questions than in providing (premature) answers. We believe that it would be short-sighted to consider education at the interface without also considering the direction(s) in which the larger discipline of psychology seems to be moving. Such directions were considered by the National Conference on Graduate Education in Psychology, held in June of 1987 at the University of Utah, Salt Lake City. In addition to specific resolutions endorsed by the conference participants, a number of scholars critically considered the present and future of the discipline (e.g., Altman, 1987).

Resolutions

There were 11 major resolutions, all containing subresolutions and proposed mechanisms by which the various resolutions could be implemented:

1. On the matter of a core curriculum, although breadth of curriculum and coverage of essential basic content areas appeared to be well accepted, definitions of a core were left up to individual departments and schools.
2. Support was given to broad liberal arts training for undergraduate psychology majors, with increasing specialization through postdoctoral work.
3. Although psychology doctoral work is usefully taught in a number of settings (e.g.,

arts and sciences, education, business), non-university-affiliated freestanding professional schools were discouraged.

4. Program quality control is necessary; however, there are diverse criteria for measuring quality. Accreditation by the American Psychological Association is one (but only one) such criterion.

5. Psychology should be involved in assisting its graduates to market themselves successfully in both the academic and nonacademic work worlds.

6. Psychology needs to focus strongly on both recruitment and retention of graduate students, particularly those students from underrepresented groups.

7. There needs to be increasing attention to cultural diversity in psychology (in students, faculty, and curricula).

8. It is psychology's responsibility to aid in the informal socialization of its students.

9. Participants affirmed differences between and value in the Ph.D., Ed.D., and Psy.D. degrees.

10. Greater communication among subfields of psychology is essential.

11. Although attention has been focused on psychologists as researchers and practitioners, the psychologist as educator is extremely important.

Though all of these resolutions seem reasonably congruent with psychology as we know it, four of them appear particularly appropriate to education at the interface. Resolutions 1 and 2, supporting broad undergraduate education and increasing (though not narrow) specialization through postdoctoral work, as well as a psychology core curriculum, means that students trained at the interface need thorough grounding in traditional psychology before venturing too far into interface work. The necessity for psychology to market its graduates seems wholly congruent with interface training, itself designed to equip students well for either academic or more service-delivery roles. The resolution perhaps most important to the interface is that calling for greater communication among psychology's subfields. That in fact is one primary basis for the interface; the bone and sinew of interface education is collaboration.

Learning From the Past

If we do not learn from the past, we are doomed to repeat it, a sage once said. In dis-

cussing the forces for convergence and divergence in psychology over the past 100 years, Altman (1987) commented that there is a natural ebb and flow to this process. Outlining a number of the professional, social, and political forces influencing the process, Altman observed that psychology exhibits the effects of substantial divergent, or "centrifugal" forces at the present time, and this direction is unlikely to change.

One of the characteristics of centrifugal forces is that they pull an organism apart, and that has been an ardent concern of many contemporary psychologists. However, an equally dangerous phenomenon occurs when such forces are suppressed in the service of "unity." Diversity can be enriching, and as Altman (1987) noted, "centrifugal trends can infuse the field with new ideas" (p. 1069). Perhaps the interface is one such new idea.

REFERENCES

Altman, I. (1987). Centripetal and centrifugal trends in psychology. *American Psychologist, 42*, 1058–1069.

Belar, C. D., & Siegel, L. J. (1983). A survey of postdoctoral training programs in health psychology. *Health Psychology, 2*, 413–425.

Belar, C. D., Wilson, E., & Hughes, H. (1982). Health psychology training in doctoral psychology programs. *Health Psychology, 1*, 289–299.

Brehm, S. S. (1976). *The application of social psychology to clinical practice.* Washington, DC: Hemisphere.

Bresler, C. (1988). Health promotion in the community: Development of a curriculum for predoctoral clinical psychologists. *Professional Psychology, 19*, 87–92.

Harvey, J. H., & Weary, G. (1979). The integration of social and clinical psychology training programs. *Personality and Social Psychology Bulletin, 5*, 511–515.

Hendrick, C. (1983). Clinical social psychology: A birthright reclaimed. *Journal of Social and Clinical Psychology, 1*, 66–87.

Hendrick, C. (1987). Perspectives on the interfaces of social, counseling, and clinical psychology: An overview. *Journal of Social and Clinical Psychology, 5*, 146–149.

Hendrick, C., & Hendrick, S. S. (1984). Toward a clinical social psychology of health and disease. *Journal of Social and Clinical Psychology, 2*, 182–192.

Hendrick, S. S. (1983). Ecumenical (social and

clinical and x, y, z . . .) psychology. *Journal of Social and Clinical Psychology, 1*, 79–87.

Hendrick, S. S. (1987). Counseling psychology in the interface. *Journal of Social and Clinical Psychology, 5*, 21–26.

Leary, M. R. (1987). The three faces of social-clinical-counseling psychology. *Journal of Social and Clinical Psychology, 5*, 168–175.

Matarazzo, J. D. (1983). Education and training in health psychology: Boulder or bolder. *Health Psychology, 2*, 73–113.

Resolutions approved by the National Conference on Graduate Education in Psychology. (1987). *American Psychologist, 42*, 1070–1084.

Sarason, S. B. (1987). A house, a home, an interface. *Journal of Social and Clinical Psychology, 5*, 222–226.

Schwartz, G. E., & Weiss, S. M. (1978). Behavioral medicine revisited: An amended definition. *Journal of Behavioral Medicine, 1*, 249–251.

Sheridan, E. P., Matarazzo, J. D., Ball, T. J., Perry, N. W., Weiss, S. M., & Belar, C. D. (1988). Postdoctoral education and training for clinical service providers in health psychology. *Health Psychology, 7*, 1–17.

Spring, B., Chiodo, J., & Bowen, D. J. (1987). The social-clinical-psychobiology interface: Implications for health psychology. *Journal of Social and Clinical Psychology, 5*, 1–7.

Stabler, B., & Mesibov, G. B. (1984). Role function of pediatric and health psychologists in health care settings. *Professional Psychology, 15*, 142–151.

Stone, G. C. (1983). Proceedings of the National Working Conference on Education and Training in Health Psychology. *Health Psychology, 2*, 1–153.

Strickland, B. R., & Halgin, R. P. (1987). Perspectives on clinical, counseling, and social psychology. *Journal of Social and Clinical Psychology, 5*, 150–159.

Strong, S. R. (1978). Social psychological approach to psychotherapy research. In S. L. Garfield & A. E. Bergin (Eds.), *Handbook of psychotherapy and behavior change: An empirical analysis* (2nd ed.). New York: John Wiley & Sons.

Strong, S. R. (1987). Social-psychological approach to counseling and psychotherapy: "A false hope?" *Journal of Social and Clinical Psychology, 5*, 185–194.

Taylor, S. E. (1987). The progress and prospects of health psychology: Tasks of a maturing discipline. *Health Psychology, 6*, 73–87.

Tipton, R. M. (1983). Clinical and counseling psychology: A study of roles and functions. *Professional Psychology, 14*, 837–846.

Weary, G. (1987). Natural bridges: The interface of social and clinical psychology. *Journal of Social and Clinical Psychology, 5*, 160–167.

Weary, G., & Mirels, H. L. (1982). *Integrations of clinical and social psychology*. New York: Oxford University Press.

Winder, A. E., Michelson, L. A., & Diamond, D. (1985). Practicum training for pediatric psychologists: A case study. *Professional Psychology, 16*, 733–740.

Winer, J. L. (1987). Counseling-clinical-social psychology: A counseling psychologist's assessment. *Journal of Social and Clinical Psychology, 5*, 216–221.

CHAPTER 40

THE INTERFACE TOWARD THE YEAR 2000

C. R. Snyder
Donelson R. Forsyth
(with commentaries by Sharon S. Brehm, John H. Harvey, Clyde Hendrick, Susan Hendrick, Robert C. Carson, Arnold P. Goldstein, Frederick H. Kanfer, Richard S. Lazarus, Mark Snyder, Bonnie R. Stricklund, and Hans H. Strupp)

THE HEALTH-HELP-HEALTH FRAMEWORK REVISITED

In Roman mythology Janus was a powerful god; only Jupiter outranked him in prestige and authority. The Romans believed it was Janus who opened and closed the gates of heaven each morning and evening, and they often portrayed him as a man with two faces; one facing east and one facing west. He was the god of all beginnings and all endings, and the Romans felt doorways and gateways symbolized Janus's power. Today, to be "Janus-faced" implies deceit, but to the Romans the two faces symbolized Janus's ability to see in two directions at once—into both the past and the future and at the good and the bad.

In this chapter we look at the interface of social and clinical psychology as Janus would. First, we look back by reviewing the foundations of the interface as explicated in the preceding chapters. Using the health-help-health framework as an organizing heuristic, we briefly consider both person-based processes such as self-maintenance systems and personality processes, as well as en-

vironment-based processes such as interpersonal relations, diagnosis, and treatment. Second, we also look forward into the future to prophesy what will happen to the interface in coming years. The interface holds considerable promise for advancing our understanding of human adjustment and dysfunction, but its viability depends on its success in the face of challenges and confrontations that lie ahead. In both our look back and look forward, we draw on the insights of a number of individuals who have played instrumental roles in social and clinical spheres. Their commentaries are interspersed throughout this final chapter.

Person-Based Processes

The health-help-health framework assumes that health, which is broadly defined as that psychological and physical state of well-being that the individual is motivated to sustain or change, is the product of both the person-based and environment-based processes. Looking first at person-based processes, past research and the preceding chapters have focused on the two major constellations of concern: (a) the self and its dynamic processes and (b) the measurement and meaning of individual differences (Snyder, 1988). The lessons learned by investigators toiling in both of these fields are considered below.

Self-Related Issues

It has long been argued that the self is a cognitive structure by which people organize information about who and what they are. William James highlighted the social foundations of the self when he wrote that if people "acted as if we were nonexisting things, a kind of rage and impotent despair would ere long well up in us, from which the cruelest bodily tortures would be a relief" (1890, p. 293). Now, a century later, researchers have revived this perspective by advocating the importance of self-schemas and self-theories as structures for knowing oneself (Greenwald & Pratkanis, 1984; Kihlstrom & Cantor, 1984; Markus & Wurf, 1987).

This reawakened interest in the nature of the self has stimulated the study of self-processes: the causal and mediational impact of the self has stimulated the study of self-processes: the causal and mediational impact of the self on thought, emotion, and action (Markus & Sentis, 1982; Markus & Wurf, 1987; Neisser, 1976; Snyder, 1989). As Markus and Wurf (1987) wrote,

> The unifying premise of the last decade's research on the self is that the self-concept does not just reflect on-going behavior but instead mediates and regulates this behavior. In this sense the self-concept has been viewed as dynamic—as active, forceful, and capable of change. It interprets and organizes self-relevant actions and experiences; it has motivational consequences, providing the incentives, standards, plans, rules, and scripts for behavior; and it adjusts in response to challenges from the social environment. (pp. 299–300)

This handbook's chapters on the self generally share this emerging "hot" perspective on the self. In other words, the processes involving the self, in many instances, are conceptualized as being intimately tied to particular types of appraisal, attention, and motives. In turn, these appraisal, attentional, and motivational processes that operate in the various self systems appear to have health-related sequelae. Indeed, a common theme is that the self processes enable us to better understand the ways that people may sustain positive health; conversely, these same self processes give us clues about poor health.

Such theories and supporting findings may provide an answer to a question that occasionally is asked by graduate students who are beginning their practicum work. The question is, "What use is it to know about the person's self?" The obvious answer is that the self processes are inextricably tied to the client's psychological and physical health. As such, this literature provides further information about the mind-body relationship. Putting this another way, some people appear to have adaptive health-help-health person-based processes. This leads us to the discussion next of the individual differences person-based processes.

Individual Differences Issues

The study of person-based processes also has been advanced by psychologists who have studied variability among people along some dimension of interest. This work is typically theory driven, and in many ways is similar to the approaches used for studying the self. Investigators usually begin with an observable dimension of comparison (e.g., gender), or a hypothesized dimension of comparison (e.g., locus of control, hope, explanatory style, etc.), and construct a theory about the nature of the principal characteristics underlying this dimension. Then, a measure (typically self-report) of the particular individual differences dimension is developed so as to meet acceptable psychometric standards. Next, the scale is validated in order to assure that it measures what it purports to measure. Lastly, the measure is used to make predictions about the particular behaviors of interest. In the case of this handbook, the behaviors predicted by the various individual differences measures involve psychological and physical health.

The interface researchers using this individual differences approach have generated an increasing number of theories and associated measures aimed at predicting health-related outcomes. What is not clear, however, is the nature of the discriminant validity of these scales. In the spirit of the interface, we would encourage the various researchers to continue their consideration of the overlap in the various theories and measures. If there are common factors underlying the various theories and related individual differences measures, then the understanding of these factors may simplify our unraveling of the most adaptive health-help-health person-based processes.

Many of the researchers exploring self and individual differences issues have typically made an implicit assumption regarding the underlying motivation for the health-help-health sequence. That is, many of these models are based on the assumption that the normal health-help-health sequence is characterized by (a) people in a positive state of health (psychological and physical) who (b) engage in natural, intrapersonal coping processes (the "help" in this framework) (c) in order to maintain their positive state of health. An implicitly assumed corollary to this pattern of normal help-health-help sequencing is that (a) when people find themselves in a negative state of health, (b) they will engage in natural, intrapersonal coping responses (the "help" in the equation) (c) in order to reestablish their positive state of health. Such intrapersonal models are thus based on the assumption that people have a propensity toward positive health, whether this means that they are sustaining or recapturing it.

One question that may arise is whether people would purposefully maintain a negative state of health, or may purposefully attempt to move from a positive to a negative state of health. In other words, is the "help" in the health-help-health intrapersonal sequence such that the person purposefully attempts to engage in self-defeating or self-destructive acts? This latter point is relevant for those people who do not evidence the adaptive aspects of the particular self or individual differences models. In a recent review of this latter question, Baumeister and Scher (1988) reviewed the available evidence with nonclinical populations. They conclude that there is no support for the notion that normal people intentionally engage in self-destructive behavior. This finding supports the implicit assumption of many of the self and individual differences models in this handbook.

Interestingly, however, Baumeister and Scher (1988) found evidence to support the fact that people engage in self-destructive behavior. This hardly comes as a surprise to anyone who reads the newspaper, or anyone who has done therapy, but based on their review of the literature, Baumeister and Scher provided the clarifying evidence that this seemingly self-defeating behavior occurs under two circumstances. They wrote,

> there was little evidence that normal people ever *desire* harm or failure. Rather, self-destruction occurs either as an unforeseen and unintended outcome of strategies aimed at positive goals or as the result of a tradeoff in which strongly desired benefits accompany the harm to self. (p. 18)

Such unintended or tradeoff motives may characterize the maladaptive "help" styles that the various authors in this handbook describe as they develop their self or individual difference models. In this latter sense, some people have naturally occurring help intrapersonal processes that are counterproductive in achieving their overall goal of remaining positive. It is important to reemphasize, however, that even such persons may well be doing the best that they can to secure a reasonably positive state of health.

Environment-Based Processes

No firm line separates the personal from the interpersonal. The self, for example, is at once a private, personal view of one's capabilities, but at the same time is influenced to an extraordinary degree by interpersonal factors. Similarly, one's health is at once a product of person-based processes and environment-based processes. We consider several of these externally oriented processes below, including interpersonal, diagnostic, and treatment issues.

Interpersonal Issues

Social psychology rests, at its core, on the assumption that an individual's thoughts, feelings, and behaviors are inexorably and ubiquitously influenced by other people. When this assumption is brought to bear on problems of adjustment and health, the result is an interpersonal view that assumes the following (Maddux, 1987):

> Psychological and behavioral problems—or problems of human adjustment—are essentially social and interpersonal processes.
>
> The distinction between normality and abnormality is essentially arbitrary and is the product of social norms that were derived in social settings and are enforced in social settings.
>
> So-called 'abnormal' social or interpersonal patterns are essentially distortions or exaggerations of normal patterns or normal patterns that are displayed at times and in places considered by those in charge (norm enforcers) to be inappropriate.
>
> Most, and possibly all, clinical interventions based on psychological principles, regardless of their theoretical foundation, focus on changing what we think about, what we feel about, and how we behave toward other people. (pp. 29–30)

Such an interpersonal approach does not transform the individual into an empty pawn caught up in the interplay of social forces. Rather the person is assumed to be an active choreographer of the interaction minuet; a sensitive perceiver who is attuned to the interpersonal meaning of the social setting; a tactful interaction partner who selects particular courses of actions depending on personal interactional tendencies and their appropriateness in the particular situation; a selective pragmatist who seeks out situations and interaction partners while avoiding others; and a stubborn negotiator bent on confirming his or her own social identity and definition of the situation.

The chapters in this handbook attest to the burgeoning study of the interpersonal processes as they operate routinely to promote and maintain health during times of stress and times of complacent calm, and how tears in the fabric of our interpersonal relations can undermine adjustment. Although social psychologists have long contented themselves to study short-term attraction, the work discussed in the chapter by Fincham and Bradbury, as well as the chapter by Jones and Carver, illustrates a growing interest in long-term relationships, loneliness, and the impact of these on health. Also, as if heeding Carson's (1969) plea for a more detailed analysis of Harry Stack Sullivan's (1953) theory of interpersonal processes, the separate chapters by Kiesler and Strong review the implications that an interpersonal approach holds for diagnosis and treatment. These efforts bespeak the considerable progress made in the last decade, but they also hold the promise of even more successful effort as we move toward the year 2000. As Berscheid (1985) noted, researchers and theorists have been content to cover their theoretical canvases with broad brush strokes, leaving whole sections of the picture unpainted. It remains for future investigators to exploit more fully the useful implications of an interpersonal approach to adjustment.

Diagnostic Issues

Beyond the new information that the authors in this handbook present in understanding the processes that underlie clinical judgments, especially the previous propensity to perpetuate a "fundamental negative person bias," the suggestions and implications of these chapters for improving the procedures and practices are noteworthy for applied psychology in general and health in particular. Many previous writings on the topic of diagnosis have taken the tact of highlighting all the pitfalls, as well as engaging in "clinician-bashing," in which practitioners are faulted for perpetuating "the problem." This handbook's authors, however, take a more constructive stance. One of the most useful messages conveyed in this set of chapters pertains to the importance and necessity of looking to the situation in order to better understand how the person is functioning. Assessment must take into account the reciprocal relationship between the person-based and environment-based forces. For all the work that has been done on the person side of this equation, including the chapters in this handbook that describe advances in self and related individual differences measures, there has been little integration of these developments into the diagnostic activities of practicing clinicians who are employing the *Diagnostic and Statistical Manual of Mental Disorders* (DSM-III; American Psychiatric Association, 1980) (Kiesler's chapter is a noteworthy exception). One obvious goal of interface scholars, especially in regard to the health perspective, will be to have an impact on the subsequent revisions of the DSM III. As such, many of the points made in the new theory and research on the self and individual differences need to be considered and incorporated in the forthcoming versions of DSM III.

Just as we need to attend more to the environmental forces, both in conjunction and in reciprocal interaction with person forces, there is also a need to consider the valence of the information. As Beatrice Wright argues in her chapter, it is appropriate to look at both the weaknesses and the strengths of the person whom we are diagnosing. By examining the strengths, the prevailing negativity bias may be balanced as we form a diagnostic impression. Taken together, as Wright reasons, it is further possible to conceptualize clients in a two-by-two matrix, in which we look at the strengths and weaknesses both of the person and the environmental levels. The literature on diagnosis suggests that one cell in this four-celled matrix has captured the bulk of our previous attention when we engage in professional assessments. This cell, of course, is the one focusing on the weaknesses in the person. Our position is not that this cell lacks important diagnostic implications, but rather that it is only part of the picture. In keeping with our focus on health as encompassing the bad and the good, the other cells in this matrix need to be considered because they contain valuable information. In fact, in the degree to which the diagnosis is linked to the treatment (see below), then these other cells are critical to the forming of the best plan for interventions.

COMMENTARY 1:

Progress Happens, But Slowly:
A Brief Personal History of the Social Animal Perspective
Robert C. Carson
Duke University

It is now a commonplace observation, despite divergences in language and emphasis, that most of what we conceive as human personality is in fact the residual scriptlike or schematic influences of the person's past interactions with others on his or her present ones. Personality is therefore an inherently social-psychological phenomenon. Perhaps because my own training as a clinical psychologist was for its day extraordinarily infused with the Sullivanian perspective, I came very early on to take this unity as a given. I was therefore most pleasantly surprised 20 years ago by the reception accorded my *Interaction Concepts of Personality* (1969), which I had viewed as a mere updating and modest systematization of the multiple intersections of social and clinical psychology, ones I had assumed to be obvious to nearly everyone. Clearly that was not the case, and in retrospect I also can appreciate that this work struck a chord in some because it offered a plausible alternative to the absurd choice of "person" versus "situation" during the opening salvos of what was to become one of psychology's most pointless but enduring controversies.

While this bit of personal history readily serves as a reminder that psychology as a discipline is not immune to the peril observed in Santayanna's gloomy forecast about forgetfulness, my main purpose in recounting it is to illustrate how far we have come over the past two decades in achieving consensus on the main components and experiential (there are, to be sure, other sources as well) roots of personhood. As I read the evidence, there is now an unprecedented and truly remarkable confluence of thinking on this topic, all of it pointing to the centrality of interpersonal history in shaping our prepotent response dispositions and hence to a degree the kinds of situations to which we expose ourselves, and indeed the manner in which we construe or process these situations in assigning meaning (including the meaning *stressor*) to them. A certain continuity of personhood, even maladaptive personhood, is assured in such a system because environmental reactions routinely confirm the person's already established interpersonal realities.

Impressive as is this convergence of thinking from many sources, however, it must be noted that the constituent ideas could hardly qualify as revolutionary, or even counterintuitive. On the contrary, when concisely stated as above, they seem today rather obvious and pedestrian—not the sort of thing to provoke either enthusiastic adoption or strong dissent. If we have come a long way then—and I believe we have—the progress has been neither rapid nor marked by anything remotely resembling a dramatic breakthrough, as happens sometimes in fields whose observational instruments more closely track what is contemporaneous high tech. Rather, we have an instance of what Meehl (1978) called "the slow progress of soft psychology."

As we approach the 21st century, and as psychology assumes what I believe to be its manifest destiny as the final frontier of medical science, I for one do not anticipate that the road will be any easier, or that genuine progress will be any more clearly marked by dramatic discoveries that presage entirely new directions. Rather, I anticipate a slow accretion of wisdom, punctuated by the exploration of many blind alleys—as, for example, has already occurred in relation to the Type A behavior pattern. Wrestling with the psychological dimensions of the immune response, already known to be incredibly complex in organization, will, I suspect, severely test both the patience and the mettle of the young investigators now being prepared for the battle. I wish them well, and I advise them not to forget that humans are, as much as anything else, social animals.

Lastly, assessment and treatment must be integrated. In a common scenario, the diagnostic procedures may play little or no role in the subsequent interventions that are employed with people. Our view, and it is a strong form argument regarding the underlying reason for professional diagnosis, is that the diagnosis must be linked to the treatment procedures in order to warrant its continued existence. Of course, we are not so naïve that we can ignore the autonomous status that diagnosis has achieved in the general mental health field. Indeed, there are large publishing industries and technologies (e.g., witness the recent emergence of computerized testing procedures) that fuel the continued existence and popularity of diagnostic tests and testing. Our point is that often the diagnostic process appears to have taken on a life of its own. Somehow, the hyphen needs to be put back in the phrase "diagnostic-treatment sequence."

Treatment Issues

Some would argue that the ultimate test of the usefulness of the social/clinical interface relates to whether it can generate therapeutic strategies that will not only be understood with regard to how they work, but they will actually be used by practicing clinicians "in the trenches" (see commentary by Mark Snyder on this point). The former goal of developing theories about how treatment works is explored by the authors in this handbook who have written about various treatment issues. The question of whether these or other procedures will find their way to "the trenches" is, at yet, unanswered.

Perhaps a good starting point in discussing treatment issues is to go to the bottom-line question, "Does it work?" The answer appears to be yes when this question is applied to the results of meta-analyses studies conducted since 1977. Us-

ing statistical procedures for collapsing across treatment outcome studies conducted by a multitude of different investigators, Smith and Glass (1977) published the initial meta-analysis study in which the benefits of psychological treatment were documented. In these meta-analysis studies, the sizes of the positive outcome changes evidenced by people receiving specific psychological treatments (varying in terms of their procedures) are compared with the sizes of positive outcome changes found in people who do not receive such treatments. Meta-analysis studies subsequent to the original Smith and Glass one consistently have provided support for the effectiveness of treatment (e.g., Andrews & Harvey, 1981; Barker,

---

COMMENTARY 2:

Social Psychology and Clinical Practice: The Therapeutic Imperative
Mark Snyder
University of Minnesota

I am of the school of psychology that takes it as an article of faith that, as Kurt Lewin proclaimed many years ago, there is nothing so practical as a good theory. As much as I have been invested in advancing the state of theory in psychology, I have always believed that one proof of the utility of developing psychological theories is in their application. This is not to say that I believe that the agenda for theoretical work in psychology should be set by applied considerations. Rather, I believe that ultimately the more we work to create better theories in psychology, the more psychology will be able to address practical concerns in people's lives and in society at large.

In recent years, much has been said and much has been done to define the "interface" of social and clinical psychology. Undeniably, this union has been a fertile one, producing much empirical and theoretical work, as this handbook attests. Those who have labored at the interface have much to say about the problems of individual and social functioning. I wholeheartedly endorse, applaud, and encourage these efforts. There is, I must admit, a somewhat self-serving edge to my words of praise. After all, I have gone to great lengths to spell out the implications of my work on self and identity for understanding the origins and treatment of problems of adjustment (Snyder, 1987) and of my work on social relationships for understanding interactions between therapists and their clients (Snyder & Thomsen, 1988).

Yet, my purpose here is not all cheerleading. As thrilled as I am by all the research generated by the social-clinical interface, and as impressed as I am with the considerable utility of social psychological perspectives to conceptualize clinical issues, I must confess that, for me at least, there is something lacking. My commitment to the "nothing so practical as a good theory" dictum compels me to speak on behalf of those who actually practice the clinical arts. If I labored in the trenches of clinical practice, if I were a therapist or counselor doing battle day in and day out with the problems that brought my clients to me, I would have one question. Where are the treatments, where are the interventions, where are the therapies generated by the interface between social and clinical psychology?

Quite simply, I am suggesting that the bottom-line consideration in evaluating the fruits of the social-clinical interface may be the therapeutic procedures it produces. Now do not get me wrong. I do expect therapies based on the theories and procedures of social psychology to be developed, just as therapies based on principles from other domains of psychology (e.g., learning, cognition) have been systematically developed and refined. And my nagging may prod things along just a bit. Of course, even if and when social-clinical therapies emerge from the interface (and I am not so impatient as to ask for immediate delivery), they will find themselves in a crowded marketplace. Already, there are hundreds of brands of psychotherapy competing for the allegiances of practitioners. Yet, when it comes to fulfilling the promise of the social-clinical interface, I cannot help but believe that the proof of the pudding just may be in the therapeutic enterprise; that is where theory and research on the interface will prove just how practical they can be.

Funk, & Houston, 1988; Landman & Dawes, 1982; Prioleau, Murdock, & Brody, 1983; Shapiro & Shapiro, 1982).

The behaviors examined in these outcome studies are many and varied. To name but a few, these have included anxieties and phobias of various types, insomnia, depression, and relational (marriage, parenting, dating) problems. Further, studies use observable outcomes, self-report outcomes, and sometimes both. Although this diversity of outcome measures is impressive, it also is the case that researchers vary widely in how they conceptualize and measure the actual outcome changes. Likewise, there is some question about the adequacy of the measures and operationalizations of change (see the commentary by Hans H. Strupp for several concerns about the way that outcome is used in research). A related point to be raised in the context of our present attention on health-related outcomes is that future researchers will need to include observable, quantifiable, and valid indexes of physical health. Self-report measures of health have been more typical, but we would recommend using these in conjunction with "harder" measures of physical health.

Although previous results provide support for the effectiveness of treatments, there is considerable room for improvement. One of the major tasks in this regard will be to maximize the change that we can engender in people through our treatments. Further work is warranted in explicating the best person by treatment matches for effecting change. Some work has been done on this topic, most notably the client-therapist matching (see Beutler and others, this volume), but there is much more that we can learn about how the person-based processes interact with the environment-based treatments. Such work may come from the individual differences researchers who will increasingly want to examine the interactions of their person-based constructs with various types of treatment. Conversely, treatment researchers will want to turn to diagnostic or individual differences variables to expand the power of their interventions.

Another set of related issues about the general power and effectiveness of treatment pertains to transfer and maintenance of change (see Karoly, this volume). Although change can and does occur in the short-term through treatment, the sobering fact is that the generalization across settings (transfer) and across time (maintenance) often is rather meager in two senses. First, the available

research suggests that generalization simply does not occur for many clients. Second, researchers tend not to take measures of change across settings and time, and as such there is not sufficient attention paid to these important issues. We would agree with the commentary by Arnold P. Goldstein. He asserts that more attention needs to be given to embedding generalization augmentation strategies into the structure of the treatment itself, and to involving the client's eco-system (parents, peers, employers, teachers, and spouses) in the treatment.

Having argued for the continued development and mapping of person-by-treatment interactions, we would like to make a closing, seemingly inconsistent comment. While we applaud and encourage the subsequent technological work that needs to be done in this regard, we would hasten to emphasize our view that it is the underlying theory that should be the focus of generalization rather than the technology. We will never achieve a level of technological sophistication whereby we can absolutely match people and treatments, but the useful theory has the inherent flexibility to be applied to a given client under given circumstances. To have a valid theoretical perspective to apply to our clients, in our estimation, is the key to the treatment processes that we employ. In this vein, we are reminded of a successful gardener who continually works with the roots of a plant rather than merely focusing on the leaves. To the credit of the authors of this handbook who have written on the topic of treatment, there is an obvious thrust in regard to the importance of theory. It is our view that the interface researchers are especially well qualified to develop and test such theories.

Caveats

Against this backdrop of encouraging theoretical growth and empirical results, we must consider limitations as well as strengths. With regard to the person-based processes, it should be noted that our individual differences measures account for relatively small amounts of self-reported health behaviors, and even less of the actual physical health markers. This is reminiscent of Mischel's (1968) earlier skepticism with regard to the predictive power of personality measures.

There are ways to increase the predictive capabilities of self-report individual differences measures to health outcomes, assuming that (a) the underlying theory is heuristic and (b) the respond-

COMMENTARY 3:

Psychosocial Treatments: Some Unsolved Problems
Hans H. Strupp
Vanderbilt University

Three critical issues continue to bedevil the measurement of change in psychosocial treatments of all kinds. First, there is the problem of outcome. Because of its central importance for all research concerned with therapeutic change, clarification of the outcome problem is urgently needed. Critical questions include the following: (a) What kinds of specific changes are expected as a result of particular therapeutic interventions? (b) Who judges whether a given change is to be characterized as an improvement or as a negative effect—the patient, society, or the therapist? (c) Is it reasonable to combine judgments derived from the foregoing domains, or should they be kept separate? (d) What instruments or measurement operations are adequate to assess changes? Across-the-board changes, as measured, for example, by the Minnesota Multiphasic Personality Inventory and other "inventories," or single indices like behavioral avoidance tests, have increasingly emerged as inadequate. As elaborated by Strupp and Hadley (1977), the issues to be resolved are research tasks only in part; they also involve to a significant degree issues of researchers' beliefs, societal standards, and public policy, which in turn call for a thorough analysis of social values and the manner in which they enter into judgments of mental health and therapy change.

A second issue involves techniques versus nonspecific factors. This issue continues to be a topic of central theoretical and practical importance. There is as yet limited evidence that specific techniques are uniquely effective apart from nonspecific factors; indeed, earlier enthusiasm about the vaunted superiority of certain techniques (e.g., systematic desensitization) has given way to more sober assessments as greater weight is being assigned to contextual factors; that is, the patient-therapist relationship in which techniques are always embedded. This point also underscores the futility of clinical trials in which techniques are decontextualized.

Third, there is the problem of diagnosis. There is a great need to describe more adequately patient populations for whom particular forms of treatment are intended. The traditional diagnostic categories, as most researchers and therapists recognize, are woefully inadequate, but so are taxonomies based purely on behavioral indicators. So-called simple phobias in a presumed "normal" personality are rare, and there is increasing appreciation that the person's total personality makeup (character) or social modes play a part in the presenting disorder. There are still only limited conceptual schemes for describing patients and their problems, a situation seriously impeding outcome assessments and treatment comparisons. In particular, we must develop better ways of assessing the totality of the patient's functioning—its strengths and weaknesses—within which descriptions of what constitutes a "problem" in need of therapeutic modification must take their place.

There is a great need for studies in which more sharply defined techniques are studied in relation to particular patient-therapist combinations, which again must be defined more stringently. Answers from such studies will not only shed light on the relative importance of particular techniques and particular combinations of personality factors, but they also have important implications for optimal assignment (matching) of particular therapists to particular patients in clinics and other treatment facilities.

ents have not been accurately accessing and reporting their self-knowledge. In this latter vein, three techniques that lead to increased predictive power between self-report and actual behavior have been suggested (see Wicklund & Eckert-Nowack, 1989; Zanna & Fazio, 1982, for expanded discussions). First, by instructing the respondents to self-report in terms of how extremely they could imagine responding to the content tapped in the items, rather than using their typical stance, the predictive power is increased (e.g., Willerman, Turner, & Peterson, 1976). Second, if the respondent is given a concrete situational context in which to imagine him or herself and is then asked to respond to the self-report items in this context, the predictive power of the measure is increased (Fazio & Zanna, 1978; Zanna & Fazio, 1982). Third, self-focused attention instructions increase the predictive capabilities of self-report indices (see Gibbons, 1983, for review).

Much of the variability in human behavior and health outcomes in particular is driven by genetics. This fact, in part, explains why relatively small amounts of variance are predicted by the psychological variables that are employed by interface scholars. What is not clear, however, is the extent to which our psychological variables somehow contain genetic underpinnings. Perhaps some of the motivational individual differences constructs (e.g., Type A behavior pattern, the agency

COMMENTARY 4:

Toward Clinical Utility:
From Theory to Technique to Situation to Person, and Back
Frederick H. Kanfer
The University of Illinois at Urbana — Champaign

Psychological treatment is a problem-solving enterprise. Therefore, a clinician must be familiar with a body of knowledge about phenomena that relates to the problem at hand, techniques for translating such knowledge into effective operations, and some rules or heuristics that include which body of scientific knowledge is most relevant to the problem. Rapprochements of social and clinical psychology that relate two or more subdomains of science (e.g., interpersonal or decision-making processes and pathological processes) have made excellent progress, as has the translation of principles into operation (see Section III of this handbook). A critical shortcoming, however, lies in providing heuristics for matching techniques to characteristics of situations and patients. Barber (1988) has called attention to this lack of guidelines on how to use models and to map problems onto them. Among others, Hayes, Nelson, and Jarrett (1987), Kanfer and Nay (1982), and Dance and Neufeld (1988) have dealt with various facets of the problem of utility (i.e., developing specific guidelines and predictors that take into account patient characteristics, problems, and situations). But to date the bridges have built mostly from theories about individual differences to treatment operations. The translation must be enriched by consideration of the realities of the context in which therapy occurs; such realities usually transcend specific psychological subdomains and unidimensional models.

Providing a fruitful interface between theory and application requires several steps. In a utopian scenario, the literature would offer, on the one hand, guidelines on how to formulate the clinical problems in the technical language of psychological science. On the other hand, the clinician would find detailed statements of the implications and applicability of research and theory to everyday problems. Once this had been achieved, a clinician would then be assisted by guidelines for selecting among the many variables those that not only have a statistically significant effect but an ecologically useful impact on the practical situation. A conceptual formulation could then be made of the problem, the desired outcome, and the interventions required to achieve it. Intervention strategies derived from this formulation would be translated into available technology and operations appropriate for the individual case. The client's life contexts and the characteristics of the therapeutic setting also would be examined to assess their probable impact in facilitating or blocking successful outcomes. Because the dynamic aspect of human existence involves continuing change in interrelationships among components of the person-environment, static models of basic psychology will have to be supplemented and expanded. To attain clinical utility, scientific enterprises cannot stop with descriptions of interrelationships of statistical significance. They must also contribute toward analyzing the relative power (utility) of principles and methods for different individual situations and the robustness of changes both over time and for different individual contexts. While current trends are moving in this direction, these efforts have just begun. Ultimately, it should be possible to train clinicians not only to be familiar with psychological science but also to behave in ways that enact the implications of theory and research in everyday practice.

component of hope) are to some degree "hardwired." The sophisticated interface studies linking genetics and the various psychological variables have yet to be done, but will be important if we are to advance our understanding of subsequently developed explanatory theories.

Another caveat involves our rather short-term temporal approach to conducting research on health-related outcomes. In other words, what we know so far is based on studies involving short temporal envelopes (anywhere from a few minutes to a few months). Health outcomes undoubtedly are derived from long-term patterns of behavior, and we heretofore have not had the time, energy,

and investment (both psychologically and monetarily) to engage in the necessary long-term analyses of health-help-health sequences. It is as if we have taken snapshots of a process that is, at minimum, a long movie. Because of this, our understanding of the health-help-health process is somewhat delimited.

Perhaps the last caveat is also the most difficult. In reading the work that the present scholars have generated, as well as other work in journals and books, it is apparent that there is no consensus on what is meant by the term "health." Our resolution, as articulated in the first chapter, was to define health as consisting of the psychological/

COMMENTARY 5:

Generating Transfer:
Toward a Technology of Transfer and Maintenance Enhancement
Arnold P. Goldstein
Syracuse University

Though the implicit belief to the contrary often remains strong, most successful psychological treatments rarely function as inoculations against the later return of the psychological states that engendered the initial seeking of treatment. The inoculatory belief is made explicit in the goal statements of some psychotherapeutic approaches, and in aspirations regarding "enduring personality change." It appears more implicitly in the "train and hope" aspiration of other approaches. Yet considerable evidence from many sources, involving diverse therapeutic approaches employed with many different types of clients, consistently reveals that both major categories of generalization — across settings (transfer) and across time (maintenance) — do not occur in a substantial proportion of outcomes. In terms of both the real-world use of, and enduringness of, therapeutic gains, much of the time we (change agent and client) have largely wasted our time and effort. That, as they say, is the bad news. The good news is that during the past decade three highly promising, complementary strategies for generating generalization of treatment gains have emerged. Each has gathered at least a moderate level of empirical support, and each is clearly a worthy candidate for both further experimental evaluation as well as continued clinical utilization.

The first generalization augmentational strategy concerns the internal structure of the treatment itself. Growing evidence suggests that generalization of gain will be more likely when the psychological treatment offered is both broad and multichannel. Band width in this context refers to the breadth or number of client qualities targeted by the treatment; multichannelness refers to the range of different modes of client response targeted, respectively, by the different components of the treatment. Our approach to chronically aggressive adolescents, aggression replacement training, consisting of separate but integrated weekly sessions of prosocial skills training (the behavior-targeted component), anger-control training (the affect-targeted component), and moral reasoning (the values-targeted component), is an example of such a broad band, multichannel treatment. Demonstrations of reductions in recidivism associated with this intervention are initial evidence of its generalization-promoting efficacy.

The second recommended strategy involves the incorporation into the structure of the treatment, or the manner in which it is delivered, of an array of transfer- and maintenance-enhancing procedures. These several methods have their initial roots in laboratory research on verbal learning, but in recent years have been examined for their efficacy in clinical contexts. The five transfer-enhancing procedures include (a) provision of general principles (general case programming); (b) overlearning (maximizing response availability); (c) stimulus variability (train sufficient exemplars, train loosely); (d) identical elements (programming common stimuli); and (e) mediated generalization (self-recording, self-reinforcement, self-instruction). The five maintenance enhancing procedures include (a) thin reinforcement (increase intermittency, unpredictableness); (b) delayed reinforcement; (c) fade prompts; (d) booster sessions; and (e) preparation for real-life nonreinforcement (teaching self-reinforcement, relapse and failure management skills, and graduated homework assignments).

The final strategy for encouraging real-world enduring use of treatment gains, overlapping in some of its particulars with those described in the previous paragraph, lies external to the treatment itself and, in one form or another, involves reaching into the client's ecosystem. Transfer and maintenance will be enhanced if the change agent, with creativity, energy, and persistence, seeks to maximize the degree to which the client's interpersonal environment (parents, peers, siblings, employers, teachers, spouse) are promotive of such reinforcement. In the relevant research and clinical efforts, such promotive behavior by the client's real-world significant others has typically been operationalized by continuation of the treatment itself with the parent, peer, and so forth serving as change agent, and/or the mobilization and programming of such persons as skilled contingency managers, providing reinforcement as appropriate for continued desirable behaviors, as well as prompting, coaching, and perhaps punishing for continued undesirable behaviors. Reaching into the client's ecosystem also may be accomplished by teaching the client to use reinforcers that occur naturally in his or her environment. The client is taught to identify easily reinforced behaviors, and use both reinforcement recruitment and reinforcement recognition.

The diverse concretizations of these three strategies constitute the current technology available to the treatment community for the purposes of generating generalization of client gain. It is an underused technology, yet one that must be employed, investigated, expanded, and promoted if we are to serve our clients in a more fully ethical and effective manner.

COMMENTARY 6:

Evaluating Psychosocial Factors in Health
Richard S. Lazarus
University of California-Berkeley

Taking care of one's health through the management of stress, and via active programs devoted to exercise, diet, and avoiding substance abuse are all the rage, and the indicated values and knowledge base have spawned a number of new disciplines sometimes identified as health psychology.or behavioral medicine. This comment affords me the opportunity — which I hasten to take advantage of — to remind health-oriented professionals about how little we know about whether and how much we can do to effect long-term health outcomes. We seem to have accepted unwarily the medical obsession that we can control health — even chronic health — and any intimation that we may have less ability to do this than is commonly presumed is offensive.

I would like to offer four reasons — essentially methodological — why it is difficult to demonstrate unequivocally that there are important psychosocial influences on health even though we all tend to believe that they exist.

First, health is affected by a great many factors over which we have little or no control, but which are probably very powerful influences nonetheless. These include genetic-constitutional factors, accidents, environmental toxins, and long-term life-styles, which involve using harmful agents as in drinking and smoking, and which are undoubtedly of transcendent importance, especially in vulnerable persons. After the influence on health variance that is played by these factors, and probably a host of others of which researchers are only dimly aware, has been taken into account, there may be only modest amounts of variance left to show the operation of psychosocial factors like stress.

Second, health is usually very stable and does not change rapidly, except under special circumstances such as aging or rapidly progressing illnesses. In our research we have found the correlation over a year — with admittedly poor measures — to be about .70. To demonstrate causal influences requires that one show that psychosocial factors produce changes in health, but because of this stability doing so is very difficult (see Kasl, 1983).

Third, to show that stress and coping affects long-term health requires that we measure stable patterns during the time interval in which we make our observations. It is not what happens in a single encounter that is important, but what happens consistently over time. The only solution is either to find processes that are stable or representative of the person — a rather unlikely state of affairs — or to monitor what happens in the time interval of interest. This means sampling what is going on repeatedly, rather than making only a single pre- and post-assessment.

Several researchers (e.g., Caspi, Bolger, & Eckenrode, 1987; Eckenrode, 1984; Stone & Neale, 1984) have begun to realize, in fact, that monitoring a relatively short time interval for stress, coping, and illness symptoms offers a more practical strategy for doing this than trying to study the problem over years of longitudinal research. Along these lines, DeLongis, Folkman, and I (1988), in research using an intra- as well as an interindividual design, showed that certain personality traits, such as the perception of poor social support and negative self-esteem, predicted a rise in illness symptoms following increased daily stress.

Fourth, I believe we will never effectively study the relationship between stress, coping, and health unless we have some conceptual guidelines for what we mean by health, which are not now in evidence. As I have noted elsewhere (Lazarus, in press), if longevity is the criterion of health, then one condition, mucous colitis, seems to have no bearing on the outcome variable, but another condition, hypertension, does; however, if social functioning is the criterion of health, then hypertension has no bearing — especially when it remains untreated by distressing drugs — but colitis does. This example is only one of many that highlights the need for a workable theory of health that would be useful in helping us create a sound measurement strategy for epidemiological and clinical research.

My reason for offering this relatively pessimistic account of our prospects for adequately supporting the contention that psychosocial factors such as stress and coping are important influences on health is not to discourage clinical, social, and personality psychologists interested in health. One hates to be a spoilsport. Rather, it seems to me that these methodological issues are so important that professionals always need to keep them in mind lest they fail to understand what is really known and not known about behavior and health, fail to understand how to go about getting valid answers, and be mistaken about the prescriptions they offer for intervention and self-help. Only sophistication about our knowledge base will help us avoid making outrageous claims that only uninformed laypeople and physicians — who undoubtedly want to believe — would be willing to accept.

physical state that the person is motivated to sustain or change. This definition is obviously an overarching one. It entails both the psychological and physical elements, it emphasizes the person's phenomenology, and it has an accompanying sense of motivation. This definition was chosen because it captures a myriad of other specific health definitions, but it has at least one flaw. Imagine, for example, the person who has a serious physical illness, but who is not yet aware of this phenomenologically. Certainly this person has a health problem from a physiological point of view, but does not have one phenomenologically. Realistically, it may never be possible to arrive at a common definition of health, and it is therefore incumbent on interface scholars to clarify for their audiences what they mean by this crucial term.

BUILDING THE INTERFACE

Challenges to Be Met

The progress that has been made with regard to social-clinical interface does not guarantee a stable future, for the problems that jeopardize its future viability are serious ones (see the commentaries by Sharon S. Brehm, Susan S. Hendricks and Clyde Hendricks, and Bonnie R. Strickland for related discussions). First, there is the historical and continued separation of the clinical and social training programs in departments of psychology. (At some universities, however, the separation is so complete that there is an entirely distinct department or division of clinical psychology. This separation includes the various levels of autonomy, for example, administration, budget, building, and courses.) Although faculty technically may be in the same department, the separations are clear. In some departments the social and clinical faculty may occupy different buildings, and even if they are in the same building, they may have separate floors. Additionally, the programs each have their faculty, students, curriculum, meetings, and administrative structures. In part, some of this separation is driven by the fact that the American Psychological Association has a detailed set of administrative and curricular criteria that must be met by clinical programs in order to attain and maintain accreditation; in contrast, social programs are under no such accreditation guidelines and as such are free to develop more varied administrative and curricular models of education.

It should be noted, also, that the length of the temporal envelope involved in securing a Ph.D. may be another stumbling block. Each program, whether clinical or social, wants us to ensure that the minimum basic entry skills and knowledge are acquired. Therefore, to produce Ph.D.s with an interface curriculum would necessitate extending the time period required to obtain the degree. Neither the faculty nor students may be willing to do this.

In addition to the aforementioned formal boundaries between social and clinical, it also should be noted that faculty members naturally tend to reproduce the education format in which they were trained. Thus, the separation of the training is a replication of "the way we did it at my school." Also, for a new assistant professor, the interface may seem especially risky because such activities do not fit the clear mold of what a "social" or a "clinical" faculty member is to do in order to get promoted. As one assistant professor put it to the editors at a recent conference on the interface, "It is easy for you guys with tenure to talk and behave this way, but I have to look at what will get me tenure." In other words, the interface individual runs the risk of being a "marginal person" who is not recognized and rewarded in the context of many present day psychology departments.

Just as the individual faculty may tend to solidify his or her "identity," support, and reward structure within a clinical or social program, the programs may continue their efforts to solidify their resources within the department of psychology more generally. This means that a particular program argues for its needs (e.g., faculty, space, equipment, etc.), and as such any jointly derived ventures are viewed as threats to the core program needs. The separation is further reinforced by professional networking systems for each subarea. For example, there are journals dedicated to each area; likewise, each has its own set of professional societies or divisions, conventions, awards, etc.

Lastly, we are presently witnessing the inability of scientist and practitioner psychologists to cooperate at the national level. The American Psychological Association has been the formal battle ground for this split, which has occurred because of the inability of various divisions in the national organization to arrive at shared goals and to make compromises. In this vein, the American Psychological Society was formed specifically to respond to the needs of the scientific psychologists. There

COMMENTARY 7:

On Winning Battles and Losing Wars
Sharon S. Brehm
The University of Kansas — Lawrence

In 1976, my book *The Application of Social Psychology to Clinical Practice* was published to what, at the time, appeared a deafening roar of indifference. I had thought of myself as carrying on the tradition of pioneers such as Frank, Carson, Goldstein, Heller, and Sechrest. Instead, I seemed to be the end of the line of descent. Fortunately, my initial optimism turned out to be a better predictor than my brief spell of pessimism. The social-clinical interface easily weathered a period of neglect to emerge full of life in the 1980s. Invigorated by creative and talented researchers, solidified by insightful books and chapters, and institutionalized by John Harvey's founding of the *Journal of Social and Clinical Psychology*, the interface prospered. All seemed well.

But was it? Certainly, the interface was firmly established in social psychology. By the mid-1980s, it was unusual to pick up any issue of any mainstream journal in social psychology without finding research relevant to some clinical topic. Although slower to develop, the interface also became increasingly important in the work of researchers in clinical and counseling psychology. As barriers fell, ease of passage could be taken for granted. Surely, all was well.

Not quite. Talking with graduate students these days is like entering a time warp. Clinical students talk "clinical"; social students talk "social." You can make them talk "interface," but for most it remains an imposed, artificial dialect. Social students are eager to conduct research on depression — without ever having seen a clinically depressed individual. Clinical students will master a narrow wedge of the social literature for a research project, but show little or no interest in the larger context. And they are amazed (or amused) if you suggest that social psychology might be relevant to their clinical work. Putting it mildly, the interface seems less than a major force in their intellectual and professional lives.

There are, of course, exceptions. I would suggest, however, that it is unwise to rely entirely on exceptions to carry on the tradition. My hope for "the interface toward the year 2000" is that we would take more seriously our responsibilities for the training of the next generation. They should be better than we are. To be better, I submit, will require a fully integrated training program where students learn "real" clinical and "real" social. True, such a program would require unusual flexibility from the faculty involved and probably an extra time investment of a year or so from the students. Would the potential benefits justify the added effort?

I believe the price would be well worth paying. Consider, for example, the kind of theory and research that would be produced by the graduates of interface programs. One might expect some new solutions to the eternally vexing problem of balancing conceptual richness and empirical precision. Consider also the possible effects on clinical practice. I am prepared to argue that the ultimate test of the clinical-social interface must occur at the level of the consumer. If so, we should not trust our ideas simply to "trickle down." We must develop interface therapeutic strategies, evaluate them, and train people to use them. Finally, consider the profession. In a time of petty quarrels within the American Psychological Association, the scientist-practitioner model is in desperate straits. Are we to retreat within our little niches? Or, shall we up the ante and make an even greater commitment to this model within the context of the social-clinical interface? It seems to me that the tradition deserves to be passed along. The battle for acceptance among our peers having long since been won, we can take the time to build a reconciliation that will endure.

has been an "us" versus "them" mentality in this debate, and as such it has many of the qualities of the problems outlined previously in this section.

Drawing a Blueprint

Against this backdrop of potential obstacles, it is important to discuss what can be done to ensure the growth of the interface. Perhaps the first task is to specify the nature of what we mean by the interface. In the past, the interface has involved an intersection of the subareas of social and clini-cal psychology. This intersection has resulted in a simple touching or connection of the boundaries of the two subareas. The aforementioned definition is reflected in writers who use the phrase "at the interface" in describing some aspect of social/clinical work. This conception of the interface was useful because it satisfied the needs of each subarea. Social psychology was searching to be relevant, to maintain and increase its attention to real-life issues; clinical psychology, having thoroughly explored some of the grand theorists of previous decades, needed new theoretical frameworks for conceptualizing people. With regard to the neces-

COMMENTARY 8:

A "Healthy" Interface:
On the Value of Professional Confidence, Listening, and Ecumenism
Susan S. Hendrick and Clyde Hendrick
Texas Tech University

If the interface is to become an increasing reality toward the year 2000, it seems to us that more psychologists must relinquish their historical arrogance (manifested by feelings of superiority toward other disciplines such as sociology, family studies, and education) and low self-esteem (manifested by feelings of inferiority toward other disciplines such as biology, chemistry, and mathematics), replacing this bipolar behavior with healthy confidence in what we can and cannot do. Once we begin accepting our limitations and honestly seeking ways in which to enrich our research and practice, we will find it easier to become ecumenical, embracing strengths of other disciplines as well as of other areas within our own discipline of psychology. Although we have espoused ecumenism throughout psychology, our focus has been on the interface of social, clinical, and counseling psychology. And our personal knowledge of these three areas involves incidents in which all three have been "guilty" of spending available energy defending turf, or else using it to devalue one of the other areas, and in both cases neglecting the more important issue of how the three areas can work together. We know that it is easier to argue than to negotiate; in fact, the two of us deal with professional competition/cooperation on nearly a daily basis. We disagree on many issues of education (i.e., what constitutes a core curriculum) and training (i.e., how much practicum training [if any] is needed before someone is ready to deal therapeutically with a client). What makes our arguments typically fruitful, however, is a basic respect for the other person as a psychologist, and for the other person's area of the discipline. Without that basic respect, creative dialogue would be impossible. Thus, we believe that every time a psychologist belittles a psychologist from another content area, the interface slips a little farther from our grasp. And every time a psychologist seeks respectful collaboration with a psychology colleague, the interface moves a little closer.

It is always easier to articulate change at the level of the institution rather than at the level of the individual, both because institutional change appears more removed and less personally demanding, and because institutional change happens so seldom that our basic desire for homeostasis is usually satisfied. Certainly, we are not disputing the value of political statements, organizations, handbooks, and the like as driving forces for professional progress. All are necessary for change to occur. However, for something like the interface, change must happen for individuals, or it cannot happen for institutions. We believe that nothing less than massive change on the part of psychologists, encompassing secure confidence about what we have to teach, and open curiosity about what we still need to learn, can provide the future for the interface that it so richly deserves.

sity of theory and subsequent experimental tests with actual people attempting to cope with the vicissitudes of life, it is important to emphasize that these latter values have formed the backbone of these previous interface endeavors.

In our estimation, the social/clinical interface will need to take on a more interactive model of intersection than has previously been the case. That is, we would advocate that the two subareas need to establish an interface in an overlapping sense (see Forsyth and Leary, this volume). In other words, however it is accomplished, what we are calling for in subsequent years are recognized arenas whereby interface psychologists can work together and be recognized and rewarded for such activities. To some extent, this is already the case in some psychology departments where people trained as clinical or social psychologists are

prospering. Such people, however, have literally evolved on their own into personifications of interface scholars in that their interests have led them to this integrative stance.

Beyond those professionals who have naturally emerged as manifestations of the interface, there have been a handful of people who have obtained training in both predoctoral clinical and social psychology programs. It is our view, and one shared by other writers (see previous Sharon S. Brehm commentary), that we can not count on this relatively small pool of interface psychologists to "carry the torch" in the manner that it deserves. What is needed are educational contexts wherein students can garner Ph.D.s in the interface. This will mean that present faculty will have to have the vision, and negotiating skills, to develop or evolve such programs in the context of

COMMENTARY 9:

The Viability of the Discipline of Psychology: A Plea for Integrating Science and Practice

Bonnie R. Strickland
University of Massachusetts at Amherst

The issues faced by psychologists as they approach the 21st century and their second hundred years will continue to focus on the growth and survival of the discipline. The first hundred years of psychology defined the science and profession. The second half of the 20th century also marked the establishment of the practice of psychology as an independent health-care profession.

Psychology has enjoyed enormous successes but these have led to the inevitable strains that occur as any science matures. With an explosion of knowledge in the science and application of psychology, it is increasingly difficult to be broadly trained, and one's interests move naturally toward specialized areas. Such evolution raises continued concerns about a core of psychology and whether the discipline can remain unified. Moreover, because psychology is so broad, we increasingly interact with other disciplines or find ourselves involved in establishing and developing new fields of inquiry, such as health psychology. Some find the new endeavors so different from their earlier experiences that they leave the field of psychology, or no longer call themselves psychologists.

Psychology has also been unique among the major sciences and professions in trying to combine the generation of knowledge with its application. Because scientists and practitioners often hold different values and work in different venues, a true integration of science and practice has often been quite difficult. Health psychologists, in particular, must of necessity be knowledgeable in both basic and applied arenas and practice their psychology, as appropriate, within the highest standards of ethical practice.

So, overriding issues, especially relevant to social and clinical, and health psychology, have to do with how we maintain and nourish the discipline of psychology so that social and clinical psychologists continue to inform and be informed by the traditional core areas of psychology. Additionally, social psychology, as both a basic and applied science, and clinical psychology as a practice, are deeply affected by the problems of integration that face psychology.

The protection and enhancement of the discipline are essential, not only for the partisan support of psychology, but because psychology is that contemporary science that is not reductionistic but gives attention to a total, organismic functioning. No other science emphasizes behavior and focuses on individual actions within a situational context. We cannot afford to lose a discipline that seems so clearly necessary for understanding and alleviating human problems. We must continue to link health psychology to both our basic and applied knowledge base in general psychology.

Social and clinical psychology seem to be uniquely poised to advance and apply knowledge of the human condition. We will need, however, to forge new models for preserving the discipline, for communicating across areas, and for integrating the science and practice of psychology.

existing departments with separate clinical and social programs. This will be no easy task. As Seymour Sarason (1987) noted with regard to such proposed changes,

> Graduate programs and departments, like the universities of which they are part, are conservative organizations that adhere tenaciously to tradition, existing practice, and the marketplace. The changing of curricula encounters a field of mines. (p. 223)

There certainly are psychology departments where an interface program might flourish, but this important task remains to be accomplished. If and when such programs are established, the true overlap in social/clinical training will be achieved. This task will involve attention to what the constituent faculties consider to be the "basics" in social and clinical psychology, with special attention also being paid to meeting the requirements of the American Psychological Association for the accreditation of clinical programs. Undoubtedly, these interface programs will require a somewhat longer period of training. It is this fact as well as the accompanying problems (e.g., securing another year of graduate student support money) will need to be resolved by the faculty.

Once established, such programs would entail a reward structure for interface faculty. Also, these programs would provide a source of employment for future interface-trained graduates. The major

COMMENTARY 10:

Roots and Growth:
The Role of Theory and Laboratory-Experimental Methodology
John H. Harvey
University of Iowa

Indeed there are issues and problems that deserve our consideration as we move toward the next century and a likely prosperous era for this interface of clinical-counseling-social/personality psychology. Editors Snyder and Forsyth were wise to include such a futuristic section in this book. The one issue I wish to emphasize (as a social psychologist) is the enduring value to clinical and counseling scholars of laboratory research on basic social and personality processes. I would be one of the first to question the external (and sometimes internal) validity of laboratory-experimental research for advancing our understanding of many complex human problems. At this border, the lab and the experiment can only serve as adjunctive approaches to surveys/interviews/archival probes of the target phenomena in relevant populations. Nonetheless, taken as an indispensable enterprise for developing basic knowledge, the lab-experimental approach can be pursued in parallel to these more naturalistic–real world approaches and should have a clear, dignified stature in the evolution of this hybrid domain of contemporary psychology. Without such an approach, the development of several major current theories in clinical psychology (e.g., attributional analysis of learned helplessness and depression) would be retarded, or nonexistent. Similarly, basic work on special topics such as cognitive dissonance, reactance, and the actor-observer hypothesis in attribution and more generally work on theories of persuasion, social perception, stigma, group process, altruism, aggression, and violence have contributed in a fundamental way to more clinically relevant research and therapy in the last three decades—as the chapters in this book attest. So as we look to the era of the 21st century, let us not forget our roots. We owe so much to the theoretical and methodological thinking that pioneers such as Kurt Lewin and Fritz Heider bequeathed us. Those traditions also speak to openness and respect for diverse points of view. My hope is not only that the interface will be flourishing in 2000, but that it also will continue to embody such traditions and respect for basic work on social and personality processes.

employment arenas, however, obviously would be traditional clinical and social programs, as well as the multitude of other jobs where present applied social and clinical psychology graduates obtain employment. Further, once graduates of such interface programs enter psychology department settings, it may be possible for them to establish more interface programs. If the interface is the viable intellectual and practical hybrid that we believe it is, then it is obvious that the key next step is to establish the first such interface predoctoral programs.

Beyond the predoctoral programs, another vehicle for expanding the pool of social/clinical interface scholars involves postdoctoral training. For the present and until such time that predoctoral programs are established, it is possible for students who have obtained their Ph.D.s in either social or clinical psychology to obtain postdoctoral experiences (1 to 3 years) in the complementary subarea. Given the sheer amount of knowledge and skills that are necessary for a person in the interface, the notion of the availability of postdoctoral experi-

ence as a supplement is important. This present "building from a base" model of education is available to potential interface students.

Beyond the establishment of interface graduate training programs, there are other available building blocks for the interface. As a means of networking and disseminating information, for example, there is a need for continued conferences of interface scholars to share ideas; similarly, the development of societies or divisions of relevant psychological associations (with the usual newsletters) may produce further opportunities. Already, many clinical and social journals are filled with contents that epitomize the interface. Additionally, the operation of the *Journal of Social and Clinical Psychology* is yet one more index of the specific development of publication outlets for interface materials.

Lastly, the interface may weather the present difficulties because some of the important developing subdisciplines of psychology are implicitly involving social, clinical, and interface scholars. As a case in point, consider the subtitle of this handbook, "The Health Perspective." As this sub-discipline has emerged, it has offered a relatively "turf-free" content arena in which there was a naturally occurring cooperation among social and clinical psychologists (as well as professionals from other disciplines). In the extent to which other new applied content areas capture the attention of psychologists in subsequent years, similar opportunities for interface scholars will appear. At this time, the health perspective provides an excellent theme for the interface, but in future years a different theme may provide a better integration.

On the Building of a Home:
The Lesson of the Three Little Pigs

This summary chapter has been filled with visions of the future for the interface of social and clinical psychology. Although there are caveats and difficulties that we must address as we face the future, it is our strong belief that we need to move beyond a shared commons from which the various subareas of clinical and social "feed." In this sense, to return to an earlier discussed definition of the term interface, we are advocating more than a simple intersect of the two subareas. Indeed, what is needed is a "house" that we can share. Although some of the "rooms may look strangely familiar," as we note in the close of the introductory chapter of this handbook, we now should build a house where the rooms are readily identifiable as "ours." This will change the house into our home. Further, as the present chapters attest, such building projects by social/clinical psychologists may contribute to our understanding and facilitation of healthy people. But, to continue the work that has been started, it is absolutely essential that we build together. In this sense, we close the *Handbook* with the following allegorical evolution (Forsyth, 1988, pp. 63–65) of the story of "The Three Little Pigs":

> Not-so-long-ago in a not-so-far-away land lived three little pigs. These three little pigs grew up in the same neighborhood, attended the same schools, and shared the same passion: houses. The three were fascinated by the various types of structures inhabited by pigs the world over, and they whiled away many a happy hour puzzling over the nature and design of such dwellings. They could think of nothing more meaningful than dedicating their lives to the scientific study of houses and the ways they can be improved and repaired.
>
> As they grew older, however, the pigs gradually grew apart in values, beliefs, and goals. The first

pig became intrigued with understanding how houses worked, and embarked on a systematic study of foundations, arches, doors, and windows. So he bought a big arm chair in which to sit in his straw house and develop theory. He converted his pig pen into an elaborate laboratory where he could test out hypotheses, and erected a large sign for all to see. The sign read: Scientific Pig. Using his armchair and laboratory, he developed a particularly interesting theory about round houses that had no windows or doors. Although no one had found any of these houses, other scientifically minded pigs thought the work was interesting.

The second pig was also interested in the theory behind houses, arches and doorways. The second pig, however, wanted to use this knowledge to improve houses; to repair misshapen houses and possibly make houses of tomorrow better than houses of today. So this pig put a sign in front of his pen that read "Practical Pig," and began helping other pigs build and repair their houses. Soon, practical pig had made so much money that he could afford to build a breathtakingly beautiful house of sticks on a large tract of land in the country.

What, in the meantime, was the third pig doing? Well, it seems that he too was trying diligently to understand the nature of houses. Although scientific pig and practical pig only spoke to one another once a year at their annual reunion, the third pig often visited each one to talk about houses and ideas for improving them. When Scientific Pig would describe his studies of round houses, the third pig would ask what the studies say about the structural dynamics of houses in general. And when Practical Pig would talk about building houses out of sticks, the third pig would ask why sticks rather than stone? After many conversations and much research on houses, the third pig managed to build a house that, though it lacked the beauty of Practical Pig's house, was more useful than the round houses that the Scientific Pig studied.

One day a pig-hungry wolf came to town. When he came to the first pig's pen the wolf said, "I am hungry, and must have a pig for breakfast."

Scientific Pig, rising up from his arm chair said, "Why eat me? Can't you see the long-term importance of my work on round houses?"

"No," answered the wolf as he bit off the poor Scientific Pig's head.

You see, although, the first pig had fashioned a marvelous round house of straw and mortar with strong arches and walls, it had no window or doors. It was a fine model to be used for testing predictions about houses, but it didn't protect him from the wolf. The third pig had warned him that building houses with doors would yield both better data as well as safety from predators, but he hadn't heeded his friend's warnings.

Sadly, the second pig was also eaten, for although he had built what seemed to be a safe house, Practical Pig decided to use sticks for the walls. Although the first pig had found that "weightbearing, rigid barriers fashioned from the woody fibers of trees and shrubs can be rendered discohesive through exposure to focused atmospheric air pressure of excessive magnitude," the Practical Pig felt that the first pig's studies were so artificial that they didn't have any relevance for "real" houses. In fact, he had let his subscription to the *Journal for Purely Scientific Pigs* (or, *JPSP*) lapse, so he didn't even know about the problems with sticks. So when the wolf huffed and puffed and blew, the house tumbled down and the second pig fell victim.

The third pig survived (of course). When he saw the wolf approach, he ran into his house and locked the door. The wolf pushed on the house, but the foundation and structure were too strong. He tried blowing on the house, but the stone walls held secure. He tried climbing on the roof, but the carefully crafted masonry gave him no purchase. The hungry wolf, relenting, then left the third pig in peace.

The moral of the story is taken from the monument that the third pig erected to the memory of his departed childhood friends. It read:

> Knowledge cannot prosper
> When science is one-sided,
> The basic and applied must be,
> United, not divided.

REFERENCES

American Psychiatric Association. (1980). *Diagnostic and statistical manual of mental disorders* (3rd ed.). Washington, DC: Author.

Andrews, G., & Harvey, R. (1981). Does psychotherapy benefit neurotic patients? A re-analysis of the Smith, Glass, and Miller data. *Archives of General Psychiatry, 38*, 1203–1208.

Barber, P. (1988). *Applied cognitive psychology: An information-processing framework.* New York: Methuen.

Barker, S. L., Funk, S. C., & Houston, B. K. (1988). Psychological treatment versus nonspecific factors: A meta-analysis of conditions that engender compable expectations for improvement. *Clinical Psychology Review, 8*, 579–594.

Baumeister, R. F., & Scher, S. J. (1988). Self-defeating behavior patterns among normal individuals: Review and analysis of common self-destructive tendencies. *Psychological Bulletin, 104*, 3–22.

Berscheid, E. (1985). Interpersonal attraction. In G. Lindzey & E. Aronson (Eds.), *Handbook of social psychology* (Vol. 2, 3rd. ed., pp. 413–484). New York: Random House.

Brehm, S. S. (1976). *The application of social psychology to clinical practice.* Washington, DC: Hemisphere.

Carson, R. C. (1969). *Interaction concepts of personality.* Chicago: Aldine.

Caspi, A., Bolger, N., & Eckenrode, J. (1987). Linking person and context in the daily stress process. *Journal of Personality and Social Psychology, 52*, 184–195.

Dance, K. A., & Neufeld, W. J. (1988). Aptitude-treatment interaction research in the clinical setting: A review of attempts to dispel the "patient uniformity" myth. *Psychological Bulletin, 104*, 192–213.

DeLongis, A., Folkman, S., & Lazarus, R. S. (1988). Hassles, health, and mood: Psychological and social resources as mediators. *Journal of Personality and Social Psychology, 54*, 486–495.

Eckenrode, J. (1984). The impact of chronic and acute stressors on daily reports of mood. *Journal of Personality and Social Psychology, 46*, 907–908.

Fazio, R. H., & Zanna, M. P. (1978). On the predictive validity of attitudes: The roles of direct experience and confidence. *Journal of Personality, 46*, 228–243.

Forsyth, D. R. (1988). Social psychology's three little pigs. *Journal of Social Behavior and Personality, 3*, 63–65.

Gibbons, F. X. (1983). Self attention and self-report: The "veridicality" hypothesis. *Journal of Personality, 52*, 517–542.

Greenwald, A. G., & Pratkanis, A. R. (1984). The self. In R. S. Wyer & T. K. Srull (Eds.), *Handbook of social cognition* (Vol. 3, pp. 129–178). Hillsdale, NJ: Lawrence Erlbaum Associates.

Hayes, S. C., Nelson, R. O., & Jarrett, R. B. (1987). The treatment utility of assessment: A functional approach to evaluating assessment quality. *American Psychologist, 42*, 963–974.

James, W. (1890). *The principles of psychology* (Vol. 1). New York: Holt.

Kanfer, F. H., & Nay, W. R. (1982). Behavioral assessment. In G. T. Wilson & C. M. Franks (Eds.), *Contemporary behavior therapy: Conceptual and empirical foundations* (pp. 367–402). New York: Guilford Press.

Kasl, S. V. (1983). Pursuing the link between stressful life experiences and disease: A time for reappraisal. In C. L. Cooper (Ed.), *Stress research: Issues for the eighties.* Chichester, England: John Wiley & Sons.

Kihlstrom, J. F., & Cantor, N. (1984). Mental representations of the self. *Advances in Experimental Social Psychology, 17*, 1–47.

Landman, J. T., & Dawes, R. M. (1982). Psychotherapy outcome: Smith and Glass' conclusions stand up under scrutiny. *American Psychologist, 37*, 504–516.

Lazarus, R. S. (in press). Stress, coping, and health. In H. S. Friedman (Ed.), *Personality and disease*. New York: John Wiley & Sons.

Maddux, J. E. (1987). The interface of social, clinical, and counseling psychology: Why bother and what is it anyway? *Journal of Social and Clinical Psychology, 5*, 27–33.

Markus, H., & Sentis, K. (1982). The self in social information processing. In J. Suls (Ed.), *Psychological perspectives on the self* (Vol. 1, pp. 41–70). Hillsdale, NJ: Lawrence Erlbaum Associates.

Markus, H., & Wurf, E. (1987). The dynamic self-concept: A social psychological perspective. *Annual Review of Psychology, 38*, 299–337.

Meehl, P. E. (1978). Theoretical risks and tabular asterisks: Sir Karl, Sir Ronald, and the slow progress of soft psychology. *Journal of Consulting and Clinical Psychology, 46*, 806–834.

Mischel, W. (1968). *Personality and Assessment*. New York: John Wiley and Sons.

Neisser, U. (1976). *Cognition and reality*. San Francisco: W. H. Freeman.

Prioleau, L., Murdock, M., & Brody, N. (1983). An analysis of psychotherapy versus placebo studies. *The Behavioral and Brain Sciences, 6*, 275–310.

Sarason, S. B. (1987). A house, a home, an interface. *Journal of Social and Clinical Psychology, 5*, 222–226.

Shapiro, D. A., & Shapiro, D. (1982). Meta-analysis of comparative therapy outcome studies: A replication and refinement. *Psychological Bulletin, 92*, 581–604.

Smith, M. L., & Glass, G. V. (1977). Meta-analysis of psychotherapy outcome. *American Psychologist, 32*, 752–760.

Snyder, C. R. (1988). From defenses to self-protection: An evolutionary perspective. *Journal of Social and Clinical Psychology, 6*, 155–158.

Snyder, C. R. (1989). Reality negotiation: From excuses to hope and beyond. *Journal of Social and Clinical Psychology, 8*, 130–157.

Snyder, M. (1987). *Public appearances/private realities: The psychology of self-monitoring*. New York: W. H. Freeman.

Snyder, M., & Thomsen, C. J.(1988). Interactions between therapists and clients: Hypothesis testing and behavioral confirmation. In D. C. Turk & P. Salovey (Eds.), *Reasoning, inference, and judgment in clinical psychology* (pp. 124–152). New York: Free Press.

Stone, A. A., & Neale, J. M. (1984). New measure of daily coping: Development and preliminary results. *Journal of Personality and Social Psychology, 46*, 892–906.

Strupp, H. H., & Hadley, S. W. (1977). A tripartite model of mental health and therapeutic outcomes. *American Psychologist, 32*, 187–196.

Sullivan, H. S. (1953). *The interpersonal theory of psychiatry*. New York: W. W. Norton.

Wicklund, R. A., & Eckert-Nowack, M. (1989). *A psychological analysis of the self-knower*. Unpublished manuscript, University of Bielefeld, West Germany.

Willerman, L., Turner, R. G., & Peterson, M. (1976). A comparison of the predictive validity of typical and maximal personality measures. *Journal of Research in Personality, 10*, 482–492.

Zanna, M. P., & Fazio, R. H. (1982). The attitude-behavior relation: Moving toward a third generation of research. In M. P. Zanna, E. T. Higgins, & C. P. Herman (Eds.), *Consistency in social behavior*. The Ontario Symposium (Vol. 2, pp. 283–301). Hillsdale, NJ: Lawrence Erlbaum Associates.

AUTHOR INDEX

Faber, S. S., 693
Fabry, J., 628, 639
Fairbairn, W. R. D., 501, 505
Fairey, P. J., 173, 175
Fairfield, M. L., 205, 211, 217
Falbo, T., 311, 323, 543, 560
Falke, R. L., 354, 374
Falkner, S. B., 54, 194
Falloon, I. R., 668, 677
Fanshel, D., 768, 772
Farber, M. L., 286–287, 289, 295, 301
Farber, S., 345
Farina, A., 363, 369
Farkas, G., 723, 733
Farmer, L., 454, 459
Farquhar, J. W., 597, 602
Farr, M. J., 694
Faught, A. K., 594, 605
Faust, D., 426–428, 432
Fava, J., 598, 605
Favero, R. V., 295, 303
Fay, M., 90, 92, 609, 621
Fazio, R. H., 140, 155, 795, 805–806
Feather, N. T., 100, 106, 111, 134, 163, 175, 204, 213
Federman, E. J., 448, 463, 542, 561
Federoff, N. A., 142, 148, 154
Feigenbaum, E. A., 681, 693, 696
Feigl, H., 484, 486
Feinglos, M. N., 594, 605
Feinleib, M., 197–198, 200, 213–214, 217
Feinstein, A. R., 425, 532
Feld, S., 319, 324
Feld, S. C., 352, 370
Feldhusen, J. F., 684, 693
Feldman, A., 672, 677
Feldman, D. A., 559, 560, 626, 629, 639
Feldman, J., 681, 693, 696
Feldman, N. S., 380–381, 391–392
Feldman, S., 474, 486
Feldstein, M., 672, 676
Felix, M. R. J., 719, 733
Felner, R. D., 224, 227, 243, 693
Felson, R. B., 163–164, 175
Fenigstein, A., 138, 142, 151–152, 154, 163, 175, 292, 301
Fennell, M. J., 145, 154
Fenner, F., 649, 663
Ferguson, M., 396, 414
Fernandez, G., 610, 621
Ferrara, N. A., 260, 262
Ferrarese, M. J., 47, 55
Ferrin, H. H., 684, 696
Ferriti, R. P., 689, 692
Feshbach, S., 378, 391
Festinger, L., 6, 15, 26, 28, 36–37, 58, 75, 79, 92, 131, 134, 377, 391, 489, 505, 525, 537, 554, 560, 628, 640, 670, 677, 675, 678
Fetzer, B. K., 162, 177

Feuerstein, M., 297, 301
Feyerabend, P., 767, 771
Fezler, W. D., 645, 660
Fibel, B., 228, 241, 288, 301, 743, 753
Fick, C., 252, 263
Fiedler, F. E., 222, 240, 674, 677, 704, 712
Fiedler, K., 324, 432, 434
Field, G., 30, 37
Field, T., 610, 621
Field, T. M., 263, 342, 346
Fieve, R. R., 343, 345, 347
Fifield, J., 90–91, 383, 390
Figley, C. R., 506
Figueroa, J., 723, 733
Filsinger, E. E., 318, 323
Finch, A. J., 224, 241, 243
Fincham, F. D., 99, 111, 311–312, 314, 318–319, 323–324
Fine, R. L., 140, 154
Fineberg, H. V., 425, 437
Finkelstein, P., 669, 677
Finman, R., 224, 241
Finn, S. E., 200, 215, 233, 241, 724, 735
Firestone, I. J., 11, 14
Firestone, P., 594, 605
Fisch, R., 624, 626, 631, 640, 643
Fischer, E. H., 353, 362, 369
Fischhoff, B., 425–428, 432, 435
Fish, B., 102, 111
Fish, R., 490, 507
Fishbein, M., 59, 73–75, 436, 523–524, 536–537
Fisher, D., 535, 539
Fisher, E. B., 581, 592, 599, 602, 604, 723, 725, 733–734
Fisher, J. D., 350, 356, 358–360, 363–364, 367–369, 370–375, 394
Fisher, L., 50, 54, 248, 263, 342, 346
Fisher, R., 484, 486
Fisher, S., 605, 682, 693
Fishman, R., 324, 349
Fiske, D. W., 276, 281, 743, 753, 760, 770–772
Fiske, S., 631, 640
Fiske, S. T., 119, 128–129, 134, 167, 175, 419, 432–433, 436, 490, 492, 505, 745, 756
Fitzgerald, R. G., 340, 347
Fitzpatrick, M. A., 317, 324
Flanagan, M. R., 11, 15
Flaner, R. C., 703, 713
Flavell, J. H., 683, 693
Flaxman, J., 648–650, 657, 663
Fleg, J. L., 200, 213
Fleming, R., 116, 134
Flemming, R., 498, 505
Fletcher, B. L., 479–480, 486–487
Fletcher, G., 610–611, 621
Fletcher, G. J. O., 318, 324
Fletcher, R. H., 200, 219
Floor, E., 50, 54

SUBJECT INDEX

Test anxiety and self-focused attention, 146
Theories:
  construction of, 541
  generalizing from research findings, 11
  Lewin's view of, ii, iii, 8, 793
  nature of, 9–10
  pyramid model, 97–102
  reasoned action, of, 73
  role of theory in science, 803
  science, in, 10
  self-efficacy as a social/clinical theory, 57–58
  usefulness during therapy, 10
Therapeutic flexibility, 730–732
Therapeutic interpretations, 500
Therapeutic process:
  confrontation, 500–501
  during cognitive-behavioral interventions, 509–518
  internalization, 504
  interpersonal transaction, as an, 444–446
  resistance, 501–502
  revision of assumptive worlds, as a, 498–504
  social influence model of, 525–526, 555–559
Therapeutic relationship, 503
Therapist characteristics:
  attitude change and, 525–526
  change in therapy groups and, 673–674
  client-therapist matching, 699–710
  trust, 558–559
Therapist-client matching:
  matching clients and treatment procedures, 704–709
  person X environment interaction, and the, 794
  pretreatment methods for increasing, 702–704
  similarity in personal qualities, 700–702
Therapist(s):
  American Psychological Association training guidelines, 7, 758–759
  clinical judgment of, 427–429
  help-seeking and the characteristics of, 358–359
  training of, 7, 783–784
Therapy effectiveness:
  determinants of, 499
  impact of techniques vs. nonspecific factors, 795
  outcome studies, 518
  paradox-based treatments, 625–627
  therapeutic change with hypnotherapy, 646–659
Therapy:
  attitudes and therapeutic change, 525–536
  client-therapist matching and, 699–710
  cognitive-behavioral interventions, 511–518
  confrontation to assumptive belief during, 500–501
  distinctions between various types, of, 513–514, 704–709
  effectiveness of, 793–794
  form of social influence, as a, 699–700
  four-step model of, 498–505
  increasing controllability through, 614–620
  inferential vs. emotional bases of change in, 502–504
  interpersonal, 444–446

interventions based on interpersonal theory, 444–446, 555–559
interventions designed to modify Type A behavior patterns, 209–211
means of dealing with loneliness, as a, 409
resistance during, 501–502
seeking, 351–367
social comparison during, 389
strategic therapy and paradox-based treatments, 630–638
technical eclecticism and treatment selection, 704–709
therapeutic advances generated by the social-clinical interface, 793
therapeutic relationship, and the, 503
the use of theory during, 10
Trust:
  close relationships, in, 316
  during therapy, role of, the, 558–559
Type A Behavior Pattern (TABP):
  assessment of, 198–201
  attributions and, 208
  cardiovascular reactivity and, 201–204
  coronary heart disease and, 197–198, 201–206, 209–212
  development of, 208–209
  group therapy as a treatment for, 210
  health-promoting behavior and, 205–206
  hostility and the, 200–201, 204–205, 208
  interventions designed to modify, 209–211
  limitations of measures of, 743–744
  narcissism and, 206
  reactions to loss of control and, 205–206
  self-awareness and, 206–207

UCLA Loneliness Scale, 396–397
Uniformity myth, 669, 691
Unrealistic optimism, 162, 495

Validity:
  analogue research ff, 11
  construct, 740, 743, 748
  external, 9–11, 740
  internal, 740
  statistical conclusion, 740, 745
  strengthening, methods of, 742, 744–750
  studies of persistence of treatment effects, of, 719–720
Value(s):
  anxiety and threats to cultural, 26–27
  personal beliefs and treatment persistence, 725
  socialization and cultural values, 23–24
  therapist values and effectiveness, 702
  threats to personal values and existential anxiety, 28–29
  versus meaning, 28–29, 31
Victimization:
  attributions and blaming the victim, 85–86, 89–90
  following negative life events, 495–498
  help-seeking and, 357

ABOUT THE EDITORS
AND CONTRIBUTORS

ABOUT THE EDITORS

C. R. Snyder received his Ph.D. in clinical psychology from Vanderbilt University in 1971. He is presently a professor in the Department of Psychology at the University of Kansas—Lawrence.

Donelson R. Forsyth received his Ph.D. in social psychology from the University of Florida in 1978. He is presently a professor in the Department of Psychology at Virginia Commonwealth University.

ABOUT THE CONTRIBUTORS

Glenn G. Affleck received his Ph.D. in educational psychology from the University of Connecticut in 1975. He is presently a professor in the Department of Psychiatry at the University of Connecticut School of Medicine.

Elizabeth M. Altmaier received her Ph.D. in counseling psychology from Ohio State University in 1977. She is presently a professor in the Coun-

seling Psychology Program of the Division of Psychological and Quantitative Foundations at the University of Iowa.

John R. Anderson received his Ph.D. in clinical psychology from the University of Kansas in 1988. He is presently the director of the American Psychological Association's AIDS Community Training Project.

Susan E. Becker received her M.A. in clinical psychology from the University of Colorado—Colorado Springs in 1989, and she is presently completing her doctorate in clinical psychology at the University of Arizona.

John Bergen is presently completing his Ph.D. in clinical psychology at the University of Arizona.

Larry E. Beutler received his Ph.D. in clinical psychology from the University of Nebraska in 1970. He is presently a professor in the Department of Psychiatry at the University of Arizona College of Medicine.

Thomas N. Bradbury received his Ph.D. in Clinical Psychology from the University of Illinois at Urbana—Champaign in 1990. He is presently an assistant professor in the Department of Psychology at UCLA.

Jonathan D. Brown received his Ph.D in social psychology from the University of California—Los Angeles in 1986. He is presently an assistant professor in the Department of Psychology at the University of Washington.

Sue Ann Ludwig Burchill completed her M.A. in clinical psychology at the University of Miami (Ohio) in 1988, where she is presently completing her Ph.D.

Melanie O. Burns is presently completing her Ph.D. in clinical psychology at the University of Pennsylvania.

John T. Cacioppo received his Ph.D. in social psychology at Ohio State University in 1977, and he is presently a professor of Psychology at the same institution.

Margaret D. Carver is presently completing her Ph.D. in psychology at the University of Tulsa.

Audrey H. Chen is presently completing her Ph.D. in clinical psychology at San Diego State University.

Charles D. Claiborn received his Ph.D. in counseling psychology from the University of Missouri—Columbia in 1978. He is presently an associate professor of Counselor Education and Counseling Psychology in the Department of Psychological and Quantitative Foundations at the University of Iowa.

Lee Anna Clark received her Ph.D. in clinical psychology from the University of Minnesota in 1982. She is presently an associate professor in the Department of Psychology at Southern Methodist University.

John F. Clarkin received his Ph.D. in clinical psychology from Fordam University in 1971. He is presently a professor of Clinical Psychology in the Psychiatry Department of Cornell University Medical Center, and Director of Psychology at the New York Hospital-Cornell Medical Center-Westchester Division.

James C. Coyne received his Ph.D. in clinical psychology from Indiana University in 1975. He is presently an associate professor in the Departments of Psychiatry and Family Practice at the University of Michigan Medical School.

Marjorie Crago received her Ph.D. in clinical psychology from the University of Arizona in 1974. She is presently a research assistant in the Department of Psychiatry at the University of Arizona College of Medicine.

Karina Davidson-Katz received her M.A.Sc. in industrial/organizational psychology from the University of Waterloo in 1987, and is presently completing her Ph.D. in clinical psychology at the same institution.

Bella M. DePaulo received her Ph.D. in social psychology from Harvard University in 1979. She is presently an associate professor in the Department of Psychology at the University of Virginia.

Kevin Doherty received his M.S. in social psychology from the University of Florida in 1989, and he is presently continuing toward his Ph.D.

Frank D. Fincham received his Ph.D. in social psychology from Oxford University in 1980. He is presently an associate professor in the Department of Psychology at the University of Illinois—Champaign.

Jeff Greenberg received his Ph.D. in social psychology from the University of Kansas in 1982. He is presently an associate professor in the Department of Psychology at the University of Arizona.

James C. Hamilton received his Ph.D. in clinical psychology from Case Western Reserve University in 1986. He is presently a visiting assistant professor in the Department of Psychology at Hamilton College.

John H. Harvey received his Ph.D. in social psychology at the University of Missouri—Columbia in 1971. He is presently a professor in the Department of Psychology at the University of Iowa.

Martin Heesacker received his Ph.D. in counseling psychology from the University of Missouri—Columbia in 1983. He is presently an assistant professor in the Department of Psychology at Ohio State University.

Clyde Hendrick received his Ph.D. in social psychology from the University of Missouri—Columbia in 1967. He is presently a professor in the Department of Psychology and Dean of the Graduate School at Texas Tech University.

Susan Singer Hendrick received her Ph.D. in counseling psychology from Kent State University in 1978. She is presently an associate professor in the Department of Psychology at Texas Tech University.

P. Paul Heppner received his Ph.D. in counseling psychology from the University of Nebraska in 1979. He is presently a professor in the Department of Psychology at the University of Missouri—Columbia.

Raymond L. Higgins received his Ph.D. in clinical psychology from the University of Wisconsin in 1973. He is presently a professor in the Department of Psychology at the University of Kansas—Lawrence.

Eric T. Hillerbrand received his Ph.D. in counseling psychology at the University of Iowa in 1988. He is presently an assistant professor in the Department of Psychology at the University of Missouri—Columbia.

Rick E. Ingram received his Ph.D. in clinical psychology from the University of Kansas in 1983. He is presently a professor in the Department of Psychology at San Diego State University.

Lori M. Irving is presently completing her Ph.D. in clinical psychology at the University of Kansas—Lawrence.

Ronnie Janoff-Bulman received her Ph.D. in social psychology from Northwestern University in 1977. She is presently a professor of Psychology in the Department of Psychology at the University of Massachusetts.

Warren H. Jones received his Ph.D. in social psychology from Oklahoma State University in 1974. He is presently a professor in the Department of Psychology at the University of Tennessee.

Paul Karoly received his Ph.D. in clinical psychology from the University of Rochester in 1971. He is presently a professor in the Department of Psychology at Arizona State University.

Philip C. Kendall received his Ph.D. in clinical psychology from Virginia Commonwealth University in 1977. Presently he is a professor in the Department of Psychology at Temple University and professor of research in Psychiatry at the Eastern Pennsylvania Psychiatric Institute of the Medical College of Pennsylvania.

Donald J. Kiesler received his Ph.D. in clinical psychology from the University of Illinois in 1963. He is presently a professor in the Department of Psychology at Virginia Commonwealth University.

Mark R. Leary received his Ph.D. in social psychology from the University of Florida in 1980. He is presently an associate professor in the Department of Psychology at Wake Forest University.

Herbert M. Lefcourt received his Ph.D. in clinical psychology from Ohio State University in 1963. He is presently a professor in the Department of Psychology at the University of Waterloo.

James E. Maddux received his Ph.D. in clinical psychology from the University of Alabama in 1982. He is presently an associate professor in the Department of Psychology at George Mason University.

Nancy L. Murdock received her Ph.D. in counseling psychology from Virginia Commonwealth University in 1986. She is presently an assistant professor in the Department of Counseling Psychology and Counselor Education at the University of Missouri—Kansas City.

Richard E. Petty received his Ph.D. in social psychology from Ohio State University in 1977, and he is presently a professor of Psychology at the same institution.

Tom Pyszczynski received his Ph.D. in social psychology from the University of Kansas in 1980. He is presently an associate professor in the Department of Psychology at the University of Colorado—Colorado Springs.

Frederick T. Rhodewalt received his Ph.D. in social psychology from Princeton University in 1979. He is presently an associate professor in the Department of Psychology at the University of Utah.

Peter Salovey received his Ph.D. in clinical psychology from Yale University in 1986. He is presently an assistant professor in the Department of Psychology at Yale University.

Barry R. Schlenker received his Ph.D. in psychology from the State University of New York — Albany in 1972. He is presently a professor in the Department of Psychology at the University of Florida.

Steven S. Schwartzberg received his M.S. in clinical psychology from the University of Massachusetts, where he is presently completing his Ph.D.

Martin E. P. Seligman received his Ph.D. in experimental psychology from the University of Pennsylvania in 1967. He is presently a professor in the Department of Psychology at the University of Pennsylvania.

Craig A. Smith received his Ph.D. in social psychology from Stanford University in 1986. He is presently an assistant professor in the Department of Psychology and Human Development at Vanderbilt University.

Timothy W. Smith received his Ph.D. in clinical psychology from the University of Kansas in 1982. He is presently a professor in the Department of Psychology at the University of Utah.

Sheldon Solomon received his Ph.D. in social psychology from the University of Kansas in 1980. He is presently an associate professor in the Department of Psychology at Skidmore College.

Nicholas P. Spanos received his Ph.D. in psychology from Boston University in 1974. He is presently a professor in the Department of Psychology at Carleton University.

William B. Stiles received his Ph.D. in clinical psychology from the University of California — Los Angeles in 1972. He is presently a professor in the Department of Psychology at Miami (Ohio) University.

Stanley R. Strong received his Ph.D. in counseling psychology at the University of Minnesota in 1966. He is presently a professor in the Department of Psychology at Virginia Commonwealth University.

Howard A. Tennen received his Ph.D. in clinical psychology from the University of Massachusetts in 1976. He is presently a professor in the Department of Psychiatry at the University of Connecticut School of Medicine.

Suzanne C. Thompson received her Ph.D. in social psychology from the University of California — Los Angeles in 1983. She is presently an associate professor in the Department of Psychology at Pomona College.

Dennis C. Turk received his Ph.D. in clinical psychology from the University of Waterloo in 1978. He presently is a professor of Psychiatry and Anesthesiology at the Pain Evaluation and Treatment Institute of the University of Pittsburgh School of Medicine.

David Watson received his Ph.D. in personality psychology at the University of Minnesota in 1982. He is presently an associate professor in the Department of Psychology at Southern Methodist University.

Gifford Weary received her Ph.D. in social and clinical psychology from Vanderbilt University in 1977. She is presently a professor in the Department of Psychology at Ohio State University.

Michael F. Weigold received his Ph.D. in social psychology from the University of Florida in 1989, and he is presently an assistant professor in the Advertising Department at the University of Florida.

Thomas A. Wills received his Ph.D. in social psychology from the University of Oregon in 1975. He is presently an assistant professor in the Department of Epidemiology and Social Medicine at the Einstein College of Medicine.

Beatrice A. Wright received her Ph.D. in psychology from the University of Iowa in 1942. She is presently a professor emerita in the Department of Psychology at the University of Kansas.

Pergamon General Psychology Series

Editors: **Arnold P. Goldstein,** Syracuse University
Leonard Krasner, Stanford University &
SUNY at Stony Brook

*Out of print in original format. Available in custom reprint edition.